Short Story Criticism

Guide to Gale Literary Criticism Series

For criticism on	Consult these Gale series
Authors now living or who died after December 31, 1959	**CONTEMPORARY LITERARY CRITICISM (CLC)**
Authors who died between 1900 and 1959	**TWENTIETH-CENTURY LITERARY CRITICISM (TCLC)**
Authors who died between 1800 and 1899	**NINETEENTH-CENTURY LITERATURE CRITICISM (NCLC)**
Authors who died between 1400 and 1799	**LITERATURE CRITICISM FROM 1400 TO 1800 (LC)** **SHAKESPEAREAN CRITICISM (SC)**
Authors who died before 1400	**CLASSICAL AND MEDIEVAL LITERATURE CRITICISM (CMLC)**
Black writers of the past two hundred years	**BLACK LITERATURE CRITICISM (BLC)**
Authors of books for children and young adults	**CHILDREN'S LITERATURE REVIEW (CLR)**
Dramatists	**DRAMA CRITICISM (DC)**
Hispanic writers of the late nineteenth and twentieth centuries	**HISPANIC LITERATURE CRITICISM (HLC)**
Native North American writers and orators of the eighteenth, nineteenth, and twentieth centuries	**NATIVE NORTH AMERICAN LITERATURE (NNAL)**
Poets	**POETRY CRITICISM (PC)**
Short story writers	**SHORT STORY CRITICISM (SSC)**
Major authors from the Renaissance to the present	**WORLD LITERATURE CRITICISM, 1500 TO THE PRESENT (WLC)**

Volume 25

Short Story Criticism

Excerpts from Criticism of the
Works of Short Fiction Writers

Carol T. Gaffke
Anna J. Sheets

Editors

GALE

DETROIT · NEW YORK · TORONTO · LONDON

STAFF

Carol T. Gaffke, Anna J. Sheets, *Editors*

Lawrence J. Trudeau, *Associate Editor*

Kathy D. Darrow, Debra A. Wells, *Assistant Editors*

Susan Trosky, *Permissions Manager*

Kimberly F. Smilay, *Permissions Specialist*
Sarah Chesney, *Permissions Associate*
Stephen Cusack, Kelly Quin, *Permissions Assistants*

Victoria B. Cariappa, *Research Manager*

Michele P. LaMeau, *Research Specialist*
Julia C. Daniel, Tamara C. Nott, Tracie A. Richardson, Norma Sawaya, Cheryl L. Warnock, *Research Associates*

Mary Beth Trimper, *Production Director*
Deborah L. Milliken, *Production Assistant*

C. J. Jonik, *Desktop Publisher*
Randy Bassett, *Image Database Supervisor*
Mikal Ansari, Robert Duncan, *Scanner Operators*
Pamela Hayes, *Photography Coordinator*

Library of Congress Catalog Card Number 88-641014
ISBN 0-7876-0757-6
ISSN 0895-9439

Printed in the United States of America
10 9 8 7 6 5 4 3 2 1

Contents

Preface

A Comprehensive Information Source
on World Short Fiction

*S**hort Story Criticism (SSC)* presents significant passages from criticism of the world's greatest short story writers and provides supplementary biographical and bibliographical materials to guide the interested reader to a greater understanding of the authors of short fiction. This series was developed in response to suggestions from librarians serving high school, college, and public library patrons, who had noted a considerable number of requests for critical material on short story writers. Although major short story writers are covered in such Gale series as *Contemporary Literary Criticism (CLC), Twentieth-Century Literary Criticism (TCLC), Nineteenth-Century Literature Criticism (NCLC),* and *Literature Criticism from 1400 to 1800 (LC),* librarians perceived the need for a series devoted solely to writers of the short story genre.

Coverage

SSC is designed to serve as an introduction to major short story writers of all eras and nationalities. Since these authors have inspired a great deal of relevant critical material, *SSC* is necessarily selective, and the editors have chosen the most important published criticism to aid readers and students in their research.

Approximately eight to ten authors are included in each volume, and each entry presents a historical survey of the critical response to that author's work. The length of an entry is intended to reflect the amount of critical attention the author has received from critics writing in English and from foreign critics in translation. Every attempt has been made to identify and include excerpts from the most significant essays on each author's work. In order to provide these important critical pieces, the editors sometimes reprint essays that have appeared elsewhere in Gale's Literary Criticism Series. Such duplication, however, never exceeds twenty percent of an *SSC* volume.

Organization

An *SSC* author entry consists of the following elements:

- The **Author Heading** cites the name under which the author most commonly wrote, followed by birth and death dates. If the author wrote consistently under a pseudonym, the pseudonym will be listed in the author heading and the author's actual name given in parentheses on the first line of the biographical and critical introduction.

- The **Biographical and Critical Introduction** contains background information designed to introduce a reader to the author and the critical debates surrounding his or her work.

- A **Portrait of the Author** is included when available. Many entries also contain illustrations of materials pertinent to an author's career, including holographs of manuscript pages, title pages, dust jackets, letters, or representations of important people, places, and events in the author's life.

- The list of **Principal Works** is chronological by date of first publication and lists the most important works by the author. The first section comprises short story collections, novellas, and novella collections. The second section gives information on other major works by the author. For foreign authors, the editors have provided original foreign-language publication information and have selected what are considered the best and most complete English-language editions of their works.

- **Criticism** is arranged chronologically in each author entry to provide a useful perspective on changes in critical evaluation over the years. All short story, novella, and collection titles by the author featured in the entry are printed in boldface type to enable a reader to ascertain without difficulty the works discussed. Also for purposes of easier identification, the critic's name and the publication date of the essay are given at the beginning of each piece of criticism. Unsigned criticism is preceded by the title of the journal in which it appeared.

- Critical essays are prefaced with **Explanatory Notes** as an additional aid to students and readers using *SSC*. An explanatory note may provide useful information of several types, including: the reputation of the critic, the intent or scope of the critical essay, and the orientation of the criticism (biographical, psychoanalytic, structuralist, etc.).

- A complete **Bibliographical Citation,** designed to help the interested reader locate the original essay or book, precedes each piece of criticism.

- The **Further Reading List** appearing at the end of each author entry suggests additional materials on the author. In some cases it includes essays for which the editors could not obtain reprint rights. Boxed material following the further reading list provides references to other biographical and critical sources on the author in series published by Gale.

Beginning with volume six, *SSC* contains two additional features designed to enhance the reader's understanding of short fiction writers and their works:

- Each *SSC* entry now includes, when available, **Comments by the Author** that illuminate his or her own works or the short story genre in general. These statements are set within boxes or bold rules to distinguish them from the criticism.

- A **Select Bibliography of General Sources on Short Fiction** is included as an appendix. This listing of materials for further research provides readers with a selection of the best available general studies of the short story genre.

Other Features

A **Cumulative Author Index** lists all the authors who have appeared in *SSC, CLC, TCLC, NCLC, LC,* and *Classical and Medieval Literature Criticism (CMLC),* as well as cross-references to other Gale series. Users will welcome this cumulated index as a useful tool for locating an author within the Literary Criticism Series.

A **Cumulative Nationality Index** lists all authors featured in *SSC* by nationality, followed by the number of the *SSC* volume in which their entry appears.

A **Cumulative Title Index** lists in alphabetical order all short story, novella, and collection titles contained in the *SSC* series. Titles of short story collections, separately published novellas, and novella collections are printed in italics, while titles of individual short stories are printed in roman type with quotation marks. Each title is followed by the author's name and corresponding volume and page numbers where commentary on the work is located. English-language translations of original foreign-language titles are cross-referenced to the foreign titles so that all references to discussion of a work are combined in one listing.

Citing *Short Story Criticism*

When writing papers, students who quote directly from any volume in the Literary Criticism Series may use the following general forms to footnote reprinted criticism. The first example pertains to material drawn from periodicals, the second to material reprinted from books:

[1]Henry James, Jr., "Honoré de Balzac," *The Galaxy 20* (December 1875), 814-36; excerpted and reprinted in *Short Story Criticism,* Vol. 5, ed. Thomas Votteler (Detroit: Gale Research, 1990), pp. 8-11.

[2]F. R. Leavis, *D. H. Lawrence: Novelist* (Alfred A. Knopf, 1956); excerpted and reprinted in *Short Story Criticism,* Vol. 4, ed. Thomas Votteler (Detroit: Gale Research, 1990), pp. 202-06.

Comments

Readers who wish to suggest authors to appear in future volumes, or who have other suggestions, are invited to contact the editors by writing to Gale Research Inc., Literary Criticism Division, 835 Penobscot Building, Detroit, MI 48226-4094.

Acknowledgments

The editors wish to thank the copyright holders of the excerpted criticism included in this volume and the permissions managers of many book and magazine publishing companies for assisting us in securing reproduction rights. We are also grateful to the staffs of the Detroit Public Library, the Library of Congress, the University of Detroit Mercy Library, Wayne State University Purdy/Kresge Library Complex, and the University of Michigan Libraries for making their resources available to us. Following is a list of the copyright holders who have granted us permission to reproduce material in this volume of *SSC*. Every effort has been made to trace copyright, but if omissions have been made, please let us know.

COPYRIGHTED EXCERPTS IN *SSC*, VOLUME 25, WERE REPRODUCED FROM THE FOLLOWING PERIODICALS:

Black American Literature Forum, v. 15, Summer, 1981 for "Aim High and Go Straight: The Grandmother Figure in the Short Fiction of Rudolph Fisher" by John McCluskey, Jr. Copyright © 1981 Indiana State University. Reproduced by permission of Indiana State University and the author.—*Chasqui,* v. XVII, November, 1988. Reproduced by permission.—*CLA Journal,* v. XXVI, December, 1982. Copyright © 1982 by The College Language Association. Reproduced by permission of The College Language Association—*The Crisis,* v. 78, July, 1971 for "Rudolph Fisher: An Evaluation" by Oliver Louis Henry. Copyright © 1971 by The Crisis Publishing Company, Inc. Reproduced by permission of the publisher and the author.—*Critique: Studies in Modern Fiction,* v. IX, 1966-67. Copyright © 1967 Helen Dwight Reid Educational Foundation. Reproduced with permission of Helen Dwight Reid Educational Foundation. Published by Heldref Publications, 1319 18th Street, N. W., Washington DC 20036-1802.—*English Journal,* January, 1967 for "The Role of Order and Disorder in 'The Long March' " by Welles T. Brandriff. Copyright © 1967 by the National Council of Teachers of English. Reproduced by permission of the publisher and the author.— *Foundation,* v. 59, Fall, 1993 for "Take-Over Bids: The Power Fantasies of Frederik Pohl and Cyril Kornbluth" by David Seed. Copyright © 1993 by the Science Fiction Foundation. Reproduced by permission of the author.—*The Hemingway Review,* v. IV, Spring, 1985 for "Voice Out of Africa: A Possible Oral Source for Hemingway's 'The Snows of Kilimanjaro' " by Alice Hall Petry, v. VIII, Fall, 1988 for "The Silly Wasters: Tzara and the Poet in 'The Snows of Kilimanjaro' " by Kenneth G. Johnston. Copyright © 1985, 1988 by The Ernest Hemingway Foundation. Both reproduced by permission of the publisher and the author.—*Hispania,* v. 65, December, 1982 for "Juan Rulfo: Dialectics and the Despairing Optimist" by Arthur Ramirez. Copyright © 1982 by The American Association of Teachers of Spanish and Portuguese, Inc. Reproduced by permission of the publisher and the author.— *Indian Literature,* v. XVI, July-December, 1973.—*Journal of Commonwealth Literature,* n. 5, July, 1968. Copyright © by the author. Reprinted with the kind permission of Bowker-Saur, a division of Reed-Elsevier (UK) Ltd.— *Journal of South Asian Literature,* v. X, Fall-Winter, 1974. Copyright © 1974 by the Asian Studies Center, Michigan State University. Reproduced by permission.—*Journal of Spanish Studies,* v. 1, Winter, 1973. Reproduced by permission.—*The Langston Hughes Review,* v. 1, Spring, 1982. Copyright © 1982 by The Langston Hughes Society. Reproduced by permission.—*Los Angeles Times Book Review,* September 12, 1993, December 11, 1994. Copyright © 1993, 1994, Los Angeles Times. Both reproduced by permission.—*MLN,* v. 101, March, 1986. Copyright © 1986 by The Johns Hopkins University Press. All rights reserved. Reproduced by permission.—*Modern Fiction Studies,* v. 18, Spring, 1972, v. 21, Winter, 1975-76, v. 23, Summer, 1977. Copyright © 1972, 1976, 1977 by Purdue Research Foundation, West Lafayette, IN 47907. All rights reserved. All reproduced by permission of The Johns Hopkins University Press.—*The Nation,* New York, v. 213, September 27, 1971. Copyright © 1971 The Nation magazine/ The Nation Company, Inc. Reproduced by permission.—*New Mexico Quarterly,* v. XXXV, Winter, 1965-66 for "Juan Rulfo: Contemporary Mexican Novelist" by Luis Harss. Copyright © 1966 by The University of New Mexico. Reproduced by permission of the author.—*The New Republic,* v. 151, December 26, 1964. © 1964 The New Republic, Inc. Reproduced by permission of The New Republic.—*New Statesman,* v. LXXIII, March 17, 1967. Copyright 1967 The Statesman Publishing Co. Ltd. Reproduced by permission.—*The New York Review of Books,* v. XXIX, April 1, 1982, v. XLII, February 16, 1995. Copyright © 1982, 1995 Nyrev, Inc., Reproduced with permission from The New York Review of Books.—*The New York Review of Books,* April 9, 1967. Copyright © 1967 by The New York Times Company. Reproduced by

COPYRIGHTED EXCERPTS IN *SSC,* VOLUME 25, WERE REPRODUCED FROM THE FOLLOWING BOOKS:

PHOTOGRAPHS AND ILLUSTRATIONS APPEARING IN *SSC,* VOLUME 25, WERE RECEIVED FROM THE FOLLOWING SOURCES:

Rudolph Fisher
1897-1934

American novelist, short story writer, and playwright.

INTRODUCTION

With the publication of "The City of Refuge" and "Ringtail" in *Atlantic Monthly* in 1925, Rudolph Fisher became the first Harlem Renaissance writer to break into mainstream publishing. Considered the most able writer of this new wave of African American authors, Fisher wrote two well-received novels, *The Walls of Jericho* (1928) and *The Conjure Man Dies* (1932), in addition to more than a dozen short stories. *The Conjure Man Dies* was the first detective novel written by an African American, and was later made into a stage play, *Conjur' Man Dies* (1936). Writing was not Fisher's primary occupation; he was also a well-respected physician whose scientific articles on the effects of ultraviolet rays on bacteria were published in medical journals during his lifetime. Fisher practiced medicine for all of his adult life, while simultaneously writing fiction. At the time of his early death at age 37, critics agreed that Fisher had yet to realize the full potential of his talent.

Biographical Information

Rudolph "Bud" Fisher was born into the black bourgeoisie of Washington, D.C. on May 9, 1897. He spent his childhood in various cities along the East Coast, as his father, who was a Baptist minister, moved the family each time he was assigned to a new parish. The family eventually settled in Providence, Rhode Island, where Fisher later attended Brown University. There he was awarded several academic prizes in addition to earning his B.A. in English and his M.A in biology. His talent and passion for both literature and biology were evident then, and the prizes he won ranged over subjects as diverse as German, composition, and public speaking. From Brown, Fisher moved on to Howard University Medical School, the only class A medical school in the United States for African Americans at that time. It was during his senior year at Howard that Fisher began work on his first short story, "The City of Refuge," which he submitted to the *Atlantic Monthly* in the spring of 1924. Also in 1924, Fisher met Jane Ryder, an elementary school teacher who he married the following year. In 1925 Fisher was awarded a National Research Council Fellowship to study bacteriology at Columbia University in New York City, and relocated to New York with his wife. He remained a New Yorker for the rest of his life, and established a private radiology practice on Long Island that relied on patient referrals from Harlem.

From the time of the publication of "The City of Refuge," Fisher continued to write short stories and sketches, including "The South Lingers On," "Ringtail," (also published in the *Atlantic Monthly*) and "High Yaller" (*Crisis*, 1925). The last of these won the Amy Spingarn Prize for fiction in 1926. By this time, Fisher had become friends with other influential figures of the Harlem Renaissance, among them singer Paul Robeson and writer Langston Hughes, with whom he collaborated on a project that set traditional Negro folk songs in a series of skits that were to be performed by Paul Robeson. The project was never realized because Robeson found success on the London stage and declined to return to America. During the later part of the 1920s and the early 1930s, Fisher spent much of his leisure time exploring Harlem's nightclubs, speakeasies, and theatres, observing the styles and customs of Harlem's denizens. It is clear that Fisher became quite familiar with the dance and theatre crowd, and used his understanding of those people to create the vivid, dynamic characters that populate his short stories. This understanding was also parlayed into stories and essays that captured the essence of Harlem in all its complexities and contradictions, in turn earning Fisher the reputation of "Harlem's interpreter."

Unfortunately, Fisher's life was unexpectedly cut short at the age of 37, when, after undergoing three operations for a stomach disorder, he died of complications on December 26, 1934. His loss was deeply felt in the African American community, and expressions of grief and sympathy poured into Harlem from across the country. Summing up the reaction of many, Zora Neale Hurston lamented in a telegram to Fisher's wife: "The world has lost a genius, you have lost a husband, and I have lost a friend."

Major Works of Short Fiction

In "The City of Refuge" Fisher began exploring themes that dominated many of his later works: the rural immigrant's adjustment to the city; race relations; tension between social classes; and "passing," which is when an African American is mistaken for white, or vice versa. This last theme, which was of great interest to Fisher, is predominant in "High Yaller" and "The Man Who Passed" (unpublished). Religious characters, most often in the form of a grandmother figure, appear throughout Fisher's short fiction as links to the traditional values of the past—a connection repeatedly placed in jeopardy by the sinful nature of Harlem. One such grandmother is the protagonist of what is probably Fisher's most widely anthologized story, "Miss Cynthie" (*Story*, 1933). Miss Cynthie attempts to protect her grandchild from the perils of Harlem, especially nightclubs, dancing, and jazz. Always present in Fisher's fiction are vivid descriptions of the multi-racial composition of Harlem—its sights, sounds, and people—portrayed clearly by the varied dialects and the jazz and blues music Fisher knew so well. Music plays an integral part of several of his stories, setting the mood or acting as a refrain that comments upon the action, as is seen in "Common Meter" (*Negro News Syndicate* 1930) and "Blades of Steel" (*Atlantic Monthly* 1927).

Critical Reception

Criticism on Fisher's work prior to 1987—when the first collection of his short stories was compiled—was focused on his most anthologized stories: "The City of Refuge" and "Miss Cynthie." John McCluskey, in the Introduction to one of the collections (*The City of Refuge*, 1987) asserts that each belongs to a different "movement" prevalent in Fisher's short fiction, and identifies the movements as "The Quest" and "The New Land." The first, characterized by "The City of Refuge," deals with newly arrived Southerners' first experiences in Harlem. The characters bring with them a great sense of hope, which they struggle to maintain in the callous environment of Harlem. The second movement turns inward as the characters now struggle to maintain personal integrity and to reconcile their traditional upbringing with the "sinful" practices of the city. The challenges these characters face form the basis of Fisher's short fiction.

In all of his stories, Fisher writes about immigrants, musicians, and the poor of Harlem. In his time, critics chastised him for not writing about African Americans of his own bourgeois class. W. E. B. Du Bois wrote to that effect in a 1928 review of *The Walls of Jericho*, asking why characters more like Fisher's actual Harlem friends (doctors, writers, and educators) never appear in his fiction. Countering that criticism, Wallace Thurman commented that "The entire universe is the writer's province and so are all the people therein" ["High, Low, Past and Present," *Harlem* 1928], and argued that it was silly for Du Bois to decree that African American writers should write about one class and not another. Both concur, however, that Fisher wrote remarkably well, and that in his descriptions of the era's Harlemites he managed to capture the elusive essence of the times.

More recent criticism tends to focus on the themes and characters of Fisher's work, including the issues of race and class, and the character of the grandmother. Much has been said about the plight of the rural southern immigrant newly arrived to the city and about the importance of the stock scene of the cabaret or dance hall. The latter is seen as a means to incorporate the African American vernacular and folk traditions into the stories. Other interpretations of his work are still emerging as it gains new attention in the 1990s. Still, critics agree that Fisher was the writer who best captured the essence of Harlem during its most vital period, deftly exploring the tensions of class and color that played beneath the surface in such stories as "High Yaller," "Blades of Steel," and "Common Meter." His understanding of Harlem and its people, and his love of blues and jazz, gave Fisher the background necessary to become Harlem's pre-eminent interpreter.

PRINCIPAL WORKS

Short Fiction

"The City of Refuge" 1925; published in *Atlantic Monthly*
"South Lingers On" 1925; published in *Survey Graphic*
"Ringtail" 1925; published in *Atlantic Monthly*
"High Yaller" 1925; published in two parts in *Crisis*
The City of Refuge (1987)
The Short Fiction of Rudolph Fisher (1987)
*"Across the Airshaft"
*"The Lindy Hop"
*"The Lost Love Blues" (three versions)
*"The Man Who Passed"
†"One Month's Wages"
†"A Perfect Understanding"
†"Skeeter"

Other Major Works

"The Caucasian Storms Harlem" (essay) 1927
The Walls of Jericho (novel) 1928

The Conjure Man Dies: A Mystery Tale of Dark Harlem
  (novel) 1932
Conjur' Man Dies (play) 1936

*These are unpublished short stories held at the John Hay Library
at Brown University.

†These are unpublished short stories held by Jane Ryder Fisher.

CRITICISM

Oliver Louis Henry (essay date 1971)

SOURCE: "Rudolph Fisher: An Evaluation," in *Crisis*, Vol.
78, No. 5, July 1971, pp. 149-54.

[*In the following essay, Henry argues that Fisher's literary merits should be judged by his short stories, which
show a keen attention to race and class consciousness.*]

Class consciousness is perhaps the single most consistent theme found in Fisher's work. He was extremely aware
of the class and color distinctions present in the black
community, especially the Harlem community, the locale of
most of his stories. And almost the entire body of his
material deals with the interaction of the various social
types and groups present in that community. What makes
Fisher so appealing is that he writes about black people
in a manner which expresses their kinship with other peo-
ples. He underscores and highlights the fundamental human condition of black Americans. And, through a close
observation of their pursuits and concerns, shows that
black men and women laugh and cry, sing and dance, work
and build, hate and destroy. He captures the historically
induced unique qualities of black people; but, and perhaps even more importantly, he writes of them basically as
people.

Fisher authored two full-length novels and a host of short
stories. The latter represents his major contribution to the
literature of the black community. He ranks as a major
black writer in the short story form. Of his novels, *The
Walls of Jericho* (1928) ranks as one of the best written
during the heyday of the Negro Renaissance. In *Anger
and Beyond*, Herbert Hill indicates that this book gave a
lift to the New Negro Movement. *The Conjure Man Dies*
(1932) represents the first detective or mystery novel written by a black American; and, according to Arthur P.
Davis who reviewed the novel for *Opportunity* (October,
1932), it represents "not merely a good Negro detective
story," but rather "is a good detective story."

Fisher's short stories and sketches reveal the same range
and variety of human experience that he captured in his
full-length novels. Criticism and evaluation of this writer
should be based primarily upon his short stories rather
than upon his novels because he was first and foremost
a writer in that genre. In no way should this sentiment

downgrade his novels; rather it maintains that the principal form in which an author writes provides a more suitable basis for criticism and evaluation. Though Fisher's
full-length novels would appear more than adequate to
establish him as a major contributor to the Negro Renaissance, his reputation must inevitably rise or fall on the
basis of the respect accorded his short stories.

In 1925 **"High Yaller"** won the Amy Spingarn Short Story
Contest sponsored by *The Crisis* magazine. The story is
very much in the "tragic mulatto" tradition, a theme formerly pursued assiduously by black writers. In this case,
Evelyn Brown, a mulatto, is accused by Mayme Jackson,
a darksome woman, of being "color struck." The accusation takes place at a dance which followed a basketball
game at the Manhattan Casino:

> The air was vile—hot, full of breath and choking
> perfume. You were forever avoiding, colliding, making
> time on the same spot. So insulating was the crush that
> you might sway for several minutes near a familiar
> couple, even recognize their voices, yet catch only the
> merest glimpse of their vanishing faces.

Concerned about the grain of truth contained in Mayme's
comment, Evelyn convinces Jay Martin, her unmistakably
black dance partner, to give her the rush. Evelyn does not
want the Jim Crow tag foisted upon her by the Mayme
Jacksons of the world. But, in assessing the reason for her
attraction to Jay, she says, "'he's so—white'." (In manner
and attitudes.)

Jay agrees to her plan and they make the Harlem scene.
During the period of their relationship, each member of the
doomed couple experiences some embarrassment and
hostility. Many persons, both Negro and white, thought
they were an interracial couple. Taboo. Crossing the color
line was frowned upon on both sides. At one point Jay
says:

> "Well, I'll tell you, Ev. This place, like some you
> already know about, has a mixed patronage, see? Part
> jigs, part ofays. That's perfectly all right as long as the
> jigs keep to their own parties and the ofays to theirs.
> But as soon as they begin to come mixed, trouble
> starts. . . . So the management avoids it."

Evelyn calls herself a misfit. And Fisher uses dream sequences to reveal the inner attitudes of both Evelyn and
Jay regarding their relationship. Evelyn's mother, an obviously black woman, restrained any impulse Evelyn may
have had to leave the race, to cross over the color line.
Eventually, the mother dies, Evelyn disappears, and the
police arrest and beat Jay. Formally charged with "resisting arrest," but in actuality detained for "messing" with a
"white" woman. And Fisher, writing of the episode from
Jay's perspective, says:

> What an enormity, blackness. . . . White, the standard
> of goodness and perfection. . . . An instinctive shrinking
> from the dark? He'd seen a little white child run in
> terror from his father once. . . . Instinctive. . . .
> Unbearable.

Writing in *The Crisis* (August, 1928), Allison Davis accused Fisher of sensationalism in **"High Yaller."** He criticized Fisher along with Langston Hughes, George Schuyler, Eugene Gordon, Claude McKay, and Countee Cullen as Negro writers who, "'confessing' the distinctive sordidness and triviality of Negro life, [make] an exhibition of their own unhealthy imagination, in the name of frankness and sincerity." The criticism is caustic, but Fisher finds himself in rather good company.

"Ringtail" (1925) did not evoke the same critical response, but it might have if some critics had displayed the same concern for the intraracial conflict which provides its motif as they showed for the rather realistic presentation Fisher made of the color consciousness pervading the black community to this very day. **"Ringtail"** involves the intraracial relationships which exist between native black Americans and other blacks, in this story, principally West Indians.

Cyril Sebastian Best is a West Indian who made his way to New York by swimming from a ship in New York harbor shortly after he was taken to task by the ship's cook. It appears that Cyril sometimes had difficulty getting along with people: he had a rather large ego. "From those who picked him up exhausted and restored him to bodily comfort," Cyril stole "what he could get and made his way into New York." Fisher describes Cyril in the following manner:

> To him self-improvement meant nothing but increasing these virtues (self-esteem, craftiness, contentiousness, and acquisitiveness), certainly not eliminating or modifying them. He became fond of denying that he was "colored," insisting that he was "a British subject," hence by implication unquestionably superior to any merely American Negro.

The hostility was more than returned. One bright Sunday afternoon as Cyril promenaded down Harlem's Seventh Avenue, he was roughed up a bit by some native black Americans who were led in this sport by Punch Anderson and Meg Minor. Resisting, Cyril was punched in the nose by Anderson who told him, "Now get the hell out o' here, you ringtail monkey-chaser!"

"Monkey-chaser" was a derisive Harlem term for West Indians, and Cyril, offended, vowed revenge. Later, Punch, Meg, and some of their friends discussed the event:

> "There ain't no such thing as a harmless monkey-chaser. . . . If you've done anything to him, he'll get you sooner or later. He can't help it—he's made that way, like a spring."

> "I ain't got a thing for a monk to do, anyhow. . . . Hope Marcus Garvey takes 'em all back to Africa with him. He'll sure have a shipload."

> "You jigs are worse'n ofays. . . . You raise hell about prejudice, and look at you—doin' what you're raising' hell over yourselves."

Though intraracial animosity provides the basic theme for the story, Fisher indicates the basic unity of black people. In describing a card game attended by Punch, Meg, and some other characters he writes: "One player was startlingly white, with a heavy rash of brown freckles and short kinky red hair. Another was almost black, the hair of an Indian and the features of a Moor. The rest ranged between."

Intraracial discord plays a less significant role in **"The City of Refuge"** (1925). For in this story the theme is simply the cruelty of one man toward another, how one man can take advantage of another's friendship. King Solomon Gillis came to New York, to Harlem from his native North Carolina because he had shot a white man. He reached Washington, D.C., where a bootlegger aided his escape with $100 and directions to the place where he longed to come. Concerning the reasons for which Gillis decided that Harlem was the place for him, Fisher writes, "That was the point. In Harlem, black was white. You had rights that could not be denied you; you had privileges, money. It was a land of plenty. . . . The land of plenty was more than that now; it was also the city of refuge."

When "Gillis set down his tan cardboard extension case and wiped his black, shining brow," [he] slowly, spreadingly, grinned at what he saw: Negroes at every turn; up and down Lenox Avenue, up and down 135th Street; big, lanky Negroes, short, squat Negroes; black ones, brown ones, yellow ones . . . here and there a white face drifting along, but Negroes predominantly, overwhelmingly everywhere. . . . This was Negro Harlem."

Early recognized as a new recruit to the Harlem community, Gillis asked a stranger for directions and, immediately, trusted him. Mouse Uggam, the stranger, is in fact from Gillis' hometown, and he helps Gillis get settled in Harlem. In reality Uggam is a dope peddler who wants to transfer his dope business to Gillis because there is some danger that the dope ring may be crashed by the police. Uggam works himself into Gillis' confidence by getting him a job and, later, offering him an opportunity to earn extra money by selling "French Medicine." Gillis, the gullible newcomer to Harlem, the type Harlem treats hard, falls for it all: "'Sure y' get the idea?' Uggam carefully explained it all again. By the time he had finished, King Solomon was wallowing in gratitude."

"'Mouse, you sho' is been a friend to me. Why, 'f 't hadn't been fo' you—'"

Gillis is in business; he learns much about Harlem life. But the ways of the city are hard on those who take it at face value. And "Mouse Uggam," his friend. "Harlem. Land of plenty. City of refuge—city of refuge. If you live long enough—." Fisher writes about life as it is to those who believe, those who dream. It is a harsh reality, but there can be good times along the way. Even Gillis was exultant in his own way, for his own reasons.

In **"The Promised Land"** Fisher explores the impact of the community on an ordinary Harlem family. This theme is similar to **"The City of Refuge"** in that Fisher in both stories reveals the smiling ruthlessness, almost diffidence, and seeming impersonality with which the metropolis, Harlem, favors or disfavors those who view her as either refuge or promise.

Mammy came North to keep house for her two grandsons Wesley and Sam. Together, the cousins left Virginia "to find their fortunes in Harlem." Wesley became a window washer while Sam earned more money as a mechanic. The competition of city life rewarded the cousins differently; it poisoned their relationship. Harlem broke the bond between Wesley and Sam, and "fashioned them a bludgeon with which to shatter their common life." The cousins utilized their new weapon. The hostilities caused by the differences in the rewards the city offered Wesley and Sam were accentuated by a dispute over the affection of a city woman who would not choose between them. Ellie wanted to "play the boobs off against each other, let them strut their stuff." And they did. Mammy just wondered how a girl in "the spring of her life" could subject romance to utility. But Mammy was from a different generation, another lifestyle, school of behavior. As she watched the new generation, a city generation, she pondered:

> But such a dance! The camel walk. Everybody "cameling." Had God wanted man to move like a camel He'd have put a hump in his back. Yet was there any sign of what God wanted in that scene. . . . Skins that he had made black bleached brown, brown ones bleached cream-color; hair that He had made long and kinky bobbed short and ironed dead straight. . . . Where was God in that?

He was somewhere, and perhaps for that reason Mammy attempted to make Ellie choose between Wesley and Sam. The bond broken by the metropolis might somehow be healed by human intervention. But, while Mammy talked of God and sin, Ellie responded, "'Say, what's the idea'?" She refuses to have anything to do with either cousin, and Sam blames Wesley who merely laughs.

> To Sam it was galling, derisive, contemptuous laughter, laughter of victory. Anger, epithets, blows he could have exchanged, but laughter found him defenseless. In a hot flush of rage he drew back a foot and kicked viciously at Wesley's legs.

Still, though the city worked its will on her family, Mammy realizes that in fact it is a promised land: "'New York. Harlem. Thought all along 'twas d' las stop 'fo' Heaven. Canaan hisself. Reg'lar promis' lan'. Well, dat's jus what 'tis—a promis' lan'. All hit do is promise'." And she wonders in the words of the old Negro spiritual:

> Bow low!—How low mus' I bow
>
> To enter in de promis' land?

"Blades of Steel" (1927) must be regarded as one of Fisher's less satisfying short stories. It contains all the elements and displays, as usual, the tremendous range of knowledge the author possessed concerning the black community. Still, the plot is rather too contrived, almost phoney.

The initial setting of the story is a barbershop on 135th Street just prior to the "Barbers' Annual Ball." The street represents the heart and soul of Negro Harlem. "It is common ground, the natural scene of unusual contacts, a region that disregards class. It neutralizes, equilibrates, binds, rescues union out of diversity." At times 135th Street does serve this function, but in **"Blades of Steel"** it serves as a setting for conflict. Eightball-Eddy Boyd and Dirty Cozzens argue as to whom is next in line for a tonsorial job. The actual reason for their dispute is the fact that Eightball Eddy dealt himself consecutive blackjacks in a darkjohn game. He won twenty dollars from Dirty who, of course, thought something was amiss. Dirty has a reputation as an evil man with a blade and he pursues his vendetta with Eightball-Eddy. Pop, proprietor of the barbershop, offers this commentary:

> "They's nineteen niggers 'round Harlem now totin' cuts he gives 'em. They through pullin' knives, too, what I mean. . . . He's that bad. Served time fo' it, but he don't give a damn. Trouble is, ain't nobody never carved him. Somebody ought to write shorthand on his face. That'd cure him."

Later that evening at the Barbers' Annual Ball, Dirty asks Effie, Eightball's girl, to dance; she refuses. Another confrontation between Eightball and Dirty seems inevitable. "Mercy—Lawd have Mercy!" A tune heard often on 135th Street.

> **As a writer, [Fisher] was principally concerned with the presentation of Negro life in Harlem, the capital of the black world, during the Negro Renaissance.**
>
> **—*Oliver Louis Henry***

The conflict which rages through and gives a dark cast to **"Blades of Steel"** transforms itself into the spirit of reconciliation in **"Miss Cynthie"** (1933) which ranks among Fisher's best works. Reconciliation between the generations is the theme of this story. At the request of David Tappen, her grandson, Miss Cynthie comes North, the first time she had been more than fifty miles away from her home town in North Carolina. As a southern matriarch, she is similar to Mammy in **"The Promised Land,"** and Miss Cynthie has something in common with King Solomon Gillis in **"The City of Refuge,"** for they both hail from the same town in North Carolina, Waxhaw. But she is different from both in her acceptance of the new generation, of the city, of Harlem. Fisher provides us with a glimpse of her basic wisdom in a conversation she has with a red-cap upon her arrival in New York:

"Always like to have sump'n in my hand when I walk. Can't never tell when you'll run across a snake."

"There aren't any snakes in the city."

"There's snakes everywhere, chile."

Indeed there are. And Miss Cynthie, who always wanted David to become either a preacher or a doctor, wonders what line of work the city has mandated for him. She had urged him to "always mind the house o' the Lord—whatever you do, do like a church steeple: aim high and go straight." The least she desired for him was that he become an undertaker. Miss Cynthia wanted him to have some contact with the church, no matter how minimal, no matter what form. And the first compliment she gives the city puts her stamp of approval on its churches "fo' colored folks." David does not tell her what his business is because he wants it to come as a surprise. But Ruth, his girl friend, warns him, "You can't fool old folks."

David and Ruth take Miss Cynthie to the Lafayette Theatre. She had always viewed the theatre as the antithesis of the church.

> As one was the refuge of righteousness, so the other was the stronghold of transgression. . . . And not any of the melodies, not any of the sketches, not all the comic philosophy of the tired—and the hungry duo, gave her figure a moment's relaxation or brightened the dull defeat in her staring eyes.

In Miss Cynthie's world, the theatre was the house of the "sinsick, the flesh-hungry mob of lost souls." But David remembered a tune which Miss Cynthie sang when he was young:

> Oh I danced with the gal with the hole in her stockin'
> And her toe kep' a-kickin'
> And her heel kep' a-knockin'
> Come up, Jesse, and get a drink o' gin,
> Cause you near to the heaven as you'll ever get ag'in—

And she understands: "'Bless my soul! They didn't mean nothin'. . . . They jes' didn't see no harm in it'" Miss Cynthie reconciles herself to David's business while David thanked her for always urging him to "aim high."

One can "aim high" in many ways, not the least of which is a rule of the road: "aim high" in steering. This is an elementary driving rule because it decreases the chance of accident, of a mistake. Fisher uses this theme, check the facts—get the big picture—of the situation before making a decision, in **"Dust"** (1931), one of his few non-Harlem stories. The action takes place almost completely in Pard's brand new black and silver roadster. He and Billie, his girl friend, are on an afternoon outing. As they travel along the Connecticut countryside, Pard notes the surprise of those in the automobiles alongside them at the appearance of Negroes in his fine car. Realizing that he and Billie are merely "niggers" to those around them, he says: "Now, damn it, eat niggers' dust.'" Easily his

roadster passes others on the road. But Billie says, "'Horrible thing, prejudice; does you all up. Puffs you out of shape.'"

Pard can outhate whites and he likes it. Still, a yellow coupe with a Georgia license plate passes him:

> "Lyncher. . . . Atta baby—go get 'im—Red-necked hillbilly. . . . Ought to run him off the road anyhow—every cracker less is a nigger more. . . . Listen. . . ."

He indulges himself in a race to catch and pass the Georgia plated car. At a fork in the road, suddenly, another car appeared from a side road, the racers hit their brakes, and the yellow coupe goes off the road. Pard and Billie drive back to see if they can help the driver. "No question of hatred." That driver astonished them.

Not very much astonishes Grammie in **"Guardian of the Law"** (1933), a story similar to **"Blades of Steel"** in that its plot is somewhat outrageous. And the theme, the protection a grandmother feels for her grandson, is a bit trite. On balance, however, the story is more satisfying than **"Blades of Steel."** Grammie, who brought up Sam, her grandson, is proud when he passes the written exam to become a policeman. Yet, she realizes that he was chosen for the appointment over Grip Beasely. For that reason, one afternoon as she watched over 133rd Street from her window-throne, Grammie becomes a bit agitated when she sees Sam go into Beasely's apartment building. As one might expect of a protective grandmother, she goes to investigate.

Gaining entry to Beasely's apartment, Grammie discovers that Judy, Sam's girl, is also there: something is amiss. And, while going through the apartment, Grammie enters like a "terrible angel of vengeance" a room where she finds Sam. Again, like a good grandmother, Grammie foils the plot concocted by Beasely to snare Sam's job. And she tells Sam:

> "You jes' ain't got no sense. Hyeh you is a rookie, on your six months' probation, when the boss-man can drop you fo' anything you do. . . . And you gettin' ready to up and tell 'em that yo' grandmammy—yo' grandmammy! had to come along and help you out. Humph!"

Grammie's account of the episode varies somewhat from the truth, and Judy reminds her of this. Grammie nods and says that when they get as old as she, they too, can lie, but not before; for there is a time and place for everything.

Rudolph Fisher looms large as a writer of stories dealing with life in the black community. He did not attempt to hide, camouflage or apologize for the lives of ordinary black men and women, no matter whether they were "dicties" or "rags." Fisher wrote about them all. As a writer, he was principally concerned with the presentation of Negro life in Harlem, the capital of the black world, during the Negro Renaissance. He knew Harlem through and through. Sometimes he satirizes, as in *The Walls of Jericho,* but at other moments he applauds the particular uniqueness of the people, black people, about whom he wrote. At all times he is honest, and true to his craft. Though basically a middle class Negro, Fisher portrayed the lives of both the classes and the masses through their hearts and languages, in their homes and cabarets, through the prism of this experience. And he, just as they, will endure.

The light touch of Fisher's style:

Rudolph Fisher, who had the lightest touch of all the Renaissance writers, managed an intermingling of kindly satire and bittersweet tensions in his fiction. Although he is well known for his novels, *The Walls of Jericho* (1928), which presents a cross section of black life, and *The Conjure Man Dies* (1932), in which he begins a black tradition of the detective story, it is in such short stories as **"Miss Cynthie," "The City of Refuge,"** and **"High Yaller"** that he achieves a tight form that renders some of the plight of the newly arrived Southern migrant and the tensions of color caste. In such a novel as *The Walls of Jericho* we have good fun and pictures of life that grow serious, but are held in check by a middle-class sense of hearty good will, exemplified by an author expert at pulling strings.

The short stories approach the stark threats of life in the destruction of the idealistic Southern migrant in **"The City of Refuge"** and the hard choices forced by the tensions of color caste in **"High Yaller."** Once again one feels oneself in the presence of a writer of potential greatness. Unfortunately, Fisher died at the age of thirty-seven, so it cannot fairly be said where his talents would have led him. During his brief life, he gave us pictures of the ordinary workaday black who was largely neglected by other Renaissance writers.

George E. Kent, "Patterns of the Harlem Renaissance," in The Harlem Renaissance Remembered, *Dodd, Mead & Co., 1972, pp. 27-50.*

John McCluskey, Jr. (essay date 1981)

SOURCE: "'Aim High and Go Straight': The Grandmother Figure in the Short Fiction of Rudolph Fisher," in *Black American Literature Forum,* Vol. 15, No. 2, Summer, 1981, pp. 55-9.

[*In the following essay, McCluskey examines Fisher's use of the grandmother figure—often in combination with music and religion—as a healing agent for African Americans new to city life.*]

To conceive the Harlem Renaissance, a cluster of socio-cultural concerns and often over-publicized activities,

without regard to the migration of thousands from the rural South and the West Indies is to reduce the Harlem era to a sputtering debate in aesthetics and social history. With hopefully fruitful results we can now build on the works of writers as diverse in method and temperament as Harold Cruse [*The Crisis of the Negro Intellectual,* 1967], Nathan Huggins [*Harlem Renaissance,* 1971], and Malcolm Cowley [*Exiles Return,* 1962], works which have enlarged our sense of the twenties. Yet one point remains clear: without the migration to and ferment in the cities, specifically in New York, there would have been neither a Harlem Renaissance nor New Negro Movement as we know it today. The figures for the migration to Harlem might be familiar now. Between 1914-1918, close to half a million blacks reached Harlem. From 1920-1930, the population of Harlem nearly tripled. The pattern for other northern cities is quite similar, if not identical.

The fiction writers of the Renaissance did not let the impact of the cities on the Southern or West Indian migrants and their institutions go untreated. In fact, well before the twenties, Paul Laurence Dunbar had dealt with the plight of the new arrival in *Sport of the Gods.* James Weldon Johnson had given a strong impression of the effects of the city—some exhilarating, some destructive—in his seemingly effortless *Autobiography of an Ex-Coloured Man,* first published in 1912. Indeed such encounters have been developed in the novels of many American writers before and, with greater consistency, after the turn of the century. The works of William Dean Howells, Frank Norris, Upton Sinclair, Henry Roth, and more recently the works of two native American novelists, N. Scott Momaday and Thomas Sanchez, demonstrate a broad range of treatment of the city's impact on the migrant. I do not argue here, therefore, that the conflict of rural and urban values is a theme unique only to Afro-American writers of the Harlem Renaissance. My concern here is with how Afro-American writers, specifically Dr. Rudolph Fisher, have come to grips with the conflict of nineteenth-century traditions of survival with the swifter, harsher rhythms of the twentieth-century city.

Though it was Harlem which was the mecca for artists, also attracting and developing an urbane and international "community," most of the Renaissance fiction focused on the glittering promises on which Harlem failed to deliver. To the writers of the Harlem Renaissance, the city was a restless temptress, bringing the naive and ambitious alike to destruction. Harlem was a cancer that burned its way into families, churches, and spirits and left them as dry husks, empty memories. The short fiction of Dr. Rudolph Fisher is centered squarely on the adjustment of the rural migrant to the ways of Harlem. In this essay I wish to discuss Dr. Fisher's works as they relate to the tragedies and possible resolutions of the problems of adjustment. I will discuss his development of grandmother figures to whom he would turn so often and consistently in order to dramatize one mode of resolution.

From Fisher's background one might expect different temperament, radically different concerns. Reared in Providence, Rhode Island, Rudolph Fisher (1897-1934) graduated Phi Beta Kappa from Brown University in English and biology. He received his M.A. in English from Brown and then entered Howard University Medical School, graduating in 1924 with highest honors. After a year's internship at Freedman's Hospital in Washington, D.C., Dr. Fisher left for New York where for two years he was a Fellow of the National Research Council, specializing in biology at the College of Physicians and Surgeons of Columbia University. Dr. Fisher then entered the practice of medicine in New York in 1927 and after specialization in roentgenology he opened an x-ray laboratory. A lover of music, he sang with Paul Robeson and arranged musical scores. He was the author of 15 published stories and two novels. Clearly a restless and versatile talent, Fisher was a man interested in many areas of experience.

The short fiction of Dr. Rudolph Fisher is centered squarely on the adjustment of the rural migrant to the ways of Harlem.

—John McCluskey, Jr.

Dr. Fisher's first story, **"City of Refuge,"** was written while he was still in medical school and published in the *Atlantic Monthly* in its February 1925 issue. The story was selected for inclusion in *Best American Short Stories, 1925.* **"Ringtail"** was published in *Atlantic Monthly* three months later. In these two early pieces, the grandmother figure does not appear and the impact of the city is not blunted. The victims are swept under by either their own vindictiveness or Harlem's callousness. The protagonists are men who have floated on seas of delusion. Though the possibilities are certainly there, the setting provides very little that roots them in the big-city reality. Without roots, these men are merely pushed from one situation to the next.

"City of Refuge" introduces King Solomon Gillis, a fugitive from North Carolina who emerges from a subway station into the blare and glare of Harlem. After he becomes accustomed to the blur of colors, the smear of sounds, he is struck by the presence of a black policeman gruffly directing traffic which, of course, includes white drivers. Gillis' thoughts approach awe: "Done died an' woke up in Harlem."

Immediately he is sized up as a "mark" by (the reader learns later) Mouse Uggams, a man who grew up in the same town as Gillis. Mouse befriends him and steers him to a rooming house. Mouse will later urge him to ease a West Indian man out of a job at an Italian grocer's store. In his new job, Gillis unwittingly becomes a contact for cocaine sales and is eventually arrested. He never realizes that he has been part of an elaborate scheme to divert attention of the police from Mouse and his narcotics-peddling partner Edwards. Gillis' demise is therefore predictable, if not inevitable. There is nothing or no one he can lean and depend on, for that figure of trust, that

"home-boy" Mouse Uggams, has been an agent in his destruction.

Two images dominate Gillis' thoughts during the course of the story: the "gal in green stockings," the glamorous promise of the city; and the black policeman, symbol of his potential manhood. Gillis' rapt attention to the girl's legs causes his crash into the Italian grocer, an accident which by a convoluted series of circumstances results in his job at the man's store. That same girl goads him to his final misdirected action, fighting police officers in a cabaret. The other dominant image has, of course, snagged his interest from the beginning. Yet it is a black policeman who has answered the call for help from his fellow officers and who will arrest Gillis. Gillis surrenders, perhaps still reaching out to the only figure still worthy of his trust and admiration. In turn, however, the city of refuge has surrendered its promise of power, sexual/romantic and political.

In **"Ringtail"** the pretty girl of Fisher's first piece and the West Indian immigrant, now the protagonist, comprise part of the dramatic tableau. Supercilious Cyril Sebastian Best has come to Harlem from the West Indies. Best is an elevator and switchboard operator in a rather pompously furnished apartment building, the pomposity easily matching the manners and attitudes of Best.

The piece opens with Best strutting to work, contemptuous of all around him. A group of young men lounge on a street corner, ogling attractive women, exchanging comments on other passersby. One of their favorite games is for one member of the group to push another into a passerby, then fake an apology. Their fun is thereby the sputtering embarrassment of the passerby. Best proves irresistible in his "wide wing-collar, with its polka-dot bow-tie matching the border of the kerchief in his breast pocket . . . his heavy straw hat with its terraced crown and thick saucershaped brim, . . . his white buckskin shoes with their pea-green trimmings . . . his silvertopped ebony cane."

Angered, Best curses Punch Anderson, the culprit. After a brief and heated exchange, Punch strikes Best. Later while at work on the elevator, Best chats briefly with the beautiful Hilda Vogel. Somewhat flattered by her coy attentions, he is about to ask permission to "call" later during the week. Before he can ask, however, she dances off the elevator with the cryptic answer to one of his questions: "I may be in love—you'd never know." Believing the words to be meant for him, Best nearly swoons. However, days later, while listening in on Hilda's telephone line, Best learns that Punch Anderson has asked her out and that she, as coyly as ever, has accepted the invitation. Enraged by the Punch who has delivered two blows to his pride, Cyril Best soon comes upon a means of revenge. Through a dramatic shift in the narrative point-of-view, the reader learns later that Punch has an accident in the elevator. Both legs have been broken. Although Cyril may not win Hilda, he has been able to effect a revenge.

In both stories Fisher rather deftly accentuates the difference between the protagonists and the street-wise Harlemites. He accomplishes this through skillful narrative description and the use of dialogue. On the run from the South where he has shot a white man, King Solomon Gillis steps onto the Harlem pavement. He meets a "little, sharp-faced yellow man" (Mouse Uggams) who gives him a card with the address of a nearby rooming house. Gillis asks for directions.

> "See that second corner? Turn to the left when you get there. Number forty-five's about halfway the block."
>
> "Thank y', suh."
>
> "You from—Massachusetts?"
>
> "No, suh, Nawth Ca'lina."
>
> "Is 'at so? You look like a Northerner. Be with us long?"
>
> "Till I die," grinned the flattered King Solomon.

The contrast in voices, Uggams' transparent flattery about Gillis' place of origin, Gillis' trust of a sharp-faced stranger—all work to show and foreshadow the fugitive in an alien and manipulative environment. Still later, in the final cabaret scene, Gillis spies the girl in green stockings and cannot identify the race of her escort. When he bothers Mouse with the question, Mouse shrugs as if the point is unimportant in the scheme of things.

In **"Ringtail"** the friction between Afro-West Indian and Afro-American is heightened by the dialect and attitudes of Cyril Best. Best is out of touch, his clothes out of style and, even among his West Indian brothers, he seems out of reach, nursing his fantasy of Hilda's love for him. Yet it is the narrator's opening description that best summarizes his personality.

> He became fond of denying that he was "colored," insisting that he was "a British subject," hence by implication unquestionably superior to any merely American Negro. And when two years of contact convinced him that the American Negro was characteristically neither self-esteemed nor crafty nor contentious nor acquisitive, in short was quite virtueless, his conscious superiority became downright contempt.

In both cases Fisher has established distance of the protagonists from the surrounding community. Cyril Best gains a revenge far greater than the insults and still winds up empty-handed. Gullible Gillis has fled a racist South only to be jailed in the city of refuge.

In other short stories Fisher would identify elements that might soften the impact of Harlem on the new arrival. The use of music, specifically the blues, is crucial here and this subject needs close critical attention in its own right. Fisher also addresses the effectiveness of the church and religious attitudes in preserving and keeping intact a moral core in the dizzying whirl of Harlem life. But the subject here is the use of the grandmother figure as it demonstrates the enduring qualities of Southern folk tradition and its ability to touch the lives of the young migrants. Moreover, in subtle ways, the grandmother figure combines Fisher's interests in both music and religion as healing agents.

Sandwiched between the publications of **"City of Refuge"** and **"Ringtail"** was a series of sketches entitled **"The South Lingers On,"** published in *Survey Graphic* in March 1925. With one sketch deleted, the series was reprinted in Alain Locke's *New Negro* as **"Vestiges."** The sketch **"Majutah"** introduces us, albeit briefly, to our first grandmother in Fisher's published fiction. Grandmother is responsible for the upbringing of her granddaughter Majutah ("Jutie," as her grandmother calls her; "Madge," as she prefers to be called by the smarter set). One night Jutie tries to sneak out past her dozing grandmother, but is caught. Fidgeting as she thinks of her date waiting downstairs, she lies about where she is going. Again she is caught.

Yet we learn that somehow Jutie manages to get away and go to the cabaret with her Harry. Much later that night, while Jutie dances to a sinful blues in the cabaret, Grandmother finishes her Bible and broods over her granddaughter and Harlem, "this city of Satan." Harlem has changed Jutie and thousands of others. Where there had been naturalness of expression and feeling, there was now only artificiality, lies. Grandmother cries and prays for Jutie's "lost soul."

In the **"Promised Land"** (*Atlantic Monthly* January 1927), the grandmother figure witnesses a much more dramatic example of destruction. The story—the title of which is freighted with as much irony as **"City of Refuge"**—focuses on two cousins, Wesley and Sam, who vie for the attentions of the attractive Ellie. Their grandmother who has come from the South to live with them is witness to the triangle and is quite aware of the tension mounting between Wesley and Sam. At the outset of the story she watches the activities of a rent party that is taking place directly across the airshaft from her apartment. With horror Grammie then sees her two grandsons square off over Ellie. Grammie hurls her Bible through the window, startling the cousins and temporarily diverting them from self-destruction. When Grammie confronts Ellie about the necessity of making a decision about the two men, she learns that for Ellie there is no urgency. She will judge them ultimately by their capacity to show her a good time.

The day after the confrontation between Ellie and Grammie, Wesley is washing the windows of their fifth floor apartment. Sam enters the room and an argument over Ellie quickly ensues. Sam aims a kick at the one leg Wesley has used to brace himself. After a silent, desperate effort, Wesley loses his balance and falls to his death. Grammie has witnessed his struggle before the fall and perhaps out of her own sense of desperation and despair holds out hope that he is still alive. He had died instantly, however.

The story ends with Grammie reading her Bible at the window. Voices drift up the airshaft from a rent party somewhere below. Sam is with Ellie. Grammie has sworn to the police that Wesley's fall was accidental. She now blends her hymn with the blues drifting up the airshaft. The story ends tragically. Clearly, Grammie's promised land is not the city, but an escape from its sin and raucousness.

Like Majutah's grandmother, Mammy seems quite bewildered by the cold ways of the city. The callousness of Harlem is personified best by the character of Ellie, perhaps a future version of Majutah. When Grammie confronts Ellie with the hope of averting tragedy, Ellie seems indifferent and explains quite calmly how it is to her benefit not to make a decision between Sam and Wesley. Mammy is incredulous.

> Mammy looked at Ellie as she might have looked at the armadillo in the zoo—this strange, unbelievable creature who in the spring of her life subjected romance to utility. For Mammy saw that the girl really preferred Wesley to Sam, yet had no apology of word or manner in prospectively renouncing Wesley's character for Sam's superior pay. Young, pretty, live girls like Ellie should have to be told to consider their suitors' pay. With them it ought to be secondary to youth's more compelling absurdities. But here was a slip of a girl who spoke like a thrice-married widow of fifty.

Mammy proceeds to berate Ellie about the sins of gross materialism, about the greed for money that brought many migrants to the North seeking fortunes. Such a greed forces them away from the matters of the spirit.

> "Hit's sin. Dat's whut 'tis—sin. My people done fo'got dey God, grabbin' after money. I warn 'm fo' dey all lef'. Longin' fo' d' things o' dis worl' an' a-fo'gittin' d' Lawd Jesus. Broke up dey homes in d' country—lef' folks behind sick an' dyin'. . . ."

But Ellie is not moved by this. She suggests that Mammy not meddle in her affairs, curses her, and leaves the room.

Both **"Majutah"** and **"The Promised Land"** present Grandmother figures who look to their Bibles for resolutions that they themselves are unable to effect. In future writings, however, Fisher would attempt to develop more active and complex grandmother characters. There is an identifiable progression from relatively passive grandmothers to those so active the stories border on melodrama. In the later stories, Harlem's glitter still tempts; family stability is still threatened. However, resolutions would be worked out in the context of the stories themselves without much recourse to outside forces, heavenly or otherwise.

In the first scene of **"Lindy Hop,"** an unpublished story presumably written during 1932-1933, young Tillie is explaining to Grandma the importance of her winning a lindy hop contest to be held that night. A glamorous job as a cabaret hostess will be her reward. Grandma hesitates, for she remembers the fate of Tillie's mother, who, after coming to New York, found work in a dance hall and died young. Certainly Grandma does not want Tillie to follow in her mother's footsteps. Like Majutah, however, Tillie

sneaks out anyway and Grandma, unlike Majutah's grandmother, follows her to the ballroom. The older woman balks at the entrance when she hears the music blaring from within. Then, erect, she walks into "the mouth of hell" to rescue her Tillie. She watches the couples transformed by the music from overworked laborers to "jubilant spirits of freedom." Still, however, the dancing and the music are signs of the Devil at work.

By the time the contest begins, Grandma has surrendered to an urge to end the dancing. As Tillie and her partner Solo dance, Grandma has her hand on the fire alarm and hesitates. Solo begins to falter, his steps grow confused. They lose the contest and at the story's end, a weeping and repentant Tillie is comforted by Grandma.

In a second draft of **"Lindy Hop,"** a love triangle is introduced. With Tillie at the center, Pep, a "class" young man with virtuous ambitions, is pitted against Solo, the sport. As Solo and Tillie rehearse for the dance, Pep is growing jealous despite the fact that Solo has taught Pep a few dance steps. Yet, what is more significant about this version of the story is the action of Grandma. After she enters the ballroom, she finds Pep and enters the contest! The crowd is at first bewildered, then delighted. Grandma dances the traditional dances: the reel, quadrille, schottische, and cake-walk. Pep dances the turkey, scrunch, Charleston, and camel. Agility, speed, and gusto are offset by precision, steadiness, and grace. Youth is balanced by age. This theme of balance is the one which Fisher had been working so consistently to integrate into much of his short fiction. The final performance of Grandma and Pep demonstrates the theme quite well. Tillie does not get her hostess job but she is reunited with Pep around a slumbering and triumphant Grandma. Grandma has plunged into the den of iniquity to help her granddaughter and she has taught a younger generation a lesson in dance history and the possibility of fusing the traditional with the modern. She has also summoned strength and memories from reserves of which she was not aware. She emerges unscathed, but weary.

In the last two published stories to include the grandmother figure, we find two characters equally spirited. **"Guardian of the Law,"** published in *Opportunity* in March 1933, presents the loving and feisty Grammie. As a result of hard work and study, her grandson Sam has just won an appointment to the police force. He has begun his six-month's trial work during which he will be closely watched and evaluated by his superiors. Grammie is understandably proud of his achievements, but wary of Grip Beasley who did not get the appointment. To further aggravate Grip, Judy, a mutual interest of Sam and Grip, has announced that she is Sam's girl exclusively. (The romantic triangle is a standard device in much of Fisher's short fiction.)

Grammie's fears are realized when, as she stands at her apartment window, she sees Sam rush into Grip's apartment building. Like Grandma in **"Lindy Hop,"** Grammie does not hesitate to rush down after her grandson. When she gets inside the building she finds that Judy has been forced by Grip and his partner Cowley to lure Sam within. Cowley pulls a gun on Sam, disarms him, and they force him into a distant room of the apartment. Their plan is to force him to drink whiskey and thereby embarrass him in the eyes of his superiors. He would lose his appointment and Grip Beasley with help of his contacts would get the appointment.

Spurred even further by her memory of her days as a fearless youth, Grammie comes to the rescue. With a squirt from a snuff box she momentarily blinds Cowley. Then Sam and Grip wrestle as Grammie shouts directions to Sam.

"Sam, you fool you, turn 'im loose so you can hit 'im. You huggin' 'im like you love 'im. Let him do the huggin'—you hit.—That's better, see? He can outhug you but you can outhit him.—I declare that po'chile look mo' like a gorilla 'n he do like a man. Look out— he'll bite you if he get a chance!—Now—that's it— that's it—now you got 'im. Tho'w 'im down and sit on 'im. Fine. . . ."

Judy returns with two policemen and the day (and the appointment) is saved.

Grammie then weaves a tale for the arresting officers, a story in which Sam has single-handedly freed himself. Her purpose is to erase her presence in the rescue; for Sam's fellow officers to know that he was saved by his arthritic grandmother might prove too embarrassing. When Sam and Judy later protest the yarn in the privacy of Grammie's apartment, she silences them.

"Hush up! . . When y'all get old as I is, y'all can lie too." She considered this a moment, then added, "But not befo'."

By 1933 Fisher's grandmothers are as religious as they were in his stories of the late twenties, though now more quickwitted and physically more assertive. They are not overwhelmed by the evil ways of the city and realize that they cannot wait for good to expel evil. Evil must be actively confronted and rooted out; in this struggle even lies in the service of good are permitted.

Rudolph Fisher's finest short story is **"Miss Cynthie,"** published in June 1933 in *Story* magazine and later reprinted in *Best American Short Stories, 1934.* Since its first publication, the story has been included in countless anthologies of Afro-American literature. In **"Miss Cynthie,"** Fisher avoids the melodrama of **"Guardian of the Law"** and creates a tender portrait of the tough-spirited Miss Cynthie. Plot, theme, and characterization merge to make an entertaining and memorable story.

Miss Cynthie comes to New York to visit her grandson Dave Tappen. She has never been to New York, indeed has never traveled before, though unlike King Solomon Gillis she is blessed with a great deal of mother-wit. At the train station she tells a redcap that he may take her bags but that she will hold on to her umbrella.

"Always like to have sump'm in my hand when I walk. Can't never tell when you'll run across a snake."

"There aren't any snakes in the city."

"There's snakes everywhere, chile."

Such a descriptive stroke distinguishes her instantly from the naive Gillis. Like Gillis, however, she has brought her baggage of idealism to the city. She knows that Dave is a success and she anticipates a respectable profession. He invites her to a theater where she is to learn that he is a highly successful dancer and singer. She gasps at the notion and enters the theater with as much trepidation as the grandmother in **"Lindy Hop."** "She entered the sudden dimness of the interior as involuntarily as in a dream."

Fisher's grandmothers have memories of more secular . . . times of their own youth and these memories permit them to identify more closely with the struggles of Harlem's young.

—John McCluskey, Jr.

She is shocked by what she considers the sinful nature of the music revue and the crowd's response. She is even more surprised when Dave and his girlfriend Ruth cavort on stage. After thunderous applause, Dave reappears on stage. He taps out a rhythm and sings a song taught to him years before by Miss Cynthie. Then he quiets the audience to tell them of the source of his success. It is Miss Cynthie who has taught him to do "like a church steeple—aim high and go straight." He may not have succeeded in a field of which she approved, but he has achieved nonetheless.

As Dave is singing his secular childhood song, Miss Cynthie watches its effect on the audience. They are transformed from a loud and sinful crowd to children, children who share in Dave's memory and remember perhaps a similar song, a similar love and caring. Miss Cynthie concludes that "they didn't mean no harm" in their fervent appreciation of the revue. The crowd, Dave, and Miss Cynthie are brought together in a magic moment of love. Her understanding of an essential innocence and idealism, including her own, that can endure the whirl of the city is important for her acceptance of Dave's work. Dave's singing has allowed all of them in the room to touch and recall an important dimension of themselves. It is Fisher's unmistakable implication that such a dimension is significant enough for hope for a new community in the urban North.

Throughout these stories Fisher does not idealize the South: he does not insist on a return to a lush garden of innocence. The move to the city, the search for a better place, is inevitable. What is crucial is that the positive attributes of the Southern experience—suggested in brief strokes as family and group loyalty, attention to spiritual values—be transplanted in the city.

For the young Harlemites, however, the grandmothers are from another time, relics. The migrants see only their strange old-fashioned habits, smile at their superstitions. Fisher develops this initial distance effectively to show the chasm which must be bridged. For example, Miss Cynthie sees her first talkie film and considers it a "miraculous device of the devil." Majutah's grandmother doesn't permit a telephone in the apartment; she's afraid it would draw lightning. Again, all the grandmothers are steeped in religion and the clash of their beliefs with those of their younger charges creates effects sometimes comic, often poignant.

Miss Cynthie told Dave before he left the South that he could be a preacher or a doctor. If he chooses not to doctor the soul, then he should "doctor the body." If he can't be a physician, he should be a "foot-doctor" or a "tooth-doctor." Failing these, the least he could be is an undertaker. The latter work would keep him "acquainted with the house of the lord."

Except for Ellie's cursing of Mammy and Majutah's and Tillie's plots to flee to the delights of the cabarets, the grandmothers are generally listened to and their corrections, even of strangers, are met with soft-spoken respect. When the redcap says quite innocently that he bets Miss Cynthie will have a good time while visiting New York, she replies, "Musn't bet, chile. That's sinful." In **"Guardian of the Law,"** one policeman responds to Grammie's protecting yarn with an honest, "Well, I'll be doggone." She scolds him, "Muss'n cuss, chile . . . Cussin's a sin." The policeman is humbled briefly, "'Scuse me, ma'am."

All of these touches—the gentle reproaches, the superstitions, the religious beliefs, the caring—work well to characterize the older women and their distance from city ways. In his last three published pieces, Fisher's grandmothers emerge as more than types. They are not developed as saints; they have memories of more secular, sometimes riotous, times of their own youth and these memories permit them to identify more closely with the struggles of Harlem's young.

It might be useful here to note a similar use of female characters in the work of a contemporary Afro-American writer, Ernest J. Gaines. "Auntie" figures appear throughout Gaines' short fiction and novels. Generally they function as the voices of caution and restraint for the driven male protagonists. Yet in his important *Autobiography of Miss Jane Pittman,* Jane learns from the reckless courage of Ned Douglass and Jimmie; she integrates the necessity of direct struggle into her being. At that novel's end, this woman, over a hundred years old, becomes one with a struggle generations old.

As a Harlem Renaissance writer, Rudolph Fisher is unique in his dramatizations of encounters that still shape the

personalities of urban black communities and their institutions. The impact of black migration on the cities and the impact of the cities on blacks have been profound. Despite the seeming euphoria of the white night-visitors and both black and white publicists for Harlem cabarets and the Renaissance, there were sides of Harlem life that were not so well-known. In his first autobiography, *The Big Sea,* Langston Hughes said, ". . . ordinary Negroes hadn't heard of the Negro Renaissance. And if they had, it hadn't raised their wages any." We are indebted to Fisher for giving us a glimpse of that side far from the glitter, indeed for showing both the anguish and the comedy of new arrivals trying to find their balance and seek clarity and purpose in a new and often indifferent city.

While Jean Toomer presented his messianic figures and arresting images which only suggested a possible harmony of rural and urban sensibilities, while Zora Neale Hurston barely engaged the urban setting, while Nella Larsen chose to deal with the dilemmas of characters in the context of a professional class, Rudolph Fisher treats the concerns of the workaday Harlemite. As a fiction writer he joins Langston Hughes in shaping a significant body of work which consistently reflects the trials and triumphs of the early urbanization of Black America. In Fisher's more mature short fiction, bridges are sought and a dialogue develops. In the dialogue between young and old, between traditional and modern, the result can be understanding and growth.

John McCluskey, Jr. (essay date 1982)

SOURCE: "Healing Songs: Secular Music in the Short Fiction of Rudolph Fisher," in *CLA Journal,* Vol. 26, No. 2, December 1982, pp. 191-203.

[*In the following essay, McCluskey argues that Fisher transplants folk vernacular, through music, to the urban setting, and incorporates it into his stories where it serves as both a framing device and a refrain.*]

In the preface to the first edition of the *Book of American Negro Poetry,* published in 1921, James W. Johnson insisted that the black American poet find a form "that will express the racial spirit by symbols from within rather than symbols from without, such as the mere mutilation of English spelling and pronunciation." Johnson proceeded to relate the stifling effects which the minstrel and Plantation School traditions had on the use of dialect. Perhaps a time would come when attitudes toward the use of dialect would mature, but that time, at least to Johnson's way of thinking, was not the decade of the twenties. Yet, Johnson continues, "There is no reason why these poets should not continue to do the beautiful things that can be done, and done best, in the dialect."

Johnson's statement is interesting for both the sense and the timing of it. Coming as it did in the first years of one of the most eventful decades in Afro-American cultural history, the statement both reviews past difficulties in utilizing the raw materials of Afro-American folk life in poetry and anticipates the extensive attempts of younger poets such as Langston Hughes and Sterling Brown to use folk materials honed to a sharp political cutting edge. If we can broaden Johnson's "dialect" somewhat to "vernacular" in order to include not only folk speech, but also elements of black folk life (religious sermons, sacred and secular music) articulated by that speech, we can further appreciate the implications of this statement. At the turn of the century that group of writers that appropriated black folk materials for literary uses emphasized the bizarre and the folksy, utilizing the double vision of the anthropologist and the sentimentalist longing for the "good ole days befo' de wah." Further, if we can substitute "writer" for Johnson's "poet," then the charge for a new generation of black writers, based primarily in the cities, comes clearer: how could the vernacular be rescued from the exhausted soil of rural local color and transplanted in the urban hot houses in poetry, fiction, and drama? Still further, after the transplanting, how do these writers nurture the forms that speak more broadly (and Johnson clearly insisted upon the ideal of universality in his preface and in all his critical statements) and yet retain a cultural integrity?

As suggested above, some members of a younger generation of poets responded to Johnson's call in vigorous and exciting ways. The early experiments of Langston Hughes are well known and have been commented upon fruitfully. Johnson himself would create a new form without the use of dialect in his *God's Trombones* (1927). In his *Southern Road* (1932) Sterling Brown created blues ballads which, in ways often humorous, indicated Southern racial mores and celebrated the toughness of black traditions. Johnson's challenge was met most consistently in the poetry of the period.

In fiction, however, the experimentation with vernacular beyond background and local color was rare. Jean Toomer in 1923 would burst on the scene with *Cane,* the haunting imagery of which was able to shrewdly suggest a different coloring of the Southern landscape. There were other prose writers of the period who, incidentally, were more familiar with black idioms than Toomer and attempted extensive applications of black oral expressions to creative prose. They included most prominently Langston Hughes, Zora Neale Hurston, and Rudolph Fisher. Though Hughes seemed equally at home in urban and small-town settings and though Hurston would work exclusively with the rural South, Rudolph Fisher would consistently choose the city, or, more specifically, Harlem, to work out the problems of a rhetoric of vernacular that would not limit his theme. It is the purpose of this paper to call attention to his specific uses of music in short fiction. His early attempts at involving the vernacular in direct and fresh ways, coupled with his concern for the plight of the Southern migrant in Harlem in a period of extensive urbanization of black America, mark him as a writer and chronicler far more important than critical attention has thus far suggested.

Born in Washington, D.C., and reared in Providence, Rhode Island, Rudolph Fisher (1897-1934) graduated Phi Beta

Kappa from Boston University in English and biology. He received his M.A. in English from Brown and then entered Howard University Medical School, graduating in 1924 with highest honors. After a year's internship at Freedman's Hospital in Washington, D.C., Dr. Fisher left for New York, where for two years he was a Fellow of the National Research Council, specializing in biology at the College of Physicians and Surgeons of Columbia University. Dr. Fisher then entered the practice of medicine in New York in 1927, and after specialization in roentgenology, he opened an x-ray laboratory. A lover of music, he sang with Paul Robeson and arranged musical scores. He was the author of fifteen published stories (several of them for juvenile audiences) and two novels, *The Walls of Jericho* (1928) and *The Conjure Man Dies* (1936). Fisher's writing career had an auspicious beginning. His first published piece, **"The City of Refuge,"** was written while he was still in medical school and published in *The Atlantic Monthly* in February 1925. The story was selected for inclusion in *Best American Short Stories, 1925.* His last piece was published one month after his death. The piece was **"John Archer's Nose"** and was published in *Metropolitan Magazine* in its first and only number, January 1935. Between the piece on the fall of King Solomon Gillis, a newly arrived Southern migrant to Harlem, and the detective story, most of Fisher's pieces dealt with the struggle for the achievement of a humane ethic in the seemingly indifferent yet tantalizing Harlem. This struggle was informed by memory of a more tightly knit Southern community. The Southern traditions is often symbolized by lyrics from spirituals; the Northern urban tradition, by the raucous cry of blues, the siren call of jazz. The setting for the secular music was usually a cabaret, speakeasy, or ballroom.

. . . . .

By the time Fisher developed his pieces in the mid-twenties, there was no shortage of the cabaret-dance scenes in American fiction. How he would extend the possibilities of that stock scene, how he would attempt to incorporate music more deeply into the fabric of his short stories is what is at issue here. Throughout his brief writing career, Fisher would address the problem of the meaningful uses of vernacular. His growth in this direction was steady.

> **Most of Fisher's pieces dealt with the struggle for the achievement of a humane ethic in the seemingly indifferent yet tantalizing Harlem.**
>
> —*John McCluskey, Jr.*

In **"City of Refuge,"** King Solomon Gillis' final betrayal and fantasy is played out against the background of jazz, for it is in a speakeasy that he sees the girl with the green stockings dancing with a white man. It is there, after a struggle with the police, that he confronts his adopted symbol of manhood, the black policeman, before he ceases his confused struggle. In **"High Yaller,"** published nine months later, a popular lyric operates as a mocking refrain which establishes the plot's ultimate irony.

"High Yaller," one of Fisher's few pieces to treat the passing theme, centers on the frustrations of the fair-skinned Evelyn. Eager to be accepted more fully into the black community, Evelyn seems embarrassed by her light skin. In the story's first scene, while dancing with her darker-skinned escort, Jay Martin, she is stung by a remark she has overhead. A lyric from the bandstand forces the pain even deeper.

> Oh Miss Pink thought she knew her stuff,
> But Miss High Brown has called her bluff.

Bristling, Evelyn asks Jay, "Can you imagine what it's like to be white?" Despite her initial hurt, however, she decides Jay is quite "white" after he has forced a loud-talking ruffian from their presence. She soon insists on immersing herself in the life of Harlem—in blackness, if you will. While visiting an after-hours joint, the couple is subtly deflected to a side-room; the dinner-coated attendant has mistakenly identified Evelyn as white and the presence of mixed couples would surely bring trouble in the shady establishment. When Jay reveals this to Evelyn, she wails. Drifting from below "like a snicker" comes the fragment of the song "Yaller Gal's Gone Out o'Style."

In a later scene while visited by a phantom nightcaller, a nightcaller (her conscience?) who taunts her for her decision not to pass for white and thereby end her anguish, Evelyn pauses. The bizarre dialogue has been interrupted by the whistling of a nightwalker on the street below. Evelyn recognizes the melody fragment as "Yaller Gal's Gone Out o'Style."

Soon afterwards Evelyn's mother dies and Evelyn disappears. Jay is picked up by racist police who believe that he is publicly dating a white woman. After a beating in the police torture-chamber and a warning to leave white women alone, Jay is released. In the story's last scene, thoughts of racial friction flit through his mind as he sits in a movie theater. With a start he notices Evelyn in the audience. Her escort is white: Jay realizes that she has decided to pass for white. He rushes from the theater with the orchestra's familiar refrain "like a loud guffaw," "Yaller Gal's Gone Out o'Style."

Music in this early piece functions as an ironic frame about—and refrain within—the story. The pain of the passing dilemma has shifted from Evelyn to Jay in his consequent sense of loss. Indeed the "yaller gal" is no longer out of style but also out of his life. The song line cruelly mocks the tragic motions of their lives.

A similar refrain-and-frame mode is at work in **"The Promised Land,"** published in January 1927. Mammy has moved from the South to live with her two nephews in Harlem. She witnesses the decadence of Harlem street life, wit-

nesses the developing jealousy over the attractive, though heartless, Ellie. As the piece progresses, the reader watches the conflict between the two men deepen. In a playful scuffle, one of the nephews falls from a window to his death. In shock, Mammy is helpless. The piece is framed by the raucous blues from a rent party and the triumph of the secular music over Mammy's softly hummed spiritual. In the opening scene, Mammy sits in a window, her Bible in her lap, and watches her two nephews in an apartment across an air shaft. As they prepare to fight over Ellie, Mammy hurls her Bible into the room, temporarily ending their conflict. In the final scene the laughing Ellie dances with Sam, and Mammy can only hum her tune in defeat. She can only witness and warn; she cannot direct the lives of her nephews. In this piece Mammy, the attendant to a sacred flame, to a tradition of warmth and close kinship ties, retreats in horror and in seeming resignation before the destructive forces of city life.

What is unique about this piece is the foreshadowing of an issue that Fisher would continue to inspect: the conflict between the fast-paced urban and secular life and the traditional ties with family and church in the South. The piece also introduces for the first time in his fiction the important Grannie figure, who would represent the South, memory, and humanity in the Fisher equation.

"Common Meter" (1930) and **"Blades of Steel"** (1927) develop in their separate ways concerns already established in **"High Yaller"** and **"The Promised Land."** Yet in these two pieces, Fisher utilizes secular music in ways significantly different from before. In **"Common Meter"** the business of Bus Williams, the darker-skinned protagonist, is music. Bus Williams and Fessenden "Fess" Baxter are rivals for the crowd's adulation and the affections of Miss Jean Ambrose. Again, as in **"High Yaller,"** the opening scene is a dance hall and Fisher swiftly uses the setting to introduce the conflict. While Bus's orchestra plays a rather popular "She's Still My Baby," Fess first sights the attractive Miss Ambrose, who is working as a hostess. His interest soars. However, he soon learns that Bus has gotten Jean the job and that Bus has romantic designs on her. Undaunted by her possible allegiance to Bus, Fess dances with her and makes a pass. Jealous of her apparently rapt attention to Fess's whispers, Bus watches helplessly from the bandstand and sends his orchestra through two blues numbers. The sincere emotion of the blues instantly counters the earlier relatively innocuous tune and, of course, reflects Bus's hurt. Its power strikes a responsive chord, however, in the audience's collective soul.

The climax of the story is the jazz contest a few nights later, a contest in which the winner will receive the large victory cup and, presumably, the undivided attention of Jean Ambrose. The reader learns that the drum sheets on the trap and bass of Tappen, Bus's master percussionist, have been cut, rendering his drums useless. It is obvious that the devious Fess will stop at nothing to win. With poor audience response to the first two of the scheduled three numbers, Bus is desperate to find a means to catch up with and surpass Fess's score.

Sharing his desperation, Jean provides the key: play a blues and turn the blues into an old-fashioned shout in which the audience can join with claps and stomps. The stomping feet of the musicians would substitute for the pulse of the bass drum. The transformation of the audience is instantaneous. They become one with the music and, surprisingly, one with their pasts:

> They had been rocked thus before, this multitude. Two hundred years ago they had swayed to that same slow fateful measure, lifting their lamentation to heaven, pounding the earth with their feet, seeking the mercy of a new God through the medium of an old rhythm, zoom-zoom. They had rocked so a thousand years ago in a city whose walls were jungle, forfending the wrath of a terrible Black god who spoke in storm and pestilence, had swayed and wailed to that same slow period, beaten on a wild boar's skin stretched over the end of a hollow treetrunk.

Bus's orchestra reconstructs that moment that profoundly ties past to present. The blues statement, "St. Louis Blues," taps a socio-historical chord which stretches to the sacred.

Needless to say, the villain Baxter in his final number cannot touch the depths that Bus's authentic blues have reached. Flashy craft without the emotional commitment cannot do the trick. Though by a final ruse Baxter manages to win the victory cup, Jean Ambrose renounces any claim he might make on her attention. Bus's group strikes up "She's Still My Baby" as a final mocking retort.

Far more than a frame and internal refrain, secular music here binds and connects an individual call of romantic distress with collective memory. Interestingly enough, he has foreshadowed such an effect on the audience in the first scene. However, at that time, the effect was specific to the pain of lost love. In the final scene the effect goes beyond the secular-romantic mode to a sacred moment suggesting a larger spiritual tie. Though thematically curative it is technically unsatisfactory here given its quickness. The attempt is notable, for it signals a gesture toward the use of music as a bridge which would not be fully developed until quite late in his brief career as a writer.

In **"Blades of Steel"** another rivalry between two young men is worked. Once again, the darker-skinned protagonist, in this case "Eight-Ball" Eddie Boyd, is countered by the much lighter-skinned Dirty Cozzens. And once again the essential conflict is suggested early. On the eve of the Barber's Annual Ball, Eight-Ball has stopped in a crowded barbershop to get the necessary trim for the dance. As he is about to climb into the barber's chair, Eight-Ball is stopped by Dirty Cozzens, who claims that it is his turn. A scuffle is averted by the pretty Effie, who runs a beauty parlor across the street from the barbershop. Later, Eight-Ball escorts Effie to the dance, where they meet Cozzens

again. Rebuffed by Effie when he asks for a dance, Cozzens deftly slashes Eight-Ball's coat while the couple dances. The reader soon learns the root cause of the conflict: Cozzens is still angry at losing too much money to Eight-Ball in a crap game. A skilled veteran with the razor, Cozzens wants to push Eight-Ball into a fight. The stage for the showdown is Teddie's place. A blues, its lyrics the combination of the secular and sacred, establishes background.

> My man was comin' to me—said he'd
>   Let me know by mail,
> My man was comin' to me—said he'd
>   Let me know by mail—
> The letter come and tole me—
> They'd put my lovin' man in jail.
>
> Mercy-Lawd, have mercy!
>   How come I always get bad news?
> Mercy-Lawd, have mercy!
>   How come I always get the blues?

Cozzens demands the money he has lost and the fight ensues. Eight-Ball gains the upper hand and is about to deliver the finishing blow when his arm is stopped in mid air by the lyric "Have Mercy—Lawd, Have Mercy." He spares Cozzens and sends him slinking off to the nearby hospital. The reader observes that Eight-Ball has beaten Cozzens with the aid of the street-wise Effie.

Fisher's short fiction demonstrates an often entertaining approach to weaving the vernacular into the fabric of creative prose.

—John McCluskey, Jr.

Though relatively minimal in the story, the blues-line has entered the plot and helped direct its essential action. This blues by Tessie Smith, "a curious mingling of the secular and religious," speaks to dual experiences: the anger of Eight-Ball at the hi-jinks of Dirty Cozzens and the resolution which, oddly in a blues tune, approaches prayer. Although the tale is thoroughly secular, it is interesting that the song's final plea, seemingly out of context, is so logical for the action.

Fisher's choice of lyric is important in the way in which it demonstrates his notion of the unity of the sacred and secular modes of experience. That unity is built on a tension that characterizes Fisher's mature fiction: that struggle is between the actions and sensibilities (violence and indifference to family or ethnic loyalties) shaped by the urban context and the more traditional ethic of intragroup caring and generosity. However, the mode for bringing these actions into some constructive merger was not completely clear to Fisher when he wrote **"Blades of Steel."** As short fiction the piece remains a compact melodrama of

Harlem street life. In the evolving Fisher canon, both **"Common Meter"** and **"Blades of Steel"** introduce ways in which a music lyric can directly enter the narrative and alter the action.

The sacred-secular tension, the grandmother figure who symbolizes the Southern tradition hoping to transplant human concerns in Harlem, the lyric which drives the plot toward a wholesome resolution—all of these are brought together in one of Fisher's last published pieces, the popular **"Miss Cynthie."** The story was published in *Story* magazine in June 1933 and reprinted in *Best American Short Stories, 1934*. Since that time, the piece has been included in numerous anthologies of Afro-American literature. In the opening scene, Miss Cynthie arrives in New York to visit her grandson Dave Tappen. She has never been to New York; indeed, she has never traveled far from her hometown in North Carolina. She has learned that Dave is a success and she anticipates his achievement within a respectable profession. When he invites her to the theater to watch the musical review in which he stars, she is disappointed. A stage career is not her idea of a respectable profession. Her disappointment quickly shifts to shock as she watches Dave and her girl friend cavort on the stage much to the delight of the crowd. After a thundering ovation, Dave reappears on stage. He taps out a rhythm and sings a song taught to him years ago by Miss Cynthie. The song is instantly recognized by the audience. He then quiets the crowd to explain the true source of his success: the feisty Miss Cynthie, who has instructed him to do "like a church steeple—aim high and go straight."

As Dave sang his childhood song, Miss Cynthie has watched the lyric's effect on the crowd. The young men and women have been transformed from a loud and sin-loving crowd to children, children who share in Dave's memory and perhaps recall a similar song and caring from their pasts. The movement is from the throes of decadence to relative innocence. Miss Cynthie concludes that "they didn't mean no harm" in their fervent appreciation of the musical revue. In addition, the song seems to have unlocked a door to Miss Cynthie's secular past, for as she moves out of the theater, she pats her foot in time to the jazz rhythms of the orchestra's recessional.

The transformational and binding aspect of black music functions credibly in this place, since it operates through an agent who comprises the dual aspect in dynamic, comic, and moving ways. Miss Cynthie's thinking is not so rigid that she cannot accept an aspect of her own past. Incidentally, there were at least two other models for Miss Cynthie in two earlier, though less successful, stories. Grammie in **"Guardian of the Law"** takes matters into her own hands and rescues her nephew, a rookie policeman, from the clutches of two thugs. In an alternative ending in an unpublished story, **"Lindy Hop"** (c. 1932-33), Grandma wins a dance contest in order to indirectly dissuade her granddaughter from working as a ballroom hostess. She dances the traditional dances (reel, cake-walk, etc.) while her much younger partner dances the modern danc-

es (Charleston and turkey trot). Youth is balanced by age here. For both stories, the older female figure is driven to seemingly unlikely actions through love.

It is Miss Cynthie's love that insists on forgiving both Dave for his choice of profession and simultaneously the young crowd for their seeming fixation with decadence. The snatch of children's rhyme is part of an informing tradition that can open up a different aspect of their lives, can deflect them from a headline flight to moral chaos, can summon the memory and possibility of love.

The capacity of a lyric to function in this way is far more credible and effective in **"Miss Cynthie"** than in **"Common Meter."** The sacred-secular duality only described in **"Blades of Steel"** is affectingly personified with Miss Cynthie, and as a result, the latter piece brings the duality into far better focus. The concerned Grandmother in **"The Promised Land"** has provided the key to deliverance in **"Miss Cynthie."** Interesting though rather contrived elements in the earlier stories are better integrated in the more mature work.

Fisher's development of music in his short pieces—the evolution from simple background and mood-setting to active agent—signals his consistent interest in demonstrating the importance of music and myth in the lives of ordinary folk. In this connection one thinks of Sterling Brown's moving tribute of Ma Rainey and the power of her performances:

> I talked to a fellow, an' the fellow say,
> "She jes' catch hold of us, somekindaway.
> She sagge Backwater Blues one day:
>
> And den de folks, dey natchally bowed dey heads
>   an' cried,
> Bowed dey heavy heads, shet de moufs up tight
>   an' cried,
> An' Ma lef' de stage, an' followed some de folks
>   outside.
>
> Dere wasn't much more de fellow say.
> She jes gits hold of us dataway.

The performance and the lyric are more than entertainment; they touch a profoundly collective chord.

The notion of blues/jazz-as-statement might be obvious enough to us today, informed as we have been by close studies of secular music forms by numerous writers. However, during the Harlem Renaissance few writers and intellectuals took the evolving form of jazz and urban blues seriously. Nathan Huggins has commented on the matter in *Harlem Renaissance:*

> Of course, they [Harlem intellectuals, except Langston Hughes] all mentioned it as background, as descriptive of Harlem life. All said it was important in the definition of the new Negro. But none thought enough about it to try and figure out what was happening. They tended to view it as folk art—like the spirituals and the dance—the unrefined source for the new art. Men like

James Weldon Johnson and Alain Locke expected some race genius to appear who would transform that source into *high* culture. That was, after all, the dream of Johnson's protagonist in *Autobiography of an Ex-Coloured Man* as he fancied symphonic scores based on ragtime.

Notwithstanding the purpose of the protagonist in his only novel, Johnson does seem to have taken ragtime and blues more seriously as forms by the time he wrote his preface. However, the spirit of Huggins' argument is accurate when applied to both Alain Locke and W. E. B. DuBois. In addition, Huggins singled out Langston Hughes as the only writer to take the new forms seriously. Rudolph Fisher must be credited with that same seriousness. His short fiction demonstrates an often entertaining approach to weaving the vernacular into the fabric of creative prose. Though perhaps infrequently, Johnson's challenge was nevertheless met in both prose and poetry before the lights of the Renaissance grew dim.

Eleanor Q. Tignor (essay date 1982)

SOURCE: "The Short Fiction of Rudolph Fisher," in *Langston Hughes Review,* Vol. 1, No. 1, Spring, 1982, pp. 18-24.

[*In the following essay, Tignor traces the principal themes, character types, and settings in Fisher's short fiction.*]

In 1925, Rudolph Fisher broke into the predominantly white publishing world with his short story **"City of Refuge,"** a triumph commented upon in this letter from Arna Bontemps:

> I saw and talked with Rudolph Fisher frequently between the date of publication of his story **"City of Refuge"** in the *Atlantic Monthly* and August 1931 when I left New York. Earlier Countee Cullen had told me that someone had told him about a young writer from Washington who had just sold two stories to the *Atlantic.* This news had gone around literary circles in Harlem, because up to that time none of the young writers of the New Negro Movement had been able to break into that magazine. So the stage was set, and **"City of Refuge"** created something of a sensation.

Bontemps further remarked:

> I met Bud, as we called Fisher, some months later, and I remember when he set up his practice on 7th Avenue. . . . Bud was clever, facile. . . . His health seemed exceptional, so his early death was more than shocking. He was indeed part of the spirit of the Harlem Renaissance.

Before his premature death at age thirty-seven, seventeen other of Dr. Fisher's short stories had been published, five of which are vignettes with the all-inclusive title **"South Lingers On"** (called by Alain Locke **"Vestiges, Harlem Sketches"** and given four subtitles: **"Shepherd, Lead Us," "Majutah," "Learnin'," and "Revival"**), published in the

1925 special issue of *Survey Graphic* and two of which are little known children's stories with the same young boy (Ezekiel) as the central character, published in *Junior Red Cross News.* The other published stories came out in subsequent issues of *The Atlantic,* in *McClure's, The New York News, Opportunity, Crisis,* and *Story.* Through a communication with Rudolph Fisher's sister, Pearl Fisher, I discovered four unpublished stories: **"The Lost Love Blues,"** a three-part, 46-page story; **"The Lindy Hop,"** a story in three versions (an incomplete handwritten manuscript of fourteen pages, with many revisions, and two typewritten manuscripts of three parts each, with major differences only in the ending, one having twenty-five pages and the other, which seemed to be Fisher's preference, having twenty-three); a 19-page story, **"Across the Airshaft,"** and the 24-page **"The Man Who Passed"** or **"False Face"** (with both titles and a third undecipherable one deleted). These manuscripts, as well as a slightly modified version of **"Miss Cynthie,"** better known in its published form, are all undated but were typed by the same Broadway typing and mimeographing service.

Thematically, Fisher's short fiction might be grouped in five somewhat overlapping categories: vestiges of the South and the promise of Harlem (**"City of Refuge," "Lost Love Blues,"** and the five-part **"South Lingers On,"** including **"Shepherd, Lead Us,"** the Jake Crimshaw sketch, **"Majutah," "Learnin'," and "Revival"**); the conflict of generations (**"Fire by Night," "The Lindy Hop,"** and **"Miss Cynthie"**); foul play in Harlem (**"Guardian of the Law," "The Backslider," "Blades of Steel," "Across the Airshaft,"** and **"Common Meter"**); problems of prejudice (**"High Yaller," "The Man Who Passed"** or **"False Face," "Dust,"** and **"Ringtail"**); the child in Harlem (**"Ezekiel"** and **"Ezekiel Learns"**).

All of the stories except **"Dust,"** set on a Connecticut highway, take place in Harlem. To establish setting and atmosphere, the author often began with extensive descriptive detail, as in **"Fire by Night"**:

> Lenox Avenue arises in a park, flaunts a brief splendor, dies and is buried in a dump. From 110th Street it marches proudly northward with the broad grandeur of a boulevard. Fatal pride. Within half a dozen blocks comes sudden hopeless calamity—a street-car line slips in from a side street . . . deals the highway its deathblow. . . . Ugly, cheap little shops attack it, cluster brutally over it, subway eats wormily into it. Waste clutters over it, odors fume up from it, sewer-mouths gape like wounds in its back. Swift changes of complexion come—pallor—grayness—lividity. Then, less than a mile beyond its start, the Avenue turns quite black.

A few pages later, he embellished the description:

> Between Lenox and Seventh Avenue lives Harlem's middle class, flanked on the east by rats, dicties on the west. . . . This central strip is in truth the colony's backbone. Here live its laborers, haulers, truck-drivers, carpenters, chauffeurs, mechanics; here live its steady, dependable, year-around wage-earners, family providers.

Its businesses fringe and invest this strip and subsist largely upon it. But those who own the businesses and the strip have moved across Seventh Avenue, occupying the so-called private houses of the upper two hundreds. When they move, they move westward and northward: Edgecombe, St. Nicholas, Morningside . . .

Though some of the stories allude to Strivers Row and Sugar Hill, making the unknowing reader aware of their existence, his stories were usually not set in these dickty sections. While Tom Edwards' home in **"The Man Who Passed"** was an attractive yellow brick house on a quiet street, most of the dwellings Fisher made use of were single rooms, sometimes with one window opening onto an airshaft, from which emerged the noises and odors of many families, and small flats. The passing Perryn Joel went into a crowded, dingy, cheap apartment building with unkempt backyards.

Harlem was referred to as a "city of Satan," a "great, noisy, heartless, crowded place where . . . night was alive and morning dead." Through the stories, one gets an excellent indication of the places of nighttime entertainment: the cabarets, the center of Harlem's 1920's night life, often located in basements, blasting with blues and jazz, and featuring a brown-skinned female vocalist. Fisher set his dances at the Manhattan Casino and the Arcadia Ballroom, which featured dance and jazz contests, as in the stories **"The Lindy Hop"** and **"Common Meter."** The Savoy Ballroom is also alluded to. Dance halls were frequently the gathering places for the Negro masses in the 1920's. Popular dances performed or referred to are the Charleston, camel, fishtail, turkey, geche, blackbottom, scronch, skate, and lindy hop. One theatre is shown, the Lafayette, with a stage show featuring a Negro tap dancer and his female partner, managed by two white men. Only one movie house serves as a setting for a Fisher scene, but it is not associated with an actual place.

The pool parlor, often with a gambling room in the rear, and the bar are shown as major social centers for men— places for talking, drinking, gambling, sometimes arguing and fighting. The barbershop is also a place of gossip and in one story (**"Blades of Steel"**) a place of discord. A realist, Fisher did not cover up the fact that Blacks in Harlem sometimes used razor blades and knives as weapons (e.g., Dirty Yaller in **"Blades of Steel"**). His stories reflect the widespread existence of bootlegging and dope peddling, but he did not attack these practices as social evils. They were interwoven into the narratives without much exact detailing. Two bootleg victims died (a child in **"Lost Love Blues"** and a man in **"Fire by Night"**). A naive migrant (Gillis of **"City of Refuge"**) was shown as the dupe of a dope racketeer; Tom Edwards, the dope peddler in the same story, received police protection. The white policemen were shown as condoners of crime or as aliens in Harlem. Fisher pictured them as patrolling the streets in a group, never singly. It was said in **"The Man Who Passed"** that a new police captain "made the mistake" of sending some white policemen on a raid. One character (Jay in **"High Yaller"**) was à victim of police injustice and brutality.

Storefront churches or house churches, popular when Fisher was writing, are seen in his stories, for example, in **"The Backslider."** No scenes were set in the large Negro-owned churches, but these were observed with delight by Miss Cynthie upon her arrival in Harlem. A camp meeting of the time was shown in **"Revival."** The services were emotional ones at which a usually eloquent but unsettled minister preached of the wrath of a demanding, unmerciful God and of what one might expect if His will were not heeded: "maddening thirst for the drunkard; for the gambler insatiable flame, his own greed devouring his soul," to which his flock responded with amens of approval, loud moans, nodding of heads, rhythmic swaying, and "Help him, Lord!" "Preach the word!" "Glory!" No cultists found their way into Rudolph Fisher's narratives; Father Divine did not become extremely popular until 1935 and Daddy Grace until even later.

Allusions are made to the Garvey Movement. Roanna in **"The Man Who Passed"** asked the white Perryn if he had heard of the Movement. While some non-American Blacks in **"Ringtail"** differed in their opinions about going back to Africa, in the same story some American Blacks wanted to see them sent to Africa during the Movement.

Harlem was further shown through Fisher's characterizations. Gillis, in the **"City of Refuge,"** in Harlem for the first time, saw:

> big, lanky Negroes, short, squat Negroes; black ones, brown ones, yellow ones; men standing oddly on the curb, women, bundle-laden, trudging reluctantly homeward, children rattle-trapping about the sidewalks . . .

Miss Cynthie could tell, because of the people, that she was in Harlem:

> Not just a change of complexion. A completely dissimilar atmosphere. Sidewalks teeming with leisurely strollers . . . Boys in white trousers, berets, and green shirts, with slickened black heads and proud swagger. Bare-headed girls in crisp organdie dresses, purple, canary, gay scarlet . . .

Fisher sometimes seemed to revel in his descriptions of the diverse colors, sizes, and shapes of his Negro Harlemites.

There were certain types of characters, however, whom he favored. One was the naive Southerner who came to Harlem, usually expecting it to be the promised land, the land of plenty, sometimes a city of refuge. This type of character seemed to have heard the call of Northern newspapers. "Come North, where there is more humanity, some justice and fairness." Once in New York, however, he generally had difficulty finding work because of a lack of "city" skills. And too trusting, he was often victimized by a scheming Negro Harlemite. The best examples of the naive Southern migrant were Jed and Cinnamon, in **"Lost Love Blues,"** who enthusiastically accepted their landlord's offer of a share in a bootlegging business, foolishly thinking he was being generous when in actuality his aim was self-protection; King Solomon Gillis, in **"City of Refuge,"** who thought that he was being given the opportunity to earn some money by merely distributing some pills, when in reality he was peddling dope; Ebenezer Grimes, in **"The Backslider,"** who when voted out of a Baptist church, did not realize that this was not an act of God, but thought, instead, that God had forsaken him. Similarly, Jake (part II of **"South Lingers On"**), though rejected everywhere he sought employment, refused to believe that Harlem, the perfect place for Negroes, had nothing to offer him, and Wesley (**"The Promised Land"**), who earned little money and was naive about Harlem's fun-loving, materialistic girls, tried to gain the love of one of them, not realizing that she was primarily interested in the money that he could spend on her.

The grandmother was another frequently delineated character. Strong, usually wise and witty, she was often portrayed as head of the family, a then authentic characterization stemming from this role during slavery when she was also the repository of the accumulated lore and superstition of the slaves, and just after Emancipation when she acted as family midwife, cared for the orphaned and abandoned children, and kept the generations intact. In the 1920's, the grandmother "unawed and still with her ancient dignity," in the words of E. Franklin Frazier, watched over her children in the strange world of the city, maintaining her traditional role as guardian of the younger generation. The grandmother in **"The Promised Land,"** for instance, came from Virginia to New York to care for adult grandsons. Majutah's grandmother in the **"South Lingers On"** (part III) was a mother-substitute, too, as were Tillie's in **"The Lindy Hop,"** Sam's in **"Guardian of the Law,"** and David's in **"Miss Cynthie."** These old ladies were generally religious, much given to reading the Bible and praying. But they were also practical; Sam's grandmother, as an illustration, rescued Sam, who was being held at gunpoint, by throwing snuff into the eyes of his enemy. Miss Cynthie, who decided that singing and dancing on a stage were not as sinful as she had thought in the South, was the wittiest and most funloving of these Black matriarchs.

Fisher made use of two contrasting types of preachers—the faithful, courageous, sincere old minister, on the one hand, and the hypocrite, on the other. The best examples of the first were the Reverend Ezekiel Taylor (**"Shepherd, Lead Us"**), who followed part of his congregation to Harlem in order to establish a church, and the Reverend Zachary Pride, (**"Fire by Night"**), who prayed fervently for his wayward son though his prayers seemed in vain, and who assumed the burden of the social and economic, as well as the religious, problems of his flock. In contrast stood the hypocritical Senior Deacon Crutchfield, in **"The Backslider,"** a gambler and bootlegger, and Brother Ealey, of **"Shepherd, Lead Us,"** whose goal was that of Chaucer's Pardoner, self-gain.

Another recurring character in Rudolph Fisher's short stories is the fun-loving, pleasure-seeking girl, earlier alluded to. Usually rebellious against parental rule but not a violator of the Christian Commandments, she might be contrasted with Claude McKay's street girls, who "enjoyed life in their own way, without claiming virtue and without consciousness of vice." Fisher's young women enjoyed dancing and cabaret life. Ellie (**"The Promised Land"**) was the most materialistic and the boldest. Majutah, in the story of the same title, was determined to dress in the 1920's style, to use make-up, and to go to a cabaret despite her grandmother's objections. In **"The Lindy Hop,"** Tillie, a very similar character, entered a dance contest though her grandmother disapproved.

Also represented several times were scheming racketeers: the bootleggers Turpin and Strut, in **"Fire by Night"** and **"Lost Love Blues,"** respectively, the highjacker in **"Across the Airshaft,"** Tom Edwards, the dope peddler in **"The Man Who Passed"** and **"City of Refuge."** Fisher liked to set "good" characters against "bad," with the good usually winning. For example, in **"The Lindy Hop"** Pep rather than Solo won Tillie's favor. In **"Common Meter"** Bus Williams rather than Fess Baxter won Jean and got the cup for being the best jazz musician. Eight-Ball in **"Blades of Steel"** got revenge on Dirty Yaller and was the man Effie preferred. In **"Guardian of the Law"** Sam, instead of Grip, got the position as rookie policeman and won the affection of Judy.

Rudolph Fisher moved most of his short stories toward a happy or optimistic resolution, frequently with an O. Henry-style surprise twist. Detached but at the same time accepting of human foibles and able to see the comic side of human nature, Fisher was a sympathetic recorder and translator of Harlem life of the 1920's and early 1930's. As Arna Bontemps stated, "He was indeed part of the spirit of the Harlem Renaissance."

Fisher's relationship to Harlem:

In a 1933 radio interview, Fisher responded to a question on whether he intended to write of Harlem exclusively in the future. His answer is important: "I intend to write whatever interests me. But if I should be fortunate enough to become known as Harlem's interpreter, I should be very happy." At a time when the general strategy in black fiction seemed to oscillate too often between a dramatic indictment of a racist society in a strict realist mode and a too facile celebration of black urban life, Dr. Rudolph Fisher kept steadily to the task of probing and exploring. With both affection and a critical eye, he presented a symmetrical portrait of the Afro-American encounter with the modern city. It is Rudolph Fisher's achievement to have given us some of Harlem's possibilities so entertainingly, so carefully and wisely, beyond mere cleverness and glibness, during his short time on this earth.

John McCluskey, Jr., "Introduction," in The City of Refuge, *University of Missouri Press, 1987, p. xxxix.*

John McCluskey, Jr. (essay date 1987)

SOURCE: "Introduction," in *The City of Refuge, The Collected Stories of Rudolph Fisher,* University of Missouri Press, 1987, pp. xi-xxxix.

[*In the following excerpt, McCluskey suggests that Fisher's short stories explore the tension arising between arriving African Americans and the modern city.*]

The short fiction of Dr. Rudolph "Bud" Fisher might be neatly categorized for presentation to a contemporary audience, but like all categories these would be merely for convenience, for the noting of emphases. In this volume, I have grouped the short fiction into two movements—"The Quest" and "The New Land." The first movement offers portraits that treat first or early encounters with Harlem. The new arrivals are rushed through the blur, screech, and bumps of the city and are still feeling their way. Most often, blind trust and intuition are their only guides. They have arrived with great hope, and they struggle to maintain that hope despite disappointments. The conflict of values is sharply drawn in these pieces, and in this battle zone Fisher's use of satire is most effective. The second movement presents those stories in which the principal characters are more familiar with Harlem and its codes. The struggles of these characters often involve salvaging personal integrity from a corrosive cynicism.

Within these movements it is possible, of course, to identify even narrower concerns. However, none of these concerns or emphases is discrete. Throughout this body of work there are overlapping emphases, as there must be in the collected works of any writer, emphases that haunt the specific artistic imagination with the ease of dreams.

One group of stories focuses on city etiquette and generally dramatizes the ambitions and woes of the newcomer to Harlem. I suggest especially **"City of Refuge," "Ringtail," "Promised Land," "South Lingers On,"** and the two children's stories, **"Ezekiel"** and **"Ezekiel Learns."** A second group deepens the theme of transition by introducing the specific figure of the ancestor who actively struggles to keep some sense of integrity clear to her young charges. The stories **"Promised Land," "Guardian of the Law,"** and **"Miss Cynthie"** are representative of this category. A third group treats the problems of Harlemites without the influence of the ancestor and with violence a real threat to personal and communal unity. Common to these pieces is the active force of music, whether as foreshadowing agent, as metaphor, or as balm. In some cases the wisdom of the musical statement substitutes for that of the ancestor. Equally common is the collective cabaret/dance-hall scene. **"Common Meter," "Backslider,"** and **"Blades of Steel"** include most of the elements defining this series. A fourth group, much smaller than the other three, contains stories that treat caste and class as areas of tension. **"High Yaller," "Fire by Night,"** and **"Dust"** emphasize these aspects most explicitly. Each of these groups of stories will be discussed in greater detail below.

Finally, there is the long detective story **"John Archer's Nose,"** which is a sequel of sorts to Fisher's second novel, *The Conjure Man Dies.* It is so unlike the rest of the fiction that I will discuss it with the novel. I also urge that the piece, taken with the second novel, offers the fullest persona Fisher was able to develop.

In **"City of Refuge,"** King Solomon Gillis has fled to Harlem from the fictional Waxhaw, North Carolina, home also of Miss Cynthie in a later story. (In **"Ezekiel,"** the home is Waxhaw, Georgia.) As he emerges from the subway, he is assaulted by the blur of Harlem sounds and colors. He is too quickly befriended by Mouse Uggams, a "home-boy," and is soon working in a grocery store. Mouse has arranged for Gillis to sell dope, though Gillis has no idea he is doing anything illegal. He believes firmly in the down-home commitments to friends, newfound or otherwise. Gillis is caught at this trade, arrested in a cabaret, and, after a struggle, led toward jail at the story's end. Throughout this quickly moving story, Fisher supplies many flashes of humor. One of the best examples exploits the clash of dialects so keenly shown in the piece. Gillis has stopped on the street to figure out the direction of a rooming house. Mouse eases up to give directions and eventually befriends him for his own purposes.

> "See that second corner? Turn to the left when you get there. Number forty-five's about halfway down the block."
>
> "Thank y', suh."
>
> "You from—Massachusetts?"
>
> "No, suh, Nawth Ca'lina."
>
> "Is 'at so? You look like a Northerner. Be with us long?"
>
> "Till I die," grinned the flattered King Solomon.

The joke, of course, rests on the crude drawl of the outsider in the face of the street-wise ex-immigrant's slick come-on. Similarly, Fisher juxtaposes the voice of the West Indian stockboy ("Who you call nigger, mon?") with that of Gillis ("How you know dis' is me?"). He even introduces the voice of the Italian immigrant, Gabrielli ("Dope?. . What's a dis, dope?"). The dissonance of this ensemble of urban immigrant voices defines the relationships among the characters and their limited understanding of the codes of the streets. In this piece only the voices of Mouse and the policeman ("Are you coming without trouble?") communicate with a complete knowledge of that code, even if antagonistic.

Two images of power and possibility especially snag the imagination of Gillis: the flashing green stockings of a passing woman and the sight of a black policeman directing traffic, gruffly giving directions to white folks. With these twin images—sexual glitter and reversed authority—overriding the most powerful ones from the rural South he had known—mob violence and economic repression—Gillis takes on the twentieth-century city.

Many of the ingredients common to Fisher's stories are provided in this first published piece—the displaced person, the quick-paced action, the cabaret scene, and swift violence. What is missing here that was present in another 1925 piece, **"The South Lingers On,"** is the ancestor—the steadying voice of tradition. In **"City of Refuge"** that voice is partially played out in Gillis's consciousness as he reflects in fragments on the hostile South:

> "Know whut dey done? Dey killed five o' Mose Joplin's hawses 'fo he lef'. Put groun' glass in de feed-trough Sam Cheevers come up on three of 'em one night pizenin' his well. Bleesom beat Crinshaw out o' sixty acres o' lan an' a year's crops. Dass jess how 't is. Soon 's a nigger make a li'l sump'n he better git to leavin.' An' 'fo long ev'ybody's goin' be lef'!"

But Solomon is alive with no guide except a con man who deserts him at the end.

Beneath it all is a subtle, yet devastating, critique of the city and the tragedy of self-delusion. Posing no rural and sentimental alternative, this story is an early statement on personal disintegration. Yet the specific flashes of humor overwhelm the tragedy.

The tableau of the outsider trying to maneuver among those more familiar with the city code is similar in Fisher's next published pieces. **"Ringtail," "The South Lingers On,"** and **"High Yaller."** Originally published in a special edition of *Survey Graphic* in March 1925, **"The South Lingers On"** is a series of five sketches that introduce the difficulty of communication among the generations, among urban Northerners and transplanted rural Southerners, among the devoutly religious and their exploiters or detractors. The second vignette was deleted when the series was published as **"Vestiges"** in *New Negro* late the same year.

Both **"Ringtail"** and **"High Yaller"** introduced the notion of vengeance, which will be taken up in the discussion of a later piece. What is interesting in these first pieces are the tensions between the Afro-American and the West Indian, which force the action for **"Ringtail,"** and the tensions of color, which are the cause of distress in **"High Yaller."** Fisher did not return to either theme as a dominant factor in any later published fiction. The latter story echoes the familiar theme of a black passing as nonblack handled in earlier works by William Wells Brown, Charles Chesnutt, James Weldon Johnson, as well as by Fisher's contemporary, Nella Larsen. Considered as too long for H. L. Mencken's *American Mercury*, the story was introduced to *Harper's* with the help of Walter White. The piece eventually appeared in *The Crisis*, where it later won the 1926 first-place Amy Spingarn Prize in the fiction contest sponsored by that magazine. It is interesting to note that the three judges for that contest were Charles Chesnutt, Sinclair Lewis, and H. G. Wells. Both Lewis and Wells placed the story well ahead of three other submissions. Chesnutt praised the plot and Fisher's ambitions

for the piece, but, before offering his rankings, said, "To me at least the theme is not convincing."

In one of his most daring unpublished stories, **"The Man Who Passed,"** Fisher treats the passing theme humorously, but from another angle. Peuryn Joel is a white reporter sent to Harlem to pass for black. His editor wants a "descriptive article with plenty of local color." A series of sobering experiences sends Joel back downtown with a more sympathetic view of black life. Incidentally, by the end of the decade the passing story and the theme of color obsession with their attendant oversentimentality were ripe for the swords of the satirists George Schuyler (*Black No More*) and Wallace Thurman (*The Blacker the Berry*).

The majority of Fisher's short fiction, however, sought to portray black intragroup dilemmas involving areas beyond skin color, with class conflict frequently more important than color. We see that in his first four published pieces, all appearing in 1925, when, again, he was also an intern and later a research fellow, he was to stake cut the territory he would explore, often with the eye of a skillful and affectionate surveyor. There is the estrangement often compounded by age and by culture, and the destructive impulses of revenge and social violence with their potential for communal disintegration. In his more mature pieces Fisher would seek ways to bond the community, to heal the rifts and tensions that Harlem experienced while defining itself as a community. To this end I suggest that he was aiming to paint a broad canvas—wedding the best in the traditional ethos with the promise of the modern age as experienced in the city.

The second group of stories involves the presence and force of the ancestor in all cases an older female figure, a grandmother. Though the grandmother figure does not always explicitly describe the communal loyalties and cohesion of the black community in the rural South, she does occasionally comment on this in the context of urban violence and fragmentation. In most cases she leans on the steadying chords of spirituals, which are occasionally drowned out by the blare of the blues.

Fisher's first portrayal of the grandmother figure was in the vignette **"Majutah"** in **"The South Lingers On."** In this sketch as well as in **"The Promised Land,"** the older woman appears helpless to guide her young charges around the snares of city life. In **"The Guardian of the Law,"** the grandmother is far more active and emerges as a savior in several ways. This series culminates in the wonderful **"Miss Cynthie."** Easily as popular as **"City of Refuge,"** this story was first published in *Story* magazine in June 1933 and has since appeared in numerous anthologies of Afro-American literature. In **"Miss Cynthie,"** Fisher avoids the melodrama of **"Guardian of the Law"** and the resignation of both **"Majutah"** and **"Promised Land,"** creating a tender portrait of the tough-spirited Miss Cynthie.

Miss Cynthie comes to New York to visit her grandson, Dave Tappen. She has never been to New York, indeed has never traveled out of the South before, though, unlike King Solomon Gillis, she is blessed with a great deal of mother-wit. At the train station she tells a redcap that he may take her bags but that she will hold on to her umbrella.

> "Always like to have sump'm in my hands when I walk. Can't never tell when you'll run across a snake."
>
> "There aren't any snakes in the city."
>
> "There's snakes everywhere, chile."

Such a caution distinguishes her instantly from Gillis. Like Gillis, however, she has brought her baggage of hope and faith to the city. She knows that Dave is a success, and she anticipates a respectable profession. He invites her to a theater where she learns that he is a highly successful dancer and singer. At first, she enters the theater with much trepidation: "She entered the sudden dimness of the interior as involuntarily as in a dream." She is shocked by what she considers the sinful nature of the musical revue and the crowd's response. She is even more surprised when Dave and his girlfriend, Ruth, cavort onstage. When he first appears onstage, after thunderous applause, Dave taps out a rhythm and sings a song taught to him years before by Miss Cynthie. Then he quiets the audience to tell them of the source of his success. It is Miss Cynthie who has taught him to do "like a church steeple—aim high and go straight." He may not have succeeded in a field of which she approved, but he has achieved, nonetheless.

As Dave is singing his secular, childhood song, Miss Cynthie watches its effect on the members of the audience. They are transformed from a loud and sinful crowd to a gathering of children, children who share Dave's memory and remember perhaps a similar song, a similar love and caring. Miss Cynthie concludes that "they didn't mean no harm" in their fervent appreciation of the revue. The crowd, Dave, and Miss Cynthie are brought together in a magic moment of love. Her understanding of an essential innocence and idealism, including her own, that can endure the whirl of city life is important for her acceptance of Dave's work. Dave's singing and recognition of Miss Cynthie—the recognition of a caring tradition—have allowed all present to touch and recall an important dimension of themselves.

In the second draft of an unpublished story entitled **"Lindy Hop,"** probably written during 1932-1933, the grandmother enters a dance contest. It is a desperate gesture to save her granddaughter from winning and reaping awards that will surely lead her to a life of sin. While the grandmother's younger partner dances the contemporary dances, the grandmother dances the traditional dances: the reel, quadrille, schottische, and cakewalk. To the delight of the crowd, agility, speed, and gusto are offset by precision, steadiness, and grace. Youth is balanced by age. It is Fisher's unmistakable point throughout this series of stories that the achievement of this balance—between the insights of tradition and the bold restlessness of the new age—is a significant basis for optimism about the directions of a new community.

The stories in the third group look even more closely at the rift within the community. Humor fades into the background; melodrama, already introduced in the earliest stories, steps forward, center stage. While they explore the theme of personal vengeance, the pieces I have grouped together here seek not only the resolution of personal fragmentation but also a means of communal healing. In these pieces we have a typical, though not stock, cabaret dance scene. As related earlier, in **"City of Refuge"** this setting is the backdrop of Gillis's final confusion. In **"High Yaller,"** the music from the cabaret operates as an ironic frame around, and refrain within, the story. **"Backslider"** (1927), **"Blades of Steel"** (1927), and **"Common Meter"** (1930) develop in their separate ways concerns already well established in the earlier stories. Yet, in these two pieces, Fisher utilizes secular music in ways significantly different than before.

I will focus on **"Common Meter"** here. In this story the business of the protagonist Bus Williams is music. Williams and Fessenden "Fess" Baxter are rivals for the crowd's adulation and the attention of Miss Jean Ambrose. As in **"High Yaller,"** the opening scene is a dance hall and Fisher moves swiftly to introduce the main conflict. The climax of the story is the battle of the bands, with the leader of the winning band to receive a large victory cup and, presumably, the undivided attention of Miss Ambrose. The reader learns that the drum heads of Tappen, Bus's master percussionist, have been sliced, rendering the drums useless. The devious Fess will stop at nothing to win. When the audience responds poorly to the first two of the scheduled three numbers, Bus is desperate to find a means to catch up with and surpass Fess's score. Identifying with his desperation, Jean provides the key: play a blues tune and turn it into an old-fashioned shout in which the audience can join in clapping and shouting. The stomping feet of the musicians thus take the place of the pulse of the bass drum. The transformation of the audience is instantaneous. They become one with the music and, further, one with a collective past.

> They had been rocked thus, before, this multitude. Two hundred years ago they had swayed to the same slow fateful measure, lifting their lamentation to heaven, pounding the earth with their feet, seeking the mercy of a new God through the medium of an old rhythm, zoom-zoom. They had rocked so a thousand years ago in a city whose walls were jungle, forefending the wrath of a terrible Black God who spoke in storm and pestilence, had swayed and wailed to that same slow period, beaten on a wild boar's skin stretched over the end of a hollow tree trunk.

Bus's orchestra reconstructs the moment that profoundly ties past to present. The blues tune, "St. Louis Blues," strikes a sociohistorical chord that resonates toward the sacred. Far more than serving as a frame and internal refrain then, secular music here explicitly connects an individual's call of romantic despair with the response of control. Here ritual summons collective memory. One recalls similar effects frequently dramatized is narrative poetry. Sterling Brown's "Ma Rainey," for example, portrays the effect of the great blues artist's performances on the crowd:

"O Ma Rainey
Sing yo' song;
Now you's back
Whah you belong,
Git way inside us,
Keep us strong."

True ritual defines and strengthens the group.

In **"Blades of Steel,"** song lyrics help to color, if not direct, the story's central action, and "a curious mingling of the secular and religious" is achieved. Both **"Common Meter"** and **"Blades of Steel,"** however, used secular lyrics not only to reflect the deepest yearnings of the group but also to alter group and individual consciousnesses in seemingly indifferent or antagonistic contexts.

The fourth group of Fisher's stories concerned caste and class as areas of tension. In one of the few discussions of the short fiction of the Harlem Renaissance, Robert Bone emphasizes the pastoral as a means by which black writers reconciled a number of issues: the conflict of cultures (urban North and rural South), the conflict of classes, and the conflict of races. The result of all this, Bone contends, is the suspension of class divisions. "In recoiling from the values of the white middle-class, black writers sought an alternative value system in the 'lower' world of negro folk culture. Pastoral, with its characteristic inversion of values, was an ideal instrument for this theme."

When he applies this notion to Fisher's work, Bone is correct in identifying the healing spirit as an emphasis. However, he overstates the case when he describes the extent to which Fisher is "torn" between two value systems, that of the street and that of middle-class respectability. This theory might apply to, say, **Fire By Night,** but the greater part of Fisher's work, not to speak of the several accounts of his life, does not bear this out. Indeed, as I attempted to suggest earlier, personally and professionally the alliance was an easy one.

Bone's notion of an inversion of values is equally misleading. Reading the pieces in this group, and in fact all the stories, I see not the attempt to show the superiority of black life, as Bone calls it, but a self-assured effort to view the black urban experience as worthy of exploration in its own right. We do not get exotics ready to Charleston at the first lick from a hot trumpet, nor do we get the stereotyped country cousins sitting in the shade and humming all day. We do get vital statements on individuals searching for an ethic in a time of rapid socioeconomic change. Fisher did not view the modern city as a symbol of civilization or hell. I suggest he viewed the city as frontier, that space between wilderness and civilization. Only through the humanizing and clarifying effect of specific traditional elements as demonstrated in the stories could the urban experience be a liberating and enlightening one. Though the pace may be more leisurely in his two novels, the tensions identified within the short stories are still evident.

A mixed review of *The City of Refuge*:

Although this work is little read today, Dr. Rudolph Fisher once held a prominent place among that pantheon of writers and artists whose reputations blazed during the Harlem Renaissance. And justifiably so, since his writing effortlessly captures the spirit and vitality of the Harlem he experienced in the 1920's and early 30's. Taken individually, the short stories collected in *The City of Refuge* show Fisher's remarkable command of both standard English and various dialects. One feels, smells and tastes his Harlem; its people come alive and one cares about them. Unfortunately, when read over a short time span, these parts seem to diminish the volume as a whole. They tend to follow the same depressing theme: Harlem crushing the spirit of the naïve newcomer. In fact, there is only one somewhat positive piece, **"Ezekiel,"** in the 15 that make up this book. Most of Fisher's tales are about Southern immigrants coming to black America's Promised Land, Harlem, and how these honest, hard-working, God-fearing country people are swept away by the cynicism of the mean uptown streets. Fisher, a physician who died in 1934 at the age of 37, certainly deserves to be read, and this collection is as good a place to start as any. But I suggest you start slowly and take the good doctor in small doses.

Stephen C. Miller, review of The City of Refuge,
in The New York Times Book Review,
Vol. XCII, No. 51, December 21, 1987,
pp. 16-17.

Margaret Perry (essay date 1987)

SOURCE: "A Fisher of Black Life: Short Stories by Rudolph Fisher," in *The Harlem Renaissance Re-examined,* AMS Press, 1987, pp. 253-62.

[*In the following essay, Perry observes that Fisher was a satirist and social historian whose stories were traditional in style—in the mode of Poe, Gogol and James—yet were still able to capture the spirit of Harlem.*]

It is not surprising that little of the work done in the short story form by Rudolph Fisher (1897-1934) is known; there has never been a collection of all his short stories, and this hampers the scholar in pursuit of a unified view of Fisher's themes and style. In the early part of our century, short stories written by black authors had little appeal to the primary reading public, which was white; Fisher seems to have been the exception to this, however. Although his stories were published frequently in Negro publications, he also appeared in non-Negro publications such as *Atlantic Monthly* and *McClure's,* and thus was able to reach a wider audience of short-story readers. Despite this, little space is devoted to Fisher in critical histories of the American short story. Indeed, the central metaphor of

Black Invisibility can be said to have been operating among critics of the short story in America. In an effort to rectify this neglect, the present article explores the stories of Rudolph Fisher, both published and unpublished, and places them within the context of the times in which he lived. The precise time in history, as well as the place—Harlem, its spirit—were significant elements in Fisher's fiction; indeed they were perhaps the reasons he felt impelled to capture his world within the strictures of the short-story form. Full of wit, irony, humor, and some acerbity, Fisher has enriched the world of literature in a medium Frank O'Connor has called our "national art form."

Rudolph Fisher, born in Washington, D.C. on 9 May 1897, was brought up mainly in Providence, Rhode Island, where he completed his studies at Classical High School in 1915 with high honors. In 1915 Fisher matriculated at Brown University, majoring in English and biology. Following graduation, Fisher remained at Brown through the next academic year in order to get his M.A., then attended Howard University Medical School, where he graduated with highest honors in 1924. Beginning private medical practice in 1927, he later specialized in roentgenology and opened an X-ray laboratory. Fisher died on 26 December 1934, after his third operation for an intestinal ailment.

Fisher's first published story, **"City of Refuge,"** was written while he was still in medical school, and appeared in *Atlantic Monthly* during February 1925. In addition to unpublished stories, Fisher wrote two plays, "The Vici Kid" and "Golden Slippers," neither of which was ever published or produced. According to his sister, the late Pearl M. Fisher: "like most writers, Dr. Fisher's ambition was to write the great Negro novel." Though Fisher did publish two novels—his second one, *The Conjure Man Dies,* was the first detective novel by a Black American—it is through his short stories that he presented the widest view of Black American life in Harlem. In a radio interview, Fisher stated the following: "Harlem is the epitome of American Negro life . . . I intend to write whatever interests me. But if I should be fortunate enough to become known as Harlem's interpreter, I should be very happy."

Harlem's interpreter—this was his expressed desire, and this was the goal he achieved through all of his fiction, as well as in his articles. The reading public responded to Fisher's role as a reflector of the life in the nation's Black capital during the 1920s, for one newspaperman wrote: "De Maupassant used Paris for his chess-board, while Fisher moves his dusky pawns over the field of Negro Harlem, a location quite as interesting as 'dear Paree.'" At last the reading public would be entertained with literature that reflected the informing spirit of the Afro-American race, the cultural *temenos* sustaining the unique character of Black life from country to town to city, in particular, Harlem. The model of life, the white life, was to be just another version of real life rather than the version that would overpower the Black reality of living. Sometimes, of course, the evil or injustice evolving from what white *could impose* upon blacks is treated with satiric strokes by Fisher, such as in **"High Yaller."** Still, Fisher seems, in his portraits of life in Harlem, to have realized what

Octavio Paz observed when writing about the majority and minority in Mexico: "Without otherness there is no oneness." So Fisher was, indeed, "Harlem's interpreter."

Fisher's fascination with Harlem came with the times, and his only regrets seemed to be the effects of white incursion into Harlem's places of entertainment. He hoped that the whites would also venture to explore more than this obvious part of Harlem and learn to understand Black life in general: "Maybe," he wrote, "they are at least learning to speak our language." Not really—but as long as the writings of Rudolph Fisher exist, everyone, Black and white, can learn to enjoy the sighs and sounds of Negro Harlem during the 1920s, the city that King Solomon Gillis first viewed with wide-eyed joy and fascination by saying: "Done died an' woke up in Heaven." It was a little of everything, and Fisher's canvases faithfully paint the people and places in its mosaic of dark and light hues.

The short stories of Rudolph Fisher have a sense of literary history behind them, for he ploughed the same fields as the masters of this art, such as Poe, Gogol, and James. There are times, indeed, when Fisher gives the impression that he went from studying the nineteenth-century writers directly to his desk to write, ignoring practitioners of the art who were his own contemporaries. In an earlier review of Fisher's work I noted that "Both stories [**"City of Refuge"** and **"Miss Cynthie"**] illustrate Fisher's ability to transform life into art through control of characterization, plot, and diction, and insistence on a single effect at the story's conclusion." Fisher was a traditionalist in form, then; but he was also one in point of view, in his themes, and in the values he stressed through the major characters he created. One might also venture to say that Fisher often wrote in the mode of dramatic comedies, eschewing tragedy in any case even in the stories that end unhappily.

Fisher writes comedy in the classical sense, as Gilbert Murray states in *The Classical Tradition in Poetry,* comedy that has at its core "a union of lovers." This re-creation of acts and emotions, mimesis, moves from conflict to resolution within the very special milieu of Black Harlem. The over-all impression one gets of Fisher's use of the short story form is that he engages the reader in a positive, comic view of life which arises from the lyric impulse to sing mainly about triumph, about the possibility of being saved or renewed. Once again, to quote Murray: "Tragedies end in death. Comedies end in marriage." Murray is not referring to marriage as a legal procedure, but is alluding to the joy that issues from a harmonious end to the strife and conflict within the imaginative work. It seems he is seeking not only the melody but also the harmony, as Shelley wrote in his famous *Defence of Poetry.* One is always conscious of an ordered universe in Fisher's world; he writes about the ruptures that are brought on by disharmony, the disjointedness that must be replaced at the denouement by order.

There are important non-literary elements in Fisher's stories that should also be noted, because he emphasizes them consistently. He was a satirist and social historian through the medium of the short story; thus, we have an accurate portrait of Harlem during the 1920s, whether or not one believes this is the proper function of imaginative literature. Fisher portrays the life of the "rats" and the "dickties" as well as the criminal element and the ordinary wage-earner. We see how life is played out in the cabaret, at rent parties, and we witness the city version of religion as it struggles to recapture the joy and spontaneity of the "down home" mode of expression. As a critic of the city—the city as duper, the city as destroyer of the immigrated Black—Fisher's stories act out the ritual of ruin in which so many men and women were immolated. For some, the family unit is disrupted, as in **"The Promised Land"** or in **"The South Lingers On"**; while others, seeking safety and freedom, like King Solomon Gillis in **"City of Refuge,"** find that exploitation, confinement and racism are not limited to the South. In the latter story, Gillis encounters a new sort of racism, explored in several other Fisher stories—the prejudice of black against black, particularly Afro-American vs. British West Indian.

The relationship, or more aptly, the animosity, between the American Black and the West Indian Black is portrayed sharply in several of Fisher's stories; indeed, this topic is the major element of conflict in **"Ringtail."** Sociologically, there were several reasons for this real and sometimes imagined dislike among the two groups: to many American blacks it seems that the West Indians were arrogant about their "British" background—and many West Indians, like Cyril Sebastian Best in **"Ringtail,"** lorded this so-called advantage over American Blacks. Then, it did appear that West Indians who immigrated to the United States fared better economically and in a shorter length of time. As one character in **"Ringtail"** says: "'. . . they stick too close together an' get ahead too fast. They put it all over us in too many ways . . . Same as ofays an' Jews.'"

There was also the movement of "Back to Africa," carried on with parade and pomp, electrifying the masses with a thesis none of them wanted in reality. Going back to Africa and "chasing monkeys" wasn't the dream of American Blacks; so the detractors had a ready-made phrase to coin about Marcus Garvey, leader and symbol of this abortive movement. His fellow-West Indians fell prey to the same expression and it is still used privately to this day by many American blacks (and probably less privately in non-bourgeois society).

There are strains of satire, light in most cases, lurking among Fisher's descriptions of life in Harlem. The picture of Cyril Sebastian Best (**"Ringtail"**) is satirical, particularly at the opening when he is parading in his finery. Fisher mocks the concerns of the "dickties" for the false trappings of bourgeois habits, such as the So-and-So's "supper dansant" described in **"Fire by Night."** He mocks the fragility of the dickties further in this story when, at the height of a brawl at the "dansant," the women scurry to save their fur coats from invading pool-hall scavengers: "girls who had saved for two years to buy seal wraps; wives who had wheedled for months to get a caracal like Mrs. Jones; women who had undertaken payment for their

Persian lambs by installments." There is the hypocrisy of the religious exposed in **"The Backslider,"** and even a hint of satire in the minor appearance of the Goldman brothers in **"Miss Cynthie."**

Imagery of a world of confinement and darkness—the black world on earth, not Hell (although that is one point, i.e., that Harlem frequently is Hell)—characterizes Fisher's fictional domain. Sometimes there is no value judgment implied in the painting he presents, e.g., "The pavement flashed like a river in the sun" (**"Ringtail"**); but most often his images and figurative language are undergirded by Fisher principles and points of view. A large proportion of Fisher's imagery derives from his use of similes and metaphors such as "the thoughts that gathered and throbbed like an abscess were suddenly incised" (**"High Yaller"**); the "roadster . . . snorted impatiently" (**"Dust"**); "A young bronze giant" (**"Guardian"**); or, the "ambulance gong was like receding derisive laughter." (**"Ringtail"**). In a comprehensive sense, the image we have of Harlem is one of "a stage upon which one looked as from an upper box" (**"Guardian"**). Fisher places Harlem in an open-air theatre so the reader can view the high and the low, the very fine Seventh Avenue as well as Lenox Avenue, "the boulevard of the unperfumed." In painting scenes with colors as well as with sound, Fisher gives the reader what Mammy, in **"The Promised Land,"** sees from her window: "a screen upon which flashed a motion picture oddly alive and colorful." Often Fisher invests inanimate objects with human traits (e.g., the "keyboard grinned evilly"—**"Guardian"**) to indicate a point of view, the author's moral stance. The Blacks, frequently living in "hencoops," the white downtown in "kingly dwellings," the good and the bad, common and uncommon, the city itself, all enter upon a stage set up by Fisher and perform their roles in a pageant of contrasts and disharmonies that will eventually end in an orderly resolution. It is difficult to categorize Fisher's treatment of the rent party phenomenon, whether it is sadness or satire when he writes (in **"The Promised Land"**), "You provide music, your friends provide advertisement, and your guests, by paying admission, provide what your resources lack." Certainly, Fisher saw that the underlying reason for this Northeastern version of the "shinding" was in most instances exploitation, because people were having to pay more than a fair price for apartments. In any case, Fisher was unable to avoid the satiric touch from time to time as a technique for pointing out the meaninglessness of certain habits and concerns in the Black community.

In highlighting the special qualities that composed life in Harlem at every stratum, Fisher dramatically portrayed the obsession of blacks with their color. He turned this self-absorption into an artistic mode with moral as well as social implications. It has been noted by another critic that Fisher uses color to differentiate between good and bad characters, that "the lighter the skin color the lower the moral character of the individual." This differentiation is made in several of Fisher's stories, notably **"Blades of Steel"** and **"High Yaller."** Fisher offers readers a gallery of "good" guys and "bad" ones, most often designated by skin color—dark equaling good and yellow for the low-down cad. Consider for example, the following characters:

> "His coarse granular skin was dingy yellow and scarred . . ."
> **("Fire by Night")**;

> "Eight-ball . . . was as dark as it is possible for skin to be, smooth and clean as an infant's . . ."
> **("Blades of Steel")**;

> "Bus Williams' jolly round brown face beamed down on the crowd . . ."
> **("Common Meter")**.

In between the absolute dark and light we have women who are "amber" (**"Common Meter"**), or "red-brown" (**"Guardian of the Law"**), or "golden-skipped" (**"Miss Cynthie"**); the women, in any case, are never black. The darkest woman of importance in his short stories is Effie Wright in **"Blades of Steel,"** who is described as having an "almost luminous dark complexion called 'sealskin brown'." With this obvious attention to color, Fisher reflects the self-consciousness of the decade toward the various shades of 'Blackness.'

It cannot be said that Fisher accomplished every goal he attempted in his short story writing, for there are some structural and linguistic imperfections that do not go undetected. Fisher, with his balanced and sane approach to the difficulties in life, wanted to demonstrate the effects of illusion on individuals. People continually misread the motives of self and other, and thus the seeds for conflict are scattered. Here we have the necessary elements for a good story—action, reaction, and resolution. If the exposition complements these elements, then the production proceeds as it should to a successful completion. This does not always occur, however, in Fisher's stories; there are some weaknesses that are apparent.

One weakness, which appears to derive from Fisher's occasional desire to preach or educate, is that of author intrusion. In **"Dust,"** which is one of his least effective stories, he succumbed to the urge to teach rather than to entertain, he did not move toward the effect he wanted, he commenced with it and rode it to death.

Adopting the role of the totally omniscient author, of course, allowed Fisher to write as he pleased. Still, he was good enough as a short-story writer to understand the necessity of removing unneeded words, the necessity of keeping the movement "tight" yet, more than once, he placed himself as writer into the middle of a story.

Another weakness was a general tendency to write by formula, making a Fisher situation and/or ending predictable, and sometimes too slick or facile. As one critic has written about **"Common Meter"**: "To the cynical modern reader, the outcome is possible only in a fairy tale. The winner is the most noble and upright character, the jazz musician who prizes rhythm above all else and the man

whose skin is darkest." Of course, this conforms to Fisher's basic comic style, which anticipates the "happy ending."

Generally, however, Fisher goes swiftly to the heart of his story—moves the reader into the conflict, clearly points to the cast of characters and their features, and concludes the story tidily—leaving no doubt in the mind of the reader concerning the meaning of the tale. A certain stylistic stiffness in Fisher's expository mode sometimes impedes the smooth movement of the story, but this is an authentic feature of his writing. His use of idiomatic Harlem language is another characteristic feature, a strength in terms of authenticity, but also another weakness if taken as it has been by one critic in the following observation: "his use of the Negro idiom, Harlemese, (is) . . . self-conscious."

Despite these weaknesses, Fisher was successful in portraying his fellow black Americans from all strata of Negro life, from the "rats" to the "dickties," and he achieved this goal to a greater degree than any other writer of this period. The last of Fisher's short stories to be published in his lifetime, **"Miss Cynthie,"** leads one to postulate that he was moving closer to the real art of short fiction writing. As Robert Bone has noted, "'**Miss Cynthie**' constitutes . . . a psychological as well as an artistic triumph. Published in the shadow of impending death, it testifies to Fisher's inner growth and aggravates our loss of his maturing powers."

The importance of **"Miss Cynthie"** in the canon of Fisher literature does not obscure his lesser tales; but this story is the exemplum of Fisher's overriding concern for the motifs of love and reconciliation, of harmonious union between opposing elements, for that "union of lovers" in the most boundless sense. To say that "Class consciousness is perhaps the single most consistent theme in Fisher's work" is to mistake the means for the goal. Other themes are also found among Fisher's major concerns, such as the futility of prejudice (the irony of it, the waste), or the effects of the lure of the city upon people and the city's power to destroy individuals. Added to his themes is Fisher's employment of language to underscore the characterizations and settings. This wholeness of themes, characterizations, settings, and language exemplify the concerns of Rudolph Fisher to render the life he witnessed and lived in the transformed manner of mimetic art through the short story.

Fisher is predictable and consistent in his language, in descriptions, exposition, and dialogue. He uses words of confinement frequently, e.g., hencoop, airshaft, underground railroads, suffocation, a religious vocabulary in connection with characters acutely aware of sinfulness, and lastly—Fisher's special forte (or, as has been pointed out, also a weakness)—the language of Black Harlem, "Contemporary Harlemese," to use his own expression.

"City of Refuge" demonstrates Fisher's concern for the tidy progression of a tale from beginning to middle to end; the six sections of the story each lead Gillis closer to his fate. Just as he emerges like Jonah from the whale into Harlem (after being in the "hell" of the subway), he is caught at the end in a cabaret, which is another hell, and truly the place for the lost victims of the city, such as Gillis. The end of **"The City of Refuge"** reflects the tendency of the modern short story, starting in the 1920s in fact, to place the protagonist in a situation where he receives some illumination as to the truth of his actual plight—a mini-epiphany, as it were—a moment of obvious reversed fortunes but without the insight into his own flawed character as one would have it in Aristotelian tragedy. There is passivity in King Solomon's acceptance of his "mistakes"; that his character has weaknesses does not occur to this protagonist, however. In this fashion, Fisher was certainly part of the mainstream of short story writers during his period of creativity—a time when there was, in short story writing, an under-playing of plot, reversals, total change, or complete insight into the self (or a need to do anything about an internal problem when it was discovered). In part, then, Fisher was writing in the mode of his contemporaries. Also, the fact that **"The City of Refuge"** has a comic rather than a tragic ending does not lessen the emotional poignancy of Gillis's situation unless, of course, the reader finds untenable Gillis's naiveté and gullibility.

Optimism is integral to the fiction of Fisher, a bourgeois-based belief that an optimistic philosophy of life, a firm Christian faith, and clear comprehension finally of human needs and motives can result in a harmonious conclusion to life's inversions. Because Fisher's aim was to be instructor as well as interpreter, this adoption of a positive and sanguine attitude gave him a limited point of view and made some of his work press too hard upon "a willing suspension of disbelief." Rather than demonstrating alienation from or despair with his group, Fisher—even when satirizing his race—chose to construct his stories around moral principles that served to emphasize the redemptive spirit. As in the case of all writers, of course, the choice was his to make; but the choice vitiated the effectiveness of his avowed wish to be an interpreter of his people.

The intent of his writing, however, cannot be overlooked at any time; and, apparently because he kept his aim clearly in mind, he succeeded. In a sense, he made the leap from individualizing his artistic concerns to informing about a group experience in his literary corpus; he sought to apply universal qualities to a special group and thus tamed "The artist's struggle with his vocation . . . a version of a universal human struggle: of genius with Genius, and of genius with genius loci (spirit of place)." And in demonstrating a manner of bond between his characters and their setting Fisher captures the cultural *temenos* of that Black capital.

What we have in Fisher's stories, then, is a polished portrait of the varied life in Harlem, written in a quick, sometimes witty, sometimes satiric, sometimes acerbic-sounding style. The conflicts between social and moral questions inform many of Fisher's stories—e.g., **"The Backslider," "High Yaller,"** or **"The Promised Land"**—which highlights his aim to be not only entertaining, but enlightening as well. The social historian works hand-in-

hand with the creative artist; the man of conscience stands behind the stories. A descendant of Emerson, Fisher stresses in his stories the notion that the God-loving, God-fearing person can triumph over adversity. If the short story is, as Mark Schorer has said, "an art of moral revelation" (whereas the novel is "an art of moral evolution"), then Fisher accomplished what he wished as an artist practicing this literary genre. His keen observations of life and manners in Harlem, couched in a literary form, demonstrate his very American concern for probing those flaws in our character which he felt could be ameliorated. The personal conflicts of his characters illustrate, once again, a major American concern—the problems stemming from belief versus action; a testing, it seems, of the theory of the American way of life versus the reality of how life is acted out day by day.

> **What we have in Fisher's stories . . . is a polished portrait of the varied life in Harlem, written in a quick, sometimes witty, sometimes satiric, sometimes acerbic-sounding style.**
>
> —*Margaret Perry*

Unlike many of the white writers of the 1920s (e.g., Sherwood Anderson, Hemingway), who frequently chose protagonists who were unattractive and second-rate, Fisher for the most part eschews this sort of character in a principal role and emphasizes the redeeming features of the "good guy." One prominent exception is **"Ringtail,"** although it is not clear to me what attitude Fisher has or the precise point of a story such as this, where the main character certainly succeeds in evil-doing. But in each case where there is a repugnant individual in a Fisher story, a contrasting figure is provided in the balance to represent the author's moral point of view. This, too, is an essential element of his art—to make sure that nothing, then, is left to the reader's inference: characters, setting, theme, point of view, resolution of the plot come together in a conclusion calculated tidily to furnish a panorama of Harlem as painted by a master interpreter of black life in this mecca of multicolored inhabitants.

FURTHER READING

Criticism

Chamberlain, John. "The Negro As Writer." *The Bookman* LXX, No. 6, (February 1930): 603-11.

Chamberlain surveys "Negro fiction," and writes of Fisher as the "most able craftsman among the Negro novelists."

Brawley, Benjamin. *The Negro Genius.* New York: Dodd, Mead, & Company, 1937, 366 p.

Brawley contextualizes Fisher within the "New Realists" of African American fiction and praises his short stories for their vivid "transcriptions" of urban life.

Additional coverage of Rudolph Fisher's life and career is contained in the following sources published by Gale Research: *Black Literature Criticism*; *Black Writers*; *Contemporary Authors,* Vols. 107, 124; *Dictionary of Literary Biography,* Vols. 51, 102; *DISCovering Authors: Multicultural Authors Module*; **and** *Twentieth-Century Literary Criticism,* Vol. 11.

Elizabeth Gaskell
1810-1865

English novelist, short story writer, biographer, and essayist.

INTRODUCTION

One of the most popular writers of the Victorian era, Gaskell is principally remembered for her portraits of nineteenth-century provincial life in the novels *Cranford* (1853) and *Wives and Daughters: An Every-day Story* (1866). An esteemed storyteller, she also wrote a considerable assortment of short fiction, much of which was published in the weekly journals of Charles Dickens. Dickens, who had read Gaskell's popular social novel *Mary Barton: A Tale of Manchester Life* (1848), asked her to submit her new work to his *Household Words*. This encouraged her to write "Lizzie Leigh: A Domestic Tale" and provided her with a rewarding publishing outlet. Other short works, including "Lois the Witch" and "The Grey Woman" were originally published in Dickens's *All the Year Round*, prior to being released in collections. In all, Gaskell wrote over forty short stories and sketches, and several novellas. Many of these works are genre pieces—Gothic mystery stories or historical fiction—and many are comedies or darker tales of varying quality, which until recently have been somewhat neglected by critics in favor of her longer works, particularly *Cranford*.

Biographical Information

Elizabeth Cleghorn Stevenson was born September 29, 1810 in Chelsea, London, but following her mother's death thirteen months later, moved to the quiet town of Knutsford in Cheshire with her aunt. She had little contact with her father from that time on, but the town of Knutsford became central to much of her writing and the principal location for her novels *Cranford* and *Wives and Daughters*. While on a visit to Manchester—the setting for her first novel, *Mary Barton*—she met the Unitarian minister, William Gaskell, whom she later married. She became active in the liberal Unitarian community and occupied herself with her domestic duties, including raising four children, and traveling. One of her trips took her to Haworth where she met Charlotte Brontë. The two became close friends, and Gaskell later undertook the writing of her biography, though its publication in 1857 was marred by charges of misrepresentation. Mortified by allegations of dishonesty, Gaskell did not attempt another full-length work until 1863, instead focusing on her production of shorter fiction. In 1865, exhausted from continuous work and persistent ill-health, Gaskell collapsed suddenly while visiting her

Hampshire country home. She died of heart failure, leaving her novel *Wives and Daughters* unfinished.

Major Works of Short Fiction

While predominately concerned with social issues, especially the role of women in Victorian society, Gaskell's many other interests often surfaced in her shorter works of fiction. "Mr. Harrison's Confessions," like the later *Cranford*, reveals her ability to capture the nuance of a small and vanishing town's way of life. The story, which relies on misunderstood gossip, demonstrates Gaskell's characteristically light and gently ironic humor. "Curious, If True" represents Gaskell's exploitation of a fantasy motif, as its somewhat dim-witted narrator fails to recognize that he has stumbled into the dwelling of several aging fairy-tale characters, including Snow White and Cinderella. "The Old Nurse's Story," a tale of ghosts told from a feminine perspective, exemplifies Gaskell's work in the gothic mode, while "A Dark Night's Work" details a murder motivated by the inequities of social class. In "Lois the Witch" Gaskell demonstrates her talent for historical fiction. Inspired by the Salem witch trials, the story dramatizes themes of intolerance and fear. Among her novellas, *Cousin Phillis* resembles such realistic works as *Mary Barton* and *North and South,* and like them illustrates Gaskell's concern for social reconciliation during the industrial revolution. Its story follows the changes brought about by the construction of a railroad near the quiet, pastoral Hope Farm. The heroine of *The Moorland Cottage* (1850), Maggie Browne, faces a conflict between her social responsibilities and her own personal fulfillment. Certain elements of the story appear in Gaskell's later works of realistic fiction, especially *Wives and Daughters.*

Critical Reception

Despite her popularity in the mid-1800s, for the first century after her death critics tended to view Gaskell as a limited writer whose novel *Cranford* alone kept her in the English canon. Her work, however, has since been reappraised. Scholars have noted her ability to convincingly convey the emotional states of her characters and have recognized that she indeed wrote in the mode of Realism even before its proponents, like her friend George Eliot, had articulated its tenets. Feminists have seen in Gaskell's short stories a sustained examination of the situation of women in a patriarchal society, especially in characters such as Thekla of "Six Weeks in Heppenheim" and Ellinor Wilkins of "A Dark Night's Work." And, while a portion of her short fiction has been perceived as ephemeral in nature, evidence both of the lasting appeal of much of her work and of the historical realities of her writing—she faced tremendous difficulties in a literary world dominated by male publishers and critics—has, according to modern critics, only magnified Gaskell's considerable achievements.

PRINCIPAL WORKS

Short Fiction

The Moorland Cottage (novella) 1850
Hands and Heart and Bessie's Troubles at Home 1855
Lizzie Leigh and Other Tales 1855
My Lady Ludlow (novella) 1858
Right at Last, and Other Tales 1860
Lois the Witch and Other Tales 1861
Cousin Phillis: A Tale (novella) 1864
The Grey Woman and Other Tales 1865
Mrs. Gaskell's Tales of Mystery and Horror 1978

Other Major Works

Mary Barton: A Tale of Manchester Life (novel) 1848
Cranford (novel) 1853
Ruth (novel) 1853
North and South (novel) 1855
The Life of Charlotte Brontë (biography) 1857

Sylvia's Lovers (novel) 1863
Wives and Daughters: An Every-day Story (novel) 1866

CRITICISM

The Athenaeum (review date 1850)

SOURCE: Review of *The Moorland Cottage,* in *The Athenaeum,* No. 1208, December, 1850, pp. 1337-8.

[*In the following assessment, the anonymous critic praises* The Moorland Cottage *for its "wholesome moral."*]

There is little risk in predicting that this Christmas book will divide public favour with the Rhenish adventures of 'The Kickleburys.' Nor is there much hazard in saying that *Mary Barton* was not more unlike *Becky Sharp* than Combehurst is dissimilar to Cologne, Coblenz, Caub, and all the other C's of the Rhineland to which Mr. Thackeray has done the honours.

The Moorland Cottage, like *Mary Barton,* is a tale of passion and feeling, developed among what may be called every-day people:—but, unlike *Mary Barton,* it is not a tale of class-sufferings and class-interests. It is merely a story intended to soften the heart and sweeten the charities at Christmas time by the agency of pity and sympathy. The idea is simple, but the execution is of no common order. The characters are nicely marked. Mr. Buxton, the great man of the village-town,—his saint-like invalid wife—Mrs. Browne, with her jealous hardness towards her daughter and her credulous indulgence of her son—are as well made out as they are artfully, because artlessly, contrasted. Perhaps the following scene will bring the manner of our authoress and moreover the heroine, as pleasantly before the public as any in the book. The delicate and pious Mr. Buxton has become aware that Maggie Browne is insufficiently prized at the Moorland Cottage, and has tempted the child over to Combehurst to see her. This the grudging mother has reluctantly permitted.—

"It needed a good deal of Nancy's diplomacy to procure Maggie this pleasure; although I don't know why Mrs. Browne should have denied it, for the circle they went was always within sight of the knoll in front of the house, if any one cared enough about the matter to mount it and look after them. Frank and Maggie got great friends in these rides. Her fearlessness delighted and surprised him, she had seemed so cowed and timid at first. But she was only so with people, as he found out before his holydays ended. He saw her shrink from particular looks and inflections of voice of her mother's; and learnt to read them, and dislike Mrs. Browne accordingly, notwithstanding all her sugary manner towards himself. The result of his observations he communicated to his mother, and in consequence he was the bearer of a most civil and ceremonious message from Mrs. Buxton to Mrs. Browne, to the effect that the former would be much obliged to the latter if she would allow Maggie to ride down occasionally with the groom, who would bring the newspapers on the Wednesdays (now Frank was going to school), and to spend the afternoon with Erminia. Mrs. Browne consented, proud of the honour, and yet a little annoyed that no mention was made of herself. When Frank had bid good-bye, and fairly disappeared, she turned to Maggie. 'You must not set yourself up if you go amongst these fine folks. It is their way of showing attention to your father and myself. And you must mind and work doubly hard on Thursdays to make up for playing on Wednesdays.'—Maggie was in a flush of sudden colour, and a happy palpitation of her fluttering little heart. She could hardly feel any sorrow that the kind Frank was going away, so brimful was she of the thoughts of seeing his mother; who had grown strangely associated in her dreams, both sleeping and waking, with the still calm marble effigies that lay for ever clasping their hands in prayer on the altar-tombs in Combehurst Church. All the week was one happy season of anticipation. She was afraid her mother was secretly irritated at her natural rejoicing; and so she did not speak to her about it, but she kept awake till Nancy came to bed, and poured into her sympathising ears every detail, real or imaginary, of her past and future intercouse with Mrs. Buxton. And the old servant listened with interest, and fell into the custom of picturing the future with the ease and simplicity of a child.—'Suppose, Nancy! only suppose, you know, that she did die. I don't mean really die, but go into a trance like death; she looked as if she was in one when I first saw her; I would not leave her, but I would sit by her, and watch her, and watch her.'—'Her lips would be always fresh and red,' interrupted Nancy.—'Yes, I know; you've told me before how they keep red,—I should look at them quite steadily; I would try never to go to sleep.'—'The great thing would be to have air-holes left in the coffin.'—But Nancy felt the little girl creep close to her at the grim suggestion, and, with the tact of love, she changed the subject.—'Or supposing we could hear of a doctor who could charm away illness. There were such in my young days; but I don't think people are so knowledgeable now. Peggy Jackson, that lived near us when I was a girl, was cured of a waste by a charm.'—'What is a waste, Nancy?'—'It is just a pining away. Food does not nourish nor drink strengthen them, but they just fade off, and grow thinner and thinner, till their shadow looks grey instead of black at noon day; but he cured her in no time by a charm.'—'Oh, if we could find him.'—'Lass, he's dead, and she's dead, too, long ago!'—While Maggie was in imagination going over moor and fell, into the hollows of the distant mysterious hills, where she imagined all strange beasts and weird people to haunt, she fell asleep. Such were the fanciful thoughts which were engendered in the little girl's mind by her secluded and solitary life. It was more solitary than ever now that Edward was gone to school. The house missed his loud cheerful voice and bursting presence. There seemed much less to be done, now that his numerous wants no longer called for ministration and attendance. Maggie did her task of work on her own grey rock; but as it was sooner finished, now that he was not there to interrupt and call her off, she used to stray up the Fell Lane at the back of the house; a little steep stony lane, more like stairs cut in the rock than what we, in the level land, call a lane: it reached on to the wide and open moor, and near its termination there was a knotted thorn-tree; the only tree for apparent miles. Here the sheep crouched under the storms, or stood and shaded themselves in the noontide heat. The ground was brown with their cleft round foot-marks; and tufts of wool were hung on the lower part of the stem like votive offerings on some shrine. Here Maggie used to come and sit and dream in any scarce half-hour of leisure. Here she came to cry, when her little heart was over-full at her mother's sharp fault-finding, or when bidden to keep out of the way and not be troublesome. She used to look over the swelling expanse of moor, and the tears were dried up by the soft low-blowing wind which came sighing along it. She forgot her little home griefs to wonder why a brown-purple shadow always streaked one particular part in the fullest sunlight; why the cloud-shadows always seemed to be wafted with a sidelong motion; or she would imagine what lay beyond those old grey holy hills, which seemed to bear up the white clouds of Heaven on which the angels flew abroad. Or she would look straight up through the quivering air, as long as she could bear its white dazzling, to try and see God's throne in that unfathomable and infinite depth of blue. She thought she should see it blaze forth sudden and glorious, if she were but full of faith. She always came down from the thorn comforted and meekly gentle."

If joy came of Maggie's pony rides with such an escort, on the other hand the poor girl was called on to bear cruel trial because of Edward. He from being his mother's pride, became the disgrace of the family,—chose the law for his profession, because of its advantages, and grew up a flashy and fraudulent attorney,—repaying Mr. Buxton's friendly interest in him by disgraceful offence. Nor was this made easier to bear by Maggie and Frank having become be-trothed lovers,—to the displeasure of the ambitious old man. The poor girl, as too often happens, had to stand between these conflicting impersonations of selfishness, under deadly peril of the happiness and joy of her life being trampled out in the struggle. Rarely has woman drawn a fairer study of self-sacrifice in woman than our authoress in Maggie Browne; and if we refrain from quot-ing some of the scenes in which this is developed, it is simply because we will not take the edge off the reader's curiosity with regard to a story of such deep interest and wholesome moral:—for wholesome beyond the usual fash-ion of novelists is the form of Maggie's self-sacrifice, and her standing up for those rights which in Life count for so much while in Fiction they are disregarded as it were by receipt. That there is a touch of the *Deus ex machinâ* in the catastrophe no one can question:—but the final scenes are so clear of all the exaggeration with which they might have been overlaid and overcoloured, that it would be hypercriticism to reckon severely with the au-thoress for introducing what belongs to the class of *coups de théâtre* at the close of a story so unforced yet so forc-ible, so natural yet so new, as **The Moorland Cottage**.

The Bookman   **(review date 1908)**

SOURCE: Review of *Cousin Phillis*, in *The Bookman*, Vol. XXXV, No. 206, November, 1908, pp. 98-9.

[*Below, the anonymous critic favorably reviews* Cousin Phillis.]

To most of us the name of Mrs. Gaskell has hitherto spelt *Cranford*. Comparatively few of us have any personal knowledge of this fragrant idyll, ***Cousin Phillis***, which first saw light in the *Cornhill* in the early 'fifties, and is now ably and tenderly introduced by Mr. Thomas Seccombe to a forty-five-year-later audience. To read *Cranford* and ***Cousin Phillis*** now, and realise their respective dates, is to pause surprised at their order of production. *Cranford* came first—came, indeed, among Mrs. Gaskell's earliest writings, and Mr. Seccombe remarks: "Based upon generalised reminiscences of early childhood and youth, *Cranford* is coloured too with the riper tints of autumn, and the wonder is that these hues of sadness should be manipulated to so exquisite an issue by so fair, so sanguine, and so youthful a hand." The hand, however, was over forty years old when it began these finely artistic sketches of an avowedly inartistic period; and in forty years there is much opportunity to learn observation and suffer experience. The wonder lies even more, it seems to us, in the spontaneous radiance, the young glamorous youth and freshness of the later story, which gleams as if steeped in early morning sunshine, and is fragrant as a garden of dew-washed gillyflowers. Its charm is so elusive and delicate that the idyll seems passively to refuse detailed criticism; scenes, characters, phrases, captivate us, but in spite of this it stands to be judged whole, it appeals as a young, living thing.

Mr. Seccombe's Introduction could not be bettered; we have read it four times, out of sheer pleasure. In five-and-twenty pages he is reminiscent, enthusiastic, critical, enlightening; he tells us the history of the story in England and on the Continent; he shows us the growth of Mrs. Gaskell and of ***Cousin Phillis***. To his own work he has brought thought and knowledge; to Mrs. Gaskell's work affection and understanding. And as an annotator does any one surpass Mr. Seccombe in his own way? There are just four notes to this Introduction, and each is a model of generous conciseness, each is apt, helpful, graphic.

The story of ***Cousin Phillis***, "that flawless, radiant idyll," is of a kind but rarely achieved with full success. Perhaps they achieve it more often in America than here, though one such triumph was certainly attained by Mr. Walter Raymond some years ago in "Tryphena in Love"—a *Queen's Treasure*, too, which would not be out of place in this series. Numberless new readers will now make acquaintance with Mrs. Gaskell's heroine, as Cousin Paul did, when, as he says, "the westering sun shone full upon her, and made a slanting stream of light into the room within. She was dressed in dark blue cotton of some kind; up to her throat, down to her wrists, with a little frill of the same wherever it touched her white skin. . . . She had light hair, nearer yellow than any other colour. She looked me steadily in the face with large quiet eyes, wondering, but untroubled by the sight of a stranger." And they will leave her, as we have done, languid after her sorrowful illness, her heart bruised by an unmeant hurt, her hands holding the blue ribbons which her pitiful father had bought in his almost childlike endeavour to please and rouse her, and in her heart a new germ of courage.

Margaret Ganz (essay date 1969)

SOURCE: "The Humorist's Vision," in *Elizabeth Gaskell: The Artist in Conflict,* Twayne Publishers, 1969, pp. 132-81.

[*In the following excerpt, Ganz studies Gaskell's use of humor in two of her short works, "Mr. Harrison's Confessions" and* My Lady Ludlow.]

"Mr. Harrison's Confessions" is indeed a remarkably enlightening introduction to *Cranford,* for it not only anticipates Mrs. Gaskell's basic approach in that work, but also the Cranford setting, characters, and situation. Less subtle in approach and less whimsical in characterization, it enables us to assess the fruition of her powers in *Cranford* where a fine discrimination is unerringly at work to suggest the humor and pathos of provincial existence.

Like *Cranford,* **"Mr. Harrison's Confessions"** treats us to a picture of small-town life in which a self-sufficient society largely composed of widows and maiden ladies pursues a well-regulated round of tea-drinkings, card-playings, shopping trips, and outings, and indulges in its favorite pastime of gossip (mostly matrimonial conjectures). Specific characters in *Cranford* are already suggested: Miss Tomkinson, the Roman-nosed "grenadier" whose gruff appearance belies her kind heart is an appropriate predecessor for the assertive bluestocking Miss Deborah Jenkyns . . . busybody Miss Horsman anticipates Miss Pole.

Though Mrs. Gaskell handles the at once absurd and endearing attributes of the "Amazons" ruling the provincial world with far greater skill and diversity in *Cranford,* she already irradiates them with humor in this early story. Even here the Duncombe ladies' gossip is not seen as just a silly, or even malicious, way of filling up idle time in a society where little work is performed. As she will show more subtly in *Cranford,* such conduct has its whimsical, appealing side because it reflects some basic contradictions and incongruities in the nature of its inhabitants and thus documents that eternally humorous contrast between the dictates of reason and the claims of the imagination. We already witness in **"Mr. Harrison's Confessions"** the comic and touching spectacle of a society whose behavior is confined within exact rules and ceremonies but whose imaginative life transcends those restrictions, appropriating to itself all external events and performing upon them those distortions and magnifications which bring them into line with their (often unconscious) aspirations and apprehensions.

The town's ludicrous misunderstandings regarding the marital intentions not only of young Doctor Harrison, a newcomer, but of Mr. Morgan, the older doctor who prides himself on his knowledge of the town's ways, could easily have been merely a series of farcical *quid pro quos*. But the author's whimsicality enriches the comic situation by sometimes giving the silly pretensions of the town ladies a certain baroque charm. Thus Miss Tomkinson makes a stab at culture and sophistication by naïvely assuring the young doctor that "We have been all anticipating an Apollo . . . and an Aesculapius combined in one; or, perhaps I might confine myself to saying Apollo, as he, I believe, was the god of medicine!" Mrs. Bullock strives for exquisite taste by objecting to the chemical symbols in her husband's manual because "they give the page a very ragged appearance" and by praising her father's contempt for "variety" in books.

The tendency of Duncombe residents to deny reality and yield to their imagination is charmingly suggested in the narrator's comments on the practice of calling the police:

> Now there was no police, only a rheumatic constable, in the town; but it was the custom of the ladies, when alarmed at night, to call an imaginary police, which had, they thought, an intimidating effect; but, as everyone knew the real state of the unwatched town, we did not much mind it in general.

Yet the womanly dependence displayed here and in matrimonial aspirations that contrast so humorously with the ladies' generally self-sufficient behavior is not as subtly suggested as in *Cranford*. There is none of that naïve unconsciousness of motivations which lends ineffable pathos and sweet humor to Miss Matty Jenkyns' nervous exclamation upon hearing of an impending Cranford marriage: "Two people that we know going to be married. It's coming very near!"

Part of the qualitative difference between the two worlds is due to the vantage point from which they are each observed. And the choice of narrator is not as skillful in the earlier work. In *Cranford,* Mary Smith's sympathetic (if intermittent) participation in the town's activities guarantees an intimate knowledge of its assumptions, while her sophisticated insight into its lovable absurdities (her greatest charm) allows her to view these foibles at an affectionate remove and exercise her humor and irony upon them. The very technique of depicting Duncombe life from the point of view of Harrison, a genuine outsider by virtue of being both a *man* and a stranger to the community, effects the kind of distance which precludes, doing justice, whether seriously or humorously, to the point of view of a feminine society. The self-absorption of such a society, its self-satisfaction regarding rules and traditions—its whole ethos in fact—is so effectively celebrated in *Cranford* because Mary Smith is partially committed to it, yet unerringly senses its limitations. But the logical outcome of confronting Harrison—a dashing young doctor—with the society of Duncombe is that its mores are seen from an alien vantage point and that the emphasis falls on his plight as an eligible bachelor in a society of largely ineligible ladies.

The temptation to treat such a situation in a farcical manner is irresistible. That in **"Mr. Harrison's Confessions,"**

unlike *Cranford,* actions rather than the life of imagination are a frequent source of laughter is evident in the behavior of the ladies who do not merely dream of a changed status but embrace any opportunities to achieve their matrimonial goal. Thus Miss Caroline Tomkinson exploits her supposed ill-health to win Mr. Harrison's interest, and Mrs. Rose uses her position as housekeeper to further her mistaken hopes. The former's silly frivolity and selfishness, the latter's absurd malapropisms and coyness make them unsubtle subjects for laughter.

> **We witness in "Mr. Harrison's Confessions" the comic and touching spectacle of a society whose behavior is confined within exact rules and ceremonies but whose imaginative life transcends those restrictions.**
>
> *—Margaret Ganz*

"Mr. Harrison's Confessions" is thus basically a comedy of *situations* rather than a humorous exploration of *character* and *temperament*. The ludicrous deductions which characters make from misinterpreted appearances are not such imaginative delusions as, for example, the wild suspicions of Miss Pole in *Cranford* regarding the true identity of the female tramp, but traditional farcical misunderstandings. Mr. Harrison, who loves Sophy, the charming daughter of the Vicar, is thought to be wooing Miss Caroline Tomkinson when he is in fact on his knees only to examine her heart with his stethoscope; he is believed to be courting Mrs. Rose because he gives her a sewing table, whereas he is merely trying to get rid of an unfortunate purchase.

The farcical aspects of Harrison's situation are heightened by his active part in his own victimization; after all it is he who, right after buying the table, has tantalized Miss Horsman, the town gossip, by suggesting that he is indeed beginning to furnish a household and has a specific lady in mind. And he unwittingly reinforces Mrs. Rose's mistaken hopes by going out of his way to absolve himself of dallying with someone else. This scene in which Mr. Harrison by trying to solve one problem lays the foundation for a new one (there are echoes in the situation of that famous imbroglio which eventually landed Mr. Pickwick in prison) is a good example of the author's farcical approach to romantic misinterpretations in her story. Blind to the meaning of Mrs. Rose's coyly keeping "the fire screen . . . as yesterday, between me and her," Mr. Harrison blunders on in his presentation of what he conceives to be a reasonable, obvious justification:

> The most unfortunate misunderstanding has taken place. Miss Tomkinson thinks that I have been paying attention to Miss Caroline; when, in fact—may I tell you, Mrs. Rose?—my affections are placed elsewhere. Perhaps you have found it out already?' for indeed I thought I had been too much in love to conceal my

attachment to Sophy from anyone who knew my movements as well as Mrs. Rose.

She hung down her head, and said she believed she had found out my secret.

'Then only think how miserably I am situated. If I have any hope—oh, Mrs. Rose, do you think I have any hope'—

She put the hand-screen still more before her face, and after some hesitation she said she thought 'If I persevered—in time—I might have hope.' And then she suddenly got up and left the room.

Almost invariably actions and situations rather than character are exploited for laughter. Thus Harrison's ludicrous predicament of being romantically identified with *three* ladies (Mrs. Bullock has been pushing her daughter's claim) when he has merely heeded his superior's advice to be generally friendly is intensified by the bad reputation he owes to the mischievousness of his rowdy friend Jack. The latter's reckless conversation convinces the ladies that their new doctor has a prison record ("in Newgate for three months" is the Duncombe version) when in fact he has only once briefly appeared before a magistrate, and he compounds Harrison's romantic difficulties by secretly sending a valentine to Miss Caroline. The subtle handling of a practical joker in *Cranford* reveals the psychological poverty of a character like Jack, a mere tool to complicate the intrigue.

In keeping with the farcical mood, the depiction of characters is, as we have suggested, far less indulgent and affectionate: failings seem too often ridiculous mannerisms rather than endearing, psychologically convincing foibles. The mellow mood of *Cranford,* investing so many of the characters with lovable attributes, is absent here; even gossip is not always a harmless, amusing weakness but can be dangerously malicious; eventually assumptions are made about Mr. Harrison's character that are not entirely digestible through laughter:

. . . . I found that my practice was falling off. The prejudice of the town ran strongly against me. . . . It was said—cruel little town—that my negligence or ignorance had been the cause of Walter's death; that Miss Tyrell had become worse under my treatment; and that John Brouncker was all but dead, if he was not quite, from my mismanagement. All Jack Marshland's jokes and revelations, which had, I thought, gone to oblivion, were raked up to my discredit. . . .

In short, so prejudiced were the good people of Duncombe that I believe a very little would have made them suspect me of a brutal highway robbery, which took place in the neighbourhood about this time.

Eventually of course, in the tradition of farce, all the problems are ironed out, not without the assistance of a crop of marriages. Harrison wins the pretty and virtuous Sophy whose life he has saved by racing to a distant town to secure the necessary medicine. Mr. Morgan condescends to marry Mrs. Rose as an "efficacious contradiction" of rumors linking him with Miss Tomkinson, and Miss Caroline elopes with a rich and old tallow-chandler, having first convinced her sister that her hysteria at Harrison's supposed engagement to Mrs. Rose merely resulted from "eating pickled cucumbers."

Whereas the suggestions of pathos are in *Cranford* often an intimate function of the humorous vision of life, they are here barely perceptible in the harsher and more unsubtle atmosphere of farce; only Miss Tomkinson is sometimes touching in her selfless concern for her worthless sister. The intrusion of tragedy (the sudden death of little Walter, Sophy's appealing brother) seems therefore particularly inappropriate. In *Cranford,* where the whimsy so often has pathetic undertones, even the totally unexpected death of Captain Brown seems psychologically tenable. Humor has widened the range of possible feelings and thus reduced the gap between tears and laughter. . . .

The persistence of that inspiration which transfigured Knutsford life in *Cranford* is most dramatically evident in Mrs. Gaskell's crowning work, *Wives and Daughters* (1864-66). For, as we shall see later, though both the scope of her observation and the depth of her psychological insight have increased in that novel, her basic approach to provincial life has not really changed. She has never ceased to feel for the patterned, circumscribed way of life celebrated in *Cranford* the understanding and loving tolerance which allowed her effortlessly to do justice to the humor and pathos of its vicissitudes.

A story written seven years after *Cranford* already testifies to the continuing claim of this material on her imagination. It is true that in ***My Lady Ludlow*** (which like *Cranford,* first appeared in *Household Words*—from June 19 to September 25, 1858) her emphasis has shifted somewhat; since her heroine is a member of the aristocracy, not a genteel rector's daughter like Miss Matty, she faces different problems in relating to the little community of which she is the most august member. And yet Lady Ludlow's basic conflict is not so different from that of *Cranford*'s real heroine. For if only one has a title, both are "ladies" in the higher sense (Miss Matty, we have been told, is in contrast to the Honorable Mrs. Jamieson, "a true lady herself") and find the claims of this natural nobility often hard to reconcile with traditional allegiances.

Undoubtedly, Lady Ludlow's plight does not possess the timeless attributes of Miss Matty's dilemma. For she quite specifically represents both in her narrow-mindedness and generosity the weaknesses and strengths of an aristocracy whose way of life is on the wane. The constant clash between her resistance to change and her benevolent instincts documents a social more than a psychological phenomenon. Of course we have never been unaware of the threat of social change in old-fashioned Cranford; it is to a certain extent true that, as Paul Elmer More says, the "charm" of that book does "depend largely . . . on a feeling of unreality, or, more precisely, of proximity to the great realities of Manchester"; that the "grace" of *Cranford* "is of something that has survived into an alien age, and is about to vanish away." Indeed Mrs. Gaskell's sensitive description of the decay into which the Cranford Assembly Rooms have fallen is a moving reminder of how much "grace" (and indeed grandeur) has already vanished. But, as we have attempted to show, the author's humorous vision often transcends her specific subject to suggest in the unsophisticated Cranford ways eternal human eccentricities, thereby endowing a transient way of life with timeless, universal attributes. She is less successful in *My Lady Ludlow*, for, however humorous and touching the conflicts of "the high-bred and high-spirited, but at heart God-fearing and humble *châtelaine*" are, those conflicts most often grow out of her particular social position, whereas Miss Matty's are the natural function of her basic temperament, whose sweetness, innocence, and diffidence would be tried by the demands of conformity in almost any social situation.

Given that qualitative difference, there are remarkable resemblances in Mrs. Gaskell's approach to the social viewpoints governing the worlds of Cranford and Hanbury. Here again flourish those class distinctions which nourished many a Cranford conversation, that religious intolerance of Dissenters which the Aga Jenkyns so slyly ridiculed in Mrs. Jamieson, that conservative suspicion and hatred of all things French which Mrs. Forrester so amusingly exemplified during the Cranford "panic." And even though Lady Ludlow is the most spirited exemplar of such attitudes, neither the members of her household nor the town's inhabitants are exempt from convictions which the author, as in *Cranford,* handles with light humor or irony through the medium of a narrator. Though not as subtly conceived as the at once "prim" and shrewd Mary Smith, Margaret Dawson is nevertheless lively and observant as she reminisces on her youth when, one of a select group of young ladies, she was educated in Lady Ludlow's household. Like Mary Smith, she chronicles her former sympathies with the assumptions of that world, even as she reveals its humorous limitations. Thus as she recalls Lady Ludlow's indignation at the news that a neighboring estate "was bought by a Baptist baker from Birmingham," she goes on to display the absurdity of her own prejudices at that time:

> "A Baptist baker!" I exclaimed. I had never seen a Dissenter, to my knowledge; but, having always heard them spoken of with horror, I looked upon them almost as if they were rhinoceroses. I wanted to see a live Dissenter, I believe, and yet I wished it were over. I was almost surprised when I heard that any of them were engaged in such peaceful occupations as baking.

It is of course in Lady Ludlow that such conservative views assume their most whimsical form. For her, the wearing of one's "own hair" is a sinister repercussion of the French Revolution since "To be without powder . . . was in fact to insult the proprieties of life by being undressed. It was English sans-culottism." Because she is suspicious of widespread education as "levelling and rev-

olutionary," she will not hire servants who can write; young Harry Gregson's boast of having read a letter before delivering it to her provokes a lengthy tale of woeful adventures during the French Revolution illustrating the dire results of educating the lower classes. The Vicar Mr. Gray, who is eager to establish a Sunday school in the village, is accordingly a sore trial to her after the comforting presence of the former clergyman, Mr. Mountford, who, as the narrator informs us, "was true blue, as we call it, to the backbone; hated the dissenters and the French; and could hardly drink a dish of tea without giving out the toast of 'Church and King, and down with the Rump'."

What the story documents is the humorous and touching way in which Lady Ludlow comes to terms with the threatening inroads of change upon those principles which are her way of life. Invariably, like Miss Matty, she triumphs over her deeply ingrained traditionalism through a kind heart.

Even her opposition to the Sunday school is eventually overcome as, almost in spite of herself, her natural feelings go out to the very people who had so uncomfortably challenged her. Her regard for her steward; her growing fondness for young Harry Gregson, his protégé (whom at some sacrifice she has helped financially after an accident); her increasing admiration and affection for the shy clergyman, Mr. Gray, whose courageous refusal to obey her has both outraged her pride and stimulated her liking—all these emotions triumph over her wish to assert authority by achieving a general subservience to conservative principles.

Though Lady Ludlow's apprehensions and prejudices sometimes possess the whimsy and absurd charm of private eccentricities rather than conventional snobberies, her capitulations to the dictates of the heart are viewed more often through sentiment than humor. Only one whimsical instance of true charity deserves to take its place with the best examples of the author's humor in *Cranford;* it is that in which Lady Ludlow's exquisite tact and tenderness triumph over her commitment to social graces as she rescues from public ridicule Mrs. Brooke, the wife of that same "Baptist baker from Birmingham" whose arrival in the community had so outraged her sensibilities. Margaret Dawson's correspondent describes for her the following scene at Lady Ludlow's tea party:

> ". . . all the parsonesses were looking at Mrs. Brooke, for she had shown her want of breeding before; and the parsonesses, who were just a step above her in manners, were very much inclined to smile at her doings and sayings. Well! what does she do but pull out a clean Bandana pocket-handkerchief, all red and yellow silk; spread it over her best silk gown. . . . There we were, Tom Diggles even on the grin . . . and Mrs. Parsoness of Headleigh—I forget her name, and it's no matter, for she's an ill-bred creature . . . —was right-down bursting with laughter, and as near a hee-haw as ever a donkey was; when what does my lady do? . . . She takes out her own pocket-handkerchief,

all snowy cambric, and lays it softly down on her velvet lap, for all the world as if she did it every day of her life, just like Mrs. Brooke, the baker's wife; and when the one got up to shake the crumbs into the fireplace, the other did just the same. But with such a grace! and such a look at us all."

It is appropriate that this instance of Lady Ludlow's capacity to love (which puts to shame the coarser snobbery of those far less entitled to scoff at ill-breeding than she) should be recounted by Miss Galindo, the kind-hearted eccentric. From the moment this seemingly "queer, abrupt, disagreeable, busy old maid" appears on the scene (and she does so only halfway through the story), she brings with her direct reverberations from the Cranford world. Devoid of the aristocratic dignity and grace which make her august patroness Lady Ludlow a rather difficult subject for humor, Miss Galindo allows the author to illustrate with zest and whimsy those grotesqueries of behavior which distinguish the lovable Cranford eccentrics.

Nor is Miss Galindo, with her brusque frankness and outlandish generosity, a mere echo of such characters as Miss Deborah Jenkyns or Miss Pole. There is in her an added dimension of intelligence and self-consciousness which makes her both the subject of laughter and the conscious perpetrator of it. If she is, like Miss Jenkyns, committed to the proposition that women can do more than hold their own with men, she obviously enjoys her whimsical ways of abetting men's erroneous sense of self-importance. So that, when she undertakes, at the request of Lady Ludlow, the position of clerk to Mr. Horner, her attempts to allay his suspicions of womanly incompetence satisfy her playful instincts:

> "I see he [Mr. Horner] can't find a fault—writing good, spelling correct, sums all right. And then he squints at me with the tail of his eye, and looks glummer than ever, just because I'm a woman—as if I could help that. I have gone good lengths to set his mind at ease. I have stuck my pen behind my ear; I have made him a bow instead of a curtsey; I have whistled—not a tune, I can't pipe up that—nay, if you won't tell my lady, I don't mind telling you that I have said 'Confound it!' and 'Zounds!' I can't get any farther."

That her own eccentricities often imply some shrewd comment on human failings is evident when she describes a short-lived literary career, started by providing herself with "paper and half-a-hundred good pens, a bottle of ink, all ready," and abruptly terminated by "my having nothing to say, when I sat down to write." She finds the logic of that decision questionable, however, for, as she puts it, "sometimes, when I get hold of a book, I wonder why I let such a poor reason stop me. It does not others." Even wholly absurd comments reveal some sharp power of observation turned to comic use. Thus she defends her assumption that Lady Ludlow's acquaintance, a retired captain in the navy, is the possessor of a wooden leg by indisputable evidence: ". . . sailors are almost always wounded in the leg. Look at Greenwich Hospital! I should say there were twenty one-legged pensioners to one with-out an arm there."

Since Miss Galindo shares both Lady Ludlow's conservative principles (her objection to mass education takes the comic form of indignation that her little servant should be "seduced" from her daily work by the clergyman's attempts to save her soul) and her innate generosity of soul, but is more shrewd and realistic about the challenges of change, she serves as an appropriate mediator in reconciling Lady Ludlow to its demands. She herself has placed love above propriety by taking into her home the illegitimate child of a man she once hoped to marry (like Miss Matty, she has been condemned to spinsterhood by social prejudice). Her admiration for the Vicar's kind-heartedness has led to an emotional acceptance of his liberal views on education, an acceptance not without its effect on Lady Ludlow. It is Miss Galindo who, in her whimsical way, also reconciles Lady Ludlow to the final indignity of Captain James's marriage with the daughter of the Baptist baker. Of the actual choice made by the two partners she has this to say:

> "Indeed, my lady, I have long left off trying to conjecture what makes Jack fancy Gill, or Gill Jack. It's best to sit down quiet under the belief that marriages are made for us, somewhere out of this world, and out of the range of this world's reason and laws. I'm not so sure that I should settle it down that they were made in heaven; t'other place seems to me as likely a workshop; but at any rate, I've given up troubling my head as to why they take place."

How fully Lady Ludlow finally comes to share her opinion has already been demonstrated in the little scene described by Miss Galindo to Margaret Dawson. Both characters testify to the transcending power of human sympathy over social conventions, once again reasserting the author's central message not only in *Cranford,* of course, but in her social novels.

Though **My Lady Ludlow** lacks that sustained vision of human eccentricities and effortless control over plot and atmosphere which give *Cranford* its artistic coherence, it nevertheless provides another significant instance of the author's ability to make meaningful—especially through humor—those struggles and conflicts which do not take place in the dramatic arenas of the great world but in the confines of that provincial one whose secrets she had been able so early to discover.

Claire Tomalin   (review date 1978)

SOURCE: "Fireside Frissons," in *Times Literary Supplement,* No. 3983, August 4, 1978, p. 881.

[*In the following review of* Mrs. Gaskell's Tales of Mystery and Horror, *Tomalin suggests that the twentieth-century impulse to classify Gaskell as a "mystery" or "horror" writer is misleading.*]

Elizabeth Gaskell's friends spoke of her as a teller of ghost stories at the fireside; and she once lightly claimed to have seen a ghost. Her biographer, Winifred Gérin, reminded us of her Celtic origins but had little more to say about her interest in the supernatural: hardly surprising, since the great mass of her work, including the majority of the stories in this slim collection, was firmly built on earthly premises.

Of the seven tales here, only one is a ghost story proper—**"The Old Nurse's Story."** Written in 1852 at the invitation of Dickens for the Christmas number of *Household Words*, it is a stock tale of a small orphan sent with her nurse to a lonely mansion below the Fells; they encounter weird music from a ruined organ, a locked east wing and whispers of old family scandals. The conclusion is crude melodrama, but there is one powerful touch which must surely be cribbed from Emily Brontë: a ghostly waif who is heard "crying, and beating against the window-panes, as if she wanted to be let in."

For the following Christmas Mrs Gaskell offered Dickens a wholly unremarkable tale of a highwayman, buttressed by a verse translation of a contemporary Breton poem on a folk theme, which was not even her own work but her husband's. It can hardly have been what Dickens had in mind (but Michael Ashley prints it here). The next few years saw her preoccupied with *North and South* and her *Life of Charlotte Brontë;* then in 1859 Dickens again asked for a ghost story to be run as part of a series in his new magazine, *All the Year Round.* This time Mrs Gaskell sent him an extremely fine piece of writing, **"The Crooked Branch."** Its drawback was that there was nothing supernatural about it; but he tacked on an introductory paragraph to remedy this and changed the title to **"The Ghost of the Garden Room."** Since the change was made purely to suit the series, it is hard to see why Mr Ashley uses the Dickens title here except to support his claim that this is primarily a tale of mystery and horror.

But **"The Crooked Branch"** does not trace its ancestry to *The Castle of Otranto* or *Frankenstein* It is the fruit of Mrs Gaskell's abiding interest in locality—in this instance a North Riding farm, exactly and affectionately delineated—and in the unredeemed miseries of the poor. Here her imagination is at its most fertile, as she shows the old couple uneasily watching their spoilt son leave for London and return again with a different accent: they know very little, but enough to sense that their story has taken a wrong turn and this is "not a true prince." Her feeling for the working of their minds is remarkable again when she shows the farmer and his niece puzzling over a dead letter returned by the postman, half convinced that the phrase signifies the death of the intended recipient.

The story embodies another of Mrs Gaskell's favourite themes, that of the fresh, vulnerable girl forced to await her destiny quite passively and gradually losing youth and smiles and hope. This figure of the good girl blighted appears again in **"Lois the Witch,"** a novella written in the same year and the longest piece of this group. **"Lois"** is not a story of the supernatural, as Mr Ashley claims,

but a careful piece of historical fiction based on the Salem witch trials (and surely owing something to Hawthorne's *Scarlet Letter*). It is painful, even gruesome to read but scrupulously based on fact and a clear grasp of the way in which hysteria can run through a family. One critic (Coral Lansbury) has suggested that Mrs Gaskell was drawing on some of her knowledge of Haworth Parsonage; and while this does not really fit the case—neither the rigidity nor the hysteria were of the same kind—there is no doubt that the springs of the story are in human psychology, not the occult.

Mr Ashley's determination to claim these stories as offspring of the Gothic novel (which he describes as having been given a "seal of approval" by *Northanger Abbey*) does not lead him into any illuminating comments upon them. He tells us that Mrs Gaskell emphasized the personal aspect of the supernatural, as opposed to male writers who were more interested in its scientific aspect Yes; and a case could be made for printing *Mary Barton* and *Ruth* as more tales of mystery and horror. But Mrs Gaskell is a writer so subtle and exciting that any refloating of her stories is welcome, even under these somewhat strange colours.

Ina Ferris (review date 1979)

SOURCE: Review of *Mrs. Gaskell's Tales of Mystery and Horror,* in *Nineteenth Century Fiction,* Vol. 34, No. 1, June, 1979, pp. 95-6.

[*Here, Ferris faults Gaskell's ability to portray the non-rational motivations which give rise to fantasy, mystery, and the Gothic.*]

This collection of six Gaskell stories [**Mrs. Gaskell's Tales of Mystery and Horror**] appears as part of the Gollancz Library of Fantasy and Macabre. But only two of the stories (**"The Old Nurse's Tale"** and **"Curious If True"**) venture into the supranatural world of fantasy, and none generates the crawling horror of the genuine macabre. Readers hoping to discover exotic depths in a Gaskell released from the confines of realism will be disappointed. These tales come from the same world and the same mind as do the novels, so offer no startling insights into Gaskell as a fiction writer. Her novels, despite their diversity, draw sustenance from a firm belief in reason and history, and it is no accident that the most powerful story in this volume, **"Lois the Witch,"** turns to history and reconstructs the collective loss of reason in Salem in 1692. But the emotional sanity and fundamental rationality that make Gaskell so attractive as a realist prevent her from handling effectively less rational modes of narrative. The language of understanding lacks the psychic resonance and dramatic power needed to convey the edge where rational and nonrational converge, the edge which is the source of tales of mystery. And a mind as committed to civil society as that of Gaskell cannot penetrate the anarchic primal impulses that feed fantasy and horror. Not only does Gaskell repeatedly defuse the irrational world but she fails to imagine convincingly that world itself. She contains her ghost story ("**The Old Nurse's Tale**") within a moral commonplace, but her ghosts are easily contained because they never move beyond the function of moral exempla to begin with.

As with most Victorian novelists, Gaskell's is an expansive imagination, and compression crushes its vitality. The economy of the short story requires a suggestive concentration alien to Gaskell.

—Ina Ferris

The stories, then, should be seen not as departures from but as extensions of her work as a realistic novelist. But here, also, they are generally disappointing. "**The Ghost in the Garden Room**" (more commonly known in its shorter version, "**The Crooked Branch**") is typical in offering a well-worn tale conventionally handled. This predictable story of a spoiled son who goes bad is illuminated fitfully by Gaskell's characteristic strength in handling dialect and her ability to convey the pathos of the inarticulate. But Wordsworth did it all much better in "Michael," and we sense that Gaskell herself is not fully engaged in her narrative. This suspicion is reinforced by the knowledge that "**The Ghost in the Garden Room**," like most of the stories collected here, was written for one of Dickens's Christmas issues, an enterprise that Gaskell never took very seriously. Furthermore, the technical clumsiness of the tales, particularly in pacing and structure, illustrates Gaskell's incompatibility with the mode of the short story. As with most Victorian novelists, hers is an expansive imagination, and compression crushes its vitality. The economy of the short story requires a suggestive concentration alien to Gaskell. Whereas her novels, for example, handle the problem of betrayal with rich insight, the stories offer a routine, thin treatment of the same theme.

Only when Gaskell finds space and a subject that sparks her historical imagination does her writing achieve force. In the lengthy "**Lois the Witch**" she produces a gripping tale of a community out of control, sustaining here the intensity essential to shorter fiction. The image of Salem, enclosed by the dark forest, cut off by winter snows, and left "to prey upon itself," is masterfully created. In this story Gaskell's complex historical intuition of the connection between environment and sensibility takes control, and she defines the morbid Puritan culture generated as a defense against the pressures of pioneer experience, a culture breeding the self-destructive "corruption of imagination" that infected Salem so dramatically. The word "imagination" tolls through this narrative, rendering explicit the fear of the imagination that underlies a good deal of Victorian writing. In "**Lois the Witch**" the imagination is a dark force capable of transforming reality and destroying whatever it finds uncongenial. Gaskell links its power to the introversion, individualism, and transcen-

dence of the Puritan code, expressing the rationalist's distrust of a mind that sustains itself on a nonempirical reality. Although the story maintains the classic realist pattern of the defeat of idealism, its emotional core is charged with a fear that empirical reality is indeed vulnerable, malleable. The ground, as in much Victorian fiction, may not be so solid, after all.

"**Lois the Witch**" is an important, impressive addition to the Gaskell canon, and Michael Ashley has performed a valuable service in rescuing it from the out-of-print files. If none of the other stories matches its achievement, the collection is nonetheless useful in aiding students of Elizabeth Gaskell to clarify the still nebulous understanding of the nature of her fiction.

George Levine   (essay date 1981)

SOURCE: "The Landscape of Reality," in *The Realistic Imagination: English Fiction from Frankenstein to Lady Chatterley,* University of Chicago Press, 1981, pp. 204-26.

[*In the following excerpt, Levine analyzes the narrative of Gaskell's novella* Cousin Phillis, *placing the work within the Victorian realistic tradition.*]

Since, in keeping with the compromises realism entails, the landscape of the real is consistently rather flat, or at best rolling, a topographical survey of the Victorian novel would produce a large and unilluminating catalogue. It is worth pausing, however, for a glance at a characteristically low and domesticated landscape in order to gather some sense of the way such a landscape at once denies and imitates more absolute and more frightening realities, and accommodates itself to the more subtle shades, the less checkered patterns of the novelist's reality. A convenient place to look for such a landscape—although it is also the landscape of George Eliot's midlands, of Hardy's Wessex, of Trollope's Barsetshire—would be in the works of Elizabeth Gaskell, a writer who stands with Trollope as one of Victorian realism's most consistent practitioners. In Gaskell, as in Trollope, there are moments of violence and suggestions of extremes; but few writers stay more firmly within the limits Charlotte Brontë advocated but could not herself accept.

In her short novel *Cousin Phillis*, Gaskell confines her narrative to a sharply imagined place that has the virtue, for my purposes, of neatly focusing the dominant landscapes of the Victorian realistic tradition. Hope Farm seems to imply all the qualities that led early modern writers to reject Victorian realism as prudish and sentimental. The very name contains a suggestion of allegory which might seem inconsistent with the most rigorous realistic techniques, but is in fact consistent with its practice. (Think of Trollope's Mrs. Proudie, or the Duke of Omnium, of George Eliot's Middlemarch and Lowick, of Thackeray's Newcomes or, for that matter, Pen; it is not by any means only Dickens who uses names in this way.) Mr. Holman (again allegorical, of course) is both farmer and minister, an apparently complete man of learning and of physical power. But what Gaskell is giving us here is something very precisely individualized while also typical. Hope Farm seems almost the ideal of the old English countryside, showing evidence of its history and of an earlier grandeur ("two great gates between pillars crowned with stone balls for a state entrance"), but now entirely functional and unpretentious. "It's an old place," we learn early, "though Holman keeps it in good order."

All the action occurs at the farm, in the widely interspersed visits of the narrator, Paul Manning, and, in effect, very little happens, for the narrative is marked by the absence of finality. The farm is governed by the rhythms of the seasons, in a characteristic mid-nineteenth-century fashion; and with quietly mythic implications "there was a garden between the house and the shady, grassy lane." Almost everything is understated or deflected, and the expected romance between Paul and Cousin Phillis is dismissed very shortly, for Paul finds it uncomfortable to imagine a wife in a beautiful young woman "half a head taller" than he, who reads books "I had never heard of" and talks about them too, "as of far more interest than any mere personal subjects." One senses, of course, that something dangerous enters the garden and threatens the carefully cultivated paradise; but it is difficult to find a clear villain. It has as much to do with the inevitable rhythms of natural growth and change—which are assimilated to the growth and change going on in society as whole—as with "plot" in any ordinary sense.

The critical scenes in the narrative are all imagined very carefully in the landscapes, which are conceived subtly as both highly cultivated and vulnerable to natural violence. Holdsworth, the railroad engineer Paul introduces into the family, is the alien element in the garden that finally disrupts its peace, and he is the subject of the only abrupt intrusion into the narrative's direct movement through time that Paul (or Gaskell) chooses to make. Before the crisis comes, Paul writes, "It is many years since I have seen thee, Edward Holdsworth, but thou wast a delightful fellow! Ay, and a good one too; though much sorrow was caused by thee." The effect, of course, is to disallow any absolute imagination of evil—Holdsworth is no snake in the garden—before we have a chance to feel his behavior as such. But the critical scene in which Holdsworth evokes Phillis's love has about it the ominousness of evil's inobtrusive entrance into the garden. Interestingly, although the landscape is low, it is at least a bit higher than its surroundings. Paul goes to find his friends

> out on to a broad upland common, full of red sand-banks, and sweeps and hollows; bordered by dark firs, purple in the coming shadows, but near at hand all ablaze with flowering gorse, or, as we call it in the south, furze-bushes, which, seen against the belt of distant trees, appeared brilliantly golden. On this heath, a little way from the field-gate, I saw the three. I counted their heads, joined together in an eager group over Holdsworth's theodolite.

The scene is ominously pretty, quietly suggestive of disruption, and that disruption comes physically in a violent electric storm. Of course, Holdsworth himself is the disruption, and in several ways. First, we have already learned that there is something "foreign" about him. "He cuts his hair in a foreign fashion," Paul had told Phillis earlier, and she had answered with, "I like an Englishman to look like an Englishman." But the foreignness of Holdsworth has not merely to do with Italian haircuts. He brings the machine to the garden for he is learned both in languages and in the technology of the railways. Mr. Holman suggests that "there is a want of seriousness in his talk at times," but, Holman goes on to say, "it is like dram-drinking. I listen to him till I forget my duties, and am carried off my feet. Last Sabbath evening he led us away into talk on profane subjects ill befitting the day." Not accidentally, Holdsworth's first act with Phillis is to help her translate Dante's *Inferno*! The obviously symbolic collocation of facts is so muted in the text that it is easy to read over them and miss it, and in a way it is important that one do so. Holdsworth is not, we are early warned, a devil, but a "delightful fellow." The scene in the heath, in any case, wonderfully and subtly enacts the complexities and shadings Gaskell seeks.

While Holdsworth satisfies Holman's thirst for knowledge, they all fail to notice the upcoming storm—the rain came "sooner than they had looked for." Holman, who keeps his lands "in order" and is learning from Holdsworth how to "survey" it, opens himself to the disorder and violence of nature itself when it is not comfortably regulated in relation to home and garden. And it is here, after Phillis rushes to rescue Holdsworth's "apparatus," that we are allowed to see Phillis's own potentiality for sexual energy. "She came running back, her long lovely hair floating and dripping, her eyes glad and bright, and her colour freshened to a glow of health by the exercise and the rain." Holdsworth then, in a spirit of badinage that Phillis does not quite understand, calls her "Willful" and "Unchristian." The misunderstanding provokes Holdsworth to say "something gravely" to her, "and in too low a tone for me to hear." The snake has entered the Holmans' garden, and it has done so in an exposed geography, where forces beyond the control of cultivation are released. At the same time, it is important to note that the release of those forces is very much Holman's responsibility, intoxicated as he is with knowledge. It is equally important to see that on this only slightly raised elevation Holman's failure is barely evil at all. Through most of the novel, knowledge is not sinful; and, indeed, until the end a rigorously antiintellectual and puritanical reading is disallowed in the cold comfortings of Brother Hodgson and Robinson. They ask Holman, with a subtle significance for the text, whether "this world's learning has not puffed you up to vain conceit and neglect of the things of God." Holman's answer is, I think, decisive, and central to our experience of realism and of the natural landscape. "I hold with Christ that afflictions are not sent by God in wrath as penalties for sin."

The other crucial scene is also set deliberately out-of-doors where nature can do its worst; once again, however, it is not a place of wilderness and desolation but a great stack of wood in the orchard. There Phillis sits on a log in the snow on a "bitter cold day," and there Paul hears her "making a low moan, like an animal in pain, or perhaps more like the sobbing of the wind." Her pain and her direct assimilation to wild nature are the result of Holdsworth's departure. Significantly for our sense of realism's landscape, he has gone to foreign places—to Canada—there to help build a railway, that powerful emblem of the new knowledge and the new culture. Paul, to relieve Phillis's pain, then tells her that Holdsworth, before his departure, had said that he loved Phillis and wished to marry her. Again, the new knowledge has ambiguous value. It suddenly rescues Phillis from the anguish of her simple animality, allows her to resist the deadly cold and to return to the warmth of the hearth. Yet it also implicates the "innocent" narrator, for when Holdsworth, inevitably in that foreign place, falls in love with another Lucy (Paul had noted how Phillis reminded him of Words-worth's poem) and marries her, the effect on Phillis is even more deadly. It finally saps her of all energy. The literal cold returns as a spiritual cold.

But what is perhaps most striking about *Cousin Phillis* is that its obvious mythic structure, which gives it a stunningly un-Trollopian shapeliness and coherence, finally undercuts itself. The violence of the weather that threatens with each critical access of knowledge in the novel's rarely exposed geography is ultimately understood to be both significant and random. Holman's humane faith that afflictions are not sent as penalties disorders the universe which was, apparently, so firmly and mythically ordered by the novel's garden, by Dante's Inferno, by Holman's and Phillis's acquiescence in Holdsworth's seductive attractiveness. In its quiet way the novel abstains from moral judgment—of Holdsworth, or Holman, or Paul, or Phillis. What happens is felt to be quite natural and unforced despite Gaskell's wonderful shaping art. At the same time, in the storm on the heath, in the cold at the woodpile, in the depths of Canada, there are energies beyond the control of either characters or author. When Phillis recovers at the end, we are reminded that in the ordinary world tragedy is never absolute; and we understand that she does so by force of will. Everyone has done for her what is possible. The servant, Betty, tells her: "Now Phillis! . . . we ha' done a' we can for you, and th' doctors has done a' they can for you, and I think the Lord has done a' He can for you, and more than you deserve too, if you don't do something for yourself." Finally, there is nothing but individual human will in a world where the natural, however securely domesticated, moves inevitably to disruption. When Phillis concludes by asking for a "change of scene," we know that the mythic expulsion from the garden is completed. "Only for a short time," she says, "Then—we will go back to the peace of the old days. I know we shall; I can, and I will!"

The will is all that can do it; but it cannot do it. Paradise, surely, will not be regained. Moreover, as we examine the energies of nature quietly manifest in the book, and as we consider how implicated in them are the very figures whose force of will has brought order to the countryside, we recognize that it was no paradise in the first place—attractive though it may have been. The powerful father is less competent than the ignorant mother, and his interests are absolutely different. He had tried artificially to keep the family knit together—almost as the Frankenstein family did in its domestic haven in Geneva. The inevitable intrusion finds him unprepared. Only in Gaskell's quietly confident muting of the extremes does she avert the full implications of Mary Shelley's romance. Holdsworth, after all, is a "delightful fellow," and Phillis, as Thackeray and Trollope both would have known, does not die of a broken heart. The monster is in the garden, but Gaskell's realism dulls his ferocity sufficiently to make a life of quiet, wary compromise possible.

Gaskell, in demythifying the landscape and her narrative, implies that experience is an endless and disenchanting process, but avoids dissolution into sheer multiplicity. She stays within one sharply delimited narrative, and contains the monstrous energies figured by wilder landscapes. The effect is achieved in part by the continuities among the personal, social, and natural worlds; the precisely located place in which the action evolves implies the nature of the characters who live there, of the culture they represent (as opposed to that of the railroad people who visit them), and of the natural world that encroaches on its borders. But that place is clearly not the Alps. Its gentler outlines metaphorically imply a quiet Wordsworthian world of feeling. If the very prettiness implicitly hides the symbol of suffering that George Eliot places in the landscape of *Adam Bede,* we are not allowed to see the symbol. It is a sad domestic story, not a romantic tragedy.

Barbara Weiss (essay date 1984)

SOURCE: "Elizabeth Gaskell: The Telling of Feminine Tales," in *Studies in the Novel,* Vol. 16, No. 3, Fall, 1984, pp. 274-87.

[*In the following essay, Weiss maintains that the short tales within Gaskell's larger fiction work out "the anxieties and ambiguities inherent in the role of the female artist."*]

In considering the works of Elizabeth Gaskell, the critic is immediately confronted with those twin damning adjectives, "charming" and "minor," which have clung to the reputation of Gaskell in the present century and prevented a balanced and serious consideration of her works. Discussions of her talent usually suggest her marginal status, protraying her as a homemaker and an amateur, rather than as a serious professional writer. And no quality has been held against the author more than her natural gift of storytelling. Her love of plot-making, her appreciation of the good anecdote, story, or melodrama has been cited against her, as if her very charm and natural ability as a spinner of tales were evidence of an absence of art and purpose in her works. In particular, the interpolated tales which frequently crop up in all but her most mature works are likely to strike the modern critic as disruptive and unnecessary. In recent years, however, feminist criticism has shed a new light on the act of storytelling and its psychological implications for the female artist. Sandra Gilbert and Susan Gubar, for example, in *The Madwoman in the Attic* have explored the difficulties inherent in the position of the woman writer in an age in which ideal women were supposed to have no stories and in which the act of making stories of one's own life or the lives of other women could be considered a subversive activity. In a tradition of patriarchal literature, great anxiety and self-doubt seem to have been the portion of those women who attempted to give a feminine shape to reality by telling their own tales. Viewed in such a context, then, the interpolated tales in Gaskell's works may have been the means through which the author was able to work out the anxieties and ambiguities inherent in the role of female artist. Indeed, in the seemingly artless and random tales which her characters tell to one another, Gaskell may well have explored her own attitude toward fiction and the act of making fiction, and her perceptions about the difference between the fiction of men and the fiction of women.

Gaskell's life-long love of a good story is well documented; her letters attest to an early interest in local customs, legends, and superstitions. Her dramatic skill as a raconteuse was valued by the Howitts, who praised her ability to tell ghost stories around the fire, while her friend Charles Eliot Norton wrote, "She is a wonderful storyteller . . . always dramatic." Several of her published stories suggest her delight in a rattling good ghost story (**"The Old Nurse's Tale"** and **"The Poor Clare"**) and many reflect her interest in local folklore, embroidering or reworking local tales with an introduction tracing something of their origins. But it is her fondness for interpolating a seemingly unrelated tale into the midst of an ongoing narrative that has marked Gaskell in the eyes of her critics as a naturally gifted but essentially artless amateur. Even Edgar Wright, who in *Mrs. Gaskell: The Basis for Reassessment* makes the most persuasive case for her "unity" and "development" as an important writer, is forced to take her to task for her interpolated tales: "Mrs. Gaskell was one of those who find it difficult to resist a digression; to this extent her fondness for reminiscence and local tales affects the mechanics of her art as well as the tautness of her style." And indeed it cannot be denied that Gaskell was sometimes guilty of interrupting the continuity of her work with an unrelated tale or anecdote. The gentle, pastoral tone of **My Lady Ludlow**, for example, is seriously disrupted by the gory tale of Clément, a melodrama which occupies about one-third of the book with only the lamest excuse of connection to the main plot. More often it was the comic anecdote which tempted Gaskell from the flow of her narrative. In *Mary Barton*, for example, Margaret tells an involved story of a seemingly dead scorpion her grandfather brought home, only to have it thaw out by the fire. Often such stories are put in the mouth of a local character to serve the function of local color as well as comedy. One of the delights of *Ruth* is to be found in the comic stories of the servant Sally, which cannot fail to entertain the reader, even if they do nothing to speed the progress of the narrative. In one

memorable and long-winded tale, Sally tells of the clerk who got down on his knees while she kneeled at her cleaning tasks and proposed marriage instead of the "Methodee" prayer she had expected. The story meanders on for eleven pages; its avowed purpose, which it accomplishes, is to "talk" Ruth to sleep. Other equally verbose tales include Sally's recovery of Christian cheerfulness after causing Mr. Benson's accident and the making of her will, in which she pays an extra sixpence for each fancy "law-word" included. Such comic tales serve as the very staple of *Cranford,* which consists largely of remembered anecdotes of such local and domestic events as the old woman dressing her cow in flannel, or the cat swallowing the old lace. The verve of such anecdotes cannot fail to amuse the reader, but it is their seemingly random quality which has earned their author the epithets "charming," "minor," and "artless."

To defend Elizabeth Gaskell fully from such pejorative terms, it would perhaps be necessary to prove that she did indeed possess a conscious aesthetic in the creation of literary fiction, a task made difficult by the author's own self-effacement as a writer. Seldom in her letters did Gaskell discuss the artistic principles of her work; she was, of all Victorian authors, perhaps the least likely to make grand pronouncements upon her own art. For this reason it will be necessary to turn to the work itself to discover what Gaskell considered to be the function of fiction, and an interesting starting point is a seldom remarked episode in *Sylvia's Lovers,* in which the hero Phillip finds consolation for his troubles in the reading of old tales. Estranged from Sylvia by his own failure of truth and her lack of charity, Phillip goes off to war, returning home poverty-stricken and disfigured, to take refuge as a bedesman. Seeking diversion, he immerses himself in a "tattered old volume" of the *Seven Champions of Christendom* and reads of how Sir Guy, Earl of Warwick, came home from war disguised as a beggar and was unrecognized by his own wife until he sent for her to come to his deathbed. There "they had many sweet and holy words together, before he gave up the ghost, his head lying on her bosom." Obsessed with this literary image, Phillip dwells upon it as comfort and inspiration: "All night long, Guy and Phillis, Sylvia and his child, passed in and out of his vision." The story of Sir Guy and his wife, of course, neatly forecasts and encapsulates the destiny of Phillip and Sylvia, who will be reunited in compassion and forgiveness on Phillip's deathbed. Gaskell had this ending firmly in mind from the very beginning of the composition of *Sylvia's Lovers:* she seems to have felt that the emotional truth of her tale was embodied in this ending, for she wrote to her reader, W. S. Williams at Smith and Elder, asking him not to judge the book until he could see how it would be justified by the ending. The function of the story from the *Seven Champions of Christendom,* then, is to foreshadow the reconciliation and Christian harmony in which *Sylvia's Lovers* is destined to conclude. This connection is significant, for it seems to suggest that literary fictions, such as the story of Sir Guy, can convey the hard-won emotional lessons which characters are often too blind to recognize clearly. The telling of a tale can often encapsulate emotional truths which function as either warning or inspiration, functions which Gaskell, like her Victorian contemporaries, would have considered to be the first obligations of literature. Seen in this light, then, the tales and anecdotes which interrupt the flow of a narrative are hardly likely to be random or artless, and an examination of the other interpolated tales of *Sylvia's Lovers* should bear out this theory.

Though assuredly not a feminist writer, no Victorian woman writer of major stature was more aggressively *feminine* than Gaskell.

—*Barbara Weiss*

Unlike the tale of Sir Guy, which comes from a "tattered old volume," the other tales of the novel come from an oral tradition of legends and local history; one of them is clearly an indulgence by the author in her weakness for ghost stories—a sailor's tale of how his uncle was saved from robbers by his brother's ghost. Other stories, however, are more closely related to the theme and unifying images of the novel. Kinraid, for example, first impresses Sylvia with his tales of the sights he has seen on his whaling voyages. As she listens in "fascinated wonder," he tells her what seems to be a typical sailor's tall tale about his glimpse of the "mouth o' hell"—a wall of ice seventy miles long with burning flames inside it, and black demons darting about it. The story is significant, for it marks the first impression which Kinraid makes upon Sylvia; but it also is significant for the way in which its fiery images seem to jar with the pastoral milieu of Sylvia's life. Kinraid's suggestion that it was the daring of the sailors which led them to "peep at terrors forbidden to any on us afore our time" hints of a wild and reckless nature in the young sailor; while he is not developed as an evil or demonic character, the nature of his tale certainly suggests that he is neither destined nor suited to be the hero of the pastoral romance in which Sylvia is casting him. Similar in nature is the tale which Daniel Robson uses to cap the young sailor's story, also a sailor's yarn and one with which the young Robson first fascinated and courted Sylvia's mother years before. Like Kinraid's tale, Robson's nautical story about a wild ride upon the back of a whale suggests a nature unsuited for domestic harmony and responsibility, and perhaps forecasts Robson's reckless end, riding on and at the same time imprisoned by a wave of mob violence.

Opposed to these stories of terror, wonder, and adventure told by male characters, there is the simple anecdote of local history told by Sylvia's mother. The story of poor "crazy Nancy" has an obvious reference to the romance of Sylvia and Kinraid. A young man, "as nobody knowed" but who had "summat to do wi' the sea" turns the head of a young serving girl "just to beguile the time, like," and then he abandons her. Poor Nancy can no longer

perform her tasks and ends her days chained to the kitchen dresser of the workhouse, unable to utter anything but one phrase: "He once was here." Mrs. Robson's story is a warning which Sylvia chooses not to hear, but its message is clear to the reader. A woman who abandons herself to an unwise love risks abandoning her duty, her serenity, and even her sanity. Madness is another "doorway to hell," as fearsome as that glimpsed by Kinraid or Robson in their travels, and closer to the truth of Sylvia's own life than any image of masculine adventure, for with Kinraid's abandonment Sylvia will come precariously close to madness and to abandoning her Christian path. Her mother's story clearly embodies the same emotional truth which the novel embodies for the reader; the function of the telling of tales, then, can clearly be the same as that of writing novels—to reach the heart of the listener with a symbolic truth made powerful by imagination and art. In addition, there seems to be a special truth concerning the nature of women's lives which can only be conveyed by the fiction-making powers of a woman who tells tales for other women.

If such a large claim may be made for most of the interpolated tales of *Sylvia's Lovers,* then it would seem worth the reader's while to consider the function of the tales which the characters tell to one another in other works of Gaskell, and it would seem valid also to consider what role the sex of the storyteller plays. For it is apparent from even a cursory look at the interpolated stories in *Sylvia's Lovers* that there is a great difference between the tales that men tell and the tales that women tell, a difference which is surely significant in an age when the function of the female writer was much in doubt.

The attitude of Gaskell concerning her role as a woman writer was at best problematical. Her letters reflect a recurring conflict between what she called "home duties" and "the development of the individual," (i.e., her work as a writer) and her anxieties, which she referred to as "my puzzle," apparently were never resolved. Modern attemps to portray her as a feminist seem equivocal or exaggerated. In spite of her acknowledgment of the special disadvantages under which a talented woman labored, Gaskell was far from a doctrinaire supporter of feminism; it was only with reservations that she signed a petition for the Married Women's Property Act, and her advice to an aspiring woman writer was to concentrate on household duties. Nevertheless, she was vocal on the need for meaningful work for women and was anxious that her writing be taken seriously. Like Mary Ann Evans and the Brontë sisters, who published under masculine or neutral names, she washed to avoid the connotation of frivolity and sentimentality which plagued works by "lady" novelists. Gaskell consulted her publisher about the possibility of using a masculine pseudonym and eventually published her first novel anonymously. But in spite of her desire to have her writing judged apart from considerations of her sex, Gaskell was far from disclaiming sexual differences in literary perspective. No critical praise for *Mary Barton* pleased her more than that of Thomas Carlyle, who began his letter with an intuition of the novel's female authorship, and Gaskell was extremely chagrined to discover that she had guessed wrongly at the sex of the author of *Adam Bede.* Though assuredly not a feminist writer, no Victorian woman writer of major stature was more aggressively *feminine* than Gaskell. Active and even strenuous as her life as a writer and minister's wife was, it seems to have convinced her that the feminine sphere of interest was not only different from that of men—it required a different literary perspective, an act of feminine fiction-making, to give reality and shape to it. Such an attitude may be discerned in the voice of the feminine narrator of *Cranford,* who dismisses a letter from her father, noting disdainfully that it was "just a man's letter; I mean it was very dull and gave no information beyond that he was well, that they had had a good deal of rain, that trade was very stagnant, and there were many disagreeable rumors afloat." The letter from Mary Smith's father is not unimportant, for the "disagreeable rumours" pertain to the imminent failure of Miss Matty's bank, a key thread in the plot of *Cranford.* But the narrator's disdain for this "man's letter" is significant in an author who was herself a prolific and accomplished letter-writer. What a "woman's letter" might have contained is suggested by the collected letters of Gaskell herself and by the closely observed feminine perspective of the narrator of *Cranford:* domestic details, gossip, the trivia of human connectedness, and hints of the rich inner emotional life. Mary Smith's father warns of the failure of a bank, but only Mary herself can report on the effect of this event on Miss Matty's character, on her relationships with the community, and on her view of herself and of her world. To say that *Cranford* could have been written and observed only by a woman writer is not to trivialize the book, but to suggest that there existed in the nineteenth century a world of domestic concerns, human relationships, and inner needs which could scarcely have been attained from a masculine literary perspective.

It is little wonder, then, that in the works of Gaskell, the stories that women tell differ greatly from those of men. As the stories in *Sylvia's Lovers* have already suggested, the tales of men are likely to be filled with adventures, journeys, and marvels—like the sailor's ghost story or the nautical tall tales of Kinraid and Daniel Robson. Edgar Wright has detected in the scene in *North and South* in which Mr. Thornton first impresses Margaret with the chronicle of his early struggles, a suggestion of Othello's seducing Desdemona with his marvelous tales. The Othello courting motif is observable in the interpolated tales of other Gaskell heroes; as has already been noted, Kinraid in *Sylvia's Lovers* first impresses Sylvia with his nautical tales, just as Daniel Robson had once courted Sylvia's mother. Similarly, in *Mary Barton* Will Wilson comes home from the sea to make an impression on the heart of Margaret Legh with his fireside tales of flying fish and mermaids with bright green hair. Again, in *Cranford,* the old bachelor Peter comes home from his travels to enchant the ladies of Cranford with "more wonderful stories than Sinbad the Sailor." Other tales that men tell are likely to revolve around some great journey or adventure. In *Mary Barton,* John Barton tells how the workmen took their petition to London, only to have Parliament refuse to hear it, and Job Legh tells a comic epic of two old men bringing

back an infant granddaughter from London. The tales of these men are not at all random or unrelated to the progress of the narrative. Barton's adventure is a key motivation for the eventual murder of the millowner's son, and the whole episode of the workmen's petition is crucial to the theme of the misunderstanding between the working men and the managerial class. Job Legh's comic tale embodies another of the novel's themes, the compassion and humanity of the poor for one another. The comic journey of the two grandfathers to rescue an infant echoes other acts of charity which the poor perform for one another in *Mary Barton.* The old men's ignorance and incompetence at child care are the stuff of high humor, but the readiness with which their own class, and particularly the women of their class come to their aid, is a recurring motif in the works of Gaskell. These masculine stories of adventure are thus hardly random or without purpose. Exciting yarns in their own right, they are also a part of the cumulative method by which Gaskell piles up her novels' impressions. The stories are chosen deliberately to display something of the teller's character; moreover, they generally reflect the broader themes and images of the novel.

Unlike the adventure stories of the masculine characters, on the other hand, the tales that women tell, like Mrs. Robson's story of Crazy Nancy, usually convey an emotional truth about the lives of women. Their messages in themselves are not likely to be overtly subversive; often in fact they reinforce prevailing stereotypes of the ideal Victorian "angel in the house." The mere act of female storytelling, however, becomes a means, not unlike the writing of novels, by which the female characters may name and give shape to the reality of their lives in a patriarchal society. Often the stories are told by one woman to another, to inspire her, to warn her, or to serve as some sort of clue by which she may find her path in the midst of the perplexities and trials with which feminine lives are fraught. In Gaskell's earliest novel, for example, almost every story told by a woman is told to Mary Barton herself, or is intended for her benefit, and each of them contains some feminine guidance about the duties and needs of a womanly life which the heroine desperately needs to hear. Left motherless at an early age, Mary is in danger of abandoning domestic duties and family ties for the empty flattery and false temptations offered to her by Harry Carson. (The luxury and idleness of the life of a "lady," which Mary hopes to attain through Carson, are embodied in the ironic portrait of Carson's sisters; in *North and South,* Mr. Thornton's sister and Margaret's cousin are similar portraits which suggest that the vain and idle life of a lady is not the ideal of the true woman.) With her mother dead and her father increasingly absorbed by his obsession with the workers' struggle, Mary has only the guidance of the other women in her life, and in their tales and conversation, these characters often act as surrogate mothers by suggesting to Mary the advice which her own mother might have provided had she lived. Old Alice Wilson, for example, relates the story of her youth to Mary and Margaret Legh, both young and motherless girls. Alice tells of leaving her home in the country to go into "service" in Manchester and of how it hurt her own mother that she was so willing to go. In subsequent years she often plans to go home again, but is unable to do so before her mother's death. The motif of Alice's futile desire to see her old home once more is repeated again and again throughout the novel; it serves as a warning to Mary about the value of the "home ties" she is tempted to abandon. Even the ballad which Alice sings about "the golden hills o' heaven" which remind her of the hills of her country home serves as a veiled warning to Mary and Margaret. The old folk ballad is about "a lover that should hae been na lover" and about the girl who succumbed to him and was therefore barred forever from the golden hills, a tale which forecasts presciently the danger that Mary herself will skirt. Another tale is offered to Mary by Mrs. Wilson, who is destined to become Mary's mother-in-law. She tells Mary of the time early in her marriage when, in her domestic ignorance, she boiled potatoes all day until she had produced "a nasty brown mess, as smelt through all the house." Mrs. Wilson is a weak and foolish character, and her recital of small domestic tribulations is comic, but the implications of her tale are serious and are intended for Mary's instruction. Mary has already neglected her social duties and domestic ties by failing to visit this old family friend more often, and her failure is symptomatic of the fact that she is neglecting the honest love of Jem Wilson for the false blandishments of Harry Carson. Mrs. Wilson's story, then, is a reminder of the importance of women's true duties. The subsequent discussion about the tendency of factory women toward "putting their little ones out at nurse, and letting their house go all dirty, and their fires all out" serves as another reminder of where Mary's true duty and true fulfillment lie. But the novel's most important tale is clearly the one told by Mary's Aunt Esther. The story of Esther's life cannot, of course, be told directly to Mary, for Esther is a prostitute, and Mary must be protected from such contact and from the direct knowledge of such a sordid tale. But Esther tells her chronicle of seduction and betrayal with the express intention of preventing Mary from following such a course, and thus she seeks out first Mary's father and then Mary's suitor, Jem Wilson, to force them to listen to her story in the hopes that they can prevent a similar fate from befalling Mary. Like the Ancient Mariner accosting wedding guests, Esther forces her listener to hear the truth about her ruin in the hopes that it will serve as guidance for Mary's path in life. (Indeed, it is not unlikely that Esther's tale forecasts Gaskell's purpose in her own tale of a seduced woman, her novel *Ruth*.) As in other stories that women tell in *Mary Barton*, Esther's tale is intended to convey the same symbolic truth about women's lives as the novel itself, indeed the same truth that Victorian society heartily endorsed—that true fulfillment comes from the emotional and spiritual ties that bind a woman to hearth and family. The very telling of such tales, however, seems to suggest the existence of a feminine community of interests which differ radically from those of men, a community which supports and gives validity to the act of feminine fiction-making.

The stories that women tell each other in *Ruth* seem to perform a similar function. Once again a motherless young heroine is embarked upon a life fraught with moral peril,

and once again she finds solace and guidance in the tales of the women she meets. Ruth's first storyteller is a fat old lady who comforts the weeping girl on a coach journey by telling of her own lost sons, "soldiers and sailors, all of them," all very far from home, "and yet, you see, I can laugh and eat and enjoy myself." The sympathy of this traveller suggests a community of women sharing the values of nurturing, love, and compassion and linked by the common bond of motherhood which Ruth is about to share. The existence of such a bond is demonstrated again toward the end of the novel when Ruth's son hovers on the verge of death and an old crippled woman comes to inquire and pray for him, "stirred with a sharp pang of sympathy, and a very present remembrance of the time when she too was young, and saw the life-breath quiver out of her child." Later, after Leonard's recovery, Ruth listens, weeping at the old woman's story of how her own child had sickened and died, "and the two were henceforward a pair of friends." Significantly, the old woman herself no longer sheds tears, but sits "patient and quiet, waiting for death." The jolly woman traveller and the crippled old woman are both linked to Ruth through their common motherhood, and the stories they tell of the loss of their sons imply a Christian resignation in the face of life's adversity, which is surely the novel's most prevalent theme. Their resignation, however, is at least partially belied by the relish with which they make stories and dramas out of their lives and use those stories to create a bond with other women. But the supreme storyteller of the novel is, of course, the servant Sally, and it remains for Sally to tell the tale which drives the moral of the novel home to Ruth. Watching Ruth perform household tasks with a languid and depressed spirit, Sally tells of her own experience as a young servant girl. Despondent over the accident which had crippled Master Thurstan, Sally "took to praying and sighing, and was careless about dinner and the rooms." She is reprimanded by her mistress, who points out that Sally's beloved Master Thurstan cannot eat the sodden pudding, and asks her if she thinks we are put into the world to "do nothing but see after our own souls? or to help one another with heart and hand, as Christ did to all who wanted help?" Sally's tale, and her accompanying admonition that "making a bed may be done after a Christian fashion," remind Ruth that she must find her proper work in the world through Christian love and resignation, the tale thus encapsulating in comic form the central theme of the novel. Indeed, the character of Sally is pivotal to this theme, and all of her tales suggest the same motif, even when they are intensely comic. The story of Sally's refusal of a proposal of marriage from the kneeling clerk is really the proof of her devotion to her master, whom she will not leave even for a life and home of her own, and the story of the drawing up of her will, with its fancy "law-words," is the tale of another act of Christian love and charity, for she is leaving her savings to her master. Thus Sally endorses the typically Victorian role of the selfless heroine; her triumph lies in her ability to give purpose and dimension to her life by her own considerable verbal powers.

The tales that women tell to the heroines of *Ruth, Mary Barton,* and *Sylvia's Lovers* are all aimed at conveying the central truths about the lives of women that the novels themselves embody; in each case the interpolated tale reflects upon the shared experience of women in a way that mirrors the novels' larger themes and, by implication, the very function of the female novelist. In other Gaskell works, the tales of women are not central to the development of a heroine, but nonetheless are in keeping with the concern of the novels with the emotional drama of women's lives and their attempts to gain some control over this drama by makng it the stuff of their tales. *Cranford,* as has previously been observed, is a collage of stories told by the ladies of the town and by the female narrator, comic and slight in their effect, but slowly creating a portrait of a stable, traditional, nurturing, and *feminine* community, as opposed to the masculine world of the neighboring city. Nina Auerbach has pointed out the role of "fancy" (i.e., tale-telling) in uniting the feminine community of Cranford in such a way that a private, feminine, fictional vision is created out of magic burglars, ghosts, spies, Frenchmen, witches, and the "white lies" told to Miss Matty to preserve her dignity, all acts of feminine fiction-making which in the end subvert "public, masculine truth." The only story which jars in this stable, communal experience is the wild adventure related by the conjuror's wife, but the "Signora," as she is called, is another woman bonded by the common experience of motherhood, for she has lost six children and possesses, as the narrator observes, "those strange eyes that I've never noticed but in mothers of dead children." The feminine community of Cranford rallies itself to her aid, with even the formidable Miss Pole drawn into this sisterhood of compassion and humanity. The tale of the conjuror's wife concerns her journey through India to save the life of her last surviving child, and the kindness that she receives along the way, particularly from an officer's wife whose own children have died. The story is remarkably similar to the story in *Mary Barton* in which Job Legh takes his infant granddaughter home from London, helped along the way by women who have lost their own children. (Job, of course, is a masculine taleteller, but he is more of a nurturing figure than the other male storytellers, being older and having raised his granddaughter alone.) In any case, the story of the conjuror's wife is decidedly a contrast to that of the other traveller returned from India to Cranford, Miss Matty's brother. Peter returns home to tell such traditionally masculine tall tales as the one about shooting a cherub off a mountain top, whereas the story of the "signora" revolves around the feminine themes of sacrifices made for a child and the bond between women who have suffered loss. Like the other ladies of Cranford, the conjuror's wife uses storytelling to impose verbal control on a life in which she otherwise has little power.

There are fewer interpolated tales in *North and South.* Mr. Thornton's recital of his early struggles, which fits into the Othello-Desdemona pattern of courting noted in Gaskell's works, is an integral part of the developing of the hero's personality and the theme of the harsh, sturdy Northern character. But there is one clearly anecdotal story of great interest in the novel, and it is told by Margaret Hale herself. A sturdier heroine than those of Gaskell's previous novels, Margaret Hale does not seek much guidance from other women and specifically rejects the advice of such surrogate mothers as Mrs. Thornton and her own Aunt Shaw. Margaret relies, sometimes to her regret, largely upon her own judgment, and the story she tells is interesting in that it contains her own vision of the inner reality of women's lives. The story emerges in the midst of a heated discussion between Margaret and Mr. Thornton about the conduct of the masters toward their workers. Mr. Thorton compares the workers to children and declares himself in favor of governing such children by autocratic laws. Margaret responds with a strange story of a wealthy man in Nuremberg, who lived for many years with a child he kept shut up in his immense mansion. Upon the death of the father, the son is discovered to be "an over-grown man, with the unexercised intellect of a child," who is unable to take care of himself in the world and falls prey to every bad counsellor and evil influence. Eventually this "great old child" must be cared for by the city authorities, for "he could not even use words effectively enough to be a successful beggar." Margaret's story is clearly related to the political and economic discussion at hand, for it suggests that the workers, deprived of education and independence, will grow to be both ignorant and dangerous. Margaret implies that in order to be capable of governing themselves rationally, the workingmen must be educated to understand the economic conditions which govern their lives and must be given some control over their own destiny. Such an argument is clearly central to the major economic theme of the novel, but it is related as well to an equally central theme: the dilemma of women's lives. As John Pikoulis has noted, in *North and South* "the theme of women searching for an expansion of the possibilities for living that are open to them is combined with the theme of the dispute between masters and men." In the discussions between Margaret and Mr. Thornton, Gaskell depicts an intricate blending of economic and sexual tensions; as a woman suffering the limitations forced upon her by male society, Margaret identifies strongly with the equally powerless industrial workers. Her anecdote serves a double function, then; it establishes her political position in opposition to Mr. Thornton and it also suggests Margaret's clear-sighted vision of the central problem in the lives of nineteeth-century women—the lack of experience and education which might teach them to function independently. With Margaret Hale, Gaskell seems finally to have created a heroine strong enough to articulate her own visions in fictions of her own making.

In view of Gaskell's increasingly subtle use of the feminine anecdote or tale to convey the central concerns of her novels, it is interesting to note that there are fewer and fewer interpolated tales in her later works. *Cousin Phillis* contains almost no tales, although, of course, it is, like *Cranford,* a narrated reminiscence. Peter Keating has pointed to a significant difference between the female narrator of *Cranford* and the masculine narrator of *Cousin Phillis* which is consistent with the way that Gaskell used male and female storytellers in other works: "whereas Mary Smith had embodied Mrs. Gaskell's own perceptions of Cranford, [the narrator of *Cousin Phillis*] lacks any truly sympathetic understanding of the lives and events he describes." (The measure of the gulf between Mary Smith and Paul Manning as narrators may be gauged by the effect of their respective interventions in the events of their stories. Mary Smith arranges for the return of Peter from India, and intuitively suggests the perfect genteel employment for Miss Matty in her reduced circumstances; Paul's well-intentioned intervention in his cousin's love affair, on the other hand, brings about the bleak ending of **Cousin Phillis**.) But aside from the blundering ignorance of the masculine persona of her narrator, Gaskell shows little interest in the act of tale-telling in **Cousin Phillis** and none at all in her last novel, *Wives and Daughters.*

It is apparent that the dwindling role of the interpolated tale in Gaskell's later work is related to some development in her ideas about her role as a woman writer; just what this development might have been is difficult to document. Aina Rubenius has postulated a change in Gaskell's writing from the publication of *The Life of Charlotte Brontë,* which "marks the transition in Mrs. Gaskell's authorship from the writing of novels with a purpose, such as *Mary Barton, Ruth,* and *North and South,* to the writing for art's sake." According to Rubenius, Gaskell later came into contact with ideas about women's rights and Goethean ideas of self-development, and thus came to regard the demands of her art as paramount. Although evidence for such an intellecutal change is hard to pinpoint, it is at least certain that her literary success in later years brought her economic confidence and independence. Her letters show that by the end of her life she had taken control of her own income generated from writing and had no qualms about using it at her own discretion. It is possible that in later years her admiration for Charlotte Brontë may have inspired her with greater self-assurance about the role of the woman writer, or that the very act of writing the biography (the story of a woman who outwardly had no story) may finally have laid to rest her doubts about the validity of women creating stories out of the reality of feminine lives.

Whatever the cause, at the end of her career, Gaskell seems to have had less need to work out a justification for feminine fiction-making through the interpolated tale. *Wives and Daughters,* in particular, is imbued with such a forceful vision of the painful inner drama of seemingly prosaic feminine lives, that the author seems not to have needed the help of her characters to tell stories which hammer home her themes. And yet, to say that there are no tales and stories in Gaskell's most mature work is not to suggest that the tales are necessarily random or intrusive in the earlier works. Rather, they seem to be the mark of a growing artist, striving to control her material and her artistic vision within the bounds of an exuberant and bountiful talent, and striving also to justify the very act of feminine creation. Taken as a whole, the stories and tales of these novels show an astonishing range of fiction-making, from the comic and the marvelous to the pathetic. Each is appropriate in some way to the character of its narrator, and each in some way reflects upon the major concerns of the novels. The act of storytelling in Gaskell's works, particularly when the teller is a woman,

is an artistic and literary act of faith—the passing on of tradition, the sharing of experience or vision, the strengthening of communal bonds—in the same way that writing a novel is, for a woman, an act of faith. Each of the storytellers of these novels is a literary artist in his or her own right; and in particular, the female tellers of tales seem to convey the inner truths of feminine experience which Gaskell would have considered to be the particular province of the woman novelist. Far from being artless or intrusive, then, the interpolated tales of Gaskell's novels are a measure of the author's early power to absorb the broadest possible range of life's experience, to make it serve the purposes of her art, and to work out the implications of a uniquely feminine making of fiction.

Coral Lansbury (essay date 1984)

SOURCE: *"Cousin Phillis,* the Short Stories, and *Cranford,"* in *Elizabeth Gaskell,* Twayne Publishers, 1984, pp. 48-77.

[*In the following excerpt, Lansbury presents an overview of Gaskell's short stories.*]

It was not unusual for the short story in [the mid-nineteenth century] to be a prelude, a testing piece for a subsequent novel. Themes were tried out on the public in one of the weekly or monthly magazines and, if the response were favorable, then a novel would follow in due course. Dickens's own short fiction frequently enunciates situations and expresses moods that were later developed in longer works. Thackeray's snobs, grimacing and strutting through the pages of *Punch,* can be found refined and humanized in *Vanity Fair.* Most Victorian novelists moved easily between journalism and fiction, frequently conflating the two forms.

Gaskell had begun her public career as a writer of short stories and essays, and she continued composing them to the end. **"Libbie Marsh's Three Eras"** (1847) had established a setting and provided characters who then moved onto the larger stage of Manchester in *Mary Barton* (1848). When this novel received critical acclaim Dickens wrote to Gaskell requesting a contribution for his journal *Household Words.* From the cast of *Mary Barton* she selected Esther and changed her to Lizzie Leigh, the errant daughter of a devout farming family that has emigrated to Manchester. **"Lizzie Leigh"** (1850) shows Dickens's hand guiding the plot at every turn and producing a sentimental and predictable conclusion. It was Dickens who altered the grimly laconic **"A Night's Work"** to **"A Dark Night's Work"** (1863) and changed the title of **"The Crooked Branch"** (1859) to **"The Ghost in the Garden Room,"** a catchy, glib, and deceptive invitation to the reader that failed to produce either a ghost or even a garden room. What worked so well for Dickens often resulted in something resembling flashy advertising copy for other writers.

Nevertheless, despite Dickens's frequent and unfortunate

influence upon her work, Gaskell's short stories display at their best a psychological intensity and graphic singularity of theme that set them apart from contemporary fiction. Where Dickens was sentimental, she was tough-minded and shrewd; where he constructed explosive denouements she instinctively sought the wry unfoldings of passion and conscience. The rub was that her area of greatest weakness, the external delineation of event and character, was most susceptible to Dickens's influence. It was not a ghost that returned to rob and destroy Nathan and Hester Huntroyd in **"The Crooked Branch"** but their only son, Benjamin, who was quite prepared to murder them for their money. This is the truth more horrifying than any visitation of the supernatural.

Indeed, like those of Sheridan Le Fanu, Gaskell's ghosts are more often the expression of a troubled mind rather than an invading diabolical force. One is reminded of the old North Country saying that it is not the dead who should be feared, but the living. So in the delightful **"Curious if True"** (1860), the narrator, Richard Whittingham, who may possibly be a figure of fairy tale himself, dreams of, or perhaps actually attends, a ball where Blue Beard matches wit with Tom Thumb and a little girl hurries past with a repentant wolf. And the Gothic conclusion of guilt and revenge in **"The Old Nurse's Story"** (1852) is deliberately related by a practical, unimaginative woman who comes under the spell of her young charge Rosamond, a child capable of evoking the passions of the past and imposing them on all around her. The source of the supernatural is as subtly evaded in this story as in Henry James's "The Turn of the Screw." Generally, the seemingly supernatural is a manifestation of individual and social hysteria where madness can extend from a family to a whole community. **"Lois the Witch"** (1859) is not a study of the occult in Salem, but the delineation of a religious fanaticism leading irresistibly to mass lunacy and bloody persecution.

Unlike many of her contemporaries, Gaskell never saw the patriarchal family as the ideal, or even natural, ordering of society. Instead she offered unusual groupings of people spanning sex, age, and class, frequently women capable of sustaining each other under the same roof after the fashion of her own Aunt Lumb. George Eliot in *The Mill on the Floss* recounts an accepted relationship between a brother and sister—Maggie is dominated by Tom and her life is inevitably ruined by men unworthy of her love. When Maggie confronts Tom with the bitter reproach ". . . You are a man, Tom, and have power, and can do something in the world" he replies bluntly, "Then, if you can do nothing, submit to those who can." But not even a brother's threats of physical violence and a mother's tears can make Gaskell's Maggie in *The Moorland Cottage* reject the man she loves. She answers them both simply:

> "I cannot give up Frank," said she in a low, quiet voice. Mrs. Browne threw up her hands, and exclaimed in terror—"Oh, Edward, Edward! go away—I will give you all the plate I have; you can sell it—my darling, go!" "Not till I have brought Maggie to reason," said he, in a manner as quiet as her own, but with a subdued

ferocity in it, which she saw, but which did not intimidate her. (chap. 9)

There is no appeal to the ways of the world and of society here in Eliot's customary fashion, simply the conviction that it is often a woman's duty to deny the assumed moral authority of a man. In *The Moorland Cottage* Maggie resists all threats and eventually her courage triumphs over the opposition of family and friends. Whereas Eliot shows women demeaned and diminished by their need for love, Gaskell insists that women are capable of challenging male authority and surviving to assert their independence like Margaret Hale in *North and South* and Mary Barton. The most extraordinary expression of love and courage in all Gaskell's work is not between a man and a woman, but between two loving women in a relationship that can be seen as a most unconventional family.

"The Grey Woman" (1861) is one of Gaskell's most remarkable and perceptive studies of female psychology. It has always been overlooked because the story makes use of the conventional forms and devices of the Gothic novel, and it is only recently that the Gothic has come to be seen as something more than a clattering of chains and piercing shrieks from the east wing. The Gothic is an expression of female manipulative power moving between the climacterics of sexuality and terror. There is the narrative perspective of the young virgin who confronts a dark and Satanic lover in a house isolated from the world. The heroine's love is obsessive and is set against the terrifying reality of a mad wife and elements of the supernatural. Charlotte Brontë's *Jane Eyre* with its countless imitators can be seen as the classic of this form. In order to be fulfilled sexually the mad wife must be disposed of and the lover transformed into a less dominating figure. Only then can the heroine say, "Reader, I married him." Gaskell takes all these conventions and deliberately sets them at odds in **"The Grey Woman"** to make a new and compelling statement about the nature of woman and love.

The work is set within the frame of cheerful travelers taking shelter in a German mill from a thundering storm. There the narrator sees the portrait of a gray woman whose unearthly beauty and pallor of grief cannot be concealed by the inept brush of a provincial artist. The miller produces a chronicle written by the woman in the portrait, a woman now long dead and almost forgotten by her own family. Anna Scherer, the mill owner's daughter, had been a great beauty with an aversion for men and the sexuality they represented. Karl, the oldest apprentice, loved her and wanted to make her his wife but "she had no notion of being married, and could not bear anyone who talked . . . about it." (chap. 1)

When her brother marries, Anna is dispatched to the home of her friend Sophie Rupprecht in Carlsruhe. At first, she is only amused and occasionally bored by the attention of her many admirers until a strange young man arrives and immediately captivates her by his appearance. At this point the conventions of the Gothic are adjusted for a subversive and radical theme to emerge: it is not the traditional hero of darkly virile masculine strength who charms Anna but a man of title, de la Tourelle, who seems like a young girl. He has features "as delicate as a girl's" and his manners are soft and effeminate. The initial charm vanishes when de la Tourelle proposes marriage and Anna recognizes the man beneath the feminine appearance. It is seen as a good match and Anna is compelled to accept.

Tourelle's chateau in the Vosges is a mysterious castle with winding corridors and locked doors where Anna finds herself a prisoner attendant upon the moods of her strangely feminine jailer. Desperate with fear and loneliness, a protector of strength and courage arrives when Amante, a Norman servant, is brought to be her maid. Immediately there is the distinction of appearance between her husband and Amante. Anna is drawn to her at first sight: "She was tall and handsome, though upwards of forty, and somewhat gaunt." Here indeed is the Gothic hero, older than the heroine, resourceful, and a little contemptuous of Anna's childlike fears.

Servant becomes protector and lover when the two women accidentally discover Tourelle's real avocation as leader of a gang of brigands, the dreaded *Chauffeurs,* who rob, torture, and murder their victims. They escape and take refuge in an old mill where Amante disguises herself as a tailor wearing male dress, while Anna darkens her face and cuts her hair to seem like a tailor's wife. Anna has not told her husband that she is with child for he has sworn to destroy it or any others she may have. Soon Anna and Amante come to see and speak of the unborn child as their own as they flee from one hiding place to another with Tourelle and his men in pursuit.

The women take refuge in Frankfort, where Anna's child is born.

> At length my child was born—my poor, worse than fatherless, child. It was a girl, as I had prayed for. I had feared lest a boy might have something of the tiger nature of its father; but a girl seemed all my own. And yet not all my own, for the faithful Amante's delight and glory in the babe almost exceeded mine; in outward show it certainly did.

Amante is now husband and father, going out to work in neighboring houses until the day comes when she is recognized and murdered by Tourelle and his henchman, Lefebvre. Eventually Tourelle is brought to justice and Anna marries the doctor who attended Amante in her last hours. Within a very short time Anna is a widow and later records the story of her daughter, thus successfully preventing her marrying the man she loves. By cruel coincidence the daughter has fallen in love with the son of one of her father's victims, but again there is an enigmatic thrust to this incident. Is it conscience that dictates the marriage should not take place, or the mother's desire that her daughter remain single, aloof from all masculine passion?

"The Grey Woman" challenges many of the implicit assumptions of the Gothic form in a reversal of customary sexual roles: Tourelle, the effeminate and dangerous lover; Amante, the masculine and faithful husband. Because the story concludes with Anna's voice to the reader, there is no opportunity for the narrator's comment or explication, and in this way many of the questions the reader might wish to ask are left unanswered. Unquestionably, **"The Grey Woman"** is a powerful story that successfully uses and subverts the accepted Gothic tradition. Students of the Gothic would be well advised to consider it in the light of contemporary fiction.

In so many of the short stories conventions are deliberately set at odds by new and disturbing insights into character and society. **"Morton Hall,"** for example, first published in November 1853 in *Household Words,* brings a new focus to the traditional tale of terror with its inevitable curse that ruins a noble house. Harrison Ainsworth (1805-1882) had given Scott's historical novels a popular cast with *Rookwood* in 1834, and stories of Cavaliers and Roundheads continued of flourish in novels and short stories. Depending on the religious and political temperament of the writer, either the Cavaliers or Roundheads were made the heroes of these accounts. Cromwell was a grave upholder of public and private morality or a fanatical zealot in these tales, and a romantic and sentimental cast was thrown over the whole period. The setting was always a stately home, with lovers from the contending parties and a curse.

Just as she was capable of subverting the Gothic by means of a particular narrative voice in **"The Grey Woman,"** Gaskell uses a garrulous old woman in **"Morton Hall"** to imply that the Cavaliers and Roundheads were rather less heroic than the versions imposed on the reading public by popular fiction. The narrator in this case is a Cranfordian lady, Miss Bridget Sidebotham, who lives with her sister Ethelinda in the vicinity of Morton Hall, once the finest and most powerful estate in the neighborhood. The occasion for Miss Sidebotham's history of Morton Hall is her return from having helped at the laying out of the last of the Mortons, a Miss Phillis Morton, who had died of starvation in the old house while clinging to the last vestiges of her name and ancestry. Genteel poverty indeed!

At the heart of the story is the marriage between the royalist Sir John Morton and the daughter of the Puritan who had supplanted him as the owner of Morton Hall during the Interregnum. The quarrels between husband and wife, bitter and vindictive, reflect the issues of their opposing parties. The climax comes when Sir John refuses shelter to his wife's brother, condemning him to death as an enemy. Lady Morton then pronounces a curse on all of her husband's line that is fulfilled when Miss Phillis Morton's shriveled body is laid to rest.

Clearly this is as melodramatic as any of the popular renditions of the period, but there is a dislocation between the story and its rendering by Miss Sidebotham's recollection of what Mrs. Dawson, the Morton housekeeper, had told her mother. It is made apparent by this indirect irony, so typical of Gaskell, that stories that filtered down through the servants' hall will always find an eager audience in the general reading public, however inaccurate they may be. Less obvious is Gaskell's inference that the Civil War was not really an occasion for romantic taletelling, being more a time when sordid domestic differences were magnified to national causes. Admittedly, this is a questionable stance to take, but Gaskell was never moved by the pomp and circumstance of war, and, in a sense, **"Morton Hall"** is her response to the glamour given armed conflict. Typically Gaskell accomplishes this by means of a narrative voice that has more in common with the persona of Browning's dramatic monologues than the omniscient narrator of so many novels of the period.

Bridget Sidebotham's fortunes have sunk perilously close to the condition of Phillis Morton, and possibly for the same reasons. Pride and poverty often go hand in hand, and a disinclination for work can be a certain recipe for ruin. Bridget is so effective as a narrator because she shares a great many of the attitudes evidenced in the story of the curse. Breathlessly she tells the reader that perhaps her own lack of fortune may also be the result of a "curse":

> . . . were the Sidebothams marked with a black mark in that terrible mysterious book which was kept under lock and key by the Pope and Cardinals in Rome? It was terrible, yet, somehow, rather pleasant to think of. So many of the misfortunes which had happened to us through life, and which we had called "mysterious dispensations," but which some of our neighbours had attributed to our want of prudence and foresight, were accounted for at once, if we were the objects of the deadly hatred of such a powerful order as the Jesuits, of whom we had lived in dread ever since we had read the "Female Jesuit."

All that Miss Sidebotham requires is that life should be accounted for in terms of a popular Gothic novel, and then she proceeds to relate the downfall of the Mortons in precisely that fashion. Like so many of her readers, Miss Sidebotham prefers prejudice to reasoned opinion and high romance to history. She states very firmly: "If there is one thing I do dislike more than another, it is a person saying something on the other side when I am trying to make up my mind—how can I reason if I am to be disturbed by another person's arguments?" It is the failure to reason, or even to listen to the other, that sets Sir John and Lady Morton at odds and extends to Roundhead refusal to countenance the views of Cavalier. This is not Harrison Ainsworth, or any of the more popular versions of the Interregnum, but it does reflect Gaskell's disinclination for any kind of historical romance that overlooks the reality of suffering and death.

One of Gaskell's most effective personae was that of a young ingenuous man, of the kind who was to relate the story of his cousin Phillis in the novella of that name. However, these young men who travel and observe are not all as artless as Paul Manning in *Cousin Phillis*. The narrator of **"Six Weeks at Heppenheim"** (1862) is a shrewd young Oxford graduate who deftly sets about matchmaking in the hotel at Heppenheim, where he arrives suffering from fever and slowly recuperates from his illness. Throughout the story there is his concern for Thekla, the maid who nurses him with such tenderness.

Thekla still loves the wastrel of her childhood, Franz Weber, and has unwisely refused an offer of marriage from Fritz Müller, the widower innkeeper. It is a simple story made complex by the narrator's condition and intentions.

At first, Thekla's predicament is little more than an interesting entertainment for the invalid made petulant and irritable by his disease; later, her happiness is to be the expression of his gratitude to her. The story begins with the statement of a remarkably practical and shrewd young man, clearly not the type to engage in romantic fancies or become interested in the plight of lovesick maids:

> After I left Oxford, I determined to spend some months in travel before settling down in life. My father had left me a few thousands, the income arising from which would be enough to provide for all the necessary requirements of a lawyer's education, such as lodging in a quiet part of London, and fees in payment to the distinguished barrister with whom I was to read; but there would be a small surplus left over for luxuries or amusements; and, as I was rather in debt on leaving college, since I had forestalled my income, and the expenses of travelling would have to be defrayed out of my capital, I determined that they should not exceed fifty pounds. As long as that sum would last me I would remain abroad; when it was spent my holiday should be over, and I would return and settle down somewhere in the neighbourhood of Russell Square, in order to be near Mr.——'s chambers in Lincoln Inn.

With his life planned in such orderly fashion, the narrator is justifiably upset when illness throws everything into disarray. It should be apparent from these opening lines that he is a young man who prizes neatness and order, one who will never hesitate to set the lives of others to rights even when his own has been disrupted by circumstance. He has all the makings of an admirable lawyer!

When he first becomes aware of Thekla it is through the mist of sickness, and even then he is caught between two moods: one of embarrassment that this hard-working young woman should spend her hours of well-earned rest at his side, the other, a childish fear that he is in no condition to be left untended through the night. It is these modulations of thought and feeling, which are so often at variance, that most characterize Gaskell's definition of character:

> Night came on; the sounds of daily life died away into silence; the children's voices were no more heard; the poultry were all gone to roost; the beasts of burden to their stables; and travellers were housed. Then Thekla came in softly and quietly, and took up her appointed place, after she had done all in her power for my comfort. I felt that I was in no state to be left all those weary hours which intervened between sunset and sunrise; but I did feel ashamed that this young woman, who had watched by me all the previous night, and, for aught I knew, for many nights before, and had worked hard, been run off her legs, as English servants would say, all day long, should come and take up her

care of me again; and it was with a feeling of relief that I saw her head bend forwards, and finally rest on her arms, which had fallen on the white piece of sewing spread before her on the table. She slept; and I slept. When I wakened dawn was stealing into the room, and making pale the lamplight. Thekla was standing by the stove, where she had been preparing the bouillon I should require on wakening. But she did not notice my half-open eyes, although her face was turned towards the bed. She was reading a litter slowly, as if its words were familiar to her . . .

With all an invalid's singleminded concern with trivialities, the elucidation of this letter becomes the narrator's major concern. Slowly he is drawn into Thekla's story and his health improves as he is able to convince Thekla that she is not morally bound to marry a man who had once rejected her and now returns, expecting her to be his wife and support. When Max Müller's little boy also succumbs to the fever, Thekla's doubts are swept away and she remains to nurse the child back to health.

The plot is predictable in the context of Victorian attitudes toward health and sickness, but Gaskell's vision goes beyond the merely trite when she sets out to analyze the feelings of her staid narrator. Only when he has brought peace and happiness to the lives of the simple folk at Heppenheim does he find his health restored. From being a tiresome guest at the inn he had become a member of Müller's family, holding a picture in his mind that is to become the future at Heppenheim:

> As I sat down in my easy-chair close to the open window through which I had entered, I could see the men and women on the hill-side drawing to a centre, and all stand round the pastor, bare-headed, for a minute or so. I guessed that some words of holy thanksgiving were being said, and I wished that I had stayed to hear them, and mark my especial gratitude for having been spared to see that day. Then I heard the distant voices, the deep tones of the men, the shriller pipes of women and children, join in the German harvest-hymn, which is generally sung on such occasions; then silence, while I concluded that a blessing was spoken by the pastor, with outstretched arms; and then they once more dispersed, some to the village, some to finish their labours for the day among the vines. I saw Thekla coming through the garden with Max in her arms, and Lina clinging to her woollen skirts.

It is this scene that later becomes a central figure in *Cousin Phillis*, where Ebenezer Holman stands bareheaded among his workers in the field at Hope Farm, giving thanks to God. Holman's prayers fall on deaf ears in *Cousin Phillis*, but **"Six Weeks at Heppenheim"** ends in peace and with a blessing for all.

Gaskell can often be seen reworking scenes and characters from one story to the next in this fashion. **"Crowley Castle"** (1862), for example, uses characters that recall **"The Grey Woman,"** but whereas the latter is a Gothic tale, **"Crowley Castle"** belongs to the popular mode for sensational fiction, those narratives that sent the reader into spasms of terror and dread. Mrs. Braddon and Har-

rison Ainsworth are not regarded as major writers today, but they enjoyed an enormous vogue in their own day. Their influence was pervasive in the writing of the period, and generally deleterious; however, Gaskell is unusually successful in this sensational mode. By emphasizing character and locality she manages to breathe life into mechanically predictable events.

Victorine is a diabolical Amante, a devoted servant who obligingly murders so that her mistress may become free to marry a rejected suitor, and then demands her mistress's love as the price of her silence. It is melodrama, but melodrama that works within the context of the medium. When Victorine cries out in baffled fury to Therese of the dark services she has rendered, her words carry the appropriate shuddering force:

> "And is that what it has come to!" exclaimed Victorine. "In my country they reckon a building secure against wind and storm and all the ravages of time, if the first mortar used has been tempered with human blood. But not even our joint secret, though it was tempered well with blood, can hold our lives together!"

Like most political radicals, Gaskell always felt comfortable contemplating the downfall of ancient houses and their aristocratic owners. She never stood among ruins in the manner of Scott and Carlyle and contemplated a happier age. In temperament she was closer to Macaulay, who considered the Middle Ages a time of blight and oppression, and all periods prior to the present a pale foreshadowing of the prosperity of the future. Gaskell uses the convention of the ruined house to illustrate the follies of past times: the people she describes are foolish and arrogant and deserve no more than a place in the world of romance. For a writer who could be as discursive as Thackeray, Gaskell's description of her arrival at Crowley Castle is remarkably concise and effective:

> We drove from the little sea-bathing place in Sussex, to see the massive ruins of Crowley Castle, which is the show-excursion of Merton. We had to alight at a field-gate, the road further being too bad for the slightly-built carriage, or the poor tired Merton horse; and we walked for about a quarter of a mile, through uneven ground which had once been an Italian garden; and then we came to a bridge over a dry moat, and went over the groove of a portcullis that had once closed in massive entrance, into an empty space surrounded by thick walls, draperied with ivy, but unroofed and open to the sky.

It is often overlooked to what extent murder was a recurring theme in Gaskell's work. In her first novel, *Mary Barton*, she had shown murder to be a social act and then traced its psychological implications for the individual. Two of her stories deal explicitly with murder within the family, crimes committed with deliberate intent in one case and as the result of aberrant passion in the other. Both **"The Crooked Branch"** (1859) and **"A Dark Night's Work"** (1863) are explorations into the nature of murder, but in each case the crimes are seen to be a disturbing extension of everyday life.

Nothing could be more disarmingly tranquil than Nab's-End Farm of Nathan Huntroyd, who married his old sweetheart, Hester Rose, when he was a man in his middle years. They had one son, Benjamin, a child of astonishing beauty and intelligence who was admired by all who saw him, and an idol (that fatal Gaskell term!) to his parents. Benjamin grew up with Bessy Rose, Hester's orphaned niece, and the parents cheerfully contemplated the day when the two young people would marry and carry on the farm. Admiration and indulgence, however, had their usual effect on the son and he grew up to be an ingrate and wastrel who returned one night with accomplices to murder his parents and steal their savings.

Told so baldly the story seems little more than a crime taken from the pages of any newspaper; what removes it from the merely sensational is its rendering of character. With the best possible intentions the Huntroyds have created a monster in their son, a boy who resembles the dandified Pip, who lives for the great expectations promised by his supposed patron, Miss Havisham. It is as though Gaskell had taken Pip from Dickens's *Great Expectations* (1861) and translated his character into everyday terms. In a sense **"The Crooked Branch"** is a commentary upon Dickens, suggesting that instead of repentance and redemption Pip may well have returned one night to murder Miss Havisham for her money. Gaskell was often sentimental in her admonitions to the reader, but seldom so in her perception of character.

Benjamin grows up despising his parents for their lack of gentility even as he expects them to support him in a station of life to which he has previously been unaccustomed. The role of a gentleman without recognition of its duties and obligations to others was a hollow sham—a license to impose upon others, in Gaskell's opinion.

Benjamin has acquired the accent of a gentleman, which alone is enough to enrage his father. Like Joe Gargery in *Great Expectations* he finds that he no longer speaks the same language as the young man who is now a gentleman. When Benjamin coolly demands three hundred pounds from his father the old man cannot contain his anger:

> He was out of breath by this time. His son took his father's first words in dogged silence; it was but the burst of surprise he had led himself to expect, and did not daunt him for long.
>
> "I should think, sir"—
>
> "'Sir'—whatten for dost thou 'sir' me? Is them your manners? I'm plain Nathan Huntroyd, who never took on to be a gentleman; but I have paid my way up to this time, which I shannot do much longer, if I'm to have a son coming an' asking me for three hundred pound, just meet the same as if I were a cow, and had nothing to do but let down my milk to the first person as strokes me."

Bessy's quick wits and courage save her uncle and aunt

when she hears intruders in the house. She runs to the neighboring farm where John Kirkby and several of his men are tending a sick cow. They arrive with pitchforks and attack the burglars, leaving two men wounded. Benjamin escapes and flees the country, a fugitive from justice. The horror of the crime is only elicited from the taciturn Nathan at the trial when his wife is called upon to say what she heard the third person left downstairs shout to his companions on the stairs:

> "It wur my son, my only child, as called out for us t'open door, and who shouted out for to hold th' oud woman's throat if she did na stop her noise, when hoo'd fain ha cried for her niece to help."

The serious flaw in this story is Gaskell's determination to wring the last drop of feeling from the trial scene. This was always a set piece in contemporary fiction and Gaskell clearly falls into a conventional mode at the expense of the realism she has previously established. Nathan, Bessy, and Hester have depth and complexity; the judge and the lawyers are cut from cardboard and creak accordingly. The judge weeps, the jury sniffles, and we have that Victorian predilection for handing the reader a handkerchief and offering to blow his nose for him. Overwritten and vapid, these passages are in stark contrast to the rest of the story. What one remembers is Nathan courting his elderly sweetheart, dressed in his Sunday best and presenting himself at Mrs. Thompson's back door in Ripon, where Hester Rose is employed as a cook:

> Hester stood there, in answer to the good sound knock his good sound oakstick made: she, with the light full upon her, he in shadow. For a moment there was silence. He was scanning the face and figure of his old love, for twenty years unseen. The comely beauty of youth had faded away entirely; she was, as I have said, homely-looking, plain-featured, but with a clean skin, and pleasant frank eyes. Her figure was no longer round, but tidily draped in a blue and white bed-gown, tied round her waist by her white apron-strings, and her short red linsey petticoat showed her tidy feet and ankles. Her former lover fell into no ecstasies. He simply said to himself, "She'll do"; and forthwith began upon his business.

The spare, laconic excellence of this prose does not require judges whose faces quiver all over and authorial comments describing the pitiable presence of Hester Huntroyd confronted by the jury.

Again, just as Dickens, with his customary regard for a good title at the expense of the story, had magisterially changed **"The Crooked Branch"** to **"The Ghost in the Garden Room"** when it first appeared in the Extra Christmas Number of *All the Year Round* in 1859, he altered Gaskell's chosen **"A Night's Work"** to the present title, **"A Dark Night's Work"** when the long short story first appeared in *All the Year Round* between January and March 1863. Gaskell and Dickens were both critical of the other at this time, preferring to correspond through intermediaries. She had determined never to publish with him again, and was outraged when he changed her title

(G.L. No. 524). Dickens in turn complained that Ellinor Wilkins, the heroine of her work, was intolerably like Mrs. Gaskell. Ellinor is, of course, strong minded, resourceful, and intelligent, qualities that had little appeal to a writer who preferred his heroines to be "little."

Edward Wilkins is a tragic figure and as much a victim of his society as John Barton. Indeed, if Gaskell had revealed the miseries of the poor in *Mary Barton,* in **"A Dark Night's Work"** she shows how oppressive the rural gentry can be to a man who has every right to be numbered among them, save one thing only, his father's and his own profession—that of conveyancing attorney. The father had made the irremediable error of sending Edward to Eton, educating him as a gentleman, and then, instead of permitting him to go to university, forcing him "to return to Hamley to be articled to his father, and to assume the hereditary subservient position to lads whom he had licked in the playground, and beaten at learning."

It is this circumstance that inevitably leads to Wilkins's ruin and act of murder. No matter that he is rich, cultivated, and marries a young woman of aristocratic background, Miss Lettice Lamotte; he is still regarded as an upstart by the local squires, who envy his money and sneer at his lack of breeding. After his young wife's death, he finds little comfort in Hamley and makes even longer trips to London, where he can find company and friends. His only tie to the country is his daughter Ellinor and his failing and neglected practice.

In Hamley, Wilkins affects to despise the men and the society to which he passionately yearns to belong, a condition that causes him to spend more time at sport and in drinking than is wise for a solicitor. Only Anthony Trollope has surpassed Gaskell in the ability to describe the attraction and essential boorishness of the rural gentry at this time. It was an easy matter to deride the gentry, as Gaskell made clear in *Wives and Daughters,* but everyone in the county wanted to be their friend. The feeling of being only grudgingly accepted in this society extends to Ellinor, who can force herself to believe that she is happy while being politely snubbed at the Assembly balls.

> Ellinor stood by her father watching the dances, and thankful for the occasional chance of a dance. While she had been sitting by her chaperone, Mr. Wilkins had made the tour of the room, dropping out the little fact of his daughter's being present, wherever he thought the seed likely to bring forth the fruit of partners. And some came because they liked Mr. Wilkins, and some asked Ellinor because they had done their duty dances to their own party and might please themselves. So that she usually had an average of one invitation to every three dances; and this principally towards the end of the evening. (chap. 5)

Ellinor's love is divided between her father and Ralph Corbet, an aspiring lawyer, who, being a prudent young man, is not unmindful of Ellinor's being an only child and heir to the fortunes of a rich widower. Unfortunately, Mr. Wilkins's wealth is being steadily diminished as he neglects his practice and finds more solace in the bottle

than in his clients' affairs. Reluctantly appreciating that he needs a clerk to set his affairs in order he hires Dunster and immediately dislikes the man for his competence and his obvious disregard for the hallmarks of a gentleman: he is industrious, devout, and shabby. Gaskell shows Wilkins developing an intense loathing for Dunster because the latter embodies the image of what the county gentry would like to see in a local attorney—Dunster is the man Wilkins imagines that others see when they look beyond the fine horses and rare paintings to the local conveyancing attorney. His detestation for Dunster becomes obsessive at the same time as his reliance upon him grows and develops. Dunster is no Uriah Heep, simply a hardworking clerk who dreams of a partnership with Wilkins and a steady income in a respectable profession. Wilkins chafes under Dunster's control of his affairs, but he can only rage inwardly and turn for comfort to the bottle. What infuriates him is that Dunster is never openly critical of him, and he construes this as silent insolence:

> Mr. Wilkins himself winced under his new clerk's order and punctuality; Mr. Dunster's raised eyebrows and contractions of the lips at some woeful confusion in the business of the office, chafed Mr. Wilkins more, far more, than any open expression of opinion would have done; for that he could have met and explained away, as he fancied. A secret respectful dislike grew up in his bosom against Mr. Dunster. He esteemed him, he valued him, and he could not bear him. Year after year, Mr. Wilkins had come to be more under the influence of his feelings, and less under the command of his reason. He rather cherished than repressed his nervous repugnance to the harsh measured tones of Mr. Dunster's voice; the latter spoke with a provincial twang which grated on his employer's sensitive ear. He was annoyed at a certain green coat which his new clerk brought with him, and he watched its increasing shabbiness with a sort of childish pleasure. But by-and-by Mr. Wilkins found out that, by some perversity of taste, Mr. Dunster always had his coats, Sunday and working-day, made of this obnoxious colour; and this knowledge did not diminish his secret irritation. (chap. 3)

Ralph Corbet and Ellinor are unofficially engaged to be married, and her life is a pleasant round of domestic duties marred only by concern for her father's increasing dissipation. When troubled she can always console herself with planning for the time when she will be the wife of Ralph Corbet. One night she is disturbed by sounds of men arguing in the garden. A few moments later she hears furniture falling and goes downstairs to find Dunster lying dead in the living room. Wilkins could no longer bear the man's authority over his affairs and had killed him in a bout of drunken anger. Then ensues one of the most remarkable scenes in the literature of the period, for Ellinor, Dixon the gardener, and Wilkins drag Dunster's body out across the lawn and bury him.

Possibly it was this action on Ellinor's part that so affronted Dickens. After all, Esther Summerson, the heroine of *Bleak House* (1853), buries a doll, but that any of his heroines should be an accessory to murder is unthinkable. Gaskell was aware of the singularity of the incident and observes in her narrative that

> Ellinor could not have told whether it was reason or
> instinct that made her act as she did during this awful
> night. When afterwards, notwithstanding her shuddering
> avoidance of it, the haunting memory would come and
> overshadow her, during many, many years of her life,
> she grew to believe that the powerful smell of the spilt
> brandy, absolutely intoxicated her—an unconscious
> Rechabite in practice. (chap. 7)

Wilkins explains Dunster's absence by declaring that his
clerk has absconded with funds stolen from the office,
and it is assumed that he has fled to America. Ellinor
promptly falls ill, the traditional response to extreme stress,
and on her recovery finds that her adored father has become a stranger to her. Neither Wilkins, Ellinor, nor Dixon
can tolerate the other's presence without being reminded
of the murder. Whenever they meet, the shadowy presence of Dunster is at their side. They are haunted by
something more terrifying than a ghost, and that is the
awareness of their guilt, which becomes more anguished
when they are together.

Wilkins becomes a drunkard and Ellinor desperately tries
to conceal his infirmities and his crime from others. Ironically, it was this concern for her father that caused Mr.
Livingstone, a young clergyman staying in the area, to
fall in love with her. One evening at dinner, to divert
attention from her father's blurred speech and changed
demeanor, she had chatted brilliantly with Livingstone
and riveted his attention. However, if Livingstone dreamed
of making Ellinor his wife, Ralph Corbet is unconsciously seeking a plausible reason for ridding himself of her.

Corbet is not presented unsympathetically. There are excellent reasons why he would not wish to make Ellinor
his wife. His father disapproves. He is painfully aware of
Wilkins's failings and suspects that he will be unable to
provide a marriage settlement, but above all, Ellinor's
rustic charms are beginning to pall on a young man grown
accustomed to the bright conversation of London.

> It had become difficult for Ralph to contract his mind
> to her small domestic interests, and she had little else
> to talk to him about, now that he responded but curtly
> to all her questions about himself, and was weary of
> professing a love which he was ceasing to feel, in all
> the passionate nothings which usually make up so much
> of lovers' talk. The books she had been reading were
> old classics whose place in literature no longer admitted
> of keen discussion; the poor whom she cared for were
> all very well in their way; and, if they could have been
> brought in to illustrate a theory, hearing about them
> might have been of some use; but, as it was, it was
> simply tiresome to hear day after day of Betty Palmer's
> rheumatism and Mrs. Kay's baby's fits. There was no
> talking politics with her, because she was so ignorant
> that she always agreed with everything he said.
> (chap. 9)

It is with considerable relief that Corbet makes the occasion of a quarrel with the drunken Wilkins the reason for

his breaking the engagement. He is further convinced of
his good judgment when Wilkins dies, leaving Ellinor
almost penniless—aspiring young barristers cannot afford
poor wives.

Ellinor realizes that she must rent Ford Bank, the family
home, but how can she leave Dunster's grave? Miss
Monro, her old governess, has taken a residence in East
Chester Close, but the care of the grave remains her despairing concern. It is Dixon who remains as custodian of
the crime. Over the years her fears subside and she suggests that Dixon should make his home with her. The old
man shakes his head and mutters that:

> At times I dream, or it comes into my head as I lie
> awake with the rheumatics, that some one is there,
> digging; or that I hear 'em cutting down the tree; and
> then I get up and look out of the loft window—you'll
> mind the window over the stables, as looks into the
> garden, all covered over wi' the leaves of the jargonelle
> pear-tree?

The years pass and Corbet becomes an eminent barrister,
making a brilliant marriage and being appointed to the
bench. Livingstone has just been made a canon at East
Chester Cathedral when Ellinor takes a holiday in Rome
to restore her failing health. It is there in the middle of
the Carnival that she learns that Dixon has been arrested
for murder or manslaughter. The railroad navvies had
uncovered Dunster's body and, alongside the corpse, a
horse-lancet with the name of Abraham Dixon engraved
on the handle.

With Livingstone's help, Ellinor returns to England and
determines to go alone to London and plead Dixon's innocence to Judge Corbet. The interview between the two
is compounded of alternating moods of regret and satisfaction on Corbet's part: relief that he did not involve
himself with the daughter of a murderer and regret that he
had refused to marry this quiet, disarming woman instead
of his imperious and demanding wife. The story concludes
with the chagrin of Judge Corbet and the content of Ellinor, who marries Canon Livingstone and takes Dixon
into her home:

> Those who pass through the village of Bromham, and
> pause to look over the laurel-hedge that separates the
> rectory garden from the road, may often see, on summer
> days, an old, old man, sitting in a wicker-chair, out
> upon the lawn. He leans upon his stick, and seldom
> raises his bent head; but for all that, his eyes are on a
> level with the two little fairy children who come to
> him in all their small joys and sorrows, and who learnt
> to lisp his name almost as soon as they did that of
> their father and mother. (chap. 16)

There is a remarkable social and moral logic to this story,
which accords with Gaskell's conviction that there is no
such quality as absolute evil. Wilkins is a murderer but
his crime is made to seem a natural response to psychological pressures that he is only dimly aware of himself.
He is never conscious, for example, that Dunster has come

to embody for him all the injustice of his position in the county and the snubs he has received over the years from a thick-headed gentry, men who were inferior to him in every way save that of birth.

Because Gaskell's fiction was moved less by well-designed plots than by the natural progress of thought, she was often at a loss to fill a required space with the appropriate number of words [when writing for serial publications].

—*Coral Lansbury*

So often in Gaskell's short stories, a clumsy expression or lurch into sentimentality can be forgiven because she has the courage to take up questions of considerable moral and social complexity. Even the most lachrymose Sunday School story is enlivened by a sudden pungent thought and glint of humor that comes from an "unenchanted eye" looking at people and events.

Many of Gaskell's failings in the short stories and novellas can be attributed to the requirements of serial publication and editors who wanted to package prose like boxes of biscuits. Because Gaskell's fiction was moved less by well-designed plots than by the natural progress of thought, she was often at a loss to fill a required space with the appropriate number of words. The Victorian novelists have their descendants in the writers of television soap operas who know the precise amount of emotion to be squeezed into each episode. It is this lack of competence that accounts for the number of "baggy monsters" that found their way into print under her name. *My Lady Ludlow*, first published in *Household Words* in 1858, later became the central story in the *Round the Sofa* volumes of 1859, and it cannot be fairly argued that there is any reason for publication in this form except the demand for a book and the advice of the ubiquitous Dickens.

If a counterpart for her stories is found then one must look across the Channel to George Sand, evoking the truth of feeling in her provincial stories. In both writers commonplace events have a luminosity and moral dimension that set them between narrative and poetry. These qualities define *Cousin Phillis* and redeem the most discursive stretches of *My Lady Ludlow*, where Gaskell pauses and makes the change between two estate managers an occasion for discussion of time and memory:

> And Mr. Horner was dead, and Captain James reigned in his stead. Good, steady, severe, silent Mr. Horner with his clock-like regularity, and his snuff-coloured clothes, and silver buckles! I have often wondered which one misses most when they are dead and gone— the bright creatures full of life, who are hither and thither and everywhere, so that no one can reckon upon their coming and going, with whom stillness and the long quiet of the grave, seems utterly irreconcilable,

so full are they of vivid motion and passion—or the slow, serious people, whose movements, nay, whose very words, seem to go by clockwork; who never appear much to affect the course of our life while they are with us, but whose methodical ways show themselves, when they are gone, to have been intertwined with our very roots of daily existence. I think I miss these last the most, although I may have loved the former best. Captain James never was to me what Mr. Horner was, though the latter had hardly exchanged a dozen words with me at the day of his death.

For Sand, it is the heart that speaks to the essential nature of reality, and only through feeling can the world be known. Wordsworth's romantic thesis is tempered in Sand by a consistent irony of vision, whereas for Gaskell romance is always fortified by a tough Mancunian shrewdness. If she is only rarely profound, she is never silly. Nonetheless, both writers believed that the world can only be experienced and understood by the responsive heart, and the source for this belief is, of course, Wordsworth.

Tessa Brodetsky (essay date 1986)

SOURCE: "A Mixed Bag—Short Stories," in *Elizabeth Gaskell*, Berg Publishers, 1986, pp. 80-8.

[*In the following essay, Brodetsky surveys Gaskell's work as a writer of short stories and novellas.*]

> An honest tale speeds best being plainly told.
>
> Shakespeare: *Richard II*

During the whole period of her literary output, Elizabeth Gaskell was publishing short stories and novellas, from **"The Three Eras of Libbie Marsh"** in 1847 to *Cousin Phillis*, finished in 1864. That she had skill in telling a gripping tale is obvious from the fact that she never had difficulty in getting her stories published; indeed, they were often commissioned, particularly by Dickens, who usually paid generously for them.

These stories present some practical difficulties for the modern reader. In the first place, there are problems in getting hold of some of them, as there is no readily available complete edition. Secondly, in many cases they are much longer than the commonly accepted 'short story' of today, an important characteristic of which is surely that it can be conveniently read at a single sitting; this is frequently impractical with Elizabeth Gaskell's stories. The length may partly be explained by the serialisation of many of them in a variety of contemporary periodicals, and a further consequence of this is often evident in a lack of structure, for example, in *My Lady Ludlow*, **"The Poor Clare"** and **"The Doom of the Griffiths."**

Many of the stories are concerned with themes and situations explored more fully in her novels: **"Lizzie Leigh"** deals with the plight of the unmarried mother; **"Mr Harrison's Confessions"** centres on life in the small community of Duncombe, which is reminiscent of Cranford; whilst the problem of the woman unwittingly committed to two lovers, which occurs in **"The Manchester Marriage,"** is developed in much greater depth in *Sylvia's Lovers*. She did not, however, restrict herself to such themes in these shorter works, but often ranged much more widely in both subject-matter and settings. Whilst *Sylvia's Lovers* is the only novel with an historical setting, quite a number of the shorter stories are set in the past; these include *My Lady Ludlow*, **"Lois the Witch," "An Accursed Race," "The Doom of the Griffiths"** and **"The Squire's Story."** None of her novels is concerned with the supernatural, yet this is the theme of such stories as **"The Old Nurse's Tale," "Curious if True"** and **"The Poor Clare."** Rather than touch superficially on a great number of these tales, let us consider four in more detail, and from these appreciate some of her achievements and shortcomings in this field. **"Half a Life-Time Ago"** was published in October 1855, *My Lady Ludlow* between June and September 1858, **"Lois the Witch"** in October 1859 and *Cousin Phillis* between November 1863 and February 1864. **"Half a Life-Time Ago"** tells the story of Susan Dixon, a strong-minded woman, who promises her dying mother to look after her younger brother, Will, who becomes seriously deranged after a bad dose of fever. Susan's lover, Michael Hurst, loathes Will and makes his confinement in a lunatic asylum a condition of marrying Susan. She does not hesitate to put her promise to her mother and love for her brother first and, as a result, she lives a hard, grim life, whilst Michael marries another local girl. He does not, however, prosper. When Will dies, Susan is left lonely and isolated. One November night, years later, she finds Michael buried in a snow-drift. With a superhuman effort she drags him to her home, but he is already dead. The following day, she goes to tell Michael's widow what has happened, and finally takes the widow and children to live with her.

The plot is simple enough, but the quality of this story lies in the finely-drawn character of Susan. We are made painfully aware of the suffering she experiences in giving up Michael for Will. After their final separation, she remembers poignantly places they had been to and things they had done together, and each evening she imagines she hears him approaching:

> She would wonder how she could have had strength, the cruel, self-piercing strength, to say what she had done; to stab herself with that stern resolution, of which the scar would remain till her dying day. It might have been right; but, as she sickened, she wished she had not instinctively chosen the right.

Her life with Willie is far from easy; he becomes increasingly violent, and she not only has to contend with this, but also, in order to prevent his being consigned to a madhouse, to keep his condition hidden:

> The one idea of taking charge of him had deepened and deepened with years. It was graven into her mind

as the object for which she lived. The sacrifice she had made for this object only made it more precious to her.

Her devotion to her mad brother is complete, and when he dies she experiences the worst fate of all: '. . . there was no one left on earth for her to love'. She develops into a 'tall, gaunt, hard-featured, angular woman—who never smiled, and hardly ever spoke an unnecessary word . . .' whose home and farm are models of cleanliness and efficiency, but lack any human touch. She works tirelessly and uncomplainingly in her utter loneliness, having lost first Michael and then Will.

Mrs Gaskell achieves a moving but unsentimental ending by writing simply of Susan's change of life-style. There is a feeling of completeness, of the wheel coming full circle, in the apt conclusion to this story:

> When she returned to Yew Nook, she took Michael Hurst's widow and children with her to live there, and fill up the haunted hearth with living forms that should banish the ghosts.

> And so it fell out that the latter days of Susan Dixon's life were better than the former.

My Lady Ludlow is also notable for fine character drawing, in particular of Lady Ludlow herself and of Miss Galindo. There is present as well a little of the humour and sparkle of *Cranford,* but as Margaret Dawson, the narrator, explains: 'It is no story: it has, as I said, neither beginning, middle, nor end'. Within the tale is contained the story of Clément de Créquy, set in Paris during the French Revolution; this is a diffuse, irrelevant interlude, which could well have been developed into a separate story, but as it stands, it certainly endorses the claim that *My Lady Ludlow* is no story! Lady Ludlow, in whose home Margaret Dawson spends her adolescence, lives in Hanbury Court in Warwickshire. She is a small, dignified, elegant, old-fashioned lady, who rules her household and the local villagers on feudal principles; she is a firm believer in the distinctions of rank and class, and assumes that her judgement will be accepted, partly owing to her experience of life, but more especially because of her station in society. In particular, she deplores the idea of educating the 'lower orders':

> It was a right word . . . that I used, when I called reading and writing 'edge-tools.' If our lower orders have these edge-tools given to them, we shall have the terrible scenes of the French Revolution acted over again in England.

The boy who occasions these reflections, Harry Gregson, later breaks his thigh, and Lady Ludlow explains that: 'It all comes from over-education'. The story within a story about the French Revolution, in which two aristocrats are guillotined, is also used to illustrate the dangers of teaching the lower classes to read, for it is through this that the aristocrats are betrayed. But Lady Ludlow is shown gradually modifying her principles. We have seen that Susan Dixon is portrayed as both a stern upholder of moral behaviour and a woman of great compassion, and we find that Lady Ludlow, as she deals with individual instances, changes her attitude, so that her behaviour too is eventually both morally sound and humane. For example, at first she refuses to intercede on behalf of Job Gregson (Harry's father) who, she is told, has been wrongly committed to gaol for stealing; she has a stormy interview with the new parson, Mr Gray, refusing to accept his opinion, but as she finally admits: ' "It so happened that I saw Job Gregson's wife and home—I felt that Mr Gray had been right and I had been wrong".'

However, it takes her years to alter her views on education, but she does eventually withdraw her opposition to a village school, provided that:

> . . . the boys might only be taught to read and write, and the first four rules of arithmetic; while the girls were only to learn to read, and to add up in their heads, and the rest of the time to work at mending their own clothes, knitting stockings, and spinning.

Lady Ludlow is too wealthy, too influential and too much of an aristocrat to have fitted into Cranford society, but Miss Galindo would have been quite at home there. We are given a lengthy, rambling background history of Miss Galindo, although she only appears in the latter part of the story, when she comes as a clerk to help Lady Ludlow's steward. She is a poor gentlewoman, who keeps one servant: 'invariably chosen because she had some infirmity that made her undesirable to every one else'. She has a peppery temper, and delights in scolding her servants, who are nevertheless greatly attached to her. As she explains: ' "I must have something to stir my blood, or I should go off into an apoplexy; so I set to, and quarrel with Sally" .' She tells us that as a young girl she thought of becoming an authoress, but after collecting paper, pens and ink

> . . . it ended in my having nothing to say, when I sat down to write. But sometimes, when I get hold of a book, I wonder why I let such a poor reason stop me. It does not others.

Her inexhaustible kindness, talkativeness and wit add a much-needed sparkle to the second half of the tale.

Although Mrs Gaskell never visited the United States, the story of the Salem witch hunt of 1692 obviously fired her imagination, and she uses this setting for the story of young Lois Barclay. The actual episode, in which a fanatical delusion led to the arrest of hundreds and the eventual death of twenty, does indeed seem to have been precipitated by several young girls and an American-Indian servant in the house of the local pastor, elements which Mrs Gaskell weaves into her story of **"Lois the Witch."** However, by introducing a young English girl, brought up happily and normally in an English country parsonage, into the household of her bigoted Puritan relations in Salem, their fanaticism and wildly emotional behaviour is highlighted.

It is a beautifully constructed, tautly-written story with no extraneous material. There is an inevitability in the outcome in which Lois, with no one to befriend or support her, is finally denounced as a witch, and hanged. From her very arrival in New England, Lois's thoughts are directed towards witchcraft; she even relates the story of old Hannah: ' . . . a poor, helpless, baited creature', who, in her home village of Barford, had cried out to Lois:

> 'Parson's wench, Parson's wench, yonder, in thy nurse's arms, thy dad hath never tried to save me, and none shall save thee when thou art brought up for a witch.'

The four relations with whom she goes to live in Salem are all depicted as somewhat abnormal. From her aunt, Grace Hickson, who 'had a kind of jealous dislike to her husband's English relations' she experiences 'positive, active antipathy to all the ideas Lois held most dear'. Grace comes to believe that Lois has bewitched her beloved son, Manasseh, and begs her to release him from the spell. When Lois protests her innocence, her aunt curses her most terribly and, throwing a handful of dust at her, leaves her to await execution the following morning.

The three cousins, Faith, Prudence and Manasseh, exhibit varying degrees of unbalance. Faith, at first the kindest and most sympathetic towards Lois, eventually becomes insanely jealous of her, believing she is her rival in love, and begins to think of her and refer to her as a witch. Prudence, portrayed as an impish child devoid of any feelings, behaves (according to the Indian servant, Nattee) as one possessed. It is she who finally, mercilessly, accuses Lois of witchcraft. The completely mad member of the family is Manasseh; he has had fits of insanity which his mother has kept secret, even having to tie him down with cords because of his violence. He believes he hears a voice telling him to 'Marry Lois!' and plagues her to agree to this. He admits that:

> 'At times I feel a creeping influence coming over me, prompting all evil thoughts and unheard-of deeds, and I question within myself, "Is not this the power of witchcraft?" and I sicken, and loathe all that I do or say, and yet some evil creature hath the mastery over me, and I must needs do and say what I loathe and dread.'

Lois, a gentle, kind, loving, normal girl, is relentlessly swept along in this alien, fanatical environment by forces she can neither understand nor resist. The mass hysteria and inhumanity of the inhabitants of Salem form a poignant contrast with the well-balanced, warm-hearted young English girl, as her death draws inexorably nearer.

Mrs Gaskell's skill is revealed in this powerful, well-constructed story, in which all the elements blend convincingly, so that we are compelled to accept Lois as the foredoomed victim of the Salem delusion. Mrs Gaskell's love of justice is illustrated in the way she ends the story by including the historical fact that Judge Sewall acknowledged his error in 1713 and prayed publicly for forgiveness. However, as Hugh Lucy, Lois's English lover, truly says, 'All this will not bring my Lois to life again, or give me back the hope of my youth'.

In *Cousin Phillis*, which was written as a four-part serial, Mrs Gaskell returns to her Cheshire roots. She evokes the rural setting deliberately and carefully, and describes with poignancy Phillis Holman's deep love for Holdsworth, a clever, attractive railway engineer. Paul Manning, the narrator, is a distant cousin of Phillis; like Mary Smith in *Cranford,* he not only narrates, but also participates in the action, and it is he who introduces Holdsworth to the Holman family. He describes effectively the beauty and serenity of Hope Farm:

> The many-speckled fowls were pecking about in the farmyard beyond, and the milk-cans glittered with brightness, hung out to sweeten. The court was so full of flowers that they crept out upon the low-covered wall and horse-mount, and were even to be found self-sown upon the turf that bordered the path to the back of the house. I fancied that my Sunday coat was scented for days afterwards by the bushes of sweetbriar and the fraxinella that perfumed the air.

Phillis's life is no idyll, but is rooted in the practical daily tasks of a farmer's daughter: we see her picking peas, peeling apples, mending socks, knitting. She is an intelligent girl who loves studying with her father, with whom she has a great affinity: he is both a farmer and a nonconformist minister, a man of considerable learning, of deep sympathy and love. Holdsworth is able to share in their intellectual pursuits, using his knowledge of Italian to help Phillis translate Dante. Phillis's mother and Paul are simpler people, not widely educated, and thus excluded from many of the interests of the other three; it is perhaps the main deficiency in Phillis's character that she is unaware of her mother's isolation and feelings of inferiority which this has occasioned.

Holdsworth leaves unexpectedly to take up a post in Canada; just before his departure, he admits to Paul that he loves Phillis and hopes to return in perhaps two years and tell her so. It is, however, obvious to the reader that he is more superficial than Phillis, more extrovert, less serious, and that this will be reflected in the quality of his feelings. This turns out to be the case, and it is not long before he writes from Canada telling of his marriage there. Unfortunately, Paul has already told Phillis of Holdsworth's love, to comfort her, as he becomes aware of her deep feelings for his friend. The news of Holdsworth's marriage therefore comes as an even greater shock to her, and results in a brain fever from which she makes a very slow, painful recovery.

We are given some moving insights into the character of Phillis's father, who has never fully accepted the fact that his beloved daughter is no longer a small child: indeed, she is nineteen before she stops wearing childish pinafores. When he learns that Paul has told her of Holds-

worth's love, he is enraged:

> 'So young, so pure from the world! how could you go and talk to such a child, raising hopes, exciting feelings—all to end thus; and best so, even though I saw her poor piteous face look as it did. I can't forgive you, Paul; it was more than wrong—it was wicked—to go and repeat that man's words.'

And when Phillis then upbraids her father for blaming Paul, explaining that she has indeed loved Holdsworth, he is unable to understand:

> 'Phillis! did we not make you happy here? Have we not loved you enough? . . . And yet you would have left us, left your home, left your father and your mother, and gone away with this stranger, wandering over the world.'

Although Phillis regains her physical strength, she remains languid, uninterested in the life around her, till the old family servant, Betty, reprimands her:

> 'If I were you, I'd rise and snuff the moon, sooner than break your father's and your mother's hearts wi' watching and waiting till it pleases you to fight your own way back to cheerfulness. There, I never favoured long preachings, and I've had my say.'

Mrs Gaskell excelled in her portrayals of the outspoken old servant, full of commonsense and ready to give good advice; other examples are Dixon in *North and South* and Kester in *Sylvia's Lovers,* and we have already seen Sally upbraiding Ruth in a manner similar to Betty's.

Phillis does indeed, a day or two after this, show enough strength of character to tell Paul: ' "We will go back to the peace of the old days. I know we shall: I can, and I will!" ' We admire her determination, but are not totally convinced by it. We must also admire the splendid rural setting and the well-drawn characters in this finely written story and, especially, the portrayal of Phillis's maturing emotions.

The four stories we have just considered illustrate Elizabeth Gaskell's skill in creating credible characters, and in evoking convincingly a particular mood and setting. On the other hand, *My Lady Ludlow* demonstrates her inability on occasions to construct a well-shaped story. She was by no means always successful as a short-story writer, but it is evident, from reading **"Lois the Witch"** and *Cousin Phillis* that she could and did master this genre.

Patsy Stoneman (essay date 1987)

SOURCE: "Two Nations and Separate Spheres: Class and Gender in Elizabeth Gaskell's Work," in *Elizabeth Gaskell,* Indiana University Press, 1987, pp. 45-67.

[*In the following excerpt, Stoneman investigates the means by which Gaskell blurs traditional gender roles across class divisions and criticizes patriarchal authority in her short fiction.*]

The society in which Elizabeth Gaskell lived and wrote was intersected horizontally by class and vertically by gender divisions. Critics have created a divided image of her work by focusing on one or other of these axes— 'industrial' or 'domestic'—and we can simply, but radically, revise this view by considering their interaction. I want to begin by drawing examples from Elizabeth Gaskell's lesser-known fiction, in which the issues are often very clear, but which critics have less completely labelled and categorised; this discussion will then serve as a context for a rereading of the familiar works in subsequent chapters.

What emerges from her work as a whole is that, at subsistence level, gender divisions are blurred: women exercise responsibility; men give basic nurturance. In the middle class, ideology heightens differentiation, producing infantilised women and authoritarian men.

Because Elizabeth Gaskell's studies of working-class life are read as 'industrial' novels, criticism has focused on factory-workers like John Barton and Nicholas Higgins. Her work as a whole, however, highlights working women—not just factory workers like Bessy Higgins but seamstresses, milliners, washerwomen, 'chars,' a tailor, beekeepers, farmers, housewives and domestic servants. Her very first publication is a verse portrait of an old working woman ('Sketches Among the Poor', *K*1: xxii-xxv). Her first published story, **"Libbie Marsh's Three Eras"** (1847), is about the friendship of an unmarried seamstress and a widowed washerwoman. These stories are remarkable for their focus on the physical detail of working-class life. Her Sunday-school stories, **"Hand and Heart"** (1849) and **"Bessy's Troubles at Home"** (1852), bring home the sheer effort required to produce the simplest results—a cup of tea, for instance—in the working-class homes of the 1840s.

Yet work is not seen primarily as a hardship in these stories but as a means to self-sufficiency and mutual support. In **"The Well of Pen-Morfa"** (1850) an unmarried mother supports herself by beekeeping; in **"The Manchester Marriage"** (1858) a widow, her mother-in-law and their servant keep themselves by running a boarding-house; in **"The Grey Woman"** (1861) a servant supports her former mistress by working as a tailor. As Anna Walters says in her splendid introduction to the Pandora *Four Short Stories* 'we are left as so often in Gaskell's writing with the impression of what women *can* do rather than the reverse.'

Perhaps the most impressive example of self-sufficiency is that of Susan Dixon the Cumbrian 'states-woman' in **"Half A Lifetime Ago"** (1855). As manager and later owner of the farm where she works alongside the labourers, she seems to epitomise Mary Wollstonecraft's ideal: 'how many women . . . waste life away the prey of discontent, who might have practised as physicians, regulat-

ed a farm, managed a shop, and stood erect, supported by their own industry.' Susan's life, however, is grim and lonely until she takes to live with her the widow and orphans of her former lover; 'and so it fell out,' the story succinctly ends, 'that the latter days of Susan Dixon's life were better than the former.'

Although three of Elizabeth Gaskell's best-known novels (*Mary Barton, North and South* and *Wives and Daughters*) end with a love-match, most of the short stories, together with *Cranford, Ruth, Sylvia's Lovers* and *Cousin Phillis*, stress the unreliability of sexual love and the durability of female friendships. Libbie Marsh and Margaret Hall agree to live together; Mrs Leigh sets up house with her 'fallen' daughter Lizzie; Nest Gwynne in **"The Well of Pen-Morfa,"** betrayed by her lover, takes in an idiot woman 'on the parish'; in *My Lady Ludlow* (1858) an aristocratic lady 'adopts' half-a-dozen needy young gentlewomen; in **"A Dark Night's Work"** (1863) Ellinor sets up house with her former governess; in **"The Grey Woman"** (1861) a servant disguises herself as a man and lives with her former mistress as her husband.

Female alliances occur naturally in the working-class, where needs are urgent and neighbours close by, but for Elizabeth Gaskell's middle-class women, help comes less from friends than from servants. Like Mary Wollstonecraft, she believed that good sense and heroism were more likely where people were forced to confront real crises. 'With respect to virtue,' says Wollstonecraft, 'I have seen most in low life . . . gentle-women are too indolent to be actively virtuous.'

The revolutionary function of domestic servants in Elizabeth Gaskell's work has been largely over-looked; critics seem blinkered by the stage convention that servants are comic, colourful 'characters.' Yet they provide practical, moral and psychological decision in situations which are sometimes deadly serious. Adrienne Rich argues that 'because the conditions of life for many poor women demand a fighting spirit for sheer physical survival, such mothers have sometimes been able to give their daughters something to be valued far more highly than full-time mothering.' Elizabeth Gaskell's middle-aged servants are generally childless, but they function as 'fighting mothers' for the middle-class woman in their care. It is Peggy who sustains Susan Dixon, and Betty Cousin Phillis, after the defection of lovers; it is Sally who teaches Ruth to survive by putting effort into proximate tasks; Miss Monro, the governess in **"A Dark Night's Work,"** not only works for Ellinor but stops her going mad; Norah, in **"The Manchester Marriage,"** takes on the moral dilemma about disclosing a family secret; in *Cranford*, Martha becomes her former mistress's landlady to save her from penury; and Nancy is the moral backbone of the Brown family in *The Moorland Cottage* (1862). When Mrs Buxton in that tale tells stories of saints and heroines to the little girls, she includes servants.

All these situations blur class boundaries, and although Elizabeth Gaskell herself had a number of servants, her behaviour throughout her life defines their relationship as one of function rather than immutable class distinction.

When Marianne was a baby, she wrote, 'we have lost our servant Betsy. . . . But we still keep her as a friend, and she has been to stay with us several weeks this autumn.' After all the girls were grown up their governess, Hearn, stayed on as 'a dear good valuable *friend*.' In **"French Life"** Elizabeth Gaskell praises the French habit of living in flats because 'there is the moral advantage of uniting mistresses and maids in a more complete family bond . . . . [a] pleasant kind of familiarity . . . which does not breed contempt, in spite of proverbs.' A contemporary conduct-book, declaring it 'highly improper for young people to associate with their servants,' emphasises her unconventionality.

In **"The Old Nurse's Story"** (1852) this theme is given a 'gothic' treatment. A 5-year-old girl, the youngest of a decayed aristocratic family, is poised between the drawing-room, occupied by a silent great-aunt, and the warm life of the kitchen. Tempted to her death by a phantom child, she is rescued by her nurse. Under the supernatural surface we can read the author's resistance to aristocratic values—patrilineal pride of possession, sexual rivalry and the ethic of revenge. Hester the nurse and the other working people provide an alternative pattern for personal relationships, unstructured by kinship but united by common nurturance and co-operation.

The care of children is Elizabeth Gaskell's crucial test of moral values; seen as a communal duty (though undertaken by individuals), it takes precedence over all other responsibilities and is never restricted to biological mothers or conventional households. Servants act as 'fighting mothers' to their charges; widows and unmarried mothers cope alone; Libbie Marsh devotes herself to a neighbour's child; Susan Palmer, in **"Lizzie Leigh"** (1850), brings up a baby thrust at her in the street; Bessy looks after her brothers and sisters; Miss Galindo, in *My Lady Ludlow*, adopts her dead lover's child; Lady Ludlow adopts a houseful of girls; in *Mary Barton*, Alice Wilson brings up her brother's son. Everywhere in Elizabeth Gaskell's work the maternal instinct flourishes, inside and outside marriage, with and without biological ties. . . .

Elizabeth Gaskell's Sunday-school stories are where we would expect to find most explicit didacticism about social role-playing, and each of them stresses gender-role reversal. Bessy learns 'the difficult arts of family life' from an older brother, and in **"Hand and Heart,"** the 'ministering angel' is a little boy. Tom Fletcher creates the sort of domestic peace we associate with Dickens's child-heroines; when orphaned he derives comfort from nursing his aunt's baby, and eventually he reforms the whole rowdy, quarrelsome household:

> His uncle sometimes said he was more like a girl than a boy . . . but . . . he really respected him for the very qualities which are most truly 'manly'; for the courage with which he dared to do what was right, and the quiet firmness with which he bore many kinds of pain.

In **"The Half-Brothers"** the slow-witted Godfrey gives his life to save the brother entrusted to him by their dying mother, protecting him from freezing with the warmth of his own body; like Tom Fletcher's, his action is both 'manly' and physically succouring. Elizabeth Gaskell's middle-class heroes are often doctors, who have professionalised the nurturing role.

Gender roles in these tales are not only blurred in general but shift according to circumstances. When the hero in **"Six Weeks at Heppenheim"** is nursed by the servant Thekla, her 'support was as firm as a man's could have been,' yet when she is distressed he invites her to ' "tell me all about it, as you would to your mother." ' Later Thekla, though 'strong as a man', is fed like a baby by Herr Muller, while her hands are busy nursing his little boy. . . .

Despite her uncertainty about the means, however, Elizabeth Gaskell's vision of the caring father remains a valid and vital goal, which modern feminists with sharper analytic tools are just beginning to recognise.

. . . . .

Mary Wollstonecraft saw the tradition of educating girls only to please, as responsible for women's narcissism, deviousness, sensuality and irrationality. The conduct-books 'render women more artificial, weak characters, than they would otherwise have been . . . [they] degrade one-half of the human species, and render women pleasing at the expense of every solid virtue.' Similarly, Elizabeth Gaskell shows that this ideology distorts parental feeling, making parents protect girls rather than educate them. Mr Wilkins in **"A Dark Night's Work"** is a rich and doting father but tells the governess to teach Ellinor ' "only what a lady should know," ' an attitude repeated by Mr Holman and Mr Gibson. As Peter Cominos points out, although 'a conscious struggle was waged on behalf of their moral purity by overprotective parents and chaperons', the girls themselves were kept 'innocent' and hence irresponsible. But, as these stories show, daughters cannot be protected from every moral decision. Each heroine acquires the strength and knowledge to cope with adult life, often with the help of servants rather than parents, but at unnecessary emotional cost. Elizabeth Gaskell's own daughter, by contrast, was left at 4 years old 'to judge if such an action be right or not . . . [to] exercise her conscience.'

The last part of **"Morton Hall"** is an attack on conduct-book education; three maiden aunts try out different 'systems' on their niece. The eldest models herself on Lord Chesterfield, whose 'unmanly, immoral system' is, according to Wollstonecraft, second only to Rousseau's in perniciousness: 'instead of preparing young people to encounter the evils of life with dignity, and to acquire wisdom and virtue by the exercise of their own faculties, precepts are heaped upon precepts, and blind obedience required when conviction should be brought home to reason.' Accordingly, Cordelia in **"Morton Hall"** is subjected to arbitrary rules; she must eat her meals standing, drink cold water before pudding, and never say 'red' or 'stomach-ache.' Although Miss Morton poses as a strong-minded woman who despises mere beauty, she is careful that Cordelia preserves her complexion. Wollstonecraft points to similar hypocrisy in Dr Gregory's renowned *Legacy to His Daughters,* where daughters are taught that though it is 'indelicate' *obviously* to want to please men, 'it may govern their conduct.'

Cordelia's second aunt, who educates her 'sensibilities,' is subjected to gentle satire which is nevertheless in line with Wollstonecraft's attack on sensibility, which 'naturally relaxes the other powers of the mind, and prevents intellect from attaining that sovereignty which it ought to attain to render a rational creature useful to others.'

The third aunt has no system but frightens Cordelia with dogmatic and unpredictable ways. This tale is very light humour, but it shows that Gaskell concurred with the Wollstonecraft thesis that conduct-book education based on obedience or sensibility was debilitating and that the marginalised role of many middle-class women made them into dogmatists, invalids or eccentrics.

. . . . .

The facile assumption of much Gaskell criticism has been that she 'looked up to man as her sex's rightful and benevolent master.' But many of her 'horror' stories depend on the inhuman possibilities of authority. In the early part of **"Morton Hall"** a sane Royalist lady is consigned to a mad-house by her Puritan husband; in **"The Grey Woman"** the heroine is married by a well-intentioned father to a man who proves to be a brigand who tortures victims on a heated iron floor; in **"French Life"** (1864) an aristocratic lady is poisoned, forced from a high window and repeatedly stabbed by her male relatives with the connivance of a priest. In **"Lois The Witch"** (1859) several hundred people, mostly women, are imprisoned and nineteen executed during the Salem witch hunt with the approval of every authority figure from fathers, guardians and ministers of the Church to judges and politicians. Although Basch claims that 'Mrs Gaskell and the majority of feminist reformers . . . blamed husbands abusing their powers and the law rather than accuse the powers and the law themselves,' Gaskell returns so often to the abuse of authority that her work as a whole does constitute a challenge to patriarchy itself, which confers on one set of people the right to command, and on another the duty to obey.

There are rather few 'orthodox' families, with father, mother and two or more children, in Elizabeth Gaskell's work, but when they do appear, *paterfamilias* is always a source of oppression and misery. Lizzie Leigh is driven into prostitution when her father disowns her; the Rev. Jenkyns, in *Cranford,* banishes his son Peter for half a lifetime; Mr Bradshaw, in *Ruth,* tyrannises his family. In **"The Heart of John Middleton,"** the hero begins life as 'Ishmael', the outcast, and only gradually validates his masculine status in the community by proving his ability to earn his living, fight his rivals and support his wife. But whereas as an outcast he had lived in love of his father and fellowship with other poachers, as a church-

goer and upholder of the law he lives by the ethic of 'an eye for an eye.'

Bourgeois men in Elizabeth Gaskell's works are not only tyrannical but culpable. Edward in **The Moorland Cottage** and Richard in *Ruth* both exploit positions of trust to embezzle funds; in **"The Squire's Story"** (1858) the heroine's husband turns out to be a highwayman; Mr Wilkins, a lawyer and the heroine's father in **"A Dark Night's Work,"** kills his clerk in anger.

Not only individuals, however, but the law itself is fallible. In **"The Grey Woman"** the heroine escapes her brigand husband but, as an absconding wife, can claim no protection from the law and spends years in flight and disguise. In both *Mary Barton* and **"A Dark Night's Work"** the courts are ready to execute an innocent man. The whole of *Sylvia's Lovers* is a protracted protest against the legal injustice of the press-gang. Frederick Hale's mutiny against unjust naval officers in *North and South* is surely meant as a redeeming analogy for the workers' riot against the threat of the militia. **"An Accursed Race,"** dealing with the persecution of the 'Cagots' in France and Spain, shows legalised injustice on the scale of genocide. As [one critic] puts it, 'obedience to law is simply not a reliable guide to moral behaviour.'

Lady Ludlow exposes the contingent nature of 'the law' when she bursts out' "Bah! Who makes laws? Such as I, in the House of Lords—such as you, in the House of Commons," ' and repeatedly the stories endorse the distinction between 'justice' and 'the law.' In **"The Crooked Branch"** (1859) a mother, forced to testify against her son, is seized with a stroke, and her husband tells the court: ' "now yo've truth, and a' th' truth, and I'll leave yo' to th' Judgment o' God for th' way yo've getten at it."

The contrast between justice and the law is most developed in **"Lois the Witch,"** where the authority-structures of a whole nation are complicit in cruel persecution. The story ends with a confession of guilt and fallibility by the judge and jury responsible for the executions. Two other stories also deal with supposed witches: **"The Heart of John Middleton"** (1850) is set on Pendle Hill, and **"The Poor Clare"** (1856) in the Trough of Bolland—both districts historically associated with witch hunts—and each concerns an independent old woman whose psychology Elizabeth Gaskell analyses in a realistic way. In **"Lois the Witch,"** among various psychological determinants of the mass delusion of Salem, she emphasises the gullibility of people who are used to deferring to authority; a powerful preacher like Cotton Mather could influence thousands, and Lois herself begins to wonder whether she is a witch when authoritative voices tell her so. The Unitarian Charles Upham, whose *Lectures on Witchcraft* (1831) were Elizabeth Gaskell's source, attacks 'the leaders of opinion' who constitute 'the law' in its widest sense:

a physician gave the first impulse to the awful work
. . . the judges and officers of the law did what they

could to drive on the delusion . . . the clergy were also instrumental in promoting the proceedings. Nay, it must be acknowledged that they took the lead.

Upham concludes that Salem forces everyone to think about 'the cultivation and government of his own moral and intellectual faculties, and . . . the obligations that press on him as a member of society to do what he may to enlighten, rectify and control public sentiment.' . . .

Jane Spencer (essay date 1993)

SOURCE: "Household Goodness: 'Cousin Phillis', *Wives and Daughters*," in *Elizabeth Gaskell,* St. Martin's Press, 1993, pp. 116-40.

[*In the following excerpt, Spencer argues that Gaskell's later works, "Curious, If True" and* Cousin Phillis, *illustrate the melding of her social conscience with her escapist tendencies.*]

Towards the end of her writing career, Gaskell gained a new sense of confidence in her work. *Cousin Phillis* (1863-4) and *Wives and Daughters,* the enchanting 'everyday story' which she had not quite finished when she died, display a new and dazzling sureness of artistic control. Edgar Wright explains this development in terms of a move from direct authorial commentary to more impersonal narrative methods. In *Cousin Phillis* the narrator is a major character in the story, and in *Wives and Daughters* the omniscient narrator withdraws to the background, leaving Molly Gibson, in Henry James's terms, the 'fine central intelligence' that gives the novel a unified viewpoint. (As Wright points out, James admired Gaskell's final novel). This artistic development is sometimes assumed to entail a movement away from the social commitment of her earlier fiction. Wright praises her for dropping the 'didactic element' in her later work, and sees *Cousin Phillis* and *Wives and Daughters* as a return to 'the Cranford world', a place whose values are so much 'part of her own nature' that she does not need to judge it in social, moral or religious terms: 'she needs only to demonstrate'. Thus Gaskell seems to achieve artistic greatness at the expense of social analysis. Yet *Cousin Phillis* and *Wives and Daughters* contain social commentary all the more telling for being subtly rendered. Patsy Stoneman offers a more helpful approach to Gaskell's later achievements when she argues that in *Wives and Daughters* Gaskell uses the authority of a realist stance to make the 'Woman Question', which had been present, but unfocused, in earlier novels, into a central issue, 'the acknowledged subject of debate'.

Gaskell's late work shows the fruits, not of a movement from anxious social commitment to artistic freedom from commitment, but of a transformed view of the artist, and especially the woman artist. She is no longer fundamentally split into dutiful and escapist halves. That earlier view, articulated in her correspondence with a fellow woman artist in 1850 haunts much of Gaskell's work, but

the later Gaskell is able to imagine a healing of the split, so that social commitment and enchantment need not preclude each other.

We can find her considering the possibility of this new synthesis in one of the short stories she wrote for the *Cornhill Magazine* in 1860, '**Curious, If True**'. The mode of expression is itself an indication of the later Gaskell's greater confidence: whereas her earlier doubts about the artistic vocation were anxiously expressed in private letters, the later work publicly presented a kind of parable about artistic vocation, delivered in a light, playful manner. Praised for its delicacy of humour, this 'lively *jeu d'esprit*' is worth examining for its dramatisation and visionary healing of the split within the artist.

Subtitled 'Extract from a letter from Richard Whittingham, Esq.', the story consists of this gentleman's narrative of a 'curious' and 'dream-like' experience that happened to him one summer evening in France. The narrator is visiting that country to pursue some research into his own family history. He is a descendant of Calvin's sister, and believes that he may find some distant relatives, also collateral descendants of Calvin. What he finds instead is a group of strange people who claim kinship with him on a very different basis. One evening when he is staying in Tours he takes a walk in the woods and gets lost. Just as he is resigning himself to a night in the open he sees a large château in the distance, and goes to ask for shelter. Identifying himself as 'Richard Whittingham, an English gentleman', he is immediately welcomed as a long-expected guest by the porter, who incidentally is as large as a giant. When the porter goes on to ask whether he has brought 'Monsieur le Géanquilleur' with him, it becomes clear to the reader what is going on. Richard Whittingham has been mistaken for Dick Whittington (someone later asks him how his cat is getting on) and has been admitted into a reunion of some of the best-known characters from fairy-tales. Our literal-minded narrator does not recognise this, and much of the fun in the story comes from the reader's being able to work out from the narrator's detailed, realistic but uncomprehending descriptions who the various people are. Cinderella, the Sleeping Beauty, Puss-in-Boots, Tom Thumb, Beauty and the Beast, and many more, are there. The hosts of the party are Bluebeard's surviving wife and her second husband. The narrator's strange experience ends with the appearance of a 'little old lady, leaning on a thin wand'. All the characters greet her in 'shrill, sweet voices', signalling that they belong to the world of faery, and they call her 'Madame la Féemarraine' (fairy godmother). Immediately afterwards the narrator finds himself lying in the wood. It is morning, and we can believe, if we like, that he has been asleep and dreaming all night.

Richard Whittingham, pursuing his historical research, can be seen as a representative of one part of Gaskell the writer—the careful, accurate social historian. He has known what Gaskell called the 'hidden world of art', but has grown out of it, as we see when he gets into a conversation about Jack the Giant-killer:

Jack the Giant-killer had once, it is true, been rather an intimate friend of mine, as far as (printer's) ink and paper can keep up a friendship, but I had not heard his name mentioned for years; and for aught I knew he lay enchanted with King Arthur's knights, who lie entranced until the blast of the trumpets of four mighty kings shall call them to help at England's need. (253-4)

Like Gaskell, he has experienced the fascination of Arthur's hidden world, but he does not think of it as a realm he can re-enter. His relationship to and admiration for Calvin underlines his difference from the fairy-tale world. Significantly, he refers to Calvin as the 'Great Reformer'. Gaskell herself hoped in some way to be a reformer through her realistic writing, and in creating this narrator she is commenting on her own aspirations.

The story suggests two possible ways of responding to the characters Whittingham encounters in the château. In his account of them, the creatures of fairy-tale are comically diminished. They have apparently been stuck in the château since their creation by the French writers Charles Perrault, Madame de Beaumont and Madame d'Aulnoy in the seventeenth century. Their immortality does not include immunity to decay. Cinderella is 'a very sweet-looking lady, who must have been a great beauty in her youth', but she is now 'extremely fat', and her feet, so swollen that she cannot walk, are taking revenge on her, she says, for forcing them into such tiny slippers in her youth. The romance belonging to the characters' original stories is fading faster than their looks, and the worldly-wise narrator describes them in a way that reduces them to mundane contemporaries. The Sleeping Beauty is introduced as a lady

> beautiful, splendid as the dawn, but—sound asleep on a magnificent settee. A gentleman who showed so much irritation at her ill-timed slumbers, that I think he must have been her husband, was trying to awaken her with actions not far removed from shakings.

Other fairy-tale characters are shown similarly doomed to repeat gestures that have lost their original meaning. The story can be read as a witty, realistic glance at the fairy-tale world that finds it charming, but inadequate.

On the other hand, we might find the narrator's response itself inadequate. In a place where the reader of fairy-tales knows that magic and marvel exist, Whittingham can only find ordinary people. However, he is uneasily aware that he has no right to the welcome he is being given, suggesting that at some level he recognises that he has entered an enchanted world where he has no place. The appearance of Madame la Féemarraine at the end of the story hints at the limitations of the realistic picture the narrator has given us of the château's inhabitants. This is the climax of the short piece, revealing that it is fairyland Whittingham has strayed into and simultaneously banishing him from it:

> And just as I spoke, the great folding-doors were

thrown open wide, and every one started to their feet to greet a little old lady, leaning on a thin, black wand—and—

> 'Madame la Féemarraine,' was announced by a chorus of sweet shrill voices.

> And in a moment I was lying in the grass close by a hollow oak-tree . . .

The fairy godmother, of course, is the benign if enigmatic ruling figure of one of the fairy-tales alluded to here, *Cinderella*. She rules the world of **'Curious, If True'**, commanding the allegiance of everyone in the château, and returning the narrator to the real world. She has sometimes been identified with Madame d'Aulnoy, writer of fairy-tales, but more helpful than a particular identification is the idea that Gaskell wants to give this enchanted world a female creator. Most of the tales to which she alludes in this story are versions written by a man, Charles Perrault, but they were popularly associated with female story-telling, having been published as *Tales of Mother Goose* with a frontispiece engraving of a woman telling stories to children.

The mother-figure who tells enchanting stories might be an appropriate image for Gaskell herself. Among her friends she was a famous story-teller from her girlhood. She particularly liked to tell tales of the supernatural, and 'no one ever came near her in the gift of telling a story', claimed Susanna Winkworth. Later, Dickens associated her with a woman of legendary story-telling power when he called her 'my dear Scheherezade'.

In **'Curious, If True'** the figure of the writer is split into the 'sensible and historical' but somewhat blinkered narrator Whittingham, and the old lady with a wand, who does not speak at all, but seems to be the source of the enchanted world that the narrator is trying to decipher. Here Gaskell is dramatising the self-splitting that she had articulated ten years earlier in her letter to Eliza Fox. The truth-seeking researcher, whose pursuit of his connections with Calvin suggests stern duty and self-denial, is imagined as male, just as earlier, when writing *Mary Barton,* Gaskell had thought of adopting a male pseudonym. Gaskell is here imagining the artist split into masculine duty, feminine pleasure; masculine reality, feminine fantasy.

However, the split between Richard Whittingham and the fairy-tale world that he visits is far from total. When he wakes up back in reality, it feels like anything but a banishment:

> I was lying in the grass close by a hollow oak-tree, with the slanting glory of the dawning day shining full in my face, and thousands of little birds and delicate insects piping and warbling out their welcome to the ruddy splendour.

Reality itself has become enchanting through the experience of the fantasy world. The misanthropic Whittingham, who only explored the countryside because he wanted to avoid his unprepossessing fellow guests, has been altered by his experience in the château. He has refused to adopt the cynical approach to its inhabitants displayed by one of the fairy-tale characters himself, M. Poucet (hero of the tale of the seven-league boots), and he has been given a vision. During his time in the château, he looks out of the window, back into the wood where he lost his way, and sees the ghost of a little peasant girl who is said to have been eaten by a wolf. This, of course, is Red Riding Hood, who in Perrault's version of her story is not rescued by the woodcutter. In death she is reconciled with her killer, for she appears with the wolf, which seems to be 'licking her hand, as if in penitent love'. Red Riding Hood then has a peculiar status: having died in a fairy-tale, she is a ghost to a world that is itself a fantasy. She seems doubly removed from reality, yet she is also used as an image of ordinary country life, 'a little girl, with the "capuchon" on, that takes the place of a peasant girl's bonnet in France'. The narrator's companion at the window (Beauty from *Beauty and the Beast*) exclaims:

> There, we have seen her! . . . Though so long dead, her simple story of household goodness and trustful simplicity still lingers in the hearts of all who have ever heard of her; and the country-people about here say that seeing that phantom-child on this anniversary brings good luck for the year. Let us hope that we shall share in the traditionary good fortune.

This phantom-child recalls not only Red Riding Hood but Wordsworth's Lucy Grey, the lost child who can still be seen tripping along in the lonesome wild. The good fortune that the sight of her brings is a very Wordsworthian blessing; Whittingham's return to the real world with 'the slanting glory of the dawning day shining full in [his] face' is like a restoration of the 'visionary gleam' whose loss is lamented in the Immortality Ode.

The narrator's experience of the fantastic, then, has sent him back to the real world with a renewed sense of wonder in everyday reality. Here is an imaginative resolution to Gaskell's sense of artistic split. The real, but enchanting world Whittingham returns to can be compared with the world Gaskell creates in late works such as *Cousin Phillis* and *Wives and Daughters,* works that present as their reality the natural beauty of the countryside and the 'household goodness and trustful simplicity' of young women like Phillis Holman and Molly Gibson, and invest that reality with a sense of wonder that is Gaskell's legacy from a lifetime of excursions into her 'hidden world of art'.

Wordsworth's 'Lucy' poems, with their idea of the young woman as 'child of nature', are often brought to mind in Gaskell's later work. Lucy is alluded to in connection with both Phillis Holman and Molly Gibson: the narrator of *Cousin Phillis* quotes two lines from 'She dwelt among th'untrodden ways' in evocation of the heroine, while in *Wives and Daughters* the heroine herself feels, at one point, that she is being 'rolled round in earth's diurnal course,/ with rocks, and stones, and trees' like Lucy in 'A

Slumber did My Spirit Seal'. It is worth considering Gaskell's use of Lucy figures in the light of recent feminist criticism of the Lucy poems. Lucy is sometimes a child (as in 'Lucy Grey') and sometimes the poet's lover (as in 'Strange Fits of Passion I have known'), and sometimes she is unnamed (as in 'A Slumber did My Spirit Seal'), but she is always associated with loss. Either she is dead or (as in 'Strange Fits of Passion') the threat of her death hangs over the poet. As Meena Alexander explains, 'Whether adult or child, named or nameless, she is bound to the natural landscape. She crystallises loss, intense longing. She is the impossible object of the poet's desire an iconic representation of the Romantic feminine.' In losing Lucy, and thus his own connection with the feminine nature he so desires, the poet gains a major theme for his Romantic writing, and a place in masculine culture. He writes about her loss. Mary Jacobus, pointing out that in 'Three years she grew' Lucy becomes a part of the landscape, adds that her death and assimilation into nature enable the poet to assume his identity:

> Lucy here is not just a memory; she becomes the ground or background for Wordsworthian figuration. He writes on her. However loving, all acts of naming or poetic naming such as those lavished on Lucy might be said to involve the constitution of the speaking or writing subject at the expense of the silenced object.

The male narrator's experience in **'Curious, If True'** is comparable to that of the Romantic poet as described by Alexander and Jacobus. His vision of the lost Lucy figure frees his creative imagination, allowing him to become more than merely 'sensible and historical' and able to write of enchantment.

If Whittingham, like the Romantic poet, depends on the icon of the innocent, dead young female for the grounding of his creativity, where does that leave Gaskell, who is, I have suggested, using his story as a way of dramatising her concerns about her own creative role? She, too, might be said to be gaining her creative identity through the objectification and silencing of the Lucy figure. There is, however, a difference. Gaskell is not to be identified with Whittingham; rather the story contains projections of two aspects of her creative personality. She is equally to be found in Madame la Féemarraine. The parable is not about the birth of a Romantic poet but about the renewal of a realistic prose writer; and the emphasis is not on the loss of the Lucy figure but on her rediscovery. Only by being reminded of the everyday enchantment of her household goodness can the sensible writer gain a poetic sense of the real world where he belongs.

'Curious, If True' is thus a transposition of the story of the Romantic poet's development onto the concerns of the Victorian novelist. In so far as Gaskell uses the story as a way of resolving her own artistic conflicts by constructing an aesthetic in which Wordsworthian nature, fairy-tale enchantment and realistic narrative can harmoniously combine, she, like the male poet, depends on the icon of the lost female. Yet in the mature work that follows this story, Gaskell uses her new aesthetic confidence to rescue the Lucy figure from silence and death. *Cousin Phillis* and *Wives and Daughters* both return to the figure of the innocent young female, but in these narratives she is not lost or silenced. Unlike the male Romantic poet, the female Victorian novelist is interested in 'Lucy's' subjectivity and survival. These late works resist the sacrifice of the young woman. Gaskell's last heroines are like Lucy, but a Lucy with a difference.

Paul, the narrator of *Cousin Phillis*, compares Phillis—without realising it—to Wordsworth's Lucy.

> My cousin Phillis was like a rose that had come to full bloom on the sunny side of a lonely house, sheltered from storms. I have read in some book of poetry—
>
> A maid whom there were none to praise,
>   And very few to love.
>
> And somehow those lines always reminded me of Phillis; yet they were not true of her either. I never heard her praised; and out of her own household there were very few to love her; but though no one spoke out their approbation, she always did right in her parents' eyes, out of her natural simple goodness and wisdom.

Phillis, like Lucy, is compared to a sheltered flower; but she is not completely the secluded child of nature. Her world, however small, is a social world of parents and household, and her relationship is to the social world, whereas Lucy exists only in nature and for the poet who writes of her. Paul's relationship to Phillis is like and unlike Wordsworth's to Lucy. Like, because he creates her story in his words, and because she represents for him a lost world of harmony with the natural. His first sight of her is so vivid in his memory that it remains a living vision: 'I see her now—cousin Phillis'. As the Wordsworth of the Lucy poems may be said to be creating himself as poetic subject in writing on Lucy, so Paul is writing of his own coming into manhood as he narrates his cousin's story. The first two pages of the story are devoted to recollections of Paul's first job, first lodgings away from home and his relationship with his father. After mentioning a family dispute of later years, when Paul 'really offended against [his] father's sense of right', an incident never further explained, the narrator suddenly recollects that he is supposed to be writing about cousin Phillis, not himself. It still takes a few more pages before he gets to her. Even then Phillis's story is occasionally interrupted by references to Paul's, and we learn, in passing, about his meeting with his own future wife.

Yet Paul's relationship to Phillis is unlike Wordsworth's to Lucy because it is not exclusive. Instead of being the only one to appreciate her, he is an onlooker on the intense drama of her relationships with her father, Minister Holman, and Edward Holdsworth. Holdsworth, the managing engineer for the new railway line between Eltham and Hornby, disrupts the Holmans' quiet, pastoral existence with his talk of modern technology and foreign countries. He loves Phillis but leaves her for a chance to

further his career in Canada. The pathos and necessity of cultural change is a familiar Gaskellian theme, and the railway a common Victorian figure for all that is modern. In *Cousin Phillis*, though, social transformation is mainly there as a metaphor for personal changes. The railway is not in itself a threat. Holman has built a life combining Christianity, strong family ties, classical learning and consciously Virgilian agricultural labour. He is quite capable of absorbing technological advances into his rounded existence, as his enthusiasm for Paul's father's invention shows; but his daughter's growth to maturity is another matter. Holman's idyll depends on the presence of a daughter to share the intellectual pleasures that his wife cannot understand. Phillis is infantilised, wearing childish pinafores at an age when other girls have given them up; her Lucy-like seclusion is unnaturally induced. When she falls in love with Holdsworth her father's dreams are shattered.

Phillis's lover and father both think of her as an unconscious innocent. Holdsworth, leaving for Canada, compares her to Sleeping Beauty and imagines that he will return in a couple of years to wake her to love. Because he has not told her of his love he does not feel any guilt when he marries another woman instead—another Lucy figure, 'Lucille, the second daughter . . . curiously like Phillis Holman' as he tells Paul in his letter. Lucille is clearly a substitute not just for Phillis herself but, through her friendly, rural yet cultured family, for the ideal pastoral existence represented for Holdsworth by the Holmans. When Phillis's father finds out about her heartbreak he blames Paul for telling Phillis about Holdsworth's love. To him his daughter is 'So young, so pure from the world! how could you go and talk to such a child, raising hopes, exciting feelings'. Her declaration that he is wrong, that she loved Holdsworth before Paul spoke, is the crisis point for both of them. The stress of revealing her sexual feelings to a father who feels betrayed by their existence brings on a collapse and a long illness.

Phillis's sexuality is pinpointed as the element neither father nor lover can incorporate into their idealised visions of her. The Lucy figure is revealed as a masculine fantasy based on seclusion of and total possession of the desired object. The logic of the narrative would seem to support Brother Robinson's stern admonition as he tells the anxious father to examine 'whether you have not made an idol of your daughter?'; but the brethren's punitive theology is rejected. Gaskell holds with Holman, who 'hold[s] with Christ that afflictions are not sent by God in wrath as penalties for sin', and Phillis recovers. Unlike Lucy, she is not dead or lost. For all the intense nostalgia of the narrative tone when first introducing Phillis, Phillis at the end of Paul's narrative is still a presence in his life. The words that describe her as changed also indicate her survival into the narrative's present: 'I sometimes grew desponding, and feared that she would never be what she had been before; no more she has, in some ways'.

The ending of the story achieves a fine balance between the pathos of Phillis's illusory hope that she can 'go back to the peace of the old days', and the reader's understanding that her efforts to take the servant Betty's good advice, and do something for herself, may enable her to go forward into a changing world. At one point Gaskell thought of spelling out more of Phillis's future, having her carry out drainage work in the village. Thus she would have become a moderniser like Holdsworth, but with more care for the people's existing way of life. This union of social and personal development, and representation of a woman grown up into public action, was probably rejected as too schematic: the later ending is effective in its open-endedness. There is just the hint of a wider life for Phillis, a 'change of thought and scene'. . . .

Jenny Uglow (essay date 1993)

SOURCE: "A Habit of Stories," in *Elizabeth Gaskell: A Habit of Stories*, Faber and Faber, 1993, pp. 236-58.

[*In the following excerpt, Uglow explores the fifteen year period (1850-1865) during which Gaskell associated herself with Charles Dickens and wrote most of her short fiction.*]

> 'I did feel as if I had something to say about it that I *must* say, and you know I can tell stories better than any other way of expressing myself'.

This was how Elizabeth would explain *Ruth* to her friend Mary Green. Her new fame forced her to ask herself why she wrote. Until the late 1840s writing had been a private hobby, and she could justify the publication of the *Howitt's* stories and *Mary Barton* by her Unitarian belief in the moral function of art and in the duty to state the truth and expose social evils. Writing fiction was permissible as a branch of philanthropy. But what if it was just fun in itself? A personal need? A virtual career? While part of her shrank from the taint of professionalism, at the same time Elizabeth was briskly counting her earnings, studying her contracts and moaning about her publishers.

1850 was the year of her letters to Eliza Fox about the conflict of home duties and art. It was also the year she met Charlotte Brontë, and the year that she began to write for Dickens. A good time, then, to consider how completely she lived in an atmosphere of stories. In 1850 she published **'Lizzie Leigh'**, **'The Well of Pen-Morfa'** and **'The Heart of John Middleton'** and a novella, *The Moorland Cottage*. These were forerunners of a wealth of shorter works, stunningly varied and accomplished, which would pour from her pen in the next fifteen years, most of them destined to appear in Dickens's *Household Words*.

From time to time after *Mary Barton* was published Elizabeth would proclaim to the world at large that she was *not* working on another book. The fact was, however, that she simply could not cease writing. Stories were intrinsic to her cast of mind. Her letters are studded with swift character sketches and condensed narratives. Some flash past in a few suggestive phrases, like the placing of the yet unknown Charlotte Froude as a heroine of romance,

or this description of a local murder in 1850: 'such a tragedy here yesterday, which you will see in the papers. We knew Mrs Novelli! She was a madonna-like person with a face (and character I believe) full of thought and gentle love, Miss Maistaid's faithful servant and friend.' Other letters are instinctively composed to produce an effect, like the long description of giving Tennyson's poems to Bamford, with its structure of quest, discovery, climax and final tableau. She told Forster of her great joy in hunting across Manchester for the 'great, grey stalwart man', pouncing on him as he emerged from a pub and leaving him, red with pleasure, reading aloud in the middle of the street in a 'sleep-walking state', in grave danger, she feared, of being run over.

The habit marked her talk as well as her letters, as Emily Winkworth had noted when Elizabeth visited Catherine at Southport in 1848: 'all those nice long stories and that very factual style of conversation that Katie likes so much'. In late 1849 Emily mentioned this again, bemoaning the fact that she could not entertain her sick sister half so well: 'Oh! what would I give to be able to tell long stories like Lily, or to speak out all my actual present little feelings in that simple picturesque way she does'.

Elizabeth loved rich, wide-ranging talk, as full of stories as a Christmas cake is of fruit, nuts, spices and peel. Her idea of social misery was a stuffy dinner party, or a 'grave and serious' tea of the kind she described in **'Company Manners'** in 1854. At this tea-party the talk was as heavy as the food, and in every ponderous silence the hostess would say, 'eat another macaroon'. The first macaroon she revelled in, the second she enjoyed, the third she got through—but after the sixth she got up to go. She was met with a burst of indignant surprise: ' "You are surely never going before supper!" I stopped. I ate that supper, hot jugged hare, hot roast turkey, hot boiled ham, hot apple-tart, hot toasted cheese. No wonder I am old before my time'. It was not the food which weighed on her so much as the boredom. She longed for word-games to be played—'Wit, Advice, Bout-rimés, Spanish Merchant, Twenty Questions'. She yearned for rules to be transgressed. She delighted when one of these 'rational parties', where everyone wore sedate, anxious expressions, was brilliantly disrupted by 'a beautiful, audacious but most feminine romp' who made them play a ridiculous game of puffing to keep a feather in the air. A far better use of their breath, in Elizabeth's view, than earnestly reporting new scientific discoveries ('the details of which were all and each of them wrong').

What she liked best was 'a slightly gipsy and impromptu character' and in **'Company Manners'** she gave an example of her ideal five o'clock tea. It was held in a large old schoolroom, which could have been doleful but was thoroughly romantic: the trees moaned outside, Irish staghounds bayed in the stables, a Spanish parrot talked continuously from its perch in a dark corner and 'the walls of the room seemed to recede as in a dream, and, instead of them, the flickering firelight painted tropical forests or Norwegian fiords, according to the will of our talkers'. The old black kettle, long banished from the kitchen, sputtered and leaked, and 'did everything that was improper'. They ate only thick bread and butter:

> 'Who ate it I don't know, for we stole from our places round the fireside to the tea-table, in comparative darkness, in the twilight, near the window, and came back on tiptoe to hear one of the party tell of wild enchanted spicy islands in the Eastern Archipelago, or buried cities in farthest Mexico; he used to look into the fire and draw and paint with words in a manner perfectly marvellous . . . Our host was scientific; a name of high repute; he, too, told us of wonderful discoveries, strange surmises, glimpses into something far away and utterly dream-like. His son had been in Norway, fishing; then, when he sat all splashed with hunting, he too, could tell of adventures in a natural racy way'.

But in the formal dining-room that night the magic vanished:

> 'At dinner the host talked of nothing more intelligible than French mathematics; the heir drawled out an infinite deal of nothing about the "Shakespeare and musical glasses" of the day; the traveller gave us latitudes and longitudes, and rates of population, exports and imports, with the greatest precision; and the girls were as pretty, helpless, inane fine ladies as you would wish to see'.

Conversational storytelling can take many forms. At its simplest it is just recounting what has happened, to oneself, one's family, one's friends. A degree further on these accounts become embroidered and shaped—memories crystallize into anecdotes through frequent repetition. At some stage in this process, in the hands of particular people, storytelling becomes an art and the teller is valued for the gift, especially when the tales conjure up different worlds, like the travellers' yarns, or re-create a vanished past. This latter quality was what Elizabeth treasured as a girl in Knutsford, where, as she says in 'The Last Generation', 'the old ladies were living hoards of tradition and old custom'. At another remove some stories become increasingly fantastical in the telling, slipping from experience towards fantasy. Such are the ghost stories and wild tales Elizabeth swapped with Mary Howitt and her cousins, but even here the tellers would still claim truth to 'fact' as a pledge of authenticity.

Because her conversation vanished with her, critics tend to ignore the links between Gaskell's spontaneous, spoken stories and her written work. Yet she herself often refers to this context. She saw social storytelling as an art and in her view one of the great qualities of Mme de Sablé and her circle (the starting point for **'Company Manners'**) was that 'they knew how to narrate':

> 'Very simple, say you? I say, no! I believe the art of telling a story is born with some people, and these have it to perfection; but all might acquire some expertness in it, and ought to do so, before launching out into the muddled, hesitating, broken, disjointed, poor, bald, accounts of events which have neither unity,

nor colour, nor life, nor end in them, that one sometimes hears'.

Hard words.

In her own short stories and novellas Gaskell likes to present herself and her narrators as telling stories to a friend by the fire, or as part of a community of storytellers, like those who gather in Mrs Dawson's salon in *Round the Sofa,* each promising to 'narrate something interesting, which we had either heard, or which had fallen within our own experience'. A convention like this—used in so many Victorian collections—reflected real social practice. Skilfully used, this context of talk, of unplanned entertainment, allowed freedom from strict rules of form. The varied personalities of the 'speakers' hover behind each piece and the unspoken story of their own lives enriches the readers' response to their narration—one 'teller' might present something as dense and tight as an academic paper, like an **'An Accursed Race'**, while another might spin a long, loosely structured tale of reminiscence, like *My Lady Ludlow,* which Mrs Dawson declares to be 'no story: it has, as I said, neither beginning, middle, nor end'.

Part of the fun of reading Gaskell is watching her subtle play with the figure of the narrator, and with the inevitable claims of veracity: there is a tongue-in-cheek irony in the very title of a comic story like **'Mr Harrison's Confessions'**. She knew the lure of the good story, and in real life she was alert to the perilous frontier between accuracy and invention, the slippery, heady slide from dramatic reporting to a heightened and selected version of the truth and finally to a lie.

In 1859 she wrote a worried letter to her young friend Charles Bosanquet about the danger of getting the 'bible-women' who were encouraging the poor to subscribe to bibles, to keep journals 'of more than mere statistics'. She noticed that when this happened, the temptation was that conversations were 'thrown into dramas, as it were— with little accounts of looks, & gestures which seemed "touched up" as it were'. Instead of an accurate picture of the poor, all individuality was lost—they all seemed to say the same thing. She explained her odd fear—for she supported the cause—by referring to her disillusionment with 'a *very* good man' (almost certainly her old friend Thomas Wright). Some years ago, she said, he was

> 'brought into much notice for his philanthropy, and many people were only too glad to learn something of the peculiar methods by which he certainly *had* reclaimed the erring. So he was asked about his "experiences", and told many *true* interesting histories. Lately I have observed that it was difficult to "bring him to book" as it were about his cases, he would tell one of a story that made one's heart bleed,—tell it dramatically too, which faculty is always a temptation, & when, unwilling to let emotion die without passing into action, one asked for the address &c,—it always became vague,—in different ways. For some time I have suspected that he told *old* true stories, as if they were happening *now,* or had happened *yesterday.* And

just lately I have found that this temptation to excite his hearers strongly, has led to *pure invention*'.

Wright knew how to narrate too well. Storytelling gives power, and power corrupts the teller.

When she laid passionate claim to the truth of her own controversial novels, *Mary Barton* and *Ruth,* Gaskell was, of course, appealing not to the accurate representation of facts—although she felt these were not distorted—but to a truth of feeling, attitudes, experience. And within her fiction lies are a major cause of psychic crises. Often these untruths are not wilful inventions, but 'white lies' forced on people to *cover up* the truth: Thurstan and Faith Benson inventing a past life for Ruth to protect her and her illegitimate child; Margaret Hale lying to protect her brother from arrest; Ellinor Wilkins in **'A Dark Night's Work'** colluding with her father's lies after he has killed his clerk, Dunster. The pressure is terrible: the truth will out. As Ellinor says, after eighteen years of suppression, 'I knew it would come out in the end.'

In a more light-hearted vein in her short stories Gaskell plays knowingly with that borderline between invention and fact (fact which we, as readers, and she, as author, already know to be fiction). In **'My French Master'**, for example, a Paris friend tells the narrator about the marriages which, as in a Shakespearian comedy, end the sad exile of the hero, M. Chalabré, and return him to his ancestral estates. The teller bears a marked resemblance to Elizabeth's own friend, Mary Clarke Mohl—'English by birth, but married to a German Professor, and very French in manners and ways'. Mme Mohl had a well-known love of matchmaking and we are warned, in the story, against this narrator's inevitable claims of truthfulness since 'she was rather in the habit of exaggerating trifles into romances'. We are also alerted to other perils:

> 'I sank back in my easy chair. Some of my friends are rather longwinded, and it is well to be settled in a comfortable position before they begin to talk.'

The real danger of such talk is that it trembles on the edge of gossip, turning private tragedy or triumph into public entertainment. Gaskell was well aware of this. She gives us splendid gossips, both malicious and harmless, like the cynical Miss Horsman of **'Mr Harrison's Confessions'** and the bustling Miss Pole of *Cranford*. Both are a-quiver with nosiness, bursting to be first with the news. On one dreadful occasion in *Cranford* when Mrs Forrester arrives at Miss Matty's house in the midst of the gratifying excitement caused by Miss Pole's announcement of Lady Glenmire's engagement to Mr Hoggins, the unhappy Miss Pole is seized with a terrible fit of coughing. Knowing her so well, Matty and Mary Smith generously hold back the news, until her choking has passed:

> 'I shall never forget the imploring expression of her eyes, as she looked at us over her pocket handkerchief. They said, plain as words could speak, "Don't let Nature deprive me of the treasure which is mine, although for a time I can make no use of it." And we did not'.

Elizabeth herself was not a compulsive gossip, but she could certainly identify with *Cranford*'s narrator Mary Smith, who confesses:

> 'In my own home, whenever people had nothing else to do, they blamed me for want of discretion. Indiscretion was my bugbear fault. Everybody has a bugbear fault; a sort of standing characteristic—a *pièce de resistance* for their friends to cut at; and in general they cut and come again'.

Her own indiscretions sometimes tripped her up. In 1851, for instance, she was happily passing on rumours about the splendour of Dickens's house. Writing to Emily Tagart, she hotly disputes the notion that her informant is an ignoramus from, of all places, Lancaster. 'Tell Helen', she writes, 'my informant, who lives in *London* I beg to say, and in a capital circle in London too, writes me word that the Dickens have bought a dinner-service of *gold* plate. My informant dined with the Dickens the very day when he wrote to me, and told me this; so after *that,* let Helen doubt me as she will'. She should have known better: Dickens added a teasing postscript to his next letter:

> 'We have just bought a neat little dinner service of pure gold for common use. It is very neat & quiet'.

He kept the joke running for months, from references to Catherine and Kate Dickens wearing dresses of gold and silver thread to the tender announcement of the birth of Edward Dickens in 1852 as a golden baby, 'his silver skin laced (internally) with his golden blood'.

Elizabeth did not learn from experience. In 1855 she was caught repeating some scandal about 'Mr Hawkes' 2 wives', which seems to have started with Jane Carlyle and Fanny Wedgwood and found its way back to Thomas Carlyle via Mazzini, who demanded an explanation. A more serious tangle arose in 1859 when she was swept into the controversy about the authorship of *Scenes of Clerical Life* and *Adam Bede*. One camp (led by Florence Nightingale's friends Charles and Selina Bracebridge, and abetted by the imposter himself) declared George Eliot to be a certain Joseph Liggins of Nuneaton. Elizabeth was taken in, reluctant, at first, to believe that the books she so admired were written by the Marian Evans who lived openly with G. H. Lewes (of whom, by then, she thoroughly disapproved). She was desperately curious and soon her whole network of contacts was humming. Her 'informants' were legion, but all her evidence was second, third or even fourth hand. She relied on vague contacts such as Miss Ewart's cousin-in-law, Mr Bacon, a clergyman near Nuneaton, or Mrs Sandars's friend Mrs Fisher, 'unknown to me', who had allegedly sat next to Liggins at dinner. To explain her credulity she was reduced to citing Blackwood's bookseller in Edinburgh, who had been sharply cross-examined by Meta:

> 'And Meta (1st week in August, when everyone was

discussing Miss Evans' claims) being in Blackwoods shop, plumped the question to the head young man "Who wrote Adam Bede" "I do not know. But I know it was not written by a lady—" (observe this last clause was volunteered.) Meta said "Do you *know* it was not written by a lady?" "Yes, I do".'

Harriet Martineau, the recipient of this story, had taken a great interest in the affair: letters flew back and forth (with Elizabeth's handwriting becoming faster and larger in every one). By October 1859 Harriet, and other friends, including Elizabeth's current publisher, George Smith, had convinced her of her error. When she knew the truth, she was full of remorse. The whole incident gives a gripping impression of Elizabeth's burrowing curiosity and love of a good story, and also of the extraordinary intensity of such rumourmongering. At one point we find members of a house-party busily copying letters to one of the guests and bearing them off to show other friends and relations, thus spreading the ripples of falsehood wider and wider. This was an accepted practice, but when one realizes how busily these worthy Victorians talked about each other and how freely letters could become public property, Elizabeth's adamant instructions to Marianne make very good sense: '*Pray* burn my letters. I am always afraid of writing much to you, you are so careless about letters'.

She was not alone in her fears. R. K. Webb describes the same fierce anxiety in Harriet Martineau: 'Injunctions about her letters went out to all her correspondents: they were either to return them or suffer excommunication, and she did what she could to prevent any publication of her letters after her death. 'Letters are talk', said Harriet. How could she write freely if all the world might read them? Victorian correspondences, especially those of women, are littered with urgent notes like Geraldine Jewsbury's to Jane Carlyle: 'for pity's sake take care of your letters. I have burned all yours which could be misunderstood'. Elizabeth herself carefully edited the letters of Charlotte Brontë when she presented her life to the public, but in private she was as great a sinner as any. In one letter to John Forster she enclosed not only Charlotte's intensely personal note about her engagement to Arthur Nicholls ('to make up for my dull letter') but also two of Mary Mohl's letters from Paris: 'Don't you like reading letters? I do, so much. Not grand formal letters; but such as Mme Mohl's I mean'.

She was on safer ground, one would think, when she passed on stories which were *not* about people she knew, like wild adventures or ghost stories. She told these constantly, with great relish. Charlotte Brontë once had to stop her hastily when she was about to launch into a particularly dismal ghost story, just before bedtime, by explaining that she was superstitious and dreaded 'the involuntary recurrence of any thoughts of ominous gloom which might have been suggested to her'. (The *frisson* of ominous gloom was just what thrilled Mrs G.)

One of Elizabeth's own special tales was about a young married woman haunted to the point of illness and breakdown by the face of a man. Eventually, while convalesc-

ing in Rome, she vanishes completely, last glimpsed weeping in a carriage—and 'by her side there sat a strange man, with the face she had so often described'. Elizabeth saw such stories as heirlooms, treasures like old lace or family jewels, to be protected and cared for and handed on to the next generation. Three weeks before she died she told this tale to A. C. Hare, saying that it had been told to her as a girl in Knutsford. She impressed on him that

'she felt so greatly the uncertainty of life, that she wished a story which might possibly be of consequence, and which had been intrusted to her, to remain with someone who was certain to record it accurately'.

Her strong feelings over this particular story led to a dusty exchange with Dickens, who also loved to talk about 'the latest murder and the newest thing in ghosts'. When she discovered that he had included a version (getting the ending wrong) in 'To be Read at Dusk' for *Heath's Keepsake* (Christmas 1851), she was furious: 'wretch that he is to go and write MY story of the lady haunted by the face; I shall have nothing to talk about now at dull parties'. Dickens sent flamboyant, comic apologies, pleading in mitigation: 'I never yet met anybody who read the Keepsake'. He clearly felt no guilt and pointed out that the same thing had happened to him: 'Yet I never complained!' Casting a sideways glance at Catherine Crowe's immensely successful two-volume anthology of 1848, *The Night Side of Nature,* he went on:

'More than that, Crows have plucked at the fleeces of other Ghosts of mine before now—but I have borne it meekly. Ghost stories, illustrating particular states of mind and processes of the imagination, are common property, I always think—except in the manner of relating them, and O who can rob some people of *that*!'

The rebuke was fair. Such tales were indeed common property, and if Dickens pinched one, Gaskell had more to hand.

Dickens was right to point out the collective ownership of stories. He was right too in his throw-away words about the 'manner of relating them'. Gaskell's stories, spoken and written, always bore the stamp of her style and were invariably recast to bring out the ideas that most preoccupied her. Many were based on real life. She could be extremely discreet, but she could also be free with people's private lives if she found a good story or a colourful detail; the danger she saw in Thomas Wright was not altogether absent in herself. When *Cranford* was published, the good folk of Knutsford fell over themselves in their eagerness to find the originals of her characters. Part of the 'evidence' in the Liggins affair in 1859 would turn on the eager pursuit of local models for George Eliot's characters, and Elizabeth told Harriet Martineau (who had experienced the same fuss after *Deerbrook*) that she herself had been

'complimented or reproached, as the case might be,

with having used such or such an incident, or described such & such a person, & never seem able to understand how one acquires one's materials unconsciously as it were'.

1850 offers two examples of the way Elizabeth acquired her materials 'unconsciously as it were' and used real lives imaginatively—one in fiction, the other, more dubiously, in biography. The first is a young prostitute, whom we know only as Pasley. Elizabeth had visited her in Manchester's New Bailey Prison in 1849 and when Tottie came to stay that December, she too became concerned with Pasley's case; Elizabeth later wrote to her about 'our girl'. On 8 January 1850 she wrote to Dickens, at the suggestion of his brother-in-law Henry Burnett, who lived near her in Manchester. She knew of Dickens's involvement in the refuge for fallen women that he had established with Angela Burdett Coutts at Urania Cottage in Shepherd's Bush. Could he or Miss Coutts advise her, she asked, or accept Pasley in one of their emigration schemes?

Elizabeth's letter, while accurate (as far as we know), gives a distinctive Gaskellian shape to the girl's life. Pasley is a girl of good family; her father is an Irish clergyman who dies when she is two, and her mother ignores her, remarries and sends her out to nurse. At six her uncle puts her in an orphanage and at fourteen she is apprenticed to a dressmaker. When the business fails, her employer sends her to another dressmaker, who connives at her seduction by a doctor, called in when she is ill. Pasley appeals to her mother in vain, and in her despair enters the penitentiary. There she is picked up by a woman who visits specifically to decoy the inmates into prostitution. For months she has lived on the streets

'in the hopes, as she tells me, of killing herself, for "no one had ever cared for her in this world"—she drank, "wishing it might be poison", pawned every article of clothing—and at last stole.'

Almost as if for effect, after signing the letter, Elizabeth scrawled "Turn over". Now comes a postscript, a dramatic, ironic coda: 'I have not told you one incident'. In prison Pasley is confronted 'face to face' by her seducer, now the prison doctor. As she faints, he whispers, 'Good God, how did you come here'. (Gaskell adds, in good storytelling vein: 'The chaplain can guarantee the truth of all I have said'.)

It may be unfair to stress the style of narration and structure, since there is no doubt of Elizabeth's real concern. Dickens replied at once, using a wonderfully suggestive image: Miss Coutts could not take responsibility, since 'the Voyage Out has been, and still is, our great difficulty'. He did, however, send a page of advice from Angela Burdett Coutts which Elizabeth gratefully took. She found a couple sailing for the Cape, organized the master of a local ragged school to take her to London and found a 'whole *nest* of good ladies' to take care of her until the ship sailed. What became of the real Pasley we do not know, but her plight, and some aspects of her story, took fictional shape in Gaskell's next novel, *Ruth*.

The second figure, by odd coincidence, was also the daughter of an Irish clergyman: Charlotte Brontë. She too had a hard childhood, although of a different kind, and she too, in Elizabeth's eyes, appealed in some ways to be 'rescued'. If Pasley was cast as heroine-victim (under the heading 'fallen woman'), so was Charlotte (under the class of 'lonely genius'). The image was fixed before Gaskell even set eyes on her.

The writers already admired each other's work: Gaskell was fascinated and puzzled by *Jane Eyre* and Brontë thought *Mary Barton* 'a clever though painful tale', but feared its theme might anticipate *Shirley,* which she was working on at the time. Before *Shirley* was published, in November 1849, she sent an early copy to Gaskell and was moved by her prompt letter of congratulation: 'The note brought tears to my eyes. She is a good, she is a great woman'. The support of writers like Mrs Gaskell and Harriet Martineau, she said, took the sting out of other criticism. Meanwhile (despite her rage at the impertinence of those who had tried to pierce her own anonymity) Elizabeth was, of course, consumed with curiosity about Currer Bell. She pursued her quest through Tottie and other friends, and by late November was telling Catherine Winkworth: 'Currer Bell (aha! what will you give me for a secret?) She's a she—that I will tell you—who has sent me "Shirley".' In December, her goal reached, she was able to tell Annie Shaen about Charlotte's meeting with Harriet Martineau, describing her (unseen) as 'a little, very little, bright haired sprite, looking not above 15, very unsophisticated, neat & tidy . . . Her father a Yorkshire clergyman who has never slept out of his house for 26 years; she has lived a most retired life'. When she read the romantic account in the biography, describing how Charlotte, after slight hesitation, went straight to her side, Harriet—who was very deaf and well known for her bizarre ear-trumpets—just wrote tartly in the margin: 'Seeing the trumpet'.

Charlotte and Elizabeth were finally brought together in the summer of 1850 by Sir James Kay-Shuttleworth, the James Kay who had tackled the Manchester cholera in 1832; he had since been knighted and added his wife's surname to his on inheriting the Shuttleworth estates. Assiduous in pursuit of the famous, he called at Haworth after the publication of *Shirley* and invited a reluctant Charlotte to their splendid Elizabethan house, Gawthorpe Hall, near Burnely, on the East Lancashire border. She went in June. The stay was not as bad as she feared and she agreed to stay with them at Windermere that summer. By then Lady Kay-Shuttleworth, a small, energetic woman of thirty-two, had met Elizabeth, while staying at Capesthorne. They had exchanged long letters, about the restless age, the search for purpose, the growth of sisterhoods—and about Charlotte Brontë, to whom Elizabeth said she was drawn not only by her books but by 'the glimpses one gets of *her,* and her mode of thought, and, all unconsciously to herself, of the way in which she has suffered. I wonder if she suffers *now?*' In August Lady Kay-Shuttleworth gave her the chance to find out, by inviting the Gaskells to Brierley Close.

William has just returned from Scotland and was about to set off for Birmingham so Elizabeth went alone. Both she and Charlotte found the worldly, talkative Sir James hard to take. (Marianne Gaskell later got the measure of his self-importance perfectly: 'watch his left eye, & provide him with Savoy biscuits'.) Charlotte particularly disliked him. She respected his intellect and 'marked kindness', but decided that 'the substratum of his character is hard as flint' and that he had a natural antipathy to imaginative writers: 'Their virtues give him no pleasure—their faults are as wormwood and gall in his soul: he perpetually threatens a visit to Haworth—may this be averted!'

Brierley Close stands on the hillside above Lowood, just south of Ambleside, looking westward to the fells across the shimmering lake. As their hostess had a cold, Charlotte and Elizabeth were thrown together, talking over needlework in the drawing-room, driving in the countryside and boating on the lake. They also paid a visit to the Arnolds at Fox How, which revealed Charlotte's chronic shyness. In long conversations they explored each other's tastes, finding that they agreed on some things, such as liking Ruskin, but were far apart on others. Afterwards Elizabeth told Charlotte Froude: 'she and I quarrelled & differed about almost everything—she calls me a democrat, & can not bear Tennyson—but we like each other heartily / I think / & hope we shall ripen into friends'. In her turn Charlotte Brontë found Elizabeth 'a woman of the most genuine talent—of cheerful, pleasing and cordial manners and—I believe—of a kind and good heart'. On returning home they immediately wrote to one another and Charlotte sent Wordsworth's *Prelude* and a 'little book of rhymes'—the *Poems* of Ellis, Acton and Currer Bell.

By virtually the same posts that carried her mail to Haworth, Elizabeth was dispatching a flurry of letters to different friends, including Charlotte Froude and Tottie, describing her Windermere stay. In these, her first introduction to Charlotte has the sense of a puzzle, a dark shape she cannot yet make out: 'a little lady in black silk gown, whom I could not see at first for the dazzle in the room'. As she wrote her letters the picture became focused and detailed, and she mixed what she had learnt of her past directly from Charlotte with the untrustworthy gossip of Lady Kay-Shuttleworth, much of it gleaned from 'an old woman of Burnley' (an embittered nurse dismissed by Patrick Brontë in his wife's last illness). Miss Brontë, Elizabeth reported, was 'altogether *plain*' (like many Gaskell heroines), tiny, 'undeveloped'. She saw a child within the woman:

> 'Her hands are like birds' claws, and she is so shortsighted that she cannot see your face unless you are close to her. She is said to be frightfully shy, and almost cries at the thought of going amongst strangers.'

Patrick Brontë was already defined, sight unseen, as 'strange and half mad'. He sawed up chairs and set fire to hearthrugs when enraged, ate by himself, did not educate his daughters and ignored their writing; Mrs Brontë had died of a broken heart; Emily and Anne had been denied a doctor's care and Charlotte herself had been stunted by starvation at school and was probably 'tainted with consumption', living in the lonely Parsonage, so bleak that no flowers could grow because of the biting winds: 'the wonder to me is how she can keep heart and power alive in her life of desolation'. Seen thus, it was undoubtedly a tragic story; the pattern was set for the *Life*.

Elizabeth could not help turning lives into stories, and Charlotte Brontë's seemed the opposite of her own. Charlotte wrote in solitude, in the wild isolation of the moors, while she scribbled amid the chaos of family life in the heart of a city. In 1850 the puzzle was not only how to find time but whether she could, or should, try to reconcile her 'selfish' compulsion to write with the demands of motherly, wifely and parish duties.

Charles Dickens had written in early January, asking if she would contribute to the new weekly journal he was planning, *Household Words,* declaring: 'there is no living English writer whose aid I would desire to enlist, in preference to the authoress of *Mary Barton* (a book that most profoundly affected and impressed me)'. (This tribute is often quoted to illustrate Dickens's high opinion of Gaskell, but, alas, he wrote in this vein to all his potential contributors.) In addition to flattering her, he cleverly appealed to her conscience as well as her pride. The aim of his journal, he said, would be 'the raising up of those that are down, and the general improvement of our social condition'. The causes Dickens particularly wanted to publicize—education, housing, sanitary reform—were dear to the Gaskells' hearts. But Elizabeth still felt torn between home and writing, a dilemma which Dickens (who had no such worries) smartly brushed aside, saying that he was 'not at all afraid of the interruptions necessary to your domestic life, and that I think you will be far less sensible of them in writing short stories than in writing a long one'. For this year, at least, she took his advice, and wrote shorter—if not short—fiction.

In response to his January request she sent **'Lizzie Leigh'**. This tale of prostitution, sombre in tone, seems a strange offering for a family journal, but she knew of Dickens's interest and had only recently written for advice about Pasley. She may not have known, however, that just before her story arrived he had promised Angela Burdett Coutts he would try to deal with the 'sad' subject in *Household Words*. Gaskell's timing was good—she did the work for him. The truth was, also, that the magazine was flung together in something of a rush, and Dickens, who wrote much of the paper himself, was grateful for a lead story.

'Lizzie Leigh' appeared in the first issue, dated 30 March 1850, following, appropriately, immediately after the stirring 'Preliminary Remarks', where Dickens proclaimed that 'in all familiar things, even in those which are repellent on the surface, there is Romance enough, if we will find it out'. The rest of the issue was made up of an article by Dickens and Wills on the new General Post Office, another Dickens piece on popular theatre, a dramatic poem by Leigh Hunt, a profile of the French tragedienne Clairon and 'A Bundle of Emigrants Letters' by the campaigning Caroline Chisholm. For her story, which ran for three issues, Elizabeth received £20, a generous payment by contemporary standards. She was delighted: 'I stared, and wondered if I was swindling them but I suppose I am not; and Wm has composedly buttoned it up in his pocket. He has promised I may have some for the Refuge.'

This little incident has been taken to show that William ruled his wife and took her earnings. Given his character, what it really shows is how he liked to tease in the face of her excitement. While he helped to manage her affairs, signing contracts and receipts, William certainly never asserted his legal right over Elizabeth's property; many payments were sent straight to her. Over the years the small sums from *Household Words*—10 guineas here, £5 there—were a useful bonus, and she would later dash off a quick story or two when she needed money urgently. Dickens's magazine promised to be an ideal outlet. Payment was good, publication swift and, since the articles carried no names, she was freed from fear of criticism. In fact, as Dickens was mentioned on every page as 'Conductor' (not anonymous but '*mono*-nymous throughout', said Douglas Jerrold), most stories were credited to him, and **'Lizzie Leigh'** even appeared under his name in the American *Harper's* that June.

Although she liked the idea, Elizabeth had little time to write for *Household Words* in early 1850. Plaintively, Dickens wrote in July:

> 'This is a brief letter, but—if you only knew it!—a very touching one in its earnestness.
>
> Can't you—won't you—don't you ever mean to—write me another story?'

It was not until early November that she dug in her desk and sent him **'The Well of Pen-Morfa'**. Until then her attention had been occupied elsewhere. To her own annoyance she had promised Edward Chapman a Christmas book. When she finished it in August, she told Tottie it had been 'a *very foolish* engagement of mine, which I am angry with myself for doing, but I promised it and I have done it'. The whole affair irritated her. She was sore with Chapman, who never told her about sales or new editions of *Mary Barton*. She felt that he simultaneously ignored her and bullied her. He asked her to write, she complained, 'recommending benevolence, charity, etc . . . However I could not write about virtues to order, so it is simply a little country love story called Rosemary'. The title was the next battle. Chapman discarded 'Rosemary' for 'The Fagot', at which Elizabeth was understandably appalled: 'I will disown that book if you call it The Fagot;—the name of *my* book is December Days'.

In the end it was called *The Moorland Cottage*. It is, as she said, a country love story, telling of the slow-growing romance between the daughter of a clergyman's widow and the local squire's son, threatened by the squire's pride and the criminal activities of the heroine's spoilt brother, but dramatically saved by her unselfish courage. The melodramatic climax packs in a fire and a shipwreck, but on the whole the pace is leisurely, with the moorland landscapes lovingly described. It could not have been more different, in subject and tone as well as setting, from *Mary Barton,* and some of her friends were disappointed; Emily Winkworth dismissed it as 'a sweet, poetical, simple, sketchy story' which she could safely give her younger sister. Other readers, however, bathed happily in its sentiment. Matthew Arnold's sister, Mary Forster, told a friend how he was spending the week after Christmas at Fox How: 'Matt is stretched out full length on the sofa, reading a Christmas tale of Mrs Gaskell's which moves him to tears, and the tears to complacent admiration of his own sensibility'. It was redeemed in Elizabeth's eyes by the fact that Charlotte Brontë liked it, declaring that it opened like a daisy and 'finished like a herb—a balsamic herb with healing in its leaves . . . The little story is fresh, natural, religious. No more need be said'.

The Moorland Cottage is a gentle book, with an interesting feminist tinge, but there was no gentleness in **'The Heart of John Middleton'**, which Gaskell sent to Dickens in early December. This is a sternly moral tale in which a fierce man is turned from vengeance on an old enemy by the intervention of his dying wife. In a central incident, before they marry, Nell is crippled when hit by a sharp stone aimed at John by his rival. Gaskell's fondness for such accidents made Dickens sigh. He had already had the death of little Nanny in **'Lizzie Leigh'** and the crippling of Nest in **'Pen-Morfa'**. He also thought the death of Nell unnecessary. He told Wills that he found the story 'very clever'—

> 'I think the best thing I have seen, not excepting Mary Barton—and if it had ended happily (which is the whole meaning of it) would have been a great success. As it is, it had better go in the next No., but will not do much, and will link itself painfully, with the girl who fell down at the well and the child who tumbled down stairs. I wish to Heaven, her people would keep a little firmer on their legs'.

Writing to Elizabeth, he diplomatically called it 'a story of extraordinary power, worked out with a vigour and truthfulness that very very few people could reach', but he still said he wished she had not killed the wife, an infliction of unnecessary pain.

'The Heart of John Middleton' is indeed powerful and, as Dickens also acknowledged, very clever. In it Gaskell works out with a single stroke how to dramatize the conflict of (masculine) revenge and (feminine) love, making her narrator-hero the son of a violent father who never knows his mother and who comes to religion through falling in love with a tender, pure woman. At first his religion is still vengeful: he becomes a 'ranter', a member of a fanatical sect, wishing he had been present at Christ's death to take vengeance on 'the wicked Jews'. He is drawn naturally to the old stories of Ishmael, Joseph and Pharaoh, Jael and Sisera, taking the Bible's message as a personal one and reading 'the mighty act of God's vengeance, in the Old Testament, with a kind of triumphant faith that, sooner or later He would take my cause in hand and revenge me on mine enemy'. Only when he is given this chance, and rejects it, following the spirit of his wife's dying words, is he redeemed: 'the burning burden of a sinful, angry heart was taken off'.

The story is set on the high moors near Pendle Hill, which separate Yorkshire from Lancashire, and Gaskell gives it a regional quality by combining the Old Testament references with a north-country proverb which Charlotte Brontë had told her: 'Keep a stone in thy pocket for seven years; turn it, and keep it seven year more; but have it ever ready to cast to thine enemy when the time comes'. The stone that wounds Nell is also the stone in John's heart. His narration blends the language of the Authorized Version easily with the local dialect, as he himself explains— 'for we, in Lancashire, speak a rough kind of bible language'—and with the rhythms of the books he finds in the travelling pedlar's packs: *Pilgrim's Progress, Paradise Lost,* Byron's *Narrative.* As the moment of confrontation approaches the writing gains a particular intensity which Gaskell would only find again when she came to describe a similar fanatical Puritan, Manasseh in **'Lois the Witch'**. Romantic personification of nature fuses with Gothic supernatural and with apocalyptic language in a fearful image of that recurring figure in her fiction, the Grim Father:

> 'The wind came sweeping down from the hill-top in great beats, like the pulses of heaven; and, during the pauses, while I listened for the coming roar, I felt the earth shiver beneath me. The rain beat against windows and doors, and sobbed for entrance. I thought the Prince of the Air was abroad; and I heard, or fancied I heard, shrieks come on the blast, likes the cries of sinful souls given over to his power.

> The sounds came nearer and nearer. I got up and saw to the fastenings of the door, for, though I cared not for mortal man, I did care for what I believed was surrounding the house, in evil might and power'.

From this year on Dickens became the chief publisher of Gaskell's shorter works, and to start with he proved a shrewd and tactful editor. He soothed her initial anxieties about her tendency to detail and her inability to write to a prescribed space: 'Allow the story to take its own length and work itself out', he said (having complained privately to Wills a week earlier that **'Lizzie Leigh'** was 'very good, but long'). His editorial suggestions were sensible—that Lizzie herself should put the baby into Susan's arms, so that the contrast between her abandonment of her baby and her mother's maternal tenderness would not disconcert the reader, or that Nell Middleton should not die but live on to be a good influence. Gaskell accepted the first suggestion and would have done the second if it had reached her in time. She was due to come to London the following week and Wills, thinking she was already there, chased all over town to find her. As Dickens was in his usual hurry, he printed it as it stood; by the time she got the message it was too late. Dickens alleged that he rushed to see if he could alter it, but found the mag-

azine 'at Press, and 20,000 copies already printed . . . Never mind. It is a very fine story, nobly written,—and you can put a pleasanter ending to the next one!'

Dickens always tried to avoid depressing his family readership and this mild admonition was in line with his appeal to Wills about the magazine in general: 'Brighten it, brighten it, brighten it!' As it happened—though probably not because of this rebuke—most of what Gaskell sent him over two years was to be much brighter in tone. This was especially true of the Cranford sequence, but also of potentially serious articles like 'Disappearances', written in response to his own pieces on the new detective system:

> 'Once more, let me say, I am thankful I live in the days of the Detective Police. If I am murdered, or commit bigamy, at any rate my friends will have the comfort of knowing all about it'.

For the first couple of years their relationship was good and, as far as was possible for an editor with such itchy fingers, he left her work alone. The honeymoon did not last. They disagreed, gently, over the first Cranford episode in 1851, then fiercely over **'The Old Nurse's Story'** in 1852 and eventually clashed violently, with endless, hair-tearing wrangles, over the serialization of *North and South* in 1854. What began as a friendly, even flirtatious relationship finally settled into a wary and stubborn truce. But of over forty stories and articles written by Elizabeth Gaskell between 1850 and her death, two-thirds were published by Dickens, either in *Household Words* or its successor, *All the Year Round.*

Gaskell's lesser works are inevitably overshadowed by her novels, but a quick glance forward shows what an inventive and innovative short-story writer she was. To call these stories 'short' is somewhat misleading since few are under thirty pages, most are well over fifty and at least five are novellas, like **The Moorland Cottage**, of over a hundred pages. They vary in subject, style and setting from moral tales to Gothic mysteries and brilliant small-scale comedies. Their relative simplicity allows central themes and favourite character types to leap swiftly into view: wayward sons, stern fathers or husbands, motherless children, ailing wives, returning wanderers (for good or ill), stalwart servants, heroines forced into self-sufficiency or finding solidarity with other women.

Stories could lie in Elizabeth's mind for years, but she usually wrote the final versions very fast and rarely troubled to correct, which led to her sometimes muddling the characters' names, forgetting the number of their children or repeating favourite details (in *Cranford* almost everyone drums their fingers on the table). Sometimes, with hindsight, the stories seem sketchy in a different sense, a first outline of ideas developed more thoroughly later: thus **'Martha Preston'** is reworked in **'Half a Lifetime Ago'**, the stone-throwing incident from **'The Heart of John Middleton'** becomes a key scene in *North and South,* the character groupings from **The Moorland Cottage** reappear in *Wives and Daughters.* In her short stories we see Gaskell consciously practising her craft, playing with it and expanding its possibilities. She mixes real and surreal, comic and tragic. She explores the possibilities of language—making bold use of the vernacular in **'The Heart of John Middleton'** and **'The Crooked Branch'**, or creating a period speech for **'Lois the Witch'**. She experiments with structure, from the play-like **'Mr Harrison's Confessions'** to the sweeping historical **'Morton Hall'** or the loose, enfolding form of *My Lady Ludlow*.

Beneath these variations lies an underlying pattern, which seems to mirror the process of creation, the engagement and full release of her imagination. In almost all Gaskell's works, short or long, author and reader slowly approach the subject and learn the lie of the land until, at a moment of crisis, a door suddenly seems to open, like Sesame, and we step into new terrain—melodrama, mystery, intense emotion or fantasy. Some openings embody the movement into fiction physically—the Bartons and Wilsons walking from Greenheys into Manchester—while others provide a social map, so to speak, of the territory, like the description of the 'Amazons' in *Cranford*. Sometimes map and movement are combined, as in the panorama of Monkshaven and Sylvia's walk into the town with her butter in *Sylvia's Lovers,* or the railway journey to Keighley and the fierce habits and customs of Yorkshire in *The Life of Charlotte Brontë*. The early stages establish the milieu, the characters and their way of life until at some central point narrative itself takes over. From that point on 'truth' is displayed not in realism or analysis but in the symbolic workings of the plot.

Only once did Gaskell suggest what it means to cross this threshold into a self-governing world of fiction. She did so—naturally—in a story, one that is not serious but playful and ironic. In 1860 she wrote her first piece for Thackeray's *Cornhill,* a *jeu d'esprit* whose ambiguous title, **'Curious if True'**, questions the usual storyteller's claim to be curious *but* true. An earnest Englishman, Richard Whittingham (first clue), travels to Catholic France to trace his solid, austere Calvinist ancestry; but the ancestors he finds are rather different. One night, lost in a dark wood, he sees a lighted château through the trees with 'pepper boxes, and *tourelles* and what not, fantastically growing up into the dim starlight'. A great entertainment is in progress and to his surprise he is greeted as if expected. But where, he is asked, is his friend, Monsieur le Geanquilleur? The bemused Whittingham cannot think who this can be, even when he learns that he is also known as Le Grand Jean d'Angleterre. Can they mean John Bull? John Russell? John Bright!

The guests seem familiar but exceedingly odd: M. Poucet, with whiskers and very old boots; a beautiful lady 'splendid as dawn' fast asleep on the settee; a fat old lady of twinkling charm, who long ago married a prince despite the efforts of two unkind half-sisters. The hostess is a Madame de Retz, who weeps over the memory of 'the best of husbands', killed in haste by her brothers, and fondly shows the visitor his portrait:

"You observe the colouring is not quite what it should be."

"In this light the beard is of rather a peculiar tint". said I.

"Yes; the painter did not do it justice. It was most lovely, and gave him such a distinguished air, quite different from the common herd. Stay, I will show you the exact colour, if you will come near this flambeau!" And going near the light, she took off a bracelet of hair, with a magnificent clasp of pearls. It was peculiar, certainly. I did not know what to say. "His precious, lovely beard!" said she. "And the pearls go so well with the delicate blue!"

'Curious if True' is Gaskell's tribute to the most haunting and popular (in all senses) of storytelling genres. Within its mansion it is the imaginary characters who live 'real' lives, domestic, bustling and down to earth, growing old with their memories, which are also our favourite fairy tales. When, for once, they tell their own tales, these turn out to be different from what centuries of 'gossip' would have us believe. They inhabit the house of story, which is different from the house of dreams, for listeners to stories are wide awake. This house exists in the middle of the dark wood of life, throughout time, alongside the daily rush. Yet some 'rational' people, like Whittingham, will never understand how the imagination can whisper of an ideal world where 'everybody would have their rights and we should have no more trouble'. 'If I were in England', Whittingham says, 'I should imagine Madame was speaking of the Reform Bill or the millennium; but I am in ignorance'.

When the folding doors are thrown open and the long-awaited Madame la Féemarraine finally arrives, Whittingham is still in ignorance, denied revelation. He awakes on the grass in the clear light of morning to find that the château has vanished. Elizabeth Gaskell, however, gathering her 'materials unconsciously as it were', with her lifelong passion for stories and magical gift for telling them, could find and re-enter the castle of fiction at will, unlocking a different door each time. And although she returns to certain themes, characters, incidents and images, the cumulative effect is not of repetition but of subtle variation and advancing skill—no story 'feels' the same as any other. No wonder Dickens pressed her to write for him and called her his 'dear Scheherezade'—because, as he said,

'I am sure your powers of narrative can never be exhausted in a single night, but must be good for at least a thousand nights and one'.

Philip Rogers   (essay date 1995)

SOURCE: "The Education of Cousin Phillis," in *Nineteenth Century Literature,* Vol. 50, No. 1, June, 1995, pp. 27-50.

[*In the following excerpt, Rogers contends that Phillis's male education in* Cousin Phillis *is not liberating, as other critics have argued, but prescriptive and ultimately damaging.*]

For Elizabeth Gaskell the story of Phillis Holman's disappointment in her first love in **Cousin Phillis** (1865) is inseparable from the process and content of her unusual education. As both daughter and lover—the only roles open to her as learner—Phillis is inescapably a pupil of men who control her education in ways that serve their interests. Learning from men what men traditionally have taught other men does not make her, as her cousin Paul naively supposes, "more like a man than a woman." On the contrary, the lessons of her reading and the experience of male tuition inculcate contradictory and damaging definitions of womanhood, diminishing her independence and sense of self. Like Gaskell's narrator, most critics of **Cousin Phillis** have interpreted Phillis' learning simply as evidence of her superior intelligence and promise rather than as allusive commentary on her predicament and that of educated women generally. Far from liberating her from the conventional constraints of Victorian womanhood, Phillis' readings in Virgil, Dante, and Alessandro Manzoni comprise no less prescriptive guides to woman's behavior than her mother's conduct book, the "Housewife's Complete Manual." The shame-sickness of her breakdown is thus as much a product of her male education as of her loss of Holdsworth.

Learning in **Cousin Phillis** is the province of men. Gaskell's representation of teaching and learning among the male characters—a pervasive concern of Paul Manning's frame-narrative—defines the social context in which the nature and ends of Phillis' education are explored. Just as Maggie Tulliver's "yearning for effectual wisdom" in George Eliot's *The Mill on the Floss* (1860)—Maggie is a probable model for Gaskell's heroine—is fully understood only in relation to her brother's education and apprenticeship, Phillis' learning is defined by contrast with that of her cousin and the other men. Relationships among men in **Cousin Phillis** all possess a tutelary component. Holdsworth learns about driving wheels from Paul's father; Paul, in turn, is Holdsworth's apprentice. The friendships that form between Paul, Holdsworth, Mr. Manning, and Minister Holman are confirmed in scenes of mutual instruction. In her analysis of male learning Gaskell is especially attentive to issues of authority. The mutual esteem of men depends on their possessing exclusive knowledge and being able to tell others something that they do not know. Their knowledge, like Manning's winch, is patented, a possession exchangeable for the knowledge of others. Thus, in his first visit to Hope Farm, Mr. Manning must display his expertise as inventor; in response, Holman explains the fine points of the cow. Holdsworth teaches Holman "the practical art of surveying and taking a level," and Paul reinflates his Phillis-punctured ego by showing her and the minister that he knows "something worth knowing" about engineering. And in the central action that all this teaching activity points toward, the minister teaches Phillis Greek and Latin and Holdsworth instructs her in Italian, providing texts, dictionaries, les-

sons, and marginal annotation.

Paul represents this round-robin of instruction approvingly. To him the participants are all engaged in wholesome self-improvement, Phillis also evincing "manly" eagerness to expand her intellectual horizons in the realm of male knowledge. However, an important difference is evident, if unremarked by Paul: Phillis' participation in learning, unlike that of the men, is never mutual. Although she is distinguished by her educational attainments and ambition, Phillis holds no patents and remains invariably the pupil. Paul, her only potential student, will not subject himself to the teaching of a younger, taller woman and disparages the utility of her kind of knowledge as "dead-and-gone languages." In subjects that the men view as specifically male concerns, Phillis' status is even less than that of the pupil: when Holdsworth and Manning instruct Holman in surveying and dynamics Phillis is merely an onlooker, struggling to hear what is said. Her father is "almost unconscious" of her presence as she peers over his shoulder, "sucking in information like her father's own daughter," as Paul aptly notes, unconscious of the irony. Even in Phillis' study of language and literature, Gaskell implies, "her father's own daughter" has been permitted access to male knowledge only by default. The minister's motive in teaching Phillis arises not from a belief in his daughter's unique promise or the desirability of her knowing Latin and Greek but rather from his having made her a son-surrogate. Mr. Manning accounts for Phillis' anomalous education by noting that "she is the only child of a scholar." Paul observes that Phillis becomes more and more "the very apple of her father's eye" as she grows to resemble the little boy who died. Had Brother Johnnie lived, Sister Phillis would instead have been the apple of her mother's eye.

A second aspect of male learning against which Gaskell measures Phillis' education is its emphasis on utility. In particular, the engineering-inventing-agricultural institutions to which the men each belong stress concrete outcomes. For them knowledge is the production of driving wheels and turnip cutters, hay and milk. Even the minister's literary studies reflect a utilitarian motive; his Virgil is the *Georgics,* read for its shrewd advice on "rolling and irrigation . . . choice of the best seed . . . keep[ing] the drains clear." Gaskell also stresses the utility of learning for males in its direct connection to social advancement; learning is rising and "manning": promotion, partnership, the boss's daughter, and one's own carriage.

In contrast to the purposes of men's learning, Phillis' studies relate to no apparent institution or end. As Gaskell observed in distinguishing the Brontë family's attitudes toward Branwell and his sisters, men are "expected to act a part in life; to *do* while [women] are only to *be*." The only image in the text of Phillis' reading represents it as an awkward distraction from a more pressing responsibility—paring apples in the kitchen. Her father's pupil, she is more fundamentally her mother's apprentice. In contrast to the tool-equipped men, whose spades, rulers, theodolites, burnt sticks, and pencils (noticeably not ungendered implements) serve as emblems of authoritative, engaged male knowledge, Phillis wields only a paring knife and produces only pies. Gaskell defines the Holmans' social position in order to emphasize the detachment of Phillis' learning from necessary ends. As the only child, she will inherit the family farm; thus she has no need for teaching credentials, the motive for learning for a Jane Eyre or Lucy Snowe. Further, given the limited opportunities of a country town and the personal constraints implied in the Holman family religion, any future application of Phillis' education appears improbable. Indeed, in Mr. Manning's opinion, her being a scholar is worse than pointless, the sole flaw in her eligibility for marrying his son. His prediction defines her problem unsympathetically: "once she's a wife and a mother she'll forget it all." Gaskell resents Manning's glib certainty, yet in the text she nonetheless wonders what difference Greek and Latin can make to a wife and mother in a world harmonized by Minister Holman's spade and propelled by Inventor Manning's driving wheel.

What then does Gaskell imply Phillis' aim to be in seeking to educate herself? Gaskell denies her male characters—and especially her narrator—any insight whatever into the nature or object of Phillis' intellectual ambitions. As Gaskell's title implies, Paul Manning writes about Phillis not as a person in her own right but as his cousin. His narrative (manifestly driven by self-exculpatory motives) defines her in terms of his own indiscretion, the sole unhappy episode in an otherwise successful *Bildung*. He writes to put her behind as well as beneath him. Readers of Gaskell's subtle, ironic text are consequently invited to reshape a Phillis from the evidence of Paul's ignorance and distortions, to recover Phillis' inner life from small revelations that Gaskell permits to leak through the fine filters of male bias and obtuseness.

That Phillis views her education, despite its inutility, as a kind of liberating self-fulfillment, a way to "be," is implied in the intensity of her desire to learn in spite of the frustrations she encounters, always doing "two things at once." That she wishes to escape the limits of her father's tutoring, to reject the intellectual pinafore and achieve an independent sense of self as an adult woman (possibilities unrecognizable by Paul) is especially evident in her attempting to read in Italian, a language unknown to her father. In undertaking the *Inferno* she too, like Dante, seeks a new life. Paul, of course, has not glimpsed her "dark wood" or the leopard blocking the way; he can only make out the connection of inferno to "infernal," an association sufficient to alert readers to the ominous import of Gaskell's allusion. For Phillis, however, the aim of entering the *Inferno* is to abandon not hope but Hope Farm. She recognizes that in learning Italian the "meaning of the hard words"—her father's knowledge, the parental definition of her—no longer suffices. Her attraction to a new text, a foreign language, and a man with foreign knowledge and experience implies not merely her sexual coming of age but also the desire to escape the limitations of Heathbridge, a "dark wood" indeed for an ambitious, educated woman. The arrival of the railroad bringing Holdsworth to Heathbridge also offers Phillis the means to a way out. Phillis' interest in Holdsworth, as her father

immediately recognizes, implies a desire to leave: "you would have left us, left your home, left your father and your mother, and gone away with this stranger, wandering over the world."

But Gaskell implies no liberation for Phillis in her reading; undertaking the new language does not lead her to independent individuality and travel, because dictionaries and passports, like most of the tools in her world, are male possessions. Even Phillis' vocabulary is monitored. Holdsworth's intrusive annotation of the hard words in her text comprises subtle censoring: knowing a range of possible choices, he chooses for her, "writ[ing] down the most accepted meanings." Virgil's presence in the *Inferno* as Dante's guide implies not a successful escape for Phillis into a new text but rather the repetition of Phillis' Latin texts and paternal limits in a less spacious setting; in learning Italian, Phillis merely substitutes a lover-tutor for a father-tutor, a development that appears to deny her education any moment of self-direction or even the privacy expressive of independent womanhood. That Phillis and Holdsworth's love blossoms in their sharing of books, in their reading together of Dante and Manzoni, suggests that Gaskell's allusion to the *Inferno* points in particular to its best-known episode, the tale of Paolo and Francesca—whose illicit love was also mediated by fiction, the tale of Lancelot and Guinevere. Gaskell thus associates Phillis not with Dante, the pilgrim passing through the Inferno on an upward journey, but with the book-betrayed Francesca, a permanent resident.

Yet while learning in *Cousin Phillis* is the province of men, Gaskell shows it to be a realm beyond their mastery: men know less than they suppose. In spite of Paul's talking up the triumphs of engineering and invention, his meeting his cousin emerges as the consequence of an engineering failure: Phillis enters Paul's and Holdsworth's lives at that point in the building of the railroad where the engineers are puzzled and brought to a halt. The Heathbridge myrtle bogs, while "very wild and pretty" country, prove to be "shaking, uncertain ground," lacking a "steady bottom"; no sooner is one end of the line weighted down than the other goes up. The Heathbridge myrtle bog may be bridged but not tracked. Gaskell represents engineering to be a visual science; Holdsworth surveys, maps, sketches. But the uncertain depths of the bog are invisible to theodolites, and the engineers are obliged to abandon Heathbridge to lay their track on firmer ground. One need not know (as Virgil notes at the beginning of Holman's favorite text, the *Georgics*) that myrtle is Venus' plant in order to see the failure of the Heathbridge line as emblematic of Phillis' abandonment by the unsuccessful engineer. Yet the tracking-of-the-myrtle bog metaphor suggests a reading of Phillis and Holdsworth's relationship quite different from the narrator's. Paul's narrative—which bridges rather than tracks his cousin—stresses Phillis' failures: she cannot hold Holdsworth, cannot control her feelings for him after he leaves, and cannot, as is implied in the unspecific account of her later years, establish a new life worthy of Paul's mention. In the context of Victorian fictional convention this implies a woman's ultimate failure—to become a wife and mother. The impossibility of laying track in the bog, on the other hand, invites readings that identify the failures in *Cousin Phillis* not as Phillis' but as those of men out of their depth.

Paul presents Holdsworth's abandonment of Phillis as merely circumstantial, the consequence of his departure for a new job. Yet the story of Paul's own aborted interest in courting his cousin clearly anticipates and comments on Holdsworth's. Paul's dread of a wife who knows more than he does might appear to be the opposite of Holdsworth's encouragement of Phillis' learning, yet the scenes of Holdsworth's wooing of Phillis similarly prefigure his abandoning her for Lucille Ventadour. Holdsworth's abortive sketching of Phillis exactly parallels the railroad failure; the analogy of his attempt to map her surface to the process of survey and measurement by theodolite (scenes that Gaskell juxtaposes) is evident in his abstracting her as Ceres. Since, like the bog's, Phillis' depths are invisible to him, Holdsworth can deal with Phillis only by defining limits: he marks her off within the boundaries of a mythological parcel; he takes her level in "most accepted meanings." But just as she resists his suggestive whispers in the theodolite episode, Phillis will not return the engineer-portraitist's surveying gaze or submit to his command ("Please look at me for a minute or two, I want to get in the eyes"), nor will she hold the assigned pose. The track cannot be weighted down, the sketch is abandoned. Holdsworth has not succeeded in mapping Phillis' depths. He understands her resistance only in clichés; he would make her an English fertility goddess if she would submit, but she is innocent, passionless, an unawakened sleeping beauty. Thus his sketch of her is incomplete, lacking "shading or colouring." Reading backward from Hardy, we recall Tess' annoyance at Angel Clare's mythologizing her as Artemis and Demeter. Like Angel's, Holdsworth's stereotypes are as inherently contradictory as they are wrong, celebrating Phillis simultaneously as the essences of both chaste innocence and natural sexuality: "What a sweet innocent face it is! and yet so—Oh, dear!" No sooner is the sweet, innocent-faced end of Holdsworth's track weighted down than it is destabilized by ("Oh, dear!") her "pretty mouth." Holdsworth's failure to recognize qualities in Phillis other than these stereotypes explains his abandoning her. Any other woman can serve such interests as Holdsworth's, and indeed, to him, Lucille Ventadour "is curiously like" Phillis.

Minister Holman's learning is no more efficacious than Holdsworth's in tracking Phillis. From the first it is apparent that the coherence of Holman's learning, the system of his knowledge as it relates to his daughter, depends on suppressions: he seeks to deny his daughter's adult sexuality, to keep her in pinafores. Less obvious in Holman's attempts simultaneously to educate and to control Phillis are the contradictory premises of his teaching. Gaskell undermines the validity of Holman's claim of authority over his daughter by showing his knowledge to be not in fact "whole" but rather an unstable pairing of conflicting halves. The two ends of Holman's track are apparent first in his dual roles as minister and farmer. The introduction to Holman in Paul's narrative implies the potential incompatibility of the two. Both before and after

Paul's first visit Holdsworth questions the minister-farmer pairing: "It is not often that parsons know how to keep land in order, is it?"; "how do preaching and farming seem to get on together?" Gaskell also stresses centripetal tendencies of preaching and farming in the incident of Holman's prayer for his sick cow. In asking a blessing for Bessie, Holman forgets to order her "warm mash," the means to cure her: "here was I asking a blessing and neglecting the means, which is a mockery."

The cover illustration of the 1867 edition of *Cousin Phillis and Other Tales* represents Holman's halves in a memorable emblem. Grouped in the stubble field, Phillis and two workmen sing the psalm "Come all harmonious tongues" as the minister beats time with his spade and Paul looks on. The scene's implied harmonizing of the minister's two "tongues"—preaching and farming linked by an act of devotion in the fields—is rendered discordant by its most trenchant detail, the incongruous spade that beats time. This staff, which seeks to harmonize and control by main force the orders of nature and grace, soon bifurcates (like the engineers' unbalanced tracks) into dual, not ungendered staves specific to Holman's halves: the minister's parish rod of discipline and the farmer's parish bull—images expressive of the contrary modes of authority implicit in preaching and procreation, the blessing and the means.

The bearing of Holman's unharmonious tongues on the education of Phillis is evident in the texts that voice their respective practices—the Bible (and Holman's religion generally) and Virgil's *Georgics,* which articulates the tongue of agriculture. In making her minister-farmer also a student of the classics, Gaskell accomplishes various purposes. Most obviously, the classical knowledge allows her to explore the implications of Phillis' receiving from her father a man's education. Then, by linking Holman's Latin teaching to Virgil's *Georgics,* his agricultural "Bible," Gaskell extends the thematic implications of the minister-farmer duality to include the opposition of Christian and pagan texts, a conflict especially relevant to Phillis' learning the contradictory lessons that men teach men about women: "the true adornment is a meek and quiet spirit," yet oh, dear!—her pretty mouth. As the Heathbridge community walks to church the minister contemplates his discourse, and the young men, like Holdsworth, "cast admiring looks" on Phillis. The opposition of Virgilian and Christian sexual mores is underscored in Holdsworth's ironic reply to Paul's doubting the minister's willingness to have Phillis read novels: "You don't suppose they take Virgil for gospel?"

Ironically, for Holman the *Georgics is* gospel. He values Virgil not as poetry but for its present-time accuracy of observation and its practical advice to farmers: "It's wonderful . . . how exactly Virgil has hit the enduring epithets, nearly two thousand years ago, and in Italy; and yet how it describes to a T what is now lying before us in the parish of Heathbridge, county—, England Undermining Paul's defensive dismissal of Latin as a "dead-and-gone" language, Gaskell quite insistently stresses the relevance of the minister's and Phillis' classical readings to their own present-day lives, especially to Phillis' relationship with Holdsworth. As the minister notes, Holdsworth's talk of Italy "makes Horace and Virgil living, instead of dead, by the stories he tells me of his sojourn in the very countries where they lived, and where to this day, he says—." "Where to this day, he [and Virgil and Horace] says—" what?, the reader is made to wonder. Gaskell's allusions, reinforced by Paul's frequent protests of his ignorance of languages and hymns, plainly direct the reader to consider the relevance to **Cousin Phillis** of Virgil, Horace, Dante, and Manzoni, as well as the "profane" but suggestively suppressed subjects of Holdsworth's Italian anecdotes.

FURTHER READING

Bibliography

Selig, Robert L. *Elizabeth Gaskell: A Reference Guide.* Boston: G. K. Hall & Co., 1977, 431 p.
A comprehensive bibliography of critical commentary on Gaskell's life and works published from 1848 to 1974.

Criticism

Duthie, Enid L. *The Themes of Elizabeth Gaskell.* Totowa, NJ: Rowman and Littlefield, 1980, 217 p.
Thematic study of Gaskell's works that includes chapters on nature, society, family, religion, and industry.

Easson, Angus. Introduction to *Cousin Phillis and Other Tales,* by Elizabeth Gaskell, pp. vii-xiv. Oxford: Oxford University Press, 1981.
Summary of contemporary critical response to Gaskell's fiction.

———, ed. *Elizabeth Gaskell: The Critical Heritage.* New York: Routledge, 1991, 595 p.
Compilation of the enormous body of early criticism on Gaskell.

Fisher, Benjamin Franklin, IV. Review of *Mrs. Gaskell's Tales of Mystery and Horror. Studies in Short Fiction* 18, No. 1 (Winter 1981): 110-11.
Briefly evaluates several of Gaskell's genre stories, noting that "none of these tales is likely to enhance Mrs. Gaskell's literary standing."

Laun, Ellen M. "A Missing Gaskell Tale Found." *Studies in Short Fiction* 15, No. 2 (Spring 1978): 177-83.
Investigates "The Poor Clare" as "an important story for scholars interested in tracing Elizabeth Gaskell's growth as a writer."

Low, Frances H. "Mrs. Gaskell's Short Tales." *Fortnightly Review* LXVI (1899): 633-43.
Includes favorable estimations of *Cousin Phillis,* "The Crooked Branch," and "Mr. Harrison's Confessions."

Lumpkin, Ramona. "(Re)visions of Virtue: Elizabeth Gaskell's *Moorland Cottage* and George Eliot's *The Mill on the Floss." Studies in the Novel* 23, No. 4 (Winter 1991): 432-42.
Traces affinities between Gaskell's novella and Eliot's later novel.

McVeagh, John. "Notes on Mrs. Gaskell's Narrative Technique." *Essays in Criticism* 18 (1968): 461-70.
Examines Gaskell's use of a "static narrative technique," which eliminates the necessity of undue structural organization in her works.

———. *Elizabeth Gaskell.* London: Routledge & Kegan Paul, 1970, 104 p.
Provides a series of key extracts from Gaskell's complete works.

Schor, Hilary M. *Scheherezade in the Marketplace: Elizabeth Gaskell and the Victorian Novel.* New York: Oxford University Press, 1992, 236 p.
Examines Gaskell's position as a woman writing at a time of intense social upheaval and traces the figure of the heroine throughout her fiction.

Williams, Merryn. "Elizabeth Gaskell." In *Women in the English Novel, 1800-1900,* pp. 106-18. London: Macmillan Press, 1984.
Summarizes Gaskell's oeuvre, including brief discussions of her short stories "Libbie Marsh's Three Eras," "The Well of Pen-Morfa," and "Lizzie Leigh."

Wolfreys, Julian. "Critical Nationalism and the 'Truth' of (Identity in) Elizabeth Gaskell." In *Being English: Narratives, Idioms, and Performances of National Identity from Coleridge to Trollope,* pp. 81-102. Albany: State University of New York Press, 1994.
Argues that Gaskell's writings cannot be read from any single political position, and illustrates this statement by using her short texts "Round the Sofa," "An Accursed Race," and *Cousin Phillis.*

Additional coverage of Gaskell's life and career is contained in the following sources published by Gale Research: *Concise Dictionary of Literary Biography, 1832-1890*; *Dictionary of Literary Biography,* Vols. 21, 144, 159; *DISCovering Authors*; and *Nineteenth-Century Literature Criticism,* **Vol. 5.**

"The Snows of Kilimanjaro"
Ernest Hemingway

The following entry presents criticism of Hemingway's short story "The Snows of Kilimanjaro." For an overview of Hemingway's short fiction, see *SSC,* Volume 1.

INTRODUCTION

One of the best-known writers of the twentieth century, Hemingway played a crucial role in the development of modern fiction. In his renowned short stories, including "The Short Happy Life of Francis Macomber" and "The Snows of Kilimanjaro," he drew from his own experiences to create fiction that was praised as direct, immediate, and powerful. Hemingway consciously adopted the central Modernist tenet that form expresses content, and he strove to imitate the rhythms of life in his fiction, augmenting meaning through repetition, counterpoint, and juxtaposition. "The Snows of Kilimanjaro" offers numerous examples of this literary style, with collage-type effects employed to convey the protagonist's vivid memories of his childhood and youth.

Plot and Major Characters

The epigraph to "The Snows of Kilimanjaro" describes the frozen carcass of a leopard preserved near the icy summit of Mount Kilimanjaro, the highest peak in Africa. This image stands in startling contrast to the opening details of Hemingway's story. Stranded on the hot African plain, within sight of the snow-capped mountain, the protagonist, Harry, suffers from a gangrenous leg wound. He is accompanied by his wealthy lover, Helen, on whom he is financially dependent. As they await rescue by plane, Harry bitterly reflects on his once-promising writing career. He realizes that he has sacrificed his talent for the material pleasures offered by Helen. Filled with rage and self-disgust, Harry responds with sarcasm to Helen's thoughtful ministrations. The couple fruitlessly bicker, and as they argue he has a premonition of his own death. He wistfully recalls his life, packed with experiences he once planned to translate into art: the purity of skiing in the Austrian alps; the torment of first love; the charm and absurdity of bohemian Paris; the stark beauty of his grandfather's farm in Michigan; and the horror of trench warfare during World War I. As night falls and a hyena flits past the camp, Harry once again senses the approach of death. He feels a sudden sensation of weight on his chest, but as he is carried to his tent his discomfort is abruptly relieved. The following morning the rescue plane arrives and Harry is airlifted to apparent safety. However, as the plane rises into the clouds, he suddenly realizes that he is headed not for the hospital but for the blindingly white

summit of Kilimanjaro. At this moment, the story abruptly cuts to the sound of Helen's sobs as she discovers Harry's corpse and we realize that the "plane trip" was, in fact, the final flight of Harry's imagination.

Major Themes

"The Snows of Kilimanjaro" reveals the preoccupation with mortality common to much of Hemingway's fiction. As in his novel *The Sun Also Rises,* a significant distinction is drawn between spiritual and physical death. By compromising his literary talent, Harry has already embraced a kind of death-in-life. The corruption spreading from his gangrenous leg simply makes manifest his moral decay, an irony of which he is painfully aware. Elsewhere in the Hemingway canon the theme of death is examined with an almost journalistic realism. "The Snows of Kilimanjaro" presents a fascinating exception to this rule by making use of a group of recurrent symbols. The figures of the frozen leopard and scavenging hyena contrast two attitudes to death: while the leopard's preserved corpse suggests the possibility of permanence through fame, the hyena signifies the inevitability of death. Kilimanjaro it-self offers a powerfully multifaceted symbol. Its dazzling heights provoke a wealth of associations from Chaucer's House of Fame to Shelley's Mont Blanc. Most important-ly, however, the mountain represents the mystery of death, a mystery underlined by the double closure of "The Snows of Kilimanjaro."

Critical Reception

Hailed by critics as one of Hemingway's greatest short stories, "The Snows of Kilimanjaro" has garnered a wealth of interpretations in the past half-century. In general, dis-cussion has focused on two related issues: the signifi-cance of the epigraph and the meaning of Harry's final death-flight. While some commentators have found paral-lels to the frozen leopard in Dante and in biblical passag-es, others have viewed the frozen leopard as an uncom-plicated symbol of heroic perseverance. It also has been asserted that the association of the leopard with idealistic aspiration reinforces the story's rejection of material plea-sures. However the reader views the leopard, the question of Harry's success or failure remains. Most critics have perceived the final scene as a moral triumph, as the pro-tagonist Harry rises above a lifetime of failure in his final moments, imaginatively matching the leopard's achieve-ment. Others have rejected this view, arguing that Harry miserably fails to redeem himself. Additional critical stud-ies have examined the story's autobiographical elements and misogynist qualities, as well as identifying the possi-ble influences on Hemingway's work.

CRITICISM

Carlos Baker   (essay date 1952)

SOURCE: "Lesson from the Master," *in Hemingway: The Writer as Artist,* Princeton University Press, 1963, pp. 191-96.

[*In the following excerpt, which was originally published in 1952, Baker explores the autobiographical aspects of "The Snows of Kilimanjaro."*]

"The Snows of Kilimanjaro" is a tragedy of a different order [from "The Short and Happy Life of Francis Ma-comber"]. Its setting is the final afternoon and evening in the second life of a writer named Harry, dying of gan-grene in a camp near the edge of the Tanganyika plains country. "Francis Macomber" proceeds through and by action; "The Snows of Kilimanjaro" is an experiment in the psychology of a dying man. Like *Across the River and Into the Trees*, it contains almost no overt physical activity, though much is implied. Judged in terms of its intention, it is a triumphant piece of writing.

Hemingway's own experiences on safari help to account for the origin of the story. The undeveloped germ of "Francis Macomber" may have been the occasion when Hemingway and M'Cola entered a bush-covered area in pursuit of a lion they heard but never saw. The general outline of "The Snows" was almost certainly suggested by Hemingway's own grave illness, the flight out of the plains country, and the distant view of the enormous, snow-capped mountain of Kilimanjaro. During the flight east, and no doubt also during the period of treatment in Nairo-bi—his head aching and his ears ringing from the effects of emetine—Hemingway had ample time to reflect on a topic which would naturally occur to him in such a situ-ation: the death of a writer before his work is done. As in "Francis Macomber," however, most of the other cir-cumstances of the story were invented.

Like Hemingway, the writer Harry in the story has been "obsessed" for years with curiosity about the idea of death. Now that it is close he has lost all curiosity about it, feeling only a "great tiredness and anger" over its inex-orable approach. "The hardest thing," Hemingway had written in *The Green Hills of Africa,* is for the writer "to survive and get his work done." This is mainly because the time available is so short and the temptations not to work are so strong. Harry has succumbed to the tempta-tion *not* to work at his hard trade. Now his time is over, and possessive death moves in.

The story gains further point and poignancy from another obsession of Harry's, the deep sense of his loss of artistic integrity. Despite the difference between London and Tanganyika and the lapse of time between the rule of Edward VII and that of Edward VIII, Hemingway's posi-tion is that of Henry James in "The Lesson of the Mas-ter." Harry's dying self-accusations are well summarized in the words of Henry St. George, the sold-out novelist in James's novelette. "Don't become in your old age what I have in mine," he tells his young admirer, "—the depress-ing, the deplorable illustration of the worship of false gods . . . the idols of the market; money and luxury . . . everything that drives one to the short and easy way." The dying writer in Hemingway's story has followed that route, and his creeping gangrene is the mark he bears. He knows that he has traded his former integrity for "security and comfort," destroying his talent by "betrayals of him-self and what he believed in." Henry or Harry, England or Africa, the lesson of the master is the same: Thou shalt not worship the graven images of false gods, or acquiesce in the "life of pleasant surrender."

Although the setting of "The Snows of Kilimanjaro" is as completely un-Jamesian as one could possibly imag-ine, the themes which the story engages are, on the con-trary, very close to those regularly employed by James. "I wonder," Hemingway once ruminated, "what Henry James would have done with the materials of our time." One answer might be that a modern James would simply have altered the costume, the idiom, and certain of the social customs which appear in his novels. The themes, which were matters of greatest interest to him, would scarcely need to be changed at all. The close reader of "**The Snows**

of Kilimanjaro" easily recognizes and responds to its theme of confrontation. The dying writer is far different from the ghost of his former self, the young, free, unsold writer who took all Europe as his oyster and was seriously devoted to his craft. As he listens to the self-accusations with which Harry tortures himself, the reader acquainted with James may be reminded of "The Jolly Corner." In this long story, an American expatriate, returning to his old and empty house at the corner of the American city street, finds himself beleaguered by the ghost of his other self, the ravaged man he might have been had he not followed his esthetic ambitions to Europe. Although the situation is obviously quite the opposite of the one detailed by Hemingway, the strategy is exactly the same: the face-to-face confrontation of an ego by an alter ego. The corner of the tent in which Harry finally dies might well be called, in an echo of Jamesian irony, the jolly corner.

The story is technically distinguished by the operation of several natural symbols. These are non-literary images, as always in Hemingway, and they have been very carefully selected so as to be in complete psychological conformity with the locale and the dramatic situation. How would the ideas of death and of immortality present themselves in the disordered imagination of a writer dying of gangrene as he waits for the plane which is supposed to carry him out of the wilderness to the Nairobi hospital? The death-symbols were relatively easy. Every night beasts of prey killed grazing animals and left the pickings to those scavengers of carrion, the vultures and the hyenas.

It is entirely natural that Harry, whose flesh is rotting and noisome—is, in fact, carrion already—should associate these creatures with the idea of dying. As he lies near death in the mimosa shade at the opening of the story, he watches the birds obscenely squatting in the glare of the plain. As night falls and the voice of the hyena is heard in the land, the death-image transfers itself from the vultures to this other foul devourer of the dead. With the arrival of his first strong premonition of death, which has no other form than "a sudden, evil-smelling emptiness," Harry finds without astonishment that the image of the hyena is slipping lightly along the edge of the emptiness. "Never believe any of that," he tells his wife, "about a scythe and a skull." His mind has been far away in the days of his former life in Paris, and now it has come back to Africa. "It can be two bicycle policemen as easily, or be a bird. Or it can have a wide snout like a hyena." Death has just come as if to rest its head on the foot of the cot, the direction from which the infection will rise up towards the vital center. Presently it moves in on him, crouching on his chest so that he cannot breathe.

Harry's dying directive, "Never believe any of that about a scythe and a skull," is an important commentary on Hemingway's own habitual approach to the development of natural symbols. He is prepared to use, where they conform to the requirements of an imaginary situation, any of the more ancient symbols—whether the threes and nines of numerology, or the weight of the Cross in Christian legend. But the scythe and the skull, though ancient enough, simply do not fit the pattern of Harry's death and are therefore rejected in favor of the foul and obscene creatures which have now come to dominate Harry's imagination.

Like the death-symbol, the image for immortality arises "naturally" out of the geography and psychology of the situation. When the weight leaves his chest, Harry finds that morning has brought the rescue plane to carry him to Nairobi. Helping him aboard, Old Compton says that they will have to refuel at Arusha. Everything happens as if it were actually happening—the take-off, the long view of the plain and its moving animals, the hills and forests to the east passing in slow majesty under the belly of the plane—until it dawns on Harry that for some reason they have by-passed Arusha. At first he does not know why. But as the plane emerges from a rain-squall, he suddenly sees ahead of them the square top of Kilimanjaro, "wide as all the world," incredibly white in the sun. "Then he knew that there was where he was going."

While he was in Africa Hemingway learned that the Masai name for the western summit of Kilimanjaro is Ngàje Ngài, which means "House of God." The association between mountainous terrain and the idea of home was, however, already an old one in his mind. He had used it symbolically in the Burguete section of *The Sun Also Rises* and also, far more extensively, in the Abruzzi and the Montreux locale-images of *A Farewell to Arms*. "I will lift up mine eyes to the hills," runs the Psalm, "from whence cometh my help." But there is no psalm-quoting in the back-to-earth dénouement of Hemingway's story. There is only Harry's wife Helen, waking in the middle of the night down in the flat plains-country, far from Kilimanjaro, and calling to a husband who does not answer.

Anyone interested in the methods by which the patterns of experience are translated to the purposes of art should find abundant materials for study in the three stories—non-fiction and fiction—which grew out of Hemingway's African expedition. The foreword to *The Green Hills of Africa* contains an implicit question. Given a country as interesting as Africa, and given the shape of a month's hunting-action there, and given the author's determination to tell only the truth, the question then becomes this: Can such a book possibly compete on equal terms with a work of the imagination? The answer is that it certainly can *compete*, provided always that the narrative is managed by a very skilled writer who takes both truth (the truth of "the way it was") and beauty (the extremely careful formal construction) as his watchwords. Yet the experiment proved also that the narrator who takes no liberties with the actual events of his experience, who tells things exactly as they were, who invents nothing and suppresses nothing important, will place himself at a real disadvantage in the competition. He gives the opposition too large a handicap. Good as *The Green Hills of Africa* is in two respects (verisimilitude and architectonics), it lacks the intensities which Hemingway was able to pack into **"The Short Happy Life of Francis Macomber,"** and it cannot possibly achieve anything like the genuine pathos of **"The Snows of Kilimanjaro."** The experience of wrestling with the African book, followed as it was with the writing of the two short stories, undoubtedly established one esthetic principle very firmly in Hemingway's mind. The highest art must take liberties, not with the truth but with the modes by which the truth is projected. This was no new discovery for Hemingway. But for any serious writer it is a useful maxim.

Marion Montgomery   (essay date 1961)

SOURCE: "The Leopard and the Hyena: Symbol and Meaning in 'The Snows of Kilimanjaro'," in *The University of Kansas City Review,* Vol. XXVII, No. IV, June, 1961, pp. 277-82.

[*In the following essay, Montgomery analyzes the significance and implications of the central symbols in "The Snows of Kilimanjaro."*]

In **"The Snows of Kilimanjaro"** Ernest Hemingway employs specific symbols—a mountain, a hyena, a leopard—to dramatize a favorite theme: heroic perseverance. But the symbols' relationship to the action of the story arouses questions of interpretation which are not easily resolved. It is the purpose of this [essay] to analyze the story to see just where the symbols, the leopard and hyena particularly, raise problems in the dramatic structure and the meaning of the story and to consider to what extent the problems are solved by the story.

The center of dramatic conflict in **"The Snows of Kilimanjaro"** is the protagonist's mind, which is constantly agitated by a contrast between the present ignoble situation and the memory of a more heroic past. Harry, a writer, at the point in his life where he should have realized his ideal or should at least find himself still devoted to the ideal, lies dying of gangrene because of his carelessness in not treating a scratch got on a hunt. He knows that he is dying physically, but he knows also that he has died spiritually long before, through his choice of carrion comfort over the lean joys of more dangerous pursuit. Like Eliot's old man in "Gerontion," he remembers his failures sardonically. He adds up the actions of his life, the motions and facts, that have brought him to a cot in the dry plains of Africa, and he faces despair self-condemned.

If Harry judges himself by his actions, the fact that he does so indicates a positive code against which he measures them. What is that positive code, which he has forsaken? To approach a statement of it, we must make use of two keys which Hemingway provides: one is the leopard described in the headnote to the story; the other is the hyena which functions dramatically in the story. The headnote reads:

> Kilimanjaro is a snow covered mountain 19,710 feet high, and is said to be the highest mountain in Africa. Its western summit is called Masai "Ngaje Ngài," the House of God. Close to the western summit there is

the dried and frozen carcass of a leopard. No one has explained what the leopard was seeking at that altitude.

This is the only direct reference to the leopard, and therein, perhaps, lies a weakness of the story, a point to be considered later. What is important to note at this point is that a contrast seems to be implied between the leopard of the headnote and the hyena that slinks through the story itself. The hyena's first appearance occurs just at dark when "there was no longer enough light to shoot." Had there been enough light, one may venture to suppose from Harry's attitude that he would certainly have shot the loathsome creature. From this point on, as Harry continues to judge and condemn himself, the hyena plays an important role in his thoughts. For instance, when Harry realizes beyond all doubt that he is going to die, we are told that the realization "came with a rush . . . of a sudden evil-smelling emptiness and the odd thing was that the hyena slipped lightly along the edge of it." To extract Harry's code from the story, we must explain the relationship of the leopard frozen on the mountain to the hyena attracted by the smell of Harry's decaying flesh.

Now the quotation just cited might naturally lead one to suppose that the hyena functions in the story as a symbol of death, but its symbolic function is, I think, more complex. Harry has, as a writer, already been considering death's symbols. He has watched the vultures collect, also attracted by the smell of decay. He thinks of death at one point, after remembering his life in Paris, as something that "went on bicycles and moved absolutely silently on the pavements." And late in the story he says to his wife: "Never believe any of that about a scythe and a skull . . . It can be two bicycle policemen as easily, or be a bird. Or it can have a wide snout like a hyena." At this point Harry is already drifting into a dream-like state which will be consummated by his flight to the House of God. He has felt death come and rest its head on the foot of the cot, "and he could smell its breath," this after having just heard the hyena in the darkness. Here Harry is losing control of his thoughts as he drifts into death. His speech and reflections become less clear, less rational, and his association of the hyena with death seems once more quite simple. But death has not been a hyena up to this point; it has been "a sudden evil-smelling emptiness." And the hyena has been to Harry a symbol of a particular kind of life, the life he has followed to that morally "evil-smelling emptiness." We must remember that Harry is a writer, but more importantly we must remember that he is a hunter. What game is to the animal predator, the book is to Harry. But to Harry the captured game, the finished book, is really of secondary importance. He does regret that he has never written about those things which are clearly important, but even more does he regret having lost sight of their importance. Harry has ceased to be the kind of hunter he holds ideal. To make this point clear, we must note that, while Harry does lament his artistic failure, he judges himself in other terms. In the first part of the story he is angry "that this was the end of it [life]." He is angry, not because his failure as writer, but because of a moral failure: because he has not been the good hunter.

There are two streams of Harry's consciousness presented in the story, distinguished by typography, in which he considers himself primarily as hunter. The one is in italics, the other in Roman type. The italics embody Harry's reflections concerning the past he approves of; the material in Roman type embodies the past and present he disapproves of. The two play against each other, giving rise to the story's internal and external dramatic tension. For instance, at the end of the first scene, Harry's wife protests against the fate that has caused Harry's discomfort. "What have we done to have that happen to us?" He answers, "I suppose what I did was to forget to put iodine on it when I first scratched it." A whole train of half measures has led to the decaying leg, and Harry's sardonic tone as he relates the neglect reflects a judgment on his failure. But the sardonic tone reflects on more sins than a failure to use iodine. The half measures that have led him to a spiritual rot are gnawing at him, and he remembers himself in a more worthy state in the italicized passage which follows this scene. We do not know at first just what those spiritual half-measures were, because Harry's thought skips that portion of his history for the moment, leaving us to deduce the comparison of the half-measures from the sardonic tone he uses with his wife and the heroic tone of the italicized reflection. (Just so may we deduce Harry's ideal code from the hyena's, the negative code.) Harry recalls a retreat from Thrace and the snow on Bulgarian mountains which brought death to those trapped in their heroic attempt; he recalls the aid given a deserter who won admiration through his courage. He recalls the full-spirited skiing and gambling, and in contrast he recalls Barker who machine-gunned helpless enemy officers. Those were the good days of pursuit for the sake of pursuit which demanded a worthy victim, not the helpless game which scavengers like Barker come by.

Harry breaks his reflections to ask his wife "Where did we stay in Paris?" His mind has turned now, suddenly for the reader, to his own infamous life with his rich wife in a comfortable section of Paris—in-famous because it was a life content with an easy pursuit. He is vicious in his repartee with his wife, leading her to ask: "Do you have to kill your horse and your wife and burn your saddle and your armour?" She is a simple woman whose main talent is the bed, and she cannot see that he is scourging himself more than her. She has made possible his comfort and decay through her money, and his desperate, destructive words are his way of "trying to kill to keep . . . alive." When he speaks the cruel truth of his failure, she mistakes his sardonic tone for sarcasm and his words for an attack upon her, and so he slips back into "the familiar lie he made his bread and butter by": he tells her he loves her. He reflects that "If he lived by a lie, he should try to die by it," an attempt to regain some nobleness of spirit. It is not the woman's fault that he has traded on his talent, accepting the unworthy pursuit of the hollow, decayed rich, telling his conscience that his end was to write about those spiritually decayed beings. That, then, was the beginning of the half-measures ending in the spiritual rot which left him dead long before the infection of his leg. Harry, alone on his cot, recalls how lies became life. "You

kept from thinking and it was all marvellous." In other words, Harry began stalking dead game, as Barker did in strafing the helpless enemy officers and as the hyena stalks Harry outside the fire's circle. He recalls next how he was in turn stalked by the woman, as if she caught the scent of his decay. They are alike, he concludes, and in resignation he accepts her again, lying on the cot by the fire while she talks, still unable to reclaim the old ideal that might purge him of the smell of moral decay. It is at this moment in his thought that "it occurred to him that he was going to die," a fact that has already occurred to him and been accepted but which becomes terrifyingly impressive because it is at this point that he senses death as "a sudden evil-smelling emptiness and the odd thing was that the hyena slipped lightly along the edge of it."

The end of "The Snows of Kilimanjaro," one suspects, is not metaphysical so much as it is sentimental. It gives the story a happy ending, useful to lesser attempts of Hollywood, but not justified by Harry's nature. It seems void of any real meaning.

—*Marion Montgomery*

Harry remembers next, in contrast to his wife, those women he loved too much, how through the corrosion of quarrelling he and they "killed what they had together." There was unhappiness as a result, but there was no living of a lie. It was a cleaner death he pursued. But now his cruel honesty cannot kill what he and his wife have together any more than the hyena can kill the carrion it stalks. From this point in the story the hyena and the woman are associated, but the equation implied in Harry's thinking is complex—hyena: carrion:: Harry: wife:: death: Harry. In sharp contrast to that animal creature, the Armenian slut, Harry's wife is soft and yielding, the easy death he has sought. "And as he looked and saw her well-known pleasant smile, he felt death come again." He associates the smell of his physical death and the look of his wife, which remind him of his moral decay.

Harry is, by this time, approaching a moral rejuvenation through self-condemnation. He has come to Africa in the first place to work the fat off body and soul, to give up the easy comforts in an attempt to regain the old hunting form, and it is a wry irony of fate that threatens to destroy him before he can reclaim himself. But in spite of fate, he begins an affirmation. Now rejecting the code of life corresponding to the hyena's in the animal world, he reaffirms that corresponding to the leopard's. He summons memories to strengthen him. There are his grandfather's guns, burned when the family cabin burned. His grandfather, he recalls, refused to let the boy disturb them in their ashes. The image of the burned guns in ashes suggests the leopard of the headnote: there is an unexplained steadiness of devotion in the old man's attitude that is of the same order as that which led the leopard beyond its element. Harry remembers, too, his destitute neighbors in the Place Contrescarpe where he lived before he began living the lie. He recalls those drunkards who killed their poverty with drink and the "sportifs" who "took it out in exercising" by bicycle racing. Here are the hyenas and leopards of the Paris slum, and Harry, in his reflections, judges the drunkards much as he judges Barker and himself and the hyena. He remembers the half-wit chore boy in Wyoming who remained constant to duty to the point of foolishly shooting a man to protect some hay, and there is in Harry's remembering a note of approval of the boy's action. The full-hearted deed is important to him, not the consequences of appearing ridiculous by defending burnt guns or winning third prize in a bicycle race, or being jailed, perhaps hanged, for shooting a man, or ending up with an Armenian whore instead of a respectable wife.

When his present wife interrupts these reflections of past events to bring Harry more broth, to insist that he do what is good for him, he resists her, more determined than ever, because what she means by *good* is, to Harry, *easy*. Death is Harry's chance of self-recovery. He will not care for death, he reflects, and thus he will overcome it. He is determined he won't spoil this experience as he has so many others. He fears only pain, not the idea, and the pain itself does not bother him now. He drifts into death thinking that he has waited too long and too late, and that his life is therefore wasted. "The party's over and you are with your hostess now." But he is bored with his hostess death. "He looked at her [wife's-death's] face between him and the fire . . . He heard the hyena make a noise." He feels death creep up his leg again and "he could smell its breath." It had no shape. "It simply occupied space," negative being. "You've got a hell of a breath," says Harry, his last words as he feels death crouching on his chest. Then he has the sensation of the cot's being lifted as he is carried into the tent, after which everything becomes "all right." His last thoughts show no fear.

So far the story has held together, but the final two sections are crucial to its success, and it is at this point that the story falls apart. It does so, partly because the device of the fantasy flight to Kilimanjaro seems an artificial contrivance, following as it does the realism of the rest of the story, and partly because the final section, shifting back to the level of conscious reality, also shifts the point of view and seems intended primarily to prevent a possible misunderstanding of the story's outcome, as a sort of footnote to the story.

The next to the last section, Harry's flight to Kilimanjaro, takes us back to the headnote with which the story begins and to the question of the story's basic weakness. It is easy enough to accept the plane ride as a possible death

dream Harry experiences, for it has been prepared for all along in the story. His wife hopefully argues that the plane will come for him in time to save him, and Harry's rational thought throughout has been patterned by association—the good life with the bad, a good woman with bad, and so on. The plane-ride dream, then, is a psychological possibility which one can accept. Further, one is prepared for a psychological use of the mountain, though Kilimanjaro itself does not figure in the story until the dream passage, for Harry's thoughts run to the cool snows of his heroic yesteryears as he lies on the cot on the hot African plain. However, one is not sufficiently prepared for the rather sudden symbolic use of the mountain, for the relationship of the mountain to Harry's moral code is inadequately prepared for in the story itself. One surmises that the leopard's relation to the mountain is in some manner paralleled by Harry's relationship to it, but it is an unclear relationship, whereas Harry's relationship to the hyena and carrion is not.

Further, the use of the mountain as symbol is confused by the last three lines of the headnote as contrasted with the events of the flight and with Harry's self-evaluation. What is the "House of God?" Some positive level of achievement on Harry's part is suggested since he apparently is taken to the summit, some achievement which transcends death on the slopes. Throughout the story the emphasis has been on the ideal of attempt, not on accomplishment; then suddenly one has Harry's final thought on seeing "the square top of Kilimanjaro," the House of God: "And then he knew that there was where he was going." Has Harry, by his act of renouncing the hyena's way for the leopard's, gained salvation? Is that salvation anything more than the soothing balm of the snows of yesterday recovered through the force of desire? The story's end, one suspects, is not metaphysical so much as it is sentimental. It gives the story a happy ending, useful to lesser attempts of Hollywood, but not justified by Harry's nature. It seems void of any real meaning. The problem is further complicated by the fact that the reader has expected the leopard to become an integral part of the story. When one sees the mountain, first described in the headnote, looming rather suddenly out of the story, he expects to see the leopard also. Then, too, the final line of the headnote keeps bothering the reader. "No one has explained what the leopard was seeking at that altitude." Harry knows the answer to the question in terms of other hunters: his grandfather, the half-wit boy in Wyoming, himself in happier days. And Harry obviously knows the mountain: why does the mountain not appear in his consciousness as would naturally be likely; why is there no thought of the leopard, the natural opposite of the hyena, in the mind of this symbol-conscious writer? As hunter he knows the worthy leopard, even as he knows about that most hated of all animals, the hyena. The answer to these questions seems to be simply that Hemingway does not make efficient use of the leopard and mountain, whereas his use of the hyena is extremely skillful. The headnote and the final two sections protrude from the story, making it an awkward iceberg.

Oliver Evans (essay date 1961)

SOURCE: "'The Snows of Kilimanjaro': A Revaluation," in *PMLA: Publications of the Modern Language Association,* Vol. LXXVI, No. IV, December, 1961, pp. 601-07.

[*In the following essay, Evans delineates the differing critical interpretations of various symbols in "The Snows of Kilimanjaro," in addition to offering an alternative reading of his own.*]

When "The **Snows of Kilimanjaro**" first appeared in *Esquire* (August 1936), it attracted immediate attention. It was promptly reprinted (in *Best American Short Stories of 1937*) by Edward J. O'Brien, who, praising it in his preface, remarked: "Nothing is irrelevant. The artist's energy is rigidly controlled for his purpose." Since then it has been anthologized many times, and now it is probably safe to say that, with the possible exception of **"The Killers,"** none of Hemingway's stories has enjoyed greater popularity than this one. Hemingway's own opinion was that it was "about as good as any" of his shorter works.

In the last ten or fifteen years, however, **"The Snows"** has come in for considerable disparagement, mainly from the so-called New Critics and their followers. In 1945 Ray B. West, Jr., wrote in *The Sewanee Review* [January-March issue]: "While I consider this story one of Hemingway's best . . . it is spoiled for me by the conventionality of its leading symbol: the White-capped mountain as the 'House of God'." In 1950 Allen Tate and Caroline Gordon, referring to it in *The House of Fiction* as a "magnificent failure," complained that it lacked "dramatic force" and objected that the symbolism was not properly integrated with the action. And in 1956 William Van O'Connor characterized it as a "rather puzzling story" and expressed dissatisfaction with the ending [*The History of Ideas Newsletter,* Vol. II].

Even critics who have praised the story without reservation have differed widely in their interpretation of it, so that one might well wonder if the symbols through which it communicates its meaning are indeed as conventional as Mr. West has found them. The fact is that no other story of Hemingway's has caused quite so much critical controversy, and the main reason for this is disagreement on the meaning of the symbols.

II

A brief summary of the story may be helpful at this point. It will be remembered that it is preceded by an epigraph in which the reader is told that the snow-covered western summit of Mount Kilimanjaro, in Africa, is called by the natives the "House of God"; that the dried and frozen carcass of a leopard was once found there; and, thirdly, that "no one has explained what the leopard was seeking at that altitude." We are then introduced to the main characters, a writer named Harry and his wife, Helen, who are on a safari in Africa. They are encamped on a plain, and

Harry, who has received a scratch on his leg a few days earlier, is dying of gangrene: although the infection is painless, the odor of his rotting flesh has attracted several vultures, who "squat obscenely" in the glare of the plain, waiting for him to die. Helen attempts to reassure him by telling him that the plane for which they have sent will arrive at any moment, but Harry knows that it is too late. He does not fear death, but he is filled with a sense of unfulfilled ambition: "Now he would never write the things that he had saved to write until he knew them well enough to write them well."

In a series of flashbacks, Harry's past is then unfolded. We learn that Helen is the last of several women in his life; and that, though she loves him, he has never really loved her but married her for her money, whereupon he ceased to write and squandered his energies among the very rich, the people of his wife's set. Now, on his deathbed, he realizes that he has traded for security his integrity as a writer—and as a man as well, for his relationship with his wife is based upon a lie, "the familiar lie he made his bread and butter by." It is natural that he should feel resentment toward her now, and he expresses this resentment in a number of ill-tempered and consciously cruel remarks: he tells her, among other things, that he has never loved her. But the next moment he begs her forgiveness: "Don't pay any attention, darling, to what I say. I love you, really. You know I love you." But when she answers "You're sweet to me," he lashes out again: "You bitch. You rich bitch." Honesty, born of the desperation of the situation, struggles with habit and achieves a few temporary victories. In his calmer moments, however, he realizes that he is being unfair, and that he can blame no one but himself for his failure: "She shot very well, this rich bitch, this kindly caretaker and destroyer of his talent. Nonsense. He had destroyed his talent himself. Why should he blame this woman because she kept him well?"

The flashbacks alternate with the level of present action, and contrat the happiness he has once known, when he was wholly alive and writing well, with the sickness, frustration, and impotence of the moment. The impotence is physical as well as literary (at one point he tells Helen, "The only thing I ever liked to do with you I can't do now"), and is, of course, a consequence of his infection. The incidents which his memory selects from these earlier, happier days involve scenes in which snow figures prominently: the mountain tops of Bulgaria; the skiing slopes in Bludenz and Schrunz, where the snow was "as smooth to see as cake frosting and as light as powder"; and a snow-bound ranch in the United States. All of these reminiscences are by no means idyllic: there is the sordid scene in which he fights with a British gunner over a "hot Armenian slut," the ghastly incident in which his friend Williamson is disembowelled by a German stick bomb, and the shocking massacre of the inexperienced Greek troops in Anatolia. But they are all scenes of action, contrasting by their very violence with the slow rot of which he is now dying, and they are connected with the vitality which has deserted him: then, at least, he was alive and living life up to the hilt.

When evening comes, Harry sees a hyena skulking near-by; shortly after this, he feels for the first time the certitude of his approaching death: "It came with a rush; not as a rush of water nor of wind; but of a sudden evil-smelling emptiness and the odd thing was that the hyena slipped lightly along the edge of it." Later he has another vision of death, as a pair of policemen on a bicycle (this has been prepared for by a flashback in which he recalls his career as a struggling young writer in Paris). After dark he becomes delirious, and Helen has the servant, Molo, move his cot inside the tent. In his final delirium, he dreams that the plane has come for him; the pilot lifts him in; they fly through clouds and rain; and then he sees, looming ahead of them, the snowcovered peak of Kilimanjaro shining whitely in the sun: "And then he knew that there was where he was going." At this point the hyena makes a "strangely human, almost crying sound"; Helen wakes up, and, going to Harry's cot, discovers that he has died. Hemingway has so contrived the ending that the reader is unaware, until Helen makes her discovery, that the plane trip never took place except in the mind of the dying man: the details of it are rendered with the utmost realism.

The level of present action in the story is negligible; most of the action occurs in the past, at various levels, but **"The Snows"** is not, primarily, a story of action at all: its interest lies in the *situation,* and in the conflict between idealism and materialism that takes place within the protagonist. To charge that the story lacks "dramatic force" is to conceive of drama solely in terms of external action, and this does not do justice to Hemingway's intention.

III

As for the symbols, there is, first of all, Africa itself, the Dark Continent, which stands in the story for the mysterious nature out of which man comes and into which he returns at last. Since the natural and the good are, in Hemingway's system of values, usually identified, this symbol has a moral significance; to Harry, Africa means the hope of moral regeneration: "Africa was where he had been happiest in the good time of his life, so he had come out here to start again. . . . He had thought he could get back into training that way. That in some way he could work the fat off his soul the way a fighter went into the mountains to work and train in order to burn it out of his body."

It will be seen that Harry here associates Africa with the creative phase of his life, when he was leading a "natural" existence before the corruption of money set in. Since he was happy there, he thinks of it nostalgically as a kind of spiritual home, to which he returns now in the hope of recovering something of his lost integrity. The therapeutic value of nature is, of course, an obsessive theme with Hemingway: it occurs in many of the stories in his first book, *In Our Time* (1925), and in the novel which he published the following year (*The Sun Also Rises*), where Jake revives himself, after his dissipations in Paris, by going on a fishing trip with Bill to a remote spot in Spain.

Spain, indeed, had for Hemingway in the 'twenties something of the symbolic value that he later attached to Africa: W. M. Frohock, speaking of the Basque peasants in *The Sun Also Rises,* comments, "We get the feeling that to Hemingway, unspoiled people of this sort are always good," and notes the admiration which Hemingway expresses, in *Green Hills of Africa,* for certain African tribes.

The main symbol, of course, is the snow-covered mountain top. To say (as do Tate and Gordon) that it represents death is to misread the meaning of the story, for while it is true that the mountain stands for a kind of perfection that is attainable only in death, through union with nature (the peak, as has been mentioned, is called by the Masai the "House of God"), it operates in the story not as a symbol of death but of life-in-death. The snow with which it is covered is, of course, a traditional symbol of purity: this is the reason it figures so importantly in Harry's recollections of his early life, when he was still happy in the possession of his integrity. It is associated in the story with life, not with death—or with death only in the sense that it is the means of achieving eternal life.

As the mountain symbolizes life-in-death, the plain on which the man is dying symbolizes death-in-life, and the essential contrast in the story is between the two. The plain is hot and full of glare (we are told this several times), and it is associated with the joylessness of his recent existence, an existence which is in fact a form of death-in-life. Mountain tops and hilltops are traditionally symbolic of the ideal (one *strives* toward them), and low-lying plains, by contrast, symbolize earthly and material values; it is by these that Harry has lived, and on his deathbed his mind dwells wistfully on thoughts of snow and high places. The situation is coherent also on the realistic level, since a feverish man might be expected, in his delirium, to think of coolness. Cold and hot; high and low—these are the two extremes that Hemingway chooses to dramatize Harry's situation, and they are admirably illustrated in the symbols of mountain and plain.

I tend to agree with Charles Walcutt [in *The Explicator,* April 1949] that "the conflict in the story is between a fundamental moral idealism and the corrupting influence of aimless materialism." Harry's idealism reveals itself in his sense of frustration and despair, and it contrasts oddly with the mechanistic views which he expresses from time to time. Thus, when Helen asks, speaking of his illness, "What have we done to have that happen to us?" he answers, "I suppose what I did was to forget to put iodine on it when I first scratched it." His wife replies, "I don't mean that," whereupon he says: "If we would have hired a good mechanic instead of a half baked Kikiyu driver, he would have changed the oil and never burned out that bearing in the truck." Helen says again, "I don't mean that," and Harry continues: "If you hadn't left your own people, your goddamned Old Westbury, Saratoga, Palm Beach people to take me on. . . ." Here he refuses to acknowledge a plan, an intention in the scheme of things, and clings stubbornly to the view that all is accident. Again, several pages later, he reflects that "now this life she had built again was coming to a term because he had not used iodine two weeks ago when a thorn had scratched his knee as they moved forward trying to photograph a herd of waterbuck standing, their heads up, peering while their nostrils searched the air, their ears spread wide to hear the first noise that would send them rushing into the bush." This is the habit of thinking, in terms of mechanical cause and effect, into which he has fallen since his association with Helen, and it is only occasionally that his old idealism asserts itself. It must be remembered too that Harry is a sick man, the external illness being but a symbolic manifestation of the sickness of the soul from which he has long been suffering: these are the thoughts of a man without faith, a man who is morally ill.

The gangrene symbol has been chosen as carefully as the others: for rotting flesh, read rotting soul. The story begins with Harry's remark, "The marvelous thing is that it's painless. That's how you know when it starts." The death-in-life which Harry has been living was an easy, comfortable one, and the moral disintegration, like the physical, occurred stealthily and by degrees: "But he would never do it, because each day of not writing, of comfort, of being that which he despised, dulled his ability and softened his will to work so that, finally, he did no work at all."

Contrasted with the symbol of the man rotting away in the heat of the plain is the symbol, in the epigraph, of the leopard which, having attained the summit—and died in the effort—leaves his body preserved immaculately and eternally in its snows. The contrast may be merely ironical, in which case the epigraph appears rather gratuitous, justifying the objection of Tate and Gordon that the symbolism "seems something the writer has tacked on rather than an integral part of the story." It is probable, however, that Hemingway intended to identify the man in some way with the leopard. What has happened to the leopard is a pretty obvious example of life-in-death, and what has happened to the man is, as has been noted, a form of death-in-life. The man has two dimensions, spiritual and material, and the leopard symbolizes the former: thus, Harry too achieves life-in-death, through union with what is ideal and eternal, but only (like the leopard) at the cost of his earthly existence. It should also be noted that the leopard, being a *spotted* animal, is peculiarly appropriate as a symbol of Harry's moral identity: what is maculate, both in the beast and in the man, has become immaculate in eternity.

Of all Hemingway's symbols, the leopard in this story has provoked the most controversy. Ten years ago, Alfred G. Engstrom [in *MLN*, March 1950] asked rhetorically, "As for the other symbol in the epigraph, can there by any doubt as to its meaning?," and went on to declare: "The leopard is Dante's—the symbol of worldly pleasure and lechery—one of three beasts, in the first Canto of the Inferno, that stood between the medieval poet and his own Delectable Mountain." It did not require much ingenuity for Douglas Hall Orrok, the following year [*MLN*, November 1951], to refute this interpretation, but the one with which he attempted to replace it called for a great deal: he suggested that the leopard symbol was taken from Revelation xiii.1, in which there is mention of a beast

"like a leopard" which is blasphemy, and that Harry, by neglecting his talent, has been guilty of literary blasphemy. **"The Snows of Kilimanjaro,"** he wrote, "is a fable of literary integrity. The artist who blasphemes against the Gods of Parnassus is sacrificed in the ascent of the mystic peak." This theory does at least establish an identity between the man and the beast, but it breaks down when we apply it to the contrasting set of circumstances under which Harry and the leopard meet their death, nor does it fit into the total symbolic framework of the story. Charles Walcutt, in 1949, was the first critic to suggest that the leopard was a "symbol of Harry's moral nature," but he was unable to integrate the symbol into the story satisfactorily because his conception of the mountain did not include the associations of life-in-death; he thought of the peak merely as "a symbol of Truth, meaning—or an incarnation of the ideal." Agreeing with this view, E. W. Tedlock, Jr., pointed out [in *The Explicator*, October 1949] the "leopard and mountain represent those things which do not decay" in contrast to the man who is dying on the plain; he did not, however, explore the implications of this contrast. In 1952, Philip Young, whose book on Hemingway [*Ernest Hemingway*] has the kind of biographical emphasis that enables him to view **"The Snows"** as "a fictionalized purge, in this case of a whole set of guilty feelings . . . an exercise in personal and aesthetic hygiene," identified the leopard with the kind of literary work that Harry (i.e., Hemingway) would like to leave behind him: "He dreams of immortality for some of what he has done; he thinks, that is, of writing prose that will be so pure that it can never spoil, that will be permanent." Besides limiting the meaning of the story rather narrowly, this interpretation does not sufficiently account for what happens in it: Harry's integrity as a man as well as a writer is involved in **"The Snows,"** and his situation has universal moral interest and application. Curiously enough, Young also accepted Engstrom's theory that the leopard symbolizes the worldly pleasure that stood between Dante and the Holy Hill, as well as the notion (also from Engstrom) that one of Flaubert's letters was the source of the mountain symbol: how these can be reconciled to the idea that the beast represents Harry's unaccomplished literary ambitions is by no means easy to see. In the most recent (1956) analysis of the story, Carlos Baker, agreeing with Walcutt and Tedlock, fitted their interpretation of the leopard into his theory that the mountain as Home, and plain as Not-home, underlies most of Hemingway's early work. Baker succeeded brilliantly in correlating the story with the Hemingway *Weltanschauung*, but he did it insufficient justice in its own right.

The vultures and the hyena, of course, are symbols of death, and they are associated with the death-in-life of the second phase of Harry's career, after he has made the fatal sacrifice; they are contrasted in the story with the leopard, which is associated with the earlier, purer phase of his life, the period of idealism, and also (as we have seen) with the eternal life which is achieved only in death: life-in-death. Few creatures could be more unlike, on the realistic level, than the skulking, cowardly hyena, which feeds chiefly on carrion, and the bold and graceful leopard which attacks living prey.

What has apparently escaped all the critics is that Harry's wife, Helen, is herself a symbol—and by no means the least important one in the story. Beyond noting that her influence is generally inimical (Edmund Wilson was the first to do this), no one has shown how skilfully and how consistently Hemingway employs her throughout as a symbol of death, or rather of death-in-life. Take for example the following passage: "Drinking together . . . he could feel the return of acquiescence in this life of pleasant surrender. She *was* very good to him. He had been cruel and unjust in the afternoon. She was a fine woman, marvelous really. And just then it occurred to him that he was going to die."

This is his first premonition of death, and note that it occurs immediately after his reflection that his wife is a "fine woman." Helen *is,* of course, a "fine woman" in the sense that she is "very good to him," but it is exactly this which is fatal for Harry—the comfort and security which she represents result in a "pleasant surrender" on his part, and lead to death-in-life. A few pages later we read: "She looked at him with her well-known, well-loved face from *Spur* and *Town and Country* . . . and as he looked and saw her well known pleasant smile, he felt death come again."

The fact is that no other story of Hemingway's has caused quite so much critical controversy, and the main reason for this is disagreement on the meaning of the symbols.

—Oliver Evans

This is his second premonition, and again it occurs while he is with the woman, watching her "pleasant smile." Shortly before he enters his final delirium, we find the following: "He looked at her face between him and the fire. She was leaning back in the chair and the firelight shone on her pleasantly lined face and he could see that she was sleepy. He heard the hyena make a noise just outside the range of the fire."

The contiguity of this description of the woman with Harry's intuitions of his approaching death, and with the hyena, make it probable that Hemingway is using Helen quite consciously as a symbol of death-in-life. Finally there is the passage:

> . . . if it was no worse than this as it went on there was nothing to worry about. Except that he would rather be in better company.

> He thought a little about the company he would like to have.

No, he thought, when everything you do, you do too long, and do too late, you can't expect to find the people still there. The people are all gone. The party's over and you are with your hostess now.

His "hostess," on the realistic level, is Helen; on the symbolic, it is death. It is, after all, only right that Helen should have this function in the story, since Harry's moral infection, the gangrene of his spirit, dates from his association with her. Of the various death symbols, Helen is the most important: the vultures and the hyena are waiting in the hope that he will die; Helen is waiting in the hope that he will live—but live a death-in-life. In this context, Harry's reflection, that "She shot very well, this good, this rich bitch, this kindly caretaker and destroyer of his talent," takes on a strong ironical significance.

In describing the early relationship of Harry and his wife, Hemingway writes: "The steps by which she had acquired him and the way in which she had finally fallen in love with him were all part of a regular progression in which she had built herself a new life and he had traded away what remained of his old life." The inference is that what has been bad for Harry has been good for Helen: she has thrived at his expense. But she does not thrive on his *vitality*; she thrives, as would the hyena, on *what is dead* in him: "The people he knew now were all much more comfortable when he did not work at all." This conception of women, that they can live comfortably with their men only when the latter are dead morally, may be found also in that other, simpler story about Africa that Hemingway wrote about the same time, **"The Short, Happy Life of Francis Macomber,"** where Margot, when her husband belatedly asserts his identity, shoots him. According to Edmund Wilson, "the emotion which principally comes through in **'Francis Macomber'** and **'The Snows of Kilimanjaro'**—as it figures also in *The Fifth Column*—is a growing antagonism to women." Indeed, the women characters of Hemingway's early and middle period frequently have a menacing quality: they interfere with the pursuit of masculine ideals, whether aesthetic or athletic. In as early a book as *The Sun Also Rises* we find the innkeeper, Montoya, a dedicated *aficionado* of the bullring, fearful of Brett's influence over the toreador Romero; and when Pop, in the autobiographical *Green Hills of Africa,* asks the author, "What are the things, the actual, concrete things that harm a writer?," Hemingway replies: "Politics, women, drink, money, ambition."

IV

If the New Critics, preoccupied with surface technique, have failed to evaluate **"The Snows"** properly, other critics, preoccupied with biographical considerations, have succeeded scarcely better. It is true that, as in almost all of Hemingway—especially the early Hemingway—the biographical element looms large. Philip Young, the champion of this school, states that in 1936 Hemingway, who had been "chasing about Europe and Africa with the very rich and drinking too much," felt depressed about his own work; he asserts that the model for Helen was Hemingway's second wife, Pauline Pfeifer, a wealthy fashion writer for *Vogue*; he points out that much of the material in the flashbacks came straight from Hemingway's own experience (the fishing and skiing episodes, the descriptions of Paris neighborhoods, and the incidents in the Turkish-Greek War and on the Austro-Italian line in World War I); and he notes that the "Julian" of the story was F. Scott Fitzgerald, that in the first printing of **"The Snows"** (in *Esquire*) he is called Scott Fitzgerald instead of Julian, and that Hemingway himself once made the reply, "Yes, they have more money," to Fitzgerald's observation, "The rich are very different from you and me," attributed in the story to Julian. And Carlos Baker tells us that in January 1934 (only two years before **"The Snows"** was written), Hemingway was taken seriously ill of amoebic dysentery in Tanganyika while on safari and was flown past Kilimanjaro to Nairobi for treatment: "During the flight east, and no doubt also during the period of treatment in Nairobi . . . Hemingway had time to reflect on a topic which would naturally occur to him in such a situation: the death of a writer before his work is done."

Now all of this may be true—some of it certainly is—but Hemingway intended **"The Snows"** to be more than a slightly fictionalized diary, and the perceptive reader will find that he succeeded in that intention. *In Our Time*, *A Farewell to Arms,* and *The Sun Also Rises* are also to a large extent personalized fiction, but the critic is dangerously myopic who sees in them only, or chiefly, the biographical element. It also limits the story, though much less narrowly, to regard it merely as a parable of the artist. Engstrom makes this mistake, as do also Orrok, Tate and Gordon, and, to a certain extent, Baker, who states that the central theme is the same as James's in "The Lesson of the Master."

I have suggested that the theme of **"The Snows"** involves a contrast between life-in-death, of which the leopard and mountain are symbols, and death-in-life, with which is associated a group of symbols that includes Harry's wife, Helen, and the physical illness from which he is suffering. To appreciate fully the moral meaning of the story, it is necessary to understand the conditions under which Harry first contracted his spiritual sickness. Hemingway tells us that when Harry met Helen he had already exhausted his capacity for love: "It was not her fault," he has his protagonist reflect, "that when he went to her he was already over," and again: "He had never quarreled much with this woman, while with the women that he loved he had quarreled so much they had finally, always, with the corrosion of the quarreling, killed what they had together. He had loved too much, demanded too much, and he wore it all out." It is this inability to love which is his real sickness, and it is aggravated by the deception which he practices—and practices successfully—upon his wife: "But when he no longer was in love, when he was only lying, as to this woman, now . . . it was strange that when he did not love her at all and was lying, that he should be able to give her more for her money than when he had really loved." The definition of love that he frames now, in his sickness ("Love is a dunghill. And I'm the cock that gets on it to crow") contrasts powerfully with

the wistful, almost sentimental manner in which, in the flashbacks, he recalls his early love affairs.

Life without love is death-in-life: this is the real moral of the story, as it is the moral of "The Ancient Mariner"; Hemingway's protagonist, however, is less lucky than Coleridge's, for it is only in death, or life-in-death, that he will recover his integrity and achieve identification with that which is infinite and perfect. It is significant that Harry's disintegration as a writer began at the moment he felt himself incapable of love: when he stopped loving, he stopped creating. This is the reason, too, for the boredom he now feels about almost everything, even death: "For this, that now was coming, he had very little curiosity . . . I'm getting as bored with dying as with everything else, he thought." When he lost his ability to love, he lost his curiosity about life as well as his capacity for it.

It is very important to realize that the story ends on a note of triumph. Harry does gain the mountain top, not merely *in his delirium,* as William Van O'Connor thought, but *in death.* It is because O'Connor did not, apparently, understand this that he found the story "puzzling." Had Harry's delirium been merely that, and had it not been followed by his death, **"The Snows"** would indeed have been puzzling, but Hemingway is careful to depict the delirium in such a way that its climax is synchronous with Harry's death: "And then he knew that there was where he was going." Death is the price that he must pay, but life-in-death, Hemingway is telling us, is preferable to death-in-life at any cost. "Only in fantasy does he escape from the nature that pulls him down," O'Connor objected, but Harry's escape from the plain to the peak is real and absolute: it is there, in the "House of God," that he is reunited to that which is ideal and permanent, to that which never rots.

"The Snows of Kilimanjaro" is Hemingway's most religious story. For man, the only alternative to love is death, as W. H. Auden has often insisted; and this is the lesson which Hemingway's parable dramatizes. It is a larger lesson than that which Henry St. George, in James's story, gives to his disciple, and it is essentially a religious one. Hemingway's religion, like that of the American Transcendentalists with whom he has more in common than has usually been supposed, is to a large extent a religion of nature, containing elements of pantheism and Platonism. From the point of view of the latter doctrine, **"The Snows"** is the story of a man who, having lost contact with divinity when the spark of human love (an emanation of divine love) is extinguished within him, is returned to the Original Source of all love. From the time of his first novel, *The Sun Also Rises,* one of Hemingway's most consistent convictions has been that to the extent man is in tune with nature he fulfills the divine plan and his own proper destiny: this is the reason for his insistence on the therapeutic value of nature, and I think it explains also, at least partially, his obsessive interest in those activities which he regards as "natural," such as hunting and fishing. This is, of course, a romantic attitude, and indeed the number of critics is increasing who would agree with Malcolm

Cowley that Hemingway is only superficially a realist. There are other romantic themes in **"The Snows,"** such as that of the *femme fatale,* which, as Mario Praz has shown in *The Romantic Agony* (where he traces it to Greek mythology), is one of the most characteristic preoccupations in the literature of Western Europe. Hemingway has less in common with Dreiser than with Hawthorne and Melville—the men, as Cowley puts it, "who dealt in images that were symbols of an inner world"—which is merely another way of saying that he writes, as nearly all important romantic authors have written, out of an obsession. To the extent that this "inner world" resembles the outer one, and its symbols are intelligible, the romantic writer succeeds. Hemingway, of course, has been unusually successful.

R. W. Stallman   (essay date 1961)

SOURCE: "A New Reading of 'The Snows of Kilimanjaro'," in *The Houses That James Built: And Other Literary Studies,* Ohio University Press, 1961, pp. 173-99.

[*In the following essay, Stallman provides a structural analysis of Hemingway's story.*]

> *When in doubt, it seems, when in fear, when taken by surprise, when lost in bush or desert and without a guide, the human, the animal, heart prescribes a circle. It turns on itself as the earth does and seeks refuge in the movement of the stars.*
>
> —Laurens Van Der Post: *Venture To The Interior* (1951)

What has not been noticed about **"The Snows of Kilimanjaro"** is how it is designed. Scenes of external reality alternate with juxtaposed scenes of internal monologue, reminiscences of Harry's past life that Harry failed to utilize as writer. These cutbacks—they are set into italics—are not dreams, but rather they are recollected reality; the point is that they relate thematically. They are not irresponsible reminiscences. They are relevant in that they elicit, albeit obliquely, one motif or another relating to the plight of the protagonist. The narrative progression moves now forward in present reality and now backward to recollected reality.

The story is about an artist—or potential artist—who died spiritually the day he traded his integrity for security, and here he is dying now with a gangrenous leg whose stink has symbolic import. You begin to stink when you sell yourself out. Then is when moral gangrene sets in; after that, well, life becomes painless. "The marvellous thing is that it's painless," says Harry about his gangrenous leg. "That's how you knew when it starts." His gangrenous leg is token symbol of his moral gangrene as creative writer. Obversely put, writing is a struggle, an act of labor and pain. Stephen Crane had the same theory: "*The Red Badge of Courage* . . . was an effort born of pain—despair, almost; and I believe that this made it a better piece of literature than it otherwise would have been. It

seems a pity that art should be a child of pain, and yet I think it is." But Harry never exerted himself, never tried because he feared he might fail; instead of using his talent he traded on it. He blames the rich bitch Helen ("You rich bitch. That's poetry. I'm full of poetry now. Rot and poetry. Rotten poetry"), but he admits: "He had destroyed his talent himself. Why should he blame this woman because she kept him well? He had destroyed his talent by not using it, by betrayals of himself . . .". Harry's dying now of gangrene counterpoints with Harry's dying of spiritual gangrene years ago. He kept from thinking, "and it was all marvellous"—marvellous because painless. His painless death implies his painless life. Ironically, while dying he can't help *not* to keep from thinking. That he recollects his fragmented past, experiences he failed to recreate into formed literary works, that he recollects all that he has missed out on as potential artist, evokes the ironical poignancy of Harry's situation. What's painful about his present plight is just *that*. "Now he would never write the things that he had saved to write until he knew enough to write them well. Well, he would not have to fail at trying to write them either."

Like Kurtz in Conrad's "Heart of Darkness," Harry incriminates himself as failure. By his own self-admission Harry has sold Conscience short. So, too, does Doctor Diver in *Tender is the Night*: "My politeness is a trick of the heart." It is the characteristic Hemingway division and conflict between internal code or conscience and an external and meretricious code of manners or social front, a division and conflict exploited notably in *Huckleberry Finn.* One exemplar of integrity or conscience is Francis Macomber in Hemingway's **"The Short Happy Life of Francis Macomber."** Whereas at the start Macomber is presented in mock triumph, at the end he attains a moral triumph; the story is thus plotted with a reversal of the initial situation. "Francis Macomber had, half an hour before, been carried to his tent from the edge of the camp in triumph on the arms and shoulders of the cook, the personal boys, the skinner and the porters. The gun-bearers [however] had taken no part in the demonstration." Reversal of situation is obtained by the Conradian device of a wrenched chronology, the opening scene relocated so as to begin the story on the note of mock triumph. Because Macomber has defaulted in the lion hunt, he has lost face; the gun-bearers shun the false demonstration. The story begins with Macomber asking: "Will you have a lime juice or lemon squash?" The guide Robert Wilson says: "I'll have a gimlet," rejecting thus Macomber's kind of drink. "'I'll have a gimlet too. I need something,' Macomber's wife said, 'I suppose it's the thing to do,' Macomber agreed, 'Tell him to make three gimlets.'" Mrs. Macomber, ashamed of her husband, drinks Wilson's kind of drink; and Macomber, ashamed of himself, follows likewise the leader. But when Wilson later defaults on the hunter's code by chasing in the automobile the buffalo they hunt, he loses face; this reversal is spelled out by Macomber: "Now she [Margot] has something on you." The story began with Macomber in the power of Wilson and Mrs. Macomber; it ends with Wilson and Mrs. Macomber in the power of Macomber—he triumphs morally over them. As in **"The Short Happy Life of Francis**

Macomber," reversal of situation defines the structure of *The Portrait of a Lady, The Ambassadors, The Return of the Native,* "The Bride Comes to Yellow Sky," and *Tender is the Night.*

"The Snows of Kilimanjaro" is constructed very differently, the various parts being related not logically but psychologically:

> *That was one story he had saved to write. He knew at least twenty good stories from out there and he had never written one. Why?*

> 'You tell them why,' he said.

> 'Why what, dear?'

> 'Why nothing.'

The narrative shifts from recollections, from the mind of Harry, back to reality; here the transposition is clearly managed by the linked "Why?" Harry's memoried experiences furnish a kind of scrapbook of images which Harry had intended to recast into stories; they are all fragments, disjointed episodes, not yet organized into dramatic wholes because Harry never converted them into works of art. They are the unformed life he failed to form. Harry has not organized them, but Hemingway has.

While their sequence is seemingly haphazard, these internal monologues progress toward the climactic and final image of Williamson who was hit by a German bomb as he crawled through the trench's protective wire, *"with a flare lighting him up and his bowels spilled out into the wire, so when they brought him in, alive, they had to cut him loose. Shoot me, Harry. For Christ sake shoot me."* It is as though Williamson's plea were Harry's own death-wish, and almost immediately subsequent to this image of death-by-agony Harry himself dies—in contrast to Williamson, however, Harry does not die in agony. When "the weight went from his chest," Harry dies in his sleep. "It was morning and had been morning for some time and he heard the plane." Harry at the moment of his dying dreams that Compton comes to take him away by plane. "It was difficult getting him in, but once in he lay back in the leather seat, and the leg was stuck straight out to one side of the seat where Compton sat." All of this dream episode is set in Roman type so as to distinguish it from the italicized passages of Harry's recollections of the past; they are not dreams. The transition from reality to dream is as adroitly managed here as in Bierce's "An Occurrence at Owl Creek Bridge," Hemingway's device deriving from Bierce's famous story. In both stories the ending returns us to that point in the narrative where the death-dream began. Harry's wife, awakened by an hyena's almost human crying sound, discovers by flashlight in the dark tent that Harry's leg hangs down alongside his cot. "The dressings had all come down and she could not look at it." Harry does not answer her cry, "and she could not hear him breathing." Dream and reality—point-present-reality as distinguished from recollected reality—are rendered as blending almost unnoticeably one with the other,

the projected leg in Harry's death-dream connecting with the projected leg in Harry's cot. Harry has no last name, and his wife is named only once, *only* in his dream: "Helen had taken Compton aside and was speaking to him." She's not exactly Helen of Troy, but she links with Helen of Troy inasmuch as loving her—Harry's way of loving her—is destructive: "That's the good destruction." The Elizabethan meaning of *to love* in its double sense of *to love* is *to die* is exploited also in *A Farewell to Arms.*

Caroline Gordon in the textbook anthology *The House of Fiction* (1950) opines that Hemingway "has made no provision for the climax of his symbolic action. Our attention is not called to the snow-covered peaks of Kilimanjaro until the end of the story; as a result we do not feel that sense of recognition and inevitability which help to make a *katharsis*." At the end of Harry's dream, during which the perspective is from the airplane with images evoking a sense of Harry's belated nostalgic love for life, "all he could see, as wide as all the world, great, high, and unbelievably white in the sun, was the square top of Kilimanjaro. And then he knew that that was where he was going." But he isn't going there, not at all; because he has not earned admission to the heights, admission to "the House of God," as the western summit of Kilimanjaro is called.

> *Kilimanjaro is a snow covered mountain 19,710 feet high, and it is said to be the highest mountain in Africa. Its western summit is called the Masai 'Negàje Ngài,' the House of God. Close to the western summit there is the dried and frozen carcass of a leopard. No one has explained what the leopard was seeking at that altitude.*

The story opens with this italicized passage, which I presume is one of Harry's recollections since all his other recollections are likewise italicized passages. So, then, the symbol is not "something the writer has tacked on" (*contra* Caroline Gordon); but rather it is an integral part of the story. "He uses the snow-covered mountain of Kilimanjaro as the symbol of death, but the symbolism . . . is not part of the action and therefore does not operate as a controlling image. . . ." She damns the story as a magnificent failure, whereas I see it as a magnificent success.

Harry's "vision" of Kilimanjaro in his death-dream returns us at the end to the opening passage and shapes the whole in circular form. Immediately following that italicized image of the Kilimanjaro summit, which in effect is a riddle to be unriddled, Harry says: "The marvellous thing is that it is painless." But it wasn't painless for that leopard to ascend the summit, an ascent which Harry never attempted; he has attained an immortality which Harry never earned. The symbol is far more than simply a symbol of death. That leopard exceeded the nature and aspirations of his kind: *"No one has explained what the leopard was seeking at that altitude."* Well, he wasn't seeking immortality, being only a dumb beast; but he got just that in attaining the heights, admission to "the House of God."

In contrast to the noble leopard is the hyena which Harry imagines as death. Death "like a hyena"—but now suddenly shapeless, crouches and weighs down on his chest. "'You've got a hell of a breath,' he told it. 'You stinking bastard'." In addressing the stinking hyena Harry is addressing himself; Hyena Harry—a cowardly and carnivorous beast. Or he is addressing himself as vulture, since he imagines death also as a bird. "'Love is a dunghill,' said Harry. 'And I'm the cock that gets on it to crow.' 'If you have to go away,' she said, 'is it absolutely necessary to kill off everything you leave behind? I mean do you have to take away everything? Do you have to kill your horse, and your wife and burn your saddle and your armour?' 'Yes,' he said. 'Your damned money was my armour. My Swift and my Armour'." She is his Armour, a pun on his *Amour*. Not Helen of Troy, but rather Helen of Swift & Armour, the Chicago slaughter house; and as for Harry, he's Slaughter House Harry, as it were, slaughtering not only his wife but his "horse."

In the second Internal Monologue or stream of consciousness interlude Harry remembers an old man looking at the snow falling in the mountains of Bulgaria. Nansen's Secretary asks him "*if it were snow and the old man looking at it and saying, No, that's not snow. It's not snow and them all saying, It's not snow we were mistaken. But it was snow all right and he sent them on into it when he evolved exchange of populations. And it was snow they trampled along in until they died that winter.*" It is an incident depicting flight, retreat, betrayal; hence it mirrors Harry's own plight—Harry in flight from himself, Harry betraying himself. Like Nansen's Secretary, Harry betrays his trust.

Death by snow sums up that memoried image, but it is the snow that saves the deserter in the episode immediately subsequent: "*the deserter came with his feet bloody in the snow. He said the police were right behind him and they gave him woolen socks and held the gendarmes talking until the tracks had drifted over.*" Here again is flight, and in both actions snow is deceptive.

Next comes an image of skiers on snow "*as smooth to see as cake frosting and as light as powder and he remembered the noiseless rush the speed made as you dropped down like a bird.*" But "the snow was so bright it hurt your eyes"; so again snow is deceptive. And again the action is of flight.

Next comes the story of Herr Lent who lost at card-playing "*Everything, the skischule money and all the season's profit and then his capital.*" It occurs in a snow-blizzard, when they were snow-bound a week in the Madlener-haus, and Harry "*thought of all the time in his life he had spent gambling.*" Harry, too, has gambled on life and lost.

The fifth recollected experience evokes again the motif of betrayal. "*But he had never written a line of that, nor of the cold, bright Christmas day with the mountains showing across the plain that Gardner had flown across the lines to bomb the Austrian officers' leave train, machine-gunning them as they scattered and ran.*" He broke faith

during the Christmas truce. When he returned to his own men, somebody said: "*You bloody murderous bastard.*" Here again snow, though not mentioned, is implied; thus again the motifs of snow and death, snow and betrayal. Also, here again is an action of flight. The final two scenes are again reminiscences of skiing, of snow—"the fast-slipping rush of running powder-snow on crust"—as life. Thus Harry figures in these reminiscences as all these things: the betrayer, the deserter, the skier, the gambler, the murdering betrayer of code. And snow, figuring in all these scenes, associates with the title of the story and the snow-covered Kilimanjaro with its leopard as mock commentary on Harry's plight. He's no leopard transcending reality; Harry's merely the common bestial man devoid of transcendent virtues.

"The Snows of Kilimanjaro," says our biased critic, "lacks tonal and symbolic unity," but a close reading disproves that claim. "Its three planes of action, the man's intercourse with his wife, his communings with his soul, and the background of Enveloping Action, the mysterious Dark Continent, are never integrated." Well, let us examine what's what.

As the image of the leopard on Kilimanjaro's summit is integrated with the various incidents in the above recollections of Harry, so is it integrated with what Harry recollects in the subsequent italicized passage, Internal Monologue 3. It is again counterpointed against Harry as betrayer. Harry as two-timer writes the woman he loves that he cannot bear life without her, and her letter in reply is discovered by his wife: "'*Who is that letter from, dear?' and that was the end of the beginning of that.*" Even that same night he wrote her from the Club he went out and picked up a girl and took her out to supper, but he two-timed her: "*left her for a hot Armenian slut, that swung her belly against him so it almost scalded. He took her away from a British gunner subaltern after a row.*" Another incident he remembers has to do with artillery firing into its own troops, a metaphor of Harry destroying himself.

The fourth section of italicized reminiscences presents in contrast the happy Paris life when "*he had written the start of all he was to do. There never was another part of Paris that he loved like that,*" etc. He hadn't yet sold himself out to the rich; but he never got around to writing about the Paris he loved, nor in fact about any of the rest of his experiences.

Internal Monologue 5 follows close upon the previous recollection, and the final one of Williamson follows almost immediately. Their frequency increases towards the end of the narrative when Harry approaches death. Now he recalls the murder of an old man by a half-wit boy, whom Harry betrays. He gets the boy to aid him in packing the old man's body ("*frozen in the corral, and the dogs had eaten part of him*") onto a sled, "*and the two of you took it out over the road on skis, and sixty miles down to town to turn the boy over. He having no idea that he would be arrested. Thinking he had done his duty and that you were his friend and he would be rewarded. . . .*"

That was one story he had saved to write. Why?" Why Nothing sums up Harry. (Why Nothing sums up Dick Diver in *Tender is the Night,* who likewise sold himself out to the rich.) Harry remembers "poor Julian and his romantic awe of them and how he had started a story once that began, "'The very rich are different from you and me.' And how some one had said to Julian, Yes, they have more money. But that was not humorous to Julian. He thought they were a special glamorous race and when he found they weren't it wrecked him just as much as any other thing that wrecked him."

The fifth monologue spells out Harry as betrayer and links thus with the second and third italicized recollections. Again, it is a scene of death in snow and thus links with the second internal monologue. All six sections of italicized recollections present a death scene and link thus with the plight of the protagonist. Again, actions of betrayal are recurrent—in monologues number 2, 3, 4, and 5. To say that "Our attention is not called to the snow-covered peaks of Kilimanjaro until the end of the story" is to ignore these multiple interrelationships of recollected scenes with their recurrent motifs of death, deception, betrayal, and flight. The final death-dream is itself a scene of flight, flight from the Dark Continent to the House of God. The leopard made it there, but not Harry. To say that the leopard symbolism "is not part of the action and therefore does not operate as a controlling image" is to ignore the whole substance of Harry's recollected incidents; they furnish obliquely linked analogies with Harry himself and thematically they are counterpointed against the opening image of the leopard dead in the snows of Kilimanjaro's summit. Man betrays man; only the leopard is true. That opening image of the miraculous leopard operates, by my reading, as controlling and focal symbol. Don't underrate Hemingway!

William Van O'Connor (essay date 1962)

SOURCE: "Two Views of Kilimanjaro," in *The Grotesque: An American Genre and Other Essays,* Southern Illinois University Press, 1962, pp. 119-24.

[*In the following essay, O'Connor places "The Snows of Kilimanjaro" within the context of the genteel tradition in American literature.*]

In the early 1850's, Bayard Taylor made a trip to Africa, traveling in Egypt, Soudan, and Ethiopia. He wrote a book about his travels entitled *A Journey to Central Africa, or, Life and Landscapes from Egypt to the Negro Kingdoms of the White Nile.* He also wrote a number of poems, including one called "Kilimanjaro." In the early 1930's, Ernest Hemingway was hunting in Africa. Out of his experiences came *The Green Hills of Africa,* as well as **"The Short Happy Life of Francis McComber"** and **"The Snows of Kilimanjaro."** It is merely fortuitous, of course, that two American writers, almost a century apart, chose to write about the great African mountain. The coincidence, however, affords an oppor-

tunity to examine two separate traditions in the American literary mind.

It so happens that Hemingway made a statement in *The Green Hills of Africa* about the "genteel tradition." He said the genteel writers were "good men with the small, dried, and excellent wisdom of the Unitarians. . . . They were all very respectable. They did not use the words that people always have used in speech, the words that survive in language. Nor would you gather that they had bodies. They had minds, yes. Nice, dry, clean minds." Presumably Hemingway would call Taylor's "Kilimanjaro" a genteel poem. And of course it is.

The opening lines of the poem are designed to humanize the great mountain, to bring it into a proper relationship with man and civilization:

> Hail to thee, monarch of African mountains,
> Remote, inaccessible, silent, and lone,—
> Who, from the heart of the tropical fervors,
> Liftest to heaven thine alien snows,
> Feeding forever the fountains that make thee
> Father of Nile and Creator of Egypt.

In the second stanza the mountain is clearly placed inside the orbit of civilized doings:

> The years of the world are engraved on thy
>   forehead;
> Time's morning blushed red on thy first fallen
>   snows;

On the other hand, there is an acknowledgment of the mountain's foreign otherness: once she was lost in the wilderness, unknown, unnamed. Even so, Taylor implies, nature is under *our* spell:

> Knowledge alone is the being of Nature,
> Giving a soul to her manifold features,
> Lighting through paths of primitive darkness
> The footsteps of Truth and vision of Song
> Knowledge had born thee anew to Creation,
> And long-baffled Time at thy baptism rejoices.

Taylor, as poet, relates how floating in a boat on the Nile he scoops up water, "a magical mirror," and sees therein a vision of the mountain "supreme in the midst of her co-mates." He sees her as exhibiting, at various heights, the several seasons of the year:

> There, in the wondering airs of the Tropics
> Shivers the Aspen, still dreaming of cold:
> There stretches the Oak, from the loftiest ledges,
> His arms to the far-away lands of his brothers,
> And the Pine-tree looks down on his rival, the
>   Palm.

If the mountain is a little mysterious, it is none the less as orderly as the coming of the seasons. Comparing Mont Blanc and other great mountains with Kilimanjaro, Taylor says thay were "baptized." In other words, and unlike a later American poet, Wallace Stevens, he could not conceive that the gods of Africa would be appropriate to Africa. In Taylor's mind Kilimanjaro is seen as having been reduced to the jurisdiction of the European community.

Taylor was willing to have Kilimanjaro exotic, strange, and mysterious—but not too mysterious ("unseen but of God") and certainly not an object to contemplate with fear or terror. Taylor's own civilized order is interposed between himself and the great mountain rising from the hills and plains of central east Africa.

Near the end of December, 1933, Hemingway was in Tanganyika, where he fell ill with amoebic dysentery. He continued to hunt, but after a short period it was clear that he was too ill to remain. In mid-January a two-seater plane carried him 400 miles north for medical treatment, past Ngorongoro Crater and the Rift Escarpment to the town of Arusha and from there past the huge bulk of Kilimanjaro to Nairobi in Kenya.

In his **"The Snows of Kilimanjaro,"** a rather puzzling story, Hemingway makes use of the mountain as symbol. The oft debated epigraph to the story is this: "Kilimanjaro is a snow-covered mountain 19,710 feet high, and is said to be the highest mountain in Africa. Its western summit is called the Masai 'Ngaje Ngaji,' the House of God. Close to the western summit there is the dried and frozen carcass of a leopard. No one has explained what the leopard was seeking at that altitude."

The narrative itself recapitulates the life of Harry, a highly gifted writer. One learns that he has written a few good things, but mostly he has taken the easy way, even to marrying for money. Now, at the moment of the story's action, during a safari in Africa he is dying from gangrene. Half delirious, he picks quarrels with his wife, and he recalls many of his experiences. Suspense is maintained by the promised arrival of a plane that will pick him up and carry him to a town where his leg can be treated. There are several quite startling images of death. Finally, he dies. In the moments before he dies he has a fantasy in which the night has passed, the plane arrives, and he is put aboard and carried out (the reader, for the moment, thinks this is actually happening, but then learns that it is still night, Harry's wife has awakened and sees that he is dead). A part of the fantasy is this:

> And then instead of going on to Arusha they turned left, he [the pilot] evidently figured that they had the gas, and looking down he saw a pink sifting cloud, moving over the ground, and in the air, like the first snow in a blizzard, that comes from nowhere, and he knew the locusts were going to the East it seemed, and then it darkened and they were in a storm, the rain so thick it seemed like flying through a waterfall, and then they were out and Compie [the pilot] turned his head and grinned and pointed and there, ahead, all he could see, as wide as all the world, great, high, and unbelievably white in the sun, was the square top of Kilimanjaro. And then he knew that there was where he was going.

Man, like the leopard frozen near the western summit, pushes upward. As C. C. Walcutt has put it, all reason is against the leopard being found at that height and all reason is against Harry's ambition to rise above an "aimless materialism." Whatever it was that drove the leopard up there "is the same sort of mystery as the force that keeps idealism alive in Harry." But man is in material nature. The story tells us that Harry did capitulate. He had not written the true and beautiful stories it was in his power to write. He did not live to achieve what he might have achieved. Only in fantasy does he escape from the nature that has pulled him down. In his delirium, he believes he has escaped into the mysterious beauty that Kilimanjaro symbolizes—but he has not escaped. Among the final images in the story is one almost equally vivid with the white brilliance of the mountain: "She could see his bulk under the mosquito bar but somehow he had gotten his leg out and it hung down alongside the cot. The dressings had all come down and she could not look at it." Idealism does not always win. She has an implacable foe in physical decay which succeeds in winning major victories, perhaps the major victories.

Within Taylor's vision of civilization there is a far greater assurance of strength and abiding influence than there is in Hemingway's vision. Historically, it is that the affirmations of the "genteel tradition" gave way, as everyone knows, to affirmations of a more qualified sort. Taylor, the nineteenth-century visitor to Africa, was assured that the primitive could be civilized, whereas Hemingway, the twentieth-century visitor, feels or knows that the "primitive" is a part of civilization. To develop this point much further would entail an examination of the "genteel tradition" and certain of the reactions to it. Perhaps it is sufficient to observe, once more, that Taylor, the genteel poet, superimposed a civilized order of things on a nature that the twentieth-century man sees as alien or at least as apart from him. Taylor was in awe of the mountain, but not so profoundly in awe of it as Hemingway was.

Between Bayard Taylor and Hemingway lay the breakup of the genteel tradition. George Santayana, in his brilliant lecture, "The Genteel Tradition in American Philosophy," says "the three American writers whose personal endowment was perhaps the finest—Poe, Hawthorne and Emerson—had all a certain starved, abstract quality. They could not retail the genteel tradition; they were too keen for that. But life offered them little digestible material, nor were they naturally voracious." Santayana is saying that Poe, Emerson and Hawthorne tried to turn away from the genteel tradition, and in doing so had to become highly subjective writers.

James, he says, treated the matter differently. "Mr. Henry James has [freed himself] by turning the genteel American tradition as he turns everything else, into a subject-matter for analysis. For him it is a curious habit of mind, intimately comprehended, to be compared with other habits of mind, also well known to him. Thus he has overcome the genteel tradition in the classic way, by understanding it."

James's "The Madonna of the Future" (1873) is an excellent example of what Santayana means. James was only thirty when he wrote it—and obviously he had been thinking about his future as an American writer. His father's generation had aspired to create the Beautiful, and most of them managed to achieve little or nothing, because the Beautiful as a transcendental entity does not exist. Undoubtedly James feared this could happen to him. It was also, one would guess, a reason why he chose to live in Europe.

James invents a painter, an old man, an American exile. The scene is Florence. The old painter dreams of the great madonna he will one day produce. He sits in a shabby room before a canvas, getting ready to paint it. Meanwhile his "beautiful" young subject has aged twenty years, becoming stout, coarse and vulgar. The painter "sees" her as she was. It would never occur to him to paint her as she is. When forced to see her as she actually is, he is shocked and shortly thereafter dies.

There is a second artist, a cynical Italian, who is the woman's lover. He does obscene statuettes of monkeys and cats in amorous relationships. He says, "The idea's bold; does it strike you as happy? Cats and monkeys— monkeys and cats—all human life is there! Human life, of course I mean, viewed with the eye of the satirist! To combine sculpture and satire, signore, has been my unprecedented ambition. I flatter myself I have not egregiously failed." The young American admits they are "strikingly clever and expressive."

James is saying that beauty must come fron lived experiences, and these may include the sordid and the ugly. Human life isn't all cats and monkeys—but they are a part of it. A dream of art separated from actuality is unnatural and doomed to failure. That is why, as James implies in "The Author of Beltraffio," the genteel tradition produced no serious art.

The genteel writers, and Taylor is an example, turned their backs on actuality. They separated love from sex, tried to separate the ideal from the forces of materialism and nature, and to create an art that ignored commonplace and sometimes unpleasant or distressing human impulses or actions. Howells, Crane, Dreiser, Anderson and others struggled to free themselves from the genteel. One might almost say that for Hemingway in **"The Snows of Kilimanjaro"** the process is reversed: sex struggles to relate itself to love, and materialism and nature struggle to relate themselves to the ideal. Human impulses, pleasant and unpleasant, are the material of the art, and contribute to its beauty.

William Goldhurst   (essay date 1963)

SOURCE: "Ernest Hemingway," in *F. Scott Fitzgerald and His Contemporaries,* The World Publishing Company, 1963, pp. 155-216.

[In the following excerpt, Goldhurst compares the figure of the failed writer in works by Hemingway and F. Scott Fitzgerald.]

The destroyed writer is an American phenomenon and something of an American preoccupation. The fate of such literary artists as Edgar Allan Poe and Hart Crane seems more typical, to many observers at least, than the opposite image of established solidity typified by William Dean Howells. Van Wyck Brooks, for example, has commented at some length upon what he calls "the abortive career" of the American literary artist. The same theme has attracted the attention of some of our leading fictionists: Henry James remarked that the American writer seemed destined to follow a pattern of "broken careers, orphaned children, early disasters, violent deaths." James's comment is but one of many that stress the native tendency toward unfulfilled talent, alcoholism, and suicide—comments that seem to culminate in Fitzgerald's "Crack-Up" essays. "No one of us escapes it," said Sherwood Anderson, speaking of the "tragedy" of the creative man in America. "How can he?"

If Anderson's remark is exaggerated, it is nevertheless true that many American writers, among them Ring Lardner and Scott Fitzgerald, reveal a tendency toward tragic misfortune in their personal and professional histories. It is also true that the theme of the ruined writer has received considerable attention from many of our critics and fictionists. Hemingway appears to have been much interested in this theme in the mid nineteen-thirties, but his fullest and most important treatment of it occurs in **"The Snows of Kilimanjaro"** (written in 1936). The hero of the story, a man named Harry, has for a number of years entertained a profound desire to write about his experiences, vividly remembered from his wanderings in Europe and America. But he has never realized this ambition; instead, he has gradually yielded to his preference for the pleasures of love-making, the company of rich women, and the life of ease that has softened his determination to exercise his literary talent. It is Harry's failure, treated in a tone of overwhelming regret, that Hemingway dramatizes in **"The Snows of Kilimanjaro."**

The story is set in Africa, where Harry and his wealthy American wife have set out upon a hunting expedition; Harry has the idea that the rigors of the trip will help toughen him up and restore his creative powers, or at least restore his ability to apply himself to his work. But the safari breaks down when one of the native guides burns out a bearing in the truck and Harry discovers that a cut on his leg has become infected and gangrenous. Now, as he lies dying of his wound—a symbol of the decay of his talent—Harry relives in his mind those experiences he has wanted to record on paper. He also tries to define the reasons for his failure to do so.

> Now he would never write the things that he had saved to write until he knew enough to write them well. Well, he would not have to fail at trying to write them either. Maybe you could never write them, and that

was why you put them off and delayed the starting. Well he would never know, now.

What was his talent anyway? It was a talent all right but instead of using it, he had traded on it. It was never what he had done, but always what he could do. And he had chosen to make his living with something else instead of a pen or a pencil.

We must all be cut out for what we do, he thought. However you make your living is where your talent lies. He had sold vitality, in one form or another, all his life and when your affections are not too involved you give much better value for the money. He had found that out but he would never write that, now, either. No, he would not write that, although it was well worth writing.

She shot very well this good, this rich bitch, this kindly caretaker and destroyer of his talent. Nonsense. He had destroyed his talent himself. Why should he blame this woman because she kept him well? He had destroyed his talent by not using it, by betrayals of himself and what he believed in, by drinking so much that he blunted the edge of his perceptions, by laziness, by sloth, and by snobbery, by pride and by prejudice, by hook and by crook.

If Harry's tragedy sounds somehow familiar to readers of the fiction of the period, it is because Scott Fitzgerald had rehearsed the same story a few years earlier in *Tender Is the Night*. Dick Diver, too, has "sold vitality, in one form or another"—to the group of expatriates who are drawn to his control and charm, and to his wife Nicole, whom he has been "hired" to love and protect. Like Harry, Diver has undergone emotional and professional deterioration because his wife's wealth has made effort unnecessary; like Hemingway's hero, Dick Diver has become accustomed to the comfort that corrupts the will and destroys ambition. Like Harry, too, Diver is ambivalent about the reasons for his deterioration: he vacillates between placing the blame upon his own weakness and the seductive leisure purchased by the Warren fortune: "I can't do anything for you any more," says Diver to Nicole near the end of the novel. "I'm trying to save myself."

"From my contamination?" [asks Nicole.]

"Profession throws me in contact with questionable company sometimes."

She wept with anger at the abuse.

"You're a coward! You've made a failure of your life, and you want to blame it on me."

Diver and Harry also share similar attitudes, in their decline, toward the wealthy class of American idlers with whom they have been associated. "The rich were dull and they drank too much," Harry reflects near the end of Hemingway's story. "They were dull and they were rep-

etitious." In one of the concluding chapters of Fitzgerald's novel, Mary Minghetti tells Dick Diver: "Nobody cares whether you drink or not. Even when Abe drank hardest, he never offended people like you do." Diver replies: "You're all so dull."

Finally, for all the surface description of Diver's professional involvements with psychiatry, the hero of *Tender Is the Night* may be accurately considered a ruined artist of the sort Hemingway writes about in **"The Snows of Kilimanjaro."** By making his hero a doctor rather than a writer Fitzgerald no doubt hoped to gain distance and detachment. But his efforts were not completely successful. Biographical data support the notion, already mentioned by several students of Fitzgerald's fiction, that in *Tender Is the Night* the novelist was projecting his anxiety about his own career and emotional instability. There is, furthermore, strong internal evidence that Fitzgerald conceived of Dick Diver's career as parallel, in many respects, to his own. All through *Tender Is the Night* there are references to Diver's literary activity. An early episode mentions his publication of an extremely popular medical treatise ("The little book is selling everywhere," says Nicole. "They want it published in six languages.")— an obvious counterpart to Fitzgerald's best-selling novels. And during the central sections of *Tender Is the Night* Diver struggles, at times aimlessly, to complete another medical text. Finally, in the last chapter Fitzgerald returns to the unfinished manuscript to give particular emphasis to Diver's loss of ambition, the decline of his professional dedication: "he always had a big stack of papers on his desk that were known to be an important treatise on some medical subject, almost in process of completion."

Thus Fitzgerald's *Tender Is the Night* traces the same pattern as **"The Snows of Kilimanjaro"** and reveals, indirectly at least, the same interest in the blighted artistic career and the decay of a writer's talent. An important aspect of Diver's tragedy, like Harry's, is that "he would never write the things he had saved to write until he knew enough to write them well." It might also be worth repeating, in conclusion, that Harry and Dick Diver have been victimized by the same forces. Temperamental weakness, to be sure, plays a part in the misfortunes of both heroes. But Hemingway and Fitzgerald have stressed as well the ruinous influence of a luxurious life provided by wealthy American women.

Earl Rovit (essay date 1963)

SOURCE: "The Real Thing," in *Ernest Hemingway*, Twayne Publishers, 1963, pp. 35-9.

[*In the following excerpt, Rovit examines the theme of artistic failure in "The Snows of Kilimanjaro."*]

Although many of Hemingway's heroes might nominally qualify as artists—Jake Barnes, writer; Nick Adams, writer; Frederick Henry, architect; Richard Cantwell, expert in general; Robert Jordan, writer—only Harry of **"The**

Snows of Kilimanjaro" is presented convincingly as a writer; and only he seems actively concerned with the problems created by his calling. Structurally the story is rather simple—a variation on Ambrose Bierce's classic "An Occurrence at Owl Creek Bridge." Harry, the writer, tries to come to terms with the fact of his approaching death; he has a badly gangrenous leg which is too far advanced to be cured, even though a rescue airplane is expected on the following day to carry him out of the African bush to the nearest hospital. He spends the afternoon and early evening quarreling with his wealthy wife, berating himself for having wasted his talents, remembering sharp vignettes of the past that he had always intended to use in his writing but never did. The last section of the story (as in Bierce's model) is a description of the arrival of the airplane and its ascent to the top of Kilimanjaro: "great, high, and unbelievably white in the sun." Then the story flashes back to the dead Harry discovered by his wife, and we realize that the airplane ride was Hemingway's trick on the reader. The story is prefaced by the following epigraph: "Kilimanjaro is a snow-covered mountain 19,710 feet high, and is said to be the highest mountain in Africa. Its western summit is called the Masai 'Ngaje Ngai,' the House of God. Close to the western summit there is the dried and frozen carcass of a leopard. No one has explained what the leopard was seeking at that altitude."

Thematically the story is also relatively simple, and it is reminiscent of Henry James's "The Middle Years" in which another writer confronts the fact of death and berates himself and life for not having time enough to write the things he is now ready to do. If we approach **"The Snows of Kilimanjaro"** from the special view with which we have been concerned, we will see that Hemingway used a traditional structure and a conventional theme to achieve his own peculiar ends; and we will also see that Harry is a kind of extended portrait of the artist, similar in attitude to the portrait of Belmonte previously cited.

First, there are some obvious, paired contrasts within the story: the snow, clean and cold on the mountain top and in Harry's reminiscence, as against "the heat shimmer of the plain" which becomes associated with the ugly rotting leg. Similarly, "the dried and frozen carcass" of the leopard is contrasted to the wide-snouted hyena which is the harbinger and final announcer of Harry's death. Through various devices, Helen is contrasted with Harry and associated with the heat, the plain, the gangrene, and the hyena. The contrasts are all neat and in balance, with the exception of Harry; he, of course, is connected to the leg, Helen, and the hyena—even as he dreams of the snow and the ascent beyond the plain. And it is Harry's character that provides the key to the story. He is not, at all, a nice man. He is a liar, a quarreler, and a traitor to himself as well as to other people. "He had sold vitality, in one form or another, all his life and when your affections are not too involved you give much better value for the money." He had married Helen, he tells us, for security and comfort, and he had never loved her. And yet, "it was strange . . . that he should be able to give her more for her money than when he had really loved."

Several things should be obvious. Harry is egocentric, hypocritical, and morally as well as physically rotten; and yet the thrust of values in the story elevates him to the snow-capped summit and forces the reader to accept him as a superior man. Helen, on the other hand, is honest, generous, and reasonably intelligent; yet she is left at the end of the story with the unbandaged leg that she cannot bear to look at. Harry disposes of her for himself and for the reader in one sentence: "She was always thoughtful, he thought. On anything she knew about, or had read, or that she had ever heard." On normal standards of valuation, this would seem to be generous praise; but in terms of the story, it is clear that this is enough to make Helen despicable. Harry, it would seem, is thoughtful on things he *doesn't* know about, *hasn't* read, and *hasn't ever heard*. He is justly contemptuous of artists, like Julian (F. Scott Fitzgerald), who have been wrecked. He is justly contemptuous of Helen and her total *milieu*; he is "a spy in their country" and, by implication, a mysterious stranger in all countries save that which he shares with a frozen leopard at an altitude of almost 20,000 feet. And the only source of his marvellous superiority is that "for years it [death] had obsessed him; but now it meant nothing in itself." That, and the fact that in the face of death, he performs his craft; *he writes*. This is what makes him superior; this is what gives him "the feeling of immortality" which is vouchsafed to him in his ascent to the mountain.

It is fair to say that Hemingway succeeds in "The Snows of Kilimanjaro" in insulting his audience beyond endurance, in making the audience eat its own wounds, and like it.

—*Earl Rovit*

The portrait of Harry is thus very similar to the earlier picture of Belmonte [from *The Sun Also Rises*]. Both are sick with disgust at their unknowing audiences (Helen is Harry's audience), but both, presumably, attain a level of inner possession which can only be called beatific. Harry differs from Belmonte in that he manages in an offhand way to satisfy his audience even with the gangrene. The remarkable *tour de force* of the story is that Hemingway is able to present a thoroughly upside-down world to readers who must not be very different from Helen—and to make them like it. And here we must mention the hyena in order to appreciate the full resonance of the *tour de force*. The hyena is introduced into the story in such a way as to connect it to the obscenely squatting vultures which sit with their "naked heads sunk in their hunched feathers," presumably waiting for Harry's death. It, like them, is called "a filthy animal" and a "bastard," and it is quickly associated with the "sudden evil-smelling emptiness" that characterizes the approach of both the gangrene and death in the narrative. But *after* Harry dies, the hyena appears again: "Just then the hyena stopped whimpering in the night and started to make a strange, human, almost crying sound." He continues to do this until Helen wakes up and discovers the corpse. If the hyena were simply meant to stand for death, its continual symbolic use is a foolish distraction which dissipates the force of the story. And why the emphasis on "human," especially since the hyena's crying is almost the first "human" sound in the story?

It is possible to suggest an interpretation for the hyena which will be in keeping with the reading of the story and the portraiture of the artist that we have been examining, if we call to mind Hemingway's description of the "highly humorous" hyena in *Green Hills of Africa*. The hyena is a source of much amusement in that book because of the obscenely funny contortions that he goes through when he is shot.

> . . . the pinnacle of hyenic humor, was the hyena, the classic hyena, that hit too far back while running, would circle madly, snapping and tearing at himself until he pulled his own intestines out, and then stood there, jerking them out and eating them with relish. . . . Fisi, the hyena, hermaphroditic, self-eating devourer of the dead, trailer of calving cows, ham-stringer, potential biter-off of your face at night while you slept, sad yowler, camp-follower, stinking, foul . . . Mongrel dog-smart in the face . . .

The despicable hyena joins Helen in weeping for the dead artist, because the hyena becomes a distended identification of the audience that the artist must serve. Fickle, treacherous, stupid and cunning at the same time, it is quick to lament the loss of the artist, even as it is quick to harry him down when he is alive. Without pushing the metaphor too far, it is fair to say that Hemingway succeeds in this story in insulting his audience beyond endurance, in making the audience eat its own wounds, and like it. There is surely a more than savage irony in the "human, almost crying sound" that ends the tale; and the reflection that Hemingway was reputed to have received $125,000 for the movie rights to this story merely compounds the irony.

Robert W. Lewis, Jr. (essay date 1965)

SOURCE: "Woman or Wife?" in *Hemingway on Love*, Haskell House Publishers, 1973, pp. 97-110.

[In the following essay, originally published in 1965, Lewis explores the relationship between Helen and Harry, concluding Harry is portrayed as a tragic romantic.]

"The Snows of Kilimanjaro" is in some ways similar to **"The Short Happy Life of Francis Macomber."** It was published a month before the Macomber story, and both are set in East Africa while an American couple is on safari. On the surface, **"The Snows"** seems to have as its theme the corruption of the American writer, but although this approach to the story is a profitable one, the fact that Harry is a writer is not of great consequence. Harry's role transcends his particular profession, and his story may also be read as one of the corruption of love. As Carlos Baker has said about the Macomber and Kilimanjaro stories:

> Both deal . . . with the achievement and loss of moral manhood. Both look further into the now familiar men-without-women theme. The focal point in each is the corrupting power of women and money, two of the forces aggressively mentioned in *Green Hills of Africa* as impediments to American writing men.

Aside from the obvious differences in the action of the two stories, **"The Snows"** differs from **"Macomber"** chiefly in the variations of the men and women's characterizations. Both Margot Macomber and Helen of **"The Snows"** are dominating women who are good at and enjoy love-making, but Helen's dominance is passive—it does not take the form of the active bitchery of Margot. Harry has willingly submitted to the protection and power of wealthy Helen, while it was Margot Macomber who stayed with Francis because he had money. Helen is "tolerant" of Harry's male bitchery, while it was Francis Macomber who was tolerant of Margot. Helen reads "enormously" and is overly influenced by books, while Francis was the bookworm of the Macombers. And finally, if one applies the Tristan myth to **"The Snows,"** a different role is seen for the Hemingway woman. Helen can be read as a type of Iseult of the White Hand, while Margot, if anything, was the other, first Iseult, Iseult the Fair. (Iseult of the White Hand was Tristan's unsatisfactory substitute for Iseult the Fair; he married Iseult of the White Hand but never loved her, and in revenge she finally betrays him. The name Helen may justifiably suggest the Trojan Paris' wife.)

These variations on a theme suggest several things: Hemingway was intent upon following through with some of the ideas suggested to him by *Green Hills of Africa*. But he was not sure what the best embodiment of his ideas would be, or, perhaps, he did not know until he wrote both stories what he wanted to say. He had recognized a fertile situation for good fiction in his exotic African setting, and, in the manner of some of his earlier fiction, he chose to write more than one story about the material, as if approaching it in two ways would get more out of it or guarantee that he had missed nothing of importance in the imaginative situation. See the uses of the Italian wound, for instance, in *The Sun Also Rises, A Farewell to Arms, Across the River and into the Trees,* and several short stories.

"The Snows" is not, therefore, a simple preface to or a superfluous variation of **"Macomber."** It is a very good story that embodies ideas of its own. My point here is simply that it is a better story when read in the light of comparison with and contrast to *Green Hills of Africa* and **"Macomber."** And like those two works, **"The Snows"** is largely concerned with a romantic vision of life and love.

Like the Macombers, Harry and Helen would seem to be an ideal couple with "everything to live for." But Harry is a morally sick man; his physical wound is symbolic of his inner illness. The wound to his leg epitomizes his sickness, for it is a type of castration wound and had been subconsciously self-inflicted. (Harry had neglected a thorn scratch and then treated it improperly.) Like Francis Macomber he has been partially responsible for the loss of his manhood, and he has, or imagines he has, a devouring mate eager to seize any sexual advantage.

Harry himself regards his life as a failure. He has prostituted his art: "each day of not writing, of comfort, of being that which he despised, dulled his ability and softened his will to work so that, finally, he did no work at all." The months and years of idleness slip by. He never acts, he never loves, he never carries out his plans. He returns to Africa simply because he had once been happy there, and he thinks perhaps there he can "work the fat off his soul." Scorning the challenge of real life all around him, he postpones writing the stories he knows, and he postpones loving an eminently lovable woman simply because she is his and is available at the present moment.

His is the sickness of Tristan; his end is the obscene, filthy, diseased product of a romantic dream in which the present is bitter and only the past contains any happiness. Thus the flashbacks and the action in them and in the fantasy death-flight at the end of the story. Present time in the story is static, passive. Yet in his sickness, bitterness, and remorse, where is Harry? Irony of ironies, he, like Melville in *Typee*, is in the Garden of Eden. He had returned to Africa because "Africa was where he had been happiest in the good time of his life, so he had come out here to start again." But the myth of the eternal return, the recapturing of the "good times," is destroyed by the gangrenous wound that attracts vultures and hyenas. Here on the beautiful, teeming plain near Mt. Kilimanjaro and its western summit, called the House of God, Harry is to die with his dreams unfulfilled.

"This was a pleasant camp under big trees against a hill, with good water, and close by, a nearly dry water hole where sand grouse flighted in the morning." And here too are Adam and Eve back in the Garden, trying desperately to pretend they are something else, and Harry feeling very sorry that the only way to the House of God is death.

The epigraph to the story has caused some uneasiness, but as soon as one accepts the possibility of a mythic dimension in the story, it seems rather obviously a device to alert the reader to a point contained within the story, a point which follows Harry's death but which is to be kept in mind throughout the story. Kilimanjaro is a sacred mountain, a type of the sacred mountains widely used in ancient myths and familiar to our culture through Biblical mountains, Dante's Mount Purgatory, Bunyan's Delectable Mountains, and others. It is the meeting point of heaven, earth, and hell from which the universe spreads out. At its base the earthly Paradise is traditionally located, and the road to the center of the universe and this sacred mountain is always a difficult one.

That Kilimanjaro "is said to be the highest mountain in Africa," that a leopard's body lies near the western summit, the House of God, and that "no one has explained what the leopard was seeking at that altitude," all indicate the sacred nature of the mountain and the religious or mythic nature of Harry's fantasy at the end of the story. In addition to having a Sacred Mountain, Dante's *Commedia* also has a leopard, a symbol of worldly pleasure and lechery, the values that Harry has traded his art for. Thus the appropriateness of Harry's flight to join the leopard in death at the top of the mountain. Clearly, what both the leopard and Harry were seeking is the House of God, the summit to which the leopard has irrationally climbed and to which Harry flies at his death, finally achieving in his longed-for death that happiness which he never permitted himself in life: "There, ahead, all he could see, as wide as all the world, great, high, and unbelievably white in the sun, was the square top of Kilimanjaro. And then he knew that there was where he was going."

The day before his death Harry had resolved that "because no thing could hurt him if he did not care . . . he would not care for death." Thus he would conquer death; it would have no dominion. The death that had obsessed him all his life would die. In five flashbacks Harry returns to his past, and each time his thoughts turn to scenes of death or love. The combination is significant.

It has been noted before that death and eros are somehow related. The Greek sculptor modeling Eros and Death with similar features and the metaphysical poet punning with "die" to mean sexual intercourse are followed by the popular song and the popular novel that sentimentalize death. The first of Hemingway's flashbacks tells of death and suffering that Harry has seen. All the scenes are of winter, and snow is instrumental in the death of the fleeing Greek refugees, though it covers the tracks of the deserter. Harry remembers too the skiing he enjoyed so much. These random thoughts, reminding us of the title and the epigraph, prepare for the denouement, because snow is a death symbol and skiing is both a type of the death flight (which is explicit at the end of the story) and a type of the sexual act.

In the second flashback the combination of eros and death or violence is elaborated. Here Harry clarifies what the earlier loves of his life were, those loves that he can never find in Helen. The Tristan syndrome is at work again: Harry has had a succession of lovers, but it is only his first love, his unrequited love, that is real for him. The flashback begins with Harry alone and lonely in Constantinople, apparently covering the Greco-Turk War, as Hemingway did in the fall of 1922. Harry had left Paris after a quarrel with his wife (not his lover), "whored the whole time" in a futile attempt to "kill his loneliness, but only made it worse," and then "had written her, the first one, the one who left him, a letter telling her how he had never been able to kill it." He writes to her that he thought he once saw her in Paris, and followed the woman, and felt "faint and sick inside," and all the women he had slept with since knowing her only made him miss her more, and "he knew he could not cure himself of loving her."

After sending the letter, asking her to write, "and that night missing her so much it made him feel hollow sick inside," he takes a hot Armenian belly-scalding slut away from a British subaltern after a fist fight and sleeps with the "smooth, rose-petal, syrupy, smooth-bellied, big-breasted" woman who "needed no pillow under her buttocks. . . ."

The next day he accompanies a Greek attack that is horribly botched—the new officers are incompetent, the artillery fires into its own troops, the Greeks run and are shot by their officers, and there follows things that are "much worse." In contrast to this elemental struggle, he returns to Paris and finds a stupid-looking, potato-faced American poet talking about Dada to the affected Roumanian Tristan Tzara, founder of the Dada movement.

Harry is in love again with his wife, their quarrel is over, the madness all over, but the "first one," the one he gets sick over, answers his letter, and his wife finds out about his "sickness," and "that was the end of the beginning of that."

Harry concludes his reverie by remembering all his numerous quarrels with women, quarrels that always took place when he was feeling best. He had seen the world change and a "subtler change" that it was his duty to write of, but now he never would.

In this flashback are revealed Harry's real problem and the concepts of eros, agape, and romantic love. Contrary to the popular image of the Hemingway hero as a free lover, we see here sexual indulgence with an important qualification or reservation. Eros, Harry finds, is no remedy for romantic love. It is hard to overemphasize the importance of Harry's thinking he could not cure himself of love.

The irony of longing for a woman in the past who rejected him is beyond Harry's grasp, but at least he recognizes it as a sickness, and he also returns un-Tristan-like to a wife whom he also loves. When the flashback ends, we can see Harry repeating himself. In Africa he quarrels with another woman whom he thinks he does not love. But what might he have thought of Helen had he lived another ten years and found himself with another woman? He would have thought of Helen as a woman he once loved; he would remember with longing those "good breasts" and "useful thighs" that he looks on rather academically now.

A further irony which Hemingway must consciously intend is his use of the real name of the affected Roumanian in Paris. Tristan Tzara is obviously too sophisticated to have an Iseult.

The flashback has another interest in its biographical parallels. Not only was Hemingway a war correspondent in the Greco-Turk War, but he was also caught in a compromising situation much as Harry was. Hemingway's "first one"—Iseult—was Agnes II. von Kurowsky, the real-life counterpart of Catherine Barkley of *A Farewell to Arms*. When he was married to Hadley Richardson, his first wife, he reportedly wrote a "fond letter" to Agnes, and incompatibility eventually led to his divorce from Hadley. One biographer, Milt Machlin [*The Private Hell of Hemingway*] even assumes that Hadley, like Helen in **"The Snows,"** knew of a reply from Agnes, but there is no evidence for assuming the historicity of every event in the story. From Hemingway's "true" account of the African safari, *Green Hills of Africa,* we may read of his warm, happy relationship with P.O.M., Pauline Pfeiffer, his second wife. Hemingway later said that he, like Harry, had been happiest in Africa, but, unlike Harry, he said that Pauline was the best wife he ever had. Thus the changes in the Macomber and Kilimanjaro stories must be considered major. Is the legal relationship of man and woman also changed?

Both Carlos Baker [in *Hemingway: The Writer as Artist*] and Philip Young [in *Ernest Hemingway*] tacitly assume that Harry and Helen are man and wife; both critics refer to Helen, in passing, as "wife." And, indeed, if one reads the story casually, there is little reason to suppose that they are not married. Engstrom [in *MLN*, 1950] however, refers to Helen as Harry's mistress: "His wealthy mistress is with him." Although Engstrom is writing about the mountain and leopard symbolism, he goes on to quote a passage from the story which contains the hints "this rich bitch" and "she kept him well."

If Harry and Helen are not married, a further variation on the situation common to *Green Hills of Africa* and **"Macomber"** would be established and would be of importance to a consideration of Hemingway's love ethic. The evidence is this: at the outset of **"Macomber"** it is clearly established that the Macombers are man and wife. In **"The Snows"** Helen is never directly referred to as Harry's wife, and there is only one allusion to her as a wife. That allusion, significantly, comes from Helen's own lips. After the first flashback Harry asks Helen where they stayed in Paris.

> "At the Crillon. . . ."
>
> "There and at the Pavillion Henri-Quatre in St. Germain. You said you loved it there."
>
> "Love is a dunghill," said Harry. "And I'm the cock that gets on it to crow."
>
> "If you have to go away," she said, "is it absolutely necessary to kill off everything you leave behind? I mean do you have to take away everything? Do you have to kill your horse, and your wife and burn your saddle and your armour?"
>
> "Yes," he said. "Your damned money was my armour. My Swift and my Armour."

The soft woman uses the euphemism "go away" for "die" and sentimentalizes his death to produce an ironic effect for the reader and for Harry, one which he seizes upon in his pun. She seriously envisions Harry as a medieval knight, but her history is not accurate if she thinks of him as a Tristan and of herself as his legal wife. It was Iseult the Fair, the adulteress, who died at Tristan's death, not his wife, Iseult of the White Hand. But if Helen thinks metaphorically of her relation with her Tristan Harry, then indeed they are man and wife, married in spirit and undying devotion if not in fact. Harry's bitterness toward her and the corrupting influence on his art of her wealth is thus capsuled in his pun. While she romanticizes, he plays to the groundlings, and the pun has a nice appropriateness as it links the names of two large meat-packing houses, in which Helen might possibly have had a financial interest, with Harry, another piece of meat, no longer much of a man, decaying and dying in the pre-eminent land of carnivores, with hyenas and vultures waiting for their Treet.

At least Helen's remark establishes the possibility that Harry and she are married. Contrary evidence would include Harry's remark, "'If you hadn't left your own people . . . to take me on—'" and the previously cited "she kept him well." In other places "he went to her," and "she had acquired him." Never is it "married me" or "married him." In indirect discourse Harry usually thinks of her as "the woman," "the rich bitch," or simply "she." The other characters, the servants and the pilot, Compton, use the indeterminate "Memsahib." In speaking or thinking of him, Helen uses "dear," "darling," and "Harry," but never "husband."

When one notices the ambiguity of the relationship, as indicated by these names and phrases, the contrast with **"Macomber"** is striking. In that story the marriage of the pair was painful, emphatic, and clear. The conclusion that might be drawn is that if Harry and Helen are married, as probably most critics and readers assume, phrases like "take me on," "kept him," and "acquired him" connote the cheapness and shallowness of their marriage, which is in fact more like a prolonged affair than a marriage. (Such a view is sensible and would gain some support from Hemingway's position as a defender of marriage in his own life. The state of marriage apparently had value for Hemingway, and he respected it through four marriages.) Perhaps the reader who assumes that marriage binds Harry and Helen believes so because Harry is so manifestly unhappy, and no such couple would stay together except for moral and legal sanctions. Such reasoning would have greater merit if Harry and Helen were pictured as creatures of traditional Anglo-Saxon morality, but they are not. Such reasoning also underestimates both the power of money, the armour that Helen supplies so abundantly, and the weakness of Harry. Harry is poor but dishonest, willing to let Helen believe he loves her for the sake of his security.

"It was strange that when he did not love her at all and was lying, that he should be able to give her more for her money than when he had really loved." If he were married to her, he would perhaps have no reason to sham his love to keep his material position except for the reason of common decency that would not allow him to hurt the naive woman who had bounced about from man to man and now thinks she has found her true love. On the other hand, she tells him once that the money "'was always yours as much as mine'."

In any event, the ambiguity of their relationship indicates the relative unimportance to them of the technical state of marriage and the breakdown, by extension, of the institution of marriage. For the Macombers and for Harry and Helen it is hard to see where adultery leaves off and marriage begins, where hate leaves off and love begins.

Harry's feelings for Helen are violently mixed. Although he had "sold vitality" in exchange for security and comfort, he had received a bonus along with his regular dividends.

> She was still a good-looking woman, he thought, and she had a pleasant body. She had a great talent and appreciation for the bed, she was not pretty, but he liked her face, she read enormously, liked to ride and shoot and, certainly, she drank too much. . . .

> She was a damned nice woman too. He would as soon be in bed with her as any one; rather with her, because she was richer, because she was very pleasant and appreciative and because she never made scenes.

> She looked at him with her well-known, well-loved face from *Spur* and *Town and Country*, only a little the worse for drink, only a little the worse for bed, but *Town and Country* never showed those good breasts and those useful thighs and those lightly small-of-back-caressing hands, and as he looked and saw her well-known pleasant smile, he felt death come again.

Quite fittingly he feels death at the same moment that he feels eros.

Yet he hates Helen for another reason than that he fears death and associates love for her with it. He has a deep-seated malaise that prevents him from enjoying this kind, somewhat groping and distressed woman who waits only on him, who seems in fact to have an obsessive regard for him, who possesses him just as she possesses her money. The night Harry dies, Helen has a dream about her daughter and her very rude father. That night Harry has been rude to Helen too, and a likely excuse for the presence of the dream in the story is that Helen has an Electra complex.

Like the Macombers, they are repeatedly quarreling, or rather Harry is, since Helen tries her best to avoid disputes. Harry insists on being brutally realistic about his gangrenous wound, but Helen would rather not recognize the odor and pain and the hyenas and the vultures, signs of Harry's death and her loneliness. His resignation bewilders her. Her hopefulness is only bitter irony for him who has already felt death and knows its closeness. He hates Helen for being rich, for putting him in an inferior role, being dominated by her money; but of course it is himself he must ultimately hate for succumbing to her temptations. And he must hate, too, the example of her selflessness which she thrusts upon him, even if he knows it stems from her fear of being left alone.

Although he cannot see it, this romancer who thinks he is being cruelly realistic is destroying Helen's love for him, just as his quarrels destroyed his previous loves.

> "Why, I loved you," Helen protests. "I love you now. I'll always love you. Don't you love me?"
>
> "No," said the man. "I don't think so. I never have."

His love is the "first one," or the last one, but always a phantom.

He thinks to himself:

> He had never quarreled much with this woman, while with the women that he loved he had quarrelled so much they had finally, always, with the corrosion of the quarrelling, killed what they had together. He had loved too much, demanded too much, and he wore it all out.

What a commentary on true love! Since Harry doesn't love Helen, they don't quarrel much. She is "a fine woman, marvellous really." "He had been cruel and unjust," but he doesn't love her!

Both Helen and Harry affect the Tristan-Iseult pose, but in different ways. It has been noted that Harry has been bitterly realistic about his imminent death that started with an innocent-seeming thorn scratch. That bitterness, however, is not the opposite of romance. He says he loved Paris and Africa and all the places where he had been happy, but most of his flashbacks to the scenes he has never written about are to scenes of death, violence, and destruction; fire, suicide, poverty, murder, and an agonizing wounding. His only remedy for these calamities that marked his life and spirit was romance, which was for him a necessary illusion.

At his death, when the world of pain and suffering seems dominant to him, he thinks that romance has somehow cheated him or escaped him. "So this was the way it ended in a bickering over a drink." When Helen reminds him that he loved Paris, there is a saving recognition when Harry says, "Love is a dunghill." What has he known of the mutual need and help that Helen thinks he is scorning? Harry is referring instead to that emotion of his that he feels cheated him. It is not eros at all, for the Armenian slut and Helen herself did very nicely for that. But Harry is still lonely and empty after that lovemaking which he does almost compulsively. Harry is a Tristan reacting against his sick vision which ends in memories of death and violence and obscene vultures and hermaphroditic hyenas waiting for him to die.

It is Helen who makes the chivalric allusion to Harry as a dying knight, but she is essentially criticizing his romantic disillusionment by her tacit preservation and use of the "necessary illusion," if it is that. She clings to love, she clutches love to her in the person of Harry, giving him everything she has—her wealth, her body, her devotion. Can she help it if Harry resents the first, recognizes

the second as universally available, and grudgingly, dog-in-the-manger accepts the third? Being a Tristan, he wants nothing that can be his. He wants none of this Iseult of the White Hand, this "rich bitch." He has used her money for his armour, to protect his emotions, to keep himself from becoming truly involved with another person.

The repulsion that he rightly feels is due to her dominance over him. Everything that she gives him increases her power over him. Unlike Margot Macomber, Helen does not complain; she endures, forgives—even in his death fantasy Harry puts her in a kindly role—and so she dominates him as she loves him and sucks off the energy that he would have channeled into his art. Harry has been, like Francis Macomber, a coward, though not in the physical way that Macomber was. Harry wants death to come and get it over with, but he has not the moral courage to obtain his freedom by loving Helen. He had made himself nothing more than a gigolo.

His concern for himself distinguishes Harry from Helen and is also the cause of his failure to write. Helen says,

> "You can't die if you don't give up."
>
> "Where did you read that? You're such a bloody fool."
>
> "You might think about some one else."
>
> "For Christ's sake," he said, "That's been my trade."

Harry tries to make a Robert Cohn-like figure out of Helen by attributing her idealism to too much reading. Later Harry thinks, "She was always thoughtful. . . . On anything she knew about, or had read, or that she had ever heard." And later, "she read enormously. . . ." But the burden of their problem rests with him, and because he no longer cares for others, he is no longer a writer. In flashback three we learn that he used to be kind—when he was poor and unknown. Fame nourished his self-esteem and killed his friendships. "No, he thought, when everything you do, you do too long, and do too late, you can't expect to find the people still there. The people all are gone. The party's over and you are with your hostess now."

But Helen is kind in many little things, is thoughtful, and wants desperately to be loved and loving because, a little like Robert Jordan's Maria, she has had a bad time—not the hell of war, violence, and slow death that Harry remembers, but the equally crippling agony of a struggle with oneself, a struggle that Harry has postponed until the infected scratch makes it too late, except to regret having avoided the battle for the sake of his security and comfort.

Her struggle had started when her comfortable, tranquil world was, like Harry's, touched by death, the death of her husband when she was still "comparatively young." As in Hemingway's earlier story **"The Gambler, the Nun, and the Radio,"** her history was a search for opiates, first, devotion to her children, then horses (phallic totems), then books, then bottles, then lovers. But none of these, and least of all the lovers, who bored her, was a permanent deadener. She was still alive, a raw nerve, and "acutely frightened of being alone."

Because she admired Harry's writing and envied him his independent life, she "acquired him" and then, second step, fell in love with him, thus regaining some semblance of the human solidarity she had had with her husband. The cost for Harry was a trade of freedom for security and comfort. Ironically, the very qualities Helen values and acquires are also security and comfort, but she has seen into a void during *her* freedom. She wants none of it and no doubt is puzzled at Harry's esteem for independence, which he obviously regrets having lost.

Helen asks Harry not to quarrel with her anymore. She places an overpaid value on his affection and is willing to settle for simple toleration because she is neurotically afraid of being alone.

> "You don't have to destroy me. Do you? I'm only a middle-aged woman who loves you and wants to do what you want to do. I've been destroyed two or three times already. You wouldn't want to destroy me again, would you?"
>
> "I'd like to destroy you a few times in bed," he said.
>
> "Yes. That's the good destruction. That's the way we're made to be destroyed."

She has known the agony of loneliness and the destruction that is worse than loneliness, the discovery of hate or indifference in the men she thought loved her but who were, alas, only lovers. But even here at Helen's moment of high seriousness, Harry can think of destruction only as eros.

"Macomber" had ended with Margot exhorting Wilson to stop his accusations. She succeeded when she used the word "please." **"The Snows"** begins with Helen exhorting Harry to "Please don't" refer so casually to the odor of his gangrenous leg, and it ends with Helen crying, "Harry! Please, oh Harry!" Please, Harry, she means, don't leave me, for I will be alone. Both women are left alone, but Helen is crying her "please" to her dead man.

Harry is flying to the House of God. It is a trip that crosses many hazards, just as every journey to a Sacred Mountain traditionally does. The "old cock" Harry is put in the Puss Moth, where there is, naturally, room for only one. The pilot says, "'I'll be back for the Mem',," as indeed he may. Getting Harry in the plane is difficult; he has not made things easy for such a momentous flight. There are wart-hog holes and a bumpy field on take-off, a heavy forest, high hills, columns of rising heat that bump the plane, a blizzard of locusts, and a heavy rainstorm, but having met and passed these hazards of life, Harry bursts through the storm to see "as wide as all the world, great, high, and unbelievably white in the sun . . the square top of Kilimanjaro. And then he knew that there was where he was going."

In these terms his death must be considered a victory— as senseless as the leopard's perhaps, but a victory. Death, the "stinking bastard," the hyena that lay upon his chest, is done with. The leopard's frozen carcass on top of Kilimanjaro, the Sacred Mountain, knows no decay or violation by the scavengers of the plains. The hyena makes "a strange, human, almost crying sound." Helen wakes and Harry is gone.

Carlos Baker   (essay date 1967)

SOURCE: "The Slopes of Kilimanjaro: A Biographical Perspective," in *Novel: A Forum on Fiction*, Vol. I, No. 1, Fall, 1967, pp.19-23.

[*In the following essay, Baker identifies the various influences on "The Snows of Kilimanjaro."*]

> This much is known, moreover, that at times people ascend the mountain, and descend again in safety, if they but choose the right season; of which, indeed, they are mostly ignorant, and hence many have perished in the attempt.
>
> —John Rebmann's *Diary of a Journey to Kilimanjaro*, 1849.

In August, 1935, Ernest Hemingway completed the first draft of a story about a writer who died of gangrene on a hunting trip in what was then Tanganyika. The non-fiction "novel," *Green Hills of Africa,* was already in press and due for publication in October. But the book had not used up all the material which Hemingway had accumulated in the course of his shooting safari of January and February 1934. The new story was an attempt to present some more of what he knew, or could imagine, in fictional form. As was his custom, he put the handwritten sheets away in his desk to settle and objectify. Eight months later, on a fishing-trip to Cuba, he re-examined his first draft, modified it somewhat, got it typed, and gave the typescript one final working over. Then he mailed it to Arnold Gingrich for publication in *Esquire* magazine in August, 1936, exactly a year after its inception. Although he had sweated mightily over the title, as he commonly did with all his titles, his ultimate choice displayed the true romantic luminosity. It was called **"The Snows of Kilimanjaro."**

The new story was curiously and subtly connected with Henry David Thoreau's *Walden.* Thoreau had lately been in Hemingway's consciousness. "There is one [author] at that time [of the nineteenth century] that is supposed to be really good," he had asserted in *Green Hills of Africa.* "I cannot tell you about it [*Walden*] because I have not yet been able to read it. But that means nothing because I cannot read other naturalists unless they are being extremely accurate and not literary. . . . Maybe I'll be able to [read it] later."

If he ever read the second chapter of *Walden,* "Where I Lived and What I Lived For," Hemingway would certainly have been struck by Thoreau's statement about his reasons for the sojourn at Walden Pond. He took to the woods in order "to live deliberately, to front only the essential facts of life." He wanted to learn the lore of nature as early as possible so that he would not reach the point of dying only to discover that he "had not lived" in any real sense at all. It is of course a far cry from Thoreau's asceticism to Hemingway's aggressive hedonism. Yet the passage from *Walden,* slightly modified, embodies the theme of **"The Snows of Kilimanjaro."** For Hemingway's protagonist, dying of a noisome infection on the plains of Africa, is made to reflect bitterly upon his failure to set down the results of his experience of life in the forms of fiction. Although Hemingway wisely changed his mind before the story appeared, it is a curious fact that his original name for the dying writer in **"The Snows"** was Henry Walden.

The revised typescript of the story was garnished with a pair of epigraphs, neither of them from Thoreau, but both from "other naturalists." One was drawn from a remarkable book called *Speak to the Earth: Wanderings and Reflections among Elephants and Mountains* (1935). Its author was a naturalized Englishwoman named Vivienne de Watteville, an exact contemporary of Hemingway's, a friend of Edith Wharton's, and a Fellow of The Royal Geographical Society. She was the daughter of Bernard de Watteville, a distinguished Swiss naturalist from Berne. She had been orphaned at the age of 24 when her father was mauled to death by an African lion. She had been with him when he died and subsequently wrote a book called *Out in the Blue,* based on her diaries from that safari. She returned to Africa again four years later, recording her adventures in a second volume, *Speak to the Earth.* Hemingway's first epigraph was drawn from this book. Miss de Watteville spoke of her determination to climb Mount Kilimanjaro. An adviser who had already made the ascent drew her a rough map of the trail up the mountain and told her that she "could pick up a guide and porters at Moshi." "This," she said, "fired me more than ever to make the attempt. I had, of course, no climbing outfit with me; but the difficulties, he said, were not in the actual climbing. It was a long grind, and success depended not on skill but on one's ability to withstand the high altitude. His parting words were that I must make the attempt soon, before there was any risk of the rains setting in."

Hemingway's second epigraph, composed by himself, stated simply that "Kilimanjaro is a snow-covered mountain 19,710 feet high, and is said to be the highest mountain in Africa. Its western summit is called [by] the Masai 'Ngàje Ngài,' The House of God. Close to the western summit is the dried and frozen carcass of a leopard. No one has explained what the leopard was seeking at that altitude." Hemingway had gleaned his facts from the guidebooks he had used in preparing for his trip to Kenya and Tanganyika. He had heard the story of the leopard (whose carcass was still there in 1967) from Philip Percival, his white hunter, during an evening's conversation on safari in 1934.

The two epigraphs had in common the idea of immense height. Both Miss de Watteville's anonymous adviser and the example of the dead leopard indicated that the chief problem for the mountaineer on Kibo Peak of Kilimanjaro was "the ability to withstand the high altitude." Ernest's dying protagonist, Harry, was obliged to confront the fact that never in his life had he attempted to climb that high. His bitterness arose from the realization that he was now literally rotting to death without ever having attained the heights of literary achievement to which he had once aspired. In the end, Ernest deleted the epigraph from Vivienne de Watteville, retaining the one he had himself composed.

Harry tries to assuage his bitterness by making a scapegoat of his pleasant wife Helen. He blames her wealth for his own esthetic decay. Because of it he has followed a life of ease and sloth instead of realizing his former ambition to be a great writer. More than twenty years after the story first appeared, Hemingway explained how he had arrived at his portraits of Helen and Harry and his conception of the central theme. "If you are interested in how you get the idea for a story," he wrote, "this is how it was." On returning to New York after the African trip early in April, 1934, he was met at the pier by ship news reporters who queried him about his future plans. He told them that he was going to work until he had accumulated enough money to go back to Africa. When the story appeared in the newspapers next morning, "a really nice and really fine and really rich woman" invited him to tea. After "a few drinks," she said that she "had read in the papers about the project." She was unable to see any reason for delay. "She and my wife [Pauline] and I could go to Africa any time and money was only something to be used intelligently for the best enjoyment of good people." The offer struck Ernest as "sincere and fine and good," and he liked the lady "very much." But for various reasons he felt obliged to decline her invitation.

Back in Key West he began to reflect upon what might have happened to "a character like me, whose defects I know, if I had accepted the offer." Out of these reflections gradually arose a portrait of the lady, whom he named Helen, and one of Harry, the dying writer, to whom she was married. To describe "the dying part" was no problem for Hemingway. "I had been through all that," he wrote:

> Not just once. I got it early, in the middle, and later. So I invent how someone I know who cannot sue me—that is me—would turn out, and put into one short story things you would use in, say, four novels if you were a careful [sic] and not a spender. I throw everything I had been saving into the story and spend it all. . . . I make up the man and the woman as well as I can and I put all the true stuff in, and with all the load, the most load any short story ever carried, it still takes off and flies. This makes me very happy. . . . Any questions? The leopard? He is part of the meta-

physics. I did not hire out to explain that nor a lot of other things. I know, but I am under no obligation to tell.

Among the "other things" that Hemingway felt no obligation to explain was the fact that Helen was a composite of at least two women. One, if we can trust the story, was the munificent lady in New York. The other was his own second wife, Pauline. He had seen her in action during the recent safari, nor could he forget that her father was among the wealthiest citizens of northeastern Arkansas or that her paternal uncle, Gustavus Adolphus Pfeiffer, was a millionaire who had generously underwritten the trip to Africa with a grant-in-aid of twenty-five thousand dollars. While Hemingway had not by any means surrendered his integrity as a writer in the presence of riches, and while he often complained at this period about his shrunken bank balance, he knew very well that among his "defects" was a liking for the pleasures wealth could buy. The dying writer in his story was an image of himself as he might have been if the temptation to lead the life of the very rich had ever overcome his determination to continue his career as a writer.

At the time when Hemingway wrote this story he knew very well that he had climbed no farther than the lower slopes of his personal Kilimanjaro.

—*Carlos Baker*

A similar mixture of "true stuff" and invention appears in the stream-of-consciousness monologues which periodically interrupt the surface movement of the story. These represent Harry's memories of his past life, and many of them, naturally enough, are Hemingway's own. It is only by knowing the course of his life in some detail that one can sort out truth from fiction. As in any process of free association of ideas and scenes, the episodes Harry recalls ignore strict chronology. Yet if they are arranged in historical sequence, they provide a rough running account of scenes from the life of the author. The earliest of Harry's internal landscapes reveals "a log house, chinked white with mortar, on a hill above the lake." The lake is Walloon, nine miles from Petoskey, Michigan, where Hemingway spent the seventeen summers of his boyhood, beginning in 1900. The house is that of Grandpa Bacon, an aged patriarch with a red beard who was still alive when the Hemingway children were growing up. References to the first world war are brief. There is one to the fighting around Monte Corvo on the Italian-Austrian front, a passage at arms that Hemingway had heard of but not seen, and another about trench warfare, presumably in France, in which an officer named Williamson is disemboweled by a German stick-bomb in the tangled barbwire of No Man's Land.

Hemingway returns to his own experience with a graphic cityscape—the hilltop on the Left Bank in Paris where he lived with his bride Hadley in a walk-up flat in the rue Cardinal Lemoine from the spring of 1922 until they left for Toronto in the summer of 1923. There is also a reminiscence of their fishing vacation in the Black Forest of Germany in August, 1922. Hemingway romanticizes and fictionizes his trip to Constantinople and Adrianople to cover the Greco-Turkish war as correspondent for the *Toronto Star*. He also goes out of his way to insult the Left Bank literati by retailing a trivial incident connected with Harry's homecoming from the Middle East. On the way back to his apartment the day of his return, Harry passes a café and glances inside. There sits "Malcolm Cowley with a pile of saucers in front of him and a stupid look on his face talking about the Dada movement with . . . Tristan Tzara." Hemingway deleted Cowley's name before the story appeared. Harry's wife forgives him for going to Constantinople, just as Hadley forgave Ernest that October morning in 1922, though she had refused to speak to him for three days before his departure because she was afraid to be left alone in the rough neighborhood of the rue Cardinal Lemoine and the Place Contrescarpe. Hemingway seems to have invented the episode in which Harry's first wife discovers a love-letter from another girl in the morning mail, though something not unlike this may have happened while Ernest was conducting a surreptitious liaison with Pauline Pfeiffer before she became his second wife. But the allusion to the *femme de ménage* and her views on the disadvantages of the eight-hour working day, is a direct quotation from Madame Marie Rohrbach, who was in service to Ernest and Hadley during most of their time in Paris.

The apartment in the rue Notre Dame des Champs, where Ernest, Hadley, and their infant son John lived after their return from Toronto, does not figure in this story because Hemingway had already used it in a flashback in *Green Hills of Africa*. But it was from this apartment, in the early winters of 1924-1925 and 1925-1926, that the Hemingways twice left for the village of Schruns in the Austrian Vorarlberg so that Ernest could write and ski in comparative peace. Harry is made to recall the village and to use the actual name of Walther Lent, who operated a ski-school in Schruns and played poker with Ernest at the Madlenerhaus, an Alpine hut high in the Silvretta Range. Another of Hemingway's favorite locales which comes into Harry's mind is the valley of the Clark's Fork branch of the Yellowstone River in Wyoming. Harry is made to remember "the silvered gray of the sage brush, the quick, clear water in the irrigation ditches, and the heavy green of the alfalfa." The violent anecdote of the halfwit chore-boy who murdered his cantankerous employer is an invention of Hemingway's, and brings to an end the pastiche of truth and fiction which courses through Harry's memory as he lies dying, full of vain regret that he has not used enough of what he knows in what he has written.

For the climactic scene of his story, Hemingway drew upon yet another autobiographical episode. Though actually on the very brink of death, Harry is made to imagine that an airplane has arrived to carry him back to the hospital in Nairobi. Hemingway was flown out of the plains country to Nairobi on January 16, 1934, in a Puss Moth biplane for treatment of a severe case of amoebic dysentery. Harry recalls in detail the arrival of the plane, the appearance of the bush pilot, the look of the land, and the behavior of the grazing animals as the plane takes off for the long flight to the north, passing on the way the enormous snow-capped western summit of Kilimanjaro. This was where the adventurous leopard had succumbed to the altitude, only to lie preserved forever in his "metaphysical" fastness. But Harry has died without having attained a similar height.

One of Hemingway's recurrent motivations to literary creativity throughout his life was the conviction that he might soon be going to die without having completed his work or fulfilled his unwritten promise to his talents. At the time when he wrote this story he knew very well that he had climbed no farther than the lower slopes of his personal Kilimanjaro. It is at least a legitimate speculation that he read the passage in Vivienne de Watteville in a symbolic as well as a literal sense. Although he ultimately rejected it as an epigraph for his story, he must have been struck by the statement that success depended "on one's ability to withstand the high altitude" as well as the warning that the attempt must be made "soon, before there was any risk of the rains setting in" to destroy his plans. This was one of the things he knew but felt "no obligation to tell" as he stood poised upon the slopes of the mountain in the midst of his career.

Gloria R. Dussinger (essay date 1967)

SOURCE: "'The Snows of Kilimanjaro': Harry's Second Chance," in *Studies in Short Fiction,* Vol. V, No. 1, Fall, 1967, pp. 54-9.

[*In the following essay, Dussinger emphasizes the significance of the final death scene of "The Snows of Kilimanjaro," concluding that this scene validates the protagonist's quest for truth and identity.*]

The similarity of Harry's memories in **"The Snows of Kilimanjaro"** to those of Hemingway in *A Moveable Feast* reveals the autobiographical intensity of this short story. When Hemingway speaks through his protagonist, *"He had seen the world change. . . . He had been in it and he had watched it and it was his duty to write of it . . . ,"* he makes clear that Harry's story is his professional manifesto. In his narration of the experiences of a dying man, Hemingway proves by example the one thing needful to the writer's pursuit of his hallowed calling. Hemingway embodies in **"The Snows of Kilimanjaro"** his idea of the writer's vocation, the artistic form giving it a validity that public, non-fictional statements lack.

If **"The Snows of Kilimanjaro"** expresses Hemingway's artistic credo, why has the story been so variously interpreted and even rejected by Hemingway critics? An ob-

vious answer lies in the symbolism; Hemingway, with uncharacteristic directness, included the symbols of the mountain and the leopard in an epigraph, where they cannot be ignored. Most of the criticism of this story founders on the two symbols: commentators have made numerous attempts to locate literary and natural sources for them, to discover their meaning, and to evaluate their success.

When passing an aesthetic judgment on the symbols in **"The Snows of Kilimanjaro,"** students of Hemingway follow one of three courses. The first is to grant the leopard and the mountain their full idealistic value, but to deny Harry a place among them. Only by reading the story ironically, by regarding the symbols of permanence and purity as a mockery of Harry's unwholesomeness, can one maintain this critical position. It ignores the formal characteristics of irony, the implied meaning of snow and mountains in Harry's honest past, and the self-evident validity of Harry's final vision. Although Hemingway has made Harry's ascension to the House of God true by *seeing* Kilimanjaro through the eyes of his protagonist, these critics refuse to believe.

A second critical group, accepting the metaphysical meaning of the symbols and also accepting the apotheosis of Harry, cannot reconcile the two. Feeling that Hemingway has insufficiently proven Harry's worthiness, these critics call **"The Snows of Kilimanjaro"** a magnificent failure. Gordon and Tate accuse Hemingway of tacking on the symbol of the mountain for which they fail to find a counterpart in the action. Montgomery insists that Hemingway has not related Harry's moral code to the mountain, nor integrated the leopard into Harry's death-dream. Consequently the end of the story appears to Montgomery sentimental and inorganic.

The third approach to **"The Snows of Kilimanjaro"** subscribes unreservedly to both the transcendental import of the symbols and the transfiguration of the protagonist. Critics who follow this approach see the significance of the snowy mountains of Harry's reminiscences and the truth of his recognition of Kilimanjaro as his goal. To justify Harry's spiritual elevation, they point out that, in spite of self-betrayal, Harry retains enough honesty to judge himself rightly in his last hours. He strives to write then all that he had evaded earlier, assured that quality more than makes up for quantity. Moreover, Harry matches the leopard in surmounting the naturalism of his contemporaries. The riddle of the epigraph is analogous to the surprising fact that Harry, despite the destruction of his talent, despite the changing of the world, has never lost his curiosity. The willingness to go on experiencing, even when experience must serve as its own end—this is Harry's affirmation.

If the obvious meaning of the symbols in the epigraph and the equally obvious linking of them with Harry's past and Harry's death were all that Hemingway offered in support of his writer-hero, critics would be justified in questioning the organic soundness of the symbols. Were such the case, it would be plain that Harry has not earned the redemption Hemingway awards him. But Hemingway, with superb artistry, has developed Harry's value through the narrative structure and then firmly established that value by subjecting it to a test. Harry's death-dream is a brilliantly contrived technique for measuring the intrinsic worth of the protagonist. In his flight toward death, Harry's behavior achieves Hemingway's personal standard; therefore, that section of the story simultaneously vindicates the hero and voices the author's creed: to be true to the senses is the writer's ultimate duty.

An analysis of the narrative will make clear Hemingway's design. From the beginning of the story, Harry knows that he is dying but knows it with an intellectual detachment. His relationship with the woman is that of the friendly enemy—a quarrelsome, superficial connection. Within the first series of reminiscences, Harry's thoughts turn to snow scenes, mountains, betrayal, good skiing, and the birth of God (four Christmases are mentioned). This juncture of disparate topics mirrors the chaotic world of the war generation. The topics are somewhat general; Hemingway indicates that they do not touch the inner Harry by causing Harry to break them off, returning the story to the present. The memory of the German inn triggers Harry to ask Helen about a Paris hotel. His willingness to exchange the past for idle chatter with the woman proves his lack of commitment to it. Moreover, the past has not yet cauterized Harry's festered spirit: he slips easily into the familiar lie that symbolizes his lost integrity.

Between the first and second sets of flashbacks, Harry makes plain to the reader the determinism that permits him so easily to deceive himself: "We must all be cut out for what we do, he thought. However you make your living is where your talent lies." On two previous occasions Harry had revealed a deterministic philosophy: by reasoning, "Maybe you could never write them, and that was why you put them off and delayed the starting" and by his strictly naturalistic answers to Helen's metaphysical question: "What have we done to have that happen to us?" Soothed by determinism, which makes no demands upon the moral responsibility of the individual, Harry slips again into the lie.

The second set of recollections uncovers the real Harry; it deals with his loves and with his wartime trauma, "the things that he could never think of." In the section following these memories, one can note several changes in the protagonist: he passionately desires to write, he no longer falls back on deterministic reasoning, he associates the woman with death and therefore cannot maintain the lie, and he feels death with his senses. The narrative reflects the nearer approach of death by dwelling increasingly on the past and shortening the present passages to interludes.

A third group of reminiscences contains a brief reference to the castration theme but centers on Harry's vocation and its beginning in Paris. Hemingway shows the renewed sensitivity of Harry to physical phenomena in the Place Contrescarpe section: Harry cannot dictate these memories because they are not actions but raw, unclassified

sensations—sights, sounds, smells. The accuracy of the sense impressions signifies the rebirth of Harry's artistic integrity, for the Hemingway hero holds to the truth of the sensations, honesty perceived and recorded. Additional proof of Harry's forsaking the lie can be found in the fourth flashback. Here Harry names himself the betrayer, an admission he had skirted in the first series, pointing at Nansen and Barker instead.

Harry in his restored honesty straightens out his false relation to the woman. He acknowledges that he will never write about her, and thus cuts himself off forever from his conscience-salving rationalization. By portraying the gradual retreat of Harry into the truth of his past, away from the woman and the falsehood of the present, Hemingway reveals his understanding of the psychology of a dying man. Harry is left with his naked self, the irreducible *I am* that defies chaos: "He could beat anything, he thought, because no thing could hurt him if he did not care." Realizing now that the power to mold reality lies within the self, Harry has transcended the scientific materialism to which he was prey at the beginning of the story. His final memory takes the form of a death-wish, for Harry guesses that his state of self-illumination is threatened by time: "It's a bore. . . . Anything you do too bloody long."

Had **"The Snows of Kilimanjaro"** ended here, the reader would remain unimpressed by Harry's conversion. True, he had established honest relations with his fellow man (represented by Helen) and with himself, both of which were founded on the clarity of his senses. But what dying man, if he had the time, would not do as much? The test of Harry's integrity, the ordeal which proves his sincerity, is a second chance. Up to the paragraph beginning "It was morning," this has been the story of a man convinced that he must die. From that paragraph forward to "the square top of Kilimanjaro," it is the story of a man confident of living. By structuring the story in this way, Hemingway gives his writer-protagonist what Dencombe pleaded for in James's short story "The Middle Years," and, in so doing, makes manifest the value of Harry.

Scrutiny of Harry's response to his second chance will settle the question of his merit. Toward others the redeemed Harry shows a sympathetic understanding that contrasts with his previous egocentricity: he twice offers breakfast to Compton rather than trying to hurry him; he calls the woman by her name, acknowledging her separate identity. What Harry does *not* do is lie. He does not tell himself that the rich are worth writing about after all; he does not try to avoid writing by reasoning naturalistically that he lacks talent; he does not tell Helen he loves her in order to insure his job after the hospital stay; he doesn't sell his spiritual vitality for physical comfort. What Harry *does* do is record faithfully and in precise detail the sensory impressions of his journey. The passage narrating the flight contains colors, textures, motions, temperatures conveyed in the incisive Hemingway prose style. It is the restoration of the seeing eye, which perceives the final flight with as much sensory accuracy as the flashbacks, that announces Harry's victory.

Chaman Nahal (essay date 1971)

SOURCE: "The Short Stories," in *The Narrative Pattern in Ernest Hemingway's Fiction*, Fairleigh Dickinson University Press, 1971, pp. 80-120.

[*In the following excerpt, Nahal examines the tension between life and death in "The Snows of Kilimanjaro."*]

"The Snows of Kilimanjaro" was first published in 1936. By then Hemingway was moving slowly to the realization that the larger life of the universe must include an intuitive awareness of the mystery of Death; as early as 1932, in *Death in the Afternoon* he had commented on it. For the cosmic order of the universe could be maintained only through as powerful a balancing force on the other side as life on this one. Here Hemingway goes very close to the Christian mysticism of Boehme, where duality is seen at the center of everything. In the latter half of his creative career, Hemingway concerned himself with death in an increasingly intense fashion. *Across the River and Into the Trees* and *The Old Man and the Sea* are fine studies of death and are powerful, creative reconstructions of the force of death. But in **"The Snows of Kilimanjaro"** we have a good foretaste of this.

The systolic-diastolic rhythm is most consummately presented in **"The Snows,"** so much so that, by giving some of the passages in the story in a different type face, in italics, Hemingway himself seems to be subscribing to the theory. There is hardly any physical action in the story, as our hero is confined to bed with gangrene and cannot move. His mind is wandering and there are series of flashbacks, through which we see his earlier life and his relationships. But slowly in the story even the minimal systolic action is further reduced and then totally abandoned. By the time the story is over, diastolic action has taken over completely. And so has death taken over from life. And in a way the story becomes, in the series of clashes between the systolic and the diastolic actions, a struggle between life and death.

But the italicized passages are not to be seen as flashbacks, strictly speaking. For flashbacks imply a psychological departure into the past, which is not the aesthetic design followed by Hemingway in his fiction. For Harry, the hero of the story, these are very real moments, indicative of the present tense rather than the past. The passages are italicized by the author to give the reader the feel of an altered rhythm. The subject of these passages is not a vicarious longing for the past, but something very much alive to Harry. The subject is death.

On the surface it looks as though Harry in these passages is thinking of his early life. Memories of the war, his earlier love affairs, his fishing and hunting trips of the past, his days in Paris, do come and crowd his mind at the moment. But these images he recalls not to find refuge or support for his present fate.

These passages are representative of Harry's departure into another type of consciousness, and the memories are rather a symbolic projection of his current awareness. Right from the beginning of the story, we see Harry's intuitive feeling that he is going to die. While traveling through the African bush in Tanganyika, a writer has hurt himself. A thorn scratched his flesh and the wound became septic and now gangrene has set in too. The man knows that this is the end. "I'm dying now," he tells his wife and the vultures gathered round him seem to support his fears.

But these fears of his are thus far at the systolic level. Thus far he is thinking of death merely as an event in time. Like every other human, he is afraid of it; like everyone else he wants to avoid it and save his life. And since he knows he cannot, since he knows that gangrene is usually fatal, he is bitter with himself and his wife—more than usually bitter.

A very remarkable thing now happens in the story. But before we take note of it, it is worthwhile to consider the epigraph with which the story begins and which has been interpreted variously by Hemingway scholars. The epigraph gives a composite image of a snow-covered mountain peak, a peak called "the House of God," and "the dried and frozen carcass" of a leopard. It is essential not to split up the image into two units, as some critics have done ("fundamental moral idealism" versus "aimless materialism," or "integrity" versus "carelessness"). The snow-covered mountain and the carcass of the leopard represent a single image having a plural significance. The single composite image that the epigraph presents is that of Life-and-Death, *not* taken separately but *together*. Life is beautiful and great. But death walks hand in hand with it.

The remarkable development that takes place in the story is that Harry, instead of considering death as an event in time as he had to begin with and perhaps has done all his life, comes to look upon it as a living presence. The story thereafter unfolds the slow arrival of death at his side—its physical arrival. With the onset of gangrene the physical pain has stopped, and he no longer has that pressure on his nervous system to keep him in fear of the event. "Since the gangrene started in his right leg he had no pain and with the pain the horror had gone and all he felt now was a great tiredness and anger that this was the end of it." We read: "For years it had obsessed him; but now it meant nothing in itself."

So the fear of the event has actually stopped, at least for the time being. But at the other level, the diastolic level, another kind of awareness is coming into existence. It is slow in appearing, but once the process has started it gathers momentum. His death is now not an event for him in time, but a weird companion of life, and just as at one time life had possessed the soul of Harry completely, now death was going to take possession of him as completely.

This realization is made final for him through a clever factual insertion by Hemingway in the plot of the story, and by his tying up this factual bit with the awareness of death in Harry's consciousness. Harry is a professional writer, and it is not the loves of his life, or his quarrels, for that matter (the last of them, with his present wife Helen, still with him), or his days in Paris, or his fishing and hunting expeditions, or his adventures in the war—it is none of these things that at heart he cares about. What he really cares about is his writing, his ability to transmit or communicate experience through words. He sees clearly that with death around he would never be able to communicate life any longer. He is thus in a state of ultimate knowledge, when he knows that he is entering a new region that has its own terms of reference. Death is not an event that will just cut him off from life; death is a territory imposing its own aesthetic requirements.

Those are requirements of an unfamiliar order and Harry realizes that "now he would never write the things that he had saved to write." At the systolic level, this realization emerges in the form of self-accusations: "He had destroyed his talent by not using it, by betrayals of himself and what he believed in, by drinking so much that he blunted the edge of his perceptions, by laziness, by sloth, and by snobbery, by pride and by prejudice, by hook and by crook." But at the diastolic level he has no doubt about his ability; he is conscious of things that he still might have done had he been spared. His talent has not altogether vanished or been destroyed. Only a bigger thing has now come along, this death, and it wants to take him along with it.

None of the five italicized passages in the story represents "memories," but subjects on which Harry could still write. These passages by implication show his realization of death. They—those subjects—are remembered by him in the context of the impending end, which is going to remove him from them. The diastolic reality subjects him to a wider vision, in which he sees the vaster potentialities which remained unfulfilled. "But he had never written a line of that," is his response—not a line. While at the systolic level he blames himself for the delay; at the diastolic level he accepts the delay as perhaps inevitable, as a period of preparation—for all the time he knew that he "would write it finally."

> There was so much to write. He had seen the world change; not just the events; although he had seen many of them and had watched the people, but he had seen the subtler change and he could remember how the people were at different times. He had been in it and he had watched it and it was his duty to write of it; but now he never would.

"But now he never would." The phrase strikes one as not a statement of regret so much as of a weird realization of the approach of that other master force, the master companion of life—death.

As the story proceeds, Harry's awareness of death becomes sharper. His wife has just returned with some game for him which she has shot, and in the evening they are having a drink together. Harry is feeling remorseful for having been so bitter to her in the morning. He thinks she *is* a good woman, considerate all the time—"marvellous really." And then, for the first time in the story, his diastolic realization of death comes on him. He is in fact at the moment talking of other things, his mind not preoccupied with dying. But all at once he senses death:

> It came with a rush; not as a rush of water nor of wind; but of a sudden evil-smelling emptiness and the odd thing was that the hyena slipped lightly along the edge of it.

The parallel images of the "rush of water" or the "rush of wind," and their rejection as suitable similes is purposeful. For with this rejection Hemingway is trying to establish the "otherness" of death. Even "evil-smelling emptiness" is not enough, so that another image, that of the hyena slipping "lightly along the edge of it," has to be brought in to establish the reality which cannot be communicated through words or language. But that Harry does sense a presence near him and is startled by it, we are left in no doubt. His wife notices this, and asks: "What is it, Harry?" And he answers: "Nothing . . . You had better move over to the other side. To windward."

But from now on, he cannot seem to get rid of the sense of death. His wife goes away to have her bath and when she returns and they are about to eat, he senses it once again. "This time there was no rush. It was a puff, as of a wind that makes a candle flicker and the flame go tall." The whole thing is done very inventively, bordering on the occult. Harry realizes that there is going to be a meeting, a strange meeting. "So this was how you died," he tells himself, "in whispers that you did not hear." But lying as he is in the diastolic peace, there is no fear of the unexpected. There is even a joy, an expectancy. After all, death is copartner of life, and this copartner was now going to manifest itself to him.

In none of his reactions in the diastolic period do we notice any misgivings in Harry: "The one experience that he had never had he was not going to spoil now." This establishes the utter strangeness of what is happening—a welcome strangeness. So he promises himself that he will do nothing to spoil the new feelings that were coming. He also tells himself: "He probably would. You spoiled everything. But perhaps he wouldn't."

But an even more monumental transformation comes to pass at this stage. For years, as he has been reprimanding himself, Harry had written nothing. For years he had frittered away his creativity. But with the near arrival of death, with the arrival of something so new and so powerful, what happens is that his creativity also returns to him. He suddenly wants to write—this minute—now.

> "You can't take dictation, can you?"
>
> "I never learned," she told him.
>
> "That's all right."
>
> There wasn't time, of course, although it seemed as though it telescoped so that you might put it all into one paragraph if you could get it right.

The systolic mood returns, and he again wants to hang on to life; he is by turns afraid of death and also attracted to it. "He lay still and death was not there. It must have gone around another street. It went in pairs, on bicycles, and moved absolutely silently on the pavements." His wife nags him about his drinking but, unconcerned, he lapses into the diastolic mode and his mind roams over some of the stories that he could have written but never did. Once again he returns to the systolic mood and once again he does not wish to die. "He would rather be in better company."

We are now very near the end of the story, and diastolic action almost completely takes over from the systolic. Death finally is back with him and the hour of the meeting has come. "Do you feel anything strange?" he asks his wife.

"No. Just a little sleepy."

"I do," he said.

He had just felt death come by again.

The movement now resembles a nocturnal dance. Death keeps advancing at him and the scene of his surrender to that great power is vivid and powerful. He keeps talking to his wife, but his intuition is sharp. "What is that?" he asks himself,

> Because, just then, death had come and rested its head on the foot of the cot and he could smell its breath.

The moods come and go in flashes, and he tries to explain death to Helen. He is consciously aware by now that death has not one image but many, and none of the metaphors that he might employ would quite communicate what he is experiencing. It is like Wallace Stevens's "Thirteen Ways of Looking at a Blackbird." Death is not merely "a scythe and a skull"; it could as easily be "two bicycle policemen," or "a bird," or the "wide snout" of a hyena. But he knows that it has many shapes, or rather no formal shape at all, which is another way of saying the same thing. "It had moved up on him now, but it had no shape any more. It simply occupied space."

In the ultimate meeting with death, the systolic and the diastolic moods mingle intimately. At the systolic level, Harry wants to fight death. At the diastolic level he knows, it will offer him peace as nothing else ever had or ever could.

First comes the systolic fight. He tells his wife aloud to ask this thing to go away. But it "moved a little closer." And he can smell it now and he shouts: "You stinking bastard."

> It moved up closer to him still and now he could not speak to it, and when it saw he could not speak it came a little closer, and now he tried to send it away without speaking, but it moved in on him so its weight was all upon his chest, and while it crouched there and

he could not move, or speak, he heard the woman say, "Bwana is asleep now. Take the cot up very gently and carry it into the tent."

The fight, however, is soon over. But this story, or this kind of Hemingway story, must be distinguished from the story in which there is a clear division between the two movements. In the stories considered in the previous section, once we enter the diastolic mood, we stay there. Here the two movements alternate.

Harry is still not quite dead, but he has given himself over now to death in acceptance—in diastolic acceptance. In the long passage where the arrival of Compton and the subsequent departure of Harry by plane are narrated, Harry is still alive. It is Harry's consciousness which is conjuring up these pleasant images. And it is Hemingway's method of making us aware of the newness of the experience. No didactic passage in praise of death or its glory is ever introduced by Hemingway. The purity of the moment is never presented rhetorically. It comes to us in the form of narrative, and has to be known at the aesthetic level alone. But we see that Harry finds death a uniquely new experience from the fact that he is at least at peace with himself. While flying high in his imaginative vision, he looks down and sees "a new water that he had never known of." The plane then passes through a black waterfall, which is only rain falling very thickly. Once out of the rain, Compton turns his head toward Harry and points out to him their destination in the distance. And what does Harry see there? The square top of Kilimanjaro, "as wide as all the world, great, high, and unbelievably white in the sun." Compie here is death who is taking Harry to the mountain of life. Harry dies with this knowledge, and the epigraph of the story becomes his epitaph.

Scott MacDonald   (essay date 1974)

SOURCE: "Hemingway's 'The Snows of Kilimanjaro': Three Critical Problems," in *Studies in Short Fiction*, Vol. II, No. 1, Winter, 1974, pp. 67-74.

[*In the following essay, MacDonald offers a stylistic and thematic analysis of "The Snows of Kilimanjaro," contending that contrary to other critical interpretations, the protagonist does not transcend artistic failure.*]

In spite of the unusually large amount of criticism that has been devoted to **"The Snows of Kilimanjaro"** during the last thirty-five years, several of the most fundamental critical problems posed by the story remain unsolved. Recent criticism indicates that there is still no adequate general understanding of the significance of Harry's imagined flight to Kilimanjaro near the end of the story, of the specific reasons for Hemingway's extensive use of italics, or of the exact implications of the brief epigraph of the story.

The flight to Kilimanjaro which Harry dreams he takes near the end of Hemingway's story has been interpreted in a number of different ways. The majority of critics, however, have seen Harry's journey as a kind of spiritual elevation, as Hemingway's method of indicating that at least at the moment of his death, Harry has become a superior man. The only widespread disagreement on this point, in fact, has resulted from varying opinions as to whether Hemingway's elevation of his protagonist is justified by Harry's actions during the story. [In the *University of Kansas City Review,* Summer 1961] Marion Montgomery feels that Harry's "salvation" is not justified by his nature and that his journey to Kilimanjaro is, thus, a sentimental attempt to give the story a happy ending. [In *Ernest Hemingway,* 1963] Earl Rovit goes further. He believes that Harry is a despicable character, but that Hemingway awards salvation to him in order to insult the reader. Other critics see Hemingway's elevation of Harry as perfectly justifiable. [In the *Texas Quarterly,* Winter 1966] Max Westbrook, for example, feels that Harry's flight metaphorically indicates that Harry has received redemption from moral and physical decay by honestly recognizing his failures and thereby coming to a "knowledge of the real." According to Oliver Evans [in *PMLA,* December 1961], Harry's loss of the ability to love during his recent life has brought him to what Evans calls a state of "death-in-life." The flight to Kilimanjaro at Harry's death, however, indicates that divine forgiveness has enabled Harry to return "to the Orginal Source of all love" and be reunited "to that which is ideal and permanent." [In *Studies in Short Fiction,* Fall 1967] Gloria Dussinger agrees that Harry achieves salvation, but she is more specific as to the reason why. The plane flight is, she feels, Hemingway's method of giving Harry a "second chance." During the flight, according to Ms. Dussinger, Harry accurately records "the sensory impressions of his journey" and, as a result, regains his artistic integrity and comes to deserve the salvation he is subsequently awarded. Although some of these critics argue with considerable ingenuity, there is a fundamental weakness in all of their interpretations and, really, in all other interpretations of **"The Snows of Kilimanjaro"** that view Harry's trip to the mountain as an indication of his achievement of salvation. The problem is that such interpretations ignore the implications of the way in which Hemingway carefully limits his presentation of the events of the story.

Until the flight to the mountain, every detail of **"The Snows of Kilimanjaro"** is presented from the protagonist's perspective. What Harry does not think about, perceive, or remember, in other words, is not presented. That the reader sees only what Harry sees becomes especially obvious during Harry's last waking moments. When "death" is described as resting its head on the foot of Harry's cot and as moving up on Harry until it crouches on his chest, the reader understands that the animal Harry sees exists only in his imagination, that it is the psychological projection of a mind that is growing delirious. The animal seems real enough, but this is because it is described as Harry sees it. The "hell of a breath" that Harry thinks death has is actually the odor from his putrefied leg. The beast's sitting heavily on Harry's chest is Harry's projection of internal pain. In other words, while death does come to Harry, the form in which the reader

sees it results from the fact that Hemingway is limiting his presentation of events to Harry's perspective. This same narrative strategy is used for the presentation of the imagined flight to Kilimanjaro. As most critics have understood, Harry does not really see Kilimanjaro. The flight seems real enough, but this is because the reader sees only what the protagonist sees. That Harry in reality doesn't take a plane flight is made perfectly clear in the final section of the story, when Helen wakes us and sees Harry on the cot. When Harry dreams he sticks his leg straight out to the side of Compton's seat, he is actually moving his leg out of the cot. It is even likely that when Harry dreams he is being carried to the plane, he is actually being carried into the tent.

While most critics have realized that the flight to Kilimanjaro does not really occur, however, the important implications of this fact have often been ignored or evaded. Because the flight is something Harry dreams, there is no justification for interpreting the story as though Hemingway were awarding immortality to Harry by taking him to the mountain. As every critic has suggested, Harry's journey to Kilimanjaro has metaphoric value. However, whether the flight to the mountain is thought of as a metaphor for the achievement of one of the kinds of salvation defined by Montgomery, Rovit, Westbrook, Evans, or Ms. Dussinger, or whether it is thought to have some other type of metaphoric significance, the fact remains that the flight occurs only in Harry's imagination and that whatever moral or artistic integrity is suggested by his reaching the mountain is something Harry wishes he were attaining, not something he actually attains. In other words, the flight to Kilimanjaro may suggest an ennobling of Hemingway's protagonist, but Hemingway is not ennobling Harry, Harry is deliriously ennobling himself.

Those critics who see the flight to Kilimanjaro as Hemingway's method of rewarding Harry seldom mention the final section of the story. That this is the case is understandable, for whatever ennoblement Harry dreams he undergoes during his last moments is harshly undercut when Helen is awakened by the hyena. Evans, Ms. Dussinger, E. W. Tedlock [in *The Explicator,* October 1949], and others contend that **"The Snows of Kilimanjaro"** ends on a note of triumph. The real ending, however, is a good deal less than triumphant. As William Van O'Connor mentions [in *The Grotesque: An American Genre and Other Essays,* 1962] among the final images in the story, one is nearly as memorable as the white brilliance of the mountain. When Helen wakes up, she can see Harry's "bulk under the mosquito bar but somehow he had gotten his leg out and it hung down alongside the cot. The dressings had all come down and she could not look at it." Clearly, the final emphasis of the story is not on Harry's achievement of some sort of salvation, but on the finality of his decay and death, on those very limitations on human life that give significance to the difficult struggle for immortality in art.

The meaning of Harry's death is further clarified by an examination of another frequently discussed aspect of the narrative strategy of **"The Snows of Kilimanjaro"**: Hemingway's extensive use of italics. At first glance, the italics seem merely a means for isolating Harry's memories of his past life from other kinds of thinking and from the action that is occurring on the hot African plain. That more is involved in the use of italics, however, is made clear by the fact that some of Harry's memories—those of his life with Helen and of "poor Julian"—are presented during unitalicized sections of the story. Montgomery suggests that the italicized sections embody "Harry's reflections concerning a past he approves of; the material in Roman type embodies the past and present he disapproves of." While it is true that in a general sense Harry approves of his early life and disapproves of the recent past and present, however, Montgomery's distinction does not account for the kinds of memories that are included in the italicized sections. Harry certainly doesn't approve of those portions of the past represented by incidents such as the one in which Williamson is *caught in the wire, with a flare lighting him up and his bowels spilled out into the wire . . .*", or the one in which Barker bombs the Austrian officers' leave train on Christmas day. It is also unlikely that Harry approves of his own conduct in all instances. Surely, the episode in which Harry writes a passionate letter to his first wife, only to forget about it later, is not included because Harry sees himself playing a particularly admirable role during the incident. More is involved in Hemingway's use of italics, in other words, than the question of Harry's approval or disapproval of the things he remembers.

The specific nature of the distinction between italicized and unitalicized sections becomes more understandable when the reader realizes that, as R. W. Stallman suggests [in *The House that James Built and other Literary Studies, 1961*] all of the incidents included in italics are memories of experiences that Harry remembers he *"had saved to write,"* experiences he *"had always thought that he would write"* but now never would. The last italicized section in the story, in fact, is the only section during which some direct statement to this effect is not included. That even this section presents memories Harry wishes he had written, however, is indicated by the fact that during the conversation that immediately follows the section, Harry tells Helen that he has been "writing." Harry has not really been writing, of course. He is beginning to grow delirious, and he confuses his dreams of creation with the act of creation. However, the fact that he wishes he were writing the events he has just remembered indicates that, like all previous italicized sections, the brief final section presents experiences Harry had saved to write. Harry's procrastination, however, is not *per se* the criterion for Hemingway's use of italics. In at least one instance an experience Harry had thought he would write is presented in Roman type. Harry remembers that after his marriage to Helen, he considered himself a "spy" in the "country" of the rich and presumed that once he knew the country well enough, he would "leave it and write of it and for once it would be written by some one who knew what he was writing of." However, unlike every other incident Harry had thought he would write about, unlike all the incidents in italicized sections, Harry's plan to tell

the truth about the rich proved ultimately not worth carrying out. When Harry came to know the rich, he found that his experiences in their "country" were not worth writing. As he thinks to himself, "The rich were dull and they drank too much, or they played too much backgammon. They were dull and they were repetitious." The specific criterion for the distinction between incidents in italics and incidents in Roman type, then, becomes clear. The episodes in italics are experiences Harry had put off writing and which, indeed, were worth writing about. The italicized sections, in other words, portray those experiences which *should have been* used in the creation of fiction.

Critics have generally agreed that the division of **"The Snows of Kilimanjaro"** into italics and Roman type results in a meaningful contrast between Harry's "present ignoble situation and the memory of a more heroic past." The specific basis for the use of italics, however, causes the division of the story to have more specific implications. For one thing, the alternation of italics and Roman type keeps the reader constantly aware of the degree to which Harry has failed to fulfill his obligations as a writer. The episodes that make up the italicized sections illustrate the beauty and power of the things Harry has seen and, as a result, emphasize the loss of the fiction that Harry might have produced. The fact that some of the episodes represent numerous incidents, all of which should have become fictional material, emphasizes the extent of Harry's failure.

Another implication of the use of italics in **"The Snows of Kilimanjaro"** involves the fact that in the final analysis the italicizing of memories is more than merely a reflection of Harry's judgement. Were the italicized episodes presented in Roman type, it would still be clear which memories Harry had saved to write and which are best forgotten. The change would in no way detract from the presentation of Harry's thinking. The fact is that in general the changes from Roman type to italics (and the breaks between the different sections) create very noticeable interruptions in the otherwise smooth process of Harry's thought, interruptions which draw the reader's attention away from Harry and toward the emphasis by the narrator which is implicit in the changes. What would really be lost if the italics were omitted is Hemingway's own emphasis that Harry should have used the episodes of the italicized sections as the raw material for fictional creation. In other words, though Hemingway does not enter **"The Snows of Kilimanjaro"** as an omniscient narrator in order to comment on the meaning of Harry's life, he uses italics in a way which emphasizes the fact that his protagonist has failed to fulfill his potential and that strongly confirms Harry's judgement as to which experiences he would have written about had he maintained his integrity.

One further implication of Hemingway's use of italics seems to follow. Hemingway's emphasis on the value of Harry's experiences as potential fictional material and on the protagonist's failure to capitalize on this potential makes particularly obvious the fact that at least in one sense some of the protagonist's memories *have* become fictional material. Harry's failure adequately to fulfill the duty of a writer is made clear, after all, not only by the story's catalogue of many of those specific incidents to which Harry neglected to apply his talent, but also by Hemingway's use of some of those incidents as fictional material. By drawing attention to his own act of creation through his use of italics, in other words, Hemingway subtly implies a contrast between the fate of a fictional character who has lost his moral and artistic integrity and the achievement represented by his own story, by a work of art which itself gives evidence of the fact that Hemingway's integrity as a writer remains intact. To put it another way, the achievement represented by the writing of **"The Snows of Kilimanjaro"** is itself the ultimate standard against which the reader can measure Harry's failure.

> **By presenting a man who has procrastinated the writer's job until he must be satisfied with only the dream of attaining immortality as an artist, Hemingway illustrates the kind of self-indulgence and self-deception the real artist must avoid. Hemingway's story, however, does more than portray one artist's failure**.
>
> *—Scott MacDonald*

Once the implications of Harry's "flight" to Kilimanjaro and of Hemingway's use of italics are understood, it becomes possible to clarify the meaning of the epigraph that precedes the body of the story. Most critics have seen the leopard of the headnote as a metaphor for Harry, and they have interpreted the leopard's climb up the mountain as Hemingway's metaphoric way of indicating Harry's achievement of moral or artistic integrity during the final hours of his life. Not only does this interpretation ignore the emphasis of the story on Harry's failure, however, it is also based on a distortion of the implications of the epigraph itself. In order to interpret the leopard's climb as an indication of Harry's success, it is necessary to see the animal's attainment of the mountaintop as a worthwhile achievement. The fact is, however, that the leopard is only successful in a most limited sense. The animal's attainment of the mountaintop is clearly a prodigious feat. At the same time, however, by making the journey the leopard leaves its natural habitat and places itself in an environment in which it is not able to survive. The leopard's successful journey, in other words, is ultimately nothing more than a means to failure and death. It is, in fact, the leopard's inability to survive in its new environment which enables the reader to understand the relationship between the epigraph and Harry's story. Harry is like the leopard in failing to withstand the "high altitude" he

achieved as a result of his struggles as a young writer. During his early years as an artist, Harry endured many hardships in order to maintain his integrity and create worthwhile literature. The artistic success Harry achieved, however, brought with it financial rewards and their accompanying temptations, temptations which finally resulted in the death of Harry's integrity and in his abandonment of the difficult creative life. It is true that Harry has returned to Africa in order to try to "work the fat off his soul," but his attempt clearly comes too late. As Hemingway says in *Green Hills of Africa,* "The hardest thing" for a writer "because time is so short, is for him to survive and get his work done." Unfortunately, Harry has failed to work during his life, and the result is that when the end comes, he must die with only the dreams of writing and of being flown to Kilimanjaro and immortalized, rather than with the real immortality he might have achieved had he maintained or re-won his integrity. Thus, like the physical journey of the leopard of the epigraph, Harry's early successful journey as a creative artist is ultimately nothing more than a means of creative failure and death.

Though both Harry's struggle and the leopard's ultimately end in failure and death, however, both the animal and the man do receive one kind of immortality. The leopard's struggle and failure are immortalized by the preservative powers of the mountain snow. The animal's dried and frozen carcass is made permanent, in fact, by that very element which the animal was unable to conquer. In a similar manner, Harry's failure to fulfill the duties of a true artist by enduring the temptations which resulted from his early success is immortalized through the creation of fiction, by that very "element," so to speak, which Harry was unable to conquer. Just as the leopard's failure is preserved by the snows of Kilimanjaro, in other words, Harry's failure as an artist is preserved through Hemingway's creation of a story about Harry. That Hemingway's story is entitled **"The Snows of Kilimanjaro,"** in fact, emphasizes its preservative function.

"The Snows of Kilimanjaro" does not communicate Hemingway's vision of the artist's responsibilities, as most critics have supposed, by portraying a man who fulfills these responsibilities durng the story. Instead, by presenting a man who has procrastinated the writer's job until he must be satisfied with only the dream of attaining immortality as an artist, Hemingway illustrates the kind of self-indulgence and self-deception the real artist must avoid. Hemingway's story, however, does more than portray one artist's failure. By using italics to emphasize his feeling that many of the events Harry remembers should have become the basis for artistic creation, Hemingway reminds the reader that in fact these events have been the basis for a work of art, the one the reader is reading. In other words, Hemingway contrasts Harry's failure to make the creative effort necessary for real immortality with the positive creative effort represented by **"The Snows of Kilimanjaro."** Finally, Hemingway uses the epigraph of the story to emphasize his ideas. He develops a parallel between the preservation in the snows of Kilimanjaro of the carcass of a leopard which failed to stay alive on a high peak and the preservation in **"The Snows of Kili-**

manjaro" of the story of a writer who failed to stay artistically alive at the high level represented by his early writing. In the final analysis, **"The Snows of Kilimanjaro"** not only describes Harry's failure to win immortality, it also enables Hemingway himself to achieve the only immortality a true artist need consider, that which is given him by his work.

Kenneth G. Johnston (essay date 1984)

SOURCE: "'The Snows of Kilimanjaro': An African Purge," in *Studies in Short Fiction,* Vol. XXI, No. 3, Summer, 1984, pp. 223-27.

[*In the following essay, Johnston perceives Hemingway's story as an attempt to confront fears of literary failure.*]

> The ethics of writing are fairly simple but very confusing to the public. The fact that a man lies, is cruel, betrays his wife, gets drunk, betrays his friends, has this or that odd or ugly sexual habit does not mean that he is not as honest in his writing as any Sir Galahad. No matter what lies he tells in his life he is an honest writer as long as he does not lie to or deceive the innermost self which writes.
>
> —Ernest Hemingway

When Hemingway returned from his African safari in April 1934, he told reporters in New York that he planned to return to Africa as soon as he had earned enough money. A wealthy woman read the remark in the papers, invited him to tea, and offered to finance the trip. Hemingway politely refused. When he got back to Key West, he started "to think what would happen to a character like me whose defects I know, if I had accepted that offer. . . . So I invent how someone I know who cannot sue me—that is me—would turn out, and put into one short story things you would use in, say, four novels if you were a careful and not a spender. I throw everything I had been saving into the story and spend it all." At least that is how Hemingway remembered it some twenty-five years later.

Hemingway, one strongly suspects, wrote **"The Snows of Kilimanjaro"** to exorcise his guilt feelings for having neglected his serious writing, and to re-dedicate himself to his craft. He had not published a novel since *A Farewell to Arms* in 1929. His production of short fiction had been slight since the publication of *Winner Take Nothing* in 1933; during the next three years, before the appearance of **"The Snows,"** he would publish only three new pieces of short fiction: **"One Trip Across," "The Tradesman's Return,"** and **"The Horns of the Bull"** (later retitled **"The Capital of the World"**). But during that same three-year period, he would publish the following nonfiction: *Green Hills of Africa*; a letter on mutilated fish; a recipe for a "Death in the Afternoon Cocktail"; an article on the purchase of Joan Miró's painting "The Farm"; an angry article for *New Masses* on the veterans who died in the 1935 Florida hurricane; and twenty-seven articles

for *Esquire* on fishing, hunting, prize-fighting, Paris, international politics, and other assorted topics. "At the time when he wrote the story of the dying writer on the plains of Africa," writes Carlos Baker [in *Ernest Hemingway: A Life Story,* 1969], "he knew very well that he had climbed no farther than the lower slopes of his personal Kilimanjaro." His neglect of his serious craft, and the fact that his African safari had been paid for by his wife's very rich uncle (it cost about $25,000), probably preyed upon Hemingway's conscience. In short, **"The Snows of Kilimanjaro"** has a firm autobiographical base, and it may be read as a report on the artistic and spiritual health of its author.

"The Snows of Kilimanjaro" is concerned primarily with a dying writer's attempt to explain, to rationalize, to evade full responsibility for his failure to fulfill his early promise as a writer. He admits in a moment of candor that he has "destroyed his talent by not using it, by betrayals of himself and what he believed in, by drinking so much that he blunted the edge of his perceptions, by laziness, by sloth, and by snobbery." Yet it is quite clear that deep down he blames the corrupting power of money and the seductive life of hedonism, which the wealth makes possible, for sapping his artistic vitality. Thus in his final hours, his considerate, loving wife Helen, whom he characterizes as "this rich bitch, this kindly caretaker and destroyer of his talent," becomes the target for his bitterness and frustrations, and the scapegoat for his artistic demise.

Harry's death, which will occur before the night is out, is caused by gangrene: the local death of soft tissues due to the loss of blood supply; the death of one part of the body while the rest is still alive. The word "gangrene" derives from the Greek *gangraina,* meaning "eating sore," from *gran,* "to gnaw." With moist gangrene, the kind that Harry is afflicted with, there is not much pain, but the decaying tissues give off a very offensive smell. It seldom occurs, according to *Black's Medical Dictionary,* "save in people of very low vitality." Figuratively speaking, Harry has been suffering from a gangrenous condition for many years. His literary self has been "dying" for a long time. No longer is writing a vital part of his life. But his artistic conscience, although feeble, is still alive, gnawing at his soul. His failure to care for a thorn scratch on his knee two weeks ago fits into the pattern of his small neglects, over the years, of his artistic talent. In both cases, physical and artistic, the fault is clearly his.

The safari is self-prescribed treatment to recover his artistic health. "Africa was where he had been happiest in the good time of his life, so he had come out here to start again. They had made this safari with the minimum of comfort. There was no hardship; but there was no luxury and he had thought that he could get back into training that way. That in some way he could work the fat off his soul . . .". And for a short while, "he had felt the illusion of returning strength of will to work." But the disease has spread too far and too deep for such superficial treatment. The only "writing" he does is in his mind, as he recalls the people, places, and events of earlier years, the stories he might have written but now knows he never will. His memories center on scenes of snow, of poverty and innocence, of violence and quarrels, of mistakes and betrayals. These narrative memories are fragments and sketches; they have not been developed or structured. It would take a great deal of hard work still to shape and expand them into short stories, or chapters in a novel, or sections in a book of memoirs. (Hemingway eventually will include many of these memories in *A Moveable Feast*.) Harry's belief that they are ready for dictation is yet another illusion.

The snow-capped Mt. Kilimanjaro of the epigraph looms over the story, and at the end it is apparently Harry's spiritual destination. In reality, the rescue plane does not arrive in time, and Harry's corpse is discovered by his wife in the tent. The rescue and the flight to Kilimanjaro are only what-might-have-been. When he was young and dedicated, the journey was a real possibility. But in recent years, Harry has abandoned all preparations for the difficult ascent to the top of Mt. Kilimanjaro; he does not even attempt to write the many stories, locked in his memory, which might have gained for him a permanent place in literature, an immortality such as the leopard has achieved. Unlike the leopard, whose frozen and dried carcass is near the western summit, the middle-aged writer does not adventure forth from his "safe" and comfortable habitat to risk the unknown; to test his strength, endurance, and discipline. The unchanging, cold purity of the higher elevations is in sharp contrast to the decay, the stench, in Harry's tent, pitched in the sweltering heat of the plains. The tent, the abode of the transient, is fitting shelter for the artistic failure.

"Ah, Madame," confided Hemingway in *Death in the Afternoon,* "it is years since I added the wow to the end of a story." But four years later he attached a "wow" ending to **"The Snows of Kilimanjaro."** It is an ending that cannot be supported by the narrative. Harry's few bitter regrets and remarks in his dying moments concerning his betrayal of craft and self do not atone for a wasted artistic life. Clearly he has not earned the flight to Mt. Kilimanjaro. Perhaps the imagined flight was intended to reveal Harry's final illusion, but since the writer is already dead, the reader is left to struggle with the logic.

Hemingway's original choice for the name of his protagonist in **"The Snows of Kilimanjaro"** was Henry Walden; thus one is not surprised to detect echoes of Thoreau's philosophy and writings throughout the story. Harry's minimum-comfort safari and his recall of the happy days of relative poverty, when he and his first wife had "slept on mattresses filled with beech leaves" in the woodcutter's house in the mountains of Austria, are reminiscent of Thoreau's call for Spartan simplicity. Several other Thoreauvian themes may also be detected in **"The Snows"**: the folly of flight, the quest for self-knowledge and the limitations of wealth. Why go to Africa, asked Thoreau, when one's own interior is "white on the chart"? Harry has journeyed to Africa for reasons rather similar to those that drew Thoreau to Walden Pond: "I went to the woods," declared Thoreau, "because I wished to live deliberately,

to front only the essential facts of life, and see if I could not learn what it had to teach, and not, when I came to die, discover that I had not lived." Thoreau knew from the start what Harry is just beginning to comprehend: that "money is not required to buy one necessary of the soul"; that the rich, that "most terribly impoverished class of all," have "forged their own golden or silver fetters." Harry, as he lies dying on the low-lying plain, ponders the Thoreauvian balance sheet of his life. But too late he understands that "a man is rich in proportion to the number of things which he can afford to let alone." Too late he calculates the cost of his "acquiescence in this life of pleasant surrender." The smell from his gangrenous leg drifts across the campsite. "There is no odor so bad," wrote Thoreau, "as that which arises from goodness tainted. It is human, it is divine, carrion."

The approach of Harry's death is signaled by the emboldened vultures, which have been attracted to the vicinity of the camp by the scent and/or sight of the dying man. The description of their movements subtly links them to the death plane and its frightening shadow at story's end: the vultures "sailed" in the sky, "making quick-moving shadows as they passed"; they "planed down" to a landing. But the hyena, which also feeds on carrion, soon becomes the main symbol of death. At dusk, when "there was no longer enough light to shoot," a hyena crosses in the open near the camp. "'That bastard crosses there every night,' the man said. 'Every night for two weeks'." Harry's first realization that he is going to die "came with a rush; not as a rush of water nor of wind; but of a sudden evil smelling emptiness and the odd thing was that the hyena slipped lightly along the edge of it." Soon, death, which has "a wide snout like a hyena," comes and rests "its head on the foot of the cot and he could smell its breath." It moves in and crouches like a smothering weight on his chest. It is the hyena's "strange, human, almost crying sound" that awakens Helen in the night to discover that Harry is dead. This eerie sound, which closes out the story, serves as a kind of death wail, a hyenic lamentation for the dead.

"The pinnacle of hyenic humor," Hemingway wrote in *Green Hills of Africa,* "was the hyena, the classic hyena, that hit too far back while running, would circle madly, snapping and tearing at himself until he pulled his own intestines out, and then stood there, jerking them out and eating them with relish." Harry, too, may be seen as playing this "comic" role in **"The Snows of Kilimanjaro."** Instead of a "comic slap of a bullet," there is the comic scratch of a thorn. But both show "agitated surprise" to find death inside them. Both "start that frantic circle," racing death; and both devour themselves with relish. If viewed in this light, the hyena in **"The Snows"** symbolizes not only death but also the particular manner in which Harry dies—his frantic circling back to feed upon his dead past and his dying self. Thus, the sound of hyenic "laughter" is a most fitting note on which to end the story.

"The Snows of Kilimanjaro," which Michael F. Moloney has called [in *Hemingway and his Critics: An International Anthology,* edited by Carlos Baker] "the tragedy of a man who lacked the courage to reject the world," was not simply the tragic tale of an American writer. It spoke across national boundaries to men and women everywhere who were struggling to defend the idealism and the promise of their youth against the forces of materialism—as well as to those who had already lost the battle and, thus, found some sad consolation and justification in witnessing another man's doomed struggle to purge himself of the blunders and the betrayals of his past. The snows became "las nieves," "les neiges," "der schnee," "ta chionia," "de sneeuw," "snön," "snegovi," "silge," "snega," "sneen," and so on as the story, like dozens of others by Hemingway, was translated to reach an international audience. [In his *The Literary Life and the tell with It*, 1938] William Saroyan, who early on ranked **"The Snows of Kilimanjaro"** as "one of the few truly great stories of our time," wrote that he could "give odds of one hundred to one . . . to every publisher in America that in one hundred years it will have been read by more people than any top-selling novel now on the market." Not quite a half a century later, it is clear that Saroyan was betting on a sure thing.

Alice Hall Petry (essay date 1985)

SOURCE: "Voice Out of Africa: A Possible Oral Source for Hemingway's 'The Snows of Kilimanjaro'," in *The Hemingway Review,* Vol. IV, No. 2, Spring, 1985, pp. 7-11.

[*In the following essay, Petry uncovers a link between Hemingway's story and the reminscences of an early female aviator.*]

Ever since it was first published in *Esquire* in August of 1936, Ernest Hemingway's **"The Snows of Kilimanjaro"** has consistently enjoyed popular acclaim and scholarly attention. A generous portion of the interest which the story continues to generate focuses on its possible sources—more precisely, the sources of the epigraph and the various elements within it (such as the frozen leopard). But the long-running epigraph controversy has tended to overshadow an equally fundamental critical problem in **"The Snows"**: the source of the dramatic situation Hemingway depicts of a woman attempting to comfort a dying, delirious man. Is this purely Hemingway's imaginative rendering of his fate with the anonymous woman who offered to finance another safari for him in April of 1934? Or does it owe something to sources—written or oral—outside of his imagination? It is possible that an important unrecognized source of **"The Snows"** is the orally-transmitted stories of Beryl Clutterbuck Markham (b. 1902), a Kenya-based flying ace who had met Hemingway during his African safari of 1933-34.

Until now, one of the few commentators to focus on the source of more than just the epigraph of the story is Robert W. Lewis, Jr., in his "The Texas Manuscript of 'The Snows of Kilimanjaro': Part II: Vivienne de Watteville, Hemingway's Companion on Kilimanjaro." [in the *Texas Quarterly,* Winter 1966]. Lewis points out that Hemingway

had read Watteville's African memoirs, *Speak to the Earth,* shortly after its publication in 1935; that the Texas manuscript of **"The Snows"** proves that originally the story featured an epigraph from her book; that Watteville recounts how, suffering from malaria, she found that her mind "'floated away independently' to scenes of her past life"; and that in her book *Out in the Blue* she describes sitting by the bed of her father, who was dying after being mauled by a lion. Lewis's provocative essay suggests convincingly that Watteville's African memoirs were a likely written source for **"The Snows,"** but there does exist another possible source: the stories of Beryl Markham, whose autobiographical *West With the Night* was a best-seller in 1942.

West With the Night is a dramatic, anecdotal, non-chronological account of Markham's childhood in East Africa on her father's thoroughbred ranch, and of her adventures as a private pilot in Kenya. Chapter II, "Men with Blackwater Die," recounts her meeting with a dying man, and it contains many elements which are strikingly reminiscent of **"The Snows."** In this chapter, Markham describes flying with a tank of oxygen on a medical emergency to the outpost of Nungwe. She is detained there by a Mr. Ebert, who begs her to speak to Mr. Bergner, an immigrant who is dying of blackwater fever. Even before depicting her bedside encounter with Bergner, Markham sets the tone of the meeting by describing the environment in which he is dying:

> In the path of the rising sun, scattered bush, and tufts of grass lay a network of shadows over the earth, and, where these were thickest, I saw a single jackal forage expectantly in a mound of filth. . . .
>
> The sight of the jackal had brought to mind the scarcely comforting speculation that in Africa there is never any waste. Death particularly is never wasted. What the lion leaves, the hyena feasts upon and what scraps remain are morsels for the jackal, the vulture, or even the consuming sun.

The atmosphere which Markham depicts is strikingly similar to that of **"The Snows,"** wherein so many elements— the gangrene, the vultures, the hyenas—are associated with filth and death. Indeed, even Markham's grim personification of death—"Death, or at least the shadow that precedes him, seemed to have stalked far and wide that morning"—calls to mind Harry's observation that "death had come and rested its head on the foot of the cot and he could smell its breath."

Further, Markham speculates on the psychology of death as she attempts to prepare herself emotionally for her encounter with the dying stranger:

> Wherever you are, it seems, you must have news of some other place, some bigger place, so that a man on his deathbed in the swamplands of Victoria Nyanza is more interested in what has lately happened in this life than in what may happen in the next. It is really this that makes death so hard—curiosity unsatisfied.

This sense of missing out on life and the refusal to speculate on "what may happen in the next" nicely encapsulates the mental situation of Harry, who recognizes that his past experiences and feelings will die with him, and that his marriage to Helen—apparently intended to give him the financial security necessary for writing—had effectively insulated him from more recent experiences which he might have transmuted into art.

The bedside scene in *West With the Night* is itself highly reminiscent of **"The Snows"**:

> I pulled up a chair and sat in it near the head of Bergner's bed and tried to think of something to say, but he spoke first.
>
> His voice was soft and controlled, and very tired.
>
> "You don't mind being here, I hope," he said. "It's been four years since I left Nairobi, and there haven't been many letters." He ran the tip of his tongue over his lips and attempted a smile. "People forget," he added. "It's easy for a whole group of people to forget just one, but if you're very long in a place like this you remember everybody you ever met. You even worry about people you never liked; you get nostalgic about your enemies. It's all something to think about and it all helps."
>
> I nodded, watching little beads of sweat swell on his forehead. He was feverish, and I couldn't help wondering how long it would be before the inevitable delirium overtook him another time.

As a dying man far from home, Bergner finds himself thinking about individuals from his past, including enemies, because "it all helps" him to block out "the simple fact that now he is dying"—a fact which comes to him (as to Harry) "with ceaseless repetition." He particularly thinks about an old friend, a white hunter named Carl Hastings:

> ". . . I wonder if he ever married? He used to say he never would, but nobody believed him."
>
> "He did, though," I said. It was a name I had never heard, but it seemed a small enough gesture to lie about a nebulous Carl Hastings—even, if necessary, to give him a wife.

The conversation between Bergner and Markham rapidly becomes a tissue of well-intended lies—strikingly like the conversation between Harry and Helen ("The plane will be here tomorrow. . . . Then, in town, they will fix up your leg and then we will have some good destruction.") Further, as Gloria R. Dussinger suggests in her analysis of **"The Snows"** [in *Studies in Short Fiction,* Fall 1967], "By portraying the gradual retreat of Harry into the truth of his past, away from the woman and the falsehood of the present, Hemingway reveals his understanding of the psychology of a dying man," and in fact Bergner—like Harry—lapses into delirium-induced, jumbled recollections of a more "truthful" past:

> A fleck of spittle formed on his lips and he began to talk in meaningless garbled words.
>
> I couldn't understand all of what he said, but even in delirium he was neither sobbing nor complaining very much. He mumbled only about small things, people he had known, places in Africa, and once he mentioned Carl Hastings and Nairobi together in an almost intelligible sentence. I had come closer to the bed and leaned down over it, feeling a wave of sickness in my own body. Trying to quiet him, I talked, but it was a wasted effort . . .
>
> I wanted to call out for Ebert, for anyone. But I couldn't say anything and no one would have heard, so I stood there with my hands on Bergner's shoulders feeling the tremor of his muscles pass through my fingertips and hearing the rest of his life run out in a stream of little words carrying no meaning, bearing no secrets— or perhaps he had none.

Markham leaves Bergner as he dies, and the question naturally arises as to why she did not attempt to fly him to Nairobi for medical attention. But as Markham points out, she had in fact attempted such a rescue on an earlier occasion:

> All I could think of was the time I *had* moved a blackwater patient from Masongaleni in the elephant country to the hospital at Nairobi.
>
> I never knew afterward for how many hours of that journey I had flown with a corpse for company because, when I landed, the man was quite dead.

The idea of having a dead passenger aboard one's airplane is very reminiscent of the twist ending of **"The Snows,"** an ending which heretofore has been attributed solely to the influence of Bierce's "An Occurrence at Owl Creek Bridge."

West With the Night was not published until 1942; and despite its strikingly anecdotal nature, I have found no evidence that any of it was published piecemeal before 1942. Clearly, then, it could not have served as a written source for **"The Snows"**; but Markham herself may well have been the *oral* source. Hemingway had met Markham during his safari in East Africa (November, 1933 to February, 1934), and it is quite possible that she had acquainted him with the materials which she included in her book nearly a decade later. As Hemingway wrote to Maxwell Perkins in August of 1942:

> Did you read Beryl Markham's book, *West With The Night*? I knew her fairly well in Africa and never would have suspected that she could and would put pen to paper except to write in her flyer's log book. As it is, she has written so well, and marvelously well, that I was completely ashamed of myself as a writer. I felt that I was simply a carpenter with words, picking up whatever was furnished on the job and nailing them together and some times making an okay pig pen. But this girl who is, to my knowledge, very unpleasant, . . . can

write rings around all of us who consider ourselves as writers. The only parts of it that I know about personally, on account of having been there at the time and heard the other people's stories, are absolutely true. So, you have to take as truth the early stuff about when she was a child which is absolutely superb. She omits some very fantastic stuff which I know about which would destroy much of the character of the heroine; but what is that anyhow in writing? I wish you would get it and read it because it is really a bloody, wonderful book.

Sadly, the only person in a position to shed further light on the parallels between **"The Snows"** and *West With the Night,* Mrs. Markham herself, is unable to respond to my inquiries. In a letter dated May 15, 1984, her attorney in Nairobi states that her memory is "now very bad" and that she is "extremely vague" about Hemingway. One can only lament that Mrs. Markham's encounters with Hemingway in Africa were not recorded when she was in the prime of life.

The possibility of oral sources for **"The Snows"** was raised in 1970 by Jurgen K. A. Thomaneck [in *Studies in Short Fiction,* Spring 1970], who argues convincingly that A. E. Johann's *Gross ist Afrika,* although not published until 1939, contains information about leopards on Kilimanjaro which Hemingway probably heard about during the 1933-34 safari and incorporated into **"The Snows"** in the Spring of 1936. That Beryl Markham was possibly another oral source does not negate the importance of written sources such as Vivienne de Watteville's *Speak to the Earth* or *Out in the Blue.* Rather, it suggests that Hemingway was able to use both personal and vicarious experience, both the written and the spoken word, in the creation of one of his most powerful stories.

Jeffrey Meyers (essay date 1985)

SOURCE: "Tolstoy and Hemingway: 'The Death of Ivan Ilych' and 'The Snows of Kilimanjaro'," in *Disease and the Novel, 1880-1960,* Macmillan, 1985, pp. 19-29.

[*In the following essay, Meyers compares "The Snows of Kilimanjaro" to Tolstoy's "The Death of Ivan Ilych," maintaining that it is a modern, non-religious version of Tolstoy's tale.*]

The unexamined life is not worth living.
Plato, *Apology*

I

Tolstoy was Hemingway's literary hero, for both men had fought in battles and written a great novel about war and love. Despite his apparent deference, Hemingway matched his own short story masterpiece against Tolstoy's finest work in that genre when he consciously imitated and transformed "The Death of Ivan Ilych" (1886) in **"The Snows**

of Kilimanjaro"** (1936). In both stories the heroes are dying in early middle age of a smelly disease, which has trivial origins (a knock on the side, a scratch from a thorn) and symbolizes the corruption of their personal and professional lives. Both stories employ a suffocating symbol (the black sack and the hyena) to represent encroaching death. Both Ivan and Harry betrayed themselves for security, comfort and material success. Both never loved and now hate their wives, who encouraged their corruption and remain attached to the values their husbands have renounced. Both vacillate between self-loathing and self-pity. Both temporarily escape from their present torments by recalling happy memories (of childhood and early manhood) when they still possessed innocence and a sense of morality. As disease sharpens their insight both heroes reject the familiar lies and comforting deceptions about their recovery, suddenly accept the awful fact that they are going to die and by doing so lose their fear of death. The dreadful confrontation with mortality forces them to repudiate their past—which has been nothing more than a living death—and allows them to gain, in their final moments, spiritual conversion and self-redemption.

In Tolstoy's tale Hemingway recognized a sympathetic temperament and a literary form that enabled him to recreate in the modern tradition his own story of disease and dying, revelation and redemption. **"The Snows of Kilimanjaro"** is a triumphant example of what Eliot calls "Tradition and the Individual Talent": "The historical sense involves a perception, not only of the pastness of the past, but of its presence; the historical sense compels a man to write not merely with his own generation in his bones, but with a feeling that the whole of the literature of Europe from Homer and within it the whole of the literature of his own country has a simultaneous existence and composes a simultaneous order."

Hemingway's references to Tolstoy in four of his books and a major interview show that he used Tolstoy as an artistic standard, but retained sufficient critical judgment to avoid his dogmatism. Hemingway took Tolstoy's early accounts of combat in the Crimea and Caucasus on his first African safari, and in *Green Hills of Africa* admires his ability to evoke the Russian landscape: "I still had the Sevastopol book of Tolstoi and in the same volume I was reading a story called 'The Cossacks' that was very good. In it were the summer heat, the mosquitoes, the feel of the forest in the different seasons, and that river that the Tartars crossed, raiding, and I was living in that Russia again." In *A Moveable Feast* he tests Tolstoy's fiction against his own experience and praises the realistic portrayal of war: "the movement of troops, the terrain and the officers and the men and the fighting in Tolstoi. Tolstoi made the writing of Stephen Crane on the Civil War seem like the brilliant imagining of a sick boy who had never seen war. . . . Until I read the *Chartreuse de Parme* by Stendhal I had never read of war as it was except in Tolstoi."

In a reminiscent *Esquire* article, "Old Newsman Writes," Hemingway makes an important distinction between the didactic and imaginative passages in Tolstoy's greatest novel: "Read another book called *War and Peace* by Tolstoy and see how you will have to skip the big Political Thought passages, that he undoubtedly thought were the best things in the book when he wrote it, because they are no longer either true or important, if they ever were more than topical, and see how true and lasting and important the people and the action are." And in his Introduction to the anthology *Men at War,* his most substantial discussion of the master, he analyzes Tolstoy's account of Bagration's fighting and the battle of Borodino, his contempt for generals, his prolixity and the limitations of his thought. Hemingway learns an important lesson from the crucial weakness (accentuated in the late phase) of Tolstoy's art, and states his own artistic credo: "He could invent with more insight and truth than anyone who ever lived. But his ponderous and Messianic thinking was no better than many another evangelical professor of history and I learned from him to distrust my own Thinking with a capital T and to try to write as truly, as straightly, as objectively and as humbly as possible."

In Lillian Ross' *New Yorker* profile—which portrayed Hemingway as a pugnacious philistine, drinking heavily and grunting in pidgin English—he used art as a weapon for competition and combat. His vainglorious boast began with a handsome (self-reflective) compliment to the Slavic slugger, but provoked disastrous retaliation from the critics and seriously damaged his own reputation:

> Tolstoy [was] an artillery officer who fought at Sevastopol, who knew his stuff, who was a hell of a man anywhere you put him—bed, bar, in an empty room where he had to think. I started out very quiet and I beat Mr. Turgenev. Then I trained hard and I beat Mr. de Maupassant. I've fought two draws with Mr. Stendhal, and I think I had an edge in the last one. But nobody's going to get me in any ring with Mr. Tolstoy unless I'm crazy or I keep getting better.

II

In virtually all novels disease is evil and has negative effects; in "The Death of Ivan Ilych" it is positive and causes good. The spread of Ivan's abdominal cancer leads to a parallel growth in self-awareness. In the course of the novella he moves from worldly corruption to spiritual consciousness, from a decomposing body to an awakening soul. Disease, pain and the fear of death force him to struggle from a commonplace existence to an extraordinary conversion, insight, self-judgment and understanding of the nature of God.

There is a close correspondence between Ivan's character and career, the nature of his incurable disease, the treatment of the incompetent doctors, and the stages of his gradually increasing insight. The life of Ivan Ilych—dominated by propriety, comfort, ambition and vanity—"had been most simple and most ordinary and therefore most terrible." For his success and complacency never allowed him to examine the meaning and value of his life. Tolstoy emphasizes at the outset of the story that Ivan is "an intelligent, polished, lively and agreeable man . . . capable, cheerful, good-natured, and sociable." But his excruciating, purgatorial pain, which at first seems inappropriate to his venial sins, is necessary to jolt him into revelation and repentance.

Ivan, who is swallowed up by the material possessions that occupy a good deal of his leisure time, becomes incapable of perceiving reality (his cancer). He ironically attributes the etiology of his disease to a knock on his left side that he received while hanging drapes in the drawing room: "It is really so! I lost my life over that curtain as I might have done when storming a fort." The pressure and discomfort in his side gradually increase, and are accompanied by irritability and ill humor. His mouth tastes bad and his breath smells disgusting. He is unable to sleep at night as the poison penetrates more and more deeply into his whole being. His brother-in-law notices an immense physical change and pronounces him "a dead man." The gnawing disease—the ultimate truth—soon becomes a tangible enemy that drains his strength and will while it reveals his impotence and fear: "*It* would come and stand before him and look at him, and he would be petrified and the light would die out of his eyes, and he would again begin asking himself whether *It* alone was true. . . . He would to go his study, lie down, and again be alone with *It*: face to face with *It*. And nothing could be done with *It* except to look at it and shudder."

In Tolstoy's "The Death of Ivan Ilych" Hemingway recognized a sympathetic temperament and a literary form that enabled him to recreate in the modern tradition his own story of disease and dying, revelation and redemption.

—*Jeffrey Meyers*

In the third month of his disease he is given opium and injections of morphine, but they bring little relief and soon grow worse than the pain itself. He is tormented by the smell, uncleanliness and humiliation of his own excrement. The persistent pain never ceases for an instant and, as his life inexorably wanes, he clearly sees the approach of death. His mental sufferings become his chief torture, his sparks of hope are drowned in a sea of despair and he is acutely frightened of being alone. Finally overcome by unendurable agony, his screaming "continued for three days, and was so terrible that one could not hear it through two closed doors without horror."

Ivan's doctors cannot agree about the nature, treatment and prognosis of his disease. At first it does not seem a question of life or death, but a diagnosis of a floating kidney or appendicitis. (Ivan's internal organs have failed to do their "duty." But appendicitis is unlikely if he has injured his *left* side.) When a celebrated physician is consulted, Ivan experiences an annoying reversal of roles, for the doctor "put on just the same air towards him as he himself put on towards an accused person" in court. And when Ivan tries to ask if his case is serious, the doctor considers the question inappropriate and ignores it. The deluded Ivan attempts to follow the doctor's directions, but discovers there is no relation between the hopeless treatment and the dreadful disease. As his condition deteriorates, a specialist is called in. But he is also self-important, confused about the nature of the illness, unwilling to give a precise diagnosis, unable to state if it is possible for Ivan to recover.

The egoistic and hypocritical response of Ivan's friends and family exacerbates his condition. He first inspires fear and horror in his friends, but they are pleased that *he* is the one who is sick and soon begin to anticipate promotions to the position he has involuntarily vacated. Their condolences are manifestly insincere and—when Peter Ivanovich bounces on the springs of the pouffe—absurd. Ivan's wife and daughter—still very much attached to the world he has been severed from—are also fundamentally indifferent to his illness. They are more concerned with the annoying effect on their own lives than with the mortal danger to his. Ivan's wife "began to feel sorry for herself, and the more she pitied herself the more she hated her husband. She began to wish he would die; yet she did not want him to die because then his salary would cease." Ivan, who cannot stand her health and hypocrisy, warmly returns her hatred as she kisses him goodnight.

When Ivan, who childishly desires their pity, begins to relate the doctor's grim prognostications, his wife and daughter feel he is poisoning their lives and cannot bear to hear the end of his tedious tale. Neither physician nor family dare acknowledge the reality of his cancer. Both collaborate in lies, encourage his self-deception, blame Ivan for his illness and reduce the significance of his death to a casual, unpleasant, almost indecent incident: "Those lies—lies enacted over him on the eve of his death and destined to degrade this awful, solemn act to the level of their visitings, their curtains, their sturgeon for dinner—were a terrible agony for Ivan."

The family prospers as Ivan declines, and his daughter becomes engaged as he searches for the meaning of his misery. Just after the specialist has failed to help him, she appears in full evening dress, ready to leave for the theater. Her young exposed breasts mock Ivan's wasted flesh just as her self-absorption ignores his agony. She is "impatient with illness, suffering, and death, because they interfered with her happiness," and selfishly exclaims: "I am sorry for papa, but why should we be tortured?"

Ivan's stages of awareness develop as the estrangement from his family becomes complete. He begins his illness, as he has lived his life, in a state of self-deception; and assures himself that everything is or soon will be well. But when the doctors fail and his brother-in-law forces him to accept his immense physical change, he rejects the facile explanation of appendix or kidney disorders, and admits that he will be dead in a matter of weeks or even

days. At this point he begins to question the meaning of life. But he still protests his innocence, craves pity, blames others, hates his family and despises *their* lies.

The metaphor of Ivan pushed deeper and deeper into a suffocating black sack, without ever reaching the bottom, effectively symbolizes his meaningless past life and present search for truth through severe self-examination. As Georg Lukacs observes [in *Studies in European Realism*, 1964]:

> [Tolstoy] turns the inevitable isolation of the dying Ivan Ilyich into . . . an island of horror, of a horrible death after a meaningless life—and inspires with a terrible dark poetry all the figures and all the objects through which the human relationships are conveyed. The fading world of court sittings, cardparties, visits to the theatre, ugly furniture, down to the nauseating filth of the dying man's bodily functions, is here integrated to a most vivid and animated world in which each object eloquently and poetically expresses the soul-destroying emptiness and futility of [middle-class life in materialist society].

Ivan cannot yet find the truth. He accuses God of cruelty while doubting His very existence, and challenges his Creator to strike him dead. Stimulated by intense pain, he finally perceives that his personal relations, his callous official life and his obsession with material things has led him to kind of death in life: that he has not lived as he ought to have done. He now realizes that he has suppressed all his generous and humane impulses and accepted a corrupt system of values: "It occurred to him that his scarcely perceptible attempts to struggle against what was considered good by most highly placed people, those scarcely noticeable impulses which he had immediately suppressed, might have been the real thing, and all the rest false."

As the story focuses on the internal drama of death, Ivan perceives that the true meaning of life has been hidden by falsehood, that God is a hound of heaven who mortified his sinful body in order to shut out the world and turn him inward. He works out his salvation by affirming his belief in God's goodness despite the terrible sufferings he has been forced to endure. He achieves a life-deepening and life-extending insight, and finds some relief by confessing to a priest.

Ivan is led back to the ultimate truth through the humble ideal of his servant and his son, who appear briefly as symbols of innocence in the opening chapter. His servant Gerasim—a sharp contrast to the corrupt city folk—is an efficient, cheerful and healthy peasant. He accepts death as the natural conclusion of life (just as he accepts excrement as the natural product of ingestion), and says of Ivan's death: "It's God's will. We shall all come to it some day." Gerasim is the only person who brings relief during Ivan's suffering. He feels better when Gerasim holds his legs; and his strength and vitality (which Ivan resents in other men) comfort him.

Ivan learns to recapture that childhood purity through his own son—the only one in the family who understands and pities his frightened and pathetic father. Two hours before his death, when Ivan is still desperately screaming, his son creeps softly into the room and receives his father's benediction. At this very moment Ivan sees the light—which was extinguished from his eyes and could not be found at the end of the black sack—and realizes that his life can still be rectified. For the first time, he abandons his lifelong self-absorption and feels sorry (not for himself) but for his weeping son. He asks forgiveness, knowing God will understand, accepts his punitive pain, and loses his fear of death in the hope of eternal salvation.

As his emaciated body twitches and dry throat rattles, someone at his bedside echoes Christ's last words about His suffering in human life: "It is finished" (John 19:30). Ivan's last words, an *imitatio Christi,* refute the terrible *It* that had pursued him earlier in the story: "Death is finished . . . It is no more!" Then, actively rather than passively: "He drew in a breath, stopped in the midst of a sigh, stretched out, and died."

The story begins, as it ends, with the death of Ivan Ilych. But it is not until his sudden but efficacious deathbed conversion that we understand why the dead Ivan, who smells (like the story) of incense and carbolic, seems "much changed": "his face was handsomer and above all more dignified than when he was alive. The expression on the face said that what was necessary had been accomplished, and accomplished rightly. Besides this there was in that expression a reproach and warning to the living"— which the living (like Ivan himself) choose to ignore until faced with the Four Last Things: death, judgment, heaven and hell.

The extreme repetition, moralistic tone, dogmatic message and deathbed conversion all characteristically convey the religious doctrine preached by Tolstoy during the last phase of his career, when he tried to repudiate both his art and his sensual self. He believed that life was a gift of God and a preparation for death, which released the soul for judgment. And he reveals how Ivan's response to disease teaches him how to die and—paradoxically—how to live. Tolstoy uses illness to devalue the physical side of life and suggest that vanity and ambition lead straight to a smelly death. But he also distances the effects of disease by drawing a distinction between the material reality, in which Ivan had placed so much emphasis, and the wisdom of the soul. The paradigmatic illumination in "The Death of Ivan Ilych" is Tolstoy's noble contribution to the *ars moriendi* and the literature of salvation—a tradition which begins with the death of Socrates in *Phaedo* and Cicero's *De Senectute,* reaches a peak in Taylor's *Holy Dying,* progresses with Young's *Night Thoughts* and Beddoes' *Death's Jest-Book,* and continues after Tolstoy in Lawrence's "The Ship of Death" and Hemingway's **"The Snows of Kilimanjaro."**

III

In **"The Snows of Kilimanjaro"** Hemingway secularizes "The Death of Ivan Ilych," replaces faith in God as the

highest good with fidelity to Art, removes the "Messianic thinking" from his fiction and creates a work that is technically superior to—though less ambitious and profound than—Tolstoy's story. Harry is a much more substantial, insightful and interesting character than the archetypal Ivan; the illusory dream of the plane rescue is far more effective than the sudden deathbed conversion. By eliminating the didactic element and objectifying his own emotions, Hemingway also purged the radical defect—the arrogant posturings and tedious pontifications—that marred his major works of the mid-1930s: *Death in the Afternoon* and *Green Hills of Africa.* Edmund Wilson (with a notable mixed metaphor) identified this crucial weakness: "As soon as Hemingway drops the burning-glass of the disciplined and objective art with which he has learned to concentrate in a story the light of the emotions that flood in on him, he straightaway becomes befuddled, slops over. . . . As soon as Hemingway begins speaking in the first person, he seems to lose his bearings, not merely as a critic of life, but even as a craftsman."

Hemingway achieves his inspiration by imitating Tolstoy and his originality by diverging from him. His subject and theme are the same, but his style and emphasis are different. Ivan is led to God by the innocence of his son and the primitive Christianity of his servant; Harry is led to the pure snows of Mount Kilimanjaro, which the Masai call "the House of God," by the frozen leopard who sought the heights that Harry abandoned and whose clean carcass is contrasted with Harry's rotting leg. The light that Ivan sees at the end of the sack becomes the vision of the plane that transports Harry to the top of Kilimanjaro: "great, high, and unbelievably white in the sun."

Tolstoy's hero is an ordinary man; Hemingway's—through the brilliant flashbacks of his experiences in love, sport, travel, violence and war—is extraordinary. Ivan justifies himself; Harry condemns himself. Ivan's disease is agonizing; Harry's painless. Ivan goes through a shattering trauma before achieving a calm detachment from life; Harry begins with detachment, and calmly but regretfully waits for death. Tolstoy's setting is interior and Ivan looks inward to save his soul; Hemingway's setting is exterior and Harry gazes outward to find the truth. (The description of the African animals and landscape is one of the great strengths of the story.) Harry, isolated in the wilderness, rejects his wife; Ivan, surrounded by family and friends, is rejected by them. Ivan could say, in the words of the Psalmist: "My heart is sore pained within me: and the terrors of death are fallen upon me" (55:4); Harry could say: "I will lift up mine eyes unto the hills, from whence cometh my help" (121:1).

Tolstoy's expansive story is an apologue for the edification of others; Hemingway's taut tale is an autobiographical laceration for the benefit of himself. Ivan, who led a tranquil existence, ignored death until stricken by disease and then became obsessed by it; Harry, who led a violent life, was obsessed by death and then got "as bored with dying as with everything else." Though both deaths are purgatorial punishments, Ivan's is divinely designed while Harry's is absurdly accidental. The most meaningful aspect of Ivan's life is the anticipation of his future salvation; the most significant aspect of Harry's life is the recollection of the past—when he tested his courage and achieved fulfillment, before abandoning his creative gift and surrendering to a life of luxury.

Harry's wife Helen is the richest and least-loved of the women in his life. Harry thinks she is the instrument of corruption and self-betrayal, and connects her to the story of "poor Julian" ("Scott Fitzgerald" in the original *Esquire* version of the tale) that expressed his romantic awe of the wealthy. In "The Rich Boy" Fitzgerald confidentially remarks: "Let me tell you about the very rich. They are different from you and me. They possess and enjoy early, and it does something to them, makes them soft where we are hard, and cynical where we are trustful," But it is actually the gangrenous Harry—not the hard-boiled Helen—who becomes soft and cynical. His excessive comfort "softened his will to work" and he became defensively cynical when confronted with the ultimate truth about his life.

The ironic theme of **"The Snows of Kilimanjaro"** is that the dying Harry "would never write the things that he had saved to write until he knew enough to write them well." Harry's mental flashbacks contrast his potential with his tragic failure, connect the image of snow with the theme of death, portray a truthful natural life and the enjoyment of pleasures not bought by money but earned by war. The flashbacks also reveal that the threat of death has concentrated Harry's mind, that he had a great and genuine talent, and that he could have fulfilled his promise and ensured his salvation (for Hemingway equates artistic with moral effort) if he had only been able to record the vivid memories that show him at the very height of his powers.

Both Tolstoy and Hemingway use disease and dying realistically and symbolically. Both heroes feel responsible for and guilty about their sickness and try to blame their wives, who resent the hostility of the dying. Both heroes connect their decay and destruction to their spiritual states. But disease and morality are not scientifically related: bacteria and virus are impartial, good and evil men equally subject to death.

Hemingway adapts the subject of Tolstoy's moral fable—the death of the central character, his reflections on the past, his insights while dying—to the poignant situation of his typical hero, who betrayed his own stoical code and is condemned by his own moral weakness. The tragedy expressed in Tolstoy's morbid imagery and claustrophobic interiors is relieved by Ivan's joyful encounter with God. Hemingway's natural imagery and vital description of the Masai country—"There was a pleasant camp under big trees against a hill, with good water, and close by, a nearly dry water hole where sand grouse flighted in the mornings"—intensify Harry's tragic sense of waste and final loss of life. Hemingway removes Tolstoy's story from the Christian context, stresses self-fulfillment rather than faith in God, emphasizes the individual rather than the social background, and gives it a bitter

modern tone, but he retains the same redemptive pattern and the same exemplary mode.

Jerry A. Herndon (essay date 1986)

SOURCE: "'The Snows of Kilimanjaro': Another Look at Theme and Point of View," in *The South Atlantic Quarterly,* Vol. LXXXV, No. 4, Autumn, 1986, pp. 351-59.

[*In the following essay, Herndon reevaluates thematic and structural aspects of "The Snows of Kilimanjaro," asserting that Harry does achieve moral redemption at the conclusion of the story.*]

In the long-running critical debate about the resolution of Hemingway's **"The Snows of Kilimanjaro,"** a number of critics have maintained that Harry's dream of flight at the end of the story—at the end of *his* story, at any rate—is the self-indulgent delusion of a failure. Others, like Max Westbrook, for instance, insist that the dream flight to Kilimanjaro, the Masai "House of God," signifies a moral triumph [in the *Texas Quarterly,* Winter 1966]. Westbrook sees Kilimanjaro as "an appropriate image of Harry's moral achievement," which consists in his coming to an honest awareness of his moral corruption and of his "apartness from the permanence symbolized by Kilimanjaro." His self-awareness, in Westbrook's view, purges Harry of "the sickness of temporal rot," and, in conjunction with his "redemptive knowledge of the real," prepares him for death.

I am in agreement with Max Westbrook and the other critics—Oliver Evans, for example, who see the dream-flight as a vision of redemption. I propose to reexamine some elements in the story which lend credibility to this interpretation, looking at these elements more closely than has previously been done.

I

It is clear from the outset that Harry, the protagonist, sees life as essentially pain and loss. He has been obsessed with death for years, but its coming as the result of infection from an accidental scratch underlines his bitter assessment of life's unfairness as he thinks over his losses. It is this intense preoccupation with the failures of his past life that wrings from him his last bitter retort to Helen, when she naively remarks, "'You've never lost anything. You're the most complete man I've ever known.'" "'Christ,'" Harry remarks, "'How little a woman knows.'" Helen, of course, has not been aware of his thoughts about his past.

Harry's thoughts are not merely of personal loss, but are also about the pain and the losses he has witnessed in the lives of others, even in the lives of nations. Thus, his vision of life is a universal one, and hence is a significant comment on human life, not just a personal petulance. The first item in his meditations on "the things he had saved to write" is a memory of the retreat of the Greeks from Eastern Thrace to Macedonia in 1922, before the invading Turks. Hemingway had witnessed this retreat, observing the sufferings of the civilian refugees which affected him so strongly he could never forget them. He does not let his alter ego think of the civilians' misery and suffering, but he no doubt felt, on his principle of selective omission, that these events were still "there," and still felt by both protagonist and reader as a part of the context of the memory.

The next memory Harry recalls is an instance of the horrors wrought by complacent men in charge, even when motivated by idealism. He thinks of the destitute civilians who died in the winter snows when Fridtjof Nansen, the implacable Norwegian humanitarian, in his role as League of Nations High Commissioner for Refugees, ordered "exchange of populations" in the countries of the Balkan Peninsula after the First World War. By agreement with the Greek and Turkish governments, Nansen moved half a million turks out of Macedonia to make room for the Greeks fleeing from Turkish territory. He also resettled some of the Greeks in Western Thrace. Harry remembers the arrogance of the "old man" when he denied that the snow clearly visible on the mountains in Bulgaria was really snow. He said, "It's too early for snow."

Nansen did not want the elements to interfere with implementation of his humanitarian plan. Perhaps Hemingway means to suggest that the old man had received too much praise for his previous humanitarian efforts, those involving repatriation of prisoners of war from the Far East and famine relief in Russia, and had been corrupted by the adulation. Over-confidence in his own wisdom and humanity had made the plan he conceived more important than the people it was designed to help. It is interesting to note that the sympathy of Hemingway's protagonist extends to the Turkish refugees as well as to the Greek noncombatants whose flight Hemingway had witnessed. This is a point worth noting, since it indicates that Hemingway is broadening Harry's awareness of the pain and suffering at the heart of human life to include both sides in the Greco-Turkish war. Other critics note only Hemingway's sympathy with the Greeks, though one of his dispatches filed with *The Toronto Daily Star* had mentioned the Turks being driven out of Thrace by the Greeks, and the random, senseless brutality practiced against some of them. Hemingway's sympathy lay with the suffering noncombatants on both sides.

Harry goes on to think sardonically of how eager people are to be lied to by those they worship because of their power. Nansen's secretary immediately repeats the old man's pronouncement to the other girls, "No, you see. It's not snow . . . ," and they chorus in unison, "It's not snow we were mistaken." But, Harry recalls, "it was . . . snow all right and he sent them on into it. . . . And it was snow they tramped along in until they died that winter." The old man got the Nobel Peace Prize for his earlier humanitarian efforts, and further adulation for the genius of "exchange of populations."

One notes several interesting things about Harry's meditations in this first italicized passage. For one thing, he thinks of snow-covered mountains, not only in Bulgaria but also in Austria. One set of reminiscences, those of Austria, recalls times of great happiness and exhilaration. But these memories are mingled with awareness of the pain of others—of the deserter whom Harry and his wife helped escape, and of Herr Lent's losing at cards his profit and capital for his skiing school. Thus, both aspects of life, the sweet and the bitter, are reflected in these memories.

It seems fitting to point out here that the view that Kilimanjaro does not appear in the story until the end, in Harry's dream, a view that is a critical commonplace, may not be correct. Harry's first meditation practically begins with snow-covered mountains associated with pain and death, associations appropriate to his situation. Perhaps, like Hemingway himself, Harry has seen snow-covered Kilimanjaro on the way to his hunting camp, and perhaps it is the memory of Kilimanjaro that brings snow-topped mountains and the ecstasies and agonies of human life he associates with them to his mind. Hemingway may expect the reader to realize this, and to connect the mountain with the idea of eternity. Given this assumption, one realizes that Hemingway's principle of selective omission, his "iceberg principle," is operative here, and, though the great mountain is not mentioned within the story until the end, it is there as an unspoken mental reality, provoking Harry's brooding reflections on his past and the tragic changes he has seen in the world.

It is worth noting that Harry's initial meditation on experiences worth writing about focuses on Christmas Day. In this context, he recalls both the ecstasy of a perfect skiing run in postwar Austria and the murderous attack by Baker on the Austrian officers' leave train during the war. Barker performed his assassination run on a "cold, bright Christmas day" when "the mountains [were] showing across the plain . . .". Thus, there is a connection between this initial meditation and the last one, in which Harry thinks of the officer disemboweled by a stick bomb in the barbed wire, and remembers a debate about whether "our Lord" ever sent a man more pain than he could bear. Harry is asking himself, by implication, these questions: "What is the meaning of all this? And what is the relevance of the supposed truths of Christianity to the savagery of man's life?" It is natural for Harry to reflect on these questions in his last hours, especially if he, like Hemingway in 1933, has passed Christmas in his hunting camp.

Harry's second meditation sequence drifts to personal losses, to the quarreling with a first wife which caused her to leave him, and the loneliness he had felt for her thereafter. He thinks of how he tried to pick up the thread with her after quarreling with his second wife and how the first one's letter ruined his reconciliation with the second. Mixed in with the memories of the multiple loss of love are memories of the universal pain of the World War. He remembers Greek artillery units firing into their own troops, and a British observer crying like a child at their tragic, bloody incompetence. And he remembers

Greek officers shooting into their own men as they broke and ran before a Turkish advance, then breaking and running themselves.

The third meditation is a series of images of pain and loss, beginning with the memory of Grandfather's log house in Michigan, and its burning. After the fire, the burned, twisted barrels of the old man's guns lay on the ash heap, but he refused to let the children play with them. Too many irreplaceable memories were connected with the guns, so he never let anyone touch them to profane those memories. And he never bought any more guns and never hunted again. The memories of the past were burned to ashes with the house, in a sense.

Harry's memory switches to the Black Forest and the delights of trout fishing after the war, but the black depths of life are indicated in his memory of the Triberg hotel proprietor who hanged himself after being ruined by post-war Germany's runaway inflation. Then he remembers wistfully the Paris of his first writing and first love, and the happiness he enjoyed there in the midst of poverty. He recalls that life lived close to the bone as infinitely preferable to the soft, rich life that trading on his talents has bought him.

In the fourth meditation, Harry recalls the beauty of a ranch in Wyoming, with "the silvered gray of the sage brush, the quick, clear water in the irrigation ditches, and the heavy green of the alfalfa." Significantly, in connection with the symbolism of the great African mountain in this story, he also recalls "behind the mountains, the clear sharpness of the peak in the evening light and, riding down along the trail in the moonlight, bright across the valley." Then, as if it is recalled by this image of beauty, he remembers the tragedy of "the half-wit chore boy" who thought he was doing his duty to protect the ranch's hay by killing a man who stopped to get some feed. The man had beaten the boy when he had worked for him, and he threatened to beat him again when the boy told him he could not have any hay. Harry remembers the boy's bewildered horror when he was arrested for doing what he thought was his duty. This stark image of pain and loss, Harry reflects, is only one of "at least twenty good stories" he might have written "from out there" and never had. One assumes that all the stories would have the same meaning, emphasizing the loss and pain inseparable from life.

Harry, one recalls, felt that if one could do it, if one had time enough, his perception of the essence of life "telescoped so that you might put it all into one paragraph if you could get it right." Thus, it is not surprising that his last meditation puts it all—all the pain and the questioning—into one paragraph. So far as I know, no other critic has commented on this aspect of the story. Harry remembers Williamson, the disemboweled officer caught in the barbed wire so that they had to cut him loose, and Williamson's begging him to shoot him "For Christ sake. . . ." As he remembers bitterly how long it took the morphine to work, he recalls their argument about whether "our Lord [ever sent] you anything you could not bear," and someone's theory "that at a certain time the pain passed

you out automatically." Williamson had received no such mercy.

Ironically, Harry's own pain, the physical pain, *has* stopped, just as "he had felt it breaking him." But the psychic pain remains, and the bitterness at his approaching death which cuts short his effort at artistic and moral redemption. But he has gotten his view of life's essence—its pain and loss—and all his questioning about its meaning, into one paragraph. So it is appropriate that he tells Helen shortly afterward, "'I've been writing.'" He won't see it in print, but mental creation precedes the physical act of writing, and he has condensed the questioning implicit in the multiple-paragraph meditations into just one. Thus, if, as Max Westbrook suggests, salvation is "a state of being," Harry has redeemed himself as an artist, given the short time left to him. He has no time to write, only time to think out verbally what he would write, if given time. I agree with Westbrook that "Harry's expiation in consciousness is as genuine as the redemption through courage in hunting that is achieved by Francis Macomber. . . ."

II

Harry achieves redemption not merely as an artist, but as a man as well. This can be seen in his moving from the bitter verbal brutality directed against the woman who is his current companion to compassion for her. His sarcastic reply to her statement that "'There must be something I can do'" is the suggestion that she cut his leg off herself or shoot him. When she tells him he can't die if he doesn't give up, he calls her "'a bloody fool.'" He twists the knife when she asks if he loves her: "'No,'" he replies, "'I never have.'"

Following his first meditation about the losses he has seen others suffer, and those he has experienced himself, he tells her that "'Love is a dunghill'" and that she used her "'damned money'" to buy him. He relents briefly when she begins to cry, and tells him he is having no fun in what he is doing, that he is "'trying to kill to keep [himself] alive. . . .'" Then he tells her he loves her. But her soft, appreciative reply evokes his bitterness again and he calls her a "'rich bitch.'" When she asks him why he has "'to turn into a devil,'" he says, "'I don't like to leave anything. . . . I don't like to leave things behind.'"

After this, Harry falls asleep, and when he awakes, he learns that "'Memsahib's gone to shoot.'" Harry reflects on her thoughtfulness, knowing that she "had gone well away" from the camp to hunt so that she would not disturb the game in his view, knowing how well he liked to watch it.

Harry next reflects that "it was not her fault" that "he was already over" when he had accepted a liaison with her. He reflects on the sapping of his will to work by his subsidized way of life, and tells himself honestly that "It wasn't this woman's fault." She is only the last in a series of wealthy paramours who have made possible the rich living which has dulled his will to write.

Then Harry slips and thinks of Helen as "this rich bitch, this kindly caretaker and destroyer of his talent." But he tells himself immediately, "Nonsense. He had destroyed his talent himself." He had done so, he reflects, "by not using it, by betrayals of himself . . . by drinking so much that he blunted the edge of his perceptions, by laziness, by sloth, and by snobbery . . . ." Then with complete honesty, he thinks, "We must all be cut out for what we do. . . . However you make your living is where your talent lies." That is to say, people do not define themselves by their supposed "potential"—but by what they actually do. People *are* what they *do*, not what they *promise* to do.

Harry's achieving complete honesty with himself is an aspect of his moral redemption. So is the compassion, the pity, he develops for Helen. Earlier, when she had said that even if he didn't care whether the truck came, she did, he had told her, "'You give a damn about so many things that I don't.'" Her reply was, "'Not so many, Harry.'" In effect, Harry acknowledges this, and admits that Helen is, after all, not so very different from himself, as he thinks of the pain and the losses she has suffered in her own life. She "had had a husband and children . . . had taken lovers and been dissatisfied with them, and . . . loved him dearly as a writer, as a man, as a companion and as a proud possession . . . ."

Harry remembers that Helen's "husband had died when she was still . . . comparatively young" and that she had tried to fill the void in her life with devotion to "her two just-grown children, who did not need her. . . ." So she turned for solace to absorption in "her stable of horses, [and her] . . . books," and to alcohol. She drank in order to be able to sleep, so that she could forget her pain and emptiness. He continues to reflect,

> That was before the lovers. After she had the lovers she did not drink so much because she did not have to be drunk to sleep. But the lovers bored her. She had been married to a man who had never bored her and these people bored her very much.

> Then one of her two children was killed in a place crash and after that was over she did not want the lovers, and drink being no anaesthetic she had to make another life. Suddenly, she had been acutely frightened of being alone.

She needed "some one . . . she respected with her," and she had chosen Harry, ironically under the impression that "he did exactly what he wanted to." With him, "she had built herself a new life. . . ." Harry realizes, with genuine feeling *for* her, that his accidental infection and approaching death has the result of bringing the new life she has built to an end. He thinks of the irony of the deadly scratch, seemingly so insignificant at first, which he got while trying to slip up on a herd of waterbuck for a picture. "They had bolted, too, before he got the picture." The author suggests with this little vignette, by the way, the theme of the story: that in life, the ideal can never be captured.

When the woman returns from her hunt, performed for the purpose of getting an antelope so that a broth can be made

for Harry, he greets her pleasantly, compliments her on her shooting, and, when she asks him to promise not to talk brutally to her again, he pretends not to remember what he has said. He cautions her to put on her mosquito boots, then, while she is bathing, he thinks of his losses in love. When she returns, she asks him how he feels. He says he feels "'all right'" and she asks him to "'take some broth.'" He doesn't want it, and tells her bitterly that he is going to die. When she says "'please,'" however, he drinks it, even though it almost gags him to get it down, in order to please her. Then he tells her, "'You're a fine woman. . . . Don't pay any attention to me.'"

Their conversation continues, spaced by intervals of Harry's silent meditation, but Harry is kind, and does not say anything brutal or sarcastic to her again. Thus, having achieved complete honesty with himself, and compassion for this woman who loves him, Harry is morally ready for death. Since perfect fulfillment is impossible for man, Hemingway implies, acceptance of one's limitations and compassion for others is the best one can do. As Hamlet puts it, "'readiness is all.'" Harry's flight toward the ineffable—toward whatever lies beyond life's foredoomed strivings toward the ideal—is presented symbolically, the only way in which the ineffable can be presented. Kilimanjaro represents death, and whatever lies beyond.

At the end of the story, the point of view shifts, necessarily, from the dream-vision of Harry's last few moments of consciousness, to the earth-bound viewpoint of Helen, who has also been dreaming. This return to the reality of time, decay, and death, does not, as Scott MacDonald insists [in *Studies in Short Fiction,* Winter 1974], "undercut" the nobility implied in Harry's death-dream. It is made necessary by the fact that Harry is now dead, and Helen is still alive with all her disappointments and fears. She is not yet at the point of death, not yet ready for *her* flight into the unknowable.

Helen has been dreaming that she is at her house on Long Island "the night before her daughter's début." Her father is there, and he has been "very rude." When the hyena outside the tent wakes her, the influence of the dream lingers, and she is "very afraid." One realizes which daughter she was dreaming of: the one who died in the plane crash and whose death had left her "acutely frightened of being alone." She awakes, with the dream's fear in her heart, only to discover that the new life she had built after her daughter's death has been destroyed. Harry is dead, and this woman, presented very compassionately by Hemingway through the protagonist's consciousness, awakes from *her* dream to life's bitter reality. The hyena cries outside the tent again, but she cannot hear him. All she can hear is the pounding of her own heart, as she stares in terror at Harry's motionless body awkwardly sprawled on his cot.

Kenneth G. Johnston (essay date 1988)

SOURCE: "The Silly Wasters: Tzara and the Poet in 'The Snows of Kilimanjaro'," in *The Hemingway Review,* Vol. VIII, No. 1, Fall, 1988, pp. 50-6.

[*In the following essay, Johnston discusses Hemingway's treatment of Dadaism—particularly its most important figure Tristan Tzara—in "The Snows of Kilimanjaro."*]

When Ernest Hemingway arrived in Paris at the end of 1921 to launch his writing career, another expatriate, Tristan Tzara, was already there making a circus of the literary scene. It would be hard to imagine two more disparate artists: the quiet, unknown American, shy and serious, totally dedicated to his craft, slowly and meticulously shaping his "true sentences" in the solitude of a rented room; the brash, notorious Romanian, bold and mischievous, totally dedicated to the demolition of traditional art and literature, chanting his Dada sense and nonsense in the streets and at public *soirees*.

The antics and manifestoes of the Dadaists were bound to arouse the suspicions of any aspiring, serious young writer. "We are circus directors," Tzara announced in his first manifesto, "whistling amid the winds of carnivals convents bawdy houses theatres realities sentiments restaurants HoHiHoHo Bang." And what a circus it was! The Dadaists created "poems" by picking words at random out of a hat: they shouted others—often nonsense verbal collages—to the deafening accompaniment of saxophones and bass drums and bells; they published the alphabet in the form of a poem and entitled it "Suicide"; they printed a random extract from the telephone book under the title "Psst"; Tzara and two others once presented a "simultaneous poem"—a recitation of three separate texts, in three different languages, read simultaneously; they presented "plays" that consisted of only two lines of unrelated dialogue; they held art exhibitions in public urinals; they so shocked, outraged, and taunted their bourgeois audiences that often their public festivals ended in near riots, and once the Dada performers were pelted with eggs, tomatoes, and, if Tzara is to be believed, beefsteaks. "I am an idiot, I am a clown, I am a faker," Tzara proclaimed in his "Manifesto of mr. aa the antiphilosopher." "You are all idiots . . . Give yourself a poke in the nose and drop dead. dada."

Little wonder, then, that the dapper little Romanian with the monocle made a deep impression on the young Hemingway, who scorned the poseurs and fake artists that crowded the streets and cafes of Paris.

Hemingway was probably dismayed when Ford Madox Ford placed four Dada fragments by Tzara immediately ahead of his untitled short story ("**Indian Camp**") in the April 1924 issue of the *transatlantic review*. Tzara's contribution, entitled "Monsieur Aa L'Antiphilosophe," opens with a dire warning to a "Captain" that fire and flood threaten, that "the knot of serpents, the lash of chains, advance triumphantly through the land contaminated by perpetual rage." The anti-philosopher cautions the Captain to beware: "all the accusations of the mistreated animals, in bites above the bed, yawn like rosettes of blood, the rain of stone teeth and the stains of excrement in the cages bury us in cloaks endless like the snow." Apparently Hemingway wanted to distance himself from this extravagantly provocative prophecy of revolution and/or

doomsday, for in the next issue of the review he expressed his disdain for the man and his work:

> Dada is dead although Tzara still cuddles its emaciated little corpse to his breast and croons a Roumanian folksong, written by Princess Bibesco, while he tries to get the dead little lips to take sustenance from his monocle.

And in the August issue, which Hemingway edited in Ford's absence and which printed an absurd, Dada-like play by Ring Lardner, he continued his attack: "How very much better dadas the American dadas, who do not know they are dadas . . . are than the French and Roumanians who know it so well."

Tzara's name surfaced again—as a synonym for the frivolous—in a letter Hemingway wrote to John Dos Passos in 1932 in which he expressed his concern over the forthcoming critical reception of *Death in the Afternoon*:

> God damn but I'm glad you liked it. If Malcolm Cowley or one of those recent converts pans it in New Republic or Nation or New Masses in the name of their newly risen Lord . . . you might write that letter. . . . It's damned funny when I used to get the horrors about the way things were going those guys never took the slightest interest nor even followed it. They were all in Europe and got worked up over Tristan Tzara when the god damndest things were happening— then when you've gotten . . . completely disillusioned on the *working* of anything but intelligent political assassination then they start out and say, "Don't you see the injustice, the Big Things that are happening. Why don't you write about them etc."

As Hemingway anticipated, Cowley did raise the question of social injustice in his lukewarm review of *Death in the Afternoon*:

> Bull-fighting really does imply a certain attitude toward life, a willingness to accept things as they are, bad as they are, and to recompense oneself by regarding them as a picturesque tragedy. Bull-fighting does, I think, imply an aristocracy, an established Church, a proletariat resigned to suffering pain in return for the privilege of seeing pain inflicted on others, and a rabble of gladiators, bootlickers and whores; but I am just as glad that Hemingway does not consciously draw these implications.

This social-conscience commentary on the bullfight was the sort of nonsense guaranteed to enrage Hemingway. To make matters even worse, Cowley chided Hemingway for having "fallen into the habit of writing with his eyes turned backwards. This habit, revealed engagingly in all his books, is now becoming a vice."

Three years later Hemingway would give us a fictional glimpse of Tzara, and once again his contempt spilled over to include an American friend of the Romanian poet/essayist/playwright. In a flashback section in "**The Snows of Kilimanjaro**" the dying writer, Harry, remembers seeing in a Paris cafe "that American poet with a pile of saucers in front of him and a stupid look on his potato face talking about the Dada movement with a Roumanian who said his name was Tristan Tzara, who always wore a monocle and had a headache." What is remarkable is not that Hemingway took his final jab at Tzara, but rather that the allusion—if one accepts Hemingway's judgement of Tzara and the Dada movement—enriches the story's central theme of the wasted life. Harry has betrayed his talent and, implies Hemingway, so has Tzara. It is no accident that the reference to Tzara appears in a section filled with memories of various mistakes and betrayals.

The glimpse of Tzara in **"The Snows"** is both well informed and cleverly satirical. Hemingway's wording casts doubts on the authenticity of Tzara's name and, thus, on the credibility of the man himself. Tristan Tzara (1896-1963) was born Sami Rosenstock in Moinesti, Roumania; sixteen years later in Bucharest, he was calling himself S. Samyro; by 1916 in Zurich he was known to the Dada group as Tristan Tzara. Hemingway's reference to Tzara's constant headache may also be more subtly informed than openly contemptuous. Tzara did suffer from severe and frequent headaches, but the inclusion of that fact may also have been intended as an allusion to the Dadaists's assault on reason. In his important "Dada Manifesto 1918." Tzara urged the "abolition of logic, which is the dance of those impotent to create." Moreover, Tzara's first major Dada work was a short play entitled *La Premiere Aventure Celeste de M. Antipyrine* (1916). "Although it has been translated as the *First Celestial Adventure of Mr. Fire-Extinguisher*," writes Elmer Peterson, "it seems it would be proper to substitute Aspirin for Fire-Extinguisher, as Antipyrine was a popular headache remedy at the time in France and Switzerland."

The identity of the American poet in **"The Snows of Kilimanjaro,"** another work in which Hemingway had "his eyes turned backwards," is now known. In the Texas manuscript of the story, Harry remembers seeing "Malcom [sic] Cowley with a pile of saucers in front of him a stupid look on his face." Hemingway later lined out "Malcom Cowley" and penciled in "that American poet" and inserted the word "potato" before the word "face".

I wrote to Malcolm Cowley to ask if he knew why Hemingway had attacked him in **"The Snows"** Did you two quarrel about this time (1992 or 1935-36), I asked? (The time reference in the story is November 1922, but the story was written in 1936-36.) Cowley replied as follows:

> I don't know why Hemingway took that crack at me. We had no quarrel in 1922-23 and none in 1935-36. In fact I didn't know he had made the crack until Philip Young unearthed it in a Hemingway manuscript. . . . I had thought the poet with a potato face was Matthew Josephson. Thinking back on the episode, I felt that Hemingway probably resented me in 1922-23 for being a good friend of the French Dadaists, particularly Tzara and [Louis] Aragon. In 1935-36 he had something of a hate on the *New Republic*.

The Americans who were in Paris in the 1920's give us a varied picture of Tzara and the Dada movement. Janet Flanner, writing in 1925, believed Tzara to be "probably the most sensitive and original French poet today, aside from being not French at all, but Rumanian. No one has written more foolishly at times, but many have written almost as foolishly and never once so well. . . . Tzara is a great man of small stature and wears a monocle. Gertrude Stein, mistress of the putdown, wrote that she found it difficult to understand the stories of Tzara's violence and wickedness for when he came to her house he sat beside her at the tea table and talked to her "like a pleasant and not very exciting cousin. Harold Loeb described "the papa of Dada" as "pompous, dignified, monocled" (*The Way It Was*). John Dos Passos got caught up in a *Manifestation Dada* involving "a prime collection of zanies" led by Tristan Tzara. "It turned into a game of follow the leader," Dos Passos wrote in his memoirs. They paraded through the streets of Paris executing "idiotic maneuvers," chanted Dada, Dada, and ended by marching pokerfaced through a Turkish bath. "It certainly wasn't very funny," recalled Dos Passos. Robert McAlmon thought that many of the Dadaists enjoyed being Dadaists "because Dada is nothing, so they could do nothing and feel fine about it. It was impossible to know them, and to glance at their work, and to come away impressed". Certainly, Hemingway was not favorable impressed; in a letter to Ezra Pound in May 1924, he characterized Tzara's work as "shit in French". Even Cowley, whom Tzara once introduced as "a poete Dada americain," was puzzled by the poverty of the movement:

> Nobody can read about the Dada movement without being impressed by the absurd and half-tragic disproportion between its rich, complicated background and its poor achievements. Here was a group of young men, probably the most talented in Europe: there was not one of them who lacked the ability to become a good writer or, if he so decided, a very popular writer. They had behind them the long traditions of French literature (and knew them perfectly); they had the examples of living masters (and had pondered them); they had a burning love of their art and a fury to excel. And what, after all, did they accomplish? . . . They wrote a few interesting books, influenced a few others, launched and inspired half a dozen good artists, created scandals and gossip, had a good time. Nobody can help wondering why, in spite of their ability and moral fervor and battles over principle, they did nothing more.

Dada was an *avant-garde* artistic and literary movement that flourished in Western Europe, and to some extent in New York City, between 1916-1923. Its aim was to discredit all previous art and literature, and to discover reality by a technique of comic derision in which irrationality, chance, and intuition were the guiding principles. Its sweeping aesthetic and philosophic nihilism probably contributed to the eventual demise of the Dada movement itself. "The true dadas are against DADA," Tzara proclaimed. Tzara, who played a leading role in the movement both in Zurich and Paris, has been described by a fellow Dadaist as a "self-styled barbarian, who wanted to put to fire and sword the things that we had designated as the goals and objects of necessary annihilation . . . The various demonstrations that Tzara led in Paris testify to this philosophy. And it wasn't a joke, it wasn't a sentimental and ironic assault on the *status quo* it was a revolution, a total physical and mental revolution. Writing in 1948, Tzara confessed to Dada's "impertinence." "We were bound to scandalize society," he admitted, "to scandalize it so drastically that it could only regard us as criminals or imbeciles." In his nostalgic review of the past, Tzara modestly characterized Dada as "a brief explosion in the history of literature".

Hemingway and Tzara were light-years apart concerning the literary tradition, the role of the artist, and the creative process. Hemingway did not reject the tradition; instead, he saw himself in competition with the great writers of the past. "The only people for a serious writer to compete with," he wrote, "are the dead that he knows are good. It is like a miler running against the clock rather than simply trying to beat whoever is in the race with him. Unless he runs against time he will never know what he is capable of attaining." Tzara, the "literary terrorist," would demolish the past: *DADA: abolition de la memoire: DADA; abolition de l'archeologie.* He made the *tabula rasa* into a guiding principle of his activity, and took Descartes' phrase—"I do not even wish to know if there have been other men before me"—as a motto and emblazoned it on the cover of *Dada 3.* Hemingway believed that the whole object of the writer was to "convey everything, every sensation, sight, feeling, place and emotion to the reader." But Tzara declared: "Art is a private affair, the artist produces it for himself; an intelligible work is the product of a journalist." Hemingway, moreover, was a meticulous craftsman who revised and revised his work. "Most writers," he said, "slough off the toughest but most important part of their trade—editing their stuff, honing it and honing it until it gets an edge like the bull fighter's *estoque,* the killing sword." But Tzara elevated spontaneity to a guiding principle. "The thought," he declared, "is made in the mouth." A champion of the fortuitous, he offered this formula for writing a Dada poem:

> Take a newspaper. Take some scissors. Pick out an article which is as long as you wish your poem to be. Cut out the article. Then cut out carefully each of the words in the article and put them in a bag. Shake gently. Then take out each piece one after the other. Copy them down conscientiously in the order in which they left the bag. The poem will resemble you and you will find yourself to be an infinitely original writer with a charming sensitivity even though you will not be understood by the vulgar.

Cowley himself may have been responsible for freshening Hemingway's memory about his association with Tzara and the Dada movement—and even linking it with the idea of betrayal—by the publication in 1934 of *Exile's Return,* The Dada group, he wrote, were "the most amusing people in Paris" in 1922.

> They believed that life should be rash and adventurous, that literature should be freed from all impure motives, and especially from the commercial motive. . . . But in practice they could not do what they preached. They did not live in a free society. . . . For the most part they were poor young men of middleclass families

with their own way to make. They sooner or later had to betray their high principles; not many of them chose to starve.

This statement comes very close to describing the life and career of Hemingway's writer in **"The Snows,"** a writer who sold out for a life of comfort and "bloody money."

The disgust of the Dadaists was so deep, recalled Cowley, "that they no longer trusted in words to express it: manifestoes must give place to manifestations and poems to deeds, to 'significant gestures." He then gave an account of his own "significant gesture," his punching the jaw of the proprietor of the Cafe Rotonde on Bastille Day, July 14, 1923. Cowley was more or less convinced that the proprietor was a paid police informer. Later in the day, while walking with Tristan Tzara, Cowley was arrested for the assault and spent the night in jail. Most probably it was this "gesture," along with his association with the Dada crowd, which prompted Hemingway to describe the look on the poet's face as "stupid." Harold Loeb, who witnessed Cowley's gesture, admitted that there had been "much drinking among us." The stack of saucers in front of the poet at the cafe in **"The Snows"** serves to remind us that the poet, as well as the dying writer, had "blunted the edge of his perceptions" by drinking too much.

It is not clear why Hemingway described the American poet in **"The Snows"** as having a "potato face." "Poor potato" and "small potato," of course, are slang terms of disparagement, listed in *The American Thesaurus of Slang* along with many others, including "twirp," "damn fool," and "dada." Hemingway, it is interesting to note, characterized Cowley as a "twirp," and a "fool" in letters written to Dos Passos in 1932. But "potato" and "potatoes" are also slang for "dollar" and "money." Perhaps Hemingway meant to suggest that Cowley, like the writer in **"The Snows,"** had sold out. Cowley had returned to New York from Paris in 1923 to become "another advertising copywriter who hated his job." Then in 1926 he bought some garden tools, moved to a farm in the Connecticut Valley, and began supporting himself by "doing translations from the French and writing for magazines." "We all admired Thoreau in a distant fashion," Cowley wrote in *Exile's Return:*

> The trouble was that we didn't carry his doctrine to the same extreme of self-dependence. Some of us accepted too much from publishers and Wall Street plungers—too many invitations to parties and weekends, too many commissions for work we didn't really want to do but it paid well; we took out little portion of the easy money that seemed to be everywhere, and we thereby engaged or committed ourselves without meaning to do so. We became part of the system we were trying to evade, and it defeated us from within, not from without. . . .

Hemingway, whose original choice for the name of the dying writer in **"The Snows"** had been Henry Walden, may have inserted the word "potato" into the poet's sketch to mock Cowley for his half hearted embrace of the Walden lifestyle. Thoreau, one recalls, in order to meet the "unusual expenses" of his move to Walden, had planted potatoes and other crops.

Although in **"The Snows"** Hemingway did not identify by name the Paris cafe where Tzara and the American poet talked, one can now be quite certain he had the Cafe Rotonde in mind. From the very beginning of his sojourn in Paris, Hemingway had disparaged the crowd of "American bohemians" who patronized that establishment: "you can find anything you are looking for at the Rotonde—except serious artists," he wrote in a newspaper article published in 1922.

> They are nearly all loafers expending the energy that an artist puts into his creative work in talking about what they are going to do and condemning the work of all artists who have gained any degree of recognition. By talking about art they obtain the same satisfaction that the real artist does in his work. That is very pleasant, of course, but they insist upon posing as artists. [The real artists of Paris] resent and loathe the Rotonde crowd.

The author of **"The Snows"** would forever associate Malcolm Cowley in the 1920's with a crowd that he would later call the "silly wasters." In a letter written in 1951 Hemingway remembered Cowley as running with the "idiot fringe," unaware of the solid working Paris of committed artists and writers. In another letter written the same year, he scornfully mentioned Cowley's significant gesture of striking the proprietor of La Rotonde, in order to contrast the poet's frivolous behavior with his own dedication to hard work. Hemingway, who once boasted to Maxwell Perkins that he had "a rat trap memory," never forgot—nor ever forgave—the poet's "stupid" Dada gesture or his friendship for a "waster" named Tristan Tzara.

FURTHER READING

Criticism

Bache, William B. "*Nostromo* and 'The Snows of Kilimanjaro'." In *Modern Language Notes* LXXII, No. 1 (January 1957): 32-4.

Finds parallel systems of realistic symbolism in Conrad's novel and Hemingway's story.

Elia, Richard L. "Three Symbols in Hemingway's 'The Snows of Kilimanjaro'." In *Revues des Langues Vivantes* XXXXI, No. 3 (1975): 282-85.

Discusses the symbols of the leopard, the hyena, and the mountain in Hemingway's story.

Howell, John M. "Hemingway's Riddle and Kilimanjaro's Reusch." In *Studies in Short Fiction* VIII, No. 3 (Summer 1971): 469-70.

Briefly comments on the origins of the leopard symbol in "The Snows of Kilimanjaro."

Kolb, Alfred. "Symbolic Structure in Hemingway's 'The Snows of Kilimanjaro'." In *NMAL: Notes on Modern American Literature* I, No. 1 (Winter 1976): np.

Claims that Hemingway deliberately contrasts Afro-Arabian and Judeo-Christian mythologies in his story.

Lewis, Robert W., and Max Westbrook. "The Texas Manuscript of 'The Snows of Kilimanjaro'." In *Texas Quarterly* IX, No. 4 (Winter 1966): 66-101.

Provides a full account of Hemingway's creative process in writing "The Snows of Kilimanjaro."

Stephens, Robert O. "Hemingway's Riddle of Kilimanjaro: Idea and Image." In *American Literature* XXXII, No. 1 (March 1960): 84-7.

Discusses the conflict between physical and spiritual desire in "The Snows of Kilimanjaro."

Taylor, J. Golden. "Hemingway on the Flesh and the Spirit." In *The Western Humanities Review* XV (1961): 273-75.

Views "The Snows of Kilimanjaro" as a secular revision of Christian redemption.

Wilson, Edmund. "Hemingway: Gauge of Morale." In *The Wound and the Bow: Seven Studies in Literature,* pp. 174-97. Farrar, Straus, Giroux, 1978.

Examines the theme of misogyny in "The Snows of Kilimanjaro."

Young, Philip. "The Hero and the Code." In *Ernest Hemingway: A Reconsideration,* pp. 74-8. University Park: The Pennsylvania State University Press, 1966.

Asserts that Hemingway conceived of "The Snows of Kilimanjaro" as a literary exorcism.

R(asipuram) K(rishnaswami) Narayan
1906-

Indian writer of short stories, novels, essays, and memoirs.

INTRODUCTION

Widely considered India's foremost author writing in English, Narayan is noted for his creation of Malgudi, a fictitious village set in southern India, which most critics consider a composite of his birthplace of Madras and his adult residence of Mysore. Writing in a spare, straightforward style derived from India's oral and literary traditions, Narayan uses wry, sympathetic humor to examine the universalized conflicts of Malgudi, usually focusing on ordinary characters who seek self-awareness through their struggles with ethical dilemmas. All of Narayan's characters, in accordance with principles of Hinduism, retain a calm, dignified acceptance of fate.

Biographical Information

Narayan was born into an aristocratic Brahmin family. He learned English at school, where he performed poorly despite family pressure to excel. Narayan received his B.A. from Maharaja College at 24, after which he tried his hand at a number of jobs without much success. About this time Narayan began contributing articles to the English-language newspaper *Hindu*. In 1933 he met and fell in love with a woman named Rajam. Narayan befriended her father and eventually won his consent for the marriage, but an astrologer, who was consulted in the traditional manner, declared that Narayan and Rajam should not wed. Angered, Narayan bribed a friend to find them compatible. The couple was married in 1935. That same year, Narayan published his first novel, *Swami and Friends: A Novel of Malgudi*. Warmly received by critics abroad, most notably Graham Greene, the novel ensured Narayan's success as a professional writer. He has since produced twelve more novels, numerous short story collections, essays, and travel guides. In 1939 Narayan's wife died of typhoid, leaving him with a young daughter. Narayan mourned his wife deeply and has never re-married. In 1994 he was awarded a literary prize for lifetime achievement in India.

Major Works of Short Fiction

All of Narayan's stories, like his novels, exhibit his natural and unaffected language, his subtle humor, and his ability to transform a particular lifestyle into a universal human experience. His style, like his village of Malgudi, is seem-

ingly untouched by the events of the twentieth century. Politics and national issues rarely appear in his fiction. His touch is light, his jests are careful not to offend, and he refrains from judging his characters. In his early fiction Narayan often drew from personal experiences to address conflicts between Indian and Western culture. In "Iswaran," for example, the student protagonist contemplates suicide after repeatedly failing to pass government exams. The clash between Indian and Western cultures are again examined in a number of stories portraying middle-class Indian characters who must reconcile Western ideals of financial and personal success with everyday reality. "Forty-Five a Month" and "Fruition at Forty" both depict white-collar gentlemen who must endure tedious employment in return for desirable middle-class wages.

The majority of Narayan's later short fiction, however, features common heroes from India's streets—pick-pockets, black-marketeers, and performers. In "Under the Banyan Tree" an illiterate storyteller relates colorful tales inspired by divine imagination, while in "The Mute Companions" a mute beggar discovers his humanity when he teams up with a monkey. Animals are frequently depicted in Narayan's short fiction. In "Chippy," "At the Portal," and "Flavour of Coconut" Narayan makes use of Indian legends and folktales to suggest that animals may be as capable of thought and feeling as human beings. Children, too, appear in Narayan's stories regularly. "The Watchman" features a young woman desiring to become a doctor who drowns herself to avoid an arranged marriage. In "A Shadow" a boy watches a film of his dead father daily in attempt to avoid the reality of death.

Critical Reception

Narayan's early popular success abroad attests to the universal appeal of his fiction. As Sita Kapadia wrote, Narayan is capable of "expressing something long-felt and long-understood." Even so, critical response to Narayan's fiction is largely divided. While many reviewers have praised his works for their gentle characterizations and vivid descriptions of rural India, an equal number have found his fiction simple and ineffectual. As M. K. Naik noted, "Narayan . . . appears to fight shy of a tragic ending even when the logic of events in a story seems to demand it." Still other reviewers complain that Narayan's language is textbook-like and replete with clichés. According to Shashi Tharoor, "though he writes in English, much of his prose reads like a translation." Yet even Narayan's detractors have recognized Narayan's unique gift as a storyteller. As Avadhesh K. Srivastava and Sumita Sinha asserted in *The Journal of South Asian Literature*, "Narayan is essentially a short story teller and the one element that stands out even in his novels is the story element."

PRINCIPAL WORKS

Short Fiction

Malgudi Days 1941
Dodu and Other Stories 1943
Cyclone and Other Stories 1944
An Astrologer's Day and Other Stories 1947
Lawley Road 1956
Gods, Demons, and Others 1964
A Horse and Two Goats 1970
Under the Banyan Tree and Other Stories 1985
The Grandmother's Tale: And Selected Stories 1994

Other Major Works

Swami and Friends (novel) 1935
The Bachelor of Arts (novel) 1937
The Dark Room (novel) 1938
The English Teacher (novel) 1945
Mr. Sampath (novel) 1949
The Financial Expert (novel) 1952
Waiting for the Mahatma (novel) 1955
The Guide (novel) 1958
My Dateless Diary (memoir) 1960

The Man-Eater of Malgudi (novel) 1961
The Sweet Vendor (novel) 1967
The Painter of Signs (novel) 1967
My Days (memoir) 1974
A Tiger for Malgudi (novel) 1982
Talkative Man (novel) 1987
The World of Nagaraj (novel) 1990

CRITICISM

Stanley Kauffmann (review date 1964)

SOURCE: A review of *Gods, Demons, and Others,* in *The New Republic,* Vol. 151, No. 26, December 26, 1964, pp. 21-23.

[*In this review of* Gods, Demons, and Others, *Kauffmann discusses the characteristics of the mythological tales that form the basis of the stories in this collection.*]

The most admirable Publisher's Note I have ever read is on the jacket of R. K. Narayan's *The Printer of Malgudi,* issued by Michigan State University Press in 1957. The note explains that, five years before, they took the unusual step for a university press of publishing this author's first novel in America after trying to persuade a commercial publisher to take it on; they then published four more of his novels, each with critical success.

> "And now, with the publication of *The Printer of Malgudi,* we are happy to be able to announce that this is the last of Mr. Narayan's novels we will publish. In the future he will be published by The Viking Press, one of the finest houses in American publishing. We feel that we have done our duty in introducing Mr. Narayan to the American public and that The Viking Press will be able to carry his books to a wider public than we could ever reach."

It might almost have been written by a Narayan character. One hopes it has proved true, that many have discovered Malgudi, the town in Southern India that Narayan has created in his novels with affectionate humor and an eye to historic changes.

Now Viking presents, in an attractive volume illustrated by the author's brother, fifteen very old Indian tales retold by Narayan. He explains that these are truly storytellers' stories. Every village has such a storyteller, usually an old man. "When people want a story, at the end of their day's labors in the fields, they silently assemble in front of his home, particularly on evenings when the moon shines through the coconut palms." These stories, traditional like those of all the world's village storytellers, have certain particularities. First, they are steeped in religion. They exemplify divine attributes, mortal virtues and failings *vis-à-vis* religious precept, demonic schemes, basic moral unity.

Chesterton said of Aesop that there is only one moral to all the fables because there is only one moral to everything. This is sound Hinduism, but Aesop is dramatized homily in which the point is not clear until the end. These Indian stories start, grow, and conclude in a numinous ambience. As in Greek myths, a line between man's free will and the gods' determination is never firmly drawn. And as in those myths and the Old Testament, man's confrontation with the divine is constant, both in dialogue and influence. Throughout these stories man is learning his place, hierarchical and moral, in the cosmos; and the stories live because each new generation must learn the same cosmogony, simultaneously certified and imposed by the billions who have preceded them. In these stories are both the strengths of tradition and a hint of the past as burden.

A second particularity of these stories is the way they use time, neither in a linear way nor in the variations of the linear by flashback and vision to which we are accustomed. Speaking of *The Ramayana*, the great epic by Valmiki from which some of these stories derive, Narayan says:

> "The time scheme of the epic is somewhat puzzling to us who are habituated to a mere horizontal sequence of events. . . . One has to set aside all one's habitual notions of movement and get used to a narrative going backwards and forwards and sideways. When we take into consideration the fact that a king ruled for sixty thousand or more years, enjoying an appropriate longevity, it seems quite feasible that the character whose past or middle period is being written about continues to live and turns up to have a word with the historian."

The explication is helpful, but let it not sound forbidding; the adjustment is not difficult. In fact the West has, in its technology, a kind of lubricant of the imagination. In these days of stratospheric weightlessness, of circling the globe in two hours—indeed, in the stopping, reversal, dilation of time in the cinema—the flights of Hindu imagination are apposite. A man who can see other men's past incarnations is not so remote from men who have made fine wires into brains with histories and judgments; both are acts of intense imaginative will.

The stories are divided into five groups, each with a topic: adventures of mortals; sublimation; God in action; wifely devotion; kingly principle. They are told by Narayan with an uncoy simplicity. (The dialogue has its own archaic charm. A highwayman, asking his victims to hand over their money: "You are seven and may be hiding something among yourselves. Immediately deliver it, will you?") Almost every story starts with an ostensible intent, then, as Narayan promised, refocuses, flowers unexpectedly along its tangents. There is a slight, pleasant tedium to most of the longer ones, like just a bit too much lovely sightseeing.

All travelers convert currency in their heads as they go; so with trips into foreign myth. There is no question of reducing the unfamiliar to the familiar, for we do not live in One World and "they" are not, at bottom, just like "us." But there is a lingua franca in mythology, and familiar themes give us a ground from which to assimilate the less familiar. The theme of wifely devotion through dreadful adversity (in **"Nala"** and **"Shakuntala"**) is already part of our tradition through the *Arabian Nights*. **"Harischandra"** and **"Sibi"** are versions of the Job theme, man being tested by Heaven (in more ways than Heaven sometimes seems aware of). **"Lavana,"** in which ages pass in an instant, is like the legend, retold by Stevenson, of the monk who grew old while listening to a bird's song. **"Savitri"** is, essentially, Orpheus and Eurydice with the roles reversed. There is just enough echo in it all to give us some paradoxical feeling of rediscovering the new.

It ought also to be noted that, as in Japan, another country whose immense past is greatly involved in its busy present, the old tales of India are very much a part of their films. *Harischandra* was one of the first long films made in India. *Shakuntala*, dramatized 1,500 years ago by Kalidasa, was made into one of the major postwar Indian films. *Savitri* was filmed in the silent days and has subsequently appeared in six different sound versions.

Narayan provides some explanatory material both before and after the tales, helpful because profusion is the essence of both the terminology and the religion. Nothing need be memorized though certainly not all the names and traits and epochs can be remembered. Despite the profligacy of odd terms, the book appeals and illuminates, though, unlike other myths, it never deeply moves us. Two impressions are dominant: this religion of serenity and peace has a legendary base of bloodshed that makes the Norse sagas look mild. Women, who are of course inferior, have humbly to be wiser than the wise men; there are several women in these stories who want children by sages and have to entice the men into fatherhood.

And there is one unforgettable parenthetical comment at the end of a passage about a certain king:

> He was childless. He devoted all his hours to praying for issue. . . . The goddess Savitri, whose hymn he recited a hundred thousand times as a part of his prayer, appeared before him and conferred on him the boon of a daughter (although he prayed for a son). . . .

How can their religion fail a people so ancient in acceptances?

Perry D. Westbrook (essay date 1968)

SOURCE: "The Short Stories of R. K. Narayan," in *The Journal of Commonwealth Literature*, No. 5, July, 1968, pp. 41-51.

[*In this seminal essay, Westbrook focuses on the human quality of the short stories in Narayan's first two published collections.*]

The first of R. K. Narayan's three volumes of short stories, *An Astrologer's Day and Other Stories* (1947), contains thirty pieces, all of which had previously appeared in the Madras *Hindu*. Thus they had been written for, and presumably read and enjoyed by, the readership of one of India's greatest English-language newspapers. Though this readership would include most of the British, Anglo-Indians, and Americans living in South India, it would be made up overwhelmingly of true Indians. It is an important point. Narayan is an Indian writing for Indians who happen to read English. He is not interpreting India for Westerners. In Europe and America, of course, Narayan's reputation rests upon his novels. The publication in London of *An Astrologer's Day* followed two well-received novels, *Swami and Friends* and *The English Teacher,* but long before he was a novelist with an enthusiastic Western following, Narayan was an Indian journalist loved by his fellow-countrymen.

Paradoxically, however, though Narayan's short pieces have been welcomed in the *Hindu* for over thirty years, his novels have never been popular in India; indeed, I myself have found that they are obtainable there only with the greatest difficulty. Another book-hunter reports that in the leading bookshop of Bangalore in Narayan's own Mysore State not a single book by Narayan was available. On being queried, a clerk replied that there was no demand for Narayan's works. Narayan himself has stated that in the city of Mysore, where he has lived most of his life, perhaps only 200 of the population of 275,000 have ever read any of his books. And yet Mysore justly has the reputation of being an important centre of education and culture. The fact is that Narayan's books have first been published in England, and more recently in the United States, and have only later appeared in Indian in unattractively printed paperback editions.

Any reader of Narayan is aware that his stories are cut from very much the same cloth, both in quality and in pattern, as his novels. There is no intrinsic difference to explain why in the same cities where his novels are obtainable, several thousand or more subscribers to the *Hindu* read him with gusto. It becomes even more of a puzzle when we consider that the Indian booksellers do a brisk business in British and American novels and in continental novels in English translation. The most cogent explanation seems to be that of lingering cultural colonialism on the sub-continent. Too many educated Indians simply will not accept the possibility of excellence of style in the English writing of a compatriot. In the early years of the independence of the United States much the same prejudice existed. Publishers and readers alike preferred to read books—at least in the category of *belles lettres*—imported from the 'old country'; American authors were deemed to produce something less than the authentic product.

The newspaper origins of the short stories would tend to place them in the category of reporting on Indian life and thus make them more acceptable to readers who would ignore his longer and more ambitious works. The reportorial quality is especially marked in his second collection, *Lawley Road,* in which the selections are sketches and vignettes rather than plotted stories. In *An Astrologer's Day* the tales also accurately mirror Indian life and character, but most of them appear to have been chosen for the ingenuity of their plots. The title story, '**An Astrologer's Day**', is a good example. The description of the astrologer pursuing his profession on the sidewalk provides an entirely typical glimpse of Indian street life. The astrologer himself, a fake driven into imposture by hard luck, is well drawn. The trickiness of the plot (its O. Henry quality) results from the coincidence of the astrologer's being requested, during a day's business, to forecast the fortune of a man he recognizes as one whom he had stabbed and left for dead years ago. It was this crime that had forced the astrologer to flee from his village. But the victim recovered, as he informs the astrologer, and has been devoting his life to tracking down his assailant so as to get revenge. The astrologer, who recognizes the man without himself being recognized, informs him that his enemy has died beneath the wheels of a lorry. Thus the astrologer saves himself from attack and learns, to his great relief, that he is not a murderer after all. Though such situations do credit to an author's ingenuity, they do not suit modern taste. Yet they are in a long and honoured tradition, that of Chaucer's 'The Pardoner's Tale', itself derived from the Sanskrit. As a part of ordinary life, coincidences are legitimate material from any story-teller. At any rate, more than half the tales in *An Astrologer's Day* depend on such twists for their effect. Many of them have other merits as well, such as compelling atmosphere or a memorable character, but perhaps the most justifiable of them are those which present ghosts. '**An Accident**' vividly conjures up on a lonely mountain road the ghost of a man killed in an automobile accident who now devotes himself to helping other motorists in distress. '**Old Man of the Temple**' evokes the mystery and desolation of one of the ruined temples along the South Indian highways. '**Old Bones**' exploits the atmosphere of the more isolated of the *dak* bungalows (government-operated overnight hostels). These are skilfully told stories of pure entertainment.

But some of the stories in *The Astrologer's Day* do not depend upon coincidence or some strange circumstance. The most impressive are those that open a window on to the bleak, tedious lives of the white-collar workers of India, that large segment of the population who drag out their lives at forty or fifty rupees a month in government or business employment. Examples are '**Forty-Five a Month**' and '**Fruition at Forty**', accounts of dreary, lifelong wage-slavery. In depicting such prisoned lives Narayan is at his best, even in stories freighted with 'surprise endings'. Thus in '**Out of Business**' the destructive mental effects of unemployment on a former gramophone salesman are vividly presented, though the suicide that he narrowly escapes would have been a more convincing conclusion than the gratuitous turn of luck that saves him from it. More believable is the fate of Iswaran in the story of that name. Iswaran, a representative of the vast army of Indian students whose sole goal in life is the passing of government examinations, is driven by repeated failure to a suicide that even his last-minute discovery that he has finally passed with honours cannot deter his crazed will from carrying out. Most prominent in all these stunted lives is the intolerable humiliation that is part of the daily routine. The insults endured by a jewelry-shop clerk in **'All Avoidable Talk'** and the clerk's feeble attempt to rebel are unparalleled even in Gogol's and Dostoevsky's fiction on similar themes. Indeed a comparison with the insulted and injured in the works of the great Russian authors is inevitable. The tutor in **'Crime and Punishment'**, the twentyninth story in Narayan's volume, suffers true Chekhovian and Dostoevskian indignities, as does also the porter in **'The Gateman's Gift'**, whose employer speaks to him exactly twice in twenty-five years of service. Blighting frustration, of course, figures in all these tales but most severely in **'The Watchman'**, one of the most powerful short stories Narayan has written. Here a young girl wishes to study medicine but her poverty-stricken family try to force her into a marriage she abhors; she drowns herself at night in a temple tank—at the second attempt, as a watchman stopped her the first time. The pathos lies in the inability of even the best-intentioned person to help a fellow human being in distress. This is the ultimate frustration.

Narayan's second volume of stories appeared in 1956, almost ten years after *An Astrologer's Day*. It is also compiled from writings previously printed in the *Hindu*, but contains fewer elaborately contrived stories. Named *Lawley Road* after a typical thoroughfare in the typical, though fictitious, South Indian city of Malgudi, the volume is made up of sketches, character studies, and anecdotes indigenous to just such a street in such a town. They are the more powerful for the absence of gimmicks, and are marked by naturalness, by the easy pace of Narayan's novels, and the informal style of a leisurely raconteur.

Thoroughly typical of this collection, and indeed of all of Narayan's best short work, is **'A Breach of Promise'**. It begins:

> Sankar was candidate 3,131 in the Lower Secondary Examination and he clearly saw his number on a typed sheet, announcing the results, pasted on the weather-beaten doors of the Government Middle School. That meant he would pass on to High School now. He was slightly dizzy with joy.

By way of celebration the boy and two of his companions go first to a restaurant and then to the local cinema. At four the next morning they climb the thousand steps carved a millennium ago in the rocky side of a nearby hill to the temple of the Goddess Chamundi. Thrice the boys make the circuit of the temple and then enter the shrine and remain there while the priest presents their offerings to the Goddess. They give thanks for having passed their examinations and pray for success in all future ones. As they prostrate themselves before the Goddess, Sankar suddenly recalls that before taking his examinations the preceding year he had vowed to the Goddess that he would kill himself if he failed to pass. He had in fact failed that year, but had self-protectively kept the memory of the vow suppressed in his sub-conscious. But now, overwhelmed by his memory, he leaves his friends on the pretence of buying some jaggery in the temple shop. Actually he

climbs ten ladders to the top of the lofty gate-tower of the temple, crawls out into the mouth of the huge demon that caps the pinnacle, and is about to jump. At that instant he notices a bleeding scratch on his elbow, and his determination to leap vanishes. Carefully he crawls back into the tower and descends, vowing to give the Goddess two coconuts a year instead of his life. At the bottom he hurries to get the jaggery and resumes a boy's normal existence.

Narayan says that **'A Breach of Promise'** is 'almost his first tale', and describes it as being 'very truthful—autobiographical, you know'. Narayan was himself adept at flunking school examinations and after one of his failures he actually did climb to the tower room of Chamundi Temple with the idea—but not, he emphasizes, the intention—of suicide. 'The whole thing was farcical', he says. 'That's the way life is in our temples and our houses'.

If there is an all-pervasive theme in Narayan's work it is that human beings are human beings, not gods.

—Perry D. Westbrook

This is the way life is in most of Narayan's novels and early stories. What more absurd than the ease with which an irrelevance diverts a boy from a solemn vow and makes him substitute an utterly commonplace one? But what is important is that one doesn't feel contempt for the boy; one is delighted that he is saved, and is something of a humbug. He is very human as he celebrates his successful examinations by gorging in a restaurant, attending the cinema, and only as an afterthought running up the hill to give thanks to the goddess Chamundi. In retaining Sankar's humanity, Narayan secures the reader's sympathy, for we see life re-asserting itself against absurdity and solemnity.

If there is an all-pervasive theme in Narayan's work it is that human beings are human beings, not gods. Men and women can make flights toward godhood, but they always fall a bit short. Even Gandhi in the novel *Waiting for the Mahatma* displays an occasional human foible. Other aspirants fall much wider of the mark, of course. In the novel, *Mr. Sampath* (entitled *The Printer of Malgudi* in the United States edition), Srinivas tries with his newspaper *The Banner* to arouse the soul of India, but he is sidetracked, at least temporarily, into movie-making. Nataraj, the printer in *The Man-eater of Malgudi*, futilely combats the principle of evil as embodied in the demonic Vasu. Indeed in that novel all of Indian society, as allegorically represented by a poet, a journalist, an inn-keeper, a civil servant, a veterinarian, and a temple dancer, fail to curb Vasu, who is endowed with the strength, cunning and malice of a mythological *asura*. Even the Gods had trouble overcoming the *asuras*. How could a mere human, or nation of humans, even 450,000,000 of them, be expected to blot out evil? Yet Narayan finds the efforts laudable—and at times amusing.

The foibles that Narayan records may be specifically Indian, but they are also generically human. Sometimes they are public and political, as in the title piece of *Lawley Road*, which recounts the agonizings of the municipality of Malgudi over the statue of an Englishman, Sir Frederick Lawley, who had been prominent in the city's history. When Indian independence came, the presence of this statue at a main intersection could not be tolerated, especially as it was discovered that Sir Frederick was 'a combination of Attila, the scourge of Europe, and Nadir Shah, with the craftiness of a Machiavelli. He subjugated Indians with the sword and razed to the ground the villages from which he heard the slightest murmur of protest. He never countenanced Indians except when they approached him on their knees'. The narrator of the story, a private citizen, buys the statue and at great expense removes it to his own premises, where it not only fills his house but protrudes into the road. In the meanwhile the Municipal Chairman receives telegrams from all over India pointing out that there were two Sir Frederick Lawleys—one a despot, the other a humanitarian and an advocate of Indian independence. The statue at Malgudi was of the latter. The result is that the Central Government orders it to be set up again. The owner sells the statue to the Municipal Chairman, who pays for it from his own pocket, thus insuring his victory at the next election.

The story is obviously good-natured spoofing, a rollicking satire on the confusion of the public mind at the time of transition from the British raj to independence. Somewhat more serious as satire is **'The Martyr's Corner'**. Rama, a small entrepreneur of the type that abounds in socialist India as in no capitalist country in the world, has for years made a living selling *chapatis* and other dainties on an advantageously located street corner which he has managed to reserve for himself by a little judicious bribing of the constable and the health department officer. Rama's working day, what with cooking his wares and vending them, begins at three or four in the morning and extends till late at night. His net earnings average five rupees a day. One evening a riot flames up in the town, its cause unknown even to the rioters. A man is killed on Rama's corner, which is then designated as the site for a statue to the martyr in an unknown cause. Rama is of course ousted from this 'holy' ground; in a new location his business falls off to nothing, and he is forced to take a job as a waiter at twenty rupees a month. Who is the martyr? The brawler to whom the statue is erected or Rama who is reduced to penury?

Narayan's fiction is not especially preoccupied with politics; in fact his attitude towards it approaches disdain. (Among his novels *Waiting for the Mahatma* is the only one that is appreciably political.) But disdain becomes dismay in the story **'Another Community'**, where he writes on religious rioting. Bigotry, fear, ignorance, hate explode into a massacre that sweeps an entire city. Obviously Narayan has in mind the frightful outbreaks between the Hindus and Muslims in 1947. The smouldering engulfing hate, ready at any moment to erupt into violence, is presented through the consciousness of an educated, rational man, untouched by the popular passions, who considers the whole state of affairs 'absurd'. Detachedly wondering who will spark the conflagration, he unwittingly does so himself in a bicycle collision with a stranger in a dark alley. They quarrel and exchange blows. Unfortunately the stranger turns out to be a member of the other community. With typical restraint Narayan declares that the results 'need not be described . . .'

Narayan has said, 'My focus is all on character. If his personality comes alive, the rest is easy for me.' Certainly in the *Lawley Road* collection, the stories of character are the most absorbing, and where other considerations obtrude, character usually remains the dominant interest. Thus in 'The Martyr's Corner' the focus is always on the *chapati* seller rather than on the rather violent action; always before the reader's eyes is the little vendor—his drab monotonous life, his comments on his customers, his manipulation of the officials who could ruin him, above all his attitude towards existence, his sense of occupying a niche in the social order, the sense of dignity and satisfaction that transforms sheer dreariness into human significance. On every market street in every city, town, and village in India these curb-side merchants spread out their wares—old bottles, tin cans converted into cups and cooking utensils, baubles, and edibles of every kind. What sort of people are they? What can life mean to them? **'The Martyr's Corner'** contains at least the beginnings of answers to these questions.

Another ubiquitous frequenter of Indian streets is the beggar. There is one in the story **'The Mute Companions'**, which records the way of life of a mute mendicant who for a time enjoys the company and added income brought to him by a monkey he accidentally captures and successfully trains. Performing on the streets and in the homes of the wealthy, the mute companions share a good life together till one day the animal escapes and disappears. There is pathos in this story in the dependence of man and beast on one another, despite the unbridgeable differences of species. Narayan skilfully presents the process by which this speechless, gurgling, subhuman wanderer of the streets (one of the homeless, maimed, and starving of the world) regains his humanity through his association with a monkey, and becomes an object of concern and compassion. As for the characterization of the monkey, Narayan has here too achieved a minor miracle. Throughout his work Narayan's skill in depicting animals is noteworthy. In *Lawley Road*, there are several other memorable stories of animals: **'Chippy'**, which presents two dogs; **'At the Portal'**, an account of two squirrels; **'Flavour of Coconut'**, in which the protagonist is a rat! But the most remarkable of all of Narayan's animal portraits is the revered invalid elephant in *The Man-eater of Malgudi*. Narayan certainly bears out the belief that Indians are more understanding than Westerners are of non-human forms of life.

In addition to street-vendors and beggars a score of other types are represented in *Lawley Road,* highly individualized characters like the pick-pockets in **'The Trail of the Green Blazer'**, the 'coolie' in **'Sweets for Angels'**, the black-marketeer in rice, who appears during every famine, in **'Half-a-Rupee Worth'**, the illiterate *ayab* or nursemaid of **'A Willing Slave'**, who is a slave first to the family in which she works and later to her husband.

In his first novel, *Swami and Friends,* Narayan proved himself a skilful portrayer of children. In **Lawley Road** there are at least half a dozen stories of children, in addition to **'A Breach of Promise'**. **'Dodu'** tells of a boy who has heard that the local museum has purchased some Palmyra-leaf documents, so he takes ordinary palm leaves to sell to the curator. In **'A Shadow'** a boy, Sambu, daily attends a movie in which his dead father played the star role. In the film the father teaches arithmetic to a little girl in exactly the way he had taught it in real life to Sambu. Death is no longer a reality to the watching boy. In **'The Regal'** we enter into the activities of a boys' cricket club and share their efforts to find a place where the adults will let them play. In **'The Performing Child'** a precocious little girl dancer with a strong instinct for self-preservation refuses to dance before a movie director who her exploiting parents hope will hire her at a large salary. In **'Mother and Son'** an adolescent runs away from his mother's home when she is too insistent about his marrying his fourteen-year-old cousin; after spending a night by the temple tank he is found by his mother and returns.

Lawley Road has not been published in the West: it is unobtainable in even the greatest libraries in the United States, nor is it listed in the printed catalogue of the British Museum. Two of the stories have been printed in America: **'The Trail of the Green Blazer'** under the shortened title **'Green Blazer'**, and **'At the Portal'**, the squirrel story, under the title **'The Mother Bit Him'**. Two other stories by Narayan have appeared in American periodicals: the sensitive and humorous **'A Bright Sunday in Madison'** (about an American child who gets lost temporarily) and **'A Horse and Two Goats'**, a piece of humour underlining the lack of communication between East and West.

In 1964 Viking Press published the United States edition of Narayan's third collection, **Gods, Demons, and Others**, a volume that marks a radical departure from his previous tales. Instead of drawing upon contemporary Indian life, Narayan in this book retells myths and legends from the *Ramayana,* the *Mahabharata,* and several other ancient Indian works. In an article in *The Atlantic* Narayan once wrote: 'All imaginative writing in India has had its origin in the *Ramayana* and the *Mahabharata.*' The English influence, to be sure, opened up an entirely new perspective on literature and established a vogue for Western modes and genres. Yet, Narayan believes, the great religious and mythological writings still hold sway over the Indian literary mind, as can be seen in the numerous and usually unsuccessful attempts to reproduce the old legends in cinema form, attempts that Narayan lampoons in several novels, especially *Mr. Sampath*. Re-tellings of the great epics or parts of them are commonplace in Indian literature. In the present generation Aubrey Menon's

version of the *Ramayana* is notorious for its irreverence, which caused its sale to be banned in India, and C. Rajagopalachari's versions in Tamil of the *Ramayana* and the *Mahabharata* were later translated into popular English editions. So Narayan's reworking of the age-old stories is completely in the tradition of Indian literature and art.

In his earlier stories Narayan did make some use of legendary material, as in **'The Image'** (**Lawley Road**) and **'Such Perfection'** (**An Astrologer's Day**), both of which are accounts of sculptors whose skill is regarded as divine rather than human. More important, Narayan's conception of the nature and function of literature seems throughout his writing career to have been influenced by ideas about the nature and function of the epics in Indian life that have been commonly accepted through the ages. In **Gods, Demons, and Others** he describes the composition of the *Ramayana* by Valmiki, 'The greatest story-teller of all times'. According to Narayan, 'Rama, the hero . . . was Valmiki's creation, although the word "create" is not quite apt . . . Rama was not a "character" created by a story-teller and presented in a "work". The "work" in the first place, was not "written"; it arose within the writer. The "character" was not conceived but revealed himself in a vision.' Now this notion, which has much in common with the Greek concept of the Muses and with later theories of the artist as a mere channel for divine revelation, was the theme of **'Under the Banyan Tree'**, in the final story in *An Astrologer's Day*. Far back in the forested hills, in the sleepy and illiterate village of Somal ten miles from the nearest bus stop, the story-teller Nambi holds sway over the imaginations of the villagers. Illiterate himself, Nambi attributes his stories to 'the Goddess', who causes them to spring up in his own imagination and provides him with the words with which to pass them on to his audience. Nambi's stories are pure flights of fancy, coloured and suggested by the whole body of Indian religious writing. The impression is that Nambi is a lesser Valmiki, in whose mind the Gods have decreed that certain persons and events will spring into being. Later, when Nambi's imagination dries up, he ascribes his failure to the Goddess's pleasure and resigns himself to her will. What Narayan is apparently conveying in this story of Nambi and in his comments on Valmiki is that all creativeness, even that of the humblest village story-teller, depends on something other than the teller's mental energy. Ved Mehta reports Narayan as saying: 'I can't like any writing that is deliberate. If an author is deliberate, then I can't read him . . . ' He says of himself, that he is 'an inattentive, quick writer, who has little sense of style'. With him, as Ved Mehta says, 'a novel well begun writes itself', and elsewhere, as we have seen, he claims: 'I can write best when I do not plan the subject too elaborately . . . If (my protagonist's) personality comes alive, the rest is easy for me.' Narayan's account in *My Dateless Diary* of how he started on his novel *The Guide* bears out these statements.

The art of narration, then, is a talent given to man by God for the benefit of all humanity, for their amusement and edification. In India even at present (as in all other cultures in the past) story-telling is an oral art, an activity in which the listeners and, very likely, the teller are unlettered. The tales in *Gods, Demons, and Others* are presented as told by a village story-teller—in this case, a well-educated one, of whom Narayan gives a detailed and interesting description. But even the stories in the two earlier collections are in many cases told in the words of **'The Talkative Man'**, a garrulous raconteur of Malgudi who is always ready with some account of personal experience if an audience of one or more is at hand. Narayan believes that modern writers, especially those of the West or under Western influence, have strayed far from their original function of providing pleasure and instruction to the masses. He is uncomfortable about recent academic interest in his own writing. 'Literature', he asserts, 'is not a branch of study to be placed in a separate compartment, for the edification only of scholars, but a comprehensive and artistic medium of expression to benefit the literate and illiterate alike.' Though far from achieving this purpose himself in his own country, where he writes in a tongue known mainly to the educated elite, perhaps he comes nearest to it in his short stories, at least those of the first two volumes, which first appeared in a widely circulated newspaper.

In his preface to *The Bachelor of Arts,* Graham Greene writes of the strange mixture of humour, sadness, and beauty in Narayan's novels, 'a pathos as delicate as the faint discolouration of ivory with age'. In the same preface he comments on Narayan's 'complete objectivity, complete freedom from comment'. Like many critics Greene sees a Russian quality in Narayan: 'Mr Narayan's light, vivid style, with its sense of time passing, of the unrealized beauty of human relationships . . . often recalls Tchekhov.' The vastness of the Indian geography, in which friends are separated never to see each other again, the irrelevance of Indian education which prepares students for nothing: these too remind Greene of the Russia of the tsars and the great novelists. In his introduction to *The Financial Expert,* Greene comments on Narayan's gift of comedy with its undertone of sadness, its gentle irony and absence of condemnation—a type of comedy virtually extinct in the West, where farce, satire and boisterousness are substituted for true comedy. At the basis of Narayan's comedy, Greene points out, is 'the juxtaposition of the age-old convention and the modern character . . . The astrologer is still called to compare horoscopes for a marriage, but now if you pay him enough he will fix them the way you want: the financial expert sits under his banyan tree opposite the new Central Co-Operative Land Mortgage Bank'. Mr Greene's comments are in the main just; and they apply as much to Narayan's short stories as to his novels.

Laurence Lafore (review date 1970)

SOURCE: "A review of *A Horse and Two Goats,*" in *The New York Times Book Review,* January 25, 1970, p. 5.

[*Below, Lafore argues that the unifying theme of Naray-*an's stories is the failure of people to communicate with one another.*]

This is a collection of short stories, the first to be published in the United States, by the distinguished Indian novelist R. K. Narayan. Like his novels, they deal (with the exception of the title story) with life in the city of Malgudi, which is Mr. Narayan's Yoknapatawpha County. They are all very specifically Indian, richly adorned with picturesque native customs and vivid local color, so that the casual reader with a limited appetite for folklore might well form the misleading impression that this is all they are. He might also be misled by their brevity and simplicity into supposing that they belong in the category of Theophrastian vignettes.

They are, in fact, something quite different. Picturesque they may well seem to an American reader, but they are no cliché. Except in the title story, there are none of those distressing encounters between East and West that have become so dominant (and tiresome) a theme in most of the fiction written in or about India. It is also refreshing to find that Mr. Narayan, who writes in English, does so with a perfect American accent, equally free from both the Anglicisms and the brand of folkloristic archaism frequently judged appropriate by authors and translators dealing with Asian subjects.

Much more important, Mr. Narayan is not really concerned with character sketches or with anthropological particularities. He is concerned with ideas, and with dramatic structure. His stories are not particularly novel in their themes, but they are certainly universal in their application. The collection adds up to a consistent and coordinated expression of his view of the world and its inmates.

The subjects are various. An interchange between an unsuccessful goat-herd who wants to sell his two goats to an uncomprehending American tourist and the tourist who wants to buy an antique piece of sculpture that he thinks belongs to the goatherd. A gardener, who doesn't know the name of any flowers, who moves in on a householder one day and then abruptly departs many years later. A male nurse subject to hallucinations. A child raised in affection by his parents' murderer. A devoted husband who sets out to be unfaithful to his wife because an astrologer tells him infidelity is necessary to save her life. But the unifying theme is very strong. Mr. Narayan is dealing with the failure of people, in the word of current cant, to "communicate." But his is an original approach to the subject. He is saying that if people *do* "communicate" they destroy each other.

Men live, in short, by illusions which, being peculiar to themselves, insulate them effectively against reality and everyone else in the world as well. The illusions are widely assorted, some diabolic, some funny, some tragic. Some involve submission to traditional mythology, some are the mistakes of very ignorant people, some the fantasies of madmen, some the fecund imaginings of intelligent and educated men. But in every case they are the motive and means of staying alive and of taking action.

The lives they make possible are unsatisfactory. The action they cause is usually unfruitful and sometimes terribly destructive, but all of them are necessary. Thus the rational man who despairs of his wife's life is driven to accept the astrologer's receipt that she can be saved from the baleful horoscopic prophecy of Mars in the Seventh House only if he sleeps with another woman. He believes this not because he is a fool but because he requires hope.

All meanings, all beliefs, and all hopes, Mr. Narayan tells us, are insulating illusions. They can be swallowed whole by children or forced down by young people, ignorant people and desperate people. For mature people, the presence of lethal reality stands always at their shoulders, dimly perceived and ready to undo the life-prolonging therapies of self-deception. This existentialist notion may strike some readers as rather bleak. I found it an invigorating change from the current belief (illusion, Mr. Narayan would say) that human beings could live in love and harmony if only socially induced hostilities, or capitalism, or *something,* did not stand in the way of "communication." He presents his argument in finely subtle and forceful dramatic form.

H. G. Trivedi and N. C. Soni (essay date 1973)

SOURCE: "Short Stories of R. K. Narayan," in *Indian Literature,* Vol. 16, Nos. 3 and 4, July-December, 1973, pp. 165-79.

[*In the following essay, the authors review Narayan's short stories, first by collection, then by character type.*]

R. K. Narayan, one of the most famous Indo-Anglian writers, author of *Mr. Sampath* and *The Guide,* is famous in the western world more for his novels than for his short stories or for other forms of literature that he has tried. Apart from his ten novels, a volume of fifty-five sketches and essays, stories retold from India's immense store of myths and legends, books conveying his travel impressions, Narayan has written quite a large number of short stories which have been collected and published in six volumes—*Dodu and other Stories, Malgudi Days, Cyclone and other Stories, Lawley Road and other Stories, Astrologer's Day and other Stories, A Horse and Two Goats.*

Many of the stories in these collections were first published in the leading Madras daily, *The Hindu.* Narayan also contributed some stories to leading American journals like *The Reporter, The New Yorker, Vogue* and others. The stories published in *The Hindu* were meant largely for the Indian readers. And comprehension of Narayan's fiction presents no problems, it only needs a vocabulary of 5,000 words. These stories belong to the Indian soil and are redolent of its culture. In the main they depict South Indian life and clearly expressing Narayan's view of the world and those who live in it. Simple but fascinating plot, lively characterization, strict economy of narration

and elegant simplicity of language are features of these short stories. They serve as a good introduction to the foreigner who wants to know Indian life.

Narayan does not give the date of publication of these collections. *An Astrologer's Day and other Stories* was first published by Eyre and Spottiswoode, London, in 1947, and then by Narayan's own publishing unit, Indian Thought Publications, Mysore. *Lawley Road* has been brought out by Hind Pocket Books of Delhi. The other collections have been published by Narayan himself. And since they are published in India, readers abroad know very little about the first three volumes.

Dodu is a collection of seventeen short stories based on themes like the innocence of childhood, the financial worries of the middle class, the gullibility of the poor, the naivete of the uneducated, motherly love, problems of South Indian marriages and so on. Narayan has an eye for the minor details of life and an ear for the language of the common people.

In **"Dodu,"** the title story, Narayan mildly satirizes the attitude of the elderly people towards the child. The "treasures" collected by the boys Dodu and Ranga remind us of Tom Sawyer and his choicest possessions.

"Ranga" presents Narayan at his best. Though one of his early tales, it shows that the author had matured soon in his career. It is a simple and moving tale of a motherless child who develops into a frustrated and disillusioned youth, good for nothing. Even the minor characters—a peon, a vagabond, a teacher, a coolie, a loving father, and a kind merchant—spring to life. Narayan has a knack of turning a serious situation into a light one. The significance of the story lies in the presentation of the author's point of view: We often do what we really should not and are consequently miserable. **"Ranga," "A Change"** and **"The One-Armed Giant"** should be read together to understand the message that the author has to give to his readers. Eastern philosophy of reconciliation is reflected in Narayan's fiction. In **"A Change"** which describes how an omnibus ruffles the tranquillity of the life of a coachman, we hear unmistakably the author's voice in the words of the protagonist's wife: "The Merciful will save one who doesn't defeat His Plan." Samad wants to survive and hence giving up the job of a coachman, he becomes a vendor of sweets. "Man should do what he can and be contented with what he gets" seems to be the message of **"The One-Armed Giant." "Blessings of Railway"** bears some resemblance to the first chapter of Jane Austen's *Pride and Prejudice.* Its theme is hunting for a son-in-law. The beginning of the story is reminiscent of the sparkling, dialogues between Mr. and Mrs. Bennet. **"Gandhi's Appeal"** is a noble tribute to the Mahatma's effective elocution and irresistible hypnotism which made his listeners absolutely forget themselves in making gifts. Stories like **"Forty-five a Month," "Ranga," "Mother and Son,"** and **"The Broken Pot"** bring out the intense awareness of human loneliness. Venkat Rao, Ranga, Murugan, Lakshmi and Kannan feel utterly lonely and form, with some others, Narayan's "submerged population group." Stories like

"Leela's Friend" reveal Tagore's influence on the author. The story bears a close resemblance to "The Cabuliwallah." True, Sidda does not stand comparison with the Cabuliwallah, a man of spirit. Tagore's Mini is more real and more appealing than Narayan's Leela. **"The Broken Pot"** is the only story of its type in all the six collections of the author. Hence, its significance. It is the tragic tale of an unfortunate man who could not keep the pot boiling because he was ostracized. The story ends in two suicides and a murder. It brings out the evil consequences of hatred, ill-well and enmity.

Malgudi Days

Malgudi Days is another collection of nineteen fresh and original stories out of which two stories—**"Old Bones"** and **"Neighbour's Help"** deal with the supernatural element. The collection contains delightful stories like **"The Gold Belt," "The White Flower," "An End of Trouble,"** and **"Under the Banyan Tree."** **"The Gold Belt"** seems to be a continuation of **"Blessings of Railway"** in the previous collection. The significance of the stories lies in the criticism against the dowry system and the presentation of the South Indian customs associated with marriage. Humour blends with sadness and the story ends in a pleasant surprise. We hear Sambasivan's wife telling her husband:

> Do you know what Sharda (the bride) has done? These girls are cleverer than we were in our days. She had an hour's talk with her husband . . . and he (the bridegroom) has offered to send the money for the belt in two or three days. . . .

We smile when Sastri, the most practical man in the story remarks:

> You must really be proud of a daughter like Sharda. If she can do so much in a hour's interview . . . she shows great promise and will go very far.

"The White Flower" is a mild satire on superstitions and blind belief in astrology. Sentimentalism has spoilt the effect of **"An End of Troubles"** which introduces to us a rickshaw puller who is deprived of his means of livelihood with the advent of omnibuses. He finds the struggle of life rather unbearable. An accident provides an end of all troubles. **"Under the Banyan Tree"** is an idyll of pastoral life. The story takes us into the old pastoral world of peace and tranquillity inhabited by selfless, sober, sympathetic, co-operative people. The atmosphere of the story is strange and yet beautiful. The charm of the story lies in the remoteness of the setting. Nothing endures. And so Nambi's remarkable ability to tell tales deteriorates slowly but steadily. Narayan often introduces the Talkative Man to narrate the story. Like Maugham, Edgar Allan Poe and others, Narayan, too, favours this device of the first person singular narration. As Maugham says in the Preface to the second volume of his short stories: "This is a literary convention which is as old as hills." Its object is to achieve credibility and it would be unfair to Narayan to say that the object is not realised in his stories as well.

Narayan does achieve credibility but this "Sir Nameless" is too abstract an entity for grappling "to our souls with hoops of steel." **"Gardens"** introduces sparrows and **"The Mute Companions,"** a monkey. Narayan introduces items from Indian languages when he feels that these can be adequately translated into English. The dialogues are natural, suggestive and often forceful.

Cyclone and other Stories

This collection brings us a fresh stock of eighteen stories that mirror quite accurately Indian life and character. The remarkable quality of these stories is the ingenuity of their plots. **"The Doctor's Word," "An Astrologer's Day," "The Roman Image"** are good illustrations of this fact. Stories like **"A Parrot Story," "Chippy"** and **"The Blind Dog"** introduce birds and animals and impress us on account of the most accurate and vivid descriptions of the behaviour of these species. **"An Astrologer's Day"** and **"Fellow-Feeling"** are rib tickling. Guru Nayak, an attempt on whose life was made by the fake astrologer; the seller of fried nuts with a gift of the gab; the archaeologist who advances in vain the theory of the origin of the image obtained from the Sarayu by his assistant; the accountant who saves the life of the gateman on the verge of insanity, these are some of the many memorable minor characters. The skilful manipulation of the plot very often depends upon coincidence. The collection provides a good illustration of Narayan's descriptive power. The astrologer's equipment; the marriage pander in **"Missing Mail"**; the Doctor's efforts to save Gopal his bosom friend; and the mental tension that he is subjected to; the dog's behaviour and the blind beggar's greed in **"The Blind Dog"**; Iswaran's strange behaviour after getting his examination result and the unbearable psychological tortures that Govind Singh suffered after receiving the envelope from the manager of the institute he had served—These have been very vividly described. **"A Night of Cyclone"** and **"Such Perfection"** describes the storms in a superb manner. Here is one such description:

> At this moment a wind blew from the cast. The moon's disc gradually dimmed. The wind gathered force, clouds blotted out the moon; people looked up and saw only pitch-like darkness above. Lightning flashed, thunder roared, and fire poured down from the sky. It was a thunderbolt striking a haystick and setting it ablaze. Its glare illuminated the whole village . . . Another thunderbolt hit a house. . . . The fires descended with a tremendous hiss as a mighty rain came down. It rained as it had never rained before. The two lakes. . . . filled, swelled, and joined over the road. Water flowed along the street.

Nature in its tranquil beauty—though not so prominent in Narayan's fiction—is certainly not beyond his reach. The author delineates his characters vividly. For instance, the character of the astrologer sitting under the tamarind tree on the sidewalk:

> His forehead was resplendent with sacred ash and vermilion, and his eyes sparkled with a sharp abnormal

gleam which was really an outcome of a continual searching look for customers, but which his simple clients took to be a prophetic light and felt comforted. The power of his eyes was considerably enhanced by their position—placed as they were between the painted forehead and the dark whiskers which streamed down his cheeks; even a half-wit's eyes would sparkle in such a setting. To crown the effect they wound a saffron-coloured turban around his head.

The description provides a glimpse into a typical Indian street life.

"Iswaran" is a psychological study of the behaviour of a diffident boy who is mocked by others. He gains unexpected but brilliant success in the Intermediate examination. This rouses his feelings to a fever pitch. The boy jumps into the Sarayu and dies. Whether it is an act of suicide or an accidental death due to frenzy of exuberance is something very difficult for us to say. Narayan, as we have already seen, is against suicide.

An Astrologer's Day and other Stories

Those who have read the earlier collections may not find this volume very interesting inasmuch as twenty-four stories out of the collection of thirty have been reproduced here. Of the six remaining stories **"The Tiger's Claw,"** **"The Watchman,"** and **"Crime and Punishment"** deserve careful consideration. **"The Watchman"** brings out Narayan's message on how "to bear the slings and arrows of outrageous fortune." **"Crime and Punishment"** is the story of a poor teacher, ambitious parents, and a naughty child with a below-average ability. For only thirty rupees a month, the teacher patiently puts up with the lectures on child psychology delivered almost everyday by the educated parents.

Lawley Road and other Stories

The volume contains twenty-eight stories out of which fourteen have been reprinted from the earlier collection. However, stories like **"Lawley Road,"** **"The Martyr's Corner,"** **"Wife's Holiday"** and **"Half-a-Rupee"** are really good. **"Uncle's Letters"** and **"Another Community"** mark a departure from the traditional stories. In the former story an Uncle writes letters to his nephew and affords us an insight into the life of an average South Indian. The latter story is without a hero. It reveals Narayan's hatred of communal riots. Narayan often writes stories where plot is less important than the ideas presented. The plot never disappears altogether but it is generally subordinated to the situation. The significance of the collection lies in the presentation of well-drawn character-sketches or vignettes.

A Horse and Two Goats

The volume was first published by Viking Press, Inc., N.Y. in 1970 in which year the first Indian edition was also brought out. The collection comprises five stories with rich comic characters and to know them is to love them. The confusion created by the language in which the two

main figures, Muni and the American, speak to each other is the pivot round which the action of this, rather too long a story, revolves. At the end of the story we feel like asking ourselves if the American is really so foolish as to consider a shepherd to be the owner of the equestrian statue on the edge of the village. Muni's wife serves as a foil to other female characters of Narayan. She leads Muni by the nose. When Muni grumbled at the food-stuff—spinach and the drumsticks—served to him every day, his wife commented:

> You have only four teeth in your jaw, but your craving is for big things. All right, get the stuff for the sauce, and I will prepare it for you. After all, next year you may not be alive to ask for anything.

We wonder if any Indian woman uses this kind of language when she talks with her husband. The story, however, provides us with a subtle and real entertainment. It is artfully told and carefully plotted.

The next story, **"Uncle,"** is a masterpiece. It presents two worlds, two levels of consciousness. Narayan takes us into the world of childhood and shows what "the distorting mirrors of adolescence" could do to reality. This mysterious story set in Malgudi presents a loving, old man whose day passes between "munching and meditation"; a lady who advises the innocent child bursting with curiosity to know whether his uncle is really a "murderous imposter" to forget what he heard from others, particularly, from the photographer, Jayraj, and not to ask his uncle a single question. The child took the advice and never asked anything about his parents.

> I maintained the delicate fabric of our relationship till the very end of his life.

Here we enter *once again* into Narayan's *familiar* enchanting world, full of life and activity:

> The crowd passing through the market gateway, shoppers, hawkers, beggars, dogs and stray cattle and coolies with baskets on their heads, all kind of men and women, jostling, shouting, laughing, cursing and moving as in a trance . . .

"Annamalai" and **"A Breath of Lucifer"** deal with two simple, uneducated, sincere, hard-working, faithful servants. Annamalai is a household servant. Sam is a Christian male nurse or attendant. Both leave the scene rather too abruptly. There is "something fierce as well as soft" about them. They serve their masters with scrupulous care throughout. But both are governed by their own impulses and leave their masters in the end in an unceremonious way. Their company and conversation inspire their masters to narrate these stories.

"Seventh House" seems to be a continuation of **"The White Flower."** Here Krishna takes us into confidence and reveals a secret which he kept from us even in *The English Teacher*. His marriage was an unconventional love marriage. To avert the influence of Mars in the Seventh House of his horoscope and thereby to save the life of his ailing wife, he tries in vain, as advised by his astrologer, to transfer his love even to a prostitute and temple dancer.

Each one of these stories is a character study, a glimpse of mankind and "an infusion of India."

In his article entitled "The Fiction Writer in India" (*Atlantic Monthly,* 1953) Narayan writes, "Every writer. . . . hopes to express through his novels and stories the way of life of the group of people with whose psychology and background he is most familiar, and he hopes that this picture will not only appeal to his own circle, but also to a larger audience outside."

In his short stories, Narayan has depicted familiar situations and explored ways of life with which he was intimate. But the people here represent humanity at large and hence Narayan's novels and short stories have universal appeal.

Some of Narayan's short stories contain parallel characters, i.e. characters appearing in his stories and novels and bearing the same nature if not always the same name. For instance, **"The White Flower," "Seventh House"** and *The English Teacher* have Krishna as their hero.

Sambasivan appears in **"The Gold Belt"** as well as **"Blessing of Railway."** The action in **"The Antidote"** reminds us of a similar situation in *Mr. Sampath.* **"The Shelter"** reminds us of Rosie, the heroine of *The Guide.* **"Gandhi's Appeal," "The Trail of the Green Blazer"** and **"The Gold Belt"** contain the seeds of his novels like *Waiting for the Mahatma, The Guide,* and *The Bachelor of Arts.* Raju of **"The Trail of the Green Blazer"** reminds us of Raju, the Guide.

Narayan's novels are set in Malgudi, but Malgudi is not the locale of all his short stories. Sometimes the action takes place in Mysore, sometimes in Bangalore, Madras, Kritam and other places.

Narayan's characters are illiterate. Characters like Doctor Raman form an exception. As Frank O'Connor says: "The short story has never had a hero. What it has instead is a submerged population group." Narayan also has his own waifs. He presents poor artists, neglected workers, pedlars, astrologers, beggars, rickshaw pullers, lock repairers, servants and attendants and other homeless, helpless persons. What Narayan says for the vendor in **"The Martyr's Corner"** is applicable to him also. "His custom was drawn from the population swarming the pavement." Quite a number of his stories are character studies, "a glint of mankind." The characters are both believable and likeable. Narayan loves them all and it is this that illumines them.

Narayan's minor characters are more assertive than many of his major characters. In the brief precious moments allowed to them they act their part exceedingly well. With the deft strokes of a clever artist, Narayan creates living and breathing characters which haunt our memory long after we have finished reading his stories. He describes Bamini Bai, for instance, as "the vision of beauty and youth—a young person, all smiles, silk and powder." Can there be a better description of a film-actress?

Narayan's sympathy is extended even towards the dumb animals, birds and insects. A rat, a monkey, snakes, an elephant, dogs, squirrels, parrots and tigers—these play important part in stories like **"The Mute Companions"; "Attila"; "Chippy"; "The Blind Dog"; "Flavour of Coconut"** etc. Even while depicting a hateful character, Narayan wins our sympathy for it by underlining some of the relieving features. In **"Wife's Holiday,"** for instance, Kannan breaks open the cigarette tin in which his son had put his savings for safe-keeping. He loses the cash in gambling. Kannan's act is in no way praiseworthy, and yet we do not hate him. For he feels qualms of conscience at the sight of the tin. He remembers how he himself had encouraged his son to use the tin as his money-box. When the lid does not give way, he plucks out a nail from the wall and puts the picture of god on the floor. Then he feels uneasy and presses his eyes to the feet of the god in the picture. He goes to the Mantapam not only to play the game of dice but also to enjoy the muddy smell of the place and the sight of the sky and the hillocks seen through the arches of the Mantapam. How can we dislike a man of this type?

Narayan's major characters can be divided into three or four categories as under:

Idealists:

We meet idealists like Sekhar (**"Like the Sun"**); Doctor Raman (**"The Doctor's Word"**); Soma (**"Such Perfection"**); Vijaya (**"The Comedians"**); Gopal (**"The Antidote"**); Sambasivan (**"The Gold Belt"**); Kutti (**"The Performing Child"**); Krishna (**"The Artist's Turn"**) etc. These characters are self-willed or wayward. Sekhar would not tell a lie on the day devoted to the practice of truth, though his vow drives him into a corner. Doctor Raman has developed a blunt truthfulness. He does not believe that agreeable words ever save life. It is none of his business to provide an "unnecessary dope" when Nature would tell the truth presently. Soma, the sculptor, would not main the image of God though perfection infuriates nature. Vijaya, the comedian, would not accept the compliments and a gold medal when he knows that he has failed miserably to make the people laugh. Krishna, the poor artist, would not accept anything from the greedy publisher and faultfinder who knows little about art. Kutti hates the "cinema men" and would not dance or sing for any film. Gopal would do nothing disagreeable on his birthday. He would at least shake his head and open his right eye though he has to play the part of a dead man.

Practical:

We come across practical people like Sastri (**"The Gold Belt"**); the Astrologer, (**"An Astrologer's Day"**); Thanappa, the postman (**"Missing Mail"**); the Priest (**"The White**

Flower"); and the Watchman in a story, titled, **"The Watchman."**

Sastri advises Sambasivan to satisfy the demand of the bridegroom's people, when he finds that the marriage of Sambasivan's daughter, Sharda, may be called off if a gold belt is not given. "Don't think of the payment now," says Sastri to Sambasivan, "we can always arrange it to suit our convenience." The astrologer accepts Guru Nayak's challenge without being intimidated, names his antagonist, takes him into confidence, inspires faith in his knowledge of astrology and makes the antagonist flee homeward by employing a clever trick. Thanappa, the postman, does not deliver a letter and a telegram to Ramanujam. For he knows that the marriage of Ramanujam's daughter must not be postponed under any circumstances. It was only after Kamakshi's marriage that Ramanujam learnt about the sad demise of his uncle. Krishna wants to marry the girl whom he loved. But the horoscopes do not match. The priest asks a child to pick up one flower out of the two presented to her and to put it on the door-step of the sanctuary. The girl picks up the white flower which stands for God's permission for the wedding.

Sentimentalists:

Sentimentalists like Govind Singh (**"The Gateman's Gift"**); Iswaran, Sankar (**"The Evening Gift"**); and the girl in **"The Watchman"** also play their part in Narayan's short stories. Govind Singh does not follow the advice of the people to open the registered letter that he has received and to read the contents. The presumption that it is from a lawyer unhinges his mind. Iswaran presumes that he has failed at the Intermediate examination and behaves like a desperado. He hates the idea of going to the Senate Hall to know his examination result. Sankar does not tell his employer a word about his problem but leaves the wealthy drunkard at the moment when Sankar's company was badly required. A police complaint was lodged and Sankar who "felt sick of his profession of perpetual cajoling and bullying" the wealthy drunkard, got into hot water. The girl in **"The Watchman"** considered herself to be a burden. She did not want to live on anybody's charity. She had lost hope of getting a scholarship and someone was coming to have a look at her. She felt she had no home and wanted to plunge herself into a watery grave.

Servants:

"Household" servants in Narayan's fiction are, broadly speaking, honest, hardworking and sincere but rather simple to a fault. Some extraneous element, some unusual event, lures them off the beaten track. Consequently they become unhappy and make their masters also miserable. Mr. Jesudasan, a kind, middle-aged Christian, employed Ranga to work in his store. Ranga slowly rose to the position of a bill collector. One day he met his old friend, a servant in a doctor's house, who gave an exaggerated account of the advantages that betting in a race brought to men who ventured to take part in this game. Ranga thought he was only temporarily investing his master's money in the race but was soon disillusioned and shocked.

He could not face his master. He went to the sea with a view to committing suicide. Of course, he did not do so. Ramu (**"A Career"**), a frustrated servant falls in love with a girl from Hyderabad, squanders his master's money and ruins his credulous master completely. We have already seen how Annamalai and Sam, the Christian male nurse, leave their masters in the lurch.

The beggars that we come across in short stories are, as a rule, cheats. Pachai, the blind beggar is not really blind.

Heroines:

Narayan has heroes; no heroines. His female characters are passive and unimpressive. Rare exceptions like Bamini Bai in **"Dasi, the Bridegroom"** only prove the rule. Many of his female characters are like those of Dickens. Narayan hardly cares to mention them by their names. He does not assign to them any important role. They do not have independent existence. Yet they all bear some feminine traits. They obey their husbands; circumambulate the tulsi plant; eat betel leaves and areca-nuts and are easily susceptible to feelings of joy, sorrow, surprise and anger. At times they do resist but it is only a weak resistence that they offer. Lower-class women often dominate their husbands though they too light the fire, fetch water and cook food.

Children in his stories are playful, innocent, intelligent, resourceful and mischievous. They are against conventional discipline and hence often ill-treated by superior parental or educational authority.

Narayan's stories produce one single vivid effect. They seize the attention of the reader from the outset. Like Kipling, Narayan has translated the language of his Indian characters into English. Narayan's purpose does not seem to be moral and didactic like that of Aesop's or Tolstoy's. Yet some of his stories do suggest various truisms. For example, "As you sow, so shall your reap" is the implied moral of **"A Career."** **"The Snake-Song"** tells us, "Kind words cost nothing." **"A Change"** emphasizes the need for adaptibility to changing circumstances. If **"The Gold Belt"** wants us not to create imaginary troubles, **"Out of Business"** tells us, "Life is a struggle: face it." If **"Four Rupees"** points us to the self-evident truth, "No risk, no gain," **"Sweets for Angels"** and **"Another Community"** warn us not to rush into action in blind haste. Narayan is not a fatalist like Hardy. However, fate does play its part in stories like **"The Martyr's Corner," "The Level Crossing," "An End of Trouble,"** and **"The Broken Pot."** In **"Martyr's Corner,"** Rama says "God is jealous of too much contentment." Does this belief of Rama explain the tinge of sadness in his humour?

The titles that Narayan gives to some of his stories are ironical. For example, in **"Father's Help,"** the help given to Swami by his father is only a hindrance from the son's point of view. In **"The Attila,"** the dog Attila is not a scourge but only a commonplace cur. In **"The Comedian,"** Vijaya succeeds only in bringing tears into the eyes of his audience. Swami in **"A Hero"** is only a coward. The doll in **"Unbreakable Doll"** is brittle!

In Narayan's fiction blessings and good wishes may or may not come true but oaths taken by the characters always materialize.

Seenu, for instance, vows a Friday visit to God Anjaneya and a gift of an anna at every visit if his missing valuable pen is found again. The same evening Seenu's father calls him, asks him for the pen, and gives it back to him after explaining how he bought it from a pickpocket for eight annas. (**"The Birthday Gift"**).

Narayan's handling of the supernatural creates the proper atmosphere. His ghost stories deserve admiration for their appropriate atmosphere, telling phrases and vivid descriptions. When we read them there is a willing suspension of disbelief. Narayan has humanised the ghosts and so they listen to reason, argue, and cause no harm. We wish Narayan will give us many more ghost stories.

Avadhesh K. Srivastava and Sumita Sinha (essay date 1974)

SOURCE: "The Short Fiction of R. K. Narayan," in *The Journal of South Asian Literature,* Vol. X, No. 1, Fall, 1974, pp. 113-19.

[*In this essay, the authors describe Narayan's purely artistic approach to his writing, and compare his style to that of other Indian authors writing in English.*]

Almost every Indo-Anglian writer of fiction has tried his hand at short stories in addition to novels, and none perhaps quite so successfully as R. K. Narayan. Mulk Raj Anand, Raja Rao and Narayan form the "Big Three" of Indian English writing. Santha Rama Rau has gone so far as to assert that Narayan is "the best novelist that India has produced and probably among the most entertaining and distinguished of contemporary writers anywhere." Narayan himself records in *A Dateless Diary* that in America some people place him with Hemingway and Faulkner as one of the three greatest modern writers of the world. And Graham Greene, probably Narayan's most enthusiastic champion and admirer in the West, holds him up as a model for other writers when he says: "if he [an author] allows himself to take sides, moralise, propagandise, he can easily achieve an extra-literary interest, but if he follows Mr. Narayan's methods, he stakes all on his creative power." Apparently, it would appear that the critical estimates of R. K. Narayan, the writer, are made only on the evidence of his novels. Such an estimate can at best be one-sided. R. K. Narayan's short stories are artistically as distinguished as his novels, and in any general estimate of his writings they cannot be ignored. In fact, one might go so far as to say that Narayan is essentially a short story teller and the one element that stands out even in his novels is the story element.

Narayan's complete dependence on a purely artistic ap-

proach to literature sets him apart from other Indian writers in English. For instance, Mulk Raj Anand's avowed purpose in his novels and short stories is to teach men "to recognize the fundamental principles of human living and exercise vigilance in regard to the real enemies of freedom and socialism." He is ever conscious of the need ". . . to help raise the untouchables, the peasants, the serfs, the coolies and the other supressed members of society, to human dignity and self-awareness in view of the abjectness, apathy and despair in which they are sunk." But Anand's heavy emphasis on the didactic quality of art stands in the way of his attainment as a novelist; for obtrusive propaganda makes his novels suffer from an inability to visualize clearly the objective situations of his characters. Anand, Bhabani Bhattacharya and Kamala Markandaya have dealt quite forcibly with the theme of hunger and the concomitant theme of human degradation in some of their works.

Narayan, however, presents social evils without any emotional involvement and with no overt aim to reform or change existing conditions. Khushwant Singh's chief concern as a writer is sociological. As Chirantan Kulshrestha has pointed out:

> His socio-cultural preoccupations define the nature of his fiction: clash of sensibilities and life styles in modern India, tensions in families on account of the conflict between tradition and modernism, emotional responses to the Partition by different communities—these are some of the elements which form the matrix of his plots.

Narayan's themes likewise are also mostly sociological, but he is a novelist with a vision, with equipment that enables a good artist to convey, beyond the deterministic control of his milieu, a transcendence which invests the whole narrative with a sense of significance—a quality that Khushwant Singh altogether lacks.

Narayan differs from another major Indian writer, Raja Rao, in that he does not concern himself unduly with man's relationship to God, with mysticism and a philosophical interpretation of life, Narayan's attitude to the interplay of good and evil cosmic forces is one of wonder at the intellectual level and acceptance at the physical. What Narayan says of his character Srinivas in *Mr. Sampath* is an apt description of his own mental approach:

> His mind perceived a balance of power in human relationships. He marvelled at the invisible forces of the universe which maintained this subtle balance in all matters. . . . For a moment it seemed to him a futile and presumptuous occupation to analyse, criticise and attempt to set things right anywhere. . . . If only one would get a comprehensive view of all humanity, one would get a correct view of the world: things being neither particularly wrong nor right, but just balancing themselves.

In fact, Narayan perceives this balance in every aspect of

man's life—social, political and moral and the perception leads to his own detached observation of the human scene. It is this quality more than any other that distinguishes Narayan from the other writers.

Among the more important figures of Indian English fiction, Narayan is the most prolific, having published ten novels and seven volumes of short stories. His fame, however, rests almost entirely on his attainments as a novelist. As suggested earlier, it is one of the ironies of literary history that while so much is made of Narayan's novels, the short stories which have the unmistakable stamp of the artist in him should be relatively neglected. Perhaps it is due to the fact that the short story is essentially a modest art and has none of that ponderous air of significance so dear to the critic and the literary historian. Nevertheless, Narayan is basically (and also in his novels) a story-teller, one of the very few in the context of Indian English fiction. The air of apparent disengagement and delicate charm invest his stories with such perfect artistic unity which Poe would have commended and which Henry James would have found specially enchanting. As P. D. Westbrook has noted, [*The Journal of Commonwealth Literature,* 5, July 1968] "Any reader of Narayan is aware that his stories are cut from very much the same cloth, both in quality and in pattern, as his novels." Yet he finds that in many important cities of India Narayan's novels are not available and his stories are only read because they had originally appeared in *The Hindu,* one of the India's foremost English-language newspapers. The reason, he thinks, lies in the "lingering cultural colonialism on the sub-continent," the refusal of educated Indians to accept the possibility of excellence of style in the English writing of a compatriot. This is a Westerner's point of view and he tells us that "in Europe and America, of course Narayan's reputation rests upon his novels." The same is true in India if what we gather from the critical material available is any indication of the trend of public taste.

Narayan's short stories form a considerable bulk in his writings as compared to Raja Rao's single collection, *The Cow of the Barricades,* Kushwant Singh's *A Bride for the Sahib and Other Stories* and Bhabani Bhattacharya's *The Steel Hawk and Other Stories.* Only Mulk Raj Anand has five volumes of short stories to his name, but they do not compare with those of Narayan in variety of theme and character and beauty of presentation. Raja Rao's stories present rustic characters embodying the virtues of faithfulness, devotion and love. His "Javni" and "Akkayya" symbolise the silent heroism and selfless sacrifice of Indian womanhood, while "Narsiga" symbolises "the beauty of an unspoilt shepherd-boys abiding life-loyalties." Anand's stories are more in the nature of character sketches, caricatures mostly, aiming at social satire. Some of his famous creations are Chandu the barber in "The Barber's Trade Union," Dhandu the carpenter in "A Rumour," the Nawab of "A Kashmir Idyll" and the criminal in "The Maharaja and the Tortoise." Khushwant Singh's stories such as "The Constipated Frenchman," "Rats and Cats in the House of Culture" or "Mr Kanjoos and the Great Miracle" are burlesques or extravaganzas and lack a serious artistic purpose.

Narayan's stories, like his novels, deal with themes of common life and simple people. They are not of topical interest and rarely does Narayan deal with the world-shaking events of the 1930s and 1940s or the political and social upheavals in India during and since independence. What he excels in doing is to select incidents and people that reveal the human comedy. In his novels Narayan shows himself a clever manipulator of plot and character, an artist whose main concern lies in projecting, through the unrippled flow of his narrative, an amused (through non-condescending) and amusing view of life. The larger canvas and a different art form do not seem to signal in Narayan the requirement of an artistic function different from the one realized in the short stories. One might even go so far as to suggest that the short stories and the novels of Narayan are made of the same artistic material except in so far as the former exploit plot or character and the latter the interplay of the two.

> **Narayan is essentially a short story teller and the one element that stands out even in his novels is the story element.**
>
> —*Avadhesh K. Srivastava and Sumita Sinha*

In recent years, the rapidity with which Indian writing in English has established itself as a subject of academic study has not been matched by an equally impressive body of critical commentary. We find ourselves "in a literary climate in which good writing is praised for wrong reasons, mediocrity is bloated up, and adulation subsumes all critical distinctions." As David McCutchion says, "From the beginning the judgement of Indian writing in English has found itself beset with peculiar hazards." It has been treated as a phenomenon rather than a creative contribution, its "Indianness" and not literary merit being considered. In what way is the treatment Indian? Does the language have an Indian flavor? Are the metaphors taken from Indian life and nature? Such questions may be expected of the outside enquirer, but Indianness does not lie in "exotic" content as in the mind behind the organization of that content. "Whether one writes about apples or mangoes, roses or hibiscus, is not the point but 'life attitudes', 'modes of perception'—which is where Dr. Mokashi finds the Indianess of Lal in his recent *Appreciation.*" But the deliberate pursuit of this intangible quality may result in a kind of self-mystification, vagueness being disguised as "Indian" resistance to form, sentimentality as "Indian" gentleness. Raja Rao's *The Cat and Shakespeare,* like his *The Serpent and the Rope,* purports to depict a different kind of mind—outside Western categories, beyond Western criticism. With R. K. Narayan or B. C. Rajan's *Too Long in the West,* the supposed inconsequentiality or incongruous naivete of the Indian mind become frankly a comic device.

In Narayan's stories the evidence of "Indianness" is not

as obtrusive as in Raja Rao's fiction, but it has its own distinctive character. Narayan is not writing for Westerners; that is why his Indianness is not self-conscious like Rao's. Because he has a native reading public in view, there is no deliberate pursuit of indigenous elements which he might fuse into his literary style. What he authentically presents is his own experience as a man educated to think and feel in Western categories confronting the radically different culture all around him or confronting himself or any experience so far as he himself responds to it. And apart from the success or otherwise of his books as art, the documentation of his own attitudes is valid to the extent that it stems from an experience he has lived through honestly faced, and expressed in the language which provided the thought-structure of that experience.

Narayan reduces to the minimum the problem of conveying an Indian sensibility in a foreign tongue by remaining faithful to the bare facts of narration and describing what is essentially true to human nature.

—*Avadhesh K. Srivastava and Sumita Sinha*

Narayan's self-discipline is more than evident in his short stories, which are written with extreme simplicity and purity of diction. He reduces to the minimum the problem of conveying an Indian sensibility in a foreign tongue by remaining faithful to the bare facts of narration and describing what is essentially true to human nature. N. Mukerjee, in an article in *The Banasthali Patrika* states his opinion that, "R. K. Narayan is undoubtedly the most distinguished contemporary Indian novelist writing in English. In the course of these thirty-two years of literary career Narayan has not only matured in his vision, he has also perfected his craft." Margaret Parton in her review of *Grateful to Life and Death* says, "No better way to understand what Mr. Nehru means by 'the tender humanity of India' than to read one of Mr. Narayan's novels." The characters of Narayan are rooted to the soil of Malgudi, which is there creator's most outstanding contribution to the world of fiction. "Keen observation, sympathy, unfailing good humour and gentle satire wrapped up in leisurely meditativeness are some of his most serviceable tools in establishing the intimate sense of reality in his saga of Malgudi." We can go out, in Graham Greene's words, "into those loved and shabby streets and see with excitement and a certainty of pleasure a stranger who will greet us we know with some unexpected and revealing phrase that will open a door on to yet another human existence." Narayan has achieved this verisimilitude in his works because the situations he portrays not only combine the probable and the possible, they also reveal habits, nuances and modes of thought that are of universal signifi-

cance. It is because Narayan is not preoccupied with projecting a vision of the typical India, but rather with depicting the foibles and eccentricities, the hopes and aspirations, the sorrows and disappointments of the average man anywhere. George Eliot once remarked:

> Depend upon it, you would gain unspeakably if you would learn with me to see some of the poetry and the pathos . . . lying in the experience of the human soul that looks out through dull grey eyes, and that speaks in a voice of quite ordinary tone.

It is this poetry and pathos of everyday life that Narayan has succeeded in discovering in his novels and short stories. Samuel the Pea in Narayan's earliest novel, *Swami and Friends,* becomes a symbol of an outlook on life, "an attitude which cherishes and explores the unnoticed, subtle possibilities of the average and the unremarkable."

Narayan's use of the English language in his short stories has answered many a question that is raised on the adequacy of a foreign language being the medium of Indian writers. The problem of adapting and suiting the English language for literary purposes is one that every writer of Indian English finds himself faced with. Arguments for and against this medium of expression have been advanced at all stages of the history of Indo-English fiction and we need not go into this debate at this point. Narayan has mastered the English language sufficiently well to be able to convey the essence of his thought and describe the intricate social patterns of the life he is depicting with ease and assurance. The short stories are written in simple, direct prose that reads smoothly and lucidly. Moreover, they appeal to a wide and catholic taste because the English Narayan employs here is devoid of verbal cliches, Indianisms, coinages and startling imagery of far-fetched symbols. Narayan is never strident or emphatic; he works for the most part by under-statement or by implication. In each story there is a measured simplicity, an idiomatic naturalness that shows the perfect adapting of content with the medium of expression. In its nice modulations, Narayan's style is to be appreciated throughout his work—relaxed yet always disciplined to its purpose, easy but never slack, occasionally using "the formal word precise but not pedantic."

Fiction has always been a powerful means of man's exploration of the human situation. This exploration is of a special kind; it takes its origin in the depths of the human psyche which cannot be easily reached and cannot be easily expressed except in a special kind of language. And the language can be adequate to convey the perception of an author, his vision of reality when its tone and texture reveal how the author experiences his characters. R. K. Narayan is a great writer not because he succeeds in depicting Indian life accurately without exploiting its linguistic patterns, but because he succeeds in impressing upon us the fact that human culture, human experience, reality itself, transcends the barriers of language. And nowhere is this more evident than in his delightful short stories.

V. Panduranga Rao (essay date 1978)

SOURCE: "The Craftsmanship of R. K. Narayan," in *Indian Writing in English,* edited by Ramesh Mohan, Orient Longman Ltd., 1978, pp. 56-64.

[*In this essay, Rao describes Narayan as somewhat of an anomaly in Indian literature: an author at peace with himself, his society and his God. He further argues that this inner peace gives Narayan the ability to create sympathetic, believeable characters.*]

Foregrounding

Too many of our novels and stories written in English, it seems to me, exhibit poor craftsmanship. Their authors labour under an inability to spin a simple yarn; they are handicapped by a serious want of invention—of scene and situation, of character and action. With talent that is probably too queasy to generate 'an appetite for the illustrational,' too many of our second line fiction-makers (a couple of our diligent women novelists in particular) appear to practise a curious Penelope effect: weaving and unweaving, weaving . . . : till the innocent reader, led up the garden path, outraged at this literary coquetry, puts down the book in frustration. But perhaps the failure is at the very roots of artistic inspiration: a failure of sensibility which alone can achieve a creative intimacy—a live-coal brush—with experience; it is a too common lack, ultimately, of the gift of vision, 'a vision prompted by life.' This radical penury is reflected in their language as surely as disorder in the blood; they write a poetical, levitated language.

But consider the Nigerians, our Commonwealth cousins in colour and culture. Their first novels appeared less than two decades ago. In this short span they have produced a body of fiction which is remarkable for its breadth as well as depth. Beginning with Amos Tutuola, their pure primitive, with his half-light twilight tales (twilight tales are in the oral tradition of the tribes), we have Chinua Achebe in the very centre of the field, a Commonwealth gift, a novelist in the humanist tradition of the novel; at the other extreme, we have the poets Wole Soyinka with his *Interpreters* (a novel about young modern Nigerians) and Gabriel Okara with his gem of a novel, *The Voice.* There are others vigorously filling up this mosaic, like Ekwensi, Aluko, Nzekwu and Nwankwo. There are other African examples: Ngugi, the Kenyan; Peter Abrahams, Alex La Guma and Ezekiel Mphahlele, the South Africans: but the Nigerians already seem to have given their novel in English a homogeneous pattern of collective achievement, an African iridescence.

This is not to denigrate the Indian performance. While only a naive mind would overlook the solid contributions of the Big Three, we have competent novelists in Malgonkar and Arun Joshi. Nagarajan's *Chronicles of Kedaram* and Attia Hosain's *Sunlight on a Broken Column* are notable novels; even Nityanandan's unpretentious novel, *The Long, Long Days* is at least readable. Khushwant Singh is a clever story-teller (but to gauge his shortfall in

Train to Pakistan we must read Ved Mehta's account of the experience in his *Face to Face;* or we probably cannot do better than read Balwant Singh Anand's *The Cruel Interlude.*) And we have remarkable achievements in Ahmed Ali's *Twilight in Delhi,* Desani's *Hatterr* and Anantanarayanan's *The Silver Pilgrimage,* alongside the expatriate excellence of Sudhin Ghose. The total effect is none the less an irresistible feeling that we have more successful novels than novelists. We cannot help wondering if the history of the Indian novel in English is not the sad story of individual achievement and collective failure.

Focus

Since writing last about Narayan's art as a novelist and, especially, after meeting him and conversing with him, the conviction has grown in me that he is a creative writer who has come to terms with himself and has no fierce quarrel with man, society or God. Narayan's novels reveal a creative intelligence enjoying inner harmony evolved rather early in life, though not without struggle and suffering. The house of fiction that Narayan built is built on the bedrock of his faith (Whatever happens India will go on, he told Naipaul). This, I thought, was my complaint against Narayan: he is unique, human and not so accessibly human. The distance between the world immediate to me and that of Narayan's later novels is the distinction between the Inferno and the Purgatory. I, of course, believe that the Inferno—the world of Narayan's *Dark Room*—is too much with us. But I give credit to Narayan for his achievement: he makes his Purgatory credible (if not acceptable) to us of the Pit, both in the East and in the West. There is a muted contradiction in Narayan's later novels, between the humour which is humanizing and the grand Narayan vision which is so far above the merely human.

Then Narayan's *A Horse and Two Goats* appeared, a slender collection of five stories. I believe that two stories in this volume are among the best written by an Indian in English. It is in these stories—the title story, **'A Horse and Two Goats'** and **'Annamalai'**—that Narayan truly evokes memories of the great Russian master, Chekhov. They are to me a marvellous re-affirmation of Narayan's (at) oneness with man; an orchestration of the merely human, inevitably rooted in the actual. I offer below an analysis of **'A Horse and Two Goats'** in a small bid to peep behind the curtains and see Narayan at work.

The opening lines:

> Of *the seven hundred thousand villages* dotting the map of India, in which *the majority of India's five hundred million live, flourish and die,* Kritam was *probably the tiniest,* indicated on the district survey map by a microscopic dot, the map being meant more for the revenue official out to collect tax than for the guidance of the *motorist,* who in any case could not hope to reach it since it sprawled far from the highway at the end of a rough track furrowed up by the iron-hooped wheels of bullock carts. *But its size did not prevent its giving itself the grandiose name Kritam,*

which meant in Tamil "coronet" or "crown" on the brow of this subcontinent. The village consisted of less than thirty houses, only one of them built with brick and cement. Painted a brilliant yellow and blue all over with gorgeous carvings of gods and gargoyles on its balustrade, it was known as the Big House. The other houses, *distributed in four streets,* were generally of bamboo thatch, straw, mud, and other unspecified material. *Muni's was the last house in the fourth street,* beyond which stretched the fields. (Italics mine)

We notice the easy, unselfconscious narrowing down of the focus from *seven hundred thousand villages* and *five hundred million* (lives) to Kritam, the tiniest village, and Muni the least of its villagers. The phrase *live, flourish and die* is not as much of a cliche as it appears; there is an unsuspected, seemingly endless agony between *flourish* and *die*: Muni in the story has had his halcyon days and is yet to die—we are going to witness him caught in that infernal suspension when living ends without death. Further there is the casual *motorist;* it is going to be a chance motorist that sets up ripples in the stagnant pond of Muni's life. And we also notice the touch of humour in the comment on the name Kritam; and as Muni is the least of the villagers his hut is the last in the last street of the village. (This is about two-thirds of the opening paragraph of the story. Further in the same paragraph we are also introduced to the 'horse' of the title; we are told that the horse is, unexpectedly, made of clay. The horse is a 'horse.')

So Muni is poor. A definition of his poverty follows, in the second para of the story:

> His wife lit the domestic fire at dawn, boiled water in a mud pot, threw into it *a handful of millet flour,* added salt, and gave him his first nourishment for the day. When he started out, she would put in his hand *a packed lunch,* once again the same millet cooked into a little ball, which he could swallow with a raw onion at midday. *She was old, but he was older and needed all the attention she could give him in order to be kept alive.*

This seems as good an account of Indian poverty as any (isn't Indian poverty a prime export item for many of our novelists in English?). But let us pause at the *packed lunch.* To commuters in India it might evoke associations of tiffin carriers; for westerners it could mean a nice fat carton of selective (watch your calories) snacks. We have already been told that Muni's first nourishment could not be more than *a handful of millet flour;* and when we are told that Muni's wife put in his hand *a packed lunch* it might conceivably rouse our expectations for Muni. But having roused our expectations, Narayan dashes them in the very next breath (just with the interruption of a comma): *once again the same millet cooked into a little ball, which he could swallow with a raw onion at midday.* And this is poverty pared of sentimentality because it is, illustrationally, the definition of Muni's poverty; but here is how, to cap it, Narayan concludes his statement:

> *. . . She was old, but he was older and needed all the attention she could give him in order to be kept alive.*

This is a sudden lighting up; coming through the old woman's point of view, it is her casually muted, endearingly cynical expression of her love for her old man. This unobtrusive surfacing of the love between this old man and this old woman, the beauty of their relationship, in spite of the enormity of their indigence, is what gives the entire passage the sound of being merely factual and unsentimental; neither shutting his eyes to the presence of the wolves at the door nor spurning sentiment within the hut, Narayan gives character and dignity to the couple's poverty. The last sentence breaks through the crust of the preceding lines even as their humanity does through their sub-human living.

Narayan's invention moves ahead to illustrate and dramatize, to root his characters and their setting firmly in the actual. Here is the second half of the next paragraph:

> . . . And so the two goats were tethered to the trunk of a drumstick tree which grew in front of his hut from which occasionally Muni could shake down drumsticks. *This morning he got six.* He carried them in with a sense of triumph Although no one could say precisely who owned the tree, it was his because *he lived in its shadow.*

First, Narayan has initiated action with *This morning he got six.* For these six precious drumsticks Narayan sends Muni a little later to the shopman of the village who helps reveal a new dimension of Muni's poverty. And meanwhile there is the last sentence. *Although no one could say precisely who owned the tree, it was his because he lived in its shadow.* This is the drumstick tree. I believe that Narayan could have planted with equal facility any other vegetable tree or plant here; for example, a jack fruit tree or a gourd creeper. But it has to be the drumstick tree; for of course any South Indian with half Muni's weakness for drumstick sauce will know that a drumstick tree, as trees go, casts pretty little shadow; its small sparse leaves don't help, unlike say a banyan tree, shelter anybody that 'lives' in its shadow. We normally have to take the idiomatic meaning of the phrase, but I think in the given context it acquires literal overtones. Thus we see that Narayan's invention is very economical—the crafty artist not only makes use of the drumsticks but also the drumstick leaves.

When Muni asks his wife for drumstick sauce, she orders him out to somehow procure the groceries for making the sauce; and Muni approaches the village shopman. The shopman helps Narayan throw light on Muni in a couple of ways. First we come to know of the 'daughter.'

> 'I will pay you everything on the first of the next month.' 'As always, and whom do you except to rob by then?' Muni felt caught and mumbled, 'My daughter has sent word that she will be sending me money.'

> 'Have you a daughter?' sneered the shopman. 'And she is sending you money! . . .'

The Munis have no children, as a little later on we come to know. In the Indian context even if one has many daughters (not a welcome proposition) one rarely expects to receive monthly allowances from any one of them—where's your self-respect? But even daughters will do for Muni, childless, would very much like to have some.

> He recollected the thrill he had felt when he mentioned a daughter to that shopman; although it was not believed, what if he did not have a daughter?—his cousin in the next village had many daughters, and any one of them was as good as his; he was fond of them all and would buy them sweets *if he could afford it.* Still, everyone in the village whispered behind their backs that Muni and his wife were a barren couple. . .

The non-existent daughter thus adds a new dimension to Muni's poverty; he is not only poor in money and material possessions, he is also utterly poor—in progeny. This sort of freckles Muni's character, this old man, and he is insinuated fully into our sympathy.

Muni may be poor but he still has vestiges of dignity and self-respect. Here is the conclusion of his unsucessful mission to the shopman who indulges in Muni-baiting giving him nothing but mockery and scorn.

> . . . Muni thought helplessly, 'My poverty is exposed to everybody. But what can I do?'
>
> 'More likely you are seventy,' said the shopman. 'You also forget that you mentioned a birthday five weeks ago when you wanted castor oil for your holy bath.'
>
> 'Bath! Who can dream of a bath when you have to scratch the tankbed for a bowl of water? We would all be parched and dead but for the Big House, where they let us take a pot of water from their well.' After saying this Muni unobtrusively rose and moved off.
>
> He told his wife, 'That scoundrel would not give me anything. So go out and sell the drumsticks for what they are worth.'

Muni may not have got much out of the shopman but Narayan has. Narayan's art is rich in the invention of the actual. But let us now move on to the farcical scene that is central to the action of the story. This is the scene between Muni and the foreigner. Basically Narayan is exploiting a device from the slapstick drama of our popular theatre. It is the humour of situation and dialogue that two deaf people create when they encounter each other in earnest business.

> . . . Now the other man (the foreigner) suddenly pressed his palms together in a salute, smiled and said, 'Namaste! How do you do?'
>
> At which Muni spoke the only English expressions he had learnt, 'Yes, no.' Having exhausted his English vocabulary, he started in Tamil. . .

And while 'The foreigner nodded his head and listened courteously though he understood nothing,' he is anxious that the Indian should understand him; he has already set his heart on the statue. He is puzzled that Muni doesn't understand English. He says:

> ' . . . I have gotten along with English everywhere in this country, but you don't speak it. Have you any religious or spiritual scruples against English speech?'

Not an incapable man. But with Muni he seems to be getting nowhere; the two are on two different wave-lengths. Here is more evidence of Narayan's shrewd exploitation of the linguistic curtain between the two:

> Noting the other's interest in his speech, Muni felt encouraged to ask, 'How many children have you?' with appropriate gestures with his hands. Realizing that a question was being asked, the red man replied, 'I said a hundred,' which encouraged Muni to go into details. 'How many of your children are boys and how many girls? Where are they? Is your daughter married? Is it difficult to find a son-in-law in your country also?' (p. 23)

So they go on, representatives of two civilizations, failing to establish contact except by the sheerest accident when the result as in the climax, is comic catastrophe.

> The foreigner followed his look and decided that it would be a sound policy to show an interest in *the old man's pets*. He went up casually to them and stroked their backs with every show of courteous attention. Now the truth dawned on the old man. His dream of a lifetime was about to be realised. He understood that the red man was actually making an offer for the goats.

Thus Muni and what's-his-name. But what is the foreigner's name? He is unnamed. He is the red-faced foreigner, the red man, the foreigner without a name. But how marvellously Narayan invents the American with the very quirk and tang of the American's speech:

> ' . . . I assure you that this will have the best home in the USA. I'll push away the bookcase, you know, I love books and am a member of five book clubs, and the choice and bonus volumes mount up to a pile really in our living room, as high as this horse itself. But they'll have to go. Ruth may disapprove, but I will convince her. The TV may have to be shifted too. We can't have everything in the living room. Ruth will probably say what about when we have a party? I'm going to keep him right in the middle of the room. I don't see how that can interfere with the party—we'll stand around him and have our drinks.'

This is expert literary ventriloquism and it helps superbly concretize the image of the American. Still, this is a case of a character being endowed with more than a local habitation—and that without a name: purposely. His speech, his manner and his actions typify him as a westerner (and who is more western in modern times than a New Yorker?); and the elision of his name, perfectly natural in the situation, is just the deviation to endow him with more than ordinary significance. He had told his wife in America, 'We will visit India this winter, it's time to look at other civilizations.' The unnamed foreigner is a typical representative of his civilization. He is *the* westerner.

The other civilization is India and of course who more true to her than Muni? To begin with he comes from *probably the tiniest village* of India. Narayan has always believed that India is her villages. (We remember *The Guide;* it is the rural India that traps Raju and positively sublimates him.) Narayan has already indicated this in his opening lines. 'Of the seven hundred thousand villages dotting the map of India, in which the majority of India's five hundred million live . . . ' Not simply quantitatively; even qualitatively India is her villages. *The tiniest* (and *microscopic dot*) is thus microcosmic and the name Kritam with that selective touch of humour Narayan honours it with emphasizes the same symbolic value, with *the four streets* as likely standing for the four chief castes of the traditional Indian society. Muni may not know more than 'Yes, no' of English (the only one who knows English in Kritam, the postman, has not prospered much—he is fighting shy of the shopman to whom he is indebted and his wife has run away with somebody); but he has imbibed the puranas through the oral tradition, and the *Ramayana* and the *Mahabaratha* and the legends of the land, can talk no end of them. He is poor *and* dignified; unlettered *and* well-drilled in the country's rich lore. Muni is as Indian as one in the centre of the society can realistically wish. He is the Indian delegate; he represents India for Narayan.

Here of course is the East-West encounter, so dear to our writers and critics—with a vital difference: it is offered to us through the prism of Narayan's vision, humanized by his humour.

But that is not the end of the story's potential for significance. The statue of the horse and soldier too is subject to just that accretion of meaning which marks it out as a metaphor. Narayan's careful and elaborate description of the statue—running into 24 lines—is supported by Muni's attempt at estimating its ancestry:

> ' . . . I was an urchin this high when I heard my grandfather explain this horse and warrior, and my grandfather himself was this high when he heard his grandfather, whose grandfather. . . .'

In the heightened context of the encounter between India and the West, the Horse stands for India's ancient heritage. But there is no sentimental mushing up here. We come back to the title. **'A Horse and Two Goats.'** A Horse made of clay; Muni sees no value in it; though he has moved in its shadow ever since he can remember, he is not aware of any special value attached to it; but the appreciative American businessman is eager to possess it—even if he has to build his cocktail parties around it. Two Goats; made of poor (metaphorical) clay, probably far below the stipulations of a Chicago butcher. The gawky goats are Muni's only property, his only capital and not the horse; the American of course has no use for them, except

to ingratiate himself with—for he has concluded they are Muni's *pets*. Each thinks the other values what he himself values; each doesn't value what the other does. In the event both leave with an absurd sense of business well—and hardly—done.

Atma Ram (essay date 1981)

SOURCE: "Introduction," in *Perspectives on R. K. Narayan,* Vimal Prakashan, 1981, pp. xvii-xxxi.

[*This essay examines the general characteristics of Narayan's fiction, including his realistic rendering of day-to-day life, the importance of family relationships, and the role of the caste system in Indian society.*]

Rasipuram Krishnaswami Narayan, one of the most prominent Indians writing in English, was born in Madras on 10 October 1907. He remained in Madras with his grandmother for some time when the family shifted to Mysore. The grandmother supervised with great care the education of children:

> Grandmotherhood was a wrong vocation for her; she ought to have been a school inspectress. She had an absolute passion to teach and mould a young mind. In later years after my uncle was married and had children, as they came of a teachable age, she took charge of them one by one.

Narayan had his school and college education in Madras. He disliked the present system of education and felt that it seriously hampered free thinking and natural play of fancy. He "instinctively rejected both education and examinations, with their unwarranted seriousness and esoteric suggestions." As an open revolt in the family was not possible, he went through it without any enthusiasm or distinction. He failed in Arithmetic repeatedly and did his graduation in 1930 when he was twenty-four.

R. K. Narayan tried a number of professions. He worked in the Mysore Secretariat for some time but found his work tedious. Then he became a teacher, but the vocation did not suit him. Thereafter, he was a correspondent of *Madras Justice,* and a sub-editor, At last he left all work and took to creative writing. He would often incorporate material from day-to-day observations:

> I had started writing mostly under influence of events occuring around me and in the style of any writer who was uppermost in my mind at the time. My father had lost a dear friend, which affected him deeply. Moved by his sorrow I wrote ten pages of an outpouring entitled "Friendship," very nearly echoing the lamentations of 'Adonais' but in a flamboyant poetic prose.

In the beginning many of his writings were rejected outright which naturally had a dampening effect on the young author. However, he was convinced that he should go on writing in his own way:

> I offered samples of my writing to every kind of editor and publisher in the city of Madras. The general criticism was that my stories lacked "plot." There was no appreciation of my literary values, and I had nothing else to offer. Malgudi was inescapable as the sky overhead.

He had resolved to live on writing alone, but his earnings were very meagre. We are told that in his first year of writing he earned nine rupees and twelve annas; the second year a story was sold for 18 rupees, the third a children's tale fetched 30 rupees. His first novel, *Swami and Friends,* was declared satisfactory by a young collegian. (This boy later became a constant critic and adviser of Narayan):

> Years ago when I wrote my first novel, *Swami and Friends,* and found none to read it, a very young-college friend came forward to go through the manuscript; he read and certified it as readable which was very encouraging.

Later, Graham Greene was impressed by Narayan's fiction. He wrote "introductions" for *The Bachelor of Arts* and *The Financial Expert,* and also persuaded a leading publisher to bring out his first four novels.

In 1933 Narayan met a handsome, tall, slim girl, Rajam, and fell in love with her. He describes the episode in his autobiography:

> After the false starts, the real thing occurred in July, 1933, I had gone to Coimbatore, escorting my elder sister, and then stayed on in her house. One day, I saw a girl drawing water from the street tap and immediately fell in love with her. I could not talk to her. I learned later that she had not even noticed me passing and re-passing in front of her while she waited to fill the brass vessels. I could not really stand and stare; whatever impression I had of her would be through a side-glance while passing the tap. I suffered from a continual melting vision. The only thing I was certain of was that I loved her, and I suffered the agonies of the restraint imposed by the social conditions in which I lived.

Narayan befriended her father and in course of time announced his intention to marry his daughter. But their horoscopes didn't tally. The infatuated lover bribed his pundit who compared the horoscopes and declared them all right. Narayan thus married Rajam in 1935. Rajam helped her husband in his creative work. But, unfortunately, after a brief married life of over five years she died in 1939 of typhoid, leaving behind a daughter. Rajam could see the publication of only first three novels, and is reflected in some detail in Sushila in *The English Teacher* and Srinivas's wife in *Mr. Sampath.*

Narayan is now a prolific and eminent writer; he has published eleven novels, over two hundred short stories and four books of non-fiction. He has received a number of literary awards and distinctions: National Prize of Indian Literary Academy 1958, Sahitya Academy Award on *The Guide,* 1960; Padma Bhushan, 1964; National Association of Independent School Award, 1965; Litt. D.: University of Leeds, 1967; D. Litt.: Delhi University 1973.

As a man, Narayan is quite simple, unassuming and gentle. He is often reluctant to speak on his writing. He is a "very considerate author, never referring to my works unless I am forced to." He believes that a work of literary art should be self-explanatory. It should also be not confused with reality as in it everything passes through the crucible of imagination. Its incidents and characters are deeply rooted in the world of fiction. *The Guide,* therefore, need not be regarded as "typical":

> I had to repeat here, and later, everywhere that a novel is about an individual living his life in a world imagined by the author, performing a set of actions (up to a limit) contrived by the author. But to take a work of fiction as a sociological reality or a social document could be very misleading. My novel *The Guide* was not about the saints or the pseudo-saints of India but about a particular person.

R. K. Narayan's observations on his art and craft are revealing. Like many other Indian-English authors, he enjoys writing intensely. As he once pointed out: "The pure delight of watching the novel grow, can never be duplicated by another experience." Common occurrences provide sufficient material for his writings. Whereas Fielding finds "ridiculous" a perennial source of humour, Narayan describes trivial eccentricities of characters. As he remarks: "But I am more interested in, and would like to portray people with small eccentricities." These characters undergo little development and remain essentially the same beings. Says Narayan: "It is not the enlightened self they carry, but an unchanged, unchanging old self. It's part of their nature which cannot be transformed." Such characters engage their creator's sympathy but there is little involvement:

> "I don't take them seriously, I have ample sympathy for them. Still there is no involvement. I am detached."

When he begins a story, he is not aware how it will end. Nor does he impose any external pattern on it, he lets the incidents invent themselves: "Each day as I sat down to write I had no notion of what would be coming."

One general reaction to R. K. Narayan's fiction is: "Oh, how real it is!" One feels that his works embody the reality of life in India so easily and adequately. For example, the opening scene in *The Guide* is at once realistic in tone and description. The foreign readers are particularly struck with the element of social realism in Narayan's writing. The novelist has to stress time and again that his characters and situations belong to a work of fiction.

"Do brothers quarrel in India?"

"Of course, brothers would quarrel anywhere in the world," I said, and delivered a long discourse on joint family living in India. About fifty answers, always reminding the audience in conclusion that *The Financial Expert* was a work of fiction, not a treatise or a document, and the story was about an individual and was not portraying a type.

Narayan's stories have a specific fictional locale—Malgudi, an imaginary town in South India. Like Hardy's Wessex, Malgudi has a life of its own. However, Hardy shows the disappearance of the rural mode of living and the urban culture impinging upon rustic life, whereas Narayan describes both the old and the new existing side by side. There exist pastoral simplicity as well as contemporary complexity of life. The era of science and technology has set in, yet the old way of life has also its votaries. Margayya in *The Financial Expert,* for example, wishes to start again his old business under the banyan tree towards the close of the novel. Graham Greene aptly observes: "But the life of Malgudi—never ruffled by politics—proceeds in exactly the same way as it has done for centuries, and the juxtaposition of the age-old convention and the modern character provides much of the comedy."

Narayan's work is deeply rooted in Indian soil and mode of existence.

—*Atma Ram*

R. K. Narayan concentrates on orthodox family and incorporates numerous features of Indian life. He deals with middle and lower middle classes who constitute the bulk of India's population. He studies various relationships in his novels with family as the nucleus. There is a strong sense of kinship in his fiction, and the equation between Margayya and his brother in the *Financial Expert* is a telling example in point. It is a patriarchal society where father's influence is immense and all-pervasive. In *Swami and Friends,* the father is an archetype of all father-figures in Narayan's later novels. Chandran's father in *The Bachelor of Arts* behaves like a medieval knight. Ramani in *The Dark Room* is a tyrant who represents cruel men in India dominating over women.

Man-woman relationship occupies an important place in Narayan's fiction. In *The Bachelor of Arts* the Chandran-Malathi affair is warm and romantic. In *The Dark Room,* however, the obvious movement is from a tragedy to a dramatic anti-climax. Savitri is not blind to the faults of her husband, though she meekly gives in and keeps quiet. Srinivas in *Mr. Sampath* has no inclination for the normal husband and wife relationship and he doesn't hold it sacred. Shanti comes to live with him as his mistress, and he justifies his conduct: "Every sane man needs two wives—a perfect one for the house and a perfect one out for the social life. I have the one. Why not the other?"

Bullying husbands like Ramani and meek wives like Savitri are a common feature of our traditional society. Woman is a helpless creature to be guarded by her father as a child, by her husband in her youth and by her son when she is old and a widow. A female child is ever a liability. In Sushila the novelist portrays an ideal Hindu wife rooted in Indian culture. According to Indian custom, a guest is a god, and a typical Indian woman, like Savitri, has "a genius for making the existing supply elastic and transforming an ordinary evening course, with a few hurriedly fried trimmings, to a feast."

Paternal love is one of the significant refrains in Narayan's fiction. Here, no character despises children, at least his own. In *Swami and Friends,* when Swami is not back till nine at night, his mother anxiously waits for him and stands like "a stone image looking down the street." Chandran's parents love him intensely. His father languishes when he is away for eight months. Ramani is genuinely concerned about his children. Savitri's maternal instinct compels her to return home and submit to the brutalities of her husband. Krishnan of *The English Teacher* loves his daughter immensely. The parents miss their daughter in their hunting expedition. When she falls ill, they suffer quietly. Srinivas in *Mr. Sampath,* too, loves his son. Margayya in *The Financial Expert* is chiefly interested in his son, who has come as a result of many prayers. Jagan of *The Sweet Vendor* pins high hopes on his son. Vasu, the man-eater of Malgudi, is the only major character who dislikes children, but he is held up to ridicule.

Then, Granny is an inevitable part of the Indian household, an integral feature of extended family. Narayan maintains that in a joint family children are well brought up as there is a congenial home atmosphere for them.

> . . . . the children do not feel lonely, as they generally spend their time with their cousins; uncles or grandparents. As a matter of fact, in a big household children hardly ever cling to their parents. They get a balanced training as they are always watched by someone or the other.

Swami's grandmother in *Swami and Friends* is benign, talkative and ignorant, and she influences him in his formative period. After the night meal, "with his head on his granny's lap, nestling close to her, Swami felt very snug and safe in the faint atmosphere of cardamom and cloves." She is a prototype of thousands of Indian grannies, who uphold the values of traditional society. Sriram's granny in *Waiting for the Mahatma* is a woman of strong will and rectitude. She scrupulously sends to the bank every pie she receives on behalf of her grandson and gives the entire amount to him the day he attains maturity. A pious Hindu, she cannot touch the skin of a dead animal.

Indian society is down deep traditional and caste-ridden. In this country arranged marriage is a common phenomenon and horoscopes are often compared. This happened in Narayan's own life. Chandran in *The Bachelor of Arts* could not marry the girl he loved because the horoscopes did not tally. This problem crops up in *The Financial*

Expert as well. The astrologer who thinks that the horoscopes of Balu and Brinda do not match is dismissed with a fee of one rupee, whereas the one who testifies that the horoscopes match perfectly is rewarded with a fee of Rs 75/-. Raju's mother in *The Guide* is first sympathetic towards Rosie. But she changes her attitude completely when she learns that Rosie belongs to the dancing girls class. Srinivas's wife does not take food cooked by a non-Brahmin. It is difficult for Jagan (in *The Vendor of Sweets*) to accept a non-Hindu girl as his daughter-in-law. Raman's aunt in *The Painter of Signs* decides to go on a pilgrimage when she learns that Raman is going to marry a Christian girl. Belief in supernatural communications, such as we find in *The English Teacher,* is prevalent all over the world. However, in the traditional society of India even educated people have implicit faith in such things.

Narayan's novels describe many other characteristics of Indian society. For example, it is repeatedly shown that in India it is a disgrace to fail in an examination. Here many young persons suffer mental agonies when they cannot pass an examination. In **'Isawaran'** the protagonist is a student who drowns himself in the Sarayu river when he fails in the intermediate examination for the tenth time. He feels that his life is meaningless: "If I can't pass an examination even with a tenth attempt, what is the use of my living and disgracing the world?" In another story entitled **'Breach of Promise,'** a youth resolves to end his life in case he does not pass an examination. It is also a fact that most students in India depend on "Guides" and "critics", and don't study the "texts" critically. In 'On the Abuse of Criticism' Narayan laments that our students read Verity and Bradley, not Shakespeare. Gajapali in *The Bachelor of Arts* refers to Dowden and Bradley quite frequently. The vagaries of private buses are treated realistically in *Waiting for the Mahatma,* and *The Man-Eater of Malgudi.*

Narayan's work is deeply rooted in Indian soil and mode of existence. Here distinctive features of Indian life are artistically treated, nothing remains undigested. To take two examples. After Rajam's death Narayan felt intensely sad and lonely. It was a grief beyond description. He was asked to describe his experiences in his next novel, but he could not. Later he had an experience of telepathy through Dr. Paul Brunton and was convinced that a communication with an individual after death is possible. He practised psychic contacts and felt relieved as he found a satisfying pattern operating in his life. *The English Teacher* is the literary result. In the novel, Krishna is a lecturer in English in a college. He lives with his wife, Sushila and small daughter, Leela. They plan to own a house, and at last select one. However, Sushila dies of typhoid and Krishna feels isolated and crestfallen. He sends his daughter to school and through her is acquainted with the Headmaster. Incidentally Krishna is spiritually connected with his wife, through letters she sends him messages to be careful and have interest in life. Here Narayan's experience has been converted into an aesthetic one. The novel turns out to be a powerful work of literary art. Says Lily Blair:

". . . . but let me tell you, in future you may do well or ill, but to have written *The English Teacher* is enough achievement for a lifetime. You won't do it again and can't even if you attempt."

The novelist had heard reports of famine and an episode in which some Brahmins prayed to God for rains in knee-deep water for twelve days, and then it rained. This is really the starting point of *The Guide.* As Narayan reports:

> At this time I had been thinking of a subject for a novel: a novel about someone suffering enforced sainthood. A recent situation in Mysore offered a setting for such a story. A severe drought had dried up all the rivers and tanks; Krishnaraja Sagar, an enormous reservoir feeding channels that irrigated thousands of acres, had also become dry, and its bed, a hundred and fifty feet deep, was now exposed to the sky with fissures and cracks, revealing an ancient submerged temple, coconut stumps, and dehydrated crocodiles. As a desperate measure, the municipal council organised a prayer for rains. A group of Brahmins stood knee-deep in water (procured at great cost) on the dry bed of Kaveri, fasted, prayed, and chanted certain mantras continuously for eleven days. On the twelfth day it rained, and brought relief to the country side.

At that time he had the idea of *The Guide* in his mind. In the novel the main motif is made operative unobtrusively. Narayan writes with deftness and control. When Raju comes out of the jail, he has nowhere to go. In a village he is taken for a saint. He stays on and befriends the village folk. After some time there is a drought in that region. The villagers quarrel with one another. Through the wrongly delivered message, Raju has to carry on a fast for rains. He becomes famous, people from far and near come to see him. In the end he looks about and says, "Velan, it's raining in the hills. I can feel it coming up under my feet, up my legs—" He sags down. Narayan, here manages by a miracle of perception and choice of detail to convey the Indian reality without a single false feeling or gesture.

His narrative technique enables Narayan to present a microcosm of Indian society. He avoids authorial comments and employs irony as a vision, not as a device. His humour is never satirical. He tries to offer an objective viewpoint and includes comments as a part of description and narration. For instance, the growing relationship between Rosie and Raju is mentioned in this manner:

> At the door of number 28, I hesitated. She opened the door, passed in, and hesitated, leaving the door half open. She stood looking at me for a moment, as on the first day.
>
> "Shall I go away?" I asked in a whisper.
>
> "Yes. Good night," She said feebly.
>
> "May I not come in," I asked, trying to look my saddest.

"No, no. Go away," She said. But on an impulse, I gently pushed her out of the way, and stepped in and locked the door on the world.

Narayan narrates the story at two levels: the superficial stage where the locale is dominating for proper interpretation of the episodes, the deeper stage where general truths are incorporated in artistic terms. To give an example, the progress of Raju from a scout boy to Raju the guide and Swami is gripping. The novelist employs here the oral method of story-telling which is most effective. As he points out: "My manuscript being what it is, I had to resort to the ancient system of oral story-telling. I think a story acquires an extra-dimension in this kind of narration and it is such a labour-saving device." But when this is read as the story of what circumstances make one do, it acquires greater depth and meaning. The charm of Narayan's art lies in the fact that at both the levels the story holds the wedding guest. The casual reader is happy to meet Sushila's ghost in *The English Teacher* or to learn of the heavy rains in *The Guide*. However, a serious student of Narayan is left thinking whether the ghost is a real one, whether the rains referred to are only a coincidence or a figment of Raju's imagination.

The novelist calmly views life from an aesthetic distance as a movement. While standing at a crossroad, he gets sufficient material for his writing. As he once observed: "I have to just stand at the market road for my material." The general pattern embodied in his novels is that of a circle—an order, a disturbance for some time; and later the order regained with some modifications. The protagonist in Narayan works within the framework of the traditional society. There exist situations with tragic implications. However, the novelist, a comic genius, escapes this aspect because he accepts life as such. Despite difficulties, there is something mysterious in Indian life which keeps it going. It is the innate zest for life, pleasure in sheer living, its religious routine. This is what enables Indians (and the novelist) to take a quiet and generous view of life. As he remarked: "Most Indians pray and meditate at least for a few minutes every day, and it may be one of the reasons why, with all our poverty and struggle, we still survive and are able to take a calm view of existence."

Narayan's locale is Tamil Land, and life in Malgudi primarily refers to life in South Indian villages. However, village reality in India is easily a prototype of national life. Narayan thus presents a viable portrait of India. Now a great artist transcends the limitations of a regional writer. "All great art," says T. S. Eliot, "has something permanent and universal about it, and reflects the permanent as well as the changing. . . . no great art is explicable simply by the society of its time." Narayan's theme is basically Indian but truly universal. 'The Astrologer's Day' is Indian in tone and setting, yet the ending imparts to it a universal significance. *The Guide* depicts the progress of a tourist guide to a *Swami* in Indian context. But the inherent theme—that man in the crowded world is all alone, and he

is what circumstances make of him—is true for every man on the earth.

Influences on Narayan's characters:

Narayan's ever-alert eye for the comic does not spare even the epics—the Ramayana and the Mahabharata. His *Gods, Demons and Others* (1964), an earlier work, is not really noted for any reinterpretation of myth or legend, but neither is it a mere paraphrase of the stories found in the Indian Puranas. There is an unmistakable freshness of approach and insight in the presentation of some characters. It is interesting to note that Narayan, more than any Indian novelist except Raja Rao, has been inspired to a considerable extent by the Puranas, not merely in the ingenious way one of the legends is adapted in *The Man-Eater of Malgudi* (1961), but also in the art of storytelling. His essay "The World of the Storyteller" reveals the secrets of his own success as storyteller. The essay has a poetic appeal while it evokes an atmosphere by creating the widening circles around the focal point—namely, the storyteller. The seeming naïveté of such an approach should serve as a corrective to the high-strung intellectual of modern times who is eager to present a theory of fiction.

C. N. Srinath, "R. K. Narayan's Comic Vision: Possibilities and Limitations," in World Literature Today, *Vol. 55, No. 3, Summer, 1981, pp. 416-19.*

M. K. Naik (essay date 1982)

SOURCE: "Malgudi Minor: The Short Stories of R. K. Narayan," in *The Laurel Bough*, edited by G. Nageswara Rao, Blackie & Son Publishers Private Limited, 1982, pp. 195-202.

[*In this essay, Naik criticizes the lack of tragic irony and imagination in Narayan's short stories, but finds that his tight form and structure result in a well-constructed story.*]

The short stories of Narayan are remarkable more for their workmanlikeness and finish than for the quality of the reading of life they offer; and one of the chief reasons for this is the limited role played by irony in them, though a persistent ironic note is by and large, their distinguishing feature. Narayan's short stories number more than four score, and are included in the following collections: *Malgudi Days* (1941); *Dodu and Other Stories* (1943); *Cyclone and Other Stories* (1944); *The Astrologer's Day and Other Stories* (1947); *Lawley Road* (1956) and *A Horse and Two Goats* (1970). A few uncollected stories like **"The Cobbler and the God"** have also appeared recently.

A sizable number of these stories are built round the principle of simple irony of circumstance, leading to the shock of discovery or surprise or reversal at the end. In **"An Astrologer's Day"**, a town astrologer meets a client and reads his past correctly, saying that a man had knifed him in a village brawl years before. He tells the man that the person who knifed him is dead and adds. "I see once again great danger to your life if you go from home." The story ends with the shock of the discovery that the astrologer was himself the person who had knifed that man and then the irony of both his reading of the past and his advice to his client is brought home. In **"Mother and Son"** the mother of an unemployed and unmarried youth, who quarrels with her and does not return at night fears that he has gone and drowned himself in a tank nearby but is finally relieved to find him next morning sleeping on a bench near the tank-bund.

A final shock of surprise is the main point of stories like **"Missing Mail"** and **"Out of Business"**. In the first story, an altruistic postman, conceals the news of a near relative's death from a family in order that a wedding, which for certain urgent reasons cannot be postponed, can take place on the appointed day. The bride's father comes to know the truth only at the end. In **"Out of Business,"** Rama Rao, who is broke, wants to commit suicide by falling before a railway train, is saved because it is running late and returns home to find his financial problems temporarily solved.

Ironic reversal is the basic structural principle behind some of the stories. In **"Father's Help"**, which is a "Swami" story, young Swami armed with his father's letter of complaint against the teacher Samuel addressed to the head master deliberately courts punishment at Samuel's hands, hoping to have his revenge at the end of the day when he would hand over the letter to the headmaster. His hopes are suddenly frustrated when he comes to know that the headmaster is on leave that day and hence the letter has to be given to his assistant—viz., Samuel himself! **"Trail of the Green Blazer"** operates on the same principle. Raju, the pickpocket expertly picks the purse of the man in the green blazer and removes the cash from it. As he is about to throw the purse away, he notices a toy baloon folded and tucked away inside it and filled with thoughts of affection and pity for the child for whom it is meant, tries to put the purse back in "Green Blazer's" pocket and is caught red-handed!

In all these stories there is a single stroke of irony each. Occasionally, ironic complications ensue in a linked chain, enhancing the comic effect. **"Engine Trouble"** provides an excellent example. The winner of a steam engine in a lottery finds that the prize is a perfect white elephant for him. It lands him into all kinds of trouble and expense when he tries to get it moved. He is charged rent for parking it; and in the attempt to get it moved by the temple elephant, a compound wall is demolished and the elephant injured, involving further damages. In the end, there is a lucky earthquake during which the engine falls into a dilapidated well, which solves at one stroke the problems of the owners of both the engine and the well.

In addition to the motif of the irony of circumstance, in a few stories, the irony is linked with a revelation of human psychology, though in a rather limited way. **"Gandhi's Appeal"** shows the transition from simple irony of situation to ironic revelation of psychology. Padma, moved by Gandhiji's appeal for funds at a public meeting, parts with her gold bangles and apologetically informs her husband about this. When, however, she learns that he too has given away the fifty rupees earmarked for rent to the same cause, she scolds him indignantly, while he has already forfeited his own right to do so! Dr. Raman in **"The Doctor's Word"** has the reputation of being always brutally frank and truthful in dealing with his patients. When his best friend is dying of a heart attack, however, the doctor deliberately lies to his patient, telling him that he will live and such is the force of his reputation for truthfulness that the patient does recover, to the astonishment of the doctor himself. In **"Gateman's Gift"** an illiterate watchman receives a registered letter and assumes the worst ('only lawyers send registered letters') so much so that he goes mad, and his sanity is restored only on learning that the letter contains a cheque presented to him by his boss.

> **Narayan . . . appears to fight shy of a tragic ending even when the logic of events in a story seems to demand it.**
>
> —*M. K. Naik*

Tragic irony does not seem to appeal to Narayan to the same extent as comic irony, and the few examples of its kind in his repertoire hardly rank among the best of his efforts in shorter fiction. Even among them he appears to prefer the gentler evocation of pathos to the sterner effects of tragedy. **"Iswaran"** presents a college student, who, after repeated examination-failures, writes a suicide note to his father before proceeding to the river to drown himself; on the way, he casually checks upon his result, discovers that he has passed in second class, goes mad at the shock of joy and drowns himself in the river; and no one knows the real reason why he died. The ironic double-twist at the end seems to interest the author more than the psychology of the protagonist. In **"Seventh House,"** the revelation of psychology is far more important. A young and devoted husband whose wife lies dying of a serious disease is assured by an astrologer that if he is unfaithful to her, that could propitiate the evil planets and thus save her. The husband's timid attempts to visit a prostitute are frustrated by a well-meaning horse-carriage driver whom he engages to take him to his desination, and finally, unable to explain his reasons to this cruel Good Samaritan, the husband pathetically resigns himself to his fate. Narayan also appears to fight shy of a tragic ending even when the logic of events in a story seems to demand it. In **"The Gateman's Gift,"** which has already been cited, the protagonist's sudden return to sanity at the end is not adequately motivated; in fact, the edge of the irony in the story is blunted by this denoument, while a tragic ending would certainly have added to the final effect.

Considering the large number of eccentrics that figure in Narayan's novels, it is significant that he does not have many short stories-dealing with the comic exposure of eccentricity. This is perhaps another indication of the fact [that] in the short stories his finer artistic resources do not appear to have been brought fully into play. The half-wit in **"Dasi the Bridegroom"** has a trick played on him by people who tell him that a cinema star who has recently come to stay in the locality is his destined bride. The ensuing comic complications yield humour of a rather elementary variety, and the narrator's neutral tones leave no room for the possibility of the narrative developing an extra dimension of pathos. **"Annamalai"** is a fuller sketch. This old man who attaches himself to the narrator one day has had a colourful history. Running away from home at the age of ten, he has worked as a coolie in Ceylon and Malaya and has escaped from a Japanese prison there. A self appointed gardener at the narrator's house, he is guided more by whim than by the logic of his profession in carrying out his duties. His general ignorance (his response to a trunk call is 'No trunk or baggage here. Master is sleeping') and his complicated financial dealings with the people back at his village provide the comedy. But considering the space given to him (the story runs to 37 pages), Annamalai hardly emerges as a more memorable character than the eccentrics in say, *The Man Eater of Malgudi,* who are drawn with a few rapid strokes.

Not many of Narayan's stories can be classified as stories of character in which the psychology of the protagonist is the chief point. And even in the few examples of this genre, the author does not appear to exploit fully the opportunities offered by his subject. **"A Willing Slave"** is a case in point. Here, Ayah, the old servant who looks after young Radha, always frightens her ward by telling her about the 'Old Fellow' (meaning Ayah's husband) who wants to carry away his wife. One day the 'Old Fellow' actually arrives to carry Ayah away and Radha, who is mortally afraid of him does not even come out to bid Ayah goodbye. The situation here is reminiscent of that in Tagore's "Cabuliwallah," but the psychological richness of Tagore's story is hardly in evidence in Narayan's which remains at the anecdotal stage only. The same appears to be the case with **"The Axe,"** the story of an old gardener attached to a sprawling house, who is dismissed when the ownership changes hands. The gardener leaves as the garden is being demolished a situation reminiscent of *The Cherry Orchard,* but here again, the reader gets the impression that in contrast to Chekhov, Narayan has not adequately met the challenge of his tragic theme here, and that there is a failure of the imagination in apprehending with the requisite power the experience sought to be conveyed.

This failure of the imagination is also evident in the group of 'Animal stories,' some of which seem to follow the creed: 'triteness is all.' **"The Blind Dog"** is a rather simplistic presentation of canine affection, which offers no

variation on a commonplace theme. And in **"Attila,"** the story of a dog, the fierce exterior of which conceals an extremely friendly disposition so that when it catches a thief it actually does so in spite of itself the irony does not rise above simple comic incongruity. Stories dealing with animals other than dogs too are in the same class, and the performing monkey in **"Mute Companions"** and the little mouse in **"Flavour of Coconut"** can offer only passing amusement. The squirrel story, **"At the Portal"** makes a half-hearted attempt at allegory which is frustrated because simple situational irony breaks in towards the close. Here we have a mother squirrel teaching her young one to climb up a wall, while the latter has its own fears and anxieties. The faint suggestion that this incident may have a larger significance on the human plane with an implied parallelism is nullified by the author's ironic comment in the end: "Watching him I felt here was an occasion for me to address an appeal to the university authorities to reduce the height of portholes on their compound walls" (*Lawley Road And Other Stories*). The intrusive presence of the author as observer in the story further destroys all chances of an allegorical content. In contrast with this, in Liam O'Flaherty's "His First Flight," the purely objective narration of the first flight of a blackbird takes on a great allegorical significance in human terms while the story, at the same time, remains on the primary level a 'bird story' told with accurate realism.

Another group of stories which also betrays the same disastrous failure of the imagination comprises the more then dozen exercises in the supernatural Narayan has attempted. The ghost stories—**"The Level-Crossing," "An Accident," "Old Bones"** and **"Old Man of the Temple"**—fail to rise above the level of travellers' yarns, and **"The Snake Song,"** the tale of a Sadhu's curse, deserves the same verdict. The limitations of Narayan's imagination and his verbal resources are painfully evident in "Such Perfection" in which a sculptor fashions an all too perfect image of Nataraja, which, true to the belief that such perfection spells danger for this imperfect world, produces a cataclysm. Narayan's description of this is as follows:

> The Moon's disc gradually dimmed. The wind gathered force, clouds blotted out the moon; people looked up and saw only pitch-like darkness above. Lightning flashed, thundered, roared and fire poured down from the sky. It was a thunderbolt striking a haystack and setting it ablaze. . People ran about in panic searching for shelter. The population of ten villages crammed in that village. . Women and children shrieked and wailed. . . . It rained as it had never rained before. The two lakes, over which the village road ran, filled, swelled and joined over the road. . . . 'This is the end of the world!' wailed the people (*An Astrologer's Day and Other Stories*).

This is hardly "the end of the world"—only the end of a rather poor paragraph in which drab, matter-of-fact details are fondly expected to produce an effect which only a powerful imagination could have evoked, employing appropriate linguistic resources. Contrast this with Manjeri Isvaran's description of the same phenomenon in his short story, "Dance of Siva" in which an Englishman sees the great God's Dance Destruction in a dream: "He wakes up to see a gigantic figure towering to the skies with eyes like fiery globes, its matted locks a whirl with the whirling inky clouds. . . . Its forehead burst open in the middle like a smoldering planet, and pillars of flame shot forth and a wilderness of arms with lethal weapons. . . . A dread combustion roared, with the thunder of a billion rockets exploding; and every thing was an endless, immeasurable furnace into which the hounds of hurricane swept and swirled." Isvaran's description too has its own limitations (like its wordiness, for example) but it does stir the reader's imagination in a way which Narayan's tame effort totally fails to do.

Narayan's stories are normally built around either situation or character and occasionally when he discards these props and tries his hand at a different kind of a short story he is immediately seen to be out of his depth. **"Fruition at Forty"** offers little more than the somewhat trite reflections of an office clerk on his fortieth birthday. **"Uncle's Letters"** traces the life of a man from birth to his eightieth birthday by means of the letters written by an uncle to his nephew but the description here too clings obstinately to conventionalities. **"A Night Of The Cyclone"** is also a simple piece of description which is extremely pedestrian.

Narayan's technique of the short story clearly shows him subcribing to the idea of the "well-made short story". Almost all his short stories are compact and neatly structured. The only exceptions are some of the later stories like **"Uncle," "Annamalai"** and **"A Horse and Two Goats,"** which tend to be rather "discursive," as C. V. Venugopal has rightly pointed out. The omniscient author's method of narration is obviously the most suitable one for his well-ordered narratives. The narration is sometimes put into the mouth of the "Talkative Man" in the manner of P. G. Wodehouse's 'Oldest Member' Stories. A variant device is to use the autobiographical 'I' for narration. Most of the stories with a supernatural motif employ either the 'Talkative Man' or the autobiographical "I" as a narration in the hope of ensuring greater credibility for the yearns told, though they fail for other reasons, as already shown. The epistolary form is tried only once, in **"Uncle's Letters."**

In the 'well-made short story' the beginning and the end are of crucial importance and Narayan, like O'Henry, rarely fumbles in handling either. A typical Narayan story may begin in a variety of ways but it almost always carefully establishes what H. E. Bates, referring to O'Henry described as "an instant contact between reader and writer." One method of doing so is to plunge straight into the action as in "Such Perfection": "A Sense of great relief filled Soma as he realized that his five years of labour were coming to an end" (*An Astrologer's Day and Other Stories*). In the case of a story in which the center of interest is the depiction of an unusual character, Narayan introduces the protagonist straightway as in **"Dasi the Bridegroom"**: "His name was Dasi. In all the extension there was none like him," Sometimes an apt generalization relevant to the central situation makes a convenient starting

point as in **"Gateman's Gift"**: "When a dozen persons question openly or slyly a man's sanity he begins to entertain serious doubts himself." The autobiographical narrator may naturally begin by explaining his situation as in **"Uncle"**: "I am the monarch of all I survey, being the sole occupant of this rambling ancient house. . . ." (*A Horse and Two Goats*). Alternatively, he may start the narration at a convenient point, as in **"Chippy"**: 'I cannot give a very clear account of Chipp's Early Life' (*Lawley Road And Other Stories*). The Talkative Man enjoys the same privilege, and sometimes starts his yarn in a manner reminiscent of the folk tale which begins with 'once upon a time'. Thus, **"The Roman Image"** begins with: "The Talkative Man said: 'Once I was an archaeologist's assistant" (*Cyclone and Other Stories*).

Narayan's stories are normally built around either situation or character and . . . when he . . . tries his hand at a different kind of short story he is immediately seen to be out of his depth.

—*M. K. Naik*

The endings of Narayan's short stories show a strong influence of O'Henry's celebrated technique of the trick finale. All the stories in which irony either comic or tragic—plays a shaping role naturally have a suprise ending, as already pointed out. The twist at the end is normally a single one, as in **"An Astrologer's Day," "Missing Mail," "The Doctor's Word," "The Gateman's Gift"** etc., but occasionally as in **"Iswaran"** it is, as noted earlier, a double twist, another example of which is provided by **"A Career"** the story of a trusting shopkeeper swindled by his assistant, who has run away. Year later the shopkeeper meets the man now a blind beggar, sitting in front of a temple. The second twist follows when the shopkeeper in a fit of pity for the man places a rupee on his outstretched palm thus adding a touch of irony to the shock of discovery. In one story, however, in an obvious attempt to trick the reader by not ending the story in an expected manner, Narayan resorts to a rather tame finale. **"The Antidote"** presents Gopal, a film actor, asked to enact a death-scene on his fortieth birthday which, he has been warned by an astrologer, is a crucial day for him, because it might really see him die. The imperatives of the shooting schedule, however, make all his protestations futile. Compelled to enact the death scene, he finds a solution to his problem: "Though he was supposed to be dead, he shook his head slightly, opened his right eye and winked at the camera, which he hoped would act as an antidote to the inauspicious role he was doing" (*Lawley Road and Other Stories*). One wonders whether a further twist resulting in Gopal's actual death, in spite of the "antidote" would not have given the story a sharper point.

Where irony is absent, the stories peter out into equally tame endings. In **"Wife's Holiday,"** Kanan, the gambler, seized the opportunity offered by his wife and child's temporary absence, to smash the little money box in the house and remove all the coins. As he returns home having lost the money, he meets his family coming back, and is now afraid of facing the consequences. The total lack of irony in the ending which rests upon a simplistic cause and effect relationship makes the story almost pointless. Equally pedestrian is **"The Performing Child."** Kutti, the talented little girl here is to act in a film, though she hates the idea. On the day the film people come for her, she hides herself in a linen basket and the parents abandon the project. What precisely is the point of the story is difficult to say, since no attempt has also been made to probe into the mind of Kutti which at least could have given the story an artistic centre.

The setting for most of Narayan's stories is Malgudi, but it is interesting to note that unlike his novels, some stories are enacted entirely against a background other than that of Malgudi. Madras provides the backdrop for five stories—**"All Avoidable Talk," "Fruition At Forty," "A Willing Slave," "Sweets for Angels"** and **"Man-hunt"**. In **"Chippy," "The Regal," "Dodu"** and **"Mother and Son,"** the setting is Mysore, while the action in **"A Night of Cyclone"** takes place against the background of Vizagapatnam.

The thematic connections between the short stories and the novels of Narayan are interesting. Some of these have been noted by P. S. Sundaram. Situations, characters and motifs from each novel by Narayan except *The Painter of Signs* appear in the short stories also, though in some cases the stories belong to an earlier date. As already noted, the exploits of the school-boy hero in *Swami and Friends* have spilled into **"Father's Help"** and **"The Hero,"** and twelve year old Dodu in *The Regal* with his passionate devotion to cricket is only another incarnation of Swami. The failure of marriage negotiations owing to the incompatibility of horoscopes in *The Bachelor of Arts* is a motif repeated in **"The White Flower."** Savitri's attempt to drown herself into the river, her rescue by Mari and her final reluctance to repay her debt to him in *The Dark Room* are parallelled in **"The Watchman."** And *The Dark Room* situation of a husband throwing his wife out of the house also appears in **"The Shelter."** Krishna, in **"Seventh House"** finds his wife dying of typhoid like Krishnan in *The English Teacher,* though the remedy suggested by the astrologer in the short story naturally has no place in the novel. ('The White Flower' motif reappears in this story also.) In *Mr. Sampath* Srinivas, goes to see the British Manager of the Engladia Banking Corporation. Govind Singh in **"The Gateman's Gift"** has spent twenty-five years in the service of **"Engladia's."** (Ramani in *The Dark Room* is local Branch Manager of the Engladia Insurance Company). The relationship between the private tutor and his truant charge in **"Crime and Punishment"** was later to be echoed in the dealings of young Balu with his tutor in *The Financial Expert*. Most of the women who attend Gandhi's meeting in *Waiting For The Mahatma* are without ornaments, knowing Gandhi's aversion to all show and luxury. Padma in **"Gandhi's Appeal"** also goes to hear Gandhi, without her jewels on, the reason however being

the fear that he may ask her to donate them to his fund. (The meeting in the novel takes place on the bank of the Sarayu, but that in the short story is held on the beach). In **"Four Rupees,"** Ranga finds the role of the 'well-man' thrust upon him, and is compelled to undergo the ordeal of descending into a well sixty feet deep, to recover a brass pot from it, though he has no experience of the job. He comes through the ordeal, unscathed, unlike poor Raju in *The Guide* whom compulsion drives to martyrdom. Rangi the temple dancer, who plays so crucial a role in *The Man Eater of Malgudi* is still plying her trade eight years later in **"The Seventh House,"** though the timidity of the hero prevents, her from delivering the goods. Finally, **"Such Perfection,"** only spells out in full Chinna Dorai, "Story of the dancing figure of Nataraj, which was so perfect that it began a cosmic dance and the town itself shook as if an earthquake had rocked it, until a small finger on the figure was chipped off" in *The Vendor of Sweets*.

While Narayan has practically written no story which can be called dull, one might well ask at the same time whether he has written any which can truly be called a major achievement to rank with Maupassant's "Ball of Fat," Chekhov's "The School Mistress," Maugham's "Rain," Hemingway's "The Short Happy Life of Francis Macomber" or Katherine Mansfield's "The Garden Party"—to mention only a few memorable examples. Even the most striking of Narayan's efforts like **"The Doctors Word,"** **"Engine Trouble"** and **"Seventh House"** do not appear to deserve to be ranked with these universally acknowledged masterpieces. To compare Narayan, the short story writer, with his Indo-English peers is also to realize that he has produced nothing in this genre to match Mulk Raj Anand's "Birth" and "The Lost Child" or Raja Rao's "Javni" and "The Policeman and the Rose."

One explanation for this may be found in the fact that Narayan began his career as a a short story writer by contributing stories to *The Hindu* and it was difficult for him, under these conditions, to escape the influence of the slick 'magazine story' which has manifestly the limited purpose of providing the average reader with his dose of an hour's amusement alone. The well-made story technique encouraged him to be mostly satisfied with surface irony and snap ending, while depth and complexity of experience and subtlety of response were clearly elements not quite necessary. In the 'narrow plot of ground' of the short story Narayan's talent did not develop much, although, given the longer freedom of full-length fiction, his irony did mature in strength and purpose.

This perhaps accounts for the extremely limited thematic range of his short stories though, paradoxically enough, they evince a great variety of characters, drawn from all the strata of society except the highest. In these short stories we meet clerks, doctors, archaeologists, tutors, school and college students, housewives, shopkeepers, film actors, artists, sculptors, journalists, astrologers, postmen, ayahs, house-servants, gardeners, tree-climbers, food-vendors, coolies, beggars, vagabonds, pick-pockets and rustics apart from dogs, squirrels and parrots. This variety is, however, hardly matched by a corresponding thematic richness, because though all these characters are present-ed realistically, their dilemmas, as their creator sees them, are hardly meaningful enough in thematic terms and the author is mostly satisfied with the ironic twist these petty dilemmas provide. This makes for a general lack of social, political and even existential awareness and urgent emo-tional involvement in these short stories. The satire on the ways of the Municipality in **"Lawley Road"** and **"Engine Trouble,"** and that on blackmarketing in **"Half a Rupees worth"** is slight and in **"Gandhi's Appeal,"** Gandhism is only a prop to support the situational irony of the trick ending. Even when he deals directly with a communal riot in **"Another Community,"** Narayan's tones remain so neutral that only the irony of the misunderstanding result-ing in the death of the protagonist in a clash which soon develops a communal colouring is highlighted at the ex-pense of the potentiai tragic effect.

Narayan's short stories therefore appear to be, by and large, a museum of minor motifs. They lack the kind of thematic weight and the richness of experience which the major short stories of the world invariably possess. The shorter fiction of Narayan generally reveals the artist as Autolycus—"A snapper up of unconsidered trifles," and not as Jacob, wrestling with the angel. In the major novels, Narayan rises to his fullest stature as a master of existen-tial irony; in the short stories he mostly remains a small time ironist.

Robert Towers (review date 1982)

SOURCE: "The Old Country," in *The New York Review of Books,* Vol. XXIX, No. 5, April 1, 1982, pp. 21-2.

[*In the following review of* Malgudi Days, *Towers asserts that Narayan's writing style is as traditional and un-changed as the culture of rural India, and examines several passages that support that belief.*]

While changes on the macrocosmic scale in India have been tumultuous since R. K. Narayan's first novel, *Swami and Friends,* appeared in 1935, the imaginary South Indian town of Malgudi—the microcosm of his fiction—has un-dergone little transformation. To be sure, it is more crowd-ed. The population continues to increase at an alarming rate, and advocates of birth control and vasectomy have appeared on the scene, their presence an affront to the old Hindu notions of fertility, sex, and decency. The British have gone; Coronation Park (just *whose* coronation is no longer remembered) has become Hamara Hindustan Park and the statue of the Victorian military governor, Sir Fre-derick Lawley, has been pulled down from its pedestal (only to be re-erected elsewhere). Hippies sometimes join the mendicants on the temple steps. But cobblers and knife-grinders and the vendors of sweets still go about their business much as their grandfathers had. Marriages are still arranged, horoscopes consulted. Though there are more cars, the cries of the tradesmen, the dust, and the

pungent smells of the place are those that struck the senses of the boy Swami fifty years ago.

> **The new stories in *Malgudi Days* confirm the impression that Narayan's mild and delicate craft has changed over the decades almost as little as Malgudi itself.**
>
> **—*Robert Towers***

Once (in *Waiting for the Mahatma*) Gandhi himself paid a visit to Malgudi, with momentous results for the novel's protagonist and his aged Granny, but then the Mahatma returned to the national stage and final apotheosis. For the most part, the shocks of the new India, though duly registered, are so muffled and attenuated by the time they reach Malgudi that they are easily assimilated into the world of slowed time and become the source of much of Narayan's comedy. The new stories in *Malgudi Days* confirm the impression that Narayan's mild and delicate craft has changed over the decades almost as little as Malgudi itself. Early in his career he found—and quickly perfected—a narrative mode that has remained untouched by all that we think of as modernism. Nowhere in his fiction do we encounter the dissonance, the structural disjunctions, the obscurity, or multilevel wordplay—in-deed any of the radical techniques—by which the great writers of this century have jolted the reader from his sense of literary security.

Narayan's mode is that of a shrewd and ironic teller-of-tales whose aim is to beguile his listeners, to share with them his appreciation—sympathetic though slightly with-drawn—of the oddities of human (and animal) behavior. Here is the beginning of **"Cat Within"**:

> A passage led to the back yard, where a well and a lavatory under a large tamarind tree served the needs of the motley tenants of the ancient house in Vinayak Mudali Street; the owner of the property . . . had managed to create an illusion of shelter and privacy for his hapless tenants and squeezed the maximum rent out of everyone, himself occupying a narrow ledge abutting the street, where he had a shop selling, among other things, sweets, pencils and ribbons to children swarming from the municipal school across the street. When he locked up for the night, he slept across the doorway so that no intruder should pass without first stumbling on him; he also piled up cunningly four empty kerosene tins inside the dark shop so that at the slightest contact they should topple down with a clatter: for him a satisfactory burglar alarm.
>
> Once at midnight a cat stalking a mouse amidst the grain bags in the shop noticed a brass jug in its way and thrust its head in out of curiosity. The mouth of the jug was not narrow enough to choke the cat or wide enough to allow it to withdraw its head. . . . It began to jump and run around, hitting its head with a

clang on every wall. The shopkeeper, who had been asleep at his usual place, was awakened by the noise in the shop. He peered through a chink into the dark interior. . . .

An evil spirit is clearly at work. An exorcist is summoned, and the fabliau-like story proceeds through several vicissitudes to its entirely satisfactory conclusion.

Storytellers appear with some frequency in Narayan's fiction: sometimes as the figure known as the Talkative Man, sometimes (as in *The Painter of Signs*) in the person of a temple *pandit* who recites to an audience of old women the fantastic tales culled from the *Ramayana,* the *Mahabharata,* and the cycle of the Lord Krishna; Narayan himself has engagingly retold episodes from this vast body of legend in **Gods, Demons, and Others**. In his own fiction, however, Narayan largely avoids the supernatural and the fantastic while retaining the classical right to *tell* rather than merely show, to manipulate rather than merely render, to propel an action and to assert an ending.

This display of a firm narrative hand works in conjunction with a perfected simplicity of style, a limpid English prose that is adequately sensuous without ever becoming lush, a prose of the sort that Graham Greene and the early Waugh achieved for their very different purposes. This combination is admirably suited to Narayan's evocation of a way of life—a way of perceiving human relations and human destinies—that has more in common with Chaucer's world than that of Jane Austen or Proust or Saul Bellow. The inhabitants of Malgudi still partake of what might be called the "old consciousness," in which men and women define themselves (and are perceived by others) more in terms of their occupations, their roles, or stations in society than as the embodiments of individualized psyches. The major transactions of life are public, externalized; what happens in the marketplace is deemed more significant than the private exchanges of the bedroom. (In any case, there is little privacy in a Malgudi home and often no bedroom—people sleep in odd corners, on porches, on mats that can be rolled up and carried away.)

In New York the same person might be sequentially (or even simultaneously) a teacher and editor, a lawyer and writer, a PhD and a cabdriver; in Malgudi the occupations are fixed (sometimes hereditarily, by caste), and each occupation is likely to be associated with a particular personality. A painter of signs is perceived as being in some way different from a vendor of sweets, though their economic status may be exactly the same; both are identified with their trade—find their identities in it—as no television repairman in Milwaukee or Liverpool is identified with his. Poverty is more likely to be regarded as a fate than as an economic condition. Indeed, the notion of karma or destiny pervades much of the Malgudi response to the accidentals of life.

Of course, given the chasm between Hinduism and the Judeo-Christian outlook, comparisons with the pre-Reformation West are of limited, even dubious validity.

But one of the charms of Narayan's fiction for a contemporary Western reader is precisely this evocation of an older consciousness—now mostly lost to us but still recognizable, in some sense still remembered—that offers a degree of relief from the burdens of personal choice and relentless self-assessment. In Malgudi specified activities and duties are rigidly assigned.

"No one in the house knew her name," begins the remarkable story called **"A Willing Slave"**; "no one for a moment thought that she had any other than Ayah [nurse]. None of the children ever knew when she had first come into the family. . . ." The Ayah's existence is so woven into the fabric of the family she serves that she can be separated from it only by a summons to an even more sanctified set of duties—in this case to a wizened old husband who unexpectedly reappears after many years of absence as a worker in the tea gardens of Ceylon. She must return to her village to cook for him and look after him.

With great subtlety Narayan plays off one traditional role against another, leaving the Ayah's inner feelings in a mysterious realm of their own—perhaps no more consciously accessible to the old woman than to ourselves. We see her avert her face and shake with laughter when her mistress asks her if she wants to go. And we also see her waiting outside the kitchen door to take leave of the child Radha whom she has nursed and played with—waiting in vain, for the child has identified the old husband with the mythic "Old Fellow" shut up in the dog house, whom the Ayah had often invoked to frighten the children into obedience.

> When the Ayah stood outside the kitchen door and begged her to come out, Radha asked, "Is the Old Fellow carrying you off?"
>
> "Yes, dear. Bad fellow."
>
> "Who left the door of the dog house open?"
>
> "No one. He broke it open."
>
> "What does he want?"
>
> "He wants to carry me off," said the Ayah.
>
> "I won't come out till he is gone. All right. Go, go before he comes here for you." The Ayah acted on this advice after waiting at the kitchen door for nearly half an hour.

In Malgudi the old ways are often tested but seldom ruptured by the more personal expectations of a new era. A number of the stories (and the novels too) deal with a single young man tended by a widowed female relative who is at once the sustainer and burden of his life. More often than not, the mother or grandmother or aunt is plotting an arranged marriage for the good-for-nothing young man, who has imbibed other, more Western ideas. Though the sons are likely to be sexually shy and inexperienced, they dream of movie stars and are repelled by the idea of marriage to a fourteen-year-old girl with a protruding tooth (as in **"Mother and Son"**).

In **"Second Opinion"** the feckless son Sambu, who fancies himself an intellectual and reads the weighty volumes of the *Library of World Thought,* is subjected to extreme pressure. He has just been informed by his mother that he was betrothed in childhood to a girl only a few hours old at the time.

> "It's idiotic," I cried. "How can you involve me in this manner? What was my age then?". . .

> "Old enough, about five or six, what does it matter?"

> "Betrothed? How? By what process?"

> "Don't question like that. You are not a lawyer in a court," she said. . . .

> I remained silent for a while and pleaded, "Mother, listen to me. How can any marriage take place in this fashion? How can two living entities possessing intelligence and judgment ever be tied together for a lifetime?"

> "How else? . . . No one marries anew every month."

> I felt desperate and cried, "Idiotic! Don't be absurd, try to understand what I am saying. . . ."

> She began to wail loudly at this. "Second time you are hurling an insulting word. Was it for this I have survived your father? How I wish I had mounted the funeral pyre as our ancients decreed for a widow; they knew what a widow would have to face in life, to stand abusive language from her own offspring." She beat her forehead with such violence that I feared she might crack her skull.

"What a civilization," says the cornered and exasperated son to himself. *A Wounded Civilization,* he adds, revealing that he has read V.S. Naipaul's despairing book on India. But at the end he agrees at least to go to the bus station to meet the girl's father, who is arriving from the ancestral village to complete arrangements for the marriage.

As a narrator, Narayan remains detached, refusing to take sides in the tension between the old ways and the new and conveying his sly enjoyment of the absurdities that arise. In **"The Edge,"** an elderly knife-grinder, who has fathered seven children (six dead), narrowly escapes vasectomy when he is lured into a government-sponsored birth control unit by a promise of thirty rupees. In **"God and the Cobbler,"** a poor, hard-working cobbler fixes the sandal strap of a hippie whose face has been tanned by the sun and whose dusty clothes ("a knee-length cotton dhoti and vest") have "acquired a spontaneous ochre tint worthy of a *sanyasi*." Glancing up, the cobbler reflects,

> "With those matted locks falling on his nape, looks like God Shiva, only the cobra coiling around his neck missing." In order to be on the safe side of one who looked so holy, he made a deep obeisance.

Meanwhile, the hippie, who romanticizes the poor in India, feels an admiration for the cobbler:

> "He asks for nothing, but everything is available to him." The hippie wished he could be composed and self-contained like the cobbler.

Narayan pays a certain price for the mildness of his fictional demeanor. I find that, because of their relatively low intensity, his stories and novels tend in retrospect to blur, to lose definition. While a strong sensory impression of Malgudi remains, the characters and situations of the individual works sink back into their collective existence—perhaps a very Hindu effect. In the near view, however, each piece has a distinct shapeliness and coloration of its own. Though some are slight, hardly more than bright flutterings quickly caught and fixed upon the page, a high proportion of the new stories are expertly wrought, full of interest and charm. Like other good Indian writers, Narayan has had to fight against an apparently ingrained reluctance of Americans to include India (as distinct from Anglo-India) within the geography of their literary imagination; *Malgudi Days* should advance his cause.

R. K. Jeurkar (essay date 1985)

SOURCE: "Narrative Techniques in R. K. Narayan's Short Stories," in *Indian Readings in Commonwealth Literature,* edited by G. S. Amur et al., Sterling Publishers Private Limited, 1985, pp. 106-16.

[*In this essay, Jeurkar explores the three narrator-types found in Narayan's fiction: the "Talkative Man," the third-person narrator, and the omniscient narrator.*]

Among the Indo-English fiction writers Narayan is the most prolific, having published twelve novels and seven volumes of short stories besides a travelogue, *A Dateless Diary,* and an autobiography, *My Days.* His fame, the critics contend, rests almost entirely on his achievement as a novelist. However, "it is one of the ironies of literary history that while so much is made of Narayan's novels, the short stories which have the unmistakable stamp of the artist in him should be relatively neglected." The estimates of Narayan would be one-sided since "Narayan's short stories are artistically as distinguished as his novels, and in any general estimate of his writings they cannot be ignored. In fact, one might go so far as to say that Narayan is essentially a story-teller and the one element that stands out even in his novels is the story element."

P. D. Westbrook [*The Short Stories of R. K. Narayan, the Journal of Commonwealth Literature,* July 5, 1968] states that "any reader of Narayan is aware that his stories are cut from very much the same cloth, in quality and pattern, as his novels." Narayan is "a story teller nothing less and seldom more", says Uma Parmeshwaran. Some of his stories are novels in a nutshell. For example, **"The White Flower"** and **"The Seventh House"** remind us of the theme of his *The English Teacher*, **"Dodu"** and **"Father's Help"** give glimpses of his *Swami and Friends*.

Narayan employs three kinds of narrators, namely the first person narrator who is the Talkative Man of Malgudi, the third person narrator and the omniscient narrator.

The Talkative Man is, Narayan tells us,

> . . . a part and parcel of the Indian village community, which is somewhat isolated from the mainstream of life. . . . He is the source of enhancement in the village, a grand old man who seldom stirs from his ancestral home on the edge of the village . . . except on some very special occasion calling for his priestly services in a village home. When people want a story, at the end of their day's labours in the field, especially on evenings when the moon shines through the cocount palms . . . on such occasions the story teller will dress himself for the part by smearing sacred ash on his forehead and wrapping himself in a green shawl. . . . When the story teller enters to seat himself in front of the lamps, he looks imperious and in complete control of the situation. . . . He can never really be handicapped, through the lack of an understudy of assistants, as he is completely self-reliant knowing as he does by heart all the twenty-four thousand stanzas of The Ramayana, 100,000 stanzas of The Mahabharata, and the 18,000 stanzas of The Bhagwata. . . . Every detail of his life is set for him by what the shastras say: that is the reason why he finds it impossible to live in a modern town.

Narayan once expressed his desire to become a Bhagvatar himself. The talkative man resembles the modern prototype of the Bodhisatva of *Jataka Tales*.

The method of the Talkative Man is a dramatised mode of narration; an effective way of achieving objectivity which provides the writer with special advantages like commenting upon the characters and sometimes laughing at their follies with superb detachment. It is a mode of depersonalization for achieving that sophistication of objectivity which demands detachment, the key word we find in Narayan's fiction. He presents the things as they happened or are happening without any recourse to theorising or taking sides. It is left to the good sense of the reader to perceive irony which is the essential tool Narayan employs throughout his fictional narrative. The ironic vision which rests upon the duality of objects grants him detachment. The narrator takes us directly to the heart of the dramatic action of the story without any editorials. Narayan presents situations in such a convincing manner that the characters emerge naturally. His emphasis is always on characterization. Narayan mentions this fact to Wolsely in a letter: "All my novels have been written in this manner. All I can settle for myself is my protagonist's general type of personality—my focus is all on character. If his personality comes alive, the rest is easy for me;

background, and minor characters develop as I progress." The same principle is applicable to his short stories wherein his emphasis is always on characterization. The 'I' of the narrator should not be taken for the autobiographical 'I' of the author, though **"A Breach of Promise,"** his very first story, which has an autobiographical element, is narrated by the omniscient narrator. About the story **"A Breach of Promise,"** Narayan told Mehta in an interview, "it is very truthful—autobiographical, you know. It concerns a student, myself, who fails a lot of examinations." The first person narrator or precisely for that matter the garrulous raconteur of Malgudi who associates himself with the incidents in which he participated, gives him the authority of a reliable narrator with intense emotional attachment. The aesthetic distance is properly maintained since he is at the helm of affairs. He does not talk about himself more than what is absolutely necessary. His focus is always on an incident and the study of the character's response to it. the character's intuitive reactions enable us to understand the character. The narrator is always in the middle of the action and does not allow one's attention to be diverted. His convincing narration gives no scope to the reader to doubt the veracity of his narration as he is giving his own responses and the reader has to believe it.

The talkative man of **"The Roman Image"** informs us that he got himself appointed an archaeologist's assistant. The archaeologist

> was a famous person called doctor something or other. He was a superb, timeless being, who lived a thousand years behind the times, and he wanted neither food nor roof nor riches if only he was allowed to gaze on undisturbed at an old coin or chip of a burial urn.

The talkative man narrates the story and like most of the Narayan's first person narrators he is more of a method and less of a character. He is the medium through which our interest in the story is aroused. As a good raconteur, he is always witty enough to compel our attention. His situation in this respect is analogous to that of a public speaker who is always well advised in making his seriousness palatable through a proper seasoning of wit.

Most of Narayan's narrators are guides, reminiscent of *The Guide,* who are themselves misguided. They are either helpers like the present one employed by the archaeologist to assist him in his "digging work" and was in a month able to lead him by the hand, or spiritual guides like the astrologer in **"An Astrologer's Day."** During their search, they were camping at Siral—a village sixty miles away from the town, the Sarayu river winds its way along the northern boundary of the village. One day, after a good day's work, while assisting the doctor to clean up and study a piece of stained glass picked up in a field outside the village, he constantly shook his head and said:

> This is easily the most important piece of work which has come under my notice. This bit of glass you see is not an ordinary archaeological stuff, but a very

important link. This piece of glass is really Florentian, which went out of vogue in A.D.5. How did this come here . . . If the identity of this is established properly we may ultimately have a great deal to say about the early Roman Empire and this part of India.

With these thoughts in his mind he dived deep into the water and suddenly his hand struck against a hard object in the sandy bed. He came to the surface with the object, a stone image. Without drying himself he handed over the image to the doctor whose reactions were: "this takes us to an entirely new set of possibilities." The archaeologist keenly examines it: "This was a Roman statue. How it came to be found in these parts is an historical fact we have to wrest from evidence. It is going to give an entirely new turn to Indian history." On the basis of their recent findings, it was decided to publish a monumental work covering over a thousand pages of demy size, full of photographs and sketches. The assistant pores over books for months in libraries, burns the midnight oil, and is about to give finishing touches to what might become a monumental contribution to the country's history. All the while, the whole country was impatiently waiting for its publication. It was then that the assistant, in need of some vital information, visits the spot where they had unearthed the image, and in a casual conversation with a man of the locality, learns that the image had nothing Roman about it. It was just an ordinary *Dwarpalaka* of a Mari temple situated nearby. As for its antiquity, he was the very man who had commissioned it for the temple. The shocking news was delivered to the doctor who asked him: "drown it. After all you picked it up from the water—that piece of nonsense." He also requests him to "throw all that rubbish into the fire before we are declared mad." The archaeologist's dream, "to have a monopoly of the earliest known civilization and place it where he chose," was shattered.

The sudden denouement has indeed all the ingredients of a conclusive impact not only on the work of the archaeologist, but on the story itself and reminds us of O. Henry's technique of surprise at the end. O. Henry achieved this effect by employing an omniscient narrator who reserves some vital information and releases it at the end of the narrative, thereby producing a surprise. Narayan has achieved this effect by employing the first person narrator. Godknoff approves of this when he says:

> . . . there remains to be one of the most fascinating aspects of the subject—that first person narration may be used to produce directly opposing results. The narrator may, through his direct appeal to our attention, grab us by the sleeve, so to speak and haul us immediately into the narrative situation. The narrator forces us to evaluate the situation through him and succeeds in presenting us the desired effect.

The story is a satire on the research which is futile, a waste of time, money and energy. The narrator creates an atmosphere of curiosity with an ascending degree of emotional attachment to the events. Narayan could have achieved unity of effect by avoiding the description spread over two and a half pages on the responsibility of telling the reader how the temple image came to be associated with the river-bed. The narration is deceptively simple since it is ironic in tone. Narayan always speaks with his tongue in his cheek, intending not to criticise but to show things as they are, achieving thereby brilliant effects.

Narayan's employment of the third person narrrator gives him an advantage of both the first person narrator and the omniscient narrator. When the feelings of the characters are presented directly to the reader without the commentary of the narartor, we get the feel of the first person narrator. His position for the time being becomes that of the witness recording the experiences of the character.

The third person narration is also called limited omniscience in the sense that the focus is on the protagonist. Sometimes the author intrudes on the narration but only a perceptive reader will notice the intrusion. The intrusion checks the imaginary flights of the narrator and brings him down to the level of reality so that an illusion of reality can perfectly be maintained. It helps the reader to understand the clues. The intrusion also serves another purpose so dear to the reader, it reveals the character of the protagonist.

Narayan's employment of the third person narrator gives him an advantage of both the first person narrator and the omniscient narrator.

—R. K. Jeurkar

The story **"An Astrologer's Day"** opens with brief editorial remarks of the author which serve as the background for the enactment of the future drama. The story is filtered through the mediation of the third person narrator. The focus is on the protagonist, an astrologer, who transacted his business by the

> light of a flare which crackled and smoked up above the groundnut heap nearby . . . one or two had hissing gas lights, some had naked flares stuck on the poles, some were lit up by old cycle lamps, and one or two, like the astrologer's, managed without lights of their own

The astrologer "had not in the least intended to be an astrologer when he began life." It was a life forced upon him, for once in the village when he was a silly youngster he left a person for dead in a well and fled for life to the city. One day as he was to move after the day's business, a stranger comes to him and requests him to foretell whether he would get at the person, who tried to kill him to take revenge. The astrologer refused as it was getting late and was in a hurry to go home. When his credibility was challenged by the stranger he (astrologer) asked for more money which was agreed upon subsequently. "The astrologer sent up a prayer to the heaven, the other lit a cheroot. The astrologer caught the glimpse of his face by the match light." The astrologer felt very uncomfortable and tried desperately to free himself. After a good deal of haggling the astrologer took courage and said:

"You were left for dead, Am I right?"

"Ah, tell me more."

"A knife had passed through you once," said the astrologer.

"Good fellow." He bared his chest to show the scar.

"What else?"

"And then you were pushed into a well nearby in the field. You were left for dead."

"I should have been dead if some passerby had not chanced to peep into the well," exclaimed the other overwhelmed by enthusiasm. "When shall I get at him?" he asked, clenching his first.

"In the next world," answered the astrologer. "He died four months ago in a far-off town. You will never see any more of him." The other groaned on hearing it.

The story ends with a brief conversation between the astrologer and his wife. The astrologer after dinner, sitting on the pyol, told her:

"Do you know a great load is gone from me today? I thought I had the blood of a man on my hands all these years. That was the reason why I ran away from home, settled here, and married you. He is alive."

She gasped, "You tried to kill?"

"Yes in our village, when I was a silly youngster. We drank, gambled, and quarrelled badly one day—why think of it now? Time to sleep," he said.

P. D. Westbrook (1968) criticises the story for its element of unconvincing coincidence. He does not seem to have properly understood the importance of coincidence in a story. As Brooks and Warren argue:

Coincidences do occur in real life, sometimes quite startling ones, and in one sense every story is based on a coincidence namely, that the particular events happen to occur together, that such and such characters happen to meet, for example. But since fiction is concerned with a logic of character and action, coincidence in so far as it is purely illogical, has little place. Truth can afford to be stranger than fiction, because truth is "true"—is acceptable on its own merits—but the happenings of fiction must justify themselves in terms of logical connection with other elements in fiction and in terms of meaningfulness.

It is quite logical that the stranger, a gullible rustic in search of his assailant to take revenge may call upon an astrologer and request him to foretell if he would be successful in his mission or not. Even educated people in India approach astrologers to know their future. The use of coincidence gives substance to the story.

The story can be read as a metaphor. The astrologer was a rogue and "knew no more of what was going to happen to others than he knew what was going to happen to himself next minute." Moreover, he was forced to take up this job which needed "a working analysis of mankind's troubles: marriage, money, and the tangles of human ties, long practice had sharpened his perception." He took to astrology to hide his identity with whiskers which streamed down his cheeks, and the saffron coloured turban he wound around his head prevented him from being recognised by others. The author has succeeded in achieving the aim of objectivity by incorporating the crisp conversation between the astrologer and the stranger, and the man and his wife.

"Our friend felt piqued." The remark is addressed to a hypothetical spectator, a device whereby Narayan is able to maintain the indirection or objectivity. This is a guise under which the omniscient narrator speaks, a substitute for the intuitions and the speculative commentary of the first person narrator. The story is praised for its dialogue between the astrologer and the stranger in the beginning, and the astrologer and his wife at the end. The dialogue reveals the character and motivation of the protagonist and furthers the dramatic action of the story.

The telling of a story by the author himself is as old as the genre of the story itself. Most of Narayan's stories are narrated by the omniscient narrator. This device helps him in establishing direct rapport between the teller and the reader, while it also offers him the God's eye-view from where he can narrate the story, sketch the characters and details of incidents, probe the psyche of the characters while giving his own commentary. This is the oldest technique a fiction writer has the use of. The sophisticated techniques of which we talk earnestly are a recent phenomenon.

In Narayan's stories the emphasis is on omniscience rather than on omnipresence in correspondence to the oral narration of the folktales. The narrator is out of the narrative world, at the peripheral level and would always be roving from one point to another giving details of his narration.

The story, **"A Breach of Promise,"** describes how the dizzy joy of a young boy who passes Lower Secondary Examination turns into fear as he appears before the Goddess Chamundi and is reminded of his precious promise of ending life if he failed. Thinking that he has committed a great sacrilege by not keeping the promise, he decides to end his life. On a second thought, as he has passed his examination, he brushes aside such a rash decision and substitutes it by promising the goddess an offering of a coconut thrice a week which was more convenient. The story is told by the omniscient narrator with the main focus on Sanker who was "a candidate, 3,131 in Lower Secondary Examination." The way in which the excitement of Sankar and his friends is described is realistic. It is quite natural that these students climb the Chamundi Hills with their offerings to the goddess with whose blessings they pass the examinations and pray for future: "Mother, we have passed our examination through your grace. Bless with success all the examinations hereafter." It is the innocent world of a child having deep psychological basis. Narayan has gone through the agony himself and has brilliantly communicated it to us.

In Narayan's stories the emphasis is on omniscience rather than on omnipresence in correspondence to the oral narration of the folktales.

—*R. K. Jeurkar*

Narayan has employed the device of foreshadowing which serves as a clue to the reader's understanding, if he is alert. Sankar would have remembered the vow he had taken "if two of his best friends had not failed with him, if he had not gone away, after the results, to his sister's place for a month or two and spent a most exhilarating holiday there, and if he had not passed this year," These thoughts show how man tries to find out pretexts to evade the pledge he has taken. That sounds quite realistic. The author is filtering for us the intutive response and feelings of the characters of life without editorials. He is not diverting his omniscience to dictate the thoughts and feelings of his characters. The narrative also has the advantages of the first person narration which gives authenticity of information and reliability of reportage.

In conclusion it can be said that Narayan is a very conventional story-teller and uses traditional methods of narration. There is no attempt to exploit sophisticated techniques such as the stream of consciousness, interior monologue or the retrospective flashback. The characters do not suffer modern maladies as psychic imbalance or schizophrenia. They are ordinary, of the earth and earthly. Hence, as Brunton has pointed out, Narayan seems "lacking in the national self-consciousness of Raja Rao or the social radicalism of Mulk Raj Anand. His work is unpretentious, untheoretical, fluently professional."

This apparent lack of technical sophistication has led many critics to accuse him of incapacity to probe the deeper issues of life. He skims over the surface of life and leaves the profound questions of life—death, fate, freedom, self—alone. The contradictions of life emerging from man's relation to God, to society and the self do not seem to enlist his creative attention.

Narayan does not seem to have felt the impact of the great social, political and economic changes of our century. All these factors should normally make a writer severely limited in his appeal. On the contrary, we find that Narayan's short stories as well as novels are immensely popular. This is because his strength comes from the very integrity which makes him accept his limitations. He himself has pointed out that he cannot write about life and character with which he is not thoroughly familiar:

> "I must be absolutely certain," he said, "about the psychology of the character I am writing about, and I must be equally sure of the background, I know the Tamil and Kannada speaking people best. I know their brckground. I know how their minds work and almost as if it is happening to me, I know exactly what will happen to them in certain situations and under certain circumstances. And I know how they will react. I do not feel I have this kind of knowledge about Americans and America in spite of the time I have spent in that country. And anyway there is so much to write about right in India. There is so much diversity and individuality that almost any one I meet provides me with material for a story or a novel."

Narayan's stories must be read, therefore, in the context of his felt experience and the sense of life which emerges from this. One quality which emerges from this is detachment, detachment which leads to sympathy divorced from condescension. Even when the stories deal with complex problems of life, they refuse to take sides. They are not loaded with any aggressive notions of social reform or muted nostalgia about a vanished, allegedly glorious past. This is because Narayan has the capacity to contain the usual annoyance at the complexity of human life—the duplicity and deception—through the comic sense. This comic sense, as William Walsh (1972) has noted, is rooted in the "inclusive nature" of the Indian tradition itself.

Alfred Kazin (review date 1985)

SOURCE: A review of *Under the Banyan Tree,* in the *New York Times Book Review,* July 21, 1985, pp. 1,19.

[*Kazin's review of* Under the Banyan Tree *focuses on the seemingly limitless wealth of material available to Narayan in course of everyday life.*]

Rasipuram Krishnaswami Narayan is on the threshold of 80 still India's most notable novelist and short-story writer in English. Quite apart from the beautiful traditionalism of his middle name, there is good reason to note his full Indian name. Mr. Narayan is an elegant, deceptively simple stylist who cleverly reports—or translates—the speech of his Indian characters into inflated schoolroom English. "How can we blame the rains when people are so evil-minded?" "A good action in a far-off place did not find an echo, but an evil one did possess that power." Yet everything he describes is intensely local, reflecting his long residence in Mysore and the intricacy of continuing and conflicting traditions throughout modern India.

Mr. Narayan's strength is that his material seems inexhaustible. He clearly feels he has only to look out his window, take a walk, hire a servant, to pick up story after story. The American reader may not know exactly where all this is taking place, but the world is so intensely visualized and comprehended—without any particular judgment made on so many daily uproars and disasters—that he finds himself surrounded by brilliant pinpoints of life in the vast, steamy, unknowable land mass that is the foreigner's India.

Storytelling becomes inevitable in such a world, and storytellers themselves become characters. In the most arresting piece of the collection, **"Annamalai,"** Mr. Narayan returns to his favorite subject, the uneasiness of educated English-speaking Indians in relating to their "inferiors." Mr. Narayan shows himself overwhelmed by the servant whose character he has been trying to decipher for 15 years. In the title story, the last in the collection of 28, the great spreading banyan tree is the ritual setting for an illiterate but highly professional village storyteller who always takes 10 days to narrate a tale to the villagers. Perhaps reflecting Mr. Narayan's awareness of age, this storyteller suddenly finds himself unable to carry on and makes a public profession of weakness that is of course another story, his last.

Mr. Narayan is an almost placid, good-natured storyteller whose work derives its charm from the immense calm out of which he writes. It has all happened before, it happens every hour, it will happen again tomorrow. But there are levels of irony, subtle inflections and modulations in his easy, transparent style, meant to show the despair—usually economic panic—driving his characters. In **"A Horse and Two Goats,"** Muni, an old peasant who has lost everything but his goats, tethers them to the trunk of a "drumstick tree that grew in front of his hut and from which occasionally Muni could shake down drumsticks. This morning he got six. He carried them in with a sense of triumph. Although no one could say precisely who owned the tree, it was his because he lived in its shadow."

Muni and his wife are straight out of the Brothers Grimm— Muni "always calculated his age from the time of the great famine when he stood as high as the parapet around the village well, but who could calculate such things accurately nowadays with so many famines occurring?" In the morning of the day covered in the story, before Muni meets the red-faced American who will apparently change their fortunes, his wife scolds him: "'You are getting no sauce today, nor anything else. I can't find anything to give you to eat. Fast till the evening, it'll do you good. Take the goats and be gone now,' she cried, and added, 'Don't come back before the sun is down.'"

They have no children. "Perhaps a large progeny would have brought him the blessing of the gods." But the American passing through their village mistakes the statue of a horse on the outskirts for Muni's property and buys it for 100 rupees. Muni returns with the money to his incredulous wife, believing he has sold his goats to the foreigner. They turn up bleating at his door, and the old woman to whom he has been married since they were both children some 60 years earlier threatens to go off to her parents.

The story is totally without condescension or sentimentality, does not even linger satirically on the acquisitive American. But the transparency with which it discloses the totally abject condition of Muni and wife is all the more striking because there is no visible moral. What usually interests Mr. Narayan is the chance to make a story, not a point, out of anything that comes his way. His is a cult of observation for its own sake, and his stories are always even-tempered and benign in a way that reflects the author's lack of political edge and his "British" culture. Reading him, I remember Nehru saying "I am the last Englishman to rule India." Mr. Narayan's stance is not what you get from the so much more penetrating and politically sharp mind of V. S. Naipaul. But of course Vidiadhar Surajprasad Naipaul, in spite of the name, is not from India.

"Annamalai," the most troubled and dramatic story in this collection, shows Mr. Narayan transcending himself under the pressure of a character not to be contained by routine observation. Annamalai is presented as the author's gardener, watchman, "and general custodian of me and my property." He is of course illiterate "in any of the fourteen languages listed in the Indian Constitution"; he dictates wild unfathomable letters for the village scribe to write down. He is sensitive to names and wants his master to remove his own name from the gate: "All sorts of people read your name aloud while passing down the road. It is not good. Often urchins and tots just learning to spell shout your name and run off when I try to catch them. The other day some women also read your name and laughed to themselves. Why should they? I do not like it at all."

Annamalai, a demon for work, "came in only when he had a postcard for me to address. While I sat at my desk he would stand behind my chair, suppressing even his normal breath lest it should disturb my work, but he could not help the little rumbles and sighs emanating from his throat whenever he attempted to remain still." Anything Annamalai relates (he often talks for the pleasure of talking aloud, needing no listener) becomes a story in itself. He recounts Japanese brutalities during the war, and tells a long story about a tailor and his sewing machine that I did not understand and that, I suspect, is meant to be understood as a reflection of Annamalai's capacity for storing grievances.

Sometimes, however, one of his tales is sufficient unto itself: "I was sitting in a train going somewhere to seek a job. I didn't have a ticket. A fellow got in and demanded, 'Where is your ticket?' I searched for it here and there and said, 'Some son of a bitch has stolen my ticket.' But he understood and said, 'We will find out who that son of a bitch is. Get off the train first.' And they took me out of the train with the bundle of clothes I carried. After the train left we were alone, and he said, 'How much have you?' I had nothing, and he asked, 'Do you want to earn one rupee and eight annas a day?' I begged him to give me work. . . . The lorry put me down late next day on the mountain. All night I had to keep awake and keep a fire going, otherwise even elephants came up."

After 15 years, the author loses him. "Why do you have to go away like this?". . ."He merely said, 'I don't want to die in this house and bring it a bad name. Let me go home and die.'" Nowhere else in this fine book does Mr. Narayan so interestingly submit to his material. He claims in his foreword that "the short story is the best medium for utilizing the wealth of subjects available. A novel is a different proposition altogether, centralized as it is on a major theme, leaving out, necessarily, a great deal of the available material on the periphery. Short stories, on the other hand, can cover a wider field by presenting concentrated miniatures of human experience in all its opulence." But the opulence of India includes a lot of misery and confusion. Though a miniature, **"Annamalai"** bursts the bonds of that predictable form, the short story. It brings a human strangeness home to us, as only a novel usually does—and that is the unexpected effect of Mr. Narayan's collection.

Sita Kapadia (essay date 1994)

SOURCE: "The Intriguing Voice of R. K. Narayan," in *R. K. Narayan: Critical Perspectives,* edited by A. L. McLeod, Sterling Publishers Private Limited, 1994, pp. 66-75.

[*In this essay, Kapadia examines the sources and qualities of Narayan's literary voice.*]

Among writers writing in English anywhere, R.K. Narayan has a distinctive voice. A lively storyteller, he sprinkles his tales with humour but withholds the derisive sting; while he is engagingly realistic in his descriptions, his words are not cut-and-dry; while he vividly portrays the failings and foibles of his townsfolk he never fails to extend to them his humane indulgence. He draws to his writing the stalwart literary critic as well as the undergraduate student of literature; he engages the sophisticated and the discerning as well as the casual, untutored reader. The voice of such a person, the voice of such a writer, is naturally intriguing.

What is the basis for this voice? How is it created? Narayan himself may have the best answers to these questions, if he chooses to engage in the necessary vivisection. To me, it is an engrossing subject—engrossing because challenging, and a challenge worth taking up because it yields richer than usual rewards. Voice, in literature, may be defined as an elusive and distinctive combination of a certain preferred syntax, a choice of words, a pattern of rhythms, and an attitude towards the reader and the world. Voice, in a singer, is resonance in sound; all singers do not have it. Narayan does have it, and it has long captivated me; finally, I can say I have uncovered its likely source.

Webster's New Universal Unabridged Dictionary offers a succinct and pertinent dictionary definition of *voice:* "the characteristic speech sounds normally made by a certain person." We know the voices of familiar people on the telephone before they say who they are. This is because each person has a voice as distinctive as fingerprints. When the term "voice" is applied to written literature, it signifies the characteristic speech sounds conveyed through writing. A writer, however, may not be as easily identified unless he is eminently distinctive. This is so because (beyond the literal, obvious subject matter) writing conveys emotional and philosophic meaning. As John Dewey says, "Poets and philosophers may democratically share accent and rhythm as ways of shaping communication." Our author is both poet and philosopher by virtue of his shaping voice.

This shaping quality comes from the voice of the storyteller, who speaks in the rhythms of everyday speech, the natural iambic rhythm, direct and comfortable, marking the interactions of real persons with their real surroundings. The natural tempo, following by and large the basic syntax of English (the subject-verb-object order), places events authentically in the rhythm of life. Unlike the periodic sentence, with its limited academic appeal, and the cumulative sentence, with its artful rhetoric, it imparts immediacy and easy intimacy to the writing and thereby creates a bond between the writer and his readers.

Further, the fluid interaction engendered by natural rhythm is enhanced by Narayan's "real voice." In *Writing with Power,* the most imaginative and extensive study that explores voice, Peter Elbow says that real voice comes from real self. Real voice has liveliness and energy, as well as power and resonance. Adding to this idea, Elbow says, "I see that when people start using their real voice, it tends to start them on a trend of growth and empowerment in their way of using words—empowerment even in relating to people." I believe Narayan has the spontaneous intimacy with his reader that comes from such empowerment.

His bond with the reader strengthens because he writes about the living world he witnesses. The subjects of Narayan's works may best be described in his own words: "The material available to a story writer in India is limitless. Within a broad climate of inherited culture there are endless variations: every individual differs from every other individual, not only economically, but in outlook, habits and day-to-day philosophy. It is stimulating to live in a society that is not standardised or mechanised, and is free from monotony" (*Malgudi*). Though Narayan is speaking here in the context of the difference between the arduous task of crafting a novel and simply looking out of a window and picking up a story, what he says about the individual and freedom from monotony holds true of characters in his novels as well.

Finding out all about his characters, with their individual idiosyncrasies, he does not feel the need to invent the absurd, to promote social theory, to seek sensational subjects, or to delve into abnormal psychology to get his reader's attention or to be regarded as a writer of consequence. It takes a great deal of courage and self-possession in a writer—especially a modern writer—to write about ordinary, everyday occurrences in the lives or ordinary, everyday people; it takes a great deal of talent and truth to keep the reader interested in and enthralled by such writing, story after story, book after book. It must take more than syntax, word choice, presentation of ideas, or some undefined expectation to keep interest mounting. I think it has to do with the writer's voice. We want to listen to him, to his voice.

The spoken charm or oral quality of Narayan's writing is unmistakable. Most of it comes to us in first-person narrative. Whether it be poignant nostalgia, sombre recollection, self-justifying reverie, compulsive talk, or comical recounting, it has the intimacy of the talking voice. It is distinctly not the voice of a distant and stern adjudicator of human predicament; rather, it is confiding, spontaneous—as though unedited, full of warmth and verve.

Furthermore, Narayan's world is very much like the world of his storyteller in *Gods, Demons, and Others*:

> Everything is interrelated. Stories, scriptures, ethics, philosophy, grammar, astrology, astronomy, semantics, mysticism, and moral codes—each is part and parcel of total life and is indispensable for the attainment of a four-square understanding of existence. Literature is not a branch of study to be placed in a separate compartment, for the edification only of scholars, but a comprehensive and artistic medium of expression to benefit the literate and the illiterate alike.

In the world of the imagination, if it is necessary to have a prerequisite (the willing suspension of disbelief), then in Narayan's imaginatively recreated world of real, everyday characters there is another given: the willing suspension of harsh indictment. This is not to say that there is no moral or intellectual discrimination as to the chasm between the saint and the scoundrel; it is, in fact, keenly present, but dispensed with clarity, humour, and faith that the scoundrel—and even savage—may someday become a saint. Raju, the unscrupulous guide, with holiness thrust upon him, does become a caring, self-sacrificing saviour. The once-wild tiger, becoming a non-violent sojourner in Malgudi, is assured of *moksha* (salvation). This is not a pattern in Narayan's novels, though, for there are others that remain incorrigibly greedy, habitually deceptive. The imposter Dr. Rann (in *Talkative Man*) and Sampath (in *Mr. Sampath*) are two such irreversibles.

There is, then, not a pattern in plot that gives resonant voice to Narayan's writing but a pattern of faith. I believe that it is worth exploring the content of Narayan's work by applying the "neti, neti" (not this, not this) method of negation in Indian metaphysics to discover the truth. Many a nineteenth—and twentieth-century writer of eminence points a finger at society for the evil that men do. Dostoevsky's protagonist in *Crime and Punishment*, outraged at a society that robs people of human dignity, becomes a murderer. Apparently no such thesis underlies Narayan's plots; nor is there an existential finger waving about, exposing absurdity, the meaninglessness of life. Narayan

does not perplex. We do not tease our minds as we do with Albert Camus over the senseless actions in *The Stranger* or cogitate with Franz Kafka about *The Metamorphosis* or wonder why a whole village in Japan shovels sand all night, every night, in Kobo Abe's *Woman in the Dunes*. Narayan's characters do not stand for anything other than themselves, individuals free of the monotony of modernisation and standardisation.

A variety of issues (modernisation, Westernisation, caste, prejudice, violence, urban dehumanisation, oppresssion of women, injustice, and many more) form part of the human drama energising the story. But nowhere, not even in *A Painter of Signs* or *The Dark Room*, does the theme (feminism, in these two novels?) overshadow the story. And the story is not an excuse for sizzling social issues as we often find in the novels of Kamala Markandaya or Chinua Achebe or Buchi Emecheta, nor for imaginative predictions of the future as in the works of Isaac Asimov. But social awareness and vivid imagination are ever-present in the very tone and turn of phrase of the narrative.

For instance, Srinivas brings up the matter of Sampath's affair:

> At first Sampath pooh-poohed the entire story. But later said, with his old mischievous look coming back to his eyes: "Some people say that every sane man needs two wives—a perfect one for the house and a perfect one for outside social life. . . . I have the one, why not the other? I have confidence that I will keep both of them happy and if necessary in separate houses. Is a man's heart so narrow that it cannot accommodate more than one? I have married according to Vedic rites: let me have one according to the civil marriage law. . . ."

What I see running through Narayan's work is a pattern of faith. In *Swami and Friends* it was intuited. It became explicit in *My Days: A Memoir* and in *The English Teacher* (alternatively titled *Grateful to Life and Death*, a title that bears significance to all of Narayan's work). The boy in the memoir, more at ease with the peacock and the monkey than with other boys, grows up into a young man steeped in literature, with a preference for reading and writing at Kukkanhalli Tank to teaching some meaningless things by rote to uninterested schoolboys. An absence of worldly wisdom, a pervasive listlessness, as well as an emptiness, seems to hover over his life, even when he is seemingly happily married. It is only after his wife's death, when he is intuitively drawn to the life of spiritual living, that he finds fulfilment in non-attachment, sacrifice, and service, maturing thus far beyond his earlier self-absorption. He accepts circumstances with peace in his heart, grateful to life and death. A close parallel to this memoir is evident in *The English Teacher*. Perhaps not so obviously, but similarly and subtly in every story, whether there is a radical transformation or not, a movement, a magnetic pull, toward the spiritual is discernible. Religion is not a theme; it is not even obliquely presented through Narayan's characters or zealously debated by them. However, a strong spirituality, a Hindu awareness, is latent. *The Vendor of Sweets* begins with an apparently flippant remark by the universal cousin about giving up over-fondness for food; the essence of the novel is the resilience of a broken paternal heart that learns non-attachment, letting go, and contemplation. It is as central to the Hindu way was anything can be. It is the premise of many a Narayan novel that, even when not explicitly stated, informs the argument or the core of the story. It resonates clearly in *A Tiger for Malgudi, The Financial Expert, The Guide* and *The Vendor of Sweets*. The choice of subject is an index. In the *Ramayana,* the incarnate Rama is goodness itself, but whereas he is not always infallible, he is always endearing, And there is a significant connection between character portrayal and the voice of the writer, for the voice expresses philosophy and faith, thought and feeling.

Many of Narayan's stories are recollections of the protagonists; they are narrations that express the quiet wisdom of hindsight. This is radically different from the time-reversed, attention-grabbing technique of plunging headlong into the fray at a point of conflict, developing a complication, and manoeuvring a resolution. Not so the voice of reveries, which is couched in the attitude of live-and-let-live. In **"Uncle,"** the little boy's attachment to Uncle and his growing awareness of the sinister history of that adored elder is told from the contentment and comfort of an easy chair. The narrator is himself the beneficiary, the inheritor of Uncle's presumably wicked spoils. As a young man supported by apparently the most gentle of souls, the God-loving, plant-cultivating imposter, he dispenses with moral issues with convenient speed. When he tells the story, he is indolent, indulgent, and certainly not given to either self-doubt or self-blame; it is the voice of calm-of-mind-all-passions-spent. The voice of torture is absent; the voice of philosophy is low-key but strong. It is typical of Narayan. It explains, partly, the importance of **"Uncle"**; the ambivalence of the genre label (short novel or long short story), to which our author is probably quite indifferent, is symptomatic of the freedom from moral dogma. All comes from a place in peace.

Literature must at once entertain and uplift. Narayan never loses his hold on those perennial essentials of great literature. The story is primary; we clamour for more, more! In terms of outer action, the stories are simply and traditionally crafted. The progression is generally chronological and often presented as events recollected by the protagonist. The English teacher, Raju, TM, the nephew in **"Uncle"** are some of them. While there is a deliberate self-awareness on their part, there is not the rush and plunge, and back-swirl of the stream of consciousness. The narrative moves along naturally, as though effortlessly in a quiet yet lively tempo of natural (by which I mean oral) expression. Reading any page, even a randomly opened page of Narayan's writing, assures the reader that wit and style are not lost but enthrallingly present. Here are the opening lines from *Talkative Man*:

> They call me Talkative Man. Some affectionately shorten it to TM: I have earned this title, I suppose, because I cannot contain myself. My impulse to share an experience with others is irresistible, even if they sneer at my back, I don't care. I'd choke if I didn't talk

. . . perhaps like Sage Narada of our epics, who for all his brilliance and accomplishments carried a curse on his back that unless he spread a gossip a day, his skull would burst.

Who can resist reading on? Who is not enchanted by the wit and style, the ambiance of his words?

Every page delights the reader. From Susila's two-digit accounting in **"Grateful to Life and Death"** to the half-uttered, oblique and inconclusive dialogues between Nagaraj and his wife Sita in *The World of Nagaraj,* we read and keep reading and want more. Why? It is, perhaps, because they provide present comfort to our own uneventful mental joggings on the spot, our own seemingly momentous though philosophically inconsequential involvements in our own world. The reason, however, is neither the comfort nor the empathy it provides; it is located in the voice.

There are two basic modes, two generic voices in Narayan's writing: the first person and the third person. The first is intimate, confiding, explicating and self-indulgent. The third person, radically different in theory, is objective, omnisciently commanding a cosmic picture. There is between them the usual intellectual and emotional difference, but essentially a vital concurrence of spirit. The omniscient voice—wiser, brighter, more sophisticated—is none the less just as indulgent, tolerant of human weakness and individual peculiarities as any self-aware and self-absolving first-person oration.

I give below one example of each of these two voices. The first person is beautifully used in this passage from *The Guide*:

> The gentle singing in the bathroom ceased; my mother dropped the subject and went away as Rosie emerged from her bath fresh and blooming. . . . She was completely devoted to my mother. But unfortunately my mother, for all her show of tenderness, was beginning to stiffen inside. She had been listening to gossip, and she could not accommodate the idea of living with a tainted woman. I was afraid to be cornered by her and took care not to face her alone. But whenever she could get at me, she hissed a whisper in my ear, "She is a real snake-woman, I tell you. I never liked her from the first moment you mentioned her."

The third person is also well illustrated from the same novel: He felt enraged at the persistence of food-thoughts.

> With a sort of vindicitive resolution he told himself, "I'll chase away all thought of food. For the next ten days I shall eradicate all thoughts of tongue and stomach from my mind. . . ." Lack of food gave him a peculiar floating feeling, which he rather enjoyed, with the thought in the background, "This enjoyment is something Velan cannot take away from me."

There is here a crucial connection, a vital unity of voice that is more significant than the difference in narrative standpoints.

Again, within the third-person narrative, typically and intimately, the reader comes upon the internal monologue, "the internal controversy" as it is called in *The Bachelor of Arts,* in which Chandran argues with himself:

> Chandran steadily discouraged this sceptical half of his mind, and lent his whole-hearted support to the other half. . . . His well-ironed chocolate tweed was sure to invite notice. He hoped that he didn't walk clumsily in front of her. He again told himself she must have noticed that he was not like the rest of the crowd. And so why should he not now go and occupy a place that would be close to her and in direct line of her vision? Staring was half the victory in love. His sceptical half now said that by this procedure he might scare her off the river for ever. . . .

Further, along with these fictional voices resonates the voice of the writer of *My Days*: "The postman became a source of hope at a distance and of despair when he arrived. My interest in him continues even today. In every country I visit I habitually watch the postman. It's probably a conditioned reflex, like Pavlov's salivating dog."

R. K. Narayan has that full-tone voice expressing something long-felt and long-understood.

—*Sita Kapadia*

John Knowles's protagonist, Gene Forrester, in *A Separate Peace,* says, "I knew what I said was important and right and my voice found that full tone voices have when they are expressing something long-felt and long-understood and released at last." R.K. Narayan has that full-tone voice expressing something long-felt and long-understood. Coming thus from a contemplation in the heart as well as the head, it is spiritually mature, free of hatred, contention, resistance, unrest, indignation—howsoever righteous. All one mode or another of reaction to the world, it comes out of wholeness and wholesomeness; it simply tells a story; it tells it with wisdom; it tells it as *leela.*

The writer is a compassionate and joyful witness; what he writes about is the spectacle of life, simply as spectacle, as *leela,* the spontaneous play of the impersonal Being in the universe. It is another way of saying that this is writing without a bias: no urgent need to drive home a point of view, no bitterness, no nostalgia, no anger, no anxiety, no socio-psycho convolutions, no talisman, and no utopia. Perhaps this is the reason Americans, with their overwhelming civil rights consciousness, their constant vigil to guard personal freedom, find Narayan so refreshingly unique, so purely entertaining. Through his writing

many a reader, especially many an undergraduate student, has come to understand and love India, its colours and flavours, its variegated humanity who have a local habitation and a name in Malgudi as well as a universal habitation in the minds and hearts and experiences of people everywhere.

The speaking voice is all-important to Narayan himself. He said in *My Days* of Keats, Shelley, Byron, and Browning: "They spoke of an experience that was real and immediate in my surroundings and stirred in me a deep response." The same is true of himself for us. He, too, evokes in us a deep response by speaking to us of the real and the immediate in that voice that comes from the centre.

Peter Elbow says, "Often words from the center are quiet. Their power comes from inner resonance. . . . I would point to the central characteristic of real voice: the words somehow issue from the writer's center . . . and produce resonance which gets the words more powerfully to the reader's center."

What a multitude of characters come to mind when we think of Narayan's writing! How engaging are their voices in memoirs, stories and novels! The resonance that comes from witnessing and delighting in life's *leela* comes from the centre. It makes of all these intriguing voices one real voice. It is an endearing voice, the voice of R.K. Narayan himself.

Shashi Tharoor (review date 1994)

SOURCE: "Comedies of Suffering," in *The New York Times Book Review,* September 11, 1994, pp. 40-1.

[*In this review of* The Grandmother's Tale, *Tharoor claims that the simple and straightforward style that gives Narayan's stories their charm also weakens the overall effect due to inadequacies of language.*]

"Some time in the early 30's," Graham Greene recalled, "an Indian friend of mine called Purna brought me a rather traveled and weary typescript—a novel written by a friend of his—and I let it lie on my desk for weeks unread until one rainy day." The English weather saved an Indian voice: Greene didn't know that the novel "had been rejected by half a dozen publishers and that Purna had been told by the author . . . to weight it with a stone and drop it into the Thames." Greene loved the novel, *Swami and Friends,* found a publisher for it in London, and so launched India's most distinguished literary career of recent times, that of Rasipuram Krishnaswami Narayan.

The author, now 87, went on to publish 25 more books, including 12 more novels. This year he was awarded a literary prize in India for outstanding lifetime achievement by a South Asian writer. The jury's citation declared Mr. Narayan "a master storyteller whose language is simple and unpretentious, whose wit is critical yet healing, whose characters are drawn with sharp precision and subtle irony, and whose narratives have the lightness of touch which only a craftsman of the highest order can risk." In the West, Mr. Narayan is widely considered the quintessential Indian writer, whose fiction evokes a sensibility and a rhythm older and less familiar to Westerners than that of any other writer in the English language.

The Grandmother's Tale: And Selected Stories appears in this country at the culmination of Mr. Narayan's long literary career. Fortunately, it effectively showcases all of his many strengths, as well as his considerable limitations.

The title story was published in India in 1992 by the author's own press, Indian Thought Publications, as a novella with illustrations by his cartoonist brother, R. K. Laxman. Mr. Narayan's American publisher, rightly judging that *The Grandmother's Tale* did not have the heft to stand on its own, has dispensed with the drawings and added instead a selection of Mr. Narayan's best short stories culled from the last five decades of his work.

The old favorites are all here: the classic tale **"An Astrologer's Day,"** perhaps his most famous and widely anthologized short story, about an astrologer coming face to face with the man he thought he had murdered years earlier; **"A Horse and Two Goats,"** a hilarious account of the encounter between an American tourist and a desperately poor and illiterate Indian peasant, though one in which the joke is stretched to the breaking point; **"The Blind Dog,"** about a blind man and his dog, a moving meditation on free will, dependence and greed; and **"Emden,"** an affecting story of an old man reaching out for elusive wisps of his past.

In other stories, an aspiring woman novelist finds that her husband's recipes are more publishable than her fiction; a judge acquits the defendants in a murder trial when a monkey in a temple makes off with his glasses; a village storyteller loses his narrative gift and summons his audience to hear his most important story. Though there are some that seem merely anecdotal or half-realized, this collection represents Mr. Narayan at his best as a consummate teller of timeless tales, a meticulous recorder of the ironies of human life, an acute observer of the possibilities of the ordinary: India's answer to Jane Austen.

But they, and the stories that accompany them in this collection, also point to the banality of Mr. Narayan's concerns, the narrowness of his vision, the predictability of his prose and the shallowness of the pool of experience and vocabulary from which he draws. Like Austen's, his fiction is restricted to the concerns of a small society portrayed with precision and empathy; unlike Austen's, his prose cannot elevate those concerns beyond the ordinariness of its subjects. Mr. Narayan writes of, and from, the mind set of the small-town South Indian Brahmin, but his writing does not suggest that he is capable of a greater range.

The gentle wit, the simple sentences, the easy assumption of the inevitabilities of the tolerant Hindu social and philosophical system, the characteristically straightforward plot-

ting are all hallmarks of Mr. Narayan's charm and help make many of these stories interesting and often pleasurable.

Yet Mr. Narayan's metronomic style is frequently not equal to the demands of his plots. Intense and potentially charged situations are rendered bathetic by the inadequacy of the language used to describe them. The title story, an autobiographical account of the author's grandmother, abandoned by the man she had married as a child, who travels hundred of miles and brings him back 20 years later after befriending and betraying his second wife, hints at extraordinary possibilities. But it is told in flat, monotonous sentences that frustrate rather than convince, and in a tone that ranges from the clichéd to the flippant.

The author has said in interviews that he is indifferent to the wider canon of English fiction and to the use of the English language by other writers, Western or Indian; indeed, his indifference is something of which he is inordinately proud. He says he doesn't read modern fiction: "I avoid every kind of influence." This shows in his writing, but he is defiant: "What is style?" he asked one interviewer. "Please ask these critics to first define it. . . . Style is a fad."

The result is that he uses words as if unconscious of their nuances: a distraught girl, who faces social ostracism and fears her husband dead, "threw a word of cheer to her mother and flounced out of the house." "Flounced" is a favorite Narayanism; it recurs in a man "slapping a face and flouncing out in a rage." Flowers grow "wildly" when the author means "wild"; a man whose wife and daughter upbraid him in indignation protests, "Everyone heckles me"; a village medicine man is called a "local wiseacre," though Mr. Narayan does not intend to be disparaging. Clichés and banalities abound—"kith and kin," "spick and span," "odds and ends," "for aught it mattered," "caught his fancy" and a proliferation of "lest"—as if the author learned them in a school textbook and is unaware that they have been hollowed by repetition. Mr. Narayan's words are just what they seem; there is no hint of meanings lurking behind the surface syllables, no shadow of worlds beyond the words. Indeed, though he writes in English, much of his prose reads like a translation.

Such pedestrian writing diminishes the stories, undermines the characters, trivializes the concerns: it confines R. K. Narayan to the status of an exotic chronicler of the ordinary. And it is not only the language that seems impervious to the existence of a wider world. Mr. Narayan's writing is blissfully free of the political clashes, social conflicts and historic upheavals that dominated Indian life during the more than half a century of his career; yet it is authentic in reflecting faithfully the worldview of a self-obsessed and complacent Brahmin caste. "I write primarily for myself," Mr. Narayan has said. "And I write about what interests me, human beings and human relationships. . . . Only the story matters; that's all." Fair enough: one does not expect Austen to be Orwell. But one does expect an Austen to enrich the possibilities of language, to illuminate the tools as well as the craft, Mr. Narayan's is an impoverished English, limited and conventional, its potential unexplored, its bones bare.

And yet—and yet. How can one fail to be charmed by an illiterate gardener's pride at mastering the telephone? ("In distinguishing the mouthpiece from the earpiece, he displayed the pride of an astronaut strolling in space.") Or by a storekeeper's prattle about baldness? ("God gives us the hair and takes it away when obviously it is needed elsewhere, that is all.") Or to admit the aptness of Mr. Narayan's un-self-conscious description of villagers who "never noticed their surroundings because they lived in a kind of perpetual enchantment"? There *is* enchantment in Mr. Narayan's world; his tales often captivate, and perhaps one should not pay too much attention to their linguistic surroundings.

The world that emerges from these stories is one in which the family—or the lack of one—looms as the defining presence in each character's life; in which the ordinary individual comes to terms with the expectations of society; and in which these interactions afford opportunities for wry humor or understated pathos. Because of this, and because of their simplicity, the stories have a universal appeal, and are almost always absorbing. They are also infused with a Hindu humanism that is ultimately Mr. Narayan's most valuable characteristic, making even his most poignant stories comedies of suffering rather than tragedies of laughter.

In this joyous and frustrating book, the author has given himself the last word. "The only way to exist in harmony with Annamalai," his narrator says of a servant, "was to take him as he was; to improve or enlighten him would only exhaust the reformer and disrupt nature's design." Even the most grudging critic would not deny R. K. Narayan this self-created epitaph.

Tone Sundt Urstad (essay date 1994)

SOURCE: "Symbolism in R. K. Narayan's 'Naga,'" in *Studies in Short Fiction,* Vol. 31, No. 3, Summer, 1994, pp. 425-32.

[*In the following essay, Urstad describes Narayan's literary technique of juxtaposing modern life with elements of myth. Urstad sees "Naga" as representative of this technique and analyses its effectiveness in short fiction.*]

R. K. Narayan is generally acknowledged as the most outstanding of the three major Indian authors writing in English to emerge in the 1930s (R. K. Narayan, Mulk Raj Anand, Raja Rao). His works have been described as "an original blend of Western method and Eastern material." His material is "Eastern" not just in the sense that he describes Indian characters in an Indian setting, but in the way that he uses references to Hindu mythology and the Indian epics to lend depth to his own works. He has what Britta Olinder has called "a singular power of joining his

fresh and humorous view of the ordinary world with the deeper meaning and larger perspectives he finds in the mythical treasures of his own religion." In *The Man-Eater of Malgudi,* for instance, the comic conflict between the good-natured but ineffectual Nataraj and Vasu, his taxidermist lodger, is on a deeper level a struggle between the forces that sustain life and those hostile to life. The struggle is brought to a happy conclusion because Vasu, like the *rakshasa* to which he is compared, carries within him the seeds of his own destruction.

Narayan's basic technique of ironically juxtaposing scenes of modern life with the exploits of gods, demons, and heroes of old, is well known and, in the case of some of his novels, well documented. **"Naga"** shows to what effective use Narayan can also put the same basic technique within the tighter form of the short story.

"Speaking for myself," Narayan has said, "I discover a story when a personality passes through a crisis of spirit or circumstances." A character "faces some kind of crisis and either resolves it or lives with it" (**Malgudi Days**). **"Naga"** certainly conforms to this simple pattern. A young boy faces two crises. When the story begins, he has already lived through the first one. Abandoned by his father, he has been forced to face life on his own. He has discovered that he has sufficient knowledge to carry on the family trade of snake charming, performing with Naga, the cobra the father has left behind. The story starts at a point close to the second crisis, which occurs when Naga—old and tired—has become a burden. The boy tries unsuccessfully to rid himself of his dependent by setting him free, only to find that Naga cannot survive on his own. The boy finds that he is incapable of purchasing his own liberty at the price of Naga's life and resumes responsibility for the snake. This is a variation on a theme that often appears in Narayan's works: an individual's impulse towards greater independence or individuality is hampered by forces within his immediate or extended family. Naga is family, as the father has made clear: "He is now one of our family and should learn to eat what we eat."

When the father abandons his son, he takes with him the "strumpet in the blue sari" and the performing monkey, and leaves behind in the hut the wicker basket containing Naga. The interpretation of the short story hinges partly on the answer to one question: why does the father leave the serpent rather than the monkey for his son? After all, when they performed for people, the father and the cobra functioned as one team, and the boy and the monkey as another. One could, of course, see the father's decision in terms of a selfish act: he takes the monkey because its earning power is far superior to that of the cobra, leaving his son to fend for himself as best he can (whereas the monkey is "popular," the father has to go through with his snake act "unmindful of the discouragement" initially met with from householders). Somehow this interpretation of the father's motives does not quite agree with the facts as we know them. The father is not described as an evil man. Admittedly, when under the influence of alcohol, he handles his son roughly. He also, by all accounts, has bad taste in women. However, in the few brief glances that we are given of him at the beginning of the story, he is presented as a sympathetic character. He teaches his son respect for animals; he shows imagination in his conversations with the child and a certain amount of sensitivity in his dealings with the animals. He has taken care of his son during the years of total dependence and has taught the boy his own trade, thereby ensuring that the child will one day be able to stand on his own feet. That the boy can, in fact, manage on his own is proven by events.

How, then, are we to interpret the father's act of leaving Naga—already an old snake and soon to become a burden—for the boy, while making off with the commercially viable monkey himself? After all, we are told that "the boy never ceased to sigh for the monkey. The worst blow his father had dealt him was the kidnapping of his monkey." At this point, one of the story's most striking features takes on a deeper significance: the use of names, or lack of them. The main character is known simply as "the boy"; neither the father nor the father's new consort has a name; her former husband and/or pimp is described only as "a hairy-chested man"; the neighbor who informs the boy of what has happened and who tries to comfort him is simply "a woman," and so on. There is a significant contrast here between the human beings, none of whom has a name, and the animals, who do: Naga, the snake; Rama, the monkey; Garuda, the kite. This serves to focus attention on these names, forcing the reader to consider the special significance that attaches to them.

A basic knowledge of Hindu mythology is indispensable to an understanding of most of Narayan's works, and this short story is no exception. Naga means, quite simply, "snake." Since ancient times snake divinities, known as "nagas," have been worshiped in India. In Indian architecture nagas are represented as beings with halos consisting of an uneven number of expanded cobra hoods.

The nagas are basically benign deities. They are guardians of the life-giving moisture of the earth, and dwell at the bottom of ponds and rivers and seas, where they are thought to have their own underworld realm (*Nagaloka*) full of beautiful palaces. Nagas are also thought to live among the roots of trees, since a tree is living proof that there is water in the ground. Because of their connection with the moisture in the earth, nagas are also the guardians of all metals and precious stones in the ground.

The nagas have a reputation for wisdom and knowledge and are associated with the act of protection. On Hindu and Buddhist monuments—one of Narayan's special interests—nagas are often depicted as worshiping and even protecting the gods and their incarnations. There are several old myths that illustrate this protective function. When the Buddha, after the Enlightenment, fell into a state of meditation that lasted for several weeks, the great naga Muchalinda protected him from the inclemencies of the weather by coiling itself around him and spreading its hood over his head like an umbrella.

The nagas protect not only superior beings but also mere

mortals. Nagas live close to humans and, in some areas, have become popular household patrons. They are numbered among "the guardians of life" who together have the power to bestow on human beings "all the boons of earthly happiness—abundance of crops and cattle, prosperity, offspring, health, long life."

A basic knowledge of Hindu mythology is indispensable to an understanding of most of Narayan's works, and ["Naga"] is no exception.

—*Tone Sundt Urstad*

From the beginning of the story, it is clear that the father looks upon Naga not just as an ordinary snake, but as a serpent deity. To his audience he describes a snake as "a part of a god's ornament, and not an ordinary creature," referring specifically to images of Vishnu, Shiva, and Parvati. Voicing a widespread popular belief, he asserts that a serpent is "a great soul in a state of penance." The father expects great things from Naga, telling the boy,

> We must not fail to give Naga two eggs a week. When he grows old, he will grow shorter each day; someday he will grow wings and fly off, and do you know that at that time he will spit out the poison in his fangs in the form of a brilliant jewel, and if you possessed it you could become a king?

Again the father is voicing popular beliefs. A naga was supposed to carry a precious jewel in its head, and was often willing to grant jewels and other boons to deserving mortals. There is no reason to think that the father does not literally believe that Naga will eventually provide for his son's material welfare.

This image of Naga as a future dispenser of wealth is later reinforced by that of Naga as the protector of precious metals when the father leaves 80 paise in small change for his son, placed—significantly—on the lid of Naga's wicker basket. Naga's function as protector of coins is ironically alluded to in the boy's plans to sell Naga's skin "to the pursemakers" if the snake dies. Even the location of the hut is significant. It belongs to a "colony of huts, which had cropped up around the water fountain," situated "beside the park wall, in the shade of a big tamarind tree"—just the kind of place where one might expect to find a naga. Since he functions as a kind of household deity, Naga must obviously remain with the property that he protects, even after the little household has split up.

Clearly the father's motive in leaving Naga with the boy was a wish to obtain protection, in every sense of the word, for his son. The associations of the naga with protection in one form or another are very strong in Hindu mythology. If Narayan had wished to avoid these associations, surely he would have found a more neutral name for the snake. Instead he actually named the story after this "character."

The irony of all this is, of course, that Naga is quite simply a snake and thus vulnerable, and once he becomes old and sluggish he proves incapable of protecting even himself, let alone the boy. This becomes evident when the boy tries to set him free. Naga is oblivious to the threat to his life from the Brahmani Kite Garuda flying high above, "its shadow almost trailing the course of the lethargic snake." The boy sees that Naga is incapable of surviving on his own and resumes responsibility for him. Thus the protector becomes the protected as the boy and the snake reverse roles, and the boy reaches a new stage in his development towards greater maturity when, no longer protected by his father, he takes on the involuntary role of protector of his dependent, Naga.

It is noteworthy that although the boy sees unblinkingly that Naga is just a worn-out old snake, he also sees Naga partially with his father's eyes, as something more than just that. The boy's last words to Naga show that he still thinks of the snake both as serpent and divinity: "If you don't grow wings soon enough, I hope you will be hit on the head with a bamboo staff, as it normally happens to any cobra. . . ." On a more subtle level, we notice it in the way the boy talks to Naga when he lets the snake loose in a lonely spot with many "mounds, crevasses and anthills":

> You could make your home anywhere there, and your cousins will be happy to receive you back into their fold. . . . You should learn to be happy in your own home. You must forget me. You have become useless, and we must part. I don't know where my father is gone. He'd have kept you until you grew wings and all that, but I don't care.

The mention of Naga's "cousins" and "their fold," the repeated references to Naga's "home," and, a little further on in the paragraph, to Naga's "world," do not merely allude to the fact that an attempt has been made to return Naga to nature. Within the context of the naga myths it is clear that the boy wishes the snake to return to the realm of the nagas, *Nagaloka,* with its bejeweled palaces and comfortable life, which, it is believed, can be reached via anthills and caves.

Notwithstanding the fact that the boy also thinks of Naga as a serpent deity, we see that Naga means two different things to the father and the boy. For the former, Naga represents protection for his son; but for the latter, the snake represents unwanted responsibility. Naga causes unnecessary expense in the form of food and stands between the boy and total liberty of movement. As long as the boy is responsible for Naga he will be unable to realize his dream of perhaps getting on a train "someday and out into the wide world."

For the boy there is an opposition between Naga and Rama, just as the two are described as incompatible because the snake terrifies the monkey when it rears itself up. While Naga means age and dependence to the boy, the monkey represents youth and freedom. When Rama first turns up he is described as "a tiny monkey gambolling amidst the branches of the tamarind tree," the boy watching "with open-mouthed wonder." He says, "Father, I wish I were a monkey. I'd never come down from the tree." Subsequently we hear of the monkey's "endless antics," and even after the monkey is caught, taught to perform, and made to wear clothes, he is described in terms of playfulness and spontaneity. In the evenings, when his clothes are removed, Rama does "spontaneous somersaults in sheer relief." Early in the mornings he performs "many fresh and unexpected pranks." Even during performances the monkey does not only act rehearsed scenes, but does "what was natural to him—tumbling and acrobatics on top of a bamboo pole."

What does the monkey represent to the father? Again, the man follows standard Hindu mythology when he says that Rama is "gentle and wise." Monkeys are also symbols of wealth and fertility, and it is therefore appropriate that the father, setting off for his new existence together with the new woman in his life, should bring the monkey with him. Significantly, in northern India, the monkey-warrior Hanuman "presides over every settlement, the setting up of his image being a sign of its establishment." Just as Naga protects the established household, the monkey protects the new settlement. Significantly, a new trained monkey features prominently in the boy's dreams for a new life.

The father names the monkey "Rama," after the avatar of Vishnu who is the hero of the *Ramayana,* explaining: "Rama, name of the master of Hanuman, the Divine Monkey. Monkeys love that name." In this way the basic story of the *Ramayana* is evoked: how Rama sets out to find and bring back his wife Sita, the model of wifely fidelity and modesty, who has been abducted by the evil king of Lanka, Ravana. In his quest Rama is joined and helped by Hanuman and his monkey warriors. Together they defeat Ravana and bring back the virtuous Sita. In "Naga," one of the tricks that Rama the monkey performs for the spectators is to "demonstrate how Hanuman, the Divine Monkey of the *Ramayana,* strode up and down with tail ablaze and set Ravana's capital on fire." All of the references to the old epic, with its heroic tale of courage, ideal love and virtue, serve to create an ironic background to the sordid details of the father's relationship with the "strumpet in the blue sari." In this modern tale of love the hero, whose lack of courage makes him avoid any confrontation with the "hairy-chested man," sets out accompanied by his monkey to liberate a latter-day Sita who is a prostitute (she stands at the door of her house "like a fixture") from a Ravana who is her husband and/or pimp. This Sita, who calls her lover's child "bad mischievous devil, full of evil curiosity," is certainly no model of chastity and purity.

In the passages that describe the boy's attempt to set the snake free, Narayan alludes to other Hindu myths that help to deepen our understanding of the boy's predicament. The scene is Nallappa's Grove (In Tamil Nallappa means "good father," an implied compliment to the boy for his handling of his dependent). When the boy sees that Naga is in imminent danger of being killed by the bird Garuda, he offers this touching prayer: "You are a god, but I know you eat snakes. Please leave Naga alone."

Narayan constructs a mythical framework within which the humans merely act out age-old patterns and conflicts.

—Tone Sundt Urstad

In Hindu mythology Garuda, the sun bird, is constantly at war with the nagas, who symbolize the life-giving waters, acting out the unremitting conflict between the sun and the water in a hot climate. In this battle Garuda is the stronger since the sun dries up the moisture in the earth. On the other hand, the serpents are thought to be tenacious of life (typically, Naga refuses to die). One myth relates how Vishnu rescued an elephant captured by the nagas. He came on his mount Garuda, but no battle was necessary because the nagas immediately fell down and worshiped their lord. At Puri in Orissa people who have been bitten by snakes are brought to a pillar in the temple and made to embrace the figure of the Garuda.

Vishnu is thus the lord of Garuda, which carries him through the air, but also of the nagas since he reclines upon the cosmic serpent Ananta. As "the Absolute, the all-containing Divine Essence," Vishnu must take up into himself all dichotomous aspects of life.

In Hindu mythology the opposition between Garuda and the nagas is seen in terms of the opposition between the sun and the water. In Western thought, however, the bird symbolizes "father Heaven . . . the unfettered far-flying celestial bodies . . . the spirit freed from the bondages of earth . . . divine eternal being." The serpent, on the other hand, represents mother Earth and a life tethered to worldly considerations. This is an opposition that Narayan clearly makes use of to lend depth to the ending of the story. Naga and Garuda are acting out the age-old battle for survival, in which Naga would not stand a chance without the boy's protection. At the same time, the bird "sailing in the blue sky" symbolizes complete freedom, unhampered by responsibilities and other earthly considerations, while the snake, on the other hand, symbolizes a life bound to the earth. The boy is forced to make a choice at this point, and, since he is not ruthless enough to sacrifice Naga, he remains bound by the snake's dependence on him. He is unable to do to Naga what his father did to him because, unlike the boy, Naga is incapable of surviving alone, while, unlike his father, the boy is not driven by a sufficiently strong human need to override the consideration.

It is in this context that Narayan's decision to give names to the animals but not to the human beings must be seen.

Through the ancient myths evoked by the names of the animals, Narayan constructs a mythical framework within which the humans merely act out age-old patterns and conflicts: the tension between the father's duty towards his offspring and his own sexual and (perhaps) emotional needs, differs only in degree from the conflict in the boy's mind between duty toward a dependent and a desire for personal freedom from responsibility. These tensions are only variations of an eternal pattern of life in which there will always be a conflict between the Sun-bird and the snakes, and in which Vishnu is lord over both Garuda and the nagas.

Judith Freeman (review date 1994)

SOURCE: "May You Always Wear Red," in the *Los Angeles Times Book Review,* Dec. 11, 1994, p. 9.

[*This review of* The Grandmother's Tale *highlights the subtlety, elegance, gentleness, and profundity of Narayan's work.*]

There is a saying in India, "May you always wear red," a phrase spoken among women, and offered as a sort of benediction. Widows, who do not have an easy time of it in India, are prohibited by custom from wearing the color red. And so what this saying means is: May you die before your husband. May you be spared the indignities of a solitary old age.

It's the sort of detail, a way of looking at things, that an American might never think of but which is an integral part of the world of R. K. Narayan, who has for many decades, in 13 novels, a half a dozen story collections, and in his memoirs and essays, described the nuances of his native culture with unparalleled tenderness and irony.

Narayan was once hailed by Graham Greene as "the novelist I most admire in the English language," a remarkable compliment considering the source. Reading Narayan is a bit like reading Greene. Both writers belong to a generation of elegant storytellers, masters of their craft. Along with V.S. Pritchett, Narayan is one of the last remaining voices from this era. And as his new collection of stories makes clear, age has not diminished his talent but simply added an extra dimension of wisdom to his remarkable and enduring vision.

Some of the stories in *Grandmother's Tale* are new, some have been collected from earlier works. A number are extremely short—a mere three or four pages; others, like the title story, have the weight of a novella. In each we find ourselves once again in the town of Malgudi and its surrounding villages, Narayan's equivalent of Faulkner's Yoknapatawpha County, where the majority of his fiction has been set.

Faulkner once wrote that "the primary job that any writer faces is to tell you a story out of human experience. I mean by that universal mutual experience, the anguishes and troubles and griefs of the human heart, which is universal, without regard to race or time or condition. He wants to tell you something which has seemed so true, so moving, either comic or tragic, that it's worth preserving."

It is precisely the combination of the comic and tragic that makes Narayan's stories worthy of the label "universal." That, and the very ordinariness of the lives he so lovingly renders in fiction. He takes a Western reader into the very heart of an Indian village and the family compounds where the little dramas of marriage and money and kinship inevitably result in a tangle of human ties. The foreignness of the setting, rituals and traditions may seem to us exotic, but the underlying humanity of Narayan's dramas can't fail to strike a familiar chord.

His characters are mirrors of history, men and women betrothed to each other as children, raised up in a post-colonial India, who find that their own children, infected by the evils of modern education, Western influence and torrid Hindi films, no longer wish to abide by the old rules. In **"Second Opinion,"** a profligate son discovers his widowed mother has long ago arranged his marriage to a village girl when he was only 5. At first he rebels against the alliance, then, thinking his mother is on the verge of death, acquiesces, only to discover too late that his mother is in perfect health.

One finds this sort of ironic O. Henry twist in many of these stories. In **"Lawley Road"** the mayor of Malgudi feels he has not done enough to celebrate independence and orders that all British names be removed from road signs. A statue of Sir Frederick Lawley, perceived as the very incarnation of colonial evil, is torn down. The story is a sort of riotous sendup of forced political correctness: not only does the town become "unrecognizable with new names," but Lawley is discovered to have been one of the most enlightened men of his era, championing independence early on. The statue, very difficult to remove from its lead pedestal (Britain had erected herself on "no mean foundation") is put up again and newly venerated.

"A revolutionary change is needed in our society," says a character in the story **"Guru,"** but what comes through in these tales is how firmly the old traditions prevail in modern India. Ninety percent of the marriages in India are still arranged with astrologers determining whether an alliance is propitious. The wheel of progress turns slowly, and yet the creaking can be heard. Annamalai, the gardener in the story of the same name, considers it a triumph that he can handle the telephone. In being able to distinguish the mouthpiece from the earpiece, he displays "the pride of an astronaut strolling in space."

Dowries, gossip, the favor or disfavor of family deities and all sorts of superstitions command a center place in the lives of Narayan's characters. These are simple people, shepherds and knife sharpeners, child brides, housewives yearning to be novelists, yet beneath the simplicity of their lives is a rich tapestry of emotion. No story displays this better than **"A Horse and Two Goats,"** a story I first read some years ago in V. S. Pritchett's anthology, *Best English Short Stories*. In it, an Indian couple, childless, destitute and reaching the end of their lives, encounter a New Yorker on vacation in India ("I told my wife, 'Ruth, we'll visit India this winter, it's time to look at other civilizations'"). Muni, the old man, is tending his two remaining goats in a field near an ancient statue of a horse when the New Yorker stops to ask directions. Prevented by a language barrier from understanding each other, they nevertheless engage in a long and extremely funny conversation, in which the New Yorker tries to negotiate a price for the horse statue in English, while Muni retells the tale of the Mahabaharata in Tamil.

The story reveals the depth and subtlety of Narayan's fictional sensibility, which is never overtly polemical, yet leaves a reader with much to think about—in this case, the irony of cultural misperception. Like all good stories, it is layered with meanings. What is so lovely about Narayan's work, and what makes it so valuable in a world torn by racial misunderstanding, is the gentleness of his vision, the way he makes each of us a member of his wondrous universe. He left me longing to return to his country and yet feeling that I had already done so, simply by reading his stories.

Hilary Mantel (review date 1995)

SOURCE: "Real Magicians," in *The New York Review of Books,* Vol. XLII, No. 3, February 16, 1995, pp. 10-11.

[*This review of* The Grandmother's Tale *discusses Narayan's delicate treatment of his characters.*]

R. K. Narayan is a writer of towering achievement who has cultivated and preserved the lightest of touches. So small, so domestic, so quiet his stories seem; but great art can be very sly. Born 1906, publishing his first book in 1935, he is generally acknowledged to be India's greatest living writer. His writings span an age of huge social change, and in his stories and novels, set in the imaginary town of Malgudi, he has built a whole world for his readers to live inside. Graham Greene said, "Narayan wakes in me a spring of gratitude, for he has offered me a second home. Without him I could never have known what it is like to be Indian."

Can we know, if we are not? For the non-Indian reader, part of the fascination of Narayan's work is that he can make his world familiar to us—and yet within that familiarity, the exotic is preserved. He can do this because he has such a sharp eye. He never takes anything for granted: that this must be so, should be so, has always been so. Life surprises him; he allows himself to be surprised. Any day, any street, any room in an accustomed house, any face known since childhood, can suddenly be fresh and strange and new; one reality peels away, and shows another underneath.

Most of the nineteen stories in *The Grandmother's Tale* are set in or around Malgudi, or a place very like it. It is Anyplace, really; to villagers a vast metropolis, but of little account to those used to the sophistication of Madras. Luckily for us, it is peopled by gossips, bystanders, doorstep-lurkers, and window-peerers. No one really has a private life; every street contains a by-the-way nephew, a remote uncle, or roundabout cousin, all of them with flapping ears and a loud mouth. The people of Malgudi are insurance clerks, photographers, shopkeepers, doctors, beggars, astrologers, and professional exorcists. Their wives rise at dawn to cook for them, scold and harry them through their days, and wait up at night to berate them and give them hot drinks.

One surprising wife, in **"Salt and Sawdust,"** writes a novel. The hero is to be a dentist—an original touch—who has trained in China, which accounts for many odd facets of his character. He falls in love with the heroine while he is making her a new set of teeth, though how she lost the originals is exterior to the text. Fact and fiction get mixed up in the nightly discussions Veena holds with her husband. They plan lavish meals for the characters and write out the recipes. Veena's novel finds no substantial public, but she becomes a best-selling author of cookbooks and travels the country giving popular demonstrations. It is a result gratifying and disappointing in equal measure.

Dreams, aspirations: that is what Narayan deals in. Small men, and small women, have great ambitions inside them. The illiterate knife-grinder in **"The Edge"** wants his daughter to be a "lady doctor." He lives on handouts of food and sleeps in a derelict building so that he can send money back to her, though his wife wants to take her away from school and get her earning a living in the fields. Another story, **"A Horse and Two Goats,"** is about Muni, a starving goatherd—who has only two goats left. He engages in a comical transaction with an American tourist, who wants to buy a statue of a horse and rider which stands on the outskirts of the poor man's village. Finding the goatherd crouching under the horse's belly seeking shade, the red-faced stranger decides that Muni must be the statue's owner. He offers money; Muni is at first baffled, but concludes the man is trying to buy his goats. After all, has he not fattened the animals against the day when some fool will come along with a wallet full of rupees, and make him an offer for them? It is a dream come true.

"Carry them off after I get out of sight, or they will never follow you, but only me . . . ," Muni advises; but since he and the American do not have a word of any language in common, the mutual mystification runs its course. While Muni is at home gloating over his money and boasting to his wife, the American carries off the statue in his truck. Muni is stunned when, that night, the unwanted and abandoned goats bleat their way home to his door. Next morning, when he wakes, he will have more, and less, and just the same, as yesterday.

It is an empty enterprise to single out stories in this collection, to claim that they do this or that in particular. Narayan does not bother to wrap up his tales neatly. Life goes on, the stories flow on, one into another, as if tributaries could loop back and feed the greater stream. Only the title story is a little disappointing. The narrator, a would-be writer, coaxes out of his grandmother the story of her own mother, Bala, married at seven to a boy of ten. The boy disappears, having followed a gang of pilgrims who were passing through his village; when Bala grows up she decides to track him down. She takes to the road, begging when necessary, surviving all manner of dangers, and at last finds him, a prosperous man married to another woman. The story of Bala's journey, and of how she traps and manipulates her husband into coming home with her, has many piquant details, but it must be said that Grandmother is not a natural storyteller, and we grow impatient with her vagueness and the gaps in her memory, however true-to-life her deficiencies are.

> **Narayan does not bother to wrap up his tales neatly. Life goes on, the stories flow on, one into another, as if tributaries could loop back and feed the greater stream.**
>
> *—Hilary Mantel*

Elsewhere, as ever, the master is in charge of his material—his hand delicate, his methods douce. His characters, self-absorbed, are often blind to real events, and stalk the town by the light of their own egos. They are touchy, raw-nerved people, yet often grossly insensitive to the feelings of others; perhaps we all suspect ourselves of this failing, and with some reason? Narayan is the bard of marital strife. Paradoxically, it is the details that make for universality. Are married people's quarrels the same, all the world over? Time after time, you come across conversations you could swear you have heard, from your neighbors beyond the bedroom wall. Then the horrible realization strikes: Have I myself, perhaps, said such things? And had them said to me? Such absurd things—so passionate and so meant and so howlingly funny?

Narayan's humor almost defies analysis—but not quite. He can make you laugh out loud, but he never imposes a joke—all the humor arises from character, and much of it from the self-importance and the affectations of his people. There is always someone lurking—a wife or a donkey, a cat or a dark room—that will cut the pompous down to size. Yet the fun is very gentle, and predicated on absurdity, on the careful observation of workaday human foolishness. Unforgettable is the old man—formidable in his day, but not feeble—who takes the same walk every afternoon:

Before six-thirty, he would be back at his gate, never

having to use his torch, which he carried in his shirt pocket only as a precaution against any sudden eclipse of the sun or an unexpected nightfall.

At the heart of Narayan's achievement is this: he respects his characters, respects their created natures. This is why he can make jokes about them and stay friends with them. In one story after another he offers them a change of fortune, a change of heart. He allows them insights, illuminations, epiphanies, yet he does not despise their unenlightened, less fortunate state. There is nothing cozy about his fiction. He may be gentle, but he is too clever to be bland. What he depicts is a complex, plural, everchanging society. As his characters are so strange to each other, is it a wonder that they are fresh and new to us? In **"Annamalai"** a man employs a gardener who begs him to take down a signboard on his gate that bears his name:

> "All sorts of people read your name aloud while passing down the road. It is not good. Often urchins and tots just learning to spell shout your name and run off when I try to catch them. The other day some women read your name and laughed to themselves. Why should they? I do not like it at all." What a different world was his where a name was to be concealed rather than blazoned forth in print, ether waves, and celluloid!

In Malgudi and environs, cause and effect do not operate as in the West. Reality looks quite different where horoscopes govern lives—yet fate is partly negotiable. Bureaucrats, too, have their own lunatic rules, yet each man and woman, self-willed and go-getting, is at one time or another a master or mistress of destiny. Seldom has an author been less of a puppet-master; within the country Narayan has invented for them, his people live freely. They live on close terms not only with their neighbors, with the stray dogs in the street, the donkeys who stand about the fountains, but with their memories and their gods. Celebrant of both the outer and inner life, he makes us feel the vulnerability of human beings and of their social bonds. Here is the town with its daylight bustle, its hawkers, beggars, shoppers, porters: outside, and within, are the deep forests, where tigers roar in the night.

FURTHER READING

Biography

Pontes, Hilda. *R. K. Narayan.* Atlantic Highlands: Humanities Press, 1983, 170 p.

Comprehensive profile and bibliography of the author.

Criticism

Graubard, Stephen R. "An interview with R. K. Narayan." *Daedalus* 118, No. 4 (Fall 1989): 233-37.

Interview in which Narayan discusses literature, travel, and his writing habits.

Olinder, Britta. "Aspects of R. K. Narayan's narrative technique." *Actes du Congrès d'Amiens,* (1982): 463-72.

A discussion of Narayan's novels that is also pertinent to studies of his short stories.

Sah, Prajapati P. "R. K. Narayan's 'Gateman's Gift': The Central Theme." *Literary Criterion* XV, No. 1 (1980): 37-46.

Focuses on the efforts of an individual struggling to break free from socio-economic constraints.

Vanden Driesen, Cynthia. "The Achievement of R. K. Narayan." *Literature East and West* 21, Nos. 1-4 (Jan.-Dec. 1977): 51-64.

Asserts that Narayan's works combine local and universal characteristics.

Venugopal, C. V. "R. K. Narayan." *The Indian Short Story in English,* pp. 75-89. Bareilly: Prakash Book Depot, 1976.

Compares Narayan to other Indian writers, describing him as an author who has no "angle," but who sees a story from a journalistic perspective.

Walsh, William. *R. K. Narayan.* London: Longman Group Ltd., 1971, 26 p.

A clear and comprehensive introduction to Narayan's life and works.

Additional coverage of Narayan's life and career is contained in the following sources published by Gale Research: *Contemporary Authors,* Vols. 81-84; *Contemporary Authors New Revision Series,* Vol. 33; *Contemporary Literary Criticism,* Vols. 7, 28, 47; *DISCovering Authors*; *Major Twentieth-Century Writers*; and *Something About the Author,* Vol. 62.

Margaret Oliphant
1828-1897

Scottish short story writer, novelist, essayist, biographer, and critic.

INTRODUCTION

Margaret Oliphant was an extremely prolific and popular writer in her day, publishing almost a hundred novels as well as collections of short stories, many books of history, travel essays, and a biography. Many of her works are notable for their depiction of her native Scotland, though she travelled widely and is not exclusively a regional writer. Her female characters are often remarkable for their strength and independence, and in much of her work she satirized English society. Most of her fiction is long out of print and unavailable, but recent critical interest has brought about new editions of some of her novels and short stories. The works best known to modern readers are her stories of the supernatural, such as "The Library Window" and the novella *The Beleaguered City*.

Biographical Information

Margaret Oliphant was born Margaret Wilson in 1828 at Wallyford, Scotland. Her father was a customs official, and the family had two boys older than Margaret. Her father was a retiring and unsociable person, and Margaret was chiefly raised and educated by her mother. She was not allowed many amusements besides reading, and developed into a serious and responsible young person. Around the age of sixteen, Margaret's mother became ill, and Margaret began to write as something to while away long hours in the sick-room. She completed a novel, which was appreciated by her mother, but was never published. By the time she was twenty, however, she had finished another novel, *Margaret Maitland,* which was promptly accepted and published by a London firm. This book was quite successful, and quickly ran into three editions.

It has often been assumed that Oliphant wrote so prolifically because she had dire financial need. Yet the day she finished *Margaret Maitland* she began a new novel— long before she knew her first book would be acclaimed and earn money. She seemed to have a voracious need to write. The fact that she could earn a living this way certainly encouraged her, but it was not the sole reason for her immense literary productivity. Nevertheless, her family soon began to depend on the income her writing brought. Her brother Willie drank and fell into debt as a student in London, and Margaret was dispatched to look after him. In London she met her cousin, Frank Oliphant, a painter and stained glass artisan, whom she married a few years later.

Oliphant moved to London with her husband, where her income from her novels chiefly supported them. She had three children in quick succession, but her second daughter died at eight months, and her third died shortly after birth. Oliphant's beloved mother also died around this time. She continued to write through these tragedies, and a little boy, Cyril, was born some years later. In the late 1850s her husband developed consumption, and his health rapidly declined. In an effort to save him, the family left for Italy in January, 1859. They took rooms in Florence, but were apparently shocked to find that Italy was not warm and sunny year round. Oliphant supported the family with money she earned from stories and essays she published in *Blackwood's Magazine,* a journal she would write for until the end of her life. By October it was clear her husband would not live. He died and was buried in Rome, where a few weeks later Oliphant gave birth to a son, Francis.

Now a widow with three children, it was absolutely necessary for Oliphant to write to support the family. She returned to England, where she conceived of a series of novels about country clerics, her Chronicles of Carlingford. These novels were enormously successful, and are still considered among her finest works. On a trip to Italy in 1864, her oldest child, her daughter Maggie, died suddenly of a short illness. Oliphant's burdens only increased after this tragedy. Her brother Frank's wife died, and Oliphant took over the support of his family of three children. In spite of precarious finances, she determined to send her sons to the best schools. They went to Eton and Oxford, while their mother wrote unceasingly. In 1877 Oliphant published three "three-decker" (three volume) novels as well as three academic books for a series for young people; the next year one three-decker, and in 1879 two three-deckers and a collection of short stories. Her industry never failed, though the work was not of uniformly high quality. Her two sons died young, their intellectual promise unfulfilled, and a nephew she had raised also died as a young man. After the tragic deaths of all these children, she began to write some of her most enduring works, fascinating stories of the supernatural. Her popularity was in decline at the end of her lifetime, as the three-decker form she had excelled at became outmoded. Yet she never stopped writing, and even on her death-bed was editing proofs of her two-volume history of Blackwood's publishing house.

Major Works of Short Fiction

Of Oliphant's 98 novels, few are consistently praised by modern critics. The novels of her early series, The Chronicles of Carlingford, are among her best. *Miss Marjoribanks* is especially noted for its sharp examination of social relations and its complex female characters. A late novel, *Kirsteen,* has often also been singled out by critics as an outstanding work of Victorian realism. The story of a Scottish woman, *Kirsteen* also exhibits Oliphant's deft depiction of her native region. But Oliphant is best known today for her novellas and short fiction that deal with "the unseen." Her novella *A Beleaguered City* caused a sensation when it was first published, and is still appealing to present-day readers. It tells the story of the town of Semur, in France, which is taken over by its dead residents. The ghosts expel the living, who are not sufficiently pious. The tale is remarkable for its atmosphere of mystery—the strange events of Semur are never categorically explained, but only hinted at by different narrators. *A Beleaguered City* is a spiritual story, suggesting that those who do not strive to discover "the true meaning of life" are living in sin and darkness. Yet the story is free from pat religious morals or sanctimonious pieties.

"The Library Window" and "Old Lady Mary" are two other highly respected ghost stories. "The Library Window" tells of a young girl who sees an image of a man writing through a window in an adjacent building. She cannot contact the man, and others convince her that the window is only a figment. "Old Lady Mary" tells of a selfish old woman whose whim to hide her will robs her ward of her inheritance. Lady Mary returns as a ghost, to try and rectify her misdeed, but she is unable to communicate with the living. Like many of Oliphant's supernatural stories, these show with great poignancy the barriers between the living and the dead. Another notable story of the afterlife is "The Land of Darkness." Oliphant's vision of Hell as an urban, industrial landscape prefigures Orwell and Huxley. Though the bulk of Oliphant's fiction is realistic, "The Land of Darkness" shows she had an extraordinary imaginative power as well.

Critical Reception

Oliphant was a popular and respected writer at the height of her career. Her novels, particularly her Chronicles of Carlingford, were well received. She was adept at the three-volume "triple decker" novel that was the staple of Victorian publishing. But by the end of her life, the triple decker form had practically disappeared, and Oliphant's writing was no longer the height of fashion. After her death, her fiction was mostly dismissed by critics as the work of a hack who wrote too quickly and too prolifically. This sentiment was passed down without much further examination until recent decades, when a few critics worked to bring some of her best stories and novels back into print, and to re-evaluate her career. The idea that Oliphant only wrote as much as she did because she had to support her family is one notion modern critics have unseated. Oliphant mentions several times her unquenchable need to write for its own sake. Contemporaries described her vivid intellect and sparkling energy, suggesting that she may have created just as much literature even if she had had no need for the income it brought. And though she was a popular writer, modern critics assert that her fiction shows little conformity to Victorian attitudes towards piety and sentimentality. Her female characters are often uniquely self-reliant and resourceful. Her supernatural tales, which are all available in modern editions, are highly regarded. After a long decline, Oliphant's reputation, at least in a limited academic circle, is on the rise. With reprints of her work now available, Oliphant may enjoy a small popular revival as well.

PRINCIPAL WORKS

Short Fiction

Passages in the Life of Mrs. Margaret Maitland 1849
The Rector and the Doctor's Family [Chronicles of Carlingford series] 1863
A Beleaguered City and Other Stories 1879
The Two Mrs. Scudamores 1879
Two Stories of the Seen and the Unseen 1885; expanded edition, *Stories of the Seen and the Unseen* 1902
The Land of Darkness, along with Some Further Chapters in the Experience of the Little Pilgrims 1888
Neighbours on the Green: A Collection of Stories 1889
The Two Marys 1896
The Lady's Walk 1897
The Ways of Life: Two Stories 1897
A Widow's Tale and Other Stories 1898
That Little Cutty and Two Other Stories 1898

Selected Stories of the Supernatural [edited by Margaret
   K. Gray] 1985
The Doctor's Family and Other Stories [edited by Mer-
   ryn Williams] 1986

Other Major Works

Katie Stewart (novel) 1853
The Athelings; or, The Three Gifts (novel) 1857
Chronicles of Carlingford (novel series): *Salem Chapel*
   1863; *The Perpetual Curate* 1864; *Miss Marjoribanks*
   1866; *Phoebe, Junior* 1876
A Son of the Soil (novel) 1865
The Minister's Wife (novel) 1869
The Three Brothers (novel) 1870
*Memoirs of the Count de Montalembert: A Chapter of
   Recent French History* (biography) 1872
The Curate in Charge (novel) 1876
*The Makers of Florence: Dante, Giotto, Savonarola, and
   their City* (history) 1876
A Little Pilgrim in the Unseen (novel) 1882
It Was a Lover and His Lass (novel) 1883
The Wizard's Son (novel) 1883
*The Makers of Venice: Doges, Conquerors, Painters, and
   Men of Letters* (history) 1887
*Kirsteen. The Story of a Scottish Family Seventy Years
   Ago* (novel) 1890
The Heir Presumptive and the Heir Apparent (novel)
   1891
Jerusalem, the Holy City: Its History and Hope (history)
   1891
The Railway Man and His Children (novel) 1891
*Annals of a Publishing House: William Blackwood and
   His Sons, Their Magazine and Friends.* 2 vols. (histo-
   ry) 1897
The Autobiography and Letters [edited by Mrs. Harry
   Coghill] 1899; revised edition 1899; *The Autobiogra-
   phy* [edited by Elizabeth Jay] (autobiography) 1990

CRITICISM

Vineta and Robert A. Colby (essay date 1966)

SOURCE: "The Seen and the Unseen," in *The Equivocal
Virtue: Mrs. Oliphant and the Victorian Literary Marketplace*, Archon Books, 1966, pp. 88-107.

[*In this excerpt, Vineta and Robert Colby review the
varied qualities of Oliphant's supernatural tales.*]

Early in her career, in her novels and in her biography of
Irving, Mrs. Oliphant had revealed a sympathy for the
visionary mystic, the prophet without honor in his country—just such a figure as is represented in the tragic Paul
Lecamus of *A Beleaguered City*. Her study of Montalembert brought her into contact with the French monastic
revival, the continental counterpart of the Oxford Move-

ment. The interest she developed in the ideas of
Montalembert and his fellow crusaders Lamennais and
Lacordaire account in particular for the French setting of
A Beleaguered City as well as for the socio-religious
milieu of that impressive story. Moreover, one of her closest friends, Principal Tulloch, was the leading Scotch
churchman of the age and an eloquent apologist for the-
ism against skepticism and rationalism. In the light of this
background one can account for an important theme that
underlies all the Stories of the Seen and the Unseen—the
affirmation of the existence of an immanent and transcendental Creator and of the immortality of the soul in the face
of the growing number of agnostics, scientists, aesthetes,
hedonists, and materialists who were undermining traditional faith.

In her 1862 *Maga* article on "Sensation Novels," Mrs.
Oliphant had protested against the *outré* in fiction. It is
significant that in her own supernatural tales her spirits
are beneficent ones, not demons, the emotion she arouses
being awe rather than terror for the world beyond. For the
same reason, the Stories of the Seen and the Unseen
generally avoid lurid incident of any sort, achieving their
effects rather through delicacy of feeling and sympathy
with man's longings for transcendental experience. Her
reviews in *Maga* of spiritualistic novels like *The Gates
Ajar* by Elizabeth Stuart Phelps and *Hitherto* by Mrs.
Adeline Whitney give us some idea of the popular stories
that Mrs. Oliphant was to imitate and excel in her own
writing. Another influence came from one of her favorite
novelists, Edward Bulwer-Lytton. Writing an obituary article on him for *Maga* (March 1873), she classified his
versatile output into stories of life and manners, historical
romances, crime novels, and tales of magic and mystery.
The latter—as represented particularly by the theosophical novels *Zanoni* and *A Strange Story*—she reserved for
the last, remarking in words that make clear her own affinity for them that "the mysterious unseen world which
surrounds us, of which we know so little by our reason,
and so much by our fancy, about which every one believes much which his mind rejects, and feels much which
his senses are unconscious of, must ever have a charm,
not only for the fanciful and visionary, but for all to whom
fact and certainty do not sum up the possibilities of existence."

Through all these observations we can feel Mrs. Oliphant
groping her way towards her own tales of "magic and
mystery." The sudden intimation of immortality, the eva-
nescent inner light that is extinguished as suddenly as it
is ignited—these are the spiritual phenomena that lie at
the center of her religious consciousness. Like Dickens
and Wilkie Collins, she tried to awaken readers to the
romance of real life, but through spiritualizing rather than
sensationalizing the mundane world. Behind her supernatural fiction, as with that of many forgotten writers then in
vogue, lay the need articulated by theologians and ministers and felt by sensitive laymen for a general revival and
revitalization of the religious emotions. Also hovering in
the background is the contemporary interest in the phenomena of parapsychology, or what we speak of today as
extra-sensory perception. The baffling experiences of such

characters as Martin Dupin in *A Beleaguered City*, Colonel Mortimer in **"The Open Door,"** Edmund Coventry in **"Earthbound,"** while leading them to a new religious insight, bring out the inability of the human reason to account for the nature of ultimate reality. Mrs. Oliphant refers to the supernatural simply as the Unseen, with the implication that our failure to achieve mystic insight is due to an obfuscation of our faculties, a spiritual blindness that results from living too much in the realm of the Seen. Significantly, the vision denied to the more intellectual and sophisticated characters of these stories is imparted to children like Connie in **"Old Lady Mary,"** to the pure in heart like Madame Dupin in *A Beleaguered City*, or to innocents like the elderly heroine of *A Little Pilgrim in the Unseen*, "a gentle soul which never knew doubt." These are, as with Wordsworth, the "first philosophers." For the old, the learned, or the worldly to gain so much as a glimpse into the Unseen is an arduous process of removing mists and lifting veils.

Mystery and wonder suddenly obtruding themselves in the midst of the bustle of ordinary life, the depths of spiritual life concealed beneath the placid surface of familiar things, but momentarily emerging to jolt us out of our dull complacency—such is the keynote sounded by *A Beleaguered City*, the first and most ambitious of the *Stories of the Seen and the Unseen*. The story begins on a late afternoon in June 1875. Martin Dupin, Mayor of Semur, a prosperous farm town in the Haute-Bourgogne, is returning home from an inspection of the vineyards in the country when he witnesses a shocking incident. As Monsieur le Curé leads a procession along the Grande Rue carrying the rites of the church to a dying man, an atheist of the village tries to block his path and shouts sacrilegious words. Dupin, like all the others present, is shocked at the outrage, though it is rather his social sense than his religious feeling which is wounded. One of the more religious townspeople is moved to exclaim: "'It is enough to make the dead rise out of their graves!'" Shortly afterwards a strange pall settles over Semur. Various explanations are offered for this phenomenon. The superstitious of the town suspect witchcraft, the rationalists attribute it to an eclipse or a horde of insects, while the pious immediately conclude that all of the people of Semur are being punished for the blasphemy of the few. Mayor Dupin wavers between the religious and scientific viewpoints as he struggles to take control of the situation.

Meanwhile, mysterious sights and sounds pervade the atmosphere. Boats sail down the river propelled apparently by nothing but air; various citizens claim to have seen their dead beloved; the bells of the cathedral are heard to toll, though nobody is known to be inside; the cathedral suddenly becomes ablaze with light. Soon all the inhabitants feel themselves being pushed out of the gates of the town, and they encamp before the walls of Semur, refugees from an unknown, unseen, vaguely felt enemy. In time the stranded populace are confronted by the town pariah, the discredited visionary Paul Lecamus, who claims to have had contact with the unearthly visitants and to have recognized among them some of the dead of Semur. He assures his fellow citizens that the spirits have come

to save them, not to destroy them. Persuaded by Lecamus, Mayor Dupin and Monsieur le Curé form an embassy of good will to the visitors. They grope their way through the quiet, seemingly empty town to the cathedral where the priest performs the Mass. Suddenly the darkness is dispelled, and Semur is bathed once more in radiant sunlight. The citizens re-enter, raising hosannas, and the town is swept by a religious revival. Then all settles back into normal routine, while Mayor Dupin ponders the significance of these "remarkable events."

Mystery and wonder suddenly obtruding themselves in the midst of the bustle of ordinary life . . . momentarily emerging to jolt us out of our dull complacency—such is the keynote sounded by *A Beleaguered City*, the first of the *Stories of the Seen and the Unseen*.

—Vineta and Robert A. Colby

The cumulative power of *A Beleaguered City* derives in part from the contrast between the surface simplicity of the narrative and its larger implications. The subtitle—"A Narrative of Certain Recent Events in the City of Semur in the Department of the Haute Bourgogne"—suggests a document to be filed in a government archives; indeed one of the Mayor's alleged motives for telling his story is to set the record straight. While aware that "the faculty of imagination has always been one of my characteristics," Dupin hastens to assure his readers that, "Had it been possible for me to believe that I had been misled by this faculty, I should have carefully refrained from putting upon record any account of my individual impressions." His narrative, in accordance with this preamble, is remarkable for its lucidity and objectivity (resembling in this respect Defoe's *The Apparition of Mrs. Veal*). The mode of narration of *A Beleaguered City*—the most intricate Mrs. Oliphant ever attempted—contributes further to its texture and stature. It is the only one of her stories told by multiple narrators, a method of presentation justified again by Martin Dupin's fidelity to facts. As "one who is the official mouthpiece and representative of the commune, and whose duty it is to render to government and to the human race a true narrative of the very wonderful facts to which every citizen in Semur can bear witness . . . it has become my duty so to arrange and edit the different accounts of the mystery, as to present one coherent and trustworthy account to the world." This device has been likened by some critics to the assemblage of the testimony of the various witnesses in Wilkie Collins' *The Moonstone*, but Mrs. Oliphant was probably influenced here more by Browning's *The Ring and the Book*, which she very much admired. At any rate, the several eyewitnesses of the "extra-ordinary events" of Semur contribute not so much different information as diverse viewpoints towards the confusing circumstances, giving Mrs. Oliphant opportunity for varied and dramatic characterization.

Dupin carries the burden of the narration. With his combination of pride, humility, officiousness, and sensitivity he emerges as one of Mrs. Oliphant's most complex portraits. Most moving is the growth of a religious consciousness in this *honnête homme* intended to represent the *haute bourgeoisie* mind of modern France—rationalistic, materialistic, state-centered and man-centered. But dimension is added to the story by the superposition of other religious attitudes. Mrs. Oliphant's sublimest style is reserved for the account by the mystic Paul Lecamus, befriended by the Mayor, though shunned by the others as "a dreamer of dreams." The language in which he describes his reunion with his dead beloved is at once Dantean and apocalyptic: "Her presence wrapped me round and round. . . . She was more near to me, more near, than when I held her in my arms. How long it was so, I cannot tell; it was long as love, yet short as the drawing of a breath. . . . We said to each other everything without words—heart overflowing into heart. It was beyond knowledge or speech."

At the opposite extreme is Monsieur de Bois-Sombre, a *déclassé* aristocrat and retired *mousquetaire,* humane, but snobbish and obtuse, who looks upon these same untoward events as connected somehow with the unleashed forces of republicanism. As a worshipper of reason and "the logic of circumstance," he sees Lecamus as "a harebrained enthusiast." One gathers that so far as Monsieur is concerned, Church and State alike exist mainly to control the canaille. The two women who contribute accounts, Mayor Dupin's wife and mother, represent two antithetical types of piety. Madame Dupin is the serene, cheerful Christian, quite removed from the turbulent spiritual world of Lecamus. She is the simple, charitable, saintly soul who grasps religion mainly by intuition. Madame Veuve Dupin, on the other hand, is the stern evangelical, ever walking in "the light of reason" and recalling others to their sense of duty. It is significant that it is not she but Madame Dupin who sees the heavenly emissaries.

The various figures of *A Beleaguered City* seem to be intended as archetypes of religious and intellectual positions rather than as individualized personalities. Minor figures in the story are given generic names, such as the timorous *adjoint* M. Barbou, the miser Gros-Gain, and the ironically named M. Clairon, the ineffectual scientist from the Musée who is as baffled as the rest when challenged to explain the "miracle" of Semur. Even a place-name like Bois-Sombre (Dante's "selva oscura") has symbolic overtones. It is possible, in fact, to read the story throughout as a parable of the human faculties, with Jacques the atheist and the other peasants representing the irrational part of the soul, Dupin representing reason and courage, Madame Dupin natural piety, and Lecamus spiritual wisdom. The sparseness of setting, the lack of extensive physical topography in Mrs. Oliphant's fictitious Semur, as well as the confinement of sensuous impressions to light and darkness, music and silence, all make for a concentration of effect characteristic of a fable.

Apart from its literary quality, *A Beleaguered City* is endowed with remarkable depth of feeling. The ultimate effect of the miracle of Semur is to strengthen the Dupins in their marital devotion. Before the story opens, they have suffered the death of a young daughter, Marie. (Thus the author projects her grief over her own Maggie.) In the course of the visitation of the spirits, Madame Dupin is consoled by her communion with the spirit of Marie. Martin Dupin, lacking his wife's spiritual faculty, never gets to see Marie, but at one point, while he is groping about the house in the darkness, he suddenly discovers an olive branch hanging over her veiled portrait. His final narrative ends when he and Madame Dupin pay obeisance at the grave of Lecamus, the one citizen of Semur who apparently grasped the full significance of the return of the dead. Dupin is deeply moved when he notices that carved on the cross of Lecamus' tomb is an olive branch—a replica of the one he had seen suspended over the portrait of the dead Marie. Gazing at his wife, he muses: "Who but she could have done it, who had helped him to join the army of the beloved?" His wife seems to have read his mind. Her explanation brings the story to its muted end: "'This was our brother,' she said, 'he will tell my Marie what use I made of her olive leaves.'"

Despite this touching close, the tone of *A Beleaguered City* is not predominantly sentimental. It offers no easy consolation in the manner of so much of the more conventional religious fiction of the period. Mrs. Oliphant makes it clear, for one thing, that it is not open to all to see the angels. Not only is Monsieur le Maire denied the privilege, but Monsieur le Curé as well. She also is aware that the way to mystic revelation is a thorny one, and that such vision brings its pains as well as its pleasures. Although Paul Lecamus, for example, achieves ecstasy, the experience proves so shattering that he dies as a result of it. Also, the inhabitants of Semur are not permanently converted by the visitation to a Christian way of life. When Monsieur le Maire and Monsieur le Curé walk courageously hand in hand through the gates into the benighted city to confront the spirits, Mrs. Oliphant seems to be offering the hope that Church and State may come to support each other, instead of working at cross purposes. But such is not to be. Once the threat is removed, Dupin finds himself again scoffing at superstition, as he sees Monsieur le Curé too ready to accept insincere devotion for true religion. The wave of religion that momentarily swept Semur proves to be but an epidemic of hysterical evangelism and a reign of false prophets. Nevertheless, she leaves us with some hope at the end of her story, through the image of the domestic and temporal orders, personified by the Dupins, bowing before the spiritual order—in awe of Last Things.

The tautness of structure and beauty of style of *A Beleaguered City*, shaped by a controlling idea, make this story something unique in Mrs. Oliphant's writings. It was produced out of a rich fund of experience, from her life as well as from her reading. And, as happened rarely with her, her emotions, her mind, and her imagination were equally and simultaneously engaged in the creation of a work of fiction. That it was a labor of love for her is apparent from the unusual amount of time and effort she expended upon it. One regrets she could not allow herself this luxury more often, for the account of the strange events in Semur lends support to those critics who contend that Mrs. Oliphant might have been a major writer had economic pressures not forced her to write too much and too quickly. On the whole, posterity has rewarded her for her pains. *A Beleaguered City* has been the most frequently reissued of her books and one of the few to see print in recent years.

Two years after the appearance in book form of *A Beleaguered City*, Mrs. Oliphant published a shorter and simpler tale, **"The Open Door,"** in the January 1882 issue of *Maga*. Quite possibly because it is the most "Gothic" of her supernatural stories, it has been the one most frequently anthologized, and it has therefore maintained something of a reputation among connoisseurs of horror stories. But **"The Open Door"** is not a mere ghost story. The effect it leaves on the reader is more of pathos than of horror. It is related in theme to *A Beleaguered City*, as an attempt by a spirit to communicate with the living. Like its predecessor it is told by a character who stands midway in attitude between credulity and skepticism towards the inexplicable events described. The narrator, Colonel Mortimer, is a retired gentleman recently returned from India with his family. They settle in an old country house near Edinburgh to permit the young son, Roland, who is in frail health, to go to school while remaining under his parents' surveillance. On the grounds are some old ruins of unknown origin, including the remains of a door. Shortly after the family arrives, young Roland begins to show alarming symptoms. It develops that he has heard a wailing sound in the vicinity of the ruins which leaves him physically weak and emotionally shattered. Upon investigating the grounds, Colonel Mortimer also hears this eerie noise, which sounds to him like a plea of a homesick youth crying to be let back into the house. Fearing for the possibly fatal effect of this disturbance upon his sensitive little boy, he is determined to get at the source and rid the neighborhood of it. After various unsuccessful attempts to find the mysterious wanderer or to account for his presence, he summons the minister, Dr. Moncrieff, who has lived in the vicinity for many years. Upon hearing the voice, the minister recognizes it immediately as that of a young man, presumed dead, who had lived on these premises but who had run away from home years before. He gathers that this spirit is trying to make amends belatedly for desertion of his family, and he speaks gently to him, trying to persuade him of the futility of knocking on the door of his former house of which nothing remains and telling him that his mother has long since gone "home" to a distant place where he is now free to seek her out. Apparently placated, the spirit is heard no more and young Roland is restored to health.

Embedded in this strange tale are personal preoccupations never far removed from Mrs. Oliphant's heart—the grief of parents, the erring son. She writes here of a sensitive boy in delicate health, reflecting her constant concern about the health of her own children. Her giving the name Willie to the vagrant, "weak, foolish, easily imposed upon and

'led away,'" who returns as a spirit, indicates how she could wear her heart on her sleeve at times. However, just as she so beautifully transmuted her grief over Maggie's death in *A Beleaguered City*, in **"The Open Door"** she is able to elevate her private sorrows into something close to poetry. The reader is left by this plaintive tale with a haunting sense of that loneliness, alienation, and remorse that fall to the general human lot.

"The Open Door" is generally associated with the later story **"Old Lady Mary"** because the two were republished together in the volume called *Two Stories of the Seen and the Unseen* (1885). Two years separated the original serial publication of the tales, and, for all evidence to the contrary, they may well have been conceived independently of each other. Nevertheless, the stories serve as pendants to one another, **"The Open Door"** being concerned with the efforts of one who is living to alleviate the suffering of a dead person, **"Old Lady Mary"** being concerned with the attempts of a dead person to bring succor to a loved one who has survived her. On the whole, **"Old Lady Mary"** is superior, more deeply moving, warmer and mellower in its pathos, and finer in characterization—qualities, one gathers, that have not commended it to compilers of collections of ghost stories. Its theme is the recurrent one in Mrs. Oliphant's supernatural fiction of the struggle of spiritual beings to 'get through' to earthly ones, but this time the spirit is made palpable; in fact, it is the central character of the story. In this respect **"Old Lady Mary"** is transitional between those supernatural stories already considered that take place on earth, and the dream-vision type, represented by the "Little Pilgrim" series, which depict the voyages of spirits in the after-world.

"She was very old and therefore it was very hard for her to make up her mind to die," begins this tale in a gently foreboding tone. Lady Mary is caught in the situation of Everyman, overtaken by Death summarily and without previous preparation. Her predicament is all the more unfortunate because she is carried off so suddenly that she is unable to make known to her executor the provisions she has made for her young god-daughter and companion who is dependent upon her. However, she is allowed the unusual dispensation of returning to the land of the living in order to rectify this oversight, and her frustrating attempts to make restitution to her god-daughter are the burden of the story.

Lady Mary has much reason to cling to life. She has reached that silver age when all strong emotions have subsided, when pain and sorrow are absorbed into muted memory, and when one is content to sit back as a calm witness of the passing scene. "To passion, to joy, to anguish, an end must come," the author comments, "but mere gentle living, determined by a framework of gentle rules and habits—why should that ever be ended?" In one of the loveliest passages in all her writing, Mrs. Oliphant gives us a composite of Lady Mary's pleasant regimen. Lady Mary has had her share of cares and vexation, youthful vanities and sorrows, but now:

> She had a pretty house full of things which formed a

graceful *entourage* suitable, as she felt, for such a woman as she was, and in which she took pleasure for their own beauty—soft chairs and couches, a fireplace and lights which were the perfection of tempered warmth and illumination. She had a carriage, very comfortable and easy, in which, when the weather was suitable, she went out; and a pretty garden and lawns, in which, when she preferred staying at home, she could have her little walk or sit out under the trees. She had books in plenty, and all the newspapers, and everything that was needful to keep her within the reflection of the busy life which she no longer cared to encounter in her own person. The post rarely brought her painful letters; for all those impassioned interests which bring pain had died out, and the sorrows of others, when they were communicated to her, gave her a luxurious sense of sympathy yet exemption.... She came down-stairs at a certain hour, which she kept to as if it had been of the utmost importance, although it was of no importance at all; she took just so much good wine, so many cups of tea. Her repasts were as regular as clockwork—never too late, never too early. Her whole life went on velvet, rolling smoothly along, without jar or interruption, blameless, pleasant, kind. People talked of her old age as a model of old age, with no bitterness or sourness in it. And, indeed, why should she have been sour or bitter? It suited her far better to be kind. She was in reality kind to everybody, liking to see pleasant faces about her. The poor had no reason to complain of her; her servants were very comfortable; and the one person in her house who was nearer to her own level, who was her companion and most important minister, was very comfortable too.

But the calm balance of Lady Mary's gentle sybaritism is destined to be upset. With all her virtues she has a streak of stubbornness and perversity in her nature which is responsible for her being unprepared for death, although she is over eighty. She refuses to yield to the continued importunings of her lawyer to allow him to draw up her will for her signature. Instead, as a little joke on him, she writes her own will one night, signs it in the presence of two illiterate servants, and hides it in a cabinet. Her intention is to surprise the lawyer by producing this will the next time he broaches the subject. But one winter day she catches a chill while out on a carriage ride and dies suddenly, apparently intestate since she has not confided her prank to anybody.

Lady Mary awakens in a vast, unfamiliar place which she cannot identify, although she recognizes among the strangers here the face of a friend who, she is certain, had died. "'I suppose,'" she inquires of this friend, "'that we are not in—what we have been accustomed to call heaven?'" "'That is a word,'" he replies, "'which expresses rather a condition than a place.'" Lady Mary infers that she is not yet ready for this "condition." In this penitential hall, akin to Dante's Purgatorio, she is stung with remorse for her sins of omission as she realizes that her young companion, whom she knows as little Mary, as well as her servants, are left destitute. She gains permission to return to earth briefly to right her wrong to these people, although warned that the path back is a "dark and dreadful way," and that the journey is likely to be a fruitless one.

We are spared Lady Mary's perilous voyage, picking her up as she arrives one winter day, a lonely spiritual derelict, in her home village. Although she is overjoyed to be back, we soon feel with her a sharp sense of isolation as she recognizes former friends with whom she cannot now establish communication because they are completely unaware of her presence. "It is hard to be left out in the cold when others go into their cheerful houses," Mrs. Oliphant comments, "but to be left thus outside of life, to speak and not to be heard, to stand, unseen, astounded, unable to secure any attention! She had thought they would be frightened, but it was not they who were frightened. A great panic seized the woman who was no more of this world." Lady Mary's return to earth proves to be a journey through the Valley of Humiliation. She must overhear herself upbraided by her former servants for her thoughtlessness without being able to plead her extenuating circumstances. She re-enters her former house to find it now occupied by *nouveaux riches*. Young Mary has been taken in by neighbors until she can find suitable employment. She finds young Mary but is unable to convey any message even to her. However, she does have the deep satisfaction of discovering that her god-daughter, the one she has most wronged, remains faithful to her memory, never once speaking out against her. Ironically, the only character in the story who can see Lady Mary is little Connie, daughter of the new tenants of her house, whom young Mary is hired to tutor. But the child's vision is dismissed as hallucination by the village doctor. In a scene of almost unbearable anguish, Lady Mary tries in vain to reveal herself to her erstwhile ward, but is finally forced to give up in despair:

> "I have failed. What am I that I should do what they all said was impossible? It was my pride, because I have had my own way all my life. But now I have no way and no place on earth, and what I have to tell them will never, never be known. Oh my little Mary a servant in her own house! And a word would make it right! but never, never can she hear that word. I am wrong to say never; she will know when she is in heaven. She will not live to be old and foolish, like me. She will go up there early, and then she will know. But I, what will become of me?—for I am nothing here, and I cannot go back to my own place."

> A little moaning wind rose up suddenly in the dark night, and carried a faint wail, like the voice of some one lost, to the windows of the sleeping house. It woke the children, and Mary, who opened her eyes quickly in the dark, wondering if perhaps the vision might come to her. But the vision had come when she could not see it, and now returned no more.

In time, presumably, justice is done. Some months afterwards, in the course of the removal of Lady Mary's furniture from her old house, the cabinet is opened by some boys: "And there the paper was found in the most natural way, without any trouble or mystery at all." It was far from Mrs. Oliphant's intention to write just another story of secreted wills and their unexpected discovery. Such was the staple of all too much murky sensational fiction at which she had scoffed. God's mysteries are made of subtler stuff, and so the story takes a different turn at its conclusion. Lady Mary, it develops, not her ward, is the principal gainer from her earthly mission. Upon her return "home," one of her companions in the after-life asks her if she has accomplished her goal:

> She had come to herself by this time, and the dark lines were melting from her face. "I am forgiven," she said, with a low cry of happiness. "She whom I wronged loves me and blessed me; we saw each other face to face. I know nothing more."

> "There is no more," said all together. "For everything is included in pardon and love."

One is tempted to read into the description of Lady Mary's round of life before she is taken off an idyll of the kind of old age Mrs. Oliphant herself longed to enjoy; just as the story that follows might be taken as a dramatization of her perpetual fears of leaving her own dependents in a state of poverty. Old Lady Mary in fact had a real-life prototype—a Scotch *grande dame*, "that dear and bright old lady" Mrs. Duncan Stewart, whose London salon in Sloane Street, was often filled with luminaries of the day. Mrs. Oliphant recalls her in a charming sketch in the *Autobiography*. By coincidence, Mrs. Stewart's death occurred shortly after the publication of **"Old Lady Mary"** in *Maga*. "Even in the shock of loss," writes Mrs. Oliphant, "it was impossible not be consoled by the thought of that vivid curiosity and interest and enjoyment with which she would find a new sphere before her, with everything to be found out." Subsequently, when the story was reprinted in *Two Stories of the Seen and the Unseen*, it bore the dedication: "To An Old Lady Ever Young, Harriet Stewart Now Gone Where Youth and Age Are No Distinction."

Mrs. Oliphant achieves a fine balance of tough-mindedness with tender feeling, sophistication with pathos, and affirmation of faith with a sense of man's spiritual limitations.

—*Vineta and Robert A. Colby*

Another Story of the Seen and the Unseen in which a phantom is made palpable is the enigmatic Hawthornesque tale **"Earthbound,"** first published in *Fraser's Magazine* (January 1880). Like many ghost-spirit stories, it has a Christmas connection, beginning at a Christmas party in a country house. However, this is not a gay time for the hosts, the Beresfords, who are in mourning for the death of their young son. The narrative centers on one guest, Edmund Coventry, who is engaged to the Beresfords' daughter Maud. While strolling about the grounds alone, Edmund sees a strange young woman moving lightly along the lime tree walk. From a distance she resembles Maud,

but her dress is old fashioned, suggesting a figure posed for a formal portrait. She disappears as suddenly as she had appeared, and Edmund makes futile inquiries about her throughout the neighborhood. Eventually he meets her again on the walk and this time engages her in conversation. He learns that her name is also Maud, her age a perpetual nineteen. She refers vaguely to having been condemned to remain indefinitely on earth because she had loved it so much. She disappears again, and Edmund confides this conversation to his host, Sir Robert Beresford. A skeptic, Sir Robert has a rational explanation. He shows Edmund an album of portraits of ancestors, among them one done by a pupil of Sir Joshua Reynolds a century earlier which looks exactly like the figure Edmund saw. Sir Robert assumes that Edmund had seen the portrait before and that it had impressed itself on his mind as a vision. Left alone with the portrait as night falls, Edmund kneels before it. Suddenly the subject materializes again. He pleads with her to promise that they will meet again in death if not in life. This she refuses to do, affirming that the future is not at her disposal, but she takes a fond farewell of him. Shortly after, Edmund is found in a coma. In time he recovers and marries Maud Beresford. The other Maud never returns. "Perhaps the time of her willing punishment is over, and she is earthbound no more," the author conjectures.

It is possible to interpret Edmund Coventry's shattering experience, as does Sir Robert, as hallucination. Just what his vision is supposed to signify is not altogether clear, but Mrs. Oliphant has left a clue. The influence of Dante, implicit in most of the *Stories of the Seen and the Unseen*, is explicit in this one. Maud's cryptic words to Edmund are glossed by these lines from Dante:

> Prima vuol ben; ma non lascia il talento
> Che divina giustizia contra voglia,
> Come fù al peccar, pone al tormento. . . .

> (*Purgatorio*, XXI, 64-66)

> It wills indeed before, but is not free
> From that desire, God's justice against will
> Sets, as toward sin once, now to its penalty. . . .

> (Binyon translation)

These are the words addressed to Dante and Virgil by the poet Statius, now on his way to everlasting bliss after having lain for five hundred years in penance, to account for the readiness of penitent sinners in Purgatory to accept what seems unendurable suffering. The desire which formerly inclined them towards sin, Statius explains, is turned in this state of penance towards its expiation. Apparently it is with this in mind that Mrs. Oliphant refers to Maud's "willing punishment." Presumably Edmund, represented earlier as a somewhat callow though sensitive young man, rather "earthbound" too in his love of nature and of the things of this world, goes to his wedding a sadder and a wiser man.

Concurrently with these stories in which dead people return to the world of the living, Mrs. Oliphant wrote a group of fantasies centered on the dead and taking place in the after-world. The central figure of these tales is a gentle, saintly lady whom Mrs. Oliphant called "the Little Pilgrim." After first appearing in various magazines, they were collected in two volumes, *A Little Pilgrim in the Unseen* (1882) and *The Land of Darkness, along with Some Further Chapters in the Experience of the Little Pilgrim* (1888). With an exception to be noted, the Little Pilgrim series is inferior work. In her best writing in this genre, we have observed, Mrs. Oliphant achieves a fine balance of tough-mindedness with tender feeling, sophistication with pathos, and affirmation of faith with a sense of man's spiritual limitations. By contrast, the adventures of the Little Pilgrim soon cloy with an over-sweetness smacking too much of consolation literature. While the various realms through which the Little Pilgrim travels have their obvious parallels in the Inferno, Purgatorio, and Paradiso, Mrs. Oliphant's attempts to give topography to the world beyond the grave merely betray the deficiencies of her imagination. These superterrestrial travels evoke not so much the poems of Dante as the hymns of Adelaide Procter and the stained glass of the Gothic Revival.

A Little Pilgrim in the Unseen, like "Old Lady Mary," had its inception as a tribute to a friend. This was a neighbor called Aunt Nelly by Mrs. Oliphant's sons (she herself refers to the lady as "Little Nelly" in her *Autobiography,* but does not identify her), known for her self-effacing charity to family and friends. "She was far from being wise or clever," Mrs. Oliphant wrote, "generally reputed rather a silly little woman; but with a heart of gold, and a straightforward, simple, right judgment, which was always to me like the clear shining of a tiny light." She later describes Aunt Nelly's "dying in her sleep without so much as the movement of a finger," just such an easy passing away as is experienced by her fictional counterpart. When the story was published in book form, Mrs. Oliphant spoke of it in the dedication as "little more than a wistful attempt to follow a gentle soul which never knew doubt into the New World, and to catch a glimpse of something of its glory through her simple and child-like eyes."

The adventures of this innocent in the New World demonstrate that the pure in heart will see God and remind us that nothing evil can happen to a good person. Our sympathies are enlisted for the fate of proud Old Lady Mary as she is progressively humbled, but the Little Pilgrim is already among the saved when she arrives in the upper regions; therefore little distance remains, spiritually, for her to travel. As a result, her journey through the afterworld turns out to be an extended and monotonous anthem in praise of the Almighty, as she brings solace to various sinners and sufferers, is accompanied into Heaven by the Lady Ama, and becomes herself a welcoming angel to the newly arrived souls released from earthly bondage.

This apotheosis of Aunt Nelly was obviously intended to confirm the pious in their faith and to bring comfort to the

aggrieved, but it becomes evident in places that it served Mrs. Oliphant as a personal catharsis also. In one episode early in her adventures, the Little Pilgrim meets an apparition in the form of a child and holds a conversation with her:

> "Are you a child?" said the Little Pilgrim, "or are you an angel? Sometimes you are like a child; but then your face shines and you are like—You must have some name for it here; there is nothing among the words I know." And then she paused a little still looking at her, and cried, "Oh, if she [the Little Pilgrim's friend on earth] could but see you, little Margaret! That would do her most good of all."

> Then the maiden shook her lovely head: "What does her most good is the will of the Father," she said.

Just as she places her dead daughter among the angels, Mrs. Oliphant finds a place for her unfortunate late husband within Heaven's many mansions. In the second part, called **"The Little Pilgrim Goes Up Higher,"** the Little Pilgrim, having been brought into the presence of the Father, wanders about the Holy City and there meets a painter. He is apologetic about his limitations, telling her that he gains his satisfaction from drawing figures for a greater master who fills in the faces and endows them with life. One's own work always falls short of one's ambitions, the artist explains, "whereas in your master's work you have full content, because his idea goes beyond yours, and as he makes every touch, you can feel 'that is right—that is complete—that is just as it ought to be.'" If this is intended as Francis Oliphant's reconciliation to his failure on earth, perhaps here too Mrs. Oliphant offers her own apologia for the literary artist whose reach exceeds his grasp.

A Little Pilgrim was among the most popular of Mrs. Oliphant's books. Macmillan printed over 20,000 copies—a considerable figure for that time. It was frequently reprinted in America. Obviously feeling that this record warranted a return engagement, Mrs. Oliphant wrote to Macmillan's editor George Lillie Craik three years after its original publication to ask if he was willing to bring out a second series. This is the first we hear of the sequel volume, published in 1888—something of a hodgepodge made up of three magazine pieces, **"The Land of Darkness," "The Little Pilgrim in the Seen and the Unseen,"** and **"On the Dark Mountains."** After what has been said, a modern reader may feel that he has had a sufficiency of Aunt Nelly, alias the Little Pilgrim. However, as with many a greater writer, sin challenged Mrs. Oliphant's imagination more than virtue could. As a result, **"The Land of Darkness,"** which begins this volume, stands out in stark contrast to the inanity of the rest of it. A macabre fantasy, the nightmare that offsets the dream vision to follow, it is a chilling picture of human degeneration and evil that anticipates some contemporary dystopias. "I found myself standing on my feet, with the tingling sensation of having come down rapidly upon the ground from a height," begins the unidentified narrator. "There was a similar feeling in my head, as of the whirling and sickening sensation of passing downward through the air, like the description Dante gives of his descent upon Geryon. . . ." Mrs. Oliphant clearly intends this as her version of the Inferno, but the woes of this Land of Darkness stem from modern spiritual ills. We accompany the narrator through a busy, populous city which proves to be a kind of Beleaguered City without hope of redemption. In this diabolical metropolis, each man is sufficient unto himself. Traffic moves along at a dizzy pace without regulation. People greet each other and part company with curses instead of "hello" and "goodbye." To see a sick wretch lying in the street is to make one take satisfaction in his own health rather than pity on the sufferer.

At times this Land of Darkness, intoxicated with science and technology, seems like a forerunner of Aldous Huxley's Brave New World. At other times it is a Kafkaesque world of unmotivated brutality and imprisonment. The narrator, seeking escape, comes to the startling discovery that he is really trying to run away from himself. Hell, we soon realize, is humanity purged of morality and affection, knowledge pursued to no end or purpose, art and beauty debased by materialism, perpetual desire and dissatisfaction. After a number of harrowing adventures, this sufferer eventually succeeds in wresting himself free from the city—or state of mind—of aimless hedonism and endless torment.

The connection of **"The Land of Darkness"** with the Little Pilgrim series is tenuous. A brief epilogue explains that it does not belong to the adventures of the Little Pilgrim as such, but "is drawn from the Archives in the Heavenly City, where all the records of the human race are laid up," and is included to give the reader a full understanding of her experience. What follows, as we expect, is the presentation af the blissful state of the saved in contrast to the despair of the damned. The Little Pilgrim briefly returns to earth, her wish being granted to become an emissary to the grief-stricken who are left behind. She learns that God forgets nobody, not even sinners, so that the Way is always open. In the concluding portion of her adventures, called **"On the Dark Mountain,"** she becomes a guide to those stumbling on the stony peak that leads heavenwards, helping those who have managed to struggle out of the Land of Darkness to make their painful journey into the Light. In what is perhaps intended as a symbolic self-effacement, Mrs. Oliphant indicates that one of the travellers supported by the Little Pilgrim has come from the City of Art, where men have wrought everything in beauty only to find that the aesthetic life leads to vanity, greed, and discontent.

Considered out of their time, Mrs. Oliphant's stories of the supernatural are striking fables of the unsatisfied yearnings of the spirit and of the frustrations of communication between human beings. In their own age they were part of the religious ambience that included the Dante Revival, the Oxford Movement, and Ritualism, making their modest contribution to the protest against an emergent scientism. *The Stories of the Seen and the Unseen* assert the power of the mysterious and the supra-rational in the face of those who sought to or claimed to be able to bring all

phenomena within the realm of the knowable. The central characters of her supernatural stories struggle with various degrees of success to free themselves from imprisonment in the world of the senses. Their difficulties lie typically in trying to reach others through "non-conductors"—mists, darkness, thick foliage, stone walls—suggesting that Mrs. Oliphant was well aware of the new discoveries in physics concerning light waves and sound waves and optical and aural illusions. But telepathic rather than telegraphic communication was what preoccupied her—the *cor ad cor loquitur* which penetrates the most impermeable of media. In this respect, *A Beleaguered City*, **"Old Lady Mary,"** and the other tales of this group reflect the spiritualism that swept over England during the 1880's and 1890's. The breakdown of traditional faith, along with dissatisfaction with "rational" explanations of phenomena undeniably contributed to the theosophical societies, "miracle clubs," Swedenborg and Madame Blavatsky circles that burgeoned during this period. It was an age when, as a literary historian has recently remarked, "those who felt that Christianity was almost bankrupt turned eagerly to the study of Eastern philosophies and to the exploration of occult forces of all kinds." In this period of disruption and ferment, Mrs. Oliphant, rather than turning to new religions, clung to the old one.

Douglas Gifford (essay date 1971)

SOURCE: Introduction to *Scottish Short Stories, 1800-1900*, edited by Douglas Gifford, Calder & Boyars, 1971, pp. 12-13.

[*In the following excerpt, Gifford gives a brief analysis of "The Library Window."*]

Margaret Oliphant's **"The Library Window"** is a deceptively slight story. At first it seems close to James's *Turn of the Screw* in method; but it becomes even more disturbing and demoniac on reflection, and its links are rather with the ambiguity of *Wandering Willie's Tale* or Hogg's frequent tales with dual interpretations.

On one level, it is almost a modern version of the good fairy, bad fairy tales; with Aunt Mary set against Lady Carnbee. There is an implication that Lady Carnbee, while ironically protesting her youthful virtue, is that evil woman who has caused the death of the young man who now haunts the library. And Lady Carnbee is frequently alluded to by the girl as a witch; she has darker knowledge of the window's history, she "bewitches" the girl, and her diamond stings, or blazes in malediction. At this level, the story takes place "between the night and the day, when the fairy folk have power", and Lady Carnbee passes on the curse of her guilt to the girl. But Aunt Mary too has deeper knowledge than she reveals, and shares the girl's pain, bonding them in the phrase "women of our blood", recognising the spell, banishing it temporarily with her murmured "like a dream when one awaketh", which turns the window blank again. And to round out this fairy-tale aspect, the girl himself, being pure in her love, awakes the writing figure and by communicating with him, breaks the curse and sees him no more. Only the ring, malignant, remains. And on this level, the theme of guilt, together with a slighter demonism, runs through the story.

But on another level, the story is about a feverish and over-imaginative young girl who *creates* her dream world—the figure of the poet is obviously an idealisation of an unattainable love. The older folk are thus merely people who remember or don't remember the heartsickness of youth; who sympathise with the delusions of a sick girl. Thus the story is exactly like Hogg's *Justified Sinner* where the sinner may actually meet the devil, or may merely create him.

Whatever the interpretation we put on the story—and I think both are intended—the relationship with the themes of the major Scottish fiction is still apparent. Excessive imagination and sensitivity, demonism, and on the other hand worldly folk who refuse to share dreams but, like Aunt Mary or Mr. Pitmilly, retreat behind the *Times* to forget them for the news of the world—however slightly presented, these are the elements of the major fiction.

Robert and Vineta Colby (essay date 1979)

SOURCE: "Mrs. Oliphant's Scotland: The Romance and the Reality," in *Nineteenth-Century Scottish Fiction,* edited by Ian Campbell, Barnes & Noble Books, 1979, pp. 89-103.

[*In this essay, Robert and Vineta Colby discuss Oliphant's mission to educate her readers to the ways of Scottish life in her stories and novels.*]

> The wandering Scot, patriotic and energetic, pushing his fortunes at the ends of the earth, canny and practical, yet moved always by the memory of his old home, is a familiar figure in the real life of experience and in the imaginary life of literature.
>
> Lionel Johnson, "R. L. Stevenson",
>
> *The Academy,* 3 June 1893

In a literal sense Margaret Oliphant (1828-1897) was a "wandering Scot". She left the land of her birth at about the age of ten, returned in 1860 as a struggling young widow to live in Edinburgh for less than a year, and thereafter knew Scotland only as a visitor on business and summer holidays. No doubt a good measure of her devotion to Scotland was as practical as it was sentimental. Working throughout her life under almost incredible financial pressures and family responsibilities, she exploited her native land as marketable literary material. It was by natural right her heritage; and the post-Sir Walter Scott revival of interest in Scottish history and culture that came with Queen Victoria's choice of Balmoral for her summer retreats made it a likely source for Mrs. Oliphant to tap, turning her knowledge and experience (much of them acquired not at first-hand but from her Scottish mother to

whom she was devoted) into articles and books.

More important—Scotland fired her imagination. Though remote, it was alive with subjects that appealed to her. Family-minded, a dedicated mother with a fierce loyalty to all her kin, she found in the close ties and strong matriarchal figures of the Scottish family a source of personal as well as artistic inspiration. Scotland stimulated her highly developed sense of history, and most of her Scottish novels, from the early *Katie Stewart* to the late *Kirsteen,* are set in the past. It offered colourful personalities—the strongly individualistic, ruggedly independent characters, eccentric, sometimes comic, almost always sympathetic, that she found in Walter Scott and John Galt. Although Mrs. Oliphant's public image was strictly proper and conventional, we know from her letters and autobiography that she was an independent thinker who always had a lurking admiration for non-conformists and rebels. And finally, Scotland offered a spiritual appeal. Not herself drawn to superstition or spiritualism, she nevertheless was fascinated by Scottish folklore and legends.

The portrait medallion of Mrs. Oliphant in St. Giles' Cathedral in Edinburgh is inscribed: "That we may remember her genius and power as a novelist, biographer, essayist and historian"—a tribute to her literary fertility and versatility. In all these *genres* Scotland figures prominently from the beginning of her career to the end. She made her debut as a novelist at the age of twenty-one with a feigned memoir of a pious spinster "of discreet years and small riches", *Passages in the Life of Mrs. Margaret Maitland of Sunnyside* (1849). Her first contribution to *Blackwood's Magazine* was *Katie Stewart* (1852), a short fictional reminiscence of the days of Bonnie Prince Charlie. John Knox is depicted in her early historical novel *Magdalen Hepburn: A Story of the Scottish Reformation* (1854). From a long list spread out over four more decades such titles as *The Laird of Norlaw* (1858), *A Son of the Soil* (1866), *The Minister's Wife* (1869), *The Primrose Path: A Chapter in the Annals of the Kingdom of Fife* (1878), *It Was a Lover and His Lass* (1883), *The Wizard's Son* (1884), *Effie Ogilvie* (1886), *Kirsteen* (1890), and *That Little Cutty* (1898), reflect a continuing and complex relationship to the home of her ancestors.

Furthermore, as a biographer Mrs. Oliphant produced studies of important Scottish theologians and religious leaders—Edward Irving, Thomas Chalmers, Principal John Tulloch. Among her historico-travel books is *Royal Edinburgh: Her Saints, Kings, Prophets, and Poets* (1890); and one of her last books was *A Child's History of Scotland* (1895). As a reviewer for numerous magazines she grappled with important historical, religious, and polemical works by Scottish writers of the order of John Hill Burton, Dean Ramsay, John Stuart Blackie, the Rev. Robert Story, and Lord Archibald Campbell. The most tangible evidence of her attachment to her native land was her life-long relationship with the firm of William Blackwood and Sons, the most enduring of a career which brought her into business association (not always on the best of terms) with many other publishers, British and American. She worked for several generations of Blackwoods—as writer, reviewer, editor, manuscript reader, adviser (sometimes her advice was unsolicited but she gave it), and finally as their historian, reading proof for her *Annals of a Publishing House* (1897) on her deathbed. Her career indeed encompassed nineteenth-century literary Scotland. She was nurtured on Scott and Galt. As a girl she was tended by the physician-writer David Macbeth Moir ("Delta"). In her youth she met Christopher North. As an established writer she helped George MacDonald to get his first novel published. She interviewed Carlyle while she was at work on her biography of Edward Irving ("I bearded the lion in his den," as she phrased it). In 1849 that formidable critic Francis Jeffrey had hailed the author of *Margaret Maitland* as a fresh new voice; in her last years she in turn saluted two promising young Scottish writers—Robert Louis Stevenson and James M. Barrie.

It is, unfortunately, for quantity rather than quality that Mrs. Oliphant is remembered. Her ironic gift of facility in words, "that strange faculty of expression—which is as independent of education, knowledge, or culture as any wandering angel"—which produced 125 books and innumerable periodical articles and enough income to support a dying husband, two improvident brothers, two brilliant but unlucky young sons, a nephew, a houseful of nieces and cousins, and a fairly high personal standard of living—also produced a cynical and embittered woman who was forced to acknowledge early in her life that whatever talents she had would be compromised and traded off in an unfair deal with life: "It has been my fate in a long life of production", she wrote in 1892, "to be credited chiefly with the equivocal virtue of industry, a quality so excellent in morals, so little satisfactory in art" (Preface to *The Heir Presumptive and the Heir Apparent*).

Whether we read Mrs. Oliphant as a Scottish writer or an English writer we must recognise in her work the dominating presence of what, in quite another context, Matthew Arnold called "the personal estimate". Out of her massive bibliography the work that remains the most beautiful and moving is her posthumously published *Autobiography and Letters* (1898), written and carefully filed away to pay off her debts and provide for her dependents. It is her best work because it is an expression of the heart, full of flashes of wit, shrewd intelligence, the ability to catch the essence of a personality or a scene, and her endless grace and facility of language. To read Mrs. Oliphant *into* her novels is not the futile and *naïve* exercise it would be with the major Victorian novelists who could transcend themselves in their art. Her life itself was dramatic, even tragic, offering better material than any plot she ever devised. And her imagination, if not of the highest order of creativity, was lively. She was in fact a novelist by default. She never wanted to be one; she admitted that she preferred writing biography and criticism she was obliged by circumstances and by the nature of the nineteenth-century novel itself (its popularity, the steady demand for it) to be a novelist, just as she was obliged to capitalise on Scotland, to squeeze every memory and impression until bone dry for whatever charm, interest and information it would offer.

Scotland gave Mrs. Oliphant a pride and distinction that otherwise, being of undistinguished family background with no education or social position, she would not have possessed. As Henry James discerningly observed in an obituary on her in his *London Notes* (August 1897): "She showed in no literary relation more acuteness than in the relation—so profitable a one as it has always been—to the inexhaustible little country which has given so much, yet has ever so much more to give, and all the romance and reality of which she had at the end of her pen. Her Scotch folk have a wealth of life, and I think no Scotch talk in fiction less of a strain to the patience of the profane".

The bulk of her fiction was not regional. The most popular of her works was a semi-sensation novel *Salem Chapel* (1863), one of a series of novels about an imaginary community, Carlingford. The several novels that constitute her obviously Trollope-inspired "Chronicles of Carlingford" are set in a provincial English town. Some of them are delightful social satire (*Phoebe Jr., The Perpetual Curate, Miss Marjoribanks*), but they were ephemeral, quickly overshadowed by the competition of Collins, Dickens, Mrs. Henry Wood (from whose *East Lynne* she borrowed several details for *Salem Chapel*). Oddly enough, some of her Scottish novels, though written more from memory than observation and carefully tailored to the demands of the marketplace, survive the erosion of time better—perhaps because their regional details give them freshness and colour. Apart from Susan Ferrier, who until recently has been even more neglected than Mrs. Oliphant, she is the only woman novelist whose pictures of Scottish life are today remembered. Although she refreshed her memory by trips to Scotland, she was not writing out of the immediate experience that shapes the genuine regional novelist. Hers is a mixture of purely cerebral knowledge and sentiment—family pride based on a dim connection with the ancient Oliphants of Kellie in Fife, who traced their lineage back to The Bruce, and a kind of misty-eyed tribute to her warm-hearted, sharp-tongued Scottish mother.

Mrs. Oliphant's Scottish novels, no less than much other Victorian fiction, could be characterised as "novels with a purpose"—a purpose never very adroitly concealed and occasionally bobbing to the surface. In one of the last, *Kirsteen,* which looks back like *Vanity Fair* to the "teens" of the century—the turbulent times between Elba and Waterloo—she refers to another altercation, "the standing feud between Scotch and English, and the anger and jealousy with which the richer regarded the invasions of the poorer . . ." (Ch. XXIII). Among the ordeals endured by the courageous young heroine of this novel (who has left her native Argyllshire to seek her livelihood in London) are the taunts of her new compatriots: "Fierce jests about the Scotch who came to make their fortune off their richer neighbours, about their clannishness and their canniness, and their poverty and their pride, and still lower and coarser jibes about their supposed peculiarities . . ." Whether or not Mrs. Oliphant was recalling her own experience as expatriate, she exerts one of her self-imposed functions as novelist—to set the Sassenachs straight about their kin north of the Tweed.

Actually the novels transfer to the realm of fiction a campaign she conducted intermittently through the pages of *Maga* to break down what she regarded as *naïve* stereotypes retained by English readers about Scotland and the Scottish people based on prejudice or on accounts by unreliable witnesses. "There are few subjects of study so interesting and pictures que as that of national character . . . There is so much attraction in this kind of study, that everybody dabbles in it more or less", she wrote in an article in 1860, "and even harmless tourists who have had a summer's holiday in Switzerland feel themselves warranted henceforward to deliver verdicts upon the 'character of the people'". The book she was reviewing, *Reminiscences of Scottish Life and Character,* by E. B. Ramsay, Dean of Edinburgh, established her point that only one born and bred in Scotland can really speak for its "natural character", that there can be no substitute for "intercourse of people who have the gift of eyesight, without having added thereto the dangerous advantage of that traveller's pen, of which haste and exaggeration are the attendant sprites". Hard as she could be on the Cook's Tour pundit hot for "beauties" and quaintness, she was no less scornful of a scholar like the historian Buckle who, "instead of seeking his evidence in the golden Lothians, headquarters and stronghold of superstition as they are . . . has found a safer and less troublesome field of observation in the British Museum", from which he documents his characterisation of the Scottish people as self-mortifying ascetics. She was equally unhappy with the caricature perpetuated by hack English journalists of "a nation of adventurers, bound upon getting all the good things that come within their reach, and not at all over-scrupulous as to the means by which they obtain them . . . high cheek-boned, red-haired—covetous, but enterprising . . ."

It may be true, as Stevenson observed, that being born in Scotland does not guarantee one's looking good in a kilt, but Mrs. Oliphant seems to have assumed that being born in Musselburgh gave her a special *cachet* as cultural ambassador from Midlothian. Populariser of learning and mediator of issues of the day to readers of *Maga* for nearly half a century (1852-1897), the role of preceptress came as easily to Mrs. Oliphant as it had to her Mistress Margaret Maitland. Along with such recondite interests as Italian poetry and the French monastic revival, she early turned her attention to what she called "the national heart" of her own people.

In one of her reviews Mrs. Oliphant commended the historian John Hill Burton for his factual approach to Scotland's past, his scrupulousness with evidence, rejecting legend and antiquarian lore. With her own passion for fact, her sense of her audience nevertheless did not allow her to let slip the opportunity offered by her native land as "a field of amusing and picturesque observation first opened by Sir Walter". As early as *Adam Graeme of Mossgray* (1852) she was recognised for her "admirable pictures of Scottish life and scenery".

In an early historical novel, *Magdelen Hepburn,* she strains after the picturesque in this so-called "grand scene" that begins a chapter:

Grey and muffled in the morning mist, like some ancient mariner watching by the sea, North Berwick Law lowered dimly into the white haze which overspread the Firth. Still and dreaming by its foot, the fisher cottages sent up no household smoke, gave forth no household sounds upon the unawakened morn (Ch. VII).

Not so self-consciously grandiose and more akin to genre painting is this setting for Kellie Mill in *Katie Stewart:*

The mill lay at the opening of a little uncultivated, primitive-looking valley, through which the burn wound in many a silvery link between banks of bare grass, browned here and there with full sunshine which fell over it all the summer through, unshaded by a single tree (Ch. I).

She had an eye for landscape but was convinced that "readers prefer people to trees", as she remarked in one of her omnibus reviews of fiction for *Maga*. Accordingly she laid stress on the figures in the landscape. "Few countries, perhaps, have been placed in a position so well adapted for the development of *character,* as distinguished from merely intellectual gifts or outside customs, as this our kingdom of Scotland, ancient, hardy, pugnacious, and poor . . ." she declared in her review of Dean Ramsay's domestic history. Her Scottish novels, in line with this conviction, might well have been subtitled in a way familiar to Victorian readers, "Illustrations of Scottish Character".

Author of a book called *Dress* (in MacMillan's *Art at Home Series,* 1876), Mrs. Oliphant never neglected to clothe her figures carefully. We learn what Mistress Margaret Maitland wore at her nieces' wedding: "I was laying by my gown (it was silk, of a silvery gray colour, like the bark of a beech tree, and was the same as Mary, my sister's—we had both got them from Edinburgh for the occasion . . .)" (Ch. XXII). Katie Stewart and her sisters "are all dressed in a very primitive style, in home-made linen, with broad blue and white stripes; and their frocks are made in much the same form as the modern pinafore" (Ch. I). In her late novel *Kirsteen,* where the heroine becomes a professional mantua maker, she early practises her skill by indulging her father's aristocratic taste for fine linen: "Kirsteen's hemming was almost invisible, so small were the stitches and the thread so delicate. She was accomplished with her needle according to the formula of that day" (Ch. VII).

Intent on her mission of educating readers to the ways of Scottish, life, Mrs. Oliphant furnishes houses, calls attention to matters of etiquette, sometimes to quaint customs. Her best gifts, however, were displayed more in her appeals to the ear than to the eye. Her attempts to recover archaic speech in her historical novels could be as stilted as those of G. P. R. James whom she was undoubtedly emulating ("'You maun e'en do your war yourself, boy, if words are the weapons . . . My day of sword and buckler is well nigh ended, but none shall say of Roger of Lammerstane that he left a knight's arms for a priest's . . . '") (*Magdalen Hepburn,* Ch. I). But she could also render colloquial Scots speech with a ring authentic-sounding at least to outsiders:

> But matrimony is an honourable estate, Miss Margret
> . . . in especial with a licentiate—I am meaning with
> a placed minister of the Kirk. The leddy of a minister
> may haud up her head with any leddy of the land, and
> you ken it is far otherwise with a single woman, living
> her lee-lane in the world . . . (*Margaret Maitland*, Ch.
> XXII).

> He's maybe no' a' that folk could desire, this king, but
> he's a decent man, sae far as I can hear; and anyway,
> he's better than a Papish. Onything's better than a
> Papish. (*Katie Stewart*, Ch. XXII)

> No that I mean to say I believe in fate . . . though there
> is little doubt in my mind that what happens is
> ordained. I couldna tell why, for my part, though I
> believe in the fact—for most things in life come to
> nothing, and the grandest train of causes produce nae
> effect whatsoever; that's my experience (*A Son of the
> Soil*, Ch. VI).

Such externals help to vivify Mrs. Oliphant's people and
scenes, but her main interest was in personifying "Scottish National Character". She manages to do this at times
even in her polemical journalism, especially when she
domesticates Anglo-Scottish relations—poor Scotland
"always dwelling next door to the rich brother, who vexed
her soul with ostentatious display of his greater wealth",
until she is compelled to fall back on "the pride and brag
of a poor gentlewoman wrapping herself in her pinched
cloak in self-defending bitterness, while her plump neighbour laughs beside her, full and lavish, mocking the pomp
of poverty". Elsewhere she likens the uneasy union of the
two countries to a marriage in which the husband, while
loving his wife, enjoys casting aspersions on her ancestors and relatives.

Largely defences of Scotland's people and traditions, Mrs.
Oliphant's Scottish novels are not belligerent in tone but
tend to make virtue out of necessity, stressing the strength
of character that has grown out of the poverty and inferior
position to which, she believed, the Scottish nation had
been traditionally reduced. What survived and endured
was Scottish piety, pride, and resourcefulness, centered
most strikingly in the institutions of the Family and the
Church, representing a kind of collective Scottish consciousness exemplified. "How real, how living, are our old
fathers and mothers in their old Scotland younder, so
much poorer a Scotland than it was in our days!" she
wrote in *Maga*. "We cannot imitate them; but the only
way to preserve the distinct character of our country, as
of every other, lies in the truth, reality, and spontaneous
nature of individual life".

One of the "distinct character" types she brings to life is
the Scottish spinster, to whom she pays special tribute in
her essay on "Scottish National Character":

> In no other region has the genus 'old-maid' developed
> itself so notably . . . These were not the gentle souls

of modern romance, benign sufferers from some
youthful disappointment, spending their placid lives in
recollection of a lost love . . . So far from conceiving
themselves set apart into such a mild twilight of
retirement by their unwedded condition, this class of
celibates behaved themselves with great energy and
emphasis in the world, and have worked their
reminiscences into the history of their time with a
force and clearness not to be surpassed.

In a humbler sphere are Marg'ret Brown, the stoical, resourceful servant who comforts Kirsteen Douglas in her
family distress and stands by her during her "exile" in
London, and Marg'ret's sister Jean, who employs Kirsteen
in her London shop. But the prototype of the spinster-
matron in Mrs. Oliphant's fiction is Mistress Margaret
Maitland, an old maid by choice, content with her "lone
tabernacle at Sunnyside". She has refused one suitor
because his principles were not of the strictest. (Mistress
Maitland comes from a clerical family, her father, brother,
and nephew all ministers.) A far remove from "the gentle
souls of modern romance, benign sufferers from some
youthful disappointment, spending their placid lives in
recollection of a lost love", this spinster heroine is distinguished for her mental energy, spark and independence.
She has had some formal education, befitting her social
rank, "with a Miss Scrymgeour, a discreet gentlewoman,
who kept a genteel school for young ladies, to learn
divers things that were thought needful in those days,
and also how to behave myself in polite society", but
adds candidly that "I aye found the breeding of the Manse
of Pasturelands to serve me better than what I got in the
school at Edinburgh" (Ch. I). She seems to lean heavily on
native wisdom in her capacity as mentor to the young (in
the tradition of the didactic novels of the time), and she
guides her two young nieces into suitable marriages.

The wise Scottish spinster had her fictional uses and her
charms, but essentially Mrs. Oliphant's sympathies were
with the matron-mother: "Capable women, unswayable by
circumstances, queens of their position—imperative Spartan mothers, sparing of indulgence, willing their own will
and having it . . . knowing neither age nor weakness when
succour was needed, brave to do all and bear all". In her
Autobiography she was to memorialise her own mother,
who had kept the household together, as "all in all".
Significantly Mistress Maitland recalls of her mother: "Truly
she was of a most uncommon spirit, being more like a
lanthorn holding a great light than any other thing; for she
was gifted with a mind that drew others to it, as the load-
stone that bairns play with draws the needle . . ." (Ch. I).

The mother keeps the fires burning in Mrs. Oliphant's
Scottish households where fathers tend to be either absent or silent. Katie Stewart's mother,

> a little fair-haired woman, rather stout nowadays, but
> a beauty once, and with the pretty short-gown, held
> in round her neat waist by a clean linen apron, and her
> animated face, looked yet exceedingly well, and
> vindicated completely her claim to be the fountain-
> head and original of the beauty of her children (*Katie

Stewart, Ch. I).

She is "absolute sovereign of Kellie Mill". (There is a father named John, but "muckle he kens about the role o' a household", Mrs. Stewart says [Ch. VIII].) As quintessential mother, she upholds the traditional rural virtues. She is torn between family pride and ambition for her daughter as she confronts Lady Betty Erskine who has invited Katie to be part of the retinue at Kellie Castle:

> "You see, my lady, we have nae occasion to be indebted to onybody for the upbringing of our bairns. My man, I am thankful to say, is a decent man, and a well-doing, and if we're spared, we'll have something to leave to them that come after us; but I dinna dispute the advantage of being brocht up at the Castle. The Castle's ae thing, the mill's anither . . .".

However, she lays down her conditions firmly:

> "She mustna be learned to lightly her ain friends—they're a creditable kind no better than . . . her ain sisters. She's to come to the mill aye when she can win, to keep her frae pride she has nae right to . . . And she's to get to the kirk . . . She's at no hand to gang down to Pittenweem, to the English chapel; I couldna suffer that . . . And she's to get nae questions but the right question book. It's easy bending the minds of bairns, and I canna have her turned to the English way, my lady" (Ch. II).

An especially memorable figure is Jeannie Campbell, a farmer's wife, mother of the idealistic young minister Colin of *A Son of the Soil.* Unlike some of the Spartan matriarchs who dominate Mrs. Oliphant's hearths, she is outwardly delicate, "gentle-voiced", with "soft, dark, beaming eyes . . . the softest pink flush coming and going over her face . . .", but she is buttressed from within by her strong will and her faith. This "mistress of Ramore Farm" encourages her son's intellectual aspirations: "I hear there's some grand schools in England . . . no that they're to compare wi' Edinburgh", she inquires at the beginning of the novel of a wealthy young friend of Colin's who has been to Eton; "You'll be at ane o' the great schools, I suppose? I aye like to learn what I can when there's ony opportunity. I would like my Colin to get a' the advantages, for he's well worthy o' a good education, though we're rather out of the way of it here" (Ch. I). Colin goes on to university (first to Glasgow, later to Oxford), with the predictable result that he becomes filled with immortal longings somehow not satisfied in Ramore. Most touching is Mrs. Campbell's perplexity, "pondering with a troubled countenance upon this new aspect of her boy's life. Amid the darkness of the world outside, this tender woman sat in the sober radiance of her domestic hearth, surrounded and enshrined by light; but she was not like Hero on the tower" (Ch. XII). The greatest upset to her is Colin's momentary doubt as to his vocation for the ministry; and she tries to call him back to a fundamental faith: "Eh, Colin, sometime ye'll think better . . . after a' our pride in

you and our hopes! . . . It's mair honour to serve God than to get on in this world . . . It's maybe nothing but a passing fancy—but it's no what I expected to hear from any bairn of mine . . ." (Ch. XII).

"What life, what force, what a flood of vital power!" proclaimed Mrs. Oliphant of the daughters of Scotland, a country noteworthy, she contended, for women "not of genius but of character". Women tend to dominate her novels, but to at least one class of men—the clergy, and especially the Scottish clergy—she allotted a share of sensitivity and wisdom. In one of her essay-reviews she observes that whereas the French *curé* and the Italian monk figure frequently in fiction and travel diaries, "the Scotch minister has, almost up to the present time, been a personage almost as unknown in England as is the unpolemical priest of a Catholic country, unfretted by heresy, and calm in his own established rights and duties". Here she identifies another "distinct character" who emerges in her fiction.

The minister as a presence in Scottish society is related to larger religious controversies in which Mrs. Oliphant became engaged through her journalism. "There is a great deal of bad taste, to use the lightest expression, in the attitude assumed by English Churchmen generally towards the Church of Scotland", she complained in one of her reviews in *Maga.* On religious as well as secular questions Mrs. Oliphant acted as something of a national apologist. The Church of Scotland, in particular, was a subject of lively interest during the 1850s and '60s when the best of her Scottish novels were written, the Free Kirk movement of 1843 having taken place within the recent memory of many of her readers. In *The Minister's Wife,* published in 1869 but looking back to the time when Edward Irving's influence had been strong, she takes her readers inside a Kirk Session, which she reminds them was "the vestry, the guardians, the churchwardens of a Scotch parish all in one . . . And at the period of which we write, before any great rent had been made in the Church of Scotland, its authority was real and considerable" (I, Ch. XI). Earlier on, Mistress Maitland had made veiled reference to this "rent", her own family having been involved:

> . . . it is not my purpose to speak of the solemn and great things of the Kirk in a simple history like this . . . But my brother, the Minister, and Claud, my nephew, and many of their brethren . . . left their temporal providing at the appointed time, and came out with the pure and free Kirk into the wilderness; for who would heed to green pastures and still waters, if the light of the Lord's countenance was lifted away? (Ch. XXII).

Her nephew Claud adopts an ecumenical attitude towards this disruption (echoing, one suspects, Mrs. Oliphant's own): "Certainly I hold leaving the church, and leaving the establishment, to be two very different things; but the servants of the church are not confined to one locality. I may serve my Master as well in another place" (Ch. XXII).

With *A Son of the Soil* a new generation has superseded

the old:

> When Sunday morning dawned upon the Holy Loch, it did not shine upon that pretty unanimous church-going so well known to the history of the past. The groups from the cottages took different ways . . . The reign of opinion and liking was established in the once primitive community. Half of the people ascended the hillside to the Free Church, while the others wound down the side of the Loch to the Kirk, which had once accommodated the whole parish (Ch. III).

Through the hero Colin Campbell, who comes of age in this period of transition, a part of "the advanced party, the Young Scotland of his time", we get one of Mrs. Oliphant's most searching fictional inquiries into the nature of the minister's vocation—its conflicts, frustrations, and rewards.

Son of a farming family, poor but proud, Colin is the archetypal minister of the Church of Scotland as Mrs. Oliphant represents it—humble in origin and of the people. With his sensitivity and idealism, his ambition to "be a prince in his own country without, at the same time, following anything for his own glory or advantage", he answers to her characterisation of its ministry as "pervasive and profound . . . [in] its influence—working, as every good agency works, not always to the glory of the instrument, but through many disappointments and trials, to the benefit and improvement of the country". Young Colin has his share of "disappointments and trials", including a romantic infatuation for an aristocrat who spurns him for one of her own class, and a certain disenchantment with his home parish after travel to Italy and a taste of the intellectual atmosphere of Balliol College. Mainly, like a number of Mrs. Oliphant's young clergymen, he is beset with doubts as to his calling. "If I cannot bear the yoke conscientiously I cannot bear it at all", he protests in a moment of pique to his sceptical friend Lauderdale; ". . . and as for ambition . . . what does it mean?—a country church, and two or three hundred ploughmen to criticise me, and the old wives to keep in good humour, and the young ones to drink tea with—is that work for a man?" (Ch. XLVI). His greatest trial derives from the very democratic nature of the Church of Scotland—his being subjected to "the bar of the presbytery". He makes his initial appearance in the pulpit in the parish of Afton "not to instruct the congregation, but to be inspected, watched, judged, and finally objected to" (Ch. XLV). At a crucial moment he is struck with a "sudden sense of incapacity", preaching his sermon "with pale lips and a heart out of which all the courage seemed to have died for the moment" (Ch. XLVI).

Eventually Colin weathers this crisis. At first distrusted by his congregation for his lofty ideas and his English university background, he is finally accepted, and settles into the quiet round of a rural ministry. It is possible to read Colin's history as a tale of disillusionment—his discovery, as the narrator puts it, of "the impossibility of the fundamental romance which at the bottom of their hearts most people like to believe in". But at the same time we are left

to infer also that Colin's self-doubts, questionings, and spiritual pains (and a less than happy marriage) may have made him all the more fit for his calling in a religious society grown unsure of itself but still in need of guidance. "You'll no make Scotland of your way of thinking, Colin", his friend and tutor consoles him, "but you'll make it worth her while to have brought ye forth for a' that" (Ch. XLV). After his ordeal Colin discovers that "he had begun to stretch out hands for his tools almost without knowing it, and to find that, after all, a man in a pulpit, although he has two flights to ascend to it, has a certain power in his hand" (Ch. XLVI). Mrs. Oliphant herself concluded her article "Clerical Life in Scotland": "The pastor of the poor, himself not rich, may link the peasants in the highest bonds of Christian friendship and kindness with the great and gifted".

With fictional heroes like Colin Campbell and Arthur Vincent of *Salem Chapel*, Mrs. Oliphant came as close as ever she could to portraying a complex, conflicted character caught in the struggle between intellect and emotion. As a novelist she almost but never quite succeeded in creating a tragic hero. But in a single work of biography, her *Life of Edward Irving, Minister of the National Scotch Church, London. Illustrated by his Journals and Correspondence* (2 vols., 1862), she achieved what so much of her fiction aspired to—a portrait of a noble Scot self-betrayed by his idealism. Her heart, she once confessed to her publisher William Blackwood, had "sickened" at the traffic of novel writing, the formulas and conventions that the literary marketplace and the endless urgent needs of her family demanded. Criticism, literary history, and biography especially engaged and stimulated her mind as fiction never could, and *The Life of Edward Irving* is by far the best of her books. No small measure of its success is its Scottish-ness. Here truly Mrs. Oliphant went back to her national roots, not in an artificial reconstruction of the historical past, but in a labour of conscientious research, interviewing witnesses who had known Irving, including Henry Drummond, a founder of the Irvingite Church who had commissioned the book in 1858, and Jane and Thomas Carlyle, friends of his youth. In search of letters, journals, documents, she travelled to Rosneath where Irving's friend Dr. Robert Story had lived, and she visited every Scottish and English scene with which he had been connected.

Out of all this effort came not only a colourful portrait of her subject but a vivid, sensitive picture of the remote provincial Scotland from which Irving had emerged. With more life than her fictional Carlingford or Afton, she created the real rural Annan of 1792—"this little neutral-coloured community, living in a little round of social gaieties" (Ch. I); and the Kirkcaldy where, brilliant and ardent, young Irving preached his first sermons to simple, puzzled parishioners: "The people listened doubtfully to those thunder-strains which echoed over their heads . . . 'He had ower mickle gran'ner,' the good people said, with disturbed looks" (Ch. IV). As Irving moves on to Glasgow and then to London, winning more converts, stirring up controversy and notoriety, Scotland looms as his nemesis:

> Wherever he went, crowds waylaid his steps, turning

noble country houses into impromptu temples and seizing the stray moments of his leisure with jealous eagerness. His own Church was crowded to overflowing at those services which were least exclusively congregational. Amid all this his own eyes, burning with life and ardour, turned not to fashion or the great world, not to society or the givers of fame, but were bent with anxious gaze upon the "grey city of the North," where the Scotch Assembly gathered. . . . (Ch. XVI).

When finally in 1833 Irving's preaching the identity of Christ's nature with all human nature and the practice of glossolalia in his congregation were declared heresy—on charges, among others, that he had allowed his services to be interrupted "by persons not being either ministers or licentiates of the Church of Scotland"—it was by the Presbyters of his own church in Annan. Mrs. Oliphant rises to dramatic heights she never achieved in her fiction as she describes him walking out of this church in which he had been baptized and ordained—

> through crowds of confused and wondering spectators . . . contemporaries of his own, who had watched his wonderful progress with a thrill of pride and amaze . . . to this bleak afternoon of March, slowly shadowing, minute by minute, upon those clouds of eager faces growing pale in the darkness, what a brilliant interval, what a wonderful difference! (Ch. XVIII)

A broken man, Irving did not long survive his downfall. Mrs. Oliphant measured him sympathetically but realistically as a man who "looked for suffering on an heroic scale, not the harassing repetitions of Presbyterial prosecution" (Ch. XII), a tragic figure reduced to failure by his self-delusion: "Unconsciously his thoughts elevated themselves, and grew into fuller development; unconsciously he assumed in his own person the priestly attitude, and felt himself standing between God and the people" (Ch. XII). The delusion was perhaps more romantic than theological or philosophical, a blindness that Mrs. Oliphant significantly links with a word of Scottish origin, *glamour,* the magic that transforms those over whom it is cast:

> Irving had so much of the "celestial light" in his eyes, that he unconsciously assigned to everybody he addressed a standing-ground in some degree equal to his own. The "vision splendid" attended him not only through his morning course, but throughout all his career. The light around him never faded into the light of common day. . . . This *glamour* in his eyes had other effects, melancholy enough to contemplate; but even though it procured him trouble and suffering, I cannot find it in my heart to grudge Irving a gift so noble (Ch. XII).

Realistic and clear-eyed as she could be, Mrs. Oliphant herself retained a lingering love for the romance of Scotland. The terrible blows of her own life, the deaths of her husband and her children, the grinding schedule of hard work that never produced as much money as she needed, the grim realisation that with all her talents and efforts she would never rank as a first-rate writer—these were endur-

able only because she was sustained with a belief in what she called "the Unseen". She was not, however, a mystic, nor did she seek comfort in any of the flourishing spiritual movements of her day. Her stories of the supernatural range from bland dream visions like *The Little Pilgrim in the Unseen* to the sublimity of **"A Beleaguered City"**. In between are ghost stories like **"The Secret Chamber"** and **"The Open Door"**, and novels like *The Wizard's Son* which draw on Scottish folk traditions.

In one of her best ghost stories, **"The Library Window"**, she conjures up a fable of the life of the imagination out of an atmosphere of Scottish glamour. A late story (first published in *Maga* in 1896), it is told in retrospect by an elderly widow returning to her homeland after years abroad and recalling a strange episode from her youth. Delicate in health, bookish and shy, the girl is visiting with an aunt in St. Rule's, surrounded by a circle of genteel elderly Scots folk. She spends hours staring out of the window at the College Library across the road and gradually becomes fascinated by a strangely illuminated window there through which she sees a man writing busily. The vision is neither morbid nor frightening. Rather it possesses a curious kind of fascination that she associates with the hazy lights of the long Scottish midsummer evenings— "daylight, yet it is not day, and there is a quality in it which I cannot describe, it is so clear, as if every object was a reflection of itself"—and the peculiar glinting lights of an old diamond ring worn by one of her aunt's guests, a sybilline figure, Lady Carnbee. Of course there is no window and there is no writing man. And the girl's aunt, alarmed by her fantasies, sends her back home. But for years the vision haunts her, the man appears to her in crowds "as a face I knew", but then vanishes.

There is no resolution, no dramatic climax, in **"The Library Window"**. The writing man remains anonymous, and we never even learn what he was writing—certainly not poems, the narrator concludes, "because no one could possibly write poems like that, straight off, without pausing for a word or a rhyme". Such a writer could only have been one gifted (or perhaps cursed) with the facility of words, "the equivocal virtue of industry", that marked the writer Margaret Oliphant herself. But she was also the ageing widow telling the story, recalling her early life in Scotland, the enchantment of which haunted her through all her years as "a wandering Scot".

Margaret K. Gray (essay date 1985)

SOURCE: Introduction to *Selected Short Stories,* by Margaret Oliphant, edited by Margaret K. Gray, Scottish Academic Press, 1985, pp. vii-xii.

[*In the following excerpt, Gray explains Oliphant's conception of evil in relation to her supernatural tales.*]

Margaret Oliphant Wilson Oliphant was born on 4 April 1828 in the small village of Wallyford, East Lothian, the youngest of the three surviving children of six born to the

Wilson family; she died on 25 June 1897 in Wimbledon. In almost half a century of literary production Mrs Oliphant published ninety-three novels, at least thirty-six short stories, several biographies and histories—notably *Annals of a Publishing House: William Blackwood and his Sons, their Magazine and Friends* (1897)—and various critical appraisals of writers of the past. She contributed over three hundred articles to *Blackwood's Edinburgh Magazine* as well as writing critical reviews for such periodicals as *Fraser's Magazine, The Edinburgh Review, Scribner's Magazine,* and *The Spectator.*

Oliphant's sad history is reflected in her fiction in a preponderance of male characters who disappoint or fail their women, and in the alcoholics, moral degenerates, or physically ill characters who hold back the women or drag them down.

—*Margaret K. Gray*

Such a vast production inevitably resulted in a certain amount of hack writing, and also clouded the judgement of later critics who were content to dismiss both her finest and poorest work. Why, then, did she write so much? Firstly, it is quite clear that she had to write. An insatiable, almost compulsive urge to write literature of every type was part of her psychological make-up. 'I must work or die' she told Blackwood her publisher; and, like her literary predecessor and idol, Walter Scott, she felt that 'it seems to suit my demon best to let it have its own way'. Money, however, was also an overriding consideration. She travelled extensively for pleasure, for material for her books, and in the constant search for cures for her sons. There was her sons' education to pay for—Eton and then Oxford—and ponies for them, and clothes, so that the money her novels brought in was generally eaten up before she had even been paid. Pride—family and personal—had a lot to do with living at such a pitch. Scott might have had his Abbotsford, but Mrs Oliphant had her two boys, and there was nothing she would deny them. And then there were the interminable friends and relations who lived, parasitically, off her writing talent. Her favourite, beloved brother Willie was an alcoholic who, after an abortive attempt at the ministry, was sent by his sister to Italy where she provided for him until his death in 1885. Mrs Oliphant's other brother, Frank, ruined his own business and then was quite content to have her take care not only of him but also of his young family. When she married her cousin, Frank Oliphant, in 1852 it was with the hope that at last she had found security—but it was not to be. Steeped in ecclesiastical art which was already in decline before he was qualified to practise professionally, Frank had to resort to glass painting to make a living, and within seven years of their marriage he was dead of tuberculosis, leaving Margaret in debt, pregnant, and with two children under the age of six. From then on Mrs Oliphant wrote

continually—even correcting the proofs of *Annals of a Publishing House* on her death-bed—yet in spite of all her self-sacrifice and self-denial she died barely solvent. Her children, for whom she had so often prostituted her writing talent, were no longer there to appreciate her endeavours. Her daughter Maggie died at the age of eleven from gastric fever; her two sons, Cyril and Francis—always known by their childhood nicknames of Tids and Cecco—were a disappointment. Immensely gifted as young boys, their talent came to nothing despite their mother's fond hopes. Tids drifted into bad company and wasted the remains of his young life in contented indolence, dying of tuberculosis at the age of thirty-four. Cecco never really enjoyed good health and, though he attempted to find regular employment, he too finally succumbed to tuberculosis at thirty-five. Even Mrs Oliphant's nephew, Frank Wilson, whom she had educated at her own expense, died of fever on his first appointment abroad.

This sad history is reflected in her fiction in a preponderance of male characters who disappoint or fail their women, and in the alcoholics, moral degenerates, or physically ill characters who hold back the women or drag them down. But it was also this sad history that occasioned Mrs Oliphant's best fiction—both in the supernatural genre and in other types of fiction: while pecuniary difficulties resulted in imitative or expedient literature, great heartbreak and pain brought forth superb work, as though her fiction at those times was not only a solace but also a positive channel through which her deep-seated emotions could be drawn.

Margaret Oliphant's fiction can be divided into four categories. There are the well-known 'Chronicles of Carlingford'—a series that was once published as a set and should be again. She also wrote Scottish fiction, the best examples being *Harry Muir* (1853), *A Son of the Soil* (1866), *The Ladies Lindores* (1883), *It was a Lover and his Lass* (1883), and the excellent *Kirsteen* (1890). Then there are novels in which she looks at English society with a sharply satirical Scottish eye. The most notable of these are *The Curate in Charge* (1876), *Within the Precincts* (1879), *Hester* (1883), and *The Cuckoo in the Nest* (1892). Lastly, there is her supernatural fiction, a blend of the mystical and the rational that still retains its power more than a century later.

With two exceptions—the short stories **"A Christmas Tale"** (1857) and **"The Secret Chamber"** (1876)—the three novels and twelve short stories which constitute Mrs Oliphant's production in the genre of supernatural fiction were all published during the last seventeen years of her life. In several of these works she attempted to formulate a theology which would not only prove consolatory for her personal unhappiness but would also serve as a bulwark against the increasing materialism and scepticism of her age. Having lost so many members of her family in tragic circumstances, she tried to rationalise what she believed to be God's purpose in leaving her bereft, and endeavoured to bring herself to acceptance of her personal bereavement. In conjunction with this personal search for solace, Mrs Oliphant was aware that the 1880s and

1890s were decades of debate and uncertainty for many of her contemporaries. The dominance of the Anglican church in Victorian England had been progressively lessened by the growth of other denominations, but none of these movements seemed capable of providing the absolute certainty many Victorians craved. The credibility of the Old Testament account of the Creation was assailed by Darwin's theory of evolution, and this led to increasing scepticism concerning the plausibility of the entire Bible. Many Victorians believed that the whole foundation of their society was being attacked. It seemed that Man, who had previously been considered to be God's supreme creation, could no longer be said to hold the central place in the universe if he was merely the product of evolution; and it appeared that science was now able to provide rational explanations for hitherto inexplicable phenomena, and to offer a certainty which religion no longer seemed to possess. Such religious uncertainty, coupled with an increasing awareness on the part of many socially-conscious Victorians that their society was founded not upon Christian principles but upon materialism, resulted in a search by many to discover something tangible or spiritual in which they could believe. This search explains to some extent the wave of interest in science on the one hand and spiritualism on the other which swept the 1880s, as many attempted to find an unimpeachable conviction which neither the established church nor the new denominations could provide.

In this search Mrs Oliphant was, in many ways, a woman of her age. Brought up in the faith of the Free Church of Scotland, she quickly became disenchanted with its narrowness. Of the orthodox denominations, she had 'strong leanings towards the Catholic Church'—as is clearly demonstrated in several of her tales of the supernatural, in which she patently accepts the Catholic belief in purgatory. In all conventional denominations, however, she felt there was an incompleteness, a contraction, and above all an unutterable boredom. She wrote in 1862:

> Except in the case of some lucky people in some favoured localities, most men tacitly or otherwise admit to themselves, that an hour or half an hour's tedious listening is the necessary penalty which they must pay for the privilege of worshipping God with their fellows, and remaining devout members of their mother-church. . . . We must go through that farce of teaching and being taught, to our mutual pain, fatigue, and dissatisfaction.

Philosophy held no attraction for her. All other forms of knowledge, she believed, had contributed something to man's quest for enlightenment; only philosophy

> has given us nothing. She has bidden us believe that we live as shadows in an unreal world—that nature and all her glories are but the phantasmagoria of a dream . . . She has groped on from one darkness to another, losing a faculty, a faith, a scrap of feeble certainty, at every step.

Mrs Oliphant also considered that the interest in spiritu-

alism of many of her contemporaries contained an element of fraudulent sensationalism. She clearly believed in the existence of spirits yet was appalled that anyone should attempt to contact them. Such an encroachment into God's realm was 'folly' and she rejected 'contemptuously . . . the freaks of table turning and rapping'. For Mrs Oliphant, Faraday's explanation of spiritual phenomena—that they were simply the result of electrical energy—was 'trivial', and Darwin's theory of evolution was 'as foolishness to our incapable faculties'. Finding no solution or solace in science, philosophy, spiritualism, or conventional religious denominations, she formulated a theology of her own, a simple faith in which God's existence was affirmed, with the most important facet of His nature being that He was a God of Love, an ever-forgiving, consoling deity, willing to open His Kingdom to all who truly regret their past way of life. Mrs Oliphant accepted that most mortals would have to undergo a form of penance for their misdemeanours on earth in a kind of purgatory, but she believed that only those who deliberately and consciously chose evil to the exclusion of everything else were beyond reclamation. This simple theology lies behind her various tales of the supernatural.

The prose tale of the supernatural had been a flourishing genre since at least Defoe's 'A True Relation of the Apparition of One Mrs Veal'. However, where other writers (for example Poe, Le Fanu, and Mrs Radcliffe) were largely concerned with the mysterious and the suspenseful, Mrs Oliphant—apart from the youthful Gothic experiment **"A Christmas Tale"**—takes us beyond such limitations. Mere spine-tingling horror is not the object of her fiction but rather she sought, like Mrs Gaskell and Bulwer-Lytton, to make the reader examine his own beliefs and values, and to create in the reader feelings of sympathy and understanding for the beings who cross back into the world of the living. Her spirits are not cyphers included merely to engender terror but beings with rounded personalities who take active—and, in the case of Lady Mary, central—roles in the tales, much as Dickens's spirits do. Like the appparitions in "A Christmas Carol" and the ambiguous being who haunts Redlaw in "The Haunted Man", many of Mrs Oliphant's beings from beyond the grave have a mission to help mortals in some specific way, or attempt to bring humans to a clearer understanding of the inevitable consequence of their present way of life. Where she did write of evil spirits that attempt to manipulate mankind, as in **"The Secret Chamber"**, she clearly viewed the evil (as James Hogg and Nathaniel Hawthorne did) as a real consuming agency which robbed the individual of his identity; but she also believed that there was an even greater evil than demonic forms—a hidden, insidious evil emanating from man's desire for scientific knowledge. A demonic spirit could rob an individual of his identify, his soul; and obsession with scientific advancement could do similar damage to society in general. Mrs Oliphant believed that science, unrestrained by any tempering humanity, had the potential for the greatest evil the world had ever seen. It had replaced God as a religion but it was a false god, a god of no substance, and over and over again in her tales the sceptic, the non-believer, the man of science, is brought to see the limitations of his new 'faith'.

Such an idea was not a new one—for instance, Franken-stein's monster in Mary Shelley's novel is no supernatural agent but the invention of a modern scientist—but seldom had such a judgement been propounded as graphically as in Mrs Oliphant's **"The Land of Darkness"**.

It is clear that Mrs Oliphant was influenced by Dante—"Earthbound" is based on lines from his "Purgatorio", as are the descriptions of several of the cities of **"The Land of Darkness"**. The Scottish ballad tradition was clearly also a formative creative impulsion on her just as it has been for her literary descendant George Mackay Brown, a writer whose work often echoes themes propounded by Mrs Oliphant. However, it is the sheer range of her super-natural fiction that sets Mrs Oliphant apart from so many of her predecessors and contemporaries. She writes of spirits who are 'earthbound', as well as spirits who return to earth in the hope of helping mortals, and she takes us beyond the grave to heaven and to purgatory, all with a delicacy of touch and feeling that is all the more effective because of its apparent simplicity. . . .

Gerald Mangan (review date 1986)

SOURCE: "The Earthy and the Unearthly," in *Times Liter-ary Supplement,* No. 4,349, August 8, 1986, p. 870.

[*In this review of* Selected Short Stories, *Mangan finds the stories sometimes interesting and probing, though the prose is often padded.*]

During a career spanning almost half a century, Margaret Oliphant (1828-97) published a prodigious body of fiction which included, among ninety or so other novels, *The Chronicles of Carlingford* and *Kirsteen.* In her introduc-tion to six of Oliphant's supernatural tales, Margaret K. Gray portrays a strong-willed literary workhorse, widowed in her youth, who was obliged to support a family of ailing and feckless menfolk. Her fluent but undistinguished prose often betrays her need to calculate income by the para-graph; too many paragraphs demand to be skimmed ("Time flew by on gentle wings . . ."); and her recourse to the traditional Gothic properties too often recalls Peacock's parody in *Nightmare Abbey:* gloomy mansions, dusty portraits, secret chambers, crotchety patriarchs and ro-mantically susceptible youths are here in abundance, and in exhaustive detail.

In **"Earthbound"** (1880), a weak-minded youth is unwit-tingly infatuated by a beautiful apparition. In **"The Secret Chamber"** a nervous noble squirms under the thumb of the family demon; and in **"The Portrait"** an irresolute heir falls under the spell of his dead mother's portrait. The spinelessness of Oliphant's male characters must have had its origins in experience; and the hint of sternness in her tone often combines with a vein of implicit snobbery. When an aitch-dropping family of *nouveaux riches* in **"Old Lady Mary"** pride themselves on having acquired an upper-class ghost along with their rented manor, she miss-es the opportunity for comic relief. Her spectres are all

notably well-heeled according to the convention, and in-variably reluctant to reveal themselves to the lower orders.

The stories are more interesting when she expands the conventions to embody her personal theology. In one case, the central character is the dead woman herself, on a ghostly mission to right a previous wrong, and its idea of purgatory is developed at length in **"The Land of Darkness"**—a vivid nightmare inspired by Dante, which unfortunately collapses under the ponderous weight of her prose. The best of them, and the only one previously reprinted, is **"The Library Window"** (1896), in which a girl grows enamoured of a mysterious figure, glimpsed behind a bricked-up window across the street. Although tortu-ously hesitant, in a rather late-James manner, its evocation of troubled adolescence shows a certain delicacy of per-ception, not unworthy of *The Turn of the Screw,* which it anticipates by two years.

Sandra M. Gilbert and Susan Gubar (essay date 1988)

SOURCE: "Forward Into the Past," in *No Man's Land: The Place of the Woman Writer in the Twentieth Century,* Yale University Press, 1988, pp. 172-73.

[*In this excerpt, Gilbert and Gubar explore the theme of the "literary father" in Oliphant's story "The Library Window."*]

In 1896, Mrs. Margaret Oliphant published a semi-autobio-graphical Gothic fantasy that seems to define the literary father as no more than a ghostly precursor. **"The Library Window"** recounts the obsession of an imaginative young woman with a hallucinatory male figure whom she thinks she glimpses in the window of a men's college across the road from the home of some relatives she is visiting. Night and day, brooding on the absent presence of this literary father, whose intellectual labors she consistently associ-ates with the work her own "papa" does in his library, she watches him "writing, always writing. . . ." Like Hardy's passionately imaginative heroine, she becomes so com-pletely fixated on the phantom man of letters who is her hero that her aunt must explain that the female line of her family has been haunted for generations by visions of a "Scholar [who] liked his books more than any lady's love," and who was evidently murdered by the brothers of a female ancestress of the girl, who seductively "waved to him and waved to him" from her own window.

Like Hardy's Robert Trewe or, for that matter, Huxley's Richard Greenow, Oliphant's scholar seems uncannily insubstantial. Indeed, alluding by implication to the nineteenth-century female novelistic tradition in which heroines are haunted by demonic masters and their mysteries, Oliphant suggests that the imaginative woman may all along have been constructing a fiction of the heroism of the man of letters in order both to romanticize and to rationalize her own sense of secondariness. Nevertheless, if one compares Oliphant's man of letters to Hardy's Robert Trewe, whose story **"The Library Window"** might almost be glossing, one perceives at once that Hardy's hero is still aesthetically supreme, despite the urgency of his struggle with "John Ivy," while Oliphant's male author is anxiety-producing precisely because he is no more than a figment of the female imagination.

Esther H. Schor (essay date 1993)

SOURCE: "The Haunted Interpreter in Margaret Oliphant's Supernatural Fiction," in *Women's Studies,* Vol. 22, No. 3, 1993, pp. 372-86.

[*In this excerpt, Schor compares* A Beleaguered City *and the story "Earthbound," finding that each uses the confrontation with the supernatural as a metaphor for reading and interpretation.*]

In this essay, I will consider two of Oliphant's supernatural fictions from the late 1870s as highly experimental narratives about interpretation. In both **"Earthbound"** and *A Beleaguered City*, the encroachment of the Unseen on the Seen causes an interpretive crisis. While Oliphant's haunted interpreters enact our task as readers by confronting an uninterpreted "text," they also interrogate Oliphant's own authority as an interpreter of literature. As John Blackwood's "general utility woman"—her own phrase—Oliphant had published nearly ninety critical essays on literature, art, and history by the late 1870s. Merryn Williams's bibliography reveals that in the 1870s Oliphant published essays on an extraordinarily varied group of English and Continental writers, in addition to seventeen books of fiction. By the end of this decade, Oliphant was writing fictions in which the meanings of signs and figures are radically indeterminate. Creating apparitions which stubbornly resist definitive interpretation, Oliphant foregrounds the interpretive strategies of the haunted. In **"Earthbound,"** a hermeneutic romance worthy of late Borges, she demonstrates a congruence between interpretive and sexual mastery. In *A Beleaguered City*, Oliphant presents a public crisis of interpretation, considering how both gender and class are implicated in authorizing interpretations. Allegorizing the interpretation of texts as an affair between persons, Oliphant deftly conflates the discourses of interpretation and social relations. For Oliphant's haunted interpreters, confronting the unexplained figure often leads to an uncanny exchange of roles: as the ghostly figure assumes authority, the interpreters take on the aura of the irrational. By means of such transfigurations, these fictions reconfigure—surprisingly, and even subversively—familiar relations between interpreters and texts, interpreters and other interpreters, and interpreters and themselves.

From the start of **"Earthbound,"** Oliphant estranges her reader from the set-piece of a Victorian Christmas:

> There was but a small party for Christmas at Daintrey. The family were in mourning, which meant more than it usually means, and the whole life of the place was subdued . . . Christmas was coming; and though there could be no Christmas festivities in the ordinary sense of the word, one or two old friends and connections were invited.

Commonly understood terms and conventions are first rendered uncertain, then shown to have multiple meanings. Mourning, as it happens, "usually" means something quite different to men, to women, and to children. Lady Beresford's "heart was still bleeding," though she seldom takes a moment away from her family to mourn her son; Sir Robert, however, become "morose with his grief," while the children appear to be less encumbered by grief than either parent. Accordingly, the young and the old celebrate "Christmas festivities" rather differently:

> The commonplace ghost-stories which are among the ordinary foolishnesses of Christmas did not suit with the more serious tone in which their thoughts flowed; but there was some talk among the older people about those sensations and presentiments that seem sometimes to convey a kind of prophecy, only understood after the event, of sorrow on the way; and the young ones amused themselves after a sort with discussions of those new-fangled fancies which have replaced that old favourite lore. They talked about what is called spiritualism, and of many things, both in that fantastic faith and in the older ghostly traditions, which we are all half glad to think cannot be explained.

As the spiritualism of the young supplants their elders' ghostlier lore, Oliphant identifies a common satisfaction in things inexplicable. Like the inscrutable loss of Willie Beresford, which initiates the family's mourning, the talk of ghosts and spirits motivates a social discourse in which the generations meet. Though the unexplained may generate a variety of responses, Oliphant places it within the public domain.

At the Beresford estate, Edmund Coventry is something of an outsider. Beyond his ties to Sir Robert, his former guardian, Edmund has a shadowy past with "no relations to speak of."

> He was a young man of excellent character and very fair fortune; and, if the truth must be told, the heads of the house at Daintrey had concluded that he would be a very convenient match for Maud, who was the second girl. Perhaps it would be better to say that one of the heads of the house had already perceived and accepted this view.

While Lady Beresford observes that Edmund and Maud "were like brother and sister," she maintains that "there was always a possibility of something more." Still, the "self-indulgent" Sir Robert, evidently made uncomfortable by the prospect of Edmund's visit, is reluctant to "perceive and accept" the anticipated marriage. Indeed, the "possibility of something more" points ironically toward an incestuous link between Sir Robert's daughter, Maud, and the suggestively named Edmund.

Oliphant's tacit questioning of Edmund's paternity may seem tentative compared to Emily Brontë's devious insinuations about Heathcliff's paternity; unlike Catherine and Heathcliff, Maud Beresford and Edmund do eventually marry. But the relationship between Edmund and Maud Beresford is secondary to that between Edmund and a mysterious woman in white, who cryptically reveals that "I was Maud." Insofar as Edmund's desire for this woman prevents his desire for Maud Beresford, it displaces and absorbs the transgressive alliance for which Lady Beresford hopes.

In **"Earthbound,"** the polysemous word "Maud"—a single name that refers to two very different women—mocks the desirous Edmund's attempt to learn the identity of the woman in white. Only by identifying her can he marry her and legally consummate his implicitly transgressive desire. Unwilling to accept her resistance, Edmund attempts to bring his ethereal visitant into the mundane, natural world. Her mobility itself is a threat, albeit an alluring one, which he counters by trying to arrest her and affix her to him. At Maud Beresford's suggestion, he seeks her in the keeper's cottage, as though wanting to transfer this "kept" woman to his own safekeeping. The more elusive she is, the more he delights in "the little mystery"—an ambiguous term referring to both her identity and, deprecatingly, her person. Perplexed by her willfulness, Edmund reassures himself that "she did not look at all like one of those women who assert a right to walk alone, and to do whatever pleases them."

Edmund's behavior is, at best, paradoxical: he seeks to legitimate the apparition only so that he may then cancel her autonomy through sexual mastery. Thus, to legitimate the woman in white—to confer upon her the status of legal person—would be to determine and constrain her significance by an act of will. Oliphant, by linking interpretive will with sexual mastery, dramatizes the consequences of taking the inexplicable out of the public domain and into the realm of the private. Edmund's will to possess the mysterious woman produces a mode of reading that Oliphant finds too close for moral comfort.

Even a brief account of Edmund's confrontations with the female figure will suggest how masterfully Oliphant sustains her discursive *double entendre*. For Edmund, the tantilizing female "figure" is simultaneously a woman to be possessed and a text to be interpreted. His initial impulse, for example, is to determine what genre of female she is: woman? or lady?

> But when he had crossed that bridge of light he was still more surprised to see in front of him, at the end of the avenue, a woman, a lady, walking along with the most composed and gentle tread. The road was not exactly a private road—all the people from the village . . . used it . . . The dress, too, struck him with great surprise. It was a white dress, with a black mantle round the shoulders, and a large hat: not unlike the costume which people in aesthetic circles begin to affect, but far more real and natural, it seemed to him.

Her social class is not so easily read. As Maud Beresford points out, even a dressmaker "may walk like a lady and dress like a lady." Clad in black and white, the illegible figure is unwittingly associated by Edmund with the artistry of "aesthetic circles." Though he realizes how unnatural white garb is for winter, Edmund resists interpreting her costume as a sign of artfulness. She always *seems* to be "far more real and natural"; as Edmund tells Maud Beresford, "she did not look like art-needlework—she looked quite natural." He pursues her "composed and gentle tread" down well-worn paths like a reader making the public space of a text his own private property.

What Edmund neglects—and what Oliphant insists upon—is the mysterious figure's own authority to signify. While enjoying Edmund's company, the female figure thwarts his attempts to identify her, showing her face reluctantly. His persistence drives her to respond to his gaze by gazing—and speaking—back: "'So you see me!' was in tones of gentle pleasure, what she said." In the allusive lime-tree grove, she permits him to walk beside her for the first time. Earthbound yet liminal, the female figure recalls the lamed Coleridge wandering imaginatively between his embowered "prison" and the sublime hilltops:

> [Edmund] walked on beside her confused, trembling, afraid, yet full of a strange happiness; and the moon, which had been rising all the time, came shinging upon them through the lofty, slender lime branches. It seemed to him, in his bewildered condition, that it was like some poem he had read, or some dream he had dreamt, to walk thus in this measured soft cadence, with the moon upon their heads all broken and chequered by the anatomy of the great trees, like dark lines traced upon the sky.

For once, Edmund keeps pace with the "measured soft cadence" of the figure—here, creative and luminous—as they pass together through the "dark lines." The idyll occurs under the aegis of the moon, associated earlier with both female creativity and liminality: "an early pale-eyed young moon, with a certain eagerness about her, as though full of impatience to see what was going on in the earth, had got up hastily in a bit of blue. She touched the mists, and made them poetical." Momentarily, Edmund seems to join the figure in her own context, sensing that "it was like some poem he had read." But this romance of reading merely leaves Edmund lusting to read still more closely:

> "Give me your hand. Won't you give me your hand?"
> . . .

> She shook her head gently, standing so near him, her hands crossed, clasping each other. He had only to put out his arms and take her into them, but he could not. She was close, close to him, and yet—what was it that stood between?

The female figure, refusing her marital hand, clasps not his hand, but her own instead. Unable to consummate his love, Edmund begins virtually to impersonate her. He "haunts" the lime-tree grove in her absence. While entertaining the possibility that she is a madwoman (for, like

Maud Beresford, he has evidently read his Wilkie Collins), Edmund comes perilously close to losing his own reason. He becomes incapable "of cool judgment or criticism," and is thought mad by young Fred.

Sir Robert shows Edmund an eighteenth-century portrait of a woman and explains that Edmund, having seen the portrait in the family gallery, is now simply deluded. Edmund resists Sir Robert's historicism, and with good reason: the framed and dated portrait parodies his own desire to contain a ghost within the structure of marriage. He even misreads the portrait's date, "1777": "'Seven, seven, seven,' he said to himself; 'seven is one of the numbers of perfection'." But perhaps it is more than Sir Robert's historicism that disturbs Edmund. For Sir Robert's revelation simultaneously legitimates the apparition as a Beresford ancestress, and implicitly initiates Edmund into the family circle as the illegitimate son of Sir Robert. Whereas Edmund proves illegitimate, the figure proves legitimate; since they are *both* Beresfords, his desire for her proves patently incestuous. Knowing himself powerless to possess her, Edmund pleads with her to possess him—to transform *him* into *her* text:

> 'Touch me—mark me, that I may be yours always. If not in life, yet in death. Say we shall meet when I die.'

> Once more she shook her head. 'How can I tell? I do not know you in the soul . . . Goodbye, brother—good bye!'

> 'I will not let you go!' he cried; 'I will not let you go!' and seized her in his arms.

> Then in Edmund's head was a roaring of echoes, a clanging of noises, a blast as of great trumpets and music; and he knew no more.

This sisterly farewell—"goodbye, brother"—makes literal the transgressive closeness of Edmund's embrace. As though Edmund's readerly grasp were not sufficiently dubious, Oliphant shows that this violent mode of reading is tantamount to rape—the rape, in Edmund's case, of his own consciousness.

Inscribed in the denouement of **"Earthbound"** is a pathetic desublimation of another, more famous, literary embrace. In Canto XXI of the *Purgatorio* (which canto Oliphant quotes in a footnote), Dante reveals to the poet Statius that his interlocutor has been none other than Virgil himself. When Statius attempts to embrace his beloved precursor, Virgil prevents him, saying, "Frate, non far, che tu se'ombra e ombra vedi" (Brother, there's no need—you are a shade, a shade is what you see.") Statius replies:

> And, rising, he: "Now you can understand how much love burns in me for you, when I forget our insubstantiality, treating the shades as one treats solid things." (Mandelbaum trans.)

Embracing Virgil, the loving Statius feels them both to be more substantial than the shades—or texts—they are; but

Edmund's possessive embrace routs his beloved figure, leaving Edmund himself a senseless body on the attic floor. Statius' sublime love of Virgil is grotesquely deflated in what one might call, after Susan Sontag, Edmund's "erotics of reading." Edmund's close reading dismantles the dialectic between reader and text enacted by Dante and Virgil, a dialectic which, as Oliphant suggests in the lime-tree grove idyll, constitutes the loving act of reading well. Moreover, Edmund's attempt to displace the inexplicable figure from the public to the private realm only reveals harshly his own tenuous linkage to the social order. Both as a reader and as a lover, Edmund Coventry fails.

A Beleaguered City, written in 1878, concerns the possession not of an individual, but of the Burgundian city of Semur. In this novella, the strange reversal of roles that is so gradual in **"Earthbound"** is abrupt and peremptory. One evening, a mysterious sign on the cathedral door declares Semur's residents to be dwelling there illegitimately; soon the populace is silently and summarily expelled. The town's mayor, Martin Dupin, reflects that "It was rather as if the world had become a grave in which we, though living, were held fast." Ironically, the possession of Semur *dis*possesses its inhabitants, most of whom weather the three-day ordeal outside the city walls. For the predominant portion of Semur's populace, the city's besiegers remain entirely inaccessible, unseen, unheard, and distant; throughout the episode, Semur remains shrouded in clouds. Unlike **"Earthbound,"** which dwells chiefly on the tantalizing proximity between the haunted interpreter and the unexplained, *A Beleaguered City* subordinates confrontations with the unseen to the public drama of interpretive debate.

Whereas in **"Earthbound,"** gender and class articulate relations between the interpreter and his "text," in *A Beleaguered City* differing interpretations articulate the town's complex and often occult relations of class and gender. The novella comprises Dupin's official compilation of discrete documents by himself and four other narrators, a procedure designed "to present one coherent and trustworthy chronicle to the world." But even Dupin acknowledges that the account becomes less coherent as it becomes more complete:

> The narratives which I have collected from the different eye-witnesses during the time of my own absence, will show how everything passed while I, with M. le Curé, was recovering possession of our city . . . [I]n their accounts there are naturally discrepancies, owing to their different points of view and different ways of regarding the subject.

Readers who attempt to "decide" Oliphant's moral message in *A Beleaguered City* attribute to her the same interpretive absoluteness which she labors here to undermine. In this novella Oliphant broods on the ways in which public and private authority are mutually implicated in the social matrix.

In what Dupin calls "the first important incident in this

narrative," Oliphant foregrounds interpretation. Dupin beholds a mysterious sign on the facade of the cathedral:

> It was as I have seen an illumination of lamps in a stormy night; one moment the whole seems black as the wind sweeps over it, the next it springs into life again; and thus you go on, by turns losing and discovering the device formed by the lights. Thus from moment to moment there appeared before us, in letters that seemed to blaze and flicker, something that looked like a great official placard. 'Sommation'—this was how it was headed. I read a few words at a time, as it came and went . . . It was a summons to the people of Semur by name—myself at the head as Maire (and I heard afterwards that every man who saw it saw his own name, though the whole *façade* of the Cathedral would not have held a full list of all the people of Semur)—to yield their places, which they had not filled aright, to those who knew the meaning of life, being dead. NOUS AUTRES MORTS—these were the words which blazed out oftenest of all, so that every one saw them. And 'Go!' this terrible placard said— 'Go! leave this place to us who know the true signification of life.' These words I remember, but not the rest; and even at this moment it struck me that there was no explanation, nothing but this *vraie signification de la vie.*

While in **"Earthbound,"** the female figure is difficult to read, she is at least a figure in black and white; here, the luminous text is even less integral, not inscribed, but variously blazing and flickering. Insofar as each witness reads his own name on the sign (and Dupin is vexed to find his own name so prominent), the text's instability becomes politically ominous. Dupin, at the center of political authority, trusts that the terrible phrase, "NOUS AUTRES MORTS," will ensure an interpretive consensus, even as it polarizes the human and the supernatural realms. Oliphant imbues our own reading with some of the strangeness of Dupin's by using "gigantic" upper-case letters and, more importantly, by including the French version of the sign. The sign's indeterminacy is signified by its reduction to "nothing but" the inexplicable and untranslated phrase, "*vraie signification de la vie.*" Paradoxically, the sign's meaning is only intelligible to one who knows the meaning of life; but the monition only exists because Semur's residents do not. The enigmatic "meaning" of the sign, in other words, is that none of its readers are able to interpret it.

To resist the imposing apparition, the people of Semur do the one thing in their power: transform themselves from objects into subjects by reading the sign. In the resulting welter of interpretation, the community's central political tensions are expressed. Dupin, ever conscious that he is "at once the representative of the popular opinion and its guide" refuses to "yield credence to a miracle." Sending for the scientist, M. Clairon, Dupin pledges his own allegiance to materialism; in the preceding chapter, he comforts himself with the knowledge that "all sensations of the body must have their origin in the body." By his own account, Dupin is "a man of my century," unwilling to close ranks with the clerical party, though tolerant of "conscientious faith." While awaiting the arrival of Clairon,

he reveals his prejudices against the Curé by accusing him of an imposture: "'M. le Curé,' I said, 'this is a strange ornament that you have placed on the front of your church.'" The Curé, for his part, surprises Dupin by casting suspicions on the nuns of the Hospital of St. Jean: "'It is never well to offend women, M. le Maire,' he said." Dupin realizes for the first time that the Curé and the *réligieuses* are not aligned, as he had previously supposed. On the contrary, the women of the hospital (angered by complaints that their masses are disturbing patients) are suspected by the clerical and secular authorities alike. It is hardly coincidental that Dupin's initial response to the strange sign—"What is this? is it some witchcraft!"—points in the same direction as the Curé's. Dupin's own interests, as he relates in Chapter I, lie in the preservation of the patriarchal order; though a bourgeois, he is heir to "the position held by the Dupins from father to son." He abominates that "class" of women "who profess the same freedom of thought as is generally accorded to men," and maintains that it is incumbent upon women to compensate with piety for their lesser "weight" in the world. Semur's nuns unsettle Dupin's idée fixe about women expressly because they enlist religious faith in the service of secular power. Fearing an alliance between Semur's women and the unseen powers, Dupin retorts to his wife, "You love these dead tyrants . . . You love them best."

As for the nuns, they find a curious source of support in the money-worshipping underclass which Dupin disdains: "The men would all sell their souls for a *grosse piece* of fifty sous." As the refractory *vaurien* Jacques Richard declares, "*L'argent c'est le bon Dieu.*" Unlike Semur's more affluent, educated and enfranchised bourgeoisie, these men prove to have a "religious" culture; just as they had made a cult of silver, they now make a cult of the nuns. While Dupin excoriates their profane materialism (unwilling to acknowledge his own loftier scientific materialism), they are readier than many of Semur's women to credit the nuns' claim that the dead have risen angrily on the nuns' behalf. Finally, the "enlightened" Clairon arrives to offer the least persuasive interpretation of all:

> [M]any of us thought that when science thus came forward capable of finding out everything, the miracle would disappear. But instead of this it seemed to glow brighter than ever. That great word '*Sommation*' blazed out, so that we saw his figure waver against the light as if giving way before the flames that scorched him. He was so near that his outline was marked out dark against the glare they gave.

Dupin, hoping to support and be supported by a definitive interpretation, finds Clairon transformed into a figure of darkness—yet another figure whose meaning is uncertain.

While the incident of the sign provides a colorful mapping of the city's class, religious and gender relations, it is nonetheless a map drawn by Dupin, who insists on preserving the normative shape of authority in Semur throughout the crisis. By contrast, the import of interpretive difference in Dupin's compilation is both to undermine his authorial control of the document, and to question the adequacy of his centrist, tolerant notion of government. Chapters V through IX, which treat the period of Dupin's return to the occupied town with the Curé, are framed on both ends by the Mayor's narration. Dupin also narrates Chapter VI, but here his account stands beside that of the four other narrators whom he recruits for assistance: Paul Lecamus; M. de Bois-Sombre; Dupin's wife, Agnès Dupin; and his mother, Madame Veuve Dupin. Dupin regards Lecamus as "something of a visionary, though his conduct is irreproachable, and his life honourable and industrious." Dupin's tentative tolerance for Lecamus reflects his ambivalence about his own "faculty of imagination"; just as Dupin assures himself that Lecamus is "quite free from revolutionary sentiments," he assures his reader that, in writing his account, Dupin himself has kept his imagination firmly in check. Still, in an earlier chapter, it is Lecamus who ventures outside the city walls with Dupin, where both men uncannily sense the presence of an unseen crowd. Dupin's response is duplicitous: in public, he announces staunchly that he has seen nothing, then shakily asks Lecamus in private, "How do you explain—." That Dupin requests Lecamus to write an official account of his sojourn among the Unseen suggests that Dupin expects the visionary to say what he as Mayor cannot. Lecamus does exactly that, narrating his ravishment by the soul of his departed wife—a sublimer embrace, perhaps, than that of Edmund Coventry, but ultimately an *amour fatale*. Of Dupin's other surrogate, Bois-Sombre, he remarks that he "is an excellent fellow; but he smells a little of the *mousquetaire*." The aristocratic Bois-Sombre, his family holdings having been drastically reduced during the Revolution, resents having to forfeit his sole residence "probably to the licence of a mob—for one can never tell at what moment Republican institutions may break down and sink back into the chaos from which they arose." An essentialist in matters of class, Bois-Sombre dismisses Dupin's foolish attempt to transfer his scarf of office to him; blood, after all, will tell. Whereas Lecamus enacts Dupin's imaginative impulses, Bois-Sombre enacts Dupin's defense of the official authority against the leftist threat posed by the self-authorized "hare-brained enthusiast," Lecamus.

In its first published version, *A Beleaguered City* includes only the additional narrative of Agnès Dupin; Oliphant added the narrative of Madame Veuve Dupin while revising the novella for publication as a book. The revision (and Oliphant made but a handful of extensive revisions during her prolific career) is crucial: taken together, Chapters VIII and IX undermine powerfully Dupin's complacent relegation of women to "the devout sex." The object of Oliphant's criticism is not Dupin as husband, son, father, Mayor, or even Dupin as self-proclaimed "man of my century," but Dupin as a man of the future—as *historian*. Dupin expresses an ideology which, according to the historian Peter Brown, has pervaded British historiography since the Enlightenment. In *The Cult of the Saints,* Brown describes the persistent "two-tiered model" used by Hume, Gibbon, the early Newman, and numerous 20th century historians, to interpret the history of religious cultures:

The views of the potentially enlightened few are thought of as being subject to continuous upward pressure from habitual ways of thinking current among "the vulgar."

Brown argues that this model expresses the biases of Protestant ideologues, who exploited it to stress affinities between benighted, pagan forms of worship and Roman Catholicism.

Rather than present the rise of the cult of the saints in terms of a dialogue between two parties, the few and the many, let us attempt to see it as part of a greater whole—the lurching forward of an increasing proportion of late-antique society toward radically new forms of reverence . . . deriving its momentum from the need to play out the common preoccupation of all, the few and the "vulgar" alike, with new forms of the exercise of power, new bonds of human dependence, new, intimate, hopes for protection and justice in a changing world.

Perhaps Oliphant's extended sojourn in Italy and her study of the French monastic revival left her impatient with this historiographical bias against Catholicism. But in *A Beleaguered City*, Oliphant shrewdly intuits the bias against *women* implied by the "two-tiered model," which, in Dupin's hands, relegates females to a superstitious underclass. *A Beleaguered City* articulates a rich spectrum of difference among Semur's women, most of whom would probably describe themselves as "devout." While Agnès Dupin claims to have witnessed the spirits, her testament differs from that of Mère Julie.

In the night the Mère Julie had roused us, saying she had seen a procession of angels coming to restore us to the city. Ah! to those who have no knowledge it is easy to speak of processions of angels. But to those who have seen what an angel is—how they flock upon us unawares in the darkness, so that one is confused, and scarce tell if it is reality or a dream; to those who have heard a little voice soft as the dew coming out of heaven! I said to them—for all were in a great tumult—that the angels do not come in processions, they steal upon us unaware, they reveal themselves in the soul.

Agnès Dupin's intimation challenges her to accept an unfamiliar mode of consciousness neither fully wakeful nor fully dreamlike. Whereas Mère Julie's vision is derived heavily from scripture, Agnès's more idiosyncratic vision involves a paradoxical exertion of faith in the self. Her mother-in-law, who cannot perceive the angels, strives toward a faith expressed in good works:

God, He knows what it is we can do and what we cannot. I could not tell even to Him all the terror and the misery and the darkness there was in me; but I put my faith in Him . . . We are not made alike neither in the body nor in the soul.

Whereas Agnès Dupin's account concentrates on spiritual issues, Madame Veuve Dupin's explains in detail the administration of a large, diverse community of women and children. Crucially, Madame Veuve Dupin supplies the social context for the women's various responses to the crisis. Her portrait of Sister Mariette, who smiles resignedly throughout, is implicitly critical: "She had no son, no husband among the watchers," observes Madame Dupin curtly. Even Mère Julie's prophecy is compromised by her having knowingly sold inferior pears to the Dupins. Though proud of her son, Madame Veuve Dupin is openly critical of him for opposing the nuns of the Hospital. Oliphant, by revising, substitutes for a pious version of the female voice, a pluralistic array of female voices.

Dupin's document reveals a greater ambivalence toward pluralism by simultaneously authorizing and repressing other voices. For even as his four surrogates suggest Dupin's pluralistic tolerance of several interpretive positions in the social spectrum, they also suggest that any single interpretation advanced by Dupin entails the subordination of others *within his own consciousness*. Dupin's two male surrogates suggest his need to repress both his imagination and his love of control; while both qualities remain obscured to him, he inscribes them in his document through the narratives of others. Dupin fails as well to acknowledge his own femininity, as we learn during his climactic journey into the possessed town. On entering the library "where my father and grandfather conducted their affairs," he finds a change:

> The old bureau which my grandfather had used, at which I remember standing by his knee, had been drawn from the corner where I had placed it out of the way . . . and replaced, as in old times, in the middle of the room . . . Some of the old drawers were open, full of old papers. I glanced over them in my agitation, to see if there might be any writing, any message addressed to me; but there was nothing, nothing but this silent sign of those who had been here.

Finding no patriarchal message addressed to him, Dupin is placed in much the same position as his mother, who locates herself at the margins of written language. Dispossessed in the library of his male predecessors, Dupin finds himself possessed by "an inspiration from above." He hears the strange Latin words, *"Laetatus sum,"* spring from his tongue—"no thought of mine." Impulsively and silently, he and the Curé serve mass:

> The days of my childhood seemed to come back to me. All trouble, and care, and mystery, and pain, seemed left behind. All I could see was the glimmer on the altar of the great candle-sticks, the sacred pyx in its shrine, the chalice, and the book. I was again an *enfant de choeur* robed in white, like the angels, no doubt, no disquiet in my soul—and my father kneeling behind among the faithful, bowing his head, with a sweetness which I too knew, being a father, because it was his child that tinkled the bell and swung the censer . . . My heart grew soft within me as the heart of a little child.

Weeping at the altar, Dupin finds his habitual demeanor softened and made "childlike." While he never speaks of himself as effeminized, he describes in unaccustomed terms his paternal role as one of "sweetness," a role related not to patriarchal inheritance, but to parenting and the giving of nourishment.

Narrating the aftermath in Chapter X, Dupin thoroughly denies this experience of masculinity. Describing a visit to the cathedral after the ordeal, Dupin recurs to his accustomed construction of gender:

> The great Cathedral walls seemed to throb with the sound that rolled upward *mâle* and deep, as no song has ever risen from Semur in the memory of man . . . Such a submission of our intellects, as I felt in determining to make it, must have been pleasing to heaven. The women, they are always praying; but when we thus presented ourselves to give thanks, it meant something, a real homage; and with a feeling of solemnity we separated, aware that we had contented both earth and heaven.

Earlier, Dupin supposes charitably that "The *bon Dieu*—if, indeed, that great Being is as represented to us by the Church—must naturally care as much for one-half of His creatures as for the other." Here, presuming to please both the city of God and the city of man, Dupin constructs the former on the model of the latter. The distance traveled between Dupin's two remarks suggests his clearer awareness *after* the ordeal that the Church represents God with its own masculinist bias. Semur's nuns have already realized that the Hospital would be more hospitable to them than the Church; even there, male patients attempt to circumscribe their freedom to worship. *A Beleaguered City* suggests that the enfranchisement of religious women is not simply a matter of where one stakes a claim. According to Madame Veuve Dupin, the religious life of Semur's female encampment revolves around a God different from the Curé's:

> One cry seemed to rise round us as we went, each infant moving the others to sympathy, till it rose like one breath, a wail of 'Maman! Maman!' a cry that had no meaning, through having so much meaning . . . The Holy Mother could not but hear it.

Indeed, Semur's women seem to address themselves to a female God. Oliphant is at her shrewdest in having this cry originate in the lungs of infants. For while "Maman" is perhaps a far cry from mariolatry, it suggests that belief in the *Bon Dieu,* the *fils de Dieu,* and even the *Saint-Père* is only learned later—at the behest of the Church.

When Madame Veuve Dupin asks her son, "Why is it that you look so unfavourably upon everything that comes from the community of St. Jean?" he replies resonantly, "What have I to do with the community?" It may be true that Martin Dupin survives as Semur's public authority only by refusing to answer this question. But he survives as an author only by including the answer within the leaves of his file. Dupin's multi-vocal document, by enfranchising a wider spectrum of the community than Dupin does as mayor, deconstructs his own interpretive authority. The document of Semur's ordeal bespeaks a far more radical conception of both political and interpretive authority than Dupin's centrist, tolerant, but patriarchal rhetoric can sustain. More importantly, it suggests that such rhetoric can only legitimate itself as part of a varied and differentiated social discourse. In the gap between Dupin's rhetorical stance and those others voiced in his document, Oliphant exposes the conceptual threads that link psychological repression to social oppression. Oliphant's **Beleaguered City** is not a hotbed of political unrest, but a place in which the fuller enfranchisement of the social body depends on fuller and more complex recognitions of the self. What the inexplicable makes impossible is a mechanistic, rationalized view of the social body. The populace of Semur see themselves inscribed in the mysterious sign because they, too, cannot be interpreted by a univocal, authorized rhetoric, however benign or humane.

In her introduction to *The Autobiography and Letters of Mrs. Margaret Oliphant*, Q. D. Leavis describes Oliphant's supernatural fiction as "overrated":

> Though Mrs. Oliphant valued them highly herself and some have Dantean overtones, they represent a self-indulgence, the complement of her hard-headed professional self which required some non-dogmatic vaguely religious sustenance.

Clearly, Leavis gets it wrong: as both **"Earthbound"** and *A Beleaguered City* demonstrate, fiction can be non-dogmatic, yet hard-headed; "vaguely religious," but not self-indulgent. And yet, Leavis also gets it right by observing that Oliphant's supernatural fictions are the "complement of her hard-headed professional self." Having lived so much of her life as a reader on the public pages of *Blackwood's,* Oliphant was keenly aware of her own authority as an arbiter of literary fates and fortunes. A writer of fiction since her twenties, Oliphant had realized early that such critical pronouncements as she was paid to deliver had consequences for writers and their books. But by the late 1870s, she had come to reckon with her own power as a critic to shape the tastes and expectations of a nation's readers. In the mode of supernatural fiction, Oliphant explored her ambivalence about her own critical professionalism. What does it mean, these fictions ask, to use a rhetoric of distinctions, decisions and determinations to account for a literary text? to assimilate one's mixed and perhaps irreconcilable responses to a single, morally viable and socially responsible position? to authorize and canonize the reading of a single reader? In **"Earthbound"** and *A Beleaguered City*, Oliphant provisionally views the burden of interpreting literary texts—those linguistic apparitions that resist explanation—as a shared burden. In **"Earthbound,"** Edmund's close reading—an attempt to possess meaning by transforming a text into private property—renders illegitimate his claims as reader. In *A Beleaguered City*, on the other hand, Dupin's political authority is legitimated only because his interpretive authority is dialectical. If, as these fictions suggest, the way we love and the way we govern are crucially linked to the way we read, we can see why Oliphant found the task of being a critic formidable.

Finally, the "vaguely religious" quality of Oliphant's supernaturalism, as Leavis would have it, deserves a clarifying comment. Oliphant's supernatural fictions are indeed "religious" insofar as they provide a phenomenology of faith in that which cannot be fully grasped. But I would argue that these fictions are not, except idiomatically, Christian. Her last supernatural tale, **"The Library Window"** (1896), finds Oliphant veering away from faith in a Christian God, toward an entirely secular faith in what we might call (in an age in which authors are wanted more dead than alive) the "afterlife" of the author. The narrator, a dreamy, bookish girl visiting her elderly aunt, sees an old man writing ceaselessly in a window across the street, only to discover that the window is a *trompe l'oeil*. Though the panes of the window prove fictitious, the girl clings to her faith in the real pains of the writerly apparition. Late in the story, the aunt "explains" the apparition by spinning a gothic tale replete with a thwarted mistress, vengeful brothers, and a magic ring, but the girl prefers her own naturalized faith in what she cannot explain. Of the magic ring, which she inherits but will not wear, the narrator remarks, "If any one would steal it, it would be a relief to my mind." With cunning and wit, Oliphant saves the inexplicable from being reduced to a supernatural mode or subgenre—that is, to yet another authorized interpretive instrument. Bidding farewell to the supernatural, she dispenses with both gothicism and Christian piety as so many magic rings. Oliphant's supernatural fictions, far from being the "vaguely religious sustenance" of a self-indulgent journalist, are incisive essays in the cultural practice of interpretation.

Elisabeth Jay (essay date 1995)

SOURCE: "A Scottish Widow's Religious Speculations," in *Mrs. Oliphant: 'A Fiction to Herself,'* Clarendon Press, 1995, pp. 157-68.

[*In this excerpt, Jay asserts that Oliphant's supernatural tales challenged Victorian constructions of gender.*]

It was in the world of fancy, or fantasy, in her *Stories of the Seen and the Unseen*, in the liminal spaces between the here and the hereafter, in the uncharted regions of the hereafter itself, that Mrs Oliphant discovered a place to ponder further upon irresolvable paradoxes and gender-related confusions. These uncolonized spaces permitted an indirectness of approach that itself proves disruptive of reader expectation. Within a particular tale two stories often compete for our attention: a male protagonist and narrator, for instance, may stake a claim while a female ghost's silent presence intrigues in direct correlation to the suppression of her narrative.

The first problem that arises in trying to discuss Mrs Oliphant's *Stories of the Seen and the Unseen*, perhaps the least contentious title in that it sidesteps matters of genre, is the difficulty of agreeing what is covered by this collective name: the American (1889) and British (1892) versions of this anthology included different tales and the earlier publication conflated the kinds of narration that twentieth-century critical procedures would encourage us to distinguish. While it is clearly the case that all the stories from *A Beleaguered City* (1879) onwards fulfil the basic requirement of fantasy in expressing or telling of a dimension of experience not available within the prevailing realist tradition, not all of them attain that further resistance to meaning and closure that keeps the reader in a creative sense of dissatisfaction and avails the writer of a chance to express or rid himself of intransigent problems and subversive concepts. Those that do make out a space, hovering between the limitations of the terrestrial and the freedom of the supernatural, enable the exploration of problems that might be self-destructive or blasphemous in real life. A mechanical division could easily be made between those tales that chart the landscape and activities of the afterlife and those where the story makes sorties into an alternative world from an earthbound base. Such a division, however, neither accounts for the difference in the power to disturb, exerted by different stories in the first class, nor, when we come to the second class, does it distinguish sufficiently between largely allegorical tales, such as **"A Visitor and His Opinions"**, and a tale like **"Old Lady Mary"**, which includes a dimension more akin to the tales of the afterlife. Since their very variety (surprising in so small a corpus) resists theoretical categorization, it is more rewarding to consider the impulse that generated these ventures into an alternative mode from the general tenor of her realistic fiction, and the nature and chronology of the problems and anxieties explored in these tales. The enterprise seems to receive further justification from her own sense of these stories as different in kind and origin from her usual fiction. 'Stories of this description,' she wrote to William Blackwood, 'are not like any others. I can produce them only when they come to me. I should be glad to do one for the New Year number, but nothing suggests itself.' A month later she referred to **"Old Lady Mary"** as a tale that had 'presented itself' unexpectedly.

It has been traditional to ascribe Mrs Oliphant's turning to the supernatural as a source of inspiration to commercial perspicacity. The 'Little Pilgrim' tales were certainly a financial success, and her very first venture into the genre followed a vogue for comic responses to the 'Christmas fantasy' originated by Dickens's *Christmas Carol* (1843). In some ways her **"Christmas Tale"** was too carefully contrived a piece of literary parody, one suspects, to be readily enjoyed by the average periodical reader, and so when Blackwoods came to republish it the tale was retitled **"Witcherley Ways: A Christmas Tale"** to alert the reader to its deliberately playful use of the supernatural. The game that the narrator has played with us only becomes clear in retrospect when he wakes from a dream that we have been led to conceive of as taking place in his waking life: the tale explodes, or rather fizzles out, at the point of crisis just as the narrator is to meet a parricide, and we realize that the extravagances of the Gothic setting have been employed to lead us away from an allegory demonstrating that the New Year can only come of age at the expense of the death of the Old Year. Mocking allusion is made to *Wuthering Heights* in the name and character of the old servant, Joseph, and in the tale's dream and nightmare sequences, which are fed by the narrator's reading

habits, but the essentially parodic nature of the whole is given away by the mingling of devices from different genres: the tale starts at the fairy-tale time of *undermeles,* alludes to desolate wasteland landscapes opening up at street corners, involves family curses, and makes passing reference to Rosicrucian ancestors.

It was another twenty years before Mrs Oliphant appeared to realize the non-parodic potential of these devices, and market forces may again have played their part. Ghost stories were in vogue in the second half of the nineteenth century. Their appeal may have lain in the disruptions they offered to a mechanistic explanation of a world increasingly dominated by sceptical materialism. A spate of non-fictional books appeared, attempting to bridge the gap between science and spiritualism: R. D. Owen, *The Debatable Land between this World and the Next* (1872), A. R. Wallace, *Modern Spiritualism* (1874), Balfour Steward and P. G. Tait (anon.), *The Unseen Universe* (1875), and this area of investigation was given respectability when men like Leslie Stephen, Ruskin, and Symonds founded the Society for Psychical Research. Gladstone, an honorary member, made the astonishing observation that psychical research was 'the most important work, which is being done in the world'. As a reviewer Mrs Oliphant noted the warm reception given to two recent American books: E. S. Phelps's whimsical exploration of the afterlife, *Gates Ajar* (1868), and Mrs Whitney's, *Hitherto: A Story of Yesterday,* which she put down to 'the extraordinary pressure of the unseen everywhere, without, however, any relapse into the vulgar supernatural'. In the following month's number of *Blackwood's* she embarked upon a reappraisal of Coleridge and singled out *The Ancient Mariner* for its 'crossing the borders of the unseen' and 'Christabel' for its investigation of 'the mystery of evil, an unseen harm and bane'.

The title of her second tale of the supernatural, **"The Secret Chamber"**, is itself an indication that she had begun to see how she might use the genre as a literary equivalent to those Sunday evenings she had long set aside as a time to 'fantasticate' about the perplexities of her private life. The concept of 'the secret chamber' as a receptacle for a woman's inmost concerns and anxieties probably stemmed from the biblical account of Mary, of whom we are told that, unlike the shepherds, who blazoned abroad the tale of angelic appearances and Christ's nativity in a stable, 'Mary kept all these things, and pondered them in her heart'. Mrs Oliphant literalized this image in *Lucy Crofton* (1859), where the heroine, unbeknown to her husband, regularly retreats to a secret room which she has turned into a shrine for her dead baby. The allegorical application of 'The Innermost Room' in a house to represent that portion of a woman's life accessible only to the beloved dead or Christ Himself occurred in her poem of this title, published in *Blackwood's* in March 1867.

The cumulative resonance of these usages is present in a later tale of the supernatural where we are told of Old Lady Mary,

> She did not forget the dark day when her first-born

was laid in the grave, nor that triumphant and brilliant climax of her life when every one pointed to her as the mother of a hero. All these things were like pictures hung in the secret chambers of her mind, to which she could go back in silent moments, in the twilight seated by the fire, or in the balmy afternoon, when languor and sweet thoughts are over the world.

Like its predecessor, **"The Secret Chamber"** was also a Christmas tale for *Blackwood's*. Ostensibly it is concerned with a turning-point or rite of passage: the coming of age of young John Randolph, Lord Lindores, who is to be initiated by his father in a family secret. In the middle of the night Lindores is taken by his father to an old lumber-room in the heart of the family portion of the castle through which he enters 'a little intermediate place—this debatable land between the seen and the unseen' *en route* to the innermost chamber where he encounters the ancestral head of the family, Earl Robert. Lindores is offered power in return for his unquestioning allegiance to Earl Robert in all matters of family business, which will always be directed 'for the furtherance of the race'. Young Lindores is enabled to overcome this vampiric wizard, but there can be no final exorcism, partly because Lindores' father, who had succumbed to Earl Robert, still lives, and partly because the secret chamber has no identifiable material location.

As Mrs Oliphant was writing this tale she was experiencing her first real problems with her eldest son, who was, like Lindores, on the brink of his majority and an under-graduate at Oxford. Cyril was exhibiting those tendencies described in the Randolph race as making 'quite a wonderful start' and then 'falling back into mediocrity'. In November 1876 Cyril told his mother that he was 'gradually giving up all hopes of my first'. Had he, his mother must have wondered, fallen prey to the losing streak that bedevilled her brothers? It is at the moment when Lindores looks into the mirror and sees not himself, but an innumerable company of his ancestors looking back at him, 'some mournfully, some with a menace in their terrible eyes', that he comes closest to paralysis of the will. But the story is also one about a boy achieving freedom from a possessive power, and Lindores' response to Earl Robert, 'Is it for this that you oppress a race, and make a house unhappy', for all its Gothic overtones carries within it the nub of the struggle that was to smoulder for the rest of Cyril's life between the son and his mother. There is a lingering sadness to this tale, whose plot does not end with Lindores' victory over Earl Robert but with his father's denial of what has taken place. His attempt to hide the truth of the family secret from the castle guests and ultimately from himself must deprive him forever of the solace of sharing his burden.

Such anxieties lie hidden deep within a tale whose ghost-story features are crafted with a sure hand. The narrator adopts the stance of an educated man of the world, well aware that secret chambers and family ghosts are a commonplace of the folklore surrounding Scottish castles. Lindores arrives by courtesy of the Great Northern Railway to encounter an ordeal in which even at the heart of

his adventure 'a gleam even of self-ridicule took possession of him, to be standing there like an absurd hero of antiquated romance' with a 'rusty, dusty sword' in his hand. When he first sees Earl Robert he reviews the logical explanations for the phenomenon: 'what could it be but optical delusions, unconscious cerebration, occult seizure?' Cheek by jowl with the world of nineteenth-century sceptical materialism exists the castle whose architecture displays the remnants of Celtic art and Runic cords. The entrance to the secret chamber is effected via the lumber-room containing the rubbish jettisoned as outmoded by successive generations: it is from this supply of relics that Lindores' father takes 'an old sword with a cross handle' and gives it to his son, 'whether as a weapon, whether as a religious symbol, Lindores could not guess'. The narrative never discloses whether the old symbol really has potency or whether it merely serves as a visual encouragement to Lindores to pray to God.

Little over a year later Mrs Oliphant began work on *A Beleaguered City*, envisaged again as a Christmas story. It was a tale over which she took unusual pains, revising it carefully, and consequently she was fiercely proud of it. Formally the piece is experimental: a succession of narrators recount this tale of a French city, possessed by the spirit of materialism, which is then briefly taken over by the 'unseen forces of those who knew the meaning of life being dead'.

It has been customary to point to Mrs Oliphant's own knowledge of the French religious scene, gleaned whilst working on Montalembert during the 1860s and 1870s, supplemented by her acquaintance with the work of the French biblical critic Renan, to account for the setting and format of this book, whose narrative deliberately raises questions as to the status and reliability of eyewitness accounts akin to those posed by the Gospels. Actually, Mrs Oliphant knew little of Renan, other than mediated through the work of her friend Tulloch, and is as likely to have grasped the complicating possibilities of the split narrative from Wilkie Collins's *The Moonstone* or Browning's *The Ring and the Book*. The literary nature of her inspiration in this piece is beyond question. She herself cited De Quincey as her source, claiming to have found a passage in his work 'about the possibility of the dead coming back, besieging the living and turning them out of their places', and her recent efforts at popularizing Dante had exposed her to a method of embodying spiritual truth in contemporary clothing. Ostensibly the story is concerned with the inadequacy of the polite bourgeois morality, in the ascendant in France, to cope with the sudden irruption of spiritual concerns that have hitherto been dealt with by institutionalizing them. The tale's French setting allowed the Victorian reader the instant pleasure of xenophobic outrage at a country where enlightened scepticism and bourgeois respectability are openly privileged; the disconcerting parallels with British middle-class attitudes are slower to emerge. At the allegorical level the tale's disclosures are unspectacular: unthinking idolaters easily change their god when circumstances prove him inefficacious, and the humble and naturally devout, rather than those honoured by the human community, are the only ones to whom the unseen visitation comes as a delight. The tale derives its impact from the specificity with which the various narrators endeavour to communicate the inarticulable experience at its centre, from the fussy pomposities in the self-congratulatory account of M. le Maire, to the visionary narrative of Paul Lecamus, who despite his unique responsiveness 'to those mysteries which have been my life-long study' can find no metaphor or literary analogue adequate to conveying his experience. Time and again his narrative stumbles against the barriers of articulation: 'It was beyond knowledge or speech.' Moreover, the intensely personal nature of his encounter with these unseen forces, amongst whom he feels his dead wife's presence, leaves him hesitant as to the 'public signification' of the account that M. le Maire has requested of him. His use of the word 'signification' is intended to take us back to that phrase, 'la vraie signification de la vie', which, emblazoned on the doors of the cathedral, has been the notice served by the dead upon the uncomprehending inhabitants of Semur. Lecamus's reputation for 'impracticable and foolish opinions' has led to his status as a good citizen being brought into question: this distancing from the camaraderie of male citizenry, combined with his desolate yearning for his wife and the subsequent events of the story which bring him close to M. le Maire's wife, all serve to associate him with the female portion of Semur's population who, like him, are 'slow to understand a system that compartmentalizes private and public signification'. For the reader the fascination of this tale partly consists in the way it raises questions about an element of its signification apparently inaccessible to the narrators: the nature of the women's role.

M. le Maire's narrative repeatedly manages to associate women and religion as two aspects of life that can be accommodated within a sceptical male-dominated world by according 'respect to their prejudices'. This process is designed to neutralize their disruptive potential and to provide an agnostic with a spiritual insurance policy. He is struck by 'the extreme justice (not to speak of the beauty of the sentiment)' with which he explains to his wife, 'Take courage . . . this world will never come to anything much different from what it is. So long as there are *des anges* like thee to pray for us, the scale will not go far down on the wrong side.' His materialist understanding conceptualizes these matters as an affair of weights and balances.

> The *bon Dieu*—if, indeed, that great Being is as represented to us by the Church—must naturally care as much for one-half of His creatures as for the other, though they have not the same weight in the world; and consequently the faith of the women must hold the balance straight, especially if, as is said, they exceed us in point of numbers. This leaves a little margin for those of them who profess the same freedom of thought as is generally accorded to men—a class, I must add, which I abominate from the bottom of my heart.

Women have been given their compensatory affinity with heavenly concerns precisely because this is territory outside the pale of the known and the valued. When M. le Maire searches for explanations for the inexplicable events that ensue he automatically turns first to the women's part in their causation. Yet his sceptical rationalism prevents him from giving serious weight to their imprecations. He sees their instinctive revulsion at impiety, repeatedly expressed in the words 'It is enough to make the dead rise out of their graves', as a merely coincidentally apt use of cliché rather than as a formula encoding deeper truths. The trickery that he initially assumes must account for the supernatural inscription on the cathedral doors is attributed, by M. le Curé, to the nuns who are attempting to 'move heaven and earth' to prevent the secularization of their hospital. The official representative of the Church makes even M. le Maire uncomfortable when he appears to be 'abandoning his own side' by speaking of the nuns as if, like witches, they cannot be trusted to use their spiritual powers responsibly: 'It is never well to offend women . . . Women do not discriminate the lawful from the unlawful: so long as they produce an effect it does not matter to them'. The agnostic had been happy to accord them (meaningless) angelic status, but the world of official religion is driven to finding a more remote diabolic territory for them to inhabit.

At every point of the tale the women are marginalized. Structurally their narratives are left to the end, but not allowed a conclusive voice since the final chapter is given back to M. le Maire. Moreover, the two female voices, empowered only by virtue of their relation to M. le Maire, declare themselves hesitant witnesses. Madame Dupin, his wife, whose maiden name, Champfleurie, suggests the pastoral complement she was to provide to her husband's urban status, would have liked to be the representative chosen to re-enter the occupied city but she accepts that 'perhaps it was better that the messenger should not be a woman; they might have said it was an attack of the nerves. We are not trusted in these respects, though I find it hard to tell why'. His widowed mother acknowledges her triple inadequacy as a female narrator 'because in the first place I have not the aptitude for expressing myself in writing, and it may well be that the phrases I employ may fail in the correctness which good French requires; and again, because it is my misfortune not to agree in all points with my Martin'. As the plot unfolds the women are evacuated to the surrounding countryside where they care for the young, the old, and the infirm with a growing disregard for the insistence upon social hierarchy that underpinned all male planning. Here they are condemned to await the outcome of an affair negotiated by a man whom even his own mother acknowledges as an unlikely intermediary given that he is 'a person of the world and secular in all his thoughts'.

Readmitted to the now totally deserted city, M. le Maire goes to the male enclave, the library, 'where my father and grandfather conducted their affairs', in search of a message from the unseen visitors. He finds an implicit message to heed the past, conveyed in the restoration of his grandfather's desk to its central position, but looks in vain for 'any writing, any message to me'. Instead he finds the sign of the angelic visitation in his wife's rooms where the embroidered veil she has wrought for their dead child's shrine has been folded away and an olive branch laid in its place. That a non-verbal communication should have been employed by angelic forces, using a woman's handiwork and a woman's space, sets the seal upon the association patronizingly alluded to by M. le Maire's compliment to women as 'des anges'. In a moment of illumination, when the cathedral towers first pierce the sepulchral gloom surrounding the beleaguered city, the Mayor suddenly experiences a moment of conversion: 'I have loved, I have won honours, I have conquered difficulty; but never had I felt as now. It was as if one had been born again'. As an agnostic he associates his rebirth with the re-emergence of a patriarchal landmark 'which we had been born to love like our father's name', but for the reader the significance of his conversion lies in the following paragraph:

> When we had gazed upon them, blessing them and thanking God, I gave orders that all our company should be called to the tent, that we might consider whether any new step could now be taken: Agnes with the other women sitting apart at one side and waiting. I recognised even in the excitement of such a time that theirs was no easy part. To sit there silent, to wait till we had spoken, to be bound by what we decided, and to have no voice—yes, that was hard. They thought they knew better than we did; but they were silent, devouring us with their eager eyes. I love one woman more than all the world; I count her the best thing that God has made; yet I would not be Agnes for all that life could give me. It was her part to be silent, and she was so, like the angel she is. . . . *Mon Dieu!* but it is hard I allow it; they have need to be angels.

As M. le Maire himself points out, the conversions effected by this abrupt collision with another world are short-lived and his is shorter than most. His brief moment of enlightenment is quenched when, as the populace re-enter the city, he remembers that he is still wearing 'my scarf of office, which had been, I say it without vanity, the standard of authority and protection during all our trouble: and thus marked out as representative of all, I uncovered myself after the ladies of my family had passed, and without joining them, silently followed with a slow and solemn step'. Vesting himself in officialdom once again, he resumes his patronizing 'respect' for the ladies. At the celebratory service he and his brother citizens displace the female worshippers and make the walls ring to a sound 'Mâle and deep, as no song has ever risen from Semur in the memory of man'. He is oblivious to possible ironies in the women's remarks: 'The *bon Dieu* is not used to such singing . . . It must have surprised the saints up in heaven . . . It is not like our little voices, that perhaps only reach half-way'. On this occasion their words coincide with his prejudices and so they are allowed 'signification'.

> This was figurative language, yet it was impossible to doubt that there was much truth in it. Such a submission of our intellects, as I felt in determining to make it, must have been pleasing to heaven. The women, they are always praying; but when we thus present ourselves to give thanks, it meant something, a real homage.

The occupation of the city soon becomes entwined in myth, superstition, and self-interested deceit and this in turn returns M. le Maire to the fold of bigoted agnosticism: 'though gentle as a lamb and open to all reasonable arguments, I am capable of making the most obstinate stand for principle'. Now that he takes the religious threat seriously, women find themselves placed beyond the bounds of his tolerance: he is outraged that the male-led cathedral celebration is not perceived as sufficient, and when some of the citizens suggest that the chapel should be restored to the convent hospital this is his reaction: 'And now they would insult the Great God Himself by believing that all He cared for was a little mass in a convent chapel. What desecration! What debasement!' Ironically he now finds himself isolated from the majority and patronized in the very terminology he had formerly applied to women: 'The best men have their prejudices. M. le Maire is an excellent man; but what will you?' He finds himself condemned to bear the women's lot and suffer from knowing that his perceptions will go unheard and disregarded. Almost despite himself he ends his account with a tribute to the disregarded: Lecamus the visionary, and Agnes his wife. In her silent ministrations and his tombstone lie the only meaningful record of these experiences.

This tale of reversals, of the dead displacing the living, of the unseen dictating terms to a secular community, had afforded Mrs Oliphant the opportunity to explore the fears and prejudices which lurk beneath and support any dominant ideology. The exceptional nature of the events that take place provides its own commentary upon the seismic proportions of the revolution in contemporary thought that would need to occur before male complacency is shaken into taking account of the forces it has tamed by institutionalization. *A Beleaguered City* had not attempted a vision of an alternative society; rather, the incursion of these mysterious discomforting powers that the community is afraid to face had laid bare the assumptions upon which a supposedly rational, materialist society based itself. Contemporary women readers, though they might not agree with her analysis, were not slow to perceive the point of her tale. One of her correspondents, a Blanche Airlee, who disapproved of the notion that souls remained gendered in the afterlife, chose the xenophobic option the tale offered in an attempt to deflect its implications: 'I do not quite like the divisions you have made between men and women. I daresay it is true in France'. The story was written at a point in Mrs Oliphant's career when private concerns forced her to take stock of the position in which women found themselves: her nieces returned from their German boarding-school in the spring of 1879 and a future needed to be planned for them. In the couple of years that this tale took to come to fruition she published two novels that reflected many aspects of its feminist concern: *Within the Precincts* and *The Greatest Heiress*, and in the year after the tale's publication she first offered a cautious tribute, on behalf of 'voiceless women', to those feminist campaigners who had brought 'into the open the superior patronizing way in which some men regard women'.

The next tale of the unseen, **"Earthbound"**, further explores issues raised in **A Beleaguered City**, such as maternal anxiety and the need for men to be educated or jolted into seeing women as being as various in temperament and role as men. M. le Maire's two female relatives had both been mothers, but whereas his wife saw only the goodness of God in the visit of the Unseen, the mother feared a God who might require 'us to give up all if we would be perfected'. The death abroad, in October 1879, of Mrs Oliphant's nephew, Frank, had reopened the wounds of bereavement and confronted her with a picture of herself as a woman who cared too passionately about her loved ones to entrust them willingly to God's care. The Gospel tale of Mary and Martha lurked behind the contrasting pair of women, united only in their love of Martin Dupin, and was to surface openly in novels and tales from this point. **"Earthbound"** voices Martha's anxieties in a variety of ways: in the image of the bereaved mother with whom the tale opens, forced to reserve her grief for her locked room while organizing a Christmas house-party that will include a suitor for her younger daughter. Her family preoccupations link her to their eighteenth-century ancestress who haunts the grounds, condemned to the vicinity because she had been overfond 'of the house and the trees, and everything that was our own. I thought there was nothing better, nothing so good'.

The quest of Edmund Coventry, the male protagonist in this tale, has also to do with discrimination. M. le Maire has been briefly jolted into a glimpse of women as other rather than necessarily inferior, but there is no evidence that he perceives the distinctions the reader is led to make between, say, the nature of his mother and his wife. Edmund Coventry has to learn to discriminate between the unavailable spirit bound forever to her obsession with the place and the younger daughter of the family with whom he is staying and, like her ancestress, also called Maud. His meetings with the apparition, visible only to him, have aroused him from the easy indolence of bachelor life to a state where he sees 'that one ought to select one's path, to settle, to take up the more serious part of life', and like some knight of medieval romance he wanders the neighbourhood trying to find a mortal woman who incarnates the girl of his dreams. The living Maud is understandably displeased by the sense that Edmund has been aroused by the notion 'of a different kind from any he had met before: a new woman, a creature born to influence him', and proceeds to lecture him upon a young man's commonest error, that of judging women by their dress alone. From his description of the visionary girl's attire he hypothesizes that he has encountered the keeper's niece, a London dressmaker. 'A girl like that may walk like a lady and dress like a lady. She has got to be among ladies most of her time . . . Indeed, sometimes they talk even, just as nicely as we do'. Armed with this advice Edmund goes to see the young dressmaker and emerges 'pleased with his own discrimination'. At the crisis of the tale Mrs Oliphant invokes Dante to signal the story's meaning. Alluding to an embrace refused in purgatory because such a thing between shades is impossible, though the desire is itself a measure of love, the apparition tells Edward, 'You will do what is appointed; but do not be sorry, you will like to do

it'. It still remains for him to learn to discriminate between fraternal and conjugal love, as is emphasized by her farewell, 'Goodbye, brother—goodbye!' When Edmund recovers from his traumatic encounter he is ready to recognize in the living Maud not the 'sister' with whom he has grown up as her father's ward, but a potential wife. The apparition's deliberate retreat from Edmund is immediately succeeded by 'a roaring of echoes, a clanging of noises, a blast of great trumpets and music' in Edmund's head: a mental echo of the shout of triumph that marked the liberation of earthbound souls at this point of Dante's *Purgatorio*. The story does not reveal whether the ghostly visitant has been liberated from her earthly sojourn by her educative role, but Edmund learns to distinguish between the comfort and pleasure provided by the women of his guardian's demesne and the possibility of married happiness offered by a particular girl whom he must love for herself. So great has been his previous confusion that after his marriage to Maud he never revisits Daintrey.

"The Open Door", of January 1882, again used the challenge to conventional assumptions afforded by the supernatural, to investigate Victorian middle-class constructions of gender. By now Cyril was 25 and well embarked upon a career of idle dissipation much resembling brother Willie's, and Cecco had begun to show signs of following suit. The story's narrator, a brusque military man, is frankly puzzled by young fellows of 25 'with no notion of what they are going to do with their lives'. His unconscious answer is to oversee the upbringing of his delicate surviving son with a great emphasis upon 'manly' behaviour. Mrs Oliphant was well aware that even her friends had begun to attribute her sons' indolence to the pampering lavished upon them by their widowed mother. The comments so frequently proffered to single mothers about the need boys have for a strong male presence, even if galling to a woman of her particular experience, must have given her pause for thought. The fictional parents decide, like Mrs Oliphant, upon a day-boy's career for their delicate son; nevertheless the child falls ill from concern at hearing a ghostly voice in the ruined part of their rented Edinburgh estate. The voice, finally audible even to his father and the sceptical local doctor, can be heard by the sill of an open door in the ruins of the former house crying, 'Oh, mother, let me in'. The child recovers when the elderly local minister exorcizes the spirit of a former parishioner, 'Willie', by telling him to 'Go home to the Father'—a feat only accomplished when he prays to God to let the dead mother 'draw him inower'. The prodigal son, suggestively named after Mrs Oliphant's brother, is saved through the mother. Yet, as so often in her tales of the supernatural, the enigma is provided, not so much by the surface plot of ghostly visitation, but by the reader's disconcerting suspicion that the real centre of interest lies elsewhere. Thirty years' experience in learning to subvert her male persona in *Blackwood's* reaps its reward in tales like **A Beleaguered City** and **"The Open Door"**. It is the Colonel, rather than his son, who is most enduringly affected by this encounter with the unseen. To preserve his position as the decisive and effective parent the Colonel is forced to confront those very irrational forces he most distrusts and dismisses as feminine. His narrative has already dismissed 'that fool of a woman at the gate' and proclaimed that the most effective way of allaying his wife's anxieties is to refuse to take any notice of them. Events force him both to recognize the inadequacy of 'manly' fortitude as a code to life and to accommodate previously denied or suppressed facets of life within his definition of 'manliness'. Physical courage, embodied in his soldier-butler, gives way before the unseen. The local doctor's scientific materialism makes no headway with his son's health and moreover begins to irritate the Colonel by its obstinate reductionism. Only his son and the elderly minister, unembarrassed by his tearful tussle with the wandering spirit, seem free from terror and able to concentrate upon 'succouring' a poor fellow creature in misery. If by the end of the tale the Colonel's fear of 'the hysterical' is no less, at least he has been convinced that his former 'male' template does not meet all cases and his narrative ends with the sentence, 'Things have effects so different on the minds of different men'. (A far less subtle tale, **"The Portrait"** of 1885, was to investigate the spiritual sterility of the male ethos by alternately removing and replacing feminine influence in a young man's life.)

"The Lady's Walk", a short story of the same year as **"The Open Door"**, repeated these concerns and introduced a new theme that was also to haunt the next tale of the supernatural, **"Old Lady Mary"**: the power to provide for the next generation. As in **"Earthbound"** and **"The Portrait"**, we have a tale of female doubling. The spirit of an ancestress walks the ground of the Ellermore estate anxious to alert the family to impending threats. There is a strong physical resemblance between her and the current mistress of Ellermore, Charlotte, the eldest daughter, who vowed to her dying mother to devote herself to the care of her siblings. Eventually the ancestress and her descendant have to accept that they cannot avert the series of disasters that occur, but Charlotte exorcizes or liberates the ghost by distinguishing between legitimate self-sacrifice for those entrusted to one's care and attempting to usurp God's position by playing Providence. The departing ghost's rueful reflection, 'I have never done any good—just frightened them, or pleased them', is an uncomfortable echo of Mrs Oliphant's private lamentations over her inability to influence her obstinately indifferent sons. The tale is told, however, by a bachelor barrister intent on marrying Charlotte. His wishes lead him to interpret Charlotte's role as virgin-mother as enslavement,

'a poor sort of reward for a good woman. There is such a thing as being too devoted to a family. Are they ever grateful? They go away and marry and leave you in the lurch.' In the course of the tale the narrator learns 'to bear the woman's part': although he is allowed to provide sympathy from the sidelines he begins to feel 'rage at his impotence to help'. Finally, he finds himself in a position to provide the money to save the family estate but can only do so as an altruistic sacrifice since he is not to be rewarded by marriage to Charlotte, whose undivided attention seems so important to her immediate family.

FURTHER READING

Biography

Stebbins, Lucy Poate. "Margaret Oliphant." In *A Victorian Album: Some Lady Novelists of the Period,* pp. 155-91. New York: Columbia University Press, 1946.

   A complete and readable biographical essay, offering a conventional picture of the lady novelist.

Williams, Merryn. *Margaret Oliphant: A Critical Biography.* London: Macmillan Press, 1986, 217 p.

   The first full biography of Oliphant.

Criticism

Dickerson, Vanessa D. "Angels, Money, and Ghosts: Victorian Female Writers of the Supernatural." In *Gender, Culture, and the Arts: Women, the Arts, and Society,* edited by Ronald Dotterer and Susan Bowers, pp. 87-98. Selinsgrove: Susquehanna University Press, 1993.

   Explores issues of money and power through this study of the ghost stories of Oliphant and two female contemporaries, Charlotte Riddell and Florence Marryat.

Trela, D. J., ed. *Margaret Oliphant: Critical Essays on a Gentle Subversive.* Selinsgrove: Susquehanna University Press, 1995, 190 p.

   This collection of essays on Oliphant's reputation, relationship with her editor, autobiography, and many other topics, challenges the presumption that Oliphant was over-productive and over-rated.

Additional coverage of Oliphant's life and career is contained in the following sources published by Gale Research: *Dictionary of Literary Biography,* Vols. 18, 159; and *Nineteenth-Century Literary Criticism,* Vol. 11.

Frederik Pohl
1919–

American novelist, short story writer, editor, nonfiction writer, and memoirist.

INTRODUCTION

A major figure in the science fiction genre, Pohl is best known for the novel he cowrote with C. M. Kornbluth, *The Space Merchants* (1953), and his short stories of the 1950s, 1960s, and 1970s, including "The Midas Plague," "The Tunnel under the World," and "Day Million." His work of this period marked a new direction in science fiction, which, up to this time, consisted primarily of space adventure stories. Pohl, instead, satirized American consumer culture, incorporated politics and psychology into his works, and brought an element of social criticism to the genre. In addition to his writing, Pohl has edited such major American science fiction magazines as *Galaxy* and *If* as well as numerous science fiction anthologies. Considered to have profoundly influenced the development of science fiction, Pohl was once described by Kingsley Amis as "the most consistently able writer science fiction, in the modern sense, has yet produced."

Biographical Information

Born in New York City, Pohl grew up in Brooklyn during the Great Depression. His father was often unemployed, and his family moved frequently, with Pohl attending school only intermittently until he was eight. In his memoir *The Way the Future Was* (1978), Pohl recalls the homeless and destitute people he encountered as a child, and some critics have speculated that such experiences have profoundly influenced his fiction. Pohl began reading science fiction when he was about ten years old; he read all the extant back issues of the famous pulp magazines of the day, including *Amazing Stories, Science Wonder,* and *Weird Tales.* In his teens, Pohl was active in science fiction fan clubs and wrote for and edited fan magazines. After joining a group of would-be science fiction writers called the Futurians, Pohl became friends with Isaac Asimov and met Kornbluth and Jack Williamson, both of whom he collaborated with on later projects. Before he was twenty, Pohl was selling his own short fiction, working as a literary agent, and editing two pulp magazines, *Astonishing Stories* and *Super Science Stories.*

Pohl served in the Air Force in Italy during World War II and later worked in a Madison Avenue advertising agency. He continued to write short stories in science fiction and other pulp genres during this period. Pohl's career took off in the 1950s when he produced several books a year, often in collaboration with other writers. His first short fiction collection, *Alternating Currents,* was published in 1956. Pohl edited *Galaxy* and *If* from 1961 to 1969, before resigning to devote more time to his own writing. As an editor, he tried to encourage more socially conscious writing; he also both supported and decried the "New Wave" writers of science fiction, a group that borrowed literary techniques from mainstream literature and attempted to eliminate what they saw as the genre's clichés. Pohl applauded their efforts to make science fiction more literary, but he disapproved of what he considered their emphasis on sex and their aesthetic excesses. Pohl served as executive editor at Ace Books in the early 1970s and later worked as an editor at Bantam. He has since participated in numerous international science fiction conferences, lectured at colleges throughout the United States and abroad, and served as the president of Science Fiction Writers of America. Pohl has won numerous literary prizes, including a Hugo Award for best short story of 1972 for "The Meeting" and again in 1986 for the story "Fermi and Frost."

Major Works of Short Fiction

Pohl's short stories of the 1950s frequently satirize and attack American consumer culture. For example, in "The Tunnel under the World," collected in *Alternating Currents,* a town of 21,000 people is destroyed in an industrial accident. It is then rebuilt in miniature, and the minds of its former inhabitants are implanted in miniaturized robots of themselves. The experiment is run by an advertising executive who uses the model town as the perfect market research arena for outrageously abusive advertising campaigns. Another of Pohls's most notable stories from the 1950s is "The Midas Plague." In this story, the lot of the poor is to endlessly consume opulent and useless goods foisted on them by robot servants until one ingenious man, Morey Field, gets his robots to consume for him. Other significant stories from this period include "What to Do till the Analyst Comes," which presents a world transformed by the effects of Cheery-Gum, a harmless and physically nonaddictive happiness drug, and "The Census Takers," one of several Pohl stories in which an alien who comes to warn the human race of danger is nonchalantly killed.

Although Pohl spent much of the 1960s editing *If* and *Galaxy,* he did experiment with what he called "velocity exercises," short stories in which he de-emphasized plot to focus on thematic and satiric concerns. He also began to incorporate aliens and other elements of outer space into his works. The story "Earth 18," for example, includes a tourist guidebook to Earth's attractions developed by alien entrepreneurs. "Day Million" is a love story set in the future when, according to critic David N. Samuelson, "genetic engineering and social change have modified the meaning of gender, the forms human bodies can take, and the immediacy and exclusiveness of a love relationship."

Pohl's short fiction of the 1970s and 1980s is less satirical and more pessimistic and introspective than his earlier works. In these stories, he examined the negative effects of science and technology, including overpopulation and the exploitation of natural resources. He also experimented with style and structure, using more complex characterization, multiple viewpoints, and unreliable narrators. Noteworthy stories include "We Purchased People" and "Spending the Day at the Lottery Fair," both of which are collected in *Pohlstars* (1984). "We Purchased People" is the story of a couple who are found guilty of horrible crimes. Sold to aliens, who then use them for their business dealings on earth, the man and woman seldom meet, except when the aliens want to observe them to learn more about human sexuality. In the latter story, a family ambles through an amusement park where randomly selected visitors are killed throughout the day and put on display as an antidote to overpopulation. Following the publication of *Pohlstars*, Pohl focused primarily on novel writing.

Critical Reception

Before he published *The Space Merchants* with Korn-

bluth, Pohl was considered a talented but unexceptional science fiction writer. *The Space Merchants,* however, brought him unprecedented popular and critical acclaim. In one of the first serious critical works about science fiction, *New Maps of Hell* (1960), Kingsley Amis found *The Space Merchants* "the best science fiction novel so far"; he also praised Pohl's "consumer" stories of the 1950s. Later critics also focused on these early stories, heralding Pohl for his humor and satire, his inclusion of personal experience and everyday problems, his believable characters, and his focus on complex social concerns. Writing about Pohl's collaboration with Kornbluth, Charles Platt stated that the two writers "pioneered and excelled in a completely new kind of science fiction. They invented and played with 'Sociological SF'— alternate futures here on Earth, exaggerating and satirizing real-life social forces and trends." Robert Scholes and Eric S. Rabkin also emphasized Pohl's contribution to the evolution of science fiction when they asserted that he is one of the few writers to "make a genuine impact on the science fiction field."

PRINCIPAL WORKS

Short Fiction

Alternating Currents 1956
The Case against Tomorrow 1957
Tomorrow Times Seven 1959
The Man Who Ate the World 1960
Turn Left at Thursday 1961
The Abominable Earthman 1963
Digits and Dastards 1966
Day Million 1970
The Gold at the Starbow's End 1972
The Best of Frederik Pohl 1975
The Early Pohl 1976
In the Problem Pit 1976
Critical Mass [with C. M. Kornbluth] 1977
Pohlstars 1984
The Gateway Trip: Tales and Vignettes of the Heechee 1990

Other Major Works

The Space Merchants [with C. M. Kornbluth] (novel) 1953
Gladiator-at-Law [with C. M. Kornbluth] (novel) 1955
Slave Ship (novel) 1957
A Plague of Pythons (novel) 1965
The Age of the Pussyfoot (novel) 1969
Practical Politics (nonfiction) 1972
Man Plus (novel) 1976
Gateway (novel) 1977
The Way the Future Was (memoir) 1978
JEM (novel) 1979
Beyond the Blue Event Horizon (novel) 1980
The Cool War (novel) 1981
Syzygy (novel) 1981
Midas World (novel) 1983

CRITICISM

Kingsley Amis (essay date 1960)

SOURCE: "Utopias 2," in *New Maps of Hell: A Survey of Science Fiction,* Harcourt, Brace and Company, 1960, pp. 118-33.

[*In the following excerpt, Amis examines the themes of production and consumption in the stories "The Midas Plague," "The Wizards of Pung's Corners," and "The Tunnel under the World."*]

We have now reached the point of departure for the consideration, in some detail, of the work of Frederik Pohl, the most consistently able writer science fiction, in the modern sense, has yet produced. His field of interest is contemporary urban society and its chain of production and consumption. He is thus in some sort a novelist of economic man, or, rather, of two overlapping personages within that concept, the well-to-do consumer and the high-level executive who keeps the consumer consuming. An occasional space-ship flashes across his page, but no BEM ever raises its heads there and aliens do not appeal to him; the adventure-story component of his work is incidental. His mode is typically the satirical utopia, with comic-inferno elements rarely absent; his method is selective exaggeration of observable features of our society, plus the concrete elaboration noted in Sheckley. These are well illustrated in a story from his aptly named collection *The Case Against Tomorrow*. This story, **"The Midas Plague,"** is a straight comic-inferno satire on the social effects of overproduction. We open with a wedding reception in the quarter-acre, fountain-studded ballroom of the gigantic mansion owned by the hero, Morey Field, complete with its nine special-function robots. The bride's parents, wearing rented garments, eventually drive off in a miniature runabout to their five-room cottage, full of foreboding about the advisability of rich folks marrying poor folks. After a short round of fantastic luxuries, Cherry, the wife, tires even of the expensive companion-robot's anecdotes and bursts into a tearful tirade against the miseries of poverty, for in this society the poor man is he who must consume more than his neighbour. And consumption must be genuine, the Dionysian meals really consumed, the sports gear really worn out in exercise with the sparring-robot, or there will be trouble with the Ration Board, a vast

bureaucracy seen as a vigilant nuisance rather than a means of repression, this not being a political satire. Pohl quickly sketches in the domestic and social consequences of

> Limitless discovery, infinite power in the atom, tireless labor of humanity and robots, mechanization that drove jungle and swamp and ice off the Earth, and put up office buildings and manufacturing centers in their place. . . .

> The pipeline of production spewed out riches that no king in the time of Malthus could have known.

> But a pipeline has two ends. The invention and power and labor pouring in at one end must somehow be drained out at the other. . . .

> Lucky Morey, blessed economic-consuming unit, drowning in the pipeline's flood, striving manfully to eat and drink and wear and wear out his share of the ceaseless tide of wealth,

for, as he puts it to himself later, "you can't break eggs without making an omelette." The survey that follows is compact, energetic, inventive, and often comic. I cannot enumerate all the detail, but there is an account of the garishness of slums that cleverly utilises another line of satirical prediction, and a well-devised moment when Morey turns up for his regular psychoanalytic session. It is group therapy, of course, and on this occasion there are eleven in the group: "four Freudians, two Reichians, two Jungians, a Gestalter, a shock therapist and the elderly and rather quiet Sullivanite." Finally Morey brings the two ends of the production pipeline together by arranging for the robots to do all the necessary consuming after being fitted with special satisfaction circuits to obviate the normal legal and moral objections against waste. He moves up to a five-room house, is voted Consumer of the Year, and becomes reconciled with his wife. The Ration Board goes into voluntary liquidation.

> **Pohl's mode is typically the satirical utopia, with comic-inferno elements rarely absent; his method is selective exaggeration of observable features in our society.**
>
> —*Kingsley Amis*

I have outlined this story at some length because to do so goes some way to demonstrate the inventive quality I mentioned: once the specific assumption has been set up—one with a satiric value that does no violence to our notions of what is possible—the procedure of the comic inferno is to delineate the social picture by the constant introduction of novelties, these to be, where possible, witty, in the sense that they will strike by their singularity at first sight, but are on reflection found to be just. By "just" I mean that these novelties should extend the original assumption and maintain a corresponding link with the possible; they need show no individual connection with observable features of our own society. The slightest acquaintance shows that to read a science-fiction utopia as one reads the traditional allegory, alert for one-to-one correspondences, is to misread it. If this represents an impoverishment, an unwillingness to face a difficult and more serious task, something may be gained by the resulting liberation of the fancy. If, again, I seem to be justifying a flight from reality and thus from satire, it can be argued that from the good comic inferno, as here, more generalisations than one may emerge. **"The Midas Plague"** does not merely inform us that the results of overproduction may be fantastic, or hilarious, or desperate; it also comments on the revolutions in manners which human beings will swallow—in Morey Field's world you show your politeness by letting the other fellow pick up the restaurant or bar bill—and something too is being said about our adaptability in applying unchanged moral attitudes to changed moral forms—Morey's father-in-law treats a joke about waste with the reluctant abandonment of tolerance with which others might treat a joke about religion. I am not trying to solemnise a *jeu d'esprit,* but considerations like these, along with judgment of the inventive flow, are what enable us to grade science-fiction stories, to decide, for instance, that **"The Midas Plague"** is superior to another by the same author, **"The Wizards of Pung's Corners."** Here the techniques of consumer-oriented production are applied to the armoury of the United States forces, with an advertising agency occupying the fifth side of the Pentagon. After some Parkinson's-Law satire on the multiplication of auxiliaries—there are Historical Section tape recorders in every foxhole—the main thrust is reached with the description of the weapons, all of which, naturally, have built-in consumer-dissatisfactions. The 105-mm explosive cannon with Zip-Fire Auto-Load and Wizard-trol Safety Interlock turns out to be no good, the E-Z-Fyre Revolv-a-Clip Carbine is too complicated, and even the "full-color, glossy-paper operating manual— *The Five-Step Magic-Eye Way to New Combat Comfort and Security*" is no help to the troops, who are easily disarmed by a few farmers with shotguns. Though moving at a splendid pace in this scene, invention is rather sparse earlier on, apart from some very funny, but utterly irrelevant, speculation about the selling value of pornographic subliminal commercials on television. Above all, unless I am being unduly optimistic, the initial premise of this story seems too far from plausibility to permit of anything very relevant being said about our own time, and the tendency of soldiers to go on being soldiers even when tinkering with the E-Z-Fyre Carbine is hardly edifying. That rare personage, he who knows something of serious literature and something of science fiction, would conclude that **"The Wizards of Pung's Corners"** is entertaining but frivolous. But, once more, entertaining; we have not got so much of that in science fiction yet that we can afford to be patronising about it.

So much for the comic inferno, a mode of writing that is clearly older than science fiction, but makes its own hum-

ble claim to originality here, in that the absurdities it envisages rest upon conceivable developments in technology: this is an invariable rule. Its moral value, if one must be contrived, is that it ridicules notions which various heavy pressures would have us take seriously: pride in a mounting material standard of living, the belief that such progress can be continued indefinitely and needs only horizontal extension to make the world perfect, the feeling that the accumulation of possessions is at once the prerogative and the evidence of merit. When the science-fiction writer moves from dealing with the effects of these assumptions to the forces which manipulate them, his tone will become notably less jaunty. We have already referred to another story by Frederik Pohl, **"The Tunnel Under the World,"** in which a township is reduced to the status of a human laboratory for testing sales-reaction. One extra point emerging from it, in the hero's appalled realisation that what has been done to him and his friends could be done to the whole world if need be, reflects a widespread anxiety about the possible political uses of discoveries made in the commercial field. The fear that some physicist may accidentally blow the Earth into the sun is evidently being overhauled by the fear that some researcher working on consumer resistance will stumble on a subliminal technique which can be adopted by authority. This is the overt theme of a dull story called **"Take a Deep Breath,"** where the success of a hypnotic technique on television induces the manufacturer to give up making horrible cigarettes and stand for President. I mention this only because, as before, the distribution of an idea can best be gauged by its spread downwards. To return to Frederik Pohl and his tunnel: the most disturbing part of the story is not so much the horror-loaded climax as a brief scene in which the controlling power tries out a new advertising procedure. It starts with a van driving into a residential area playing at top volume a tape-recording of fire engines answering an alarm. Then:

> The bellow caught him from behind; it was almost like a hard slap on the ears. A harsh, sneering voice, louder than the archangel's trumpet, howled:

> "Have you got a freezer? *It stinks!* If it isn't a Feckle Freezer, *it stinks!* If it's a last year's Feckle Freezer, *it stinks!* Only this year's Feckle Freezer is any good at all! You know who owns an Ajax Freezer? Fairies own Ajax Freezers! You know who owns a Triplecold Freezer? Commies own Triplecold Freezers! Every freezer but a brand-new Feckle Freezer *stinks!*"

> The voice screamed inarticulately with rage. "I'm warning you! Get out and buy a Feckle Freezer right away! Hurry up! Hurry for Feckle! Hurry, hurry, hurry, Feckle, Feckle, Feckle, Feckle, Feckle, Feckle. . . ."

The effectiveness of that presumably derives not only from the way it dramatises the coercive tendency of some actual advertising, nor from the reflection any of us might have that this is how they would like to talk to us if they dared, but also from its having touched on a truth about the whole advertising idea, that it is an outrage, an assault on people's mental privacy. Here certainly, to my mind, one carries away that residual uneasiness which I mentioned before as the inverted catharsis good science fiction can provide, and which seems to contradict those critics who find in it an oversimplifying complacency posing as moral concern. One would have the best of reasons for disliking the kind of future described in this story, even without reading its entirety as an allegorical account of the thraldom of economic man.

Frederik Pohl with Paul Walker (interview date 1970)

SOURCE: "Frederik Pohl," in *Speaking of Science Fiction: The Paul Walker Interviews,* Luna Publications, 1978, pp. 129-43.

[*In the following interview, which was conducted in September-October 1970 and first published in* Moebius Trip *in 1971, Pohl discusses such topics as his writing and editing careers, his collaboration with Cyril M. Kornbluth, and the effects of technology on literature and society.*]

[Walker]: *On your Grand Tour of 2527, in* The Age of the Pussyfoot, *you suggest (if I understand you correctly) that for the future we may expect even more of today. Capitalism moves ever onward in its ever-changing guises, motivated by man's desire for material goods. Socialist idealism gives way to the "corporate state," and the wonders of a Gernsbacchanalian technology are bent to the frivolous demands of a middle-class society. Is this to be, sir?*

[Pohl]: First off, Paul, we're not going to get along very well if you ask me to defend my stories as predictions of "the" future. That's not what they're meant to be. For one thing, there is no single future. By the time our possible options are reduced to one, it isn't the future any more, it's the present. While it is the future, it is plural.

My stories are not predictions at all, they are cautionary tales (or else, rarely, they are Utopian tales), describing one possible set of future events.

I don't feel any obligation to answer questions of the form: "do you really think this is what's going to happen?"; or to defend myself against charges of inconsistency between stories. Of course, each story has an internal logic, and I must defend that if pressed.

Do you think our current trend toward socialism will be eclipsed?

I don't think so on the grounds that there isn't any such trend visible, so how can it be eclipsed? I see no evidence for increasing degrees of socialism, whether Marxist or otherwise, anywhere in the world. I do see, of course, an increasing trend toward statism and toward the concentration of power in semi-public institutions, but I don't think this is socialism.

Some partisans on either side of the state-power issue refer to this trend as socialism, and if that's what you mean, then I must give a different answer. But it still won't be a good one, because I don't think this trend will either continue or be reversed. I simply think it will be outmoded. This is, after all, what happens to all large-scale competitions; they are hardly ever resolved, they are simply replaced by different dichotomies.

(Some people think that these competitions get resolved because they often develop into wars, and wars usually have one side labelled "winner" and the other side labelled "loser." But this is nonsense, of course. The South "lost" the Civil War, but obviously the Confederacy now owns the rest of the country in fee simple. The Germans and Japanese "lost" WWII, but what are now the two fastest-growing economies on the earth?)

What about technology? Can it—has it—altered the basic life styles, the basic elements of human nature: the physical and emotional content of love and hate, aggression and passivity? Do you see any basic changes in human nature that you would ascribe to technology?

Certainly technology can basically alter our life styles. It is doing so at a headlong pace right now: the computer, the automobile, antibiotics, TV have made 1970 more different from 1870 than 1870 was from the Middle Ages. The problem with using those things as illustrations is that we haven't the perspective to see clearly what is happening to us, so let me go to the past for an example.

If there is one "moral dogma" that is universally agreed to it is the stricture against "cruel and unusual punishment"— i.e., torture. Everybody says that is evil. It is still practiced, to be sure, quite universally, including all parts of the United States; but no public figure anywhere defends it on principle.

When we read in the history books of gladiatorial games and examinations "under duress"—that is, with rack and thumbscrews—we think how much life styles have changed. But the change is technology. Until about the middle of the last century, pain was a part of every human being's life. He expected it as a matter of course, and he got it. About the only difference between being flayed alive and a normal everyday toothache was that you could survive the second, but not the first; the degree of agony was quite close. Then along came anesthesia and analgesia, etc., and pain became remediable.

So what does one say about this particular change? That it is an improvement in morality; that we are kinder now, because we don't hurt people? That it is a matter of technology? Actually, I think the explanation is that morality follows technology; what is "good" and "right" is always limited to what is possible.

People change all the time. They are changed the most when they think themselves unchanged at all. (See **"Day Million"** on this point.) What I do think is that this change does not always involve the same parameters and that it is not always in the same direction.

I don't want to talk about my work because that sort of naked vanity is embarrassing to me, so let me give you some illustrations from the real world. Compare Communist and Capitalist. Is there a difference between a Communist apparatnik and an American management man?

They think so. If you ask them what they believe in, they would even make you think so; for one would relate his life to the solidarity of the working class and the quest for world peace, while the other would refer to God and the therapeutic effects of free markets.

In practice, however, you can't tell them apart. The Communist who occupies a middle-management position in the Soviet structure (a member of the municipal party secretariat, for instance) is identical with the GM or the National City Bank $40,000-a-year man in his terror of saying the non-conforming thing or losing sight of the organization goal. To each the central fact of the world is that *he* is better off than 99% of the people around him, and he owes it to the apparatus; and he is scared witless of jeopardizing the apparatus itself or his position within it.

If my stories show the undesirable effects of technology, and of course they do, it is because they are of concern to me. But I have never believed in throwing the baby out with the bath.

—Frederik Pohl

So from this, class, we see that where human nature appears to be most changed it may well be exactly the same. Now let us prove that where it seems to be exactly the same it may well be wholly changed. Let us consider love.

If we see romantic drama, perhaps Shakespeare's *Romeo and Juliet* or *Anthony and Cleopatra,* we nod and say, ah, yes, to be sure, I saw that in an old MGM movie on TV last night; love was exactly the same to Hermia and Cleopatra as it was a few thousand years later to Bette Davis and Toby Wing. Well, it wasn't. Classic Greece and Rome had no tradition of sentimental love at all. Their man-woman couples did not practice tender courtship or suffer agonies at separation. When, very rarely, some couple showed what we would now consider a normal man-woman infatuation, their contemporaries thought they had gone crazy. It wasn't until Eleanor of Aquitaine that mooning over a desired lover came to seem standard behavior even in the western world; and of course, it is only since MGM that it has come to seem so in most of the rest of the planet.

Well, Paul, I didn't mean to belabor the point, but what the

point *is* is that I don't think there is a specific direction or kind of change in human behavior for the future any more than I think there is a specific single future. Under certain conditions there will be change of a certain kind, and when I write about those conditions I talk about that kind of change. Under other conditions, I don't think there will be any change at all; perhaps only a relabelling as between Socialist and Organization Man, and when I write about those conditions that is what I show. And then, of course, sometimes I goof.

In my last letter, I said I thought you were less interested in the future of man than in man as he is today; is that true or not? What does a white, middle-aged, middle-class man of these 1970's, with a respect for good English and academic pursuite, have to say to, and about, these whippersnappers of the "Age of Aquarius"?

The reason I didn't say I was less interested in the future of man than in man today is that it isn't true. Nor do I think those whippersnappers are as disrespectful of my long gray beard and glittering eye as you appear to be.

The long answer is that I don't think there is an Age of Aquarius, except for a tiny few people in a very limited part of the earth. In some moods, I think it is too bad. How nice it would be if we could greet strangers in love and joy instead of looking at their hands to see if they're holding a knife. In other moods I think that even violence, repression, and industrial filth are not too high a price to pay for the rapid increase in knowledge and power the human race has experienced in the past few decades.

But when forced to think about everything together, I come back to the short answer. The Age of Aquarius is a function of surplus production, and there is little reason to think that the human race can sustain the creation of even local and temporary surpluses.

That is a most provocative response, sir. Without quibbling over any inconsistency in your remarks, I think it should be asked: What good are knowledge and power to man if they do not eradicate violence, repression, and industrial filth? In fact, are they not inimical to man if they encourage violence, repression, and industrial filth? Some suggest man would be wiser to settle for less knowledge and power.

But then, what do you mean by "knowledge"? What do you mean by "power"?

Certainly technology is a force for good. Equally certainly it produces side effects which are bad. The big job for all of us is to try to retain the good parts while suppressing the evil side effects.

Of course, there are those modern Luddites who want to give up technology completely and go on to a life of tilling the soil, sitar music, and macrobiotic wheat germ bread. God bless. I don't object to any person feeling this way, although I do object to having any person try to impose this feeling on my life; *I* don't want to give up technology.

What I want to do is separate the automobile from its exhaust and traffic jams, the air conditioner from power blackouts, nuclear power from nuclear fallout; so that we can keep the first and avoid the second, in each case. If my stories show the undesirable effects of technology, and of course they do, it is because they are of concern to me. But I have never believed in throwing the baby out with the bath.

What I mean by "power" is the ability to change the environment, and in general, to do whatever the hell one wants to do. Some environmental changes are of course lousy: the Sahara, the outskirts of any American city, Lake Erie. But most are good. We can live in deserts, at the South Pole, or on the Moon, because we can change the environment or bring a new environment with us. Even our scenic changes are often good: anyone who likes England or the Mediterranean coast of France or the Bay of Naples must agree to this, because they are all artifacts; the "natural" state of them is gone.

What I mean by "knowledge" is all kinds of knowledge— you never know what particular bit of information is going to be useful. But the particular kind of knowledge that I think is urgently required is that kind which helps predict future events. You learn to drive a car. You learn right away that if you step down on the accelerator you go faster. You learn a little bit later, and maybe only after a disastrous experience, that the other thing you accomplish when you step down on the accelerator is to increase your chances of wiping out yourself and sixteen other people in a crash.

That, too, is a matter of side effects, of course.

A couple of years ago I was asked to keynote what is called the "Goddard Memorial Conference" for the American Astronautical Society. The subject of the conference was the relationship between progress and technology. For the purpose I invented a quantum unit of progress, on the principle that you couldn't relate the two concepts unless they had a measuring unit in common. The quantum unit I used was the "option." I defined as "progressive" that kind of technological change which increased the number of options available to human beings and societies; as "anti-progressive" that which reduced them.

Knowledge and power, in any sense, but particularly in the senses above, increase options.

What about the "New Wave"?

Behavioristically, what is true of the New Wave in general is that they are deeply given to discussing their work. I'm not, or at least not in the same way. The Milford sort of thing seems to me fraught with dangers. Its attraction, to the extent that I perceive any attraction in it at all, appears to lie more in the direction of personal group therapy than in improving the individual literary skills of the participants.

I think it damages more writers than it helps, all in all, but principally I am convinced that it damages me when I engage in this sort of thing, whether in the form of physical presence in a group or sitting in my own little room and engaging in literary debates about my own work. So for a long time, Paul, I have schooled myself to disregard criticism, or at least to discount maybe nine-tenths of it. This is true whether the criticism is favorable or hostile, and it isn't so much because I consider myself stronger or above it because I am certain that I am weak. I am by nature deeply susceptible to praise or blame. Flattery turns my head. Scorn makes me angry and upset. In order to be able to function at what seems to me my best attainable level of competence, I try to exclude both from my central nervous system, or anyway admit them only in filtered and tenuous form.

What is wrong with that practice is that it is possible I miss a lot of intelligent, valuable, even helpful comment, thus failing to learn things I should know and thereby damaging myself and my work. I know this is a danger, but I have no good way to avoid it.

However, I am quite sure it is not much of a danger. Let me give you an illustration. One of the most complete and perceptive studies ever made of me and my work was Kingsley Amis's. When he said in *New Maps of Hell* that I was the best SF writer around, I wrestled with an overpowering urge to vanity for some time. After some traumatic spasms I came to the conclusion that he didn't know what he was talking about. The most he should properly have said was that I happened to be the one writer who was consistently performing well in one particular area of SF, the SF of social comment, and he happened to be interested in only that area. A few years later, Kingsley changed his wife and his politics and came to the conclusion that I was no damn good at all.

Well, he was wrong both times, you see. And, in general, SF critics are as likely to be wrong as they are to be right.

I have spent most of my life in SF, one way or another, so you are entitled to ask what I think I'm doing in it. I am trying as best I can to learn everything I can about everything there is; to assemble the information thus acquired into patterns of relevance; and to display these patterns as entertainingly as I can, to anyone who cares to read them in the form of science-fiction stories.

How well have I succeeded? About this I am both humble and vain. My humility lies in the awareness that, at the age of fifty, I still have managed to learn only very imperfectly the merest surface glimmering of the enormous variety of human knowledge. I have only partially and inadequately been able to form what I have learned into larger schemes; and I have failed almost wholly to convey them in stories. My vanity, on the other hand, lies in the perception that, inadequate as I am, I can't think of very many others who have done even as well, much less better.

Apropos of nothing, I remember the poverty so vividly described in Gladiator-at-Law, *and now here in* The Age of the Pussyfoot; *your protagonists' terror of it and their eventual realization that life goes on, regardless. I'm curious to know if this is based on personal experience.*

Have I had a personal experience of poverty? Sure. As a kid I swung with the pendulum of my father's fortunes, and he was a plunger. One week we lived in a suite in a luxury hotel, the next we were looking for a rooming house to take us in on credit. I don't think it scared me, exactly, but it did affect my attitudes, although by the time I was twelve or thirteen the swings had pretty much leveled out.

I no longer worry much about poverty, partly because I've made a reasonable amount of money and partly because money isn't what I want anyway. (The one great good thing about my life is that I don't have to do anything just for money, because it has turned out that people will give me money for doing things I would gladly have done for nothing anyway.) If I became poor I would be seriously annoyed, at least temporarily, because it would mean that I couldn't take the kids to Europe or fly the whole family to Bermuda to get out of the cold weather or keep three cars and six TV sets any more; but in the long run what it would probably mean would be that we'd sell out and move to some cheaper, but quite likely pleasanter and more interesting, place.

> **I have schooled myself to disregard criticism, or at least to discount maybe nine-tenths of it. This is true whether the criticism is favorable or hostile, and it isn't so much because I consider myself stronger or above it because I am certain that I am weak.**
>
> **—Frederik Pohl**

It is not uncommon for a writer to say he writes to clarify his thoughts to himself as well as to stimulate and entertain. On the other hand, we have D.H. Lawrence's perspective that his thoughts arose from the material at hand. Do you think of yourself as a social observer utilizing the medium to express your opinions or would you write if you had no opinions whatever?

And, speaking of media, what is your apparent fondness for the short story?

I can't imagine what I would be like if I had no opinions. (I can't believe that a person with no opinions is even human.) Someone once said that the proper title for any literary work is "How to Be More Like Me." I agree that this is so; I write for the same reason that any other writer writes: because I feel that I have something to say that should be said.

The material shapes my thoughts as much as my thoughts shape the material. I can distinguish between the two in

other people's work sometimes, I think. I am sure I can't very well in my own.

In the same way, the decision to write a novel, a novelette, or a short story is in part because of the material and in part my own. I can't give a general rule, because each case is different. Let me go back a little bit behind your question and talk about how writers write.

A professional writer seldom sits down to write because he is inspired to say one particular thing at that particular time. His head is always abuzz with bits and pieces of things he sort of wants to think out and put down, and what makes him write one thing rather than another is ordinarily an external force such as an editor or publisher: he is asked to contribute a short story to a magazine or a book, or he has to fulfill a book contract, or he sees a market and tries to find something to sell to it.

The advantages of this are two: first, financial; he stands to make more money by producing something someone is known to want to buy than by producing something that he thinks is worthwhile but that has to sell itself to a customer. Second, it causes him to write in the first place.

The disadvantages, however, are severe. I have a stack of about twenty SF novels that I've read waiting to be reviewed, and frankly I haven't the heart to review them because they are so uniformly lousy. If they have one thing in common it is that none of them, not even one of them, is quite worth the space it takes up. Most of them are worth very little because of incompetence on the part of the writers; it appears that anything that is called SF and comes out to at least 50,000 words will get published by somebody, sooner or later. But even the ones which have some good qualities are fat, bloated, stretched out, milked. The reason for this is the pressure of the market; there is little market for short stories and novelettes, an insatiable market for novels.

So if you are a writer of moderate talent and standing, what do you do with your short story ideas? Why, you do what everybody else does: you pad them out to 60,000 words, whether they can stand it or not.

For various reasons I've been under less pressure than many writers in this way, so I've been able to resist the temptation at least part of the time. I'm not really particularly fond of the short story qua short story, but I've been able to avoid the necessity of turning *all* my short story ideas into jumped-up novels.

Tell me about your collaboration with C. M. Kornbluth.

Cyril and I started working together in the Futurian days, along about 1940, when I was first editing *Astonishing Stories* and *Super Science Stories,* and all of us were first trying to write for money. Collaboration was the way of life. I suppose we all wanted support. The way we first worked together, Cyril and I, was that I would write a synopsis of the story, Cyril would rough out a draft, and I would revise it for publication. We wrote a dozen or so stories that way, most of them not very good.

About 1950, Cyril moved into my house in New Jersey, having quit his job with a news-wire service, and we began collaborating again. I had written about a third of *The Space Merchants,* and offered it to Cyril as a collaboration venture. He wrote the next third from my verbal description of where it was going, and the final third we wrote a few pages at a time, by turns. After that, we wrote almost entirely by turns. We would discuss a story idea for a few hours, just talking over situation and characters and general considerations, not putting anything on paper. Then one of us would go up to the third floor where the typewriters were and write the first five pages, stopping at the bottom of the fifth page. The other would write the next five, *und so weiter*; and ultimately we would have a book. I then did the final pulling-together and polishing myself (on all except *Wolfbane,* which Cyril polished and expanded to book length just before he died).

He was one of the most rewarding people I have ever known. He was an angry man, and his own impression of himself was that he was a cruel one; certainly he missed few opportunities of shafting a friend conversationally. But he was also enormously well informed and enormously creative. We quarreled often and vigorously, but having cleared the air we were friends again. I suppose I was too close to Cyril to evaluate him in any objective way, but if I could spend an hour with anyone I've ever known I think I would want that person to be Cyril.

Aside from short stories, you write novels, essays; you edit magazines and attend fan functions; you lecture and do stints as a panelist on radio shows: do you feel at home in any one of these activities more than the others? Or do you feel that familiar restlessness when doing one thing to be doing another?

Well, first and foremost, I consider myself a writer. Anything else I do has to accommodate itself to that fact. When occasion permits, I enjoy lecturing. I'm ham enough to get a charge out of making 1800 people laugh or think about something they've never troubled to consider before. I find a hell of a lot of useful feedback from lecturing, too; the questions from the floor, the casual comments afterwards, the opportunity to interact with non-literary types—all this is good stuff for me, and probably would be for any writer. But if lecturing interferes with writing, I lay off lecturing. In fact, I have done so for most of this year. Apart from teaching a couple of college courses and one or two previous engagements that I couldn't get out of, I've accepted only about half a dozen lecture invitations in calendar 1970, and each of them for a particular reason. It had simply reached the point where I couldn't do some of the writing I wanted. (Currently there are three books and two magazine projects, including a series of interviews for *Playboy*.)

Editing is another matter. If I had to choose between editing and writing, either one to the exclusion of the other, I would have to think a little harder. I probably would still choose writing as a general principle, but with more regret. However, I don't have that freedom of choice in any realistic sense. I gave up editing not because it was interfering with writing but because editing itself became unattractive under the conditions currently open to me.

An editor is a middleman between various pairs of imperatives. Between the publisher and the writer; between the writer and the reader; between art and the marketplace; I could go on multiplying yins and yangs indefinitely. The interests of the opposite pairs are often incompatible, so the editor has to work out the least damaging compromise.

This is pretty abrasive on him. John Campbell once lumbered over to me at a dinner party, grabbed me by the lapel and said, "Fred, do you realize that every editor who doesn't work at science with his own hands goes crazy in three years?" Well, I had several answers to make to that, of course. But editors, particularly SF editors, do operate under a witch of a strain. Half a dozen of them have cracked up one way or another, and a lot of others would have if only they had had the perception and the diligence to accept their responsibilities.

Most things worth doing include strain; but it seems to me of late the job of SF editor, at least of magazines, has become increasingly stressful and less rewarding. I may be wrong. It may be just that I'm getting older. But thirty years ago the only difficult part of the job as editor of *Astonishing Stories* and *Super Science Stories* was getting writers to give me stories I liked. Two years ago that was only one difficult task out of many. I also had, as editor of *Galaxy* and *If,* to try and get distributors to put the magazines out where people could find them, printers to set type with only a few errors and print pages without getting very many of them upside down, advertisers to kick in a few bucks for space, and so on. All of these tasks were just as difficult as dealing with writers, and an awful lot less fun.

The way around those particular tasks is to work for a large publishing house that maintains a staff of specialists to do all that miserable stuff; John has that going for him at Conde Nast, for instance. That option was not open to me, at least not without a lot of other disagreeable involvements, because I also happen to feel that there's no point being an editor unless you can make all the editorial decisions yourself. Few large publishing companies allow their editors this freedom.

At some future date I may find the right combination to edit SF, either in book or magazine form, again. When I'm not doing it, I miss it; I love the creative parts of it, the finding a format in which to publish a story for maximum effect (cf. *The Dragon Masters*), the bringing along a writer who makes it (cf. Larry Niven, R.A. Lafferty), the providing a showplace for kinds of stories that haven't been available before (cf. *International Science Fiction*), and so on.

But most of it, I don't miss at all.

While editor of If-Galaxy *you are reputed to have said*

that your readership consisted of fourteen-year-olds and their parents, and that you would print nothing that would offend the parents. Is this true or false?

Frankly, Paul, it's a damn silly question. I mean, you've seen copies of *If* and *Galaxy*. If it were true that I tried to keep out of them any matter which might be offensive to fourteen-year-olds and their parents, it is quite clear that I didn't succeed very well. I don't know of any "sensitive" subject that was not dealt with in numerous stories in *Galaxy* and *If* during my tenure. Sex, race, religion, politics—if there is something I prevented people from writing about, could you possibly tell me what it is?

I did, of course, from time to time, cut out certain specific words which seemed to be offensive. There was no hard and fast rule about this; a word that might be undesirable in one context would be obviously necessary, and therefore left in, in another. And we are talking about a time several years past now. I'm not sure I would feel as strongly today. But I'm not sure I wouldn't, either. I would have to judge each story on its own merits.

The principal reason for making editorial changes is to please readers—or to avoid displeasing readers, which comes to much the same thing. On the record, I was pretty good at that. When I took the magazines over they were bi-monthlies running in the red. When I left them, they were both monthlies running in the black. I won the editing Hugo for three years straight. Every year there were more stories from my magazines winning Hugos and Nebulas than from any other. So as far as these things can be measured, I think I did about as much as I could at pleasing readers.

As far as avoiding displeasing readers is concerned, there aren't as good measures to be made. The only way you can tell when you've really displeased readers is when they take the trouble to write you about it, perhaps cancelling subscriptions. That didn't happen often. The only story that produced any sizeable number of complaints was Brian Aldiss's "The Dark Light Years," dealing with aliens who regarded moving their bowels as a sacramental act, and the complaints were not particularly violent.

The most violent complaints we ever got were not for a story: they were about Lester del Rey's highly unfavorable review of *2001*. One of the reasons why I am not over-fond of New Wavers is the organized lynch mob that sprang up among their hangers-on at that point; we were threatened with all sorts of retribution, in violent and stupid terms. But that's a separate problem. I often disagreed with what Lester, A.J. (Budrys), and other columnists had to say; but I never censored their saying it. One columnist kept making gross factual errors until I dropped him; I seldom even changed them. I never once rejected a story because it was "too daring." Not once. Not ever.

I do feel the current emphasis on sex, for instance, in SF is a retrograde movement; damn few writers have anything original to say on the subject, and most stories in that area are pretty poor stuff. But when a writer did have anything

interesting to say about sex, I think he was more likely to be able to say it in *Galaxy* and *If* than in any other professional SF magazine. When they were good, I printed them, even if they were dirty. When they were bad, I bounced them, even if they were clean. Or anyway I came as close as I could.

Lester Del Rey (essay date 1975)

SOURCE: "A Variety of Excellence," in *The Best of Frederik Pohl*, Sidgwick and Jackson, 1975, pp. ix-xvi.

[*In the following excerpt of his introduction to* The Best of Frederik Pohl, *Del Rey gives an overview of Pohl's literary career, highlighting some of his best short stories.*]

Nothing is easy to categorize about the life and works of Frederik Pohl. His stories vary more in length, attitude, type and treatment than those of any other writer I know. About the only point of similarity is the high level of excellence to be found in everything from his short-shorts to his novels. To make things more difficult for a biographer, he has been one of the leaders in almost every activity that in any way relates to the broad field of science fiction.

Even his career as a writer falls into two widely separated periods which seem totally unrelated to each other.

He began writing professionally in the very early forties, when he was just out of his teens. A large number of his stories, under a host of pen names, were written in collaboration with one or more other authors, and nobody seems entirely sure of exactly how many people or stories were involved. There were also twelve stories under the name of James McCreigh. The work produced during this period was generally quite competent—good enough to win him welcome from a number of markets—but there was nothing about it to distinguish him from many other young writers of the period.

The second phase of his writing career began eleven years later, after a long hiatus; and his reputation was established from the first story, a serial by Frederik Pohl and C. M. Kornbluth—called *Gravy Planet* in the magazine version, but retitled *The Space Merchants* for book publication. This was unquestionably the most important novel published in 1952. It was favorably reviewed by publications that ranged from *The Wall Street Journal* to organs of the extreme political left, none of which normally gave any space to science fiction.

Pohl and Kornbluth brought the art of satire back to science fiction and were soon being widely imitated by other writers; in fact, the influence of this work reshaped much of the field during the next two decades.

This novel was soon followed by two other collaborations with Kornbluth. Some of the self-proclaimed critics in the field, who remembered Pohl's earlier stories and esteemed the independent work of Kornbluth, immediately decided that Pohl was largely dependent on Kornbluth for the high quality of their novels. They proceeded to pick the works apart, deciding who had done what—and the parts they admired were always ascribed to Kornbluth.

Kornbluth agreed with Pohl that these critics were amazingly consistent in being wrong about it, so far as could be remembered. But this didn't quiet the part-pickers. Even the publication of Pohl's first independent novel, *Slave Ship,* wasn't enough to convince them, though it certainly should have done so. However, as other works by Pohl appeared, even the most severe critics were forced to concede that he was one of the major novelists of the field.

Meantime, among the readers, he was developing a high reputation as a writer of shorter fiction, in which he had no collaborator. His novelette, **"The Midas Plague,"** was the first of his independent stories to appear in *Galaxy* Magazine, in April, 1954. This is a brilliant example of satirical writing, with the shocking bite of its main assumption muted nicely by an element of humor. It is also an extrapolation of one trend, carried just a bit further than any other writer would dare to go with it, and then justified by the other well-developed details of such a society.

I recently had an excellent chance to discover just how good Pohl is as a writer of shorter fiction. In making the selections that appear in this book, I read through every word of eight collections of Pohl's shorter works. That comes to about half a million words!

Generally I've found that reading all of any one collection of shorts and novelettes by a single writer is not to be done at a single stretch. After all, shorter works are never meant to be read together, but rather to be separated by many months in magazine publication. Most writers tend to stick to certain themes, or do certain types of stories much better than others. When read at one sitting, these become too obvious, too repetitive—boring, in fact, in such an unfair way of reading them.

For that reason, I approached the task rather reluctantly. I planned to read one book at a time, then wait a week, and try another.

It didn't work that way. I read all eight books in less than a week—and found that I thoroughly enjoyed them. I not only didn't find that the reading grew monotonous, but I began to look forward to each new volume with anticipation.

The works in this collection all appeared between 1954 and 1967; there have been outstanding stories since, but I agree with Frederik Pohl that we need more time to determine which of those should endure as his best. Meantime, these are the ones I consider his best, chosen from a rich production that can often be honestly termed memorable. Probably other readers would have made other choices—there are too many good stories to make selec-

tion simple. But I have chosen these after a great deal of consideration.

As I read, I kept a list of the stories I felt mandatory for inclusion, planning to fill the remainder with "next-best" stories. Again, it didn't work out that way. My list of "must" stories was twice as long as the limits of the book permitted. So I had to go back and weed out stories, hating to eliminate even one, to reach a manageable length.

There was no problem of balancing the book to insure sufficient variety. That took care of itself.

There seems to be no limit to the variety to be found in the shorter works of Frederik Pohl, in fact. They vary in length from 1,500 to 21,000 words, and that is the smallest element of their variety. Some of them, like **"The Midas Plague,"** might be called satirical—but not with the cold sardonic contrivance so common to this much-abused form of literature. Pohl is involved in the cultures he shows; he may be sardonic or amused, but he feels himself a part of that which he holds up to the distorting mirror of reality.

Some stories depend on a twist at the end; usually this occurs in the shorter pieces, as should be the case. However, the twist is not to surprise the reader, but to bring the idea to a quick and pointed conclusion that is completely satisfactory. And there is always more than the twist. **"Grandy Devil"** is based on a marvelous character in a family that is strangely immortal; **"Punch"** tells us more about ourselves and all intelligent life than is conveyed in many novels, short as the story is.

"Tunnel Under the World" is a story of terror and of pathos—an odd blend of emotions, indeed. It is also a fine suspense-action story. **"The Hated"** could have been a simple action story, but the heroes it presents to us are engaging in a different kind of conflict with their environment.

There are stories that would simply be sentimental in the hands of a lesser writer. **"Father of the Stars"** tells of a man who felt he had to go to the ends of explored space, and how he succeeded; we've all read that story a dozen times, but not in this form! **"Three Portraits and a Prayer"** tells of an old scientist who learned he was wrong. There's sentiment there for those who can empathize—but no sentimentality.

Some might be called "idea" stories. (All are built around ideas, of course; but some ideas tend to obtrude beyond the story, except in the hands of a very skillful craftsman.) **"The Day the Martians Came"** is one of the oldest ideas, first given acceptable form in Wells' *War of the Worlds.* The title gives it all away—or does it? All the ingredients are familiar—except the way we see it, and what we realize from Pohl's view. **"Speed Trap,"** on the other hand, is a totally new idea, so far as I can determine, beautifully turned into excellent fiction. **"The Day the Icicle Works Closed"** gives us a new service for tourists, another idea that makes me wonder why no one thought of it before.

It's hard to say whether there's a new idea in **"Day Million"**—Pohl says it's a love story, the oldest idea in literature. It is a love story, but I find nothing old in it.

And finally, skipping over a few other selections you can discover for yourself, there is an article, as a sample of several excellent pieces of science non-fiction authored by Pohl. In this day of computers, we should all master arithmetic to the base two, but most of us still cling to the decimal rut. Pohl teaches us how natural and simple the new system is—and shows us that it's the only way to master some of the ordinary problems of daily life.

Pohl's career in science fiction is at least as varied and complex as his writing.

Like so many of us, he began his public life as a "fan," a reader of science fiction who became so enamored of the literature that he had to join with others in discussing and proselyting it. In those days, there was a small number of such fans who were so well known that many became more famous in science fiction than some of the writers. Pohl rapidly joined this number, and became a leader among the others.

He was part of the movement that led to the formation of the first great fan tradition—the annual World Science Fiction Convention. As much as any single person could be, he was a moving force in the organization of the very first, held in 1939. (He didn't attend! There were feuds in those days that seemed earthshaking then, and he was too strong a fan not to take sides. Happily, those feuds are now dead, and ancient enemies are now the best of friends.)

Almost at once, he graduated to editing his own magazines. This came about before he was twenty-one. Somehow, despite a very low budget for his magazines, he managed to become a major editor, with magazines second only to the acknowledged and established leader. And when I visited New York City in those days to see John W. Campbell, the only other editor it occurred to me to see was Frederik Pohl.

He might have gone on with the magazines, but the war interrupted his career. And when he returned, he turned to another field. He opened an agency to handle the stories of other writers, and rapidly became one of the leading agents in science fiction, perhaps the leading one. His roster of clients read like a *Who's Who* of science fiction, from long-established professionals to beginners who were quickly promoted to stardom under his handling. I couldn't have issued the four magazines I was then editing without his service; his help to Horace L. Gold in the launching of *Galaxy* must have been beyond value.

It was partly as a result of his work as an agent that he returned to writing. He made a strong effort to bring back many of the writers who had dropped out of the field, among them his close friend, Cyril Kornbluth, who had begun under a number of pen-names and had been one of the better young writers before the war, but had since abandoned all writing efforts. In persuading him to return to writing, Pohl discussed many ideas for stories with him. It was during these discussions that the idea of collaborating again came up, resulting in the novel, *The Space Merchants*.

As an agent, Pohl was also instrumental in steering many writers into the book field, where publishers were then just becoming interested in science fiction. Among the writers steered into this new market was Isaac Asimov. And Asimov benefited in this partly by the fact that Pohl was also still an active and important fan! There was an organization in New York called the Hydra Club which had been founded by Frederik Pohl and me in 1947, and the monthly meetings of this club were attended by most of the major writers and editors in the field at the time. It was at such a meeting that Pohl brought Isaac Asimov together with Walter Bradbury, editor for Doubleday; the result was a contract for the first of an incredible number of books by Asimov.

Eventually, the lure of writing proved more compelling than the work as an agent, and Pohl gave up his agency to become a full-time writer. He continued to collaborate with Kornbluth, but he began to work a great deal on his own. He also collaborated on two projects with me. I can't speak for other collaborators, but in my own case, Pohl contributed fully half of the writing and all the basic ideas, while taking only half the credit. But our work was so much rewritten back and forth, and so completely the result of constant rethinking that I can't even guess who was responsible for what, in most instances. But out methods were so dissimilar that we both decided after the second attempt to abandon working together, financially successful though it had been. One lasting result, however, was that my wife Evelyn and I moved out to Red Bank, where we were always the closest of friends with Fred Pohl and his wife Carol during the next two decades.

Pohl also began a series of collaborations with Jack Williamson. It seemed an unlikely combination; Pohl's writing was accepted as somewhat sardonic and cynical (though that was an unfair judgment), while Williamson was noted for his extreme romantic euphoria about man in the future. Yet the collaboration worked well through three juvenile books and many adult serials.

Nothing ever went in a straight line in his career, however. Now that he was a successful author, it wasn't too surprising that he resumed his career as an editor. Horace L. Gold resigned as editor of *Galaxy* and *If*, and Pohl was immediately chosen as his successor.

Now he was editing two of the leading magazines in the field, with a competitive budget, quite different from his previous experience.

He proceeded to demonstrate just how good an editor he really was, and the results were quickly apparent, as he began discovering new talent and making full use of the old. Many of the leading authors today first appeared in his magazines—Niven and Tiptree, to name two quite dissimilar ones from a large group. The stories he printed won a majority of the Hugo awards in the succeeding years, and *If* was picked for the Hugo three successive years!

Then the magazines were sold to Universal Publishing and Distributing Corporation. Pohl was offered the chance to continue editing the magazines, but it would have meant full-time commuting to New York City, and he decided to go back to writing without editing. He felt there were rewards enough in that; rightly so, as it proved, since he was named as Guest of Honor by the World Science Fiction Convention in 1972 and won a Hugo for his writing in 1973—the only man to win that honor both for his writing and his editing.

There were a few other contributions during all this time, of course. He became one of the most sought lecturers on science fiction and the world of the future, addressing all sorts of groups and crusading for what science fiction had long been, but which was just being discovered by a wider audience. He helped enlarge that audience. He taught science fiction in schools for young writers. And he traveled widely (to both Russia and Japan, for instance) to deepen the international flavor of science fiction.

Harold L. Berger (essay date 1976)

SOURCE: "The New Tyrannies," in *Science Fiction and the New Dark Age*. Bowling Green University Popular Press, 1976, pp. 86-146.

[*In the following excerpt, Berger examines Pohl's heavy-handed treatment of the theme of advertising in "The Tunnel under the World" and "The Wizards of Pung's Corners."*]

Frederik Pohl's advertising agency background has evidently filled him with disdain for the business world's coercive methods, for some of his best work deals with the cupidity of the huckster and the vulnerability and vacuity of consumer-man. Pohl is far less concerned with the world being blown up than with it being turned into a marketplace for the buying and selling of men, a harvest carnival where all the cornucopias are filled with idiocy. [He] has the satirist's touch. But Pohl's matter can also try the nerve of horror: a man discovering that he and all his neighbors are merely tiny androids in an advertising experiment. A world turned into a laboratory for testing sales reactions, a public so effectively manipulated that its purchases become as inevitable as the social inclinations of B. F. Skinner's Waldenites—these are recurring themes in his stories. In **"The Tunnel Under the World"** advertisers obtain the brain patterns of a town's twenty-one thousand citizens in order to test marketing techniques. One strategem involves driving a van through residential streets as a loudspeaker bellows with rage:

"Have you got a freezer? *It stinks!* If it isn't a Feckle

Freezer, *it stinks!* If it's a last year's Feckel Freezer, *it stinks!* Only this year's Feckle Freezer is any good at all! You know who owns an Ajax Freezer? Fairies own Ajax Freezers! You know who owns a Triplecold Freezer? Commies own Triplecold Freezers! Every freezer but a brand-new Feckle Freezer *stinks!* . . . I'm warning you! Get out and buy a Feckle Freezer right away! Hurry up! Hurry for Feckle! Hurry for Feckle! Hurry, hurry, hurry, Feckle, Feckle, Feckle, Feckle, Feckle. . . ."

Pohl makes his method his point by outrageously stripping from advertising its veneer of pleasantness and reason: These *are* veneer and most advertising *is* an outrage. But the story's shock effect comes from one's realization that what successfully manipulates people in one town can be turned upon the nation and the world. As good science fiction often does, Pohl's stories, whether playful or black, leave the reader with a sense of reduced immunity.

Pohl is far less concerned with the world being blown up than with it being turned into a marketplace for the buying and selling of men, a harvest carnival where all the cornucopias are filled with idiocy.

—Harold L. Berger

"The Wizards of Pung's Corners" exemplifies the comic debacle, which Pohl's satiric talents create so well. With an advertising agency installed in the fifth side of the Pentagon, the military selects its combat ordnance like consumer-oriented salesmen. But soldiers find the E-Z Fyre Revolv-a-Clip Carbine too complicated; the Zip-Fire Auto-Load Cannon with Wizard-trol Safety Interlock is worthless; and the full-color combat manual, *The Five-Step Magic-Eye Way to New Combat Comfort and Security,* doesn't save the troops from being disarmed by a few farmers with ordinary shotguns.

David N. Samuelson (essay date 1980)

SOURCE: "Critical Mass: The Science Fiction of Frederik Pohl," in *Voices for the Future*, Volume Three, edited by Thomas D. Clareson and Thomas L. Wymer, Bowling Green University Popular Press, 1984, pp. 106-26.

[*In the following excerpt, taken from an essay first published in S-F Studies in 1980, Samuelson explores the social criticism in Pohl's short fiction from the 1950s through the 1970s.*]

The problem of determining Frederik Pohl's rank among SF writers is not a simple one to resolve. As a satirist and thinker, he is at the top of American SF writers who are "fan-oriented," but as an artist, even as a technician, he often shows significant defects. Even the best of his fiction is sometimes marred by the intrusion of melodrama, sentimentality, unrationalized fantasy, and other features more or less calculated to appeal to an addicted audience. For the most part, his work seems to lack depth, density, an authentic personal voice, and a sense of style as anything more than a serviceable medium. This makes it difficult to take him seriously as a major writer, addressing with authority matters of significance.

One reason for these "flaws," if such they are, is not far to seek. Pohl's intimate connection with commercial SF over so many years has no doubt limited him at times to what he thought his known audience was willing to accept. If it was narrow and provincial, so were his stories prior to 1952. When satire and social criticism were in, he still felt constrained to gild them with snappy patter, melodramatic plots, and irrelevant aliens. His Hugos as editor were won for a magazine committed largely to adventure stories and essentially lightweight material—*IF* or *Worlds of IF*—in which he once objected editorially to the pessimism and anarchy being brought to SF in the 1960s by the "New Wave." Yet his own work later shows signs of his having accepted without hesitation the greater freedom of content and complexity of form brought to SF by the "New Wave" controversy, not to mention the broadened audience.

The reader who comes to Frederik Pohl through his short stories anthologized by others, his novels written alone or with Kornbluth or Lester del Rey, even through most of his short story collections, is bound to recognize a critical bent, out of harmony with the simpleminded optimism of most SF adventures. The obvious butts of his criticism are individual incompetents, power-grabbing manipulators, and such communal vices as war, waste, overbreeding, and the kind of gullibility that allows manipulators to prosper. Some of these gulls and failures, wheeler-dealers and baby makers must have come from experience, however broadened and universalized. Though not alone, SF readers are addicted to power fantasies, escapism and an ever-rising material standard of living. However indirectly, then, Pohl is taking aim on his own readers, as well as the masses they look down upon. Furthermore, by acknowledging the underside of SF dreams and even by telling a familiar tale better than others have done, he implicitly criticizes his own predecessors and peers.

Over the years, the audience for SF has grown, and part of it has even grown up. Pohl himself has outgrown his role as enforcer of just such rules as hampered his own talents. But the habits of 30-plus years can be hard to break. Even some of his "mature" works continue to rely on melodramatic action, unearned sentiment, thin characterization, and a rapid pace that disallows contemplative savoring of people, places, acts and consequences. Style and structure take on more importance for themselves, realistic detail and emotional intensity have increased, and the often facetious comedy of his earlier works has turned toward an almost tragic representation of the human condition. The "great work," however, still lies beyond his grasp. . . .

Aside from the collaborations with Kornbluth, Pohl's most famous consumer story is probably **"The Midas Plague"** (1954). Positing a "utopian" economy of affluence, Pohl turns upside down the idea of conspicuous consumption: the "poor" are burdened by having to consume huge amounts of foods and products churned out by automated factories. The desultory and forgettable plot, involving a newly married couple from disparate classes, concludes with the "happy idea" (long since telegraphed to the reader) of short-circuiting the process by involving robots in consumption as well as production. Well aware that the premise (suggested by *Galaxy* editor Horace Gold) was untenable, Pohl didn't really try to shore up its believability. Instead he turned it into a "tall tale" with logically extrapolated details and a rarely flagging faculty of comic invention. Complaints of the story's impossibility or lack of verisimilitude are beside the point, which was to expose and skewer the *naivete* (or duplicity) of the attitude (not limited to the 1950s) that affluence is a never-ending spiral, meanwhile softening the blow with comic exaggeration.

Only the second story to bear his exclusive byline, **"The Midas Plague"** marked (along with *The Space Merchants*) the emergence of Pohl as comic satirist. Frequently reprinted, sometimes as "serious" utopian speculation, it was popular enough in its time to inspire three sequels. **"The Man Who Ate the World"** (1956), **"The Wizards of Pung's Corners"** (1958) and **"The Waging of the Peace"** (1959) do not come up to the original, but each has its moments of comic brilliance, as does another broadly conceived satire on the commercialization of Christmas. In **"Happy Birthday, Dear Jesus"** (1956), however, the proffered cure is a love affair between the sales-worshipping narrator and a missionary's daughter, characters too simple and cliched to shoulder the burden.

More successful as stories are four which attack, grotesquely but with less zanniness, aspects of social control. **"My Lady Greensleeves"** (1957), ostensibly about a prison riot, examines the society of which that prison is a symptom. The riot fails because the white-collar thinkers and blue-collar workers can't get together to engineer a break-out. A discordant note is provided by the fortuitous presence of a Senator's daughter, pretty and innocent, available as a hostage. Rebelling against the exaggerated system of segregation by occupational specialization which is the real issue of the story, she has to be made to fear for her life, and to recognize the "good sense" of the system, which eliminates illogical biases based on color, religion or ethnic origin.

Governmental *over*control is rejected as one solution to wasted human resources in **"Rafferty's Reasons"** (1955). The title refers to inchoate causes of homicidal tendencies in a former "artist," retrained (brainwashed) to fill a niche society finds useful. Mind-numbed by his involuntary conditioning, Rafferty finally attacks a politician with a cigar butt, thinking it a knife. The underdog draws some sympathy, but he is too pathetic and monomanical to earn much of it. The politicians, however, are much more unsavory both as characters (caricatures) and on the grounds of their "principles." They have eliminated unemployment, overproduction and economic depressions, but at the cost (lightly dismissed) of love, religion, free speech, free elections, even—as in the case of Rafferty—of anything more than a semblance of free will, except for themselves.

Without controls, however, overpopulation and/or ecotastrophe are likely, as in **"The Census Takers"** (1956) and **"The Snowmen"** (1959). The job of the census takers is to regulate and reduce population, by execution if necessary, which the protagonist-narrator, an efficient but unimaginative civil servant, carries out well and without compunction. The latter story postulates a rapid approach to the "heat death of the universe" through overuse of "heat pumps" (shorthand for any temperature-regulating device). The satire is obscured, however, rather than illuminated, by the presence in both stories of alien beings. They serve as sane viewpoints, but the reader might be trusted to develop the same on his or her own, and their presence blunts the social criticism by turning our attention from human folly to alien invasion.

Cliched responses to alien invasion are definitely germane to **"The Children of the Night"** (1964). During an uneasy armistice, the Arcturans want a base in an American small town, which requires voter approval of rezoning. The narrator is another negative hero, a high-pressure public relations man, who doesn't let misgivings about the morality of his work stand in the way of doing a job well. Manipulating the good, the bad, and the public at large, he wins the referendum for the Arcturans by uniting the electorate with the hated aliens in opposition to himself as an agent of disruption, a scapegoat. Style and structure and rapid pace are all-important to this story, but the moral is far from clearcut. Pohl exploits his reader's anticipated sympathy for vivisected children and a decent politician to make the narrator's work look bad, even though the result may be a gain in peace and communication between the races.

Manipulation need not be so overt or organized. Sedation, voluntarily chosen, can do the job, as two other stories of the 1950s point out. At first glance a space opera, **"The Mapmakers"** (1955) shows a spaceship crew suffering hallucinations, and without the services of their navigator in hyperspace. Blinded in an accident, he is heavily sedated by a solicitous medical staff, until he convinces them of the reason for his agitated condition. The technicians' complacency is upset by his "second sight," which can guide them home unerringly and offers a definitive solution to the problem of interstellar travel. Chaotic and voluntary "control" by tranquilizers is the subject of **"What to Do Till the Analyst Comes"** (1956). Before hallucinogens were in the public eye, though long after Huxley's "soma" and right after the furor over "Miltown," Pohl posited a "non-habit-forming" drug which banishes worry, simultaneously freeing society from accuracy, efficiency, productivity and safety. Only the narrator is well situated to tell the story; overdosed at the drug's inception, he is allergic to it, making him the last person left to worry about anything.

None of these stories bogs down in melodrama and sentimentality. Extrapolation leads to exaggeration, action threatens to boil over, and the reader's sympathies are openly manipulated. But the author usually pulls back from the edge of bathos or overaction, achieving an emotional tone closer to the sardonic, most evident in **"The Children of Night"** and **"What to Do Till the Analyst Comes."** **"The Mapmakers"** is almost pure wish-fulfillment, **"My Lady Greensleeves"** pushes its message too much, the overconsumption tetralogy is maybe a little too zany, and **"Rafferty's Reasons"** is almost too dispassionate. And science, for stories ostensibly of SF, is almost conspicuous by its absence; it is a prop at most, since the stories are concerned primarily with social change. Simple moral judgments are generally avoided; the issues are real, if taken beyond contemporary parameters; and the characters, for the most part, are believable, though thin, which can be blamed both on the shortness of the stories and the pointed edges of the satire. Less credible are the cardboard figures in **"Rafferty's Reasons,"** and characters in tales so zany (the tetralogy) or miraculous (**"The Mapmakers"**) as to make believability irrelevant.

Comic or serious, these stories display a consistent motif, one familiar in the satiric tradition, but also pointedly relevant to the situation of a clear-sighted individual writing in an escapist medium. This paranoid sense that only one person can see clearly in an insane world is carried to its logical extreme in **"The Tunnel Under the World"** (1955). Arguably Pohl's best short work, this may be the ultimate fictional statement against commercial manipulation. Structured as a horror story, but without Gothic trappings, the story reveals its menace gradually, as Pohl takes his hero and us through several mistaken constructions of reality before announcing the devastating truth, which justifies the apparent melodrama.

Disturbed by insultingly strident advertising techniques and some bewilderingly effective salesmanship, Guy Burckhardt discovers—seemingly by accident—that the day of his experiences is being repeated again and again. It is his efforts to find out what is really happening that lead to startling but seemingly nonsensical revelations and then to a horrifying discovery. He and all his fellow-citizens, victims of an industrial accident, have been preserved through a miracle of science to function through miniature manikins in a table-top model of their small town. As a trade-off for this involuntary half-life, they sacrifice the consciousness of the passage of time, which might alter their responses. They must live, over and over again, the day after the accident. The advertising gimmicks with which they story began are their reason for existence; the whole town is nothing but a controlled test market for an advertising research firm. And knowing the truth, Burckhardt is powerless to do anything about it.

The technical premise is hard to credit, especially within the time frame suggested by the characters' manners and mores, but the idea that advertisers would do such a thing if they could is not all far-fetched. Vance Packard's *The Hidden Persuaders* detailed practices then going on, which Pohl's own experience in the ad business could verify.

Burckhardt's nightmare of timelessness may be beyond their reach, but the advertisers' grasp is hardly exaggerated. Our contemporary fascination with designer labels worn on the outside of clothing, not to mention T-shirts and apparatus blatantly advertising other products, shows how we willingly enter into complicity with the hucksters, more today than ever.

"The Tunnel Under the World" works in part because of its continued relevance, but also because of the appropriateness of its horror conventions and the "mechanical" nature of its stereotyped characters. These might put off readers for whom the satire could be a valuable dose of medicine, but for the SF reader who chews up those features as his daily bread, the application of the story to him *as an SF reader* may not be apparent. The satire seems to be directed at those other guys, who are not aware of Madison Avenue shenanigans. But like the other stories of manipulation, **"The Tunnel Under the World"** has an uncomfortably close fit to the cottage industry of SF itself, more today than ever, as movie makers and producers of spin-offs from SF properties make millions of dollars off their "harmless" addiction.

Besides relating to its audience, Pohl's attack on manipulation parallels the task of the writer himself manipulating his characters. This was especially evident to Damon Knight, who asserted that Pohl's characters just didn't care (nor apparently should the reader). The author as puppet master was too conspicuous to Knight, but the reason could be just the opposite from what Knight implied. Pohl was not disinterested, but passionately involved, if his life and his writing have anything in common. This is a man who, however naively and lightly, was active in the Communist Party for four years, and whose liberal conscience frequently shows through his writing, perhaps nowhere more explicitly than in his political primer for the 1972 election year.

It may be that he didn't have the tools, the desire, or the "permission" of the SF field to let that caring show, except in fictional polemics which raised issues above characters, and pulp fiction conventions above both. No doubt it is also true as Pohl has said that, even in the 1950s, few people in SF were writing for the ages. Writing for a deadline, for grocery money, and for an audience with a dubious memory, they had to produce a story good enough to fill pages in a cheap monthly magazine, but not to withstand repeated and critical readings. The wonder is not that these stories have flaws, but that they stand up so well after a quarter of a century. Within the sharply limited selection considered here, Pohl's stories certainly come close to deserving [Kingsley] Amis's high praise of the time, if your taste, like Amis's, runs to SF as a social criticism. . . .

Through the 1960s, Pohl was also experimenting with "sketches" in which the story proper hardly interferes at all with the satire or speculation. Displaying a verbal economy surpassing his previous efforts, they are essentially static, crammed with information rather than action. Four of them feature aliens, but not as the melodramatic men-

aces of hoary tradition. The first of these, **"The Martian Stargazers"** (1962), comments obliquely on our history and conceit, explaining through speculative Martian star lore why they killed themselves long before men landed there. **"Earth 18"** (1964) uses the Martians as the butt of racist jokes, irrelevant to a Florida hotel-keeper, but worth their weight in gold to his black bellman. And **"Speed Trap"** (1967) implies alien involvement in a suspected conspiracy to use travel, conferences and administration to keep real research from being done.

The best of these, **"Day Million"** (1966), is a self-proclaimed lovestory imagining really altered people and conditions in the future (the millionth day, A.D.). Genetic engineering and social change have modified the meaning of gender, the forms human bodies can take, and the immediacy and exclusiveness of a love relationship. Without actually telling us a "story," the narrator presents us with two "genetic males" who "marry" by obtaining electronic replicas of each other to use for that era's version of a "full" love relationship. The jolting shift of perspective common to many Pohl stories occurs not once but several times in this story, as contemporary terminology proves inadequate, even misleading, for describing the future. The richness of this verbal experience may be marred for some readers by the narrator's direct address, even browbeating them into taking historical change into account when they look past tomorrow. The overall effect, however, is contemplation of, not recoil from, the supposedly outrageous circumstances, and vindication of the claim that this is indeed a "love story."

"Day Million" and *The Age of the Pussyfoot* suggest the maturing of Pohl and his greater control of fictional techniques during the 1960s. Editing as many as four magazines at once, he was living through a change in social conditions which, along with more important things, made all kinds of SF seem vaguely respectable, and both allowed and expected it to be all things to all people. Changes were also happening in SF, if not most overtly displayed in his magazines, as the "New Wave" writers in England and their American counterparts rebelled against the old editorial formulas.

Long considered an apostle of doom, Pohl reversed his field slightly late in the decade, calling in an editorial for more hopeful and constructive stories in SF. Backing this call with at least limited action, he printed in *Galaxy* and *IF,* as other SF magazines did also, paid advertisements for and against the American presence in Vietnam, signed by other SF professionals, and announced a contest to seek feasible solutions to this problem then ripping apart the fabric of American society. But the magazines soon were sold, and he resigned as editor, entering a stage of depression in which he claims even living lost its appeal.

Reborn in the 1970s, he began re-examining the past, present and future. From that introspection came a series of autobiographical reconstructions, at least four retrospective anthologies, and something new in his writing. No longer tied to the editor's chair, and allowed, perhaps impelled, to write what he pleased, he surprised Pohl-watchers with some of the best writing of his career. Not simply comic infernos, these are coherent works of speculation and extrapolation tied to reasonably "hard" science, something almost completely lacking in his previous fiction. Pohl regards science as a great "spectator sport." It can reveal vistas inaccessible elsewhere, supply constraints or limits to work within or against, and lend authentic or authentic-sounding details to a narrative. But though science may have an inside track to the "truth," or at least a close approximation, it is not a panacea; as Guy Burckhardt found out in **"The Tunnel Under the World,"** the truth may not set you free, but rather define the boundaries of your prison.

Ecological consciousness has long been apparent in Pohl's work; over-population and exhaustion of resources play a role in his major and minor fictions. These newer stories seem even more clearly to be rooted in such matters and the problems of social control arising out of them, what the Stanford Research Institute has designated the "World Macroproblem." Rather than simply bemoaning the crisis, Pohl's stories propose solutions. The solutions may still be fantasies, but they do not settle for aliens, ESP, or unlimited resources pulled out of a hat. Pulp conventions are subdued; he depends less on sentiment and more on emotional commitment, less on melodrama and more on plausible action. Satire is still present, but it seems more integrated into the fabric of the moral fable. The satire is still directed at human vice and folly, at insane or inhumane social arrangements, especially at our apparent incapacity to undertake coordinated activity to prevent or alleviate foreseeable disasters. Most of SF is indirectly indicted in these stories by taking easy ways out, simply crying "j'accuse" or resorting to magic formulas.

Formally, these stories are more complex, with interwoven viewpoints, narrators of questionable reliability, denser characterizations, radiating images, and an iron control of tone. Though every one of them has something resembling a "happy ending," they all approach the condition of tragedy. In **"The Gold at the Starbow's End"** (1972), for example, we have a "noble experiment" overseen by a science advisor to the President (vaguely similar to Henry Kissinger), in which ten healthy, sensible, disciplined and mathematically educated young people are sent in a starship to a nonexistent Centauran planet, in the hope that ten years' concentrated thinking will have unexpected results. It does. The adventurers develop new languages, arts and sciences, transcending contemporary scientific paradigms; they also develop hostility toward those whom they discover to have hoaxed them.

The story develops fairly slowly, however, as the narrative alternates between scenes at home and messages from space, which sets the stage for the destruction sent back by the "new, improved" species. The "final solution" engineered by the supposed subjects of the experiments makes for entertaining reading but uncomfortable reflection on our present way of doing things.

A more conventional adventure story is **"The Merchants of Venus"** (1972), which centers on the successful quest of a tour-guide and prospector to make a big strike in an undiscovered tunnel of the Heechee, an ancient alien civilization which once honeycombed the planet. This is the hellish Venus of contemporary scientific knowledge, and only the existence of the Heechee tunnels makes it possible for man to settle there, while the hope of scavenging useful artifacts makes it more or less desirable. The society is built up in the tradition of cutthroat capitalism, people preying on tourists and servicing each other, with the dangers somewhat obviated by high-powered medicine, provided you have lots of money. More prized than money is "Full Medical" insurance that covers you for anything short of resurrection of the dead (and maybe even that). The hero's health and wealth are both in bad shape when the story begins, and they get worse as he takes his tourist-employers out to the planet's surface. They turn on him, and time starts running out, but we know from the traditions of adventure fictions that he will snatch victory from the jaws of defeat. The real interest, however, is in the carefully worked out physical and social background, including the disastrous ecological-population situation implied on Earth which makes Venus even slightly attractive.

> **The reader who comes to Frederik Pohl through his short stories . . . is bound to recognize a critical bent, out of harmony with the simpleminded optimism of most SF adventures**.
>
> —*David N. Samuelson*

"In the Problem Pit" (1973) is only minimal SF and an unusually positive speculation for Pohl, in which the bad guys (and innocent bystanders) don't have to be killed off to realize some utopian results. The premise is that at regular intervals, groups of citizens, some voluntary and some "drafted" to make representative samplings of the population, be brought together and isolated with professional facilitators in a marathon problem-solving session. These rotating "encounter groups," starting from their own personal problems, also engage those of their whole civilization. Like Pohl's "sketches" of the 1960s, this is an essentially static idea—which calls for character interactions within the closed environment. But the story turns on an apparently lost member of the group, a search party, and the rescue of an attempted suicide, utilizing sentimentality and melodrama to make conventionally exciting what might have been a very moving and meaningful story.

Easily the most negative of the recent works is **"We Purchased People"** (1974), a superior narrative treatment of several recurrent themes in Pohl's work. A love story with a sado-masochistic twist, it reminds us of the possible tragic consequences for individuals in certain "utopian" solutions to social problems. Wayne Golden and Carolyn Schoerner (symbolically named "beautiful people") are would-be lovers, star-crossed in a literal sense. Found guilty by human tribunals of heinous crimes (at least Wayne was), they have been sold to aliens, who exercise remote control to use them as agents for their business dealings on Earth. They rarely meet or see each other, except when one or the other is controlled, although they do have a few "stolen moments." When the aliens themselves finally decide to bring the two together, it is not for a happy ending. The aliens wish to experiment, to learn more about patterns of human sexual behavior.

That would be bad enough as an invasion of privacy, which is what Wayne and Carolyn both think it is, but an added complication makes this story definitely not for the squeamish. Having been introduced to Wayne as a frustrated lover, we only discover just why he is a "purchased person." A homicidal maniac, he got his kicks from young girls, not exactly sexually molesting them but "watching them die." Unaware of any reform of his personality, such as the reader seems to be privy to, the aliens control him according to the "sexual behavior which has been established as his norm." Given the story's premises, the result is sick, even outrageous, but predictable, even inevitable. Moreover, a simple moral judgment is once again impossible. Unlike the protagonist of **"Rafferty's Reasons,"** Wayne had no reason to expect anything better (Carolyn's guilt is obscure, her end more pathetic). Like the earlier story, however, this one also raises the question of what price is appropriate for a society to pay for benefits received. If the politicians were suspect, what of the aliens who brought us progress as an afterthought, while buying up our primitive artworks and artifacts? . . .

There is no question that Pohl has matured as a person, grown as a writer, come close to a representative in SF terms of a tragic vision of life, without renouncing his roots, both in commercial writing, and in the mode of satire. . . . Whether he can tap more of his unconscious, incite more passion, progress beyond the confines of this still and incestuous field I cannot predict, nor can I be sure that he even wants to. SF has been good to Pohl, and he continues to return the favor. If he can get beyond this plateau, however, as he has risen past others, he may realize a mission his writings about SF seem to suggest he envisions for it. Then his work will be not only a criticism of society, and of other SF, but also a serious and constructive criticism of life.

C. N. Manlove (essay date 1986)

SOURCE: "Frederik Pohl, *Alternating Currents*," in *Science Fiction: Ten Explorations,* Macmillan, 1986, pp. 35-56.

[*In the following essay, Manlove discusses major themes in Pohl's short fiction, focusing in particular on the stories collected in* Alternating Currents.]

Pohl began his trade with conventional short stories of travel to far planets, but in the early 1950s discovered that his *métier* lay as much in this planet, in the portrayal, via

fantastic metaphors, of men caught up in social and technical changes beyond their control. Pohl did continue to write (in collaboration with Jack Williamson) plain adventure stories in the form of the *Undersea* novels (1954, 1956, 1958), but the central thrust of his work became less 'escapist', more committed to visions at once comic and nightmarish, of disasters man might bring upon himself. Pohl's primary output, and the one for which he is remembered, during the 1950s and 1960s is the short and satiric story; only thereafter did he turn to the writing of longer novels of vision. With his penchant for clarity, logic and neat plotting, Pohl is probably the most witty of the authors considered [in this book]. His warnings are real, and yet their science-fictional guise enables him to escape identification; no one yet has pinned Pohl down to a philosophy. He prefers to see himself as just one of the race of science fiction writers, whom he characterises as imbued with 'an unwillingness to accept conventional wisdom, Arnold's "divine discontent" '. Of all his fourteen collections of short stories, *Alternating Currents* is arguably the finest and most integrated.

The stories in *Alternating Currents* seem at first sight very diverse. In 'The Tunnel Under the World' (1954), a whole town which has been accidentally destroyed by an explosion is recreated in miniature with human simulacra by an advertising company so that the company can test methods of selling their products. In 'Target One' (1955), the earth has been largely destroyed in atomic warfare, and one of the few remaining scientists has assembled a mode of time travel by killer atomic particles, which will make possible the murder in his youth of Albert Einstein, whose later theories were put to use in the construction of fission bombs: but the different world thus brought into being by the protagonists turns out to be vastly overpopulated and itself on the verge of discovery of nuclear fission by another route. In 'The Ghost-Maker' (1953), a scientific fellow of a museum is sacked for publishing his belief in the efficacy of magic, and employs what is close to black magic to take revenge on the superior who sacked him, by bringing to phantom life numbers of the human and animal exhibits in the museum. 'The Mapmakers' (1955) describes how a space ship becomes lost when the steersman who could guide it through hyperspace is blinded: in the end the steersman finds that though he is totally sightless he can chart a way through space far more effectively than before, and thus brings the ship home. In 'Let the Ants Try' (1949), we start, as in 'Target One', with an atomically-devastated earth and a scientist with a time machine, but this time the scientist actually travels in the machine, forty million years into the past with eight mutant queen ants which he leaves there to develop; when he returns to his own time it is to find the world filled not with a society of ants and men together as he had hoped, but with highly-developed giant ants alone. 'Pythias' (1955) presents a man with powers of 'psychokinesis', or the ability of the mind to alter the external world directly, who can wall off the power of an exploding grenade from his body or fly across the Atlantic; when he reveals his powers to a friend the latter murders him, ostensibly to save humanity from the dangers of such power. In 'Rafferty's Reasons' (1955) a man with a lowly job in a futuristic society plots the murder of his repulsive boss. The central character in **'What To Do Until the Analyst Comes'** (1955) has discovered a revolutionary substitute for cigarettes and drink that is both harmless and non-addictive. **'Grandy Devil'** (1955), a less satisfying story, tells of a young man's discovery that his family is enormously prolific and each member immortal, so that things are set fair for them to overrun the world; and all of them are the progeny of a devil.

For all their diversity, the stories have a remarkable similarity of theme and outlook. There are numbers of recurrent motifs, which are less evident in Pohl's later writings. One of these is enclosure. The protagonist of **'The Ghost-Maker'**, Ehrlich, can release the wraiths of dead creatures when he touches their bodies with a magic ring: but if he so touches any living being it becomes dead and its ghost is released. As he wanders through the museum, aware that the task of frightening Brandon his superior is failing, and becoming addicted to bringing creatures to life purely for amusement, he casually puts his ring hand without looking against the skeletal tail of a tyrannosaurus rex to demonstrate his skill to Brandon, only to see his own dead body drop at his feet. He has touched his ring to a part of the tyrannosaurus skeleton that had been reconstructed from plaster by the museum staff, and the magic action, failing on the dinosaur, has rebounded on its wearer. Now he is shut in the ghost world, with only one or two of the human exhibits his ring released to talk to, and the growing dread of the carnivorous phantoms, harmless to humans, but real enough to ghosts, that he has made his companions in this twilight world; there is only the hope that the magician from whom he got the ring originally will be prevailed upon to release him. **'Grandy Devil'** too, ends with one of the protagonists shut in, battering at the hatch of a cess pit in which he has been confined.

'Rafferty's Reasons' (a Pohl version of [George Orwell's] *Nineteen Eighty-Four*) is a portrait of psychic enclosure. Rafferty is so consumed with hatred for his boss, 'dirty' Girty, that fantasy takes over reality and the knife with which in the end he thinks he is stabbing Girty turns out to be merely a cigar butt. Throughout the story Rafferty keeps uttering hate-filled curses at every passer-by who annoys him, but the curses are actually soundless: 'Wherever he was, Rafferty talked to himself. No one heard him, no one was meant to hear him.' The result is that we repeatedly think Rafferty has really spoken, only to realise that he has not; with a consequently more powerful sense of his enclosure:

> A man jostled him and scalding pain ran up Rafferty's wrist as the hot drink slopped over.

> Rafferty turned to him slowly. 'You are a filthy pig,' he said voicelessly, smiling. 'Your mother walked the streets.'

> The man muttered, 'Sorry,' over his shoulder.

> Rafferty sat down at another table with a party of three young Project girls who never looked at him, but

talked loudly among themselves.

> 'I'll kill you, Girty,' Rafferty said, as he stirred the coffee-beverage and drank it.

> 'I'll kill you, Girty,' he said, and went home to his dormitory bed.

And at the end, with the hapless Rafferty dragged away to prison for his feeble assault on Girty, no one will know Rafferty's Reasons. When Girty asks why Rafferty did it, 'Girty's friend could not give him the answer, though he might have had suspicions. Mudgins [the leader of the state] could have answered him, and a few others around Mudgins or elsewhere. . . . But only a few. The others, the many, many millions, they could never say what the reasons were; because some of them had never known them, and some had had to forget'. In this sense it is symbolic that Rafferty is shut off from reality, as his society is cut off from truth. But even then we wonder, after this story and the rage portrayed in it, whether Rafferty's reasons, and the very emphasis on them in the title begs the question, could properly be classified as reasons at all.

'What To Do Until the Analyst Comes' explores a situation of unwillingness rather than inability to make contact with the world. The Cheery-Gum in the story is chemically non-addictive, but people do become addicted to the happiness that comes through it, with the result that all humanity apart from the narrator, who sponsored its use, is soon enclosed within the drug, out of touch with previous reality:

> I tried to lay in on the line with the Chief. I opened the door of the Plans room, and there he was with Baggott and Wayber, from Mason-Dixon. They were sitting there whittling out model ships, and so intent on what they were doing that they hardly noticed me. After a while the Chief said idly, 'Bankrupt yet?' And moments passed, and Wayber finally replied, in an absent-minded tone:

> 'Guess so. Have to file some papers or something.' And they went on with their whittling.

The enclosure is demonstrated in the mental re-ordering of the psychoanalyst Dr Yust who admits that he himself once felt worried about the effects of Cheery-Gum on the world and on the ability of society to keep working; but says that his fears proved groundless, as people still work, if slowly, and better still, he has no more mentally disturbed clients to deal with:

> 'And what's more, they weren't morons. Give them a stimulus, they respond. Interest them, they react. I played bridge the other night with a woman who was catatonic last month; we had to put the first stick of gum in her mouth. She beat the hell out of me, Mr McGory. It had a mathematician coming here who— well, never mind. It was bad. He's happy as a clam, and the last time I saw him he had finished a paper he began ten years ago, and couldn't touch. Stimulate them—they respond. When things are dull—Cheery-

Gum. What could be better?'

The question invites us into the charmed circle also. The neatest touch perhaps is in the narrator's plight: his alienation from the gum-takers and their bovine contentment is shown to depend not on any high moral insight or principle, but on the fact that he is allergic to the drug, and whenever he takes it, it gives him hives. He is outside not because he chooses but because he cannot get in; his sole escapes are through psychoanalysis or death. By removing the narrator as a norm with whom to identify, Pohl makes his story reach out to pull us in: if there is no good reason against, what is there to stop us being 'for'?

'The Tunnel Under the World' is a fantastic vision of the enclosure of consumers by producers. Time and space are shut in to one day in the life of the town of Tylerton. It is always 15 June, and only the two malfunctioning robot humans begin to sense what is wrong. There is no escape from the town, for it is merely a model on a table-top, surrounded by what is for its mostly unknowing 'inhabitants' a huge drop; and beyond that, spotlights, and advertising personnel manipulating events. Ironically—and here the story is reminiscent of **'What To Do . . . '**, Burckhardt's rebellious consciousness makes him aware of his own helplessness and enclosure as continued ignorance would never have done: he does not break out into freedom, but into knowledge of a tighter constriction. And the reader, shut in his assumption that Burckhardt is a full-sized human being and the town a real town, suffers a further form of enclosure himself as he finds out the limiting truth.

'The Mapmakers' plays with the 'Tiresias' idea that to be blind may be to see more truly: though here the issue is physical rather than spiritual. Groden the space ship navigator, though cut off by his blindness from the normal external world, is able without eyes to 'see' the configurations of stars within hyperspace as he never could when sighted; as he puts it to the others, ' "I'm blind in normal space; you're blind in hyperspace" '.

The protagonists of **'Let the Ants Try'** and **'Target One'** find that manipulation of the past does not produce escape from a miserable present. In the former the ruthless ants are no more satisfactory an outcome to evolution's labours than were human beings. The story ends in a circular manner too. While the time-travelling scientists Dr Gordy is planting his mutated ants in the soil of the Carboniferous past, he hears what at the time he takes to be a raucous animal cry from the Coal Measure forest. On his return to 'the present' he finds himself in a strange city of ants, who first make him show them how his time machine works and is put together before preparing to kill him. With a violent struggle Gordy regains his machine and sets it once more for forty million years in the past, determined to reverse his experiment. But there is no escape from it, just as there was no real escape from grimness in the present. He finds, like Well's time-traveller, that his time machine, having been moved by the ants, has arrived at a slightly different position in the primeval forest. He emerges, and a little way on sees his time machine

and himself from his previous visit. But there is also another machine of strange design, closer to him. As he watches, a door opens in it, and a horde of giant ants races out of it towards him. Having learnt from Gordy how to make a time machine, the ants had 'infinite time' to make one of their own and realize what they had to do to prevent the destruction of their race. The story ends, 'As his panicky lungs filled with air for the last time, Gordy knew what animal had screamed in the depths of the Coal Measure forest'.

In **'Pythias'** the narrator kills the inventor Connaught (which ironically means 'know nothing') to prevent the secret of psychokinesis becoming known to man; and just as he has tried to shut in this dangerous knowledge so, as he wished, he is shut in jail for murder. His intention is to reach the final safe enclosure of death through his own execution; yet his closing assertion that Connaught could not be trusted to look after the secret 'But I can', comes over as rather sinister, suggesting that he may use his powers to defy the executioner at the last. But if the narrator may thus break the enclosure and become the path by which this knowledge is made known to the world, a different kind of enclosure is entered: that by which there is no escape from knowledge. That enclosure was also present in **'Target One'** where the destruction of Albert Einstein did not prevent the discovery of atomic fission by another route.

There are enclosure motifs in some of Pohl's later stories, several of them in the collection *Day Million* (1970). The title story (1966) in *Day Million* describes what seems a bizarre love relation between two physically transformed humans remote from us in time, only to turn and ask how we might look to them. The narrator of **'Making Love'** (1966) in the same collection prides himself on the fact that as one of the privileged classes he has a mistress who is a real human being and not a robot—or is she? The humans in **'The Snowmen'** (1958; *The Frederik Pohl Omnibus,* 1966) are cold predators shut in their houses and indifferent to the steady freezing of the Earth caused by their rapacious consumption of energy, and about to experience the consequences. **'Speed Trap'** (1967; *Day Million*) is the story of a man who discovers a means of immensely reducing bureaucratic inefficiency and thus of hastening social and economic change: he finds that one of his associates commits suicide and that he is shunted into a job where he is rendered ineffectual: the implication is that it is in Someone's interest for things to stay as they are. But most of these stories differ from those in *Alternating Currents* in that the enclosures have a moral base in human pride and self-delusion: the stories in *Alternating Currents* deal much more with people trapped in situations beyond their control; and it is perhaps in keeping with this that they contain much more in the way of imagery relating to enclosure, signifying that the environment is its source rather than the self. *Alternating Currents* has much less sense of personal responsibility than later collections: it is shot through with Pohl's sense, perhaps heightened by contrast with wartime victory, of man's powerlessness before his own creations, the atom bomb, the consumer society, conformism, drugs, advertising, and thus has a darker, more tragic vision than many of his other stories, which generally end happily or at least justly. This is highlit by the anomalous stories with happy endings (among their other different features) which were added to the US and British first editions of *Alternating Currents*—respectively **'Happy Birthday, Dear Jesus'** (1956: written by Pohl for the collection) and **'The Children of Night'** (1964).

Much of Pohl's later fiction could be said to deal with exposure rather than enclosure. In **'I Plinglot, Who You?'** (1958) and **'The Day The Icicle Works Closed'** (1959), the evil schemes of an alien and a human are unmasked. In *Drunkard's Walk* (1960) and *A Plague of Pythons* (1965), the source of human destruction in a group of power-crazy mind-rulers is discovered and destroyed. In *The Age of the Pussyfoot* (1969), the hero exposes an alien plot against Earth. *The Cool War* (1979) ends with the exposure to the world of the covert international warfare being carried on by unscrupulous politicians. Much of Pohl's fiction of the 1970s has left its previous confines of Earth, and visits other planets or roams the galaxy. In *Man Plus* (1976) the protagonist has his self and body totally altered, torn away from human identity, so that he may survive as a cyborg in the harsh environment of the Martian surface. **'The Merchants of Venus'** (1972), *Gateway* (1977), *Beyond the Blue Event Horizon* (1980) and *Heechee Rendezvous* (1984) are about a civilization of aliens nicknamed 'Heechees' who have left tunnels containing some of their artifacts on Venus and tunnels plus Heechee space ships on an asteroid; initially the urge is to open ('expose') the tunnels, but increasingly through exposure to risk (*Gateway*), the purpose becomes to discover the nature of the Heechee themselves. *Syzygy* (1981) ends with man realising that he is no longer alone in the universe. In *Starburst* (1982) a group of people is sent ostensibly to colonise a planet near Alpha Centauri, but actually to develop their minds prodigiously in the controlled environment of their space ship and give Earth the benefit. The plot is exposed, Earth punished and a new and higher human civilization actually established in Alpha Centauri. In **'The Five Hells of Orion'** (1962) captive humans are brought into increasing contact with an alien race, and as they do so their environment becomes progressively less enclosed: first the darkness with which one of them is surrounded is lightened, then doors are opened till he makes contact with another, then each is made one with the consciousness of the aliens, brought up to a planetary surface and all journey from thence to perceive the lurking threat in the far centre of the galaxy.

A second theme behind most of the stories in *Alternating Currents* is the idea that attempts at changing 'the given state of things' somehow will not work—a peculiar message for science fiction, and again one that does not occur in Pohl's later work, such as *Man Plus, Syzygy* or *Jem: The Making of a Utopia* (1979). Despite the efforts of the time-manipulators, the present stays stridently the same in degree of misery in **'Target One'** and **'Let the Ants Try'**. In **'What To Do Until the Analyst Comes'**, nothing its sponsor can do can reverse the universal use of Cheery-Gum or its social and economic effects. In **'The Tunnel Under the World'**, we think that the intrepid narrator, having discovered something odd about Tylerton, will be able in the end to right matters, but in fact his efforts only result in the revelation of his true helplessness. The same reversal of hoped-for change comes at the end of **'Let the Ants Try'**, when the narrator rushes back to the past to try to reverse his experiment. The paradox of this story is that the narrative constantly changes, the bottom falling out of it, as it were, in constant reversals, to show that there can be no change. In **'The Tunnel Under the World'**, the bottom literally falls out of Burckhardt's world when he suddenly realises that beyond Tylerton there is only an abyss. Gideon Upshur in **'Grandy Devil'** fails to halt the spread of the Orville family. Rafferty in **'Rafferty's Reasons'** fails to kill Girty. While releasing the wraiths of the museum creatures, Ehrlich in **'The Ghost-Maker'** becomes a ghost himself.

Another, related motif of these stories is the benefits of losing the separate self. If **'The Mapmakers'** is anything to go by, it is only when man is helpless, lost in space and blinded, that he can begin to see aright; for only then is he no longer separate from, but in tune with the larger patterns of the universe. The very assertion of the narrator at the end of **'Pythias'** of his mastery over his own fate poses its absence; indeed his very intended death is a paradox, since he proposes by it to destroy the mastery over fate given by Connaught's invention. It seems that peace only comes when one submerges one's mind with the collective, when one becomes in a sense unconscious. It is Rafferty's sharp sense of injustice that marks him out and dooms him to his tormented life and fate. McGory in **'What To Do Until the Analyst Comes'** longs to be part of the society taking Cheery-Gum and becoming literally unconscious of the external world, but is forced to be separate and judging. In a sense inventions prove a 'Bad Idea'—Cheery-Gum, time machines, psychokinesis. Partly this is because they are aimed at changing humanity. Pohl, in an almost eighteenth-century manner, seems to insist on the limits of the human purview. Looked at one way his stories sometimes appear to propose that we should submit, and that 'whatever'—and the whatever is often hard to take—'whatever is, is right'. Seen thus, it is 'better' that one should put up with the disasters of atomic warfare that the collective wisdom of mankind has brought about than that one man should seek to reverse them. 'Better' that one's mind should not be so abnormal, so awake, as to permit realization of the horror of one's predicament: thus with Burckhardt. 'Right' that Grandy Orville wins against Gideon Upshur, because he is part of the family and the latter an intruder. 'In Pride, in reas'ning Pride, our error lies': Pope's words might certainly be applicable to the protagonists of **'Target One'** and **'Let the Ants Try'**. Certainly it is pure hubris that brings about the doom of the narrator in **'The Ghost-Maker'**: he has already interfered with the system of things by propagating so many ghosts (upsetting the natural order was one of Pope's *bêtes noires*); and it is when he idly puts his ring to the tyrannosaurus rex without looking, while addressing 'some mocking phrase' to Brandon that he is himself ghosted. In a sense he is fittingly made a ghost, for he has just refused Brandon's offer of the return of his job, indeed he has renounced any of his former concern for scientific truth, so that he no longer belongs to the collective that previously gave him his identity. The narrator in the anomalous story **'Happy Birthday, Dear Jesus'**, by contrast, succeeds by separating himself from the collective, by abandoning his previous identification with a materialist culture, leaving his job and country, marrying into a family of people opposed to the system.

Yet it would be absurd to suggest that conservatism and submission of the self constitute the sole ethic of Pohl's stories. Pope's dogmas were directed at making men submit to a broadly happy state of affairs, with an ultimately benign creator in control of an ordered and on the whole delightful universe. It is different when it comes to atomic deserts, exclusion from happiness, manipulation by others, or rejection. We sympathise with, rather than find absurd, many of the rebellions in the stories. Submission may be 'better' but it is not always nobler. Isn't Burckhardt's struggle towards awareness of the manipulations being carried out on the model Tylerton a finer thing than stupid ignorance—even if Burckhardt himself turns out to be other than a man? Isn't McGory's sense of the degradation of humanity in **'What To Do . . . '** at least as valid as the assertion of the Cheery-Gum-chewing Dr Yust that the disasters are real only to him? Isn't Rafferty's painful hatred of Girty, however inaccurate and blindly personal, a better thing than the kind of happy acceptance of Big Brother than ends Orwell's *Nineteen Eighty-Four*?

Rebellion does not go away in Pohl's stories save in death, or, in the case of Burckhardt, when 'the maintenance crews take over'. Gideon Upshur still clamours at the lid of the cess pit, Rafferty presumably continues to express his rage at Girty from behind the bars of a prison, McGory cannot escape his isolated rejection of Cheery-Gum. Therefore several of the stories are essentially dialectical. They call for rebellion, indeed sometimes almost prescribe it, only to show it to be quite futile and dangerous. In part of course it is simply the case that without the rebellions there would be no story. But this is not quite the merely circular argument it might seem. It is often rebellion that brings the new worlds into being. Had it not been for Burckhardt, Tylerton would have remained Tylerton on 15 June to all its inhabitants: it is Burckhardt's abnormal consciousness that makes him aware of the fact that it never becomes 16 June and eventually find out what Tylerton 'really' is. It is the rebellions of the scientist protagonists of **'Let the Ants Try'** and **'Target One'** that bring about a world dominated by intelligent giant ants, and an overpopulated planet on the verge of discovering atomic fission by a different route. It is the revenge-seeking drive of Ehrlich in **'The Ghost-Maker'** that makes a little company of released spirits, the human members of which are vividly characterised. In a sense the scientist is like God: he makes (though perhaps unwittingly) a new creation; the scientist in **'Let the Ants Try'** is named Salva Gordy. The impulse of rebellion seems here directly linked to the impulse to create. The ants in **'Let the Ants Try'**, unlike Dr Gordy, do not create a time machine: they copy it. Gordy has brought them into being: they do nothing but cancel his being. Equally one can rebel at the new creation,

as do Gordy or the narrator of **'Target One'** or McGory at the invention of Cheery-Gum, or the narrator of **'Pythias'** (ostensibly) at the powers of psychokinesis.

The very existence of all these different stories depends upon a 'rebellion' against the status quo of our reality: in each of them we start from a context which is an alteration of our world as it is now—a world in which travel through 'hyperspace' is possible, or atomic wars have been fought, or magic spells work, or matter can be directly manipulated by mind, or time travel is possible. And the world of each narrative is, as it were, in 'rebellion' against that of any other, in the sense that each is an 'Alternating Current'. In **'Let the Ants Try'** human beings can travel through time, while in **'Target One'** this is 'impossible by definition; matter cannot leave its locus in the chronon', though a special destructive particle known as a K-meson can be made to span time. In **'The Ghost-Maker'** magic replaces plodding science as the wonder-worker; in **'Target One'** scientific 'explanation' is given in terms of the operation of K-mesons, reactors, and Einstein's laws; in **'What To Do Until the Analyst Comes'** the irreverent lay narrator's explanation of the process of manufacturing Cheery-Gum as told to him is by way of 'a substance in a common plant which, by cauliflamming the whingdrop and di-tricolating the residual glom, or words something like that, you could convert into another substance which appeared to have much in common with what is sometimes called hop, snow or joy-dust. In other words, dope'. Thus we have Pohl the creator 'rebelling' against the external world in writing at all; each story 'rebelling' against others; and within each individuals rebelling against the conditions, or else rebelling against the results of their own rebellion. Pohl likes the idea of Chinese boxes, of events within events, worlds within worlds, rebel/creators within rebel/creators. Pope, by contrast, insisted on our entertaining the notion of only one external world, the supposedly empirical one about us: for him the artist was not a creator but a follower of nature. The very variety of Pohl's worlds suggests the contingency of ours: it is subject to alteration with the minimum of notice, whether by the creator or his creatures. Thus the fact of change, even if it is only of the mutant type, plays against implicit criticism of change.

So far as the protagonists of the stories are concerned, another motif of the collection is alienation. Most of the central figures are alone. Gordy in **'Let the Ants Try'** has his companion De Terry only for the first part, till they arrive in the city of the ants, where De Terry is killed. Ehrlich in **'The Ghost-Maker'** is a man on his own and against society, as is Rafferty in **'Rafferty's Reasons'**. Burckhardt in **'The Tunnel Under the World'** becomes isolated from his world by his own developing knowledge. The protagonist of **'Pythias'** makes himself a condemned murderer to keep the secret of psychokinesis from mankind. McGory in **'What To Do Until the Analyst Comes'** starts as the brilliant member of an advertising team and ends as a man burdened with lonely gloom, cut off from the relief and integration with humanity that would be given by the Cheery-Gum he himself sponsored, if only he could eat it. The space ship in **'The Mapmakers'** is lost, and Groden severed from the normal world by his blindness and alone able to see his way through hyperspace. The scientists in 'Let the Ants Try' and 'Target One' refuse to accept society as they find it: one irony of this is that the alternative societies they bring into being refuse to accept them. In stories in others of Pohl's collections, such as *Tomorrow Times Seven*, *Turn Left at Thursday* or *Day Million*, by contrast, there may be several protagonists, or the protagonist is in relative harmony with society. We are with a group of Earthmen defending themselves against Martians in 'The Middle of Nowhere' (1955); the apparent tribesman in 'It's a Young World' (1941) ends by stepping into leadership of a planetary council; 'The Day of the Boomer Dukes' (1956) is told from a plurality of points of view; fellow-humans help the hero to escape from destroying Martians in 'Mars by Moonlight' (1958); in 'The Man Who Ate the World' (1956) the gross protagonist ends by reintegration with himself and society; in 'The Day the Icicle Works Closed' (1959) a lawyer exposes an international fraud that has isolated the home planet from the rest of the galaxy; in 'The Seven Deadly Virtues' (1958) a man outcast from society on Mars recovers his identity in the end. There are exceptions of course, such as 'The Hated' (1961) or 'The Fiend' (1964), but it is remarkable how consistently *Alternating Currents* is different from others of Pohl's collections.

Together with the theme of alienation goes one relating to identity. Isolated, and without a social niche, a place that gives some validation to what one is, the characters in the stories lose their selfhood. The scientist Ehrlich in 'The Ghost-Maker' sinks to vengeful magician and thence to ghost. An outsider, opposed to the family, Gideon Upshur in 'Grandy Devil' is shredded in a waste-disposal unit. The similarity of the names among several of the characters—Gordy, Groden, McGory, Girty, Grandy Orville—suggests further a dissolution of self. 'The Tunnel Under the World' explores the dissolution not only of a self but of a world. His world becomes steadily stranger to Burckhardt as the story proceeds. His wife has dreamed the same terrifying dream as he has, an outrageous voice screams commercials from a van parked in the street without the police intervening; Barth, who is never absent from the office, is so on this day; the cellar of Burckhardt's house is no longer plain concrete but a thin sheath of concrete over a floor, walls and ceiling made of copper; the interior of the boat he had built now appears unfinished; and repeatedly Burckhardt is encountered by the desperate features of an aquaintance named Swanson in the streets. And then there are the neat touches that really distinguish Pohl: it is not that Burckhardt's world is simply becoming less normal, it is also the fact that it is losing its abnormalities, that is disturbing:

> It isn't the things that are right and perfect in your life that make it familiar. It is the things that are just a little bit wrong—the sticking latch, the light switch at the head of the stairs that needs an extra push because the spring is old and weak, the rug that unfailingly skids underfoot.

> It wasn't just that thing were wrong with the pattern of Burckhardt's life; it was that the *Wrong* things were wrong.

And so the story continues until Burckhardt finds that the world he thought was his is no longer his at all, but a completely alien one with only the simulation of some normality remaining. His world drops away from him; and finally his own identity drops away from himself. He finds that he is not a man, that as a man he died in the explosion he thought he dreamt. Now he is reduced to a midget; and the humanity he thought he possessed turns out to be an electronic reproduction located in a robot. By the kind of circularity that often reinforces Pohl's coolly ironic tone in these stories, Burckhardt's own job in 'real life' was associated with the very factory that thus engineered the transference of human memories, minds, emotions and habits to vacuum-tube cells: he himself ends as one of his own factory's products.

Perhaps the fullest and most suggestive account of alienation is the least fantastic story of the collection, where we are much closer to a tormented psyche—'Rafferty's Reasons'. Rafferty has lost his former identity as an artist during the machine age, when he became unemployed: now, under the Mudgins Way, everyone is given full employment and machines are abolished. This has meant two things: first, people must do the work formerly done by machines, which means largely repetitive labour; and secondly, artists such as Rafferty will be degraded to manual workers, while morons will succeed. At least, this is what one gathers from odd hints in the story, which refuses to come clean with its own context, almost like Rafferty unable to speak or act openly, or to piece out his 'reasons'. Thus Rafferty, who once was worth something, is treated as trash by his boss Girty, who is far from being a better man. It is this refusal by Girty and the world he represents to give Rafferty his own valuation and identity that is the spring of his rage—though by the time of the story his rage has become so large and formless that it has almost lost touch with any identifiable cause (the motive has lost *its* identity) and Rafferty can only burn with fury at Girty's physical being. Rafferty has lost all notion of what 'the studio' or 'Art' were, though he senses vaguely that they were better than the New Way. The enforced sameness of the world of Mudgins and the New Way is fused with the sameness of the anger that Rafferty always feels, 'He sat down and ate what was before him, not caring what it was or how it tasted, for everything tasted alike to Rafferty'. When his fury takes him, the normally clear and neat numbers which 'the artist that lived in Rafferty' enjoys making become 'hot red and smouldering black, and they swirled and bloated before his stinging eyes'. Rafferty's words and feelings have no identity, remaining unuttered, as with his acts which remain undone. The girls at his table in the cafeteria do not notice him. His whole object in the story is to whip himself up to such a point that he will make some overt definition of himself to the world. His constant mental harping on how he will carve and slice Girty is an image for cutting his way out of himself, and for shaping himself by actually carving someone else's flesh. He fails to accomplish these dramatic acts, but in his failure he reveals a truer self, that of helpless protest.

Clearly outcasts everywhere will be inclined to identify with Rafferty: but we have to remember that he is a creature in a work of science fiction, and that his failures may not be simply psychological but created by the new machines which have been set to turn humanity into unthinkingly obedient operatives before the machines are finally dispensed with. When Girty, announcing to the workers on the Project that an important visitor is coming, tells them all to ' "try to act like human beings this morning" ', the words carry no little unintended irony. Constantly the story presents us with definition, only to pull it away. As Rafferty searches for Girty, looking in the free-market restaurants, he presses 'his forehead against the glass like an urchin on Christmas Day, only with the blackness coming out of no urchin's eyes'. That phrase 'blackness coming out of no urchin's eyes' suggests that it comes out of a nothingness, before we read it aright; and the effect of the whole has been to give us a clear scene of a street urchin and Christmas time before whisking both away. When Rafferty, who has only two dollars, takes a taxi to follow Girty, 'The driver . . . never knew that murder was right behind him. But it was only a short ride—fortunately for Rafferty's two dollars': at that 'fortunately' we think the reference will be to the taxi-driver who has escaped Rafferty's murderous intent, but in fact it is directed at the two dollars; the sentence starts in Rafferty's melodramatic idiom and then shifts to the dry tone of the author.

Throughout the story Rafferty is constantly being portrayed as saying terrible things to people, whether to Girty, a stranger, the taxi-driver or a masseur, before this is taken back and we realize that they have taken place only in his imagination, not in reality at all. Rafferty's hatred is both present and not, burdened with intent and starved of act. Lying on the massage slab in the steam baths to which he eventually follows Girty, Rafferty rages at 'the darkened, shapeless core of the light': it is as though he is raging at an image of his own hate. That hatred has lost definition as, in a different way, has Rafferty's past, of which he retains only a hazy notion: he dimly recollects having been at the baths before, but loses certainty in a thicket of vague pronouns and shuffled tenses, 'Once upon a time, it seemed to Rafferty, a long, long time ago someone who *then* had been that which was Rafferty *now* had been in a place like this. That was during what they called the "Old Way", although it seemed to Rafferty, they hadn't called it that then'.

The steam-baths where the story ends are symbolic. They are hot, like Rafferty's rage. They are impersonal, like society—functional, anonymous square rooms, functional attendants. Those in them have to go naked, which suggests revelation of the true self. Yet at the same time the steam obscures everything, reducing people to dim shapes, enabling Rafferty to conceal himself from Girty, even (for a while) when he lies down on the slab beside him for massage. This double aspect, of revelation and concealment, mirrors Rafferty's eventual revelation of his feelings to Girty and the world, and at the same time his delusion that he has revealed them far more violently than in fact he has, 'After he committed suicide, he sat there and watched his victims running about. It was several seconds

before he noticed that he wasn't dead'. When Girty suddenly recognizes Rafferty in the massage room, it is then that Rafferty reveals his true self by getting slowly off his slab, voicing his incoherent hate and assaulting Girty: as Girty penetrates through the steam to Rafferty's physical identity in the baths, so he discovers something of Rafferty's inner being.

It has taken that to bring Rafferty to act: he has been lying passively on his slab waiting for 'some sort of signal', and one may suppose that had Girty not recognized him he might never have acted at all—in short that Girty, in a way, has brought Rafferty 'into being'. Rafferty depends on the very would he hates to stimulate him: perhaps it is more a part of him than he knows. Nor can he make his act fully his own: it is always like something else, like somebody else. He uses multiple analogies, seeing his eventual movements as being 'fast as lightning or the star rays that shoot across the void', even mixing his metaphors, as when he describes himself as 'an avalanche waiting on cue in the wings of a spectacular drama'. When he attacks Girty and those about him, 'It was the moment of the knife', and

> He was a Spartacus, and a Lizzie Borden, swordsman and butcher. He stabbed every one of them to the heart and ripped them up and down, and for the first time in longer than he could know, Rafferty was Rafferty, *Mister* Rafferty, a man who had once been a human being and, God save the mark, an artist, and not a mere flesh ersatz for a bookkeeping machine. Kill and slice and tear! They overturned furniture, squealing and thundering, like a trapped horse kicking at the flaming, booming walls of its stall. But he killed them all, many times, this Rafferty who was Spartacus and Lizzie Borden—

And, at last, a warrior of the Samurai as well.

The circularity of the first paragraph suggests the isolation from reality, from which the only escape is the suicidal gesture of the final sentence, a gesture which is quite imaginary. Just as Rafferty denies his true self in these analogies, so his own words lose identity. He uses cliché throughout—'the moment of the knife', 'God save the mark'; his words are repetitive—'Dirty, dirty, dirty', 'I have a knife to cut you with and stab you with'; and they are exhausted, short-breathed, lacking the emphasis even of an exclamation mark: ' "I'll kill you, Girty" '; ' "Fat, soft thing. You're dirty, cow" '; ' "Your mother loved hogs" '. Rafferty does in his way succeed in identifying himself, but the identification is limited. How far he realized he had deluded himself about the knife we do not know, as he is carried out, weeping. As for the world, he has left little mark on it: he had hoped literally to make a mark with the knife, and Girty's death, but all he has done is give Girty's body some temporary bruises. As far as Girty's mind is concerned, to it Rafferty is mere riff-rafferty, the kind of degenerate who will snap under pressure. True, Girty is left vaguely wondering at Rafferty's reason for attacking him, but that is all. All we know is that a few others not unlike Rafferty may exist, such as Girty's friend, who dislikes the harshness of the Mudgins Way, but voices his criticism only to himself. In the last section of the story the conversation of Girty and his friend largely walls off Rafferty's act from comprehension.

In this and the other stories in *Alternating Currents* Pohl is not bent on making a point or in putting over a message, which makes them all the more effective. The story of Ehrlich in **'The Ghost-Maker'** may be shown to illustrate 'pride punished' or the Faustian theme of the perils of going beyond permitted limits of knowledge and power, but Pohl never says so, never reduces the story to these lessons, and the result is that it conveys these meanings and many more. Similarly in **'Let the Ants Try'** and **'Target One'** the moral thread may be the danger of playing God, but this is no more than hinted in the name *Salva Gordy*, which leaves the story free to work at other levels. In **'Rafferty's Reasons'** we deal with a very mixed person in Rafferty, who is not reducible to any formula. Always Pohl prefers the oblique, or the dryly detached: 'Sometimes he screams, sometimes he wheedles, threatens, begs, cajoles . . . but his voice goes on and on through one June 15th after another';

> It was entirely my own fault and carelessness; but I wish I had not been so free to conjure up the ghosts of lions and lizards; I have wished it more and more since N'Ginga came running to me, face almost pale, to show me what lizard-teeth had done to the wraith of the Boy.

(That 'almost pale' is a marvellously precise touch in the midst of horror: it suggests under-statement, until we recall that ghosts are already pale.)

In other collections of his stories Pohl sometimes does look over his shoulder at an audience, or hector his readers directly, and the result is far less potent narrative. **'Day Million'** is an example. In this story Pohl's object is to show us how provincial and contingent some of our values are. He describes the peculiar marital relationship of a couple in the far future, where the man is a one hundred and eighty-seven-year-old cyborg composed mainly of metal parts, and the woman is genetically male, seven feet tall and with a body part-seal, smelling of peanut butter; and during this absurd portrait he turns to lash us for our blinkered perspective, 'Balls, you say, it looks crazy to me. And you—with your aftershave lotion and your little red car, pushing papers across a desk all day and chasing tail all night—tell me, just how the hell you think you would look to Tiglath-Pileser, say, or Attila the Hun?' If one were to put the next story from the same collection, **'The Deadly Mission of P. Snodgrass'**, beside **'Target One'**, the point is still more evident. The Snodgrass story has its scientist protagonist return to the time of Christ with the generous object of providing the benefits of twentieth-century medicine to the suffering humanity of the time. The result is a dramatic decline in the mortality rate, and the population of the world swiftly doubles and redoubles. Pressure of population forces an early industrial revolution and scientific advance to sustain the population; but even so, by the sixth century A.D. all the available land mass of the earth is covered with humans. Eventually a time machine

is constructed to send back a man to kill Snodgrass, whereupon 'To the great (if only potential) joy of some quintillions of never-to-be-born persons, Darkness blessedly fell.' The 'story' is simply direct extrapolation of what would happen after a single dramatic event; and with its projections of how humanity would eventually outweigh the universe, it, like **'Day Million'** goes to extreme lengths. As a warning against overpopulation it is much less effective, because much more naively direct, than the more oblique **'Target One'**, which fully dramatises a situation of overpopulation and its effect on human beings, and shows us something of what it would feel like. **'The Deadly Mission of P. Snodgrass'** also limits its effect by ending with a happy reversal of the disaster, where **'Target One'** does not; one thinks too of the failure of Gordy to reverse his manipulations of the past in **'Let the Ants Try'**.

One of Pohl's *fortes* in *Alternating Currents* is the neatness with which every detail fits. The narrative of **'The Tunnel Under the World'** is written from an initial position of ignorance, where we think we know where we are but slowly discover, with the narrator, anomalous factors, such as the unchanging date and weather, the explosion remembered from the 'dream', the strange commercials for unfamiliar brands, the unusual cigarettes, the absence of Barth from Burckhardt's office and so on, all causing increasing puzzlement: and then, when this has reached a pitch, every single piece fits into one explanation, one unsuspected world which seems more real because it answers everything in the story. This is, if we like, where Pohl's stories have a further kinship with Pope: every part that seemed to stand out in the end proves to be part of a larger whole ('Parts answ'ring parts shall slide into a Whole'; 'All Chance, Direction, which thou canst not see; / All Discord, Harmony not understood'). In this Pohl is quite different, for example, from an author and a story whose publication he himself ensured—Cordwainer Smith's 'Scanners Live in Vain' (1950). In Smith's story the process of 'cranching', of coming out from being a scanner or biotelepath into normal humanity is as contingent as the name: a golden-sheathed wire is wrapped about the scanner, plugged into a control in his chest, and a wire field sphere at its end thrown into the air, where it is caught and held by the force-field round the scanner before glowing and producing the change. There is nothing necessary or even symbolic about this apparatus so far as the story is concerned, apart perhaps from its relative absurdity. With Pohl the apparently random becomes patterned: in **'The Mapmakers'**—and the title itself says it—the seeming chaos of hyperspace becomes ordered in the mind of Groden.

It is this 'fitting' that makes the new worlds of Pohl coolly attractive. One of the finest examples of this is **'Let the Ants Try'**, where, in contrast to **'The Tunnel Under the World'**, we start with an apparently all-knowing narrator, one indeed who proposes to refashion the chaos of the world into his own pattern. But the very pattern he creates contains a logic and a further pattern that he did not foresee. Intelligent ants will not coexist with humans; and events will neatly circumscribe every attempt to reverse the process by which they came into being. Things get out of hand: here the narrative is symbolic, for it suggests a runaway chain-reaction, and it is precisely away from the results of such chain-reaction, in the form of devastating atomic war, that the scientist Gordy is trying to manipulate history. (In this and such sceptical stories as 'The Ghost-Maker', 'Target One' and 'What To Do Until the Analyst Comes' Pohl is again like Pope—'Man, who here seems principal alone, / Perhaps acts second to some sphere unknown, / . . . / 'Tis but a part we see, and not a whole.') The circularity of the narrative, whereby Gordy comes to live through his own unrecognized scream, is again symbolic: he is caught in a temporal pincer-movement, just as the ants have outflanked him to catch him in their physical pincers. Somehow the story is so tightly woven, so precisely balanced, that we do not question why the ants could not have used Gordy's time machine themselves rather than build a new one, or how they knew for what he had disappeared into the past, and to what precise time in the past. If anything makes Pohl's stories 'scientific', it is that they work like equations.

Neatness, wit, clarity: it is Pohl's instinct for accuracy that makes him so able to write well about a man such as Rafferty who lives an 'inaccurate' life, a man who struggles and fails to define himself. It is because the scientists in 'Let the Ants Try' and 'Target One' do not work out the possible consequences of their actions that they meet disaster. Ehrlich in 'The Ghost-Maker' meets his fate partly because he has ceased to care for accuracy, whether the accuracy of a scientist, or that of simply looking where one is going: he himself becomes ghosted because he has refused definition. In many of the stories the characters end by coming to a clearer, if often unpleasant, awareness—Gordy, Burckhardt finding the true nature of Tylerton, the protagonists of 'Target One' realizing the real nature of the world they have made, Ehrlich coming to see that ghost-carnivores can devour ghosts, McGory doomed to be the sole clear and undrugged consciousness who at the end of 'What To Do Until the Analyst Comes' sees the full effect on the world of Cheery-Gum.

Pohl always gives the fantastic events of his stories 'definition' by tying them to the everyday and identifiable. While the captain of the space-ship in 'The Mapmakers' considers the mysteries of Riemannian space he simultaneously observes that a spaceman is out of uniform and that 'The enlisted women's quarters needed floor-polishing'. Part of Rafferty's mind is preoccupied with the price of his Swedish Rub massage as he prepares to slay Girty. No better way could have been found to convey the narrowness of Gordy's escape from the ants than the severed insect leg still thrashing about on the floor of the time machine. And Pohl has a marvellously sharp ear for tones of voice and attitude—Gordy in 'Let the Ants Try' addressing the ants like a collection of ignorant natives, the pompous formalities of the narrator in 'Target One' before he is bundled away by the dingy representatives of the new society he has brought about, the smart flippancy of Ehrlich in 'The Ghost-Maker', the wry self-exposure of McGory in 'What To Do Until the Analyst Comes'. Detail, precision, scepticism, wit, astringent irony and above all

an insider's view of *this* world—whether the interior of a steam bath, a museum or an advertising company: all these go into Pohl's tone. In some ways, as we have suggested, he is like Pope; in others, particularly in his juxtaposition of the familiar and the strange, or his carrying a situation to its logical limit, or in the interplay between serious and comic in his stories, his method recalls that of the metaphysical poets: but ultimately these likenesses serve only to point more precisely to his own individuality.

Thomas D. Clareson (essay date 1987)

SOURCE: "Interim: A Resurgence of Pessimism," in *Frederik Pohl,* Starmont House, 1987, pp. 122-38.

[*In the following excerpt, Clareson analyzes the pessimism evident in Pohl's short fiction from the 1970s and early 1980s.*]

Even while he was working on the early novels of the Heechee Quartet, in which Heechee technology and Broadhead's entrepreneurship at least began to end many of Earth's problems, when asked about the future, Pohl has repeatedly said that anyone more optimistic is foolish. One can sense a brooding pessimism in *Pohlstars* (1984), his "first short story collection in a decade"; it gains its unity from the sobriety with which he treats familiar storylines and themes. In one of the few narratives not explicitly portraying a dystopian future, "Enjoy Enjoy" (1974), Tud Coopersmith's job—with its unlimited expense account—tapes the full gamut of his reactions to a wide variety of experiences to be used vicariously by his wealthy employers. Although he is told that his clients want him to have "fun," at one point his contact person informs him that "one of our best units . . . was terminal stomach cancer". Only when he becomes bored and begins his debriefing does he learn that there is no future for him, for the aliens who have hired him keep jealous possession of his experiences by keeping his head. . . .

Against the background of a dystopian Earth, "The Way It Was" (1977) momentarily echoes "Day Million" in that it seems to be the love story of Stan and Evanie. In a vast city where most of the people have been on relief for years, to "live like a human being" and avoid going back to his housing on the fortieth floor of a dormitory, Stan agrees with Associated Medical Services to take an injection a week. If he survives, he earns a thousand dollars; if he loses, his body will supply innumerable transplants. Goaded on by his sexual attraction for Evanie, although she protests that she hates his gambling, Stan tries for a big winner against impossible odds.

In contrast "Rem the Rememberer" (1974) is a child of ten who lives perhaps a century in the future; the narrative does little more than describe the hopelessly polluted world. Sometimes he cries as he awakens because he dreams of how the world used to be; that such a life is a maddening experience is implied by his uncertainty "which was the reality and which was the dream". The inquisitive child, Chandlie, who is the protagonist of **"Growing Up in Edge City"** (1975), evades his Pal, a robot companion, and descends from the "stilted bulk of Edge City" to find a colony of "Dropouts," who have abandoned the sterile, mechanized dome where humans have been regimented by their machines. Despite his own curiosity about the natural world and the entreaties of the Dropouts, he willingly returns to the City and accepts his seven demerits—seven days without free time; twenty years later he uses the incident to gain personal political power.

Published in the same year as *Man Plus,* **"A Day in the Life of Able Charlie"** (1976) explores the several minutes when an AC-770 computer completes its analysis of a typical, married American man, makes its report, and begins "its new life" as another program—that of a teenaged girl. Pohl asserts in an introductory note that it was originally written for an advertising campaign; it does dramatize the versatility of machine intelligence and takes on something of a cutting edge when the young woman in the office—who skillfully programs the AC-770 and awaits its next printout—believes that she is alone.

Concerned with the first contact between aliens and humans, **"The Mother Trip"** (1975) proves to be one of the early stories in which Pohl offers alternate outcomes to a single incident. On the outskirts of Jackson, Mississippi, an alien dressed as a cowboy is stopped by a policeman on the empty streets and then is released. Although enraged, the alien readily accepts this act of violence. In the first scenario the aliens destroy the planet with fusion bombs. In the second, agreeing that "this complicatedly comic planet needed to be taken into the motherhood of Mawkri"—the matriarch of the ship—the aliens deliver an ultimatum in the manner of Earth's nations; the six nuclear powers cooperate, and a missile destroys the ship. In a "warmer and more loving version," the aliens decide that "Human beings . . . are clearly self-destructive . . . unchecked . . . they will wipe themselves out"; they leave humanity to its own devices. One infers that a fourth version, in which the aliens "live forever . . . locked into their own small world" may well be aimed at those persons opposed to the space program.

In these stories, except for the pathos of Rem, no human gains the reader's sympathy. Much the same can be said for the later works. Two rely heavily on plot. The perhaps overly long **"The Sweet, Sad Queen of the Grazing Isles"** (1984) concerns a power struggle for control of the "oaty boats" which attempt to feed an overpopulated Earth. The likable but naive young narrator of **"The High Test"** (1983) tells how an alien who dislikes all mammals fails to set up the conquest of Cassiopeia 43-G, if not all the worlds of the Galaxy. The third—apparently inspired by a first sentence given him by his son—gives a new twist to an old idea. In the five-hundred-word **"Second Coming"** (1983), space people who took Christ from his tomb and kept him in their zoo made up of specimens of various galactic life forms return Him to Earth; the President and his advisers are glad that "He's ours"; but after watching TV and giving a speech in prime time, Christ abandons the world because "we've spoiled His planet. . . . We've messed

everything up." He goes back to the world of the space people because "They've got a better-class zoo." It provides what is perhaps Pohl's most succinct fictional denunciation of world affairs.

In an introductory note, as Pohl hoped, a "new treatment . . . a new angle of attack" give fresh vitality to a warning about overpopulation in **"Spending a Day at the Lottery Fair"** (1983). Into the richly textured, third-person account of the holiday taken by Randolph and Millicent Baxter and their three small children, Pohl inserts details building to the final ironies. The reactions of husband and wife to the job lottery emphasizes the unemployment and financial distress of the country. Foreign tourists—personified by a Scotswoman and Mr. Katshubishi—buy unlimited tickets in their own country, thereby bringing much needed money into the U.S.; they may do whatever they wish at the fair. But U.S. citizens must pay for everything, even restrooms. One learns that a Japanese colony in the north of Scotland has improved that area "agriculturally and economically" as well as ridding Japan of some of its "surplus population without pain." Millicent insists that she and the children will pay their own ways "all the rest of the day". A Black man drops dead at a nearby booth. Randolph Baxter speaks "patriotically" as he denounces such practices as compulsory sterilization and contraceptive drugs in other countries; "American ingenuity" has developed the Fair. When they attend the Hall of Life and Death—the only free pavilion—one of her daughters thanks Millicent for not aborting her. They view the sixty bodies—including the Black man—which already fill some of the seventy-five platforms which will be/must be occupied by someone by the end of the day. When the Scotswoman thinks it odd to "glorify" death in such a manner, Randolph again explains that "the greatest minds in America"—think tanks, government agencies, and three universities—have planned the Fair. In a future where "national philosophies" differ. Americans "don't go in for . . . 'birth control'. . . . No abortion. No contraception. . . . We believe that every human being, from the moment of conception on, has a right to life, although . . . not necessarily a long one". American ingenuity has developed a method by which lethal injections from tickets will kill seventy-five citizens each day at the Fair by chance; in the Hall of Life and Death, a great machine shows that each minute the population increases by "a few more persons"—so that the lottery at the Fair is a meaningless absurdity.

David Seed (essay date 1993)

SOURCE: "Take-over Bids: The Power Fantasies of Frederik Pohl and Cyril Kornbluth," in *Foundation,* Vol. 59, Fall, 1993, pp. 42-58.

[Below, Seed discusses what he considers Pohl's "preoccupation with the working of commercial processes" in three early short stories, including "The Tunnel under the World," "The Wizards of Pung's Corner," and "Waging the Peace."]

Pohl's preoccupation with the working of commercial processes in society emerges in one form or another in most of his fiction and in 1984 he published a sequel to *The Space Merchants* entitled *The Merchants' War* which recapitulates the same themes as the earlier novel. However, three stories from the 1950s stand out as major extensions of the narrative methods used in *The Space Merchants*. **"The Tunnel under the World"** (1954) addresses the nature of the environment. It opens with an evocation of the normal day-to-day routine of a business executive, defining his environment entirely through familiar consumer objects and advertisements. Then disparities begin to multiply: a new brand of cigarettes, an unusually strident advertising jingle, and so on. The main disparity, however, comes with Pohl repeating the opening line of the story and by freezing the passage of time at a single day. So although the protagonist Burckhardt wakes up several times the date stays at June 15th. As if that wasn't enough, he even discovers that his house is a metal replica! Thus two main determinants of reality—time and place—are brought into question through a series of perceptual shocks to the protagonist. The submerged plot of the story is given a metaphorical expression in a tunnel which Burckhardt discovers. Poised to enter it, he juggles with interpretive possibilities which anticipate Pynchon's fiction in their ambiguity: "He was sure of only one thing—the tunnel went somewhere. Martians or Russians, fantastic plot or crazy hallucination, whatever was wrong with Tylerton had an explanation and the place to look for it was at the end of the tunnel." These binary alternatives (extra-planetary/terrestrial, political/psychological) keep intact the master plot of conspiracy but do not identify the third possibility which is that, as a result of a massive industrial accident, Contro (read "control") chemicals has not only rebuilt the town but has housed the brains of some citizens (including Burckhardt himself) in robot humanoid bodies. **"The Tunnel"** then dramatises the power of commercial forces to construct reality on all levels. Burckhardt tries to leave the Contro plant and finds himself staring down into a void: "He was standing on a ledge of smooth, finished metal. Not a dozen yards from his feet, the ledge dropped sharply away; he hardly dared approach the brink, but even from where he stood he could see no bottom to the chasm before him. And the gulf extended out of sight into the glare on either side of him." Burckhardt's vertigo marks the culminating point of his gradual loss of reality. Jean Baudrillard has described the modern shopping mall as an apotheosis of consumption, the "total organization of everyday life." Pohl anticipates this theoretical insight through a parable which puts the company into the position of creator not merely organiser of the environment. When Burckhardt steps out onto the ledge it is as if he temporarily leaves his own diegetic frame and gazes into a void empty of shape and dimension. Pohl thereby denies the reader the sentimental consolation of even a symbolic escape on the protagonist's part and the story concludes with a seemingly endless cycle of repetitions of one day, that is after yet one more shock—the narrator's realisation that he and his world have been miniaturised.

Such shock-effects play no part in a two-story sequence of 1959 where Pohl made his closest and most explicit connection between commerce and the Cold War. **"The

Wizards of Pung's Corner" is set in a small American town after a nuclear war has laid waste much of the country (America has won the war but the detail is played down as scarcely relevant). Pung's Corner has cut itself off from the residual federal authorities and the story essentially recounts the attempts of the latter to take over the town. The story expresses the tension between local communitarian values and government centralism in terms of military combat. The main antagonists in this struggle are Edsel Coglan for the government (a combination of tycoon, spy and electronics wizard) and the local Jack Tighe ("The Father of the Second Republic"). Coglan attempts to bring the town back into the national political mainstream by introducing subliminal advertisements on the TV and using subsonic messages to the local bank manager, but the community sees through these hidden persuaders and Coglan fails. The second phase of the action is a military offensive which goes farcically wrong when the government troops show a complete inability to handle their own technologically sophisticated weaponry. Surrender follows retreat, and Jack Tighe marches on Washington.

Pohl combines a number of important, thematic elements here. Firstly the story is told orally as a reminiscence of the "old days" to a projected reader who is assumed to have considerable knowledge of the present. This method of narration builds immediacy into the descriptions, incorporates both self-authenticating emphases, and anticipates possible queries from the listener/reader. In short the oral delivery naturalises the strange events by assuming the reader's credence from the outset. Secondly the story weaves potential resemblance between Jack Tighe and Lincoln, and between Coglan's arrival and such narratives as Twain's "The Mysterious Stranger". Thirdly Pohl transposes commerce on to military combat so that the government troops become the bemused consumers of new goods: the operating manual for their rifles is entitled *The Five-Step Magic Eye Way to New Combat Comfort and Security*. The companion story **"Waging the Peace"** develops an issue which Pohl could only glance at in **"The Wizards,"** namely the unforeseen consequences of planning by a military-industrial complex. This history remains pure exposition in **"The Wizards,"** but in its sequel the account of the dispersal and construction of underground factories, and their subsequent automation, supplies an essential context for the action. With Jack Tighe in power laws are passed forbidding advertising—"the very prescription for a Golden Age." The past, however, in the form of the "cavern factories" which are still churning out massive quantities of goods, proves to be the main obstacle to this reform. Hence the theme of the story emerges as a conflict between utopian hope, the citizens' control of their own society; and on the other hand, the unforeseen consequences of its earlier economic system. The solution is battle, hence the paradox of the story's title, a battle to wipe out the factories. Once again the action follows two stages: a frontal attack on the factory entrance and underground sabotage. The latter virtually parodies the language of military heroism; ("They were unarmed and helpless against a smart and powerful factory of machines and weapons") and appears to conclude with victory celebrations when the factory has become immobilised. Except that it hasn't. The story concludes with an ironic twist in that production is continuing, even without raw materials.

Ultimately then mankind loses the struggle with its own creations. Pohl builds both his stories on a sardonic account of the rise of business design starting from the premise that "it doesn't much matter what you build, it only matters that people should want to buy it." The inducing of unnecessary desires feeds an unquestioned imperative of production, that it should always rise, and Pohl blurs this mounting spiral into another process of military escalation:

> Against an enemy presupposed to grow smarter and slicker and quicker with each advance, just as we and our machines do. Against our having fewer and fewer fighting men; pure logic that, as war continues, more and more are killed, fewer and fewer left to operate the killer engines. Against the destruction or capture of even the impregnable underground factories, guarded as no dragon of legend ever was—by all that Man could devise at first in the way of traps and cages, blast and ray—and then by the slipleashed invention of machines ordered always to speed up—more and more, deadlier and deadlier.

Pohl brilliantly evokes increase and acceleration through repetition and even through a rhythmic pattern to his phrases which suggest a process with an internally consistent logic ("just as A, so B") based on a premise of attack which is never questioned. Pohl uses post-holocaust Detroit as an image of the ludicrous end result, above ground a blackened radioactive ruin, below ground a streamlined factory churning out motor cars which could never be used. Unfortunately in neither of these stories does Pohl allows such images their full force. Instead they are deflected into an ironic comedy of humanity's failure to regain control of its own production methods. Military combat in both stories can be read as historical prediction but also as the literalisation of the metaphor of promotion as "campaign" and competition as battle.

Pohl and Kornbluth's dramatisations of the takeover of American social and political life by advertising companies received startling factual confirmation in 1957 with the publication of Vance Packard's *The Hidden Persuaders*. He presented a well-documented argument that since World War II the techniques of motivational research and depth psychology had been used increasingly by companies to promote their goods and even to win political elections. In his note for the British edition of his book Packard strikes an explicitly emotive note by declaring that "Americans have become the most manipulated people outside the Iron Curtain." The political implications ran counter to the then ideological contrast which the United States was drawing between itself and the manipulatory Communist regimes. Packard showed that manipulation was now a routine fact of everyday life in the USA and that such practices were approaching the "chilling world of George Orwell and his Big Brother." *Nineteen Eighty-Four* indeed functions as an intertext within *The Hidden Persuaders*, supporting the latter's oppositions between secrecy and openness, depth and surface. The individual psyche becomes a politicised space which the ad-men usurp: "The most serious offense many of the depth manipulators commit . . . is that they try to invade the privacy of our minds." One year earlier than Packard's book William H. Whyte had also drawn on Orwell for a similar prediction of change in America, but this time towards a benevolent therapeutic dictatorship:

> And what a terrible world it would be! Hell is no less hell for being antiseptic. In the 1984 of Big Brother one would at least know who the enemy was—a bunch of bad men who wanted power because they liked power. But in the other kind of 1984 one would be disarmed for not knowing who the enemy was, and when the day of reckoning came the people on the other side of the table wouldn't be Big Brother's bad henchmen; they would be a mild-looking group of therapists who, like the Grand Inquisitor, would be doing what they did to help you.

Packard and Whyte both evoke a situation of brainwashing on the domestic front which reflects their perceptions of how power was shifting and in the course of a 1963 discussion on Orwellian tendencies in American life Pohl confirmed the message of *The Hidden Persuaders* by stating: "what speaks for society, first and foremost—thanks to the subliminal excavations of motivational research—is advertising."

FURTHER READING

Owings, Mark. "Frederik Pohl: Bibliography." *Fantasy and Science Fiction* (September 1973): 65-69.
    Listing of Pohl's works through the mid-1970s.

Stephensen-Payne, Phil, and Gordon Benson. *Frederik Pohl: Merchant of Excellence: A Working Bibliography.* San Bernardino, CA: Borgo Press, 1990, 109 p.
    Comprehensive bibliography belonging to the Galactic Central bibliographic series of science fiction writers.

Additional coverage of Pohl's life and career is contained in the following sources published by Gale Research: *Contemporary Authors Autobiography Series*, Vol. 1; *Contemporary Authors New Revision Series*, Vol. 37; *Contemporary Literary Criticism*, Vol. 18; *Dictionary of Literary Biography*, Vol. 8; *Major Twentieth-Century Writers*; and *Something About the Author*, Vol. 24.

Juan Rulfo
1918-1986

Mexican short story writer, novelist, screenwriter, essayist, and photographer.

INTRODUCTION

Considered one of Mexico's most notable authors, Rulfo established an international literary reputation on only two works, a collection of short stories and a novel, published within three years of each other in the 1950s. His fiction depicts the lives of people in the arid lands of central Mexico. Although local in their settings, Rulfo's works transcend contextual themes to explore universal, metaphysical, social, and political questions.

Biographical Information

Rulfo was born in central Mexico in the Jalisco region. During his early childhood, the war of the Cristeros took place. A political uprising of the Catholic clergy against the Mexican government, this event and its repercussions became a recurring theme in his later work. In the 1920s both of his parents died and Rulfo was sent to an orphanage where he remained until 1933. After a brief stint in university, he became an immigration agent. At work, a colleague encouraged his writing, which resulted in the 1945 publication of his first short story. Soon after, he founded the literary journal *Pan* with prominent Mexican writers Juan José Arreola and Antonio Alatorre. In 1952 Rulfo received a fellowship from the Centro de Escritores Mexicanos, which allowed him to finish his collection of short stories, *El llano en llamas, y otros cuentos* (*The Burning Plain, and Other Stories*). Following favorable critical reception, the fellowship was renewed, enabling Rulfo to complete his novel *Pedro Páramo,* published in 1955. A second novel was begun but never published. His later nonliterary work consisted of editing history books and working with various government agencies, primarily one that studied and attempted to alleviate the problems of Mexico's indigenous population. Rulfo later wrote film scripts, published as *El gallo de oro y otros textos para cine* (*The Golden Cock and Other Film Scripts*). In 1970 he was awarded Mexico's highest literary honor, the *Premio Nacional de Letras,* and he received Spain's *Premio Príncipe de Asturias* in 1983. Rulfo died in 1986.

Major Works of Short Fiction

The short stories in *The Burning Plain* are set in the harsh countryside of the Jalisco region where Rulfo was raised. They explore the tragic lives of the area's inhabitants, who suffer from extreme poverty, family discord, and crime. The

title character of "Macario," for example, is an orphan raised by a neurotic foster mother. The narrative voice reflects the boy's thoughts as he sits alongside a drainpipe at night, carrying out his foster mother's instructions to kill the bullfrogs, whose croaking disturbs her sleep. "Nos han dado la tierra" ("They Have Given Us the Land") depicts the results of the government's land reform program for four poor countrymen who have been given a parcel of land. They march across a barren plain to reach their property, which is located too far from any source of water to be of any use to them. "La noche que lo dejaron solo" ("The Night He Was Left Alone") tells the story of a man pursued by federal troops who kill his family members when they cannot locate him. The content and, in some cases, the narrative technique of these stories have been perceived by critics as precursors to Rulfo's artistic achievement in his novel: both works share a bleak, essentially hopeless view of the lives of their characters.

Critical Reception

Rulfo's literary reputation is based on only two works, the short story collection *The Burning Plain* and the novel

Pedro Páramo. Both garnered high critical and popular praise, first in Mexico, where Rulfo received a national literary prize, and then abroad, where his work is a component of virtually any course focusing on twentieth-century Latin American literature. Though some commentators have categorized him as a regionalist writer, many critics have acknowledged that his work transcends strictly regional concerns, embodying universal themes of dispossession, loneliness, poverty, and alienation.

PRINCIPAL WORKS

Short Fiction

El llano en llamas, y otros cuentos [*The Burning Plain, and Other Stories*] 1953

Other Major Works

Pedro Páramo (novel) 1955
Obra completa: El llano en llamas, Pedro Páramo, otros textos (novel, short stories, and essays) 1977
Antología personal (novel, short stories, and essays) 1978
El gallo de oro y otros textos para cine [*The Golden Cock and Other Film Scripts*] (screenplays) 1980
Inframundo: The Mexico of Juan Rulfo (photography) 1983

CRITICISM

Luis Harss (essay date 1966)

SOURCE: "Juan Rulfo: Contemporary Mexican Novelist," in *New Mexico Quarterly,* Vol. XXXV, No. 4, Winter, 1965-66, pp. 293-318.

[*In the following excerpt, Harss stresses Rulfo's significance as a regionalist writer, contending that his short fiction successfully incorporates political and cultural themes without using propaganda or exaggerated sentiment.*]

The current of regionalism, once a tidal flow, though somewhat diminished lately, continues to run strong in our literature. A lot of what it hauls along is old-fashioned stuff of little more than pictoric interest. The old regionalists who started producing the bulk of our literature toward the end of the nineteenth century were mediators between man and nature. Their function was less literary than agricultural. Their eye was innocent: it alighted only on surfaces. There was a wilderness to be tamed, an unmarked land to be given man's image and imprint. There

were remnants of tribal cultures to be explored, catastrophes to be recorded. Literature was part of a collective effort.

Social conflicts—in feudal fiefs, mines, tropical plantations—gave this literature urgency and momentum. A branch of it, perhaps the sturdiest, taking its cue from the venerable Alcides Arguedas, who denounced the exploitation of the Indian in the Bolivian highlands in his epochal *Raza de Bronce* (*Race of Bronze,* 1919), found its cause in protest. Another, eminently represented today in the work of Peru's José María Arguedas, a fine sociologist, subordinated the epic to the interpretive. A third, the least fruitful—one thinks of El Salvador's juicy humorist, Salarrué—petered out into folklore. But whatever the emphasis, the basic characteristics of this literature were always the same. It gave a picture, not a portrait. Its lines were general and usually at once roughly drawn and overly stylized. It had poetic moments in Peru's Ciro Alegría, a pleasant truculence in Salarrué, a militant force in Ecuador's Jorge Icaza. It became experimental with Mexico's Agustín Yañez, highly expressive with José María Arguedas, and even rose to mythological altitudes with Guatemala's Miguel Ángel Asturias, who eclipsed all his contemporaries in the genre. Recently it has had new life breathed into it by a talented Paraguayan storyteller, Augusto Roa Bastos, an excellent stylist who has known how to make regional literature carry the cross of human suffering with grace and dignity.

On the whole, regionalists today are literate writers. Their work has reached an acceptable level of achievement. But, in spite of subtle refinements in methods and techniques—which never transcend basic limitations—they are essentially in the old pamphleteering tradition. They still tend toward either the tract or the travelogue. They work from set situations which, needless to say, are often as real today as they were fifty years ago, but from a literary point of view have long been exhausted. Their faceless characters, sometimes colorful enough, but rarely more than silhouettes with a few generic traits, are soon forgotten. The stress they put on local dialect helps their work date fast. There are few exceptions. Perhaps the only one is Mexico's Juan Rulfo.

Rulfo, a thin man with a lean look, was born on May 16, 1918, in a rocky land: the state of Jalisco, some three hundred miles, as the wind blows, northwest of Mexico City. The northern part of the state, where mountain goats cling to high ledges, is densely populated, but his area, extending south of the capital, Guadalajara, is dry, hot and desolate. Life in the lowlands has always been austere. It is a depressed area long gutted by droughts and wildfires. Revolutions, crop failures, soil erosion have gradually displaced the population. Much of it has moved to Tijuana in hopes of finding migrant work across the border. It is a population largely made up of hardy Creoles—the Indians who occupied the region before the Conquest were soon exterminated—who trace their ancestry back to Castille and Extremadura, the more arid parts of Spain, and are therefore, as Rulfo says, "accustomed to work ten times harder than the farmer of central Mexico to produce the same." They are a dour people reduced to a bare subsistence, who have nevertheless given the country a high percentage of its painters and composers, not to mention its popular music. Jalisco is the cradle of the ranchera and the mariachi.

Says Rulfo in his sorrowful voice: "It's a very poor state. But the people work a lot. They produce a lot. I don't know how they manage to produce so much. They produce too much. Jalisco is the state that produces the most corn in the whole country. It's not a very large state. I think it's the eighth state in size in the country. But it produces enough corn to feed the whole of Mexico. It has more cattle than any other state. But as soon as you leave the capital, there's a lot of misery. Corn is a great destroyer of the soil. So there's no good soil left. In some areas it's completely worn out."

He sits hunched in his chair in our hotel room, off the clattering Paseo de la Reforma. The lines of his gaunt face are drawn tight, his long hands with big veins like raw nerves awkwardly folded on his lap. He talks quickly, in nervous haste, frowning painfully. He is what is known in his land as a "slow starter," he says, like one of those rifles with delayed action that often backfire. He is like his land: prematurely aged, deeply furrowed, careworn. There are blanks in his past. Rugged terrain fades into a hazy background.

"I was born in what is now a small village, an agglomeration that belongs to the district of Sayula. Sayula was an important commercial center some years ago, before and even after the Revolution. But I never lived in Sayula. I don't know Sayula. I couldn't say what it's like. . . . My parents registered me there. Because I was born at the time of the Revolution, or rather, of the revolutions, because there were a series of them. . . . I lived in a village called San Gabriel. I really consider myself to be from there. That's where I was brought up. San Gabriel was also a commercial center. In the old days, San Gabriel was a prosperous town; the royal road to Colima passed through there." San Gabriel was on the highway that led inland from Manzanillo, the port of entry used in Colonial times for imports from the Orient; in its hey-day, there was such wealth that the stores were measured by the number of doors they had. "San Gabriel and Zapotitlán were the most important towns of the region from the seventeenth century down to the Revolution." They were first settled under the "encomenderos": usually soldiers who were granted lands by the Crown in reward for their services, with the local population thrown into the bargain. These "encomenderos" concentrated the population into a few main urban centers that were relatively easy to administer. That was how San Gabriel and Zapotitlán were formed, also Tolimán, Tonaya, Chachahuatlán, San Pedro, etc. But that was long ago. Since the Revolution, there have been years of sunstroke. Nowadays, "in that zone, there are five or six villages left. They are hot lands, between 2,500 and 3,000 feet high." Changing trade routes, desert winds, have swept them into decay. There is little hope of improvement. The process is irreversible. Some villages still seem alive; but on closer inspection, nothing is going on

there any more. The few superannuated inhabitants are stolid and tightlipped. "They are a hermetic people. Perhaps out of distrust—not only toward strangers, but also among themselves. They don't want to talk about their things. Nobody knows what they do, how they make a living. There are villages devoted exclusively to graft. The people there don't like to be asked any questions. They settle their affairs in their own private and personal way, almost secretly. . . ." The landscape itself—forty-five per cent of Mexico is sheer desert—is decrepit. The living are surrounded by the dead.

The dead haunt Rulfo. Perhaps because like so many people of his antediluvian region he has been uprooted and has lost his tracks in the sand. He remembers how his childhood village was gradually depopulated. "There was a river. We used to go bathe there in the hot season. Now the river has run dry. . . ." One of the reasons why the water no longer flows is that the woods in the surrounding mountains—which enclose the area in a monolithic horseshoe—have been cut down. Most people have migrated. Those who have stayed behind are there to keep the dead company. "Their ancestors tie them to the place. They don't want to leave their dead." Sometimes when they move they actually dig up their graves. "They carry their dead on their shoulders." Even when they leave them behind, they continue to bear their weight.

> **Rulfo has not blazed any new trails; to the contrary, he has been content to tread along traditional paths. But his footsteps go deep.**
>
> —*Luis Harss*

So with Rulfo, whose ancestry seems remote, therefore perhaps doubly cumbersome. He has also dug up old family graves in search of his lost origins. "My first ancestor came to Mexico around 1790, I think, from the north of Spain." "Historical curiosity" has sent him browsing, usually in vain, through libraries, bank vaults and civil registries. Mexico is a country of missing files and misplaced documents. Particularly his area, which is buried in administrative confusion. "It was an area that didn't belong to Jalisco originally. Jalisco was called Nueva Galicia. It was conquered by Núñez de Guzmán in 1530. But my area was called the province of Ávalos. Because it was conquered by Alonso de Ávalos, the man who pacified Colima and the southern part of Jalisco. The province of Ávalos was part of Nueva España, in other words, of Mexico City, the capital of the vice-royalty. Though it was near Guadalajara, the capital of Nueva Galicia, it had no political or religious connections with Guadalajara. For many years the documentation of the province of Ávalos was lost, because most of those villages were decimated by plagues and fevers, sometimes by the Conquerors themselves. One of my ancestors on my mother's side was called Arias. . . . There's a curious fact here. Most of the Spanish conquerors were adventurers, jailbirds: monks who weren't monks, priests who weren't priests, people with criminal records. They gave themselves names that don't exist. For example: Vizcaíno. I'm called Vizcaíno on my mother's side. But Vizcaíno is a name that doesn't exist in Spain. There's the province of Vizcaya. Here the name of the province was used to coin a surname. In other words, all the Vizcaínos were outlaws. It was very common among those gentlemen to change their name. They dropped their patronymic and named themselves after their province instead. That's where genealogy breaks down." The diagnosis holds good for most families of "high birth" in Mexico today, he says. If you trace them back far enough, you invariably end up with either a priest or a criminal. "That's why 'highborn' dynasties are false, formed entirely on the basis of wealth. It's hard to draw the lines here. In Ávalos it's impossible. There the villages were razed by the Revolution; the archives were burned. The only documents available were copies on file in Mexico City. So it was difficult to get down to the bottom of things. Now, many facts can be found in banks in the U.S. Because the expeditionary forces that occupied California set out from Ávalos. So the banks there have collected the documents of the period for their own information. They have the best files. Because it was a chapter in the history of California, Texas, New Mexico and Arizona." Rulfo has carried his search to all those places.

What he knows about his family is that his paternal grandfather was a lawyer, his maternal grandfather a landowner. His parents were from the more densely populated northern part of the state, known as Los Altos (The Heights). "It's an overpopulated, very eroded zone inhabited by people who started moving south around the turn of the century. How my parents reached the south, I don't know. The highlander, besides being from the highlands, is tall. 'Longback,' people call him, because of his long waist." Rulfo inherited this trait. He wears his trousers low on slim hips. He also has light eyes. They are common in his region, where the countrygirls are often blonde and blue-eyed. They are also poor. They go barefoot. "There were never any big landholdings in that area. There were always small properties. The countrypeople have always been very poor. The only time they put on their shoes is when they go into town. . . . The habits in those villages are still matriarchal. There woman commands. As a matter of fact, the power of the matriarchy made itself felt during the revolt of the Cristeros. It was the women who led the revolt."

The hardships of the time—starting around 1926, under President Calles, a centralizer who tried to impose constitutional uniformity on the country—are one of Rulfo's childhood memories.

"The revolt of the Cristeros was an internal war that broke out in the states of Colima, Jalisco, Michoacán, Magarit, Zacatecas and Guanajuato, against the federal government. There was a decree that enforced an article of the Revolution, according to which priests were forbidden to mix in politics and the churches became the property of the state, as they are today. A set number of priests was assigned to each village, in accordance with its population. Of course, people protested. Those are very reactionary, very conservative villages—fanatics. There was a lot of conflict and agitation. The war, which was born in the highlands, in the state of Guanajuato, lasted three years, until 1928." By then it had extended to Rulfo's area. In the very first days of the war, he lost his father. Six years later, he lost his mother. He had been sent to Guadalajara to study at the age of eight, and when she died he was taken in by French Josephine nuns, who ran schools in almost all the important towns of Jalisco. He had relatives in Guadalajara: "the Rulfos, a very prolific family, especially on the female side." But somehow no one seems to have claimed him. His grandparents were all dead, except for a maternal grandmother—an old lady descended from "an Arias family that had come to settle in the area in the sixteenth century, probably from Andalucía"—who was illiterate.

Rulfo remembers the orphanage as a sort of reform school. He boarded there for several years. He says softly, lowering his eyes: "That's very common in Mexico. Still today many people in remote villages who want to educate their children and have no one to entrust them to, send them to boarding schools."

Perhaps closer to his true feelings is that line in one of his stories where he might well be evoking the loneliness of the orphanage when he says, with typical understatement: "It's difficult to grow up trying to cling to something which is dead at the root."

It was a hard struggle for the melancholy country boy transplanted among the relative splendors of a pseudo-metropolitan Guadalajara, a stiff-necked town with aristocratic pretensions which was actually, as he says, little more than an outpost of provincial snobbery living off the frayed remnants of its colonial pride. After grade school, hoping to become self-supporting, Rulfo went into accountancy. Accountants always managed to make a living, even in the most run-down times. But soon he had to cut corners. "With a cousin of mine, one of the Vizcaínos, I'd just gotten into high school when a general strike was declared. The university closed down for about three years." To continue his interrupted studies, Rulfo moved to Mexico City. That was in 1933 when he was fifteen years old.

What the first months or years must have been like in the bustling capital for an impoverished youngster without friends or connections, is something Rulfo does not talk about. But they left their mark on him. It was an itinerant life of odd jobs, always hand to mouth. Besides accountancy, Rulfo studied some law—"very irregularly." In his free time, he attended literature courses at the university. In 1935 he landed a job with the Immigration Department—an obscure, but therefore, presumably, more or less safe, bureaucratic post that he occupied for ten years. It was no sinecure. When the Second World War broke out, with Mexico keeping to the sidelines, but nevertheless sympathizing with the Allied cause, he helped process the crews of impounded refugee boats—mostly tankers—of Nazi Germany. The boats were docked in Tampico and Veracruz, and the crews, which were treated more or less as war prisoners, were interned in military camps in the interior, often near Guadalajara, which became a great center of foreigners. It was unpleasant work, and in 1947, glad to be done with it, he switched to publicity work with Goodrich. He was in the sales department there until 1954. In 1955 he was with the Papaloapan Commission, formed to implement an irrigation program near Veracruz. It was a pet project of President Miguel Alemán, who aspired to create a sort of Mexican TVA in the region. On a river with a seasonal overflow that swept away local villages, the Commission built a power center. It plotted highways. But, because of mismanagement and lack of funds, the ambitious project failed. Back in Mexico City in 1956, Rulfo helped himself along doing scripts and adaptations for commercial movies. He had hopes that something of value could be done in the medium. But that was another chimera. "The result was not too positive," he says, shrugging. In 1959 another change occurred. He worked in TV in Guadalajara. With the backing of the new Televicentro, which subsidized his effort, he began compiling yearbooks of historical illustrations that were another attempt to piece together the missing evidence of the past. "The thing is, in Guadalajara the only cultural activity is a bank, the Industrial Bank of Jalisco, which publishes a history book every year as a gift to its clients. So I had an idea: to try to incorporate the whole history of Jalisco from the days of the early chronicles, and bring it out regularly, once a year, as before, in book form. To make up for the poison people were being fed on television, they'd be given a book." It was worth a try.

Nowadays—on a job he has held since 1962—Rulfo works at the Instituto Indigenista (Indian Institute), an organization devoted to the task of protecting and integrating primitive Indian communities bypassed by progress, which has pushed them to the fringes of Mexican life, where they become fodder for political agitators. It is tiring and depressing work that keeps him constantly on the move. He disappears for days at a time on some lonely mission into the misty backlands, and returns looking haggard, as if back from a lost weekend. Every trip is an added blow to him. On off-days, he sits humped over his desk in his antiseptic office on an upper floor of the Institute, starting every time the phone rings anywhere in the building and reaching for the receiver next to him as if the call were always for him. He is forever under the pressures of waiting. At any moment he might jump up and vanish. Around him are glass walls that shake and clatter as workers bang away in the hall. When no one is looking, he slips out of the office like a shadow, rides the elevator down in silent concentration, and ducks around a street corner. Visitors who catch him on the way out, suddenly unavoidable, become honored guests. He makes an endless bustle, opening doors and pulling out chairs for them. He is excruciatingly shy, gazing out of frightened eyes at his guests. Installed at his desk in his dark suit, kneading his nervous hands, looking perpetually worried and disoriented, he is like a harried village priest at the end of a long day, sighing in the solitude of his confessional. On those rare evenings when he has time to devote to his writing, he floats out into the thin mountain air, full of whispers that drive him to the penitence of nightlong work. Though of medium height, his stoop makes him seem slight: a wisp of a man on a devious course through the shifting colors of nightfall, to a hard labor that may yield a few finished lines or simply become a sleepless cramp. He writes very little—his reputation rests on two books—probably because of some monumental block in him. Perhaps his life is not his own. Somewhere along the line—he was married in 1948, and lives in a house with many children—it fused with the life of his country, beat fast when the pulse was strong, then stopped with it. He says: "Stability in Mexico is deadlock. We've come to a complete standstill."

On a late afternoon in June, after hunting him down for a week, at home and at work, only to keep losing track of him—he has been called away, he is unavailable, he breaks an appointment—we finally meet him in the lobby of our hotel, where he arrives in trepidation, with a long shadowy face and darting eyes. He is late—by several hours—he has been held up, and is dismally embarrassed. Upstairs he sits in a low chair, staring at the floor. He is ready to make for the door. He has a thousand things to do. Besides his missions for the Institute, he has been working on an experimental film with a theme of social protest. He describes it as a series of sketches interspersed with Vivaldi music, perhaps not unlike Buñuel's famous *Las Hurdes*. Overcoming his shyness, he wanders off on a meek man's compulsive monologue, stringing disconnected thoughts together, touching on everything and nothing, then falling into a tongue-tied silence. Again and again the conversation trails off. We are in a state of suspended animation. "I only know how to express myself in a very rudimentary way," he says with a gentle smile that crinkles the corners of his eyes.

He is a man who does not quite know how he came to literature—a somewhat belated vocation with him—except that one day he simply woke up in it. Perhaps the one to blame for this is the village priest of San Gabriel, back in the days of the wars of the Cristeros. For a time, Rulfo stayed on a family farm with his grandmother, a pious lady who could hardly read anything outside her prayer book, which he suspects she recited from memory—she had once tried to go on a pilgrimage to Rome to see the Pope—but whose house contained a small library belonging to the local parish. The priest had left it there in safekeeping when the government troops turned his house into an army barracks. The Rulfo household was under federal protection, because Rulfo's mother was related by marriage to one of the colonels serving against the Cristeros. Rulfo had the books all to himself. "So I read all of them." Most of them, he says, were not Biblical texts but adventure stories. They made his thoughts run ahead of him. He has been trying to keep up ever since.

But it was not until many years later, about 1940, in the solitude of the big city, that Rulfo first put pen to paper. He produced a fat novel—which he later destroyed— about life in Mexico City. "It was a conventional sort of book, very high-strung, but at bottom no more than an attempt to express certain solitary feelings. Maybe that's why it came out so high-strung. It wasn't convincing. But that was just it. The fact that I wrote it at all seems to mean I was trying to find a way out of the solitude I'd been living in, not only in Mexico City, but for many years, since my days in the orphanage."

He describes the book as having been written in "a somewhat rhetorical language that I was perfectly well aware of myself. That wasn't the way I wanted to say things. So, practising ways to free myself of all that rhetoric and bombast, I started cutting down, working with simpler characters. Of course I went over to the opposite extreme, into complete simplicity. But that was because I was using characters like the countrypeople of Jalisco, who speak a pure brand of sixteenth-century Spanish. Their vocabulary is very spare. In fact, they practically don't speak at all. . . ." The result was his first story, **"La vida no es muy seria en sus cosas"** (**"Life Is Not To Be Taken Too Seriously"**), published in 1942 in a Guadalajaran magazine called *Pan*. Limiting his scope, withdrawing within the starkness of personal memory, he seemed to have found his way. In 1945 he published his now-famous story, **"Nos han dado la tierra"** (**"The Land They Gave Us"**). The stories of the next few years, a meager but vintage crop, were collected in 1953 under the title of one of them, *El Llano en Llamas* (*The Plain on Fire*). Between 1953 and 1954, on a Rockefeller grant—during his work on the Papaloapan project—he wrote *Pedro Páramo,* which appeared in 1955.

Rulfo's brief and bright course has been one of the wonders of our literature. He has not blazed any new trails; to the contrary, he has been content to tread along traditional paths. But his footsteps go deep. He writes about what he knows and feels, with the simple passion of a man of the land come into contact with elemental things: love, death, hope, hunger, violence. With him, regional literature loses its pamphleteering militance, its folklore. Experience is not filtered through the prism of civilized prejudice. It is laid out straight, with cruel candor. Rulfo is a man attuned to the primitive poetry of desert landscapes, dusty sun-lit villages, seasonal droughts and floods, the humble joys of the harvest, the hard labor of poor lives lived out always close to plague and famine. His language is as frugal as his world, reduced almost to pure heartbeat. He has no message. He sings the swan song of blighted regions gangrened by age, where misery has opened wounds that burn like bright sores under an eternal midday sun, where a pestilent fate has turned areas that were once rolling meadows and grasslands into fetid open graves. He is a stoic who does not inveigh against treachery and injustice, but suffers them in silence as part of the epidemic of life. His theme is simply human sorrow in dispossession. He writes with a sharp edge, carving each word out of hard rock, like an inscription on a tombstone. Therefore his work glows with a lapidary purity. It is written in blood.

"So much land, for nothing," says one of the characters in *El Llano en Llamas*, gazing around him at the desolate expanses stretching out of sight in the sweltering haze. And that sets the tone of the book. Its impressionistic sketches—it would be stretching a point in some cases to call him stories—are quick glimpses into the soul of ruin. They are not all related in time or space. But the same spirit inhabits them all. The region, generally, is that of southwestern Jalisco, extending roughly from Lake Chapala, west through Zacoalco to Ayutla and Talpa, and south through Sayula and Mazamitla toward the border that separates Jalisco from the states of Colima and Michoacán. Armed bands laid the area waste during the Revolution. Then, as the population straggled back, there was the revolt of the Cristeros, during which there was "a sort of resettlement. The army concentrated people in ranch houses and villages. When the fighting got more intense, the people were moved from the villages to larger towns. So the land was abandoned. People looked for work elsewhere. After a few years, they didn't return any more." The agrarian reform was no help. It was very disorganized. "The land was distributed among small tradesmen instead of farmers. It was given to the carpenters, bricklayers, barbers, shoemakers. They were the only ones that formed a community. To form a community, you needed twenty-five people. All those twenty-five people had to do was get together and ask for the land. The countrypeople never asked for it. The proof is that until this day they have no land. The farm worker was accustomed to being entirely dependent on the landowner he served. He was a tenant farmer who had his land on loan, cultivated it, and paid for it with half his yearly crop." The confusion favored real estate speculation. There has been no change for the better in recent years. Today the small farmers of Jalisco "have nothing to live from any more. They barely survive. They go down to the coast looking for work, or cross the U.S. border as day laborers. They come back in the rainy season to plow some little plot of land at home. But their children leave as soon as they can." There is no hope for these regions, says Rulfo. They are slated for disaster. Forty or fifty per cent of the population of Tijuana comes from there. Families are numerous, with a minimum of ten children. The only industry is mezcal, the plant from which the tequila is taken. Significantly, there is a town called Tequila, northwest of Guadalajara. The mezcal and the maguey—source of an alcoholic beverage called pulque—are classical products of impoverished lands on the road to disintegration.

Rulfo mourns these lands. *El Llano en Llamas* is a quiet funeral oration to an area that is breathing its last. A pall of doom hangs in the air like a heavy storm cloud. The rule is resignation. A rough courage under a habitually apathetic surface flares up in intermittent spurts of violence and brutality: savage banditry, predatory blood feuds. It is an area of hunted men and deserted women where "the dead carry more weight than the living." "If there's nothing to be done, there's nothing to be done," people say, bowing their heads, awaiting the relief of death. Because that is their only firm faith, their last illusion, that "some day the night will come" and peace along with it, as they are laid to rest among immemorial shadows in the darkness of the grave.

The trials begin with childhood, as in **"Es que somos muy pobres"** (**"We Are Very Poor"**), where a young girl, whose older sisters, determined to wring what pleasure they can out of their destitution, have gone the way of all flesh, is, in turn, fated for perdition as her hopes of marriage vanish when her poor dowry—a cow and a calf—is swept away in a flood. Even bleaker is the lot of the child in **"Macario"**: an orphan boy brought up in an inhospitable foster home, whose sole comfort is being breast fed by a kind cook turned wet nurse, whose milk tastes of daffodils. Macario lives under the threatening shadow of his foster mother, who wags a chill finger at him, promising him hell for his misconduct. To please her—she is a neurotic insomniac—he spends his time killing frogs in a nearby pond—their croaks keep her awake—and cockroaches in the house. Gnawed by obscure pangs that the author pinpoints in vivid images, he has seizures, hears the drums of fairs pounding in the street and beats his head against the floor. With a kind of quiet sadistic glee, he mashes bugs underfoot, littering the house with them. He spares only crickets which, according to an old wives' tale, chirp to cover the laments of souls in Purgatory.

The dark urges that propel people to their undoing are portrayed in **"Acuérdate"** (**"Remember"**), a brief sketch of a village type, a young dandy who suddenly, for no known reason, turns bad, to become a criminal and a renegade. He wants to go straight. He tries his luck as a policeman, then thinks of priesthood. But a blind force leads him on to violence, until at last he is hanged from a tree that, in a final act of free will allowed him by an ironic fate, he selects himself.

The Revolution, says Rulfo, unleashed passions that have become habits in some of these villages. Though on the whole, crime has moved toward the coast lately, certain towns in Jalisco still live from it. It is a business and a way of life. A case of this is the story, **"La cuesta de las comadres"** (**"Gossips' Slope"**), told casually, by a lackadaisical narrator, with the nonchalance of a people for whom death is always close and life has little value. A marauding gang of bandits and cattle rustlers—the Torricos—terrorizes the fertile slope of small lots that gives the story its title. It is one of those places where time has taken its toll. Over the years the population, driven by those nameless illusions that haunt all of Rulfo's characters, has disbanded. Partly to blame for the exodus are the Torricos. The narrator knows them well. He once went stealing bales of sugar with them, and nearly left his skin behind. Later, because Remigio Torrico accuses him of having murdered his brother, Odilón, who was actually killed in a brawl in town (in self-defense—he is being threatened with a machete), he kills Remigio by coolly sticking a baling needle in his ribs. All this is told in a matter-of-fact tone that adds a sinister thrill to the story. The setting is the no-man's-land around Zapotlán. The most grisly things happen in those places, says Ruflo. "A while back, in Tolimán, they were digging up the dead. No one knew exactly why or what for. It happened in stages, cyclically. . . ." A scar on the landscape may turn out to be an open sewer. "Among those villages, there's one called El Chantle, which is full of outlaws. There's no

authority there. Even government troops stay away from the place. It's a town of escaped convicts. You see that kind of people elsewhere, too. As a rule, they're the calmest people in the world. They carry no arms, because they've been disarmed. You talk to them and they seem completely harmless. They're very peaceful, usually a bit sly, never quite on the level, but at the same time, without any bad intentions. Yet behind each of those men there may be a long list of crimes. So you never know who you're dealing with, whether with a gunman for a local warlord or an ordinary farmer." Often the forces of order are no more enlightened than the delinquents they track down. In **"La noche que lo dejaron solo"** (**"The Night He Was Left Alone"**), we have a fugitive from justice doggedly stalked day and night by shadowy pursuers, who mop up his whole family. Stumbling home to his hut at night, through the smoke of a bonfire, he sees the corpses of his two uncles dangling from a tree in the corral. Troops are gathered around the corpses, waiting for him. As he blunders off into the brush to splash headlong across a river, he hears a voice say with savage logic: "If he doesn't get here before tomorrow morning, we'll knock off the first man that comes this way, that'll settle accounts."

Another man pursued is the protagonist of **"El hombre"** (**"The Man"**), whose flight sends him over horizon after horizon, carrying the weight of his guilt. He is a killer who has done away with a whole family. Shifting points of view throw light on his agony, foreshadowing techniques used later to fine effect in *Pedro Páramo*. The first part of the story is told objectively, in two times: one corresponding to the perceptions of the pursued, the other to those of the pursuer. Halfway through there is a switch to a first person narrator—the fugitive—then later to the point of view of a witness: a shepherd testifying before local police authorities. All are flighty figures with fickle gestures, flickers of life that soon fade in the vastness of the plain.

> **Rulfo writes with a sharp edge, carving each word out of hard rock, like an inscription on a tombstone. Therefore his work glows with a lapidary purity. It is written in blood.**
>
> **—Luis Harss**

In the land of the damned no one is to blame for his follies, and yet everybody is guilty. For even stripped of their humanity, men continue to pay for it. The guilt may be nameless, but no less onerous for that, as in **"En la madrugada"** (**"At Dawn"**), where a farmhand is thrown into prison, accused of having killed his master in a fight, and, though he remembers nothing, he says to himself, almost with exultance: "Since I'm in jail, there must be a reason for it;" or it may be very precise and specific, as in **"Talpa,"** where an adulterous pair—man and sister-in-law—take the deceived husband, who has been afflicted with the plague, on a long pilgrimage to the Virgin of Talpa, whom they hope to reach "before she runs out of miracles." The trip has a double intent. The sick man is a burden to them; they know that the bone-wearying trip will make him die faster. And so it happens. On the way, their charge, perhaps not unaware of their designs—which they are only half aware of themselves—becomes a sort of martyr and flagellant. In a fit of blind fervor, he rips his feet on boulders, bandages his eyes, then drags himself along on all fours, wearing a crown of thorns. His pain is also their suffering; it dramatizes a common predicament. When he dies, his survivors are not acquitted of their sin. Their love dies with him.

Guilt is again a major time in **"Diles que no me maten"** (**"Tell Them Not To Kill Me"**), a story of vengeance. An old crime, which time has not repealed, catches up with the protagonist, who is tied to a stake by the son of a man he murdered years before, given a few shots of alcohol in a moment of wry compassion to dull the pain, then summarily executed. But he might just as well have been spared. A lifelong fear of retribution has already made him die a thousand deaths before that. There is a streak of humor in his end. The bullets pumped into him settle accounts many times over. They are really nothing but so many coups de grace on a corpse.

Grief is strife. Physical poverty is moral indigence. It spreads its mortal fumes into even the most intimate recesses of personal life, polluting love, undermining trust and friendship. This is the topic of **"No oyes ladrar los perros"** (**"Don't You Hear The Dogs Bark"**), which traces the footsteps of a beleaguered father who carries his wounded son into town to see the doctor, heaping reproaches on him along the way. In Rulfo there is almost always bitterness and recrimination between parents and children; they fail each other even in helping each other. What one generation can transmit to the next is little more than an age-old impotence. The young, eternally disinherited, are cast defenseless into the world, to suffer the long agony of life. Those who have nerve and fiber make good. The others wither away, or become miscreants. "Your children leave you . . . they thank you for nothing . . . they drain you even of your memory." Relations between man and woman are no happier than those between parents and children. In **"Paso del norte"** (**"Northern Pass"**) we have the story of a young man who leaves his family to cross the U.S. border as a wetback. He is met by a hail of bullets. He returns to his village in defeat, only to find that his woman has left him. Abandoning his children, he vanishes after her, destined from then on to roam the country like a soul in pain.

There are always those who, in their own wretched way, thrive on the ills of others. A case in point are the roving bandits of the title story, who sack ranches and set fields on fire as they go galloping across the plain, chased by government forces that never seem to catch up with them, or misfire when they do. They are the verminous Zamora band who, "although we have no flag to fight for at the moment," keep fit slitting throats and hoarding booty. The leader plays "bull" with his prisoners, who are made to stand unarmed as he charges them with a sword. They

derail trains and steal women. Bad luck has the narrator serve a term in jail, from which he emerges a somewhat chastened man. Perhaps a woman who awaits him with open arms—in a somewhat sentimental ending—outside the prison gate will save him. But the chances are that he will ride again. Or he might find some other way to scrape by, as Anacleto Morones, in the story of the same name, which reveals Rulfo as a biting ironist. Anacleto, a mere derelict, makes a thriving career for himself as a "santero"—peddler of religious images—combination high salesmanship with religious quackery. He builds a fine reputation, and rakes in the profits. Among his worshipping supporters are a bunch of hypocritical old hags who have succumbed to his charm in more ways than one. He has become the "saintly child Anacleto." The women want him officially canonized, appeal to Lucas Lucatero, his son-in-law, to testify to his miracles. Ambushed by them, Lucas Lucatero refuses to cooperate: Anacleto was a fraud. His greatest miracle, it turns out, was impregnating his own daughter, Lucas' wife. Lucas has killed him and buried him under the floorboards.

Perhaps, all things considered, Lucas Lucatero, and Anacleto himself, were once no worse than the honest peasants of the moving **"Nos han dado la tierra,"** which still stands as one of Rulfo's best stories. With a sort of impersonal pity that makes the tale doubly poignant, he tells of a group of men allotted lands in a barren desert region under a government distribution program. They are sent far from the fertile fields bordering the river, which have all been commandeered by powerful landlords. The group, now reduced to four men, has trekked for eleven hours, with sinking hearts, across the empty wasteland, out of which "nothing will rise . . . not even vultures."

Yet life goes on. "It is more difficult to revive the dead than to give birth to new life," Rulfo writes somewhere, summing up the general attitude. In this faint hope, scant lives find a driving force. Tapping it at the source has been Rulfo's achievement. His sketches are quick probes. It is the small touches that count. He has weaknesses as a storyteller. Excessive poetization freezes some of his scenes. His characters are sometimes too sketchy to deliver their full human impact. They are creatures of primeval passion, entirely defined by their situation. Because of their lack of inner resource, ultimately they inspire little more than pity. And that is the danger. We are often on the verge of falling into pathos. But the attentive reader will go beyond that. There is something more—still waters running deep. To live, in Rulfo, is to bleed to death. The pulse of the days beats hard, carrying off hope, gutting life at the core, spilling forces, emptying illusions. He can evoke the fatigue of a long day's march across barren spaces in a quiet phrase: "It seems to me that we've gone a lot farther than the distance we've covered," or a lifetime's inexpressible distress and longing in the voice of a woman who says of her absent man: "It's still time for him to return." Of the mother who has lost all her children, he writes simply: "It seems she had a little money, but spent it all on burials." It is the ability to suddenly close in and strike home that at moments gives Rulfo the dignity of a tragedian. His style is as stark as his landscapes. Its marks are discipline and economy. Its impact is cumulative. It has the pull of irresistible impulse.

One of the most characteristic stories of *El Llano en Llamas* is **"Luvina,"** the name of a village on a limestone hill, laboring under its obscure curse, in an area swept by a dusty black wind that seems to carry volcanic ash. It is a "moribund place where even the dogs have died." Like the once fertile slope in **"La cuesta de las comadres,"** it is a ghost town on its way to extinction. "I'd say it's the place where sadness nests, where smiles are unknown, as if everyone's face had been boarded up," says the narrator, an ex-resident, warning a traveler away from it. He ought to know: "There I lived. There I left my life." Nowadays Luvina is populated only by "the old and the unborn . . . and lonely women." Those who have stayed are retained only by their dead. "They live here and we can't abandon them," they say. They will continue to sweat out their sentence, thinking: "It will last as long as it has to last." . . .

In a country of literary cliques and coteries, Rulfo has always pursued a lone star. He seems to have no connection with anyone. Agustín Yáñez, a distinguished colleague who is Minister of Education today, is from his home state. Rulfo hardly seems to have heard of him. It would be hard to imagine two more different temperaments. Rulfo belongs to that race of men for whom writing is a very intimate affair that takes place in the dark of night. He is superstitious and secretive about his work, which he keeps undercover. He will talk about anything but that. A guarded silence on the subject is an old habit with him. As a young man quietly learning his craft by candlelight, he knew none of his literary contemporaries. He read a few literary reviews, he says, but otherwise kept to himself. All he knew was that "it seemed I had to become a writer." Later, between about 1948 and 1952, he admits he was associated with a group called América, publishers of a magazine of the same name. "The group is necessary to launch your career," he says a bit wryly. But this was a particularly scattered group that included the most heterogenous people. About all they had in common was the urge to get together once in a while in a Chinese café to drink coffee and hold bull sessions. The circle shrank and expanded as people came and went, until finally there was no one left. Fortunately, says Rulfo, the magazine no longer exists.

What is his relation to Mexican literature as a whole?

He seems uncertain about that. Back in his school days, there was not much Mexican literature, he says. The authors read in Mexico in those days were Vasconcelos, the political writers of the Revolution, the chroniclers of the time: Martín Luis Guzmán, Mariano Azuela. "But even they weren't read much. Mexican literature had almost no value. For instance, the novel of the Revolution was considered simple reporting. A lot of books were published—proportionately speaking—but they weren't read. The tendency was to read foreign literature. In schools, Spanish literature. On one's own, Russian literature—imported from Spain, where it was translated and published, but not Spanish literature. U.S. literature, which was also published in Spain. We knew Dos Passos, Sinclair Lewis, Elmer Rice and Hemingway. There was a great vogue of translations in Spain just before the Revolution, especially works of social criticism."

From the beginning, Rulfo—a traditionalist unhampered by traditionalism—struck out in his own direction. In the few literature courses he took in his free time, he was bothered by the habit teachers had of teaching the worst of Spanish literature—"Pereda, the generation of 1898. . . . I knew that was the backwardness of Latin American literature: the fact that we were absorbing a literature that was foreign to our character and disposition." Besides, Spanish culture was decadent. "They had theologized even with mathematics." Spain had isolated itself for centuries from the world. That was one of the factors that had permitted the Latin American countries to gain their independence. But culturally they were not yet emancipated. He readily recognizes his Spanish ancestry, Rulfo tells us, seized by a sudden curious scruple as we discuss the subject. He adds, amusingly, that an early ancestor of his was even a member of the royalist forces of Callejas that fought against the Mexican Revolution. Nevertheless, he reproaches Spain with provincialism and linguistic decay. "What pains me about Spain, for instance," he says, "is that it is losing its language." This is something he often discusses with people, invariably getting himself into an argument. The case is exactly the opposite in Latin America. On the one hand, Indian dialects have enriched the language. On the other, there are isolated areas where it has preserved its classic purity. He realized long ago that "Spain had no culture to give America." He was always particularly fond of Russian literature—Andreyev, Korolenko—and, above all, a great admirer of Scandinavian literature: Selma Lagerlöf, Bjornson, Knut Hamsun, Sillanpää. "Once upon a time I had the theory that literature had been born in Scandinavia, then gone down to central Europe and spread from there." He is still an assiduous reader of Sandor Laxness, whom he considers a great renewer of European literature, from a position diametrically opposed, say, to that of French intellectualism. U.S. literature, he thinks, has also had a salutary influence in latter years. But Rulfo, with his love of the diaphanous, favors the Nordics, because of their "misty atmosphere." The same factor inclines him toward the work of the Swiss novelist, C. F. Ramuz, whose portraits of simple village souls in conflict with a hostile environment have strong connotations for him. Rulfo does not pretend his predilections are based on sound judgment. He has a curious taste for Jean Giono, whom he regards as an unappreciated talent in French letters. Giono, says Rulfo, breaks with the artifices of the Jules Romains and Mauriac tradition, which, he claims, produces works so indistinguishable that "you don't know whom you're reading. They all write the same." In any case, they all sound "written." And that is what he has always tried to avoid. "I don't want to speak as you write, but to write as you speak."

If he has come anywhere near achieving his purpose, he says, it is because he never really developed his style consciously. "It was something that was there already."

He detected it, and took it as he found it. In this, he may have helped point the way for some of Mexico's younger writers, who have begun to listen more carefully to the language spoken in the streets. Not that he has imitators. He shudders at the thought. But his work may have called attention to the literary potential of popular language. "So the person who writes that way is not influenced by *Pedro Páramo*," he says. "He simply stopped to listen to the language he was talking, and realized of what use it could be to him."

Ten years have gone by since *Pedro Páramo*, and Rulfo, a busy man in a harsh city, has been strangely silent. He is vague about what he has published, when. He seems suddenly anguished when the subject is raised. He mentions "a story in the same line as those of *El Llano en Llamas*, which was supposed to be part of the book. I don't know what happened to it. . . . It was misplaced, and then it was too late to include it in the book. . . ." According to rumors, his mildness and modesty are such that he has little control over the editorial work done on his books. The French edition of *Pedro Páramo*, for instance, is fatter than the original. What could have happened? Perhaps some papers got shuffled along the way. . . .

At the moment he has other things in mind. As people wonder whether he will ever be heard from again, he is trying to bring himself to release an eternally forthcoming novel he has finished and torn apart a thousand times, called *La Cordillera*. "I'm sort of working at it," he says. Recently he thought he was done with it, then decided to go over it once more. It had to be thought out all over again. "I thought it was a bit too dense." He would like to talk about it, but "it's a bit difficult to explain." The setting, again, is provided by the villages of Jalisco. "But taken from their base this time. Starting with the sixteenth century." Rulfo traces the lives and fortunes of a family of "encomenderos" from its origins, through generations of wars and migrations, down to the present day. As usual in his work, the voyage is mental, a memory evoked in bits and strands by the dead's descendants. "It's really the story of a woman who's the last descendant of the family. . . ." She is probably another lost soul branded by a forgotten past that she wears as a birthmark. Because the sense of history, in Rulfo, is that it may be forgotten, but not left behind. Therefore, what he has tried to do in his work is "to show a reality that I know and that I want others to know. To say: 'This is what has happened and what is happening.' And: 'Let's not fool ourselves. If it's fatal, then let's do something about it.' But I don't think I'm a fatalist at heart. . . . Above all, what I want to do in *La Cordillera* is to show the simplicity of countrypeople, their candor. The man of the city sees their problems as country problems. But it's the problem of the whole country. It's the problem of the city itself. Because, when the countryman moves to the city, there's a change. But to a certain extent he continues to be what he was. He brings the problem with him." Proof of this is the sad-eyed Rulfo, who will undoubtedly continue to live with the problem for a long time to come.

Ted Lyon (essay date 1973)

SOURCE: "Ontological Motifs in the Short Stories of Juan Rulfo," in *Journal of Spanish Studies*, Vol. 1, No. 3, Winter, 1973, pp. 161-68.

[*In the following essay, Lyon identifies and examines common motifs in* The Burning Plain.]

> "Life's but a walking shadow . . ."
> SHAKESPEARE, *"Macbeth"*

El llano en llamas dramatically affirms Zum Felde's position that "La verdadera historia—la intrahistoria—la escriben los novelistas [y cuentistas]" [*Indice critico de la literatura hispanoamericana*, 1959] Numerous critics have already called attention to the correspondences between Rulfo's stories and the real world from which they are drawn. [In *Nueva novela latinoamericana*, edited by Jorge Lafforgue, 1969] Blanco Aguinaga declares that "Los cuentos . . . se dan en una tierra concreta donde la situación de los personajes adquiere un muy particular cariz porque sobre ella pesa una muy particular condición histórica." [In *Nueva narrativa hispanoamericana*, 1971], Graciela Coulson spends an entire article arguing for the universality and "supra-realism" of Rulfo's stories but concludes that none of the characters "se libera de las limitaciones de la realidad . . . Rulfo no rechaza en ningún momento la realidad material que es su experiencia inmediata." The author himself, in one of his rare interviews, almost plays with his interlocutor in declaring the necessity of recreating a known world:

> REPORTERO: ¿Por qué usted usó siempre como escenarios los pueblecitos, las rancherías?
>
> RULFO: Porque es lo que conocí.
>
> REPORTERO: ¿Un escritor debe escribir solamente acerca de lo que conoce?
>
> RULFO: Desde luego, eso es lógico.
>
> REPORTERO: ¿Y la imaginación?
>
> RULFO: Imaginar es recrear la realidad. Para imaginar primero hay que conocer.

No serious reader can deny the function of these stories in adequately mirroring the realities of rural Mexico. Yet despite such a near-palpable observation, few critics have paused to analyze the elements Rulfo employs to achieve this unique, near life-like vision of man. Even Hugo Rodríguez Alcalá, in his fine study of four stories [in *El Arte de Juan Rulfo*, 1965], does not generalize on the nature of existence nor point to any basic unifying motifs in all of the prose. In pointing out that the most striking aspect of *El llano en llamas* is its "parquedad estilística," he does hint at the basic premise of this study, namely, that Rulfo must say much in a short compass, and as a result writes with many repeated motifs and images.

This inquiry will analyze the motifs (*recurring stylistic, syntactic and thematic elements*) common to the fifteen stories of *El llano en llamas*. But rather than emphasize style or usage, each motif will be related to being and the nature of existence portrayed in the world Rulfo creates. While the stories do not exhibit the unity common to a single novel (*Pedro Páramo,* for example), taken as a whole, they do present a singular world-view of life in rural Jalisco. The following motifs serve as basic unifiers among the stories and represent aspects of the nature of human existence: (1) walking (continual movement), (2) plaguing memory, (3) futility of effort, and (4) vision limited by darkness.

The most striking aspect of Rulfo's narrative world is that life is not static or passive acceptance, rather continual change, movement, always at a slow pace, afoot. This movement is frequently an attempted escape from the past (and even the present at times), as in **"El hombre," "En la madrugada," "Paso del norte,"** and **"Diles que no me maten."** It may also function as an expiatory march in an attempt to remove past guilt or fulfill a distant promise (**"Talpa,"** and **"No oyes ladrar los perros"**). Walking may merely function to demonstrate man's groping loneliness and isolation (**"La noche que lo dejaron solo,"** and **"La cuesta de las Comadres"**). Or it may be a futile search for a lost future as in **"Es que somos muy pobres"** (the search for the drowned cow) and **"Nos han dado la tierra."** Many of the stories are completely structured on the motif of the walk. All of **"Talpa"** takes place on the road to and from that city:

> Y yo comienzo a sentir como si no hubiéramos llegado a ninguna parte; que estamos aquí de paso, para descansar, y que luego seguiremos caminando. No sé para dónde; pero tendremos que seguir, porque aquí estamos muy cerca del remordimiento y del recuerdo de Tanilo.

"No oyes ladrar los perros" is the monologue and memory of an old man during the time he stumbles along carrying a dying, worthless son; when the painful journey ends, so too does the life of the son:

> Ya debemos estar llegando a ese pueblo, Ignacio. Tú que llevas las orejas de fuera, fíjate a ver si no oyes ladrar los perros. Acuérdate que nos dijeron que Tonaya estaba detrasito del monte. Y desde qué horas que hemos dejado el monte. Acuérdate, Ignacio . . . Me estoy cansando.

"En la madrugada" and **"El hombre"** portray man in continual movement, never resting in life: "Si me la pasaba en un puro viaje con las vacas . . . me las traía de vuelta para llegar con ellas de madrugada. Aquello parecía una eterna peregrinación." **"Nos han dado la tierra"** portrays men on the move; each step painfully confirms the futility of existence and injustices perpetuated from above. The government seat ("sedere"—to be fixed in a spot) is immovable; man, on his feet ("stare"—to stand) must give

in and move.

The above-cited quotations point not only to life as movement but to the endless nature of existence: "Camino y camino y no ando nada;" "Aquello parecía una eterna peregrinación;" "estamos aquí de paso . . . y luego seguiremos caminando." Yet, confronted with this seemingly futile march, all of Rulfo's men continue; they are, in this sense, true heroes, not giving up in despair or lethargy. Life is movement and man struggles to find purpose to existence by keeping constantly on the move. He is not "petrified [static] before an implacable destiny" as one critic asserts. Rulfo's style blends with the walking motif; verbal phrases are frequently lengthened, projecting the contemporary scene into an unending present. Forms such as *"ya debemos estar llegando," "seguiremos caminando,"* and *"me estoy cansando"* concentrate the reader's attention on the continuation or duration of the action, rather than its completion. "La Cuesta de las Comadres *se había ido deshabitando,"* emphasizes the slowness of the process as well as the fact that it continues to drag on into the present; this unending action could never be shown in a shorter, completed verb form such as "se deshabitó." George Schade's fine English translation has been able to capture this continuation in time by placing "kept on," "started to," or "began," before the main form of the verb. This technique of stretching out the present through complex verb forms is one of the constant traits of Rulfo's style (as yet not seriously studied by critics). Life then, is movement, walking, plodding, running, in a futile attempt to achieve purpose.

The second unifying ontological motif is memory and its results. As life is stretched through an endless present, in constant movement, the past returns to fill up and completely determine man's now-existence. Memory is rarely mental escape into a pleasant past, rather a subconscious life experience which makes the present unendingly intolerable and the future impossible. Graciela Coulson has noted that in **"Talpa"** "el instrumento de castigo será, pues, la propia memoria de cada uno." The same may be said for all Rulfo's stories, where memory haunts and pursues. Much like Borges' Funes who eliminates his own future in his completely "unforgettable" past, Rulfo's men bear the onerous burden of memory through their tedious lives. Some carry a crime, perhaps minor or even justifiable, that relentlessly pursues (**"La Cuesta de las Comadres," "Diles que no me maten," "El hombre," "Acuérdate,"** etc.). Memory gives the entire structure to **"El hombre"** and **"Acuérdate."** Rulfo normally begins a story in the present and then quickly lapses into the past, often the body of the narrative, to show its effect on the present (**"Diles que no me maten," "Macario," "Luvina,"** etc.). Thus, man is enslaved by oppressive memory, unable to live the present of future:

> *Me acuerdo* que eso pasó allá por octubre. Y digo que *me acuerdo* que fue por esos días, porque en Zapotlán estaban quemando cohetes, mientras por el rumbo donde tiré a Remigio se levantaba una gran parvada de

zopilotes . . . de eso *me acuerdo.*

Pero nosotros lo llevamos allí para que se muriera, eso
es lo que no se me olvida.

Every one of Rulfo's major characters is beset by haunting memories. Macario is unable to sort out the past but
intuits its effect on his tragic life. Natalia's memory of
walking her sick husband to death destroys her love for
the penitent narrator. Lucas Lucatero is bound to a small
plot of ground by the memory of killing his unholy father-
in-law and the necessity of continually stacking rocks on
the grave. In every one of the fifteen stories the words
"me acuerdo," "acordarse," "nos acordamos," or some
similar verb form depict this past-in-the-present motif.
Rulfo's men have lost freedom to control their lives by the
continuance of the past into the present. Life is remembrance of a hapless past, with no future.

A third motif related to the nature of existence is that of
futility—wasted lives, worthless lands, senseless deaths,
useless government. Human relationships, like the land,
are barren and non-productive. The family is the only
institution with any meaning. Church, neighbors, local or
federal governments provide no assistance or salvation
and serve only to exploit or burden memory. The inhabitants of Luvina consider the government as a human
entity, a bastard child: ". . . el gobierno no tenía Madre."
Spiritual help fails: Tanilo "Siguió rezando con su vela
apagada. Rezando a gritos para oír que rezaba. Pero no le
valió. Se murió de todos modos" (**"Talpa"**). The infertility
of the land is the backdrop for more than half of the
stories (**"La Cuesta de las Comadres," "Es que somos
muy pobres," "Nos han dado la tierra," "Luvina,"** etc.).
Negation is the only way to describe the land: *"No,* el
llano *no* es cosa que sirva. *No* hay *ni* pájaros. *No* hay
nada. A *no* ser unos cuantos huizaches trespeleques y
una que otra manchita de zacate con las hojas enroscadas;
a *no* ser eso, *no* hay *nada . . . No* este duro pellejo de vaca
que se llama el Llano" (**"Nos han dado la tierra"**). Human
existence values no more, and sometimes less, than a mere
animal. Tacha's future is ruined in the loss of her dowry
cow. Juvencio kills his neighbor due to the death of one
calf. Walking rarely leads to usefulness or action; the
painful miles to Talpa are slowly retraced as the expected
love vanishes. The suffering during forty years of escape
and hiding is a futile argument to an unforgiving officer:
"Dile al sargento que te deje ver al coronel. Y cuéntale lo
viejo que estoy. Lo poco que valgo. ¿Qué ganancia sacará
con matarme? Ninguna ganancia." The excruciating walk
of the father in **"No oyes ladrar los perros"** is futilely
climaxed by the death of his unworthy son. All of Rulfo's
characters strive for decency, justice, and completeness
but all are frustrated by their own past, unfeeling fellow-
men or infertile land. A few of the stories end the futility
of existence with the death of the protagonist; must simply postulate continuance in a non-ending, painful present.

Eleven of the fifteen stories take place either totally or
partially during the night. Man's physical world is thus
limited to his very immediate surroundings or to the distances he can walk. Darkness is symbolic of the limited

spiritual or intellectual reaches to which man may attain,
bound by his inability to see the future or even adequately
comprehend the eternal present in which he gropes. Rarely
is he ever lost in darkness; he stumbles, plods and continues the journey, despite a predictable, futile ending.
Seldom is man described in clear terms in Rulfo; he is most
often a shadowy, mysterious being occasionally slipping
out from dark shadows, always retreating back into them.

While all stories do not occur at night, important action is
nocturnal. The flood that destroys Tacha's cow awakens
the family by its dragging sound. **"El hombre"** sneaks
into an enemy's house and kills the whole family because
the dark did not permit him to distinguish his foe. During
the rest of his life he must hide out by day (a no-life) and
exist at night, like some nocturnal animal. In fact, man
fleeing during the interminable night, forms the entire structure of **"El llano en llamas," "La noche que lo dejaron
solo," "En la madrugada"** and **"No oyes ladrar los perros."** The day-time walking in **"Talpa"** is turned into
anguish by the night-time horrors of falling out of love.
"Luvina," already a near-ghost town, is made more terrifying by the howling wind and a "murmullo sordo," later
identified merely as "el silencio," so pounding it can be
heard by any traveller to the spectral village.

The most powerful example of limited vision in darkness
is **"No oyes ladrar los perros."** The father, doubly blinded
by the sprawling son he carries as well as the night,
anticipates only one event—that the boy will hear the
village dogs barking, a sign that he's nearly home. The
barking of the dogs not only forebodes death but also
symbolizes relief, release from anxiety. Since man's sight
is clouded, in this story as well as others, the most characteristic image is auditory. Dogs bark, wind whistles,
branches crack, frogs croak, coyotes howl, rifle shots ring
out, screams shock the night. Man's life takes on less
significance as natural and animal forces take control of
the night world; they continue their unbridled existence
while man slowly gropes through darkness. The wounded
son, Ignacio, experiences increasing difficulty in hearing
and responding to his exhausted father and the reader
realizes he will never hear the dogs. As the old man
discharges his dead load "oyó cómo por todas partes
ladraban los perros." The walk ends but the reader realizes
that night and its effects will continue to oppress and
frustrate man.

Although Rulfo's only novel, *Pedro Páramo,* employs a
dream-like, stream of consciousness technique, many of
the same motifs reflect similar realities. Juan Preciado
wanders alone, searching, always on foot; much of his
odyssey takes place at night, in darkened rooms or possibly in the visionless tomb. Pedro Páramo moves constantly about but always on horseback, indicative of his
higher status than most Rulfo characters. The whole town
of Comala gives an impression of a shadowy specter,
drifting about in the darkness. Memories have destroyed
the town's existence; Juan's mother recalled it as a paradise whereas Pedro crossed his arms and let it die, remembering the unloving treatment shown him at Susana's
death. Memories have impregnated the walls and the

ground and spring out to haunt the present. Juan Precia-do's search is futile from the beginning; his father is already dead. Pedro Páramo, inferring rocky sterile ground, is frustrated in his sincere desires for Susana since her memory does not allow her to forget her first husband, Florencio. In summary, *Pedro Páramo* projects a narrative world surprisingly similar to that portrayed in Rulfo's short stories.

These four motifs combine to present a unified vision of the nature of human existence in *El llano en llamas*. Man is a struggling, ever-moving being trying to achieve. To live is to continue. Rulfo's men are not existential or intel-lectual heroes, caught in the static and stifling paradox of making absurd choices. His *heroes,* and they justifiably deserve that term, act and strive. Life is a journey, alone, on foot, in search of refuge, a future of peace, love and decency. Manuel Durán has noted several differences between the story that closes *El llano en llamas,* "Ana-cleto Morones," and the rest of the collection [*Atlantic Monthly* 213, March, 1964]. His argument is sustained by our finding—Anacleto is the only character who passes the whole story seated, making fun of the pious women who walk so far. For the rest of the characters, life can never be static.

The rhythm of the walk seems to stimulate memory, a haunting vision that pursues man, making existence an attempted, impossible escape. In every story the past re-turns to the present, weighing it down, thwarting man. Yet despite noble efforts, man's existence is futile and hope-less. Death catches its client, land is sterile, a daughter turns to prostitution, love is drowned in remorse. Unable to see beyond the dark limited present, existence is con-tinuation for these heroic men who struggle against futil-ity, dragging the past as endless burden.

Stephen T. Clinton (essay date 1975)

SOURCE: "Form and Meaning in Juan Rulfo's 'Talpa'," in *Romance Notes,* Vol. XVI, No. 2, Winter, 1975, pp. 520-25.

[*In the essay below, Clinton offers a stylistic analysis of Rulfo's "Talpa."*]

One of the most important characteristics of Juan Rulfo's *El llano en llamas* is the way in which the local Mexican scene is used to express universal human preoccupations. The dusty Mexican flatland becomes a transcendental image of a cruel reality that is completely hostile to man; although the characters are only Mexican country people, their tortured lives mirror human problems which are com-mon to all men. Rulfo achieves this universality through the use of literary techniques that are worked and pol-ished almost to the point of perfection. This type of skilled craftsmanship can be seen in **"Talpa,"** a story in which the reader is given a moving vision of the disastrous effects of sin and guilt on the human personality. In this story, the techniques used to arrive at this vision are a circular structure and the varied repetition of certain words, de-

scriptions, events, and syntactical structures. It should be emphasized that the repetitions are varied, for they do not bore the reader in any way. On the contrary, they make him more aware of the psychological tensions underlying the narration. At the same time, the repetitions universal-ize the theme by constantly reinforcing and intensifying it.

The plot of **"Talpa"** is simple. Natalia and her would-be lover hasten the death of her husband, Tanilo, by forcing him to go to Talpa, the site of a statue of the Virgin renowned for its miraculous curative powers. Tanilo, who is also the brother of Natalia's pretender, suffers from a horrible skin disease and would have died sooner or later anyway. Nevertheless, for Natalia and her brother-in-law, the husband is a barrier separating them from the satisfac-tion of their sexual desires, and the sooner he dies, the better. But instead of making possible the consummation of their relationship, Tanilo's death only causes further alienation of the lovers, for they cannot forget they has-tened his death. They become obsessed with guilt and feel they must spend the rest of their lives trying to erase the memory of their sinful deed.

In spite of the relative simplicity of the plot, the structure of **"Talpa"** is quite complex. This structural complexity is caused principally by the use of Natalia's brother-in-law as the narrator, whose perspective over the events of the story gives us a vision of a mind in a moment of spiritual crisis. Confused and disillusioned by what has happened, the narrator perceives his past actions as if they were happening in present time. He feels it is impossible for him and Natalia to escape responsibility for Tanilo's early death. Because of his obsession with his sin, the events of the arduous journey to Talpa become mixed up in the narrator's mind, and instead of narrating them in chrono-logical order, he superimposes past time upon his present existence.

One may see the superimposition of past and present at the beginning of the story. The first scene is of Natalia crying in the arms of her mother, an event that occurs after the trip to Talpa. Thus, the action begins with an event that would fall at the end of the story were it narrated chronologically. After this initial scene, some of the cir-cumstances surrounding the burial of Tanilo and the re-turn journey to Zenzontla are described. Not until the fifth paragraph does the reader become aware of the reasons for Natalia's crying: "Porque la cosa es que a Tanilo Santos entre Natalia y yo lo matamos. Lo llevamos a Talpa para que se muriera. Y se murió. Sabíamos que no aguan-taría tanto camino; pero, así y todo, lo llevamos empuján-dolo entre los dos, pensando acabar con él para siempre. Eso hicimos."

The inverted structure of this first part of the story, the presentation of the cause, is indicative of one of the principal narrative proposals of the whole story, which is to analyze the effects of the past over present time. Given this purpose, the chronological sequence of events is of little importance. The idea of maintaining tension through traditional dramatic suspension is cast aside, since the reader knows from the beginning how things are going to turn out.

The inverted structure of **"Talpa"** is significant in itself. The world of the story is one in which there is no possibility of change. Natalia and the narrator live in a closed circumstance which offers no possibility of redemption. They are condemned from the beginning and are caught in a trap from which there is no escape: "Yo sé ahora que Natalia está arrepentida de lo que pasó. Y yo también lo estoy; pero eso no nos salvará del remordimiento ni nos dará ninguna paz nunca." The introductory revelation of the consequences of their actions reinforces this idea of the impossibility of change. The past is an absolute with which the characters will have to live eternally.

After the opening paragraphs, the story consists of a more exhaustive exploration of the events which caused an already known circumstance. The theme is intensified by means of a varied repetition of the events already described in the first five paragraphs. The narrative mode is similar to a musical composition in which a theme given in the overture is repeated in diverse forms throughout the piece.

The two descriptions of the journey to Talpa are a salient example of this technique. The first description is the shortest, being a synthetic view of what happened on the road at night. In this first description we become aware of the consuming sexual frustration of the would-be lovers. While Tanilo is alive, they can never consummate their relationship. The description ends with a return to present time in which the narrator once again speaks of the change caused in Natalia by the "gran remordimiento que lleva encima de su alma."

The second description of the same journey is longer and more detailed. In this sense, it constitutes an expansion and intensification of the first description. In this second view the narrator shifts his emphasis from the characters themselves to the dry and hostile ambiance of the road: "Y arriba de esta tierra estaba el cielo vacío, sin nubes, sólo el polvo; pero el polvo no da ninguna sombra." The view is broadened even more when the narrator describes the arrival at Talpa and the precise circumstances of Tanilo's death.

The thematic intensification culminates when the narrator describes again the scene of Natalia crying in her mother's arms. As is already known, the effects of remorse have been devastating for the lovers. The narrator has already insinuated that they are going to have to pay a price for their sin, and at the end of the story we learn what this punishment will be: Natalia and the narrator are condemned to spend their lives in directionless wandering, trying, always unsuccessfully, to escape Tanilo's memory: "Y yo comienzo a sentir como si no hubiéramos llegado a ninguna parte; que estamos aquí de paso, para descansar, y que luego seguiremos caminando. No sé para dónde; pero tendremos que seguir porque aquí estamos muy cerca del remordimiento y del recuerdo de Tanilo." The final sentence of the story echoes this idea because it expresses indirectly the lovers' hope that the burial in Talpa would

be the end of Tanilo: ". . . echamos tierra y piedras encima para que no lo fueran a desenterrar los animales del cerro."

The total structure of **"Talpa"** assists in realizing the theme of eternal wandering. The story begins and ends in the same place and temporal context. This circular structure suggests the implacability of the situation of the characters ("como si no hubiéramos llegado a ninguna parte"). No matter how much they travel, they are always going to end up where they began—with a sense of remorse for Tanilo's death. Seen in this light, the two narrations of the journey to Talpa reflect the theme of eternal wandering. The retrospective narrator, who has already experienced the spiritual effects of his actions, conceives of life in terms of an unending journey. From his perspective, the journey to Talpa was nothing more than the beginning of a pattern of existence that will continue for the rest of his life. The lovers will have to make another journey ("estamos aquí de paso") that will be as useless as the first. Seen against this background, the circular structure of the story and the two views of the journey to Talpa constitute a plastic image of the narrator's interior reality.

Besides this structure, Rulfo also uses the poetic possibilities of language to achieve thematic intensification. The style, like the structure, is based on varied repetition. Certain sentences, words, syntactical forms, and descriptions are reiterated, thus emphasizing the obsessive nature of the narrator's guilt feelings. For example, there are five graphic descriptions of the bloody wounds of Tanilo. Many times, the narrator repeats himself in the same paragraph. He cannot forget the terrible events of the journey to Talpa (the italics are mine): "*Lo que queríamos era* que se muriera. No está por demás decir que eso *era lo que queríamos* desde antes de salir de Zentzontla y en cada una de las noches que pasamos en el camino a Talpa. Es algo que no podemos entender ahora; pero entonces *era lo que queríamos*. Me acuerdo muy bien." In this particular instance the incantory effect of the repetition is increased when the next paragraph begins with the final sentence of the one cited ("Me acuerdo muy bien.").

Another form of repetition is the use of similar syntactical forms in the same paragraph. A telling example of this device is the use of unbalanced sentences in which the word "eso," which functions as the complement, is placed where the subject would normally be. For instance, seven paragraphs end with such forms as "Eso hicimos," "Eso pensaba él," or "Eso hacíamos Natalia y yo. . . ." In these and other similar sentence one detects a note of finality and of spiritual inquietude. The narrator himself is incredulous when he thinks about what happened.

Still another stylistic constant is the changing from long and elaborate sentences to short and simple ones: "Algún día llegará la noche. En eso pensábamos. Llegará la noche y nos pondremos a descansar. Ahora se trata de cruzar el día, de atravesarlo como sea para correr del calor y del sol. Después nos detendremos. Después. Lo que tenemos que hacer por lo pronto es esfuerzo tras esfuerzo para ir de prisa de tantos como nosotros y delante de otros muchos.

De eso se trata. Ya descansaremos bien a bien cuando estemos muertos." The repetition of certain words ("llegará," "después," "esfuerzo," "otros muchos") and the shifts from long sentences to short laconic ones give a rhythmical quality to the language that approximates the narrator's mental agitation.

As for the formal development of the above paragraph, one may observe that the direction of thought is more "circular" than "straight." The beginning and the end of the paragraph deal with the same idea of rest from the rigors of the journey. The word "noche," used in the first sentence, is developed until it becomes an image of death by the last sentence ("cuando estemos muertos"). The circularity of the paragraph's development is even more evident when one takes into account the syntactical paralellism between the second and the next to last sentence ("En eso pensábamos."; "De eso se trata."). In the two sentences, the word order is preposition, object, and verb. Thus the formal organization of [the] paragraph serves to intensify an idea by gradually intensifying and developing it until final clarification is made on a more transcendental level of meaning. Is should also be noted that the formal organization of the paragraph is quite akin to the process at work in the story's total structure.

As we have seen throughout this study, the overall effect of the techniques of **"Talpa"** is to intensify the emotional impact of the story. The narrator is his own judge and jury, and the structure and the use of language show his chronic tendency toward self-castigation. The two aspects are complementary in that they function in a similar manner to bring about the thematic intensification. In this sense, the complex form of **"Talpa"** is not an imposed artifice that can be separated from the essential meaning of the story. Rather, the form grows naturally from thematic necessity, thereby making it possible for the reader to appreciate the world of **"Talpa"** not as something alien to his own experience, but as an authentic reflection of universal human reality.

Howard Mancing (essay date 1977)

SOURCE: "The Art of Literary Allusion in Juan Rulfo," in *Modern Fiction Studies,* Vol. 23, No. 2, Summer, 1977, pp. 242-44.

[*In the following essay, Mancing examines Rulfo's use of literary allusion in "Diles que no me maten," and asserts that Rulfo "lifts the story onto a broader plane of meaning, linking an atemporal present to an eternal (even mythic) past in order to anticipate an inevitable future."*]

The literary fame of Juan Rulfo rests on two slim books published some twenty years ago. In both his collection of short stories, **El llano en llamas** (1953), and the novel *Pedro Páramo* (1955) Rulfo's style is stark yet poetic; his technique is surprisingly simple in spite of its relationship to the Joyce-Faulkner tradition. His evocations of the land and people of Mexico are simultaneously related to the

American *criollista* (nativist) tradition and to the *nueva novela* movement. Rulfo is a meticulous artisan, working and reworking his prose until achieving a perfect end product. He has been at work so long on his promised second novel, to be entitled *La Cordillera,* that critics are beginning to doubt that it will ever appear.

Rulfo strives to capture the essence of the geographical barrenness and spiritually impoverished lives that have long existed in his native state of Jalisco and to this end sacrifices all literary frills and adornments. His prose is characterized by short, straightforward sentences; whether narrating in third person or reproducing interior monologue or direct dialogue he employs an elemental and very Mexican vocabulary, syntax and rhythm. There is rarely, if ever, a superfluous phrase or image in his intense and moving narrations. And this is precisely why the reader is so surprised to discover in one of his stories a blatant literary allusion, an artificial intrusion of the literary past into the hermetic world of Rulfo's Mexican peasants.

"¡Diles que no me maten!" is a powerful story of passion and vengeance and a cynical statement on the brutalization and insensitivity of man. The narrator chronicles the events that lead up to the brutal murder of Guadelupe Terreros by Juvencio Nava, friends and *compadres* until a drought enables the former to take advantage of his privileged, landed position to deny use of his fenced-in grazing land to the dying cattle of the latter. One night the desperate Juvencio breaks an opening in Don Lupe's fence and leads his cattle to the grass; Don Lupe mends the fence and again Juvencio breaks in; and so it continues for a while: "Así, de día se tapaba el agujero y de noche se volvía a abrir. . . ."

The line cited merely summarizes the repeated action that leads up to the killing, but it is also a direct (and almost certainly conscious) evocation of a scene from the second chapter of the anonymous Spanish classic *Lazarillo de Tormes* (1554). In this chapter the young orphan protagonist serves an avaricious priest who nearly starves the boy while keeping some bread locked in an old chest. Lazarillo manages to acquire a key for the chest and begins to steal the bread at night, making it appear that mice have broken in and nibbled away at the loaves. The priest nails shut the holes in the chest each day and the boy uses an old knife to bore new ones at night: "y cuantos [agujeros] él tapaba de día destapaba yo de noche."

Can the reader be positive that Rulfo's allusion is specifically to *Lazarillo de Tormes*? Could the similarity be mere coincidence? Or perhaps a reference (in an author fond of mythic constructions) to Penelope's web? Either is possible, but assuming *Lazarillo de Tormes* as the direct source seems far preferable to the other alternatives. The Greek myth offers fewer specific points of similarity than the Spanish novel. While Ulysses is away and presumed dead, Penelope puts off her suitors by proclaiming that she cannot marry until finishing a certain garment that she has at hand. Moved by constancy and faith that her husband will eventually return, for some ten years she unweaves every night what she has woven during the day. Penelope's contest is one of wits and nerves with her suitors, and she herself first makes and then unmakes the web, a symbolic rather than physical barrier. In *Lazarillo de Tormes* and **"¡Diles que no me maten!"** the motivation is not love but hunger; the physical barrier is first violated and then mended; the key word *tapar* (as well as the obligatory *de día . . . de noche* antithesis) is used by both writers; the contest between the two men is more direct and elemental than the subtle, refined situation of Penelope. But that there is a basic similarity between the two situations is expressly acknowledged by the author of *Lazarillo de Tormes* ("Finalmente, parescíamos tener a destajo la tela de Penélope, pues cuanto él tejía de día rompía yo de noche"), so that even in Rulfo's story a link with the Ulysses story is implicit.

And what of the possibility of coincidence? It is conceivable, of course, but also irrelevant. Whether or not Rulfo consciously and purposefully intended to allude to *Lazarillo de Tormes,* the allusion is there for the reader to perceive. The parallels are too many and too exact to be denied.

The results of the two episodes are entirely dissimilar: Lazarillo is caught, beaten, and dismissed from the priest's service; Don Lupe kills one of Juvencio's steers and is in turn murdered. The effect of the literary allusion is not to suggest an extended parallel in action, but rather to underscore the timelessness of the themes of hunger and oppression of the weak by the strong, and to evoke an image of the wall as a universal symbol of material possessions and social inequality. Good fences do not make good neighbors when in fact the other man's grass is greener.

Since Cervantes, the theme of literature in literature has been a major preoccupation of writers. An important facet of the literary career of Azorín consisted of a series of moving evocations, recreations, reinterpretations of the literary past. Jorge Luis Borges has explored the infinite possibilities of time in literature and literature in time. Juan Rulfo consistently avoids such intellectual and artistic concerns in his works, and even the most discreet and attentive reader might well pass over this unique literary allusion. But for those readers who notice the evocation of *Lazarillo do Tormes,* Rulfo's story gains immeasurably from this sudden juxtaposition of two worlds oceans and centuries apart. Rulfo's simple line, "Así, de día se tapaba el agujero y de noche se volvía a abrir," in one swift and unexpected stroke lifts the story onto a broader plane of meaning, linking an atemporal present to an eternal (even mythic) past in order to anticipate an inevitable future.

In one of his finest short pieces, "Las nubes" (inspired by *La Celestina*), Azorín says that "Vivir es ver volver." Surely one of the values of an awareness of the past is a more profound understanding of the present. To separate a literary text from literary tradition is to impoverish it greatly. We need to remember also that literary tradition works in one direction only; we can legitimately read *La Celestina, Lazarillo de Tormes* and *Don Quijote* in ignorance of Juan Rulfo, Carlos Fuentes, Julio Cortázar, Gabriel García Márquez, *et al.* But to read the latter in ignorance of the former is to run the risk of limiting—perhaps severely—our appreciation of their works.

Paul W. Borgeson, Jr. (essay date 1979)

SOURCE: "The Turbulent Flow: Stream of Consciousness Techniques in the Short Stories of Juan Rulfo," in *Revista de estudios hispánicos,* Vol. XIII, No. 2, May, 1979, pp. 227-52.

[*In this excerpt, Borgeson delineates various stream of consciousness techniques used by Rulfo in his novel and short fiction, concluding that the author is able to transcend conventional linear narrative structures.*]

Two principal tendencies have characterized Mexican prose fiction of the twentieth century. In the first few decades, the novel and short story generally reflected the country's socio-political turmoil, as in Mariano Azuela's *Los de abajo* (1915) or Martín Luis Guzmán's *El águila y la serpiente* (1926). Such social and historical analyses dominated for the first forty years or so. Meanwhile, in Europe, prose fiction was much more concerned with new trends in philosophy and psychology, in particular the ideas of Freud and Jung. These two tendencies (among others) finally came together in Mexico in the work of Agustín Yáñez (1904) and especially Juan Rulfo (1918). These writers, and others, also deal with the themes of the earlier social fiction, but with a significant difference. Rulfo, particularly, works with regional locales and characters, yet his best work is also highly universal in its portrayal of psychological issues, such as the problem of guilt, failure, and the consequences of socioeconomic dispossession. On one level, his narratives reveal the intimate circumstances of his land, suspended between growing cosmopolitanism and its rich indigenous heritage, and still in search of its identity. But Rulfo makes this process universal by exploiting the basic concept that at the center of one man lie all men, and his protagonists and their problems transcend their clearly national character. Given the dual nature of their role (general and specific), they have very few signs of individual personality. As Rulfo exposes the psyches of his fictional people, who share the same fundamental problems and live in similar circumstances, he also exposes the central core of their humanity, producing some of the finest, and most disquieting, literature in Latin America.

Rulfo's stories are unusually disturbing reading experiences. His fictional world burdens the spirit, because it is devoid of the ordering elements of time, space, and personality, and even life and death themselves become blurred and largely meaningless. Additionally, his stories also explore radically original means of structuring fiction (in my view only Borges and Cortázar have been as successful at opening the Spanish-American short story to such new possibilities). With so many elements working against our means for imposing order on literature, Rulfo's narratives at times leave us feeling that in his fictional world absolutely nothing works,

Yet Rulfo's stories themselves, almost incredibly, do work. Rulfo leaves them trembling on the brink of literary self-destruction, but the reader, seeing his simulacra of reality crashing down about him—both in content and in literary form—cannot flee. He returns to Rulfo as does Kafka's "K" to his trial, or as Rivera's Arturo Cova returns to his jungles. How, then, does Rulfo make his stories function so effectively when what they portray is so desolate and powerless?

This [essay] seeks to identify the ways in which Rulfo's stories achieve this unsettling effect, and to analyze the balance between chaos and order in the world he depicts. To do this, I will focus on specific techniques which contribute to his stories' unique nature, and whose use reveals several of Rulfo's most significant achievements.

One of the principal experiments in the early twentieth century novel, in Europe and in the United States, was the stream of consciousness approach. For the purposes of the present essay, this narrative mode may be understood according to the characterization of [Robert] Scholes and [Robert] Kellogg:

> Stream of consciousness is any presentation in literature of the illogical, ungrammatical, mainly associative patterns of human thought. Such thought may be spoken or unspoken [*The Nature of Narrative,* 1966].

I utilize this description among the many offered, because of its flexibility, its attention to technique, and for two more significant reasons: it recognizes that stream of consciousness may be portrayed either in speech or inward thought, and it gives us the insight that in such fiction, the subject matter is left apparently free from logical control. Scholes and Kellogg further help us to realize that there is not just one technique (interior monologue), but that a multitude of techniques constitutes the stream of consciousness mode, giving it richness; for what has survived has not after all been the mode itself so much as the techniques it developed.

The challenge of stream of consciousness fiction was as great as its opportunities: the writer needed to find a way to present coherently a psychological reality which was to be portrayed as chaotic; but when successful, such a portrayal could become itself, in form, a model of an illogical and fragmented reality. Juan Rulfo's fiction is based not only on the chaotic nature of the reality which surrounds his characters, but also on a general concept of the reality of the mind. Consciousness in Rulfo is portrayed as a dynamic and unstable synthesis of oppositions. On one hand are myth and irrationality; on the other are reason and order. His stories balance the two alternatives, and his problems and possibilities are then similar to those of the earlier stream of consciousness writers.

Some statements on Faulkner by Lawrence E. Bowling may help point out the technical relationship between Rulfo and stream of consciousness literature:

> The stream of consciousness technique tends to break down three stabilizing elements traditionally considered fundamental in narrative fiction: exposition, plot and chronological order. *The Sound and the Fury* is a novel about disorder, disintegration and the absence of perspective. The novel is essentially about the internal chaos of the characters—their intellectual, moral and spiritual disorder [*Kenyon Review* 4, 1948].

The problem is to develop techniques which can be integrated into a narrative with some type of structuring (preferably all but invisible) yet reveal and even share in this disorder. A review of criticism on the stream of consciousness mode reveals that virtually all of the techniques used by these writers are also found in Rulfo; yet most of them, rather than tending to destroy the narrative structure, actually contribute to his ordering of disorder. These techniques include the following: suspended coherence, sensory impression, repetition and several recurrent devices, disjunctive figures, narrative organization itself as a model of consciousness, and impressionistic or associative techniques. Such devices, understandably, tend to occur most frequently in the stories which most deeply enter into the protagonists' minds, such as in several of the classic Rulfo narratives: **"Luvina," "La cuesta de las comadres," "En la madrugada,"** and **"El hombre."** More traditional tales such as **"El día del derrumbe"** or **"Nos han dado la tierra"** use only a few, and often for different purposes.

Association

If free or apparently free association may be taken as a basis for stream of consciousness, the critic must then find a text's thematic unity in the reasons behind such associations. In identifying the underlying relationships, one unlocks both the interior life of the characters, and the very theme and structure of the narrative itself. In order to discuss associative techniques in Rulfo's stories, it will be useful to evaluate and identify them in terms of their ordering or disordering effect on the surface narration. Thus, we may consider them as follows: conjunctive techniques, tending to bring surface cohesion; disjunctive devices, which give an appearance of disorder; and bridge techniques, which balance the two. It will be found that devices for bringing fundamental order dominate in Rulfo's fiction.

Sensory impression

The principal disjunctive device from stream of consciousness fiction also used by Rulfo is sensory impression, a technique which fragments and transforms perceived reality. This term was used for the first time (to my knowledge) by Lawrence Bowling in 1948 and 1950. He describes sensory impression as the simple recording in fiction of data perceived through the senses. He writes that "sensory impression is the writer's nearest approach to putting pure sensations on paper." This device, about as objective as can be found, is used by novelists such as Woolf and Faulkner, and by Dos Passos in his "Camera Eye." Although presented with objectivity, sensory impressions are subjective in that they are not confirmed by a narrator—they are merely the reactions of a character, and may be at odds with others' perceptions. As Scholes and Kellogg have observed, "one of the major trends in Twentieth century literature is away from the attempt to penetrate an individual psyche and toward a focus on the apprehension of 'impressions' which claim no absolute validity as fact." This is precisely the case with Rulfo, whose use of sensory impressions results in a mosaic-like fragmentation of fictional reality into small bits and pieces. As Eric Auerbach writes, this "is a method which dissolves reality into multiple and multivalent reflections of consciousness." Sensory impression, then, is a major source of the apparent discontinuity which Rulfo, like the earlier stream of consciousness writers, must delicately balance with the need to be readable.

Carlos Blanco Aguinaga observes that Rulfo, "con maestría asombrosa, ha ordenado la confusión en libertad aparente." The constant play of sensory data is one of the principal ways in which Rulfo manages this. And Hugo Rodríguez Alcalá deals extensively with what he calls "experiencias de los sentidos" or "experiencias sensoriales." The reader will undoubtedly have observed the frequent and powerful use of sense-perception in Rulfo: Rodríguez Alcalá's chapter discusses smell, feelings of cold and warmth, "internal sensations" such as nausea or physical self-awareness, taste, touch and synesthesia. Here, rather than further cataloging these sensations, it will be more to the point to demonstrate their function in the narrative.

"Luvina" is an example of a *cuento* so full of powerful sensory impressions, especially of sound (the "murmullos") and touch (such as the wind) that they overwhelm the characters, who become hypersensitized to sense-perceptions. Sound, for instance, becomes so strong a symbol of the village that the following dialogue occurs:

> —¿Qué es? —me dijo.
>
> —¿Qué es qué? —le pregunté.
>
> —Eso, el ruido ése.
>
> —Es el silencio.

Even the absence of sound becomes a type of sensory impression. Rodríguez Alcalá shows that the ghostly Rulfian world is vitalized precisely by this kind of powerful and all-consuming sense-perception, in which even silence is perceived by the senses.

One of the great frustrations which the reader often shares with Rulfo's characters is a feeling of blindness. Rulfo's visual descriptions are meager at best, and one can scarcely discern what Luvina or Comala might look like through the shadows. Luvina, for instance, is a place of wind, shadows and dust. Dust reoccurs in **"Talpa,"** here as the only characteristic of the land. The Rulfian protagonist, effectively blind, perceives his world through his other physical sensations alone, and he must communicate it to his auditor in the same way. Here, Rulfo perhaps improves on

a Dos Passos; instead of simply enumerating the sensations, he is able to achieve a like effect while integrating them into a narrative context. Such an integration helps maintain the balance between order and chaos.

The sensory nature of all perception in Rulfo's stories is so complete that at least two remarkable phenomena occur. One is that the verb *sentir* becomes a synonym of *pensar,* transforming mental perception into sensory apprehension: "Y yo comienzo a sentir como si no hubiéramos llegado a ninguna parte"; "Y Tacha llora al sentir que su vaca no volverá." Reason and abstraction, in short, give way to the senses. Secondly, Rulfo's characters, who often make striking metaphors in their speech, occasionally transfer one sense to another synesthetically. Rodríguez Alcalá points out two such cases in *Pedro Páramo*: "olor verde" and "olor amarillo." We find another in *El llano en llamas*: "Olía a eso: a sombra recalentada por el sol." It is revealing that these cases also involve the transference of *visual* sensations to other senses (smell, in the instances cited), thus further weakening the already meager sight-imagery, and contributing to the feeling of impotence projected by the protagonists.

There are also several cases of metaphors verging on full synesthesia in *El llano en llamas*: "un buche de coraje," "viento pardo," a wind stirs up (*revuelve*) sadness. Such cases of near synesthesia are far more common in Rulfo, and this type of manipulation of sensory apprehension is indeed one of his most common and effective devices. One should note in this regard that Rulfo's use of sensory descriptions is by no means a type of *preciosismo*. The characters perceive sensually, and we can only enter their world, therefore, through their senses. Sensory impression may be called *the* Rulfian descriptive technique.

Suspended coherence

As mentioned above, bridge techniques serve to reinforce the appearance of disorder in the Rulfian narrative; the key word here, however, is "appearance," since they finally contribute to the reader's apprehension of the fictional world. "Suspended coherence," a favorite device of stream of consciousness literature, is Rulfo's principal bridging technique. The term, introduced by Robert Humphrey, denotes a device in which the explanations for certain statements are given to the reader only at a later point in the narrative [*Stream of Consciousness in the Modern Novel,* 1954]. The result is that the text is temporarily incoherent. When the reader comes to the explanation, a sudden revelation comes from putting the information together. The narrative content suddenly achieves perspective. The reader then sees the whole in a sort of internal overview which may at times bridge many pages of narrative. Suspended coherence is a flirtation between literary order and chaos.

In *El llano en llamas*, the technique of suspended coherence is used on at least two levels. At times only a few lines separate the complementary pieces of information. For instance, in **"Luvina,"** the professor tells the invisible listener about the wind in the town, and says "Ya mirará usted ese viento que sopla sobre Luvina." A moment later he repeats, "Ya lo verá usted." At this point the reader does not know why the traveler will see it, but his momentary disorientation is resolved a few paragraphs late, when the professor refers to the other as "Usted que va para allá." Other such momentary confusions abound.

But whereas Humphrey's discussion of suspended coherence limits itself to the level of random associations made by a wandering mind (and a consequent minor disconnection of elements), Rulfo's use of this device goes significantly further, as we shall see is the case with several other techniques. Suspended coherence becomes an essential structuring principle of stories such as **"Talpa"** and **"Diles que no me maten."** **"Talpa"** begins:

> Natalia se metió entre los brazos de su madre y lloró largamente allí con un llanto quedito. Era un llanto aguantado por muchos días, guardado hasta ahora que regresamos a Zenzontla y vio a su madre y comenzó a sentirse con ganas de consuelo.

The reader is completely unaware of what has taken place up to this point, since the story starts not even *in medias res,* but at the very end of the action. The rest of the story answers his question, "Why?" The frightful tale unfolds in fits and starts until it again reaches the end, with the "second" return of Natalia and the narrator:

> Ahora estamos los dos en Zenzontla. Hemos vuelto sin [Tanilo]. Y la madre de Natalia no me ha preguntado nada; ni qué hice con mi hermano Tanilo, ni nada. Natalia se ha puesto a llorar sobre sus hombros y le ha contado de esa manera lo que pasó.

The fact that the end of the story marks a return to its starting point indicates the lack of real progression, stressed further by the line which follows the citation just above: "Y yo comienzo a sentir como si no hubiéramos llegado a ninguna parte." In **"Talpa,"** as in so many of Rulfo's stories, nothing happens. The protagonists, in spite of their never-ending journeys, go nowhere. The technique of suspended coherence is a major Rulfian strategy for communicating their fundamental immobility, the stagnation of his fictional world, and the discontinuity of human activities, on the level of narrative organization. It is in addition one of the ways in which Rulfo combats the linear nature of narrative, a point to be explored shortly.

Recurrent techniques

By recurrent techniques, which I consider conjunctive devices for reasons which will shortly be made clear, I refer to those devices which serve above all to provide order and coherence to a narrative, even when giving an appearance of fragmentation. They are abundant in Rulfo, and their frequent use affirms that he strives to present a coherent text. The jumpiness, the fragmentation of the text is effectively overcome through the use of these devices, which finally contribute to the reader's understanding and interpretation.

The apparent discontinuity of Rulfo's narratives is particularly well expressed through several recurrent techniques: recapitulation, modulation, counterpoint, and what Rodríguez Alcalá calls Rulfo's "técnica de enfoques repetidos," which we will discuss first.

Rodríguez Alcalá shows how Rulfo's narrative technique in **"En la madrugada"** presents the same scene as perceived two and even three different times by various narrators under differing circumstances. . . .

This same device of repeated and changing focuses is used to a lesser degree in **"Talpa"** and even in **"La herencia de Matilde Arcángel."** It shows how Rulfo's narrative depends intimately on free association, and James East Irby notes that

> La secuencia de eventos dentro del relato se pliega libremente al flujo del pensamiento del "testigo," quien, torpe para el análisis, va y viene entre el presente y el pasado y comunica sus impresiones "en bruto," sin elaboración, de acuerdo a una simple asociación de ideas, espontáneamente, tal como se le vienen a la memoria [*La influencia de William Faulkner en cuatro narradores hispanoamericanos,* 1956].

The narrative device of repeated and alternating focuses (Alcalá says Rulfo "films" his stories) brings to mind the mosaic metaphor used earlier. Irby describes it as a "mosaico de escenas fragmentarias." The narrator puts the pieces into place, but the work of art is perceived, in a sense created, only within the reader. It is a kind of impressionism, reminiscent of the *pointilliste* technique. The device of repeated focus, so characteristic of Rulfo, is related to the next device: counterpoint.

Rulfo's stories are unusually disturbing reading experiences. His fictional world burdens the spirit, because it is devoid of the ordering elements of time, space, and personality, and even life and death themselves become blurred and largely meaningless.

—*Paul W. Borgeson, Jr.*

Melvin Friedman, among others, discusses the application of musical counterpoint to literature. His observations shed light particularly on Rulfo. "The few successful attempts [at counterpoint] have constituted a literary rendering of the principle under the new relationship between time and space devised by Bergson," he writes [*Stream of Consciousness: A Study of Literary Method,* 1955]. The use of counterpoint in literature, then, implies a disjuncture of linear space and time arrangements, in that elements, instead of occurring in order, overlap and occur simultaneously. Applying this notion to Rulfo's writings, we see a strikingly integrated effort to liberate prose fiction from the bonds traditionally imposed on it by the discursive nature of language, a function, after all, of time and space.

Counterpoint is the structural basis for several of Rulfo's stories, such as **"Luvina," "En la madrugada,"** and **"El hombre."** In these tales, Rulfo alternates the planes of time, space, and narrative presentation as musical tones alternate and overlap in counterpoint. In **"El hombre,"** for instance, the point of view changes rapidly, alternating between the narrator and the two protagonists. . . .

While Rulfo's technique is not truly simultaneous, it does achieve a notably simultaneous effect. And combined with the technique of alternating focus and the other recurrent techniques we are about to examine, the effect is very like that of musical counterpoint. Irby, for one, recognizes Rulfo's use of counterpoint: "Rulfo delata cada vez más su deuda a Faulkner, alternando en contrapunto diferentes planos temporales y deslizándose entre varios puntos de vista . . ." His counterpoint is not essentially fragmentary, in that it does not carry the tendency toward discontinuity to a total breakdown of the story, just as in music the use of this technique by no means destroys the composition. Rather, this device is another expression of the delicate balance between order and chaos so characteristic of Rulfo. . . .

The other musical device which we will take up with regard to recurrent techniques is variously called "transposition of leitmotif" or "modulation"; I prefer the second term, which Northrop Frye calls "the reappearance of an image in a different context." In Rulfo, modulation is often a way of giving an appearance of chaos while again maintaining order. A few examples will illustrate his use of this apparatus. In **"La noche que lo dejaron solo,"** we read that the narrator "se arrinconó en una esquina, descansando el cuerpo, aunque sentía que un gusano se le retorcía en el estómago." Later in the same story, we read: "Feliciano Ruelas esperó todavía un rato a que se le calmara el bullicio que sentía cosquilleándole el estómago." This is an instance of the simplest reoccurrence of the image. . . . Yet another kind, a bit more easily observed, depends on the use of a key word, as in **"Luvina."** . . . Modulation in Rulfo . . . may transfer elements from one image to another, and often does so without the reader consciously noting its effect. . . .

The three recurrent techniques dealt with so far (repeated focus, counterpoint and modulation) are all means for restatement, a characteristic of almost all of Rulfo's fiction. Any reading of Rulfo reveals at once the frequent repetition, and Rodríguez Alcalá even uses it in parodying Rulfo's style. Such repetitions and restatements are one way in which Rulfo assures that the reader, like the protagonists, will "get nowhere" in his stories. More often than not, after struggling through the bog of repetitions, back-tracks ("eso le dije"; "y regresando a donde estábamos"), and unessential clarifications ("así es la cosa"), the reader comes to the end of the story only to find himself back at the beginning, as we saw in **"Talpa."** Rulfo uses repetition to slow down the narration as well, to stagnate the narrative progression even within a single paragraph.

In **"Nos han dado la tierra,"** there is a repetition in a single paragraph with the pattern ABBA:

> No, el llano no es cosa que sirva. No hay conejos ni pájaros. *No hay nada. A no ser* unos cuantos huizaches trespeleques y una que otra manchita de zacate con las hojas enroscadas; *a no ser* eso *no hay nada.*

The very first paragraph of **"La cuesta de las comadres"** also bogs down immediately. Here, the repetition is ABAB:

> Los difuntos Torricos *siempre fueron buenos amigos* míos. Tal vez *en Zapotlán no los quisieran;* pero lo que es de mí, *siempre fueron buenos amigos.* Ahora, eso de que *no los quisieran en Zapotlán* no tenía ninguna importancia.

On the surface level, such repetitions are a direct reproduction of the speaker's thought. On the level of the narrative technique, they further serve the same end as the other recurrent means used by Rulfo: to give voice to the consciousness which provides the stories' ultimate subject matter. And finally, they allow the insertion of fragmentary techniques (counterpoint, repeated focus) by slowing down the progression of the story, and "making room" for such procedures in a narrative of relatively little length.

Many of the techniques found in Juan Rulfo tend to disrupt the narrative line. Yet in reading Rulfo seriously (which is to say repeatedly), few feel that his narratives fail to hold together; rather, one asks, "How has this come about?" The unity of his stories is rather like that of a river, whose splashes, changes of direction and false channels in no way prevent it from being a river. This image was of course the one used by psychologist William James, who originated the term "stream of consciousness," later appropriated into literary criticism. Later in his essay ["Principles of Psychology," 1890], James changes metaphors, and compares the shifting of conscious states with a kaleidoscope, whose very nature is change. The apparently disruptive nature of Rulfo's stories is actually inherent to their aesthetic unity.

Such a concept of fluid unity must be captured by the student of Rulfo; either one's consciousness must intuitively respond to the patterns found in the narrative, or (even better) one must achieve a simultaneous apprehension of the whole stream, manage to see it as a whole in spite of its unstable form. The story and the reader both, then, overcome the linear nature of narrative, shattered from the start by Rulfo's ordering of chaos. Enrique Anderson-Imbert alludes to these phenomena: "Por los agujeros abiertos en esa eternidad vemos y oímos a los muertos, son prendidos en instantes que no se suceden como los puntos de una línea, sino que están diseminados desordenadamente: sólo el lector va dándoles sentido." And William James, in a footnote, reminds us of Mozart, whose manner of apprehending his own creations recognizes the fullest unity of the work of art (and which directly applies to the musical nature of Rulfo's tales):

I spread it out broader and clearer, and at last it gets almost finished in my head, even when it is a long piece, so that I can see the whole of it in a single glance in my mind, as if it were a beautiful painting or a handsome human being; in which way I do not hear it in my imagination at all in succession—the way it must come later—but all at once, as it were. The best of all is the hearing of it all at once.

The procedure used by Rulfo in the 1950s has found substantial theoretical support and justification in the 1970s, particularly in work departing from that of Saussure and Barthes. Tzvetan Todorov, and especially Julia Kristeva's ideas on intertextual relations, are most useful in constructing the aesthetic behind Rulfo's procedures. Indeed: Rulfo's disjunctive and conjunctive devices provide excellent examples of Kristeva's *ideologema,* "el encuentro de una organización textual . . . con los enunciados que asimila en su espacio o a los que remite en el espacio de los textos exteriores." Further, a work relates to "distintos tipos de enunciados anteriores y sincrónicos." The *ideologema* is the means by which the word relates to the whole text, precisely what we have been observing in Rulfo. His recurrent techniques seize the opportunities provided within the text itself, and use them to the fullest.

Additionally, Kristeva's "lectura transformacional," in which each segment "es leído a partir de la totalidad del texto," is precisely—indeed decisively—what is required in reading Juan Rulfo. Without such a reading, the text may in fact be incoherent because of its destruction of linear narrative and normal time and space relations. Rulfo had apparently realized what Kristeva now asserts: "no hay novela lineal," and he skillfully structured his texts to seize the opportunities presented by a non-consecutive narrative line.

Thus the structure of Rulfo's stories is such that it leads the reader, be it consciously or unconsciously, to pass through a process of instantaneous apprehension of the whole. This process, shown to be aesthetically coherent and also based on the purest concept of the early stream of consciousness, is the ultimate justification for all of the disordering elements which we have been examining in Rulfo's tales. Through them he attempts to present a significant way to overcome the discursive nature of narrative, to create a text which steps outside of the "bourgeois" (i.e., ordered) nature of traditional narrative, to create a text which is revolutionary in its very language and structure.

Thought and speech

Interior monologue, often alternated with omniscient narration, is Rulfo's narrative mode *por excelencia.* It is also directly related to the characteristics of stream of consciousness fiction, in that interior monologue is the typical modal narration (so much so that the two terms, unfortunately, are often used interchangeably). Friedman notes that interior monologue proceeds, ideally, in the manner of musical counterpoint, by simultaneity. The juxtaposition of scenes that is one of Rulfo's contrapuntal

devices is fundamentally an impressionistic technique, as noted above. On paper, Rulfo's stories are often a collection of brusquely juxtaposed fragments; they take form, as suggested earlier, only in the mind of the reader. As a consequence, it can be said that Rulfo has made narrative form mirror a concept of the human psyche. The inordinate and disturbing depth of his creations derives from this equation; it is as if the story were a nearly bottomless well, into whose depths we apprehensively peer, to see ourselves. Yet at the bottom of the well, which we sense more than we actually see, lies the universal core of human awareness as well.

One key to the nature of Rulfo's use of stream of consciousness devices lies in the phenomenon that his character's thought and their speech are fundamentally identical. He sets in motion a balance-wheel which moves between random and logical associations, which his characters express as they occur to them (as Irby says, "tal como se les vienen a la memoria"). Juan Preciado can "speak" in *Pedro Páramo* even while dead; we hear his protagonists' spirits think (again, *pensar* corresponds to *sentir*). The meaning of *Pedro Pármo's murmullos* is nothing less than this hearing of unspoken thoughts.

Irby has noted how Rulfo's simple and uneducated characters typically do not think before they speak, and do not, therefore, deform their statements through abstraction. Often, then, thought and speech, being one, are simultaneous in the narrative. **"La noche que lo dejaron solo"** provides a clear illustration of this identity between thought and speech in Rulfo. The narrator is omniscient, and the reader is provided with all his speech and thoughts:

> No serian muchas [noches]—pensó—si al menos hubiéramos dormido de día. Pero ellos no quisieron. "Nos pueden agarrar dormidos—dijeron—. Y eso sería lo peor."—¿Lo peor para quién?

> Ahora el sueño lo hacía hablar.

The protagonist's question responds to his own unspoken thought, in perfect sequence, and he speaks at the same instant in which the question occurs to him. It is revealing to note that in Rulfo, *decir* is frequently actually *decirse,* since his characters often speak only to themselves. Furthermore, their expression is stylistically indistinguishable from that of the narrators, so that in a real sense, almost all speech in Rulfo's stories is purely internal. This is especially true if we bear in mind that the narrated world is essentially in the mind of these characters in the first place, since we perceive it largely through them. The following lines, which occur shortly after our last citation, may illustrate this point (note that since the protagonist is alone, *dijo* here is *se dijo*):

> Se detuvo con los ojos cerrados. "Es mucho—dijo—. ¿Qué ganamos con apurarnos? Una jornada. Después de tantas que hemos perdido, no vale la pena." En seguida gritó: "¿Dónde andan?"

The shout here, following immediately the character's taking stock of his situation, is the only real act of external speech. It is significant also that the punctuation of these two cited passages follows the same pattern, further supporting the contention that speech is identical to thought here because we as readers are already inside the protagonists' minds. We hear the characters think, and it is purely coincidental to them that anyone may be present to hear them when they speak aloud.

Friedman observes that stream of consciousness fiction "characterizes the mind on the verge of dissolution into unconsciousness." This is the magical, almost mythical, area where Rulfo's people dwell, and where thought and speech become one in effect. Rulfo has developed and used devices from stream of consciousness writing to create this very special and tenuous state of existence for his characters and their uncertain world.

Objectivity in Rulfo

We have seen how Rulfo utilizes all of the important devices of stream of consciousness fiction, skillfully adapting them to his particular needs, and often in the process giving them a new or more extensive function. There is one major point of contact between Rulfian narrative and stream of consciousness writing yet to discuss: their "objective" nature.

Robert Humphrey notes that "one important achievement of Joyce's in *Ulysses* which is central to his whole purpose and which is greatly dependent on stream of consciousness [is] the marvelous degree of objectivity which he achieves." He goes on to write of Joyce's ideal narrator (as expressed in *Portrait of the Artist*), whose personality almost "refines itself out of existence." Indeed, the constant characteristic of stream of consciousness narration is an apparent total separation of the author from the narrator. The objective of this procedure is to present the character's psyche with no intermediaries between it and the reader. Yet this can never really be managed. A theoretical impasse results between the goal—objectivity—and the necessarily subjective narrative modes by which the author must create this impression. The Rulfian paradox is that although his narrators have in a sense lost real faith in their own existence, they still tenuously perceive themselves; or perhaps what they see is their own limbo, in which cause and effect, subject and object, dissolve, to lose and then regain individual identity. Irby has seen the subjective nature of Rulfo's narratives in spite of their frequently "objective" presentation, and writes of Rulfo's "concepción de forma narrative como conciencia subjetiva de una realidad caótica." All "objectivity" in Rulfo is but apparent, and it exists as a result of the very techniques we have been studying.

Psychologist William James, spoken of earlier, may help show just how close Rulfo is to the original concept of stream of consciousness. Both emphasize internal reality. "We shall see," writes James, "how inveterate is our habit of not attending to sensations as subjective facts, but of simply using them as stepping-stones to pass over to the recognition of the reality whose presence they reveal." In

fact, subjectivity is enclosed in the very sentence in which the term "stream of consciousness" is first used:

> Consciousness, then, does not appear to itself chopped up in bits. It is nothing jointed; it flows. A "river" or a "stream" are the metaphors by which it is most naturally described. In talking of it hereafter, let us call it the stream of thought, or consciousness, or of subjective life.

Rulfo's world, exclusively internal, fully conforms to this founding concept of the stream of consciousness. In the Rulfian world the only reality, being internal, is the very thoughts and sensations of the characters. It is highly ironic that such a subjective view of things should be presented in such an "objective" manner. In this paradoxical coexistence lies the essence of Rulfian narrative, and here lies also the reason for Rulfo's exploitation of the devices examined in this study: they allow the *cooperation* of the disparate elements of subjectivity and objectivity, order and chaos.

Conclusion

I conclude that Rulfo utilizes virtually all of the devices identified with stream of consciousness fiction, often on a very basic level of his narrative, and in several instances he extends their application significantly. His use of them, in fact, is closer to the original concept (as expressed by James) than many of stream of consciousness' other literary adaptations. Rulfo is not a stream of consciousness writer in the sense of the decades which preceded his work; rather, he has seized on the experiments of those times, integrating them into a narrative which shares many qualities with stream of consciousness fiction, but with far fewer limitations. In so doing, he has created a magnificently gloomy picture of his characters'—and mankind's—situation.

Juan Rulfo's use of stream of consciousness techniques allows him to produce stories whose structures support fully the image of chaos and desperation expressed through the tone of the characters' speech. He has managed to portray coherently an essentially chaotic vision by utilizing devices essayed by stream of consciousness fiction, which give an appearance of disorder, but making them contribute to the stories' unified structures. In the process, Rulfo thus moves beyond traditional linear narrative structures.

If Faulkner, according to Bowling, deals with the "intellectual, moral and spiritual confusion" of his characters, Rulfo goes a step beyond: into metaphysical despair.

Arthur Ramírez (essay date 1982)

SOURCE: "Juan Rulfo: Dialectics and the Despairing Optimist," in *Hispania,* Vol. 65, No. 4, December, 1982, pp. 580-85.

[*In the following essay, Ramírez explores Rulfo's use of*

polarities, such as chaos and order, death and life, power and powerlessness, and love and hate, and asserts that this technique illustrates Rulfo's belief in the conflictive nature of reality.]

Baudelaire finds an artistic vision is "always double, though the impression it produces is one. . . ." This can be seen in the frequently dialectical world of Juan Rulfo's short story collection, *El llano en llamas* (1953), and his novel, *Pedro Páramo* (1955), in which we encounter such dualities as life and death, Inferno and Paradise, illusion and disillusion, love and hate, and reality and irreality. Yet, despite the tension of these polarities, the total effect is one of coherence. [In *Cuadernos,* 1960] Carlos Fuentes is cognizant of this:

> . . . Rulfo llega al fondo de las grandes dualidades que impulsan a los mexicanos. ¿Dualidad? Más bien, mitades de una misma fruta: en *Pedro Páramo* toda alegría lleva su propio llanto, toda muerte su propia vida. Para los mexicanos todo acto vital supone ya la negación del mismo acto.

It might be useful, however, to reverse the order of Fuentes's sequence of affirmation and then negation. Kenneth Burke in *Language as Symbolic Action* cogently presents this opposite point of view on positive-negative polarities and their dialectical interaction:

> . . . I personally would treat the negative as in principle prior, for this reason: (1) Yes and No imply each other; (2) in their role as opposites, they limit each other; (3) but limitation itself is the negation of part of a divisible quantum.

Pedro Páramo focuses on a *cacique* who dominates and then destroys a town. It is, however, his love for a woman that causes despair, disintegration, and death. In *El llano en llamas* radical innocence allows brutality to run rampant, and hopeful illusions are invariably crushed. The key lies in "the disparity between the innocence of the hero and the destructive character of his experience. . . ."

Rulfo's world view, then, is characterized by the idealist's despair at the destruction of his illusions. But disillusion could not be a strong and natural reaction were it not for the author's dedication to the ideal. Paradoxically, Rulfo is really a despairing optimist who actually implies their opposites when he writes of hate, violence, destruction, and hopelessness.

By means of these dialectical contrasts, Rulfo is pointing to the conflictive nature of reality. Fiction is necessarily about conflicts and problems, or else it will lack interest. Life is full of tension and conflict between opposites, full of what outwardly seem to be contradictory elements. Vivid contrasts in character, setting, and structure make each of the antithetical elements stand out in sharp relief. Thus Pedro Páramo's interior sensitivity to love and beauty coexists with his exterior tendency to violent, brutal action. Each pole of his character is brought out vividly.

Ultimately, however, opposites fuse into a new synthesis, as in a montage. This is true, for example, of the dialectical basis of life and death in *Pedro Páramo*: "Porque, como nos dijo Pedro Salinas, la literatura de la muerte es, en su esencia, una desesperada lucha por encontrar la vida." In **"¡Díles que no me maten!"** death stares a man in the face and he comes to savor life fully, something he had not done in thirty-five years. Juvencio Nava, like one of Dostoevski's characters, lives life to the hilt existentially in the last moments before death. Thus seemingly contradictory elements unite in a higher synthesis and each extreme of the dialectical spectrum reveals only a partial truth. Together, however, they form a total, all-encompassing, coherent view of a fragmented and paradoxical reality.

Unlike the Mexican government's "Chamber of Commerce" view of reality, such writers as Paz, Fuentes, and Rulfo present a more complex and accurate vision of Mexico. Although each writer emphasizes his own subjective feelings about Mexican reality, a truly creative and vigorous writer can synthesize a broad vision of this realty. Bound to glorify no political creed, the writer is free to turn the spotlight of his artistic conscience on social injustices. As Rulfo puts it: "El escritor tiende a dar un testimonio de lo que anda mal."

Of course, a number of critics see only the negative and pessimistic elements in Rulfo's work: ". . . todas las esencias que Rulfo descubre en su tierra son negativas. . . ." References are made to Rulfo's nihilism, his "negative psychic states," and his "cosmic pessimism." The evidence of irrationality, disintegration, despair and anguish in Rulfo's fictional world is irrefutable; like Gorki, Rulfo is essentially pessimistic. However, if the thesis is pessimistic, the Hegelian antithesis must be optimistic. And this is the case in Rulfo's world, which is not only not lacking in love, vitality and hope, but is particularly exaltive of these positive elements of life precisely because of this backdrop of negatives.

Thus, Kenneth Burke refers to "the role of antithesis in what are often called 'polar' terms, not just Yes-No, but such similarly constructed pairs as: true-false, order-disorder, cosmos-chaos, success-failure, peace-war, pleasure-pain, clean-unclean, life-death, love-hate." Harking back to Kant and especially Hegel, Burke sets forth the Hegelian "Paradox of the Negative whereby polar terms both exclude each other and necessarily require each other." The thesis, then, is negated by the antithesis, which itself is negated in turn by reference to the original thesis. The ubiquitous presence of Death in Rulfo immediately implies Life—the Life Force—and back again. The two opposing poles—the positive and the negative—do not merely imply each other, although that is particularly significant. However, equally important is the idea that each pole limits the other. And as Burke establishes: "limitation itself is the 'negation of part of a divisible quantum.'" In this regard, Hegel's concept of the Aufheben of dialectic is quite relevant:

> Starting from A, we get a view of B in terms of A; next we advance to a view of B that transcends A; and then, looking back, we can view A in terms of B.

It is, therefore, through the theme of Death that Rulfo gives Life all its vitality. Pedro Páramo, "un rencor vivo," is precisely the character that most exalts love. Only in the hell that Comala has become can we view paradise. Ultimately, a negative theme like nothingness is transformed artistically into something not only significant but also affirmative. Rulfo, like Hemingway in "A Clean Well-Lighted Place," expresses such themes as nothingness and meaninglessness so vividly, expressively, and artistically that the negative nature of the segment of reality he chooses to illuminate achieves a kind of artistic transcendence. In Rulfo's **"Nos han dado la tierra,"** nothingness is but one-half of a pervasive double vision, at whose opposite pole is something, namely life, plenitude, vitality and fertility. An essentially similar double vision is also operative in **"Luvina"** and *Pedro Páramo*.

Consequently, Rulfo is never depressing to me, even when he pictures a hostile, bleak world. As Northrop Frye points out in *Anatomy of Criticism*: "If any literary work is emotionally 'depressing,' there is something wrong with either the writing or the reader's response. Art seems to produce a kind of buoyancy." This is not to say that Rulfo's world is a happy one, but reading him, like reading any other great artist, is exhilarating—his work exalts one's spirits, as all great art does. Paradoxically, Rulfo's aesthetic efficacy gives an affirmative order to the chaos of dissolution and negation. Out of the very depths of a hellish despair in Comala in *Pedro Páramo,* Rulfo gives an image of paradise. From the perspective of the grave we are struck with how precious life is. In the midst of death, then, we are in life.

In the final analysis, Rulfo, like Beckett, believes in the basic ontological indomitableness of the human spirit. Despite the workings of an adverse nature, despite the most negative of situations (including a portrayal of hell), despite almost incessant failures, despite an oppressive sense of impotence, man, in Rulfo's fictional world, continues to crave life—even life in a marginal or catatonic state. Man affirms at all costs the passionate desire merely to exist. The specters that roam about Comala are "ánimas en pena" that still survive as remnants of that will to live. The poverty-stricken sonambulistic peasants in **"Nos han dado la tierra"** persist in their losing battle against a sterile land and a harsh government. The purgatorial characters of **"Luvina"** continue to suffer and persist in their barren and precarious existence. Somehow, the Life Force dies hard. Indeed, the basic framework of *Pedro Páramo*—the quest of the Telemachus-like hero, Juan Preciado, for his father, the aloof and almost mythical Pedro Páramo—is an embodiment of the Life Force. As a Mexican critic points out: "Buscar al padre, conocerlo, es también un medio de asegurarnos de nuestras raíces, de nuestra identidad, en un mundo inseguro y cruel." The search, as it turns out, is doomed in the face of death and time's disintegrative effect, but the attempt itself, made in such adverse circumstances, transcends that failure.

Even the omnipresent violence in Rulfo's world is a manifestation of the Life Force. Murder in such stories as **"En la madrugada"** and **"La Cuesta de las Comadres"** is simply the basic means of affirming existence. The solitary, somnambulistic characters seem to doubt whether they exist or not, whether they are dreaming or not. In the sudden explosion into violence and murder, these characters find their place in a hostile reality. Murder also gives a kind of power to the impotent, such as Esteban in **"En la madrugada."**

[In *El laberinto de la soledad,* 1964] Octavio Paz has observed that violent crime still has meaning for the Mexican because there is a personal relationship between the victimizer and the victim:

> Para nosotros el crimen es todavía una relación—y en ese sentido posee el mismo significado liberador que la fiesta o la confesión—. De ahí su dramatismo, su poesía y—¿por qué no decirlo?—su grandeza. Gracias al crimen, accedemos a una efímera trascendencia.

Crime has a transcendental value precisely because it has meaning, as in the revenge in **"El hombre,"** or the "murder" of Tanilo in **"Talpa,"** or the assertive self-protection of Lucas Lucatero in **"Anacleto Morones."** In **"La Cuesta de las Comadres"** the amoral narrator's murder of the *cacique* Torrico is meaningful because of the personal relationship between the two. In **"El hombre"** Urquidi's murderous revenge is more than merely a dubious way to personal affirmation. "He does not kill in triumph or with satisfaction, but out of necessity. He must obey the rigorous code that demands the removal of the stain on his honor."

Pedro Páramo also wreaks vengeance through murder. Unable to locate his father's assassin, he seeks to avenge his father's death by monstrously exterminating all the guests at the wedding where his father was killed. His wanton violence, committed with cold and methodical precision, is larger than life and belongs to the realm of the epic and myth. In short, violence or its expression is an aesthetic phenomenon, as it is to the revolutionary narrator Pichón of **"El llano en llamas."** This is closely akin to Mariano Azuela's view of the Mexican Revolution in *Los de abajo,* when Solís, in spite of his disillusion, is moved to exclaim: "¡Qué hermosa es la Revolución, aun en su misma barbarie!"

While there is a certain exhilaration, a sense of power and grandeur expressed through violence, it is also a necessity given the nature of Rulfo's brutal characters and their hostile environment. There are extenuating circumstances: honor, self-assertion, and a kind of radical innocence which is the spark of humanity that saves Rulfo's characters from becoming merely monstrous murderers. Ultimately, it is not with revulsion but pathos that the reader responds. [In *Novelistas contemporáneos hispanoamericanos*] Fernando Alegría claims that Rulfo's creation of pathos in his fictional world has no equal in Spanish American literature: "Acaso porque sus personajes buscan con empecinamiento infantil la trampa que un poder sobrenatural les tiene armada desde el nacimiento."

It is also difficult to fault innocent characters like Esteban in **"En la madrugada"** or the title character in **"Macario."** Even Pedro Páramo—the very archetype of the evil, brutal, violent *cacique*—is also portrayed as a sensitive youth, an indulgent father who spoils his favorite son, and a man obsessed by a love for Susana San Juan that is based on innocent childhood happiness. The deaths of his father, his son Miguel, and his wife, Susana, leave Pedro Páramo grief-stricken. This grief, although expressed in a crazed and brutally violent manner, constitutes a positive response that proves Pedro's great love for the three central people in his life. Obviously, grief would be impossible if he did not care and love, if the losses were not deeply felt. Hence, the murderous violence that on one level seems the most fiendish negation of life can also be seen as motivated by a desire to give meaning to life through an ethereal and poignant love.

To achieve greatness, the conquering hero traditionally engages in momentous actions and situations, sometimes involving murder and violence. Pedro Páramo's epic dimension, at least in part, is an identification with both his humanity and his super-human imposition of power. However, Pedro's violence, his brutal landgrabbing and the full exercise of his power, are not without an extenuating motivation: love for Susana San Juan. This is shown in Pedro's interior monologue provoked by Susana's return to Comala: "Esperé treinta años a que regresaras, Susana. Esperé a tenerlo todo. No solamente algo, sino todo lo que se pudiera conseguir de modo que no nos quedara ningún deseo, sólo el tuyo, el deseo de ti." The means may have been unjust but the end was a noble, selfless one, the desire to give everything possible to his beloved Susana. Although Pedro's actions may have been callous, at the bottom is a very human need to love and be loved. Pursued with an intensity that is awesome, physically and emotionally, this very tender desire is at the same time spiritual and physical, selfish and unselfish, realistic and idealistic.

The highest, most noble expression of positive values in Rulfo's novel is this life-long, all-encompassing love that Pedro Páramo feels for Susana San Juan. In several interior monologues that reveal Pedro Páramo's obsessions, Rulfo distills the essence of this love. The most refined expression of Pedro's feelings for Susana is found in the first interior monologue, in which he evokes the happiness of flying a kite with Susana when they were children: "Pensaba en ti, Susana. En las lomas verdes. Cuando volábamos papalotes en la época del aire." Another important positive element here is the delicate sensitivity toward beauty that is demonstrated through the idyllic images of greenery that contrast with the suffocating aridity of Juan Preciado's Comala. Pedro sees love as the basic means of overcoming mortality and death, the ultimate saving grace. As Pedro himself puts it: ". . . acaso no era suficiente saber que [Susana] era la criatura más querida por él sobre la tierra? Y que además, y esto era lo más importante, le serviría para irse de la vida alumbrándose con aquella imagen que borraría todos los demás recuerdos." Eros

thus transcends death.

While love plays a very important role in Rulfo's novel, in his short story world it is friendship, compassion, and sympathy that mark Rulfo's optimistic side. Again, many critics maintain that there is only a negative polarity to Rulfo's short stories. For example, James East Irby [in his thesis] states: ". . . Rulfo sólo puede ver alrededor suyo la desolación, la esterilidad y el estancamiento social y no halla en su mundo valores positivos que exaltar." However, a positive and tender compassion is central to more than one Rulfo short story. In **"Es que somos muy pobres,"** the essence of the story is the tenderness in the relationship between the boy who is the narrator and his sister Tacha. In large part, the poignancy of the story lies in the boy's compassion for his sister, who seems doomed to a life of prostitution. If the boy did not care deeply about his sister's fate, it would be impossible for the reader to care. But he does, and so does the reader. Tacha's crying over the loss of a dowry cow that seems to seal her destiny on the way to perdition is also moving. As Sergio Fernández notes: "La ternura, que a veces desemboca en el llanto,—casi siempre interior, contenido—, aparece cuando más se la necesita."

The father in **"No oyes ladrar los perros"** also demonstrates the love a father feels for his son, even though it is masked by austerity and an alternately condemnatory attitude because the son, Ignacio, has become a robber and a murderer. Rescuing his wounded son, the father indirectly shows his paternal love in such solicitous questions as "—¿Cómo te sientes?" and "—¿Te duele mucho?" that he mixes with his reproaches. The father's great exertion in carrying the heavy burden of Ignacio's body a great distance in the night so he can get medical attention in Tonaya also indicates the deep love the old man feels for his son and belies his outward renunciation of his offspring.

> **In the final analysis, Rulfo's artistry transcends his despairing vision of humanity and makes manifest an embodiment of the universally acknowledged highest values of mankind.**
>
> *—Arthur Ramírez*

Rulfo's fictional world is not without sympathy, hospitality and good-naturedness. For example, Abundio, the mule-driver, before leaving Juan Preciado behind in Comala, shows his concern for the stranger when he says in his parting words: "Yo voy más allá, donde se ve la trabazón de los cerros. Allá tengo mi casa. Si usted quiere venir, será bienvenido." Basic human values are not lacking even in the inferno that Comala has become. This is further underscored when Eduviges Dyada hospitably offers food and lodging to Juan Preciado after the latter leaves Abundio and knocks at her door. The kind-hearted Eduviges also provides a sympathetic portrait of Abundio. Since Abundio has told Juan to ask Eduviges for lodging, she says: "No puedo menos que agradecérselo. Fue buen hombre y muy cumplido." She adds that he used to carry news and letters to Comala, but an exploding firecracker left him deaf. "Me acuerdo del desventurado día que le sucedió su desgracia. Todos nos conmovimos, porque todos lo queríamos." Sympathy for Abundio is general and not limited just to the kindly Eduviges. Continuing her portrait, she describes Abundio as a great conversationalist until the explosion: "Desde entonces enmudeció, aunque no era mudo; pero, eso sí, no se le acabó lo buena gente." In Eduviges's opinion, Abundio remained a good person despite the unfortunate accident that left him deaf and caused his nature to change. Delivered by an inhabitant of hellish Comala, this testimonial of another's basic decency reaffirms the endurance of humanistic values even under the most adverse circumstances. Of course, Eduviges underscores her own congeniality by stressing Abundio's good qualities.

The value of friendship, even beyond death, is also exalted by Eduviges in her conversation with Juan Preciado, the son of her good friend Dolores Preciado. Eduviges tells Juan that she and his mother wanted to die together so they would never be separated. She adds: "Eramos muy amigas," and "nos queríamos mucho. Tu madre era tan bonita, tan, digamos, tan tierna, que daba gusto quererla. Daban ganas de quererla." This kind of enduring friendship is a symbolic representation of positive values, even in the infernal world of Comala.

In his subsequent wanderings through Comala Juan Preciado encounters an incestuous brother and sister. While alone with the sister, who fears that her brother Donis has left forever, Juan says: "Quise decirle: 'Voy a salir a buscar un poco de aire, porque siento náuseas'; pero dije: '—No se preocupe. ¡Volverá!'" One critic comments on this scene: "His outward display of compassion . . . is owed to her fear that Donis will abandon her. And Juan knows full well what it is to be left alone." Juan returns the incestuous couple's hospitality by demonstrating his sympathy, understanding, and compassion.

In addition to the characters' display of compassion, the author himself reveals a compassionate spirit that filters through so gently, almost imperceptibly. As one reviewer said of *Pedro Páramo*: "The poetry is in the pity, the compassion Rulfo feels for all his lost souls." Elena Poniatowska offers a similar critical response: "Pero su aridez [de Rulfo] es sólo aparente, y de repente brota toda el agua de su ternura, esa ternura recóndita en sus páginas crueles; en *El llano en llamas,* en *Pedro Páramo*." The distinguished Mexican literary critic, José Luis Martínez, emphasizes these same qualities when he describes Rulfo's view of reality as "una visión trágica, irónica y humedecida de piedad del mundo violento de los humildes de la tierra [*Revista de la Universidad de Mexico*, 1959]."

Indeed, in Rulfo's world it is often the radically innocent that suffer: the peasants in **"Nos han dado la tierra,"** and **"Es que somos muy pobres,"** the pathetically uncompre-

hending title-character, **"Macario,"** and the murder victims in **"La Cuesta de las Comadres," "El llano en llamas,"** and **"El hombre."** The reader feels all the more deeply for them because of Rulfo's narrative technique which consists of objectivity and distance, understatement and dispassion, which produce a "vacuum of response" to pathos and tragedy that the reader himself must provide. Only through such a skillful ability to make the reader care about his characters could Rulfo secure the undeniably powerful effects and responses he elicits from the reader.

However, no matter how aesthetically capable an author is, he must also care about his created characters; otherwise, the reader will not care either, and there will be no powerful effects or responses. It is, of course, true that Rulfo is very skillful at manipulating narrative technique while appearing to remain objective and self-effaced. Yet Rulfo demonstrates that he is a highly skilled artist as well as a writer who experiences deeply and poignantly the happiness and the sorrows, the tenderness and the brutalities of his fictional creatures. We must also remember that when Rulfo began to write about this rural world of his childhood, he saw it as a golden age. Perhaps some of this resplendent aura glitters through and makes us care so profoundly for his characters and their world.

Rulfo has also expressed himself clearly on the matter of the negativeness or negation in his novel. An interviewer once asked him, "¿Diría usted que *Pedro Páramo* es novela de negación?" Rulfo responded, "No, en lo absoluto. Simplemente se niegan algunos valores que tradicionalmente se han considerado válidos." Among these values are a misplaced faith or belief that has become twisted and destructive, converted into fanaticism. Thus, a form of negation becomes a critical stance that features a negative-positive polarity, as in the formulation set forth by Kenneth Burke. Rulfo negates values that only appear to be positive; on closer examination they are found to have become distorted.

Although often pessimistic, Rulfo ultimately does have an optimistic perspective which is usually expressed in a subtle manner. Paradoxically, he often stresses the negative (death, hate, violence, etc.) to bring out all the more vividly their opposites—life, love, compassion, and hope. Rulfo's vision is such that stress on one side of the spectrum produces an equal reaction on the other side. Rulfo also would not be so disillusioned if he did not have many illusions at the outset. In the final analysis, Rulfo's artistry transcends his despairing vision of humanity and makes manifest an embodiment of the universally acknowledged highest values of mankind.

Luis Leal (essay date 1983)

SOURCE: "*The Burning Plain*: The Later Stories," in *Juan Rulfo*, Twayne Publishers, 1983, pp. 43-62.

[*In the following excerpt from his full-length study of*

Rulfo, Leal offers a thematic analysis of the more recent stories collected in his short story collection.]

Some of the fifteen stories collected in 1953 under the title of one of them, *El llano en llamas* [*The burning plain*], had appeared . . . in the journals *Pan* and *América* between 1945 and 1951. There is no appreciable difference between these stories and the others, either in style or technique. It is not known if some of the latter were written earlier, but not published. It is a possibility but difficult to ascertain, either by internal or external evidence. The problem is not serious, however, since the span of years is not broad, and all fifteen stories must have been retouched before publication in book form.

It is interesting to note that the book opens with the two *Pan* stories, **"Macario"** and **"Nos han dado la tierra."** These in turn are followed by two *América* stories (**"La cuesta de las comadres"** and **"Es que somos muy pobres"**) and two unpublished, **"El hombre"** and **"En la madrugada."** The other *América* stories appear next, in the order in which they were published in the periodical: **"Talpa,"** **"El llano en llamas,"** and **"¡Diles que no me maten!"** Finally, there are six more unpublished stories: **"Luvina,"** **"La noche que lo dejaron solo,"** **"Acuérdate,"** **"No oyes ladrar los perros,"** **"Paso del Norte,"** and **"Anacleto Morones."** Two new stories were added to the second revised edition of 1970, **"El día del derrumbe"** and **"La herencia de Matilde Arcángel,"** and one, **"Paso del Norte,"** was eliminated.

It has been observed that the story **"The Burning Plain,"** under which the collection was published, appears precisely in the middle, with seven stories preceding and seven following. From this fact it cannot be deducted, however, that the first seven stories deal with Mexico before the Revolution and the last seven with the postrevolutionary period. That would be too neat an organization. Besides, it could not possibly be determined if the events narrated in the story **"Macario"** take place before or after the Revolution. And **"Nos han dado la tierra,"** which is placed in the first part, deals with postrevolutionary Mexico. Only symbolically could the stories be interpreted as representing the two Mexicos, those in which the needs of the people are expressed (lack of land, hunger, oppression) and the others showing the failure of the Revolution to solve those problems and tend to the basic needs of the people, the *campesinos*. But even here, some of the stories from the first part (**"The Man,"** **"At Daybreak"**) do not deal with social conditions, but with psychological problems. In them the living conditions of the people are seen only indirectly; they are expressed implicitly, not explicitly. Rulfo himself has stated, although not positively, that the organization of the stories was left to the editors; the story **"Macario,"** he says, "comes first, but it could be at the end; to be sure, the organization [of the book] was left to the editors, I believe."

"El Hombre"

In **"The Man"** Rulfo has made use of an archetypal structure, that of the hunt, in this case a human hunt. The hunted "man," José Alcancía, has committed a horrible crime. He has killed Urquidi's entire family in order to avenge the killing of his own brother by Urquidi sometime in the past. Alcancía did not want to kill all of them, but it was dark and he did not want to miss Urquidi. Later he repents of his act, "'I shouldn't have killed all of them; I should've been satisfied with the one I had to kill; but it was dark and the shapes were the same size. . . . I shouldn't have killed all of them. . . . It wasn't worth it putting such a burden on my back. Dead people weigh more than live ones.'"

The theme of revenge in this story is better motivated than in **"¡Diles que no me maten!"** Juvencio Nava's crime had been committed thirty-five years earlier, and he felt that he had paid for it many times over, but Alcancía's has just taken place, and the reader can sympathize with Urquidi, who immediately sets out to avenge the crime. The death of Alcancía is not dramatized, but only verified by a third character, a shepherd who had befriended the fugitive and who later found his body, and who is now reporting the discovery to the authorities. The introduction of this third character, essential to bring together the two interior monologues of Alcancía and Urquidi, softens the impact of the killing of the hunted man by the hunter. This establishment of distance is accomplished by avoiding the description of the actual killing (the shepherd didn't see it), and by the humorous account of the shepherd when relating his story to the Señor Licenciado. Although not as dramatic a confrontation as that related in **"La cuesta de las comadres,"** the impact of the killing of Alcancía, which is left to the imagination of the reader, is nevertheless very impressive. The reader can only conjecture as to the reaction of the hunted man when he saw the hunter, whom he thought he had killed. Since the killing of Urquidi's family had already been described, a description of Alcancía's murder would have been an overstatement. There seems to be a narrative pattern in Rulfo's fiction, since the same thing happens in the story **"¡Diles que no me maten!"** wherein the killing of Don Lupe is described in detail, but not that of Juvencio. The description of their dead bodies is also similar. Juvencio's face was full of holes as if eaten by a coyote, while "the man" was found by the shepherd with "his neck full of holes as if they'd drilled him."

The archetypal structure of the hunt is reinforced by the imagery. The story opens with a description of the man trying to escape from his pursuer. "The man's feet sank into the sand, leaving a formless track, like some animal's hoof." Alcancía, like some animals, had only four toes on one foot. This is a realistic and not a fantastic motif, for it is explained in the course of the story how he had lost his toe. Urquidi, like a true hunter, studies the footprints and assures himself that he is on the right track, since he knows of Alcancía's deformation. "'Flat feet . . . with a toe missing. The big toe on his left foot. There aren't many around like that. So it'll be easy.'" The expressions he uses soon after are those of a man hunting an animal: "'I'll go down where he went down, following his tracks until I tire him out.'" And even when he thinks about the past, he compares him to a reptile: "'I waited a month for you, awake day and night, knowing you would come crawling, hidden like an evil snake.'"

"El hombre," like other stories and novels by Rulfo, contains elements of magical realism, from which it acquires its tone. In brief, magical realism, as opposed to the fantastic, can be defined as a confrontation with reality on the part of the characters. Reality, for them, is magical, and therefore it is necessary to interpret its significance, to go beyond its surface appearance and look for a deeper meaning. However, the world in which these characters move is the empirical world, not an invented world like those found in fantastic literature or science fiction. The characters take their world at face value, never believing that what is happening to them is a dream, an illusion, a vision, or any other subjective phenomena. They never doubt that what is taking place is actually happening in the objective world.

The night that his family was murdered by Alcancía, Urquidi had gone to bury a baby of his. Later, while hunting the killer, he thinks: "'I remember. It was on that Sunday when my newborn baby died and we went to bury it. We weren't sad. All I remember is that the sky was gray and the flowers we were carrying were faded and drooping as if they felt the sun's absence.'" At that moment, Alcancía was killing his family. Later Urquidi understands the significance of what had happened to the flowers. Blaming himself for having left his family alone, he thinks: "'The burial of my baby delayed me. Now I understand. Now I understand why the flowers wilted in my hand.'" He does not say what it was that he understood, but it is assumed that the withered flowers were trying to tell him that his family was being murdered, and the same can be said of the gray sky.

Other motifs of magical realism are the river, which prevents the murderer from escaping; voices, which do not seem to come from their speakers' mouths; tracks left by the fear and anxiety of the hunted one ("'fear always leaves marks'"); and finally the description of nature: the path that "climbed without stopping toward the sky"; and the river, giving the man a warning that it will swallow him like it "now and then . . . swallows a branch in its whirlpools, sucking it down without any noise of protest."

Another aspect of interest in the story **"El hombre"** is the narrative technique, which points toward the novel *Pedro Páramo*. In the short story Rulfo experimented with a dual point of view, moving from the mind of one character (the man who is being hunted) to the mind of the other (the hunter), often without any intervention on the part of the narrator to indicate who is speaking. This technique was to be employed extensively in his novel. Also, the story is fragmented, part being told by Alcancía, part by Urquidi, and part by the shepherd. The reader has to put it all together, like the pieces of a jigsaw puzzle. The events are not presented chronologically, but as they come to the mind of each speaker. In general, it can be said that **"El hombre"** contains certain innovations in content and technique which were to be developed in other stories and

finally perfected in the novel.

"En la madrugada"

Rulfo's **"At Daybreak"** is the story of the death of a farm owner, Don Justo Brambila, at the hands of Esteban, his farmhand, who is now in prison waiting to be tried and trying very hard to remember what actually took place the morning of the accident. The place where the action unfolds has the same name as that where the author himself spent his childhood, San Gabriel; and a farm owner is killed as the result of a struggle over a calf, as in the story **"Tell Them Not to Kill Me!"** **"At Daybreak"** opens with a long (long for Rulfo) description of the landscape at dawn, the town in the distance, and the actions of Esteban on his way back to the farm with his ten cows after a night's pasturing. This poetic introduction, in the third person, serves to set the tone of the story. It describes the coming of the new day, the time when the struggle between Esteban and Don Justo will take place. It is the time when nothing is clear yet; it is "at daybreak," and, just like nature, so now is the mind of Esteban, who cannot quite remember what actually took place at that hour. It is the time when the fog lifts, like a curtain, on a drama that is to take place on the stage. "The stars are turning white. The last twinkles go out and the sun bursts forth, making the blades of grass glisten."

When old Esteban reaches the gate of the corral, which has not been opened for him, he is forced to jump over the fence so as to open the gate for the cows. While he is lifting the gate bar he sees Don Justo coming from the loft with the latter's niece, Margarita, in his arms. He hides until Don Justo has crossed the corral to put Margarita back on her own bed, then opens the gate, lets the cows in, and begins to milk them. Becoming angry with a calf, he kicks it. At that moment Don Justo appears and gives Esteban such a beating that he is left, as he says, "'almost out cold among the rocks.'" And that is all he remembers, according to his account to the authorities, for Don Justo was found dead by Margarita and he was accused of the crime.

Through a flashback in third-person narrative the story is retold from the moment Don Justo placed Margarita on her bed. In the next room his crippled sister, Margarita's mother, is sleeping, but awakens just as Don Justo enters, and she asks, "'Where were you last night, Margarita?'" Justo Brambila leaves the room silently. It is six o'clock in the morning. He finds Esteban mistreating the calf and beats him. Then Don Justo feels himself "blacking out and falling back against the stone paving of the corral. . . . He didn't feel any pain, just a black thing that was dimming his thought until the obscurity became total." Old Esteban gets up when the sun is already high and goes home stumbling and moaning. At eleven o'clock Margarita discovers Don Justo's body.

Ambiguity regarding Don Justo's death is purposely introduced in the story. Although it is most likely that Esteban killed him with a stone, as others say, it is also possible, as Esteban says, that Don Justo died from internal causes. "'Well, they say I killed him. Maybe so. But he might've died from anger, too. He was very bad-tempered. . . . Everything made him angry.'" At the same time, Esteban had reasons for killing him. Inside him, resentment had been building up against his boss. He continues, saying: "'He didn't even like it that I was skinny. And how could I not be skinny when I hardly eat anything. Why, I spent all the time driving the cows. . . . It was just one eternal pilgrimage.'"

There is a great difference in the attitude toward death on the part of Esteban in this story and Juvencio in **"Tell Them Not to Kill Me!"** Juvencio wanted to live in spite of his age, while Esteban is resigned to die. "'Memory at my age,'" he says, "'is tricky; that's why I thank God that I won't lose much now if they finish off all my faculties, for I hardly have any left. And as for my soul, well, I'll commend it to Him, too.'" There is another great difference. While Juvencio is highly sensitive to his surroundings, loving the earth and life in all its aspects, Esteban is angry and displaces his internal conflicts by directing them against the animals he tends. Since his whole life has been spent with the cows, he treats them as if they were his equals, as when he wanted to enter the corral, he explained that he "'didn't say anything to the cows, or explain anything to them; I slipped off so they wouldn't see me or follow me.'"

In its structure this story is unlike any other by Rulfo. To develop the anecdote he alternates between an omniscient narrator and another narrator, Esteban, who uses the internal monologue. The characterization is done by means of the external portrait, as well as revelations by the personages themselves. There are subjective transcriptions of the characters' thoughts and feelings, a technique seldom used by Rulfo. After leaving Margarita, Don Justo ponders, "'If the priest would authorize this I'd marry her; but I'm sure he'll raise an awful fuss if I ask him. He'll say it's incest and will excommunicate us both. Better to leave things in secret.'" The omniscient narrator adds, "That's what he was thinking about when he found old Esteban struggling with the calf."

The story ends with another description of San Gabriel, this time at dusk, as if a curtain were descending upon the stage where the drama had been presented. "Over San Gabriel the fog was coming in again. The sun still was shining on the blue hills. A brownish spot covered the village. Then darkness came." That night the lights are not turned on in San Gabriel. Don Justo owned the lights.

There are certain aspects of **"At Daybreak"** that foreshadow the novel *Pedro Páramo*. Don Justo is very much like Pedro Páramo, a local *cacique* who becomes angry easily. He is in love with Margarita, a woman he cannot marry, just as Pedro Páramo is in love with Susana, a woman he cannot reach. The motif of incest appears in both works; Margarita is Don Justo's niece, and incestuous relations are suggested between Susana and her father in *Pedro Páramo*. Don Justo is killed by a cowhand, and Páramo by a mule driver. Both killers have grievances against their superiors. When Don Justo and Pedro die, the two towns

mourn. **"At Daybreak"** could very well have been a chapter of the novel; however, it has the structure of a short story, since the important thing is not the fate of the characters (Don Justo and Esteban) as it is in the novel, but the anecdote, a single incident about the killing of his boss by a servant.

"Luvina"

Of the three types of stories mentioned by critics, those of personage, action, and ambience, **"Macario"** corresponds to the first, **"El llano en llamas"** to the second, and **"Luvina"** to the third. The ambience story (*cuento de ambiente*) is a narrative form in which turning point and outcome are not the most important elements (in fact, they could even be omitted); the anecdote is so diluted that it often disappears; but the ambience receives all the attention and becomes the central element of narrative. This does not mean, however, that there is no theme or action, that it is a paralyzed story, a sketch, or a verbal landscape. In **"Luvina,"** there is a central character, a teacher who has lived in Luvina for some years and is now at an inn elsewhere, remembering and relating his experiences to another teacher who is on his way to the same town. The teacher's experiences in Luvina constitute the plot, a well-structured action motivated by the nature of the physical environment of the place, and are told by him in a long dialogue to his silent partner. Luvina, the town where the teacher had taken his wife, Agripina, and his children, had such a powerful influence on him that it changed the course of his life. The story ends when the narrator, who is drinking and finding it difficult to remember, slumps over the table and falls asleep.

There are two types of space in the story, one objective—the inn where the story is being told, and another subjective—Luvina as remembered by the teacher. A contrast is established between the two in order to bring out the stark nature of Luvina, which has become an obsession with the teacher. Luvina is a desolate place, no different from a ghost town, although some people manage to survive there in spite of its deadliness. The stark environment becomes even more fatal by the contrasting description of the place where the story is being told, a place where there is life, food, children playing, and even a river. In Luvina there is only death. In the world of the theater it would appear as purgatory, not far from hell. "'San Juan Luvina. That name sounded to me like a name in the heavens. But it's purgatory. A dying place where even the dogs have died off.'" It is located on the top of a hill, covered by the dust of a gray stone which the constant black wind blows over people and things. When there is a full moon some people can even see that black wind along the streets bearing behind it a black blanket. The narrator says that he never saw it, but he saw something that affected him much more, the ever-present image of despair. And yet, the few inhabitants dreaded the hour when the wind died, for "'When that happens,'" the people say, "'the sun pours into Luvina and sucks our blood and the little bit of moisture we have in our skins.'"

In **"Luvina"** Rulfo creates a magic atmosphere by combining realistic and fantastic elements and motifs. Luvina is "'the place where sadness nests. . . . And you can almost taste and feel it, because it's always over you, against you, and because it's heavy like a large plaster weighing on the living flesh of the heart.'" The black wind "'scratches like it had nails; you hear it morning and night, hour after hour without stopping, scraping the walls, tearing off strips of earth, digging with its sharp shovel under the doors, until you feel it boiling inside of you as if it was going to remove the hinges of your very bones.'"

As the story unfolds the reader passes from the real to the unreal, from the objective world to a phantasmagoric environment. The motifs of the real world are presented as a counterpoint to the fantastic, unreal world of Luvina. The description of Luvina anticipates, to a certain extent, that of Comala in Rulfo's novel *Pedro Páramo,* after the *cacique* has died and the community has become a ghost town, a dead town.

"La noche que lo dejaron solo"

Among the stories that have the Revolution as a subject are **"The Burning Plain,"** which treats of the struggle against Victoriano Huerta, and **"The Night They Left Him Alone,"** about the Cristero Revolt of 1926-1929, the religious war which was the result of the conflict between church and state during the presidency of Plutarco Elías Calles. In both stories the heroes are men fighting federal troops, and the action is seen from their perspective. In the first story the narrator is a common soldier, **"El Pichón,"** while in the latter the action is presented from the point of view of an omniscient narrator.

Three *cristeros,* so called because their war cry was *¡Viva Cristo Rey!* ("Long Live Christ the King!"), Feliciano Ruelas, a young boy, and his two uncles, Tanis and Librado, are bringing arms to their men, who are led by "El Catorce." Unable to stay awake any longer, Feliciano falls asleep while his two uncles keep on walking. Feliciano sleeps the rest of the night and part of the next morning. When he finally arrives at the place where they were to meet their fellow *cristeros,* he discovers that the *Federales* have captured and hanged his two uncles and are waiting for him, for they knew there were three. However, Feliciano is able to flee from them.

This simple anecdote is given significance not by the realistic incidents, as was done in **"El llano en llamas,"** or by the tragedy of the two uncles, but by the way in which Feliciano's life is saved. The story opens with Feliciano ahead, urging his uncles to hurry, "'Why are you going so slow? . . . Don't you have the urge to get there soon?'" In spite of his urgency, he falls behind. Why? Because *el sueño* ("sleep") gets on his back and forces him to stop to rest. "Sleep clouded his thoughts." Sleep gets on his back and forces him to stop walking. This could be interpreted as a natural happening—Feliciano falls asleep in spite of his desire to get the arms to his companions as soon as possible. However, the boy sees sleep "coming toward him, surrounding him, trying to find the place where he was the tiredest, until it was above him, over his

back, where his rifles were slung." He slowly falls behind, starts to nod, and "The others passed him by; now they were far ahead, and he followed, nodding his sleepy head." The weight of the rifles and the weight of sleep on his back finally make him stop, and he falls asleep leaning against a tree trunk. He does not awaken until dawn, but believing that it is night falling, he goes back to sleep and does not get up until the noise of some mule drivers wakes him up, with the sun already high.

If Feliciano is saved from the fate of his two uncles it is because, as the narrator suggests, sleep knew what awaited him if he kept going. Nor can it be said that this was a ruse on the part of Feliciano because he feared what was ahead. There is evidence in the story to show that he was a brave boy. One of the soldiers who caught his uncles says, "'They say the third one is just a boy, but all the same he was the one who laid the ambush for Lieutenant Parra and wiped out his men.'" If he remained behind it was because he was overpowered by a force beyond his control.

A possible interpretation of this story is through the concept of magical realism. The boy sees sleep, feels its weight upon his back, and falls asleep against his will. Unlike the story **"El hombre,"** wherein the perspective is that of the characters, the magical occurrences in **"La noche que lo dejaron solo"** are told by an omniscient narrator in third person, and not directly by Feliciano in an interior monologue. The introduction of this magic motif gives to the anecdote a dimension that separates it from a simple, ordinary story. If not as powerful as **"El hombre"** or other Rulfo stories, it nevertheless displays his characteristic style, conciseness, organization of material, and thematic expression.

"Acuérdate"

"Remember" is the story of a maladjusted man, Urbano Gómez, as reconstructed by one of his former classmates, the unnamed narrator, who is trying to stimulate the memory of another classmate, who remains silent. The technique is that of the small-town gossip with total recall who knows the life history of every inhabitant and assumes that others also remember it in every detail. The story opens with "Remember" and the speaker uses "Remember," "Try to remember," "Remember that," or "You ought to remember" throughout the story so that his classmate can recall what happened to Urbano Gómez, a former inhabitant of the village. "Remember Urbano Gómez, Don Urbano's son, Dimas's grandson, the one who directed the shepherd's songs and who died reciting the 'cursed angel growls' during the influenza epidemic. That was a long time ago, maybe fifteen years. But you ought to remember him." Often more details are added to help the listener remember. After describing one of Fidencio Gómez's daughters as being quite tall and having blue eyes, a girl whom the townspeople believed was not his, he adds, "and, if you want any further description, she suffered from hiccups." Thus, by adding one insignificant detail to another, the narrator ends by giving a complete picture of the town's life. Like putting together the pieces of a jigsaw puzzle, the reader puts together fragments of the story until he gets the complete picture not only of Urbano's family but also of the whole village. An amusing miniature portrait of one of the inhabitants is that of Urbano's mother:

> Remember they called his mother the "Eggplant" because she was always getting into trouble and every time she ended up with a child. They say she had a bit of money, but she used it all up in the burials, because all her children died soon after they were born and she always had masses sung for them, bearing them to the graveyard with music, and a choir of boys who sang "hosannas" and "glories" and that song that goes "Here I send thee, Lord, another little angel." That's how she got to be poor—each funeral cost her a lot because of the [cinnamon-flavored] drinks she served the guests at the wake. Only two of them lived, Urbano and Natalia, who were born poor, and she didn't see them grow up because she died in her last childbirth, when she was getting along in years, close to fifty.

After giving the life history of Urbano's family the narrator turns his attention to Urbano's private life, beginning with his schooldays, when he used to get the best of his schoolmates by selling them everything he could get his hands on. The reasons for his turning bad are not clear to the narrator, who says only, "Maybe he was just that way right from birth." Urbano is expelled from school before the fifth year "because he was found with his cousin Stuck Up down in a dry well playing man and wife behind the lavatories." He is punished at school and at home, and as a result he leaves, only to return years later as a policeman and filled with hate. He kills Nachito, his brother-in-law, after Nachito serenades him with his mandolin. Urbano tries to escape but is arrested. "They say that he himself tied the rope around his neck and even picked out the tree of his choice for them to hang him from." The story ends with the narrator telling his listener that he surely must remember Urbano "because we were classmates at school, and you knew him just like I did."

The conversational tone of the monologue adds credibility to the story. A contrast is established between the narrator, who has total recall, and the person to whom he is talking, who apparently cannot remember Urbano. The many details remembered by the narrator, often irrelevant, amusing, and insignificant, also add credibility. By this technique the author restores the life of the village as it was fifteen years earlier, and reconstructs the nature of the personal relationships existing among the inhabitants. Yet, this is not a simple social document, but a well-constructed short story centered on the character of Urbano Gómez. Although his life is a tragedy, it is told in a light, matter-of-fact style due to the attitude of the narrator toward the events he is remembering. This establishment of distance makes even the death of Urbano humorous, as it is presented in terms that border on the comic rather than on the tragic. The narrator, an expert raconteur, is also characterizing himself, and his personality comes through as clearly as that of Urbano. He is the typical small-town gossip with nothing to do but inquire into the lives of his fellow villagers. Nevertheless, he has a function in the town: remembering its history. He represents the historical consciousness of the village. Without him and his memory the village, like so many small towns everywhere, would not exist. In this character Rulfo has re-created an archetype, the storyteller who is also the small-town recorder of life in the community.

"No oyes ladrar los perros"

Conflict between father and son is common in Rulfo's fiction. **"No Dogs Bark"** is perhaps one of the most representative stories of this nature. The conflict here is between Ignacio and his father, whose name is not revealed. The structure of the story is made unique by establishing a dialogue between Ignacio, who is wounded, and his father, who is carrying him on his shoulders, at night, to the town of Tonaya. Since Ignacio's legs cover his father's ears, he cannot hear the dogs from the town barking and therefore does not know if they have arrived at the town, or if they are even close to it. He is anxious to hear the dogs, for that means that he can unload his heavy burden and that Ignacio can receive medical treatment. He does not dare put him down on the road for fear that he could never lift him up again. When he finally reaches the town and puts him down, he hears all the dogs barking. "'And you didn't hear them, Ignacio?'" he said. "'You didn't even help me listen.'" With these words the story ends. And the reader assumes, as the narrator suggests, that Ignacio is dead.

While carrying Ignacio, his father scolds him for giving his parents so much trouble. Ignacio's last words are, "'Give me water,'" and "'I'm awful thirsty and sleepy.'" After that, "His feet began to swing loosely from side to side. And it seemed to the father that Ignacio's head, up there, was shaking as if he were sobbing." When Ignacio asked for water, it reminded his father of the time when his son was born and of his being thirsty all the time. In this way a contrast is established between life and death. "'I remember,'" the father tells him, "'when you were born. You were that way then. You woke up hungry and ate and went back to sleep. Your mother had to give you water, because you'd finished all her milk.'"

Not much is revealed about how Ignacio got into trouble. After he is dead, his father feels thick drops, which may be blood, falling on his hair. He thinks Ignacio is crying, and tells him, "'Are you crying, Ignacio? The memory of your mother makes you cry, doesn't it? But you never did anything for her. You always repaid us badly. Somehow your body got filled with evil instead of affection. And now you see? They've wounded it. What happened to your friends? They were all killed. Only they didn't have anybody.'" Although he is angry at Ignacio for causing them so much grief, the father still has affection for his son. This is revealed by the alternating use of the familiar *tú* and the formal *usted*. The use of *usted* serves to establish distance. With *usted* displeasure can be expressed. When Ignacio begs his father to put him down, for he wants to sleep a little, his father tells him, "'Duérmete allí arriba. Al cabo te llevo bien agarrado'" ("'Sleep up there.

After all, I've got a good hold on you'"). But immediately after that, the father changes his tone:

> —Todo esto que hago, no lo hago por usted. Lo hago por su difunta madre. Porque usted fue su hijo. Por eso lo hago. Ella me reconvendría si yo lo hubiera dejado tirado allí, donde lo encontré, y no lo hubiera recogido para llevarlo a que lo curen, como estoy haciéndolo. Es ella la que me da ánimos, no usted. Comenzando porque a usted no le debo más que puras dificultades, puras mortificaciones, puras vergüenzas.

> ("I'm not doing all this for you. I'm doing it for your dead mother. Because you were her son. That's why I'm doing it. She would've haunted me if I'd left you lying where I found you and hadn't picked you up and carried you to be cured as I'm doing. She's the one who gives me courage, not you. From the first you've caused me nothing but trouble, humiliation, and shame.")

And then again, "'Mira a ver si ya ves algo. O si oyes algo. Tú que puedes hacerlo desde allá arriba, porque yo me siento sordo'" ("'See if you can't see something now. Or hear something. You'll have to do it from up there because I feel deaf'"). Ignacio, on the other hand, uses only the familiar *tú* when talking to his father.

"No Dogs Bark" reveals Rulfo at his best as a short-story writer. In four pages he presents a drama in which physical and emotional tensions are orchestrated with great skill. By having the narrator recall Ignacio's past life at the moment of his death, Rulfo sets in opposition two climactic moments endured by all human beings. At the same time he touches upon a deep archetypal conflict, that of father and son. By limiting the time, and by placing the events at night, under a full moon, he adds a new dimension to the simple anecdote.

"Paso del Norte"

"Paso del Norte" is the old name of Ciudad Juárez, in the state of Chihuahua, Mexico. The protagonist's experiences after leaving Paso del Norte in trying to cross the river and enter the United States without documents are recounted in a dialogue between father and son after the latter returns to his home in Jalisco. Although his trip is not dramatized in the story, there is a short scene that takes place in Tlatelolco, a suburb of Mexico City, where the protagonist works unloading freight cars in order to save up the two hundred pesos needed for the *coyote* who is to take him into the United States. However, he never reaches his destination, because, as he was crossing the river with some others, "'They peppered us with bullets until they killed all of us . . . while they flashed the lights on us when we were crossing the river.'" His companion, Estanislado, is killed in the middle of the river and he himself is wounded in the arm. He is found on the Mexican side by an Immigration officer, given the fare home, and told never to come back there again.

As do many immigrants to the United States, this man had left his family in Mexico. He entrusted his father with the care of his wife, Tránsito, and their five children, but, upon his return, he finds that his wife has run off with a mule driver and that his father has sold his house in order to take care of the children. And yet, after all these misfortunes, the protagonist has not lost faith. Since his father claims that he still owes him thirty pesos, he promises to get a job and repay him. For the time being, he is going after his wife.

In **"Paso del Norte"** Rulfo has combined several themes and motifs already present in some of his other stories: hunger, poverty, and the conflict between father and son. But there are new elements: the plight of the rural people who migrate to the United States to escape the misery in which they live; the *coyote* system, which exploits them by taking advantage of their ignorance; and the creation of a character who, in the face of severe adversity, does not lose his faith. Is he, as his father insists, too stupid to realize that he has been taken in? Or is the story an indictment against the uncaring attitude of the father toward his son and his son's family; or against the whole system that forces rural people, however ambitious and hard-working they may be, to a life of poverty, misery, and despair, without hope except for the abandonment of country, family, and friends? These are some of the questions that Rulfo raises in **"Paso del Norte."**

Unfortunately, the story was omitted from the second edition of *El llano en llamas* (1970). When asked why it was not included, Rulfo replied that it was the editor's decision but that he didn't mind since he considered **"Paso del Norte"** to be flawed. "It had two transitions difficult to unite: the moment when the man goes to look for work as a *bracero* in the United States and when he returns. There is an internal theme that is not well elaborated, that is not even worked out. I would liked to have worked on that story more."

"Anacleto Morones"

In **"Anacleto Morones,"** a story slightly different from the others collected in this first edition of *The Burning Plain,* irony predominates. The story centers upon the questionable character of Anacleto Morones, a religious leader and *curandero* who is either a fake or a holy man, depending upon whose story the reader wants to believe—that of the narrator, who was Anacleto's assistant, or that of the ten church women who want to sanctify him. These women have come all the way from Amula to Lucas Lucatero's home to ask him to testify as to the saintliness of Anacleto, since he knew him well and had married his daughter. Lucas knew Anacleto well enough to believe that he was a fraud and an evil man. His daughter, he tells the women, was even carrying his own child, that being the reason why Anacleto had married her off to Lucas. The women are openly insulted by Lucas and incensed by his blasphemies about Anacleto but insist that he accompany them back to Amula even though they know him to be a liar and a scoundrel. "'The priest recommended that we bring someone who had known him well and for some time back, before he became famous for his miracles.'"

The two perspectives in the story are completely contradictory. According to Lucas, the women want to sanctify a lecherous man. Lucas accuses him of being a religious charlatan and a living devil who "'left this part of the country without virgins.'" Before the visit is over, two of the women confess that they had spent the night, although innocently, with Anacleto, and another accuses Lucas of being the father of her stillborn child. Pancha, who had stayed behind after the other women had left, agrees to sleep with Lucas but later tells him, "'You're a flop, Lucas Lucatero. You aren't the least bit affectionate. Do you know who was really loving? . . . The Holy Child Anacleto. He knew how to make love.'" Was Pancha just trying to get even with Lucas, who had insulted her by requesting that she trim off the hairs from her lips before they make love? Or was she really telling the truth?

On the other hand, according to the women, Lucas is a born liar. "'We don't believe you, Lucas, not for a minute do we believe you. . . . You were always quite a liar and a false witness.'" And in response to Lucas's accusation of Anacleto's incestuousness, they say, "'You've always been one for making up tales.'"

However, Lucas does lie to the women when he tells them that he does not know what has happened to Anacleto. The women think that Anacleto is dead. "'He's in heaven. Among the angels. That's where he is.'" But at the end of the story, in a dialogue that had taken place between Lucas and Anacleto, now reconstructed in the mind of Lucas, the reader learns that there had been an argument between them over the property, and that now the Holy Child is buried in his son-in-law's back yard. "And now Pancha was helping me put the stones over him again without suspecting that underneath lay Anacleto and that I was doing that for fear he would come out of his grave to give me a bad time again. He was so full of tricks. I had no doubt he would find some way to come to life and get out of there."

Through a combination of techniques—question and answer; interior monologue; insinuation; ambiguity; and undocumented statements—Rulfo constructs a fast-moving story and integrates the diverse points of view, each with its own credibility, without revealing the true nature of the events that took place in the past. He skillfully treats the sensitive topics of incest and religious quacks with irony and even humor. There is also the use of a technique not often seen in Rulfo: the holding back of information in order to maintain the interest of the reader. The last question—Who is telling the truth?—is never resolved, nor are the circumstances regarding Anacleto's death.

As the longest of Rulfo's stories, **"Anacleto Morones"** has the characteristics of a short novelette, such as the introduction of several characters who have well-developed personalities, each one of whom would be worthy of using in another story. In 1960 Miguel Sabido adopted the story to the theater, and it was presented with a degree of success. A motion picture based on **"Anacleto Morones"** and another Rulfo story, **"El día del derrumbe,"** was produced in 1972 under the title *El rincón de las vírgenes*

[*The virgins' corner*]. Its director, Alberto Isaac, has said that these two stories held a great attraction for him which he could not resist. "'It was a very difficult challenge facing me,'" he says, "'since I had to find the relation between them—in other words, between **"El día del derrumbe"** and **"Anacleto Morones."** At first glance they're very different pieces and to find a connecting thread took a lot of work on my part. Certainly the central character of **"Anacleto Morones"** was played by El Indio Fernández.'" There is no question that there is some relationship between these two stories, especially the humorous aspect, but the differences predominate.

"El día del derrumbe"

"The Day of the Landslide" first appeared in August 1955 in the literary supplement *México en la Cultura* of the newspaper *Novedades* of Mexico City. It was added to the stories of *El llano en llamas* beginning with the 1970 edition. It is the only story in which Rulfo uses humor to present his subject matter. The one closest to it in this respect is **"Anacleto Morones,"** and it was perhaps this element that led Alberto Isaac to combine them into one single story in his movie *El rincón de las vírgenes*. There is, however, a great difference in the type of humor used in the two stories. In **"Anacleto Morones"** black humor predominates. Lucas ridicules religion and all it stands for—miracles, church women, saintliness, prayer, and even death. This scorn is directed toward a man who takes advantage of the religious beliefs of the people in order to deceive them for his own benefit. In **"El día del derrumbe,"** the sarcasm centers upon the inflated, insensitive, and often vulgar politician who also deceives the people for his own gain. The characterization in this story borders on caricature. The governor who visits the small town of Tuxcacuexco to survey the damage caused by an earthquake is a politician whose only concern is eating: "'People were breaking their necks straining them so much to see the governor and talking about the way he'd eaten the turkey and had he sucked on the bones and how fast he was scooping up one tortilla after another and spreading them with guacamole sauce. . . . And him so calm, so serious, wiping his hands on his socks so as not to mess up the napkin he only used to whisk his moustache from time to time.'" At speech time he delivers an oration full of meaningless rhetoric: "'People of Tuxcacuexco . . . I, considering the basis of my ontological and human concept, I say: It fills me with pain! with the pain brought on by the sight of the tree felled in its first efflorescence.'" The banquet turns into a free-for-all when the town's drunkard begins to chorus the governor's remarks with the word "'Exactly.'" When they try to stop him he takes out his pistol and begins to shoot over their heads, and the fight spreads to the street. The cost of the damage done, plus the money spent by the town to feast the governor, exceed the damage done by the earthquake.

The recounting of this simple anecdote is as important as the story itself. In the form of a dialogue between Melitón and an unnamed narrator, who is apparently talking to a group of people, Rulfo is able to create the illusion of reality. The story is unfolded by frequent inquiries on the part of the narrator, who wants to know if Melitón remembers certain details regarding the event. Melitón seems to have a good memory for he remembers the day better than the narrator and even recites the governor's speech, which he had memorized. When asked if he remembers "'what that guy recited,'" he answers, "'I remember all right, but I've repeated it so many times it's getting to be a pain in the neck.'" The story opens with the narrator's trying to remember when the earthquake took place, "'This happened in September. Not in September of this year but last year. Or was it the year before last, Melitón?'" and ends when he finally remembers, "'Now I'm beginning to remember that the roughhouse was around the twenty-first of September; because my wife had our boy Merencio that day, and I got home very late at night, more drunk than sober.'"

This story is the only one in which Rulfo uses humor to treat a political theme. Criticism of the government, which had appeared in former Mexican short stories, is not common in his fiction. There is a precedent for **"El día del derrumbe"** in stories by both Gregorio López y Fuentes and Francisco Rojas González, who used the same device of a politician visiting a small town to see how he can help the people. But Rulfo's story stands out over those of his predecessors because of its incisive humor which he applies to his characterization of the governor to a degree still unsurpassed in contemporary Mexican literature.

"La herencia de Matilde Arcángel"

This story first appeared in March 1955 in the periodical *Cuadernos Médicos* of Mexico City, was added to the collection *El llano en llamas* beginning with the edition of 1970 (145-52), and translated in 1966 by Margaret Shedd under the title **"Matilde Arcángel."** As in some other stories by Rulfo, the conflict here is between father and son, but with a variation, for the son triumphs over his father. The scene in which the body of the father, Euremio Cedillo, is brought into town by his son is reminiscent of that found in **"¡Diles que no me maten!"** However, the action here is seen through the perspective of a third party, Tranquilino Barreto, a mule driver who was Euremio's *compadre* and therefore the godfather of Euremio, Jr. He has a set mind and is very opinionated. He says to his audience, for instance, that Corazón de María, their town, is where runts come from, and adds, "I hope that none of you will be offended, but that's my opinion and I stick to it." Tranquilino is narrating an incident to these people which had occurred sometime before. He had been Matilde's sweetheart and was planning on marrying her, but he made the mistake of introducing her to Euremio, who was to be his best man. Soon after that Matilde married Euremio and later had their first child, whom they named after the father. Coming back from the church after the baptism the boy, according to the father's story, gave a hoot like an owl which frightened the horse that the mother and child were riding. Matilde fell and was killed, but managed to save the child by protecting him with her body. From that time on the father carried a hatred for his son, whom he blamed for the mother's death. Later the son, who has learned to play the flute, joins a band of

revolutionaries; and the father, to get even with him, joins the government's troops. The son survives, but the father is killed, presumably by his son, for the boy brings his father's body back to the town. "He rode the animal's haunches, and in his left hand was the flute, which he played with all his might. With his right hand he balanced a corpse slung across the saddle, his father."

Tranquilino, who never stopped loving Matilde, is biased and blames the elder Euremio for her tragic death. "We buried her. That mouth which for me had been impossible to reach was filled with earth. We watched while she sank into the pit of that grave until we couldn't even see the outline of her body. And there, standing like a tree trunk, was Cedillo. I was thinking, 'If only she had been left in peace in Chupaderos she might be alive. . . .'" The father is presented as tall and brawny, and the son as weak, "and some people thought this included his mind." His frailty, according to Tranquilino, was not only the result of the accident, but also of the psychological impact of the atmosphere prevailing in his father's home, for "if he looked limp and disjointed . . . it was because he was crushed under a hate as heavy as a millstone. I think his misfortune was to have been born." On the other hand, the father was a "lusty man, so tall it made you mad just to stand next to him and heft the strength of him, if only by looking at him." The father's hatred is so intense that the mere presence of his son seemed to make his blood curdle. In order to deprive his son of his inheritance, he sells his property bit by bit and spends the money on drinking. Yet, ironically, it is the weak son that survives, and the strong father who succumbs.

In **"La herencia de Matilde Arcángel,"** as in most of Rulfo's stories, there is not only the anecdote that is important, but also the act of narrating. The many rhetorical references to this action, on the part of Tranquilino, constitute a story in itself. He begins, as is customary in traditional stories, by stating that what he is going to tell his audience took place sometime before: "Not long ago in Corazón de María there lived a father and a son known as the hermits." After a short digression about how people felt when in the presence of Cedillo, he says, "To return to where we were, I was telling you about those men who lived in Corazón de María." In order that his audience understand the reason for the father's hatred, he must relate the accident that took Matilde's life: "To understand this we have to go back, before the boy was born." Like the traditional storyteller, common among mule drivers who often have to spend the night outdoors around the bonfire, Tranquilino promises his listeners all the details: "I have to tell you who and what Matilde Arcángel was. I won't leave anything out. I'll tell you slowly. After all, we have the whole of life before us." Often the story concerns himself, and he becomes a participant in the story that he is telling his audience. "I'm a muleteer, and it's because I like it, because I like to talk to myself while I'm walking the mountain roads. But the roads wandering in her were longer than all the others of my life and I knew I'd have to follow them because I would never stop loving her." Apparently, some of his listeners are strangers, for he finds it necessary to introduce himself, "Tranquilino

Barreto, your humble servant." As do all experienced story-tellers, he repeats some of the details for emphasis so that his audience can savor their full significance. The statement, "But what everybody always knew was that he hated his son," which has to do with the story he is telling, is followed by, "I was telling you about that at the beginning," which has to do with the structure of the tale. After another digression he goes on with the story, "Well, to get ahead with the thing, one quiet heavy night . . . some rebels rode into Corazón de María." From here on he finishes the story without further interruption. These rhetorical devices have the function of establishing distance between the audience and the event related by the story-teller, used so skillfully by Rulfo here and in most of his short stories.

Stephen Boldy (essay date 1986)

SOURCE: "Authority and Identity in Rulfo's *El llano en llamas*," in *MLN: Modern Language Notes,* Vol. 101, No. 2, March, 1986, pp. 395-404.

[*In this essay, Boldy examines the role of discourse in Rulfo's short fiction.*]

There is a point in most of the stories of *El llano en llamas* where an individual comes up against the discourse of others, in the form of an accusation or declaration, and is annulled by it. His memory, knowledge, consciousness, sanity or even identity is destroyed. My first task is to describe the mechanism of that loss of consciousness. Though the alien discourse originates in a clearly identifiable figure of authority (*cacique,* parent, priest, government, army, the law), it is usually mediated by an unidentifiable impersonal or plural voice. The second question is thus why the voice of authority has become so fragmented, impersonal and empty. Three factors recur constantly: violence, transgression of structure, often family structure, its most basic form, and the death of the father. I have found it difficult to establish any strict hierarchy between these factors, any clear process of cause and effect. Rather they seem to be linked in an ever degenerating vicious circle.

"En la madrugada" provides a labyrinthine example of the mediation of the annihilating word, when the cowherd Esteban is accused of killing his land-owner employer: "Me llegaron con ese aviso. Y que dizque yo lo había matado, dijeron los díceres. Bien pudo ser; pero yo no me acuerdo." In **"Macario"**, the repetition by the authoritarian figure of the *madrina* of the plural accusation that the boy had attacked a woman turns the report into an absolute truth for him, again to the detriment of his knowledge and memory: "Yo no sé por qué me amarrará las manos; pero dice que porque dizque luego hago locuras. Un día inventaron que yo andaba ahorcando a alguien; que le apreté el pescuezo a una señora nada más por nomás. Yo no me acuerdo. Pero, a todo esto, es mi madrina la que dice lo que yo hago y ella nunca anda con mentiras." In **"Diles que no me maten"**, the accusing voice of the colo-nel comes from inside a building, and is relayed through subalterns. The subsequent punishment not only kills, but makes the accused unrecognizable: "Tu nuera y tus nietos te extrañarán [. . .]. Te mirarán a la cara y creerán que no eres tú."

A further grade of mediation is reached when the accusation is presented only in the discourse of the accused. In **"El hombre"**, the accusations made by the "señor licenciado" which arbitrarily turn the shepherd who has just reported a crime into an accomplice are reported only in the replies of the accused, who is reduced to bewilderment and ignorance: "De haberlo sabido" is all he can repeat. "Pero yo qué sabía?"; "Soy borreguero y no sé de otras cosas." The absorption of the other's words, however, finally produces an unjustified guilt, and thus a partial acceptance of the crime: "Eso que me cuenta [. . .] no me lo perdono." In **"Es que somos muy pobres"**, the guilt of the mother at her daughters' becoming prostitutes is also expressed in terms of not knowing and forgetfulness: "Mi mamá no sabe por qué Dios la ha castigado tanto [. . .]. Quién sabe de dónde les vendría [. . .] aquel mal ejemplo. Ella no se acuerda." There is nothing for her to remember, unless it be original sin: everything, including the title, shows that it is poverty and sociogeographical determinism which produce the prostitution. The alien discourse which gives her the feeling of having forgotten a crime is totally internalized, and is clearly that of the Church: "Todos fueron criados en el temor de Dios", she muses.

An unfounded accusation may create not only guilt but an actual repetition of the crime. In **"La Cuesta de las Comadres"**, the tyrannical authority of the Torricos cancels out in the consciousness of their neighbours what the latter know to be true. The narrator says that the land distribution programme had only given the Torricos a small plot, but that "a pesar de eso, La Cuesta de las Comadres era de los Torricos. [. . .] No había por qué averiguar nada. Todo el mundo sabía que así era." The accusation by Remigio Torrico that the narrator had killed his brother does not immediately expunge the memory that he had not done so: "Me acuerdo bien de que yo no lo maté." The accused rules out any dialogue with the accuser, and kills him. He now has another memory: "Así que cuando yo maté a Remigio Torrico [. . .] Me acuerdo que había una luna muy grande"; "Me acuerdo que eso pasó allá por octubre [. . .]. De eso me acuerdo." The accusation and the memory of the crime, with the difference of a Christian name, becomes true.

"Nos han dado la tierra" and **"El día del derrumbe"** depict government authority and show it to be purely linguistic. Its word is totally empty and despite or rather because of its emptiness, its effects are devastating. In the first story it takes the form of the decree of the peasants' ownership of a barren wasteland, and the refusal of their words of protest: "Pero no nos dejaron decir nuestras cosas"; "Pero él no nos quiso oír." The result is literally a drying up of their words, described in a manically repetitive paragraph: "No decimos lo que pensamos. Hace ya tiempo que se nos acabaron las ganas de hablar. [. . .] Uno platicaría muy a gusto en otra parte, pero aquí cuesta trabajo. Uno platica aquí y las palabras se calientan en la boca con el calor de afuera, y se le resecan a uno en la lengua hasta que acaban con el resuello. Aquí así son las cosas. Por eso a nadie le da por platicar." When one character does talk, it is to repeat as his own the word of authority: "Esta es la tierra que nos han dado." Very rightly, the others consider this a sign of madness: "Yo no digo nada. Yo pienso: 'Melitón no tiene la cabeza en su lugar. [. . .] Y si no, ¿por qué dice lo que dice?'" Lacan defines madness as being spoken by language rather than speaking it. The destruction of language as communication reduces the initial solidarity of the four characters to deafness, a deafness which perpetuates and generalizes that practiced by the official: "Yo ya no oigo lo que sigue diciendo Esteban." In **"El día del derrumbe"**, the word of authority similarly swamps the individual consciousness, dislodging his most personal interests. It is the account of an incredible feat of memory by a second character called Melitón, who repeats verbatim the words of another: the speech by the governor who comes to make a lengthy but vacuous promise of aid after an earthquake. The failure to help is again perpetuated in the listeners when the narrator *forgets* to call a mid-wife for the birth of his son. Not knowing as well as memory/forgetfulness also reappears in the song which duplicates the story's content: "No sabes del alma las horas de luto."

A further insight into the process is provided by **"Talpa"** and **"En la madrugada"**. They illustrate well the discontinuity between the exercisers of force and authority (the brother and wife of Tanilo, and don Justo) and the resultant fragmented and empty word which is presented as imposing death and unconsciousness. In **"Talpa"**, the desire of the killers and of the victim is formally the same: the pilgrimage. The content of their desire is opposite: Talino seeks a miraculous cure for his illness, while the others calculate that the trip will kill him so that they will be left free to enjoy their adultery. When he does die after they oblige him to complete the journey, they are separated by guilt and cannot forget his corpse, while their positive memory is obliterated: "Y Natalia se olvidó de mí desde entonces." At the moment of his death, moreover, their desire and consciousness is replaced by a plural and impersonal discourse. While Tanilo is praying, a tear drops from his eye and puts his candle out, yet the light from a multitude of other candles in the church prevents him from realizing this. Parallel to this extinction, the prayers of the congregation cancel out his own, so that he has to shout to realize that he is praying: "Pero no se dio cuenta de esto; la luminaria de tantas velas prendidas que allí había le cortó esa cosa con la que uno se sabe dar cuenta de lo que pasa junto a uno. Siguió [. . .] rezando a gritos para saber que rezaba." When the candle as consciousness ("aquella cosa con la que uno se sabe dar cuenta"), and the discourse of desire (intercession with the Virgin for a cure) goes out, so he dies. In **"En la madrugada"**, Esteban's amnesia and loss of consciousness also coincides with the extinction of light: "Esa noche no encendieron las luces, de luto, pues don Justo era dueño de la luz." The ominously named *cacique,* don Justo, is the owner of light, of life and consciousness, yet when that power is exercised, he is dead. The word which extin-

guishes the light of consciousness becomes impersonal and plural: "Y que dizque yo lo había matado, dicen los díceres. Bien pudo ser; pero yo no me acuerdo." The father figure, the giver of language and identity, is absent and yet his force is present: he is both dead and alive. As Rulfo says of the faith of the characters of *Pedro Páramo,* his word is "uninhabited": "Aunque siguen siendo creyentes, su fe está deshabitada. No tienen un asidero, una cosa de donde aferrarse." This uninhabited word kills. The death of the father-figure thus seems to bring about a loss of identity. But, as we shall see, there is also a radical loss of consciousness and identity in the story before his death, which suggests either a previous death, or a chain of deaths.

The normal pattern, which could be adduced here, of the murder of the father and his return in the superego does not seem to operate, not least because the superego imposes prohibitions, structure, difference and thus identity, whereas all these things collapse in the stories. There is clearly a more complex and wider crisis in the role of the father and authority. **"No oyes ladrar los perros"** contains a typical inversion of the expected patterns. Ignacio has killed his *padrino,* a substitute father, and is thus the guilty party. Rulfo frequently describes guilt as a weight to be carried on one's back. Yet it is the father who carries the son on his back, and not vice-versa, as might be expected given the relation of guilt with the paternal structures of the superego.

The loss of consciousness and identity on the part of Esteban and don Justo before the latter's death foregrounds two more terms in the equation of the stories: violence and transgression against family structure. The two men, master and servant, are made identical, and thus lose their individual identities, by their transgressive actions during the early morning, which form a curious but well developed parallel. Esteban returns to the ranch with the cows; he finds the gate closed and, on receiving no answer, climbs in and opens up from inside. On glimpsing don Justo, he hides, fearing he will be rebuked: "Yo me escondí hasta hacerme perdedizo arrejolándome contra la pared, y de seguro no me vio. Al menos eso creí." He decides to separate a cow from its calf ("Ora te van a desahijar, motilona"), but reunites them out of pity. Don Justo also enters a prohibited area and separates a mother from a child: his niece Margarita, with whom he sleeps, from his invalid sister. Aware of the condemnation their relationship would bring from the priest, he decides to keep it secret: "Dirá que es un incesto y nos excomulgará a los dos. Más vale dejar las cosas en secreto." Both men thus hide from authority after breaking a family structure. Like Esteban, don Justo returns the daughter to the mother at dawn. In both cases, this precedes an explosion of verbal violence: Margarita is called "prostituta", and the calf "hijo de res", before being kicked for sucking too hard. Both men, *amo* and *criado,* are made equal by the transgression of an internalized prohibition: their breaking that structure annuls the structural difference between them. While in fear of father figures, both men are in turn nominal fathers themselves: Esteban of the calf and don Justo of the daughter of a widowed sister. They renegue on that role and leave it empty, bequeathing it in a debilitated state for others.

It is after these events that the violence takes place: don Justo beats Esteban for kicking the calf, and is later found dead, either from a blow by Esteban, which is unlikely, or from "coraje". Violence is itself a contagious force in society, dissolving of structure and identity. Whether because of this violence or the previous identification between the two men, don Justo's words are drained of meaning: "gritándole cosas de las que él nunca conoció su alcance." Within the concept of light as consciousness developed earlier, it is significant that neither can open his eyes during the fight: in the case of don Justo, "una nublazón negra le cubrió la mirada cuando quiso abrir los ojos"; and of Esteban, "no se supo cómo llegó a su casa, llevando los ojos cerrados." It is blindness, the extinction of the faculty which enables one to distinguish, to perceive differences, which confirms the loss of difference between them: "Quizá los dos estábamos ciegos y no nos dimos cuenta de que nos matábamos uno al otro."

The internalized authority of the priest and employer which was unable to check the transgression and violence, and contributes to alienate the subject from his own consciousness, becomes even more phantasmal, but more deadly, in the final extinction of Esteban's awareness of self, action, and reality: "Dicen que maté a don Justo. Bien pudo ser, pero no me acuerdo." The logic of cause and effect between the death of the father, transgression and violence is either cumulative, inverted, or circular. Circularity is suggested by the fact that at the beginning of the story Esteban's belly-button is cold: a strangely precise zone to be cold, but perhaps significantly the place where the umbilical cord is severed. It is cold after a fright from a *lechuza,* perhaps an "ánima en pena" like those which are encouraged to come out in the prayer which closes the story. The most likely "ánima en pena" is don Justo, who has not yet literally died. That previous, phantasmal death of the father-figure again produces loss of memory: "Yo tenía el ombligo frío de traerlo al aire. Ya no me acuerdo por qué."

The act of violence which is at least partially an effect in **"En la madrugada"** is the cause and starting point of the drama in **"El hombre"** and **"Diles que no me maten"**. Violence generates reciprocal violence, and the reciprocity has the effect of linking the antagonists to the extent that they lose their individual identity. In **"El hombre",** the reader experiences serious doubts as to whether the pursued and the pursuer are not one and the same, one a projection of the other's guilt, a doubt only dispelled when the pursued is found with various bullets in the back of his head. Loss of consciousness and identity is clearly shown here to be contagious: the phantasmal voice at the end accuses not one of the antagonists, but a witness, the shepherd in whom the stability of subject, truth and innocence is undermined nearly as fundamentally as in Esteban. In **"Diles que no me maten"**, a parallel situation is established between two fathers and two sons, one family in authority, a landowner and a colonel, and the other powerless. The violence of Juvencio Nava against

his *compadre* Guadalupe Terrero is reciprocated on him by the latter's son, with the result that his face, his identity, is destroyed by the bullets. The "tiros de gracia" which put him out of his thirty year long agony suggest that, like his victim, he had been virtually dead for that time. The voice which accuses him is the victim's son, the reciprocity of the violence being disguised by the impersonality of the son's official military role. The official discourse overlays the personal in the same way the opposing desires of the characters of **"Talpa"** are subsumed in their common participation in the mass pilgrimage. Given the links suggested earlier between the death of the father and the emptiness of language, it is significant that the official is an orphan. His formulation is echoed throughout Rulfo's tests: "Es algo difícil crecer sabiendo que la cosa de donde podemos agarrarnos para enraizar está muerta." This rootlessness causes and is reflected in the rootlessness of language: when the accused approaches the building where the colonel is waiting, "[estaba] esperando ver salir a alguien. Pero sólo salió la voz." The emptiness of his language annihilates the individuality of the accused, turning him into merely a body occupying a space: "No podría perdonar a ése, aunque no lo conozco; pero el hecho de que se haya puesto en el lugar donde yo sé que está, me da ánimos para acabar con él." This linguistic death foreshadows the literal destruction of the subject's face. The pattern is repeated in *Pedro Páramo*: the death of the father (Lucas Páramo) creates the annihilating discourse of the son (Pedro Páramo), which destroys the consciousness and individuality of others, reducing them to the uninhabited "murmullos" which are the truest expression of his tyranny.

In a few cases, we see the individual hit back with a counter-discourse. In **"La herencia de Matilde Arcángel"**, Euremio Cedillo's mother is dead, and his father, who considers him so little of an individual that he fails to give him a name different from his own, further attempts to annul him by consuming his inheritance, "con el único fin de que el muchacho no encontrara cuando creciera de donde agarrarse para vivir." The son's counter-discourse is the music of his flute, and for once the death of the tyrannical father seems to cause little trauma: "Venía en ancas con la mano izquierda dándole duro a la flauta, mientras que con la derecha sostenía, atravesado sobre la silla, el cuerpo de su padre muerto." Music is significantly not, however, the normal medium of the intersubjective communication which makes the individual an individual by meshing him dialectically with the discourse of others. And a more representative counter-discourse is the isolated delirium of madness, explored in the first story of the collection, **"Macario"**, and in the case of Susana San Juan in *Pedro Páramo*. After the death in life of her father in the mine-shaft, Susana loses her sanity, but gains a mad discourse of metonymical associations which is impervious to the word of Pedro Páramo and his lackey padre Rentería.

"Macario" contains all the elements of the constellation we have examined so far: the "condenaciones del señor cura", the negative authority of a substitute parent figure, *la madrina,* transgressive and basically incestuous sex between the young Macario and the maid, Felipa, the impersonal accusation of an act of violence which is not remembered. The death of parents is also present as the first element of the *histoire,* though it is characteristically placed last in the text: "sin pasar ni siquiera por el purgatorio, y yo no podré ver entonces ni a mi mamá ni a mi papá, que es allí donde están."

The text is articulated around a set of strict oppositions, starkly positive and negative. The father has been described as having a double role in the transmission of language and identity: he gives a name and a "no", an identity and the prohibitions which conform the structures within which identity is formed and developed. Though the duality of the role is inseparable in normality, when on the other hand the presence of the father is perceived as being empty, the duality increases and the "no" predominates. In various stories, after the collapse of the fullness of the father, his word polarizes into something approaching schizophrenia. In **"No oyes ladrar los perros"**, for example, the father carrying his son addresses him alternately as *tú* and *usted*; while the condemnatory *usted* voice is perceived as carrying the son sadistically to his death, the paternal *tú* carries him towards medical aid and possible recovery. Dolores Preciado similarly sends her son both to heaven and hell in Comala. In **"Macario"**, the originally whole presence of the mother is split into two opposite maternal figures: the kind and sensual maid Felipa, and the authoritarian *madrina*. Associated with this split are the oppositions between heaven and hell (where the two women pray respectively that he should go); frogs and toads (edible versus inedible); day and night; crickets and scorpions (beneficent versus maleficent). Such differences are simply exacerbations of normal conceptual and linguistic structures normally held in check by a healthy discourse.

The insanity of the protagonist, Macario, is defined only once, and a curious definition it is; he is mad because he is constantly hungry: "Dicen en la calle que yo estoy loco porque jamás se me acaba el hambre." His hunger is mad because it does not respect the oppositions described earlier as structuring the story: he eats not only frogs, but toads, "aunque no se coman"; the milk from Felipa's breasts though she is not his mother; "leche de chiva y también de puerca recién parida," both goat's milk which is normal and pig's milk which is not; "el garbanzo remojado que le doy a los puercos gordos y el maíz seco que le doy a los puercos flacos," food destined for animals not humans, and *both* strictly codified types without distinction. The curious equivalence between *comer* and *platicar* in a parallel sequence confirms that eating, like everything else in the story, becomes discourse: if he stops eating, he muses, he will die and go to hell; if he stops chatting to the listener-reader, he will fall asleep, not kill the frogs, and be taken to hell by the devils his aunt will invoke. If he does not want to go straight to hell, it is mainly because he would miss the chance of seeing his parents. His discourse is thus his only possibility of maintaining some of their vital presence. The connection between eating and thus talking and the recovery of the maternal presence is further suggested by the fact that by far his

favourite food is the milk from Felipa's breasts, "los bultos esos que ella tiene donde tenemos solamente las costillas," reflected in a far less positive manner in the "dos montoncitos" of food offered by the *madrina*.

Like his eating, the metonymic chains of Macario's *plática* are transgressive of normal difference: discrete objects become rootless signifiers which turn everything into a phantasm of the mother. The story opens with Macario out killing frogs. Abstracting phrases from the first page, we read: "Las ranas son verdes de todo a todo, menos en la panza. [. . .] Las ranas son buenas para hacer de comer con ellas. [. . .] Felipa tiene los ojos verdes como los ojos de los gatos [he means of course green like frogs]". Frogs are green; frogs are good to eat; Felipa's eyes are green . . . "Felipa is good to eat" is surely the conclusion of the sophism. And Felipa's food is the maternal milk. Macario's insatiable hunger ("Yo sé bien que no me lleno por más que coma todo lo que me den") is clearly equivalent to the absence and emptiness of the mother: this gap is a hungry vortex into which the whole of language is sucked until it signifies nothing but absence.

The story is almost entirely composed of warring discourses, one trying to cancel out the other, and corresponding to the two halfs of the word of the mother embodied by the *madrina* and Felipa. The crickets drown out the screams from Purgatory: "Felipa dice que los grillos hacen ruido siempre [. . .] para que no se oigan los gritos de las ánimas que están penando en el purgatorio." The drum stifles the condemnations of the priest: "aquel tambor se oye de tan lejos, hasta lo hondo de la iglesia y por encima de las condenaciones del señor cura." The croaking of the frogs prevents the *madrina* from sleeping: "la gritería de las ranas le espantó el sueño."

The counter-discourse of Macario's *plática* is destined to lose out. Felipa does not want him to harm the frogs, the frogs which are good to eat and lead him to the positive mother. But the language of the frogs keeps the negative god mother awake, and Macario is ordered to kill them. The reason why he must obey the *madrina* is overwhelmingly final: "Es mi madrina la que saca el dinero de su bolsa para que Felipa compre todo lo de la comedera." As the possessor of money, she is, like the "dueño de la luz" don Justo, the ultimate controller of discourse, consciousness and identity. It is also the *madrina* who decrees that Macario will go to hell for knocking his head against the floor. He beats his head because it sounds like a drum: the drum which cancelled out the "condenaciones del señor cura". To beat his head is thus equivalent to the self-destructive discourse of madness against the guilt imposed by the authoritarian father-figure. There is a typical Rulfo inversion or vicious circle here: the drumming of beating his head cancels out the condemnations, but he is condemned for it. The condemnation is previous to the guilty discourse which brings it about; as elsewhere, it is the condemnation which creates the crime. Guilt, obviously related here to the death of the parents, is previous, original, or at least inherited and self-perpetuating: hence presumably his acceptance of the accusation that he had attempted to throttle "una señora nada más por nomás".

The pattern, in this story at least, seems to be that the absence or death of the parents produces a rootlessness of language in the son, a splitting of the paternal word into positive and negative discourses, and guilt. The guilt embodied in the condemnatory paternal discourse is countered by the discourse of madness designed to recover the full presence of the mother. Because of its transgression of the categories of thought and difference, the meshing of the two languages is broken, and the individual isolated. The discourse of the other becomes fragmented and phantasmal. The "no" of the father, successively embodied in the "condenaciones del señor cura" and the financially backed injunctions of the *madrina* is finally articulated in the annihilating accusation of an anonymous and plural other, in which all notion of self is irreversibly lost: "Yo no sé por qué me amarrará mis manos; pero dice que porque luego hago locuras. [. . .] Yo no me acuerdo. Pero, a todo esto, es mi madrina la que dice lo que yo hago y ella nunca anda con mentiras."

Rulfo's own orphanhood, like that of César Vallejo, the loss of a centred, meaningful and beneficent domestic discourse, leads him to a painful but privileged consciousness of the emptiness of the language of society and authority which replaces it. All Mexicans become orphans with him, pawns in the vacuous discourse of a political power which likes to present itself as paternal. The characters of **"Luvina"** know better: "Pelaron sus dientes molenques y me dijeron que no, que el Gobierno no tenía madre." It may be over-optimistic to suggest that the awareness provoked in the reader of the extinction of the consciousness and word of the individual is in Vallejo's words "potente de orfandad".

Howard M. Fraser (essay date 1988)

SOURCE: "*Inframundo*: Juan Rulfo's Photographic Companion to *El llano en llamas*," in *Chasqui*, Vol. XVII, No. 2, November, 1988, pp. 56-74.

[*In the following essay, Fraser explores Rulfo's photographic vision of Mexico, contending that it underlies the visual qualities of the stories collected in* The Burning Plain.]

How do readers perceive literature, given the intricate linguistic process of encoding and decoding that occurs once the author places words on the printed page? It is evident that much of the "meaning" of this process, the affective value of literature, depends in large part on the visual interpretation of images and linguistic symbols. Especially during the past century, the advent of photography and cinema has served to expand the repertoire of visual stimuli in literature as well as to educate readers in the literary values of the visual media. We need only to consider the wealth of critical terms derived from the visual arts such as point of view, focus, flashback, and montage among others, to begin to appreciate the interrelationships of art forms.

In this regard, numerous literary works seem to have been written to be viewed as well as to be read. Altamirano's novel, *El Zarco* (1888), illustrates the romantic treatment of violence and the search for justice in nineteenth-century Mexico with visual contrasts between light and darkness symbolizing the eternal struggle between good and evil. This treatment is so telling that it has inspired a series of splendid woodcuts that portray the richness of visual imagery and exoticism of the original text. Azuela's *Los de abajo* (1915) is a series of vignettes of the Mexican Revolution with a vivid sense of photographic or even cinematographic framing and pacing. And Fuentes's *La muerte de Artemio Cruz* is a novelistic reworking of the film classic, *Citizen Kane,* complete with filmic techniques and entire scenes adapted to fiction.

When writers and photographers combine forces to document the world from their two perspectives, we as readers doubly profit from the experience, thanks to the illustration of the verbal images in photographs, and the captions for the illustrations in the written text. For example, the classic *Let Us Now Praise Famous Men,* the volume that James Agee and Walker Evans coauthored for the Farm Security Administration in the early forties, exposed in images and text the plight of sharecroppers during the Great Depression. In like fashion, when a single individual undertakes an exposée in both photographs and text, it is a most fortuitous event. Such is the case of the Mexican novelist and photographer Juan Rulfo, whose *Inframundo* and *El llano en llamas* can be viewed as complementary manifestations of a single reality, that of rural Mexico at midcentury. In this study, I will show how the images of Mexico contained in *Inframundo* reveal the background of Rulfo's homeland and how they underly the visual qualities of his short-story collection, **El llano en llamas**.

Inframundo is a mass-produced edition of a commemorative volume entitled *Juan Rulfo, homenaje nacional* originally brought out by the Instituto de Bellas Artes in 1980. Although conceived as an homage to Rulfo the writer of fiction, the book most likely will be prized as a showcase of the author's photographic talent that is only now being recognized on the Mexican cultural scene. According to Luis Leal [in his *Juan Rulfo,* 1983], photography was a lifetime hobby that "resulted in the publication of some photographs in magazines" and a series of photographs published in Rulfo's last book, *El gallo de oro.* One hundred photographs appear in *Juan Rulfo, homenaje nacional,* and Ediciones del Norte has republished most of these in both Spanish and English editions of *Inframundo.*

In scenes of Jalisco, his birthplace and setting of his fiction, Rulfo's lens reveals "un México inquietante . . . el drama de su Jalisco y de la pobreza." Although they were all taken during the decade and a half preceding the appearance of his two masterpieces, *Pedro Páramo* (1955) and **El llano en llamas** (1953), the photographs published in *Inframundo* have not been arranged chronologically. The editors, nonetheless, juxtapose various sequences that carry out similar ideas, and for the purposes of this "exhibition" of Rulfo's works, I have chosen to present three principal thematic areas in Rulfo's photographic vision of Mexico: Structures; Landscapes; and Portraits. It should be noted that Rulfo's work here is not staged or posed in any sense. He eschews topical groupings and captions as a clue to his pictures' power and meaning, but rather he seeks the precise visual image and frequently the photographic moment that gives definition to Mexico and its people.

Inframundo opens with a series of photographs of buildings in ashes. These striking views ("El incendio de Actipán"; "Ex-hacienda de Actipán) are appropriate depictions of the setting for *El llano en llamas*. The smoke emanating from the stately buildings indicates that there is a potentially violent story to be told here, something cataclysmic that has interrupted the order of things. The power of events has a life of its own. . . . Here, the flames of the *llano* and clouds of smoke dwarf the structure, and the aftermath of the catastrophe . . . indicates the indifference of the natural surroundings to tragedy in its midst.

Throughout this collection, Rulfo shows a profound fascination with old buildings, structures torn either by disaster . . . or by time itself. . . . His sense of contrast is wonderfully displayed . . . as he focuses on a doorway and wall whose original function, to protect the house from the elements, is now lost. Light streams through the door and open roof and illuminates the rough texture of the adobe blocks and the weathered boards around the doorway showing how the divisions between inside and out, land and man-made structure, has been erased. One photograph reveals the blurring of distinctions between the natural and man-made as a building's façade displays an anthropomorphic quality of a human face.

Crumbling structures are present in his fiction and underscore man's unrelenting struggle for survival against the elements and the sheer indifference of time itself. Reflecting this imagery of decay, one of Rulfo's stories depicts the disintegration of structures as a metaphor of the crumbling of institutions and of an entire way of life is "**Luvina.**" In the story, as he prepares to spend his first night in the remote village of Luvina, the narrator selects a place for his family to sleep, a church in ruins:

> Aquella noche nos acomodamos para dormir en un rincón de la iglesia, detrás del altar desmantelado. Hasta allí llegaba el viento aunque un poco menos fuerte. Lo estuvimos oyendo pasar por encima de nosotros, con sus largos aullidos; lo estuvimos oyendo entrar y salir por los huecos socavones de las puertas: golpeando con sus manos de aire las cruces del viacrucis: unas cruces grandes y duras hechas con palo de mezquite que colgaban de las paredes a todo lo largo de la iglesia, amarradas con alambres que rechinaban a cada sacudida del vento como si fuera un rechinar de dientes.

In several of Rulfo's photos of buildings in decay, the land seems to reclaim territory taken from it, as once-human structures dissolve into the earth. Such is the case in ["Nicho de Atlihuetzín, Tlax."], ["Bardas tiradas a la calle"], and ["Pecho de Angel"] in which the buildings

crumble revealing how the wind has worked away at the walls and shape of the structure, and plant life slowly invades the man-made space as nature reclaims it.

In *Inframundo* Rulfo expresses an adoration of the monumental in nature from lush forests and waterfalls ("Cascada de Tulantango"), to the high desert. In addition to these vistas depicting the breadth and depth of Mexico's landscape, Rulfo's photographs frequently express an interest in the angular and abstract, highlighting the resemblance between solid, man-made structures and natural forms. Note the interplay of light and dark in this view of a pyramid ("Pirámide de Tenayuca, Méx."), and the juxtaposition of the massive indigenous structure that seems to mimic the enormity and stability of a mountain ("Nevado de Colima"). Much in the way Georgia O'Keefe's paintings depict the flatness of the New Mexican desert and the abstract quality of the objects found there, Rulfo can project a flat, abstract vision of the earth, as in his bird's-eye view of a mountain range with the barrenness of a lunar landscape ("Nevado de Tolum").

Perhaps due to the aridity of his native region, Rulfo depicts the starkness of flora in his landscapes. Plants are cast in an almost pathetic, reverential pose, such as in the photograph of groping thistles rising from the desert floor, a silhouette later mirrored in the skeletal profiles of dead trees ("Tiempo de verano"; "Tiempo de sequía"). This view of the earth recurs in Rulfo's stories, as the theme of death is reflected in the landscape, such as the arid setting of "**No oyes ladrar los perros**" in which a man carries his dying son across the Jalisco desert and in "**El hombre,**" a tale of revenge, in which a man pursues the murderer of his family through the angular landscape of skeletal trees: "El cielo estaba tranquilo allá arriba, quieto, trasluciendo sus nubes entre la silueta de los palos guajes, sin hojas. No era tiempo de hojas. Era ese tiempo seco y roñoso de espinas y de espigas secas y silvestres."

This hardness and unyielding texture of the land is frequently the cause of human tragedy such as in "**Nos han dado la tierra.**" Campesinos trek across the desert to receive the piece of property guaranteed by land reform. But the story presents an ironic reversal of fate as their "promised land" becomes a hell on earth. This land is as hard as tepetate, cow's hide. The men's first glance at their territory sums up the inadequacy of the land to sustain life: "No, el llano no es cosa que sirva. No hay ni conejos ni pájaros. No hay nada. A no ser unos cuantos huizaches trespeleques y una que otra manchita de zacate con las hojas enroscadas; a no ser eso, no hay nada."

Multiple tragedies have a common stimulus in the infertility of the land in "**Diles que no me maten.**" Because his fields are too parched for grazing, a farmer breaks through a fence and neglects to secure permission for his livestock to pasture on a neighbor's field. The offended neighbor kills a steer, which results in his own death in retribution for the slaughter. The story ends with a poetic justice that recalls the problem of parched land at the story's outset. The murderer, who has been on the run from his victim's family for over thirty years, has become a reclusive farmer who finally manages to till the soil and begin to grow corn. However, he unwittingly reveals his hideaway to his pursuers when they walk through his nascent cornfield and he unsuccessfully tries to scare them off. The tragedy that started with the hardness of the earth comes full circle as a kind of curse that follows the murderer: "Quién le iba a decir que volvería aquel asunto tan viejo, tan rancio, tan enterrado como creía que estaba. Aquel asunto de cuando tuvo que matar a don Lupe."

The photography of Juan Rulfo should be viewed in two contexts: as a photographic companion to his fiction as well as a document of mid-twentieth-century Mexico.

—*Howard M. Fraser*

Notwithstanding the suggestions of mortality in Rulfo's landscape, his stark visions of the land are frequently counterbalanced by a sense of life rising from the most inhospitable surroundings such as the view of cacti flourishing . . . and the row of succulents that have the vital force of a military regiment in ["Calle de Mitlas, Oax."]. Such a treatment serves as an introduction to Rulfo's belief, manifested in his portraits, that nature is redeemable, even from the harshest torments.

A recurring quality in Rulfo's portraits is an obliqueness of the pose, the indirect glance that reveals subjects, intent in their observation of events and oblivious to the camera ("Desde el dintel de la puerta"). Most of Rulfo's subjects seek anonimity in crowds, solitude ("Desamparo"), work ("Valle de Mezquital, Hgo."; "Mercado en Zacatepec, Oax.") and their own clothing, thus reinforcing Octavio Paz's characterization of the Mexican reality as a masked one ("Todos para el Sábado de Gloria"; "Danza de moros y cristianos").

However, there may be reasons for this masked quality that go beyond the Mexican's self-effacement discussed in *El laberinto de la soledad*. Rulfo's subjects are suspicious of the camera. They are curious but innocent observers of the photographer's observing them ("Niña indígena de El Chisme, Mixes Oax."; "Indígena de Totontepec, Mixes Oax."; "Anciana de Apan, Hgo."; ["Indígena de Cotzocón, Oax."]). His subjects are also self-conscious and distrust the photographer. These people want neither to be commercialized nor capitalized upon. They refuse to be transformed into a commodity. Their distrust recalls **"Luvina"** in which newcomers are not accepted into the bosom of the town until they have proved themselves worthy of trust. And this trust may take years to establish, if it is ever established at all.

In a sense, the anonimity of Rulfo's subjects may be compared to that of the men, women and children from Walker Evans's and Dorothea Lange's photographs of sharecroppers taken during the Great Depression. But the Mexican's film reveals quite a different reality than the Americans'. While it can be said that Rulfo's subjects, like the inhabitants of the North American Dustbowl, are the poor, disenfranchised, holders of the worthless land, Rulfo's farmers, display a distrust of the camera unlike the Oakies in Evans and Lange. These characters from **"Nos han dado la tierra,"** brought to life by Rulfo's art, merely acknowledge the presence of the camera without feeling the same complicity, the baring of their abject poverty to the photographer in the Walker Evans's classic *Let Us Now Praise Famous Men.*

Rulfo's subjects attempt to create distance between themselves and the photographer in order to establish a dialectic between themselves as free individuals versus the photographer as their captor. They assert a dignity in their poverty and do not evoke raw pathos in their viewers. Some of Rulfo's most effective photos are of campesinos pausing in their daily work as they set the stage for their life's story. There is an oral quality to Rulfo's subjects, reminiscent of the colloquial tone of titles from *El llano en llamas*, that the narrators deliver with a shrug of their shoulders: **"Es que somos muy pobres,"** and **"Nos han dado la tierra."** The subject of ["Quedará alguna esperanza"] draws strength from the desolation around him like the narrator of **"Macario,"** who motionlessly waits for frogs to cross his path: "Ahora estoy junto a la alcantarilla esperando a que salgan las ranas. Y no ha salido ninguna en todo este rato que llevo platicando. Si tardan más en salir, puede suceder que me duerma, y luego ya no habrá modo de matarlas, y a mi madrina no le llegará por ningún lado el sueño si las oye cantar, y se llenará de coraje." The campesino in ["En la tierra zapoteca"] contemplates the shabby land where he scratches out a living and can be considered a depiction of the narrator of **"Nos han dado la tierra"** who surveys his brittle soil: "No decimos lo que pensamos. Hace ya tiempo que se nos acabaron las ganas de hablar. Se nos acabaron con el calor. Uno platicaría muy a gusto en otra parte, pero aquí cuesta trabajo. Uno platica aquí y las palabras se calientan en la boca con el calor de afuera, y se la resecan a uno en la lengua hasta que acaban con el resuello."

But for all their commonalities, Rulfo's fiction and photography do not complement each other perfectly. Perhaps better than his stories, which frequently end on a note of despair, Rulfo's photographs outline the theme of hope in the betterment of the human condition. The series of photographs of women tilling the fields for example, portrays the dignity of the poor and of their work and, ultimately, their pride. And so it is with the series of pictures of peasant musicians that Rulfo included in his book *El gallo de oro y otros textos para cine*. Dated 1955, and shot in Oaxaca, they are reminiscent of the scenes in . . . Luis Buñuel's film *Los olvidados,* which was shot during the same time as these photographs, that depicts a blind drummer who ekes out a living at the edge of the city peopled by an inappreciative and uncomprehending mob of dispossessed youths. In Rulfo's photographs, the musicians evoke the pathos of those trying to preserve culture on the fringes of civilization that is at the same time the frontier of a cultural desert. They must deal not only with their own poverty but also with the indifference of their sparse or nonexistent audience. What these musicians reveal to us is the value their preservation of culture holds for themselves if for no one else. They also show . . . their contentment and sense of redemption in art through their dignity, solitude, and humility.

And it is remarkable that salvation appears most often in his photographs, principally through the iconographic symbol of the cross. Although we might think that Rulfo focuses on death in his numerous pictures of graves, and on the degradation of humanity in his fiction, I feel that his interest in taking pictures of tombs belies the hope of resurrection or redemption through art, an interest that he reveals in several of his images. If we examine his photographs of crosses, we see a search for uncommon forms that can reveal an aesthetic sense that, in turn, displays a redeeming purpose to death . . . The highly ornamental crosses ("Cruz de Tepeapulco, Hgo.") and the grave sprouting lillies (similar to "Alcatraces") give a sense of a life force operating through the stimulus of death.

Not only a life force but a narrative force seems to operate in his photographs as well. Perhaps his most interesting narrative potential is in his photograph of three crosses atop a tomb ("Panteón de Huamantla, Tlax."). The setting, a precipice where graves have been placed, shows the harshness of the conditions that man lives by and the commanding natural beauty chosen for his burial. The sublime mixed with the commonplace is asserted in the composition of the crosses themselves. They are either tablelegs, chair legs, or even a disassembled bedpost, common objects with which the deceased came in daily contact. The number of crosses suggests additional elements of a story yet to be told. Multiple graves can signify multiple deaths. The viewer ponders the implications of the possibilities in the common demise of a family in a massacre such as that in **"El hombre,"** or of a struggle to the death in **"La cuesta de las comadres."**

How Rulfo's graphic production should focus on the redemptive possibilities of life when his stories so frequently emphasize the tragic may be visualized in a sequence of photographs of stairways and clothes hung out to dry in *Inframundo*. Here the simplest of materials, wet clothes hanging in the sunny patio, symbolize cleansing and purification. It is perhaps the brilliant presence of light that inevitably allows us to interpret this work as a Dantesque ascent from the infernal elements of earthly existence. . . . Rulfo deals with the theme of salvation, or more correctly the damnation of humanity, through lack of

the most common necessities in various stories. In **"Es que somos muy pobres,"** the family cow is washed away in a flood. From this simple event flow catastrophic consequences such as the loss of the dowry the cow represents, the impossibility of marriage, and the probable descent into prostitution of the young woman who, lacking a dowry, is now unacceptable as a mate. Salvation from torment is assured in the toads Macario must destroy in order to avoid the wrath of his *madrina*. And in **"Diles que no me maten,"** although the murderer is not spared the death sentence, the executioner gives a rare demonstration of charity when he orders doses of *chicha* to lessen the pain of the firing squad.

In conclusion, the photography of Juan Rulfo should be viewed in two contexts: as a photographic companion to his fiction as well as a document of mid-twentieth-century Mexico. As an illustration of stories from *El llano en llamas*, the graphic art of *Inframundo* provides a visual realization of the themes in his short stories that, in turn, can now serve as captions to the photographs. His pictures, stark, visual statements about contemporary Mexico, serve as excellent illustrations of the author's literary settings, characters and themes. In addition, as a documentary photographer, Rulfo joins the ranks of such masters of the genre as Walker Evans and Dorothea Lange. Rulfo captures the essence of the downtrodden, their innate dignity and pride, and he does so with a spirit of respect and curiosity in revealing their stories. The aesthetic value of Rulfo's work, then, lies in rendering visual images of his subjects and in revealing the narrative force of their underlying reality. In response to viewing his work, we as readers and spectators resemble the subjects . . . : we are intrigued with deeper reality that lies beyond the frame on the page. And with Rulfo's aesthetic guidance in graphic and literary form, we have entrée to this world.

FURTHER READING

Brodman, Barbara L. C. "Manifestations of the Cult of Death in the Contemporary Mexican Short Story." In *The Mexican Cult of Death in Myth and Literature*, pp. 50-7. Gainesville: The University Presses of Florida, 1976.

> Discusses Rulfo's use of setting, characterization, and plot to depict the Mexican cult of death in *The Burning Plain*.

Egeland, Marianne. "Structural Patterns in *The Burning Plain*: A Key to Juan Rulfo's Fiction." *Orbis Litterarum* 40, No. 1 (1985): 55-7.

> Examines structural and thematic aspects of Rulfo's short story collection.

Leal, Luis. *Juan Rulfo*. Boston: Twayne Publishers, 1983, 116 p.

Full-length study of Rulfo's life and work.

Thomas, Mary Lorene. "A Stylistic Study of 'Acuérdate'
by Juan Rulfo." *South Atlantic Bulletin* XLII, No. 4
(November 1977): 57-66.
    Explores Rulfo's use of humor and violence in this
    short story.

**Additional coverage of Rulfo's life and career is contained in the following sources
published by Gale Research:** *Contemporary Authors*, **Vols. 85-88, 118;** *Contemporary Authors
New Revision Series*, **Vol. 26;** *Contemporary Literary Criticism*, **Vols. 8, 80;** *Dictionary of
Literary Biography*, **Vol. 113;** *DISCovering Authors: Multicultural Authors Module*; *Hispanic
Literature Criticism*; *Hispanic Writers*; **and** *Major Twentieth-Century Writers*.

William Styron
1925-

American short story writer, novelist, essayist, and playwright.

INTRODUCTION

Styron is a highly accomplished storyteller whose fiction is remarkable for its power of characterization, the polish of its rhetorical style, and the complexity of its moral vision. Styron's fiction has been well received both in the United States and in Europe. In his stories, as in his novels, one finds Styron's preoccupation with the struggle of the individual against the corruption of societal and institutional conventions. His protagonists, through their rebellion against these strictures, confront the limitations of their own natures and ultimately achieve a redemptive self-awareness.

Biographical Information

Styron was born in Newport News, Virginia, the only child of William C. Styron and Pauline Abraham. During World War II, Styron trained as a candidate for officer in the Marine Corps while attending Duke University in North Carolina. At Duke, he became interested in literature and was encouraged to become a writer by Professor William Blackburn. Upon graduating in 1947, he worked briefly and unhappily as an associate editor for McGraw-Hill publishers in New York City. Enrolling in Hiram Haydn's creative writing course at the New School for Social Research, Styron began his first novel, *Lie Down in Darkness,* for which he received the Prix de Rome from the American Academy of Arts and Letters in 1952. Styron settled in Greenwich Village to write full time, but was forced to put his literary ambitions aside temporarily when, in 1950, the Marine Corps recalled him to serve in the Korean War. This experience inspired his drama of rebellion against military authority, *The Long March,* published in 1953. When released from active duty, Styron returned briefly to New York City and founded the *Paris Review.* After winning the Prix de Rome, he went to Europe for two years. Styron returned to the United States in 1954 and settled in Roxbury, Connecticut.

Major Works of Short Fiction

In his novella, *The Long March,* Styron skillfully uses poetic description to create a nightmarish world in which the horrors and absurdities of military life are laid bare. Scholars have noted that the novella demonstrates the development of Styron's moral vision, for the story illustrates clearly the themes of mortality and rebellion which

underlie all of Styron's fiction. Styron depicts the protagonist, Mannix, as a rebel against the dehumanizing abstractions of modern life. *The Long March,* as critics have observed, also demonstrates the evolution of Styron's artistry in his deft handling of flashbacks and dream sequences, which allow him to compress radically the time of the story's action. In the collection of stories, *A Tidewater Morning,* reviewers point out that the theme of mortality is most evident and acts as a linking device for the three short stories that comprise the collection. Originally published separately in *Esquire* magazine, the stories are united through their protagonist, Paul Whitehurst, who recounts three painful incidents from his youth. These stories examine the power of memory and the unshakable hold of the past on the present. In these coming-of-age stories, the narrator confronts and reflects on the experiences of guilt, sorrow, rebellion, and death. What the narrator gains from his harsh experiences is self-knowledge and the forbearance to face the unknown trials of the future.

Critical Reception

Early in his career, Styron met with astonishing critical

acclaim and popular success. His first novel, *Lie Down in Darkness,* garnered international accolades, and literary critics hailed him as a successor to William Faulkner. In interviews, however, Styron observed that despite his debts to Faulkner and other southern writers, he did not consider himself as belonging to any Southern literary tradition or school. Later scholars have generally agreed that although aspects of the Southern literary tradition do inform his writing, Styron is a national writer with a wider-ranging perspective. They note, for example, that Styron's use of a southern setting in *The Long March* is relatively unimportant in the novella's exploration of rebellion against authority. Critics have repeatedly returned to this early work, hailed as a minor masterpiece at the time of its publication, for what it reveals of the writer's artistic growth. Styron's aesthetics of style, imagery, and character development can be traced from this early work through *The Confessions of Nat Turner* and *Sophie's Choice* and in his collection of short stories, *A Tidewater Morning.* The cautious optimism that ends *The Long March* becomes in *A Tidewater Morning* the hopeful endurance that characterizes the viewpoint of Styron's protagonist. Reviewers of *A Tidewater Morning* have widely praised this collection for its heartbreaking examination of the individual's struggle and his ultimate discovery of meaning and affirmation in the bitterness of life.

PRINCIPAL WORKS

Short Fiction

The Long March (novella) 1953
A Tidewater Morning (short stories) 1993

Other Major Works

Lie Down in Darkness (novel) 1951
Set This House on Fire (novel) 1960
The Confessions of Nat Turner (novel) 1967
In the Clap Shack (play) 1972
Sophie's Choice (novel) 1979
This Quiet Dust and Other Writings (criticism) 1982
Darkness Visible: A Memoir of Madness (nonfiction) 1990

CRITICISM

Eugene McNamara (essay date 1961)

SOURCE: "William Styron's *Long March*: Absurdity and Authority," in *The Western Humanities Review,* Vol. XV, 1961, pp. 267-72.

[*In the following excerpt, McNamara finds that the plot,*

structure, and metaphors of Styron's novella demonstrate the author's point that both acceptance of and obedience to authority are necessary and that protest is hopeless.]

All works of art reflect and echo the tenor of their time. This is inescapable. There is a certain patterning, a certain cadence of words, a tonal quality which makes a work uniquely itself, and strangely of its time.

Such a work is William Styron's novella, ***The Long March***, called "one of the two or three distinguished novellettes of the last thirty years" by John Aldridge, but otherwise curiously ignored by the critics. I say "curiously" because the pattern of the work so closely reflects the tenor of our own time. This may not be evident after a cursory glance. But if we contrast the central character, Lieutenant Culver, with the central figure in a novel of some ten years ago, Private Prewitt in *From Here to Eternity,* then the pattern becomes increasingly clearer.

If Prewitt is the archetype of the Individual (even if he is the terminus in a long line of fictional rebels from Natty Bumppo on down), then Culver is the corresponding antithetical myth-figure; the archetype of conformity, of acceptance.

To demonstrate the intentional substructure in the work, I intend to look first of all at the plot movement, then the narrational structure, and finally at the pattern of metaphor.

On the surface, the story is about a forced march in a Marine camp in the Carolinas during the early 1950s. And it is about some of the men—retreads from World War Two who had been yanked back into a war which was not a war, from a peace which was not really a peace. The Cold War, then, with its brooding atmosphere of unease and displacement, sets the tone of the work.

The Colonel, "Rocky" Templeton, feeling that his men need some sort of manœuvre to strengthen them in *esprit* (Marine Corps jargon for a sort of super-patriotism. *Gung-ho* is a more derisive synonym), plans a thirty mile forced march at the end of a field problem. Before the march is over, tension between Templeton and Mannix, the violently vocal individualist, erupts and Mannix faces a court-martial, and by the time the march is over, Culver has come to the conclusion, reluctantly, that he must choose between the two men. As much as he loves Mannix, he must choose the Colonel. He *must.*

So much for the plot movement. But there is a careful style here, almost a mannered style, jewelled, Fauknerian. It seems to slow the reading, make it more close. It seems to say, *Wait, there is more to all this.* And so there seems to be.

Within the narrative structure, there is first of all the accidental death of eight young men in a training accident. This sets the tone of the novella—a sense of acute frustration, of questioning, of anguished waste. Culver is plunged into retrospection, and contrasts his six years of peace with his present life. The six year interlude between the end of World War Two and his being called back for the police action seems now to be a dream. He usually remembers it as winter, and sees one particular scene again and again. He and his wife are pushing the baby carriage through the park. It is cold and silent, and has "an Old World calm" and for Culver a nostalgic quality as of a world which never did exist, save in a dream. And to Culver the quality of this memory is inextricably tied up with a passage from Haydn.

> It was one happy and ascending bar that he remembered, a dozen bright notes through which he passed in memory to an earlier, untroubled day at the end of childhood. There, like tumbling flowers against the sunny grass, their motions as nimble as the music itself, two lovely little girls played tennis, called to him voicelessly, as in a dream, and waved their arms.

This vision returns three times in the novella. Each time it contrasts violently with the anguish of the present; the Marine Corps, the Cold War, the Carolina swamp, the raging tropic summer, the long march—and more particularly, the eight dead boys:

> One boy's eyes lay gently closed, and his long dark lashes were washed in tears, as though he had cried himself to sleep. As they bent over him they saw that he was very young, and a breeze came up from the edges of the swamp, bearing with it a scorched odour of smoke and powder, and touched the edges of his hair. A lock fell across his brow with a sort of gawky, tousled grace as if preserving even in that blank and mindless repose some gesture proper to his years, a callow charm.

At this sight, Mannix sobs helplessly, murmuring; "Won't they ever let us alone, the sons of bitches. Won't they ever let us alone?"

This then, is the present world that Culver is plunged back into; the dead innocents in the tropic rage of the Carolina swamps. Both Mannix and Templeton take a definite attitude in regard to the death of the young men. Mannix mourns the waste of life and smoulders in rage against the system, with its senseless juggernaut movement, its impersonality, its ritual which he finds puerile and meaningless. Templeton remains impervious, almost casual in a studied way, as if to betray human emotions or to grieve openly would not only be a sign of weakness, but would be in itself a sign that the system was wrong. So the accident to Templeton must remain a problem of logistics, an error to be justified with the others. Something else to be purged by the ritual of the long march.

On the eve of the march, Mannix and Templeton are placed in juxtaposition, seen in a conference in a tent

> . . . like classical Greek masks, made of chrome or tin, reflecting an almost theatrical disharmony; the Colonel's fleeting grin sculpted cleanly and prettily in the

unshadowed air above the Captain's darkened, downcast face, where, for a flicker of a second, something outraged and agonized was swiftly graven and swiftly scratched out.

After the meeting, Culver takes control of the radio and remains on alert alone, listening to the inhuman squawks and howls that confuse the air coming through the headset. Occasionally there is a flash of danceband music from some far off Florida hotel. This only accentuates the terrible sense of isolation, of displacement, which Culver feels. He senses that the tent is like a ship's cabin, and that the swamp is like some desolate ocean. A terrible loneliness weighs on him, and the squawks on the headset sound like the cries of the damned in Hell.

The sense of prescience which Culver feels is borne out by the march itself. It is fully as horrible as Culver imagined it would be. A nail works itself loose in Mannix's boot and lacerates his foot painfully. Before the march's end, his foot is horribly swollen, and he drags it, hobbling along in delirium. But Mannix is determined that he will finish the march, although trucks have been provided for the ill or those unable to finish. The Colonel orders him to ride in and he defiantly disobeys. He is placed under arrest and hobbles on. At this point Culver realizes:

> How stupid to think they had ever made their own philosophy; it was as puny as a house of straw, and at this moment—by the noise in their brains of those words, *you will*—it was being blasted to the winds like dust. They were as helpless as children.

This insight makes him further realize that the choice he thought had to be made between Mannix and Templeton was not a choice between good and evil, but only between two different kinds of men. And Mannix, as much as Culver loves him, is out of date, obsolete, dangerous. "He was trapped like all of them in a predicament which one personal insurrection could, if anything, only make worse." The Colonel must be obeyed, not because he is right, but because he is the Colonel.

Because of the exigencies of the Cold War, there is a terrible need for purposeful mobilization, unified movement. During World War Two, one could see the need for such stratified movement, for submergence of individual desires for the good of all. The same need was not as evident during the Korean crisis. It was less evident, but even more urgent, because of the unique nature of the new kind of war. It seemed to Culver that it reduced itself to a kind of existential choice: *Obey or Perish*. The old world of peace, of the children on the sunny lawn was just a dream, a beautiful dream, but only that. Culver, like Mannix, had lived for awhile in a world which gave him love, comfort, status, security, self-realization. This world was suddenly taken from him, and he was only a Marine again. But it is six years later, and Culver knows that he is "no longer an eager kid just out of Quantico with a knife between his teeth. He was almost thirty, he was old, and he was afraid."

Mannix sees their present situation in light of the past (the world of the children on the sunny lawn) and sees it as a complete and impossible paradox—one which he does not intend to accept.

But there is yet another layer of meaning to explore: the metaphoric. A persistent pattern of metaphor in regard to each character begins to emerge. Mannix is described persistently as a "big hairy baby, washed by elemental tides," "buck naked," "naked as the day he emerged from his mother's womb." There is a definite accretive power to this repetition of metaphor. One begins to see Mannix's rebellion in a somewhat different light. He is not merely the Individualist (Natty Bumppo, Prewitt) but is the old original Adam (or even Satan, if we take one gesture of his rebellion seriously: One drunken evening, he is restrained by Culver from setting fire to "Heaven's Gate," the officers' "country club" set incongruously in the midst of the Carolina jungle), filled with pride and defiance. And the nakedness suggests the primal quality of this pride, this self-interest, this child-like rebellion.

Templeton, too, is seen through a patterning of metaphor. He is seen as a "young ecclesiastic," who has gone through "a strange interior struggle," and has a "contemplative smile." He is "priest-like," "tenderly contemplative," a "stern father," and sometimes, flatly, "the priest." In conjunction to Mannix, then, the cluster of metaphors for Templeton make a new configuration. "Rockey" Templeton is seen as a kind of religious leader, like Moses (or *Peter*) Mannix remains the recalcitrant Old Adam, unconverted, unconvinced, while Culver, like another famous convert who saw the light while on a journey, is converted during the march.

Thus, Mannix is not only a naked baby, an obstinate child, but the unbaptised, the fallen. He rejects the ministrations of the priest and rejects the ritual of the march, which is a rite of passage intended to make Marines out of boys. Culver accepts the grace merited by the ordeal and advances in understanding. Mannix remains obdurate, accepting the ritual as an imposed duty which he will perform in "proud and wilful submission" and hence, instead of grace and cleansing, Mannix not only remains fallen, but damns himself. Templeton, the priest, directs the ritual of the march not out of hate, but, like the "stern father," out of love. But it is a kind of love which Mannix is incapable of. At the book's end, he stands "naked as the day he emerged from his mother's womb" in *individual* communication with one of the Negro maids at "Heaven's Gate," who instinctively sympathizes with him and his hurt leg. He is still incapable of the final acceptance: a higher, depersonalized love of all men, seen in acceptance of the rule. The Marine Corps, in this complex of metaphor, is a kind of monastic order united in love, symbolized by the ritual which must be entered into unquestioningly, with complete obedience. And, Styron seems to say, once we accept the essential absurdity of the modern situation, obedience becomes not only desirable, but imperative. Mannix chooses to retain the myth of free choice. But the world is closed: there is only the choice between obedience and destruction. Mannix is like Willy Loman,

who nurtured his fading dreams of a frontier forever free, of Horatio Algerism, of rugged Carnegieism in an organization world which suddenly dwarfed him. There is no place in this world for Willy Loman, and there is no place for Mannix.

Another cluster of metaphor makes this terribly clear. They are images of isolation, usually of a ship lost at sea. Culver, alone in the tent before the march, sees himself in loneliness, as in the cabin of a ship lost in a desolate ocean. During the march, they are passed by a car, "a slick convertible bound for the North, New York, perhaps." And the passengers in the car are unaware of the march going on. They are like "Ocean voyagers oblivious of all those fishy struggles below them in the night, submarine and fathomless." The officers' quarters, ironically named "Heaven's Gate," a living contradiction, a night-club in the midst of Hell, makes the existential aloneness, the anguish, even more evident. At the end of the march, Culver has accepted his baptism of sweat, and having gone willingly through the ordeal, advances to a fuller understanding of his aloneness. The dream of peace—symbolized by the recurring vision of the Haydn passage and the children on the sunny lawn—has been replaced by the dead boys in the training accident. The innocence of childhood is dead, gone. It is replaced by the hard acceptance, by the awareness that we live in a world of irrevocable choices, made even more anguishing and evident by the thermonuclear disaster which hovers over him. Peace is a dream. A new kind of peace can be attained through obedience. But rebellion on an individual level can only mean disaster.

Sidney Finkelstein (essay date 1965)

SOURCE: "Cold War, Religious Revival and Family Alienation: William Styron, J. D. Salinger and Edward Albee," in *Existentialism and Alienation in American Literature,* International Publishers Co., 1965, pp. 211-42.

[*In this excerpt, Finkelstein discusses Styron's novella in the context of the Cold War period, and he notes what he considers Styron's accurate portrayal of the military's complete disregard for the value of human life.*]

Styron's short novel, **The Long March**, has the distinction of being one of the few novels registering the actual impact on the American mind of the Korean war. In the course of this war a hysteria was whipped up such as had not been found necessary in the Second World War. In that anti-fascist war, there had been no policy of answering fascist brutality with like brutality and inhumanity. But now, under the assurance that the struggle was against communism and communism was by its very nature the worst barbarism, every barbaric tactic was justified. Overlooked was the fact that our ally, whose government we were supposedly defending, was a notorious dictator and swindler. The Nazis, who had been condemned for ruthlessly carrying the war to civilians, were outdone by napalm bombs that incinerated fields, towns and people. In the anti-fascist war, the aim had been to train an enlightened soldier. Now a soldier had to be trained to be a single-minded killer. . . .

Styron's novelette is set in a marine training camp in the United States. The Korean war is only briefly mentioned as going on at the time. What he does picture is the new carelessness of human life and brutality in the military training. At the beginning, eight men are killed during target practice by a shell that falls short, the shell being from a shipment that was known to be probably defective. The rest of the story is of a forced march of 36 miles, which the men had not been trained for adequately, ordered by the commander, Colonel Templeton. He is a martinet, whose militarism has a "priestlike, religious fervor." A Captain Mannix, who hates both militarism and the Colonel, protests against the march but goes through with it, despite a hurt foot, determined to show that he can take any ordeal. Finally he explodes in wrath against the Colonel, and is cited to be court-martialed and sent to Korea.

Significant is Styron's description of Mannix: "The man with the back unbreakable, the soul of pity—where was he now, great unshatterable vessel of longing, lost in the night, astray at mid-century in the never-endingness of war?" Like Camus's Sisyphus, Mannix rolls the rock of militarism while scorning it, and this broadens to a symbol of Styron's hatred of war while feeling that man is eternally condemned to it.

Charles Child Walcutt (essay date 1966)

SOURCE: "The Idea Men," in *Man's Changing Mask: Modes and Methods of Characterization in Fiction,* University of Minnesota Press, 1966, pp. 251-57.

[*In the following assessment of* The Long March, *Walcutt argues that the author had to sacrifice characterization and credibility to get his point across.*]

In his novelette *The Long March* . . . William Styron has gathered all his forces to dramatize an idea about Jewish character. It is as unsympathetic as it is suggestive. It generates a great deal of imaginative power; and it seems to be going deep into the roots of character until its symbolic purpose takes open charge and reduces the action to an expository contrivance. . . . The characters of significance are just three: the dedicated professional soldier, Colonel Templeton, aged forty-four; Lieutenant Culver, about thirty, who has been snatched from a happy marriage and a promising career to a nightmare of forced training; and Captain Mannix, a huge Jewish bear of a man from Brooklyn, scarred from the last war, passionately rebellious, truculent, sardonic, articulate.

About 5000 men start on the march, in bone-chilling cold and blazing sun, over sandy Carolina roads. It is described as an ordeal for which the men are not ready—certainly not soft reserve officers who have been called back from their comfortable homes—and in fact scarcely 200 of the whole battalion can finish it. After the first three or four hours they are dropping like leaves and being carried off, supine, by the truckload.

The Colonel's motives for ordering such a march are obscure, complex. He is presented as a poseur who absolutely delights in his own perfect composure. No question, no emergency can force him to speak in haste. He seems to have an inordinate vanity in his carriage, his authority, his physical sleekness. Whether he orders the march to punish certain complaining officers, notably Mannix, or to set a record, or to show off his own physical fitness, or from pure sadism—this is the question; for if sometimes he looks like a brainless dandy, at others he looks like a priest. One thing is certain: his professional competence and his authority are absolute. He leads the first hour of the march at a killing pace, and he goes the whole distance on foot.

The story is told through Lt. Culver's eyes, but it is about Mannix. Culver has left a loving wife and a good career; he loathes the military service; he is out of shape, falling asleep on his feet even before the march begins; yet he is one of the handful that finish it. If all but a few officers and about 200 young marines, who have just come out of boot camp, are unable to go on to the end, if the Colonel himself is completely exhausted, it is totally incredible that Culver could have done it. Soft, out of condition, reluctant, he could never have done it, yet the author has to have him along for the point of view, and so he provides the explanation that Culver is so much a marine that his training took over and made a will-less automaton of him. He is said to be gripped by "the old atavism that clutched them, the voice that commanded, once again, *you will.* How stupid to think they had ever made their own philosophy; it was as puny as a house of straw, and at this moment—by the noise in their brains of those words, *you will*—it was being blasted to the winds like dust. They were as helpless as children. Another war, and years beyond reckoning, had violated their minds irrevocably. For six years they had slept a cataleptic sleep, dreaming blissfully of peace, awakened in horror to find that, after all, they were only marines, responding anew to the old commands." There is nothing to show that Culver would respond like a brainwashed automaton to patterns of obedience established six years before, and thus there is no credible motive provided for his doing the impossible. Nor is there any meaning drawn from it later. Indeed, Culver's thoughts after the march *directly contradict* the motives that have been presented to enable him to do the impossible: he cannot hate the Colonel, "because he was a different kind of man, different enough that he was hardly a man at all, but just a quantity of attitudes so remote from Culver's world that to hate him would be like hating a cannibal, merely because he gobbled human flesh." But in fact the motives quoted above, which account for Culver's marching, are practically the same as the Colonel's—the total identification (or submission) of one's will to the Marine Corps. Culver was exactly this; he was exactly the same kind of man in the same world as the Colonel. The author, a sophisticated intelligence, intoxicated with words, unsure where he stands among the varieties of peace and wartime commitment, is swept one way and another by his ideas, which plainly dominate both character and action.

The idea that dominates the conception of Mannix is just hinted early in the story. He has already established his general tone of humor and bitterness; furthermore, he "despised the Colonel," and he "despised everything about the Marine Corps." When Mannix's faint protest against the length of the march is firmly but fairly rejected by the Colonel, his face shows "something outraged and agonized," and he gives "a quick look of both fury and suffering, like the tragic Greek mask, or a shackled slave."

As the march gets under way, Mannix discovers a nail in the heel of one shoe; the Colonel advises him to ride on a truck, but he refuses to give up. Rather, "with a note of proud and willful submission," he limps along mercilessly driving his company, "with the accents of a born bully." As others begin to collapse, Mannix forces his faltering men on by sheer will and abuse. He *will not* let them lag or fall. Culver is appalled by Mannix's transformation. He will not give up; though his foot bleeds and swells, he "mutilated himself by this perverse and violent rebellion." The climax comes after many hours, when the Colonel finally orders Mannix to go back on one of the trucks. Mannix refuses, the Colonel repeats his order, and Mannix blows his top: "'Listen, Colonel,' he rasped, 'you ordered this goddam hike and I'm going to walk it even if I haven't got one goddam man left. You can crap out yourself for half the march . . .'" and then he curses the Colonel. This does it, for the Colonel *has* walked the whole way. He drops his hand onto his pistol and says, "'You quiet down now, hear? You march in, see? I order you confined to your quarters, and I'm going to see that you get a court-martial. Do you understand? I'm going to have you tried for gross insubordination. I'll have you sent to Korea. *Keep your mouth shut.*'"

Tottering the last six miles, Mannix is described in sentences that evoke images of Jews in ghettos, in concentration camps, on wailing walls, Jews outraged and degraded; and the implication is very plain that these humiliations are somehow sought by the Jew, that they satisfy his arrogant need to suffer horror upon horror in order to express the enormity of his resentment against the oppressor: "Mannix's perpetual tread on his toe alone gave to his gait a ponderous, bobbing motion which resembled that of a man wretchedly spastic and paralyzed. It lent to his face . . . an aspect of deep, almost prayerfully passionate concentration—eyes thrown skyward and lips fluttering feverishly in pain—so that if one did not know he was in agony one might imagine that he was a communicant in rapture . . . it was the painted, suffering face of a clown, and the heaving gait was a grotesque and indecent parody of a hopeless cripple, with shoulders gyrating like a seesaw and with flapping, stricken arms." The author's intention of generalizing, of symbolizing his own harsh notion of the Jewish soul is clearest in the phrase "a grotesque and indecent parody of a hopeless cripple."

That is about all there is to the story. It is made clear that the Colonel is neither a fool nor a sadist but just a man doing his job, "That with him the hike had had nothing to do with courage or sacrifice or suffering, but was only a task to be performed . . . and that he was as far removed from the vulgar battle, the competition, which Mannix had tried to promote as the frozen, remotest stars. He just didn't care." Mannix has by his sick need to suffer made a ghastly, revolting parody of human dignity, and in doing so he has stripped himself of all real dignity. He has crucified himself to defy a new world of Romans—but for no Cause at all.

The idea is strong. In order to cram it into his novelette the author has to sacrifice characterization and violate probability. He *tells* his reader a number of contradictory things about the Colonel, yet in the end abandons the problem by saying that he is merely a man doing a job. He introduces Lt. Culver as if something interesting were going to happen to him, but at the end he leaves him with aching legs, exhausted, lonely—but not purged, or strengthened, or enlightened. The idea is much too big for the story. Ever so much more would have to happen to dramatize so complex a system of ideas about the alienation and masochism of the Jew in the person of Captain Mannix. He would, of course, have to discover himself to some degree while making decisions which to some degree he understood; whereas he acts like a man possessed, whose bitterness mounts through cruelty to his men, on to self-destruction.

The bare facts here could have been worked up into several different stories. Basically the rebellion against authority suggests a simple story of immaturity revolting against a paternal figure. On a more complex plane, the focus could be on the cruel tyrant and the means by which he elicits the rebellion of a naive subordinate. . . . *The Long March* does not let Mannix develop in response to changing situations. He is merely revealed as the story moves along and we are allowed to see different levels of his gaudy lust for immolation. There is no growth or discovery of the sort that we associate with human people; there is no valid conflict with the Colonel, because Mannix misunderstands him. At one point, so far is he from making a person of Mannix, the author attributes his stubborn persistence to the fact that he is still basically a marine—a notion that belies everything else he does in the course of the story!

Welles T. Brandriff (essay date 1967)

SOURCE: "The Role of Order and Disorder in *The Long March*," in *English Journal*, January, 1967, pp. 54-9.

[*In this excerpt, Brandriff describes* The Long March *as the story of one man's tortured discovery of the disorder and chaos that underlie the surface of civilization.*]

There is a natural tendency to dwell upon the one-sided antagonism which springs up between Mannix and Templeton in **The Long March**, a short novel by William Styron. The conflict between the scarred man of history, and the marine colonel who deifies a system which produced many of these scars, is developed into a major theme in the book. But to contend that this is the most significant theme in the novel is to misrepresent the facts.

Certainly, it is true that Mannix "offers the extreme reaction" to the march [Melvin J. Friedman, "William Styron: An Interim Appraisal," *English Journal,* 50 (March 1961), 155]. But it is not merely his world which comes apart at the seams; Culver's world also undergoes a chaotic transformation. And then there is another matter which must be taken into account: the significant differences between these two worlds.

Friedman has pointed out in his article that Mannix's extreme reaction to the march results "in probable tetanus, insubordination, and a very certain court martial." So Mannix has been physically disabled and is about to be socially ostracized (at least by a part of society). But there has been no comparable emotional crisis. That inner compartment of the mind where a man reacts emotionally to the external world has not undergone any great change. Mannix is still the tortured man that he was before the march began, and, more significantly, he is still the deluded man.

The same thing cannot be said about Culver, however. His illusions have disappeared by the end of the march. He is no longer deluded by the thin veneer of order called civilization, for he has seen the chaos and disorder which seethe just beneath its surface. And as the forces of disorder prepare once again to crack open this veneer (this time in the form of the Korean War), his inner world of emotional order and serenity crumbles before their onslaught.

The most significant theme in this novel, then, deals with the thin, fabricated veneer called civilization, and one man's growing awareness of the essential disorder which lies just beneath the surface of this veneer. It also concerns the state of psychological disorder into which Culver slides, as he gradually becomes aware of the presence of this disorder.

The development of this awareness, and its by-product of psychological disorder, is paralleled by the development of a foundation of symbolism, the specific function of which is to underscore the contrast between surface order and subsurface disorder. This groundwork of symbolism, though constructed of varying individual symbols, is cemented together by an adhesive of sound. And it is this recurring motif of sounds which provides the narrative with such strong symbolic support.

The first crack in the veneer of order appears in the opening scene. A hot, summer noon in a Carolina pine forest should be the last place one would expect to find the cadavers of eight young marines killed in a mortar blast,

yet there they lie. . . . Even as Culver retches onto the leaves, he is profoundly shocked by the reaction of the young marine on the field phone whose primary concern was to inform Major Lawrence that he had correctly analyzed the situation while it was in the making ("the boy's voice, astonishing even in that moment of nausea because of its clear, unhysterical tone of explanation: 'Major, I tell you . . . I was . . . I tell you . . . I knew . . . and so I hollered . . .'"). The physical and psychological shock to Culver's system produces the first, small adjustment in his thinking: he realizes that he is "no longer an eager kid just out of Quantico" with the easy confidence of that age. He is afraid, and more significantly, he is emotionally off-balance.

The first brick in the foundation of this narrative is laid in place when Styron manipulates time to achieve certain symbolic effects. This is most noticeable in the first chapter, where instead of flowing smoothly forward, time moves backward in a series of disconnected leaps.

The chapter opens at a point in time just after the mortar accident, then the present is cut off abruptly, and the setting leaps back to the day that Culver was recalled into the Marine Corps. A little farther into the chapter, time again moves backward, now to the period in his life before the arrival of his orders. The general movement, then, is backward to a time in Culver's life when everything was peaceful, pleasant, and above all, ordered. And this is the particular significance of the inverted time order. For, from now on, Culver will look backward into time more and more often, trying desperately to grasp the memory of those precious few years of "vanished simplicity and charm." Since it was during those years that Culver came closest to creating the limited kind of life and order within which he could live, Styron has carefully underscored the character of this period through the use of extensive symbolism.

Although the inverted time order is certainly important, the most significant symbolic event in the first chapter is undoubtedly the introduction of the sound motif. A phonograph that plays only "Haydn, Mozart, and Bach" sounds somewhat unusual, but in this particular case it goes far towards pointing out the need for order in Culver's life. For although music itself is the imposition of order on sound, these three men have, in turn, imposed an ultimate order on music. That is, Haydn, Mozart, and Bach wrote under the most rigid set of standards in the history of composition, and anyone whose taste can be satisfied only by their music, is reaching out for an ultimate order which exists in only a few, limited forms in modern civilization. For Culver, their music is a key which opens the locked doors of the past, taking him back to those times, "which already seemed dark ages ago," when life was more ordered, more placid, and much more pleasant.

Pick any object of Culver's reveries and take a hard look beneath its surface; there will always be the underlying order. He dwells at length on the memories of his family: on the love of a "tenderly passionate wife," the happiness which springs out of a well-adjusted and meaningful marriage, "the familiar delight of the baby's good-night embrace," the joy in the winter afternoon walks with wife, child, and pet—all the things that are unique to a climate of emotional order. It is equally significant that the waning light of a Sunday afternoon "had not spelled out the promise of Monday morning's gloom but of Monday's challenge—and this was not because he was a go-getter but because he was happy" practicing law: that is, taking an active role in maintaining that system through which order is imposed upon society.

Even things of nominal importance reveal this preoccupation with order. Culver takes great pleasure in the memory of the strolls he took with his wife and child on those winter Sunday afternoons. For only then was the city's "frantic heartbeat quieted" enough so that it "seemed to have on Old World calm. . . ."

In fact, the only disorder that does not disturb him is "the droll combat" between his two house pets. The difference is this: when he ceases to be amused by their antics, he can step in and return his household to order. It is perhaps one of the few situations over which he has any degree of personal control, and this point is emphasized throughout the novel.

The first sign of psychological disorder appears shortly after Culver receives his orders. His recall is a shattering blow to his hopes, and he experiences "an odd distress" that keeps "him wandering about, baffled and mumbling to himself, for days." The first doubts begin nagging at his mind, and he wonders if the past "half-dozen years or so" of peace and serenity weren't some "glorious if somewhat prolonged dream." The doubts return again when he is seeing his wife off at the bus station. They are "surrounded by a horde of marines . . . cheap suitcases . . . fallen candy wrappers . . . the sound of fretful children" and all the other unlovely disorder "of leave-taking and of anxiety. Of war." The driving rain outside seems an appropriate setting for this "evil day. . . ." For a moment, he hangs suspended on one of those small points of time when doubt envelops the mind; for a moment, the scene seems "to nag with both remembrance [the past] and foreboding [the future] of . . . storm swept distances. . . ."

The character of the sound motif changes sharply after Culver's recall into the Marine Corps, signaling the transition from the old world of order to this new world of forced marches and endless tactical problems, "of frigid nights and blazing noons, of disorder and movement. . . ." Moments after having heard about the mortar accident, while the shock of revelation grips the characters in a tableau of suspended action and "awesome silence . . . back off in the bushes a mockingbird commenced a shrill rippling chant and far away, amidst the depth of the silence, there [seemed] to be a single faint and terrible scream." Those sounds that fit in the order of things are still there for all to hear, but for one who will listen carefully, there is also the sound of death and disorder. It is only a faint thread of sound far off in the background, but it is there nonetheless.

Later on, Culver hears—or imagines he hears—an "echo, from afar, of that faint anguished shriek he . . . heard before. . . ." His unit has been taking part in a mock tactical problem, and he has gotten very little sleep during the past 72 hours. Deeply fatigued, he falls into a doze and begins "dreaming fitfully of home, of white cottages, of a summer by the sea." When he is abruptly awakened a few minutes later, however, his return to consciousness is accompanied not by the sound of Haydn or even the mockingbird, but by the true sounds of his world—the shriek of the scarred and the moans of the wounded.

On another occasion, Culver is assigned the radio watch. The operations tent is set up "on a tiny patch of squashy marshland. . . ." Although "it was midsummer . . . nights out in the swamps were fiercely, illogically cold. . . ." The damp chill from the marshes quickly penetrates through the extra layers of clothing he is wearing. Overhead, "a single kerosene pressure-lamp [roared] . . . like a pint-sized, encapsuled hurricane. . . ." The kerosene lamp is the key to this scene because it is an exact minature of Culver's world (as it exists at this particular moment). The imposed order is still present in the form of the thin glass shell, but the chaos beneath can be both seen and heard. The shell seems no more substantial, at this point, than the thin veneer of order in Culver's life.

The feeling of "freezing marsh and grass instead of wood beneath his feet, the preposterous cold in the midst of summer," and the fear of the long march (exaggerated by his sense of fatigue), serve to throw him into a condition in which his surroundings seem to shift "into another dimension of space and time." He now feels completely disoriented and "profoundly alone."

By this point in the story, a new awareness is beginning to awaken within him. It is still in an early stage of development, but Culver is beginning to feel that "what he had had for the last years—wife and child and home . . . existed in the infinite past or, dreamlike again, never at all. . . ." The sound motif is used once again to provide symbolic support for this new awareness.

"Almost sick with the need for sleep," Culver bends over the field desk and rests his head on his arms. The earphones are still around his head. The only sounds to be heard are the tortured wails of radio signals "an inch from his eardrum . . . mingling with the roar, much closer now, of the lamp" overhead (the sound of disorder is no longer quite so far off in the background). Caught in the grip of complete exhaustion, his imagination begins to play tricks with the sounds of the radio signals. "Cracklings, whines, barks and shrieks—a whole jungle full of noise"—echoes through his mind "like the cries of souls in the anguish of hell. . . ." The "faint fluting of a dance-band clarinet" is strung briefly across his earphones and it seems very much out of place in this "swollen obbligato of demented sounds." It comes "from Florida or New York, someplace beyond reckoning." It is important to note that Culver thinks of the fluting of the clarinet—and not the other sounds—as the "thread of insanity. . . ." It is the jungle sounds which are most appropriate for the type of world he is coming gradually to know.

Styron has begun to define mid-century civilization in far more specific terms by this point in the novel. The world he describes is characterized by disorder and violence. There is always war, although it does not often appear in the form of a hot war. It is the time of not-peace called the cold war. There is an enemy who is "labeled Aggressor" although there is "no sign of his aggression. . . ." He is an invisible, "spectral foe" who poses a threat to peace yet rarely ever commits himself. In a faint echo of the sound motif, Styron compares the state of the nation (and world) to a "distant bleating saxophone" which seems "indecisive and sad . . . neither at peace nor at war."

This theme is expanded still further in a conversation between Culver and Mannix on one of their weekly escapes to the sea. Mannix reminisces about the night, back during the war, when some marine buddies dangled him "buck naked" by the heels from a window ten floors above the street. A close parallel is drawn between this incident and the phenomenon of birth, but with one striking dissimilarity: rather than being born out of darkness into light, the situation is just the reverse. Man is born out of light (the order of some earlier existence) into "that . . . infinite darkness . . ." (the disorder of the modern war-world).

The relating of this incident further depresses Culver. "His body . . . was swept by a hot wave of anguish. . . . Across the rim of his memory . . . a shower of uncapturable musical sounds" is swept abruptly away by the "repeated echoes" of something that sounds like "far-off thunder, or guns," somewhere over the distant horizon. The sound of death and disorder is still off in the distance, but it is louder by many decibels than it was before and it is moving closer. Culver "suddenly . . . felt like Mannix, upturned drunkenly above the abyss, blood rushing to his head, in terror clutching at the substanceless night. . . ."

The sound motif has contributed substantially to the forward movement of Culver's growing awareness by this point in the book. But Styron continues to use it both to delineate and to underscore Culver's rapidly-deteriorating emotional condition.

Night is coming on, and the battalion is preparing to move out. Culver is deeply fatigued, but his mind is gripped by the realization that "for six years [he] had slept a cataleptic sleep," awakening to find the peace, order, and happiness all part of a blissful dream. The "brainless chorale" of the frogs in the swamp seems "perfectly suited to his sense of complete . . . frustration."

Shortly after the march has begun, Culver comes into temporary contact with the dream-world of peace and order again. As they move out onto the highway, a car flicks by them quietly in the night. The sound motif has now subsided to a low hum, but it takes on added significance. Culver feels that the car lends "a new sensation of unreality to the night, the march," but it is a moment of delusion, for it is the car which is unreal, not the night or the

march. It is the car which is out of place here, for the people in it are still supported by the thin veneer of civilization and order. They do not yet know about the chaos that Culver is coming to know. They are "like ocean voyagers oblivious of all those fishy struggles below them in the night, submarine and fathomless."

By midnight, his "exhaustion was so profound that it enveloped his whole spirit. . . ." He is no longer capable of putting his thoughts into any semblence of order; his impressions are fragmented and "projected upon his brain in a scattered, disordered riot, like a movie film pieced together by an idiot."

There is one impression, however, which is unaffected by this overwhelming sense of fatigue. That is "the violent and haunting picture of the mangled bodies he had seen" in the noonday heat. It hovers just beyond the rim of his memory, having followed him throughout the night into the searing, dust-choked morning of a new day. And "try as he could, to dwell upon consoling scenes—home, music, sleep—his mind was balked beyond that vision: the shattered youth with slumbering eyes, the blood, the swarming noon."

Culver has become the disillusioned man by the end of the march, for the veneer of civilization has cracked open, laying bare the chaos underneath. For the first time in the narrative, he has a clear understanding of the nature of the modern war-world in which he is forced to exist (as a result of this, he is now also the sleepless man). This awareness is underscored symbolically through the recurring vision of the young marine casualties. In fact, it is this image which returns to haunt him with "unshakable regularity" (the Haydn passage having been effectively blotted from his memory).

Off on the horizon, thunderheads are booming and preparing to "roll landward" (the chaos has broken through and is casting its darkening shadow over the shattered veneer of civilization). Culver senses they are "in for a blow," but it is no surprise to him, for he has seen the signals already. And although the building storm symbolizes the return of violence to the forefront in human affairs, it also contributes symbolic support to his new awareness.

In the past, Culver has always felt that peace and order are the reality and war merely a temporary interruption to this state. Appropriately, the Haydn passage has been used symbolically to underscore this belief. As his concept of reality changes, however, so too does the nature of the sound motif. By the end of the story, the sounds have changed in form and intensity from the soothing ordered notes of a Haydn passage to the chaotic shriek of the wounded and the roar of not-so-distant thunder.

The shattering of his illusion plunges Culver deeper than ever into a psychological morass of despair and disillusionment. A vast hunger has begun to gnaw away inside him, a hunger "for something that was as fleeting and as incommunicable, in its beauty, as that one bar of music he remembered. . . ." He has come a long way in his thinking since he was recalled into the corps; in fact, he has come a long way in those 18 or so hours since the beginning of the march. He has come to realize that he has never known "serenity, a quality of repose . . . but . . . that, somehow, it had always escaped him." He has come to the point, finally, where he can admit to himself that he has "hardly ever known a time in his life when he was not marching or sick with loneliness or afraid."

August Nigro (essay date 1967)

SOURCE: "*The Long March*: The Expansive Hero in a Closed World," in *Critique,* Vol. IX, No. 3, Winter, 1967, pp. 103-12.

[*Below, Nigro argues that* The Long March *is about the degeneration of a classical hero type into an "anti-hero" due to the corruption of the military. The critic also suggests that the military is symbolic of American society where, he argues, there is no place for the heroic personality.*]

A close examination of [**The Long March**] reveals that Styron has written a fable in which a few concrete images and symbols tell at least three related tales: the story of a forced march in a Marine camp, which demonstrates Styron's belief "that military life corrupts and we would be a lot better off without it" [William Styron, "If You Write for Television . . ." *New Republic* CXL VI (April 1959), 16]; the story of the American experience in which the individual's dream of a free and peaceful Utopia is betrayed by the suppression and bondage of a closed, tightly organized society; and finally the story of the degeneration of the hero in western civilization, from a figure who personifies the aspirations of the common man and the values of society to a grotesque anti-hero who makes a futile, but necessary, attempt to assert his personal freedom and identity in the face of a society which is consistently demanding that he sacrifice both.

The Corps and the long march become representative of a larger world, Mannix representative of a cultural hero and the encounter between the hero and the world a conflict, which once more dramatizes the discrepancy between the American Dream and the American Nightmare.

—*August Nigro*

The Marine Corps, . . . represents a social condition in which the individual is suppressed, almost enslaved, into an order which necessitates insincerity, insensitivity and subservience. The Corps uses "boy scout passwords" as "part of the secret language of a group of morons . . . who had been made irresponsibly and dangerously clever

[William Styron, *The Long March,* 1956, p. 430]. All members of the group are expected to "essay some kind of answer" when questioned about anything. Even the long march is undertaken with the provision of dog-pound trucks to pick up recruits who are expected to make a little gesture and subsequently "crap out." Not only does the Corps nurture sham and imposture, it is equally adept at desensitizing the individual. Such de-humanization is apparent in Colonel Templeton, personification of what the Corps stands for. Templeton is one "to whom the greatest embarrassment would be a show of emotion" and one who "had too long been conditioned by the system to perform with grace a human act." With his pearl-handled .38 revolver and swagger stick, "Old Rocky" is the neuter commander—the marine and not the man.

And it is against the marine, not the man, that Mannix and to a lesser extent, Culver, rebel. Early in the book, before the march commences, the fury and suffering reflected in Mannix's face are described as those of a "shackled slave" and later, after the march is well under way, the men are referred to as "zombies" and "robots" and their tired, worn expressions "like faces of men in bondage who had jettisoned all hope, and were close to defeat." Mannix's rebellion against this enforced bondage is of course ironic: on the one hand, it is an assertion of his will and pride, and regardless of his failure to bring in his company and of his impending court martial, the reader feels and sympathizes with the humanity of his suffering and the dignity of his protest. However, Mannix's endurance and rebellion as a shackled slave are incongruously and grotesquely juxtaposed to his demonic fury as a driving master of his own men. His rebellion in reverse, his "rocklike" resistance of "Old Rocky," ricochets on his men and he becomes to them what Templeton is to himself; he becomes the force against which he rebels: the enslaver.

Thus, Styron demonstrates that the Corps—all military life—corrupts. On the one hand, the Corps instills and augments the very pride that moves Mannix to rebellion, and yet it also provides the bondage and humiliation which force Mannix to rebel and become that against which he rebels. The corruption and destruction of the individual dramatized in the ordeal of Mannix is complemented by and reinforced by the lamb-like submission of Culver, who stumbles "behind the Colonel, like a ewe who follows the slaughterhouse ram, dumb and undoubting, too panicked by the general chaos to hate its leader, or care."

When the central action and main characters are viewed with more perspective and the richly suggestive images and symbols considered in their full significance, Styron's indictment of military life becomes a more general indictment of American life. The "fishy struggles" under the sea become not only the conditions of marine life, but also the general conditions that underlie the social world. The Corps and the long march become representative of a larger world, Mannix representative of a cultural hero and the encounter between the hero and the world a conflict, which once more dramatizes the discrepancy between the

American Dream and the American Nightmare.

This discrepancy between dream and nightmare is apparent from the beginning of the novella. The six years of freedom and tranquility, associated with childhood innocence in Culver's reveries, become so remote in the new world of the Corps that they become almost non-existent:

> He felt suddenly unreal and disoriented, as if through some curious second sight or seventh sense his surroundings had shifted, ever so imperceptibly, into another dimension of space and time . . . as if they were adrift at sea in a dazzling, windowless box, ignorant of direction or of any points of the globe, and with no way of telling. What he had had for the last years—wife and child and home—seemed to have existed in the infinite past or, dreamlike again, never at all . . . All time and space seemed for a moment to be enclosed within the tent, itself unmoored and unhelmed upon a dark and compassless ocean.

The preceding passage not only describes effectively how the terrible experience of Culver renders his innocent past nonexistent, but also presents a rich and suggestive metaphor of the world of *The Long March*. In the first place, it visualizes two conditions of the world in which Culver, and of course Mannix, find themselves. It is a world of containment, a world like a windowless box, but also a world which is itself a minute atom upon a compassless ocean. Such a metaphor brings to mind a similar fictional world—the ship of state used by Melville in *Billy Budd* to render the social order in microcosm. Moreover, the association extends the symbolic importance of the Corps and the march, for both become, like Melville's ship and voyage, analogous to the American experience.

This analogy between the fictional worlds of Melville and Styron is complemented by a similarity between the symbols of authority in both novellas. Templeton is to the Corps what Captain Vere is to the *Indomitable*: both represent the corruption of the individual human being by the institution. Vere is one who is "always acquitting himself as an officer mindful of the welfare of his men, but never tolerating an infraction of discipline; thoroughly versed in the science of his profession, and intrepid to the verge of temerity" [Herman Melville, "Billy Budd," *An Anthology of Famous American Short Stories* (New York, 1953), p. 154]. Moreover, he is stoical in his ability to control his emotion with his reason and will and perfect in his fidelity to the maritime law, a devotion which necessitates his sacrificing the life of Billy Budd and negating the basic human tendency towards mercy.

"Old Rocky," like Vere, has developed an impersonal detachment in his devotion to the Corps; for him the "greatest embarrassment would be a show of emotion." He too is well versed in the science of his profession, fair and adamant in his attitude toward his men, and equally intolerant of disobedience. But whereas Vere's stoic stance is explained in terms of his philosophical adherence to truth, Templeton's is explained metaphorically in terms of a religious pilgrimage. With all his emotions emanating from a "priestlike, religious fervor, throbbing inwardly with the cadence of parades and booted footfalls," Templeton is the priest leading his men to "some humorless salvation."

This extension of the metaphor of Templeton as priest and the "westward" march as a pilgrimage to some salvation suggests that the maritime ordeal described literally in *The Long March* is once again the American adventure in which an ideally conceived Christian democracy, devoted to the principle of individual freedom, has to abandon that principle in peacetime as well as in war. Even this aspect is somewhat illuminated by comparison to *Billy Budd,* in which Melville describes the efforts of the ship's clergyman to minister to the doomed hero in the following words:

> Bluntly put, a chaplain is the minister of the Prince of Peace serving in the host of the god of War—Mars. As such he is as incongruous as a musket would be on the altar at Christmas. Why then is he there? Because he indirectly subserves the purpose of the religion of the meek to that which practically is the abrogation of everything but force.

Is not this the very nature of Templeton's office and the Corps in *The Long March*? Here is the advocate of a "grandiose doctrine," the leader of a westward march to some humorless salvation, the priest who has been too long conditioned by the system to perform a human act, becoming the "creator of such a wild and lunatic punishment" as the march. Thus, the "black triangular wet spot plastered" at the back of the Colonel's dungarees, symbolic of his service to the Prince of Peace, contrasts violently with the pearl-handled revolver, emblematic of his service to the god of war.

Into the contained world of Templeton comes the expansive Mannix: a "big, relaxed mass," "huge," "enormous," "formidable," "Towering," "passionate," "sullen, mountainous," "Atlas-like,"—"a great soft scarred bear of a man." This last description of the expansive hero is only part of a consistent analogy drawn between Mannix and the bear—an analogy which calls to mind one of the most important literary expressions of the discrepancy between the American Dream and Nightmare—Faulkner's "The Bear." Examination of this analogy sheds some light on the meaning of the encounter between the expansive hero and the contained world.

Like Old Ben in Faulkner's novella, Mannix is described as a "Tormented beast in a cul-de-sac," with the "baffled fury of some great bear cornered, bloody and torn by a foe whose tactics were no braver than his own, but simply more cunning." To Culver, Mannix is an "Old great soft scarred bear of a man," who is depicted in the final scene "clawing at the wall for support." The analogy is explicit and effective: like Old Ben, Mannix represents that which is primitivistically and innately free, noble and grand in America, and he is confined, baffled and destroyed by an army of American Christian soldiers preaching a "grandiose doctrine" and practising rapine and bondage contrary to that doctrine. The Faulknerian element of the analogy is even more evident in the following passage in which the containment of the bear-like Mannix is juxtaposed with the archetypal symbol of American bondage, the Negro:

> Tormented beast in the cul-de-sac, baffled fury, grief at the edge of defeat—his eyes made Culver suddenly aware of what they were about to see, and he turned dizzily away and watched the wreck of a Negro cabin float past through the swirling dust; shell-shattered doors and sagging walls, blasting facade—a target across which for one split second in the fantastic noon there seemed to crawl the ghosts of the bereaved and the departed, mourning wraiths come back to reclaim from the ruins some hot scent of honeysuckle, smell of cooking, murmurous noise of bees.

When Mannix's size and sensitivity are seen in more human terms, the analogy is one with another noble savage, Adam. Mannix is the innocent too sensitive and honest for his own good; he is a "huge hairy baby soothed by the wash of elemental tides, ready to receive anything, all, into that great void in his soul which bitterness and rebellion had briefly left vacant . . .". Thus, Mannix is not the unfallen Adam, like Billy Budd, but rather the fallen Adam, like Ahab, who Melville writes, feels "so very, very old . . . deadly faint, bowed and humped, as though [he] were Adam staggering beneath the piled centuries since Paradise." Mannix too has suffered and his suffering has "left a persistent, unwhipped, scornful look in his eyes, almost like a stain, or rather a wound, which spells out its own warning and cautions the unwary to handle this tortured parcel of flesh with care."

Thus, extending the analogy of the Melville and Styron fictional worlds, one finds an Ahab-like hero who encounters the contained world of the Corps; and like Ahab, Mannix becomes the tyrannical enslaver of his own men. The tragic irony is explicit: the Adamic hero—sensitive, enormous, primitive, child-like—outraged by his exile from innocence and peace, tormented by the betrayal of youth around him and by his own suffering, rebels against the world that enforces bondage and nurtures insincerity and insensitivity. His rebellion is noble in that he attempts to assert the self and the natural and ideally conceived right of freedom; however, the pride and will that move him to rebellion are also the tragic flaws that blind him to his own tyranny. Thus, Mannix's defeat is ironically a self-inflicted one; and the subsequent insubordination and impending court martial are more anti-climactic, external wounds which only compound his destruction. Styron's description of Mannix's finishing the march completes the picture of the grotesque victim:

> Mannix's perpetual tread on his toe alone gave to his gait a ponderous, bobbing motion which resembled that of a man wretchedly spastic and paralyzed. It lent to his face . . . an aspect of deep, almost prayerfully passionate concentration—eyes thrown skyward and lips fluttering feverishly in pain—so that if one did not know he was in agony one might think that he was a communicant in rapture, offering up breaths of hot desire to heavens . . . it was the painted, suffering face of a clown, and the heaving gait was a grotesque and indecent parody of a hopeless cripple, with shoulders gyrating like a seesaw and with flapping, stricken arms.

This portrayal of Mannix introduces a third analogy which reinforces the dramatic presentation of the discrepancy between the American Dream and the American Nightmare: Mannix as Christ. Mannix, who is constantly invoking Christ, who is himself in his passion pierced by a nail, whose wound is described as "fat milky purple," who in a moment of agony clutches the wall, naked except for a towel around his waist, and who is identified during the march as "Christ on a crutch," does in fact become a grotesque caricature of Christ. The incongruity of Mannix as a hero is furthered when the transformation of Mannix is contrasted to the transfiguration of Melville's hero in *Billy Budd,* at whose tranquil death "the fleece of the lamb of God seen in mystical vision" hovers over the *Indomitable.*

For Melville, the hero in his death is transfigured into the resurrected Christ; for Styron, the hero's defeat suggests a beaten, whipped and spasmodic Christ. In Melville, the Christ-like resurrection of the hero contrasts with the perversion of Christian values in the microcosmic world, illustrated in the sterile service of the priest aboard a man-of-war. In Styron, the contrast becomes more violent and incongruous, as the torment of the Christ-like Mannix drastically intensifies the perverse office of the priest-like Templeton. In Melville, the individual rises above a society that seeks to destroy him; in Styron, he is crushed by that society. This is the real significance of the religious imagery throughout **The Long March**: to point out the continued crucifixion of the individual in a Christian, democratic America. . . .

The analogies of Mannix to Old Ben, Adam and Christ are only a few examples of Styron's more general application of what T. S. Eliot calls the "mythical method." According to Eliot, James Joyce's method in *Ulysses,* of "manipulating a continuous parallel between contemporaneity and antiquity," is a way of "controlling, of ordering, of giving shape and a significance to the immense panorama of futility and anarchy which is contemporary history ["*Ulysses,* Order and Myth," in *James Joyce: Two Decades of Criticism,* edited by Sean Givens (New York, 1941), p. 201]. Styron employs the same mythical method not only to bring order to the futility of contemporary life, but also to sharpen that sense of futility. Through simile, analogy and allusion, Styron identifies Mannix with a series of heroes from the literature and myth of western civilization, all of whom rebel against social and traditional authority. This identification works paradoxically: on the one hand, it transfers to Mannix an heroic tradition and heroic characteristics; but on the other hand, it sharpens the absurdity of his defeat by juxtaposing it to the grandeur of their defeats.

The first analogy is suggested in the early episode in which Mannix and Templeton are likened to Greek tragic heroes. In the tent and in what approximates a war council, Mannix, the sensitive, brooding, massive Captain, protests against the actions of his superior Colonel. The setting and the general development of verbal conflict between the warriors and the allusion to the "classical Greek masks," which their countenances suggest, convene in a drama quite comparable to the Achilles-Agamemnon conflict that opens the *Iliad*. The identification here between Mannix and Achilles is reinforced later in the march when Mannix is crippled by the wound in his heel—a wound that parallels the internal as well as the external flaw of the Greek hero. For the vulnerable heel of the Greek hero is really the physical correlative to his more significant internal flaw—his passionate *hubris*. So it is with Mannix, for the skin that is peeled away from his heel is symbolic of his heightened sensitivity, which makes him prone to rebel. Shortly after Culver notices the "sharp pinpoint of torture" on Mannix's heel, he makes this observation about the vague, unpredictable and brooding Marine: "It puzzled Culver; the explosion seemed to have stripped off layers of skin from the Captain, leaving only raw nerves exposed." Thus, Mannix, like Achilles, becomes increasingly sensitive to a subordination enforced by a military superior.

Another Greek mythic figure with whom Mannix is more directly identified is Atlas: "It was as if his own fury, his own obsession now, held up, Atlas-like, the burden of his great weariness." This comparison and the tableau in which Mannix's countenance is compared to a tragic Greek mask suggest another analogy pointed out by Hays—a similarity between Mannix and the titan-brother of Atlas, Prometheus, a Greek who rebels against divine omnipotence on behalf of suffering humanity. Still another rebel with whom Mannix is likened is Satan. Mannix's despite for "Heaven's Gate," the pleasure-dome for officers only, is figuratively as well as literally a hatred for Heaven's Gate; and Mannix's confinement to it and resentment of it echoes in essence Satan's scorn for heavenly existence: "Both Mannix and Culver hated the place," which "seemed to offer up, like a cornucopia, the fruits of boredom, of footlessness and dissolution . . . they were bound to the pleasures of the place by necessity—for there was no place to go for a hundred miles, even if they had wanted to go—and therefore out of futility."

Finally, Styron draws an analogy between Mannix and Moses. In the following passage an allusion to Exodus clearly points out that Mannix's quest is one to liberate his people from bondage: "Dust billowed up and preceded them, like Egypt's pillar of cloud, filling the air with its dry oppressive menace." But the analogy is ironically extended and just as Mannix becomes an enslaver, so his voice takes on the "sound of a satrap of Pharaoh, a galley master. It had the forbidding quality of a strand of barbed wire or a lash of thorns . . .".

This evocation of traditional heroes works contrapuntally and the reader feels the heroic dimensions of Mannix's act, but also the sharp incongruity between their grand defeats and Mannix's ignoble defeat—between Achilles' powerful lament and vengeance for the death of Patroklus, Atlas' staggering labor beneath the pillars of heaven, Prometheus' ordeal on the rock of ages, Satan's titanic fall from heaven to hell, Adam's temptation and fortunate fall, Moses' struggle in the exodus from Egypt, Christ's passion and resurrection, Ahab's magnificent failure to destroy the white whale—between all these and Mannix's paralyzed, spastic, bobbing entrance into camp. One feels with Culver that the absurdity of Mannix's defeat is compounded by the fact that his stance is "not symbolic, but individual, therefore hopeless"; nevertheless, this does not alter the basic integrity and nobility of that stance. That Mannix's rebellion is not representative of the accomodation to bondage made by the other marines is a further indictment of the meek, will-less masses who give up their freedom without even a whimper.

This protest against bondage is the main theme that emerges from Styron's fable; it is given form and vitality by the ironic and dramatic presentation of the discrepancy between the American dream of innocence and the experience of evil, between the dream of an ideal Christian, democratic America and the nightmare of an organizational America which violates Christian and democratic principles. This discrepancy is sharpened by the encounter of a primitive, expansive hero with a closed, contained society; and this American experience in turn is reinforced by and translated into more universal significance through allusion to the rebel tradition in the literature and mythology of western civilization.

Peter L. Hays (essay date 1971)

SOURCE: "Limited Man," in *The Limping Hero: Grotesques in Literature,* New York University Press, 1971, pp. 166-71.

[*In this excerpt, Hays demonstrates how Styron's language and symbolism make Mannix a mythic figure comparable to Prometheus and Christ.*]

William Styron's *The Long March* presents us with three views of rebellion: as seen by the authoritarian establishment, by the passionate rebel, and by the involved but relatively objective observer caught between the two. The novella is about life in a Marine training camp during the Korean War, especially as experienced by Lieutenant Culver and Captain Al Mannix, two World War II veterans who have been recalled from civilian life. Their upset and displacement, and a short mortar round that drops on a chow line and kills eight young soldiers, set the tone of the novel, its sense of uneasiness and horrible, futile waste. The balance of the story concerns a thirty-six mile forced march at night which the Colonel, "Rocky" Templeton, hopes will fuse his men into a self-confident, cohesive unit of fighting men.

The march is horrifying. Men collapse from fatigue, and a nail that has come through Mannix's boot cuts deeper and deeper into the Captain's foot. In defiance of Templeton, the embodiment of authority, whose apparent cold-blooded acceptance of eight boys' death as an unfortunate accident revolts him and whose forced march he considers compound stupidity, Mannix deliberately disobeys the Colonel's order to drop out of the march and ride back to the base, dragging his swollen, aching foot as he hobbles along first with, then behind, what remains of his men.

Culver is the story's narrator. He observes for us, he

comments. But he is neither man enough to join Mannix in open rebellion against the Colonel nor to quit the march. Styron shows us Culver's thoughts as he realizes that

> . . . he was not independent enough, nor possessed of enough free will, was not *man* enough to say, to hell with it and crap out himself; . . . he was not man enough to disavow all his determination and endurance and suffering, cash in his chips, and by that act flaunt his contempt of the march, the Colonel, the whole bloody Marine Corps. But he was *not* man enough, he knew, far less simply a free man; he was just a marine—as was Mannix. . . .

Eugene McNamara wrote one of the first important articles on Styron's short novel, and his title, "William Styron's Long March: Absurdity and Authority" [*Western Humanities Review*, 1961], indicates his view of Mannix's revolt. Speaking of Culver, McNamara says that "the choice he thought had to be made between Mannix and Templeton was not a choice between good and evil, but only between two different kinds of men. And Mannix, as much as Culver loves him, is out of date, obsolete, dangerous. 'He was trapped like all of them in a predicament which one personal insurrection could, if anything, only make worse.' The Colonel must be obeyed, not because he is right, but because he is the Colonel." They are in a state tantamount to war, and obedience without question to orders right or wrong is the only source of order among the chaos.

In examining the novella's metaphoric patterns, McNamara sees Mannix not only as an individualist but as the "old original Adam (or even Satan . . .), filled with pride and defiance. . . ." Colonel Templeton, in McNamara's allegorical vision, is "a 'young ecclesiastic.' . . . He is 'priest-like,' 'tenderly contemplative,' 'a stern father,' and sometimes, flatly, 'the priest.'" The Colonel is a kind of religious leader, "Mannix remains the recalcitrant Old Adam, unconverted, unconvinced, while Culver, like another famous convert who saw the light while on a journey, is converted during the march."

But if Templeton is the temple, the seat of organized religion, and Culver the convert to that religion, Mannix the rebel must be, in this play on names, the representative of man. He is lame old Adam, and nearly a cleft-foot, *non-serviam* Satan too, but he is also more: he is a Christ figure.

Styron describes Mannix, his pain, his suffering, in these terms:

> The light of dawn, a feverish pale green, had begun to appear, outlining on Mannix's face a twisted look of suffering. His eyes were closed.

> Mannix's perpetual tread on his toe alone gave to his gait a ponderous, bobbing motion which resembled a man wretchedly spastic and paralyzed. It lent to his face too . . . an aspect of deep, almost prayerful passionate concentration—his eyes thrown skyward and lips fluttering feverishly in pain—so that if one did not know he was agony one might imagine that he was a communicant in rapture, offering up breaths of hot desire to the heavens.

> His face with its clenched eyes and taut, drawn-down mouth was one of tortured and gigantic suffering.

Mannix's favorite expletive is "Jesus," even specifically, at times, "Christ on a crutch!" Mannix is a Jew; he is Old Adam and the Second Adam, the Son of Man: Jesus. The nail that pierces his foot parallels the crucifixion too closely to leave any doubt. Moreover as Caiaphas, high priest of the temple of Jerusalem, denounced Jesus, so "the Colonel looked at him steadily for a moment, coldly. Mannix was no longer a simple doubter but the heretic, and was about to receive judgment." Note Styron's use of the definite article: *the* heretic; limping anti-Christ and lame, scourged, thorn-crowned, speared, and crucified Christ have become one (Mannix was badly lacerated by mortar fragments during World War II and is also a mass of scars from head to swollen foot). The scene at the end of the novel between the maimed Jewish captain, who is wearing only a towel as a loin cloth, and the Negro maid, "the two of them communicating across that chasm one unspoken moment of sympathy and understanding," emphasizes Mannix's relationship with Christ and shows that Mannix is not just a personal rebel but a spokesman for the individual worth and human dignity of all people who have endured centuries of pain and persecution.

Styron was obviously concerned to universalize his story, to make it more than just an account of a particular contemporary event. He describes a tableau between Templeton and Mannix in the operations tent, saying that "in the morbid, comfortless light they were like classical Greek masks, made of chrome or tin, reflecting an almost theatrical disharmony." The march is an exodus: "Panic-Stricken, limping with blisters and exhaustion, and in mutinous despair, the men fled westward, whipped on by Mannix's cries. . . . Dust billowed up and preceded them, like Egypt's pillar of cloud. . . ." Like ancient sacred heroes, many of whom—including Christ—served as scapegoats, Mannix "was unable to touch his heel to the ground even if he had wanted to." Styron also says of Mannix, "He only mutilated himself by this perverse and violent rebellion," a comment that might apply to Hephaestus, Prometheus, and even Christ.

Mannix is a heretic and Templeton is a priest, but it is important to see Mannix's heresy in terms of Christ's, and to see Templeton as someone like Dostoyevsky's Grand Inquisitor. Templeton does represent order, and like the Grand Inquisitor's, his system is ultimately less painful than Mannix's; for Templeton does not force the men to march as Mannix does—the Colonel has provided trucks on which they can ride. And as Eugence McNamara has pointed out [in "William Styron's *Long March*: Absurdity and Authority"], Templeton's concern at times is paternal in nature. The conflict between Mannix and Templeton, then, is not merely the rebellion of an inferior against a superior, nor even that, as McNamara titles his article, of absurdity versus authority; Mannix and Templeton are "mighty opposites." They represent stable social order and the rebel who wants to change that order—a rebel whose actions in mild form produces progress, and in the extreme, anarchy—who wants to change things for the better or just to alter them for the sake of change.

Styron does not answer the question, which is more valuable, an orderly system or a rebel willing to challenge it; the answer of course involves knowing whether the rebel can indeed improve the system. One may consider Mannix's rebellion as a personal *non serviam* or a public proof of man's incontrovertible will and indomitable spirit in spite of pain. But however one decides, one must see Mannix as a descendent of Old Adam and Satan and Second Adam, as representative man, limited and limping.

Marc L. Ratner (essay date 1972)

SOURCE: "The Rebel Purged: *The Long March*," in *William Styron*, Twayne Publishers, 1972, pp. 57-69.

[*Below, Ratner provides an overview of the techniques and symbolism that Styron uses in* The Long March *"enlarging the narrative into his general theme of rebellion."*]

Styron's novella, . . . has been singularly neglected by most critics in its significance to Styron's development and in its thematic parallels to his other works. Generally regarded as a competent literary exercise, it has been damned with the faint praise to which Styron has been occasionally subjected; but, most often, it has been treated as a single piece.

The novella concerns a thirty-six-mile march ordered by Colonel Templeton to toughen his regiment of marine reservists called up during the Korean War. Lieutenant Culver and Captain Mannix both resent the march; but, while Culver chooses to follow orders, Mannix shows his resentment by driving his men and by cursing Colonel Templeton for his inhuman command. The plot, which seems like a stock situation in a war novel, is quite simple; but the poetic metaphors, . . . enlarge Styron's theme.

If we read the account as a realistic narrative of the conflict of two wills and if we neglect the essential mood of the novella which gives it thematic structure, then the plot does resemble a standard Hollywood product about the marines. Such a reading may lead to a misunderstanding of the story. . . . The complexity of the novel lies not in its fairly common subject but in the poetic description and structural devices which Styron utilizes in enlarging the narrative into his general theme of rebellion.

Styron has excellent control over his material, as his technique with time sequences and framing episodes indicates. Yet, for one critic, this control makes the novel "a little thematic and abstract" [Maxwell Geismar, "William Styron: The End of Innocence," in *American Moderns: From Rebellion to Conformity,* 1958]. This control affects Styron's characterizations in his first three novels, and not

until Nat Turner does he present a completely successful characterization. But Styron's poetic description and imagery are adequate compensations for his tendency toward abstract characters. Styron's use of nightmare-sharp imagery to describe Culver's feelings as observer-chorus and his use of absurd incidents to motivate Mannix's actions as a rebellious protagonist give the novel its main strength. As for Styron's controlled structure, this technique makes *The Long March* more abstract and didactic than the earlier novel. The central structure of the novel has the marks of classical Greek drama, not only in the allusions to Greek masks, in Mannix's swollen foot, and in Oedipal madness, but in the dramatic control and moral point of acceptance of the human condition. Styron does not praise that condition as must as he speaks for individual survival in a world in which the "centre cannot hold."

The Long March has, therefore, moral implications beyond its contemporary setting. Though Styron is as critical of middle-class intellectual complacency as he is of the dullness of the military mind, he at least grants Culver and Mannix an awareness of their situation and a sense of their humanity in the face of fate or necessity. Thematically, *The Long March* marks Styron's movement from the tragic hopelessness of *Lie Down in Darkness* to the affirmation of existence by survival in *Set This House on Fire* and in *The Confessions of Nat Turner*.

The novella is divided into five sections built around the framework of a forced march in a Carolina marine camp at the time of the Korean War; and the central characters, Mannix and Culver, are World War II reservists who have been called from their illusory peacetime into an illusory war. The contemporary cold war background reflects man's general sense of ineffectuality in controlling his destiny, and it is also related to Styron's general theme that Americans must forego the dream of childhood, stop mourning the loss of innocence, and begin to examine the world their naïveté has in part created. In an article about his tribulations in adapting the novella for television, Styron describes his story:

> My story's hero is also a rebellious soul, a young Marine reserve officer whose mutinous rage against authority in general, and his commanding officer in particular, leads to his downfall. . . . He resists the System and it is his ruin. You cannot buck the System—I think that is what I was trying to say—for if you do you will pull disaster down upon your head. . . . At the end of my story the captain (who is not without his foolish and impulsive moments), having faced down his commanding officer at the conclusion of a senseless and brutal hike ordered by the same CO, stands ready to receive a court martial. The tragedy is implicit here. [William Styron, "If You Write for Television . . . ," *New Republic*, CLX (April 6, 1959), 16]

In the novella, Styron neither damns nor praises the "System" particularly; he indicates the futility of rebellion without a cause. Ironically, in the course of his rebellion, *because of its pointlessness*, Mannix adapts the clichés and forms of the "System" in order to oppose it. This psychological subtlety in the novella, as much as Styron's descriptions, makes it a work of art.

Disturbed over the mishandling of his book by television writers, Styron wrote that "Divorced of its philosophical content, the narrative becomes utterly routine" and that the scriptwriters misconceived matters by the reduction of "my bedevilled, desperate captain" to a "self-pitying hero" who, far from eliciting the viewer's sympathies, deserves to be punished. At least one critic, who regards the unsympathetic attitude toward Mannix as the correct one, speaks of Styron's concept of the Marine Corps as a "kind of monastic order united in love, symbolized by the ritual which must be entered into unquestionably, with complete obedience" [Eugene McNamara, "Styron's *Long March*: Absurdity and Authority," *Western Humanities Review*, XV (Summer, 1961), 267-272]. Despite the excellent analysis of Styron's metaphors by this critic, we find little or no support for his view that Styron intended to do more than present the Marines as a system—as a "collection of attitudes," not human but mechanical ones. The humanity is found in Culver and Mannix, the observer and protagonist, respectively, of a drama of rebellion.

A close examination of Styron's techniques, his use of allusive description and economy of language, demonstrates the controlled force of the novella. The narrative opens with a scene of surrealistic horror in which the eight dead marines lie "as if sprayed from a hose, they were shreds of bone, gut and dangling tissue"; and their surviving companions moan in pain. This central image of human parts scattered among inanimate objects . . . is reworked in varied forms throughout the novel. At this point, it underscores the feelings of Lieutenant Culver who has been called back from a dream of freedom and security to the reality of contemporary existence; and it is his resentment which provides the initial consciousness of the story.

Later, the image emphasizes the thematic conflict in the novella between the mechanical coldness of Colonel Templeton and the tragic humanity of Captain Mannix. But, originally, the slaughter of the innocent soldiers clearly symbolizes the shattered sense of order in Culver's life. This sense of order is recalled through another recurring image which is juxtaposed with the scene of a winter afternoon—a Sunday stroll in which "pink-cheeked and contented" persons remain undisturbed by "crimson alarms" of headlines. Eighteenth-century music—Bach, Mozart, or Haydn—gives Culver a sense of order through which he transcends to another and happier sphere of childhood.

If we look at the first few pages of Styron's original manuscript, we find that he made a conscious effort to maintain two views of the scene: a straight naturalistic description and Culver's view. After the initial description, Styron established Culver as a focal consciousness, an observer, who in turn is observed by the reader. Though Styron described Culver's civilian life with its security and routine in sharp, distinct detail, he cut sharply into a later description of Culver's earlier experiences around the marine camp. This description would have taken the reader back to an even remoter period from the present action and would have reduced the effect of Styron's narrative. It was most important for Styron to establish the contrast between the apparent harmony of civilian life for Culver and the chaos and disorder of the present. In these first few pages, we observe also Styron's choice of words and his avoidance of awkward phrasing: "hose" replaces "flit-gun," and "blood and brain" are juxtaposed not with "pork-chops" but with "scattered mess-kits" to give the mechanistic-human contrast.

Styron pointedly contrasts this world of logic, peace, and order to the chaos of wartime life in a strange land of tourist cabins and "unlovely mementoes." His technique in this first section is to shift from the explosion as a "crazy, insulting impact at Culver's belly" to his protest at the explosion which blew up his private world, to a speculation of the illusory order, and, finally, to the chaos of war. Thus, Styron creates with skill and economy the ambiance for his novel by following the natural thought of his observer, Culver.

Styron's main theme about the shattering effects of existence and reality is developed . . . through a series of moments which develop his narrative before the actual march begins. For example, the second section returns to the sound of the explosion, reworking the image "scattered faces peering toward the noise, their knives and forks suspended," to bring Culver and the reader back to the reality of the moment. Styron then rapidly delineates the two major characters, Colonel Templeton and Captain Mannix, and the officers and men who assume varied stances in relation to the two apparently opposing points of view.

Colonel Templeton fulfills the role of a priest of war who dogmatically does his duty; a man unreasoningly in the grip of an idea, he gives little sign of humanity toward others since he has surrendered it to the marines. Indeed, he is Styron's most adamantine character. Since this work is a novella, Styron cannot develop Templeton's character as he does Helen Loftis's in *Lie Down in Darkness* or Mason Flagg's in *Set This House on Fire*; but Templeton resembles them: he is the embodiment of all the values of his community or group. . . .

Culver's early view of the Colonel's "act" as that of a rigid military type and as one that is, therefore, "less offensive, less imperious than it might be," is carried through the narrative not as a defense but as a statement of fact. For the Colonel at the end is hardly a man but is a collection of attitudes. Elsewhere, Styron has described the professional military man as unconcerned with patriotism. "His devotion is to a service not to a country"; and, says Styron, "A true military man is a mercenary . . . and it is within the world of soldiering that he finds his only home" [William Styron, "MacArthur's Reminiscences," *New York Review of Books*, III (October 8, 1964), 3-5, a review of General Douglas MacArthur's books]. The most chilling aspect of the Colonel is his utter lack of humanity, of good or evil; for he is a mechanical toy whose reaction to Mannix's challenge is the stereotype of the Western hero who reaches for his gun. That Culver loathes rather than hates the Colonel because he is nonhuman is apparent from the way he regards the Colonel's concern for Mannix's wound: "He didn't hate him for himself, nor even for his brutal march. Bad as it was, there were no doubt worse ordeals; it was at least a peaceful landscape they had to cross. But he did hate him for his perverse and brainless gesture: squatting in the sand, gently, almost indecently now, stroking Mannix's foot, he had too long been conditioned by the system to perform with grace a human act."

In an early scene Styron appears to have set Mannix and the Colonel as contrasts of human victim and inhuman torturer, respectively. But the confrontation is deceptive, for Styron subtly draws a number of comparative scenes between the two which suggest greater similarities than differences. Certainly, they are unlike physically; the Colonel's small hands and pretty face are markedly different from Mannix's huge, hairy frame. Mannix detests the Colonel as a symbol of "absolute and unquestioned authority." But, as they face each other in the tent after the Colonel has announced the march, Culver sees them as strangely similar: "In the morbid, comfortless light they were like classical Greek masks, made of chrome or tin, reflecting an almost theatrical disharmony; the Colonel's fleeting grin sculpted cleanly and prettily in the unshadowed air above the Captain's darkened, downcast face where, for a flicker of a second, something outraged and agonized was swiftly graven and swiftly scratched out."

The Colonel's face is fixed with the certitude, the equilibrium of the dogmatist who never doubts his actions, while, for an instant, the beginnings of Mannix's terrible anger are part of his mask. Styron creates the tension of their struggle by present-both men in terms of their inflexible masks. For Mannix loses his identity as surely as the Colonel. He discards his humanity, not unlike a minor Ahab; and, because of his monomaniacal hatred of the Colonel, he blinds himself to his own and to his men's suffering. However, by the end of the novel he has regained his humanity and has even given Culver a renewed sense of values. Minor characters such as Major Lawrence, a bootlicking "spoiled and arrogant baby of five" with cheeks of "peacetime fleshiness," and O'Leary, whose dedication is of a more acceptable, oxlike variety, are worthy of the Colonel's indulgence because of their loyalty; both serve as contrasts to Mannix's rebellious mood.

Additional background is supplied by Culver's drowsing dream in which he recalls Mannix's challenge and the Colonel's defense of the march. When Mannix first speaks to Culver, his "unqualified cynicism" is offset by his comic exasperation with the Colonel; but his bitter comments ultimately generate fears in Culver. There is logic in Mannix's point that a thirty-six-mile forced march without some shorter conditioning hikes is absurd, but there never seems to be any question of Mannix's "making it." The fear is Culver's, and his anxiety about the march becomes symbolic to him of the terrible load of his loneliness and isolation. Listening to Mannix renews Culver's earlier anxieties; he feels "adrift at sea . . . ignorant of any direction or of any points of the globe." He feels profoundly alone with his nameless anxiety, for the world of order is stripped away.

The pointless maneuvers, the constant movement, and the lack of sleep have disoriented time and space. The sun's blinding heat and light make the day a continual inferno; the night offers no respite; and Culver experiences the feeling of death while still subject to the terrors of life. Culver's mind is obsessed with the march and with his fear of failure. This fear is amplified after Mannix lumbers to bed while Culver sits in the "chill and cramped universe of the tent" and listens to the wailing signals of the radio. His own messages in absurd code make him feel childish, and he empathizes completely with Mannix's feelings of helplessness. Yet Culver . . . cannot bring himself to act— not even to offset his frustration.

Culver's speculations about Mannix as hero relate directly to Styron's idea of the equivalent blindness of the dogmatist and the heretic. Mannix's scarred body testifies that he has suffered as a hero, but his experiences have been absurd, not heroic. Indeed, Styron frames Mannix's brave, perilous, and rocklike rebellion with two significant episodes pertinent to the nature of his rebellion. In the first scene, Mannix yells for help into a broken telephone while being shelled by his own men; in the second, he faces death while being held outside a window by two drunken marines. Interspersed with these two episodes are a series of incidents in which Mannix rebels against the dehumanizing abstraction that is the Marine Corps. His muttering during the cliché-filled lecture and his "manifesto" that the reserves "should be home with their families" is controlled, but his passionate feeling comes through. "His words had the quality, the sternness, of an absolute and unequivocal fact, as if they had been some intercession for grace spoken across the heads of a courtroom by a lawyer so quietly convinced of his man's innocence that there was no need for gesticulations or frenzy."

Mannix thus becomes as dogmatic and as blind as his antagonist, the Marine Corps; and his rebellion is based on self-pity and personal pride. This situation is distinctly different from the two earlier ones in which Mannix had no self-pity or pride but was trying to survive. Culver sees him "projected against Heaven's Gate," the officers' club, at which Mannix beweeps his "outcast state" and troubles "deaf heaven" with his "bootless cries." The background to Mannix's voice is supplied by the distant bleating saxophone, "indecisive and sad, like the nation and the suffocating summer, neither at peace or at war"; and the pointlessness of individual protest appears to Culver to be more dangerous than absurd. The danger becomes more evident when later in the novel we see Mannix brutalized by the "System." Before his redemption at the end of the novel, Mannix must be purged of that element of the "System" within himself.

The image of Mannix, clutching the air as he hangs high

over the street while his legs slowly slip in the wet hands of the two marines, is a foretaste of the novella's end. When the moment or recollection of terror and helplessness is over, Mannix laughs listlessly; and Culver sees his bitterness melt: "he seemed no longer the man who could sicken himself with resentment, but relaxed, pliable even, like a huge hairy baby soothed by the wash of elemental tides, ready to receive anything, all, into that great void in his soul which bitterness and rebellion had briefly left vacant—all—the finality of more suffering, or even death." This view of Mannix is almost identical, even to physical description, with our final view of him at the end of the novella. Through this repetition of description Styron connects the early scene with Mannix's return from insanity.

Styron's interest in the rebel and in the idea of rebellion is twofold: personal and social. Primarily for Styron the great value of action is that, through rebellion, the rebel discovers the evils of the "System" in himself, cut through self-illusions, and exorcises his devils to become a mature person.

—Marc L. Ratner

At this point in the novel, however, Culver knows only the fear, uncertainty, and loneliness which Mannix's "resigned silence" feeds. The children on the lawn and the ordered music are lost in the chaos of his present life. At this moment, Culver, who is wakened by the noonday light, returns again to the moment of explosion, which tears into Culver's consciousness, thrusting him "back into the blinding sun, the meaningless scenery of a fantastic noon." The larger frame which encompasses parts one and two is that of the explosion scene and, with it, the horror of the young marine, his face blasted away, his head surrounded by darting insects. The explosion releases Mannix's hatred; his calmness, serenity, and humor fail him; and he becomes a furious man who blinded by his rage, cries, "Won't they ever let us alone?"

The third and fourth sections deal with the march and with Mannix's self-imposed agony when he accepts, for example, the nail in his shoe as part of his bitter fortune. Culver realizes that the explosion had left Mannix's "raw nerves exposed" and that his loss of humanity is clear not only from his lack of concern for himself but also from his bullying attitude toward his men. Throughout the march Mannix, who appears demented, loses himself in his madness as thoroughly as the Colonel does in his coolness. Pitted against such an enemy, Mannix accepts the Colonel's "challenge" as personal and answers it with his masochistic pride.

With the "bloody wasteland" as a setting and with the "brainless chorale" of frogs emanating from the swamp, the marines begin their march. Mannix's strident commands are to Culver those of a "fanatic with one idea: to last" and to spite the Colonel. Mannix's moods range from mania to depressed silences; he viciously abuses his men; and his irrationality leads to imaginary conversations with the Colonel on whom he has centered all the hatred and frustration of his rebellion. Culver, on the other hand, hopes for relief from the Colonel, whom he has hitherto regarded as a stern but merciful father. Neither Mannix nor Culver receives the desired response of wrath or mercy, for the Colonel continues relentlessly. When the Colonel stops to examine Mannix's wound, Culver sees Templeton's total lack of humanity. Culver then realizes that Templeton is as indifferent as the universe to man's pain. While this moment is one of revelation to Culver, it is the moment of battle for Mannix, who challenges the Colonel; the lack of Templeton's response only infuriates Mannix further.

The march continues; and, as dawn breaks, the lash of Mannix's voice driving his exhausted men on seems to Culver the one continuing impression of the chaotic night. Styron's description of the "almost prehistoric sun" recalls the vision of the shattered dead, the explosion which blots from Culver's memory any consoling scenes of his past. As Culver's mind slips into fevered blankness, he becomes deranged in the heat; and, for a brief space, he loses connection with reality: not stopping to help a sick marine, passing through a crowd of butterflies, being taunted by passing marines in a jeep, and finally seeing a scarlet tanager metamorphose into "eight butchered corpses."

Winding his watch brings Culver back to time and to a scene of Mannix's bullying. He intervenes, appealing to Mannix's humanity. Until this point, Mannix has been speaking to his men in the brutal clichés of the march; but, when Culver pleads with him, Mannix becomes inarticulate and turns away in bitter isolation. Determined to prove himself beyond the bounds of sanity, and with his men in bondage to his madness, Mannix has lost all sense of proportion on hearing that the Colonel may have quit. Mannix has become a fanatic prophet, a Moses, who whips his followers under the burning sun.

Culver realizes that Mannix and he have never escaped being "marines"—"The corruption begun years ago in his drill-field feet had climbed up, overtaken him and had begun to rot his brain." Paradoxically, Mannix wishes to prove this corps "*esprit*" to the Colonel. Maxwell Geismar, who refers to the captain as "Nixman," points out that Mannix's "form of rebellion is indeed simply to outdo his fantastic Colonel's wildest notions of a *Marine*" [Geismar]. By the end of the novel, Mannix is cured of his monomania—his "rebellion in reverse."

As Mannix gathers the last of his men to be marched, out of pride and spite, for the last six miles, he faces the Colonel: "Mannix was no longer a simple doubter but the heretic, and was about to receive judgment." As they confront each other, they are "twin profiles"; for each has surrendered his identity: one, to the marine "system"; the other, to sightless rage; and both men lack Culver's compassion. The Colonel's gesture of power reveals the pointlessness of Mannix's "rebellion in reverse," for Mannix's Oedipal blindness has had no more point to it than the Colonel's command to make the march. The absurdity is underscored by the description of Mannix's face as he completes the march: "it was the painted, suffering face of a clown."

At the end, Culver, unable to rest, reviews the incidents of the march and of the explosion against the setting of "Heaven's Gate." Thinking of the eight dead boys, who are now past caring and who were ignorant of what their life and death meant, Culver recalls the softness of Emily Dickinson's "Safe in their alabaster chambers . . . sleep the meek members of the resurrection." The image of the boys, which carried with it the explosion symbolizing the destruction of Culver's ordered life, now calls up a mature acceptance of real tragedy and, with it, comes the "tender miracle of pity." Culver feels a "deep vast hunger" for the peace which had always escaped him. When he considers the significance of the march, Culver can no more hate the Colonel than before; but he now recognizes him for what he is: "hardly a man at all, but just a quantity of attitudes . . . remote from Culver's world." Culver's recognition is a significant change; for, like the hero of Stephen Crane's *Red Badge of Courage*, he recognizes how disproportionate were his fears.

Mannix, the tragic-absurd hero, summons a more despairing picture to Culver, whose sympathy for Mannix increases after his "defeat" by the Colonel. Paradoxically, the Colonel's "victory" reduces Mannix to nothing less than a *true* man, and he emerges as more of a human being than the Colonel. Styron draws a final picture of suffering man when Mannix, with "taut drawn-down mouth . . . of tortured and gigantic suffering," faces the Negro maid who speaks sympathetically to him: "Culver would remember this: the two of them communicating across that chasm one unspoken moment of sympathy and understanding." For Culver, the sensitive observer, renders Mannix's redemptive act as meaningful. We see Mannix again as a man of flesh and bone; scarred and naked as Odysseus on the Phaeacian shore, he appears as possessed "not with self-pity but only with the tone of a man" who has endured and lasted. Mannix's madness is over and he is reborn through the purgatory of suffering to become a man "too weary to tell . . . anything but what was true."

Styron, who originally thought of entitling the story "A Walk Through the Night," obviously felt that "The Long March" was a better title for the implications of his story. The march brings out Mannix's rebellion against the "System" and the need to assert his own being. . . . Yet it is as important to see that Styron's interest in the rebel and in the idea of rebellion is twofold: personal and social. Primarily for Styron the great value of action is that, through rebellion, the rebel discovers the evils of the "System" in himself, cuts through his self-illusions, and exorcises his devils to become a mature person. . . .

It was to be eight years before Styron's next novel, *Set*

This House on Fire, but the similar moral concerns and themes of choice and freedom are present there in contradistinction to the fatalistic world of *Lie Down in Darkness*. *The Long March* is the first of Styron's clear-cut novels of rebellion, which were to culminate in the figure of Nat Turner.

Irving Malin (essay date 1975)

SOURCE: "The Symbolic March," in *The Achievement of William Styron,* University of Georgia Press, 1975, pp. 122-33.

[*In the excerpt below, Malin discusses symbolism, characterization, and Styron's use of body imagery and contrast.*]

The opening paragraph of *The Long March* tells us much about the symbols, themes, and characters of the entire novelette. Styron begins with "noon," the hottest part of the day; the heat is as intense and extreme as the events—and the reactions to these events—he will eventually describe. (Even *noon* is intensified by the word *blaze*.) Then Styron introduces the human element: "eight dead boys are thrown apart among the poison ivy and the pine needles and loblolly saplings." The contrasts are vivid—the boys are dead, wasted, "strewn"; the noon burns with energy. Several questions leap to mind. How do men face extinction? What is the role of accident or design? Can death be meaningful?

We would expect Styron to give us more information about the *causes* of death, but he maintains the suspense. He simply informs us in the next sentence that the boys, only "shreds of bone, gut, and dangling tissue," look as if they had *always* been dead. Their past lives have disappeared. The continuity between past and present is shattered. (This theme is one of Styron's characteristic ones.) But we do know that the accident occurs in the early 1950s under "a Carolina sun" as the Marines train for service during the Korean War.

The mystery continues, but we now meet Lieutenant Culver, the "center of consciousness." He is an alert, thoughtful observer—he, like us, will have to put the pieces into some pattern—if only to *survive*. It is interesting that his sentence is the longest one so far; it contains so many qualifications, so many turns of syntax, because he does not know how to get to the heart of the situation. He cannot act simply; he must reflect at length. Thus his "how? why?"—which occur at midpoint in the sentence—seem to capture his thoughts. His question is said to buzz furiously; it is as active as the "noontime heat" which is again mentioned. Culver identifies with the "fifteen or so surviving marines" who barely escaped death; his questions are theirs as well. His initial response to the entire scene—to the "eight dead boys" and to the survivors—is perfectly natural: he vomits. And his vomiting, like his questioning, establishes our sympathy with him.

Styron tells us more about Culver. He gives us many details which demonstrate that our guide (through the "underbrush") is both a man of action and feeling. He is not a career officer; he is, on the contrary, an ironic commentator. He has the intelligence to ask the right questions about the causes of the training accident, even though he is "pulsing" with excitement. He does not, in other words, simply react without thinking about his reactions. His age clearly demonstrates that he is "no longer an eager kid just out of Quantico with a knife between his teeth." He is a tired thirty-year-old who seems to be out of place, having been called back for service during the Korean War.

There are many images which suggest the "unreality" of the entire situation. Culver sees among the "slick nude litter of intestine and shattered blue bones" some spoons—the survivors had been eating—which peek out "like so many pathetic metal flowers." What a strange description! We don't usually expect flowers to be metallic and, of course, we don't expect them to be "pathetic." Metal, abstract emotion, and nature—the three things are thrown together. It is up to Culver to define each, or better yet, to explore what is *truly human*. The description is metaphorically precise, but it also suggests that the lieutenant is a kind of visionary. He makes "odd," poetic connections.

I want to express the visionary qualities of Culver (which, by the way, make him an even more interesting guide). We are told that before he was called back to service during the Korean crisis, he experienced an "odd distress." He was dream-ridden; he was baffled by peace. But he enjoyed one recurrent vision of Sunday strolls in the park—he saw nature then as kind and calm (in contrast to the present "noon"). When Culver remembers peacetime, he thinks of the calm city heartbeat, the "pink-cheeked" people, the "sooty white tatters" of a recent snow, and these various images contrast sharply with the explosive, fragmented, and violent scene before his eyes. And in sharp contrast to the "pathetic metal flowers," he remembers two lovely little girls "like tumbling flowers." It is significant that the first part of the novelette ends with Culver's feeling that his last day before his return to service had been an "evil" one. He had to relinquish carefully defined pleasures for the renewed uncertainty of wartime service. The last sentence stresses blurring vision—he will have to see things differently; he enters strange coasts. He is adrift.

By the end of the first part, Styron has indicated the contrasts which he will develop throughout his narrative: peace and war; thought and action; "vision" and "reality"; design and accident; humanity and nonhumanity. It is Culver's fate to see distinctions clearly and to confront, if not artistically shape, them for his future well-being.

Part two begins again with the immediate past before the explosion and this time the warning signals are emphasized: a rustling of leaves; a *crump crump* noise. The contrasts between the "earth-shaking sound" and the relative silence of mealtime, between almost-cosmic inter-ruption and daily routine, are vividly suggestive. They remind us of Culver's anxiety in the midst of peacetime—war always shatters things. And when Styron introduces the unease of a "clownish" radio corporal who is said to be usually "whimsical," we feel an "added dread."

Now we meet the colonel. His name is not mentioned at first; his rank (power) is all that is important. We are surprised that he receives the news of the explosion as if it were the most "routine of messages." He cannot feel dread. Although Culver recognizes that Colonel Templeton is probably "acting," he is irritated by the neat performance. Perhaps he would like to share the colonel's calm. (His own suspense throbs "inside him like a heart-beat.") We are not told. We sense, however, the growing conflict between them.

At this point Captain Mannix is introduced. His first word is "Jesus." This is the beginning of a later symbolic identification of the captain and Christ. (When we learn that he is a dark Jew aged thirty, we are not surprised.) Mannix is outraged by the meaningless explosion, but unlike Culver, he says something. He demands to know and to punish the agents of destruction. What will Congress do about such accidents? He seeks meaningful authority which he can understand. Thus he will be able to fight "the sons of bitches" responsible for such accidents.

The stage is set for a close view of the three men. There is tension among them because they react so differently. Culver, still the "center of consciousness," stands in awe of the others. He observes; he passively notes things. He regards Templeton ironically as a prematurely aged "ecclesiastic," but he is afraid of the man's voice "which expected to be obeyed." The colonel represents "absolute and unquestioned authority." In Freudian terms Templeton is the father as lawgiver; surely his name and the religious metaphors (like "ecclesiastic") suggest an Old Testament wrath.

Culver is "in a constant state of half amusement, half terror," not knowing how to work out his tensions. He is a weak son. (We are never informed about psychological reasons for his attitudes.) He would like to be as rebellious as Mannix, but he cannot. Thus he thinks of him not as his "sibling" or partner but as another kind of superior being. Mannix is "*man*" as rebel against authoritarian commands; he is, oddly, as mysterious as Templeton (despite all his vocal complaints.)

Culver wants to sleep—to retreat from choosing between the alternatives of Mannix and Templeton. He dreams "fitfully" of home. But sleep, peace, and home no longer exist for a marine. And when the sergeant announces a "long walk tonight," we share his anxiety and gloom. Culver is trapped, recognizing that the long march may be as explosive as the real explosion, and he resents the sergeant. He pictures him "grafted to the system as any piece of flesh surgically laid on to arm or thigh." (Culver continually thinks of the body; he is keenly aware of mortality.)

Now Culver remembers that he heard of the march the night before. There is a flashback. He recalls Mannix and Templeton acting out their psychologically determined roles. Templeton is "solitary," aloof, and amused by Mannix's hot complaints. Both men (and also Culver) seem to be puppets. Culver is "the only one in the tent who could see, at the same instant, both of their expressions. In the morbid, comfortless light they were like classical Greek masks, made of chrome or tin, reflecting an almost theatrical disharmony." These lines are important. Culver is pictured again as solitary observer; he is caught between the two men. He sees more than either one, but he cannot forcefully act. He regards himself as audience. The irony is that he is "doomed" to his role as spectator—as much as the heroes on stage. By performing their habitual roles, Templeton and Mannix are nonhuman masks. They have lost some sense of choice; they apparently *must* act as they do. They are made out of "chrome or tin"; they perform mechanically. This is not to say that Culver fails to admire them. Using such words as *devout* and *religious,* he tries to be ironic—to shield himself from commitment (running up on stage)—but his admiration shines through his own ironic mask: he is oddly in awe of these extreme, godlike figures.

Mannix wears a mask of rebellion. He smiles toughly; he curses, saying "Christ on a crutch!" His gestures and remarks are "exaggerated." We are not told why. Does he choose his part? Or is it an overcompensation for chores forced upon him? The questions are important, but Styron does not answer them, except to suggest that Mannix is not a "regular."

Mannix, however, makes Culver squirm. Culver can no longer regard the march as an "abstraction"; he surrenders his theoretical view of life—at least for the time being. The imagery is significant here. Again Culver is the symbolist, finding that his surroundings "had shifted, ever so imperceptibly, into another dimension of space and time." He scrutinizes things in a dreamlike, lurid light: Mannix's "shadow cast brutishly against the impermeable walls by a lantern so sinister that its raging noise had the sound of a typhoon at sea"; he is in a "dazzling, windowless box"; he is upon a "dark and compassless ocean." The emphasis is upon exaggerated, neurotic visions of immobility and, strangely, movement. Culver lies *between* his superiors, between *all* the opposites of life. He dangles.

Culver may be an abstractionist, but he is controlled by his body. Indeed, he is afraid of it—he would like to get out of it . . . and fly away or back in time—and we can recognize that the opening explosion is also a traumatic symbol of his psychological needs. There is a subtle interaction between the external event and the internal interpretation, a field of action. It is almost possible to say that the explosion would have to be "invented" (if it had not occurred) to satisfy Culver's imagination. He courts it as a reflection of his inner being.

Culver gradually becomes less of the careful observer we had taken him to be—he is a kind of sick symbolist, unaware of his resemblance to either Mannix or Templeton. As he broods about the forthcoming march—we are still in the lengthy flashback—he hears noises; he sees things; and he discovers meaning in the wails. The radio noises seem "like the cries of souls in the anguish of hell." We have once more the religious metaphors, but we don't know how to respond precisely to them. Why does Culver see (or hear) hell? Does he *believe* in an *actual* hell? Why should he use the word? Styron has not given us enough of Culver's background to establish the religious frame of reference. We are tempted to take the earlier words as ironic. Irony has given way—to what? Despite these questions, we are moved by the curious linkage of private and cosmic symbols, especially when Culver thinks of himself in a contained "universe" of sound.

One long paragraph makes his symbolist universe especially clear. Culver thinks of the captain as a fellow symbolist. Mannix is said to be a code maker, a creator of a different kind of language from the "secret language" of the military. In this respect he destroys such words as *hero* which means different things for marine and civilian. Mannix yearns for "pure" meanings. He tries to find these in his body scars. He is down-to-earth. What is fascinating for us, if not to either man, is that although both are symbolists, one is conscious (Culver) and the other unaware of his imaginative creations (Mannix).

There is a flashback *within* the flashback. Styron insists upon the "pastness" of events; he pictures time as an ever-receding point. The marines have to cope with a never-ending (indeed, always beginning) universe which can never escape from symbolic meanings.

We meet Mannix, Culver, and Templeton five months earlier—just after the reserves have been called back. They are slaves to a "horde of cunningly designed, and therefore often treacherous machines." *Peonage, renewed bondage,* and *oppressive weather* are some descriptive words used by Styron. Mannix is, as usual, the rebel, falling asleep during orientation meetings. He irritates the lectures, but he also "inspires" Culver. Culver is off the center stage; he sits down "during the darkness of a lantern slide." But he does not feel entirely comfortable. Styron makes much at this point of *space.* The lecture "hall" is contrasted to the "Heaven's Gate" of the officers. Culver feels trapped by both. Although he should feel at home in the latter "pleasure-dome ingeniously erected amid a tangle of alluvial swampland, and for officers only," he finds little joy in this "playground" and, of course, less joy in the dark hall. Both places—like the marines and the body itself—trap him. He would like to "burn down the place" and assert his freedom from necessity.

One incident reinforces these symbols of imprisonment. Mannix recalls a past event—notice how we move even more deeply into time; our movement is, appropriately enough, a "long march"—and we see him drunk in a hotel room in San Francisco. He emerges naked from a shower and suddenly finds himself pushed out of the window by his buddies: "Imagine being that high upside-down in space with two drunks holding onto your heels. . . . I just remember the cold wind blowing on my body and that dark, man, infinite darkness all around me." The incident is perhaps the most explosive one so far described—with the exception of the opening explosion—because it strips Mannix (and Culver, his listener) of everything. He is "less than human"; he is alone with the sense of mortality. He dangles in space; he is out of control. But there are ironies. He realizes then that he is "human" and that no other person can help him get out of his condition.

Culver does not know what to make of Mannix, the survivor; he stares at him, but he cannot completely understand him. The peaceful scene—they are near the sea—blurs before his eyes. Instead of the "promenade of waves"—so unlike the possible fall into space—he sees the "substanceless night" in which he, and all slaves, move. Blood rushes to his head.

Suddenly we are wrenched back to the "noon" of the explosion. Culver snaps awake. (But which is the dream? The past or the present?) He is, nevertheless, unable to tell where he is. Styron writes that "time seemed to have unspooled past him in a great spiral." Finally he realizes that he is listening not to Mannix but to the sergeant. He must still go on the forced march. In the jeep with Templeton and Mannix, he closes his eyes. He fights his visionary nature, not wanting to see the "ghosts of the bereaved and the departed" or the "motions without meaning." He longs for sleep.

The scene shifts. Styron moves from Culver's closed eyes to the closed eyes of one boy killed by the explosion. They are "brothers." Perhaps Mannix senses this identification (and his own) when he says in the last words of this section: "Won't they ever let us alone?"

Part three begins at twilight "just before the beginning of the march"; the time is appropriate because Culver is very unsure of his motives. The "noon" intensity has given way to dim vision. Mannix finds a nail in his shoe. The nail is, of course, an omen of doom—it functions as an almost-Greek "curse"—but it also serves to inspire his rebellious nature. He needs this "pinpoint of torture" as a kind of muse and, consequently, he refuses to listen to Culver's common sense.

What are we to make of Mannix here? He is far from the classical hero. He courts death in a "nervous and touchy way." He is "at odds with his men, to whom he usually had shown the breeziest good will." He twitches. He is, to use Styron's phrase, a bundle of "raw nerves." (The body imagery is never omitted.) But Mannix is a modern "hero" because he accepts the absurdity of things. He laughs painfully. He goes to extremes in an already extreme situation. He obsessively defies the marine obsessions of Colonel Templeton. He considers the nail as his private symbol—of "lousy luck" and also the lust for survival.

Culver recognizes the symbolic thrust of Mannix. He also sees Templeton as symbolic. When the colonel appears "neat, almost jaunty, in new dungarees and boots," carry-ing a ".38 revolver," the gun becomes Templeton's "emblematic prerogative." Note the contrast between the nail and the .38. Both objects are imbued with "power" by their owners; they become unreal and huge, carrying abstract meanings. It is also interesting to consider their metallic qualities. By surrendering to their symbolic objects, the men act mechanically—like the puppets mentioned once before.

Culver cannot explain his feelings, but he emphasizes his fears. He thinks of "helpless children," puny houses of "straw," "cataleptic sleep"—the recurring symbols capture his descent into panic. Surely Culver knows that he is involved in the march; he can no longer be out of view.

The march begins. Culver stares at the colonel who pushes "ahead in front of him with absolute mechanical confidence of a wound-up, strutting tin soldier on a table top." He cannot laugh at the metallic man. He is hopelessly involved with his own body—pains. The body, which had been pictured previously as a threatening, claustrophobic container, grows in symbolic importance. It is Culver's enemy. It forces him to do things he hates; he is thirsty; he is sweaty; he is faint. By insisting upon Culver's physical pains, Styron also makes us recognize that there is no way out of the body—symbolic meanings are physically earned: "And so it was that those first hours Culver recollected as being the most harrowing of all, even though the later hours brought more subtle refinements of pain. He reasoned that this was because during the first few miles or so he was at least in rough possession of his intellect, his mind lashing his spirit as pitilessly as his body." The "lashing," the "rough possession"—such words suggest that the master-slave relationship of Templeton and his men is mirrored privately in Culver. He cannot coexist with his body—except with great struggle. Thus before the "breather," he looks at Mannix and sees a "shape, a ghost, a horror—a wild and threatful face reflected from the glass." He identifies with him in this "absurd" universe of mirrors.

When they continue the march, Culver wonders how he will last. He is a fish under the sea—falling deeply (like Mannix in the hotel?). Then he is a "ewe who follows the slaughterhouse ram." His passivity asserts itself in such symbolic details. Consequently, when he sees Mannix limping, he shares his pain, and offers some advice. The Christ words are stressed here; both officers are in a state of communion, plagued by the crucifixions of the march (stations of the cross?).

Templeton appears to smile at them. He looks "like the priest in whom passion and faith had made an ally, at last, of only the purest good intentions; above meanness or petty spite, he was leading a march to some humorless salvation." He is the false father, hiding his intentions behind "solicitous words." He hopes to grind Mannix to dust with kindness. He tells him to *ride*, not to march any more: "Nothing could have been worse."

Culver hates Templeton not as Templeton but as "the Colonel, the marine." He considers him as the very symbol of all the "crazy, capricious punishment" imposed upon him. But he dimly understands that the colonel, like Mannix, is part of his own mind. The long march is within!

The march continues and becomes "disorganized." Styron plays with such notions as "organization" and "disorganization." One is as bad as the other. The former suggests Templeton, authoritarian principles, unquestioning allegiance; the latter hints at complete chaos. Styron apparently believes that one must be "loose," ironic, and aware of patterns or, better yet, able to shape patterns flexibly without yielding to either wildness or rigidity.

In the absence of Templeton (who has gone away in a truck), Mannix goes to extremes. He will endure the march; he will transform the pattern imposed upon him into his *own. He will create order.* What black comedy! The rebel becomes the complete organization man, despite his "terrible limp."

Styron is ambivalent about Mannix and his command. He admires—or at least Culver does—the captain's "perversity" and courage, but he suggests that he acts like a robot. (We find the same kind of situation in Ahab's "mad" march toward the whale, not knowing how to distinguish between "perversity" and "heroism.") Culver, like an Ishmael, wants to say to Mannix: "*you've lost; stop*": "Nothing could be worse than what Mannix was doing—adding to a disaster already ordained (Culver somehow sensed) the burden of his vicious fury." But he cannot vent his own rage.

Culver recognizes that he is less of man than Mannix. He lacks the power to rebel against him (as the captain did against Templeton); he remains passive. Once more he thinks of "crazy cinematic tape, chaos, vagrant jigsaw images." He even dreams of cubed ice in a carnival tent. The machine, the performance, the box (tent)—all imply that Culver regards himself as an actor in someone else's confined script. He is no longer the reflective spectator watching classical masks; he is at center stage.

Templeton returns and demands that Mannix ride in the truck. Culver again recognizes the symbolic structure: when men cannot agree upon symbols (or words like *heroism, courage,* and *devotion*), they must battle. He tries vainly to separate the two men (and thereby act powerfully), recognizing that they have lost their manhood in loyalty to abstractions. And yet, in a perverse way, he is as rigid as they. All of them—not merely Mannix—are distorted, painted clowns.

The last line of this section is "What the hell," [Mannix] whispered, "we've made it." It is ambiguous. *Have they made anything?* Have they, on the contrary, been made? And "it"? What has Mannix won—except an insane, clownlike pattern? Styron does not permit Culver to respond here. The omission is especially interesting, suggesting that there are few final solutions or victories. Each man must believe that "he has made it"—if only to go on

living—but he is finally alone without any listeners or critics. He is isolated in his symbolic universe.

Part five attempts to resolve the ambiguities. Culver lies in bed, trying to sleep. (Styron uses the contrast between the march and stasis.) He closes his eyes. But he cannot join the dead boys of the explosion because he is, after all, an aware survivor.

He keeps seeing visions—of open space and commingled "sunshine and darkness." These keep him in touch with reality; they will not permit him to drift away. The visions, like Styron's symbolic details, are full of commingled opposites. When Culver looks out of the window, he notices the officers' swimming pool ("grottoblue") and "decorous" wives. (We think of their presence in contrast to the boys' strewn bodies.) But Culver moves beyond "Heaven's Gate"; he senses the "threatful beginnings of a storm." He knows that angry thunder lurks over "peace and civilization."

Culver feels a "deep vast hunger" for some transcendental vision which will *overarch* grottolike peace and threatening storm, dead boys and "lovely little girls with their ever joyful, ever sprightly dance." The vision finally eludes him because he is caught in time. He has seen too much—or not enough. Now he knows that as an anxious man—he has not been cured by the march—he can identify with all the others who must march to satisfy their symbolic longings. His hunger dies. He must live with the "hateful contraries"—with the "somber light" *and* thunderheads, with highs *and* lows (we see a "swan-dive" and a "skyward" glance), with war *and* peace.

It is fitting that Culver's victory, as tentative as it may be, should force him to move out of his room and meet Mannix. Both men have "won" victories; they "limp" to show their wounds. (Victory for Styron implies scars.) They are able to have one "unbroken minute of sympathy and understanding"—this is how long transcendental vision lasts—before their communication is destroyed.

Culver notices the Negro maid "employed in the place." She asks Mannix: "Do it hurt?" She senses his pain (and Culver's?); she has also lived in bondage. Before he can answer she says "Deed it does" (after the two of them share one "unspoken moment of sympathy and understanding").

It is at this point that Styron uses the symbolic device: Mannix's towel falls (he is going to shower); he is "naked as the day he emerged from his mother's womb." The nakedness is, of course, a comic "accident"—as opposed to the not-very-comic accident at the beginning—but it also reinforces Styron's insistence upon human frailty (mortality): man somehow dead (or at least dead tired) and alive, "clutching for support at the wall." Finally in the last words Mannix repeats: "Deed it does."

And Culver? He does not have the final word. He will, presumably, survive this scene to create his own pattern of meaning, to perform his solitary deeds. He will march again.

William Styron with Michael West (interview date 1977)

SOURCE: An interview with Michael West, in *Conversations with William Styron,* University Press of Mississippi, 1985, pp. 217-33.

[*In this excerpt from an interview that was originally published in 1977, Styron speaks of how his resentment of authority figures has been a significant feature of his writing.*]

[West]: *The themes that have captured your imagination have driven you to complete four novels, if we consider* **The Long March** *to be a short novel, and I wonder if there are some themes that recur though the stories differ greatly. I am thinking of themes like the struggle of a man or a woman against authority or an authoritarian system, a system of values which seems to oppress.*

[Styron]: Yes, that's been remarked upon before and I think there's some truth in that—a great deal of truth. I have been more or less drawn to human relationships in which there is strong polarity of power and submission, or authority versus subservience, or if not subservience a sometimes unwilling weakness. A long, long time ago, I realized in my own character that, whether I was in the classical sense a radical, I had a very strong streak of rebelliousness in me. And when I was quite young, and in school, or later in the Marine Corps, I realized how powerfully I was repelled by authority myself. I often got into trouble. I never got into major trouble, maybe fortunately, but I had trouble with teachers. And I had trouble in the Marines with authority figures.

I remember especially when I was at Camp Lejeune on KP duty in the mess hall, I was just a buck private, and this was during World War II when I was in training. I still remember the incredible hate relationship I established with the mess sergeant who was, as I recollect, an Italian from New York. His credentials for being a mess sergeant were that he ran a large restaurant in New York. It became a well-known fact that we were at war with each other. This guy was bullying me, and I was just reacting to him. None of the other guys were having this situation. It was just me. I couldn't stand his authoritarian pose. It didn't end up in any particular dramatic crisis or anything, but it always sticks in my mind—the hatred that he had for me and I had for him, and my spurning of his authority.

Along about that time, when I was in the Marines at Duke in the V-12 program, I remember how bitterly I resented a certain mathematics teacher. . . . She was teaching mathematics, which I had no interest in whatsoever, and I was determined to read books. I was deeply immersed in the reading that one does at roughly that age.

What were you reading?

Who knows? I was reading everything at that time. I was reading Thomas Wolfe, Dos Passos, Hemingway, Faulkner. She would catch me over and over reading a book which I shouldn't have been reading behind a mathematics book. She caught me, she threatened me, and from her point of view, quite properly, reported me to the colonel, the Marine colonel who was running the show down there.

And I got in trouble with the Marine gunner who was my nemesis, a very tough character. In those days they used to call them warrant officers. It was before they began to wear those little rectangular bars. He wore a little bomb on his lapel, the symbol of a gunner—a Marine gunner—and he was tough as hell. He put me on report several times.

I'm just bringing these up to show that I always had a very strong anti-authoritarian streak in me. It's a very profound resentment of authority, and I think that has shown up in my work.

Is it authority itself, or is it an attitude that some figures in authority exhibit?

It might be a duality because there's a part of me, at least at that time, that rather respected authority. After all, I was trying to become an officer myself, and I did become a Marine officer and I rather enjoyed it. It was only a brief period, but I had my little fling with authority. And I recognized that streak in me too—a respect for authority which may be the opposite side of the coin from the rebelliousness that I've often felt.

Whenever there's a new President, I always have presidential dreams. I dreamt that I was in the White House chumming it up with Jimmy Carter not too long ago. And I remember having the same dreams about Eisenhower and Kennedy. Clearly, this is an indication that there's a part of me that very much admires authority. On the other hand, there's some sort of conflict at work, because on the more important philosophical level I think I have always despised authority, especially authority which is used in a malicious, or illegal, or inhumane way. . . .

Let's talk about **The Long March**. *Does this story derive from a personal episode? For instance, did you have to go on a forced march?*

Yes.

What was that experience?

Very similar to the one in the book.

You knew someone with a nail in his foot?

No, I didn't. Mannix was a total figment of my imagination. That part did not really happen. Nor did he really exist. The Colonel is very similar to the Colonel who ran us on this march, and the march itself was very much like the one that we all had to go on, without much exaggeration one way or another. A very, very brutal forced march.

I notice the name of the Colonel is Templeton. I wonder about the choice of his name. Is somehow the idea of a temple associated with authority? You've mentioned the White House. There was a "white house" image, a white house, or white temple that Nat Turner was dreaming about.

Sure, a white temple.

Is this an echoing of that same symbol of authority?

Well, I suppose certain aspects of formal religion I have associated with authority, usually very negatively. And it is a theme I want to develop in a novel which I will finish, God willing, after the one I am writing now, one called *The Way of the Warrior,* which I published excerpts from but then put aside. It develops the theme which begins with Templeton, namely, that there is a quasi-religious aspect to military life. I've always thought that the Marine Corps was like a religion to certain people, to certain men. And I try to emphasize in the books I'm writing now how the SS, the German SS, was actually, historically, built by Himmler around the idea of the Jesuits—I mean *consciously* on his part, with the intense loyalty and intense devotion.

That is, the worship of power, a mystique of power, which is built into authority by hierarchy.

Yeah. And so the religious motif, I think, is very—even the name Templeton, of course, with its connotations. I haven't gone over *The Long March* in a long time, but I think, if I'm not mistaken, that I allude in certain ways to the Colonel as a priestly sort of man.

Culver, the narrator, seems to have a mixed impression of the Colonel as a kind of an obstacle, but at the same time the Colonel comes across as not being particularly inhumane.

I intended that. That's a fairly early work of mine and I'm still developing that kind of theme, but I'm not a person who necessarily associates military life with evil. That's the reason I was able to see the Colonel, Templeton, as a man of some distinction, of some quality. Obviously Culver doesn't love the Colonel, but has great respect for him.

One of the liberal fallacies—and I use that word advisedly, but it is, I'm afraid, a liberal fallacy—is that the military is unmitigated evil. Especially in the United States. Well, I don't happen to believe it is. It's a necessary aspect of the world we live in. Much of military life is unpleasant, and it goes against the grain of most civilized people. On the other hand, there is much in it that is attractive. Maybe this derives from the fact that I was born and raised in Virginia and I had an uncle who was a general and I lived around military people all my life. Virginia is such a military-

conscious state, and I had ancestors who were officers in the Civil War. So, in other words, I don't have this liberal, this famous knee-jerk thing that associates the military profession with fascism or butchery or insensate cruelty or anything like that.

Judith Ruderman (essay date 1987)

SOURCE: "Styron's Farewell to Arms: Writing on the Military," in *William Styron,* Ungar, 1987, pp. 71-89.

[*Here, Ruderman observes that Mannix, by virtue of his suffering and indomitable will against the impersonality of the military, achieves a heroic triumph.*]

Three of Styron's major works of fiction are focused centrally on the military: *The Long March*, *In the Clap Shack,* and *The Way of the Warrior* (in progress). In the first two of these, published twenty years apart, war is emblematic of human existence: its bureaucracy and impersonality represent all institutions; the isolation and fear of its combatants are the primary conditions of modern life.

Lieutenant Culver of *The Long March*, like many of Styron's protagonists, looks nostalgically from a chaotic present into an Edenic past. He has left behind a law practice, his family, and the strains of Haydn, Bach, and Mozart reverberating through peaceful Sunday afternoons in New York City. Now his companions are his fellow marine reservists in the Headquarters and Service Company in rural North Carolina, his comfortable existence exchanged for endless maneuvers during frigid nights and torrid days in training for possible combat in Korea. The surrealistic pursuit of an imaginary enemy, the relentless exhaustion, and the isolation from all ordinary endeavors fill Culver with confusion, apprehension, and dismay. This sense of disorder and chaos is replicated in Styron's narrative technique, which substitutes flashback within flashback for a chronological sequence of events. The first two chapters of the novella proceed by means of flashbacks to present the central event of the novel: not the long march of the title, as one might suspect, but the event that causes the march to take on its utmost meaning—that is, the accidental short firing of rounds that kills eight soldiers in the next battalion. . . .

The novella, then, focuses on a tragedy: the slaughter of eight young marines through what would come to be known in the Vietnam War as "friendly fire." Because of this accident, and because of the stateside setting in a noncombat situation, the characters wonder about the identity of their real enemy. Who is the invisible aggressor whom the reservists relentlessly stalk, against whom the commanding officers ceaselessly warn? The state of exhaustion in which the reservists perpetually exist, for they are woefully out of shape, softened by the good life back home, makes the answer to that question unclear to Culver, who plays the role of Everyman in this story. Through Culver's eyes the reader views the man who plays the role of tragic hero, the platoon leader Al Mannix. A man of mythological proportions, compared implicitly to Atlas and to Christ, Mannix identifies the enemy as the military system itself and proceeds to knock his head against the nature of things in an effort to beat the system. Through this effort, which is ridiculous and even aberrant by standards of sanity and propriety, Mannix wrests control over his life from the powers-that-be and asserts the humanity of the boys who died as well as of the reservists he leads.

> **Human existence, Styron implies, is often an upside-down view into the abyss. Any attempt to set the world rightside up and to provide something to hold onto is a laudable, even heroic task.**
>
> *—Judith Ruderman*

The story of Mannix's perverse rebellion cannot be understood unless the nature of military service as Styron views it is first delineated. Styron does not regard the military as an inherently evil profession, but, ever suspicious of institutions, he considers it to be a bureaucracy that stifles individuality. The reservists in H & S Company must all be treated alike, as marines; all-important is the esprit de corps that bonds the many into the one. In this sense the men are nonentities rather than fully realized human beings. Sergeant O'Leary, a marine regular, is said to be grafted onto the military system like a piece of skin, and therefore molded into the image of marine. The reader is reminded that the outcome may be similarly dehumanizing: the eight dead marines look as if they've been sprayed from a hose, turned into mere shreds of skin and bone that seem never to have been alive at all. Because the reservists have known freedom, they are especially resistant to the authority wielded by Colonel Templeton and his officers.

This authority manifests itself most forcefully in Colonel Templeton's order for a thirty-six-mile march that will toughen the reservists, prepare them for actual combat, and make them more like the regulars. The order and the subsequent march fill Culver and Mannix with revulsion and fear, not merely because they doubt their ability to withstand the heat and the pain, but, more importantly, because they are loath to relinquish their free will: "How stupid to think they had ever made their own philosophy; it was as puny as a house of straw, and at this moment— by the noise in their brains of those words, *you will*—it was being blasted to the winds like dust. They were as helpless as children." The military reduces the fighting men to the state of children, belittled as it were, with the commanding officers as powerful parental figures determining the course of their charges' lives—fathers, maybe, or even priests, invested with a quasidivine authority. Culver, calling "Bundle Able" on the radio at Colonel Templeton's request, feels "juvenile and absurd, as if he were reciting Mother Goose." Mannix has only contempt for this code language of military communication that re-

places ordinary conversation with boy-scout passwords. Major Lawrence, subservient to the colonel, looks to Culver like a five-year-old child, and speaks to the colonel in the third person as if Templeton were an imperial ruler and the major his subject.

Other figures of speech, more emotionally charged than the references to children, hint at the odious status of the soldiers. Captain Mannix is compared at one point to a shackled slave, and at another to a chain-gang convict. By these means Styron conveys the idea that the military imprisons the individual and subordinates him to the system. Quite simply, the marines are not free men. Mannix despises Templeton for the authority that Templeton wields, not only because authority is anathema to this rebellious individual, but also because Mannix is all too aware of the fallibility of those who wield the power. The accidental misfiring of the missiles and the resultant death of the eight young marines may well have been caused by the decision to use old shells stored on Guam since 1945. Such disregard for the consequences of decisions bespeaks a lack of connection between those who give the orders and those who do the fighting. This lack of communication between commander and commanded—indeed, between men in general—is symbolized by the incident that Mannix relates to Culver from his buck-sergeant days during World War II. Pinned down in his shell hole under heavy fire from the Japanese, Mannix screams desperately into the telephone for assistance. Each time he hollers for aid he gets hit by another piece of shrapnel. Just before losing consciousness he notices that the telephone wires have all along been severed. There has been no lifeline between him and others. Instead, he is on his own, to succeed or fail on his own powers along with the luck of the draw. Even the radio over which Lieutenant Culver tries to make contact with Able Company emits only a banshee wail of signals, "like the cries of souls in the anguish of hell." No call to that company gets through, so isolated and uprooted are these men. To Styron, this situation of being cut off is the human condition. Alienated from his God, estranged from his fellows, the individual cannot count for aid and comfort on the ministrations of anyone else; he had best rely on himself.

And so, because the dead soldiers could not take control over their lives, Captain Al Mannix takes control over his. He does not opt out of the marines, for he has made his commitment. (This is, after all, the Korean War in the conformist 1950s; the next war, in the next decade, would tell a different tale.) Rather, he chooses to exert the full force of his individuality within the strict parameters of the military system. If Colonel Templeton, nicknamed Old Rocky because of his obdurate nature, can order thirty-year-old, out-of-shape reservists to march for thirteen hours, then Captain Mannix can find his own way of being an immovable object. He finds it in a rebellion in reverse— that is, in seeing the march through to its end and exhorting his company to do the same. Mannix accomplishes this task under especially grievous conditions; added to the fatigue and heat suffered by all the marchers is the discomfort of a nail sticking up from his boot into his foot, resisting his best efforts at removal. Marching for Mannix becomes a true torture, and thus a true test of his human capacity to endure. The nail and the injury it causes provide Mannix with an escape from the forced march if he wants it: Templeton commands him to ride in on the truck. But Mannix chooses to obey the first command, to march, rather than the second one, and thereby enacts his perverse rebellion. This "one personal insurrection" cannot hope to accomplish much good. Indeed, it turns Mannix into a taskmaster, bullying his men into completing the march with him. It injures his foot and makes every step a crucifixion. It gets him confined to quarters, and perhaps even court-martialed, after cursing the colonel. But if this insurrection is absurd it is not therefore without value. In fact, it does get Mannix from point A to point B *on his own terms.* And he does indeed carry some of his company on his back, Atlas-like, completing his superhuman task almost like a god rather than a man, elevating his men in spite of themselves. By refusing to drop out or to let them drop out (though two-thirds of them eventually do), he asserts the dignity and worth of human life and thereby wrests control for the individual from dominating outside forces. Though comical, caricatural, and even bizarre, Mannix's gesture attests to the durability of the human spirit.

If Mannix is not necessarily to be considered a fool, is he therefore to be considered a hero? Styron thinks so. In the midst of senseless slaughter and a senseless, seemingly endless march, in a war presaging the "forceless, soulless, pushbutton wars of the future," one indefatigable man with an indomitable will imprints his features on the action. By so doing he fights the battle of the luckless marine whose "face had been blasted out of sight" while he waited for his lunch. Templeton's own face is likened to a mannequin's, betokening his lack of humanity, and the loaded pearl-handled revolver he wears on his hip is a sign of the military's potential to turn humans into inert matter in one moment, as the short rounds did to the men on the chow line; the forks and spoons of the dead soldiers were turned into "pathetic metal flowers," completing the inhuman and unnatural picture. Mannix is ennobled by his suffering, which personalizes the impersonal order to march and humanizes the dehumanizing task of carrying out this order. His rebellion therefore sets the world in order, if only temporarily. The reader recalls the episode related by Mannix to Culver about his most harrowing experience during World War II. On a spree out of boot camp, on the tenth floor of a hotel in San Francisco, Mannix had been suspended for several long minutes naked and upside down from the window by a couple of drunken marines. The utter helplessness and disorientation of the situation were too horrible for bearing. Human existence, Styron implies, is often an upside-down view into the abyss. Any attempt to set the world rightside up and to provide something to hold onto is a laudable, even heroic task.

Throughout the novella Styron draws attention to Mannix's body. Whereas the other characters are clothed and protected, Mannix is often pictured naked and vulnerable. One is aware of his fleshiness, his mortality; he is massive and hairy, larger than life. Mannix points out to Culver the

many scars covering his entire body. He seems almost a mass of wounds, and he shows them off not proudly but matter-of-factly, as if to say, this is what it means to be alive. He is wounded and suffers because he dares. His emotions are not controlled, his responses are not programmed. Mannix is a man, not a machine.

The final scene of the novella drives home this point. Mannix has showered after his long march and proceeds down the hall draped only in a towel, clutching the wall for support and dragging his maimed leg behind him. His suffering is described as gigantic, befitting this man's physical and spiritual proportions. He meets the black maid, whose sympathy for his condition is immediate and genuine as she asks him if he is in pain. He communicates a complex set of emotions to the maid without jargon, without lies, almost even without words. As he struggles to remain upright the towel falls away, and for one last moment he stands naked and exposed, his body a mass of scars. Tomorrow Mannix may be court-martialed, his world turned topsy turvy again. But for today he has made it through, vulnerable and suffering as ever, but still standing. And that, at least for now, is triumph enough.

Samuel Coale   (essay date 1991)

SOURCE: "*The Long March*: A Failed Rebellion," in *William Styron Revisited,* Twayne Publishers, 1991, pp. 50-8.

[*In this excerpt, Coale examines Styron's polarized vision of rebellion and authority, particularly what he sees as Styron's confusion over whether to portray the rebellious individual as heroic or as existentially absurd.*]

The Long March . . . stands as the prototype for several of Styron's later longer novels. Besides the thrust and crisis of rebellion on which the book is based, we also find the bifurcated hero, the observant witness, and the participant rebel, what David L. Minter has described in American literature as the distinction between the man of interpretation and the man of action or design. Such dialectical characters include Ishmael and Ahab in *Moby-Dick,* Nick Carraway and Jay Gatsby in *The Great Gatsby,* Coverdale and Hollingsworth in Hawthorne's *The Blithedale Romance,* and more recently Quentin Compson and Thomas Sutpen in Faulkner's *Absalom, Absalom* [*The Interpreted Design as a Structural Principle in American Prose* (New Haven, CT: Yale University Press, 1969)].

The Long March also looks . . . closely at the individual's relationship with society, at the familiar oedipal struggles of the first novel, at the kind of Manichaean mysteries involving the confrontational polarities and unresolved oppositions in the book, and at Styron's own attempts to come to some metaphysical vision that can encompass all these many attributes and perspectives.

At the core of *The Long March* lies Styron's description of the suffering that human beings must endure. This suffering seems to be at the heart of the human condition as Styron views it through less southern-nostalgic eyes than in *Lie Down in Darkness*. Life becomes a long march, full of accident, anxiety, dread, exhaustion, pride, loneliness, and panic, filling the individual with a sense of outrage and violation, locked into some robotized routine. In short, life becomes a war in and of itself. "War was no longer simply a temporary madness into which human beings happily lapsed from time to time," Styron commented in 1963. "War had at last become *the* human condition."

Life becomes a long march, full of accident, anxiety, dread, exhaustion, pride, loneliness, and panic, filling the individual with a sense of outrage and violation, locked into some robotized routine. In short, life becomes a war in and of itself.

—*Samuel Coale*

Suffering provides the underlying motif of *The Long March*. And Mannix, the Jew from Brooklyn, becomes the emblem of "one of tortured and gigantic suffering" [William Styron, *The Long March* (New York: Random House, 1952) p. 125]. Such suffering may be part of the hero's role, and if so Mannix would certainly fill that category. And yet since Colonel Templeton firmly believes that "the hike had had nothing to do with courage or sacrifice or suffering, Styron undermines this simplistic heroic notion and leaves to the reader the task of interpreting for himself or herself the ultimate significance of suffering.

Traditional liberal values would place much of the meaning of existence upon the individual consciousness, no matter how terrible conditions had become around it. Essentially, this idea has been the key to Western tragedy as a genre and vision. And yet like suffering, the worth of the individual in *The Long March* is not taken for granted. For one thing, in Styron's novel individuals can be reduced to mere functions, men to marines, and become conformist, resigned, and even absurd when viewed as mere cogs in a wheel. And from this perspective individual rebellion or protest embodies only the absurd, since such protest can make the individual's situation not only worse but also self-victimizing and, in the end, existentially absurd: "Born into a generation of conformists, even Mannix (so Culver sensed) was aware that his gestures were not symbolic, but individual, therefore hopeless, maybe even absurd, and that he was trapped like all of them in a predicament which one personal insurrection could, if anything, only make worse."

This predicament leaves Styron's wondering about the very nature of Mannix's rebellion against Colonel Templeton's rule: "He only mutilated himself by this perverse and violent rebellion." If Mannix rebels, as he does, by willfully submitting to Templeton's long march, a kind of "rebellion in reverse," then isn't he in effect only proving how pervasive the system really is? If the self has been so

corrupted by the system that it can view itself only as a function of that system, and if its way to rebel or to conform in effect proves the same thing, then doesn't Mannix's revolt only prove that without the system, there is no self? And if this is true, then the individual self is a liberal myth that no longer exists, and any individual action, of which there can be no real example, is doomed to meaninglessness and absurdity. But if this is Styron's case, then "individual" rebellion in *The Long March* has only reinforced what we've already experienced in *Lie Down in Darkness*: the modern encapsulated self is co-cooned in so pervasive a system of social and cultural regulations that Styron's true subject is that web and its continued insidious power in trapping us—and perhaps our hopeless but nostalgic desire to escape and live without it.

Styron sets up his regulars carefully. Each acts his function as a marine, even if it seems to go against his basic instincts as a man. O'Leary believes that all are "inextricably grafted to the system" and should display "a devoted, methodical competence" despite what doubts the person might have. Bill Lawrence symbolizes the clean-cut, spoiled, and arrogant functionary in the system. And Culver even begins to think that O'Leary may be right and Mannix hopelessly, willfully wrong.

Colonel Templeton, with his set of fixed attitudes and habitualized gestures, embodies the system perfectly: "He had too long been conditioned by the system to perform with grace a human act." For him every action to be performed is a task, not a personal action involving moral value. He is as devoted as a priest to his religious rites, "almost benevolent . . . [one] in whom passion and faith had made an alloy. . . . Above meanness or petty spite, he was leading a march to some humorless salvation."

And of course Templeton is a father figure to his men, the man with the responsibility, half-feared, half-worshiped, but ultimately never really questioned. His men acquiesce to "the voice that commanded, once again, *you will*," for after all they seem to be as "helpless as children," and "they were only marines, responding anew to the old commands." This "stern father" is someone to both hate and placate. He sets the rules, and his "children" follow or disobey them, but they never question his godlike role. "Culver almost liked the Colonel, in some negative way . . . 'respect' . . . was the nearest approach." "He's not a bad guy . . . just a regular," Culver explains, reducing the father to a function and letting that function circumscribe and conjure up a world in which to function.

Styron's vision becomes confusing here. If the "old-fashioned" sense of seeing things on an individual basis—good verses evil, good guy verses bad guy—is itself absurd, because the system recognizes only functions and effects, and if in his reverse rebellion Mannix proves himself to be just a better player at Templeton's own game, then doesn't the characters'—and Styron's—"outrage . . . at the system, at their helpless plight, the state of the world" seem forced and absurd, too? Is this "real" outrage, voiced by an individual consciousness, or merely the necessary oil in the gears of functionaries going about their business and preserving the system no matter what? Can suffering be made symbolic of some larger metaphysical distress built into the human or a universal condition, or is it merely a physical given, like the necessity to eat and sleep? Is Styron himself stranded between the romantic notion of the individual's attacking the system in order to stand up for superior moral rights or reasons and the more "existential" condition of suffering as a given, with no symbolic resonance whatsoever?

In the workings out of this dilemma in *The Long March*, Styron tries to achieve a more coherently symbolic significance. Culver and Mannix, however different temperamentally, after all do not remain static. They change and develop, separately and in relation to each other. And yet they are in many ways polarized, a structural phenomenon of the novel that may be built on Styron's own dialectical or bifurcated view of systematic authority and individual conscience, complicated by the oedipal tensions we have already recognized.

The question may finally be whether or not Styron resents authority in and of itself or resents an attitude that some figures in authority exhibit. In any case in *The Long March*, as a prelude to his later novels, the polarity of vision seems to lie at the heart of the matter and helps to explain the fabric of unresolved confrontations in the novel.

Tom Culver shows all the symptoms of a contented, domesticated civilian suddenly thrust back into war. He comes to realize that all may be "astray at mid-century in the never-endingness of war" and that this atmosphere may account for his sense of anxiety, dread, solitude, and fear, and yet he is understandably at first shocked by his recall. After World War II he enjoys the civilian refuge of children, home, and classical music and fills his sweet thoughts with reveries of "two little girls playing on the sunny grass." His enforced return to military uniform fills him with resentment and dread, and he feels suddenly imprisoned in a nightmare realm of permanent disruption, adrift in the hypnagogic state "like the dream of a man delirious with fever . . . enclosed within the tent, unmoored and unhelmed upon a dark and compassless ocean." He suddenly views his new world "as if . . . through drug-glazed eyes." Displaced, uprooted, and "profoundly alone," Culver epitomizes the ordinary man trapped in a century of war.

Al Mannix is at first far more vocally disgruntled than Culver. He seems bitter, sardonic, and frank and in taking things personally despises Templeton almost on sight. He refuses to answer a colonel's questions during a lecture and decides to walk the thirty-six miles of the enforced march despite the nail in his heel. To beat the system, he feels, one must *be* the system, and Culver warily watches his transformation into a fanatic, a kind of supraorthodox heretic in the religious ranks, an absolutist bully obsessed with his own demonstration of rebellion, whatever the ultimate import. To Mannix, Templeton becomes "a prime and calculated evil" against which he (Mannix) will fight

in his own way. And very quickly "the contagion of Mannix's fear had touched [Culver]."

Significant differences proliferate between Culver and Mannix as Styron develops their characters. And in these escalating differences Styron seems to be building his polarized vision of rebellion and authority. Mannix faces death when dangled from a hotel window in San Francisco, while Culver grapples with his anxiety when faced with Mannix. When the explosion occurs and marines are killed, Culver throws up at the scene, while Mannix weeps and sees it as symbolizing a greater evil: "Won't they ever let us alone?" To Mannix, Templeton is evil incarnate; to Culver, a more or less blameless functionary and, however vaguely, a demonic father figure. At one point Culver stops Mannix in his rebellion, as if the more resigned conformist were tackling the outspoken if necessarily doomed rebel—"That's enough, Al!"—but he cries as he does it and feels his own spirit as it "sank like a rock."

Culver's confusion about the meaning of events is met and transcended by Mannix's certainty. Mannix seems to represent a tragic endurance that will continue against all odds. And despite the absurdity of Mannix's rebellion, Styron seems to want us to see an aura of Christian, classical, and humanist values hovering around that character's actions. And yet Culver's confusion proves to be far more human eventually, since he quickly sees how bullying and fanatic Mannix has become. Perhaps only victimhood is ensured when Mannix is confronted naked by the black maid at the end of the novel, as if, as each relates to the other on the basic human level of sympathy and pain, both are recognizing their roles as victims in the larger society and system.

Styron's vision may emerge more clearly in *The Long March* because he tackles his theme of rebellion and his uncertain attitude toward it more diagrammatically than in *Lie Down in Darkness*. As he himself has explained, "I wanted to free myself from Faulkner's influence before starting another full-scale book. *The Long March* was my disintoxication exercise" [Maurice Edgar Coindreau, *A French View of Modern American Fiction* (Columbia: Univ. of South Carolina Press, 1971)]. . . . he has described himself as a "provisional rebel." and that self-description certainly seems justified when seen in relation to the polarities on which *The Long March* has been built.

[*The Long March*] displays endless confrontations and juxtapositions. Chronological time from noon to noon confronts the nightmarish, hypnagogic state of dreams and anxieties. Culver's dream encompasses the night before the long march, with its tales of Mannix's past, culminating in his facing death in San Francisco. At twilight the marines start off on their trek. By 4:15 A.M. they are eighteen miles into the march, halfway to the finish line. And at noon they have arrived at Heaven's Gate, an apotheosis of sorts. The opening scene of horror reverberates throughout the entire tale, mesmerizing Culver and shaking and finally transforming Mannix. Culver experiences his three reveries involving young girls and music, the nostalgia of home and youth.

Styron arranges three friezes in the novel, two between Templeton and Mannix and one final one between Mannix and the black maid. The first emphasizes "classical Greek masks, made of chrome or tin, reflecting an almost theatrical disharmony" between the two marines, when they are viewed in Culver's mind as opposites in a dynamic tension, as polarities set up for eternal conflict: master and slave. The second frieze presents them as "twin profiles embattled," just before Mannix is court-martialed. The polarities hold, but they are now twin polarities, fellow marines upholding the same system. And the final frieze, realized on a more human scale, presents Mannix and the maid as "communicating . . . sympathy and understanding," both victims and slaves of the system that rules their lives. Styron employs throughout his images of classical tragedy and Egyptian slavery as a way of highlighting these basic confrontations.

Polarities also appear on a more thematic level. They permeate the novel like Manichaean mysteries, "Manichaean" in the sense of a pervasive, unresolved dualism, forever entangled and at war with one another, as opposed to the more orthodox Christian sense of unity and deliverance from battle. Sunshine opposes darkness, sound confronts silence, heat undermines the cold. Disruptions threaten chronological sequence and consciousness, just as Styron confronts peace with war, Heaven's Gate with prison, submission with rebellion, and Culver's reveries of classical music and sanctuary with life itself.

At times these contradictions temporarily dissolve into a kind of hypnagogic state, in which all moral categories collapse, nightmare takes over, and anything is possible. With Styron's descriptions of wails in hell in the swamp; of dark seas, spooky glows, and the green light of dawn; of the marines as zombies, ghosts, wraiths, and robots; and of night as one long nightmare of pain and exhaustion, which in Culver "enveloped his whole spirit," the novel seems to enter the disturbingly sentient universe of a Poe tale, and all morally symbolic structures or images that try to embody individual rebellion and the system nearly vanish. "Korea . . . the very idea of another war . . . possessed a kind of murky, surrealistic, half-lunatic unreality that we are mercifully spared while awake, but which we do occasionally confront in a horrible dream," wrote Styron in his introduction to the Norwegian edition of **The Long March**. "With the reality of some unshakable nightmare . . . in the summer of 1952, I found myself in Paris still unable to shake off the sense of having just recently awakened from a nightmare."

And yet even in such a clearheaded, short novel as **The Long March**, Styron has still managed to blur the significance of his tale. If it is a Gothic nightmare, then the "existential-romantic" tangle of self and society is superseded. If it is a morality tale with Gothic trappings, then can it both celebrate the individual and define him only in terms that show him to be merely a function in the larger military-social scheme of things? Is there a thin line between genuine polarities and contradictions, which seem to be at the center of Styron's vision here, and mere metaphysical confusion? Do the oedipal overtones undermine or further explain Culver's and Mannix's actions and beings?

Critics remain divided on these issues. Marc Ratner maintains that "for Styron the great value of action is that, through rebellion, the rebel discovers the evils of the 'System' in himself, cuts through his self-illusions, and exorcises his devils to become a mature person" ["The Rebel Purged: *The Long March,*" in *William Styron,* 1972]. But what are we to make of a maturity that leaves a brutal system intact with no real questions asked? Is this maturity or an evasion of the very issues the author seems to be raising? Even tone may be an issue here, as Roger Asselineau suggests: "The satirical tone of many a passage is thus neutralized by the understanding of the futile nature of revolt" [*Critical Essays on William Styron*, 1982].

Irving Malin mounts a very strong case for Culver as a "solitary observer," as a man who "lies between his superiors, between all the opposites of life. He dangles." To Malin, Culver is trapped both by the marines and by his own body. He "regards himself as an actor in someone else's script" and continues to see visions that, "like Styron's symbolic details, are full of commingled opposites." In the end "Culver feels a 'deep vast hunger' for some transcendental vision which will overarch grottolike peace and threatening storm . . . His hunger dies. He must live with the 'hateful contraries' . . . with war and peace ["The Symbolic March," in *The Achievement of William Styron*]. Culver, in effect, accepts the book's polarized view of things, which may be essentially Styron's own in 1952. And in doing so, Culver in effect changes nothing. Nothing has been so much learned as accepted.

In Culver's acceptance, however, one can't help but feel that whatever rebellious outbreak has been possible at the beginning of the novel, by the end it has fizzled out. **The Long March** may leave us as encapsulated as did *Lie Down in Darkness,* wherein even the exercise of outright rebellion only proves the existence of the walls of the prison cell, and however held up by vaunted polarities and dualistic designs, the cell remains intact. As Norman Kelvin has suggested, "We find opposites striving for union through conflict or love . . . in which heightened awareness, or an intensification of the spiritual, is attempted but unattained" ["The Divided Self: William Styron's Fiction from *Lie Down in Darkness* to *The Confession of Not Turner,*" in *The Achievement of William Styron*]. We will subsequently explore this observation in detail.

Culver and Styron seem to be straining for a vision that can unite opposites. But with the seeming acceptance of an institutionalized system with man's place faithfully circumscribed within it, the straining can seem only like carping, whining about and against what the novelist has already accepted as unalterable fact. As one critic has explained, "Styron creates his personae's visions from metaphors of reality. His characters' yearning for the 'impossible state,' for (in their terms) a finer, more desirable world, even for some glorious surceases from the anxieties and pressures of this one, are always built upon what is concrete, mundane, ordinary: as though their symbolic imagination need root itself in the solid stuff of life." That may be an inevitable human condition, but it does bring to mind Styron's more or less contented Episcopalians living contentedly with nature and their Virginian world in *Lie Down in Darkness*. Such ultimate feelings of ease in the world may dampen any rebellious quests and render them stillborn.

Nevertheless, *The Long March* lays out in fairly simple detail the developing scope of Styron's vision, stripped as it is of the organ-toned, Faulknerian presence of *Lie Down in Darkness*. Initially the second novel seems to indicate a breakthrough, a leap beyond lying to standing up. But at the last it remains curiously locked within that essentially polarized and encapsulated vision not yet jettisoned or overcome. The unresolved Manichaean mysteries are presented in all their dualistic elegance, but the nature of rebellion, individual consciousness, and society and the interactions of all of them remain blurred and confusing, if not confused.

Michiko Kakutani (review date 1993)

SOURCE: "Styron's Time Past Shows Its Hold on the Present," in *The New York Times,* September 10, 1993, p. C-27.

[*In this review of* A Tidewater Morning, *Kakutani notes Styron's skillful handling of the themes of mortality and evil, but observes that the collection is largely interesting as an index to his earlier works.*]

A key to what made William Styron a writer can be found in a passage from the title story in *A Tidewater Morning*. All three stories in the book, Mr. Styron says in an author's note, represent "an imaginative reshaping of real events" in his own life, and in this particular tale, his alter ego, a 13-year-old boy named Paul, tries to cope with his mother's cancer and his father's grief, by distancing himself from the situation.

He focuses on the music playing on the family phonograph, and recalls the headlines of that day's morning paper: "My name is Paul Whitehurst, it is the 11th of September, 1938, when Prague Awaits Hitler Ultimatum. Thus lulled by history, I let myself be elevated slowly up and up through the room's hot, dense shadows. And there, floating abreast of the immortal musicians, I was able to gaze down impassively on the grieving father and the boy pinioned in his arms." The boy will learn to use this protective detachment as a means of coping with life's hurts and losses, a means of connecting his own confusions with the alarums of the world beyond: he will become a writer.

These three stories—which depict Mr. Styron's alter ego at the ages of 10, 13 and 20—previously appeared in

Esquire magazine, and taken together they form a kind of portrait of the author as a young man growing up in the Tidewater region of Virginia. There is one vexing incongruity: In one tale, Paul's mother is depicted as a liberal Northerner, appalled at the bigoted language employed by her son; in another, she emerges as a snobbish Yankee, who must be taught racial tolerance by her Southern husband. Otherwise, the three stories knit together smoothly, cutting backward and forward in time, demonstrating, as so much of Mr. Styron's fiction does, the hold of time past over time present, the persistence and power of memory.

On the surface, these are old-fashioned coming-of-age stories. **"Love Day"** depicts the fear and excitement Paul feels as a member of a Marine battalion about to land on Okinawa and contrasts those emotions with his memories of his father working in a Virginia shipyard, readying a battleship for war. **"Shadrach"** depicts Paul's reaction to the arrival in town of a 99-year-old former slave, who has walked 600 miles from Alabama to die on the land that belonged to his childhood owner. And the title story depicts Paul's efforts to come to terms with his mother's terminal illness and his father's loss of faith in God.

All three tales are period pieces, anchored in bygone attitudes and concerns. Mr. Styron conjures up the sleepy lethargy of a small town during the Depression and its anxious collision with the reality of World War II; and he attempts to communicate to the reader the archaic state of race relations in a South only one generation removed from slavery. Indeed the language employed by the characters to talk about nonwhites is often startlingly racist: Paul describes a truckload of "farm Negroes" as a "jumble of rolling eyeballs and flashing teeth"; and his battalion commander refers to the Japanese as ''animals with rabies.''

While they're compelling enough to read, there isn't anything terribly special about any of the stories in *A Tidewater Morning*. Mr. Styron seems more comfortable with the long-distance form of the novel, and the tales here feel vaguely attenuated and speeded up, as though they were experimental sketches for something larger. Indeed their main interest lies in the fact that they are a kind of Rosetta stone to Mr. Styron's previous work, an index to his preoccupations as an artist and man.

The awakening of a young person from innocence into experience, a theme that also informs *Sophie's Choice,* lies at the heart of each of these tales, as does the theme of mortality, which rumbles ominously through these pages in much the same way it does through works like *Darkness Visible* and *The Long March*.

In many of Mr. Styron's books, an awareness of the darkness inherent in the human condition surfaces in the form of evil: slavery in *The Confessions of Nat Turner,* Auschwitz in *Sophie's Choice,* war in *The Long March*. But while war and slavery also nip at the margins of these stories, it is their cousin death that most insistently concerns Mr. Styron here. In fact, each of the stories in this volume ultimately involves Paul's recognition of the fact of mortality: in **"Shadrach"** and **"A Tidewater Morning,"** it is the death of another that shocks him into an awareness of life's brevity and pain; in **"Love Day,"** it is a premonition of his own death that both forces him to leave his childhood illusions behind and empowers him to confront the contingencies of the future.

Richard Bausch (review date 1993)

SOURCE: "'So Much Like a Lost Boy,'" in *The New York Times Book Review,* September 12, 1993, p. 15.

[*In the following evaluation of* A Tidewater Morning, *Bausch praises the way in which the three stories compliment each other and together "make one ineffable glow, like facets of the same dark jewel."*]

The three long stories that are collected in *A Tidewater Morning* appeared in *Esquire* magazine over the course of roughly a decade, beginning in 1978. In the order in which they now appear, as William Styron tells us in an introductory note, they "reflect the experiences of the author at the ages of 20, 10 and 13." This, would seem an odd juxtaposition, but curiously, when read in this sequence they appear quite linear in theme—and even, in a way, in chronology. It is as if Mr. Styron, by allowing the light of memory and imagination to play on certain crucial and painful moments, has discovered a symmetry that makes a literal recounting of his life somehow beside the point.

Mr. Styron's protagonist and speaker in all three stories is Paul Whitehurst, who, at the age of 13, loses his mother to a slow cancer. This is the calamity that informs every line of *A Tidewater Morning*, though our sense of it is somehow cumulative; we have to read on to feel it. In the first story, **"Love Day,"** we see Mr. Styron's protagonist as a "lean, mean, splendidly trained" Marine lieutenant, "hungry for Japanese heads." It is April 1, 1945, and Whitehurst is on board the troopship General Washburn.

Seeking relief from the "cramped, fetid space" of the "bowels" of the ship, he goes up on deck, where he falls asleep and dreams "the most troubled, confusing and unbearably sad dreams I could ever try to remember." They had to do, he says, "with my childhood and with my mother and father, but were resonant with no echo of serenity, no mood of repose, containing rather a vague but fearful augury of the never-endingness of war. . . . What was the message of those dreams? I wondered. Why had they made me feel so vulnerable, so helpless—so little like a marine, so much like a lost boy?"

This passage is followed by a scene in which the young man hears "scuttlebutt" that the division will not make the real assault on Okinawa, but will instead be only part of "a feint, a diversion." Whitehurst and a companion decide to speak to their commanding officer about it, and the officer, a likable man with eccentricity and flamboyance

but no ability at all when it comes to telling stories, launches into one of his endless anecdotes. Whitehurst, only half listening, sinks into a reverie about himself and his parents when he was 11 years old, and this is when we first learn of the tragedy that lies in his past. "For good reason, we were not a very happy little family. But we generally kept our tempers and were decent with one another. . . . Indeed, our love for one another had a special desperation. . . . A minor crisis other people would greet with a show of humor or equanimity made my mother and father, and eventually me, become frazzled and exhausted because of the way it represented in microcosm the on-coming disaster none of us could face or bear."

This disaster provides the thematic strand that binds the stories together, even though the specific catastrophe of the mother's death is not even mentioned in **"Shadrach,"** the second story. In each of these "tales from youth" we also feel, of course, the presence of the Depression and World War II, and the benighted history of the Virginia Tidewater as a backdrop; Mr. Styron's ability to evoke the physical reality his people move in is undiminished. If there is, in these stories, occasionally a kind of recoiling from the harshness of life, there is forbearance, too. And though the experience Mr. Styron describes is fraught with the greatest pain, he never allows his narrator the slightest note of self-pity. In fact, though we know plenty of what the young Paul Whitehurst thinks and feels, he serves more as a reliable witness to the events than as a filter for them.

In **"Shadrach,"** an aging ex-slave returns to die on the land from which he was sold as a boy, and gives himself over to the poverty-stricken remnants of the family that owned him in the dimmest past. He has come "out of no longing for the former bondage, but to find an earlier innocence . . . not as one who had fled darkness, but as one who had searched for light refracted within a flashing moment of remembered childhood." In a sense, the story of **"Shadrach"** is exactly that flashing moment in Paul Whitehurst's life, for we move from its portrayal of an innocent little boy encountering a dying old man's great dignity and endurance to the title story and the relentless delineation of the limits of dignity and endurance in the tragedy the boy himself must undergo.

"A Tidewater Morning" explores that point of suffering for which there is no earthly—and, Mr. Styron's narrator suggests, no heavenly—solace. We read it with a widening appreciation for what has transpired in the first two stories. Indeed, the anguish and sorrow that move through this last story—the cruelty and inevitability of its central event—create echoes in our experience of the whole book, so that the effect of all three tales together becomes more important than anything we might derive from each of the stories alone.

This is not to slight any of the three as stories. Even singly, they provide fine and subtle pleasures—from precise, cadenced sentences to the felt life of characters in action—and they also contain good samplings of the extravagant sensual imagery one finds in Mr. Styron's longer work. But put together in one volume, they reverberate and resonate off one another in ways that will surprise and delight the attentive reader. I believe it is a critical mistake to require that these tales stand entirely separately. They are too rich with reflected light; together, they make one ineffable glow, like facets of the same dark jewel. The effect is both heartbreaking and strangely consoling.

Richard Eder (review date 1993)

SOURCE: "A Virginia Boyhood," in *The Los Angeles Times Book Review,* September 12, 1993, pp. 3, 12.

[In this excerpt, Eder extols Styron's deft interweaving of historical occurrences, Southern legend, and his own autobiographical experiences in A Tidewater Morning.*]*

Styron has not published much since *Sophie's Choice* 14 years ago. There was a collection of essays, and a brief, lucid account of an episode of clinical depression. To revive three old short stories might be taken as a minor tidying on behalf of a remarkable but never prolific writer. In fact, read together, the "Tidewater" stories stand as one of Styron's finest works.

Two tell of events in the life of a boy named Paul [Whitehurst] one when he is 10, the other when he is 13; and both set in a small town in Virginia's flat tidewater country. In the third, Paul is 20, a lieutenant serving in the Pacific in World War II. Together they do not make a novel—they are variations on a set of themes—yet they have a compelling unity. All three take a young sensibility, portrayed in winning individual detail, through a series of large happenings: the history of the South, the meaning of war, his mother's death.

> **Styron's reshaping [of real events] is consummate and seamless, as if real events were the nymph stage in a life cycle whose adult form was fictional imagination.**
>
> —*Richard Eder*

They are autobiographical in part; Styron calls them "an imaginative reshaping of real events . . . linked by a chain of memories." The reshaping is consummate and seamless, as if real events were the nymph stage in a life cycle whose adult form was fictional imagination.

We live historically and don't perceive it. The spirit of the day enlists us completely; why, then, the restlessness, the recurrent bad dreams, the burnout? The long past has its part in us, pronouncing a continual inaudible judgment. Styron, sonorous and patrician—each story has, at some signifying moment, a great layered and stunningly articulated sentence—makes the judgment audible.

He does it most explicitly in **"Love Day."** Paul is a Marine lieutenant in the flotilla that is to land on Okinawa. He has grown out of a weedy and introspective childhood—more of that later—to become lean, fit and avid to prove himself. He and another gung-ho lieutenant pick up a rumor that their unit will not actually make the landing. They seek out their colonel—winner of the Navy Cross, an authentic hero, the supreme warrior—for consolation. He plies them with Bourbon, and recounts anecdotes of his younger days in the Marines. He is their idol; he is also dumb, and his stories meander, repeat and grow increasingly crude.

Fuddled by the whiskey, Paul drifts into a memory of a grueling midsummer car trip with his parents. The car breaks down, they chafe and bicker, and the tension mounts. His father, a ship designer at the Virginia naval works, can't repair a simple engine. His frustration and his wife's querulousness mask larger sorrows. She has cancer, and they all know it. And the father, a touchy, thoughtful man who is proud of the new aircraft carrier he has helped design, detests it at the same time.

He breaks into a bitter jeremiad. Every war in American history has claimed one of their forebears; another war is coming. His bleak vehemence reduces his wife to tears. Now, six years later, Paul is frozen into the memory of his parents' double impacted misery. His father had "allowed a meditation on war to flow to the edge of an unspoken thought—a prophecy concerning his only son and heir." In his cabin, the colonel maunders on but the warrior bond has begun to loosen.

The ending has a touch of contrivance. There is none, though, in the other two stories. The title piece is set in Paul's home, perhaps a few months after the car trip. Much of its detail is devoted to the 13-year-old's struggle with Quigley, the mean-spirited store-keeper for whom he delivers papers at $2.50 a week. Back in the dingy store after two hours in the blazing sun, Paul will fish out an occasional soda from the scummy water in the cooler. Each one is meticulously noted, and by week's end Paul gets no more than a dollar or so. Quigley never treats; never once "did he show the preferential decency, at least, that a child is supposed to receive."

The foreground is a scrim, so beautifully fashioned that it is, in a way, what the story is about. Quigley's grubby store, with the shipyard workers sitting in the back room, is a world. But history moves behind it: the Depression that for years cankered the owner's spirit; the new prewar construction boom that revives the business but not the man.

But what mainly moves through the story, and takes it over at the end, is the last days of Paul's mother. As in Agee's *A Death in the Family,* looming tragedy is the dust that settles on everything. Paul has a perpetual stomach ache; at night he covers his head with a pillow to blot out his mother's sudden shrieks of pain, and the gentle murmuring of his sleepless father and the nurse. Through the agony there is a quiet reprise of the past: the loving and combative marriage, and the musical career that Paul's mother began—there is an inscribed photograph of Gustav Mahler—and never finished. She would sing, though, for herself, her husband and the neighbors.

"Shadrach" is an enchanting raft of a story set on the somber river of Southern history. A poor white family undertakes a curious duty for a dying black man, born before the Civil War, who was once a slave on the plantation that the family's ancestors owned.

Paul is 10, a witness, and touched more lightly than in the other stories. His neighbors are the Dabneys, derelict and disreputable, with four blowzy daughters and three sons—Big Mole, Middle Mole and Little Mole Dabney—who never wash. Vernon, the father, whose own father's alcoholism and drift dropped him off the lofty Dabney family tree—scrounges and bootlegs for a living. He is spectacularly foul-mouthed, hard-pressed and narrow-minded, yet with an underlay of decency.

Shadrach, in his 90s, appears on a hot summer day, dressed in a three-piece mohair suit. He collapses in the Dabney's yard moaning for water; Dabney runs a hose into his mouth, followed by a shot of moonshine, followed by three cantaloupes, Rice Krispies and corn bread with lard. Shadrach is starving. His children, grandchildren and great grandchildren are dead or gone; he has walked 600 miles from Alabama to die and be buried on "Dabney land."

It is three generations since there were planters who were supposed to take care of their slaves, and slaves who counted on it. Suddenly, swearing and furious, Dabney reverts to an ancestral role. All the Dabneys crowd into the broken-down car and load Shadrach in with them. "Rapt in his guardian misery," Dabney drives up into the hills to the dilapidated cabin and overgrown land that was once a plantation and which he now uses for moonshining.

What follows makes a comic and touching story, marked by some of the most magical writing that Styron has ever done. Only gradually do we become aware of its intelligence and powerful anger. The beauty and humanity of the Southern tradition are evoked vividly; yet a terrible irony is at work. Shadrach's trust in feudal duty and loyalty, and Vernon's reluctant assumption of them, founder on the awful fact of betrayal: Shadrach was sold. And when Vernon rages at the end, he is raging at a double, if vastly unequal betrayal. For him and other poor whites struggling through the Depression of the '30s, the Southern legend was also a mockery.

Zachary Leader (review date 1993)

SOURCE: "Among the Whippoorwills," in *Times Literary Supplement,* December 10, 1993, p. 4732.

[*Below, Leader concludes that, in writing the stories contained within* A Tidewater Morning, *Styron sought to achieve personal integrity.*]

The pivotal moment in each of the three linked stories in William Styron's new book involves a memory of dissolution or release, one accompanied by a sudden rush of strong feeling. These are moments of breakthrough as well as breakdown, though unlike comparable fictional epiphanies (those in John Cheever's stories, for instance) the insights they offer are mostly psychological or social rather than visionary.

The memories in question belong to the narrator, Paul Whitehurst, Styron's thinly disguised fictional *alter ego*. In the first story, **"Love Day"**, set on board a troopship in the Pacific in 1945, the narrator is twenty, a Marine platoon leader, "incandescent" with health, "golden", "almost fearless". The memory that overtakes the narrator has "a luminous, mnemonic clarity", and concerns an argument between his parents, one in which his normally restrained father denounces his mother's complacent (and complicitous) idealism. The memory binds Paul to his father, flooding him with homesickness and a "ravaging", "desolate" sense of "the power of history to utterly victimize humanity", a sense that instantly undermines his boyish talk of "gallantry" and "maniacal Japs".

The second story, **"Shadrach"**, tells of an ancient black man, born into slavery, returning to die in the place of his birth. That place, a small town in Tidewater, Virginia, is the narrator's (also, presumably, Styron's) childhood home. The date is 1935, the narrator is now ten, and the moment of release he recalls involves a well-born but impoverished and overburdened neighbour, the last of Shadrach's "people". Here, again, breakdown feels like breakthrough, the narrative is suddenly suffused with emotion, and a truth about the world washes over Paul. The circumstances of the breakdown, moreover, recall those of the previous story; the outburst is precipitated by a similar combination of minor irritants and deeper-seated anxieties or instabilities, in this case a product of the Great Depression rather than war. A special virtue of the story is the child-narrator's astonished attentiveness to the old man's appearance, his description, for example, of Shadrach's unearthly hand, "warped and wrinkled with age; the bones moving beneath the black skin in clear skeletal outline".

Three years later, in the title story, the narrator's mother dies, after a long, painful illness. His father, exhausted with grief, turns on the town's well-meaning, fatuous minister and denounces ("execrates") God. The narrator's reaction to this third breakdown is revealing: "I wanted to stop my father—not for what he was saying but for fear he might become unpinned and fly out into space." This fear underlies all three memories; it also connects to the volume's epigraph, from Sir Thomas Browne's *Urn Burial*: "The long habit of living indisposeth us for dying." This is a book written out of fear of personal disintegration, in several senses.

Hence its stress on memory, which alone guarantees the self's integrity, both over time and at any one time (according to John Locke, at least). That there is an autobiographical dimension to the volume's fears of dissolution is suggested both by its immediate predecessor, *Darkness Visible* (1991), a harrowing memoir of clinical depression, and by Styron's open admission that the experiences the new book recounts "reflect the experiences of the author . . . are an imaginative reshaping of real events". The memories link not just the stories but the author-narrator's various identities—at twenty, ten and thirteen; they are attempts to anchor the self, to give it shape and meaning.

This anchoring is a matter of vital importance to Styron and his narrator, as is suggested by moments of sudden authorial intrusion. In the third story, for example, a minor character who attends the narrator's dying mother is said to possess "an arresting defect", an extra set of vestigial thumbs. "This is a grotesquerie that I almost wish I didn't have to record", the narrator tells us, anxious not to gothicize his Southern setting. "But it is an actual part of complex remembrance." In other words, the author's (or narrator's) personal needs take precedence—or are made to seem to take precedence—over artistic or aesthetic considerations.

The setting of the stories, Styron insists, "is not the drowsy Old Virginia of legend but part of a busy New South"; there are references to heavy machinery, military bases, a land "sucked dry by tobacco". But the prevailing atmosphere is pastoral, of idleness not bustle, of whippoorwills, "emerald-green" thickets, "a delicious winey smell of cedar". The setting is ultimately idealized, perhaps because it is filtered through memory; it is conventional, the South of Southern fiction, including Styron's own early novels. Also conventional is the Southern writer's tendency to see all things in Southern terms, so that the mother's complacency about war in the first story is proleptically a complacency about race. These familiar features are accompanied by the occasional cliché ("inscrutable passion", "stab of pain"), though for the most part the prose is determinedly plain, its air of transparency signalling—meant to signal—the very unity of self or personal coherence which is the narrator's great aim.

William Styron   (essay date 1993)

SOURCE: "Looking Back: *The Long March*," in *This Quiet Dust and Other Writings,* Vintage International, 1993, pp. 333-35.

[*In this essay, which first appeared as the introduction to the Norwegian edition of* The Long March *in 1975, Styron discusses the autobiographical experiences that inform his work and recounts his own artistic process of shaping these experiences into the novella.*]

Although not nearly so long nor so ambitious as my other works, *The Long March* achieved within its own scope, I think, a unity and a sense of artistic inevitability which

still, ten years after the writing, I rather wistfully admire. Lest I appear immodest, I would hasten to add that I do not consider the book even remotely perfect, yet certainly every novelist must have within the body of his writing a work of which he recalls everything having gone just *right* during the composition: through some stroke of luck, form and substance fuse into a single harmonious whole and it all goes down on paper with miraculous ease. For me this was true of *The Long March*, and since otherwise the process of writing has remained exceedingly painful, I cherish the memory of this brief work, often wondering why for a large part of the time I cannot recapture the sense of compulsion and necessity that dominated its creation.

Possibly much of the urgency of the book is due to factors that are extremely personal. As the reader may eventually begin to suspect, the story is autobiographical. To be sure, all writing is to some degree autobiographical, but *The Long March* is intensely and specifically so. I do not mean that the central figures are not more or less imaginary—they are; but the mortar explosion and the forced march, which are central to the entire narrative, were actual incidents in which I was involved, just as I was bound up, for a time, in the same desolating atmosphere of a military base in the midst of a fiercely hot American summer. If the story has a sense of truth and verisimilitude, it is because at the time of the writing all of these things—the terrible explosion, the heat of summer and the anguish of the march itself—still persisted in my mind with the reality of some unshakable nightmare.

> Even in the midst of an ultimate process of dehumanization the human spirit cannot be utterly denied or downed: against all odds, faces emerge from the faceless aggregate of ciphers, and in the middle of the march I was creating I found Captain Mannix slogging and sweating away, tortured, beaten but indomitable. A hero in spite of himself or me, he endures, and in the midst of inhumanity retains all that which makes it worthwhile to be human.
>
> —*William Styron*

Perhaps it was an even larger nightmare which I was trying to create in this book, and which lends to the work whatever symbolic power it has the fortune to possess. Because for myself (as I do believe for most thoughtful people, not only Americans but the community of peaceable men everywhere) the very idea of another war—this one in remote and strange Korea, and only five years after the most cataclysmic conflict ever to engulf mankind—possessed a kind of murky, surrealistic, half-lunatic unreality that we are mercifully spared while awake, but which we do occasionally confront in a horrible dream. Especially for those like myself who had shed their uniforms only five years before—in the blissful notion that the unspeakable orgy of war was now only a memory and safely behind—the experience of putting on that uniform again and facing anew the ritualistic death dance had an effect that can only be described as traumatic. World War II was dreadful enough, but at least the issues involved were amenable to reasonable definition. To be suddenly plunged again into war, into a war, furthermore, where the issues were fuzzy and ambiguous, if not fraudulent, a war that could not possibly be "won," a senseless conflict so unpopular that even the most sanguinary politician or war lover shrank from inciting people to a patriotic zeal, a war without slogans or ballads or heroes—to have to endure this kind of war seemed, to most of us involved in it at the time, more than we could bear. War was no longer simply a temporary madness into which human beings happily lapsed from time to time. War had at last become *the* human condition.

It was this feeling I believe I was trying to recapture when sometime later, in the summer of 1952, I found myself in Paris still unable to shake off the sense of having just recently awakened from a nightmare. My own ordeal and the ordeal of most of my Marine Corps friends (including one or two who died in Korea) was over—yet the persistent image of eight boys killed by a random mortar shell and of a long and brutal march lingered in my mind. Senseless mass slaughter and a seemingly endless march, the participants of which were faceless zeroes, were all that in retrospect appeared to me significant about this war without heroes, this war which lacked so utterly a sense of human identity, and which in so sinister a fashion presaged the faceless, soulless, pushbutton wars of the future. All right, I would write about this faceless, soulless march. Yet, all my intentions to the contrary, I began to understand, as I wrote, that even in the midst of an ultimate process of dehumanization the human spirit cannot be utterly denied or downed: against all odds, faces emerge from the faceless aggregate of ciphers, and in the middle of the march I was creating I found Captain Mannix slogging and sweating away, tortured, beaten but indomitable. A hero in spite of himself or me, he endures, and in the midst of inhumanity retains all that which makes it worthwhile to be human. I myself cannot be sure, but possibly it is the hopeful implications derived from this mystery—this kind of indefatigable man—which are all an artist can pretend to suggest, however imperfectly, in his struggle to comprehend the agony of our violent, suicidal century.

James L. W. West III (review date 1994)

SOURCE: "Tidewater Tales," in *Sewanee Review,* Spring, 1994, pp. xlix-li.

[*In this excerpt, West discusses the effect of Styron's revisions of these earlier published stories and notes that Styron's message is that art can redeem an otherwise intolerable existence.*]

It is good to see these stories made available between hard covers, but one would be mistaken to regard this small collection as a simple recycling of already-published work. The stories need to be read together, in the achronological sequence in which Styron has arranged them, if one is to experience their collective force. *A Tidewater Morning* is a small, carefully crafted volume of fiction that most closely resembles, in technique, such fictive sequences as Faulkner's *Go Down, Moses* and Hemingway's *In Our Time.* Styron has linked his stories together in ways obvious and subtle: this arrangement gives them a cumulative weight and thematic resonance that they would not possess if read separately.

All three of the stories are narrated by an autobiographical character named Paul Whitehurst. In **"Shadrach"** Paul is ten years old, in **"A Tidewater Morning"** he is thirteen, and in **"Love Day"** he is twenty. Styron might have arranged the stories in this straightforward chronological order, but he seems to have recognized that he could make his structure more dramatic and throw his themes more sharply into relief were he to take **"Love Day,"** the last story chronologically in Paul's life, and place it first in the volume.

He has made a second change as well. **"Love Day,"** in its original *Esquire* text, describes Paul as a young Marine Corps officer participating in a feigned assault on Okinawa toward the end of World War II. Paul meditates in the story about the nearness of death and the incomprehensibility of war; and, toward the end of the story, he witnesses a frighteningly swift kamikaze attack on a destroyer only a quarter of a mile away from his own ship.

When Styron took **"Love Day"** from *Esquire* and placed it in the leading position in *A Tidewater Morning*, however, he removed the kamikaze attack and ended the story ambiguously, at an earlier point, with Paul brooding about his fate and attempting to convince himself that he is where he wants to be. "*You love the Marine Corps, it's a terrific war,*" he says to himself. "*You love the Marine Corps, it's a terrific war . . .*" With these strokes of rearrangement and revision, Styron turned **"Love Day"** into a prelude for the two stories that now follow it in the volume. In these two stories he shows us how Paul did come to be standing on the deck of that troop ship on that particular day in 1945.

"Shadrach," the second narrative in the collection, leads into the final story in a similar fashion. Vernon Dabney, a down-at-the-heels aristocrat living on the remnants of his ancestral demesne in Tidewater Virginia in the mid-1930s, muses on the death of an ancient black retainer who has hobbled all the way north from Alabama to die on the plantation on which he was born a slave almost one hundred years earlier. Dabney is not much impressed. "When you're dead nobody knows the difference," he says. "Death ain't much." **"A Tidewater Morning,"** which follows immediately, shows that Dabney is mistaken. This story, which is closely autobiographical, tells of the cruelly painful death of Paul's mother in the hot Tidewater summer of 1938. The narrative, based on the death of Styron's own mother, is heartwrenching, and it must have cost Styron a great deal to write it.

The three stories in **A Tidewater Morning** are interconnected by many images and devices, some of which were present in the original *Esquire* versions but some of which were added or highlighted in revision. One discerns linked pairs of characters—old and young, black and white. One discovers repetitions that tie the tales together—odors, insects, flowers, large families, working-class people, negroes, profanity, FDR, southern food, movie stars, and commercial products of the 1930s and 40s. One sees other links as well, though they are understated: a white child who is holding the hand of an older negro, the presence of fireflies and honeysuckle, the stifling heat of the Tidewater region, the constant thirst of the characters.

The strongest cords binding these stories together are thematic. Styron is working through familiar territory for him, contemplating the fearful mysteries of grief, remorse, memory, guilt, race, rebellion, warfare, and death. The dominant theme of the related stories is that these features of human existence can be brought under control and made bearable by the power of art. At crucial points in all three of these narratives, Paul retreats into his unconscious mind, lifts himself above his doubt or pain, and fashions and imaginative rendering of the moment. This, Styron seems to be telling us, is the only way finally to address some of the almost intolerable ambiguities and injustices of our time.

Ronald Curran   (review date 1994)

SOURCE: A review of *A Tidewater Morning,* in *World Literature Today,* Vol. 68, Summer, 1994, pp. 571-72.

[*Here, Curran finds in Styron's latest collection an essential optimism that underlies the dark and painful fictionalized memories of the author's boyhood.*]

"We each devise our means of escape from the intolerable." So begins the closing paragraph in the title story of William Styron's collection *Tidewater Morning*. Each of these three tales from youth holds in its own fashion to the truth in Styron's closing observation. They evoke Styron's experience of the 1930s at ages ten, thirteen, and twenty (even though **"Love Day"** carries us up to 1945 and the invasion of Okinawa). As the author looks back on his youth, he informs it with a hindsight the appreciation of which finds what is timeless in uniquely personal moments warmly set in social and personal history. The cumulative effect of the stories is to make it painful to think that one may not have had anything comparable to cherish. Styron's is a prose that validates the bittersweet privilege of being alive. He personifies time as a heartless thief with a taste of a connoisseur.

"Love Day" finds Paul Whitehurst a twenty-year-old platoon leader in the Second Marine Division. He is ready to be a part of the largest invasion since Normandy. "Never

again," he feels, "would [his] health have such incandescence as it did at twenty." Poised for the ultimate test of his masculinity, he must come to terms with being part of a "feint, a diversion" that would never become an assault. Forced by the whim of military strategy to "chicken out" by bureaucratic design, the young officer struggles with an emotional collage of outrage, bravado, and relief. Mixing this leathery paradox of emotion with synchronous flashbacks, Styron achieves an ironic epiphany that makes Paul "sense the power of history to utterly victimize humanity, composed of forgettable ciphers like myself."

> **Styron's is a prose that validates the bittersweet privilege of being alive.**
>
> —*Ronald Curran*

In the second piece, **"Shadrach,"** "a black apparition of unbelievable antiquity," dominates the story of Styron's tenth summer, in 1935. Like a character out of Faulkner, Shadrach strikes Paul Whitehurst as a combination of Stepin Fetchit and Uncle Remus. Shad has returned to Virginia after an impossible journey undertaken in his half-blind, penniless condition. Like the huge sea turtles who use some mysterious kind of celestial navigation to find the same beaches to bury their eggs and hatch their next generation, Shad finds his way home to the Dabneys, the Virginia family who long ago owned him as their slave. He wants to die on his former owner's land. Shad hardly notices that this once-illustrious family has moved down the social ladder from Virginia gentlefolk to white trash. Reduced to bootlegging during the Great Depression, they have become "downwardly mobile." To Paul Whitehurst, they are a walk on the wild side that he savors, a counterbalance to his proper Presbyterian background that had "deprived him of a certain depravity." Striated with half-breeds at this point, the Dabneys are a parody of their former selves, with dark-skinned, voluptuous daughters; they are dysfunctional to the point of delirious amoral opportunity. But their Tobacco Road effluvium, Woolworth perfume, and sometimes "stunning ugliness" still contain a family spirit capable of reinheriting Shad once again. They do so with a "downwardly mobile" polish that manages to make a long-past noblesse oblige shine in the midst of the refuse of their messy yet vital lives. Somehow Shad manages to recapture "the one pure, untroubled moment in his life" on their property and to embrace a peace and sense of affiliation necessary for the death he seeks at home. Likewise, Styron pilfers a memory from the jumbled recollections of childhood, making it resonant with grace where one would least expect it to be.

The final tale, **"A Tidewater Morning,"** sets the end of Paul's mother's eight-year struggle with cancer amid the news of imminent war in Europe. Old marital fault lines surface as death approaches, and Adelaide the Northern reactionary materialist and Jeff the laid-back, unambitious man "of spirit and intellect" put on the cracking gloves of their cloying differences and reenact a few rounds from their former bouts. As Prague awaits Hitler's ultimatum, Adelaide slips away from her chronic pain along with other losses: world peace, Paul's paper route, and Jeff's faith. The story closes in a dissociated moment as Paul Whitehurst gazes down on himself in the arms of his grieving father. Death in this collection is in sequence evaded, dignified, and heroically suffered, as each story stands as a numinous moment of childhood or early manhood become a "means of escape from the intolerable" void of soullessness. These stories show that even in the Great Depression no darkness is so pervasive that light cannot be found in it. One wonders how much they benefit from Styron's dark descent in *Darkness Visible*. The book's epigraph from Sir Thomas Browne's *Urn Burial* says it nicely: "The long habit of living indisposeth us for dying."

Gavin Cologne-Brookes (essay date 1995)

SOURCE: "Signs of a Shift: *The Long March*," in *The Novels of William Styron: From Harmony to History,* Louisiana State University Press, 1995, pp. 45-67.

[*In this excerpt, Cologne-Brookes sees in* The Long March *signs of a change in Styron's emphases, from his earlier view that literature is a way to achieve harmony in a chaotic world to his later conviction that art is necessarily part of a dialogue with sociohistorical matters.*]

As Styron's career progressed, the discourse toward harmony was dislodged from setting the underlying direction of his fiction to being one part of a more complex dialogue. *The Long March* shows signs of this shift, since a conflict emerges between the textual movement toward verbal and social reconciliation and the novella's subject matter. As in *Lie Down in Darkness,* a struggle is waged between the centripetal and the centrifugal, this time with Tom Culver, as a "critic" ostensibly on the margins of the conflict, having a personal interest in—and as a lawyer, a professional disposition toward—finding a stable outcome. Since the novella continues the shift toward social and historical preoccupations that was incipient in the latter parts of *Lie Down in Darkness,* a conflict arises between Culver's personal drive to harmonize voices—the text's fundamental shaping movement—and the political struggle between Mannix and Templeton.

To an extent, *The Long March* is about the "intrusion of history" into private lives—as Roger Asselineau puts it—and certainly the novella embraces a wider social outlook than was apparent in the private neuroses of the Loftis family ["Following *The Long March*," in *Critical Essays on William Styron,* 1982]. Essentially a war novella, it fits Frederick R. Karl's description of such novels as *Catch-22, The Naked and the Dead,* and *From Here to Eternity*

as being "about a societal equivalent found in the military" as much as about military life [*American Fictions, 1940-1980: A Comprehensive History and Critical Evaluation*, 1983]. Culver suffers acutely from the "perpetual apprehension" that, in James Jones's novel [*From Here to Eternity*], is seen as the lot of modern man. In *The Long March*, an increased engagement with society and history begins to reshape the fixation on individual and artistic harmony in *Lie Down in Darkness*. The shift is still small, but it is enough to create tension between the discourse toward harmony and the novella's subject matter. Culver, as one critic says, tries "to put the pieces into some pattern" by attempting to reconcile the warring discourses of Templeton and Mannix [Irving Malin, "The Symbolic March," in *The Achievement of William Styron*, 1981]. But for that very reason he becomes a destabilizing figure in his overall effect on events. If in one sense *The Long March* springs from an age of conformity, of the retreat into concerns that produced, in Morris Dickstein's words, the "narrowly personal" art of *Seize the Day* and *The Assistant,* in which "the only salvation is individual or religious," at the same time the events portrayed call into question the centripetal, harmonizing measures by which Culver seeks an intermediate perch between Templeton and Mannix for personal peace [*Gates of Eden: American Culture in the Sixties*, 1977].

An examination of Culver's personal and social effort toward harmony reveals that he is not merely the "passive but sympathetic observer" of the struggle between Templeton and Mannix that some critics see him as [Marc Ratner, *William Styron*]. Rather, whether Styron intended it or not, the seemingly straightforward discourse toward harmony is complicated by Culver's effect on events. If it is partly true, as Marc L. Ratner says, that Culver "cannot bring himself to act," his inaction is itself a form of action.

At the heart of *The Long March* is the conflict between Colonel Templeton and Captain Mannix, with Mannix struggling to draw Templeton, and the authoritative discourse he upholds, into dialogue. But the conflict between Templeton's centripetal voice and the dissenting, suppressed voice of Mannix has to be seen through the figure of Culver. Thrown into turmoil from the outset, Culver is uncertain and uncommitted. He seeks to reconcile the warring voices he is caught between as well as to reassert a sense of personal stability. . . . Culver and Mannix have alike been wrenched from their domestic lives and personal ambitions and thrown into military life. Culver, however, persists in trying to find personal and social harmony, and the novella's movement reflects his aim. At the same time, the implications of his attitude—and of Styron's aesthetic—become especially apparent in virtue of the subject matter.

Bakhtin's concept of the chronotope [Mikhail] . . . can illuminate the novella's opening and overall pattern. Just as any novel is shot through with forms of language and voices, so it is also furnished with chronotopes—with spatiotemporal patterns that are the "organizing centers for the fundamental narrative events" and that "are *dialogical* in the broadest sense of the word . . . "[*The Dialogic Imagination: Four Essays,* 1981]. [In] ***The Long March*** two key chronotopes are those of domestic well-being and the military. The immiscible merging of the domestic and military worlds is at the bottom of Culver's initial distress. His mental dislocation has an underlying cause in his literal dislocation. The incommensurability of the two worlds is apparent from the start: "One noon, in the blaze of a cloudless Carolina summer, *what was left of eight dead boys* lay strewn about the landscape, among the poison ivy and the pine needles and loblolly saplings. *It was not so much as if they had departed this life but as if,* sprayed from a hose, *they were only shreds of bone, gut, and dangling tissue to which it would have been impossible ever to impute the quality of life, far less the capacity to relinquish it*" (my italics). Here one set of chronotopic details competes with another, the pleasant or pastoral giving way to the ugly reality of the military world. The details expressed by "a cloudless Carolina summer," "strewn about the landscape, among . . . the pine needles and loblolly saplings," and even "sprayed from a hose" belong to pastoral or suburban relaxation; they might be part of a summer picnic or a day lounging in a Port Warwick garden. But interspersed with these—like poison ivy, as it were—and irreversibly altering the picture are the disruptive and eventually dominant details (the phrasing of which I have italicized) of random, violent death. The remains "strewn about" are not those of a picnic—or not only of that—but of "eight dead boys": "shreds of human bone, gut, and dangling tissue." The two sets of details intermingle further in the description of human carnage literally mixed with food: a "welter of blood and brain, scattered messkits and mashed potatoes, and puddles of melting ice-cream. The unblended merging of the two chronotopes is coupled with the dialogic nature of the language, which mingles the specific, descriptive language of the dead bodies with abstractions like "departed this life." The passage is structured out of linguistic and chronotopic clashes.

The discord situates a fundamental part of Culver's sense of confusion as the story opens. "After six years of an ordered and sympathetic life," he finds himself wrenched from domestic contentment back into military life, a "new world . . . of disorder." As Ratner says, there is the "contrast between the apparent harmony of civilian life for Culver and the chaos and disorder of the present" [*William Styron*]. Culver's particular need for harmony is evident in the "moderation" of his "sensible" home life. Finding himself in a world where his idea of normal relationships between time, space, and human beings is shattered, he feels "disoriented," as if in "another dimension of space and time." He struggles to reorient himself.

The same chronotopic conflict continues to be a major cause of Culver's early "sense of disorder." He feels "adrift at sea in a dazzling, windowless box, ignorant of direction or of any points of the globe." His sense of reality is so shaken that not only does his former life of "wife and child and home" seem unreal but so does his present existence.

He moves from a "strange thicket to a stranger swamp and on to the green depths of some even stranger ravine," as if the nonsequential "dream of a man delirious with fever." For him, "all time and space" seems "enclosed within the tent, itself unmoored and unhelmed upon a dark and compassless ocean." His disorientation is literally and figuratively chronotopic, and his bearings are at this point absolutely lost.

Some critics have seen little relation between the scene of the dead boys and the rest of the march, but the march too reflects the discord that Culver will try to harmonize. Culver senses a disparity between military and civilian life, and within the military world there is the further unsettling contrast between the static, dead bodies and the constant movement of the march, an entrapping pattern of perpetual, perversely ordered movement set against chaotic stasis. In the latter, space and the time exist as a frozen instant, whereas on the march, the two are concretized in a single continuity. Templeton asserts that a certain place means a certain time, and, having begun at "nine on the dot," the group reach the highway "at ten o'clock, almost to the minute." But so imposed, so rigid is this chronotope that Culver's normal sense of spatial and temporal orientation—his memory of domestic life—is undermined. The "constant movement" makes the sun seem to come from "ever-shifting" points, so he suffers from "displacement" and "confusion," never sure if it is "morning or afternoon." His confusion amid order is worsened by the shock of seeing the human remains, which stays with him in a lingering memory that blocks any recovery of stability. If the opening explosion replays the suddenness with which Culver has been slung into this other world, the march itself functions as the novella's central chronotope; it is what moves the plot along, what brings to a head the conflicts of the participants, and what determines the outcome.

Thrown from a relatively unstructured environment into a world of strict hierarchy, Culver suffers a disorientation that is compounded by the apparent perversity of the order he observes. Like Mannix, he has a "violent contempt for the gibberish, the boy-scout passwords" that replace "ordinary conversation in the military world." The menacing childishness of those in authority is illustrated by Templeton's cowboy poses: his "pearl-handled .38 revolver," his "thumbs hooked rakishly in his belt," and his casual, squinting eyes. His cowboy mentality finds an outlet in the constant order to "saddle up." Culver and Mannix not only are in a setting that is strange to them but have to respond to, and use, a language they despise.

As the novella begins, Culver is in a state of confusion: a combination of disorientation, exhaustion, and shock only deepened by such discordant sounds as the "multitude of wails" that crackle through his radio headphones like a "jungle full of noise." Not least of these, for Culver, is the voice of Mannix himself. "Recklessly vocal," Mannix constantly feeds Culver's apprehension. But Culver is trying to bring his several vortices of verbal, chronotopic, and mental conflict under some kind of control, to rediscover orientation and stability.

If the chronotopic disorder serves as a narrative device to motivate Culver to make sense of events, it also suggests both ontological and epistemological concerns. Culver asks, How? and, Why?, yet his underlying need is to connect one reality with another, civilian with military, and to make sense of his existence. . . . The ontological concern also comes across in the textual suggestions that *The Long March* is as much about the absurdity of existence as about that of the march—an aspect of the novella that depends on Camus' voice being heard.

If the chronotopic conflicts help determine the novella's structure, its narrative interest and Culver's anguish are prolonged by the struggle between Mannix and Templeton. Their largely verbal battle, representing in microcosm the war beyond, is a struggle between the centripetal voice of Templeton and the centrifugal voice of Mannix, with Culver seeking to reconcile the two. If Templeton upholds, in a sense embodies, the authoritative discourse of the military, Mannix struggles first to bring this discourse into dialogue and then, in his frustration, to overthrow it. The irony, for Culver, is that in pursuing "individual" action, Mannix himself becomes a centripetal voice at the height of his "rebellion in reverse," when he tries to coerce others to follow his lead and carry out Templeton's orders in full.

Much of the conflict between Templeton and Mannix flows from their different dispositions toward authoritative discourse. To the degree that discourse is authoritative, any challenge to it is taboo; the authoritative word, as authoritative, is an object of reverence, a vessel of truth, beyond questioning. It might include sacred texts, the law, literature of the canon, social etiquette, or other codes of conduct. The portrayal of military discourse in *The Long March* makes it appear quasi-religious, and some of the characters, such as O'Leary and Hobbs, uphold it unquestioningly. Mannix, on the other hand, and at times Culver, try to resist its authoritative claim. But since it remains sacred for the marine regulars and rules the actions of Culver and Mannix, they can do no more than mock, parody, and profane it. They are unable to reduce its grip.

For Templeton, O'Leary, and others, marine regulations are the "special script" that governs their world view [Bakhtin, *The Dialogic Imagination,* 343]. Templeton's adherence to the word of the military is backed up by his use of a special language. But it is also apparent in his name, which reinforces the idea that military discourse is a form of religion and signals his devotion to it. Culver likens Templeton to "certain young ecclesiastics, prematurely aged and perhaps even wise." Templeton helps sustain, but also as a commanding officer embodies, an institution that does not doubt its possession of the truth and that thus smothers any possible dialogue. Templeton expects "to be obeyed." Referred to by the regulars as Old Rocky, he has a world view that precludes dialogue. The word *old* associates him with tradition, and the image of a rock captures his adamantine temperament.

Throughout there is in evidence Templeton's suppression of any true dialogue between his own voice, a vehicle for military discourse, and any voice seeking seriously to challenge it. . . . Templeton hews to the centripetal not only with others but also internally, avoiding even self-reflection unless it, like his external speech, is rigorously stylized. This is evident in his rationale for the march: "I said to myself, 'How's the battalion doing?' I mean, 'What kind of an outfit do I have here? Is it in good combat shape? If we were to meet an Aggressor enemy tomorrow would we come out all right?' Those were the queries I posed myself. Then I tried to formulate an answer." His stilted thoughts show how riddled he is with the military value system. Everything is in abstract concepts and Latinate diction. In trying to "formulate" an answer, he leaves no space for emotion but limits himself to logical, abstract thought. His Latinate diction is a way of seeking to reinforce the authority of his decisions by wrapping them in the cloak of objectivity. His internal dialogue occurs only within the bounds of his own narrow code and, unlike Culver's, is not concerned with the tension between discourses.

Any discourse that has appeal for being unified or that is vested with a monolithic truth is open to attempts by centrifugal voices to undermine it. Where such attempts seem to occur but do not is in Templeton's stylized external dialogues with regulars. O'Leary supposedly questions the decision, but his demur is mere ritual since it takes place only in the bounds of marine discourse, offering no serious challenge. O'Leary, says Culver, is "inextricably grafted to the system" like "flesh surgically laid on arm or thigh." Since he performs with "devoted, methodical competence," he can "say sarcastically, 'The Colonel's really got a wild hair, ain't he?' but shrug his shoulders and grin, and by that ambivalent gesture sum up an attitude which only a professional soldier could logically retain: I doubt the Colonel's judgment a little, but will willingly do what he says." Like the radio man Hobbs, he has "immunity," because his voicing of doubt is merely a stylized part of the system.

Mannix, in contrast, is a reluctant reservist thrust back into a military he despises. The words he utters as a partial outsider unwilling to accept the role of subordinate marine threaten to break through the accepted code. Whereas O'Leary's "incredulous whistle, right in the Colonel's face," only elicits an "indulgent smile," Mannix' murmur of "Thirty-six miles, Jesus Christ" in a tone "laden with no more disbelief or no more pain than O'Leary's whistle" brings to the colonel's face a "delicate shadow of irritation." Templeton's reacting at all opens the possibility that he will enter into dialogue with Mannix and offer some vent to the latter's frustration. But his reply "You think that's too long?" is again delivered as "merely a question candidly stated"—*stated* being the operative word. In truth, the colonel still brooks no response, and his face, having found "absolute repose," reflects this no less than his voice.

Templeton's indifference causes Mannix to look for release by trying, again and again, to engage Templeton, and in him military authority, in dialogue. The struggle advances from Mannix' comic mockery, in the early stages, to his reverse rebellion of carrying out orders even after they have been countered. But the revolt, despite Mannix' efforts, never gets beyond verbal challenge for long, since behind the colonel's indifference lies the brute force that authority can bring to bear. This is underscored by Culver's description, however satiric, of the colonel's cowboy gesture of reaching for his pistol when Mannix swears at him. Mannix, largely restricted to verbal weaponry, moves ever more recklessly from a centrifugal parody unheard by authority to outright defiance. At first he is merely "more noisily frank" than other reserves about his dislike of the Marine Corps. His antagonism comes out only in odd comments, such as his deliberately testy, colloquial reply to one of Templeton's orders: "Jesus, lemme digest a bit, Jack." At that stage, his comments, if "too often audible" for Culver's taste, are "frequently comical" and keep Culver "in a constant state of mild suspense—half amusement, half horror." They comically undercut authority but have no further effect.

Even this early there are hints that, in Culver's opinion, Mannix' revolt is doomed. Mannix seems halfway to failure already because he has begun to speak "like a marine." Thus, though Templeton can detect an extra edge to his complaints, he fits within the pattern of those whose function is to obey. Though he is trying to stand outside the stylized question-and-answer system, the seeds of his eventual capitulation are evident in his diction, for cursing and groaning serve as safety valves rather than challenge authority.

When Mannix goes on to question the length of the march, the colonel interrupts again, his voice "anticipatory, as if it already held the answer to whatever Mannix might ask." True dialogue still does not occur, and Mannix is provoked to more reckless action. Templeton remains intent in his centripetal determination to arrest any attempt at dialogue and to reposition it within the order of the discourse he adheres to. His Latinate diction, shed of emotive content, assists him in this: "They're *marines. Comprehend?*" he says. "They're going to *act* like marines.". . . Each time Mannix starts to question authority, Templeton closes up, returning "once more to that devout, ordered state of communion," with his preordained script, that Mannix' "words had ever so briefly disturbed."

The sham dialogue of authoritative marine discourse is most starkly exposed by Mannix' bid to enter into it during one of the "compulsory lectures." Lectures being, in any case, the perfect monologic structure to buttress authority, these seem specifically designed for the purpose. With "appallingly familiar" outlines, they are "doggedly memorized" ways to deliver a present message and they leave no room for innovation or discussion. Like Templeton's speech, they are dressed out in Latinate terminology and abstract concepts like that of "amphibiously integrated" group destinies, and are supported by "reams of printed and mimeographed tables and charts and résumés.". . . Most of the marines are content to discard the printed matter or simply not to listen. Mannix has to make

a gesture. Parodying the "grandiose doctrine" and "aping" the young colonel, he mutters, "Corporal, kindly pass out the atom bombs for inspection." But he does this beyond the hearing of authority, and so without engaging it in dialogue.

Later, during the question-and-answer part of the lectures, however, he exerts pressure directly on the stylized dialogue by answering "some generalized, hypothetical question" by saying that he does not have the "faintest idea." Faced with Mannix' freewheeling, the young colonel retreats deeper into formality: "I stated earlier, Captain, that I wanted some sort of answer. None of you gentlemen is expected to know this subject pat, but you can essay *some kind of answer.*" Yet the questioner clearly does not want just some kind of answer—which would allow escape from the codified marine discourse. So for a moment Mannix succeeds and the colonel is "at a loss for words."

The victory, though, is minor, a successful skirmish that punctuates overall failure. Mannix still cannot engage authority in genuine dialogue. His insistence on preserving his identity as an individual, moreover, is ironically debilitated, since the more he asserts his right to challenge, the further he reveals his adherence to the system. Becoming "more in need to scourge something," he turns to direct action but even then can only act within the code and language he is trying to fight. It is here that Culver's indecision grows problematic.

Culver has an ambivalent attitude toward both the authority of Templeton and the recklessness of Mannix. This is the strength and the weakness of his outlook. When he describes the colonel as being like "certain young ecclesiastics," he tails off with the concession that the colonel is "perhaps even wise." Culver has doubts about the worth and legitimacy of rebellion. Certainly he is skeptical of, and—when personally affected—appalled by, Templeton's fixation on order and his suppression of dialogue. Watching the colonel "squint casually into the sun" when news comes of the accident, as if he were "receiving the most routine of messages," Culver wonders "what interior struggle" has gone into the "perfection of such a gesture." In Culver's view, Templeton's stability has been bought at the price of losing the ability to feel, and so to be fully alive. "A man to whom the greatest embarrassment would be a show of emotion," he has become less a person than a "quantity of attitudes."

Still, Culver is envious of the certainty Templeton has found in accepting a code to live by. Notwithstanding that Templeton suppresses inner contradictions and bothersome emotions, Culver is drawn to the sense of order the colonel displays. Seeking stability himself, he has a kind of "respect" for the man—though he puts the word in quotation marks to distance it from his own discourse. He is caught between the language of the language of Mannix, whose rebellion upsets his desire for harmony, and the language of the military, which reinforces Templeton's authority. Sympathetic to Mannix' viewpoint, Culver is also wary of it. In order to go along with a system he dislikes, he seeks to reconcile the opposing views. . . .

It is not that Culver lacks insight or fails to question authority. But he sees that Mannix is unknowingly caught up in the system he is defying, and so realizes that the battle Mannix thinks he is engaged in is partly illusory. Culver tells himself that he despises not the "man," Templeton, but "the Colonel, the marine," since Templeton is "not himself evil or unjust" but just devoted to regulations. He is aware too that the colonel's regular subordinates have no wish to question the authority and that military speech conventions reinforce it. He sees how the major bestows on Templeton a "third person flattery," as if the colonel is beyond direct address, let alone challenge.

Since Culver's thoughts are the filter for our view of events, he does, for us, subvert Templeton's authoritative discourse. Whereas Mannix seeks to undermine Templeton through parody and then action, Culver employs irony. His narrative viewpoint supplements Mannix' actions, as when he describes the colonel's false display of emotion as "good grade-A Templeton." He sees through the "performance," and to this extent, is a centrifugal voice. In that role, he appears as an observer who, recognizing how Mannix' individualist rebellion is doomed to fail, offers sympathetic commentary on it—a commentary that makes fun of Templeton's pretensions.

But this leaves aside that because Culver never acts on his dislike of the system, he limits the shape of the action that Mannix can take and helps ensure his defeat. Culver's strength is his critical awareness, which allows him to recognize that Templeton is impervious alike to true dialogue and to Mannix' heroic challenges. What is less laudable, however, is the way the pose of critical detachment allows Culver to avoid confronting an authority he himself is unhappy with. His weakness is an ironic use of language that ends up misrepresenting the contest between Templeton and Mannix as a personal, equal one to which he is merely a detached bystander rather than letting him understand its broader, political implications.

The cowboy imagery of Culver's ironic commentary displays the conflict as a duel between individuals, even a shoot-out:

> The Captain got up, limping off toward his company, over his retreating shoulder, shot back a short, clipped burst of words at the Colonel—whose eyeballs rolled white with astonishment when he heard them—and thereby joined the battle.

> "Who cares what you think," he said.

Culver here casts the conflict of voices in terms of men in equal combat rather than as a broader social fray of which Culver himself is integrally a part. At a moment when Mannix, however recklessly, finally gets through to the colonel, Culver, the detached, passive critic—or artist—is taking a neutral stance, paring his fingernails. When he satirizes Templeton, he includes the deluded, grotesquely limping Mannix in the satire. Mannix becomes a "mammoth, gyrating" parody, with the "suffering face of a clown," who for all his heroism fails to comprehend that

"the hike had nothing to do with courage or sacrifice or suffering." Culver is content to think of Mannix' rebellion as "individual" and "therefore hopeless, maybe even absurd."

Culver's aloof complacency ensures that the dominant power remains intact. The net result of his liberal pluralism is to entrench the status quo as effectively as O'Leary or Hobbs. We are left to ponder whether it is because of him that Mannix' behavior is absurdly futile and that Templeton has his victory. Culver's chief criticism—that Mannix' actions are "hopeless" because they are "individual"—invites the obvious rejoinder that had Culver himself, and others like him, acted with Mannix, the actions would have been neither individual nor necessarily hopeless. Culver may profess sympathy for Mannix' viewpoint, but he in practice ends up supporting authority. His inaction means that he is not merely a passive witness but an active shaper of the unfolding events. At times he does physically act to shape events—when, for example, he stops Mannix from burning down the mess—but even his apparent passivity helps steer the course of the action toward the ultimate renewal of social stability.

The extent to which Styron was aware of Culver's ambivalent role is unclear. Culver is a detached artist trying to harmonize the world, and the conflicts in his role may arise from the clash between Styron's own disposition to harmonize voices and the more problematic subject matter he was canvassing, a clash not wholly muted here. Culver is distanced from the author not only because he is described in the third person but also in virtue of his job as a lawyer, which, . . . signals that he is disposed to seek order. At this stage, however, the author's dialogizing of the discourse toward harmony is not explicit, nor perhaps conscious.

Nevertheless, it is clear that the pursuit of harmony grows more questionable when, as begins to happen here and as is increasingly the case, Styron's works leave the domestic world of the larger part of his first novel and enter political arenas. The danger in trying to reconcile warring discourses is that to compromise may leave the authoritative discourse, or the power that is, intact. In *The Long March*, that is not perhaps an obvious concern, and there may be a case for arguing that, given what Mannix is up against, Culver is right to react as he does. But the political moral beneath the skin of *The Long March* rises to the surface in subsequent novels and has a bearing on some of the public controversy that attended *The Confessions of Nat Turner* . . . .

The Long March ultimately moves toward a reconciliation of conflicting voices. But a displacement in the harmonized voices reflects the discongruity between Culver's, and perhaps the author's, discourse toward harmony and the social and political questions raised by the struggle between Templeton and Mannix. Culver's viewpoint remains ambivalent to the end. He tells how Mannix himself, striving to instill marine pride in his men, becomes a centripetal voice as he works to ensure that they survive the whole march and so defy Templeton. The description of

Mannix as "rocklike," indeed, invites comparisons with Templeton. Culver thus continues to mediate, wishing "to caution" Mannix about the futility of the rebellion and to show the extremity of both men's positions.

Consumed with "one idea"—to last through the march and so defy Templeton—Mannix lets his discourse become, ironically, monologic. Coercion replaces persuasion as he proceeds to "sting and flay" his men "with the merciless accents of a born bully." As Culver sees it, Mannix' actions are part of the problem, a "part of the general scheme." It is "useless to reason" with him, since he matches Templeton in resisting dialogue:

> "See, that little jerk wants to make a name for himself—Old Rocky Templeton. Led the longest forced march in the history of the Corps—"

> "But—" Culver started.

> "He'd just love to see H & S Company crap out," he went on.

Seeing Mannix' actions as unavailing and even dangerous, Culver becomes all the less inclined to condemn Templeton. Realizing—or rationalizing—that the colonel is "as far removed from the vulgar battle" as the "remotest stars," Culver doubts that a struggle is possible and wonders if O'Leary "could be right, and himself and Mannix, and the rest of them, inescapably wrong." Subdued by weariness, he begins to fear that Mannix may instigate something worse than what he rebels against.

Mannix, for his part, battering against the impregnable wall of military discourse, becomes a caricature, "toiling down the road with hobbled leg and furious flailing arms." Physical disfigurement is matched verbally: "Let them crap out! I've did—done—" he sputters. As Ratner says, he "has been talking to his men in the brutal clichés of the march" but now "becomes inarticulate" [*William Styron*]. His language, even in rebellion, remains in the military mode he despises; outside it, his revolt loses coherence. He and Culver are, in Culver's view, above all marines, doomed to rebel only in terms of the system. Not only is Mannix' failure to breach authoritative discourse confirmed but so too, when he tells Templeton to "fuck" off, is the true nature of Templeton's discourse: "I'm not *interested* in your observations," he tells Mannix. "*Keep your mouth shut!*" After all the rhetoric, Templeton bares his intention to suppress challenging voices. What he wants from those below him is, if not stylized quasidialogue, silence.

The novella's ending, where mental and social harmony gain a hold, must be seen in light of Culver's attitude. The march seems to be a journey toward insight. Culver accepts that he cannot reconcile the interests of Mannix and Templeton, but he turns to a form of understanding between voices in the final scene, when a Negro maid asks him and Mannix, "What you been doin'? Do it hurt?" . . .

The black voice, wheeled on at the end . . . may evince a dubious attempt to parallel the suffering of the marines with that of American Negroes. But in the movement toward harmony, the maid's appearance signals a merging of voices. The "moment of sympathy and understanding" culminates, in the last line, in Mannix' echo of the woman's words, "deed it does." By using her language, he reaccentuates it, so that it links her historical situation with his immediate struggle against authority. In doing so, he invests the phrase with a new meaning that is harmonious rather than antagonistic, signaling mutual understanding. Thus the moment fulfills Culver's need to reconcile voices and end with a semblance of harmony. By using the black maid's language, Mannix suggests that they share in a struggle; the "it" that hurts transcends Mannix' situation.

The phrase is also a pun, signaling a return to the humor Mannix lost at the peak of his rebellion. The use of black discourse is integral to this since it introduces an open-ended quality. In *Black English*, J. L. Dillard discusses the ambiguity latent in black dialect. He quotes the English wife of a plantation owner, who recorded "that 'spect meaning *ex*pect, has sometimes a possible meaning of *su*spect, which would give the sentence in which it occurs a very humorous turn" [*Black English: Its History and Usage in the United States*, 1972]. Although it is the author here, rather than the black woman, who uses the dialect this way, *deed* offers a similar ambiguity, both suggesting the need to act and confirming that the struggle is unwinnable. *Indeed* confirms the pain and unendingness of the struggle, merely consoling through verbal alliance. But *deed* can be taken as reiterating the need for the kind of action Mannix takes.

The introduction of the woman's dialect allows for an ambiguous ending. The phrase flickers between pessimism and optimism. The struggle continues, but defeat is as elusive as victory, so hope is never lost. With the return of humor, both Mannix and the tone of the novella return to a healthier condition. Mannix can resume his subversive role as an overturner of language, if not, for the moment, of authority itself. Culver's movement toward harmony, and the novel's overall movement toward a reconciliation of voices, seem realized.

The verbal and social harmony reached, however, is ultimately an evasion, for to bring it about, Culver—or the author—refocuses the narrative, displacing mutual understanding from where it was originally sought, between Mannix and Templeton, to only between Mannix and the maid. The political harmony achieved permits the retention of military hierarchy. The harmony achieved on a personal level simply changes the outlooks interacting. If we see the crucial conflict as one between discourses in a society—a view encouraged by the self-containment of the world portrayed—Mannix' failure to overturn Templeton's authority through anything except parody is bleak enough. Culver's attitude near the end makes it bleaker still. If Mannix seems to Culver to prove himself part of the system he seeks to subvert, Culver himself settles for Templeton's authority, however unwanted, to achieve a "quality of repose." In other words, Culver is willing to compromise for a quiet life, content to see Templeton as someone "remote from [his] world." His personal need for harmony takes precedence over even justifiable challenges to perverse forms of authority.

The whole narrative of events shows that Culver ends up deluding himself. When he is flung from one "world" into another, where Templeton's power over him shows itself, his sense of civilian life as somehow illusory is more honest than the harmony he eventually settles for. The military, after all, has always been able to propel him out of his normal surroundings. That Templeton, contrary to Culver's conclusion, does not belong to another "world," and hence cannot be discounted, is shown in the way Culver suddenly finds himself part of Templeton's world.

Culver's thinking is dubious in a number of ways. His belief that Mannix becomes as bad as the authority oppressing them draws on one of the classic forms of argument against rebellion . . . Culver's conservative, uncombative stance ensures that the authority rankling him remains. If Mannix is reckless and lacks reflection, Culver lacks the boldness to translate reflection into action. One way or another, both try to undermine authoritarianism but neither is able to cut loose from the system. The attempts to dialogize military discourse fail because Mannix and Culver are caught up in that discourse. But they also fail because, while Mannix strives to rebel by using a marine code of heroic perseverance, Culver's urge to restore stability leads him to do what he can to quiet the centrifugal voice of Mannix, so ensuring that change does not come. The long march is to nowhere not only in that the physical journey is circular but also in its concrete results. Culver and Mannix remain firmly stuck in the hierarchical structure. If anything, Mannix will end up worse off, since the threat of court-martial hangs over him.

This relationship between the self and its sociohistorical context figures in all Styron's work from this point on, becoming a preoccupation that led to his attempt to consider two social and historical realities that have beleaguered the modern mind: slavery and its heritage, and the Holocaust. The value of Styron's voice, we can begin to see, may be precisely that it is not that of the historical or social victim—though any voice is of a potential victim—but rather that of one relatively privileged, situated somewhere between authority or power (Templeton, Mason) and the struggle of those beneath (Cass, in some ways Mannix), seeking to find his own, and by inference many of our, relationships to evil done in his, and our, name. *The Long March* involves a clash that, in *Set This House on Fire*, became a more conscious dialogue between the author's urge to harmonize conflicts and the urge to face social, historical, and political issues. Questions of wider scope began to compete with the largely personal and artistic concerns of Styron's earliest fiction.

In *The Long March*, later themes appear in embryonic form. Disjunction and discord move toward harmonious interaction, but Culver's personal and artistic commitment to such harmony results in a perpetuating of what is

objectionable. His focus away from the struggle with authority is symptomatic of an attitude that gives the personal precedence over the social. His choices thus are a good illustration of what [Georg] Lukács means when he says that a "yearning for harmony" can amount to a "faint-hearted withdrawal before the contradictory problems thrown up by life." Since the harmony achieved depends on Culver's cutting himself off "from society's struggles," it is "illusory and superficial" [*Writer and Critic, and Other Essays,* trans. by Arthur Kahn, 1978].

FURTHER READING

Bibliography

Leon, Philip W. *William Styron: An Annotated Bibliography of Criticism.* Westport, CT: Greenwood Press, 1978, 129 p.
> Detailed bibliography, including a biographical chronology, primary and secondary sources, an index of critics' names, and a subject index.

Criticism

Casciato, Arthur D., and James L. W. West III. *Critical Essays on William Styron.* Boston: G. K. Hall & Co., 1982, 318 p.
> A collection of reviews and essays, including several essays on *The Long March*.

Coale, Samuel. *William Styron Revisited.* Boston: Twayne Publishers, 1991, 149 p.
> Biocritical study of Styron.

Crane, John Kenny. "Forced Marches: 'Marriot the Marine' and *The Long March*." In *The Root of All Evil: The Thematic Unity of William Styron's Fiction,* pp. 59-77. Columbia: University of South Carolina Press, 1984.
> Discusses the contradiction of Mannix's self-canceling heroism and Templeton as a symbol of the church.

Firestone, Bruce M. "The Early Apprenticeship of William Styron." *Studies in Short Fiction* (Fall 1981): 430-43.
> Considers Styron's earliest short stories as a testing ground for new material.

Fossum, Robert H. "Christ on a Crutch: *The Long March*." In *William Styron: A Critical Essay,* pp. 20-5. Grand Rapids, MI: William B. Eerdmans, 1968.
> Discusses *The Long March* from a Christian perspective, arguing that the story suggests that when the sacred power of God has been replaced by the debased theology and dogma of war, man's rebellion is both necessary and heroic.

Friedman, Melvin J. *William Styron.* Bowling Green, OH: Bowling Green University Popular Press, 1974, 72 p.
> Favorable biographical and critical study of Styron's fiction. The work includes a brief discussion of *The*

Long March, specifically as a contribution to the "literature of violence."

Geismar, Maxwell. "William Styron: The End of Innocence." In *American Moderns: From Rebellion to Conformity,* pp. 239-50. New York: Hill and Wang, 1958.

Argues that Styron's dark view of life in *The Long March* corresponds to the bleakness of the Cold War period in the United States.

Mackin, Cooper R. *William Styron.* Austin, TX: Steck-Vaughn Co., 1969, 43 p.

Discusses Styron as a Southern writer.

Mudrick, Marvin. "Mailer and Styron: Guests of the Establishment." *Hudson Review* XVII (1964): 346-66.

Compares Styron's *The Long March* to Norman Mailer's *The Naked and the Dead*. The critic dismisses Styron's novella as imitative and uninspired.

Pearce, Richard. *William Styron.* Minneapolis: University of Minnesota Press, 1971, 47 p.

Critical overview of Styron's work, discussing themes, structure, symbolism, and influences.

Ratner, Marc L. *William Styron.* Boston: Twayne Publishers, 1972, 170 p.

Study of Styron's life and work.

West, James L. W. "William Styron's Afterword to *The Long March*." *Mississippi Quarterly* XXVIII, No. 2 (Spring 1975): 185-89.

First English reprint of the afterword to the Norwegian edition of *The Long March*, introduced by West.

Interview

West, James L. W., ed. *Conversations with William Styron.* Jackson, MS: University Press of Mississippi, 1985.

Additional coverage of William Styron's life and career is contained in the following sources published by Gale Research: *Bestsellers*; *Concise Dictionary of American Literary Biography*; *Contemporary Authors,* Vols. 5-8; *Contemporary Authors New Revision Series,* Vols. 6, 33; *Contemporary Literary Criticism,* Vols. 1, 3, 5, 11, 15, 60; *Dictionary of Literary Biography,* Vols. 2, 143; *Dictionary of Literary Biography Yearbook,* Vol. 80; *DISCovering Authors: Novelists Module*; and *Major Twentieth-Century Writers*.

Italo Svevo
1861-1928

(Pseudonym of Ettore Schmitz) Italian short story writer, novelist, playwright, critic, and essayist.

INTRODUCTION

Italo Svevo is considered the father of the modern Italian novel. He popularized the use of internal monologues as a narrative technique and was one of the first Italian authors to apply Freudian theory to his fiction, developing stories that revolve around psychological and psychoanalytical considerations. Reviewer Gian-Paolo Biasin, in his essay "Zeno's Last Bomb," wrote that "Psychoanalysis . . . provided [Svevo] with the link which he had long sought between positivism and subjectivism, between objectivity and relativity." The author's reputation outside of Italy depends largely on his novel *La coscienza di Zeno* (1923, *Confessions of Zeno*), though within his home country he is also recognized as an important playwright and short story writer. Svevo's short fiction cultivates his obsession with old age and death, often through irony and humor.

Biographical Information

Svevo's pen name reflects his dual national heritage: Italian and Austrian (Swabian). Born in Trieste to Jewish parents in 1861, Svevo was educated in a Jewish elementary school. When he was 12, he and his brother attended boarding school in Germany where Svevo grew to love literature. Upon his return home, Svevo was forced to accept a clerking position in the Trieste branch of a Vienese bank because of family financial difficulties. During this period, he became interested in the theater and also began to publish short articles in the local newspaper. Svevo married his Catholic cousin, Livia Veneziani, bowed to her pleas to be baptized into the Catholic church, and took a position in her family's successful maritime commercial painting business. In 1905 Svevo met James Joyce, who became his English tutor; the two spent hours conversing about literature. Svevo eventually became one of Joyce's models for Leopold Bloom in *Ulysses*. Joyce championed Svevo's novels and helped him obtain recognition outside of Italy. After achieving a late acceptance of his work, Svevo died of complications from a minor accident, leaving behind fragments of a sequel to *Confessions of Zeno*. On his death bed, he renounced his Catholicism, having long since become an agnostic, and asked to be buried in a traditional, Jewish burial shroud. Svevo is buried in the Catholic Cemetery of Trieste.

Major Works of Short Fiction

Except for a few uncollected pieces, Svevo came to short fiction late in his career. He attempted several plays before writing his first novels *Una vita* (1893, *A Life*) and *Senilità* (1898, *As a Man Grows Older*). Yet it was not until his third novel, *Confessions of Zeno*, that Svevo became recognized as an important Italian writer. His two collections of short fiction—*La novella del buon vecchio e della bella fanciulla* (1930, *The Nice Old Man and the Pretty Girl, and Other Stories*) and *Corto viaggio sentimentale e altri racconti inediti* (1949, *Short Sentimental Journey, and Other Stories*)—were published only after his death: Svevo's final work, *Further Confessions of Zeno* (1969), intended as a sequel to *Confessions of Zeno,* was never completed. The fragments in this volume include five narratives ("The Old, Old Man," "An Old Man's Confessions," "Umbertino," "A Contract," and "This Indolence of Mine), considered short fiction, and a play entitled *Regeneration*. These titles and many of his earlier short stories focus on old age. Svevo depicts aging men, according to G. M. A. Grube in the *Canadian Forum*, in "a pitiless picture of futility, the intense egotism, the valetudinarianism, the gradual loss of all liberty due to increasing dependence upon other people, which come upon most people during the last period of a long life." Because of his reading of Freud's psychoanalytic theories, Svevo believed character, and not plot, should determine the trajectory of a story. His witty use of irony has moved some critics to label Svevo a forefather of the Italian absurd.

Critical Reception

Svevo had difficulty gaining acceptance in Italy during his lifetime. His experimentation with language and narrative were in contrast to the fashionable classical modes popularized by D'Annunzio and Croce. Indeed, much of Svevo's success was due to the efforts of Joyce, who sent Svevo's work to T. S. Eliot and Ford Maddox Ford. Eugenio Montale, one of the finest Italian poets of the century, helped elevate Svevo's reputation by initiating the "Svevo Case," an extended public debate on the value of Svevo's work. Montale, who himself won the Nobel prize in 1975, cited "The Hoax" as "the highest point" of Svevo's macabre humor and noted that "A Short Sentimental Journey" and later stories were among the best of Svevo's work. Other critics, however, have cited Svevo's short fiction as inferior to his novels because it tends to be less experimental.

PRINCIPAL WORKS

Short Fiction

La novella del buon vecchio e della bella fanciulla [*The Nice Old Man and the Pretty Girl, and Other Stories*] 1930
Corto viaggio sentimentale e altri racconti inediti [*Short Sentimental Journey, and Other Stories*] 1949
Further Confessions of Zeno 1969

Other Major Works

Una vita [*A Life*] (novel) 1893
Senilità [*As a Man Grows Older*] (novel) 1898
La coscienza di Zeno [*Confessions of Zeno*] (novel) 1923

CRITICISM

The New York Times Book Review (review date 1930)

SOURCE: "Mellow Wisdom," in *The New York Times Book Review,* March 16, 1930, p. 6.

[*In the following assessment of "The Hoax," an anonymous critic commends Svevo's effort, asserting that, "though the story is simple, Svevo has made more of it than most writers can make with formidable and ambitious plots."*]

Ettore Schmitz, who wrote under the name of Italo Svevo, was for many years an intimate friend of James Joyce; but their work is as different as Scott's is different from Proust's. Yet, for all their dissimilarities, it is easy to understand Joyce's admiration for Svevo; it would only be difficult to understand someone who did not admire him. For here is a little book of authentic charm, full of tender humanity and ironic wisdom, and written, if we may judge by Miss de Zoete's admirable translation, in a pure and delightful Italian.

"**The Hoax**" tells the simplest of stories. It tells of a middle-aged provincial who, when he was very young, wrote one indifferent novel. But all his life, though he worked in an office and never prospered, he held himself different from those around him, considered himself an artist, and remained happy thinking of what he would some day achieve. And then a crude commercial traveler, with a love of practical joking, decided to hoax Mario, to pretend that an affluent German publisher wanted to pay a large sum for the foreign rights of his long-forgotten book. Mario fell into the trap, saw wealth and fame approaching, and felt that he was about to receive his due. There followed days of suspense shared with an invalid brother; and then the truth. It was a bitter pill, but Mario survived it, and even by an ironic twist of fate, got rich from it.

But though the story is simple, Svevo has made more of it than most writers can make with formidable and ambitious plots. He has told it with a perfect balance of irony and humanity, letting the bubble of an artist's vanity be harshly pricked, yet letting the mystery of an artist's soul maintain its radiance to the end. With the dream of this obscure provincial he has identified all those dreams which enable us to endure existence, and he has shown what a miserable blow life can deal by robbing us of our balance. Mario's story is touching by itself; but Svevo's playful wisdom carries it beyond Mario.

"**The Hoax**" is one of those books it is not possible to transmit at second hand, one of those books which does not call for discussion or analysis. How can one relay the spirit of those many little fables Mario used to write, wherein the fate and actions of sparrows signified the fate and actions of men? How can one reproduce those evenings when Giulio lay in bed and tricked Mario into reading him to sleep? One forgets the fables, but one remembers that they were wise: one forgets the details of those evenings, but one remembers their humor and their charm. It would be the gravest of critical mistakes to suppose that this book is profound, or that it reaches to the depths of our emotions. It belongs to that body of minor literature which provides a different sort of pleasure and significance. It has the mellow wisdom of the heart and head working unitedly; it is something like Anatole France of his simple and human—not his satiric or racy—little tales; its touch achieves in a different way what Chekov achieves occasionally. Reading it surrounded by so many longer, more ambitious and ebullient books, one remembers a remark of George Moore, that the 200 pages of "Manon Lescaut" are worth infinitely more than all the volumes of "Les Miserables."

The Times Literary Supplement (review date 1931)

SOURCE: A review of *The Nice Old Man and the Pretty Girl, and Other Stories,* in *The Times Literary Supplement,* No. 1510, January 8, 1931, p. 26.

[*In the following evaluation of* The Nice Old Man and the Pretty Girl, and Other Stories, *an anonymous critic finds important qualities of the Italian edition missing from the English translation.*]

The last volume of Italo Svevo's work was published posthumously in Italy in 1929; and from this volume we are now given in English translation by Mr. L. Collison-Morley three short stories and an unfinished fragment of a novel under the title of **The Nice Old Man and the Pretty Girl and Other Stories**. Except for a elever little fable of the farmyard, "**The Mother,**" which was written in 1910, the only material of the novelist's work here exhibited is "the last period of man's life, old age, with its illusions, manias and phobias and the dangers that beset it," to use the words of Signor Eugenio Montale, whose interesting and laudatory preface to the Italian edition is here also translated. This is not the place to enter into discussion of his polemical thesis that "Italo Svevo is the greatest novelist our [*i.e.,* Italian] literature has produced from Verga's day to our own"—a thesis challenged by very respectable opinion in Italy—but it may well be admitted, whatever the final verdict may be, that the importance of Svevo's work lies in what Signor Montale calls "the bare and passionate crudity of the experience, in the rigorously home-grown and independent colours in which he was able and determined to clothe it." In translation, unfortunately, the latter qualities tend to disappear; for not only is Zeno's language different in intonation from Mr. Collison-Morley's impeccable English, but the effect of contrast with tradition—very strong in the original— grows pale for English readers who are far more conversant than are Italians with the literary attitude of whimsical self-exposure.

Italo Svevo's old man who sits down to clear his mind on some important question, and thus becomes an author, is an admirable invention. The fragment of the novel here included was to be a sequel to *The Confessions of Zeno*, in which this invention was exploited to the full; and the methods of the story which gives this collection its name as also of the story **"Generous Wine"** are the same. In length and treatment the first story in this book is the most important and the most successful. Its theme is that of an old business man who is smitten with the charm of a girl driving a tramcar in wartime, and determines to have his last love affair. He seduces her, dismisses her, calls her to him again, suffers jealousy in the very moment of his embraces and preaches morality to her while he kisses her, until the girl becomes for him no longer a mistress but the symbol of a moral question that spreads and spreads till it becomes one of the whole relation of age to youth. With remarkable insight Svevo describes the stages of the obsession and the parallel progress of senile decay and of the manuscript that, in the old man's fancy, is going to solve the whole question for humanity. **"Generous Wine"** again is the description of an old man's temporary surrender to over-indulgence and the nightmare that follows. The main gist of Svevo's rueful humorous argument is that we idealize life as we describe it and therefore falsify it.

> You make no mention of your breathing there until it begins to come short, nor of all the holidays, meals and nights of sleep, until for some tragic reason they fail. And yet in real life they recur, together with many other activities, with the regularity of a pendulum and fill imperiously so large a part of our day that there is no space left for undue weeping or laughing.

The other part of his argument is that all of us, in our hearts, have the most unworthy feelings towards others, especially to our nearest relations; and his most comic effects are obtained by the detached confession of the most outrageous thoughts by his disillusioned old sinners with their passionate and always frustrated desire for greater purity and sincerity—confession to be regarded as a matter

of hygiene, "with which I shall busy myself every evening a little before taking my purgative."

Lowry Nelson, Jr. (essay date 1959)

SOURCE: "A Survey of Svevo," in *Italian Quarterly*, Vol. 3, No. 10, Summer, 1959, pp. 25-28.

[*Below, Nelson discusses various themes in Svevo's short fiction, including "canine psychology" (from a dog's point of view), the old in love with the young, and death.*]

His reputation as a short story writer must rest chiefly on **"La novella del buon vecchio e della bella fanciulla"** and **"Il mio ozio"** (the latter translated as **"This Indolence of Mine"**). They have the advantages of being completed and excellent. On a slightly lower level of achievement we may place **"Una burla riuscita"** and **"Proditoriamente."** Among other fragments of fiction one should mention **"Corto viaggio sentimentale,"** which begins splendidly as an account of the separation of a certain Signor Aghios from his wife as he is about to embark on a trivial journey; but it leads on, without concluding, to an absurd theft which would need at least all the superstructure of *Les Faux-Monnayeurs* to justify it. Two other fragments sketch the ambience of an island in the Venetian lagoon (a departure for Svevo), but they (**"Cimutti"** and **"In Serenella"**) are not long enough to come near to making any point. Their seeming concentration on plebeian milieux is interesting but inconclusive as they stand. Other fragments, such as **"Marianno"** and **"Giacomo,"** suggest that Svevo could have managed a "proletarian" novel, but it remains a question whether he could have done much with it. Of his odd sketches perhaps the most interesting is **"Argo e il suo padrone"** (**"Argo and his Master"**) which is told from the point of view of the dog Argo. Its best comparison would be some of Chekhov's early animal stories, especially "White Brow" ("Belolobyj"). Argo, with his doggish preconceptions, is not without suggestion of [an] empirical and monomaniacal approach to the world. It is quite a loss that Svevo did not give better shape or further echo to the narrative. Animal stories, between the extremes of Ernest Thompson Seton and Cervantes (between the sentimental naturalist and the brilliant parodist), are extraordinarily rare. As if prompted by some veterinarian Dr. S., Argo's "memoirs" begin: "There exist three smells in this world: the master's smell, the smell of other men, Titì's smell, the smell of different kinds of animals . . . and finally the smell that things have." The computation is accurately inexact since dogs can only count to three. At one point Argo exclaims, "So many dogs crossed our path today! Three!" Within the limits of its absurdity Svevo creates an impressive fragment of "canine psychology." Surely, however, we are justified in singling out **"La novella del buon vecchio"** and **"Il mio ozio"** as the best of Svevo in shorter form. They are purely Svevo; their pedigree is personal.

It is in **"La novella del buon vecchio"** that Svevo sounds a later rendition of the theme insistent in *Senilità*: now he can create a really old hero in love with a young girl. As in the novel, the narrative is third-person; the reflections engendered by the situation are impartially and impersonally profound in their Svevian irony. "When a really young man falls in love, his love often causes reactions in his brain that soon have nothing to do with his desire. How many youths there are who, though they could find peaceful bliss in some hospitable bed, cause havoc at least in their own houses under the impression that to go to bed with a woman it is necessary first to conquer, create or destroy. Old men, however, who are said to be better protected against the passions, surrender to them in full awareness and climb into the bed of sin only with proper precautions against catching cold." There is also in the old man of the story a sense of the ridiculous; but he hides it from himself, so that the ironic "neutral" commentary must bear the weight of total awareness. Actually, it is in this narrative that the reader will find the fullest measure in Svevo's works of knowing irony and compassion. The old hero is caught between age and youth, love and jealousy, real life and actual dreams: typical of a Svevian hero he begins to feel his mission as a writer. Somehow he must commit to writing his wisdom as a man of the world; somehow the girl must be warned against the danger of love, with the young, but especially with the old. As elsewhere with Svevo's fictional authors, the title precedes composition: in this case it is "Concerning Relations between Age and Youth." According to its "theory," youth must rely upon their healthy and wise elders to insure a utopian future. But eventually death, the resolver, writes "finis" to the unfinished and unfinishable essay.

The theme of love of the old for the young has its culmination, in Svevo's work, in **"Il mio ozio,"** in which the fear of death comes out into the open as the prime mover. In **"La novella del buon vecchio"** the absurdities of the old man's situation are expressed in his doctor's words: "You may not visit your mistress until I allow you to." He is reduced ludicrously to the status of a child, an old baby; such is the indignity of age. But in **"Il mio ozio"** love is viewed by the old man in that story more frontally as a prophylactic, a sure cure against death. We are back in the circuit of Zeno and its familiar cast of characters; it is, however, a later generation and the speaker is now a contemporary of "il buon vecchio." The whole scheme is somehow to fool mother nature. Her purpose is to keep alive an organism so long as it can reproduce itself; therefore, to take a mistress is the only way to stay alive. The crux of the comedy is the unexpected encounter between the speaker and his contemporary Misceli whom he catches as a fellow client in the rooms of Signorina Felicita. At the end all kinds of muted ironies pour forth when he is called an "old lecher" (vecchio satiro). Still, he has already set his "adventure" in perspective: almost unwittingly he exposes himself to the ultimate depredation of mother nature.

Of the two other stories worthy to be counted among his best work, **"Proditoriamente"** (**"Stealthily"** or **"Treacherously"**) is the simplest. It is a laceratingly comic treatment of death (one could imagine it illustrated by the cartoonist Steig). Signor Meier comes as a suppliant to ask a loan of Signor Reveni who is obviously going to refuse when he suddenly has a fatal heart attack. Business affairs are seen under the aspect of death. Who is better off? The man who died or the man about to be ruined? Clearly the circumstances of death could have become even more overtly than in his novels one of Svevo's masterful themes: witness also the fragment **"La morte."** But death caught the author in the act. Much richer than **"Proditoriamente"** is the long story **"Una burla riuscita"** (translated as **"The Hoax"**), in which the major theme is that dialectical relationship between literature and life. Once again the hero, Mario Samigli, has written a novel in his youth, and now he transforms his aged reality, lived out with his ailing brother, into little fables about sparrows. His spent literary ambitions are cruelly revived by a monstrous hoax perpetrated by a certain Gaia. Mario, the butt, is all the more susceptible because he has the imagination of a novelist, always ready to accept and transform *données* through artistic rationalization, through the imagination. But the crude success of the joke is tempered by Mario's mild revenge and his final transmutation of the whole affair into a fable of sparrows.

Tony Tanner (review date 1967)

SOURCE: "A Time for Heroes," in *Spectator*, Vol. 1s 6d, No. 7235, February 24, 1967, p. 230.

[*In the following review of* Short Sentimental Journey, and Other Stories, *Tanner suggests that Svevo has an "unfading fascination for the relationship between mind and body."*]

Literary success came late to Italo Svevo, for it was not until 1925 that *Confessions of Zeno* (published two years before at his own expense) suddenly earned him recognition and fame as an important modern writer with a quietly ironic-pessimistic vision all his own. This success understandably prompted him to further writing and, at the age of sixty-five, he found no subject more engaging or challenging than his own experience of growing old. 'Senility' in one form or another was, in a sense, always his subject.

The comparatively young 'heroes' of his first two novels, *A Life* and *As a Man Grows Older,* have senile souls, and at his death in 1928 he was working on a novel called *The Old Old Man*. Of the eight stories in this fourth volume **Short Sentimental Journey and other Stories** of the admirable Collected Edition of his works, five focus on the vulnerabilities, failings and sufferings of an ageing figure—all of them written (or revised) in the last three years of his life. The title story is simply an unfinished account of a train journey taken by an old man, for once in the absence of his family. The monotonies of years of domesticity have 'rusted' him over, he feels; travelling alone promises a blessed interlude of freedom. 'He wanted to live his own life—his own journey.' He relaxes and indulges his 'secret thoughts.' Cunningly he studies the reflection of a pretty girl. This, however, involves him in noticing his own 'irremediably old' features in the glass: 'he and his reflection eyed each other suspiciously.'

Unfortunately, the man opposite thinks that he is the object of this brooding and accusing scrutiny and starts to rub his face, adding apologetically: 'I think I must have some typewriter-ink on my face.' An absurd conversation, entirely removed from the old man's reveries, ensues. Such is human freedom. A man may soar unimpeded in his thoughts, but in a railway carriage there are all sorts of awkward bodies to take into account, amazing conversations to be overheard. Human flesh, in all its strangeness and frailty, is in constant collision with other human flesh. Falling asleep, the old man dreams first of all that he is flying through space, alone and free, then that he is having incestuous relations with his daughter. He wakes up to find that he has been robbed. It is a dazzling story based on the simplest situation, but evincing Svevo's matchless ability to depict the comic and painful complexity of man's private consciousness.

A more bitter tale concerns an old man who has keen sexual desires, animated cerebral theories, and an ailing body unable to sustain either impulse or intellect (**'The Nice Old Man and the Pretty Girl'**). His attempts to combine medicines, morality, and the last flickering appetites of the body are comic and sombre at the same time. But his intellectual endeavours have a more mordant conclusion. He sets out to write a thesis on 'The Relations between Age and Youth.' When should the innocent appetites of the young give way to the reponsibilities of the old? 'With whom must morality begin?' becomes a major problem in his work. But the night he dies he stares at the question, 'then he wrote wearily under it several times the word: Nothing.'

The agonies to which the failing body are prone recur throughout. In **'Generous Wine,'** a man on a diet drinks too much and as a result spends an excruciating night, during which he has a nightmare in which he offers up his own daughter to be killed to save his own life. He wakes to ask his wife: 'How can we get our children to forgive us for having brought them into the world?' In **'Death,'** an unforgettable account of a man's last moments, unfinished because of Svevo's own death, we again see physical vulnerability undermining the assertions of the mind. Roberto, an atheist stoic, intends to demonstrate to his wife, a believer, how a rational man can die. But despite his bravery and resolution, the atrocious pain which attacks his body deprives him of this last dignity and reduces him to weeping fear: 'His death was the very thing he had not wanted—a thing of terror.' As a final irony, his wife interprets his death-bed anguish as repentance and in her heart she 'converts' him. In dying, as in living, man, the thinker and dreamer, is more a victim than a master of his body. This unfading fascination of the relationships between mind and body drew Svevo to an increasing interest in psychoanalysis and the subconscious.

Dreams, with all their enigmatic revelations, clearly fascinate him in these stories. On the other hand, he was sufficiently dubious of the advantages of human mental powers to write a series of brilliant and pungent animal fables. The most famous, **'Argo and his Master,'** is includ-

ed here. In it a dog's testimony is collected by his master who learns the dog language. 'Men are much simpler animals than dogs, because they smell more than dogs, and do so more readily. When one man meets another, they touch hands and don't seem to worry about what lies behind the other man's hand. Argo, on the other hand, when he meets another dog, cautiously advances the toothed end of his own body towards the untoothed end of the other's body and sniffs. . . . '

Perhaps the sheer fact of consciousness was the ultimate mystery for Svevo—even the life of a dog, with consciousness added, becomes in his eyes not only a richly comic but also an oddly moving matter.

V. S. Pritchett (review date 1967)

SOURCE: "A Clown," in *New Statesman*, Vol. 73, No. 1879, March 17, 1967, pp. 364-66.

[*In the following review of* Short Sentimental Journey, and Other Stories, *Pritchett calls Svevo "a natural truth-teller," adding that even though it may not be apparent in the beginning, every word in Svevo's works has a purpose.*]

Svevo is a natural truth-teller who makes the professionals look like monsters of false pretension. They confused truth-telling with a passion for disgust or with personal hatreds. The paradox is that he is an egoist who is, somehow, selfless; but when one looks at his work more closely one sees that his mind hesitates on a frontier. As Ettore Schmidtz he is the Viennese Jew of the Schnitzler-Musil dispensation; as the pseudonymous Italo Svevo he is Italianate; and in writing this gave him a double vision. Where we see one emotion, he sees two: his temperament was made for tact and comedy. From the Jewish strain comes a high regard for illness, analysis and the joke; from the Italian ingenuity, realism and the heart. He seems to have done an interesting deal with his hesitancies by thinking of life as an alluring illness, the comic and touching part of it being that we do not know we are ill. His characters are born old. The important thing is to come to terms with the idea of death very early; then one's forces are freed. Svevo was a man of fables and conceits, but he was also, in the most substantial and original sense, the bourgeois clown.

Some of the stories in this collection, such as **"The Hoax"** and **"The Nice Old Man and the Pretty Girl"** are well-known to English readers; but the long **"Sentimental Journey,"** translated by Ben Johnson, the story called **"Death"** and the fable of a dog's agitated failure to learn Italian—more than a touch of Cervantes here, in fact Svevo's irony is very Cervantesque—are new. The long story is posthumous and did not get the careful polishing Svevo always gave to his work; all the same, one soon sees that, under its innocent, ambling narrative, an elaborate pattern and a dramatic story are being ingeniously created. As in all his good stories, every word, thought and incident is there for a purpose and will show its force at the end; and our first impression that we are just following the train journey of a felicitously observant and philosophising old gentleman from Milan to Trieste with a little tourism thrown in at Venice on the way, turns into the realisation that we are reading, among other things, a tale of passion, wickedness and folly. This descriptive passage lulls one into thinking we are merely starting a brilliant but languid travelogue; yet, before the end, we see that the passage is there for reasons profoundly connected with the eventual drama.

> Then Signor Aghios stopped looking at the people around him and for several minutes stood entranced, watching smoke rising thickly from the funnel of a locomotive outside the station. The wind was driving it. Coming out of the funnel in puffs, it was immediately thinned out and scattered by the wind. Each puff, as it was destroyed, seemed to lay itself bare and betray within itself the existence of a head, a mouth—an animated being. And, before disintegrating, the head strained its saucer-like eyes wide open, the better to see, and by so doing split completely, the whole head disintegrating. There was a procession of frightening, menacing heads. 'A few lines are enough to suggest the essence of life: fear or menace,' Signor Aghios moralised.

A contemporary writer might have doubts about that last sentence. I doubt if Svevo would have cut it out, though I imagine he would have removed one of those 'disintegratings' if he had revised the story. One of the points of this story, and of Svevo's outlook in general, is that moralisations are doubts; they are wise, but being wise are ridiculous; being ridiculous they are menacing and that menace is ineluctable.

The truth-telling in Svevo comes from an unusual gift not only for looking at things, people and events, but in contemplating them—an interest that has almost completely gone from literature since his time. He continually raises the question of chains and freedom; he adapts himself to his condition and sees that what is outwardly dull is animated by the comedy of rebellion and resignation. His young lovers, his staid old couples, his animals, his business partners, his philosophising old men, his cads and thieves are caught, over and over again, on this see-saw. He tells the truth because his eye is always open for all the truths. Dissimilarities, false timing, cross-purposes are the foundations of human relationships. His stories therefore abound in subtleties that are not solemnities: an old close-fisted man feels the impulse to make a wildly generous gesture, but knows that if he acts out of character in this way it will be—and prove to be—an undignified folly: he hesitates and astutely decides to put the idea into the head of his naturally generous wife, thus achieving a virtue for which he is not personally equipped. But, while hesitating, he is neatly robbed by the person he intended to benefit. Svevo's capacity for moral entanglement accounts for the gaiety and the seriousness of tales that are rich in incident but are as simple as fables, without being as platitudinous.

John Simon (review date 1967)

SOURCE: A review of *Short Sentimental Journey, and Other Stories,* in *The New York Times Book Review,* Sec. 7, April 9, 1967, pp. 4, 19.

[*In the following review of* Short Sentimental Journey, and Other Stories, *Simon describes Svevo's writing as both realistic and poetic. He concludes: "Svevo saw life as a joke Mother Nature plays on us, and his fiction laughs at it and helps all of us fellow-victims to laugh."*]

The four best pieces in Svevo's **Short Sentimental Journey and Other Stories** are those which come from the ambience, in time and sensibility, of that late masterwork, *The Confessions of Zeno.* Its protagonist is the hero as neurotic, as compulsive smoker, hypochondriac, sufferer from a premature sense of senility; but Zeno is also the man who becomes so happily absorbed with himself that his failures turn into successes, neurosis becomes livable-with, sickness becomes health. Zeno, moreover, like every other Svevian protagonist, is brazenly and brilliantly Svevo himself, or a large chunk of him. And, most important, Zeno and his book are all wit, all irony, as was Svevo himself.

In the title story, **"Short Sentimental Journey,"** a gentle, ineffectual, uxorious man in his sixties (all of Svevo's heroes are literally or spiritually in their sixties, and they are all aging babies) takes a brief trip without his wife and finds that his longed-for emancipation boomerangs on him. In **"The Hoax,"** an unsuccessful novelist is gulled into believing that an imaginary Austrian publishing house is about to make his literary fortune, but the cruel practical joker accidentally brings about his victim's financial security. In **"Death,"** a loving, elderly husband wishes to set an example of resigned dying to his fond wife, and succeeds only in undermining her simple faith. (This story, like the title one, suffers somewhat from having been left unfinished.) In **"Argo and His Master,"** a dog proves too simple-minded to understand the deviousness of human beings whose very crassness he goes on idolizing.

V. S. Pritchett once described Svevo's hero Zeno as "the clown of the inspiration and the heart," and D. J. Enright has remarked on "the quiet clarity and decency" of Svevo's novelistic style. It is that kind of hero and that kind of writing that breathe in these stories. They are both realistic and poetic, pursuing, as they do, minuscule occurrences to their ironic roots and their absurd projections on the infinitely wide screen of the universe. It is this analytical intimacy combined with universal debunking that undercut the d'Annunzianism, the grandioseness and "fine writing" of Svevo's contemporaries, and kept him from receiving his artistic due.

In a charming note to his wife, Svevo requested that his funeral be conducted "without ostentation of any kind, even of simplicity." How exquisite and deep, witty and serious that remark is! All of Svevo is. In the house of modern fiction, he is the atrium. The complex elegance of the Proust Salon, the hauntedness of the Kafka Chamber, and the many-layered dreams of the Joyce Bedroom are beyond this delightful central hall, but it opens on all of them: they can all best be reached through it.

In *The Confessions of Zeno* we read, "Life is a little like a disease, with its crises and periods of quiescence, its daily improvements and setbacks. But unlike other diseases life is always mortal. It admits of no cure. It would be like trying to stop up the holes of our body, thinking them to be wounds. We should die of suffocation almost before we were cured." Here, as elsewhere, Svevo saw life as a joke Mother Nature plays on us, and his fiction laughs at it and helps all of us fellow-victims to laugh. It is not the least profound view of life. Nor the least tragic.

Walter Guzzardi, Jr. (review date 1967)

SOURCE: "Obsessed by Death," in *Saturday Review,* Vol. 50 (L), No. 23, June 10, 1967, pp. 36-7.

[*Below, Guzzardi describes the similarities between the works of Svevo and French novelist Marcel Proust, commenting that Svevo's "contribution almost matches Proust's influence on contemporary literary currents, and it is time that Svevo's fame in the U.S. won some new boosters." In this review of* Short Sentimental Journey, and Other Stories, *Guzzardi states that the translators showed "considerable ingenuity in putting into decent English Svevo's tortured and turgid prose."*]

To call Italo Svevo the Italian Proust is to rob him of his truly original creative strength. Still, the resemblances between them—although Svevo never read Proust—conveniently position Svevo for Americans who know little about him. They were contemporaries; they both shared in shaping the new directions of the modern novel; they were both extraordinarily sensitive to and understanding about the workings of the mind, at levels to which literature had never before penetrated. Svevo's works are slimmer than Proust's, and his style less absorbing, more stilted and more precious; still, his contribution almost matches Proust's influence on contemporary literary currents, and it is time that Svevo's fame in the U.S. won some new boosters.

The University of California Press is now filling this need. Svevo's *Short Sentimental Journey and Other Stories* is the fourth volume in a uniform edition of his works being brought out by the Press, and it appears simultaneously with P. N. Furbank's *Italo Svevo: The Man and the Writer,* also published by California. Together, these volumes give new and welcome attention to Svevo and his work, and take full cognizance of his importance as a literary figure.

Italo Svevo was born Ettore Schmitz in Trieste in 1861. Being born a Jew in that city, then part of the Austrian Empire, was not necessarily a hardship; Trieste in those days was a multilingual and prosperous center of trade and commerce, Svevo's father was a well-to-do merchant, and the family lived comfortably in a residential part of the city. (Svevo has written something of his family life in an autobiographical note whose title is redolent of Proust: *L'Avvenire dei Ricordi,* "The Future of Memories"). Unlike Proust, Svevo was neither a particularly delicate boy nor a deviate. He showed some early interest in his father's business, gradually moved toward literature as his education progressed, and finally plunged into writing when a couple of his earliest articles achieved some modest recognition. Svevo lived most of his later life obsessed by the thought of death, which is one of the main themes of his work; he died in 1928, in deteriorated health, after an automobile accident.

Reading Svevo, one is reminded of other authors, and their stature is a measure of Svevo's own capacities. Passages reminiscent of Kafka (whom Svevo read and admired), streams of consciousness that summon up Joyce (a friend and sponsor of Svevo), darkness and menace that equal Chekhov, and an ability to shock and to terrify that presages William Golding are all found in Svevo's stories. Because of his constricted style Svevo cannot evoke exquisite sensations the way Proust can, but his insights into the great topics—death, old age, family relationships—are sharp and disturbing.

The main works of Svevo (*Una Vita* and *Senilità,* "A Life" and "Old Age") are contained in other volumes in this series. They, perhaps, provide better indications of Svevo's sustained strength. But the same quality can be seen in the long unfinished story **"A Short Sentimental Journey,"** which is the backbone of *Short Sentimental Journey and Other Stories*. It is the simple tale of an elderly traveler who leaves his wife in Milan to go by rail to Venice. He separates from her with feelings of guilt overlaid with pleasure, the mingling of opposites that appears so many times, in so many different forms, in Svevo's work; but soon the reader comes to understand that Signor Aghios can never be independent of his wife, despite his dreams. Nothing much happens to him in the way of external events except that he has his pocket picked, something his wife had warned him about at great length.

The incompleteness of the manuscript hardly interferes at all with the impact of the story, with its gentle ironies, edged wit, and careful accounts of the flow of Aghios's thoughts. For example, he hopes by tipping to gain some recognition of his fine qualities:

> Signor Aghios exploited his little tips like a born miser. He did not want to buy much with them—only lasting friendship. Therefore he began by paying less than the normal amount . . . then Signor Aghios would put further coins, one by one, into the other's hand, until it closed and a smile appeared on the porter's face. Thus that smile, which had been so slow to appear, was stamped the more indelibly on Signor Aghios's memory and sweetened his way for hours and miles ahead.

In **"A Nice Old Man and a Pretty Girl"** the influence of Joyce and Proust is somewhat less evident, but the foreshadowing of Golding is stronger. An old man finds for a young girl a job as a tram driver, and promptly forgets about her; only when he sees her on the tram, driving exuberantly, stamping her foot on the bell, physically active and lovely, does he invite her to his house. The clinical details are pleasingly omitted; gradually, though, a moral struggle over the decency of the relationship begins within the old man, brought on by an attack of angina (whose pain is described in frightening imagery). To clear his troubled mind he tries to write about the issues involved, finds himself putting the harder parts aside, comes to be haunted by brilliantly clear dreams, and finally "He was found dead and stiff, with the pen, over which had passed his last breath, in his mouth."

The stories are translated by several different persons; all of them have a high degree of competence, and as far as this reviewer can see they have shown considerable ingenuity in putting into decent English Svevo's tortured and turgid prose.

Svevo's contribution to psychoanalytic literature:

Svevo seriously thought he was making a contribution to psychoanalytic literature—totally obliterating from his mind the possibility that his unconscious motivations in making analysis a failure might themselves amount to resistance and hostility. Schmitz had never been analyzed, though he had toyed with the idea and respected the techniques for his literary insights. One suspects that like many creative people, he feared analysis because it might eliminate his neurosis, and therefore his creativity.

Pearlmarie McColm, "The 'Svevo Case': A New Brief," in University of Denver Quarterly, *Vol. 2, No. 2, Summer, 1967, pp. 159-60.*

Thomas G. Bergin (review date 1969)

SOURCE: A review of *Further Confessions of Zeno,* in *Saturday Review,* Vol. L11, No. 37, September 13, 1969, p. 33.

[*Here, Bergin laments that Svevo was not able to complete* Further Confessions of Zeno, *asserting that "on the evidence of these fragments it might have been Svevo's finest work."*]

Posterity has been kind to Ettore Schmitz, the disillusioned bourgeois of Trieste who chose to call himself "Swabian Italian"; it has more than atoned for the stony indifference of his contemporaries. With the sole exception of Giovanni Verga there is no other Italian prose writer of the turn of the century who can speak with familiarity and authority to readers of today. If the sponsorship of Joyce was crucial in bringing Svevo to the attention of the literary world, his survival is neverthe-

less due to his own merits, well exemplified in the book before us.

Of the six items that make up *Further Confessions of Zeno*—an omnibus title to suit the nature of the harvest—five are bits of narrative prose in which Zeno speaks for himself. The sixth is a play—the only one Svevo has left us—first published some ten years ago, three decades after the author's death. To students of Svevo it may well be the most fascinating item in this interesting anthology. The plot hinges on the "rejuvenating operation" which a seventy-year-old man is persuaded to undergo and its effect on him and his immediate circle. It is a persuasive comedy with surprisingly good dialogue (surprising because the normal Svevo opus runs to monologue and is not particularly noted for its handling of conversation), first-rate character delineation and, above all, a more outright humor than is apparent in most of Svevo's work. The sober, bourgeois background makes one think of Ibsen, but there is more than a touch of Chekhov and even a hint of the melancholy mischief of Pirandello. (This is said not to suggest "sources" but merely to indicate the tonal ingredients of the play.) "Regeneration" reads very well and might, I suspect, even act well.

But the play is not necessarily the best of the items in the book. The others are, as the editorial note tells us, "surviving fragments and drafts of the sequel to *The Confessions of Zeno* on which Svevo was working during the last years of his life," and they are excellent indeed. It is a pity that *Further Confessions* was not finished; on the evidence of these fragments it might have been Svevo's finest work.

The central figure is the same old Zeno, indolent, rather cowardly, not particularly admirable, but acute in his perception of his own nature and the circumstances of his life. "What a vast importance distant things take on when compared to those of a few weeks ago," the old man muses, thus summarizing the problems and pathos of age—and something of its poetry too. In **"An Old Man's Confessions"** he describes his well-intentioned efforts to establish a happy relationship with his son (a parable for 1970 no less than 1920); in **"Umbertino"** he makes us understand why no such efforts are needed to enjoy the company of his grandson. As for the Indian summer liaison described in **"A Contract,"** one can only admire the sophistication of the writer who can portray at one and the same time the sordid and the downright funny aspects of a senile *affaire.*

But perhaps best of all for its poetic insight is the little ten-page opener of the book, **"The Old Old Man,"** in which the brief sight of a girl on the street—recognized or merely evocative?—leads to the observation: "Time is an element in which I am not able to move with absolute sureness . . . [It] wreaks its havoc with a firm and ruthless hand, and then marches off in an orderly procession of days, months and years, but when it is far away and out of sight, it breaks ranks. The hours start looking for their place in the wrong day and the days in the wrong year."

Proust could hardly have put it better. Zeno will write no more confessions for us, but Ettore Schmitz has a long life ahead of him.

Albert N. Mancini (review date 1969)

SOURCE: A review of *Short Sentimental Journey, and Other Stories,* in *Studies in Short Fiction,* Vol. 6, No. 5, Fall, 1969, pp. 659-64.

[*In the following survey of the writings collected in* Short Sentimental Journey, and Other Stories, *Mancini concludes that to understand Svevo properly, readers must review all of his fiction, particularly his later short stories.*]

Italo Svevo's literary reputation in the English speaking world is solid and well-established. The Triestine writer was first presented with the story **"The Hoax,"** published in 1929 in England and in 1930 in America. Svevo's clear and sparse prose, his strategy and compassion and irony rendered him attractive to the English readership. The friendship with James Joyce no doubt served to endear him to the Anglo-American literati. Still, despite his sudden and early recognition, Italo Svevo so far has not attracted the same interest accorded on both sides of the Atlantic to other European writers whose careers run parallel to his. A larger audience, both scholarly and non-specialized, is Svevo's due, for he is one of the great shapers of contemporary literary taste and consciousness. To be sure, all three of Svevo's novels are currently available in English. Two of them, *Confessions of Zeno* and *As a Man Grows Older,* have been recently reprinted in paperback. But there remain in his *oeuvre* a number of *novellas,* stories, and fragments of his unfinished fourth novel that have not yet been translated or that are scattered in collections and journals limited in their appeal and not readily accessible. The selection under review, the first since 1930, has been long overdo.

One can hardly exaggerate the importance of Svevo's shorter fiction. There is, of course, no clear-cut distinction to be drawn between Svevo the novelist and Svevo the short fiction writer. Not only are the individual stories important for their intrinsic merit, but also they are invaluable for the understanding of the author. The literary output of Italo Svevo is very concentrated so that each part of it throws light on the other parts. His writing is one interpreting whole that improves with acquaintance. This presentation, therefore, of a major portion of Svevo's short fiction affords students in the field of comparative, general, and Italian literature another opportunity to re-examine the artist's worth in a new light and from a broader perspective.

True, critics in English-speaking countries have created a substantial literature on Svevo. Yet, clearly their views can stand partial corrections. For instance, one of the critical platitudes about Svevo, repeated on the jacket of this volume, is that after the publication of *A Life* and *As a Man Grows Older,* in 1892 and 1898 respectively, he gave up writing in discouragement and consecrated himself to the paint business. This makes perhaps good advertising but hardly sound scholarship and perceptive criticism. In the twenty-five years that separate his second novel from *Zeno,* Svevo had been doing more than manufacturing or selling paint and learning English. Granted that the mind defining itself under the attack of circumstance and the mind finding itself among the pressures of creation have still to be adequately brought into relationship, it is beyond doubt that this was a crucial time in the career of Svevo and impelled him to give serious consideration to the problem of the role of the narrator, the use of time, irony, and psychology in fiction. His diary, his letters, indeed his contributions to short fiction, dating for the most part from this period, reflect these preoccupations, this growing intricacy of perception and craft. But let me not add to the "Svevo case" and hasten to the writings collected for us here.

In all, this selection contains eight stories and *novellas,* written between 1910 and 1928. Of these, four had already appeared in English translation some forty years ago. The remaining four, including the unfinished title-story, are published here for the first time. The preface is only two pages long and consists of a commentary on the texts used and the English versions. It is informative, but marred by certain inaccuracies. The dating of the stories and speculations about the strata of composition still remain conjectural and must be controlled. Since the book is intended also for the Anglo-American literature audience, a more thorough introduction and abundant notes would have been helpful.

Little needs to be said about the version of **"The Hoax,"** produced by Beryl de Zoete, the official translator of Svevo (*Zeno* in 1930 and *As a Man Grows Older* in 1932). Despite minor liberties taken with the text, it is smooth yet unpretentions, making for a tone of surprising naturalness. Likewise, the translations by Ben Johnson (the first new Englishings since the memorable rendition of *A Life* by the late Archibald Colquhoun in 1963, as far as I have been able to trace) are consistently successful in conveying accurately but without awkward self-consciousness some of the distinctive flavor of Svevo's style. It is regrettable that the editors did not also include in this collection Johnson's new translation of **"The Mother."** In fact, L. Collison-Morley's renditions of **"The Story of the Nice Old Man and the Pretty Girl," "Generous Wine,"** and **"The Mother"** are the least satisfactory and attractive of the three versions. One suspects that the translator feels that he can do better than the author and must try to make what is bare, often crude, easy and palatable. In the main his language is pitched in quite a different key from the original. Of course, to echo, transpose, or emulate Svevo's voice in English is a hard task, perhaps an impossible one. It is common knowledge that Svevo is far from being a polished writer, and charges that he writes badly or even ungrammatically are still leveled at him by his compatriots. Nowadays his offhand, unofficial, even slangy manner, so immune to verbal display and 'fine writing' is not startling to us, but in early twentieth-century Italy it was stylistically, and even socially, shocking.

The editors' choices are beyond questioning. The result is a collection of stories that vary widely in length, type, and treatment. **"The Mother"** and **"Argo and his Master"** are animal fables. One of them, **"Short Sentimental Journey,"** is an unfinished short novel and two others, **"The Hoax"** and **"The Story of the Nice Old Man and the Pretty Girl,"** are longer than average. The three shorter pieces, **"Generous Wine," "Traitorously,"** and **"Death,"** are first-rate examples of Svevo's contribution to the short story, a literary form in which he showed a constant interest. Yet admittedly, one does not witness in Svevo a return to the great tradition of Italian story telling, to the Boccaccian tale with its anecdotal quality and its apparently detached reporting of an actual and memorable event.

As for the distribution of the stories, in making my own selection I might have arranged them in a roughly chronological order to allow the reader to see among the works a meaningful continuity and grouped them for convenience under two headings to bring out the links that unite the stories and the novels. These two phases, identifiable with the period 1910-1923 that precedes the appearance of *Zeno* and the period from 1923 until Svevo's death, cohere in a cycle of poetical creativity that it is by now possible to see in perspective.

After *As a Man Grows Older,* Svevo's relentless analysis tends to become more and more abstract, to be expressed or represented in very general terms, like parables and fables. In the years of self-imposed literary silence, Svevo cultivated intensively this genre. Some of these fables have been published separately, and more are to be found scattered throughout the writings of this time. As a fabulist, Svevo subjects man and life to a pitiless but passionate critique, exposing the sad and pitiful spectacle of human absurdity and self-deception. **"Argo and his Master"** tells of a man who during a stay in a mountain retreat tries to teach his dog Argo Italian. The experiment proves at least a partial failure. Though Argo never learns to speak his master's language, he teaches his teacher dog-language. The final irony is that, while the master gains remarkable insight into canine psychology, Argo dies from exhaustion. The problems and behaviour of human beings are so subjective and elusive as to defy any cold apprehension, Argo concludes. The sketch is a surprise and a delight, full of grotesque language, humorous contrasts, and whimsicalities. There are affinities with Cervantes' "Colloquy of the Dogs," but the tone strikes the reader as quintessentially Svevian. Svevo's comic inventions are not as brilliant as Cervantes', but the Triestine has none of the Spaniard's heavy mock-pedantry. His situations are more dimensional, more amusing; his style is laden with irony, but less frankly polemical and charged with overtones of an exemplary fable. Much of the force of the story comes from the easy, gay, allusive and yet heightened soliloquy of Argo. The story is told from the dog's point of view in the form of memoirs. The shortcomings of the fable are obvious: it is unfinished and certain parts are formulated according to a plan that is too sketchy and do not do justice to the dramatic intent and the artistic representation.

Almost all of the animal fables are pessimistic. **"The Mother,"** first written in 1910, is apocalyptic in mood. It relates how a brave little yellow chick sets out in search of his mother and is almost killed by the brood hen he adopts. This bitter and sardonic fable of the farmyard is a parable of alienation that not only exposes the failure of society, or the literary establishment, but also raises general problems of man's fate. With its peculiar blending of passion and skepticism, of vitality and pessimism, **"The Mother"** seems to grow out of the long and painful experiences of frustration of Italo Svevo the man and Italo Svevo the writer. The fable exhibits a Svevo too often ignored, and it asks comparison with other stories, especially **"The Evil Eye"** and **"The Very Good Mother,"** not included in this collection.

The father-son relationship will be the over-arching theme of *Zeno.* But as early as 1914, in **"Generous Wine,"** Svevo was already playing the neatest variations on the theme of the older man and his relations with the "others," particularly with those nearest to hand, his family and relatives. Svevo's argument is less the old line of *incommunicability* than a very credible reserve and a straightforward recognition of the fact that few people say what they have on their minds. At the opening of the story, the protagonist recounts candidly how during the nuptials of his niece everyone is bullying him for being senile. He decides to retaliate by indulging in food and drink, and by turning on his wife, daughter, and nephews. In typical Svevian fashion, humiliation succeeds humiliation. Inside the tipsy, sharpwitted man masquerading as a bully is a bully cunningly tricked out. Back home, the delirious old man constructs sick imaginings and rationalizations that blend one into another in a continuous flow at once humorous and clinically authentic, culminating in a climactic nightmare. The hero finds himself in a horrible cave sitting beside a coffin-like glass chest. He has been chosen to die for the sake of his closest relatives and is caught between hopes and fears. Finally, he ends up exposing himself to the supreme humiliation of proposing his own daughter for the sacrifice. We get then here, through a number of mnemonic devices, an oblique yet penetrating glimpse into the deeper layers of man's mind.

Also in **"Traitorously,"** perhaps the most strongly unified and wickedly comical of Svevo's compact short stories, we have a tale of aversion treated as meditation on the death theme. The bankrupt Signor Meier calls on an old friend to ask for a small business loan. The prosperous Signor Reveni, who is about to refuse, suddenly has a fatal heart attack. Technically, the story is hard to fault: the pace is immaculate; the moods are firmly established and differentiated; the atmosphere of potential farce sustained. Of course, **"Traitorously"** belongs to 1923, the year of the publication of *Zeno.* Svevo emerged from the conditioning of the early twenties speaking a new language of his own.

The fragment **"Death,"** composed between 1923 and 1928, deals with what might be called the *idée fixe* of the aged author: how to die well. The hero, Roberto, an atheist, explains to his wife, Teresa, the infallible system for preparing for death. In the general order of things, there can be neither pain nor fear of death. But when the stoical man becomes very ill, suffering proves too much for him: "The pain was the triumph of some other being—some being exulting in its justice. . . . His whole life had been one of guilt, guilt without end, for which he now wanted to repent. . . . His last words, tearfully, were 'I don't know.'" The effect of this confession on the pious widow is one of panic and remorse. The logical ending of the atheist's teaching is hilarious. Teresa persuades herself that "at the last moments, he had become converted". The pleasures to be found in **"Death"** are dry, intellectualized, matters of insight and understanding, not of dramatic interest; its comedy rarely seems comical. In tone and method, the story is akin to *The Old Old Man,* the unfinished fourth novel.

It is, however, the longer selections in the volume that display Svevo at his highly individual best. **"The Hoax"** concerns the last years of an elderly bank-clerk, Mario Samigli, and his bed-ridden brother, Giulio. The pair is simultaneously linked and divided. Mario in his youth had published a romantic novel that had been ignored, but now he composes only bitter animal fables. Then one day he is rudely shaken from his cosy complacencies. He is duped by his friend Gaia, a poet *manqué* turned salesman, into accepting an imaginary contract for the German translation of his youthful book. The rest of the story is about money and what it can do to a man who unexpectedly acquires a great deal of it. For, notwithstanding his ignorance of financial matters, Mario sells the royalties 'forward' and, just like Zeno in Chapter Five of the novel, makes a small fortune thanks to the inflation of the Austrian currency. There is something of the tale of practical jokes of the Boccaccian tradition in the mechanism of **"The Hoax."** But then the plot is inconsequential; it gives the non-professional Svevo the opportunity to study writers' vanity. To this extent the material is autobiographical, yet it would be easy to exaggerate in speculating on the real-life incidents and counterparts of the story.

Also the last two stories are sharply observed descriptions of the tensions and conflicts, the frustrations and self-deceptions of old age. With its central theme implied in the title, **"The Story of the Nice Old Man and the Pretty Girl"** touches on one of Svevo's favorite situations and is closely linked with the Carla episode of *Zeno.* A widowed businessman meets a young, fragile, and sensuous girl who drives a tram in wartime Trieste and decides to have one last amorous adventure. Following the usual pattern in Svevo's love stories, the nice, and rich, old man conducts his affair experimentally as if its purpose were pedagogical and love a means of therapy. At first, he is protective toward her and seems of necessity to dominate the relationship. The pretty girl responds predictably: she lies to him and betrays him while his passion persists and even grows. Tears, heart failure, and forced chastity take their toll of the nice old man. To break away, he takes the system of his two predecessors, Emilio and Zeno, to its logical conclusion by transmuting his jealousy of the girl's other lovers and

his resentment against the young and "healthy" into the moral issue of the relation of age to youth. But he makes little progress in clarifying his ideas or in putting his experience on paper. And the story ends at the beginning with the philosopher writing on the cover of his unfinished treatise: "nothing." Old age, Svevo satisfactorily proves to himself, cannot be cured by either love or art. This outline, of course, does not do justice to a novella that is essentially without plot and depends for its effects solely on the mastery with which it is presented. The interaction of narrative and theme, the counterweighting of the areas of dialogue and reflection, the various kinds and intensity of time all give the full measure of Svevo's power and charm. He manages his hero unsentimentally, with an understanding of his moods and attitudes that follows their changes and development minute by minute, yet never seems to waste time, or words, or even pity. It is at once extremely funny, and hauntingly moving.

"Short Sentimental Journey" is less intense, less elaborate, and more overtly comical. Begun before *Zeno* but written only in 1925, the "endless novella," as the author calls it in a letter to the critic Larbaud, is unfinished yet not incomplete. Old Signor Aghios embarks, his wallet stuffed with 1000-lira notes on a short business trip to Trieste, leaving behind in Milan his wife and son. At a deliberately musing rate, the story unfolds from the casual conversations with fellow-travelers to a meeting the protagonist has with an old business associate in Venice up to the long final theft episode. The business trip is clearly a dreadful failure: not only is Signor Aghios cheated and robbed, but he is also despised by some of his chance encounters. At the end, as in the beginning, of the truncated narrative, the mild-tempered and credulous Aghios seems to be in some moral danger. Structurally, the novella may break apart into two only distantly related sections. Moreover, Svevo used an anecdotal technique, piling incident on incident, and interweaving an amazing number of major and minor themes so that the reader can't tell for sure what is event, and what is context. But Svevo has a unifying center of interest in the character of his hero and in his basic tactic. As implied in the title, Signor Aghios is on a literal journey that has symbolic significance. In explanation of his quest, the protagonist says: "Even the feeling of security one enjoys in a family makes one more sluggish, more rigid; it leads to paralysis. Would he have felt more vigorous in the great world, away from his household? *This little trip would be a test;* for his business affairs would give him *a pretext for future trips.*" Rather than the details of the journey, it is, first and foremost, the moral dilemmas it causes Signor Aghios, that form the core of the novella. Evidently, the mutilation of the text corresponds to the difficulty of the subject: the terrible need for privacy coupled with the even more terrible need to have one's privacy violated. Svevo perhaps has taken on too much: the action-story lacks clarity, demanding more work from the reader than is justified; the social comedy is amusing but introduces too many shallow and forgettable characters; the travel-book element is not always integrated with the narrative; the prose is marred by lazy writing. Yet, despite its failings, **"Short Sentimental**

Journey" is an act of love, and our criticism is tinged with awe. Coming as it does in the last phase of his career, the novella goes a long way to help one interpret Svevo's writings and to appreciate his growth as an artist and as a man. With its open form and its all-accepting spirit, it represents Svevo's most rounded statement, technically and ideologically, for a lifetime of groping with the potentials of language and the absurdities of the human condition.

To conclude, both the specialist and the cultured public will welcome this present collection. It is ample enough to escape the cursoriness of a brief anthology and to permit a full encounter with Svevo as a short-fiction writer. Of course, like any partial collection, it is calculated to leave us demanding more. In presenting this selection, the editors announce that they are now at work on a companion volume that will contain other fragments of Svevo's shorter fiction in translation. We are looking forward to the appearance of this forthcoming volume. For Svevo, like Proust and Kafka, is a complex and difficult writer. We can sample him with enjoyment and profit, but we must ultimately read him in his entirety and judge him on his whole *oeuvre*.

John Simon (review date 1969)

SOURCE: A review of *Further Confessions of Zeno*, in *The New York Times Book Review*, Sec. 7, December 28, 1969, pp. 12-13.

[*Below, Simon favorably assesses* Further Confessions of Zeno, *perceiving "a cheerful banter that can swerve as easily into madcap satire as into genuine pathos, but most of the time remains just serenely and profoundly funny."*]

Readers who rightly recognize Italo Svevo's *The Confessions of Zeno* as one of the most, important novels of the century, might be put off, at first glance, by **Further Confessions of Zeno**. Bits and pieces of an unfinished novel, they might think, and a sequel at that. Bits and pieces they are, for the most part, but if that sounds uninviting, let us give them (borrowing from Svevo's favorite philosopher, Schopenhauer) the Greek words for left-overs, "parerga and paralipomena," and forthwith it all becomes respectable. Yet these fragments of a great last work are not respectable at all, merely brilliant.

Sartre has called Svevo Italy's most important contribution to modern literature, and Robbe-Grillet has hailed him as the forerunner of the new novel. Certainly Svevo's main theme—a sense of growing older, of premature senility, of sexual and existential impotence—should be of considerable interest to those of us today who cannot go along with the rock-drug-sex revolution, who cannot expand our consciousness from analphabetism to Zen, or shrink our age to under 30 and our mental age to well under half of that.

Svevo (really Schmitz), son of Italo-German and Triestine Jews, living in a city that was the battleground between a slowly dying Austrian empire and a greater Italy that took forever to get born; Svevo, a man committed to literature and a failure at it most of his life, who reprehended commerce and work yet involuntarily became a business success; Svevo, a writer who never mastered pure, literary Italian yet today outranks all the purple stylists of his day; Svevo, a timorous chap who considered himself old by the time he was 30, but in his mid-sixties wrote some of the most youthfully vigorous prose about old age and life in general—how could such a walking paradox be anything but a representative modern artist and man?

What most people who haven't read Svevo (and most people haven't) nevertheless know about him is that he had given up writing, discouraged, and was urged to resume his work (and go on to greatness) by an exile from Ireland who was teaching him English—James Joyce. They should also know that a wag has observed that Joyce's greatest achievement was Italo Svevo—and surely it was his second-greatest: a mighty close second, in my opinion. To realize this, one must read *The Confessions of Zeno*, **Short Sentimental Journey and Other Stories**, and the present volume, at last available in English.

Though these stories and fragments—all but the play "Regeneration," and that too, in a sense—were intended as parts of a sequel to Svevo's masterpiece, *The Confessions of Zeno*, they can gracefully stand on their own. For not only are they the products of Svevo's last, wisest and wittiest years (before, aged 66, he died of an auto accident in 1928), they are also the ultimate refinement of his supreme theme: growing old.

But aging for Svevo, as the critic François Bondy has remarked, "is an experience of incomparable potency, even if it is a matter of impotence, and a repertoire of new possibilities (or lacks). Above all, aging permits [him] to see different ages in a new perspective."

Although the **Further Confessions**, and even the play, "Regeneration," continue the story of the characters in *Confessions*, one finds out enough about all of them here to be able to tune in at this stage of their lives. All the more so because following Svevo's easygoing, almost rambling, narratives is an experience less like reading a structured work than like taking a walk with a vastly amusing and devilishly wise old man who never stops talking. One prefers such walks to be not too long and not at very close intervals, but regular. It is the sort of exercise that keeps the mind from going flabby.

The validity of Svevo's insights is intimately connected with that marvelous tone of his: a cheerful banter, one eye peeled on the comic absurdity of living, the other on the sad absurdity of aging and dying. A cheerful banter that can swerve as easily into madcap satire as into genuine pathos, but most of the time remains just serenely and profoundly funny:

"Oh, the only part of life that matters is contemplation. When everybody understands that as clearly as I do, they will all start writing. Life will become literature. Half of humankind will devote itself to reading and studying what the other half has written. And contemplation will be the main business of the day, preserving it from the wretchedness of actual living. And if one part of humankind rebels and refuses to read the other half's effusions, so much the better. Everyone will read himself instead; and people's lives will have a chance to repeat, to correct, to crystallise themselves, whether or not they become clearer in the process."

It is hard to say whether such a passage is inspired lunacy, gently murderous satire or sublimely smiling resignation. Probably it is all three. And what of this: "Old all day long, without a moment's respite! And aging by the second! I struggled to get used to being as I am today and tomorrow I shall have to struggle again to reseat myself in this chair, become still more uncomfortable than before. Who dares deprive me of my right to speak, to shout, to protest? All the more since protest is the shortest route to resignation." The sly, old protagonist who speaks these words is wise, ridiculous, pathetic—most important, he is laughing inexorable mortal defeat into a Pyrrhic or, more accurately, a Pyrrhonian victory.

This distillation of Svevo himself, called Zeno Cosini in the fictions and Giovanni Chierici in the no less dazzling play, is, for all his pessimism ("whenever I look at a mountain I always expect it turn into a volcano") and his comic self-pity ("Now that I am old myself I find that the only persons highly regarded are the young") capable of sympathy for all. In his rebellious son he observes "blue eyes pleading for succor and support . . when his mouth was repeating harsh words out of Marx whom he had not read and in whom he did not believe." How compassionately he puts into his recently widowed daughter's mouth the words, "It makes me more unhappy than ever, having to forget my unhappiness."

It is in his great-hearted gallows humor that Svevo and the reader snatch the best winks of comfort: "At our age a man's body maintains its equilibrium only because it cannot decide in which direction to collapse." Such laughing protest is already resignation. Or take the old man who, trying to seduce or at least subjugate a young girl, is asked by her, "How can you think of such a thing?" "There's nothing one can't think of, if one tries," he answers. "You only have to want to, and you can think the North Pole has changed places with the South. Nothing is actually changed by it, but you've had a vision; that's what makes a man strong and master of his fate." I defy anyone to pronounce this self-delusion or sagacity ridiculous or heart-rending. One can be sure only of its ludicrous magnificence.

When the protagonist of "Regeneration" undergoes a monkey-gland operation, it proves a physiological failure but, ironically, a psychological godsend. In a dream, he tells his sweet, patient, put-upon wife: "In your name I will keep and feed mankind. That is the task of us old men, us young old men, us old young men." And that is exactly

what Svevo, a man renowned for his witticisms who died with a terrific one on his lips, has done. Anybody can make us die laughing; Svevo alone can also make us laugh dying.

On *The Confessions of Zeno*, Svevo's enduring novel:

The Confessions of Zeno has kept its place among the most original pieces of writing of this century. It is half a novel, half the autobiography of an alternative self or of the many selves enclosed in an anxious, honest and ridiculous man, whose absurdity springs from the originality of his attempts to understand himself. Zeno is the stoic and bourgeois clown; the subject is egoism and the melting together of time and sensation, and he is shown enthusiastically drowning in confused intentions. One follows his career as a man trying to give up smoking, as a hypochondriac, a deluded yet crafty lover, a cruising talker and intellectual, and a gambler on the Bourse in pre-1914 Trieste; and it is all done with a verve that owes everything to Jewish sadness and Italian farce. Zeno's virtue is that when he skids into folly, he keeps his dignity. The self-centered fool is a sage. The book was a strong argument for the brilliant cosmopolitanism and café-writing which left their mark on the writing of his time.

V. S. Pritchett, "Zeno at 70," in New Statesman, *Vol. 78, No. 2007, August 29, 1969, pp. 280-81.*

Charles Lam Markmann (review date 1971)

SOURCE: "The Merchant of Trieste," in *The Nation*, Vol. 213, No. 9, September 27, 1971, pp. 277-78.

[*In the following favorable review of* Further Confessions of Zeno, *Markmann discusses the comparisons of Svevo with Marcel Proust, André Gide, James Joyce, and Luigi Pirandello.*]

Works left unfinished because of the author's death are always a calculated risk; yet there are writers who in one sense must come out ahead on such gambles, regardless of any seeming short-term loss; the very failings of the fragments drive readers into the rediscovery of the artist at his best. One could hardly assay with any justice this projected variorum of sequels to *The Confessions of Zeno* without going back first to that ancestor that reminds us once again of our debt to James Joyce the discoverer, as well as James Joyce the writer.

Zeno first confessed, it will be remembered, when he was at the peak of his powers and problems, and his psycho-analyst, pioneering that black art in Trieste before what is quaintly called the Great War, commissioned the record as part of the treatment—in which his patient never believed. The new volume contains five narrative pieces, two of which, we are told in a brief prefatory note, appear to have been alternative beginnings to the sequel, while the three other, longer pieces are subsequent fragments; there is in addition a splendid three-act play, "Regeneration," which clearly derives from the same sources and the same personages, though the names are changed.

The prose segments and the play are centered on the single obsession of the recognition of old age. Zeno is in his mid-70s now, and one can only be grateful that he was never made to taste the sententious pap of Browning ("Grow old along with me/ The best is yet to be"). Zeno is a European, not an Anglo-Saxon (or an Anglo-Saxon's idealization of a rabbi), and so he is the same realist about old age when it has caught him as he was when it relieved him of his father: it is a bore at its kindest, a degradation at its commonest, a torture at its worst. But he is an ironist too, and into his irony his creator has infused all the heady ingredients of that Trieste in which he lived and died, that Austro-Hungarian possession peopled by Slavs, Magyars, Italians and Jews in a microcosm of all that made up a now vanished *Mitteleuropa.*

No one and nothing, least of all himself and what happens to him and in him, is exempt from Zeno's sardonic analysis, in which there is now no trace of the self-pity that the younger confessor mocked in himself. Four years over his Biblical ceiling, he contemplates (in the second of the alternative opening chapters, **"An Old Man's Confessions"**) a rejuvenation operation, which in fact his counterpart in "Regeneration," Giovanni Chierici, undergoes, not least because he so wholly accepts and shares the young's impatient dismissal of the old. Which is not to say that he treats the young with any less irony.

The ironist is often a man who is frightened of his own capacity to betray himself by tenderness. Svevo, as befits the superior ironist, has no such fear. The very acuity of his insights frees him, as it does a Proust or a Joyce or a Gide or a Pirandello, for emotion without embarrassments. One is always smiling, and sometimes laughing, when reading Svevo; at times indeed one is savoring something close to *Schadenfreude.* But then, too, one is often very deeply moved. Zeno may mock his bereaved daughter's professional widowhood, as he laughs at her pompously calculating admirer, but he respects the genuine element in her paraded grief, as he cannot withhold a certain empathy from the bovine potential son-in-law whose given and family names he always prefers to forget.

Comparisons with Proust, Gide, Joyce and Pirandello, first made half a century ago, arose out of the similar attitudes of all four writers toward man's fundamental condition of often braggart helplessness, as well as their so very nearly congruent analytic sensitivities. In the play that closes this new volume, indeed, one is at times in doubt whether it is not Pirandello that one is reading: not because Svevo has borrowed or imitated but simply because psychologically and artistically they seem identical twins. Stylistically it is only Gide, among the other three, with whom Svevo has much affinity; what he shares with all, however, is point of view and perception. His prose is simple rather than ornate in its riches.

In this respect as in his insights Svevo is much more a 20th-century and even a contemporary author (in spite of his having died more than forty years ago) than that inexplicable idol of much of American youth, Hermann Hesse, to whom the young Germans very sensibly accord the charity of silence. Svevo, it is true, has nothing to say to the neo-romantics, the narcissists or the illusionists; but, if only he were brought to their attention, he should certainly have a great deal to say to perceptive minds repelled by sham and rejoiced by wit that is never dehumanized.

Svevo was always careful to make it plain that he was not a professional of literature; he was a merchant who ran a business in Trieste and who led a cultivated life there, taking no part in politics and allowing nothing of the city's ever contending allegiances even to hint its way into what he wrote for his own satisfaction. And, because he wrote for himself first, he wrote always with unswerving honesty. No fraud, however pious, was indulged—and none escaped his vision. He belonged to no school, he furthered no doctrine. It is precisely because he wrote only for himself that he wrote so splendidly for us.

This century is by now too crowded with the names of undeservedly neglected writers. It would be pleasant—though Svevo would be the first to raise an eyebrow at the notion—if the appearance of *Further Confessions of Zeno* should set off a revival of American interest in Svevo and result in new paper-back editions of all his work. None of the earlier books has been translated since 1929 (except his lecture on Joyce), and the fact reminds one of the wise proposal that every good book should be translated afresh for every generation; one would add "for every country." There is, after all, in Svevo's virile Italian no taint of the pedantic or the "literary." But there are a directness and an acknowledgment of the basic absurd that, I think, make this half-forgotten businessman who died with the 1920s a writer very much for these years.

Paula Robison (essay date 1972)

SOURCE: "*Una Burla Riuscita*: Irony as Hoax in Svevo," in *Modern Fiction Studies,* Vol. 18, No. 1, Spring, 1972, pp. 65-80.

[*In the essay below, Robison suggests that Svevo's view of art is similar to Sigmund Freud's and that "The Hoax" contains three Freudian principles that help readers to understand Svevo's fiction.*]

Those who admire Svevo most should be among the first to agree that sincerity is not one of his virtues. His tricky irony, his sly understatement, and his addiction to the *witz* delight us with the pleasures of indirection. Sincerity in any of his characters, moreover, is almost always presented as a kind of lovable folly; and the reader is invited to enjoy with Svevo the comic spectacle of the con-man outconned, the childish hero triumphing over grave authority through sheer deviousness. For Svevo loves trickery. And especially he loves to contemplate the kind of trickery that men perpetrate on themselves: the lies they tell themselves in order to disguise through rationalization the dictates of the unconscious, to preserve their self-esteem, and to continue functioning in civilized society. For the Svevo hero, lying is a means of survival.

Toward the end of his long and disingenuous confessions, Zeno Cosini argues [in *Confessions of Zeno*] that lying has its roots not in psychology but in language: "we lie with every word we speak in the Tuscan tongue," he says (in Tuscan) when his psychiatrist claims that his confessions provide evidence of an Oedipus complex. But this Tuscan version of Etimenides' Cretan paradox of truth is only one of a series of ingenious and contradictory defenses which Zeno makes against his doctor's diagnosis, and it is brought forward not to clarify but to obscure the nature of his problem. It is a lie. For surely the Oedipus complex has nothing to do with the Tuscan dialect, and this last of Zeno's defenses is an evasive action designed to throw everything into confusion, to make us conclude that it is impossible to distinguish truth from falsehood, hence impossible to assess Zeno's guilt. If we are tempted to throw up our hands in despair over the meaning of truth, to absolve Zeno of responsibility for his words and the actions and impulses to which they refer, we are the victims of *una burla riuscita*—a successful hoax. For nothing could be clearer from the novel than the fact of Zeno's Oedipus complex; underlying nearly every word and every action are grotesquely exaggerated syndromes straight out of Freud, and the Freudian point of view embodied even in the rather incompetent Dr. S. alerts us to the necessity of the psychoanalytic frame of reference. The Cretan paradox confounds the rational intelligence only because it is self-referring, because it offers no external standard for testing its validity. But Svevo's novel provides the standard of psychoanalytic theory and the additional evidence of Zeno's actions as well as his words. Despite his Tuscan paradox, then, we can determine that Zeno sometimes lies, sometimes tells truths or half-truths; and one of the novel's chief pleasures for the reader is in sorting out his various degrees of truth and falsehood. What Bergson did with the Greek philosopher Zeno, we must do with his namesake, insisting that baffling paradox is a specious invention of a mind ignorant of the ways of the world, that life triumphs over the paradoxes of the intellect, that *things move,* that *we can know when a man is lying.* Indeed, without this latter assumption, irony would be impossible, even the irony of the Cretan paradox; and equally impossible would be art itself.

If we accept the Cretan paradox, we must conclude that it is as impossible for Zeno, or any man talking about himself, to lie as to tell the truth. Some such view seems to underlie Lowry Nelson's argument [in "A Survey of Svevo," in *Italian Quarterly,* Vol. 3, 1959] that Svevo is "a universal ironist"—a writer whose work is "truly objective," impartial, employing "a narrator who is neither complacent nor superior." Again, Nelson insists on "how pervasive and untendentious [his] irony is and how it should prevent hasty attempts to crystallize Svevo's world view on the basis of this or that passage." Nelson main-

tains that "from a reading of his fiction it would hardly be possible to assert either that Svevo accepted or that he rejected 'bourgeois values.' He stays aloof as a fascinated observer." For Nelson, then, Svevo is a man without discernible opinions, preferences, sympathies, or feelings. But we may question whether this is possible, whether a man can write without tendency, and whether there can be such a thing as "a universal ironist." The answers to these questions must be no; Svevo's impartial and skeptical manner is more of his trickery. He does have a point of view and a notion of truth, and they can be inferred from the work. The truths Svevo relies on are the truths of the unconscious, the facts of human feeling. And to read him without reference to psychological fact is to be truly "senile"—comically or pathetically out of touch with the human feeling that underlies art as well as other human activities.

Three Freudian principles, in particular, form the basis of "The Hoax": the nature of art as sublimation; the connection between art, fantasy, and the unconscious; and the psychic function of comedy, wit, and humor as a means of reassuring and asserting the ego.

—*Paula Robison*

Svevo's witty story **"The Hoax"** (in Italian, **"Una Burla Riuscita"**) is an ironic *künstlerroman* which demonstrates that art has its genesis in feeling and partiality. It reveals that Svevo holds a view of art which greatly resembles Freud's, a view in which tendency and the superiority of the narrator to his tale are among the chief psychic characteristics of art. Three Freudian principles, in particular, form the basis of the story: the nature of art as sublimation; the connection between art, fantasy, and the unconscious; and the psychic function of comedy, wit, and humor as means of reassuring and asserting the ego. Each of these principles governs the artistic endeavors of Mario Samigli, the protagonist of **"The Hoax,"** and shows us how to read Svevo's fiction. Above all, a psychoanalytic reading of **"The Hoax"** shows us how intimately connected are the writer's desires and the products of his creative imagination and warns us against attributing to him a "truly objective" Olympian detachment. Whatever else literature is capable of doing, it seems, it cannot perform this miracle. And yet it strives to create the illusion of objectivity; thus the narrator's comment that "it is difficult to discover the origins of a fable" might serve as an epigraph to this and all of Svevo's work.

Mario Samigli is a study in sublimation. A life-long bachelor, an aspiring novelist doomed to clerical hack work in a business firm, author of a forty-year-old novel which has received little acclaim, and older brother to a parasitic hypochondriac indifferent to all but his own symptoms,

Mario might well be suspected of harboring vast reserves of desire, fear, guilt, and rage. His sweetness of temper and his outwardly passive acceptance of his lot cannot obliterate his feelings, but they do force them to find indirect expression. We note, of course, that except for his bachelor state, Svevo's circumstances were much the same as Mario's and that the *künstlerroman* is an especially rich form for the study of sublimated longing and rage.

A bachelor and a puritan, so innocent that he has never married a woman or entered a brothel, Mario experiments with Eros through fiction, by "fashioning . . . shadowy beings and making them live through sheer force of language." Here Mario resembles the many protagonists of the twentieth-century *künstlerroman* who, unlike many of their romantic predecessors, are surrounded by an aura not of sexual liberation in the manner of Byron or Shelley but of sexual inhibition. One thinks of Stephen Dedalus, Proust's Marcel, Paul Morel, Gustav von Aschenbach—bachelor artists whose erotic capacities are given over most fully to their art. One remembers, too, Svevo's other characters—Alfonso Nitti, Emilio Brentani, Zeno Cosini—who turn to art when sexually frustrated. And one recalls Freud's observations that "what an artist creates provides at the same time an outlet for his sexual desire" and that "the creative artist feels towards his works like a father" [*Leonardo da Vinci and a Memory of his Childhood*, trans. by Alan Tyson, 1964].

Like all the fathers in Svevo's fiction, Mario maintains an uneasy relationship with his progeny. The novel he has written in his youth is, the narrator tells us, "dead, if what has never been alive can be said to die"; and the brief and private fables he now writes are "puppets" or "tiny, rigid mummies—you could not even call them corpses, so quite without odour were they—the crevices of time began to swarm with them." These offspring are stillborn precisely because they are not real, because Mario's fear of direct contact with living beings leads him to substitute, in true "senile" fashion, intercourse with the creatures of imagination. In an extremely explicit passage, the narrator describes the psychic function of Mario's fiction:

> Often from a single gesture a novelist will reconstruct a whole character endowed with all the attributes to match such a gesture. He does not really quite believe in his creation, though he loves to imagine it living an everyday life in the world. It is of no interest to him that it may already have a counterpart in reality; wrapt up in his own thoughts, he would not recognize it if he saw it. Now Mario . . . substituted for his brother a much stronger character (though afflicted with the same disease), who loudly proclaimed his right to live just the life Giulio was living in his nice warm bed; to take his medicine and be read to, just as he was. And Mario loved his own creation, its weakness, obstinacy and patience.

The only difference between the real brother and the imaginary one, it seems, is that the real Giulio has power over Mario which is dispelled through fiction. Through fantasy Mario can ignore any threats posed by his brother to his own psychic well-being, can even safely make him "a much stronger character," and can at the same time love this brother he has rendered harmless because unreal.

The life of the imagination, Freud says, is one way of defending oneself against the threats of the real world: it "shows an intention of making oneself independent of the external world by seeking satisfaction in internal, psychical processes. . . . Satisfaction is obtained from illusions, which are recognized as such without the discrepancy between them and reality being allowed to interfere with enjoyment," [*Civilization and its Discontents,* trans. by James Strachey, 1961]. Indeed, the enjoyment is greater when reality does not intrude; just as Emilio Brentani can love the shadowy figure he calls "Ange" when he is not confronting her real-life counterpart, the heartless whore Angiolina, so Mario loves his imaginary brother better than he loves the real one. The imagination, in short, labors to bring forth the object of its desire, a fictional character it can love. And in this respect the artist is obeying, in a sophisticated manner, one of humanity's earliest impulses; Freud notes that "every child at play behaves like an imaginative writer, in that he creates a world of his own and orders it in a new way that pleases him better" ["The Relation of the Poet to Day-Dreaming," in *On Creativity and the Unconscious,* 1958].

The actual relationship between Mario and Giulio shows us what Mario fears in his brother, offers insight into the nature and importance of the "family romance" in Svevo, and demonstrates the psychic mechanisms employed by the artist who substitutes fantasy for actual experience. There is a strong element of hoax in Mario's and Giulio's seemingly amiable brotherly love. Family relationships in Svevo's work are always equivocal, ambivalent, self-deluded. In particular, the theme of sibling rivalry, appearing in relatively few modern novels, is prominent in Svevo. One thinks of Zeno's memories during psychoanalysis of his hated younger brother, of his long-lasting resentment of his brother-in-law Guido, of his own sons' intense rivalries in *Further Confessions of Zeno*, and of Emilio Brentani's precarious and ambivalent relationship with his sister in *As a Man Grows Older.* And in **"The Hoax,"** Mario and Giulio share more than "a strong mutual affection which dated from their early childhood". Their relationship is rather in the nature of a truce, grown easier by years of habit. For years, Giulio has stayed in bed and dosed himself with medicine to "combat the gout, which threatened to attack his heart"; this tenuous and probably psychosomatic illness makes him an economic and an emotional parasite, and he repays his brother for his inconvenience with an uncritical acceptance of all Mario's opinions. Mario too shows his brother the greatest deference largely, we suspect, because Giulio is the only person who shows respect for his literary achievements. But the respect is feigned, a hoax. Their evening ritual comes to symbolize the nature of the relationship: Giulio puts on his night-cap "right down over his ears and cheeks," pretends to listen to Mario reading aloud from his novel, and immediately falls asleep. The comic spectacle of Giulio using Mario's novel as a drug, Mario using his bed-ridden brother as a captive audience, belies the appearance of brotherly love and respect. The narrator describes Giulio as "the old fraud, who looked so innocent in his night-cap"; Mario is another old fraud, and their relationship is symbiotic and based on mutual deception. Indeed, the unconscious antagonism between the two becomes apparent when Mario believes that his novel will be republished. Now their separate fantasies, once complementary, come into conflict: Mario demands that Giulio listen carefully to his work, and Giulio demands that Mario show more consideration for his illness. Ironically, of course, the two fantasies are psychically identical: just as in *As a Man Grows Older,* as Gian-Paolo Biasin points out [in "Literary Diseases: From Pathology to Ontology," *Modern Language Notes,* Vol. 82, 1967], Amalia's sickness "structurally corresponds to [Emilio's] progressive decadence; her delirium corresponds to his dreams and behavior," so Giulio's illness corresponds to Mario's dream of fame. Both serve the same purpose: to defend against the possibility of failure in bourgeois life. Deprived during the period of Mario's anticipated success of the nightly readings and the ambiguous love and consideration they signify, Giulio perceives that "it was not death he was cheating by remaining alive, but life, which had no use for a miserable helpless wreck like him. And he was profoundly depressed." Mario too feels guilty, defensive, and lonely. Equivocal as their love may be, it is a necessary illusion from the point of view of the insecure ego, and it is effective only so long as the unconscious hostility is denied.

The two brothers, then, do not respect one another wholly, and it is his lack of esteem for Mario that makes Giulio dangerous to Mario's psychic well-being. By the process of fictionalizing Giulio, Mario does through art what he cannot do in life: he becomes his brother's father with all the power, authority, and respect that must be accorded to the patriarch. And this process is not confined to the brother; as Mario renders all the circumstances of his life in fiction, he becomes father of all, the lord of creation. "And Mario loved his own creation."

But the imagination has another aspect: it seeks to express not only love but also aggression. Mario's fictionalizing of his brother has a strong aggressive component, for it involves denying Giulio's existence in the real world. In his description of Mario's rival Gaia, Svevo is even more explicit on the connection between art and aggression. In Svevo's dialectic, the sexually inhibited, passive, and "senile" man of fantasy is often set against the sexually liberated, overtly aggressive, and successful rival, the man of fact: Alfonso Nitti *vs.* Macario, Emilio Brentani *vs.* Balli, Zeno Cosini *vs.* Guido. So in **"The Hoax,"** against Mario's "idealism," his sexual inhibition, his persistence in composing his modest fables at the same time as he pursues his humble career of writing business letters, and his sweetness of temper, Svevo sets Gaia's brutal realism, his familiarity with brothels, his abandoning of poetry in favor of a career as a traveling salesman, and his habit of playing cruel practical jokes. But the two men are doubles; the difference between them is largely in the manner in which they express their aggressive tendencies. Gaia has his jokes, Mario his art. And the narrator comments, "perhaps [Gaia's] love of practical joking was a relic of his suppressed artistic tendencies. For the practical joker is really an artist, a kind of caricaturist whose task is all the harder in that he has to invent and lie in such a way as to induce his victim to make a caricature of himself. A practical joke takes a lot of careful, even subtle, preparation, and a successful one deserves to be immortalized. Of course it gets more notoriety if someone like Shakespeare tells it, but they say that, even before *Othello,* Iago's was much talked about." The psychological truth underlying this typical Svevo *witz* is that art may be an outlet for aggression; for if "the practical joker is really an artist," it follows that some artists are practical jokers. And the purpose of the practical joke, Freud tells us, is aggressive [*Jokes and their Relation to the Unconscious,* trans. by James Strachey, 1960].

Although he denies it, Mario is highly aggressive. He vents his emotions and wishes through his daydreams, his dreams, and his fables; and in Freudian fashion, Svevo shows the intimate connection between fantasy, dream, and art. The daydreams, visions of himself as "a force in modern literature," the narrator says, are non-aggressive: "Mario's illusions did no harm to anyone." But the unconscious desire underlying them is aggressive as we see from his dreams:

> But apparently his dreams were less serene. His brother Giulio slept in the next room . . . he would hear strange sounds coming from Mario's room; deep and apparently painful sighs, then from time to time a loud, protesting cry. . . . It happened so regularly that one is forced to think the strange sounds which came from him when asleep were really the expression of his tortured mind. This fact would seem to cast doubt on the modern theory of dreams, which proclaims them to be the symbol of wish-fulfillment. At last, in sleep, he was free to throw off the heavy mask he had worn all day to hide his ambitious heart, and proclaim with sighs and exclamations: "I am worth more than they think! I am worth more than they think!"

The theory of dreams as wish-fulfillment, of course, is not refuted but supported by Mario's dreams, for the sighs and cries are expressions of the feelings which have been repressed during the day and which find in dreams their proper expression. These unspecified dreams are signs of the psychodynamics of Mario Samigli: his desperate need for self-esteem, his repressed struggle with the forces that deprive him of it, and his ordinary waking unawareness of his own deepest desires. As Freud remarks, "no one wants to get to know his own unconscious" [*Jokes*]; one thinks of the title *La Coscienza di Zeno* (the conscious of Zeno) which is totally out of touch with his unconscious; of Amalia Brentani's erotic dreams which contrast so strangely with her conscious maidenliness; and of Mario's dreams, symbols of the ambition and competitiveness he hides so well from others and from himself. His insistent cry, "I am worth more than they think! I am worth more than they think!" shows the extent to which self-assertion and aggression are one and the same for the competitive Mario.

Mario's aggression can be admitted to consciousness only in disguised form, and this he does through his fables. The fable greatly resembles the joke in form, tone, and function, and many of Freud's observations in *Jokes and their Relation to the Unconscious* shed considerable light on Mario's fables. Freud distinguishes between "innocent" and "tendentious" jokes and has much to say about "tendency-wit," whose purpose is to vent repressed aggression in disguised form. An incident in *Confessions of Zeno* demonstrates the tendentious possibilities of the fable form; Zeno, competing for the attentions of Guido's mistress, Carmen, and wife, Ada, is driven to compose a fable:

> *There was once a prince who was bitten by a great many fleas. He prayed to the gods to grant him one flea to himself (as large as they liked, but only one), and to distribute the others among the rest of mankind. But not one of those fleas would consent to stay alone with that fool of a prince, and he was obliged to keep them all. . . .*

It was acutely interpreted by Guido himself, who laughingly exclaimed:

"It is not a fable, it is only an excuse for calling me a fool."

I laughed too, and the pain that had inspired me to write it at once vanished.

It is the same with Mario: "his melancholy found an outlet in his bitter fables, leaving his face without a cloud." Zeno's transparent fable has little point unless we recognize it as tendency-wit; but when we identify Guido as the "fool of a prince," Carmen and Ada as the fleas, it becomes highly witty and far from innocent or pointless. And Mario's fables are no less tendentious, despite their seemingly innocuous exteriors, once we recognize their autobiographical reference and the depths of repressed aggression to which they point.

The fables mediate between conscious and unconscious. As works of art, they are highly conscious and controlled, but in their tendency and their psychic mechanisms they derive from the unconscious. Freud notes the similarity between the mechanisms of dreams and of jokes: condensation, displacement, and indirect representation. Mario's sparrow fables have all these characteristics. Two of the fables in particular show the process of distortion and transformation which marks a fable as well as the underlying aggressive content.

The first is the story prompted by Mario's embarrassment at being praised by a Slavic vendor of "fruit, eggs and poultry"; it tells of a bird which is given "some bits of bread which were too big for its beak. . . . It flew away, thinking: To receive charity from a fool is almost a misfortune." Of Mario's distortion in composing this fable, the narrator comments, "it was only the moral which fitted the case. The rest was so much altered that the donor would never have recognized himself in it; nor did Mario wish him to. He had eased his mind, and certainly had no desire

to insult his innocent admirer." He has no desire to insult him openly, that is, for to engage in overt aggression would produce guilt and perhaps punishment; but through the disguises of art all things are possible. The second is one of the fables written during the war, "which taught him he might really make use of the fable to express himself." What he expresses in his war-time fables is antagonism toward Germany, but "for safety's sake, he wrote only fables of doubtful application" like the one "about the powerful giant fighting in a marsh with animals much lighter than himself, and perishing, always victorious, in the mud which was too weak to bear him. What proof had anyone that it was about Germany?" This kind of art is literally as well as figuratively a means of "getting past the censor." It is a clear instance of tendency-wit, and, as Freud says, "the prevention of invective or of insulting rejoinders by external circumstances is such a common case that tendentious jokes are especially favoured in order to make aggressiveness or criticism possible against persons in exalted positions who claim to exercise authority. The joke then represents a rebellion against that authority, a liberation from its pressure" [*Jokes*].

Mario's fables all express rebellion against authority, against the harsh realities of life which frustrate the desires of the unconscious. If we accept the Freudian premise that "the infantile is the source of the unconscious, and the unconscious thought-processes are none other than those—the one and only ones—produced in early childhood" [*Jokes*], we can see in the fables the process of condensation which characterizes the joke. Mario's sparrow fables do seem to contain elements from infantile experience: the child's desire to be fed, his rage at being denied nourishment by seemingly capricious, oversized adults, his bewilderment, fear, and naiveté. These feelings, transferred to the struggle for success in literature, find their expression and their disguise in the fables.

And so, in his sparrow fables, Mario strikes out against the pressures and the authorities of his life—but, "for safety's sake," in seemingly innocuous terms. In these stories of simple sparrows struggling to eat, fly, and avoid traps, the drive to succeed in business and literature is exposed as a desperate struggle for survival by a helpless, harmless creature. Success is shown to be dependent on the caprices of unpredictable, indifferent, and stupid benefactors. The relations of the struggling creatures to one another are exposed as pitiless and unloving competition. The artistic impulse is described as a natural attempt at self-fulfillment—the song of a simple bird—which must be thwarted unless the singer is first rescued from starvation. Mario's plight is that of a humble but nonetheless transcendental bird—conventional romantic symbol for the artist—imperiled in a predatory world. The sparrow fables offer a bitter indictment of the struggle for success in a bourgeois world which shows neither pity nor respect for the artist.

Much of Svevo's fiction is devoted to a similar disparagement of success in bourgeois society. In contrast to the stultifying clerical hack work usually done by the Svevo hero, for instance, the successful businessman achieves his reward by following the three rules of Malfenti in *Confessions of Zeno*: "(1) It is not essential to work yourself, but you are lost if you can't make others work for you. (2) There is only one great cause for remorse—to have failed to look after one's own interests. (3) Theory is very useful in business, but only when the business has already been settled." In *A Life*, the life-long friendship between old Rultini and Ciappi is destroyed by their competition for a promotion; the job is a sinecure, and Rultini gets it because he is incompetent. Success for Svevo, it appears, is always a hoax. Occasionally, like Zeno or Mario at the end of **"The Hoax,"** the hero makes a financial profit not by his own shrewdness but because of the absurd fluctuations of a war-torn economy. When Mario first hears Gaia's lie that a Viennese publisher wants the translation rights to Mario's forty-year-old novel, he naively thinks that "he had simply got what he deserved, surely the most natural thing in the world. The only extraordinary thing was that it had not happened before." But he is all too soon undeceived as to this unenlightened assumption of the justice of bourgeois success; he makes his profit from having sold in advance Gaia's bogus check, and in accepting this money, Mario is himself the unwitting perpetrator of a hoax on the bank. Such is success.

Literary success, **"The Hoax"** tells us, is fraudulent, too. Although the narrator tells us that Mario's idea of himself as "an influence in modern literature" is one of his "flattering dreams," still the story relies on the assumption, common to the *künstlerroman* and supported by bitter experience on Svevo's part, that great and original writers are unrecognized in their time. Mario naively imagines that his novel has been discovered by an anonymous critic who is "no mere trifler, but a man of action . . . In his hands the work was rated at its true value and no more . . . [He was] the world's best critic." Puzzled, however, that the critic has not communicated with him directly, Mario concludes that he is "cold, cold like a machine that is capable of one motion. In his hands the work . . . became inert like goods passing through the hands of an intermediary, which only leave behind a monetary value." And the melancholy truth, as he discovers, is that this paragon of critical judgment does not exist and that "literature [is] a thing to buy and sell," a mere commodity on the bourgeois market.

The sparrow fables, then, clothe in Schopenhauerian, naturalistic terms, Mario's rage and resentment toward bourgeois success, which the story shows to be justified. But they also express his great desire for success, which, after all, is equated with survival. Mario, in short, is ambivalent about success. He is similarly ambivalent about his own abilities, and the fables show, in their selection and treatment of his sparrow *persona,* a simultaneous self-depreciation and self-esteem: as he thinks of the sparrows, "their weakness roused one's pity, their wings one's envy; surely these creatures were very like oneself." Despite their transcendental capacities for song and flight, Mario more often stresses their less heroic qualities, their weakness. We may wonder whether Mario's depreciation of the sparrows, which is very like his humility in daily life and like Svevo's own ironic self-mockery, is entirely genuine,

or whether it is not in part another hoax, a strategy whose aim is the ego's survival.

Two fables in particular point to the latter possibility. After Gaia's hoax has been revealed, Mario writes a fable in which he disposes of the critic he has imagined as his benefactor: "one day a tame sparrow happened to find a great many crumbs. It thought it owed them to the generosity of the biggest animal it had ever seen, a huge bull who was feeding in a neighbouring meadow. The bull was slaughtered, the bread disappeared, and the sparrow mourned its benefactor." The narrator comments, "that fable was a true expression of hatred; turning oneself into a blind fool like that sparrow only in order to make a far bigger fool still of the critic." Beneath the apparent self-mockery (the sparrow is Mario's self-portrait and the bull-critic, whom the story sends off to slaughter, is, as Mario now recognizes, only a foolish fantasy of his own imagining) is a note of triumph, for although the sparrow is a fool, the fable-maker, by virtue of his irony, is not.

Again, while he is anticipating success, Mario imagines a dialogue in which "he said to the sparrows: 'You make no provisions for the future, for you have no conception of anything but the present. How do you manage to be so happy when you expect nothing?' . . . But the birds knew better: 'We *are* the present,' they said, 'and you who live for the future, are you any happier?' Mario confessed his question was a stupid one, and promised himself to rewrite the fable so as to show his superiority over the birds." This is precisely the psychic function of the fables: to show the narrator's superiority over the figures he has invented to represent himself. By describing himself as a sparrow, Mario paradoxically and ironically assures that he is *not* a sparrow. Through fiction it is possible not only to rearrange one's world and to take revenge against one's enemies, but also to assume a position of superiority toward oneself—to transcend not only the external world but the self within. To assert one's superiority to oneself is indeed the greatest of triumphs, and it is made possible by the trick of irony.

The self-transcendence through irony which fiction affords enables Mario to confess with impunity to a number of unpleasant truths about himself. For instance, he finds it possible, by means of a fable, to admit to meager talents as a writer: "later, when the hoax was discovered, he celebrated his return to the old life by writing a fable about a song-bird in a cage, which prided itself on singing about Nature, and yet could only sing about the water and the millet in its little troughs. And it was a great comfort to him to find that he had the strength to reject, when forced to, the ridiculous notion that he deserved applause and admiration, and to accept his humble lot without repining." By seeing himself ironically, Mario turns weakness into strength, failure into success.

Again, like Zeno at the end of his confessions, Mario can offer a strong indictment of the entire human race and emerge somehow blameless, rescued from culpability by his ironic point of view. Of the fable, "a generous man had for many years regularly put out food for the birds, and was sure that they were full of gratitude to him. He must have been very unobservant, or he would have noticed that the birds looked on him as an imbecile whose bread they had managed to steal all these years without his having succeeded in capturing one of them," the narrator asks, "how came he to read such malice, such ingratitude, into the most joyous expression of Nature? It was as good as destroying it outright. Besides, to attribute such insensibility to the winged creation was really a grave insult to humanity." Precisely. By attributing malice to all creation, Mario is able to offer it "a grave insult" and at the same time to absolve himself of purely personal guilt and, by virtue of his ironic superior knowledge, to rise above the petty malice of humanity. Just so, Zeno's apocalyptic vision at the end of *Confessions of Zeno* exonerates him of personal culpability by attributing guilt and malice to the entire human race at the same time as it envisions in fantasy the destruction of humanity and elevates him to the superior status of the more-than-human oracle. Neither Mario nor Zeno could entertain these dark visions of humanity without the protection of irony.

But for the most part, Mario consistently avoids turning his sparrow-fables into tragedy; his chosen mode is not tragic but comic irony, which is more suited to consoling and asserting the ego. Once again, Svevo offers a theory of art which closely resembles Freud's. Freud remarks that the comedian who tells jokes on himself, as Mario does in his sparrow-fables, produces laughter in others "by making oneself out clumsy or stupid. . . . But one does not in this way make oneself ridiculous or contemptible, but may in some circumstances even achieve admiration. The feeling of superiority does not arise in the other person if he knows that one has only been pretending; and this affords fresh evidence of the fundamental independence of the comic from the feeling of superiority" [*Jokes*]. And so, although "all his puppets were really sad at bottom," still "Mario did not carry it to the point of tragedy," and his fables are "in a light vein." Through comedy the narrator can transcend his fundamental sadness, can pretend that he has only been pretending.

What then is "the hoax" of the story? Fame and fortune certainly, love and even art, and finally life itself as Mario's sparrow-fables seem to tell us. But the witty teller of these sad and cynical truths is himself exempt from their application; he is rescued from them by his irony and finally by his humorous attitude. Freud begins his paper on humor by telling a joke Svevo would have enjoyed: the story of the criminal being led to the gallows on a Monday who observes, "Well, this is a good beginning to the week." And Freud comments [in "Humour," trans. by James Strachey, *Collected Papers,* ed. by James Strachey, 1959], "in bringing about the humorous attitude, the super-ego is in fact repudiating reality and serving an illusion. But . . . we feel it to have a peculiarly liberating and elevating effect. . . . Its meaning is: 'Look here! This is all that this seemingly dangerous world amounts to. Child's play—the very thing to jest about!'" Just so, Mario asks, "Who knows whether our life doesn't seem to the sparrows simple enough to be expressed in a fable?" And this humorous question, so typical of Svevo's understated wit,

is the work of the super-ego, "which, in humour, speaks such kindly words of comfort to the intimidated ego . . . [and which] does try to comfort the ego by humour and to protect it from suffering" ["Humour"]. The writing of fiction which is ironic, self-mocking, and humorous serves to comfort the ego in a way which is both harmless and highly effective: it is indeed *una burla riuscita.*

"The Hoax," for all its description of an autobiographical figure's renunciation of art, is itself a work of art, highly polished, revised, and intended for publication.

—Paula Robison

Because **"The Hoax"** tells us that fiction is autobiography, self-protection, and trickery, it seems appropriate to consider the psychic function that its writing must have performed for Svevo. When we apply its theory of art to the work itself, we can only conclude that in part at least, **"The Hoax"** is a hoax. In particular, the ending of the story offers a resolution that the story itself belies. Mario sees his renunciation of "literature" written for a public audience as a realistic appraisal of his own talents and a conscious turning to true humility. The ironic narrator, of course, knows that the renunciation is still an act of pride, for by abandoning the attempt to reach a larger audience and choosing instead to read his fables for an audience of one, the uncritical Giulio, Mario again becomes independent of the external world. The ultimate extension of living the life of the imagination is to refuse to share one's literature with others, and Mario's renunciation of literature is prompted by the same motives that led him to literature in the beginning.

But Mario's solution is not Svevo's. **"The Hoax,"** for all its description of an autobiographical figure's renunciation of art, is itself a work of art, highly polished, revised, and intended for publication. It was written during a period of fearful hope occasioned by the projected French translation of *Zeno:* what then are we to think of its gentle ridicule of Mario's dreams of success, of its disparaging of bourgeois success and literary fame, and of its narrator's apparent self-transcendence? We must conclude that as Mario is to his sparrows, so Svevo is to his Mario, and we may say of Svevo what he says of Mario: "he often wrote fables on the disillusion which follows every human activity. It was as if he sought to console himself for the poverty of his own life by saying: 'I am all right. I cannot fail, because I attempt nothing.'" And when we learn that Mario's brother Giulio had his real counterpart in Svevo's brother Elio, an invalid to whom Svevo used to read his work, with whom he more than once quarreled, and who later died, we begin to suspect that the material of **"The Hoax"** is full of profound and complex feeling. If it is impossible for us to say whether love, resentment, or guilt predominates in the portrayal of Giulio/Elio, if as Nelson says it is impossible to say whether Svevo rejects or accepts bourgeois values, it is because Svevo is deeply ambivalent. Of course, he wants to succeed, to force all rivals to respect him, but we suspect that what is true of Mario's sparrows is true of Svevo as well: "their soul is a little balance, weighted on one side by fear, on the other by hunger." **"The Hoax"** attempts to assuage both fear and hunger. It is superstitious, like knocking on wood in order to assure continuing success; it consoles in the event of failure; and in the event of success, it provides for an even greater pleasure than that of desire fulfilled because its narrator assumes a stance above success or failure, beyond desire or serious aspiration. This story of failure, in short, is Svevo's success.

The appearance of objectivity, then, is very much a part of the Svevo narrator by whom, as Nelson says, "no one is judged and no one is blamed." This is simply to say, however, that Svevo refrains from editorial comment. And we must now reject Nelson's notion of "universal irony" in the light of all that **"The Hoax"** has to say about art's origins in the unconscious, which is hardly impartial and which does not ask whether its frustrations are universal, and about the self-serving, superior function of irony in consoling and asserting the ego. We see clearly the limitation of Nelson's view, its psychological naiveté, when we find that he links Svevo in "impartiality" and "objectivity" with the Hemingway who wrote *The Sun Also Rises*. For to imagine the Hemingway who wrote unceasingly of death, impotence, loss of all that matters most to the man of feeling, who spent his life seeking out danger and destruction, who admired bullfighters for the intensity of their experience as well as for the self-control that enables them to survive it, who in his last years came near to being overwhelmed by feelings of loss and terror, as unmoved and "impartial" in his rendering of the plight of Jake Barnes, is surely to insult the depths of human feeling that are Hemingway's constant subject despite the stoic tone. It would be naive and insulting, too, to read Svevo without remembering the aging Zeno's words in *Further Confessions of Zeno*: "it frightens me when I think people might after all be better than I have always thought them, or life a more serious affair than it has always seemed to me. (I feel faint, the blood rushes to my head at this thought!)." Perhaps we need no other reminder than this one passage that irony in modern literature, far from being a sign of uninvolvement, may be a strategem for concealing and surviving one's inescapable involvement in the desperate and inconclusive agonies of our times.

Peter E. Bondanella (essay date 1973)

SOURCE: "'The Hoax': Svevo on Art and Reality," in *Studies in Short Fiction*, Vol. X, No. 3, Summer, 1973, pp. 263-69.

[*In the following essay, Bondanella argues that "The Hoax" illustrates why Svevo should be considered a forerunner of the Italian absurd.*]

Though there is no longer any need to introduce Italo Svevo's major novels to informed audiences in Europe or America, few scholars have examined his short fiction in detail. What criticism does exist on the minor works often emphasizes them as autobiographical documents; and while a biographical approach to Svevo's works is often fruitful, such an approach obscures the importance of the minor works in the development of Svevo's thought. Many contemporary critics choose to read Svevo's novels as a reflection of a deep sociological crisis in twentieth-century European society. Hence, the importance of these short works is often overlooked because they do not always fit into the picture of the Svevo *engagé* proposed in many recent studies. I should like to suggest that not the least of Svevo's contributions to modern Italian fiction lies in his uniquely sensitive apprehension of the irrationality and incomprehensibility of life. If Svevo is the father of the modern Italian psychological novel, he is also—with Kafka and Pirandello—the precursor of such recognizably absurdist writers as Dino Buzzati, Italo Calvino, and Eduardo De Filippo. The lengthy story **"The Hoax,"** written in 1926 and published in 1928 by *Solaria,* a Florentine avant-guard literary journal, deserves special attention in this regard, for not only does it propose a view of reality that shows Svevo to be a precursor of the Italian absurd, but it also contains an important expression of Svevo's opinions about the nature of art and its role in dealing with the absurdity of the human condition.

Two issues are involved in **"The Hoax"**: the incomprehensibility of life and the response of the artist to this condition. To the first issue Svevo has linked the story of a cruel joke played upon Mario Samigli. This part of the story, the basis of the title, presents Svevo's view of life as absurd. Mario Samigli is an unsuccessful author whose single book, *Youth,* has been forgotten, it would seem, by all except Mario and his brother. A friend and another artist *manqué,* Enrico Gaia, plays a cruel trick on Mario by pretending to have found a German publisher for the long-forgotten novel; he hires a man to impersonate a publisher's agent who gives Mario a worthless check for 200,000 kronen. Not suspecting any deceit, Mario entrusts the worthless piece of paper to his business partner, who, thinking it to be genuine, speculates on the money market with his own money and makes a fortune for Mario by purchasing money futures on the stock exchange before the hoax is discovered.

The ontological presupposition of this short story is very simple—life is absurd, irrational, incomprehensible. Man is endowed with reason in order to understand his world, yet he discovers that reason is of no use to him. This disturbing idea is presented in such a matter-of-fact manner by the narrator that the reader can scarcely question its validity in Mario's world. Life, for Mario, is itself a hoax, a unpredictable joke played by some unknown power upon him and the human mind. This is essentially the same view of life put forth by Mario's fictional predecessor Zeno Cosini when he remarked that life is neither bad nor good but "original": "the more I thought of it the more original life seemed to me. And one did not need to get outside it in order to realize how fantastically it was put together. One need only remind oneself of all that we men expect from life to see how very strange it is, and to arrive at the conclusion that man has found his way into it by mistake and does not really belong here" [*The Confessions of Zeno*] As Albert Camus remarked in his definition of the absurd, the "divorce between man and his life, the actor and his setting, is properly the feeling of absurdity . . . the absurd is born of this confrontation between the human need and the unreasonable silence of the world" [*The Myth of Sisyphus and Other Essays,* trans. by Justin O'Brian, 1955]. Both Zeno Cosini and Mario Samigli live in a world that obeys no human laws, follows no human logic, and seems to be ordered in such a capricious manner that man is a stranger to it by virtue of his innate inability to comprehend its rules. One key distinction, however, separates Zeno Cosini and Mario Samigli, for while Zeno is presented in *The Confessions of Zeno* as being in the process of discovering the absurdity of human existence, Mario simply accepts this view of life as a fact, a natural phenomenon.

Two issues are involved in "The Hoax": the incomprehensibility of life and the response of the artist to this condition.

—*Peter E. Bondanella*

This plot of **"The Hoax"** provides a background for the second important issue in the story, the place of art in an absurd world. The response to the absurd is the true theme of this work, for whether we label life "original" or "absurd," the end result for fictional characters inhabiting such a universe is the same—they must either despair or they must seek some alternative to maintain their lives and their sanity intact. For writers of Svevo's generation, as R. W. B. Lewis has noted, art was the response given in the face of the universal pressure of death, the feeling at the bottom of the apprehension of the absurd; the protagonists of such writers of this generation as Proust, Joyce, Mann, and Svevo are often artists or men of artistic sensibility, protagonists who reflect their creators' conviction that art is the one truly redemptive power left to man. Svevo, very much a part of his day in his respect for art, thus presents the plot of the story in order to set the stage for the second and more important part of the work, the response of literature to the incomprehensibility of human life. Svevo describes Mario as having "all the dreamer's instinct to protect his dream from contact with the crude realities of life." All of Svevo's main characters—not only Mario but also Alfonso Nitti, Emilio Brentani, and Zeno Cosini—possess imaginations that allow them to reconstruct their world in such a way that it may be rendered more comprehensible and more hospitable to their own ideals. Far from being an attribute of old age, *senilità* taken in its literal rather than metaphorical sense, this quality is a positive strength in Svevo's char-

acters, enabling them to survive and even to triumph over the "reality" recognized by more normal figures in his works. Mario possesses this essentially literary imagination, compared by Freud to the child's attitude at play, an attribute which, for Svevo, was necessary for the artist: "The author's habit of scratching out a sentence that displeases him makes it easy for him to accept that others should cancel things too. He describes reality, but eliminates whatever does not conform to his reality" ["The Relation of the Poet to Day-Dreaming," in *On Creativity and the Unconscious,* 1958].

In his own literary career, Svevo first wrote within the conventions of French naturalism. After the publication of *A Life* (1892), he discovered that his talents lay in a more introspective type of psychological fiction, illustrated in his own works by *As a Man Grows Older* (1898) and *The Confessions of Zeno* (1923). **"The Hoax"** represents a rejection by Svevo of simple representational realism as the proper goal of the writer. It is not an accurate portrait of his society the artist should paint but only his own reality, his own fantasy. Life has its own rules, albeit absurd ones, but literature follows other dictates. Svevo would have agreed with his more famous contemporary, Luigi Pirandello, who drew a line between life's absurdity and the nature of art: "life, happily filled with shameless absurdities, has the rare privilege of being able to ignore credibility, whereas art feels called upon to pay attention to it. Life's absurdities don't have to seem believable, because they are real. As opposed to art's absurdities, which to seem real, have to be believable" [*The Late Mattia Pascal,* trans. by William Weaver, 1966]. Like Svevo himself, Mario Samigli (Svevo's figure of the artist) finds it impossible to repeat the realism of his earlier novel *Youth* in later attempts to compose a new book; he discovers that the tenets of realism are a restraint upon his own imagination:

> It would have been impossible for him to write another novel like the old one, which had sprung from his admiration for people who were his superiors in rank and fortune, and which he could only observe through a telescope. . . . And it never occurred to him to describe a humble sort of life like his own, exemplary in conduct and endowed with the kind of strength that came from absolute surrender, a surrender which permeated his whole being and which he would certainly never have thought of as anything remarkable. He did not know how to approach a subject which seemed to him so uninteresting, a weakness common enough among those to whom high life has remained a sealed book. So in the end he gave up writing about human beings and their way of life, be it hig or low, and devoted himself exclusively, or so he thought, to animals: he began to write fables.

To broaden Svevo's own metaphor, Mario rejects both the "telescope" of realism and the "microscope" of introspection or self-analysis in his works and follows a middle course. His animal fables, created by giving artistic form to events from his own dreary life, represents a closed world of the imagination. In his fables, biographical events, removed from their true context, become philosophical statements about the human condition in much the same manner as Svevo himself often put events or people from his own life into his works. The fables originate in Mario's life and are occasioned by his encounters with its absurdity, but such events take on meaning only when they are written down on paper in a new form where order and meaning are imposed by he artist upon the chaotic material of life. In a sense, Mario's own life is his art, but the absurdity of his life is transformed by his imagination until his writng assumes a therapeutic quality. By reorganizing his own life into an artistic pattern with his animal fables, Mario is able to come to terms with the absurd world he inhabits. The plot of each fable is the same—the description of feeding crumbs to sparrows—but no less than nineteen different statements about the human condition (each based upon Mario's own life) are wrought from this apparently banal framework.

Each time the reality of the outside world interrupts this artistic process, it becomes impossible for Mario to write. As long as he believes that his earlier novel is about to be published, for example, Mario can no longer transform events of his own life into fables: "It was weeks since he had made any or even dreamed of one. His thought had been chained by success to his old novel, which he was studying in order to rewrite it; doing it up, and filling it with new stuffing; trimming it with fresh images and turns of expression. Success was his golden cage." As soon as he learns of the hoax played upon him by his friend Enrico Gaia, Mario's creative powers return and fables again become possible for him. Paradoxically, only failure as a writer in the commercial marketplace allows Mario's literary imagination to function.

Though Mario fails to gain financial success with his novel, the absurd turn of events brought about by the hoax, his newly acquired fortune, and his ability to write fables sustains his life. He sees the conclusion of the hoax as a natural phenomenon since in his world, "aberrations from the normal had definitely become the rule." In fact, the absurdity of the human condition is so far-reaching that the hermetic world of his own fables is the only one he can comprehend: "And Mario, with his pockets full of money, looked on and studied the phenomenon with surprise. He muttered in his bewilderment: 'It is easier to understand the life of sparrows than our own. Who knows whether our life doesn't seem to the sparrows simple enough to be expressed in a fable?'" Confronted by a world ordered without any apparent rationality, it is no wonder that Mario Samigli chooses to live in a private dream world constructed by his own imagination. In the world of fables, the cruelty and pointlessness of existence is not ignored, but life is now ordered by art into a form which has some aesthetic meaning. Unlike his own life, which seems to lack any purpose whatsoever, the closed world of art has a goal, for it satisfies a human need in Mario, the need for self-expression and rationality. As Mario puts it, "you can get anywhere you like with a fable, if you know where you want to go." Knowing where one wants to go in life is much more difficult.

The two elements of the structure of **"The Hoax"** are not equally important. Though the hoax is not as central to the work as the title might indicate, the account of the trick played upon Mario and its absurd result is not "inconsequential" as one critic has claimed. It is necessary to render Svevo's opinion of the absurdity, irrationality, or, as Zeno Cosini puts it, the "originality" of life. It is precisely because of this situation that art is important. It must not be assumed that Svevo was so naive as to assert that art is a panacea for man's problems; in fact, the narrator even once calls Mario's fables "illusions." But the illusion of art is a vital part of the human response to the condition of the absurd for Svevo. One must bear in mind that **"The Hoax"** was written after Svevo had shown a serious interest in Kafka and Pirandello (two masters of the absurd) and after writing his own *Confessions of Zeno,* a work which is only now being linked with the absurdist trend in contemporary literature. Svevo became more and more philosophical during the last years of his life, and he increasingly saw art or illusion as a kind of therapeutic "cure" for the world's insanity. **"The Hoax"** is a development beyond *Zeno,* where the absurd is first recognized by Svevo as the principle of organization in the universe. In the short story, the "originality" of life is simply assumed; it no longer requires demonstration, and the conclusion of the hoax played upon Mario Samigli is hardly a surprise even to the protagonist. The story also points toward the unfinished sequel to *Zeno* that Svevo was beginning before his death in that it underlines the crucial role of art and illusion in dealing with life. In segments of this sequel that were completed, appropriately translated into English as **Further Confessions of Zeno**, there is one passage that is the continuation of Mario Samigli's reliance upon literature as a means of dealing with life and which helps to determine exactly what Svevo meant to portray in this character who wrote animal fables based upon his own life. Zeno re-examines his autobiography done during therapy and discovers that only that part of the past that he had committed to paper, only that part to which he, like Mario in his fables, had given artistic form still existed for him. The rest was dead and forgotten:

> Oh! the only part of life that matters is contemplation. When everybody understands that as clearly as I do, they will all start writing. Life will become literature. Half of humankind will devote itself to reading and studying what the other half has written. And contemplation will be the main business of the day, preserving it from the wretchedness of actual living. And if one part of human kind rebels and refuses to read the other half's effusions, so much the better. Everyone will read himself instead; and people's lives will have a chance to repeat, to correct, to crystallise themselves, whether or no they become clearer in the process.

Though Svevo sensed the absurdity of life that all modern writers feel, he drew back from the abyss of nothingness he saw. As so many of his contemporaries did, he chose to view art and illusion, with their ordering of experience, as a viable response to this human predicament. **"The Hoax"** is an important artistic statement of this response of the imagination to the absurd and is a key to the development of Svevo's thought after the publication of

The Confessions of Zeno. His views place him squarely in the generation of James Joyce and Marcel Proust, to whom he has often been compared for essentially incorrect reasons, and set him apart from another generation of writers like Camus, Silone, or Moravia who, in R. W. B. Lewis' words, tried to transcend the sense of nothingless both groups of writers felt, not by the absolute value of art but by "an agonizing dedication to life."

Roland A. Champagne (essay date 1975-76)

SOURCE: "A Displacement of Plato's *Pharmakon*: A Study of Italo Svevo's Short Fiction," in *Modern Fiction Studies,* Vol. 21, No. 4, Winter, 1975-76, pp. 564-72.

[*In the essay below, Champagne finds the ancient* Pharmakon's *dual quality in Svevo's short fiction and discusses the author's use of language as an alternate order to time and space.*]

"Il caso Svevo" bears witness to the displacement of Italo Svevo's corpus in time and place. It has not been until the 1950's, some twenty years after his death, that Svevo's work has begun to receive the attention it is due. This attention has been especially productive in university communities in and out of Italy—environments quite different from the Triestine settings of Svevo's fiction. Such a displacement of time and place has also formally and thematically existed within Svevo's short fiction. In reaction to the documentary needs for localized details so characteristic of French Naturalism, Svevo's short fiction explores a paradox implied in *La Coscienza di Zeno,* which Freccero has pointed out [in "Italo Svevo: Zeno's Last Cigarette," in *From Verismo to Experimentalism,* ed. by Sergio Pacifici, 1969]: "The paradox is a form of the ancient paradox of Zeno of Elea, transposed from the mysteries of space and motion to those of Augustinian duration and time." This paradox portrays the ambivalence of living in mixed tenses, vacillating between the oversimplified categories of past, present, and future time. In effect, Svevo's creative presentation of this condition in his short fiction is a commentary on the act of writing as a displacement of the Platonic myth of *pharmakon,* especially as Jacques Derrida has developed it for us ["La Pharmacie de Platon," in *La dissémination,* 1972]. The myth of *pharmakon* concerns the ambivalent drug which may at once be hygienic and poisonous to one's physical well-being. The very term *pharmakon* is suggested to us by the title of one of Svevo's short stories—**"Lo specifico del Dottor Menghi."** The *specifico* may be an alchemical drug that does not necessarily have to be effective. Hence, it may cause negative as well as positive reactions. The effect of deliberate falsifications in *La Coscienza di Zeno* achieves a similar ambivalence as Zeno invents several incidents as well as the order in his memoirs, according to his own admission and that of Dr. S. There are numerous other examples of the narrator's deliberate falsification of his account. These lies have personal redemptive functions for the narrator while they preclude his readers from sharing his whole perspective. Even Svevo the author participates in this insincere narrative-art as his irony often plays tricks on his characters, and sometimes even on the careless reader. As Paula Robison has presented this narrative falsification, one understands that: ". . . Svevo loves trickery. And especially he loves to contemplate the kind of trickery that men perpetuate on themselves: the lies they tell themselves in order to disguise through rationalization the dictates of the unconscious, to preserve their self-esteem, and to continue functioning in civilized society. For the Svevo hero, lying is a means of survival" ["*Una Burla Riuscita*: Irony as Hoax in Svevo," *Modern Fiction Studies,* Vol. 18, Spring, 1972]. And so is it also true for Svevo the writer who perpetrates the ambivalence of writing as *pharmakon.* Let us now examine the elements of time and place, both in their formal and thematic realizations, to exemplify this commentary on the condition of writing in the short fiction of Svevo.

I. Time as a Grammatical Entity

Time—as a linear succession of regression of moments into the tenses of past, present, and future—is questioned as an effective ordering process of human behavior by Svevo's short fiction. Continually slipping in and out of the tenses of a linear chronology, Svevo's protagonists creatively re-construct "time" to their own advantage, as Zeno tells us in **"Il Vecchione"**: "Il tempo fa le sue devastazioni con ordine sicuro e crudele. . . ." External order, whether it be naturalistic or psychoanalytical, also intimidates Alfonso Nitti, Emilio Brentani, and Zeno Cosini in the three major novels of Svevo. In the shorter fiction, this threat of external order is transformed, on the formal and thematic level, into an arrangement of "time." In effect, the Svevian "hero" internalizes "time" to create an anti-chronological order of moments. The irony of attempting to fix **"Le confessioni del vegliardo"** to the specific date of 4 April 1928 becomes underscored as the old man ponders his temporal displacement: "È quel futuro quello ch'io vivo. Va via senza prepararne un altro. Perciò non è neppure un vero presente, sta fuori del tempo. Manca un tempo ultimo nella grammatica." He feels himself carried along by the fluidity of his life. There is no formal sequence of past-present-future which certainly orders his life for him. In **"Il Vecchione,"** the old man was haunted by ". . . l'ansiosa speranza del futuro." Such a continual displacement of time causes confusion for the Svevian protagonist who seems to exemplify the Svevian realization that: "Continuo . . . a vivere in un tempo misto come il destino dell'uomo, la cui grammatica ha invece i tempi puri che sembrano fatti per le bestie." These "mixed tenses" present an ambivalent temporal awareness which becomes the privileged formal order that allows one to retreat from the external order of such categories as past, present, and future time. This theory of "mixed tenses" is a formal order insofar as it allows the suspension of sequential chronology within a Svevian narrative.

Thematically, the "mixed tenses" provide an interesting insight into Svevo's understanding of the grammatical nature of existence. Similar to Derrida's "grammatologie" ("une science de l'écriture bridée par la métaphore, la métaphysique et la théologie" [*De la Grammatologie*

1967]), Svevo's grammatical vision is also a *Weltanschauung* which comments on the very act of creative writing without the systematic implications of Derrida's proposal. Such a "grammatological" conception of the existential act of writing implies a bond between the formal presentation and the thematic discussion of "mixed tenses." Svevo's concern for old age and youth attains an added dimension with this suspension of "mixed tenses" whereby one can continually participate in both old age and youth, despite one's age. Indeed, Zeno admits in **"Umbertino"** that "io sono uomo che nacque proprio a sproposito" because in his youth old age had been respected and now in his old age youth is respected. Old age and youth seem continually to contrast with one another. However, the complementary nature of these two is vividly portrayed by the image of Zeno and Umbertino, grandfather and grandson, walking along hand in hand along some railroad tracks which, like the problem of old age and youth, seem to come together in the far-off distance. In **"La Nouvella del buon vecchio e della bella fanciulla,"** this complementary nature is specifically referred to as the old man writes in his educational treatise *Il vecchio* that an old man "è infatti . . . nient'altro che un giovine indebolito." In the same story, the doctor suggests to the old man that "la gioventú molto spesso piglia delle malattie, ma sono usualmente delle malattie prive di complicazioni, Invece nei vecchi anche un raffreddore e una malattia complicata." Because of the infirmities which degenerate both states of youth and old age, one of their common denominators is disease. It is important that the linear passage of time does not necessarily link old age to youth in an evolutionary concept, similar to Darwin's theory, with which Svevo was quite familiar.

Although time is not evolutionary, it is nevertheless a creation of fluidity by the protagonist. As Reto Fasciati noted in his thesis: "Innovatore egli è veramente quando sa fondere passato e presente in un unico tempo della coscienza, in una 'Einbildungskraft' senza limiti temporali, in un tempo che domina gli eventi e non ne è dominato" [*Italo Svevo-Romanziere Moderno,* 1969]. Indeed, Svevo's narrative art portrays the erasure of the temporal limits of past, present (and also future) so that one might escape the external determination such as that of Taine's *race, milieu,* and *moment* so respected by the French Naturalists. As in the old man's view of the ties between old age and youth, the continuity between Zeno and his son Alfio is an especially negative one: "Grave, insopportabile, quello di veder rinascere nei miei figliuoli i miei piú gravi difetti." (**"Umbertino"**). Hence, this negative continuity of internalized time tends to erase external limits and to create a dream-like "reality."

The dreams literally played an important role in **"Corto Viaggio Sentimentale," "Vino Generoso," "Una morte,"** and **"La Novella del buon vecchio e della bella fanciulla,"** among other minor roles. Perhaps it is the unconscious which may contain the secret movement of internalized time. Furbank has presented the unconscious in Svevo as ". . . the part of the mind which knows the truth but can only communicate it through the garbled and grammar-less language of dreams" [*Italo Svevo: The Man and the Writer,*

1966]. In the dream-world, Svevo's protagonists portray an associative world, unhampered by the external order of linear chronology. In the first pages of **"La Novella del buon vecchio e della bella fanciulla,"** the old man interrupts his narrative to tell of the earlier episode wherein the young girl and her mother visited him at his office. In effect, the narrator suspends his story in a future-anterior tense by postponing his future story with a previous encounter. Thus, the linear sequence of events is disturbed by associational reporting, as in a dream. The dream, however, is denied as a regression from the world by the Svevian protagonist: "Non era la mia la vita del sogno e non ero io colui che scodinzolava e che per salvare se stesso era pronto d'immolare la propria figliuola" (**"Vino Generoso"**). The dream is a creation of his world in much the same manner as the Svevian protagonist internalizes the erratic fluidity of time. The freedom of surpassing the limits of external time allows the protagonist to create his own organization of time and space, as in **"Il Vecchione"**: "ma io qui nella mia stanzetta posso subito essere in salvo e raccogliermi su queste carte per guardare e analizzare il presente nella sua luce incomparabile e raggiungere anche quella parte del passato che ancora non svani." The internal temporal order of "mixed tenses" thus organizes events and places according to an internal sense of history and geography.

II. Space and Displacement of Origin

The problem of organizing time and place in an internal sense of history and geography seems to be a spatial process of ordering for the Svevian protagonist. Space, rather than "place" which implies the definite localization of geographical position, becomes another transposition of temporal relationships for the Svevian "hero." Space, as the relative organization of place to a subjective narrator, displaces the localization of place as well as time. Hence, an origin in time and place becomes increasingly difficult to establish. As a result, "geography" is transformed into a temporal problem as the voyage and the alcoholic trance cause one to forget localization and to become displaced into a dream-like state created by an almost free association. In **"Corto Viaggio Sentimentale,"** Aghios especially feels this dislocation of geographical place, as telephone poles and landscape become fused into one another as he looks out from the train: "I pali e la campagna o una parte di vita fuggono senz'essere visti o sentiti." Indeed, the journey can substitute for the effects of wine, as in **"Vino Generoso,"** because a voyage can actually dislocate one's physical presence just as the dream displaces one's consciousness of present time: "Il vino era stato smaltito nella corsa traverso gli spazi siderei e non lo turbava piú" (**"Corto Viaggio Sentimentale"**). One may wonder what may be the positive production of such dislocations and displacements. As Furbank has explained, Svevo's narrative art is closely tied to such positive aspects in his longer novels: "As a novelist, Svevo's mind worked all the time by leaps of analogy; they became the fibre of his writing." And these leaps of analogy may provide us with insight into the organization of space within his short fiction.

Similar to Aghios in **"Corto Viaggio Sentimentale"** who "ora bisognava tentare di procurarsi un posto," Svevo also seemed to be looking for his specific place among the various possibilities of narrative form. Experimenting with the burla (**"Una Burla Riuscita"**), the novella (**"La Novella del buon vecchio e della bella fanciulla"**), the fable (**"Una Madre"**), the confession (**"Le Confessioni del vegliardo"**), the sentimental journey (**"Corto Viaggio Sentimentale"**), among other less obvious short fictional forms, Svevo appears to be playing games of the displacement of narrative space. The "leaps of analogy," whereby Svevo may be speaking of his own role as creative artist through his transformations of various formal traditions, may give us insight into the spatial intervals of his fiction. In each of the forms cited above, Svevo has lengthened the form and added elements which make the movement of his narrative extremely slow. Hence, the temporal pace of the narrative has been transformed by Svevo's experimentation with space. For example, in **"Una Burla Riuscita,"** Mario continually creates fables of sparrows to comment upon his experience. However, in contrast to **"La Madre,"** which exemplifies Professor Mancini's insight that "as a fabulist, Svevo subjects man and life to a pitiless but passionate critique, exposing the sad and pitiful spectacle of human absurdity and self-deception," Mario's fables allow for esthetic distance between Mario and the narrator, as well as between Mario and his fables. This esthetic distance allows a spatial interval to exist between the human and the animal conditions of existence. The similarities may be too obvious in an evolutionary universe as conceived by Darwin. Perhaps Svevo is implying that one should study the differences and the spatial intervals between man and animal. The narrator of **"Una Burla Riuscita"** tells us that "è difficile di conoscere le origini di una favola." And he may also be speaking of the origins of all creative writing—they are not discoverable either. We have only studied their displacements in time and place into a different spatial awareness. In effect, the writer becomes a creative historian and geographer in much the same manner as Mario who had created a new living-being with his novel *Una giovinezza*: ". . . gli appariva vitale come tutte le cose che simulano d'avere un capo e una coda" (**"Una Burla Riuscita"**). Mario had created new dimensions of time and place within which his novel could enjoy a life of its own, independent of its poor acceptance by critics in the world of three-dimensional place and linear time.

III. An Alternate Order—Language

Such a creative presentation of space precludes a mimetic esthetic. In fact, there seems to be a dissociation of sensibility operating within Svevo's narrative whereby there is no rapport between objective and subjective realities. Much irony is directed at Svevo's protagonists who seek "objective" verification of their consciousness. For example, Zeno, in **"Il Vecchione,"** is troubled by his frequent flights of imagination and looks for a mirror to localize himself: "In certi instanti impensati mi pare essa ritorni, e debbo correre allo specchio per mettermi a posto nel tempo. Guardo allora quei tratti deformati sotto il mio mento da una pelle troppo abbondante per ritornare al posto ch' è il mio." The irony of the mirror is that Zeno is merely reflecting his own subjective self back upon himself. He is using himself to verify the very existence he has created through his writings. As Zeno will later say in **"La Confessioni del vegliardo,"** "la vita sarà letteraturizzata." Life itself will become this consciousness of space transformed into writing. Svevo creates his own spatial order within which characters, who cannot find their time or place in external society, become part of the subjective time and place they have created for themselves. As Camerino has pointed out for us [in "Il concetto d'inettitudine in Svevo e le sue implicazioni mitteleuropee ed ebraiche," *Lettere Italiane,* Vol. 25, April-June, 1973], "la natura immobile è una metafora: il singolo disadattato, oppresso nei ghetti moderni, s'illude di poter evadere in qualche modo. L'individuo incapace, rifiuta la sforzo e ricerca il mito." This Svevian individual also goes further and re-constructs another myth as a substitute for the external dimensions of time and place, within which he could find no position. In writing, however, the Svevian protagonist finds a personal myth which is very different from life itself. Biasin has underscored the creativity of this myth of writing: "The words that are 'made up of letters' in space and time, the 'graphic signs,' the written words opposed to the spoken ones—all point to the difference, and *différance,* between literature and life" ["Zeno's Last Bomb," *Modern Fiction Studies,* Vol. 18, Spring, 1972]. This *différance* was conceived by Jacques Derrida to portray the *active* sense in which literature must create its own system apart from any other world that might exist. Even more than Montale's portrayal of Svevo as "the poet of our bourgeoisie—a judging and destructive poet" [*Lettere con gli scritti di Montale su Svevo,* 1966], Svevo's own short fiction attests to his creative poetic. Time and space are re-presented as functions of Svevian protagonists who posit language as an alternate order to the commonly accepted localizations of linear time and three-dimensional place.

This hypothesis about Svevo's alternate order of language is interesting since he has often been accused of writing ". . . sentences of extraordinary clumsiness, a sort of laboriousness and roundaboutness which reveals not so much carelessness as a genuine incapacity for handling syntax" [Furbank]. However, Furbank's rather negative presentation of Svevo's innovative syntax should be contrasted with Maier's view of Svevo the poet: "Poiché Italo Svevo, se non è stato un grammatico *emunctae naris* e un corretto manipolatore della sintassi, ha saputo essere qualcosa di piú: un artista autentico e, diciamo pure, in tutta l'estensione e nell'antico significato creativo del vocabolo, un 'poeta'" [*La Personalità e l'opera di Italo Svevo,* 1961]. Perhaps these negative and positive views of Svevo's style are inherent in the work of an avant-garde, "pure artist" who seeks to go beyond the esthetic of his day. Biasin tells us [in "Literary Diseases: From Pathology to Ontology," *Modern Language Notes,* Vol. 82, (January, 1967)] that the disease imagery which pervades Svevo's fiction appears to be a "gnomic category applicable to the individual and society, to the self and the world. . . ." And indeed this "gnomic category" of disease may be Svevo's awareness that writers of the early twentieth century were too occupied with a polished literary style whereby words entailed epistemological certainty. This "disease" may be his way of portraying the unfitness of society for the individual. Hence, a new order must be created wherein the individual with his consciousness may exist to experiment with all his creativity. This order, which would later become the obsession of the phenomenological school, is that aspect of language which deals with the interplay of consciousness and the unconscious.

If artistic language—as Svevo portrays it through his protagonists—is an interplay of consciousness and the unconscious, one may well wonder whether order is possible at all. Are we merely observing the negation of time and place? It seems that Svevo's protagonists are similar to Zeno (and perhaps to Svevo himself as the avant-garde writer) in that he receives energy from his process of denial. Mark Meyer observes this will in Zeno: "No longer does Zeno appear an incredulous, bemused observer, but as an almost impatient participant in an ordering process which finally can accommodate, confirm, and extend, by negating, that order" ["Zeno: His Fictions and His Problems," *Sub-Stance,* Vol. 1, Spring, 1972]. This energy had caused Zeno to set up his own subjective order with his dictionary-styled memoirs in *La Coscienza di Zeno* and with his dated confessions extending to **"Le confessioni del vegliardo."** These collections reflect unconscious needs to escape personal habit and to create a new spatial order which transcends man's tendency toward stifling habit: "M'abituo con fatica ad essere come sono oggi, e domani ho da sottopormi alla stessa fatica per rimettermi nel sedile che s'è fatto piú incomodo ancora" (**"Il Vecchione"**). Collecting his personal facts into a language which is inherently ordered rather than externally disciplined by habit, the Svevian writers, such as Zeno and Mario, exemplify the insight that "of course, writing entails order" [Albert N. Mancini, review of the Johnson-and-Furbank translation of *Further Confessions of Zeno,* by Italo Svevo, *Studies in Short Fiction,* Vol. 8, Summer, 1971]. But the Svevian order of writing is the *immanent* organization of language which implies new roles for the acts of reading and writing.

> **Svevo creates his own spatial order within which characters, who cannot find their time or place in external society, become part of the subjective time and place they have created for themselves**.
>
> —*Roland A. Champagne*

As a result of the immanent organization of language, reading becomes a manner of deciphering the spatial order of words. Mario, in **"Una Burla Riuscita,"** speaks of the role of the modern reader who must combine the images rather than the words of a particular text: "Degli scrittori il lettore frettoloso non mormora neppure la parola e passa

a segno come un viandante in ritardo su una via piana." And such a reading must be a *critical* combination of these images because a writer might very well be another Gaia who considers his art to be a practical joke, an esthetic game of one-upsmanship: "È infatti un artista il burlone, una specie di caricaturista il cui lavoro non è agevolato dal fatto ch'egli non ha da lavorare, ma da inventare e mentire in modo che il burlato si faccia la caricatura da sé" (**"Una Burla Riuscita."**) Hence, Svevo's short fiction calls upon the reader to question his previous methods of reading to see if they are still applicable in confronting Svevian writing.

Svevian writing at times seems to be a remedy for the "gnomic disease" referred to by Biasin. As the Svevian protagonist becomes aware of his own innate propensity for failure within society, he creates a subjective adjustment by internalizing and then transforming time and place into various spatial dimensions. There is an implied commentary on the ambivalent nature of Svevo's own writing in these various subjective internalizations. As an avant-garde writer, unappreciated by his own age because of his variations from the accepted esthetics, Svevo implements a writing which is a *pharmakon,* that is, a remedy and a poison for the human situation. On the one hand, many Svevian protagonists, in his major novels as well as in his short fiction, feel the need to write in order to systematize and regulate the disorder of their social lives. Hence, writing has a personally redemptive feature in its creative exploration of the human spirit and in its organization of new spatial dimensions. On the other hand, writing, as in Curra's search for his origins in **"La Madre,"** will also entail the discovery of the painful realization that it is doomed to failure and incompleteness. In the fable **"Un Artista,"** the Creator explains to the artist the nature of his artistic soul: "L'anima che ora ritorna a me, è quella di un artista ma dimenticasti di portare con te il tuo organismo perché veda perché la tua anima ne fu suffocata." Hence, the artist must necessarily seek his origins in order to complete the cycle which constitutes his very nature. However, the ultimate irony directed against the creative writer is that he is doomed to failure because such ideas as education, progress, completeness, localization, and even succession are seriously questioned by Svevo's very style. Once again, we realize that "l'ironia è ancora uno strumento-chiave della narrativa del triestino" [Albert N. Mancini, "Svevo e la recente critica anglo-americana," *Forum Italicum,* Vol. 4, December, 1970]. As readers of Svevo's short fiction, we must especially suspend our belief in life in order fully to appreciate the binary movement of writing as *pharmakon.* And suddenly we realize that our own lives have been written into that literary displacement.

Naomi Lebowitz (essay date 1978)

SOURCE: "The Fiction's Climb," in *Italo Svevo,* Rutgers University Press, 1978, pp. 154-63.

[*In the following excerpt, Lebowitz argues that Svevo's later fiction evolves into a more traditional and less dramatic form.*]

It has often been noted that the more traditional narrative modes of Svevo's shorter pieces, in relation to *Confessions of Zeno*, entail a loss of intimacy between the author and the hero. This is misleading, for there is a compensating intimacy between the favorite meditations of Svevo and the reflections of the last stories uninhibited by distracting fictional mediation. The conventional journey structure of **"Short Sentimental Journey,"** a picaresque of the vacationing mind, does not lead the hero, a likable and sensitive, but by no means extraordinary man, farther from Svevo's atmosphere than Zeno. It is only because his reflections, modest though they be, bring us so comfortably close to Svevo's mind that Signor Aghios does not destroy the new intimacy with displays of personal idiosyncrasy or calls for attention. The evolution of Svevo's fiction into a less dramatic, more casual, and static form cannot be called regressive, for it takes a kind of aesthetic confidence and security to sacrifice the seductive world of chronologically plotted anecdote and captivating personality to an unprotected reflection, dependent only upon its own quality and pace for its charm and persuasion. Some have ascribed the relaxation of narrative tension in the last Svevo, the "rassernamento dello stile" [Leone de Castris, *Decadentismo e realismo*, 1958], to the fulfillment of his latent ambition. Success brought to Svevo a diminution of the conscious struggle with technical difficulties and moral disquietude. Svevo himself, though irritated with the delays in translations and publications, admitted to Valéry Larbaud in 1926: "I am much more serene now because I have now had all I yearned for." The disappearance of contrapuntal modes of syntax seems to at least one critic a symptom of a new confidence that expresses itself in the linear and fragmented rhythms of the diary. The self-consciousness about his language, revived with his revision of *As a Man Grows Older,* is humored by the vision of Italian critics delighted to find badly written novels, and helped by a growing conviction on the part of the young critics that Svevo's language was necessary to express the Svevian consciousness. The recognition that there was a developing public acceptance, even in Italy, perhaps allowed him to assert more forcefully a vision less and less guarded by a rationalizing personality coming to terms with social acceptance. In addition, this natural development was complemented by a general atmosphere of narrative looseness and poetic structure, sensitive to the language of the mind. It was at this time too that Svevo, already very familiar with Joyce, was reading Kafka, in whose stories compulsions and dreams live autonomous lives.

But the most convincing explanation for the change is simply the fact that life is being viewed from the sixty-year-old mind, which lives without a future and in a present that draws freely from analogies with the past, rendering all experience simultaneous. Signor Aghios knows "from his personal experience of sixty years, that when one is born made in a particular way one stays like it," and Svevo himself attempts to cheer Valerio Jahier with the recognition that the intimate self never changes, nor is it cured. In the mind of old Zeno, characters assume the timelessness of states of being:

> Seventy years seem a lot when you look at them from the bottom up. Looking at them from top to bottom, they seem like nothing. . . . My father goes with me always.

Once more, in **"Short Sentimental Journey,"** Svevo chooses a hero who looks at life from the top down, imagining the impossibility of a vacation from bourgeois forms that prosaically mock the dreamed-of unity of desire and duty. Following upon the fine delineation of Signor Aghios's anxious irritability at the last goodbyes of his wife, the delusive embrace of an anaesthetic freedom, the movement from familial concern with the future of a son toward the carefree expansive flow of psychological time that is the luxury of the older man, the dreaming toward death in a railway compartment "crossing a countryside of which it was not a part," all this appears to move the story into the symbolic climate of a long line of literary sentimental journeys. But the title, like **"Generous Wine,"** with its comic reminder of limitation, snaps on the dream the typical Svevian domestic leash that guarantees to lead our animals back home. And, indeed, Svevo uses this very image to describe Aghios's failure to travel without the protection of cheating the world with words "being unused to so much liberty, like dogs kept on a chain, who tear up the gardens the moment they are set loose," The poignant recognition in *Diario per la fidanzata* of a desire for perfect intimacy and the necessity to settle for less, is fully developed and examined in the leisurely atmosphere of Signor Aghios's journey. The lyric journey to freedom, intimacy, sincerity, and kindness in a world of strangers carries its own peculiar comedy, and Signor Aghios often seems like a naughty boy running away from home in the hope of finding parents better than the ones he has and loves. His Venice will not be that of Von Aschenbach.

We are a long way too from the adolescent train ride of Alfonso that leads to a sterile suicide. The solution of suicide, as the gondolier Bortolo is fond of saying, belongs to the young: "'Ever since the world began, you young chaps have shot yourself once a day.'" In the mind of a sixty-year-old man, death has become a condition of life. Yet there is decidedly a suggestion that the older man is looking for a second childhood away from the intimidating, and sophisticated young who force him offstage. The designation of "poet" to Signor Aghios by his fellow passenger, the stolid insurance investigator Borlini, is a vacation tag worn around the neck in infantile delight as a badge of provisional parental release: "Would he have felt more vigorous in the great world, away from his household?" he wonders, and the great world grows smaller and smaller. Signor Aghios seizes upon the young generation's criticism, embodied in his son, and the old wife's devotion to her child as civilized pretexts for walking off stage to indulge his dreams: "He banished from his mind these phantoms of his wife and son." But the shadow of the bourgeois household is cast upon the entire voyage, which is constantly colored by its origin of escape rather than spiritual boldness. The controlling conscience and chronology of bourgeois morality appear only to have taken a holiday. Aghios's own conscience is eased by the recognition, ruefully and mischievously noted in Svevo's letters to Livia, that "the farther I travel from her the more I love her." With this sanction, Signor Aghios finds himself "in accord with both human and divine law, for he loved his wife sincerely." Civilization's super-ego is quieted by his debates "with that vague being who must be somewhere, perhaps in the ether (which is supposed to be everywhere) and who superintends moral law." concerning the conmandment not to covet his neighbors' wives. The first dream of release is launched, which allows "compartment theory" to smooth the tension between social conscience and desire. A civilized child, he sees himself as a classic Freudian victim of society and its discontents:

> He judged himself to be a man who desired many things which were forbidden him and which—since they were forbidden—he forbade himself, though he allowed his desire for them to continue.

Later in the journey he is captivated by a phrase used by the young thief Bacis, who refers to his passion for the girl Anna, whom he then betrays, as "the sincerity of flesh." The oxymoron opens that gap between conscience and desire, the space of mixed time, which is that of evolved man:

> The sincerity of the flesh was the sincerity of animals, but even among animals it only lasted for a flash and did not represent a commitment. Bacis, however, had tarnished this sincerity of his, because in the very moment of sincerity he had thought of playacting. Even his sincerity had only helped him to betray.

Aghios reproaches his companion with this reminder:

> "You call me a philosopher and, in the same breath, invent such a terrifying concept as that: the sincerity of flesh being contradicted by the falseness of another part of the body—flesh as well, but *evolved* flesh."

The story of Anna's seduction, most likely fictional, is already the story of the whole dead planet earth, never free from the parasites of division and destruction envisaged by Zeno. Crossing the Venetian lagoon in a gondola, Signor Aghios reflects:

> A few days before, he had read in a newspaper that it is now believed that when Earth became habitable, it was infected by some accident with life from another planet. From then on, everything followed naturally: the little animals, once here, began making love and betraying, and they invaded everything, the land and the sea, evolving, and continuing to love and betray, from stage to stage of evolution.

The bourgeois Hebraic moralism that forbids coveting the neighbor's wife has relaxed its hold as it passes through biology to psychology. Earlier in the story, upon over-

hearing the psychiatric cliché from a sophisticated youth resembling his "superior" son, that the first wounds of infancy are the most persistent and important blows to psychic health, Signor Aghios reacts in anger to a complacent theory that gives priority to the young. His leisurely sense of temporal simultaneity has been violated and he is reminded of his son's future:

> On the threshold of sixty didn't he suffer from every injury ever done him by others and from every self-doubting of his own? Flesh, composed largely of liquid, was never very resistant, and ignorance went hand in hand with it to our last breath, persuading us to attach importance to all the things that have none really, making them a burden and an encumbrance to us, and a source of distress and disease.

That flesh that wants merely to love is betrayed by psychological, social, and biological distortions of intimacy. In a wonderfully comic touch, Signor Aghios watches the young man step down from the train and disappear into the station building: "the gateway to a hamlet where the great science of psychoanalysis was arriving." Until the end, Svevo refuses to the dreams of perfect intimacy, sincerity, and kindness both romantic fulfillment and tragic collapse.

Once more, in "Short Sentimental Journey," Svevo chooses a hero who looks at life from the top down, imagining the impossibility of a vacation from bourgeois forms that prosaically mock the dreamed-of unity of desire and duty.

—*Naomi Lebowitz*

Early in the story, in a vivid scene, Signor Aghios looks at his own face in the glass of a framed photograph as he sits opposite his first acquaintance, the insurance investigator. Depressed by the strangeness of the face, he nevertheless thrills to the recognition of "the one intimate relationship existing in the whole of nature." The intimacy and honesty of the identify is counterpointed by the necessity for social lies between the two men:

> One only has to address a single word to a fellow-being and one risks telling a falsehood. Truth exists only among people who do not know each other.

The little falsehood that social kindness dictated now is rewarded by a return of kindness, which leads Aghios back temporarily from the pure contemplation of self to "the human consortium" and the acceptance of the social lie. But the dream of love persists in its antisocial tendencies:

> He couldn't exactly say he loved some*one,* but he loved, intensely, life itself—men, animals and plants—all

anonymous things, which was what made them so lovable.

Such comforting distance, unfortunately, is periodically destroyed by the existence of a beautiful woman. Indeed, had it not been that among mankind there were also beautiful women, he would have been able to await death with the serenity of a saint (the name Aghios means saint in Greek). Signor Aghios is released from a discussion on prices with the stranger by a pastoral remembrance of a day of natural happiness, "the most perfect of human intimacies." The details of the relationship between Aghios and his companion, a painter, riding in horse and buggy across the Friulian countryside, are dissolved in sunny contentment. But the painter (modeled, like Balli, on Svevo's real friend Veruda) had died and "recollection . . . is not truly a form of action" since both the "rememberer and the remembered are immobilized." They cannot stay in a world that pushes on. This dream of intimacy is harshly countered by the "intimacy of sorts" with the insurance investigator, Borlini.

And it is jolted too by two disappointed children. One, a little girl, desiring to see herself, the countryside, and the train all in one image in the train's window is surrounded by mocking laughter by an insensitive world of businessmen and parents. Aghios is touched at the child's first intimation of the cruel sundering of the original unity that prevents life from seeing itself and acting at the same time:

> Only he felt and knew what sorrow there was in not being able to see oneself while travelling. . . . To see the landscape, the train and oneself at the same time— that really would have been travelling!

The patronization of such expectation by an insensitive world of adults is continued by Borlini's stories of his younger son's dreamy nature that would seem to incapacitate him for life. "Poor Paolucci was most unlucky," thinks Aghios, "having been born into the wrong family." With the "sentimentalism of the leisurely traveller," identification with the pain of these early victims, "boundless affection for all the weak and defenseless" dreamers in a world of social and industrial insurance investigators, Aghios once again resorts to the visions that "beautify or blur" the world:

> Far off in the distance, at the foot of a mountain, one could glimpse the lights of a village. A steady, tranquil light. But for that matter, distant light is always steady and tranquil. The wind may blow, but if it does not blow it out the light remains like starlight: it shines with the tranquillity of a colour (if any colour were ever as bright). For the villagers itself, it might be blowing a hurricane; but distance is peace.

The relationship with Borlini degenerates into one as tiresome as that he left behind. "Slavery," realizes Signor Aghios, "was not only a fate, it was a habit." And as a habit, the bourgeois burdens of responsibility are desired as well as resisted. The family at this point seems infinitely preferable to Signor Borlini.

Liberated from his companion at Padua, Signor Aghios imposes his prison image upon a couple working in the fields, viewed swiftly from the window. The "sincerity of the flesh" is once again betrayed:

> They had formed an association, sexual in origin, which would degenerate into one of material interests, encompassing the field they worked in and the cottage . . . where they slept. What a colossal trick! Drawn by pleasure together, ensnared by their own natural warmth, they were loaded with chains without noticing it.

But just as quickly, in the alternation between dream and waking that dominates the rhythm of the story, he takes pride in his racial distinction in Italy (like Bloom's in Dublin):

> It's convenient . . . belonging to another race. It's as if one were perpetually on one's travels. One's thoughts are freer. And it's the same with the way one looks at things. I don't approve of the Italian way of seeing things, but neither do I approve of the Greek way.

Obviously, the sense of Triestine citizenship which, because of its estrangement from Italy, Svevo felt so keenly as both an advantage and disadvantage, is projected upon his character. But what is important here is that such a sentimental rationalization leads him into another trap of intimacy, another dream become a prison. The young Bacis calls himself a displaced traveler too, doomed as well to dialect despite some linguistic education. Once again, overwhelmed with a desire to give and receive kindness, Aghios befriends the treacherous Bacis and shows him Venice in his "barque of benevolence." But soon he marvels "how prolonged companionship even with one man was enough to deprive him of the great freedom of travel," a freedom felt only by its alternations, it appears, with slavery: "Could there be a worse slavery than having to talk of things one knew nothing about?" In a planetary fantasy on the train entering Gorizia, Aghios extends his journey to Mars, where boundless luminous space gives no resistance to his desire for freedom: "To feel it, he needed to be able to boast of it." No dream is free of the need for rhetorical witness. In an amusing reminiscence of the dreams of Svevo's nice old man, Aghios blends paternalism, "kind and virtuous," with sensual desire, as he protects the body of Anna, Bacis's willing victim of seduction, by lying on top of her. In such a dream "their posture together would last for all eternity." This is the final taunt to dreams of intimacy, which must be dressed in psychic disguises. Upon awakening, Aghios experiences the human condition, a fatal mixture of shame and joy. The stealing of his money is almost an anticlimax in this level journey of alternations between the sentimentality of freedom and the cynicism of slavery, and this impression is aided by the suggestion that Aghios's subliminal shame over his stinginess had set him up to almost will the robbery. This is also Mother Nature's way of climaxing innocent dreams of freedom, intimacy, sincerity, and benevolence. What she gives to Mario, who doesn't want it, she takes from Aghios. The cleverest of all Mother Nature's plans to prevent the saint's abstractions from dominating reality is to place in the heart of man the compulsion to be a man, half slave and half free.

The thinning of personality gives a compensatory fluidity and casualness to the sixty-year-old reflection in these last stories; we lose the delightful surprises of Zeno's improvisations born of the spontaneous debate between coveting and prohibition. It is almost as if the fictional energy that goes into creating and keeping a consistent personality on the scene had slackened, allowing the association of an older and sensitive mind, one susceptible to general motions that entail the death of personality and literary disguise, a last yearning for freedom, sweeping benevolence, and the idea of intimacy, like pictures flashing by the train window, to spread across the scene. The old irritabilities remain, and the old affections, but in attenuated form. The reflexes of reaction are slower and the mind slides off the particular, like the two children—one imagined, one seen—whose faces immediately give way to sensations of victimization. Even the Venetian tour dissolves in the general movement toward death. But the Svevian humor is still busy setting up Mother Nature's contradictions through the fluctuations of images and feelings they evoke. There is still in the Svevian world no soul large enough to be independent of the disease of being human, and fantasy is checked by its own parasitic needs to live within a social frame. There is a strong suggestion that, with a finished manuscript, the journey away from the family would have become a journey toward it. The illusions fostered by the ageless traces of "senilità" assume a naturalness here, rather than a desperate defensiveness, because the mind is not old chronologically and, unlike the mind of Mario Samigli, domestically experienced. It carries with it, for each encounter, a hundred analogies from marriage that soften experience with generalization. That the state of reflection is never given the comfort of complacency is the sign of the Svevian temperament that has aged and tired but not grown old.

Beno Weiss (essay date 1987)

SOURCE: "Short Stories," in *Italo Svevo,* Twayne Publishers, 1987, pp. 122-33.

[*In the following excerpt, Weiss explores Svevo's short fiction and finds a growing propensity toward literary experimentation.*]

It was not until 1888, that the fledgling author [Svevo] made his first appearance as a writer of fiction on the pages of *L'Indipendente,* which serialized his short story **"Una lotta"** (**"A contest"**). His "minor" narrative writings are a potpourri of mainly undated short stories and tales of different lengths, some fragmentary and others sketches of future works never brought to completion. Only seven were ever finished: **"Una botta," "L'assassinio di Via Belpoggio," "La tribù," "La madre," "Una burla riuscita," "La novella del buon vecchio e della bella fanciulla,"** and **"Vino generoso."** An eighth, **"Lo specifico del dottor Menghi,"** appears to be complete, except for a fragment missing on the first page. This narra-

tive production—in addition to his plays—belies Svevo's claim of having given up literature after the critical failure of *Senilità* and until the beginning of World War I. What is clear is that, though he may not have submitted many of his creative writings for publication, he continued to practice his craft and to experiment with new narrative forms and techniques.

Published Writings and Finished Works

"Una lotta" seems to be a parody of chivalric romance. The hero, Arturo Marchetti, is a frail, neurotic, but witty poet and theorizer, who at the age of thirty-five feels his youth is slipping away; he regards Rosina as his Dulcinea, and tries like Don Quixote to affirm his heroic spirit. His bravura in threatening his physically more powerful rival, Ariodante Chigi—a handsome, vigorous but inarticulate athlete—and the inevitable deflating result, reveal him to be a true prototype of Svevo's antiheroic characters. The story, written contemporaneously with *Una vita,* anticipates certain basic motifs and characters that Svevo will develop more fully in his novels: the dreamer, the theorizer, the individual whose propensity to think and reflect renders him unprepared for life. Indeed, Arturo resembles Emilio Brentani—both suffer from precocious "senility," both are full of unfulfilled desires. Finally, the contest between Arturo and Ariodante presages those between Alfonso and Macario, Emilio and Stefano, Zeno and Guido. The structure, the language, the intermingling of direct and indirect discourse, but above all the ironic contrast between the rivals whose characterizations are deftly achieved, all reveal Svevo's growing mastery.

Svevo's second short story is far more serious and complicated. Written in 1890 and serialized once again in *L'Indipendente,* **"L'assassinio di Via Belpoggio"** (**"Murder on Belpoggio Street"**) is clearly reminiscent of Dostoyevski's *Crime and Punishment*: an impoverished streetporter, Giorgio, kills Antonio, a casual drinking companion, and robs him of a substantial sum of money in a dark street of Trieste. Like Raskolnikov, Giorgio feels superior to his fellows and has absolutely no remorse for what he has done. Indeed, he sees himself as the wronged party: it was all the fault of Antonio who ought not have shown him the money. The murderer quickly becomes entangled in an intricate snare of motives, conscience, and fears. His true punishment is psychological; the torment of isolation from others makes him abominable to himself until he is arrested and confesses to the murder.

Giorgio is an *inetto,* at odds with both social classes, the middle class that has rejected him as an outcast, and the subproletariat that refuses to accept him. In the brutal attack on Antonio, Giorgio's monotonous and squalid life suddenly becomes dramatic. Like the servant in *Inferiorità* who kills his master, Giorgio frees himself momentarily from his sense of inferiority. The euphoria, however, is fleeting and he falls back immediately into his inherent inadequacy.

In **"L'assassinio di Via Belpoggio"** Svevo produced something more than a successful thriller. The style is simple, direct, fresh, and vigorous; the somber tone is very persuasive; and the picture of Trieste's low life is vivid and convincing. The story already reveals the mastery of psychological observation and analysis for which Svevo will eventually be esteemed.

In 1897 Svevo wrote **"La tribù" ("The Tribe")** his only political narrative. It appeared in *Critica sociale,* the prominent socialist magazine published by Filippo Turati (1857-1932), one of the founders of the Italian Socialist Party in 1892.

Svevo propounds a philosophy of sense and moderation, and his veiled message is that the functioning of any society, even a primitive and classless one, requires ideals and moral standards.

—*Beno Weiss*

The narrative, signed Italo Svevo, deals with a nomadic tribe that settles in a fertile region of the desert. The tribal tents and neat little houses soon disappear, giving way to rich mansions on the one hand and squalid hovels on the other. The tribal leader, Hussein, asks young Ahmed to help the tribe out of its predicament, but Ahmed, who has studied European economic systems, can only suggest the ways of capitalism: first factories, then exploitation, and finally equality. Hussein finds this process too long and tells the tribe that they should skip the first two phases and start with the last. Ahmed, who insists on building a factory, is expelled from the tribe, and the tribesmen thus reach a state of happiness.

Although Svevo's solution to the capitalistic system seems vague, a fabulous and ephemeral resolution to the problem, and although one may view the tale as a parody of Marxist dialectical materialism, or, as Mario Fusco suggests, "an unexpected and humorous hypothesis of Marxist doctrine," **"La tribù"** does reflect Svevo's commonsense view of morality and utopian socialism, and clearly points out the incompatibility between progress and happiness. Hussein and his people succeed in a classless society by avoiding the internecine evolutionary class struggle between capitalists and oppressed proletariat. Svevo propounds a philosophy of sense and moderation, and his veiled message is that the functioning of any society, even a primitive and classless one, requires ideals and moral standards.

"La tribù," more charming than persuasive, is memorable for Svevo's laconic wit and the irony of the political allegory.

Composing fables was one of Svevo's lifelong habits. They are central to many of his stories and particularly to his third novel, and Svevo frequently experimented with the form.

"La madre" ("The Mother") concerns several chicks hatched in an incubator who suffer because they do not have a real and nurturing mother, unlike a nearby brood with a mother hen that watches over them with great care.

First written in 1910 and revised for publication in 1927, **"La madre"** deals in allegorical form with Svevo's exclusion from the Italian literary establishment. The garden with the hen and its homogeneous population of animals represents Italy; while the one with the incubator, populated by chicks of various colors and shapes, is an obvious reference to the city of Trieste at the crossroads of *Mitteleuropa,* the melting pot of various religions and nationalities. The mother, "who was said to be able to give every delight and therefore satisfy ambition and vanity," stands for the Italian establishment, which, until the very last phase of Svevo's career, refused to acknowledge his artistic merits. Indeed, even after the so-called discovery of Svevo by the French literati and Montale, he ran into all sorts of difficulties in trying to have the second edition of *Senilità* published. Furthermore, his writings were attacked by critics like Guido Piovene, who, in a vitriolic review of *Senilità,* wrote: "What is Svevo's merit? Of having come close, more than any other Italian, to that passively analytic literature, which found its apogee in Proust; but it is inferior art, if art is meant to be a product of living and active men. . . ." And finally, the ostracism of the chick Curra reflects not only Svevo's exclusion from the strongholds of Italian culture and learning, but also his position as a Jew without a "true" sense of belonging and acceptance, particularly during the rise of fascism.

"Una burla riuscita" ("The Hoax"), completed in 1926, is a long narrative divided into eight segments; it takes place in Trieste during the last days of World War I. Mario Samigli is an unassuming but devoted office clerk who in his youth published an unappreciated novel entitled *Giovinezza (Youth)*. Forty-three years later he has still not gotten over his neglect by the critics. Though he no longer writes for publication, he secretly composes fables whose protagonists are sparrows. Gaia, a former poet who has become a successful traveling salesman, is envious of Mario's faithful commitment to literature. He decides to play a hoax on his friend, leading him to believe that an important Viennese publishing house is interested in buying the rights to his novel. Mario naively falls for the ploy and signs an attractive contract with one of Gaia's accomplices. When eventually he finds out the truth, he confronts Gaia and gives him a sound thrashing. Though the author's ego is deeply wounded, financially the hoax turns out to be rather profitable for him. A speculation performed with nonexistent funds, together with the confusion resulting from the entrance of the Italian Army into Trieste and the collapse of the Austrian currency, give the author a handsome profit of seventy thousand lire.

Aside from the obvious similarities with Svevo's own literary experiences—Lavagetto calls it "a parable of his own existence"—**"Una burla riuscita"** is extremely important in that it offers an insight into Svevo's self-image as an author right after the initially unsuccessful publication of *La coscienza di Zeno*. Like his namesake and creator, the character Samigli derives relief from the psychic pain of his existence by writing fables. Thus, literature takes on a double valence: protection and shield against the world, and escape and potential cure for his frustrations. In essence, fables are symbolic expressions of wish fulfillment akin to dreams, in which the author finds cathartic release from the tensions and anxieties produced by repressed emotions. Indeed, as the narrator says, Gaia's practical joke remains "powerless against his dreams." The story also offers a psychological study of the motives behind practical joking. Svevo echoes Freud when he explains that Gaia's love for practical joking "was a relic of his suppressed artistic tendencies"; and that he resented Mario because he had remained faithful to his art and become a "silent witness against him" for having given up and repressed his own poetry.

"La novella del buon vecchio e della bella fanciulla" ("The Story of the Nice Old Man and the Pretty Girl"), written in 1926, deals with the last love affair of an old man who is clearly the aged successor of Zeno.

During the war in Trieste, while the guns are rumbling in the distance, a rich elderly gentleman meets a young and beautiful girl who quickly becomes his paid mistress. The affair does not last very long because he suddenly falls ill, stricken with angina—no doubt precipitated by the romance—that limits all his activities. One day, as he looks out of his window, he sees her in the company of an attractive young man. Both jealous and guilty for having taken advantage of his wealth to seduce her, he sets out to reform her and write a thesis on the relations between the aged and the young, between health and disease. The girl's reeducation becomes a mere pretext for a profound and desperate examination of his own existence. The narrative ends with the old man's realization that his physical strength is insufficient to bring his thesis to completion. He wraps the pages of his manuscript in a sheet of paper on which, as a final reply to his quest, he writes several times: *Nothing*. The next day he is found dead amidst his writings, with a pen in his mouth.

The story, written in the third person with nameless protagonists, reminds us of Zeno's affair with Carla, and his attempts to appease his guilt feelings. Though similar, the two adventures differ considerably—in this narrative Svevo is merciless toward both the cynical "good" old man and the compliant, mischievous young girl. Both are willing and ready to corrupt and be corrupted by money. Love, as in *La rigenerazione,"* is seen as a cure for old age and as an escape from degrading physical and emotional conditions. Ironically, however, the cure proves to be fatal for "our old man."

Like most of the short stories written during Svevo's Zeno period, **"Vino generoso" ("Generous Wine")**, begun in 1914 and revised in 1926, is full of psychological insights and probings on the themes of disease and old age. A sickly old man narrates the story of his niece's wedding. The doctor has given him permission to break his diet and take part in the festivities like everyone less. Taking advantage of this precious and singular opportunity, the old man eats and drinks to excess not because of thirst and hunger, but "from a craving for liberty" from the pills, drops, and powders that have become part of his life. That night he has a nightmare in which all the members of the wedding party call for his death; he, however, offers his daughter's life in exchange for his own. Once awake, he blames the wine, and in order to avoid the recurrence of such a dream, decides to follow the doctor's orders and go back to his diet.

The "generous wine" of the title suggests the opening of doors leading to the subconscious. As the old man becomes more absorbed in analyzing his inner self, guilt and remorse come to the surface. He regrets, in particular, having married the wrong woman and having given up his socialist ideals. The dream clearly shows the late Svevo's familiarity with Franz Kafka's (1883-1924) work. The narrator is caught in a nightmarish tangle of guilt feelings and remorse. His lucid mind, notwithstanding the effects of the wine, finds itself confronting an incomprehensible state of existence. The simplest human conviction—that one deserves respect, affection, and good health, that one has a place in the world—has no basis in his world of altered reality.

"Lo specifico del dottor Menghi" ("The specific of Dr. Menghi"), one of Svevo's few contributions to science fiction, also concerns itself with the influence of Darwinism. The narrative, written in pseudoscientific and philosophical language, deals with the experiments of Dr. Menghi who, on his deathbed, asks his colleague Dr. Galli to read to the Medical Society a paper dealing with a special serum he has discovered. What follows is the reading in the first person of Dr. Menghi's paper.

The story, written most likely in 1904, contains in a nutshell many of Svevo's favorite themes: the elusiveness of health and the ever-lurking presence of disease, the *senectus* theme and its corresponding debilitating and degenerative effects, the death of a loved one and the ambiguous relationship between son and parent, a skeptical and ironic treatment of doctors and their magical cures. The precarious energy that fascinates Dr. Menghi and constitutes life, and the delicate physiological balance in terms of chemical, physical, and functional processes, maintained by a complex of mechanisms, is what Svevo seems to be searching for both literally and figuratively. Dr. Menghi's specifics, with their potential effect on this vital balance, are very much like the two opposite poles of the Basedowian lifeline that mesmerizes Zeno, namely, the symptomatic characteristics of Graves' disease: hypoactivity and hyperactivity. The story is also significant because it reveals Svevo's attitude toward science, and especially toward those scientists who undertake experimentation without regard for its potentially evil results. "You thought you were helping people," says the doctor's mother, "but instead your invention is nothing but a new scourge." This ominous accusation will be realized, of course, in the momentous ending of *La coscienza di Zeno*. The scientist or individual, although essentially good and well meaning, is tempted by his desire for knowledge to experiment self-ishly with life and to end up in a hell of his own making—a very timely theme indeed. Svevo remains faithful to Darwin's law of evolution and "rejects any initiative that might risk modifying the natural equilibrium of the existing forces in nature, however imperfect or unjust the equilibrium might be."

Fragments and Sketches

The sheer volume of unfinished works in Svevo's canon indicates the great difficulty he experienced in bringing his ideas to fruition. Many of these fragments abound in autobiographical data relevant to Svevo's hesitancy and ambivalence about writing, as well as to his ongoing concern with the shifting functions of reality, memory, and death. The fragment **"Incontro di vecchi amici"** (**"Old friends meet"**; ca. 1912) deals with an unsuccessful writer of unfinished stories. Roberto, like Svevo, compensates for his lack of success by becoming a businessman. The character Roberto reappears as an old man in two other unfinished stories, **"L'avvenire dei ricordi"** (**"Along memory lane"**; 1923) and **"La morte"** (**"Death"**; 1925), in which the narrator's reminiscences act as a repetition and re-creation of the past, thus slowing the approach of death. Svevo's constant focus on memory and death is also apparent in **"Proditoriamente"** (**"Traitorously"**; 1923), a drab meandering narrative—that proffers the philosophical message that death is always looming, insidiously awaiting its next victim.

Svevo also explored various theories about the nature of humankind, ranging from the tenets of natural science to the influence of superstition and psychoanalysis. **"La buonissima madre"** (**"The Very Good Mother"**; circa 1919) offers an imaginative reworking of Darwin's theory of natural selection, and echoes Svevo's suspicion—openly stated in his 1907 article **"L'uomo e la teoria darwiniana"** (**"Man and the Darwinian Theory"**)—that man has not, in fact, evolved. In **"Il malocchio"** (**"The Evil Eye"**; circa 1917), Svevo utilizes both superstition and psychoanalytic theory to depict the irrationality and absurdity of human existence, and also to express his well-founded suspicions of modern technology and scientific achievement.

Like his other works, Svevo's fragments reveal his willingness to experiment with more open narrative structures. **"Orazio Cima"** (ca. 1917) and **"Corto viaggio sentimentale"** (**"Short Sentimental Journey"**; 1925-26) are both shaped and given meaning by the consciousness and psychological attitudes of the narrators. The narrator of **"Orazio"** presents us with a tableau of conflicting values and ideologies, while in the second story the mendacious narrator offers an equally distorted picture of reality. By far the more experimental of the two stories, **"Corto viaggio sentimentale"** has no principal character other than the narrator's consciousness, no plot, and no structure. Written under the influence of James Joyce, it became Svevo's longest, albeit unfinished, short story; he referred to it as "a long, long serpent curled up in [his] desk drawer."

Svevo's Last Works

In preparation for his projected fourth novel Svevo wrote four alternative segments, in addition to the unfinished **"Il vecchione,"** that seem to be related components for a work intended to crown his literary career. According to Gabriella Contini, although these contain similarities with *La coscienza di Zeno,* and although Zeno reappears as the author/protagonist, Svevo meant to write a novel quite distinct and separate from his previous masterpiece. In her controversial book *Il quarto romanzo di Svevo* Contini argues that the projected novel consists of diverse fragmentary segments, some of which are constituent parts (**"Le confessioni del vegliardo," "Umbertino," "Il mio ozio," "Un contratto"**), while others are preparatory (*"Rigenerazione"*, **"L'avvenire dei ricordi"**), lateral (**"Orazio Cima"**), or subsidiary (**"Vino generoso," "La novella del buon vecchio," "Viaggio sentimentale," "Incontro di vecchi amici," "Proditoriamente," "La morte"**). Such a novel, according to Contini, is a work in progress, made up of interlocking segments that are readable and comprehensible only if considered in an intertextual relationship.

Regardless of whether Svevo intended these later works to form a fourth novel, it is clear that an idée fixe marks all of Svevo's works written after *La coscienza di Zeno* and serves to bind the disparate parts together. Svevo's overruling concern with old age and declining health is particularly evident in the "constituent parts" of the narrative, in which he picks up where he left off with his third novel, and in which the already-aged Zeno ages still more.

A man of leisure, cut off from all activity, Zeno turns to the past. Rereading his ten-year-old writings, Zeno realizes that what he had already narrated in *La coscienza* was not the most important part of his life. Surprisingly, he seems to have forgotten his past, except for the part recorded in the novel. Faced, however, with his previous confessions, he can suddenly recall other elements of his past. Thus, he begins to inquire philosophically about the meaning of life and to study his past objectively, as if it belonged to someone else. He asks "And now what am I? Not the one who lived, but the one I described." Zeno is surprised to see how the written word can transform life. He envisions a time when, for therapeutic reasons, everyone will be compelled to write, "life will be literalized. . . . And contemplation will be the main business of the day, shielding us from the horridness of actual living. . . ." This realization prompts Zeno to resume writing his diary, which raises the question of whether at the conclusion of *La coscienza di Zeno,* the protagonist was really cured. In any case, as he resumes writing, we may assume that Zeno's former and present writings must have some beneficial effect for him.

In **"Un contratto"** (**"A Contract"**), with the advent of peace and a bad business deal that wipes out practically all the money made during the war, Zeno realizes that he no longer has the enterprise required for the more competitive peacetime economy. Aware of his incompetence, Zeno knowingly allows himself to be manœuvered into signing a contract making young Olivi a partner of the business, and relinquishing to him virtually all control. Although Zeno regards it finally as a defeat of old age and a victory of youth, he can't help but smile at the socialist administrator who behaves like a typical capitalist, exploiting his employees and cutting their wages.

In **"Le confessioni del vegliardo"** (**"An Old Man's Confessions"**) and **"Umbertino,"** Zeno deals with family relations and attempts to fix on paper the present (with all its gradations) and the recent and distant past. Zeno, who still has virtually all of his classic foibles, tries to come to terms with his children, committing the same disastrous mistakes that marred the relationship with his own father. His docile wife Augusta, completely taken with her menagerie, fails to notice the continuous crises he endures on account of his age. Zeno's only consolations are his young grandson, Umbertino, who distracts him with his innocence and curiosity from the dreary routine of his life, and his nephew, Carlo, the son of Ada and Guido Speier.

In **"Il mio ozio"** (**"This Indolence of Mine"**) Zeno closely analyzes his inertia and discovers that even the present—himself "and the things and people round him"—is made up of various tenses. His "major and interminable present" is his retirement from business and the inertia of his daily life. In this forced indolence he becomes even more preoccupied with the degeneration of his aged body. The companionship of Carlo—very much his father's son—who has his medical degree, stimulates Zeno's curiosity, particularly with the notion that it is the sexual organs and not the heart that sustain our whole organism. According to Zeno, "Mother Nature is a maniac," who maintains life within an organism as long as it is able to reproduce itself. In view of this Zeno sets out to hoodwink Mother Nature by taking a mistress, which for him is equivalent to "going to the chemist's." The cure, however, has a sobering effect when his mistress Felicita, a tobacconist, educates him in his present role as an old man. Zeno, with his unmistakable sense of humor and lack of resolve, decides that it will be his last "fling," and then he adds slyly that he occasionally still keeps "cheating" nature.

With **"Il vecchione"** (**"The Old, Old Man"**), written in 1928 and consisting of only a few pages, we have the beginning of the proposed sequel to *La coscienza di Zeno*. A seventy-year-old Zeno, narrating in the first person, relates how on his way home from an outing he felt compelled to greet a pretty young girl as she passed near his car. When Augusta inquires who she is, Zeno explains that she is the daughter of their friend Dondi. Augusta points out that he is mistaken because Dondi's daughter is older than she, and, therefore, like herself, she too must be an old woman. This encounter triggers in Zeno a myriad of involuntary memories in which time becomes confused as he ponders his life's experiences.

Zeno finds himself constantly frustrated in an absurd and hostile world, in which he is unable to find his proper place. The trivial incident with the pretty girl, like the Proustian madeleine, evokes a rush of memories and the past floods back in its entirety, enabling him to re-create his earlier experiences, but at the same time exposing the

illusory nature of his early ideals. He discovers that the past can be recovered by memory, preserved, and even improved in his writings. As he had done once before for his failed psychoanalysis, he records his observations in great detail and analyzes his responses to them, finally rediscovering his vocation as an author. He resolves to write the book that will permit him to "pull himself together" and "rehabilitate" himself. Writing assumes a hygienic purpose, because in his memoirs time is crystallized and can always be located if one "knows how to open to the right page." By reading his former and present memoirs, he will find the past always at hand and protected from all confusion.

Zeno's constant concern with the processes of remembering and forgetting reveals his psychological sophistication. The past is forever vanishing, not only materially, but in our minds as well. Time that destroys everything is Zeno's real villain. Still, the past remains enclosed in his unconscious, waiting for the trigger that will release it. But even this recovered past is only a fragment of its totality, since each man's truth is relative to his own needs and psychological constitution.

During the last years of Svevo's life old age became the only subject of his writings. Having written so much about it as a metaphysical condition, as a psychological attitude, and mental frame of mind, Svevo now faced it also in a social and literal sense. Now that he was old and experiencing true old age, he described it as being languid, weakening, and dirty; he saw it as an abject state of enfeeblement. He acquired a new concept: no longer spiritual and emotional, but "physical and chronological" senility. The task was no longer establishing a relationship between the past, the present, and the future, but rather functioning solely in the present. "My situation has simplified itself," says the Old, Old Man, "I continue to struggle between the present and the past, but at least hope—anxious hope for the future—does not intrude. So I go on living in a mixed tense. This is man's destiny. . . ." Old age becomes a privileged point of observation from which life is examined and seen with death on one side and youth on the other. Man's condition is seen as a grammatical problem and lived in a "mixed tense," between past and present; for Svevo there is no future, no ultimate grammatical tense: the present serves only to create future memories. The aged Zeno, in all his manifestations, is a misfit because he vacillates between tenses, between youth and old age. He has always lived in the wrong tense and time.

It is difficult to arrive at an organic assessment of Svevo's numerous and fragmentary narrative writings, often marred by sketchiness, incompleteness, and incongruities. Nonetheless, both his early stories and his post-Zeno production, clearly illustrate the development of Svevo's literary experimentalism. After discovering a fully stratified dimension of memory and time in *La coscienza di Zeno*, in his later stories Svevo created a form based entirely on the present. This "presence," together with the elimination of the future, becomes the conditioning factor of Svevo the man and writer. It explains why he describes, dwells, and lingers on details, often deviating carelessly from the theme at hand. The author arrives also at a juncture where he creates not only an open-ended narrative form—innovative for his time—but also a new relationship between himself and his narrator/protagonist. Indeed, in these "further confessions" Svevo and Zeno become an organic whole no longer separate and distinct. Zeno's presence is that of Svevo, who is also beginning to be cut off from his commercial activity because of age and ill health. He too has lost the future and savors, after many years of struggle and defeat, the present fruits of his literary labors. As he tries to come to terms with his long-awaited success, he ponders his personal obsessions and philosophical anguish over the fate of man, an isolated flimsy spirit condemned to wither and die, while the world that encircles him and assails him remains in a time reduced to the present and a reality made up of a series of discontinuous moments. All this is presented by Svevo in a bristling style, in a work whose inexorable introspective analysis, tempered with irony and sagacity, presages a work to be set beside the great *La coscienza di Zeno*.

Eduardo Saccone (essay date 1989)

SOURCE: "Struggles, War, Revolution and Literature in Some Stories by Italo Svevo," in *Literature and Revolution,* edited by David Bevan, Editions Rodopi, 1989, pp. 63-71.

[*In the following essay, Saccone points to the continuous use of dramatic struggle in Svevo's work as a way to illustrate "literature as correction of life."*]

"Una lotta" ("**A Struggle**") is the title of the first story by Italo Svevo, a text of 1888, more exactly a text published in the issues of January 6, 7, and 8 of *L'In-dipen-dente*, a Triestine newspaper. It is appropriate, and almost emblematic, that the long and very consistent discourse carried on by this writer for almost forty years begins with such a word. Word and theme are to be found continuously thereafter in his texts: to mention only one example, in the conclusion of his major novel, *La coscienza di Zeno:* "Ammetto che per avere la persuasione della salute il mio destino dovette mutare e scaldare il mio organismo con la lotta e soprattutto col trionfo." More specifically, in the story so entitled—as in many other texts—struggle is opposed to contemplation, and this dichotomy, or rather this antinomy will assume different names, though equivalent and practically interchangeable. In fact Svevo will talk elsewhere of *senilità* (senility and/or old age) and *giovinezza* (youth); also, or instead, of *malattia* (illness) and *salute* (health). It is however interesting that already in the story **"Una lotta"** the opposed terms do not take on a definite—positive or negative—meaning. One term is not necessarily privileged against the other. This—and other texts—leaves the matter undecided, undecidable; and, as Svevo stated once in a letter to a young writer,

Valerio Jahier: ". . . il contemplatore come un prodotto della natura, finito quanto il lottatore".

What matters for us is that the reader is usually presented in Svevo's texts with a struggle, the origin—and the cause—of which can certainly be found in a situation of malaise, produced in turn by differences, by a condition of inequality—economic, social, moral inequality—which, in feeding resentment, creates a reservoir, as it were, of violence. A violence that may surface or be expressed in human intercourse, at times only half consciously, or may even explode: again taking by surprise the very perpetrators of such violence. It is sufficient to mention a story like **"L'assassinio di via Belpoggio"**, in which the protagonist kills, apparently in order to appropriate the money carried by his victim, an occasional drinking companion, or, in the novel *Senilità*, the antagonistic behaviour of Emilio Brentani towards his best friend Balli (and vice versa Balli's behaviour toward Emilio); or, in a play perhaps even more emblematic, very aptly entitled *Inferiorità*, what happens between a faithful servant and his beloved—and hated—master. The servant ends up killing—in earnest, not in fun as originally intended—the master.

It is this inequality that generates struggles and battles, that produces also what Svevo's texts, for instance *Una vita* and *Senilità,* call senility: a condition of insufficiency and impotence that makes one dream of, makes a myth of its opposite: *gioventù, giovanilità,* youth, youthfulness, vital energy, which are supposed to be conducive to happiness, and peace. Only to realize, soon, that the signifier opposed to *senilità* (or to *malattia* in *La coscienza di Zeno*) signifies something else, *another* youth, *another* health, *another* peace: *other* than what is commonly and properly understood with those words. (As a matter of fact words, all words in Svevo are never to be taken literally, always in quotation marks, as it were: catachreses, instead of proper words.) The Other, alternative to the world where inequality, and struggles and battles reign, is often called in Svevo's texts *dolcezza:* a condition that is literally utopian, more specifically oxymoronic. In fact, as emerges clearly from *La coscienza di Zeno*, **"La novella del buon vecchio e della bella fanciulla"**, "La rigenerazione", etc. what the Svevian character desires is a senile youth, or a sick health. Oxymorons, like the one embodied by the last cigarette game played by Zeno, or by the bird's desire in a famous little fable, twice repeated in Svevo's *œuvre,* the desire of the caged bird who refuses to leave the cage the day the gate has been left open, afraid of being deprived, once outside, of his desire: the desire to be free, to fly away.

There is one text of 1897, therefore contemporary with *Senilità,* a fable published in *Critica sociale*, the socialist journal edited by Filippo Turati, in which the perspective is not so much that of interpersonal relationship as that of sociology. It is an important text, Svevo's contribution—in the indirect ways proper to literature—to the debate raging in those years in Europe, on how to understand the destiny and outcome of socialism on the questions of reform and revolution. We are told of a tribe, that ceases to be nomadic, thus incurring immediately all the problems familiar to sedentary societies. In a short time tents give way to ". . . sumptuous palaces and filthy tumble-down hovels"; streets are walked by ". . . half-naked men and others covered with precious cloths". The change from nomadic to sedentary life has produced an ". . . agglomeration of vile slaves and arrogant masters". What should be done to change this state of affairs? The prognosis or prophecy, attributed to the member of the tribe who was sent abroad to study how the problem had been solved by more developed countries, is that one day, when the time is ripe:

> . . . the have-nots, united by the factories, their own misfortune, will form a coalition, and, full of hope, will see the new times coming and will get ready. Then, when these new times come, bread, happiness and jobs will be shared by everyone [*Vide* Italo Svevo, *I racconti,* 1988. Translations are mine].

It is the same hope that lights up the conclusion of *Senilità.* Hope as dream, as a necessary alternative: the alternative of the pleasure-principle to that of the reality-principle. Revolution and literature—because this is, essentially, what is at stake in *Senilità:* the final "dream" is the creation of literature, without which, Svevo will eventually tell us, life is impossible—revolution and literature are therefore related, go hand in hand, even in as much as they are both undertakings whose status is problematic, not to say impossible. There is really no explicit meditation by Svevo on revolution; there is something more about literature, as we shall see: about its essence and its function. But there is no doubt that there is a link between the two; and the link lies in the fact that both desire, both want to change, Svevo will say to *correct,* reality.

It is particularly in his last writings, starting with *La coscienza di Zeno*—where we also find an idea of literature as correction of life—that this notion becomes visible, and grows stronger. It is not by chance, I believe, that this idea arises against the backdrop of World War I. This war is perceived as the opposite of revolution, the opposite of an alternative to present reality. War, on the contrary, in exasperating problems, in magnifying them as it were, and upsetting the world, allows for a more vivid perception of things.

The outlook, the vision at the end of *La coscienza di Zeno* is, in a way, apocalyptic: "Io avevo vissuto in piena calma in un fabbricato di cui il pianoterra bruciava e non avevo previsto che prima o poi tutto il fabbricato con me si sarebbe sprofondato nelle fiamme." As a matter of fact, war appears to Svevo as the logical conclusion, or rather the magnification of the struggle, the exasperated sickness permeating all levels of reality. With the building in flames, about to collapse, the urgency of the "dream", the correction, the utopia of a healthy world to follow and take the place of the one that will explode becomes more evident. On the other hand it is the narrator himself who states explicitly in **"Una burla riuscita"** (**"The Hoax"**) that the reality of war is not different from everyday reality, when, writing of the "values that changed without a rule", he comments: "Cose che si erano viste sempre, ma parevano nuove perchè si avveravano in

tali proporzioni da apparire la regola della vita." It must be said, however, that in his post-war writings Svevo's literary war likes to assume different tactics which, with their limited objectives, may evoke those of guerrilla warfare. Thus literature has become an *ordigno,* an instrument of resistance: a weapon that enables one to survive, or rather to live. This new development can be observed in many of the writer's last works, but I shall limit my examples to **"La novella del buon vecchio e della bella fanciulla"** and to **"Una burla riuscita"**.

Both texts of 1926, they offer two versions, two visions, the one more, the other less desperate, of the problem: almost to give evidence of the difficulty, if not impossibility, of finding an equilibrium, an entirely satisfactory balance. If in **"Corto viaggio sentimentale"** the travelling protagonist makes the discovery of being a "poeta travestito", a poet in disguise—"a little like everybody else in this world", inasmuch as he keeps alive his desire, his dreams, preferring a short rather than a long journey—in **"La novella del buon vecchio e della bella fanciulla"** the nice old man travels back from Zeno to Emilio Brentani, from the man most able to compromise, to the romantic and deluded protagonist of *Senilità.* This new character, the nice old man, makes the mistake of living literally the oxymoron: to be a *vecchio giovine,* a young old man. The relationship with the pretty girl—which was supposed to remain simple, uncomplicated—becomes instead the opposite: too complicated for someone like him, endowed with a delicate conscience. At this point, to simplify, to go back to "calm, serenity, health" is impossible. The nice old man turns to theory, to literature, to writing. But it is the wrong kind of literature he is turning to, or rather the consolation that literature may yield is limited to the prefaces he multiplies for a certain time. Prefaces to the treatise he is trying to write, but will eventually find impossible to write, about the law that should regulate interpersonal relationships: particularly that between the young and the old. If the prefaces manage to give "much to do and much health" to the nice old man, the writing of the actual treatise is precluded by death, that overcomes the old man while vainly searching for answers to the question of what the young owe to the old.

It is a different story with **"Una burla riuscita"**, perhaps the best, the happiest, and the most Svevian of the writer's last works. The hoax succeeds, as the Italian title announces; but in what sense? Eventually, not unlike Zeno in the novel, the victim of the hoax appears to be the real winner in an absurd world. But how does this happen? Mario Samigli, the protagonist of the story, an author, like Emilio Brentani, of only one novel that, written forty years before, "might now be called dead, if what has never been alive can be said to die", has managed to live a peaceful sort of life, a life without incidents, made acceptable or rather palatable because, as the text says, it was "condita da qualche bel sogno": "seasoned with some nice dreams". The dream is that of a glorious literary future which has survived thanks to the "very inertia which, preventing him from rebelling against his lot, also absolves him from the painful task of destroying a long cherished illusion". Thus he has been able to "go through his sad life always accompanied by a feeling of satisfaction". Like Zeno, like the caged bird of the fable already mentioned, he succeeds in keeping his dreams alive: those dreams that represent his impulse, never too strong, to escape from his state of relative unhappiness. "Happily for him"—is the narrator's comment—"he was unable to find the way out of his castle of content".

This relative happiness—which includes of course a portion of unhappiness—finds one of its major supports in the short fables that he writes in his spare time. These fables, his last and by now his only literary exercise—secret, private, his private literature—are or become for Mario precisely what he says of the little birds who act in them: ". . . un complemento delle cose che giacciono o camminano, al di sopra di esse, come l'accento sulla parola, un vero segno musicale".

A complement, or, if you wish to use a word more loaded with meaning today, after Jacques Derrida's reflections, a supplement: a necessary supplement to the given reality. Complement, seasoning, supplement also because these necessary fables, in which Mario's unconscious—the reservoir of all his desires—finds its expression and its outlet, allow for a beneficial equilibrium: "I giorni di Mario dunque erano sempre lieti. Si poteva anche pensare che tutta la sua tristezza passasse nelle sue favole amare e che perciò non arrivasse ad oscurare la sua faccia." Literature, this kind of literature, has certainly for Mario a function similar to what his night dreams accomplish: his dreams, full of "loud, protesting cries", and sighs, proclaiming: "I am worth more than they think! I am worth more than they think". Cries and sighs that, beyond his consciousness, guard Mario's rest, fulfilling in a way—as the text also declares—these same desires: with rest and with the free expression of his tortured mind, precisely as the "most modern theory of dreams" mentioned therein maintains.

The delicate balance obtained by Mario, thanks to the compromises and good manners that have become almost a second nature to him, is destroyed by the hoax which, suspending it, throws back the character to the violent dimension of the struggle. What is at stake is obviously success, the pursuit of which heightens and unleashes Mario's egotism, his desire of victory, which, removing him from the world of "dolcezza", plunges him into one where difference is emphasized: difference between the weak and the strong, the inferior and the superior, the one and the other. The "sickness of success", "la malattia del successo", as it is called in the text, produces immediately and characteristically a crisis in the relationship between Mario and Giulio, the two brothers who, until then, used to take reciprocal care of each other. On the other hand it is the same logic, the logic of a world ruled by "inferiority", that originates the hoax. In fact it is the commercial traveller Enrico Gaia's envy—Enrico Gaia, who in his youth "had tried for a short time to write poetry", efforts that were eventually strangled by his profession—it is his envy, or rather his jealousy of Mario, who instead, "in the inertia of his employment had gone on living on literature, that is of dreams and fables", that sets the hoax in motion. A hoax—the text states—"intinta di vero odio", "inspired

by true hatred" . . . and the narrator adds, with words that betray the violence of this envy: "Il Gaia avrebbe voluto strappargli il sogno felice dagli occhi a costo di accecarlo". And for a certain time the hoax appears to succeed: succeed in smiting those dreams "che avevano abbellita la sua vita", after changing Mario into nothing but a successful man:

> Egli era ormai nient'altro che l'uomo del successo. Una persona in cui l'ambizione si deformava in una ridicola vanità, e che credeva che le comuni leggi della giustizia e dell'umanità non valessero per lui. [. . .] E fu poi suo grande conforto trovarsi preparato a respingere, come poi dovette, la ridicola concezione di meritare plauso ed ammirazione, ad accettare il destino che gli era imposto, come umano e non spregevole.

The hoax is ferocious because, laying bare, stripping naked as it were the subject's desire, makes him risk annihilation, the destruction of his identity through the exhibition of the self in its scarcity, in its dereliction, deprived of any mask or prop:

> Mai più gli sarebbe stato concesso di ritornare allo stato in cui era vissuto sempre, nutrendosi delle solite porcheriole condite da quel sogno alto che stereotipava il sorriso sulle sue labbra.

Luckily it will not be so. In a beautiful scene, among the most moving invented by Svevo, Mario Samigli is visited by inspiration. Three fables, like three Graces, pay a visit to the sick man, apparently wounded to death, during the night: "Erano tre le gentili soccorritrici e si tenevano per mano, ma ciascuna gli si rivelò distinta al momento opportuno per confortarlo e guidarlo." The first shows a small bird being strangled by a hawk, and registers its "short last loud protesting cry of indignation". In the second one Mario's loudly uttered resolution not to occupy himself any more with literature is corrected by a "smiling comment". The little bird of this fable, wounded by a gunshot, succeeds in "flying from the spot where it had been hit with such a loud report". Having reached the heart of a dark thicket, it manages to murmur with its last breath "I am saved", and dies. The third fable clarifies the second: "Perché celare la propria letteratura è facile. Basta guardarsi dai viaggiatori e dagli editori. Ma rinunziarvi? E come si fa allora a vivere? La seguente tragedia lo incorò a non fare quello che il Gaia avrebbe voluto." Later on, talking to his invalid brother with whom he tries to make up for the damage caused by Mario's hunger for success, he explains that *this* literature is of the domestic kind [casalinga]: it is "for the two of them, and nobody else (. . .) each [piece] a record of a particular day, or rather its correction."

Here it is again, the new idea of literature proposed by this later Svevo. Literature as "recollection" (raccoglimento) and "correction" of life; also hygiene, enema even; or better . . . seasoning (condimento), supplement, "dream", which one cannot do without.

Soon after this explanation has taken place, a soothed Giulio falls asleep and begins to snore, and Mario, delighted with his, different, success, soon falls asleep too, without difficulty, finding peace easily. A relative peace, obviously: a Svevian peace:

Poco dopo Giulio russava, e Mario, beato del suo successo col fratello, s'addormentò anche lui non molto più tardi. E al sibilo violento della bora, fecero bordone i suoni ritmici di Giulio e, presto, anche qualche alto grido di Mario, che, nel sogno, continuava ad essere convinto di meritare altro, di meritare meglio. La burla non arrivava ad alterare il suo sogno.

FURTHER READING

Bibliography

Bloodgood, Francis C., and Van Voorhis, John W. "Criticism of Italo Svevo: A Selected Checklist." *Modern Fiction Studies* 18, No. 1 (Spring 1972): 119-29.

Covers the significant scholarship on all of Svevo's works; certain important items in foreign languages.

Biography

Furbank, P. N. *Italo Svevo.* Berkeley: University of California Press, 1966, 232 p.

A well-received English-language biography of Svevo that helped Modernists in Britain and the United States present Svevo's importance in the canon.

Gatt-Rutter, John. *Italo Svevo: A Double Life.* Oxford: Clarendon Press, 1988, 410 p.

A biography that attempts to trace the public and private sides of Svevo.

Svevo, Livia Veneziani. *Memoir of Italo Svevo.* Marlboro, VT: The Marlboro Press, 1990, 178 p.

Chronicle by Svevo's widow of life with the author. A Catholic herself, Svevo's former wife ignores Svevo's Jewish heritage in this volume.

Criticism

Donoghue, Denis. "Svevo's Comedy." *The New York Review of Books* VIII, No. 8 (May 4, 1967): 29-31.

Examines the source of Svevo's comedy in his works, commenting that "most of Svevo's comedy arises from the amused consideration of man's double nature, body and spirit."

Hood, Stuart. "Smoker's Delight." *Spectator* 223, No. 7363 (August 9, 1969): 176-77.

Analyzes Svevo's themes in his writings and praises "the acute irony which makes of Svevo one of the outstanding comic writers of our time, deadpan, accurate and frighteningly precise."

Lieber, Joel. "Humanizing the Image." *The Nation* 204, No. 22 (May 29, 1967): 695-96.

Discusses Svevo's life as recounted in *Italo Svevo: The Man and the Writer* and describes Svevo's short stories in *Short Sentimental Journey, and Other Stories* as "throwbacks" to his earlier novels.

McColm, Pearlmarie. "The 'Svevo Case'—A New Brief." *The Denver Quarterly* 2, No. 2 (Summer 1967): 154-60.

A brief overview of Svevo's fiction, concluding with praise for the novels over the short stories.

Additional coverage of Svevo's life and career is contained in the following sources published by Gale Research: *Contemporary Authors,* **Vols. 104, 122;** *Major Twentieth-Century Writers*; *Twentieth-Century Literary Criticism,* **Vols. 2, 35.**

Appendix:

Select Bibliography of General Sources on Short Fiction

BOOKS OF CRITICISM

Allen, Walter. *The Short Story in English*. New York: Oxford University Press, 1981, 413 p.

Aycock, Wendell M., ed. *The Teller and the Tale: Aspects of the Short Story* (Proceedings of the Comparative Literature Symposium, Texas Tech University, Volume XIII). Lubbock: Texas Tech Press, 1982, 156 p.

Averill, Deborah. *The Irish Short Story from George Moore to Frank O'Connor*. Washington, D.C.: University Press of America, 1982, 329 p.

Bates, H. E. *The Modern Short Story: A Critical Survey*. Boston: Writer, 1941, 231 p.

Bayley, John. *The Short Story: Henry James to Elizabeth Bowen*. Great Britain: The Harvester Press Limited, 1988, 197 p.

Bennett, E. K. *A History of the German Novelle: From Goethe to Thomas Mann*. Cambridge: At the University Press, 1934, 296 p.

Bone, Robert. *Down Home: A History of Afro-American Short Fiction from Its Beginning to the End of the Harlem Renaissance*. Rev. ed. New York: Columbia University Press, 1988, 350 p.

Bruck, Peter. *The Black American Short Story in the Twentieth Century: A Collection of Critical Essays*. Amsterdam: B. R. Grüner Publishing Co., 1977, 209 p.

Burnett, Whit, and Burnett, Hallie. *The Modern Short Story in the Making*. New York: Hawthorn Books, 1964, 405 p.

Canby, Henry Seidel. *The Short Story in English*. New York: Henry Holt and Co., 1909, 386 p.

Current-García, Eugene. *The American Short Story before 1850: A Critical History*. Twayne's Critical History of the Short Story, edited by William Peden. Boston: Twayne Publishers, 1985, 168 p.

Flora, Joseph M., ed. *The English Short Story, 1880-1945: A Critical History*. Twayne's Critical History of the Short Story, edited by William Peden. Boston: Twayne Publishers, 1985, 215 p.

Foster, David William. *Studies in the Contemporary Spanish-American Short Story*. Columbia, Mo.: University of Missouri Press, 1979, 126 p.

George, Albert J. *Short Fiction in France, 1800-1850*. Syracuse, N.Y.: Syracuse University Press, 1964, 245 p.

Gerlach, John. *Toward an End: Closure and Structure in the American Short Story*. University, Ala.: The University of Alabama Press, 1985, 193 p.

Hankin, Cherry, ed. *Critical Essays on the New Zealand Short Story*. Auckland: Heinemann Publishers, 1982, 186 p.

Hanson, Clare, ed. *Re-Reading the Short Story*. London: MacMillan Press, 1989, 137 p.

Harris, Wendell V. *British Short Fiction in the Nineteenth Century*. Detroit: Wayne State University Press, 1979, 209 p.

Huntington, John. *Rationalizing Genius: Ideological Strategies in the Classic American Science Fiction Short Story*. New Brunswick: Rutgers University Press, 1989, 216 p.

Kilroy, James F., ed. *The Irish Short Story: A Critical History*. Twayne's Critical History of the Short Story, edited by William Peden. Boston: Twayne Publishers, 1984, 251 p.

Lee, A. Robert. *The Nineteenth-Century American Short Story*. Totowa, N. J.: Vision / Barnes & Noble, 1986, 196 p.

Leibowitz, Judith. *Narrative Purpose in the Novella*. The Hague: Mouton, 1974, 137 p.

Lohafer, Susan. *Coming to Terms with the Short Story*. Baton Rouge: Louisiana State University Press, 1983, 171 p.

Lohafer, Susan, and Clarey, Jo Ellyn. *Short Story Theory at a Crossroads*. Baton Rouge: Louisiana State University Press, 1989, 352 p.

Mann, Susan Garland. *The Short Story Cycle: A Genre Companion and Reference Guide*. New York: Greenwood Press, 1989, 228 p.

Matthews, Brander. *The Philosophy of the Short Story*. New York, N.Y.: Longmans, Green and Co., 1901, 83 p.

May, Charles E., ed. *Short Story Theories*. Athens, Oh.: Ohio University Press, 1976, 251 p.

McClave, Heather, ed. *Women Writers of the Short Story: A Collection of Critical Essays*. Englewood Cliffs, N. J.: Prentice-Hall, 1980, 171 p.

Moser, Charles, ed. *The Russian Short Story: A Critical History*. Twayne's Critical History of the Short Story, edited by William Peden. Boston: Twayne Publishers, 1986, 232 p.

New, W. H. *Dreams of Speech and Violence: The Art of the Short Story in Canada and New Zealand*. Toronto: The University of Toronto Press, 1987, 302 p.

Newman, Frances. *The Short Story's Mutations: From Petronius to Paul Morand*. New York: B. W. Huebsch, 1925, 332 p.

O'Connor, Frank. *The Lonely Voice: A Study of the Short Story*. Cleveland: World Publishing Co., 1963, 220 p.

O'Faolain, Sean. *The Short Story*. New York: Devin-Adair Co., 1951, 370 p.

Orel, Harold. *The Victorian Short Story: Development and Triumph of a Literary Genre*. Cambridge: Cambridge University Press, 1986, 213 p.

O'Toole, L. Michael. *Structure, Style and Interpretation in the Russian Short Story*. New Haven: Yale University Press, 1982, 272 p.

Pattee, Fred Lewis. *The Development of the American Short Story: An Historical Survey*. New York: Harper and Brothers Publishers, 1923, 388 p.

Peden, Margaret Sayers, ed. *The Latin American Short Story: A Critical History*. Twayne's Critical History of the Short Story, edited by William Peden. Boston: Twayne Publishers, 1983, 160 p.

Peden, William. *The American Short Story: Continuity and Change, 1940-1975*. Rev. ed. Boston: Houghton

Mifflin Co., 1975, 215 p.

Reid, Ian. *The Short Story*. The Critical Idiom, edited by John D. Jump. London: Methuen and Co., 1977, 76 p.

Rhode, Robert D. *Setting in the American Short Story of Local Color, 1865-1900*. The Hague: Mouton, 1975, 189 p.

Rohrberger, Mary. *Hawthorne and the Modern Short Story: A Study in Genre*. The Hague: Mouton and Co., 1966, 148 p.

Shaw, Valerie. *The Short Story: A Critical Introduction*. London: Longman, 1983, 294 p.

Stephens, Michael. *The Dramaturgy of Style: Voice in Short Fiction*. Carbondale, Ill.: Southern Illinois University Press, 1986, 281 p.

Stevick, Philip, ed. *The American Short Story, 1900-1945: A Critical History*. Twayne's Critical History of the Short Story, edited by William Peden. Boston: Twayne Publishers, 1984, 209 p.

Summers, Hollis, ed. *Discussion of the Short Story*. Boston: D. C. Heath and Co., 1963, 118 p.

Vannatta, Dennis, ed. *The English Short Story, 1945-1980: A Critical History*. Twayne's Critical History of the Short Story, edited by William Peden. Boston: Twayne Publishers, 1985, 206 p.

Voss, Arthur. *The American Short Story: A Critical Survey*. Norman, Okla.: University of Oklahoma Press, 1973, 399 p.

Walker, Warren S. *Twentieth-Century Short Story Explication: New Series, Vol. 1: 1989-1990*. Hamden, Conn.: Shoe String, 1993, 366 p.

Ward, Alfred C. *Aspects of the Modern Short Story: English and American*. London: University of London Press, 1924, 307 p.

Weaver, Gordon, ed. *The American Short Story, 1945-1980: A Critical History*. Twayne's Critical History of the Short Story, edited by William Peden. Boston: Twayne Publishers, 1983, 150 p.

West, Ray B., Jr. *The Short Story in America, 1900-1950*. Chicago: Henry Regnery Co., 1952, 147 p.

Williams, Blanche Colton. *Our Short Story Writers*. New York: Moffat, Yard and Co., 1920, 357 p.

Wright, Austin McGiffert. *The American Short Story in the Twenties*. Chicago: University of Chicago Press, 1961, 425 p.

CRITICAL ANTHOLOGIES

Atkinson, W. Patterson, ed. *The Short-Story*. Boston: Allyn and Bacon, 1923, 317 p.

Baldwin, Charles Sears, ed. *American Short Stories*. New York, N.Y.: Longmans, Green and Co., 1904, 333 p.

Charters, Ann, ed. *The Story and Its Writer: An Introduction to Short Fiction*. New York: St. Martin's Press, 1983, 1239 p.

Current-García, Eugene, and Patrick, Walton R., eds. *American Short Stories: 1820 to the Present*. Key Editions, edited by John C. Gerber. Chicago: Scott, Foresman and Co., 1952, 633 p.

Fagin, N. Bryllion, ed. *America through the Short Story*. Boston: Little, Brown, and Co., 1936, 508 p.

Frakes, James R., and Traschen, Isadore, eds. *Short Fiction: A Critical Collection*. Prentice-Hall English Literature Series, edited by Maynard Mack. Englewood Cliffs, N.J.: Prentice-Hall, 1959, 459 p.

Gifford, Douglas, ed. *Scottish Short Stories, 1800-1900*. The Scottish Library, edited by Alexander Scott. London: Calder and Boyars, 1971, 350 p.

Gordon, Caroline, and Tate, Allen, eds. *The House of Fiction: An Anthology of the Short Story with Commentary*. Rev. ed. New York: Charles Scribner's Sons, 1960, 469 p.

Greet, T. Y., et. al. *The Worlds of Fiction: Stories in Context*. Boston, Mass.: Houghton Mifflin Co., 1964, 429 p.

Gullason, Thomas A., and Caspar, Leonard, eds. *The World of Short Fiction: An International Collection*. New York: Harper and Row, 1962, 548 p.

Havighurst, Walter, ed. *Masters of the Modern Short Story*. New York: Harcourt, Brace and Co., 1945, 538 p.

Litz, A. Walton, ed. *Major American Short Stories*. New York: Oxford University Press, 1975, 823 p.

Matthews, Brander, ed. *The Short-Story: Specimens Illustrating Its Development*. New York: American Book Co., 1907, 399 p.

Menton, Seymour, ed. *The Spanish American Short Story: A Critical Anthology*. Berkeley and Los Angeles: University of California Press, 1980, 496 p.

Mzamane, Mbulelo Vizikhungo, ed. *Hungry Flames, and Other Black South African Short Stories*. Longman African Classics. Essex: Longman, 1986, 162 p.

Schorer, Mark, ed. *The Short Story: A Critical Anthology*. Rev. ed. Prentice-Hall English Literature Series, edited by Maynard Mack. Englewood Cliffs, N. J.: Prentice-Hall, 1967, 459 p.

Simpson, Claude M., ed. *The Local Colorists: American Short Stories, 1857-1900*. New York: Harper and Brothers Publishers, 1960, 340 p.

Stanton, Robert, ed. *The Short Story and the Reader*. New York: Henry Holt and Co., 1960, 557 p.

West, Ray B., Jr., ed. *American Short Stories*. New York: Thomas Y. Crowell Co., 1959, 267 p.

Short Story Criticism Indexes

Literary Criticism Series
Cumulative Author Index

SSC Cumulative Nationality Index
SSC Cumulative Title Index

How to Use This Index

The main references

Calvino, Italo
1923-1985.....CLC 5, 8, 11, 22, 33, 39,
73; SSC 3

list all author entries in the following Gale Literary Criticism series:

BLC = *Black Literature Criticism*
CLC = *Contemporary Literary Criticism*
CLR = *Children's Literature Review*
CMLC = *Classical and Medieval Literature Criticism*
DA = *DISCovering Authors*
DAB = *DISCovering Authors: British*
DAC = *DISCovering Authors: Canadian*
DC = *Drama Criticism*
HLC = *Hispanic Literature Criticism*
LC = *Literature Criticism from 1400 to 1800*
NCLC = *Nineteenth-Century Literature Criticism*
PC = *Poetry Criticism*
SSC = *Short Story Criticism*
TCLC = *Twentieth-Century Literary Criticism*
WLC = *World Literature Criticism, 1500 to the Present*

The cross-references

See also CANR 23; CA 85-88;
obituary CA 116

list all author entries in the following Gale biographical and literary sources:

AAYA = *Authors & Artists for Young Adults*
AITN = *Authors in the News*
BEST = *Bestsellers*
BW = *Black Writers*
CA = *Contemporary Authors*
CAAS = *Contemporary Authors Autobiography Series*
CABS = *Contemporary Authors Bibliographical Series*
CANR = *Contemporary Authors New Revision Series*
CAP = *Contemporary Authors Permanent Series*
CDALB = *Concise Dictionary of American Literary Biography*
CDBLB = *Concise Dictionary of British Literary Biography*
DAM = *DISCovering Authors: Modules*
    DRAM: Dramatists Module; **MST:** *Most-Studied Authors Module;*
    MULT: *Multicultural Authors Module;* **NOV:** *Novelists Module;*
    POET: *Poets Module;* **POP:** *Popular Fiction and Genre Authors Module*
DLB = *Dictionary of Literary Biography*
DLBD = *Dictionary of Literary Biography Documentary Series*
DLBY = *Dictionary of Literary Biography Yearbook*
HW = *Hispanic Writers*
JRDA = *Junior DISCovering Authors*
MAICYA = *Major Authors and Illustrators for Children and Young Adults*
MTCW = *Major 20th-Century Writers*
NNAL = *Native North American Literature*
SAAS = *Something about the Author Autobiography Series*
SATA = *Something about the Author*
YABC = *Yesterday's Authors of Books for Children*

Literary Criticism Series
Cumulative Author Index

Abasiyanik, Sait Faik   1906-1954
See Sait Faik
See also CA 123

Abbey, Edward   1927-1989...... **CLC 36, 59**
See also CA 45-48; 128; CANR 2, 41

Abbott, Lee K(ittredge)   1947-...... **CLC 48**
See also CA 124; CANR 51; DLB 130

Abe, Kobo
1924-1993.......... **CLC 8, 22, 53, 81;**
DAM NOV
See also CA 65-68; 140; CANR 24; MTCW

Abelard, Peter   c. 1079-c. 1142 ... **CMLC 11**
See also DLB 115

Abell, Kjeld   1901-1961............ **CLC 15**
See also CA 111

Abish, Walter   1931-.............. **CLC 22**
See also CA 101; CANR 37; DLB 130

Abrahams, Peter (Henry)   1919- ..... **CLC 4**
See also BW 1; CA 57-60; CANR 26;
DLB 117; MTCW

Abrams, M(eyer) H(oward)   1912-... **CLC 24**
See also CA 57-60; CANR 13, 33; DLB 67

Abse, Dannie
1923- ... **CLC 7, 29; DAB; DAM POET**
See also CA 53-56; CAAS 1; CANR 4, 46;
DLB 27

Achebe, (Albert) Chinua(lumogu)
1930- ..... **CLC 1, 3, 5, 7, 11, 26, 51, 75;**
BLC; DA; DAB; DAC; DAM MST,
MULT, NOV; WLC
See also AAYA 15; BW 2; CA 1-4R;
CANR 6, 26, 47; CLR 20; DLB 117;
MAICYA; MTCW; SATA 40;
SATA-Brief 38

Acker, Kathy   1948- .... **CLC 45**
See also CA 117; 122; CANR 55

Ackroyd, Peter   1949-.......... **CLC 34, 52**
See also CA 123; 127; CANR 51; DLB 155;
INT 127

Acorn, Milton   1923-........ **CLC 15; DAC**
See also CA 103; DLB 53; INT 103

Adamov, Arthur
1908-1970 .... **CLC 4, 25; DAM DRAM**
See also CA 17-18; 25-28R; CAP 2; MTCW

Adams, Alice (Boyd)
1926-.......... **CLC 6, 13, 46; SSC 24**
See also CA 81-84; CANR 26, 53;
DLBY 86; INT CANR-26; MTCW

Adams, Andy   1859-1935......... **TCLC 56**
See also YABC 1

Adams, Douglas (Noel)
1952-......... **CLC 27, 60; DAM POP**
See also AAYA 4; BEST 89:3; CA 106;
CANR 34; DLBY 83; JRDA

Adams, Francis   1862-1893....... **NCLC 33**

Adams, Henry (Brooks)
1838-1918 ...... **TCLC 4, 52; DA; DAB;**
DAC; DAM MST
See also CA 104; 133; DLB 12, 47

Adams, Richard (George)
1920-....... **CLC 4, 5, 18; DAM NOV**
See also AAYA 16; AITN 1, 2; CA 49-52;
CANR 3, 35; CLR 20; JRDA; MAICYA;
MTCW; SATA 7, 69

Adamson, Joy(-Friederike Victoria)
1910-1980 .... **CLC 17**
See also CA 69-72; 93-96; CANR 22;
MTCW; SATA 11; SATA-Obit 22

Adcock, Fleur   1934-............ **CLC 41**
See also CA 25-28R; CAAS 23; CANR 11,
34; DLB 40

Addams, Charles (Samuel)
1912-1988 .... **CLC 30**
See also CA 61-64; 126; CANR 12

Addison, Joseph   1672-1719 .... **LC 18**
See also CDBLB 1660-1789; DLB 101

Adler, Alfred (F.)   1870-1937 ...... **TCLC 61**
See also CA 119

Adler, C(arole) S(chwerdtfeger)
1932-....................... **CLC 35**
See also AAYA 4; CA 89-92; CANR 19,
40; JRDA; MAICYA; SAAS 15;
SATA 26, 63

Adler, Renata   1938-............ **CLC 8, 31**
See also CA 49-52; CANR 5, 22, 52;
MTCW

Ady, Endre   1877-1919 .... **TCLC 11**
See also CA 107

Aeschylus
525B.C.-456B.C....... **CMLC 11; DA;**
DAB; DAC; DAM DRAM, MST
See also DLB 176

Afton, Effie
See Harper, Frances Ellen Watkins

Agapida, Fray Antonio
See Irving, Washington

Agee, James (Rufus)
1909-1955 .... **TCLC 1, 19; DAM NOV**
See also AITN 1; CA 108; 148;
CDALB 1941-1968; DLB 2, 26, 152

Aghill, Gordon
See Silverberg, Robert

Agnon, S(hmuel) Y(osef Halevi)
1888-1970 .... **CLC 4, 8, 14**
See also CA 17-18; 25-28R; CAP 2; MTCW

Agrippa von Nettesheim, Henry Cornelius
1486-1535 .... **LC 27**

Aherne, Owen
See Cassill, R(onald) V(erlin)

Ai   1947-.................. **CLC 4, 14, 69**
See also CA 85-88; CAAS 13; DLB 120

Aickman, Robert (Fordyce)
1914-1981 .... **CLC 57**
See also CA 5-8R; CANR 3

Aiken, Conrad (Potter)
1889-1973 .... **CLC 1, 3, 5, 10, 52;**
DAM NOV, POET; SSC 9
See also CA 5-8R; 45-48; CANR 4;
CDALB 1929-1941; DLB 9, 45, 102;
MTCW; SATA 3, 30

Aiken, Joan (Delano)   1924-........ **CLC 35**
See also AAYA 1; CA 9-12R; CANR 4, 23,
34; CLR 1, 19; DLB 161; JRDA;
MAICYA; MTCW; SAAS 1; SATA 2,
30, 73

Ainsworth, William Harrison
1805-1882 .... **NCLC 13**
See also DLB 21; SATA 24

Aitmatov, Chingiz (Torekulovich)
1928-....................... **CLC 71**
See also CA 103; CANR 38; MTCW;
SATA 56

Akers, Floyd
See Baum, L(yman) Frank

Akhmadulina, Bella Akhatovna
1937-........... **CLC 53; DAM POET**
See also CA 65-68

Akhmatova, Anna
1888-1966 .... **CLC 11, 25, 64;**
DAM POET; PC 2
See also CA 19-20; 25-28R; CANR 35;
CAP 1; MTCW

Aksakov, Sergei Timofeyvich
1791-1859 .... **NCLC 2**

Aksenov, Vassily
See Aksyonov, Vassily (Pavlovich)

Aksyonov, Vassily (Pavlovich)
1932-..................... **CLC 22, 37**
See also CA 53-56; CANR 12, 48

Akutagawa, Ryunosuke
1892-1927 .... **TCLC 16**
See also CA 117; 154

Alain   1868-1951 .... **TCLC 41**

Alain-Fournier................... **TCLC 6**
See also Fournier, Henri Alban
See also DLB 65

Alarcon, Pedro Antonio de
1833-1891 .... **NCLC 1**

Alas (y Urena), Leopoldo (Enrique Garcia)
1852-1901 .... **TCLC 29**
See also CA 113; 131; HW

Albee, Edward (Franklin III)
1928-...... **CLC 1, 2, 3, 5, 9, 11, 13, 25,**
53, 86; DA; DAB; DAC; DAM DRAM,
MST; WLC
See also AITN 1; CA 5-8R; CABS 3;
CANR 8, 54; CDALB 1941-1968; DLB 7;
INT CANR-8; MTCW

Alberti, Rafael 1902- .... **CLC 7**
See also CA 85-88; DLB 108

Albert the Great 1200(?)-1280.... **CMLC 16**
See also DLB 115

Alcala-Galiano, Juan Valera y
See Valera y Alcala-Galiano, Juan

Alcott, Amos Bronson 1799-1888 .. **NCLC 1**
See also DLB 1

Alcott, Louisa May
1832-1888 ..... **NCLC 6, 58; DA; DAB;**
DAC; DAM MST, NOV; WLC
See also AAYA 20; CDALB 1865-1917;
CLR 1, 38; DLB 1, 42, 79; DLBD 14;
JRDA; MAICYA; YABC 1

Aldanov, M. A.
See Aldanov, Mark (Alexandrovich)

Aldanov, Mark (Alexandrovich)
1886(?)-1957 .... **TCLC 23**
See also CA 118

Aldington, Richard 1892-1962...... **CLC 49**
See also CA 85-88; CANR 45; DLB 20, 36,
100, 149

Aldiss, Brian W(ilson)
1925- ...... **CLC 5, 14, 40; DAM NOV**
See also CA 5-8R; CAAS 2; CANR 5, 28;
DLB 14; MTCW; SATA 34

Alegria, Claribel
1924- .... **CLC 75; DAM MULT**
See also CA 131; CAAS 15; DLB 145; HW

Alegria, Fernando 1918-.......... **CLC 57**
See also CA 9-12R; CANR 5, 32; HW

Aleichem, Sholom .... **TCLC 1, 35**
See also Rabinovitch, Sholem

Aleixandre, Vicente
1898-1984 .... **CLC 9, 36; DAM POET;**
PC 15
See also CA 85-88; 114; CANR 26;
DLB 108; HW; MTCW

Alepoudelis, Odysseus
See Elytis, Odysseus

Aleshkovsky, Joseph 1929-
See Aleshkovsky, Yuz
See also CA 121; 128

Aleshkovsky, Yuz .... **CLC 44**
See also Aleshkovsky, Joseph

Alexander, Lloyd (Chudley) 1924- .. **CLC 35**
See also AAYA 1; CA 1-4R; CANR 1, 24,
38, 55; CLR 1, 5; DLB 52; JRDA;
MAICYA; MTCW; SAAS 19; SATA 3,
49, 81

Alexie, Sherman (Joseph, Jr.)
1966- .... **CLC 96; DAM MULT**
See also CA 138; DLB 175; NNAL

Alfau, Felipe 1902- .... **CLC 66**
See also CA 137

Alger, Horatio, Jr. 1832-1899..... **NCLC 8**
See also DLB 42; SATA 16

Algren, Nelson 1909-1981 .... **CLC 4, 10, 33**
See also CA 13-16R; 103; CANR 20;
CDALB 1941-1968; DLB 9; DLBY 81,
82; MTCW

Ali, Ahmed 1910- .... **CLC 69**
See also CA 25-28R; CANR 15, 34

Alighieri, Dante 1265-1321 .... **CMLC 3, 18**

Allan, John B.
See Westlake, Donald E(dwin)

Allen, Edward 1948-............. **CLC 59**

Allen, Paula Gunn
1939- .... **CLC 84; DAM MULT**
See also CA 112; 143; DLB 175; NNAL

Allen, Roland
See Ayckbourn, Alan

Allen, Sarah A.
See Hopkins, Pauline Elizabeth

Allen, Woody
1935- .... **CLC 16, 52; DAM POP**
See also AAYA 10; CA 33-36R; CANR 27,
38; DLB 44; MTCW

Allende, Isabel
1942- .... **CLC 39, 57, 97; DAM MULT,**
NOV; HLC
See also AAYA 18; CA 125; 130;
CANR 51; DLB 145; HW; INT 130;
MTCW

Alleyn, Ellen
See Rossetti, Christina (Georgina)

Allingham, Margery (Louise)
1904-1966 .... **CLC 19**
See also CA 5-8R; 25-28R; CANR 4;
DLB 77; MTCW

Allingham, William 1824-1889 ... **NCLC 25**
See also DLB 35

Allison, Dorothy E. 1949- .... **CLC 78**
See also CA 140

Allston, Washington 1779-1843.... **NCLC 2**
See also DLB 1

Almedingen, E. M. .... **CLC 12**
See also Almedingen, Martha Edith von
See also SATA 3

Almedingen, Martha Edith von 1898-1971
See Almedingen, E. M.
See also CA 1-4R; CANR 1

Almqvist, Carl Jonas Love
1793-1866 .... **NCLC 42**

Alonso, Damaso 1898-1990 .... **CLC 14**
See also CA 110; 131; 130; DLB 108; HW

Alov
See Gogol, Nikolai (Vasilyevich)

Alta 1942- .... **CLC 19**
See also CA 57-60

Alter, Robert B(ernard) 1935-...... **CLC 34**
See also CA 49-52; CANR 1, 47

Alther, Lisa 1944-............... **CLC 7, 41**
See also CA 65-68; CANR 12, 30, 51;
MTCW

Altman, Robert 1925-............. **CLC 16**
See also CA 73-76; CANR 43

Alvarez, A(lfred) 1929-.......... **CLC 5, 13**
See also CA 1-4R; CANR 3, 33; DLB 14,
40

Alvarez, Alejandro Rodriguez 1903-1965
See Casona, Alejandro
See also CA 131; 93-96; HW

Alvarez, Julia 1950-.............. **CLC 93**
See also CA 147

Alvaro, Corrado 1896-1956 .... **TCLC 60**

Amado, Jorge
1912- .... **CLC 13, 40; DAM MULT,**
NOV; HLC
See also CA 77-80; CANR 35; DLB 113;
MTCW

Ambler, Eric 1909-............. **CLC 4, 6, 9**
See also CA 9-12R; CANR 7, 38; DLB 77;
MTCW

Amichai, Yehuda 1924- ...... **CLC 9, 22, 57**
See also CA 85-88; CANR 46; MTCW

Amiel, Henri Frederic 1821-1881 .. **NCLC 4**

Amis, Kingsley (William)
1922-1995 ..... **CLC 1, 2, 3, 5, 8, 13, 40,**
44; DA; DAB; DAC; DAM MST, NOV
See also AITN 2; CA 9-12R; 150; CANR 8,
28, 54; CDBLB 1945-1960; DLB 15, 27,
100, 139; INT CANR-8; MTCW

Amis, Martin (Louis)
1949- .... **CLC 4, 9, 38, 62**
See also BEST 90:3; CA 65-68; CANR 8,
27, 54; DLB 14; INT CANR-27

Ammons, A(rchie) R(andolph)
1926- .... **CLC 2, 3, 5, 8, 9, 25, 57;**
DAM POET; PC 16
See also AITN 1; CA 9-12R; CANR 6, 36,
51; DLB 5, 165; MTCW

Amo, Tauraatua i
See Adams, Henry (Brooks)

Anand, Mulk Raj
1905- .... **CLC 23, 93; DAM NOV**
See also CA 65-68; CANR 32; MTCW

Anatol
See Schnitzler, Arthur

Anaximander
c. 610B.C.-c. 546B.C......... **CMLC 22**

Anaya, Rudolfo A(lfonso)
1937- .... **CLC 23; DAM MULT, NOV;**
HLC
See also AAYA 20; CA 45-48; CAAS 4;
CANR 1, 32, 51; DLB 82; HW 1; MTCW

Andersen, Hans Christian
1805-1875 .... **NCLC 7; DA; DAB;**
DAC; DAM MST, POP; SSC 6; WLC
See also CLR 6; MAICYA; YABC 1

Anderson, C. Farley
See Mencken, H(enry) L(ouis); Nathan,
George Jean

Anderson, Jessica (Margaret) Queale
.... **CLC 37**
See also CA 9-12R; CANR 4

Anderson, Jon (Victor)
1940- .... **CLC 9; DAM POET**
See also CA 25-28R; CANR 20

Anderson, Lindsay (Gordon)
1923-1994 .... **CLC 20**
See also CA 125; 128; 146

Anderson, Maxwell
1888-1959 ...... **TCLC 2; DAM DRAM**
See also CA 105; 152; DLB 7

Anderson, Poul (William) 1926- .... **CLC 15**
See also AAYA 5; CA 1-4R; CAAS 2;
CANR 2, 15, 34; DLB 8; INT CANR-15;
MTCW; SATA 90; SATA-Brief 39

Anderson, Robert (Woodruff)
1917- . . . . **CLC 23; DAM DRAM**
See also AITN 1; CA 21-24R; CANR 32;
DLB 7

Anderson, Sherwood
1876-1941 . . . . **TCLC 1, 10, 24; DA;**
DAB; DAC; DAM MST, NOV; SSC 1;
WLC
See also CA 104; 121; CDALB 1917-1929;
DLB 4, 9, 86; DLBD 1; MTCW

Andier, Pierre
See Desnos, Robert

Andouard
See Giraudoux, (Hippolyte) Jean

Andrade, Carlos Drummond de . . . . . . **CLC 18**
See also Drummond de Andrade, Carlos

Andrade, Mario de 1893-1945 . . . . . **TCLC 43**

Andreae, Johann V(alentin)
1586-1654 . . . . **LC 32**
See also DLB 164

Andreas-Salome, Lou 1861-1937 . . . **TCLC 56**
See also DLB 66

Andrewes, Lancelot 1555-1626 . . . . **LC 5**
See also DLB 151, 172

Andrews, Cicily Fairfield
See West, Rebecca

Andrews, Elton V.
See Pohl, Frederik

Andreyev, Leonid (Nikolaevich)
1871-1919 . . . . **TCLC 3**
See also CA 104

Andric, Ivo 1892-1975 . . . . **CLC 8**
See also CA 81-84; 57-60; CANR 43;
DLB 147; MTCW

Angelique, Pierre
See Bataille, Georges

Angell, Roger 1920- . . . . **CLC 26**
See also CA 57-60; CANR 13, 44; DLB 171

Angelou, Maya
1928- . . . . **CLC 12, 35, 64, 77; BLC; DA;**
DAB; DAC; DAM MST, MULT, POET,
POP
See also AAYA 7, 20; BW 2; CA 65-68;
CANR 19, 42; DLB 38; MTCW;
SATA 49

Annensky, Innokenty (Fyodorovich)
1856-1909 . . . . **TCLC 14**
See also CA 110; 155

Annunzio, Gabriele d'
See D'Annunzio, Gabriele

Anon, Charles Robert
See Pessoa, Fernando (Antonio Nogueira)

Anouilh, Jean (Marie Lucien Pierre)
1910-1987 . . . . . . **CLC 1, 3, 8, 13, 40, 50;**
DAM DRAM
See also CA 17-20R; 123; CANR 32;
MTCW

Anthony, Florence
See Ai

Anthony, John
See Ciardi, John (Anthony)

Anthony, Peter
See Shaffer, Anthony (Joshua); Shaffer,
Peter (Levin)

Anthony, Piers 1934- . . **CLC 35; DAM POP**
See also AAYA 11; CA 21-24R; CANR 28,
56; DLB 8; MTCW; SAAS 22; SATA 84

Antoine, Marc
See Proust, (Valentin-Louis-George-Eugene-)
Marcel

Antoninus, Brother
See Everson, William (Oliver)

Antonioni, Michelangelo 1912- . . . . . **CLC 20**
See also CA 73-76; CANR 45

Antschel, Paul 1920-1970
See Celan, Paul
See also CA 85-88; CANR 33; MTCW

Anwar, Chairil 1922-1949 . . . . **TCLC 22**
See also CA 121

Apollinaire, Guillaume
1880-1918 . . . . **TCLC 3, 8, 51;**
DAM POET; PC 7
See also Kostrowitzki, Wilhelm Apollinaris
de
See also CA 152

Appelfeld, Aharon 1932- . . . . **CLC 23, 47**
See also CA 112; 133

Apple, Max (Isaac) 1941- . . . . **CLC 9, 33**
See also CA 81-84; CANR 19, 54; DLB 130

Appleman, Philip (Dean) 1926- . . . . . **CLC 51**
See also CA 13-16R; CAAS 18; CANR 6,
29, 56

Appleton, Lawrence
See Lovecraft, H(oward) P(hillips)

Apteryx
See Eliot, T(homas) S(tearns)

Apuleius, (Lucius Madaurensis)
125(?)-175(?) . . . . **CMLC 1**

Aquin, Hubert 1929-1977 . . . . **CLC 15**
See also CA 105; DLB 53

Aragon, Louis
1897-1982 . . . . . **CLC 3, 22; DAM NOV,**
POET
See also CA 69-72; 108; CANR 28;
DLB 72; MTCW

Arany, Janos 1817-1882 . . . . **NCLC 34**

Arbuthnot, John 1667-1735 . . . . **LC 1**
See also DLB 101

Archer, Herbert Winslow
See Mencken, H(enry) L(ouis)

Archer, Jeffrey (Howard)
1940- . . . . **CLC 28; DAM POP**
See also AAYA 16; BEST 89:3; CA 77-80;
CANR 22, 52; INT CANR-22

Archer, Jules 1915- . . . . **CLC 12**
See also CA 9-12R; CANR 6; SAAS 5;
SATA 4, 85

Archer, Lee
See Ellison, Harlan (Jay)

Arden, John
1930- . . . . . **CLC 6, 13, 15; DAM DRAM**
See also CA 13-16R; CAAS 4; CANR 31;
DLB 13; MTCW

Arenas, Reinaldo
1943-1990 . . . . . . **CLC 41; DAM MULT;**
HLC
See also CA 124; 128; 133; DLB 145; HW

Arendt, Hannah 1906-1975 . . . . . **CLC 66, 98**
See also CA 17-20R; 61-64; CANR 26;
MTCW

Aretino, Pietro 1492-1556 . . . . **LC 12**

Arghezi, Tudor . . . . **CLC 80**
See also Theodorescu, Ion N.

Arguedas, Jose Maria
1911-1969 . . . . **CLC 10, 18**
See also CA 89-92; DLB 113; HW

Argueta, Manlio 1936- . . . . **CLC 31**
See also CA 131; DLB 145; HW

Ariosto, Ludovico 1474-1533 . . . . **LC 6**

Aristides
See Epstein, Joseph

Aristophanes
450B.C.-385B.C. . . . . **CMLC 4; DA;**
DAB; DAC; DAM DRAM, MST; DC 2
See also DLB 176

Arlt, Roberto (Godofredo Christophersen)
1900-1942 . . . . . **TCLC 29; DAM MULT;**
HLC
See also CA 123; 131; HW

Armah, Ayi Kwei
1939- . . . . **CLC 5, 33; BLC;**
DAM MULT, POET
See also BW 1; CA 61-64; CANR 21;
DLB 117; MTCW

Armatrading, Joan 1950- . . . . **CLC 17**
See also CA 114

Arnette, Robert
See Silverberg, Robert

Arnim, Achim von (Ludwig Joachim von
Arnim) 1781-1831 . . . . **NCLC 5**
See also DLB 90

Arnim, Bettina von 1785-1859 . . . . **NCLC 38**
See also DLB 90

Arnold, Matthew
1822-1888 . . . . . **NCLC 6, 29; DA; DAB;**
DAC; DAM MST, POET; PC 5; WLC
See also CDBLB 1832-1890; DLB 32, 57

Arnold, Thomas 1795-1842 . . . . . . **NCLC 18**
See also DLB 55

Arnow, Harriette (Louisa) Simpson
1908-1986 . . . . **CLC 2, 7, 18**
See also CA 9-12R; 118; CANR 14; DLB 6;
MTCW; SATA 42; SATA-Obit 47

Arp, Hans
See Arp, Jean

Arp, Jean 1887-1966 . . . . **CLC 5**
See also CA 81-84; 25-28R; CANR 42

Arrabal
See Arrabal, Fernando

Arrabal, Fernando 1932- . . . **CLC 2, 9, 18, 58**
See also CA 9-12R; CANR 15

Arrick, Fran . . . . **CLC 30**
See also Gaberman, Judie Angell

Artaud, Antonin (Marie Joseph)
1896-1948 . . . **TCLC 3, 36; DAM DRAM**
See also CA 104; 149

Arthur, Ruth M(abel) 1905-1979 . . . . **CLC 12**
See also CA 9-12R; 85-88; CANR 4;
SATA 7, 26

Artsybashev, Mikhail (Petrovich)
1878-1927 . . . . **TCLC 31**

Bailey, Paul 1937- . . . . **CLC 45**
See also CA 21-24R; CANR 16; DLB 14

Baillie, Joanna 1762-1851 . . . . **NCLC 2**
See also DLB 93

Bainbridge, Beryl (Margaret)
1933- . . . . **CLC 4, 5, 8, 10, 14, 18, 22, 62;
DAM NOV**
See also CA 21-24R; CANR 24, 55;
DLB 14; MTCW

Baker, Elliott 1922- . . . . **CLC 8**
See also CA 45-48; CANR 2

Baker, Jean H. . . . . **TCLC 3, 10**
See also Russell, George William

Baker, Nicholson
1957- . . . . **CLC 61; DAM POP**
See also CA 135

Baker, Ray Stannard 1870-1946 . . . **TCLC 47**
See also CA 118

Baker, Russell (Wayne) 1925- . . . . . . **CLC 31**
See also BEST 89:4; CA 57-60; CANR 11,
41; MTCW

Bakhtin, M.
See Bakhtin, Mikhail Mikhailovich

Bakhtin, M. M.
See Bakhtin, Mikhail Mikhailovich

Bakhtin, Mikhail
See Bakhtin, Mikhail Mikhailovich

Bakhtin, Mikhail Mikhailovich
1895-1975 . . . . **CLC 83**
See also CA 128; 113

Bakshi, Ralph 1938(?)- . . . . **CLC 26**
See also CA 112; 138

Bakunin, Mikhail (Alexandrovich)
1814-1876 . . . . **NCLC 25, 58**

Baldwin, James (Arthur)
1924-1987 . . . . . . **CLC 1, 2, 3, 4, 5, 8, 13,
15, 17, 42, 50, 67, 90; BLC; DA; DAB;
DAC; DAM MST, MULT, NOV, POP;
DC 1; SSC 10; WLC**
See also AAYA 4; BW 1; CA 1-4R; 124;
CABS 1; CANR 3, 24;
CDALB 1941-1968; DLB 2, 7, 33;
DLBY 87; MTCW; SATA 9;
SATA-Obit 54

Ballard, J(ames) G(raham)
1930- . . . . **CLC 3, 6, 14, 36; DAM NOV,
POP; SSC 1**
See also AAYA 3; CA 5-8R; CANR 15, 39;
DLB 14; MTCW

Balmont, Konstantin (Dmitriyevich)
1867-1943 . . . . **TCLC 11**
See also CA 109; 155

Balzac, Honore de
1799-1850 . . . . **NCLC 5, 35, 53; DA;
DAB; DAC; DAM MST, NOV; SSC 5;
WLC**
See also DLB 119

Bambara, Toni Cade
1939-1995 . . . . . . **CLC 19, 88; BLC; DA;
DAC; DAM MST, MULT**
See also AAYA 5; BW 2; CA 29-32R; 150;
CANR 24, 49; DLB 38; MTCW

Bamdad, A.
See Shamlu, Ahmad

Banat, D. R.
See Bradbury, Ray (Douglas)

Bancroft, Laura
See Baum, L(yman) Frank

Banim, John 1798-1842 . . . . **NCLC 13**
See also DLB 116, 158, 159

Banim, Michael 1796-1874 . . . . . . **NCLC 13**
See also DLB 158, 159

Banjo, The
See Paterson, A(ndrew) B(arton)

Banks, Iain
See Banks, Iain M(enzies)

Banks, Iain M(enzies) 1954- . . . . **CLC 34**
See also CA 123; 128; INT 128

Banks, Lynne Reid . . . . **CLC 23**
See also Reid Banks, Lynne
See also AAYA 6

Banks, Russell 1940- . . . . **CLC 37, 72**
See also CA 65-68; CAAS 15; CANR 19,
52; DLB 130

Banville, John 1945- . . . . **CLC 46**
See also CA 117; 128; DLB 14; INT 128

Banville, Theodore (Faullain) de
1832-1891 . . . . **NCLC 9**

Baraka, Amiri
1934- . . . . **CLC 1, 2, 3, 5, 10, 14, 33;
BLC; DA; DAC; DAM MST, MULT,
POET, POP; DC 6; PC 4**
See also Jones, LeRoi
See also BW 2; CA 21-24R; CABS 3;
CANR 27, 38; CDALB 1941-1968;
DLB 5, 7, 16, 38; DLBD 8; MTCW

Barbauld, Anna Laetitia
1743-1825 . . . . **NCLC 50**
See also DLB 107, 109, 142, 158

Barbellion, W. N. P. . . . . **TCLC 24**
See also Cummings, Bruce F(rederick)

Barbera, Jack (Vincent) 1945- . . . . . . **CLC 44**
See also CA 110; CANR 45

Barbey d'Aurevilly, Jules Amedee
1808-1889 . . . . **NCLC 1; SSC 17**
See also DLB 119

Barbusse, Henri 1873-1935 . . . . **TCLC 5**
See also CA 105; 154; DLB 65

Barclay, Bill
See Moorcock, Michael (John)

Barclay, William Ewert
See Moorcock, Michael (John)

Barea, Arturo 1897-1957 . . . . **TCLC 14**
See also CA 111

Barfoot, Joan 1946- . . . . **CLC 18**
See also CA 105

Baring, Maurice 1874-1945 . . . . **TCLC 8**
See also CA 105; DLB 34

Barker, Clive 1952- . . . **CLC 52; DAM POP**
See also AAYA 10; BEST 90:3; CA 121;
129; INT 129; MTCW

Barker, George Granville
1913-1991 . . . . . **CLC 8, 48; DAM POET**
See also CA 9-12R; 135; CANR 7, 38;
DLB 20; MTCW

Barker, Harley Granville
See Granville-Barker, Harley
See also DLB 10

Barker, Howard 1946- . . . . **CLC 37**
See also CA 102; DLB 13

Barker, Pat(ricia) 1943- . . . . **CLC 32, 94**
See also CA 117; 122; CANR 50; INT 122

Barlow, Joel 1754-1812 . . . . **NCLC 23**
See also DLB 37

Barnard, Mary (Ethel) 1909- . . . . **CLC 48**
See also CA 21-22; CAP 2

Barnes, Djuna
1892-1982 . . . **CLC 3, 4, 8, 11, 29; SSC 3**
See also CA 9-12R; 107; CANR 16, 55;
DLB 4, 9, 45; MTCW

Barnes, Julian (Patrick)
1946- . . . . **CLC 42; DAB**
See also CA 102; CANR 19, 54; DLBY 93

Barnes, Peter 1931- . . . . **CLC 5, 56**
See also CA 65-68; CAAS 12; CANR 33,
34; DLB 13; MTCW

Baroja (y Nessi), Pio
1872-1956 . . . . **TCLC 8; HLC**
See also CA 104

Baron, David
See Pinter, Harold

Baron Corvo
See Rolfe, Frederick (William Serafino
Austin Lewis Mary)

Barondess, Sue K(aufman)
1926-1977 . . . . **CLC 8**
See also Kaufman, Sue
See also CA 1-4R; 69-72; CANR 1

Baron de Teive
See Pessoa, Fernando (Antonio Nogueira)

Barres, Maurice 1862-1923 . . . . **TCLC 47**
See also DLB 123

Barreto, Afonso Henrique de Lima
See Lima Barreto, Afonso Henrique de

Barrett, (Roger) Syd 1946- . . . . **CLC 35**

Barrett, William (Christopher)
1913-1992 . . . . **CLC 27**
See also CA 13-16R; 139; CANR 11;
INT CANR-11

Barrie, J(ames) M(atthew)
1860-1937 . . . . **TCLC 2; DAB;
DAM DRAM**
See also CA 104; 136; CDBLB 1890-1914;
CLR 16; DLB 10, 141, 156; MAICYA;
YABC 1

Barrington, Michael
See Moorcock, Michael (John)

Barrol, Grady
See Bograd, Larry

Barry, Mike
See Malzberg, Barry N(athaniel)

Barry, Philip 1896-1949 . . . . **TCLC 11**
See also CA 109; DLB 7

Bart, Andre Schwarz
See Schwarz-Bart, Andre

Barth, John (Simmons)
1930- . . . . . . **CLC 1, 2, 3, 5, 7, 9, 10, 14,
27, 51, 89; DAM NOV; SSC 10**
See also AITN 1, 2; CA 1-4R; CABS 1;
CANR 5, 23, 49; DLB 2; MTCW

Barthelme, Donald
1931-1989 ...... **CLC 1, 2, 3, 5, 6, 8, 13,
23, 46, 59; DAM NOV; SSC 2**
See also CA 21-24R; 129; CANR 20;
DLB 2; DLBY 80, 89; MTCW; SATA 7;
SATA-Obit 62

Barthelme, Frederick 1943- .... **CLC 36**
See also CA 114; 122; DLBY 85; INT 122

Barthes, Roland (Gerard)
1915-1980 .... **CLC 24, 83**
See also CA 130; 97-100; MTCW

Barzun, Jacques (Martin) 1907- .... **CLC 51**
See also CA 61-64; CANR 22

Bashevis, Isaac
See Singer, Isaac Bashevis

Bashkirtseff, Marie 1859-1884 ... **NCLC 27**

Basho
See Matsuo Basho

Bass, Kingsley B., Jr.
See Bullins, Ed

Bass, Rick 1958-................ **CLC 79**
See also CA 126; CANR 53

Bassani, Giorgio 1916-............ **CLC 9**
See also CA 65-68; CANR 33; DLB 128,
177; MTCW

Bastos, Augusto (Antonio) Roa
See Roa Bastos, Augusto (Antonio)

Bataille, Georges 1897-1962 .... **CLC 29**
See also CA 101; 89-92

Bates, H(erbert) E(rnest)
1905-1974 .... **CLC 46; DAB;
DAM POP; SSC 10**
See also CA 93-96; 45-48; CANR 34;
DLB 162; MTCW

Bauchart
See Camus, Albert

Baudelaire, Charles
1821-1867 .... **NCLC 6, 29, 55; DA;
DAB; DAC; DAM MST, POET; PC 1;
SSC 18; WLC**

Baudrillard, Jean 1929-........... **CLC 60**

Baum, L(yman) Frank 1856-1919 ... **TCLC 7**
See also CA 108; 133; CLR 15; DLB 22;
JRDA; MAICYA; MTCW; SATA 18

Baum, Louis F.
See Baum, L(yman) Frank

Baumbach, Jonathan 1933- ...... **CLC 6, 23**
See also CA 13-16R; CAAS 5; CANR 12;
DLBY 80; INT CANR-12; MTCW

Bausch, Richard (Carl) 1945- ...... **CLC 51**
See also CA 101; CAAS 14; CANR 43;
DLB 130

Baxter, Charles
1947- .... **CLC 45, 78; DAM POP**
See also CA 57-60; CANR 40; DLB 130

Baxter, George Owen
See Faust, Frederick (Schiller)

Baxter, James K(eir) 1926-1972 .... **CLC 14**
See also CA 77-80

Baxter, John
See Hunt, E(verette) Howard, (Jr.)

Bayer, Sylvia
See Glassco, John

Baynton, Barbara 1857-1929 ...... **TCLC 57**

Beagle, Peter S(oyer) 1939-........ **CLC 7**
See also CA 9-12R; CANR 4, 51;
DLBY 80; INT CANR-4; SATA 60

Bean, Normal
See Burroughs, Edgar Rice

Beard, Charles A(ustin)
1874-1948 .... **TCLC 15**
See also CA 115; DLB 17; SATA 18

Beardsley, Aubrey 1872-1898 ..... **NCLC 6**

Beattie, Ann
1947- .... **CLC 8, 13, 18, 40, 63;
DAM NOV, POP; SSC 11**
See also BEST 90:2; CA 81-84; CANR 53;
DLBY 82; MTCW

Beattie, James 1735-1803 .... **NCLC 25**
See also DLB 109

Beauchamp, Kathleen Mansfield 1888-1923
See Mansfield, Katherine
See also CA 104; 134; DA; DAC;
DAM MST

Beaumarchais, Pierre-Augustin Caron de
1732-1799 .... **DC 4**
See also DAM DRAM

Beaumont, Francis
1584(?)-1616 .... **LC 33; DC 6**
See also CDBLB Before 1660; DLB 58, 121

**Beauvoir, Simone (Lucie Ernestine Marie
Bertrand) de**
1908-1986 .... **CLC 1, 2, 4, 8, 14, 31, 44,
50, 71; DA; DAB; DAC; DAM MST,
NOV; WLC**
See also CA 9-12R; 118; CANR 28;
DLB 72; DLBY 86; MTCW

Becker, Carl 1873-1945 .... **TCLC 63:**
See also DLB 17

Becker, Jurek 1937-............ **CLC 7, 19**
See also CA 85-88; DLB 75

Becker, Walter 1950-............ **CLC 26**

Beckett, Samuel (Barclay)
1906-1989 ...... **CLC 1, 2, 3, 4, 6, 9, 10,
11, 14, 18, 29, 57, 59, 83; DA; DAB;
DAC; DAM DRAM, MST, NOV;
SSC 16; WLC**
See also CA 5-8R; 130; CANR 33;
CDBLB 1945-1960; DLB 13, 15;
DLBY 90; MTCW

Beckford, William 1760-1844 .... **NCLC 16**
See also DLB 39

Beckman, Gunnel 1910-........... **CLC 26**
See also CA 33-36R; CANR 15; CLR 25;
MAICYA; SAAS 9; SATA 6

Becque, Henri 1837-1899........ **NCLC 3**

Beddoes, Thomas Lovell
1803-1849 .... **NCLC 3**
See also DLB 96

Bede c. 673-735................ **CMLC 20**
See also DLB 146

Bedford, Donald F.
See Fearing, Kenneth (Flexner)

Beecher, Catharine Esther
1800-1878 .... **NCLC 30**
See also DLB 1

Beecher, John 1904-1980........... **CLC 6**
See also AITN 1; CA 5-8R; 105; CANR 8

Beer, Johann 1655-1700............ **LC 5**
See also DLB 168

Beer, Patricia 1924-.............. **CLC 58**
See also CA 61-64; CANR 13, 46; DLB 40

Beerbohm, Max
See Beerbohm, (Henry) Max(imilian)

Beerbohm, (Henry) Max(imilian)
1872-1956 .... **TCLC 1, 24**
See also CA 104; 154; DLB 34, 100

Beer-Hofmann, Richard
1866-1945 .... **TCLC 60**
See also DLB 81

Begiebing, Robert J(ohn) 1946-..... **CLC 70**
See also CA 122; CANR 40

Behan, Brendan
1923-1964 .... **CLC 1, 8, 11, 15, 79;
DAM DRAM**
See also CA 73-76; CANR 33;
CDBLB 1945-1960; DLB 13; MTCW

Behn, Aphra
1640(?)-1689 ...... **LC 1, 30; DA; DAB;
DAC; DAM DRAM, MST, NOV,
POET; DC 4; PC 13; WLC**
See also DLB 39, 80, 131

Behrman, S(amuel) N(athaniel)
1893-1973 .... **CLC 40**
See also CA 13-16; 45-48; CAP 1; DLB 7,
44

Belasco, David 1853-1931 .... **TCLC 3**
See also CA 104; DLB 7

Belcheva, Elisaveta 1893- .... **CLC 10**
See also Bagryana, Elisaveta

Beldone, Phil "Cheech"
See Ellison, Harlan (Jay)

Beleno
See Azuela, Mariano

Belinski, Vissarion Grigoryevich
1811-1848 .... **NCLC 5**

Belitt, Ben 1911-................. **CLC 22**
See also CA 13-16R; CAAS 4; CANR 7;
DLB 5

Bell, Gertrude 1868-1926........ **TCLC 67**
See also DLB 174

Bell, James Madison
1826-1902 .... **TCLC 43; BLC;
DAM MULT**
See also BW 1; CA 122; 124; DLB 50

Bell, Madison Smartt 1957-........ **CLC 41**
See also CA 111; CANR 28, 54

Bell, Marvin (Hartley)
1937- .... **CLC 8, 31; DAM POET**
See also CA 21-24R; CAAS 14; DLB 5;
MTCW

Bell, W. L. D.
See Mencken, H(enry) L(ouis)

Bellamy, Atwood C.
See Mencken, H(enry) L(ouis)

Bellamy, Edward 1850-1898 ...... **NCLC 4**
See also DLB 12

Bellin, Edward J.
See Kuttner, Henry

Author Index

Bessie, Alvah 1904-1985 . . . . CLC 23
See also CA 5-8R; 116; CANR 2; DLB 26

Bethlen, T. D.
See Silverberg, Robert

Beti, Mongo . . . . CLC 27; BLC; DAM MULT
See also Biyidi, Alexandre

Betjeman, John
1906-1984 . . . . CLC 2, 6, 10, 34, 43;
DAB; DAM MST, POET
See also CA 9-12R; 112; CANR 33, 56;
CDBLB 1945-1960; DLB 20; DLBY 84;
MTCW

Bettelheim, Bruno 1903-1990 . . . . . . CLC 79
See also CA 81-84; 131; CANR 23; MTCW

Betti, Ugo 1892-1953 . . . . TCLC 5
See also CA 104; 155

Betts, Doris (Waugh) 1932- . . . . CLC 3, 6, 28
See also CA 13-16R; CANR 9; DLBY 82;
INT CANR-9

Bevan, Alistair
See Roberts, Keith (John Kingston)

Bialik, Chaim Nachman
1873-1934 . . . . TCLC 25

Bickerstaff, Isaac
See Swift, Jonathan

Bidart, Frank 1939- . . . . CLC 33
See also CA 140

Bienek, Horst 1930- . . . . CLC 7, 11
See also CA 73-76; DLB 75

Bierce, Ambrose (Gwinett)
1842-1914(?) . . . . TCLC 1, 7, 44; DA;
DAC; DAM MST; SSC 9; WLC
See also CA 104; 139; CDALB 1865-1917;
DLB 11, 12, 23, 71, 74

Biggers, Earl Derr 1884-1933 . . . . . TCLC 65
See also CA 108; 153

Billings, Josh
See Shaw, Henry Wheeler

Billington, (Lady) Rachel (Mary)
1942- . . . . CLC 43
See also AITN 2; CA 33-36R; CANR 44

Binyon, T(imothy) J(ohn) 1936- . . . . CLC 34
See also CA 111; CANR 28

Bioy Casares, Adolfo
1914- . . . . CLC 4, 8, 13, 88;
DAM MULT; HLC; SSC 17
See also CA 29-32R; CANR 19, 43;
DLB 113; HW; MTCW

Bird, Cordwainer
See Ellison, Harlan (Jay)

Bird, Robert Montgomery
1806-1854 . . . . NCLC 1

Birney, (Alfred) Earle
1904- . . . . CLC 1, 4, 6, 11; DAC;
DAM MST, POET
See also CA 1-4R; CANR 5, 20; DLB 88;
MTCW

Bishop, Elizabeth
1911-1979 . . . . . . CLC 1, 4, 9, 13, 15, 32;
DA; DAC; DAM MST, POET; PC 3
See also CA 5-8R; 89-92; CABS 2;
CANR 26; CDALB 1968-1988; DLB 5,
169; MTCW; SATA-Obit 24

Bishop, John 1935- . . . . CLC 10
See also CA 105

Bissett, Bill 1939- . . . . CLC 18; PC 14
See also CA 69-72; CAAS 19; CANR 15;
DLB 53; MTCW

Bitov, Andrei (Georgievich) 1937- . . . CLC 57
See also CA 142

Biyidi, Alexandre 1932-
See Beti, Mongo
See also BW 1; CA 114; 124; MTCW

Bjarme, Brynjolf
See Ibsen, Henrik (Johan)

Bjornson, Bjornstjerne (Martinius)
1832-1910 . . . . TCLC 7, 37
See also CA 104

Black, Robert
See Holdstock, Robert P.

Blackburn, Paul 1926-1971 . . . . . . CLC 9, 43
See also CA 81-84; 33-36R; CANR 34;
DLB 16; DLBY 81

Black Elk
1863-1950 . . . . . TCLC 33; DAM MULT
See also CA 144; NNAL

Black Hobart
See Sanders, (James) Ed(ward)

Blacklin, Malcolm
See Chambers, Aidan

Blackmore, R(ichard) D(oddridge)
1825-1900 . . . . TCLC 27
See also CA 120; DLB 18

Blackmur, R(ichard) P(almer)
1904-1965 . . . . CLC 2, 24
See also CA 11-12; 25-28R; CAP 1; DLB 63

Black Tarantula
See Acker, Kathy

Blackwood, Algernon (Henry)
1869-1951 . . . . TCLC 5
See also CA 105; 150; DLB 153, 156

Blackwood, Caroline
1931-1996 . . . . CLC 6, 9, 100
See also CA 85-88; 151; CANR 32;
DLB 14; MTCW

Blade, Alexander
See Hamilton, Edmond; Silverberg, Robert

Blaga, Lucian 1895-1961 . . . . CLC 75

Blair, Eric (Arthur) 1903-1950
See Orwell, George
See also CA 104; 132; DA; DAB; DAC;
DAM MST, NOV; MTCW; SATA 29

Blais, Marie-Claire
1939- . . . . CLC 2, 4, 6, 13, 22; DAC;
DAM MST
See also CA 21-24R; CAAS 4; CANR 38;
DLB 53; MTCW

Blaise, Clark 1940- . . . . CLC 29
See also AITN 2; CA 53-56; CAAS 3;
CANR 5; DLB 53

Blake, Nicholas
See Day Lewis, C(ecil)
See also DLB 77

Blake, William
1757-1827 . . . . NCLC 13, 37, 57; DA;
DAB; DAC; DAM MST, POET; PC 12;
WLC
See also CDBLB 1789-1832; DLB 93, 163;
MAICYA; SATA 30

Blake, William J(ames) 1894-1969 . . . PC 12
See also CA 5-8R; 25-28R

Blasco Ibanez, Vicente
1867-1928 . . . . TCLC 12; DAM NOV
See also CA 110; 131; HW; MTCW

Blatty, William Peter
1928- . . . . CLC 2; DAM POP
See also CA 5-8R; CANR 9

Bleeck, Oliver
See Thomas, Ross (Elmore)

Blessing, Lee 1949- . . . . CLC 54

Blish, James (Benjamin)
1921-1975 . . . . CLC 14
See also CA 1-4R; 57-60; CANR 3; DLB 8;
MTCW; SATA 66

Bliss, Reginald
See Wells, H(erbert) G(eorge)

Blixen, Karen (Christentze Dinesen)
1885-1962
See Dinesen, Isak
See also CA 25-28; CANR 22, 50; CAP 2;
MTCW; SATA 44

Bloch, Robert (Albert) 1917-1994 . . . CLC 33
See also CA 5-8R; 146; CAAS 20; CANR 5;
DLB 44; INT CANR-5; SATA 12;
SATA-Obit 82

Blok, Alexander (Alexandrovich)
1880-1921 . . . . TCLC 5
See also CA 104

Blom, Jan
See Breytenbach, Breyten

Bloom, Harold 1930- . . . . CLC 24
See also CA 13-16R; CANR 39; DLB 67

Bloomfield, Aurelius
See Bourne, Randolph S(illiman)

Blount, Roy (Alton), Jr. 1941- . . . . . CLC 38
See also CA 53-56; CANR 10, 28;
INT CANR-28; MTCW

Bloy, Leon 1846-1917 . . . . TCLC 22
See also CA 121; DLB 123

Blume, Judy (Sussman)
1938- . . . CLC 12, 30; DAM NOV, POP
See also AAYA 3; CA 29-32R; CANR 13,
37; CLR 2, 15; DLB 52; JRDA;
MAICYA; MTCW; SATA 2, 31, 79

Blunden, Edmund (Charles)
1896-1974 . . . . CLC 2, 56
See also CA 17-18; 45-48; CANR 54;
CAP 2; DLB 20, 100, 155; MTCW

Bly, Robert (Elwood)
1926- . . . . CLC 1, 2, 5, 10, 15, 38;
DAM POET
See also CA 5-8R; CANR 41; DLB 5;
MTCW

Boas, Franz 1858-1942 . . . . TCLC 56
See also CA 115

Bobette
See Simenon, Georges (Jacques Christian)

Boccaccio, Giovanni
1313-1375 . . . . CMLC 13; SSC 10

Bochco, Steven 1943- . . . . CLC 35
See also AAYA 11; CA 124; 138

Bodenheim, Maxwell 1892-1954 . . . TCLC 44
See also CA 110; DLB 9, 45

Bodker, Cecil 1927- .... **CLC 21**
　　See also CA 73-76; CANR 13, 44; CLR 23;
　　MAICYA; SATA 14

Boell, Heinrich (Theodor)
　　1917-1985 .... **CLC 2, 3, 6, 9, 11, 15, 27,**
　　　　32, 72; DA; DAB; DAC; DAM MST,
　　　　　　　　NOV; SSC 23; WLC
　　See also CA 21-24R; 116; CANR 24;
　　DLB 69; DLBY 85; MTCW

Boerne, Alfred
　　See Doeblin, Alfred

Boethius 480(?)-524(?) .... **CMLC 15**
　　See also DLB 115

Bogan, Louise
　　1897-1970 .... **CLC 4, 39, 46, 93;**
　　　　　　　　DAM POET; PC 12
　　See also CA 73-76; 25-28R; CANR 33;
　　DLB 45, 169; MTCW

Bogarde, Dirk .... **CLC 19**
　　See also Van Den Bogarde, Derek Jules
　　　Gaspard Ulric Niven
　　See also DLB 14

Bogosian, Eric 1953- .... **CLC 45**
　　See also CA 138

Bograd, Larry 1953-.............. **CLC 35**
　　See also CA 93-96; CANR 57; SAAS 21;
　　SATA 33, 89

Boiardo, Matteo Maria 1441-1494 .... **LC 6**

Boileau-Despreaux, Nicolas
　　1636-1711 .... **LC 3**

Bojer, Johan 1872-1959 .... **TCLC 64**

Boland, Eavan (Aisling)
　　1944- .... **CLC 40, 67; DAM POET**
　　See also CA 143; DLB 40

Bolt, Lee
　　See Faust, Frederick (Schiller)

Bolt, Robert (Oxton)
　　1924-1995 .... **CLC 14; DAM DRAM**
　　See also CA 17-20R; 147; CANR 35;
　　DLB 13; MTCW

Bombet, Louis-Alexandre-Cesar
　　See Stendhal

Bomkauf
　　See Kaufman, Bob (Garnell)

Bonaventura.................... **NCLC 35**
　　See also DLB 90

Bond, Edward
　　1934- ... **CLC 4, 6, 13, 23; DAM DRAM**
　　See also CA 25-28R; CANR 38; DLB 13;
　　MTCW

Bonham, Frank 1914-1989........ **CLC 12**
　　See also AAYA 1; CA 9-12R; CANR 4, 36;
　　JRDA; MAICYA; SAAS 3; SATA 1, 49;
　　SATA-Obit 62

Bonnefoy, Yves
　　1923- ...... **CLC 9, 15, 58; DAM MST,**
　　　　　　　　　　　　POET
　　See also CA 85-88; CANR 33; MTCW

Bontemps, Arna(ud Wendell)
　　1902-1973 .... **CLC 1, 18; BLC;**
　　　　　　DAM MULT, NOV, POET
　　See also BW 1; CA 1-4R; 41-44R; CANR 4,
　　35; CLR 6; DLB 48, 51; JRDA;
　　MAICYA; MTCW; SATA 2, 44;
　　SATA-Obit 24

Booth, Martin 1944-.............. **CLC 13**
　　See also CA 93-96; CAAS 2

Booth, Philip 1925-.............. **CLC 23**
　　See also CA 5-8R; CANR 5; DLBY 82

Booth, Wayne C(layson) 1921- ..... **CLC 24**
　　See also CA 1-4R; CAAS 5; CANR 3, 43;
　　DLB 67

Borchert, Wolfgang 1921-1947 ..... **TCLC 5**
　　See also CA 104; DLB 69, 124

Borel, Petrus 1809-1859........ **NCLC 41**

Borges, Jorge Luis
　　1899-1986 ... **CLC 1, 2, 3, 4, 6, 8, 9, 10,**
　　　　13, 19, 44, 48, 83; DA; DAB; DAC;
　　　　DAM MST, MULT; HLC; SSC 4; WLC
　　See also AAYA 19; CA 21-24R; CANR 19,
　　33; DLB 113; DLBY 86; HW; MTCW

Borowski, Tadeusz 1922-1951 ...... **TCLC 9**
　　See also CA 106; 154

Borrow, George (Henry)
　　1803-1881 .... **NCLC 9**
　　See also DLB 21, 55, 166

Bosman, Herman Charles
　　1905-1951 .... **TCLC 49**

Bosschere, Jean de 1878(?)-1953... **TCLC 19**
　　See also CA 115

Boswell, James
　　1740-1795 ...... **LC 4; DA; DAB; DAC;**
　　　　　　　　DAM MST; WLC
　　See also CDBLB 1660-1789; DLB 104, 142

Bottoms, David 1949-............. **CLC 53**
　　See also CA 105; CANR 22; DLB 120;
　　DLBY 83

Boucicault, Dion 1820-1890...... **NCLC 41**

Boucolon, Maryse 1937(?)-
　　See Conde, Maryse
　　See also CA 110; CANR 30, 53

Bourget, Paul (Charles Joseph)
　　1852-1935 .... **TCLC 12**
　　See also CA 107; DLB 123

Bourjaily, Vance (Nye) 1922- .... **CLC 8, 62**
　　See also CA 1-4R; CAAS 1; CANR 2;
　　DLB 2, 143

Bourne, Randolph S(illiman)
　　1886-1918 .... **TCLC 16**
　　See also CA 117; 155; DLB 63

Bova, Ben(jamin William) 1932-.... **CLC 45**
　　See also AAYA 16; CA 5-8R; CAAS 18;
　　CANR 11, 56; CLR 3; DLBY 81;
　　INT CANR-11; MAICYA; MTCW;
　　SATA 6, 68

Bowen, Elizabeth (Dorothea Cole)
　　1899-1973 ...... **CLC 1, 3, 6, 11, 15, 22;**
　　　　　　　　DAM NOV; SSC 3
　　See also CA 17-18; 41-44R; CANR 35;
　　CAP 2; CDBLB 1945-1960; DLB 15, 162;
　　MTCW

Bowering, George 1935-........ **CLC 15, 47**
　　See also CA 21-24R; CAAS 16; CANR 10;
　　DLB 53

Bowering, Marilyn R(uthe) 1949-... **CLC 32**
　　See also CA 101; CANR 49

Bowers, Edgar 1924- .... **CLC 9**
　　See also CA 5-8R; CANR 24; DLB 5

Bowie, David .... **CLC 17**
　　See also Jones, David Robert

Bowles, Jane (Sydney)
　　1917-1973 .... **CLC 3, 68**
　　See also CA 19-20; 41-44R; CAP 2

Bowles, Paul (Frederick)
　　1910- .... **CLC 1, 2, 19, 53; SSC 3**
　　See also CA 1-4R; CAAS 1; CANR 1, 19,
　　50; DLB 5, 6; MTCW

Box, Edgar
　　See Vidal, Gore

Boyd, Nancy
　　See Millay, Edna St. Vincent

Boyd, William 1952-........ **CLC 28, 53, 70**
　　See also CA 114; 120; CANR 51

Boyle, Kay
　　1902-1992 ..... **CLC 1, 5, 19, 58; SSC 5**
　　See also CA 13-16R; 140; CAAS 1;
　　CANR 29; DLB 4, 9, 48, 86; DLBY 93;
　　MTCW

Boyle, Mark
　　See Kienzle, William X(avier)

Boyle, Patrick 1905-1982.......... **CLC 19**
　　See also CA 127

Boyle, T. C. 1948-
　　See Boyle, T(homas) Coraghessan

Boyle, T(homas) Coraghessan
　　1948- ..... **CLC 36, 55, 90; DAM POP;**
　　　　　　　　　　　　SSC 16
　　See also BEST 90:4; CA 120; CANR 44;
　　DLBY 86

Boz
　　See Dickens, Charles (John Huffam)

Brackenridge, Hugh Henry
　　1748-1816 .... **NCLC 7**
　　See also DLB 11, 37

Bradbury, Edward P.
　　See Moorcock, Michael (John)

Bradbury, Malcolm (Stanley)
　　1932- .... **CLC 32, 61; DAM NOV**
　　See also CA 1-4R; CANR 1, 33; DLB 14;
　　MTCW

Bradbury, Ray (Douglas)
　　1920- ..... **CLC 1, 3, 10, 15, 42, 98; DA;**
　　　　DAB; DAC; DAM MST, NOV, POP;
　　　　　　　　　　　　WLC
　　See also AAYA 15; AITN 1, 2; CA 1-4R;
　　CANR 2, 30; CDALB 1968-1988; DLB 2,
　　8; INT CANR-30; MTCW; SATA 11, 64

Bradford, Gamaliel 1863-1932..... **TCLC 36**
　　See also DLB 17

Bradley, David (Henry, Jr.)
　　1950- ..... **CLC 23; BLC; DAM MULT**
　　See also BW 1; CA 104; CANR 26; DLB 33

Bradley, John Ed(mund, Jr.)
　　1958- .... **CLC 55**
　　See also CA 139

Bradley, Marion Zimmer
　　1930- .... **CLC 30; DAM POP**
　　See also AAYA 9; CA 57-60; CAAS 10;
　　CANR 7, 31, 51; DLB 8; MTCW;
　　SATA 90

Bradstreet, Anne
　　1612(?)-1672 ...... **LC 4, 30; DA; DAC;**
　　　　　　　　DAM MST, POET; PC 10
　　See also CDALB 1640-1865; DLB 24

Brady, Joan 1939- .... **CLC 86**
　　See also CA 141

Broumas, Olga   1949- .... **CLC 10, 73**
See also CA 85-88; CANR 20

Brown, Alan   1951- .... **CLC 99**

Brown, Charles Brockden
1771-1810 .... **NCLC 22**
See also CDALB 1640-1865; DLB 37, 59, 73

Brown, Christy   1932-1981 .... **CLC 63**
See also CA 105; 104; DLB 14

Brown, Claude
1937- ..... **CLC 30; BLC; DAM MULT**
See also AAYA 7; BW 1; CA 73-76

Brown, Dee (Alexander)
1908- .... **CLC 18, 47; DAM POP**
See also CA 13-16R; CAAS 6; CANR 11, 45; DLBY 80; MTCW; SATA 5

Brown, George
See Wertmueller, Lina

Brown, George Douglas
1869-1902 .... **TCLC 28**

Brown, George Mackay
1921-1996 .... **CLC 5, 48, 100**
See also CA 21-24R; 151; CAAS 6; CANR 12, 37; DLB 14, 27, 139; MTCW; SATA 35

Brown, (William) Larry   1951- ...... **CLC 73**
See also CA 130; 134; INT 133

Brown, Moses
See Barrett, William (Christopher)

Brown, Rita Mae
1944- ..... **CLC 18, 43, 79; DAM NOV, POP**
See also CA 45-48; CANR 2, 11, 35; INT CANR-11; MTCW

Brown, Roderick (Langmere) Haig-
See Haig-Brown, Roderick (Langmere)

Brown, Rosellen   1939- .... **CLC 32**
See also CA 77-80; CAAS 10; CANR 14, 44

Brown, Sterling Allen
1901-1989 .... **CLC 1, 23, 59; BLC; DAM MULT, POET**
See also BW 1; CA 85-88; 127; CANR 26; DLB 48, 51, 63; MTCW

Brown, Will
See Ainsworth, William Harrison

Brown, William Wells
1813-1884 .... **NCLC 2; BLC; DAM MULT; DC 1**
See also DLB 3, 50

Browne, (Clyde) Jackson   1948(?)- ... **CLC 21**
See also CA 120

Browning, Elizabeth Barrett
1806-1861 .... **NCLC 1, 16, 61; DA; DAB; DAC; DAM MST, POET; PC 6; WLC**
See also CDBLB 1832-1890; DLB 32

Browning, Robert
1812-1889 .... **NCLC 19; DA; DAB; DAC; DAM MST, POET; PC 2**
See also CDBLB 1832-1890; DLB 32, 163; YABC 1

Browning, Tod   1882-1962 .... **CLC 16**
See also CA 141; 117

Brownson, Orestes (Augustus)
1803-1876 .... **NCLC 50**

Bruccoli, Matthew J(oseph)   1931- .. **CLC 34**
See also CA 9-12R; CANR 7; DLB 103

Bruce, Lenny .... **CLC 21**
See also Schneider, Leonard Alfred

Bruin, John
See Brutus, Dennis

Brulard, Henri
See Stendhal

Brulls, Christian
See Simenon, Georges (Jacques Christian)

Brunner, John (Kilian Houston)
1934-1995 ...... **CLC 8, 10; DAM POP**
See also CA 1-4R; 149; CAAS 8; CANR 2, 37; MTCW

Bruno, Giordano   1548-1600 .... **LC 27**

Brutus, Dennis
1924- ..... **CLC 43; BLC; DAM MULT, POET**
See also BW 2; CA 49-52; CAAS 14; CANR 2, 27, 42; DLB 117

Bryan, C(ourtlandt) D(ixon) B(arnes)
1936- .... **CLC 29**
See also CA 73-76; CANR 13; INT CANR-13

Bryan, Michael
See Moore, Brian

Bryant, William Cullen
1794-1878 ..... **NCLC 6, 46; DA; DAB; DAC; DAM MST, POET**
See also CDALB 1640-1865; DLB 3, 43, 59

Bryusov, Valery Yakovlevich
1873-1924 .... **TCLC 10**
See also CA 107; 155

Buchan, John
1875-1940 .... **TCLC 41; DAB; DAM POP**
See also CA 108; 145; DLB 34, 70, 156; YABC 2

Buchanan, George   1506-1582 .... **LC 4**

Buchheim, Lothar-Guenther   1918- ... **CLC 6**
See also CA 85-88

Buchner, (Karl) Georg
1813-1837 .... **NCLC 26**

Buchwald, Art(hur)   1925- .... **CLC 33**
See also AITN 1; CA 5-8R; CANR 21; MTCW; SATA 10

Buck, Pearl S(ydenstricker)
1892-1973 .... **CLC 7, 11, 18; DA; DAB; DAC; DAM MST, NOV**
See also AITN 1; CA 1-4R; 41-44R; CANR 1, 34; DLB 9, 102; MTCW; SATA 1, 25

Buckler, Ernest
1908-1984 .. **CLC 13; DAC; DAM MST**
See also CA 11-12; 114; CAP 1; DLB 68; SATA 47

Buckley, Vincent (Thomas)
1925-1988 .... **CLC 57**
See also CA 101

Buckley, William F(rank), Jr.
1925- .... **CLC 7, 18, 37; DAM POP**
See also AITN 1; CA 1-4R; CANR 1, 24, 53; DLB 137; DLBY 80; INT CANR-24; MTCW

Buechner, (Carl) Frederick
1926- ...... **CLC 2, 4, 6, 9; DAM NOV**
See also CA 13-16R; CANR 11, 39; DLBY 80; INT CANR-11; MTCW

Buell, John (Edward)   1927- .... **CLC 10**
See also CA 1-4R; DLB 53

Buero Vallejo, Antonio   1916- ... **CLC 15, 46**
See also CA 106; CANR 24, 49; HW; MTCW

Bufalino, Gesualdo   1920(?)- .... **CLC 74**

Bugayev, Boris Nikolayevich   1880-1934
See Bely, Andrey
See also CA 104

Bukowski, Charles
1920-1994 .... **CLC 2, 5, 9, 41, 82; DAM NOV, POET**
See also CA 17-20R; 144; CANR 40; DLB 5, 130, 169; MTCW

Bulgakov, Mikhail (Afanas'evich)
1891-1940 .... **TCLC 2, 16; DAM DRAM, NOV; SSC 18**
See also CA 105; 152

Bulgya, Alexander Alexandrovich
1901-1956 .... **TCLC 53**
See also Fadeyev, Alexander
See also CA 117

Bullins, Ed
1935- .... **CLC 1, 5, 7; BLC; DAM DRAM, MULT; DC 6**
See also BW 2; CA 49-52; CAAS 16; CANR 24, 46; DLB 7, 38; MTCW

Bulwer-Lytton, Edward (George Earle Lytton)
1803-1873 .... **NCLC 1, 45**
See also DLB 21

Bunin, Ivan Alexeyevich
1870-1953 .... **TCLC 6; SSC 5**
See also CA 104

Bunting, Basil
1900-1985 .... **CLC 10, 39, 47; DAM POET**
See also CA 53-56; 115; CANR 7; DLB 20

Bunuel, Luis
1900-1983 .... **CLC 16, 80; DAM MULT; HLC**
See also CA 101; 110; CANR 32; HW

Bunyan, John
1628-1688 ...... **LC 4; DA; DAB; DAC; DAM MST; WLC**
See also CDBLB 1660-1789; DLB 39

Burckhardt, Jacob (Christoph)
1818-1897 .... **NCLC 49**

Burford, Eleanor
See Hibbert, Eleanor Alice Burford

Burgess, Anthony
CLC 1, 2, 4, 5, 8, 10, 13, 15, 22, 40, 62, 81, 94; DAB
See also Wilson, John (Anthony) Burgess
See also AITN 1; CDBLB 1960 to Present; DLB 14

Burke, Edmund
1729(?)-1797 ...... **LC 7, 36; DA; DAB; DAC; DAM MST; WLC**
See also DLB 104

Campos, Alvaro de
   See Pessoa, Fernando (Antonio Nogueira)
Camus, Albert
      1913-1960 .... CLC 1, 2, 4, 9, 11, 14, 32,
         63, 69; DA; DAB; DAC; DAM DRAM,
         MST, NOV; DC 2; SSC 9; WLC
   See also CA 89-92; DLB 72; MTCW
Canby, Vincent 1924-............ CLC 13
   See also CA 81-84
Cancale
   See Desnos, Robert
Canetti, Elias
      1905-1994 .... CLC 3, 14, 25, 75, 86
   See also CA 21-24R; 146; CANR 23;
      DLB 85, 124; MTCW
Canin, Ethan 1960-............ CLC 55
   See also CA 131; 135
Cannon, Curt
   See Hunter, Evan
Cape, Judith
   See Page, P(atricia) K(athleen)
Capek, Karel
      1890-1938 ...... TCLC 6, 37; DA; DAB;
         DAC; DAM DRAM, MST, NOV; DC 1;
                                          WLC
   See also CA 104; 140
Capote, Truman
      1924-1984 ..... CLC 1, 3, 8, 13, 19, 34,
         38, 58; DA; DAB; DAC; DAM MST,
         NOV, POP; SSC 2; WLC
   See also CA 5-8R; 113; CANR 18;
      CDALB 1941-1968; DLB 2; DLBY 80,
      84; MTCW; SATA 91
Capra, Frank 1897-1991........... CLC 16
   See also CA 61-64; 135
Caputo, Philip 1941-............ CLC 32
   See also CA 73-76; CANR 40
Card, Orson Scott
      1951-..... CLC 44, 47, 50; DAM POP
   See also AAYA 11; CA 102; CANR 27, 47;
      INT CANR-27; MTCW; SATA 83
Cardenal, Ernesto
      1925-.......... CLC 31; DAM MULT,
                                 POET; HLC
   See also CA 49-52; CANR 2, 32; HW;
      MTCW
Cardozo, Benjamin N(athan)
      1870-1938 .... TCLC 65
   See also CA 117
Carducci, Giosue 1835-1907....... TCLC 32
Carew, Thomas 1595(?)-1640........ LC 13
   See also DLB 126
Carey, Ernestine Gilbreth 1908-.... CLC 17
   See also CA 5-8R; SATA 2
Carey, Peter 1943-........ CLC 40, 55, 96
   See also CA 123; 127; CANR 53; INT 127;
      MTCW
Carleton, William 1794-1869...... NCLC 3
   See also DLB 159
Carlisle, Henry (Coffin) 1926-...... CLC 33
   See also CA 13-16R; CANR 15
Carlsen, Chris
   See Holdstock, Robert P.
Carlson, Ron(ald F.) 1947-........ CLC 54
   See also CA 105; CANR 27

Carlyle, Thomas
      1795-1881 .... NCLC 22; DA; DAB;
                                 DAC; DAM MST
   See also CDBLB 1789-1832; DLB 55; 144
Carman, (William) Bliss
      1861-1929 .... TCLC 7; DAC
   See also CA 104; 152; DLB 92
Carnegie, Dale 1888-1955 .... TCLC 53
Carossa, Hans 1878-1956........ TCLC 48
   See also DLB 66
Carpenter, Don(ald Richard)
      1931-1995 .... CLC 41
   See also CA 45-48; 149; CANR 1
Carpentier (y Valmont), Alejo
      1904-1980 .... CLC 8, 11, 38;
                                 DAM MULT; HLC
   See also CA 65-68; 97-100; CANR 11;
      DLB 113; HW
Carr, Caleb 1955(?)-.............. CLC 86
   See also CA 147
Carr, Emily 1871-1945............ TCLC 32
   See also DLB 68
Carr, John Dickson 1906-1977 ...... CLC 3
   See also CA 49-52; 69-72; CANR 3, 33;
      MTCW
Carr, Philippa
   See Hibbert, Eleanor Alice Burford
Carr, Virginia Spencer 1929-....... CLC 34
   See also CA 61-64; DLB 111
Carrere, Emmanuel 1957- .... CLC 89
Carrier, Roch
      1937- ... CLC 13, 78; DAC; DAM MST
   See also CA 130; DLB 53
Carroll, James P. 1943(?)-......... CLC 38
   See also CA 81-84
Carroll, Jim 1951-................ CLC 35
   See also AAYA 17; CA 45-48; CANR 42
Carroll, Lewis .... NCLC 2, 53; WLC
   See also Dodgson, Charles Lutwidge
   See also CDBLB 1832-1890; CLR 2, 18;
      DLB 18, 163; JRDA
Carroll, Paul Vincent 1900-1968.... CLC 10
   See also CA 9-12R; 25-28R; DLB 10
Carruth, Hayden
      1921- ...... CLC 4, 7, 10, 18, 84; PC 10
   See also CA 9-12R; CANR 4, 38; DLB 5,
      165; INT CANR-4; MTCW; SATA 47
Carson, Rachel Louise
      1907-1964 .... CLC 71; DAM POP
   See also CA 77-80; CANR 35; MTCW;
      SATA 23
Carter, Angela (Olive)
      1940-1992 ...... CLC 5, 41, 76; SSC 13
   See also CA 53-56; 136; CANR 12, 36;
      DLB 14; MTCW; SATA 66;
      SATA-Obit 70
Carter, Nick
   See Smith, Martin Cruz
Carver, Raymond
      1938-1988 .... CLC 22, 36, 53, 55;
                                 DAM NOV; SSC 8
   See also CA 33-36R; 126; CANR 17, 34;
      DLB 130; DLBY 84, 88; MTCW
Cary, Elizabeth, Lady Falkland
      1585-1639 .... LC 30

Cary, (Arthur) Joyce (Lunel)
      1888-1957 ....TCLC 1, 29
   See also CA 104; CDBLB 1914-1945;
      DLB 15, 100
Casanova de Seingalt, Giovanni Jacopo
      1725-1798 .... LC 13
Casares, Adolfo Bioy
   See Bioy Casares, Adolfo
Casely-Hayford, J(oseph) E(phraim)
      1866-1930 .... TCLC 24; BLC;
                                 DAM MULT
   See also BW 2; CA 123; 152
Casey, John (Dudley) 1939-........ CLC 59
   See also BEST 90:2; CA 69-72; CANR 23
Casey, Michael 1947-.............. CLC 2
   See also CA 65-68; DLB 5
Casey, Patrick
   See Thurman, Wallace (Henry)
Casey, Warren (Peter) 1935-1988 ... CLC 12
   See also CA 101; 127; INT 101
Casona, Alejandro................ CLC 49
   See also Alvarez, Alejandro Rodriguez
Cassavetes, John 1929-1989........ CLC 20
   See also CA 85-88; 127
Cassian, Nina 1924-................ PC 17
Cassill, R(onald) V(erlin) 1919-... CLC 4, 23
   See also CA 9-12R; CAAS 1; CANR 7, 45;
      DLB 6
Cassirer, Ernst 1874-1945 .... TCLC 61
Cassity, (Allen) Turner 1929- .... CLC 6, 42
   See also CA 17-20R; CAAS 8; CANR 11;
      DLB 105
Castaneda, Carlos 1931(?)-......... CLC 12
   See also CA 25-28R; CANR 32; HW;
      MTCW
Castedo, Elena 1937-............. CLC 65
   See also CA 132
Castedo-Ellerman, Elena
   See Castedo, Elena
Castellanos, Rosario
      1925-1974 ...... CLC 66; DAM MULT;
                                          HLC
   See also CA 131; 53-56; DLB 113; HW
Castelvetro, Lodovico 1505-1571..... LC 12
Castiglione, Baldassare 1478-1529 ... LC 12
Castle, Robert
   See Hamilton, Edmond
Castro, Guillen de 1569-1631........ LC 19
Castro, Rosalia de
      1837-1885 ...... NCLC 3; DAM MULT
Cather, Willa
   See Cather, Willa Sibert
Cather, Willa Sibert
      1873-1947 .... TCLC 1, 11, 31; DA;
         DAB; DAC; DAM MST, NOV; SSC 2;
                                          WLC
   See also CA 104; 128; CDALB 1865-1917;
      DLB 9, 54, 78; DLBD 1; MTCW;
      SATA 30
Cato, Marcus Porcius
      234B.C.-149B.C............. CMLC 21

Catton, (Charles) Bruce
1899-1978 . . . . CLC 35
See also AITN 1; CA 5-8R; 81-84;
CANR 7; DLB 17; SATA 2;
SATA-Obit 24

Catullus c. 84B.C.-c. 54B.C. . . . . . CMLC 18

Cauldwell, Frank
See King, Francis (Henry)

Caunitz, William J. 1933-1996 . . . . . CLC 34
See also BEST 89:3; CA 125; 130; 152;
INT 130

Causley, Charles (Stanley) 1917-. . . . . CLC 7
See also CA 9-12R; CANR 5, 35; CLR 30;
DLB 27; MTCW; SATA 3, 66

Caute, David 1936-. . . . CLC 29; DAM NOV
See also CA 1-4R; CAAS 4; CANR 1, 33;
DLB 14

Cavafy, C(onstantine) P(eter)
1863-1933 . . . . TCLC 2, 7; DAM POET
See also Kavafis, Konstantinos Petrou
See also CA 148

Cavallo, Evelyn
See Spark, Muriel (Sarah)

Cavanna, Betty . . . . CLC 12
See also Harrison, Elizabeth Cavanna
See also JRDA; MAICYA; SAAS 4;
SATA 1, 30

Cavendish, Margaret Lucas
1623-1673 . . . . LC 30
See also DLB 131

Caxton, William 1421(?)-1491(?) . . . . . LC 17
See also DLB 170

Cayrol, Jean 1911-. . . . . CLC 11
See also CA 89-92; DLB 83

Cela, Camilo Jose
1916- . . . . . CLC 4, 13, 59; DAM MULT;
HLC
See also BEST 90:2; CA 21-24R; CAAS 10;
CANR 21, 32; DLBY 89; HW; MTCW

Celan, Paul . . . . . . CLC 10, 19, 53, 82; PC 10
See also Antschel, Paul
See also DLB 69

Celine, Louis-Ferdinand
. . . . CLC 1, 3, 4, 7, 9, 15, 47
See also Destouches, Louis-Ferdinand
See also DLB 72

Cellini, Benvenuto 1500-1571 . . . . LC 7

Cendrars, Blaise . . . . CLC 18
See also Sauser-Hall, Frederic

Cernuda (y Bidon), Luis
1902-1963 . . . . CLC 54; DAM POET
See also CA 131; 89-92; DLB 134; HW

Cervantes (Saavedra), Miguel de
1547-1616 . . . . LC 6, 23; DA; DAB;
DAC; DAM MST, NOV; SSC 12; WLC

Cesaire, Aime (Fernand)
1913- . . . . CLC 19, 32; BLC;
DAM MULT, POET
See also BW 2; CA 65-68; CANR 24, 43;
MTCW

Chabon, Michael 1963- . . . . CLC 55
See also CA 139; CANR 57

Chabrol, Claude 1930- . . . . CLC 16
See also CA 110

Challans, Mary 1905-1983
See Renault, Mary
See also CA 81-84; 111; SATA 23;
SATA-Obit 36

Challis, George
See Faust, Frederick (Schiller)

Chambers, Aidan 1934- . . . . CLC 35
See also CA 25-28R; CANR 12, 31; JRDA;
MAICYA; SAAS 12; SATA 1, 69

Chambers, James 1948-
See Cliff, Jimmy
See also CA 124

Chambers, Jessie
See Lawrence, D(avid) H(erbert Richards)

Chambers, Robert W. 1865-1933. . . TCLC 41

Chandler, Raymond (Thornton)
1888-1959 . . . . TCLC 1, 7; SSC 23
See also CA 104; 129; CDALB 1929-1941;
DLBD 6; MTCW

Chang, Jung 1952-. . . . . CLC 71
See also CA 142

Channing, William Ellery
1780-1842 . . . . NCLC 17
See also DLB 1, 59

Chaplin, Charles Spencer
1889-1977 . . . . CLC 16
See also Chaplin, Charlie
See also CA 81-84; 73-76

Chaplin, Charlie
See Chaplin, Charles Spencer
See also DLB 44

Chapman, George
1559(?)-1634 . . . . . LC 22; DAM DRAM
See also DLB 62, 121

Chapman, Graham 1941-1989 . . . . . . CLC 21
See also Monty Python
See also CA 116; 129; CANR 35

Chapman, John Jay 1862-1933 . . . . . TCLC 7
See also CA 104

Chapman, Lee
See Bradley, Marion Zimmer

Chapman, Walker
See Silverberg, Robert

Chappell, Fred (Davis) 1936-. . . . CLC 40, 78
See also CA 5-8R; CAAS 4; CANR 8, 33;
DLB 6, 105

Char, Rene(-Emile)
1907-1988 . . . . CLC 9, 11, 14, 55;
DAM POET
See also CA 13-16R; 124; CANR 32;
MTCW

Charby, Jay
See Ellison, Harlan (Jay)

Chardin, Pierre Teilhard de
See Teilhard de Chardin, (Marie Joseph)
Pierre

Charles I 1600-1649 . . . . LC 13

Charyn, Jerome 1937- . . . . CLC 5, 8, 18
See also CA 5-8R; CAAS 1; CANR 7;
DLBY 83; MTCW

Chase, Mary (Coyle) 1907-1981 . . . . . . DC 1
See also CA 77-80; 105; SATA 17;
SATA-Obit 29

Chase, Mary Ellen 1887-1973 . . . . CLC 2
See also CA 13-16; 41-44R; CAP 1;
SATA 10

Chase, Nicholas
See Hyde, Anthony

Chateaubriand, Francois Rene de
1768-1848 . . . . NCLC 3
See also DLB 119

Chatterje, Sarat Chandra 1876-1936(?)
See Chatterji, Saratchandra
See also CA 109

Chatterji, Bankim Chandra
1838-1894 . . . . NCLC 19

Chatterji, Saratchandra . . . . TCLC 13
See also Chatterje, Sarat Chandra

Chatterton, Thomas
1752-1770 . . . . LC 3; DAM POET
See also DLB 109

Chatwin, (Charles) Bruce
1940-1989 . . CLC 28, 57, 59; DAM POP
See also AAYA 4; BEST 90:1; CA 85-88;
127

Chaucer, Daniel
See Ford, Ford Madox

Chaucer, Geoffrey
1340(?)-1400 . . . . LC 17; DA; DAB;
DAC; DAM MST, POET
See also CDBLB Before 1660; DLB 146

Chaviaras, Strates 1935-
See Haviaras, Stratis
See also CA 105

Chayefsky, Paddy . . . . CLC 23
See also Chayefsky, Sidney
See also DLB 7, 44; DLBY 81

Chayefsky, Sidney 1923-1981
See Chayefsky, Paddy
See also CA 9-12R; 104; CANR 18;
DAM DRAM

Chedid, Andree 1920-. . . . . CLC 47
See also CA 145

Cheever, John
1912-1982 . . . . . . CLC 3, 7, 8, 11, 15, 25,
64; DA; DAB; DAC; DAM MST, NOV,
POP; SSC 1; WLC
See also CA 5-8R; 106; CABS 1; CANR 5,
27; CDALB 1941-1968; DLB 2, 102;
DLBY 80, 82; INT CANR-5; MTCW

Cheever, Susan 1943-. . . . . CLC 18, 48
See also CA 103; CANR 27, 51; DLBY 82;
INT CANR-27

Chekhonte, Antosha
See Chekhov, Anton (Pavlovich)

Chekhov, Anton (Pavlovich)
1860-1904 . . . . . TCLC 3, 10, 31, 55; DA;
DAB; DAC; DAM DRAM, MST; SSC 2;
WLC
See also CA 104; 124; SATA 90

Chernyshevsky, Nikolay Gavrilovich
1828-1889 . . . . NCLC 1

Cherry, Carolyn Janice 1942-
See Cherryh, C. J.
See also CA 65-68; CANR 10

Cherryh, C. J. . . . . CLC 35
See also Cherry, Carolyn Janice
See also DLBY 80

Chesnutt, Charles W(addell)
1858-1932 .... **TCLC 5, 39; BLC;**
DAM MULT; SSC 7
See also BW 1; CA 106; 125; DLB 12, 50,
78; MTCW

Chester, Alfred 1929(?)-1971 ...... **CLC 49**
See also CA 33-36R; DLB 130

Chesterton, G(ilbert) K(eith)
1874-1936 .... **TCLC 1, 6, 64;**
DAM NOV, POET; SSC 1
See also CA 104; 132; CDBLB 1914-1945;
DLB 10, 19, 34, 70, 98, 149; MTCW;
SATA 27

Chiang Pin-chin 1904-1986
See Ding Ling
See also CA 118

Ch'ien Chung-shu 1910- .... **CLC 22**
See also CA 130; MTCW

Child, L. Maria
See Child, Lydia Maria

Child, Lydia Maria 1802-1880 .... **NCLC 6**
See also DLB 1, 74; SATA 67

Child, Mrs.
See Child, Lydia Maria

Child, Philip 1898-1978 .... **CLC 19, 68**
See also CA 13-14; CAP 1; SATA 47

Childers, (Robert) Erskine
1870-1922 .... **TCLC 65**
See also CA 113; 153; DLB 70

Childress, Alice
1920-1994 .... **CLC 12, 15, 86, 96; BLC;**
DAM DRAM, MULT, NOV; DC 4
See also AAYA 8; BW 2; CA 45-48; 146;
CANR 3, 27, 50; CLR 14; DLB 7, 38;
JRDA; MAICYA; MTCW; SATA 7, 48,
81

Chin, Frank (Chew, Jr.) 1940- .... **DC 7**
See also CA 33-36R; DAM MULT

Chislett, (Margaret) Anne 1943- .... **CLC 34**
See also CA 151

Chitty, Thomas Willes 1926- .... **CLC 11**
See also Hinde, Thomas
See also CA 5-8R

Chivers, Thomas Holley
1809-1858 .... **NCLC 49**
See also DLB 3

Chomette, Rene Lucien 1898-1981
See Clair, Rene
See also CA 103

Chopin, Kate
.... **TCLC 5, 14; DA; DAB; SSC 8**
See also Chopin, Katherine
See also CDALB 1865-1917; DLB 12, 78

Chopin, Katherine 1851-1904
See Chopin, Kate
See also CA 104; 122; DAC; DAM MST,
NOV

Chretien de Troyes
c. 12th cent. - .... **CMLC 10**

Christie
See Ichikawa, Kon

Christie, Agatha (Mary Clarissa)
1890-1976 ..... **CLC 1, 6, 8, 12, 39, 48;**
DAB; DAC; DAM NOV
See also AAYA 9; AITN 1, 2; CA 17-20R;
61-64; CANR 10, 37; CDBLB 1914-1945;
DLB 13, 77; MTCW; SATA 36

Christie, (Ann) Philippa
See Pearce, Philippa
See also CA 5-8R; CANR 4

Christine de Pizan 1365(?)-1431(?) .... **LC 9**

Chubb, Elmer
See Masters, Edgar Lee

Chulkov, Mikhail Dmitrievich
1743-1792 .... **LC 2**
See also DLB 150

Churchill, Caryl 1938- ... **CLC 31, 55; DC 5**
See also CA 102; CANR 22, 46; DLB 13;
MTCW

Churchill, Charles 1731-1764 .... **LC 3**
See also DLB 109

Chute, Carolyn 1947- .... **CLC 39**
See also CA 123

Ciardi, John (Anthony)
1916-1986 .... **CLC 10, 40, 44;**
DAM POET
See also CA 5-8R; 118; CAAS 2; CANR 5,
33; CLR 19; DLB 5; DLBY 86;
INT CANR-5; MAICYA; MTCW;
SATA 1, 65; SATA-Obit 46

Cicero, Marcus Tullius
106B.C.-43B.C. .... **CMLC 3**

Cimino, Michael 1943- .... **CLC 16**
See also CA 105

Cioran, E(mil) M. 1911-1995 ...... **CLC 64**
See also CA 25-28R; 149

Cisneros, Sandra
1954- ..... **CLC 69; DAM MULT; HLC**
See also AAYA 9; CA 131; DLB 122, 152;
HW

Cixous, Helene 1937- .... **CLC 92**
See also CA 126; CANR 55; DLB 83;
MTCW

Clair, Rene .... **CLC 20**
See also Chomette, Rene Lucien

Clampitt, Amy 1920-1994 .... **CLC 32**
See also CA 110; 146; CANR 29; DLB 105

Clancy, Thomas L., Jr. 1947-
See Clancy, Tom
See also CA 125; 131; INT 131; MTCW

Clancy, Tom ..... **CLC 45; DAM NOV, POP**
See also Clancy, Thomas L., Jr.
See also AAYA 9; BEST 89:1, 90:1

Clare, John
1793-1864 .... **NCLC 9; DAB;**
DAM POET
See also DLB 55, 96

Clarin
See Alas (y Urena), Leopoldo (Enrique
Garcia)

Clark, Al C.
See Goines, Donald

Clark, (Robert) Brian 1932- .... **CLC 29**
See also CA 41-44R

Clark, Curt
See Westlake, Donald E(dwin)

Clark, Eleanor 1913-1996 .... **CLC 5, 19**
See also CA 9-12R; 151; CANR 41; DLB 6

Clark, J. P.
See Clark, John Pepper
See also DLB 117

Clark, John Pepper
1935- .... **CLC 38; BLC; DAM DRAM,**
MULT; DC 5
See also Clark, J. P.
See also BW 1; CA 65-68; CANR 16

Clark, M. R.
See Clark, Mavis Thorpe

Clark, Mavis Thorpe 1909- .... **CLC 12**
See also CA 57-60; CANR 8, 37; CLR 30;
MAICYA; SAAS 5; SATA 8, 74

Clark, Walter Van Tilburg
1909-1971 .... **CLC 28**
See also CA 9-12R; 33-36R; DLB 9;
SATA 8

Clarke, Arthur C(harles)
1917- .... **CLC 1, 4, 13, 18, 35;**
DAM POP; SSC 3
See also AAYA 4; CA 1-4R; CANR 2, 28,
55; JRDA; MAICYA; MTCW; SATA 13,
70

Clarke, Austin
1896-1974 ...... **CLC 6, 9; DAM POET**
See also CA 29-32; 49-52; CAP 2; DLB 10,
20

Clarke, Austin C(hesterfield)
1934- .... **CLC 8, 53; BLC; DAC;**
DAM MULT
See also BW 1; CA 25-28R; CAAS 16;
CANR 14, 32; DLB 53, 125

Clarke, Gillian 1937- .... **CLC 61**
See also CA 106; DLB 40

Clarke, Marcus (Andrew Hislop)
1846-1881 .... **NCLC 19**

Clarke, Shirley 1925- .... **CLC 16**

Clash, The
See Headon, (Nicky) Topper; Jones, Mick;
Simonon, Paul; Strummer, Joe

Claudel, Paul (Louis Charles Marie)
1868-1955 .... **TCLC 2, 10**
See also CA 104

Clavell, James (duMaresq)
1925-1994 .... **CLC 6, 25, 87;**
DAM NOV, POP
See also CA 25-28R; 146; CANR 26, 48;
MTCW

Cleaver, (Leroy) Eldridge
1935- ..... **CLC 30; BLC; DAM MULT**
See also BW 1; CA 21-24R; CANR 16

Cleese, John (Marwood) 1939- ..... **CLC 21**
See also Monty Python
See also CA 112; 116; CANR 35; MTCW

Cleishbotham, Jebediah
See Scott, Walter

Cleland, John 1710-1789 .... **LC 2**
See also DLB 39

Clemens, Samuel Langhorne 1835-1910
See Twain, Mark
See also CA 104; 135; CDALB 1865-1917;
DA; DAB; DAC; DAM MST, NOV;
DLB 11, 12, 23, 64, 74; JRDA;
MAICYA; YABC 2

Cook, Roy
See Silverberg, Robert

Cooke, Elizabeth 1948- .... **CLC 55**
See also CA 129

Cooke, John Esten 1830-1886..... **NCLC 5**
See also DLB 3

Cooke, John Estes
See Baum, L(yman) Frank

Cooke, M. E.
See Creasey, John

Cooke, Margaret
See Creasey, John

Cook-Lynn, Elizabeth
1930- .... **CLC 93; DAM MULT**
See also CA 133; DLB 175; NNAL

Cooney, Ray .... **CLC 62**

Cooper, Douglas 1960-........... **CLC 86**

Cooper, Henry St. John
See Creasey, John

Cooper, J(oan) California
.... **CLC 56; DAM MULT**
See also AAYA 12; BW 1; CA 125;
CANR 55

Cooper, James Fenimore
1789-1851 .... **NCLC 1, 27, 54**
See also CDALB 1640-1865; DLB 3;
SATA 19

Coover, Robert (Lowell)
1932- .... **CLC 3, 7, 15, 32, 46, 87;**
DAM NOV; SSC 15
See also CA 45-48; CANR 3, 37; DLB 2;
DLBY 81; MTCW

Copeland, Stewart (Armstrong)
1952- .... **CLC 26**

Coppard, A(lfred) E(dgar)
1878-1957 .... **TCLC 5; SSC 21**
See also CA 114; DLB 162; YABC 1

Coppee, Francois 1842-1908 ...... **TCLC 25**

Coppola, Francis Ford 1939-....... **CLC 16**
See also CA 77-80; CANR 40; DLB 44

Corbiere, Tristan 1845-1875 ..... **NCLC 43**

Corcoran, Barbara 1911-........... **CLC 17**
See also AAYA 14; CA 21-24R; CAAS 2;
CANR 11, 28, 48; DLB 52; JRDA;
SAAS 20; SATA 3, 77

Cordelier, Maurice
See Giraudoux, (Hippolyte) Jean

Corelli, Marie 1855-1924........ **TCLC 51**
See also Mackay, Mary
See also DLB 34, 156

Corman, Cid...................... **CLC 9**
See also Corman, Sidney
See also CAAS 2; DLB 5

Corman, Sidney 1924-
See Corman, Cid
See also CA 85-88; CANR 44; DAM POET

Cormier, Robert (Edmund)
1925- .... **CLC 12, 30; DA; DAB; DAC;**
DAM MST, NOV
See also AAYA 3, 19; CA 1-4R; CANR 5,
23; CDALB 1968-1988; CLR 12; DLB 52;
INT CANR-23; JRDA; MAICYA;
MTCW; SATA 10, 45, 83

Corn, Alfred (DeWitt III) 1943-.... **CLC 33**
See also CA 104; CAAS 25; CANR 44;
DLB 120; DLBY 80

Corneille, Pierre
1606-1684 .... **LC 28; DAB; DAM MST**

Cornwell, David (John Moore)
1931- .... **CLC 9, 15; DAM POP**
See also le Carre, John
See also CA 5-8R; CANR 13, 33; MTCW

Corso, (Nunzio) Gregory 1930-... **CLC 1, 11**
See also CA 5-8R; CANR 41; DLB 5, 16;
MTCW

Cortazar, Julio
1914-1984 ...... **CLC 2, 3, 5, 10, 13, 15,**
33, 34, 92; DAM MULT, NOV; HLC;
SSC 7
See also CA 21-24R; CANR 12, 32;
DLB 113; HW; MTCW

CORTES, HERNAN 1484-1547..... **LC 31**

Corwin, Cecil
See Kornbluth, C(yril) M.

Cosic, Dobrica 1921- .... **CLC 14**
See also CA 122; 138

Costain, Thomas B(ertram)
1885-1965 .... **CLC 30**
See also CA 5-8R; 25-28R; DLB 9

Costantini, Humberto
1924(?)-1987 .... **CLC 49**
See also CA 131; 122; HW

Costello, Elvis 1955-............. **CLC 21**

Cotter, Joseph Seamon Sr.
1861-1949 .... **TCLC 28; BLC;**
DAM MULT
See also BW 1; CA 124; DLB 50

Couch, Arthur Thomas Quiller
See Quiller-Couch, Arthur Thomas

Coulton, James
See Hansen, Joseph

Couperus, Louis (Marie Anne)
1863-1923 .... **TCLC 15**
See also CA 115

Coupland, Douglas
1961- .... **CLC 85; DAC; DAM POP**
See also CA 142; CANR 57

Court, Wesli
See Turco, Lewis (Putnam)

Courtenay, Bryce 1933-........... **CLC 59**
See also CA 138

Courtney, Robert
See Ellison, Harlan (Jay)

Cousteau, Jacques-Yves 1910-...... **CLC 30**
See also CA 65-68; CANR 15; MTCW;
SATA 38

Coward, Noel (Peirce)
1899-1973 .... **CLC 1, 9, 29, 51;**
DAM DRAM
See also AITN 1; CA 17-18; 41-44R;
CANR 35; CAP 2; CDBLB 1914-1945;
DLB 10; MTCW

Cowley, Malcolm 1898-1989 .... **CLC 39**
See also CA 5-8R; 128; CANR 3, 55;
DLB 4, 48; DLBY 81, 89; MTCW

Cowper, William
1731-1800 ...... **NCLC 8; DAM POET**
See also DLB 104, 109

Cox, William Trevor
1928- .... **CLC 9, 14, 71; DAM NOV**
See also Trevor, William
See also CA 9-12R; CANR 4, 37, 55;
DLB 14; INT CANR-37; MTCW

Coyne, P. J.
See Masters, Hilary

Cozzens, James Gould
1903-1978 .... **CLC 1, 4, 11, 92**
See also CA 9-12R; 81-84; CANR 19;
CDALB 1941-1968; DLB 9; DLBD 2;
DLBY 84; MTCW

Crabbe, George 1754-1832...... **NCLC 26**
See also DLB 93

Craddock, Charles Egbert
See Murfree, Mary Noailles

Craig, A. A.
See Anderson, Poul (William)

Craik, Dinah Maria (Mulock)
1826-1887 .... **NCLC 38**
See also DLB 35, 163; MAICYA; SATA 34

Cram, Ralph Adams 1863-1942.... **TCLC 45**

Crane, (Harold) Hart
1899-1932 .... **TCLC 2, 5; DA; DAB;**
DAC; DAM MST, POET; PC 3; WLC
See also CA 104; 127; CDALB 1917-1929;
DLB 4, 48; MTCW

Crane, R(onald) S(almon)
1886-1967 .... **CLC 27**
See also CA 85-88; DLB 63

Crane, Stephen (Townley)
1871-1900 .... **TCLC 11, 17, 32; DA;**
DAB; DAC; DAM MST, NOV, POET;
SSC 7; WLC
See also AAYA 21; CA 109; 140;
CDALB 1865-1917; DLB 12, 54, 78;
YABC 2

Crase, Douglas 1944-............. **CLC 58**
See also CA 106

Crashaw, Richard 1612(?)-1649...... **LC 24**
See also DLB 126

Craven, Margaret
1901-1980 .... **CLC 17; DAC**
See also CA 103

Crawford, F(rancis) Marion
1854-1909 .... **TCLC 10**
See also CA 107; DLB 71

Crawford, Isabella Valancy
1850-1887 .... **NCLC 12**
See also DLB 92

Crayon, Geoffrey
See Irving, Washington

Creasey, John 1908-1973.......... **CLC 11**
See also CA 5-8R; 41-44R; CANR 8;
DLB 77; MTCW

Crebillon, Claude Prosper Jolyot de (fils)
1707-1777 .... **LC 28**

Credo
See Creasey, John

Creeley, Robert (White)
1926- ..... **CLC 1, 2, 4, 8, 11, 15, 36, 78;**
DAM POET
See also CA 1-4R; CAAS 10; CANR 23, 43;
DLB 5, 16, 169; MTCW

Daudet, (Louis Marie) Alphonse
1840-1897 . . . . **NCLC 1**
See also DLB 123

Daumal, Rene 1908-1944 . . . . **TCLC 14**
See also CA 114

Davenport, Guy (Mattison, Jr.)
1927- . . . . **CLC 6, 14, 38; SSC 16**
See also CA 33-36R; CANR 23; DLB 130

Davidson, Avram 1923-
See Queen, Ellery
See also CA 101; CANR 26; DLB 8

Davidson, Donald (Grady)
1893-1968 . . . . **CLC 2, 13, 19**
See also CA 5-8R; 25-28R; CANR 4;
DLB 45

Davidson, Hugh
See Hamilton, Edmond

Davidson, John 1857-1909 . . . . **TCLC 24**
See also CA 118; DLB 19

Davidson, Sara 1943- . . . . **CLC 9**
See also CA 81-84; CANR 44

Davie, Donald (Alfred)
1922-1995 . . . . **CLC 5, 8, 10, 31**
See also CA 1-4R; 149; CAAS 3; CANR 1,
44; DLB 27; MTCW

Davies, Ray(mond Douglas) 1944- . . **CLC 21**
See also CA 116; 146

Davies, Rhys 1903-1978 . . . . **CLC 23**
See also CA 9-12R; 81-84; CANR 4;
DLB 139

Davies, (William) Robertson
1913-1995 . . . . . **CLC 2, 7, 13, 25, 42, 75,
91; DA; DAB; DAC; DAM MST, NOV,
POP; WLC**
See also BEST 89:2; CA 33-36R; 150;
CANR 17, 42; DLB 68; INT CANR-17;
MTCW

Davies, W(illiam) H(enry)
1871-1940 . . . . **TCLC 5**
See also CA 104; DLB 19, 174

Davies, Walter C.
See Kornbluth, C(yril) M.

Davis, Angela (Yvonne)
1944- . . . . **CLC 77; DAM MULT**
See also BW 2; CA 57-60; CANR 10

Davis, B. Lynch
See Bioy Casares, Adolfo; Borges, Jorge
Luis

Davis, Gordon
See Hunt, E(verette) Howard, (Jr.)

Davis, Harold Lenoir 1896-1960 . . . . **CLC 49**
See also CA 89-92; DLB 9

Davis, Rebecca (Blaine) Harding
1831-1910 . . . . **TCLC 6**
See also CA 104; DLB 74

Davis, Richard Harding
1864-1916 . . . . **TCLC 24**
See also CA 114; DLB 12, 23, 78, 79;
DLBD 13

Davison, Frank Dalby 1893-1970 . . . **CLC 15**
See also CA 116

Davison, Lawrence H.
See Lawrence, D(avid) H(erbert Richards)

Davison, Peter (Hubert) 1928- . . . . . **CLC 28**
See also CA 9-12R; CAAS 4; CANR 3, 43;
DLB 5

Davys, Mary 1674-1732 . . . . **LC 1**
See also DLB 39

Dawson, Fielding 1930- . . . . **CLC 6**
See also CA 85-88; DLB 130

Dawson, Peter
See Faust, Frederick (Schiller)

Day, Clarence (Shepard, Jr.)
1874-1935 . . . . **TCLC 25**
See also CA 108; DLB 11

Day, Thomas 1748-1789 . . . . **LC 1**
See also DLB 39; YABC 1

Day Lewis, C(ecil)
1904-1972 . . . . **CLC 1, 6, 10;
DAM POET; PC 11**
See also Blake, Nicholas
See also CA 13-16; 33-36R; CANR 34;
CAP 1; DLB 15, 20; MTCW

Dazai, Osamu . . . . **TCLC 11**
See also Tsushima, Shuji

de Andrade, Carlos Drummond
See Drummond de Andrade, Carlos

Deane, Norman
See Creasey, John

**de Beauvoir, Simone (Lucie Ernestine Marie
Bertrand)**
See Beauvoir, Simone (Lucie Ernestine
Marie Bertrand) de

de Brissac, Malcolm
See Dickinson, Peter (Malcolm)

de Chardin, Pierre Teilhard
See Teilhard de Chardin, (Marie Joseph)
Pierre

Dee, John 1527-1608 . . . . **LC 20**

Deer, Sandra 1940- . . . . **CLC 45**

De Ferrari, Gabriella 1941- . . . . **CLC 65**
See also CA 146

Defoe, Daniel
1660(?)-1731 . . . . **LC 1; DA; DAB; DAC;
DAM MST, NOV; WLC**
See also CDBLB 1660-1789; DLB 39, 95,
101; JRDA; MAICYA; SATA 22

de Gourmont, Remy(-Marie-Charles)
See Gourmont, Remy (-Marie-Charles) de

de Hartog, Jan 1914- . . . . **CLC 19**
See also CA 1-4R; CANR 1

de Hostos, E. M.
See Hostos (y Bonilla), Eugenio Maria de

de Hostos, Eugenio M.
See Hostos (y Bonilla), Eugenio Maria de

Deighton, Len . . . . **CLC 4, 7, 22, 46**
See also Deighton, Leonard Cyril
See also AAYA 6; BEST 89:2;
CDBLB 1960 to Present; DLB 87

Deighton, Leonard Cyril 1929-
See Deighton, Len
See also CA 9-12R; CANR 19, 33;
DAM NOV, POP; MTCW

Dekker, Thomas
1572(?)-1632 . . . . . **LC 22; DAM DRAM**
See also CDBLB Before 1660; DLB 62, 172

Delafield, E. M. 1890-1943 . . . . **TCLC 61**
See also Dashwood, Edmee Elizabeth
Monica de la Pasture
See also DLB 34

de la Mare, Walter (John)
1873-1956 . . . . **TCLC 4, 53; DAB; DAC;
DAM MST, POET; SSC 14; WLC**
See also CDBLB 1914-1945; CLR 23;
DLB 162; SATA 16

Delaney, Franey
See O'Hara, John (Henry)

Delaney, Shelagh
1939- . . . . **CLC 29; DAM DRAM**
See also CA 17-20R; CANR 30;
CDBLB 1960 to Present; DLB 13;
MTCW

Delany, Mary (Granville Pendarves)
1700-1788 . . . . **LC 12**

Delany, Samuel R(ay, Jr.)
1942- . . . . **CLC 8, 14, 38; BLC;
DAM MULT**
See also BW 2; CA 81-84; CANR 27, 43;
DLB 8, 33; MTCW

De La Ramee, (Marie) Louise 1839-1908
See Ouida
See also SATA 20

de la Roche, Mazo 1879-1961 . . . . . . **CLC 14**
See also CA 85-88; CANR 30; DLB 68;
SATA 64

Delbanco, Nicholas (Franklin)
1942- . . . . **CLC 6, 13**
See also CA 17-20R; CAAS 2; CANR 29,
55; DLB 6

del Castillo, Michel 1933- . . . . **CLC 38**
See also CA 109

Deledda, Grazia (Cosima)
1875(?)-1936 . . . . **TCLC 23**
See also CA 123

Delibes, Miguel . . . . **CLC 8, 18**
See also Delibes Setien, Miguel

Delibes Setien, Miguel 1920-
See Delibes, Miguel
See also CA 45-48; CANR 1, 32; HW;
MTCW

DeLillo, Don
1936- . . . . . **CLC 8, 10, 13, 27, 39, 54, 76;
DAM NOV, POP**
See also BEST 89:1; CA 81-84; CANR 21;
DLB 6, 173; MTCW

de Lisser, H. G.
See De Lisser, H(erbert) G(eorge)
See also DLB 117

De Lisser, H(erbert) G(eorge)
1878-1944 . . . . **TCLC 12**
See also de Lisser, H. G.
See also BW 2; CA 109; 152

Deloria, Vine (Victor), Jr.
1933- . . . . **CLC 21; DAM MULT**
See also CA 53-56; CANR 5, 20, 48;
DLB 175; MTCW; NNAL; SATA 21

Del Vecchio, John M(ichael)
1947- . . . . **CLC 29**
See also CA 110; DLBD 9

de Man, Paul (Adolph Michel)
1919-1983 . . . . **CLC 55**
See also CA 128; 111; DLB 67; MTCW

De Marinis, Rick 1934-.......... **CLC 54**
See also CA 57-60; CAAS 24; CANR 9, 25, 50

Dembry, R. Emmet
See Murfree, Mary Noailles

Demby, William
1922- ..... **CLC 53; BLC; DAM MULT**
See also BW 1; CA 81-84; DLB 33

de Menton, Francisco
See Chin, Frank (Chew, Jr.)

Demijohn, Thom
See Disch, Thomas M(ichael)

de Montherlant, Henry (Milon)
See Montherlant, Henry (Milon) de

Demosthenes 384B.C.-322B.C. ... **CMLC 13**
See also DLB 176

de Natale, Francine
See Malzberg, Barry N(athaniel)

Denby, Edwin (Orr) 1903-1983..... **CLC 48**
See also CA 138; 110

Denis, Julio
See Cortazar, Julio

Denmark, Harrison
See Zelazny, Roger (Joseph)

Dennis, John 1658-1734........... **LC 11**
See also DLB 101

Dennis, Nigel (Forbes) 1912-1989.... **CLC 8**
See also CA 25-28R; 129; DLB 13, 15; MTCW

De Palma, Brian (Russell) 1940-.... **CLC 20**
See also CA 109

De Quincey, Thomas 1785-1859 ... **NCLC 4**
See also CDBLB 1789-1832; DLB 110; 144

Deren, Eleanora 1908(?)-1961
See Deren, Maya
See also CA 111

Deren, Maya .... **CLC 16**
See also Deren, Eleanora

Derleth, August (William)
1909-1971 .... **CLC 31**
See also CA 1-4R; 29-32R; CANR 4; DLB 9; SATA 5

Der Nister 1884-1950........... **TCLC 56**

de Routisie, Albert
See Aragon, Louis

Derrida, Jacques 1930-........ **CLC 24, 87**
See also CA 124; 127

Derry Down Derry
See Lear, Edward

Dersonnes, Jacques
See Simenon, Georges (Jacques Christian)

Desai, Anita
1937- .... **CLC 19, 37, 97; DAB; DAM NOV**
See also CA 81-84; CANR 33, 53; MTCW; SATA 63

de Saint-Luc, Jean
See Glassco, John

de Saint Roman, Arnaud
See Aragon, Louis

Descartes, Rene 1596-1650 ...... **LC 20, 35**

De Sica, Vittorio 1901(?)-1974 ..... **CLC 20**
See also CA 117

Desnos, Robert 1900-1945....... **TCLC 22**
See also CA 121; 151

Destouches, Louis-Ferdinand
1894-1961 .... **CLC 9, 15**
See also Celine, Louis-Ferdinand
See also CA 85-88; CANR 28; MTCW

de Tolignac, Gaston
See Griffith, D(avid Lewelyn) W(ark)

Deutsch, Babette 1895-1982 .... **CLC 18**
See also CA 1-4R; 108; CANR 4; DLB 45; SATA 1; SATA-Obit 33

Devenant, William 1606-1649 ...... **LC 13**

Devkota, Laxmiprasad
1909-1959 .... **TCLC 23**
See also CA 123

De Voto, Bernard (Augustine)
1897-1955 .... **TCLC 29**
See also CA 113; DLB 9

De Vries, Peter
1910-1993 .... **CLC 1, 2, 3, 7, 10, 28, 46; DAM NOV**
See also CA 17-20R; 142; CANR 41; DLB 6; DLBY 82; MTCW

Dexter, John
See Bradley, Marion Zimmer

Dexter, Martin
See Faust, Frederick (Schiller)

Dexter, Pete
1943- .... **CLC 34, 55; DAM POP**
See also BEST 89:2; CA 127; 131; INT 131; MTCW

Diamano, Silmang
See Senghor, Leopold Sedar

Diamond, Neil 1941- .... **CLC 30**
See also CA 108

Diaz del Castillo, Bernal 1496-1584 .. **LC 31**

di Bassetto, Corno
See Shaw, George Bernard

Dick, Philip K(indred)
1928-1982 .... **CLC 10, 30, 72; DAM NOV, POP**
See also CA 49-52; 106; CANR 2, 16; DLB 8; MTCW

Dickens, Charles (John Huffam)
1812-1870 ...... **NCLC 3, 8, 18, 26, 37, 50; DA; DAB; DAC; DAM MST, NOV; SSC 17; WLC**
See also CDBLB 1832-1890; DLB 21, 55, 70, 159, 166; JRDA; MAICYA; SATA 15

Dickey, James (Lafayette)
1923-1997 .... **CLC 1, 2, 4, 7, 10, 15, 47; DAM NOV, POET, POP**
See also AITN 1, 2; CA 9-12R; 156; CABS 2; CANR 10, 48; CDALB 1968-1988; DLB 5; DLBD 7; DLBY 82, 93; INT CANR-10; MTCW

Dickey, William 1928-1994 ...... **CLC 3, 28**
See also CA 9-12R; 145; CANR 24; DLB 5

Dickinson, Charles 1951-.......... **CLC 49**
See also CA 128

Dickinson, Emily (Elizabeth)
1830-1886 .... **NCLC 21; DA; DAB; DAC; DAM MST, POET; PC 1; WLC**
See also CDALB 1865-1917; DLB 1; SATA 29

Dickinson, Peter (Malcolm)
1927- .... **CLC 12, 35**
See also AAYA 9; CA 41-44R; CANR 31; CLR 29; DLB 87, 161; JRDA; MAICYA; SATA 5, 62

Dickson, Carr
See Carr, John Dickson

Dickson, Carter
See Carr, John Dickson

Diderot, Denis 1713-1784 .... **LC 26**

Didion, Joan
1934-.. **CLC 1, 3, 8, 14, 32; DAM NOV**
See also AITN 1; CA 5-8R; CANR 14, 52; CDALB 1968-1988; DLB 2, 173; DLBY 81, 86; MTCW

Dietrich, Robert
See Hunt, E(verette) Howard, (Jr.)

Dillard, Annie
1945- .... **CLC 9, 60; DAM NOV**
See also AAYA 6; CA 49-52; CANR 3, 43; DLBY 80; MTCW; SATA 10

Dillard, R(ichard) H(enry) W(ilde)
1937- .... **CLC 5**
See also CA 21-24R; CAAS 7; CANR 10; DLB 5

Dillon, Eilis 1920-1994........... **CLC 17**
See also CA 9-12R; 147; CAAS 3; CANR 4, 38; CLR 26; MAICYA; SATA 2, 74; SATA-Obit 83

Dimont, Penelope
See Mortimer, Penelope (Ruth)

Dinesen, Isak........ **CLC 10, 29, 95; SSC 7**
See also Blixen, Karen (Christentze Dinesen)

Ding Ling............... **CLC 68**
See also Chiang Pin-chin

Disch, Thomas M(ichael) 1940-... **CLC 7, 36**
See also AAYA 17; CA 21-24R; CAAS 4; CANR 17, 36, 54; CLR 18; DLB 8; MAICYA; MTCW; SAAS 15; SATA 92

Disch, Tom
See Disch, Thomas M(ichael)

d'Isly, Georges
See Simenon, Georges (Jacques Christian)

Disraeli, Benjamin 1804-1881 .. **NCLC 2, 39**
See also DLB 21, 55

Ditcum, Steve
See Crumb, R(obert)

Dixon, Paige
See Corcoran, Barbara

Dixon, Stephen 1936-..... **CLC 52; SSC 16**
See also CA 89-92; CANR 17, 40, 54; DLB 130

Dobell, Sydney Thompson
1824-1874 .... **NCLC 43**
See also DLB 32

Doblin, Alfred .... **TCLC 13**
See also Doeblin, Alfred

Dobrolyubov, Nikolai Alexandrovich
1836-1861 .... **NCLC 5**

Dobyns, Stephen 1941-........... **CLC 37**
See also CA 45-48; CANR 2, 18

Doctorow, E(dgar) L(aurence)
1931- ..... **CLC 6, 11, 15, 18, 37, 44, 65;**
DAM NOV, POP
See also AITN 2; BEST 89:3; CA 45-48;
CANR 2, 33, 51; CDALB 1968-1988;
DLB 2, 28, 173; DLBY 80; MTCW

Dodgson, Charles Lutwidge 1832-1898
See Carroll, Lewis
See also CLR 2; DA; DAB; DAC;
DAM MST, NOV, POET; MAICYA;
YABC 2

Dodson, Owen (Vincent)
1914-1983 .... **CLC 79; BLC;**
DAM MULT
See also BW 1; CA 65-68; 110; CANR 24;
DLB 76

Doeblin, Alfred 1878-1957....... **TCLC 13**
See also Doblin, Alfred
See also CA 110; 141; DLB 66

Doerr, Harriet 1910- .... **CLC 34**
See also CA 117; 122; CANR 47; INT 122

Domecq, H(onorio) Bustos
See Bioy Casares, Adolfo; Borges, Jorge
Luis

Domini, Rey
See Lorde, Audre (Geraldine)

Dominique
See Proust, (Valentin-Louis-George-Eugene-)
Marcel

Don, A
See Stephen, Leslie

Donaldson, Stephen R.
1947- .... **CLC 46; DAM POP**
See also CA 89-92; CANR 13, 55;
INT CANR-13

Donleavy, J(ames) P(atrick)
1926- .... **CLC 1, 4, 6, 10, 45**
See also AITN 2; CA 9-12R; CANR 24, 49;
DLB 6, 173; INT CANR-24; MTCW

Donne, John
1572-1631 .... **LC 10, 24; DA; DAB;**
DAC; DAM MST, POET; PC 1
See also CDBLB Before 1660; DLB 121,
151

Donnell, David 1939(?)- .... **CLC 34**

Donoghue, P. S.
See Hunt, E(verette) Howard, (Jr.)

Donoso (Yanez), Jose
1924-1996 .... **CLC 4, 8, 11, 32, 99;**
DAM MULT; HLC
See also CA 81-84; 155; CANR 32;
DLB 113; HW; MTCW

Donovan, John 1928-1992 .... **CLC 35**
See also AAYA 20; CA 97-100; 137;
CLR 3; MAICYA; SATA 72;
SATA-Brief 29

Don Roberto
See Cunninghame Graham, R(obert)
B(ontine)

Doolittle, Hilda
1886-1961 ..... **CLC 3, 8, 14, 31, 34, 73;**
DA; DAC; DAM MST, POET; PC 5;
WLC
See also H. D.
See also CA 97-100; CANR 35; DLB 4, 45;
MTCW

Dorfman, Ariel
1942- .... **CLC 48, 77; DAM MULT;**
HLC
See also CA 124; 130; HW; INT 130

Dorn, Edward (Merton) 1929-... **CLC 10, 18**
See also CA 93-96; CANR 42; DLB 5;
INT 93-96

Dorsan, Luc
See Simenon, Georges (Jacques Christian)

Dorsange, Jean
See Simenon, Georges (Jacques Christian)

Dos Passos, John (Roderigo)
1896-1970 ..... **CLC 1, 4, 8, 11, 15, 25,**
34, 82; DA; DAB; DAC; DAM MST,
NOV; WLC
See also CA 1-4R; 29-32R; CANR 3;
CDALB 1929-1941; DLB 4, 9; DLBD 1;
MTCW

Dossage, Jean
See Simenon, Georges (Jacques Christian)

Dostoevsky, Fedor Mikhailovich
1821-1881 ...... **NCLC 2, 7, 21, 33, 43;**
DA; DAB; DAC; DAM MST, NOV;
SSC 2; WLC

Doughty, Charles M(ontagu)
1843-1926 .... **TCLC 27**
See also CA 115; DLB 19, 57, 174

Douglas, Ellen .... **CLC 73**
See also Haxton, Josephine Ayres;
Williamson, Ellen Douglas

Douglas, Gavin 1475(?)-1522....... **LC 20**

Douglas, Keith 1920-1944 .... **TCLC 40**
See also DLB 27

Douglas, Leonard
See Bradbury, Ray (Douglas)

Douglas, Michael
See Crichton, (John) Michael

Douglas, Norman 1868-1952 ...... **TCLC 68**

Douglass, Frederick
1817(?)-1895 .... **NCLC 7, 55; BLC; DA;**
DAC; DAM MST, MULT; WLC
See also CDALB 1640-1865; DLB 1, 43, 50,
79; SATA 29

Dourado, (Waldomiro Freitas) Autran
1926- .... **CLC 23, 60**
See also CA 25-28R; CANR 34

Dourado, Waldomiro Autran
See Dourado, (Waldomiro Freitas) Autran

Dove, Rita (Frances)
1952- .... **CLC 50, 81; DAM MULT,**
POET; PC 6
See also BW 2; CA 109; CAAS 19;
CANR 27, 42; DLB 120

Dowell, Coleman 1925-1985....... **CLC 60**
See also CA 25-28R; 117; CANR 10;
DLB 130

Dowson, Ernest (Christopher)
1867-1900 .... **TCLC 4**
See also CA 105; 150; DLB 19, 135

Doyle, A. Conan
See Doyle, Arthur Conan

Doyle, Arthur Conan
1859-1930 .... **TCLC 7; DA; DAB;**
DAC; DAM MST, NOV; SSC 12; WLC
See also AAYA 14; CA 104; 122;
CDBLB 1890-1914; DLB 18, 70, 156;
MTCW; SATA 24

Doyle, Conan
See Doyle, Arthur Conan

Doyle, John
See Graves, Robert (von Ranke)

Doyle, Roddy 1958(?)- .... **CLC 81**
See also AAYA 14; CA 143

Doyle, Sir A. Conan
See Doyle, Arthur Conan

Doyle, Sir Arthur Conan
See Doyle, Arthur Conan

Dr. A
See Asimov, Isaac; Silverstein, Alvin

Drabble, Margaret
1939- .... **CLC 2, 3, 5, 8, 10, 22, 53;**
DAB; DAC; DAM MST, NOV, POP
See also CA 13-16R; CANR 18, 35;
CDBLB 1960 to Present; DLB 14, 155;
MTCW; SATA 48

Drapier, M. B.
See Swift, Jonathan

Drayham, James
See Mencken, H(enry) L(ouis)

Drayton, Michael 1563-1631........ **LC 8**

Dreadstone, Carl
See Campbell, (John) Ramsey

Dreiser, Theodore (Herman Albert)
1871-1945 .... **TCLC 10, 18, 35; DA;**
DAC; DAM MST, NOV; WLC
See also CA 106; 132; CDALB 1865-1917;
DLB 9, 12, 102, 137; DLBD 1; MTCW

Drexler, Rosalyn 1926- .... **CLC 2, 6**
See also CA 81-84

Dreyer, Carl Theodor 1889-1968.... **CLC 16**
See also CA 116

Drieu la Rochelle, Pierre(-Eugene)
1893-1945 .... **TCLC 21**
See also CA 117; DLB 72

Drinkwater, John 1882-1937..... **TCLC 57**
See also CA 109; 149; DLB 10, 19, 149

Drop Shot
See Cable, George Washington

Droste-Hulshoff, Annette Freiin von
1797-1848 .... **NCLC 3**
See also DLB 133

Drummond, Walter
See Silverberg, Robert

Drummond, William Henry
1854-1907 .... **TCLC 25**
See also DLB 92

Drummond de Andrade, Carlos
1902-1987 .... **CLC 18**
See also Andrade, Carlos Drummond de
See also CA 132; 123

Drury, Allen (Stuart) 1918-........ **CLC 37**
See also CA 57-60; CANR 18, 52;
INT CANR-18

Dryden, John
1631-1700 . . . . **LC 3, 21; DA; DAB; DAC; DAM DRAM, MST, POET; DC 3; WLC**
See also CDBLB 1660-1789; DLB 80, 101, 131

Duberman, Martin 1930- . . . . **CLC 8**
See also CA 1-4R; CANR 2

Dubie, Norman (Evans) 1945- . . . . . . **CLC 36**
See also CA 69-72; CANR 12; DLB 120

Du Bois, W(illiam) E(dward) B(urghardt)
1868-1963 . . . . **CLC 1, 2, 13, 64, 96; BLC; DA; DAC; DAM MST, MULT, NOV; WLC**
See also BW 1; CA 85-88; CANR 34; CDALB 1865-1917; DLB 47, 50, 91; MTCW; SATA 42

Dubus, Andre
1936- . . . . **CLC 13, 36, 97; SSC 15**
See also CA 21-24R; CANR 17; DLB 130; INT CANR-17

Duca Minimo
See D'Annunzio, Gabriele

Ducharme, Rejean 1941- . . . . **CLC 74**
See also DLB 60

Duclos, Charles Pinot 1704-1772 . . . . . **LC 1**

Dudek, Louis 1918- . . . . **CLC 11, 19**
See also CA 45-48; CAAS 14; CANR 1; DLB 88

Duerrenmatt, Friedrich
1921-1990 . . . . . . **CLC 1, 4, 8, 11, 15, 43; DAM DRAM**
See also CA 17-20R; CANR 33; DLB 69, 124; MTCW

Duffy, Bruce (?)- . . . . **CLC 50**

Duffy, Maureen 1933- . . . . **CLC 37**
See also CA 25-28R; CANR 33; DLB 14; MTCW

Dugan, Alan 1923- . . . . **CLC 2, 6**
See also CA 81-84; DLB 5

du Gard, Roger Martin
See Martin du Gard, Roger

Duhamel, Georges 1884-1966 . . . . **CLC 8**
See also CA 81-84; 25-28R; CANR 35; DLB 65; MTCW

Dujardin, Edouard (Emile Louis)
1861-1949 . . . . **TCLC 13**
See also CA 109; DLB 123

Dumas, Alexandre (Davy de la Pailleterie)
1802-1870 . . . . . . **NCLC 11; DA; DAB; DAC; DAM MST, NOV; WLC**
See also DLB 119; SATA 18

Dumas, Alexandre
1824-1895 . . . . **NCLC 9; DC 1**

Dumas, Claudine
See Malzberg, Barry N(athaniel)

Dumas, Henry L. 1934-1968 . . . . . **CLC 6, 62**
See also BW 1; CA 85-88; DLB 41

du Maurier, Daphne
1907-1989 . . . . **CLC 6, 11, 59; DAB; DAC; DAM MST, POP; SSC 18**
See also CA 5-8R; 128; CANR 6, 55; MTCW; SATA 27; SATA-Obit 60

Dunbar, Paul Laurence
1872-1906 . . . . **TCLC 2, 12; BLC; DA; DAC; DAM MST, MULT, POET; PC 5; SSC 8; WLC**
See also BW 1; CA 104; 124; CDALB 1865-1917; DLB 50, 54, 78; SATA 34

Dunbar, William 1460(?)-1530(?) . . . . **LC 20**
See also DLB 132, 146

Duncan, Dora Angela
See Duncan, Isadora

Duncan, Isadora 1877(?)-1927 . . . . . **TCLC 68**
See also CA 118; 149

Duncan, Lois 1934- . . . . **CLC 26**
See also AAYA 4; CA 1-4R; CANR 2, 23, 36; CLR 29; JRDA; MAICYA; SAAS 2; SATA 1, 36, 75

Duncan, Robert (Edward)
1919-1988 . . . . **CLC 1, 2, 4, 7, 15, 41, 55; DAM POET; PC 2**
See also CA 9-12R; 124; CANR 28; DLB 5, 16; MTCW

Duncan, Sara Jeannette
1861-1922 . . . . **TCLC 60**
See also DLB 92

Dunlap, William 1766-1839 . . . . **NCLC 2**
See also DLB 30, 37, 59

Dunn, Douglas (Eaglesham)
1942- . . . . **CLC 6, 40**
See also CA 45-48; CANR 2, 33; DLB 40; MTCW

Dunn, Katherine (Karen) 1945- . . . . . **CLC 71**
See also CA 33-36R

Dunn, Stephen 1939- . . . . **CLC 36**
See also CA 33-36R; CANR 12, 48, 53; DLB 105

Dunne, Finley Peter 1867-1936 . . . . **TCLC 28**
See also CA 108; DLB 11, 23

Dunne, John Gregory 1932- . . . . **CLC 28**
See also CA 25-28R; CANR 14, 50; DLBY 80

Dunsany, Edward John Moreton Drax
Plunkett 1878-1957
See Dunsany, Lord
See also CA 104; 148; DLB 10

Dunsany, Lord . . . . **TCLC 2, 59**
See also Dunsany, Edward John Moreton Drax Plunkett
See also DLB 77, 153, 156

du Perry, Jean
See Simenon, Georges (Jacques Christian)

Durang, Christopher (Ferdinand)
1949- . . . . **CLC 27, 38**
See also CA 105; CANR 50

Duras, Marguerite
1914-1996 . . . . . **CLC 3, 6, 11, 20, 34, 40, 68, 100**
See also CA 25-28R; 151; CANR 50; DLB 83; MTCW

Durban, (Rosa) Pam 1947- . . . . **CLC 39**
See also CA 123

Durcan, Paul
1944- . . . . **CLC 43, 70; DAM POET**
See also CA 134

Durkheim, Emile 1858-1917 . . . . . . **TCLC 55**

Durrell, Lawrence (George)
1912-1990 . . . . **CLC 1, 4, 6, 8, 13, 27, 41; DAM NOV**
See also CA 9-12R; 132; CANR 40; CDBLB 1945-1960; DLB 15, 27; DLBY 90; MTCW

Durrenmatt, Friedrich
See Duerrenmatt, Friedrich

Dutt, Toru 1856-1877 . . . . **NCLC 29**

Dwight, Timothy 1752-1817 . . . . . . **NCLC 13**
See also DLB 37

Dworkin, Andrea 1946- . . . . **CLC 43**
See also CA 77-80; CAAS 21; CANR 16, 39; INT CANR-16; MTCW

Dwyer, Deanna
See Koontz, Dean R(ay)

Dwyer, K. R.
See Koontz, Dean R(ay)

Dylan, Bob 1941- . . . . . . **CLC 3, 4, 6, 12, 77**
See also CA 41-44R; DLB 16

Eagleton, Terence (Francis) 1943-
See Eagleton, Terry
See also CA 57-60; CANR 7, 23; MTCW

Eagleton, Terry . . . . **CLC 63**
See also Eagleton, Terence (Francis)

Early, Jack
See Scoppettone, Sandra

East, Michael
See West, Morris L(anglo)

Eastaway, Edward
See Thomas, (Philip) Edward

Eastlake, William (Derry) 1917- . . . . . **CLC 8**
See also CA 5-8R; CAAS 1; CANR 5; DLB 6; INT CANR-5

Eastman, Charles A(lexander)
1858-1939 . . . . . **TCLC 55; DAM MULT**
See also DLB 175; NNAL; YABC 1

Eberhart, Richard (Ghormley)
1904- . . **CLC 3, 11, 19, 56; DAM POET**
See also CA 1-4R; CANR 2; CDALB 1941-1968; DLB 48; MTCW

Eberstadt, Fernanda 1960- . . . . **CLC 39**
See also CA 136

Echegaray (y Eizaguirre), Jose (Maria Waldo)
1832-1916 . . . . **TCLC 4**
See also CA 104; CANR 32; HW; MTCW

Echeverria, (Jose) Esteban (Antonino)
1805-1851 . . . . **NCLC 18**

Echo
See Proust, (Valentin-Louis-George-Eugene-) Marcel

Eckert, Allan W. 1931- . . . . **CLC 17**
See also AAYA 18; CA 13-16R; CANR 14, 45; INT CANR-14; SAAS 21; SATA 29, 91; SATA-Brief 27

Eckhart, Meister 1260(?)-1328(?) . . **CMLC 9**
See also DLB 115

Eckmar, F. R.
See de Hartog, Jan

Eco, Umberto
1932- . . . **CLC 28, 60; DAM NOV, POP**
See also BEST 90:1; CA 77-80; CANR 12, 33, 55; MTCW

Farren, Richard M.
See Betjeman, John

Fassbinder, Rainer Werner
1946-1982 . . . . **CLC 20**
See also CA 93-96; 106; CANR 31

Fast, Howard (Melvin)
1914- . . . . **CLC 23; DAM NOV**
See also AAYA 16; CA 1-4R; CAAS 18;
CANR 1, 33, 54; DLB 9; INT CANR-33;
SATA 7

Faulcon, Robert
See Holdstock, Robert P.

Faulkner, William (Cuthbert)
1897-1962 . . . . . **CLC 1, 3, 6, 8, 9, 11, 14,
18, 28, 52, 68; DA; DAB; DAC;
DAM MST, NOV; SSC 1; WLC**
See also AAYA 7; CA 81-84; CANR 33;
CDALB 1929-1941; DLB 9, 11, 44, 102;
DLBD 2; DLBY 86; MTCW

Fauset, Jessie Redmon
1884(?)-1961 . . . . **CLC 19, 54; BLC;
DAM MULT**
See also BW 1; CA 109; DLB 51

Faust, Frederick (Schiller)
1892-1944(?) . . . . . **TCLC 49; DAM POP**
See also CA 108; 152

Faust, Irvin 1924- . . . . **CLC 8**
See also CA 33-36R; CANR 28; DLB 2, 28;
DLBY 80

Fawkes, Guy
See Benchley, Robert (Charles)

Fearing, Kenneth (Flexner)
1902-1961 . . . . **CLC 51**
See also CA 93-96; DLB 9

Fecamps, Elise
See Creasey, John

Federman, Raymond 1928- . . . . . . **CLC 6, 47**
See also CA 17-20R; CAAS 8; CANR 10,
43; DLBY 80

Federspiel, J(uerg) F. 1931- . . . . **CLC 42**
See also CA 146

Feiffer, Jules (Ralph)
1929- . . . . . . **CLC 2, 8, 64; DAM DRAM**
See also AAYA 3; CA 17-20R; CANR 30;
DLB 7, 44; INT CANR-30; MTCW;
SATA 8, 61

Feige, Hermann Albert Otto Maximilian
See Traven, B.

Feinberg, David B. 1956-1994 . . . . . . **CLC 59**
See also CA 135; 147

Feinstein, Elaine 1930- . . . . **CLC 36**
See also CA 69-72; CAAS 1; CANR 31;
DLB 14, 40; MTCW

Feldman, Irving (Mordecai) 1928- . . . . **CLC 7**
See also CA 1-4R; CANR 1; DLB 169

Fellini, Federico 1920-1993 . . . . . **CLC 16, 85**
See also CA 65-68; 143; CANR 33

Felsen, Henry Gregor 1916- . . . . **CLC 17**
See also CA 1-4R; CANR 1; SAAS 2;
SATA 1

Fenton, James Martin 1949- . . . . **CLC 32**
See also CA 102; DLB 40

Ferber, Edna 1887-1968 . . . . **CLC 18, 93**
See also AITN 1; CA 5-8R; 25-28R; DLB 9,
28, 86; MTCW; SATA 7

Ferguson, Helen
See Kavan, Anna

Ferguson, Samuel 1810-1886 . . . . . **NCLC 33**
See also DLB 32

Fergusson, Robert 1750-1774 . . . . . . **LC 29**
See also DLB 109

Ferling, Lawrence
See Ferlinghetti, Lawrence (Monsanto)

Ferlinghetti, Lawrence (Monsanto)
1919(?)- . . . . **CLC 2, 6, 10, 27;
DAM POET; PC 1**
See also CA 5-8R; CANR 3, 41;
CDALB 1941-1968; DLB 5, 16; MTCW

Fernandez, Vicente Garcia Huidobro
See Huidobro Fernandez, Vicente Garcia

Ferrer, Gabriel (Francisco Victor) Miro
See Miro (Ferrer), Gabriel (Francisco
Victor)

Ferrier, Susan (Edmonstone)
1782-1854 . . . . **NCLC 8**
See also DLB 116

Ferrigno, Robert 1948(?)- . . . . **CLC 65**
See also CA 140

Ferron, Jacques 1921-1985 . . . **CLC 94; DAC**
See also CA 117; 129; DLB 60

Feuchtwanger, Lion 1884-1958 . . . . . **TCLC 3**
See also CA 104; DLB 66

Feuillet, Octave 1821-1890 . . . . . . **NCLC 45**

Feydeau, Georges (Leon Jules Marie)
1862-1921 . . . . . **TCLC 22; DAM DRAM**
See also CA 113; 152

Ficino, Marsilio 1433-1499 . . . . **LC 12**

Fiedeler, Hans
See Doeblin, Alfred

Fiedler, Leslie A(aron)
1917- . . . . **CLC 4, 13, 24**
See also CA 9-12R; CANR 7; DLB 28, 67;
MTCW

Field, Andrew 1938- . . . . **CLC 44**
See also CA 97-100; CANR 25

Field, Eugene 1850-1895 . . . . **NCLC 3**
See also DLB 23, 42, 140; DLBD 13;
MAICYA; SATA 16

Field, Gans T.
See Wellman, Manly Wade

Field, Michael . . . . **TCLC 43**

Field, Peter
See Hobson, Laura Z(ametkin)

Fielding, Henry
1707-1754 . . . . . . **LC 1; DA; DAB; DAC;
DAM DRAM, MST, NOV; WLC**
See also CDBLB 1660-1789; DLB 39, 84,
101

Fielding, Sarah 1710-1768 . . . . **LC 1**
See also DLB 39

Fierstein, Harvey (Forbes)
1954- . . . . . **CLC 33; DAM DRAM, POP**
See also CA 123; 129

Figes, Eva 1932- . . . . **CLC 31**
See also CA 53-56; CANR 4, 44; DLB 14

Finch, Robert (Duer Claydon)
1900- . . . . **CLC 18**
See also CA 57-60; CANR 9, 24, 49;
DLB 88

Findley, Timothy
1930- . . . . . . **CLC 27; DAC; DAM MST**
See also CA 25-28R; CANR 12, 42;
DLB 53

Fink, William
See Mencken, H(enry) L(ouis)

Firbank, Louis 1942-
See Reed, Lou
See also CA 117

Firbank, (Arthur Annesley) Ronald
1886-1926 . . . . **TCLC 1**
See also CA 104; DLB 36

Fisher, M(ary) F(rances) K(ennedy)
1908-1992 . . . . **CLC 76, 87**
See also CA 77-80; 138; CANR 44

Fisher, Roy 1930- . . . . **CLC 25**
See also CA 81-84; CAAS 10; CANR 16;
DLB 40

Fisher, Rudolph
1897-1934 . . . . **TCLC 11; BLC;
DAM MULT; SSC 25**
See also BW 1; CA 107; 124; DLB 51, 102

Fisher, Vardis (Alvero) 1895-1968 . . . . **CLC 7**
See also CA 5-8R; 25-28R; DLB 9

Fiske, Tarleton
See Bloch, Robert (Albert)

Fitch, Clarke
See Sinclair, Upton (Beall)

Fitch, John IV
See Cormier, Robert (Edmund)

Fitzgerald, Captain Hugh
See Baum, L(yman) Frank

FitzGerald, Edward 1809-1883 . . . . **NCLC 9**
See also DLB 32

Fitzgerald, F(rancis) Scott (Key)
1896-1940 . . . . **TCLC 1, 6, 14, 28, 55;
DA; DAB; DAC; DAM MST, NOV;
SSC 6; WLC**
See also AITN 1; CA 110; 123;
CDALB 1917-1929; DLB 4, 9, 86;
DLBD 1; DLBY 81; MTCW

Fitzgerald, Penelope 1916- . . . **CLC 19, 51, 61**
See also CA 85-88; CAAS 10; CANR 56;
DLB 14

Fitzgerald, Robert (Stuart)
1910-1985 . . . . **CLC 39**
See also CA 1-4R; 114; CANR 1; DLBY 80

FitzGerald, Robert D(avid)
1902-1987 . . . . **CLC 19**
See also CA 17-20R

Fitzgerald, Zelda (Sayre)
1900-1948 . . . . **TCLC 52**
See also CA 117; 126; DLBY 84

Flanagan, Thomas (James Bonner)
1923- . . . . **CLC 25, 52**
See also CA 108; CANR 55; DLBY 80;
INT 108; MTCW

Flaubert, Gustave
1821-1880 . . . . **NCLC 2, 10, 19; DA;
DAB; DAC; DAM MST, NOV; SSC 11;
WLC**
See also DLB 119

Flecker, Herman Elroy
See Flecker, (Herman) James Elroy

Fredro, Aleksander 1793-1876..... **NCLC 8**

Freeling, Nicolas 1927-.......... **CLC 38**
See also CA 49-52; CAAS 12; CANR 1, 17, 50; DLB 87

Freeman, Douglas Southall
1886-1953 .... **TCLC 11**
See also CA 109; DLB 17

Freeman, Judith 1946-............ **CLC 55**
See also CA 148

Freeman, Mary Eleanor Wilkins
1852-1930 .... **TCLC 9; SSC 1**
See also CA 106; DLB 12, 78

Freeman, R(ichard) Austin
1862-1943 .... **TCLC 21**
See also CA 113; DLB 70

French, Albert 1943- .... **CLC 86**

French, Marilyn
1929-................ **CLC 10, 18, 60;
DAM DRAM, NOV, POP**
See also CA 69-72; CANR 3, 31;
INT CANR-31; MTCW

French, Paul
See Asimov, Isaac

Freneau, Philip Morin 1752-1832.. **NCLC 1**
See also DLB 37, 43

Freud, Sigmund 1856-1939 .... **TCLC 52**
See also CA 115; 133; MTCW

Friedan, Betty (Naomi) 1921-...... **CLC 74**
See also CA 65-68; CANR 18, 45; MTCW

Friedlander, Saul 1932-........... **CLC 90**
See also CA 117; 130

Friedman, B(ernard) H(arper)
1926-...................... **CLC 7**
See also CA 1-4R; CANR 3, 48

Friedman, Bruce Jay 1930-.... **CLC 3, 5, 56**
See also CA 9-12R; CANR 25, 52; DLB 2, 28; INT CANR-25

Friel, Brian 1929-.......... **CLC 5, 42, 59**
See also CA 21-24R; CANR 33; DLB 13;
MTCW

Friis-Baastad, Babbis Ellinor
1921-1970 .... **CLC 12**
See also CA 17-20R; 134; SATA 7

Frisch, Max (Rudolf)
1911-1991 ..... **CLC 3, 9, 14, 18, 32, 44;
DAM DRAM, NOV**
See also CA 85-88; 134; CANR 32;
DLB 69, 124; MTCW

Fromentin, Eugene (Samuel Auguste)
1820-1876 .... **NCLC 10**
See also DLB 123

Frost, Frederick
See Faust, Frederick (Schiller)

Frost, Robert (Lee)
1874-1963 .... **CLC 1, 3, 4, 9, 10, 13, 15,
26, 34, 44; DA; DAB; DAC; DAM MST,
POET; PC 1; WLC**
See also AAYA 21; CA 89-92; CANR 33;
CDALB 1917-1929; DLB 54; DLBD 7;
MTCW; SATA 14

Froude, James Anthony
1818-1894 .... **NCLC 43**
See also DLB 18, 57, 144

Froy, Herald
See Waterhouse, Keith (Spencer)

Fry, Christopher
1907- ..... **CLC 2, 10, 14; DAM DRAM**
See also CA 17-20R; CAAS 23; CANR 9,
30; DLB 13; MTCW; SATA 66

Frye, (Herman) Northrop
1912-1991 .... **CLC 24, 70**
See also CA 5-8R; 133; CANR 8, 37;
DLB 67, 68; MTCW

Fuchs, Daniel 1909-1993 .... **CLC 8, 22**
See also CA 81-84; 142; CAAS 5;
CANR 40; DLB 9, 26, 28; DLBY 93

Fuchs, Daniel 1934-................ **CLC 34**
See also CA 37-40R; CANR 14, 48

Fuentes, Carlos
1928-...... **CLC 3, 8, 10, 13, 22, 41, 60;
DA; DAB; DAC; DAM MST, MULT,
NOV; HLC; SSC 24; WLC**
See also AAYA 4; AITN 2; CA 69-72;
CANR 10, 32; DLB 113; HW; MTCW

Fuentes, Gregorio Lopez y
See Lopez y Fuentes, Gregorio

Fugard, (Harold) Athol
1932-......... **CLC 5, 9, 14, 25, 40, 80;
DAM DRAM; DC 3**
See also AAYA 17; CA 85-88; CANR 32,
54; MTCW

Fugard, Sheila 1932-............. **CLC 48**
See also CA 125

Fuller, Charles (H., Jr.)
1939-.... **CLC 25; BLC; DAM DRAM,
MULT; DC 1**
See also BW 2; CA 108; 112; DLB 38;
INT 112; MTCW

Fuller, John (Leopold) 1937-...... **CLC 62**
See also CA 21-24R; CANR 9, 44; DLB 40

Fuller, Margaret .... **NCLC 5, 50**
See also Ossoli, Sarah Margaret (Fuller
marchesa d')

Fuller, Roy (Broadbent)
1912-1991 .... **CLC 4, 28**
See also CA 5-8R; 135; CAAS 10;
CANR 53; DLB 15, 20; SATA 87

Fulton, Alice 1952-.............. **CLC 52**
See also CA 116; CANR 57

Furphy, Joseph 1843-1912....... **TCLC 25**

Fussell, Paul 1924-............... **CLC 74**
See also BEST 90:1; CA 17-20R; CANR 8,
21, 35; INT CANR-21; MTCW

Futabatei, Shimei 1864-1909 ..... **TCLC 44**

Futrelle, Jacques 1875-1912 ...... **TCLC 19**
See also CA 113; 155

Gaboriau, Emile 1835-1873 ...... **NCLC 14**

Gadda, Carlo Emilio 1893-1973 .... **CLC 11**
See also CA 89-92; DLB 177

Gaddis, William
1922-..... **CLC 1, 3, 6, 8, 10, 19, 43, 86**
See also CA 17-20R; CANR 21, 48; DLB 2;
MTCW

Gage, Walter
See Inge, William (Motter)

Gaines, Ernest J(ames)
1933- .... **CLC 3, 11, 18, 86; BLC;
DAM MULT**
See also AAYA 18; AITN 1; BW 2;
CA 9-12R; CANR 6, 24, 42;
CDALB 1968-1988; DLB 2, 33, 152;
DLBY 80; MTCW; SATA 86

Gaitskill, Mary 1954-............. **CLC 69**
See also CA 128

Galdos, Benito Perez
See Perez Galdos, Benito

Gale, Zona
1874-1938 ...... **TCLC 7; DAM DRAM**
See also CA 105; 153; DLB 9, 78

Galeano, Eduardo (Hughes) 1940-... **CLC 72**
See also CA 29-32R; CANR 13, 32; HW

Galiano, Juan Valera y Alcala
See Valera y Alcala-Galiano, Juan

Gallagher, Tess
1943-.. **CLC 18, 63; DAM POET; PC 9**
See also CA 106; DLB 120

Gallant, Mavis
1922-............. **CLC 7, 18, 38; DAC;
DAM MST; SSC 5**
See also CA 69-72; CANR 29; DLB 53;
MTCW

Gallant, Roy A(rthur) 1924- .... **CLC 17**
See also CA 5-8R; CANR 4, 29, 54;
CLR 30; MAICYA; SATA 4, 68

Gallico, Paul (William) 1897-1976 ... **CLC 2**
See also AITN 1; CA 5-8R; 69-72;
CANR 23; DLB 9, 171; MAICYA;
SATA 13

Gallo, Max Louis 1932-........... **CLC 95**
See also CA 85-88

Gallois, Lucien
See Desnos, Robert

Gallup, Ralph
See Whitemore, Hugh (John)

Galsworthy, John
1867-1933 ...... **TCLC 1, 45; DA; DAB;
DAC; DAM DRAM, MST, NOV;
SSC 22; WLC 2**
See also CA 104; 141; CDBLB 1890-1914;
DLB 10, 34, 98, 162

Galt, John 1779-1839............ **NCLC 1**
See also DLB 99, 116, 159

Galvin, James 1951-.............. **CLC 38**
See also CA 108; CANR 26

Gamboa, Federico 1864-1939...... **TCLC 36**

Gandhi, M. K.
See Gandhi, Mohandas Karamchand

Gandhi, Mahatma
See Gandhi, Mohandas Karamchand

Gandhi, Mohandas Karamchand
1869-1948 ..... **TCLC 59; DAM MULT**
See also CA 121; 132; MTCW

Gann, Ernest Kellogg 1910-1991.... **CLC 23**
See also AITN 1; CA 1-4R; 136; CANR 1

Garcia, Cristina 1958- .... **CLC 76**
See also CA 141

Garcia Lorca, Federico
   1898-1936 . . . **TCLC 1, 7, 49; DA; DAB;**
      DAC; DAM DRAM, MST, MULT,
      POET; DC 2; HLC; PC 3; WLC
   See also CA 104; 131; DLB 108; HW;
   MTCW

Garcia Marquez, Gabriel (Jose)
   1928- . . . . **CLC 2, 3, 8, 10, 15, 27, 47, 55,**
      68; DA; DAB; DAC; DAM MST,
      MULT, NOV, POP; HLC; SSC 8; WLC
   See also AAYA 3; BEST 89:1, 90:4;
   CA 33-36R; CANR 10, 28, 50; DLB 113;
   HW; MTCW

Gard, Janice
   See Latham, Jean Lee

Gard, Roger Martin du
   See Martin du Gard, Roger

Gardam, Jane   1928- . . . . **CLC 43**
   See also CA 49-52; CANR 2, 18, 33, 54;
   CLR 12; DLB 14, 161; MAICYA;
   MTCW; SAAS 9; SATA 39, 76;
   SATA-Brief 28

Gardner, Herb(ert)   1934- . . . . **CLC 44**
   See also CA 149

Gardner, John (Champlin), Jr.
   1933-1982 . . . . . **CLC 2, 3, 5, 7, 8, 10, 18,**
      28, 34; DAM NOV, POP; SSC 7
   See also AITN 1; CA 65-68; 107;
   CANR 33; DLB 2; DLBY 82; MTCW;
   SATA 40; SATA-Obit 31

Gardner, John (Edmund)
   1926- . . . . **CLC 30; DAM POP**
   See also CA 103; CANR 15; MTCW

Gardner, Miriam
   See Bradley, Marion Zimmer

Gardner, Noel
   See Kuttner, Henry

Gardons, S. S.
   See Snodgrass, W(illiam) D(e Witt)

Garfield, Leon   1921-1996. . . . . **CLC 12**
   See also AAYA 8; CA 17-20R; 152;
   CANR 38, 41; CLR 21; DLB 161; JRDA;
   MAICYA; SATA 1, 32, 76;
   SATA-Obit 90

Garland, (Hannibal) Hamlin
   1860-1940 . . . . **TCLC 3; SSC 18**
   See also CA 104; DLB 12, 71, 78

Garneau, (Hector de) Saint-Denys
   1912-1943 . . . . **TCLC 13**
   See also CA 111; DLB 88

Garner, Alan
   1934- . . . . **CLC 17; DAB; DAM POP**
   See also AAYA 18; CA 73-76; CANR 15;
   CLR 20; DLB 161; MAICYA; MTCW;
   SATA 18, 69

Garner, Hugh   1913-1979 . . . . **CLC 13**
   See also CA 69-72; CANR 31; DLB 68

Garnett, David   1892-1981 . . . . **CLC 3**
   See also CA 5-8R; 103; CANR 17; DLB 34

Garos, Stephanie
   See Katz, Steve

Garrett, George (Palmer)
   1929- . . . . **CLC 3, 11, 51**
   See also CA 1-4R; CAAS 5; CANR 1, 42;
   DLB 2, 5, 130, 152; DLBY 83

Garrick, David
   1717-1779 . . . . . . **LC 15; DAM DRAM**
   See also DLB 84

Garrigue, Jean   1914-1972 . . . . **CLC 2, 8**
   See also CA 5-8R; 37-40R; CANR 20

Garrison, Frederick
   See Sinclair, Upton (Beall)

Garth, Will
   See Hamilton, Edmond; Kuttner, Henry

Garvey, Marcus (Moziah, Jr.)
   1887-1940 . . . . **TCLC 41; BLC;**
      DAM MULT
   See also BW 1; CA 120; 124

Gary, Romain . . . . **CLC 25**
   See also Kacew, Romain
   See also DLB 83

Gascar, Pierre . . . . **CLC 11**
   See also Fournier, Pierre

Gascoyne, David (Emery)   1916- . . . . **CLC 45**
   See also CA 65-68; CANR 10, 28, 54;
   DLB 20; MTCW

Gaskell, Elizabeth Cleghorn
   1810-1865 . . . . **NCLC 5; DAB;**
      DAM MST; SSC 25
   See also CDBLB 1832-1890; DLB 21, 144,
   159

Gass, William H(oward)
   1924- . . . **CLC 1, 2, 8, 11, 15, 39; SSC 12**
   See also CA 17-20R; CANR 30; DLB 2;
   MTCW

Gasset, Jose Ortega y
   See Ortega y Gasset, Jose

Gates, Henry Louis, Jr.
   1950- . . . . **CLC 65; DAM MULT**
   See also BW 2; CA 109; CANR 25, 53;
   DLB 67

Gautier, Theophile
   1811-1872 . . . . **NCLC 1, 59;**
      DAM POET; SSC 20
   See also DLB 119

Gawsworth, John
   See Bates, H(erbert) E(rnest)

Gay, Oliver
   See Gogarty, Oliver St. John

Gaye, Marvin (Penze)   1939-1984 . . . **CLC 26**
   See also CA 112

Gebler, Carlo (Ernest)   1954- . . . . **CLC 39**
   See also CA 119; 133

Gee, Maggie (Mary)   1948- . . . . **CLC 57**
   See also CA 130

Gee, Maurice (Gough)   1931- . . . . **CLC 29**
   See also CA 97-100; SATA 46

Gelbart, Larry (Simon)   1923- . . . **CLC 21, 61**
   See also CA 73-76; CANR 45

Gelber, Jack   1932- . . . . **CLC 1, 6, 14, 79**
   See also CA 1-4R; CANR 2; DLB 7

Gellhorn, Martha (Ellis)   1908- . . **CLC 14, 60**
   See also CA 77-80; CANR 44; DLBY 82

Genet, Jean
   1910-1986 . . . . . . **CLC 1, 2, 5, 10, 14, 44,**
      46; DAM DRAM
   See also CA 13-16R; CANR 18; DLB 72;
   DLBY 86; MTCW

Gent, Peter   1942- . . . . **CLC 29**
   See also AITN 1; CA 89-92; DLBY 82

Gentlewoman in New England, A
   See Bradstreet, Anne

Gentlewoman in Those Parts, A
   See Bradstreet, Anne

George, Jean Craighead   1919- . . . . . . **CLC 35**
   See also AAYA 8; CA 5-8R; CANR 25;
   CLR 1; DLB 52; JRDA; MAICYA;
   SATA 2, 68

George, Stefan (Anton)
   1868-1933 . . . . **TCLC 2, 14**
   See also CA 104

Georges, Georges Martin
   See Simenon, Georges (Jacques Christian)

Gerhardi, William Alexander
   See Gerhardie, William Alexander

Gerhardie, William Alexander
   1895-1977 . . . . **CLC 5**
   See also CA 25-28R; 73-76; CANR 18;
   DLB 36

Gerstler, Amy   1956- . . . . **CLC 70**
   See also CA 146

Gertler, T. . . . . **CLC 34**
   See also CA 116; 121; INT 121

gfgg . . . . **CLC XvXzc**

Ghalib . . . . **NCLC 39**
   See also Ghalib, Hsadullah Khan

Ghalib, Hsadullah Khan   1797-1869
   See Ghalib
   See also DAM POET

Ghelderode, Michel de
   1898-1962 . . . . **CLC 6, 11; DAM DRAM**
   See also CA 85-88; CANR 40

Ghiselin, Brewster   1903- . . . . **CLC 23**
   See also CA 13-16R; CAAS 10; CANR 13

Ghose, Zulfikar   1935- . . . . **CLC 42**
   See also CA 65-68

Ghosh, Amitav   1956- . . . . **CLC 44**
   See also CA 147

Giacosa, Giuseppe   1847-1906 . . . . . . **TCLC 7**
   See also CA 104

Gibb, Lee
   See Waterhouse, Keith (Spencer)

Gibbon, Lewis Grassic . . . . **TCLC 4**
   See also Mitchell, James Leslie

Gibbons, Kaye
   1960- . . . . **CLC 50, 88; DAM POP**
   See also CA 151

Gibran, Kahlil
   1883-1931 . . . . **TCLC 1, 9; DAM POET,**
      POP; PC 9
   See also CA 104; 150

Gibran, Khalil
   See Gibran, Kahlil

Gibson, William
   1914- . . . . **CLC 23; DA; DAB; DAC;**
      DAM DRAM, MST
   See also CA 9-12R; CANR 9, 42; DLB 7;
   SATA 66

Gibson, William (Ford)
   1948- . . . . **CLC 39, 63; DAM POP**
   See also AAYA 12; CA 126; 133; CANR 52

Gide, Andre (Paul Guillaume)
1869-1951 . . . . **TCLC 5, 12, 36; DA; DAB; DAC; DAM MST, NOV; SSC 13; WLC**
See also CA 104; 124; DLB 65; MTCW

Gifford, Barry (Colby) 1946- . . . . . . **CLC 34**
See also CA 65-68; CANR 9, 30, 40

Gilbert, W(illiam) S(chwenck)
1836-1911 . . . . . **TCLC 3; DAM DRAM, POET**
See also CA 104; SATA 36

Gilbreth, Frank B., Jr. 1911- . . . . . . **CLC 17**
See also CA 9-12R; SATA 2

Gilchrist, Ellen
1935- . . . . **CLC 34, 48; DAM POP; SSC 14**
See also CA 113; 116; CANR 41; DLB 130; MTCW

Giles, Molly 1942- . . . . **CLC 39**
See also CA 126

Gill, Patrick
See Creasey, John

Gilliam, Terry (Vance) 1940- . . . . . . **CLC 21**
See also Monty Python
See also AAYA 19; CA 108; 113; CANR 35; INT 113

Gillian, Jerry
See Gilliam, Terry (Vance)

Gilliatt, Penelope (Ann Douglass)
1932-1993 . . . . **CLC 2, 10, 13, 53**
See also AITN 2; CA 13-16R; 141; CANR 49; DLB 14

Gilman, Charlotte (Anna) Perkins (Stetson)
1860-1935 . . . . **TCLC 9, 37; SSC 13**
See also CA 106; 150

Gilmour, David 1949- . . . . **CLC 35**
See also CA 138, 147

Gilpin, William 1724-1804 . . . . . . **NCLC 30**

Gilray, J. D.
See Mencken, H(enry) L(ouis)

Gilroy, Frank D(aniel) 1925- . . . . **CLC 2**
See also CA 81-84; CANR 32; DLB 7

Gilstrap, John 1957(?)- . . . . **CLC 99**

Ginsberg, Allen
1926- . . . . . . **CLC 1, 2, 3, 4, 6, 13, 36, 69; DA; DAB; DAC; DAM MST, POET; PC 4; WLC 3**
See also AITN 1; CA 1-4R; CANR 2, 41; CDALB 1941-1968; DLB 5, 16, 169; MTCW

Ginzburg, Natalia
1916-1991 . . . . **CLC 5, 11, 54, 70**
See also CA 85-88; 135; CANR 33; DLB 177; MTCW

Giono, Jean 1895-1970 . . . . **CLC 4, 11**
See also CA 45-48; 29-32R; CANR 2, 35; DLB 72; MTCW

Giovanni, Nikki
1943- . . . . . . **CLC 2, 4, 19, 64; BLC; DA; DAB; DAC; DAM MST, MULT, POET**
See also AITN 1; BW 2; CA 29-32R; CAAS 6; CANR 18, 41; CLR 6; DLB 5, 41; INT CANR-18; MAICYA; MTCW; SATA 24

Giovene, Andrea 1904- . . . . **CLC 7**
See also CA 85-88

Gippius, Zinaida (Nikolayevna) 1869-1945
See Hippius, Zinaida
See also CA 106

Giraudoux, (Hippolyte) Jean
1882-1944 . . . . **TCLC 2, 7; DAM DRAM**
See also CA 104; DLB 65

Gironella, Jose Maria 1917- . . . . **CLC 11**
See also CA 101

Gissing, George (Robert)
1857-1903 . . . . **TCLC 3, 24, 47**
See also CA 105; DLB 18, 135

Giurlani, Aldo
See Palazzeschi, Aldo

Gladkov, Fyodor (Vasilyevich)
1883-1958 . . . . **TCLC 27**

Glanville, Brian (Lester) 1931- . . . . . . **CLC 6**
See also CA 5-8R; CAAS 9; CANR 3; DLB 15, 139; SATA 42

Glasgow, Ellen (Anderson Gholson)
1873(?)-1945 . . . . **TCLC 2, 7**
See also CA 104; DLB 9, 12

Glaspell, Susan 1882(?)-1948 . . . . . . **TCLC 55**
See also CA 110; 154; DLB 7, 9, 78; YABC 2

Glassco, John 1909-1981 . . . . **CLC 9**
See also CA 13-16R; 102; CANR 15; DLB 68

Glasscock, Amnesia
See Steinbeck, John (Ernst)

Glasser, Ronald J. 1940(?)- . . . . **CLC 37**

Glassman, Joyce
See Johnson, Joyce

Glendinning, Victoria 1937- . . . . **CLC 50**
See also CA 120; 127; DLB 155

Glissant, Edouard
1928- . . . . **CLC 10, 68; DAM MULT**
See also CA 153

Gloag, Julian 1930- . . . . **CLC 40**
See also AITN 1; CA 65-68; CANR 10

Glowacki, Aleksander
See Prus, Boleslaw

Gluck, Louise (Elisabeth)
1943- . . . . **CLC 7, 22, 44, 81; DAM POET; PC 16**
See also CA 33-36R; CANR 40; DLB 5

Gobineau, Joseph Arthur (Comte) de
1816-1882 . . . . **NCLC 17**
See also DLB 123

Godard, Jean-Luc 1930- . . . . **CLC 20**
See also CA 93-96

Godden, (Margaret) Rumer 1907- . . . **CLC 53**
See also AAYA 6; CA 5-8R; CANR 4, 27, 36, 55; CLR 20; DLB 161; MAICYA; SAAS 12; SATA 3, 36

Godoy Alcayaga, Lucila 1889-1957
See Mistral, Gabriela
See also BW 2; CA 104; 131; DAM MULT; HW; MTCW

Godwin, Gail (Kathleen)
1937- . . . . **CLC 5, 8, 22, 31, 69; DAM POP**
See also CA 29-32R; CANR 15, 43; DLB 6; INT CANR-15; MTCW

Godwin, William 1756-1836 . . . . . . **NCLC 14**
See also CDBLB 1789-1832; DLB 39, 104, 142, 158, 163

Goebbels, Josef
See Goebbels, (Paul) Joseph

Goebbels, (Paul) Joseph
1897-1945 . . . . **TCLC 68**
See also CA 115; 148

Goebbels, Joseph Paul
See Goebbels, (Paul) Joseph

Goethe, Johann Wolfgang von
1749-1832 . . . . **NCLC 4, 22, 34; DA; DAB; DAC; DAM DRAM, MST, POET; PC 5; WLC 3**
See also DLB 94

Gogarty, Oliver St. John
1878-1957 . . . . **TCLC 15**
See also CA 109; 150; DLB 15, 19

Gogol, Nikolai (Vasilyevich)
1809-1852 . . . . **NCLC 5, 15, 31; DA; DAB; DAC; DAM DRAM, MST; DC 1; SSC 4; WLC**

Goines, Donald
1937(?)-1974 . . . . **CLC 80; BLC; DAM MULT, POP**
See also AITN 1; BW 1; CA 124; 114; DLB 33

Gold, Herbert 1924- . . . . **CLC 4, 7, 14, 42**
See also CA 9-12R; CANR 17, 45; DLB 2; DLBY 81

Goldbarth, Albert 1948- . . . . **CLC 5, 38**
See also CA 53-56; CANR 6, 40; DLB 120

Goldberg, Anatol 1910-1982 . . . . **CLC 34**
See also CA 131; 117

Goldemberg, Isaac 1945- . . . . **CLC 52**
See also CA 69-72; CAAS 12; CANR 11, 32; HW

Golding, William (Gerald)
1911-1993 . . . . **CLC 1, 2, 3, 8, 10, 17, 27, 58, 81; DA; DAB; DAC; DAM MST, NOV; WLC**
See also AAYA 5; CA 5-8R; 141; CANR 13, 33, 54; CDBLB 1945-1960; DLB 15, 100; MTCW

Goldman, Emma 1869-1940 . . . . . . **TCLC 13**
See also CA 110; 150

Goldman, Francisco 1955- . . . . **CLC 76**

Goldman, William (W.) 1931- . . . . **CLC 1, 48**
See also CA 9-12R; CANR 29; DLB 44

Goldmann, Lucien 1913-1970 . . . . . . **CLC 24**
See also CA 25-28; CAP 2

Goldoni, Carlo
1707-1793 . . . . **LC 4; DAM DRAM**

Goldsberry, Steven 1949- . . . . **CLC 34**
See also CA 131

Goldsmith, Oliver
1728-1774 . . . . . . **LC 2; DA; DAB; DAC; DAM DRAM, MST, NOV, POET; WLC**
See also CDBLB 1660-1789; DLB 39, 89, 104, 109, 142; SATA 26

Goldsmith, Peter
See Priestley, J(ohn) B(oynton)

Green, Julian (Hartridge) 1900-
See Green, Julien
See also CA 21-24R; CANR 33; DLB 4, 72;
MTCW

Green, Julien . . . . **CLC 3, 11, 77**
See also Green, Julian (Hartridge)

Green, Paul (Eliot)
1894-1981 . . . . . . **CLC 25; DAM DRAM**
See also AITN 1; CA 5-8R; 103; CANR 3;
DLB 7, 9; DLBY 81

Greenberg, Ivan 1908-1973
See Rahv, Philip
See also CA 85-88

Greenberg, Joanne (Goldenberg)
1932- . . . . **CLC 7, 30**
See also AAYA 12; CA 5-8R; CANR 14,
32; SATA 25

Greenberg, Richard 1959(?)- . . . . **CLC 57**
See also CA 138

Greene, Bette 1934- . . . . **CLC 30**
See also AAYA 7; CA 53-56; CANR 4;
CLR 2; JRDA; MAICYA; SAAS 16;
SATA 8

Greene, Gael . . . . **CLC 8**
See also CA 13-16R; CANR 10

Greene, Graham
1904-1991 . . . . **CLC 1, 3, 6, 9, 14, 18, 27,
37, 70, 72; DA; DAB; DAC; DAM MST,
NOV; WLC**
See also AITN 2; CA 13-16R; 133;
CANR 35; CDBLB 1945-1960; DLB 13,
15, 77, 100, 162; DLBY 91; MTCW;
SATA 20

Greer, Richard
See Silverberg, Robert

Gregor, Arthur 1923- . . . . **CLC 9**
See also CA 25-28R; CAAS 10; CANR 11;
SATA 36

Gregor, Lee
See Pohl, Frederik

Gregory, Isabella Augusta (Persse)
1852-1932 . . . . **TCLC 1**
See also CA 104; DLB 10

Gregory, J. Dennis
See Williams, John A(lfred)

Grendon, Stephen
See Derleth, August (William)

Grenville, Kate 1950- . . . . **CLC 61**
See also CA 118; CANR 53

Grenville, Pelham
See Wodehouse, P(elham) G(renville)

Greve, Felix Paul (Berthold Friedrich)
1879-1948
See Grove, Frederick Philip
See also CA 104; 141; DAC; DAM MST

Grey, Zane
1872-1939 . . . . **TCLC 6; DAM POP**
See also CA 104; 132; DLB 9; MTCW

Grieg, (Johan) Nordahl (Brun)
1902-1943 . . . . **TCLC 10**
See also CA 107

Grieve, C(hristopher) M(urray)
1892-1978 . . . . **CLC 11, 19; DAM POET**
See also MacDiarmid, Hugh; Pteleon
See also CA 5-8R; 85-88; CANR 33;
MTCW

Griffin, Gerald 1803-1840 . . . . **NCLC 7**
See also DLB 159

Griffin, John Howard 1920-1980 . . . . **CLC 68**
See also AITN 1; CA 1-4R; 101; CANR 2

Griffin, Peter 1942- . . . . **CLC 39**
See also CA 136

Griffith, D(avid Lewelyn) W(ark)
1875(?)-1948 . . . . **TCLC 68**
See also CA 119; 150

Griffith, Lawrence
See Griffith, D(avid Lewelyn) W(ark)

Griffiths, Trevor 1935- . . . . **CLC 13, 52**
See also CA 97-100; CANR 45; DLB 13

Grigson, Geoffrey (Edward Harvey)
1905-1985 . . . . **CLC 7, 39**
See also CA 25-28R; 118; CANR 20, 33;
DLB 27; MTCW

Grillparzer, Franz 1791-1872 . . . . . . **NCLC 1**
See also DLB 133

Grimble, Reverend Charles James
See Eliot, T(homas) S(tearns)

Grimke, Charlotte L(ottie) Forten
1837(?)-1914
See Forten, Charlotte L.
See also BW 1; CA 117; 124; DAM MULT,
POET

Grimm, Jacob Ludwig Karl
1785-1863 . . . . **NCLC 3**
See also DLB 90; MAICYA; SATA 22

Grimm, Wilhelm Karl 1786-1859 . . **NCLC 3**
See also DLB 90; MAICYA; SATA 22

**Grimmelshausen, Johann Jakob Christoffel
von** 1621-1676 . . . . **LC 6**
See also DLB 168

Grindel, Eugene 1895-1952
See Eluard, Paul
See also CA 104

Grisham, John 1955- . . **CLC 84; DAM POP**
See also AAYA 14; CA 138; CANR 47

Grossman, David 1954- . . . . **CLC 67**
See also CA 138

Grossman, Vasily (Semenovich)
1905-1964 . . . . **CLC 41**
See also CA 124; 130; MTCW

Grove, Frederick Philip . . . . **TCLC 4**
See also Greve, Felix Paul (Berthold
Friedrich)
See also DLB 92

Grubb
See Crumb, R(obert)

Grumbach, Doris (Isaac)
1918- . . . . **CLC 13, 22, 64**
See also CA 5-8R; CAAS 2; CANR 9, 42;
INT CANR-9

Grundtvig, Nicolai Frederik Severin
1783-1872 . . . . **NCLC 1**

Grunge
See Crumb, R(obert)

Grunwald, Lisa 1959- . . . . **CLC 44**
See also CA 120

Guare, John
1938- . . . . **CLC 8, 14, 29, 67;
DAM DRAM**
See also CA 73-76; CANR 21; DLB 7;
MTCW

Gudjonsson, Halldor Kiljan 1902-
See Laxness, Halldor
See also CA 103

Guenter, Erich
See Eich, Guenter

Guest, Barbara 1920- . . . . **CLC 34**
See also CA 25-28R; CANR 11, 44; DLB 5

Guest, Judith (Ann)
1936- . . . . **CLC 8, 30; DAM NOV, POP**
See also AAYA 7; CA 77-80; CANR 15;
INT CANR-15; MTCW

Guevara, Che . . . . **CLC 87; HLC**
See also Guevara (Serna), Ernesto

Guevara (Serna), Ernesto 1928-1967
See Guevara, Che
See also CA 127; 111; CANR 56;
DAM MULT; HW

Guild, Nicholas M. 1944- . . . . **CLC 33**
See also CA 93-96

Guillemin, Jacques
See Sartre, Jean-Paul

Guillen, Jorge
1893-1984 . . . . . . **CLC 11; DAM MULT,
POET**
See also CA 89-92; 112; DLB 108; HW

Guillen, Nicolas (Cristobal)
1902-1989 . . . . **CLC 48, 79; BLC;
DAM MST, MULT, POET; HLC**
See also BW 2; CA 116; 125; 129; HW

Guillevic, (Eugene) 1907- . . . . **CLC 33**
See also CA 93-96

Guillois
See Desnos, Robert

Guillois, Valentin
See Desnos, Robert

Guiney, Louise Imogen
1861-1920 . . . . **TCLC 41**
See also DLB 54

Guiraldes, Ricardo (Guillermo)
1886-1927 . . . . **TCLC 39**
See also CA 131; HW; MTCW

Gumilev, Nikolai Stephanovich
1886-1921 . . . . **TCLC 60**

Gunesekera, Romesh . . . . **CLC 91**

Gunn, Bill . . . . **CLC 5**
See also Gunn, William Harrison
See also DLB 38

Gunn, Thom(son William)
1929- . . . . **CLC 3, 6, 18, 32, 81;
DAM POET**
See also CA 17-20R; CANR 9, 33;
CDBLB 1960 to Present; DLB 27;
INT CANR-33; MTCW

Gunn, William Harrison 1934(?)-1989
See Gunn, Bill
See also AITN 1; BW 1; CA 13-16R; 128;
CANR 12, 25

Gunnars, Kristjana 1948- . . . . **CLC 69**
See also CA 113; DLB 60

Gurganus, Allan
1947- . . . . **CLC 70; DAM POP**
See also BEST 90:1; CA 135

Gurney, A(lbert) R(amsdell), Jr.
1930- . . . . **CLC 32, 50, 54; DAM DRAM**
See also CA 77-80; CANR 32

Gurney, Ivor (Bertie)   1890-1937 . . . **TCLC 33**

Gurney, Peter
See Gurney, A(lbert) R(amsdell), Jr.

Guro, Elena   1877-1913 . . . . **TCLC 56**

Gustafson, James M(oody)   1925- . . **CLC 100**
See also CA 25-28R; CANR 37

Gustafson, Ralph (Barker)   1909- . . . . **CLC 36**
See also CA 21-24R; CANR 8, 45; DLB 88

Gut, Gom
See Simenon, Georges (Jacques Christian)

Guterson, David   1956- . . . . **CLC 91**
See also CA 132

Guthrie, A(lfred) B(ertram), Jr.
1901-1991 . . . . **CLC 23**
See also CA 57-60; 134; CANR 24; DLB 6;
SATA 62; SATA-Obit 67

Guthrie, Isobel
See Grieve, C(hristopher) M(urray)

Guthrie, Woodrow Wilson   1912-1967
See Guthrie, Woody
See also CA 113; 93-96

Guthrie, Woody . . . . **CLC 35**
See also Guthrie, Woodrow Wilson

Guy, Rosa (Cuthbert)   1928- . . . . **CLC 26**
See also AAYA 4; BW 2; CA 17-20R;
CANR 14, 34; CLR 13; DLB 33; JRDA;
MAICYA; SATA 14, 62

Gwendolyn
See Bennett, (Enoch) Arnold

H. D. . . . . **CLC 3, 8, 14, 31, 34, 73; PC 5**
See also Doolittle, Hilda

H. de V.
See Buchan, John

Haavikko, Paavo Juhani
1931- . . . . **CLC 18, 34**
See also CA 106

Habbema, Koos
See Heijermans, Herman

Hacker, Marilyn
1942- . . . . **CLC 5, 9, 23, 72, 91;
DAM POET**
See also CA 77-80; DLB 120

Haggard, H(enry) Rider
1856-1925 . . . . **TCLC 11**
See also CA 108; 148; DLB 70, 156, 174;
SATA 16

Hagiosy, L.
See Larbaud, Valery (Nicolas)

Hagiwara Sakutaro   1886-1942 . . . . **TCLC 60**

Haig, Fenil
See Ford, Ford Madox

Haig-Brown, Roderick (Langmere)
1908-1976 . . . . **CLC 21**
See also CA 5-8R; 69-72; CANR 4, 38;
CLR 31; DLB 88; MAICYA; SATA 12

Hailey, Arthur
1920- . . . . **CLC 5; DAM NOV, POP**
See also AITN 2; BEST 90:3; CA 1-4R;
CANR 2, 36; DLB 88; DLBY 82; MTCW

Hailey, Elizabeth Forsythe   1938- . . . **CLC 40**
See also CA 93-96; CAAS 1; CANR 15, 48;
INT CANR-15

Haines, John (Meade)   1924- . . . . **CLC 58**
See also CA 17-20R; CANR 13, 34; DLB 5

Hakluyt, Richard   1552-1616 . . . . **LC 31**

Haldeman, Joe (William)   1943- . . . . . **CLC 61**
See also CA 53-56; CAAS 25; CANR 6;
DLB 8; INT CANR-6

Haley, Alex(ander Murray Palmer)
1921-1992 . . . . **CLC 8, 12, 76; BLC; DA;
DAB; DAC; DAM MST, MULT, POP**
See also BW 2; CA 77-80; 136; DLB 38;
MTCW

Haliburton, Thomas Chandler
1796-1865 . . . . **NCLC 15**
See also DLB 11, 99

Hall, Donald (Andrew, Jr.)
1928- . . **CLC 1, 13, 37, 59; DAM POET**
See also CA 5-8R; CAAS 7; CANR 2, 44;
DLB 5; SATA 23

Hall, Frederic Sauser
See Sauser-Hall, Frederic

Hall, James
See Kuttner, Henry

Hall, James Norman   1887-1951 . . . **TCLC 23**
See also CA 123; SATA 21

Hall, (Marguerite) Radclyffe
1886-1943 . . . . **TCLC 12**
See also CA 110; 150

Hall, Rodney   1935- . . . . **CLC 51**
See also CA 109

Halleck, Fitz-Greene   1790-1867 . . **NCLC 47**
See also DLB 3

Halliday, Michael
See Creasey, John

Halpern, Daniel   1945- . . . . **CLC 14**
See also CA 33-36R

Hamburger, Michael (Peter Leopold)
1924- . . . . **CLC 5, 14**
See also CA 5-8R; CAAS 4; CANR 2, 47;
DLB 27

Hamill, Pete   1935- . . . . **CLC 10**
See also CA 25-28R; CANR 18

Hamilton, Alexander
1755(?)-1804 . . . . **NCLC 49**
See also DLB 37

Hamilton, Clive
See Lewis, C(live) S(taples)

Hamilton, Edmond   1904-1977 . . . . . . **CLC 1**
See also CA 1-4R; CANR 3; DLB 8

Hamilton, Eugene (Jacob) Lee
See Lee-Hamilton, Eugene (Jacob)

Hamilton, Franklin
See Silverberg, Robert

Hamilton, Gail
See Corcoran, Barbara

Hamilton, Mollie
See Kaye, M(ary) M(argaret)

Hamilton, (Anthony Walter) Patrick
1904-1962 . . . . **CLC 51**
See also CA 113; DLB 10

Hamilton, Virginia
1936- . . . . **CLC 26; DAM MULT**
See also AAYA 2, 21; BW 2; CA 25-28R;
CANR 20, 37; CLR 1, 11, 40; DLB 33,
52; INT CANR-20; JRDA; MAICYA;
MTCW; SATA 4, 56, 79

Hammett, (Samuel) Dashiell
1894-1961 . . . . **CLC 3, 5, 10, 19, 47;
SSC 17**
See also AITN 1; CA 81-84; CANR 42;
CDALB 1929-1941; DLBD 6; MTCW

Hammon, Jupiter
1711(?)-1800(?) . . . . **NCLC 5; BLC;
DAM MULT, POET; PC 16**
See also DLB 31, 50

Hammond, Keith
See Kuttner, Henry

Hamner, Earl (Henry), Jr.   1923- . . . **CLC 12**
See also AITN 2; CA 73-76; DLB 6

Hampton, Christopher (James)
1946- . . . . **CLC 4**
See also CA 25-28R; DLB 13; MTCW

Hamsun, Knut . . . . **TCLC 2, 14, 49**
See also Pedersen, Knut

Handke, Peter
1942- . . . . **CLC 5, 8, 10, 15, 38;
DAM DRAM, NOV**
See also CA 77-80; CANR 33; DLB 85,
124; MTCW

Hanley, James   1901-1985 . . . **CLC 3, 5, 8, 13**
See also CA 73-76; 117; CANR 36; MTCW

Hannah, Barry   1942- . . . . . . **CLC 23, 38, 90**
See also CA 108; 110; CANR 43; DLB 6;
INT 110; MTCW

Hannon, Ezra
See Hunter, Evan

Hansberry, Lorraine (Vivian)
1930-1965 . . . . . . **CLC 17, 62; BLC; DA;
DAB; DAC; DAM DRAM, MST,
MULT; DC 2**
See also BW 1; CA 109; 25-28R; CABS 3;
CDALB 1941-1968; DLB 7, 38; MTCW

Hansen, Joseph   1923- . . . . **CLC 38**
See also CA 29-32R; CAAS 17; CANR 16,
44; INT CANR-16

Hansen, Martin A.   1909-1955 . . . . . **TCLC 32**

Hanson, Kenneth O(stlin)   1922- . . . . **CLC 13**
See also CA 53-56; CANR 7

Hardwick, Elizabeth
1916- . . . . **CLC 13; DAM NOV**
See also CA 5-8R; CANR 3, 32; DLB 6;
MTCW

Hardy, Thomas
1840-1928 . . . . . . **TCLC 4, 10, 18, 32, 48,
53; DA; DAB; DAC; DAM MST, NOV,
POET; PC 8; SSC 2; WLC**
See also CA 104; 123; CDBLB 1890-1914;
DLB 18, 19, 135; MTCW

Hare, David   1947- . . . . **CLC 29, 58**
See also CA 97-100; CANR 39; DLB 13;
MTCW

Harford, Henry
See Hudson, W(illiam) H(enry)

Hargrave, Leonie
See Disch, Thomas M(ichael)

Harjo, Joy   1951- . . . **CLC 83; DAM MULT**
See also CA 114; CANR 35; DLB 120, 175;
NNAL

Harlan, Louis R(udolph)   1922- . . . . . **CLC 34**
See also CA 21-24R; CANR 25, 55

Harling, Robert 1951(?)- . . . . **CLC 53**
See also CA 147

Harmon, William (Ruth) 1938- . . . . . **CLC 38**
See also CA 33-36R; CANR 14, 32, 35;
SATA 65

Harper, F. E. W.
See Harper, Frances Ellen Watkins

Harper, Frances E. W.
See Harper, Frances Ellen Watkins

Harper, Frances E. Watkins
See Harper, Frances Ellen Watkins

Harper, Frances Ellen
See Harper, Frances Ellen Watkins

Harper, Frances Ellen Watkins
1825-1911 . . . . **TCLC 14; BLC;**
DAM MULT, POET
See also BW 1; CA 111; 125; DLB 50

Harper, Michael S(teven) 1938- . . **CLC 7, 22**
See also BW 1; CA 33-36R; CANR 24;
DLB 41

Harper, Mrs. F. E. W.
See Harper, Frances Ellen Watkins

Harris, Christie (Lucy) Irwin
1907- . . . . **CLC 12**
See also CA 5-8R; CANR 6; DLB 88;
JRDA; MAICYA; SAAS 10; SATA 6, 74

Harris, Frank 1856-1931 . . . . **TCLC 24**
See also CA 109; 150; DLB 156

Harris, George Washington
1814-1869 . . . . **NCLC 23**
See also DLB 3, 11

Harris, Joel Chandler
1848-1908 . . . . **TCLC 2; SSC 19**
See also CA 104; 137; DLB 11, 23, 42, 78,
91; MAICYA; YABC 1

Harris, John (Wyndham Parkes Lucas)
Beynon 1903-1969
See Wyndham, John
See also CA 102; 89-92

Harris, MacDonald . . . . **CLC 9**
See also Heiney, Donald (William)

Harris, Mark 1922- . . . . **CLC 19**
See also CA 5-8R; CAAS 3; CANR 2, 55;
DLB 2; DLBY 80

Harris, (Theodore) Wilson 1921- . . . . **CLC 25**
See also BW 2; CA 65-68; CAAS 16;
CANR 11, 27; DLB 117; MTCW

Harrison, Elizabeth Cavanna 1909-
See Cavanna, Betty
See also CA 9-12R; CANR 6, 27

Harrison, Harry (Max) 1925- . . . . . . **CLC 42**
See also CA 1-4R; CANR 5, 21; DLB 8;
SATA 4

Harrison, James (Thomas)
1937- . . . . **CLC 6, 14, 33, 66; SSC 19**
See also CA 13-16R; CANR 8, 51;
DLBY 82; INT CANR-8

Harrison, Jim
See Harrison, James (Thomas)

Harrison, Kathryn 1961- . . . . **CLC 70**
See also CA 144

Harrison, Tony 1937- . . . . **CLC 43**
See also CA 65-68; CANR 44; DLB 40;
MTCW

Harriss, Will(ard Irvin) 1922- . . . . . . **CLC 34**
See also CA 111

Harson, Sley
See Ellison, Harlan (Jay)

Hart, Ellis
See Ellison, Harlan (Jay)

Hart, Josephine
1942(?)- . . . . **CLC 70; DAM POP**
See also CA 138

Hart, Moss
1904-1961 . . . . . . **CLC 66; DAM DRAM**
See also CA 109; 89-92; DLB 7

Harte, (Francis) Bret(t)
1836(?)-1902 . . . . **TCLC 1, 25; DA; DAC;**
DAM MST; SSC 8; WLC
See also CA 104; 140; CDALB 1865-1917;
DLB 12, 64, 74, 79; SATA 26

Hartley, L(eslie) P(oles)
1895-1972 . . . . **CLC 2, 22**
See also CA 45-48; 37-40R; CANR 33;
DLB 15, 139; MTCW

Hartman, Geoffrey H. 1929- . . . . **CLC 27**
See also CA 117; 125; DLB 67

Hartmann von Aue
c. 1160-c. 1205 . . . . **CMLC 15**
See also DLB 138

Hartmann von Aue 1170-1210 . . . . **CMLC 15**

Haruf, Kent 1943- . . . . **CLC 34**
See also CA 149

Harwood, Ronald
1934- . . . . **CLC 32; DAM DRAM, MST**
See also CA 1-4R; CANR 4, 55; DLB 13

Hasek, Jaroslav (Matej Frantisek)
1883-1923 . . . . **TCLC 4**
See also CA 104; 129; MTCW

Hass, Robert
1941- . . . . **CLC 18, 39, 99; PC 16**
See also CA 111; CANR 30, 50; DLB 105

Hastings, Hudson
See Kuttner, Henry

Hastings, Selina . . . . **CLC 44**

Hathorne, John 1641-1717 . . . . **LC 38**

Hatteras, Amelia
See Mencken, H(enry) L(ouis)

Hatteras, Owen . . . . **TCLC 18**
See also Mencken, H(enry) L(ouis); Nathan,
George Jean

Hauptmann, Gerhart (Johann Robert)
1862-1946 . . . . . . **TCLC 4; DAM DRAM**
See also CA 104; 153; DLB 66, 118

Havel, Vaclav
1936- . . . . **CLC 25, 58, 65;**
DAM DRAM; DC 6
See also CA 104; CANR 36; MTCW

Haviaras, Stratis . . . . **CLC 33**
See also Chaviaras, Strates

Hawes, Stephen 1475(?)-1523(?) . . . . . **LC 17**

Hawkes, John (Clendennin Burne, Jr.)
1925- . . . . . . **CLC 1, 2, 3, 4, 7, 9, 14, 15,**
27, 49
See also CA 1-4R; CANR 2, 47; DLB 2, 7;
DLBY 80; MTCW

Hawking, S. W.
See Hawking, Stephen W(illiam)

Hawking, Stephen W(illiam)
1942- . . . . **CLC 63**
See also AAYA 13; BEST 89:1; CA 126;
129; CANR 48

Hawthorne, Julian 1846-1934 . . . . . **TCLC 25**

Hawthorne, Nathaniel
1804-1864 . . . . **NCLC 39; DA; DAB;**
DAC; DAM MST, NOV; SSC 3; WLC
See also AAYA 18; CDALB 1640-1865;
DLB 1, 74; YABC 2

Haxton, Josephine Ayres 1921-
See Douglas, Ellen
See also CA 115; CANR 41

Hayaseca y Eizaguirre, Jorge
See Echegaray (y Eizaguirre), Jose (Maria
Waldo)

Hayashi Fumiko 1904-1951 . . . . **TCLC 27**

Haycraft, Anna
See Ellis, Alice Thomas
See also CA 122

Hayden, Robert E(arl)
1913-1980 . . . . . . **CLC 5, 9, 14, 37; BLC;**
DA; DAC; DAM MST, MULT, POET;
PC 6
See also BW 1; CA 69-72; 97-100; CABS 2;
CANR 24; CDALB 1941-1968; DLB 5,
76; MTCW; SATA 19; SATA-Obit 26

Hayford, J(oseph) E(phraim) Casely
See Casely-Hayford, J(oseph) E(phraim)

Hayman, Ronald 1932- . . . . **CLC 44**
See also CA 25-28R; CANR 18, 50;
DLB 155

Haywood, Eliza (Fowler)
1693(?)-1756 . . . . **LC 1**

Hazlitt, William 1778-1830 . . . . . . **NCLC 29**
See also DLB 110, 158

Hazzard, Shirley 1931- . . . . **CLC 18**
See also CA 9-12R; CANR 4; DLBY 82;
MTCW

Head, Bessie
1937-1986 . . . . **CLC 25, 67; BLC;**
DAM MULT
See also BW 2; CA 29-32R; 119; CANR 25;
DLB 117; MTCW

Headon, (Nicky) Topper 1956(?)- . . . **CLC 30**

Heaney, Seamus (Justin)
1939- . . . . . . **CLC 5, 7, 14, 25, 37, 74, 91;**
DAB; DAM POET
See also CA 85-88; CANR 25, 48;
CDBLB 1960 to Present; DLB 40;
DLBY 95; MTCW

Hearn, (Patricio) Lafcadio (Tessima Carlos)
1850-1904 . . . . **TCLC 9**
See also CA 105; DLB 12, 78

Hearne, Vicki 1946- . . . . **CLC 56**
See also CA 139

Hearon, Shelby 1931- . . . . **CLC 63**
See also AITN 2; CA 25-28R; CANR 18,
48

Heat-Moon, William Least . . . . **CLC 29**
See also Trogdon, William (Lewis)
See also AAYA 9

Hebbel, Friedrich
1813-1863 . . . . **NCLC 43; DAM DRAM**
See also DLB 129

Hollander, Paul
See Silverberg, Robert

Holleran, Andrew 1943(?)-......... **CLC 38**
See also CA 144

Hollinghurst, Alan 1954-....... **CLC 55, 91**
See also CA 114

Hollis, Jim
See Summers, Hollis (Spurgeon, Jr.)

Holly, Buddy 1936-1959 .... **TCLC 65**

Holmes, John
See Souster, (Holmes) Raymond

Holmes, John Clellon 1926-1988.... **CLC 56**
See also CA 9-12R; 125; CANR 4; DLB 16

Holmes, Oliver Wendell
1809-1894 .... **NCLC 14**
See also CDALB 1640-1865; DLB 1;
SATA 34

Holmes, Raymond
See Souster, (Holmes) Raymond

Holt, Victoria
See Hibbert, Eleanor Alice Burford

Holub, Miroslav 1923-............. **CLC 4**
See also CA 21-24R; CANR 10

Homer
c. 8th cent. B.C.-..... **CMLC 1, 16; DA;**
DAB; DAC; DAM MST, POET
See also DLB 176

Honig, Edwin 1919-............. **CLC 33**
See also CA 5-8R; CAAS 8; CANR 4, 45;
DLB 5

Hood, Hugh (John Blagdon)
1928- .... **CLC 15, 28**
See also CA 49-52; CAAS 17; CANR 1, 33;
DLB 53

Hood, Thomas 1799-1845........ **NCLC 16**
See also DLB 96

Hooker, (Peter) Jeremy 1941-...... **CLC 43**
See also CA 77-80; CANR 22; DLB 40

hooks, bell .... **CLC 94**
See also Watkins, Gloria

Hope, A(lec) D(erwent) 1907-.... **CLC 3, 51**
See also CA 21-24R; CANR 33; MTCW

Hope, Brian
See Creasey, John

Hope, Christopher (David Tully)
1944- .... **CLC 52**
See also CA 106; CANR 47; SATA 62

Hopkins, Gerard Manley
1844-1889 .... **NCLC 17; DA; DAB;**
DAC; DAM MST, POET; PC 15; WLC
See also CDBLB 1890-1914; DLB 35, 57

Hopkins, John (Richard) 1931-...... **CLC 4**
See also CA 85-88

Hopkins, Pauline Elizabeth
1859-1930 .... **TCLC 28; BLC;**
DAM MULT
See also BW 2; CA 141; DLB 50

Hopkinson, Francis 1737-1791 ...... **LC 25**
See also DLB 31

Hopley-Woolrich, Cornell George 1903-1968
See Woolrich, Cornell
See also CA 13-14; CAP 1

Horatio
See Proust, (Valentin-Louis-George-Eugene-)
Marcel

Horgan, Paul (George Vincent O'Shaughnessy)
1903-1995 ..... **CLC 9, 53; DAM NOV**
See also CA 13-16R; 147; CANR 9, 35;
DLB 102; DLBY 85; INT CANR-9;
MTCW; SATA 13; SATA-Obit 84

Horn, Peter
See Kuttner, Henry

Hornem, Horace Esq.
See Byron, George Gordon (Noel)

Hornung, E(rnest) W(illiam)
1866-1921 .... **TCLC 59**
See also CA 108; DLB 70

Horovitz, Israel (Arthur)
1939- .... **CLC 56; DAM DRAM**
See also CA 33-36R; CANR 46; DLB 7

Horvath, Odon von
See Horvath, Oedoen von
See also DLB 85, 124

Horvath, Oedoen von 1901-1938... **TCLC 45**
See also Horvath, Odon von
See also CA 118

Horwitz, Julius 1920-1986........ **CLC 14**
See also CA 9-12R; 119; CANR 12

Hospital, Janette Turner 1942- ..... **CLC 42**
See also CA 108; CANR 48

Hostos, E. M. de
See Hostos (y Bonilla), Eugenio Maria de

Hostos, Eugenio M. de
See Hostos (y Bonilla), Eugenio Maria de

Hostos, Eugenio Maria
See Hostos (y Bonilla), Eugenio Maria de

Hostos (y Bonilla), Eugenio Maria de
1839-1903 .... **TCLC 24**
See also CA 123; 131; HW

Houdini
See Lovecraft, H(oward) P(hillips)

Hougan, Carolyn 1943- .... **CLC 34**
See also CA 139

Household, Geoffrey (Edward West)
1900-1988 .... **CLC 11**
See also CA 77-80; 126; DLB 87; SATA 14;
SATA-Obit 59

Housman, A(lfred) E(dward)
1859-1936 ...... **TCLC 1, 10; DA; DAB;**
DAC; DAM MST, POET; PC 2
See also CA 104; 125; DLB 19; MTCW

Housman, Laurence 1865-1959 ..... **TCLC 7**
See also CA 106; 155; DLB 10; SATA 25

Howard, Elizabeth Jane 1923- ... **CLC 7, 29**
See also CA 5-8R; CANR 8

Howard, Maureen 1930- ..... **CLC 5, 14, 46**
See also CA 53-56; CANR 31; DLBY 83;
INT CANR-31; MTCW

Howard, Richard 1929- ...... **CLC 7, 10, 47**
See also AITN 1; CA 85-88; CANR 25;
DLB 5; INT CANR-25

Howard, Robert Ervin 1906-1936... **TCLC 8**
See also CA 105

Howard, Warren F.
See Pohl, Frederik

Howe, Fanny 1940- .... **CLC 47**
See also CA 117; SATA-Brief 52

Howe, Irving 1920-1993.......... **CLC 85**
See also CA 9-12R; 141; CANR 21, 50;
DLB 67; MTCW

Howe, Julia Ward 1819-1910 ..... **TCLC 21**
See also CA 117; DLB 1

Howe, Susan 1937-................ **CLC 72**
See also DLB 120

Howe, Tina 1937-................ **CLC 48**
See also CA 109

Howell, James 1594(?)-1666 .... **LC 13**
See also DLB 151

Howells, W. D.
See Howells, William Dean

Howells, William D.
See Howells, William Dean

Howells, William Dean
1837-1920 .... **TCLC 7, 17, 41**
See also CA 104; 134; CDALB 1865-1917;
DLB 12, 64, 74, 79

Howes, Barbara 1914-1996 .... **CLC 15**
See also CA 9-12R; 151; CAAS 3;
CANR 53; SATA 5

Hrabal, Bohumil 1914-1997..... **CLC 13, 67**
See also CA 106; 156; CAAS 12; CANR 57

Hsun, Lu
See Lu Hsun

Hubbard, L(afayette) Ron(ald)
1911-1986 .... **CLC 43; DAM POP**
See also CA 77-80; 118; CANR 52

Huch, Ricarda (Octavia)
1864-1947 .... **TCLC 13**
See also CA 111; DLB 66

Huddle, David 1942- .... **CLC 49**
See also CA 57-60; CAAS 20; DLB 130

Hudson, Jeffrey
See Crichton, (John) Michael

Hudson, W(illiam) H(enry)
1841-1922 .... **TCLC 29**
See also CA 115; DLB 98, 153, 174;
SATA 35

Hueffer, Ford Madox
See Ford, Ford Madox

Hughart, Barry 1934-............. **CLC 39**
See also CA 137

Hughes, Colin
See Creasey, John

Hughes, David (John) 1930- .... **CLC 48**
See also CA 116; 129; DLB 14

Hughes, Edward James
See Hughes, Ted
See also DAM MST, POET

Hughes, (James) Langston
1902-1967 ..... **CLC 1, 5, 10, 15, 35, 44;**
BLC; DA; DAB; DAC; DAM DRAM,
MST, MULT, POET; DC 3; PC 1;
SSC 6; WLC
See also AAYA 12; BW 1; CA 1-4R;
25-28R; CANR 1, 34; CDALB 1929-1941;
CLR 17; DLB 4, 7, 48, 51, 86; JRDA;
MAICYA; MTCW; SATA 4, 33

Hughes, Richard (Arthur Warren)
1900-1976 . . . . . . **CLC 1, 11; DAM NOV**
See also CA 5-8R; 65-68; CANR 4;
DLB 15, 161; MTCW; SATA 8;
SATA-Obit 25

Hughes, Ted
1930- . . . . **CLC 2, 4, 9, 14, 37; DAB;
DAC; PC 7**
See also Hughes, Edward James
See also CA 1-4R; CANR 1, 33; CLR 3;
DLB 40, 161; MAICYA; MTCW;
SATA 49; SATA-Brief 27

Hugo, Richard F(ranklin)
1923-1982 . . . . **CLC 6, 18, 32;
DAM POET**
See also CA 49-52; 108; CANR 3; DLB 5

Hugo, Victor (Marie)
1802-1885 . . . . **NCLC 3, 10, 21; DA;
DAB; DAC; DAM DRAM, MST, NOV,
POET; PC 17; WLC**
See also DLB 119; SATA 47

Huidobro, Vicente
See Huidobro Fernandez, Vicente Garcia

Huidobro Fernandez, Vicente Garcia
1893-1948 . . . . **TCLC 31**
See also CA 131; HW

Hulme, Keri 1947- . . . . **CLC 39**
See also CA 125; INT 125

Hulme, T(homas) E(rnest)
1883-1917 . . . . **TCLC 21**
See also CA 117; DLB 19

Hume, David 1711-1776 . . . . **LC 7**
See also DLB 104

Humphrey, William 1924- . . . . **CLC 45**
See also CA 77-80; DLB 6

Humphreys, Emyr Owen 1919- . . . . . **CLC 47**
See also CA 5-8R; CANR 3, 24; DLB 15

Humphreys, Josephine 1945- . . . . **CLC 34, 57**
See also CA 121; 127; INT 127

Huneker, James Gibbons
1857-1921 . . . . **TCLC 65**
See also DLB 71

Hungerford, Pixie
See Brinsmead, H(esba) F(ay)

Hunt, E(verette) Howard, (Jr.)
1918- . . . . **CLC 3**
See also AITN 1; CA 45-48; CANR 2, 47

Hunt, Kyle
See Creasey, John

Hunt, (James Henry) Leigh
1784-1859 . . . . . . **NCLC 1; DAM POET**

Hunt, Marsha 1946- . . . . **CLC 70**
See also BW 2; CA 143

Hunt, Violet 1866-1942 . . . . **TCLC 53**
See also DLB 162

Hunter, E. Waldo
See Sturgeon, Theodore (Hamilton)

Hunter, Evan
1926- . . . . **CLC 11, 31; DAM POP**
See also CA 5-8R; CANR 5, 38; DLBY 82;
INT CANR-5; MTCW; SATA 25

Hunter, Kristin (Eggleston) 1931-. . . **CLC 35**
See also AITN 1; BW 1; CA 13-16R;
CANR 13; CLR 3; DLB 33;
INT CANR-13; MAICYA; SAAS 10;
SATA 12

Hunter, Mollie 1922- . . . . **CLC 21**
See also McIlwraith, Maureen Mollie
Hunter
See also AAYA 13; CANR 37; CLR 25;
DLB 161; JRDA; MAICYA; SAAS 7;
SATA 54

Hunter, Robert (?)-1734 . . . . **LC 7**

Hurston, Zora Neale
1903-1960 . . . . **CLC 7, 30, 61; BLC; DA;
DAC; DAM MST, MULT, NOV; SSC 4**
See also AAYA 15; BW 1; CA 85-88;
DLB 51, 86; MTCW

Huston, John (Marcellus)
1906-1987 . . . . **CLC 20**
See also CA 73-76; 123; CANR 34; DLB 26

Hustvedt, Siri 1955- . . . . **CLC 76**
See also CA 137

Hutten, Ulrich von 1488-1523 . . . . . . **LC 16**

Huxley, Aldous (Leonard)
1894-1963 . . . . . **CLC 1, 3, 4, 5, 8, 11, 18,
35, 79; DA; DAB; DAC; DAM MST,
NOV; WLC**
See also AAYA 11; CA 85-88; CANR 44;
CDBLB 1914-1945; DLB 36, 100, 162;
MTCW; SATA 63

Huysmans, Charles Marie Georges
1848-1907
See Huysmans, Joris-Karl
See also CA 104

Huysmans, Joris-Karl . . . . **TCLC 7, 69**
See also Huysmans, Charles Marie Georges
See also DLB 123

Hwang, David Henry
1957- . . . . **CLC 55; DAM DRAM; DC 4**
See also CA 127; 132; INT 132

Hyde, Anthony 1946- . . . . **CLC 42**
See also CA 136

Hyde, Margaret O(ldroyd) 1917- . . . **CLC 21**
See also CA 1-4R; CANR 1, 36; CLR 23;
JRDA; MAICYA; SAAS 8; SATA 1, 42,
76

Hynes, James 1956(?)- . . . . **CLC 65**

Ian, Janis 1951- . . . . **CLC 21**
See also CA 105

Ibanez, Vicente Blasco
See Blasco Ibanez, Vicente

Ibarguengoitia, Jorge 1928-1983 . . . . **CLC 37**
See also CA 124; 113; HW

Ibsen, Henrik (Johan)
1828-1906 . . . . **TCLC 2, 8, 16, 37, 52;
DA; DAB; DAC; DAM DRAM, MST;
DC 2; WLC**
See also CA 104; 141

Ibuse Masuji 1898-1993 . . . . **CLC 22**
See also CA 127; 141

Ichikawa, Kon 1915-. . . . . **CLC 20**
See also CA 121

Idle, Eric 1943-. . . . . **CLC 21**
See also Monty Python
See also CA 116; CANR 35

Ignatow, David 1914-. . . . . . **CLC 4, 7, 14, 40**
See also CA 9-12R; CAAS 3; CANR 31, 57;
DLB 5

Ihimaera, Witi 1944- . . . . **CLC 46**
See also CA 77-80

Ilf, Ilya . . . . **TCLC 21**
See also Fainzilberg, Ilya Arnoldovich

Illyes, Gyula 1902-1983 . . . . **PC 16**
See also CA 114; 109

Immermann, Karl (Lebrecht)
1796-1840 . . . . **NCLC 4, 49**
See also DLB 133

Inclan, Ramon (Maria) del Valle
See Valle-Inclan, Ramon (Maria) del

Infante, G(uillermo) Cabrera
See Cabrera Infante, G(uillermo)

Ingalls, Rachel (Holmes) 1940-. . . . . **CLC 42**
See also CA 123; 127

Ingamells, Rex 1913-1955 . . . . **TCLC 35**

Inge, William (Motter)
1913-1973 . . **CLC 1, 8, 19; DAM DRAM**
See also CA 9-12R; CDALB 1941-1968;
DLB 7; MTCW

Ingelow, Jean 1820-1897 . . . . **NCLC 39**
See also DLB 35, 163; SATA 33

Ingram, Willis J.
See Harris, Mark

Innaurato, Albert (F.) 1948(?)- . . **CLC 21, 60**
See also CA 115; 122; INT 122

Innes, Michael
See Stewart, J(ohn) I(nnes) M(ackintosh)

Ionesco, Eugene
1909-1994 . . . . **CLC 1, 4, 6, 9, 11, 15, 41,
86; DA; DAB; DAC; DAM DRAM,
MST; WLC**
See also CA 9-12R; 144; CANR 55;
MTCW; SATA 7; SATA-Obit 79

Iqbal, Muhammad 1873-1938 . . . . . **TCLC 28**

Ireland, Patrick
See O'Doherty, Brian

Iron, Ralph
See Schreiner, Olive (Emilie Albertina)

Irving, John (Winslow)
1942- . . . . . **CLC 13, 23, 38; DAM NOV,
POP**
See also AAYA 8; BEST 89:3; CA 25-28R;
CANR 28; DLB 6; DLBY 82; MTCW

Irving, Washington
1783-1859 . . . . . **NCLC 2, 19; DA; DAB;
DAM MST; SSC 2; WLC**
See also CDALB 1640-1865; DLB 3, 11, 30,
59, 73, 74; YABC 2

Irwin, P. K.
See Page, P(atricia) K(athleen)

Isaacs, Susan 1943- . . . **CLC 32; DAM POP**
See also BEST 89:1; CA 89-92; CANR 20,
41; INT CANR-20; MTCW

Isherwood, Christopher (William Bradshaw)
1904-1986 . . . . **CLC 1, 9, 11, 14, 44;
DAM DRAM, NOV**
See also CA 13-16R; 117; CANR 35;
DLB 15; DLBY 86; MTCW

Kyprianos, Iossif
See Samarakis, Antonis

La Bruyere, Jean de 1645-1696...... **LC 17**

Lacan, Jacques (Marie Emile)
1901-1981 .... **CLC 75**
See also CA 121; 104

**Laclos, Pierre Ambroise Francois Choderlos
de** 1741-1803 .... **NCLC 4**

La Colere, Francois
See Aragon, Louis

Lacolere, Francois
See Aragon, Louis

La Deshabilleuse
See Simenon, Georges (Jacques Christian)

Lady Gregory
See Gregory, Isabella Augusta (Persse)

Lady of Quality, A
See Bagnold, Enid

**La Fayette, Marie (Madelaine Pioche de la
Vergne Comtes** 1634-1693....... **LC 2**

Lafayette, Rene
See Hubbard, L(afayette) Ron(ald)

Laforgue, Jules
1860-1887 .... **NCLC 5, 53; PC 14;
SSC 20**

Lagerkvist, Paer (Fabian)
1891-1974 .... **CLC 7, 10, 13, 54;
DAM DRAM, NOV**
See also Lagerkvist, Par
See also CA 85-88; 49-52; MTCW

Lagerkvist, Par .... **SSC 12**
See also Lagerkvist, Paer (Fabian)

Lagerloef, Selma (Ottiliana Lovisa)
1858-1940 .... **TCLC 4, 36**
See also Lagerlof, Selma (Ottiliana Lovisa)
See also CA 108; SATA 15

Lagerlof, Selma (Ottiliana Lovisa)
See Lagerloef, Selma (Ottiliana Lovisa)
See also CLR 7; SATA 15

La Guma, (Justin) Alex(ander)
1925-1985 .... **CLC 19; DAM NOV**
See also BW 1; CA 49-52; 118; CANR 25;
DLB 117; MTCW

Laidlaw, A. K.
See Grieve, C(hristopher) M(urray)

Lainez, Manuel Mujica
See Mujica Lainez, Manuel
See also HW

Laing, R(onald) D(avid)
1927-1989 .... **CLC 95**
See also CA 107; 129; CANR 34; MTCW

Lamartine, Alphonse (Marie Louis Prat) de
1790-1869 ..... **NCLC 11; DAM POET;
PC 16**

Lamb, Charles
1775-1834 ...... **NCLC 10; DA; DAB;
DAC; DAM MST; WLC**
See also CDBLB 1789-1832; DLB 93, 107,
163; SATA 17

Lamb, Lady Caroline 1785-1828.. **NCLC 38**
See also DLB 116

Lamming, George (William)
1927- .... **CLC 2, 4, 66; BLC;
DAM MULT**
See also BW 2; CA 85-88; CANR 26;
DLB 125; MTCW

L'Amour, Louis (Dearborn)
1908-1988 .... **CLC 25, 55; DAM NOV,
POP**
See also AAYA 16; AITN 2; BEST 89:2;
CA 1-4R; 125; CANR 3, 25, 40;
DLBY 80; MTCW

Lampedusa, Giuseppe (Tomasi) di
1896-1957 .... **TCLC 13**
See also Tomasi di Lampedusa, Giuseppe
See also DLB 177

Lampman, Archibald 1861-1899 .. **NCLC 25**
See also DLB 92

Lancaster, Bruce 1896-1963........ **CLC 36**
See also CA 9-10; CAP 1; SATA 9

Lanchester, John .... **CLC 99**

Landau, Mark Alexandrovich
See Aldanov, Mark (Alexandrovich)

Landau-Aldanov, Mark Alexandrovich
See Aldanov, Mark (Alexandrovich)

Landis, Jerry
See Simon, Paul (Frederick)

Landis, John 1950- .... **CLC 26**
See also CA 112; 122

Landolfi, Tommaso 1908-1979... **CLC 11, 49**
See also CA 127; 117; DLB 177

Landon, Letitia Elizabeth
1802-1838 .... **NCLC 15**
See also DLB 96

Landor, Walter Savage
1775-1864 .... **NCLC 14**
See also DLB 93, 107

Landwirth, Heinz 1927-
See Lind, Jakov
See also CA 9-12R; CANR 7

Lane, Patrick
1939- .... **CLC 25; DAM POET**
See also CA 97-100; CANR 54; DLB 53;
INT 97-100

Lang, Andrew 1844-1912 .... **TCLC 16**
See also CA 114; 137; DLB 98, 141;
MAICYA; SATA 16

Lang, Fritz 1890-1976 .... **CLC 20**
See also CA 77-80; 69-72; CANR 30

Lange, John
See Crichton, (John) Michael

Langer, Elinor 1939- .... **CLC 34**
See also CA 121

Langland, William
1330(?)-1400(?) ...... **LC 19; DA; DAB;
DAC; DAM MST, POET**
See also DLB 146

Langstaff, Launcelot
See Irving, Washington

Lanier, Sidney
1842-1881 ...... **NCLC 6; DAM POET**
See also DLB 64; DLBD 13; MAICYA;
SATA 18

Lanyer, Aemilia 1569-1645 ..... **LC 10, 30**
See also DLB 121

Lao Tzu .... **CMLC 7**

Lapine, James (Elliot) 1949-....... **CLC 39**
See also CA 123; 130; CANR 54; INT 130

Larbaud, Valery (Nicolas)
1881-1957 .... **TCLC 9**
See also CA 106; 152

Lardner, Ring
See Lardner, Ring(gold) W(ilmer)

Lardner, Ring W., Jr.
See Lardner, Ring(gold) W(ilmer)

Lardner, Ring(gold) W(ilmer)
1885-1933 .... **TCLC 2, 14**
See also CA 104; 131; CDALB 1917-1929;
DLB 11, 25, 86; MTCW

Laredo, Betty
See Codrescu, Andrei

Larkin, Maia
See Wojciechowska, Maia (Teresa)

Larkin, Philip (Arthur)
1922-1985 .... **CLC 3, 5, 8, 9, 13, 18, 33,
39, 64; DAB; DAM MST, POET**
See also CA 5-8R; 117; CANR 24;
CDBLB 1960 to Present; DLB 27;
MTCW

Larra (y Sanchez de Castro), Mariano Jose de
1809-1837 .... **NCLC 17**

Larsen, Eric 1941- .... **CLC 55**
See also CA 132

Larsen, Nella
1891-1964 .... **CLC 37; BLC;
DAM MULT**
See also BW 1; CA 125; DLB 51

Larson, Charles R(aymond) 1938-... **CLC 31**
See also CA 53-56; CANR 4

Larson, Jonathan 1961(?)-1996..... **CLC 99**

Las Casas, Bartolome de 1474-1566.. **LC 31**

Lasker-Schueler, Else 1869-1945 .. **TCLC 57**
See also DLB 66, 124

Latham, Jean Lee 1902-.......... **CLC 12**
See also AITN 1; CA 5-8R; CANR 7;
MAICYA; SATA 2, 68

Latham, Mavis
See Clark, Mavis Thorpe

Lathen, Emma .... **CLC 2**
See also Hennissart, Martha; Latsis, Mary
J(ane)

Lathrop, Francis
See Leiber, Fritz (Reuter, Jr.)

Latsis, Mary J(ane)
See Lathen, Emma
See also CA 85-88

Lattimore, Richmond (Alexander)
1906-1984 .... **CLC 3**
See also CA 1-4R; 112; CANR 1

Laughlin, James 1914-........... **CLC 49**
See also CA 21-24R; CAAS 22; CANR 9,
47; DLB 48

Laurence, (Jean) Margaret (Wemyss)
1926-1987 .... **CLC 3, 6, 13, 50, 62;
DAC; DAM MST; SSC 7**
See also CA 5-8R; 121; CANR 33; DLB 53;
MTCW; SATA-Obit 50

Laurent, Antoine 1952- .... **CLC 50**

Lauscher, Hermann
See Hesse, Hermann

Lowry, (Clarence) Malcolm
1909-1957 . . . . TCLC 6, 40
See also CA 105; 131; CDBLB 1945-1960;
DLB 15; MTCW

Lowry, Mina Gertrude 1882-1966
See Loy, Mina
See also CA 113

Loxsmith, John
See Brunner, John (Kilian Houston)

Loy, Mina . . . . CLC 28; DAM POET; PC 16
See also Lowry, Mina Gertrude
See also DLB 4, 54

Loyson-Bridet
See Schwob, (Mayer Andre) Marcel

Lucas, Craig 1951- . . . . CLC 64
See also CA 137

Lucas, George 1944- . . . . CLC 16
See also AAYA 1; CA 77-80; CANR 30;
SATA 56

Lucas, Hans
See Godard, Jean-Luc

Lucas, Victoria
See Plath, Sylvia

Ludlam, Charles 1943-1987 . . . . . CLC 46, 50
See also CA 85-88; 122

Ludlum, Robert
1927- . . . CLC 22, 43; DAM NOV, POP
See also AAYA 10; BEST 89:1, 90:3;
CA 33-36R; CANR 25, 41; DLBY 82;
MTCW

Ludwig, Ken. . . . . CLC 60

Ludwig, Otto 1813-1865 . . . . NCLC 4
See also DLB 129

Lugones, Leopoldo 1874-1938 . . . . . TCLC 15
See also CA 116; 131; HW

Lu Hsun 1881-1936 . . . . . . TCLC 3; SSC 20
See also Shu-Jen, Chou

Lukacs, George . . . . CLC 24
See also Lukacs, Gyorgy (Szegeny von)

Lukacs, Gyorgy (Szegeny von) 1885-1971
See Lukacs, George
See also CA 101; 29-32R

Luke, Peter (Ambrose Cyprian)
1919-1995 . . . . CLC 38
See also CA 81-84; 147; DLB 13

Lunar, Dennis
See Mungo, Raymond

Lurie, Alison 1926- . . . . CLC 4, 5, 18, 39
See also CA 1-4R; CANR 2, 17, 50; DLB 2;
MTCW; SATA 46

Lustig, Arnost 1926- . . . . CLC 56
See also AAYA 3; CA 69-72; CANR 47;
SATA 56

Luther, Martin 1483-1546 . . . . LC 9, 37

Luxemburg, Rosa 1870(?)-1919 . . . . TCLC 63
See also CA 118

Luzi, Mario 1914- . . . . CLC 13
See also CA 61-64; CANR 9; DLB 128

Lyly, John 1554(?)-1606. . . . . DC 7
See also DAM DRAM; DLB 62, 167

L'Ymagier
See Gourmont, Remy (-Marie-Charles) de

Lynch, B. Suarez
See Bioy Casares, Adolfo; Borges, Jorge
Luis

Lynch, David (K.) 1946-. . . . . CLC 66
See also CA 124; 129

Lynch, James
See Andreyev, Leonid (Nikolaevich)

Lynch Davis, B.
See Bioy Casares, Adolfo; Borges, Jorge
Luis

Lyndsay, Sir David 1490-1555 . . . . . . LC 20

Lynn, Kenneth S(chuyler) 1923-. . . . CLC 50
See also CA 1-4R; CANR 3, 27

Lynx
See West, Rebecca

Lyons, Marcus
See Blish, James (Benjamin)

Lyre, Pinchbeck
See Sassoon, Siegfried (Lorraine)

Lytle, Andrew (Nelson) 1902-1995 . . CLC 22
See also CA 9-12R; 150; DLB 6; DLBY 95

Lyttelton, George 1709-1773 . . . . LC 10

Maas, Peter 1929- . . . . CLC 29
See also CA 93-96; INT 93-96

Macaulay, Rose 1881-1958 . . . . . TCLC 7, 44
See also CA 104; DLB 36

Macaulay, Thomas Babington
1800-1859 . . . . NCLC 42
See also CDBLB 1832-1890; DLB 32, 55

MacBeth, George (Mann)
1932-1992 . . . . CLC 2, 5, 9
See also CA 25-28R; 136; DLB 40; MTCW;
SATA 4; SATA-Obit 70

MacCaig, Norman (Alexander)
1910- . . . . . CLC 36; DAB; DAM POET
See also CA 9-12R; CANR 3, 34; DLB 27

MacCarthy, (Sir Charles Otto) Desmond
1877-1952 . . . . TCLC 36

MacDiarmid, Hugh
. . . . CLC 2, 4, 11, 19, 63; PC 9
See also Grieve, C(hristopher) M(urray)
See also CDBLB 1945-1960; DLB 20

MacDonald, Anson
See Heinlein, Robert A(nson)

Macdonald, Cynthia 1928-. . . . . . CLC 13, 19
See also CA 49-52; CANR 4, 44; DLB 105

MacDonald, George 1824-1905 . . . . . TCLC 9
See also CA 106; 137; DLB 18, 163;
MAICYA; SATA 33

Macdonald, John
See Millar, Kenneth

MacDonald, John D(ann)
1916-1986 . . . . CLC 3, 27, 44;
DAM NOV, POP
See also CA 1-4R; 121; CANR 1, 19;
DLB 8; DLBY 86; MTCW

Macdonald, John Ross
See Millar, Kenneth

Macdonald, Ross. . . . . CLC 1, 2, 3, 14, 34, 41
See also Millar, Kenneth
See also DLBD 6

MacDougal, John
See Blish, James (Benjamin)

MacEwen, Gwendolyn (Margaret)
1941-1987 . . . . CLC 13, 55
See also CA 9-12R; 124; CANR 7, 22;
DLB 53; SATA 50; SATA-Obit 55

Macha, Karel Hynek 1810-1846 . . NCLC 46

Machado (y Ruiz), Antonio
1875-1939 . . . . TCLC 3
See also CA 104; DLB 108

Machado de Assis, Joaquim Maria
1839-1908 . . . . . TCLC 10; BLC; SSC 24
See also CA 107; 153

Machen, Arthur. . . . . TCLC 4; SSC 20
See also Jones, Arthur Llewellyn
See also DLB 36, 156

Machiavelli, Niccolo
1469-1527 . . . . LC 8, 36; DA; DAB;
DAC; DAM MST

MacInnes, Colin 1914-1976. . . . . . CLC 4, 23
See also CA 69-72; 65-68; CANR 21;
DLB 14; MTCW

MacInnes, Helen (Clark)
1907-1985 . . . . . CLC 27, 39; DAM POP
See also CA 1-4R; 117; CANR 1, 28;
DLB 87; MTCW; SATA 22;
SATA-Obit 44

Mackay, Mary 1855-1924
See Corelli, Marie
See also CA 118

Mackenzie, Compton (Edward Montague)
1883-1972 . . . . CLC 18
See also CA 21-22; 37-40R; CAP 2;
DLB 34, 100

Mackenzie, Henry 1745-1831 . . . . NCLC 41
See also DLB 39

Mackintosh, Elizabeth 1896(?)-1952
See Tey, Josephine
See also CA 110

MacLaren, James
See Grieve, C(hristopher) M(urray)

Mac Laverty, Bernard 1942-. . . . . . . CLC 31
See also CA 116; 118; CANR 43; INT 118

MacLean, Alistair (Stuart)
1922-1987 . . . . CLC 3, 13, 50, 63;
DAM POP
See also CA 57-60; 121; CANR 28; MTCW;
SATA 23; SATA-Obit 50

Maclean, Norman (Fitzroy)
1902-1990 . . . . CLC 78; DAM POP;
SSC 13
See also CA 102; 132; CANR 49

MacLeish, Archibald
1892-1982 . . . . CLC 3, 8, 14, 68;
DAM POET
See also CA 9-12R; 106; CANR 33; DLB 4,
7, 45; DLBY 82; MTCW

MacLennan, (John) Hugh
1907-1990 . . . . CLC 2, 14, 92; DAC;
DAM MST
See also CA 5-8R; 142; CANR 33; DLB 68;
MTCW

MacLeod, Alistair
1936- . . . . . . CLC 56; DAC; DAM MST
See also CA 123; DLB 60

MacNeice, (Frederick) Louis
1907-1963 ...... **CLC 1, 4, 10, 53; DAB; DAM POET**
See also CA 85-88; DLB 10, 20; MTCW

MacNeill, Dand
See Fraser, George MacDonald

Macpherson, James 1736-1796 ...... **LC 29**
See also DLB 109

Macpherson, (Jean) Jay 1931- ...... **CLC 14**
See also CA 5-8R; DLB 53

MacShane, Frank 1927- .... **CLC 39**
See also CA 9-12R; CANR 3, 33; DLB 111

Macumber, Mari
See Sandoz, Mari(e Susette)

Madach, Imre 1823-1864 .... **NCLC 19**

Madden, (Jerry) David 1933- .... **CLC 5, 15**
See also CA 1-4R; CAAS 3; CANR 4, 45;
DLB 6; MTCW

Maddern, Al(an)
See Ellison, Harlan (Jay)

Madhubuti, Haki R.
1942- .... **CLC 6, 73; BLC; DAM MULT, POET; PC 5**
See also Lee, Don L.
See also BW 2; CA 73-76; CANR 24, 51;
DLB 5, 41; DLBD 8

Maepenn, Hugh
See Kuttner, Henry

Maepenn, K. H.
See Kuttner, Henry

Maeterlinck, Maurice
1862-1949 ...... **TCLC 3; DAM DRAM**
See also CA 104; 136; SATA 66

Maginn, William 1794-1842 ...... **NCLC 8**
See also DLB 110, 159

Mahapatra, Jayanta
1928- .... **CLC 33; DAM MULT**
See also CA 73-76; CAAS 9; CANR 15, 33

Mahfouz, Naguib (Abdel Aziz Al-Sabilgi)
1911(?)-
See Mahfuz, Najib
See also BEST 89:2; CA 128; CANR 55;
DAM NOV; MTCW

Mahfuz, Najib .... **CLC 52, 55**
See also Mahfouz, Naguib (Abdel Aziz
Al-Sabilgi)
See also DLBY 88

Mahon, Derek 1941- .... **CLC 27**
See also CA 113; 128; DLB 40

Mailer, Norman
1923- ...... **CLC 1, 2, 3, 4, 5, 8, 11, 14, 28, 39, 74; DA; DAB; DAC; DAM MST, NOV, POP**
See also AITN 2; CA 9-12R; CABS 1;
CANR 28; CDALB 1968-1988; DLB 2,
16, 28; DLBD 3; DLBY 80, 83; MTCW

Maillet, Antonine 1929- ...... **CLC 54; DAC**
See also CA 115; 120; CANR 46; DLB 60;
INT 120

Mais, Roger 1905-1955 .... **TCLC 8**
See also BW 1; CA 105; 124; DLB 125;
MTCW

Maistre, Joseph de 1753-1821 .... **NCLC 37**

Maitland, Frederic 1850-1906 ..... **TCLC 65**

Maitland, Sara (Louise) 1950- ...... **CLC 49**
See also CA 69-72; CANR 13

Major, Clarence
1936- .... **CLC 3, 19, 48; BLC; DAM MULT**
See also BW 2; CA 21-24R; CAAS 6;
CANR 13, 25, 53; DLB 33

Major, Kevin (Gerald)
1949- .... **CLC 26; DAC**
See also AAYA 16; CA 97-100; CANR 21,
38; CLR 11; DLB 60; INT CANR-21;
JRDA; MAICYA; SATA 32, 82

Maki, James
See Ozu, Yasujiro

Malabaila, Damiano
See Levi, Primo

Malamud, Bernard
1914-1986 ...... **CLC 1, 2, 3, 5, 8, 9, 11, 18, 27, 44, 78, 85; DA; DAB; DAC; DAM MST, NOV, POP; SSC 15; WLC**
See also AAYA 16; CA 5-8R; 118; CABS 1;
CANR 28; CDALB 1941-1968; DLB 2,
28, 152; DLBY 80, 86; MTCW

Malaparte, Curzio 1898-1957 ..... **TCLC 52**

Malcolm, Dan
See Silverberg, Robert

Malcolm X .... **CLC 82; BLC**
See also Little, Malcolm

Malherbe, Francois de 1555-1628 ..... **LC 5**

Mallarme, Stephane
1842-1898 .... **NCLC 4, 41; DAM POET; PC 4**

Mallet-Joris, Francoise 1930- ...... **CLC 11**
See also CA 65-68; CANR 17; DLB 83

Malley, Ern
See McAuley, James Phillip

Mallowan, Agatha Christie
See Christie, Agatha (Mary Clarissa)

Maloff, Saul 1922- .... **CLC 5**
See also CA 33-36R

Malone, Louis
See MacNeice, (Frederick) Louis

Malone, Michael (Christopher)
1942- .... **CLC 43**
See also CA 77-80; CANR 14, 32, 57

Malory, (Sir) Thomas
1410(?)-1471(?) ...... **LC 11; DA; DAB; DAC; DAM MST**
See also CDBLB Before 1660; DLB 146;
SATA 59; SATA-Brief 33

Malouf, (George Joseph) David
1934- .... **CLC 28, 86**
See also CA 124; CANR 50

Malraux, (Georges-)Andre
1901-1976 ...... **CLC 1, 4, 9, 13, 15, 57; DAM NOV**
See also CA 21-22; 69-72; CANR 34;
CAP 2; DLB 72; MTCW

Malzberg, Barry N(athaniel) 1939- ... **CLC 7**
See also CA 61-64; CAAS 4; CANR 16;
DLB 8

Mamet, David (Alan)
1947- .... **CLC 9, 15, 34, 46, 91; DAM DRAM; DC 4**
See also AAYA 3; CA 81-84; CABS 3;
CANR 15, 41; DLB 7; MTCW

Mamoulian, Rouben (Zachary)
1897-1987 .... **CLC 16**
See also CA 25-28R; 124

Mandelstam, Osip (Emilievich)
1891(?)-1938(?) ...... **TCLC 2, 6; PC 14**
See also CA 104; 150

Mander, (Mary) Jane 1877-1949 ... **TCLC 31**

Mandeville, John fl. 1350- .... **CMLC 19**
See also DLB 146

Mandiargues, Andre Pieyre de .... **CLC 41**
See also Pieyre de Mandiargues, Andre
See also DLB 83

Mandrake, Ethel Belle
See Thurman, Wallace (Henry)

Mangan, James Clarence
1803-1849 .... **NCLC 27**

Maniere, J.-E.
See Giraudoux, (Hippolyte) Jean

Manley, (Mary) Delariviere
1672(?)-1724 .... **LC 1**
See also DLB 39, 80

Mann, Abel
See Creasey, John

Mann, Emily 1952- .... **DC 7**
See also CA 130; CANR 55

Mann, (Luiz) Heinrich 1871-1950 ... **TCLC 9**
See also CA 106; DLB 66

Mann, (Paul) Thomas
1875-1955 .... **TCLC 2, 8, 14, 21, 35, 44, 60; DA; DAB; DAC; DAM MST, NOV; SSC 5; WLC**
See also CA 104; 128; DLB 66; MTCW

Mannheim, Karl 1893-1947 .... **TCLC 65**

Manning, David
See Faust, Frederick (Schiller)

Manning, Frederic 1887(?)-1935 ... **TCLC 25**
See also CA 124

Manning, Olivia 1915-1980 ...... **CLC 5, 19**
See also CA 5-8R; 101; CANR 29; MTCW

Mano, D. Keith 1942- .... **CLC 2, 10**
See also CA 25-28R; CAAS 6; CANR 26,
57; DLB 6

Mansfield, Katherine
.. **TCLC 2, 8, 39; DAB; SSC 9, 23; WLC**
See also Beauchamp, Kathleen Mansfield
See also DLB 162

Manso, Peter 1940- .... **CLC 39**
See also CA 29-32R; CANR 44

Mantecon, Juan Jimenez
See Jimenez (Mantecon), Juan Ramon

Manton, Peter
See Creasey, John

Man Without a Spleen, A
See Chekhov, Anton (Pavlovich)

Manzoni, Alessandro 1785-1873 .. **NCLC 29**

Mapu, Abraham (ben Jekutiel)
1808-1867 .... **NCLC 18**

Mara, Sally
See Queneau, Raymond

Marat, Jean Paul   1743-1793 . . . . **LC 10**

Marcel, Gabriel Honore
1889-1973 . . . . **CLC 15**
See also CA 102; 45-48; MTCW

Marchbanks, Samuel
See Davies, (William) Robertson

Marchi, Giacomo
See Bassani, Giorgio

Margulies, Donald . . . . **CLC 76**

Marie de France   c. 12th cent. - . . . . **CMLC 8**

Marie de l'Incarnation   1599-1672 . . . . **LC 10**

Marier, Captain Victor
See Griffith, D(avid Lewelyn) W(ark)

Mariner, Scott
See Pohl, Frederik

Marinetti, Filippo Tommaso
1876-1944 . . . . **TCLC 10**
See also CA 107; DLB 114

Marivaux, Pierre Carlet de Chamblain de
1688-1763 . . . . **LC 4; DC 7**

Markandaya, Kamala . . . . **CLC 8, 38**
See also Taylor, Kamala (Purnaiya)

Markfield, Wallace   1926- . . . . **CLC 8**
See also CA 69-72; CAAS 3; DLB 2, 28

Markham, Edwin   1852-1940 . . . . . **TCLC 47**
See also DLB 54

Markham, Robert
See Amis, Kingsley (William)

Marks, J
See Highwater, Jamake (Mamake)

Marks-Highwater, J
See Highwater, Jamake (Mamake)

Markson, David M(errill)   1927- . . . . **CLC 67**
See also CA 49-52; CANR 1

Marley, Bob . . . . **CLC 17**
See also Marley, Robert Nesta

Marley, Robert Nesta   1945-1981
See Marley, Bob
See also CA 107; 103

Marlowe, Christopher
1564-1593 . . . . . **LC 22; DA; DAB; DAC;
DAM DRAM, MST; DC 1; WLC**
See also CDBLB Before 1660; DLB 62

Marlowe, Stephen   1928-
See Queen, Ellery
See also CA 13-16R; CANR 6, 55

Marmontel, Jean-Francois
1723-1799 . . . . **LC 2**

Marquand, John P(hillips)
1893-1960 . . . . **CLC 2, 10**
See also CA 85-88; DLB 9, 102

Marques, Rene
1919-1979 . . . . . **CLC 96; DAM MULT;
HLC**
See also CA 97-100; 85-88; DLB 113; HW

Marquez, Gabriel (Jose) Garcia
See Garcia Marquez, Gabriel (Jose)

Marquis, Don(ald Robert Perry)
1878-1937 . . . . **TCLC 7**
See also CA 104; DLB 11, 25

Marric, J. J.
See Creasey, John

Marrow, Bernard
See Moore, Brian

Marryat, Frederick   1792-1848 . . . . **NCLC 3**
See also DLB 21, 163

Marsden, James
See Creasey, John

Marsh, (Edith) Ngaio
1899-1982 . . . . . . **CLC 7, 53; DAM POP**
See also CA 9-12R; CANR 6; DLB 77;
MTCW

Marshall, Garry   1934- . . . . **CLC 17**
See also AAYA 3; CA 111; SATA 60

Marshall, Paule
1929- . . . . **CLC 27, 72; BLC;
DAM MULT; SSC 3**
See also BW 2; CA 77-80; CANR 25;
DLB 157; MTCW

Marsten, Richard
See Hunter, Evan

Marston, John
1576-1634 . . . . **LC 33; DAM DRAM**
See also DLB 58, 172

Martha, Henry
See Harris, Mark

Martial   c. 40-c. 104 . . . . **PC 10**

Martin, Ken
See Hubbard, L(afayette) Ron(ald)

Martin, Richard
See Creasey, John

Martin, Steve   1945- . . . . **CLC 30**
See also CA 97-100; CANR 30; MTCW

Martin, Valerie   1948- . . . . **CLC 89**
See also BEST 90:2; CA 85-88; CANR 49

Martin, Violet Florence
1862-1915 . . . . **TCLC 51**

Martin, Webber
See Silverberg, Robert

Martindale, Patrick Victor
See White, Patrick (Victor Martindale)

Martin du Gard, Roger
1881-1958 . . . . **TCLC 24**
See also CA 118; DLB 65

Martineau, Harriet   1802-1876 . . . . **NCLC 26**
See also DLB 21, 55, 159, 163, 166;
YABC 2

Martines, Julia
See O'Faolain, Julia

Martinez, Jacinto Benavente y
See Benavente (y Martinez), Jacinto

Martinez Ruiz, Jose   1873-1967
See Azorin; Ruiz, Jose Martinez
See also CA 93-96; HW

Martinez Sierra, Gregorio
1881-1947 . . . . **TCLC 6**
See also CA 115

Martinez Sierra, Maria (de la O'LeJarraga)
1874-1974 . . . . **TCLC 6**
See also CA 115

Martinsen, Martin
See Follett, Ken(neth Martin)

Martinson, Harry (Edmund)
1904-1978 . . . . **CLC 14**
See also CA 77-80; CANR 34

Marut, Ret
See Traven, B.

Marut, Robert
See Traven, B.

Marvell, Andrew
1621-1678 . . . . . . **LC 4; DA; DAB; DAC;
DAM MST, POET; PC 10; WLC**
See also CDBLB 1660-1789; DLB 131

Marx, Karl (Heinrich)
1818-1883 . . . . **NCLC 17**
See also DLB 129

Masaoka Shiki . . . . **TCLC 18**
See also Masaoka Tsunenori

Masaoka Tsunenori   1867-1902
See Masaoka Shiki
See also CA 117

Masefield, John (Edward)
1878-1967 . . . . **CLC 11, 47; DAM POET**
See also CA 19-20; 25-28R; CANR 33;
CAP 2; CDBLB 1890-1914; DLB 10, 19,
153, 160; MTCW; SATA 19

Maso, Carole   19(?)- . . . . **CLC 44**

Mason, Bobbie Ann
1940- . . . . **CLC 28, 43, 82; SSC 4**
See also AAYA 5; CA 53-56; CANR 11,
31; DLB 173; DLBY 87; INT CANR-31;
MTCW

Mason, Ernst
See Pohl, Frederik

Mason, Lee W.
See Malzberg, Barry N(athaniel)

Mason, Nick   1945- . . . . **CLC 35**

Mason, Tally
See Derleth, August (William)

Mass, William
See Gibson, William

Masters, Edgar Lee
1868-1950 . . . . . . **TCLC 2, 25; DA; DAC;
DAM MST, POET; PC 1**
See also CA 104; 133; CDALB 1865-1917;
DLB 54; MTCW

Masters, Hilary   1928- . . . . **CLC 48**
See also CA 25-28R; CANR 13, 47

Mastrosimone, William   19(?)- . . . . . . **CLC 36**

Mathe, Albert
See Camus, Albert

Mather, Cotton   1663-1728 . . . . **LC 38**
See also CDALB 1640-1865; DLB 24, 30,
140

Mather, Increase   1639-1723 . . . . **LC 38**
See also DLB 24

Matheson, Richard Burton   1926- . . . **CLC 37**
See also CA 97-100; DLB 8, 44; INT 97-100

Mathews, Harry   1930- . . . . **CLC 6, 52**
See also CA 21-24R; CAAS 6; CANR 18,
40

Mathews, John Joseph
1894-1979 . . . . . . **CLC 84; DAM MULT**
See also CA 19-20; 142; CANR 45; CAP 2;
DLB 175; NNAL

Mathias, Roland (Glyn)   1915- . . . . . . **CLC 45**
See also CA 97-100; CANR 19, 41; DLB 27

Matsuo Basho   1644-1694 . . . . **PC 3**
See also DAM POET

Mattheson, Rodney
See Creasey, John

Matthews, Greg 1949- . . . . **CLC 45**
See also CA 135

Matthews, William 1942- . . . . **CLC 40**
See also CA 29-32R; CAAS 18; CANR 12,
57; DLB 5

Matthias, John (Edward) 1941- . . . . . **CLC 9**
See also CA 33-36R; CANR 56

Matthiessen, Peter
1927- . . . . **CLC 5, 7, 11, 32, 64;**
DAM NOV
See also AAYA 6; BEST 90:4; CA 9-12R;
CANR 21, 50; DLB 6, 173; MTCW;
SATA 27

Maturin, Charles Robert
1780(?)-1824 . . . . **NCLC 6**

Matute (Ausejo), Ana Maria
1925- . . . . **CLC 11**
See also CA 89-92; MTCW

Maugham, W. S.
See Maugham, W(illiam) Somerset

Maugham, W(illiam) Somerset
1874-1965 . . . . . . **CLC 1, 11, 15, 67, 93;**
DA; DAB; DAC; DAM DRAM, MST,
NOV; SSC 8; WLC
See also CA 5-8R; 25-28R; CANR 40;
CDBLB 1914-1945; DLB 10, 36, 77, 100,
162; MTCW; SATA 54

Maugham, William Somerset
See Maugham, W(illiam) Somerset

Maupassant, (Henri Rene Albert) Guy de
1850-1893 . . . . . **NCLC 1, 42; DA; DAB;**
DAC; DAM MST; SSC 1; WLC
See also DLB 123

Maupin, Armistead
1944- . . . . **CLC 95; DAM POP**
See also CA 125; 130; INT 130

Maurhut, Richard
See Traven, B.

Mauriac, Claude 1914-1996 . . . . **CLC 9**
See also CA 89-92; 152; DLB 83

Mauriac, Francois (Charles)
1885-1970 . . . . **CLC 4, 9, 56; SSC 24**
See also CA 25-28; CAP 2; DLB 65;
MTCW

Mavor, Osborne Henry 1888-1951
See Bridie, James
See also CA 104

Maxwell, William (Keepers, Jr.)
1908- . . . . **CLC 19**
See also CA 93-96; CANR 54; DLBY 80;
INT 93-96

May, Elaine 1932- . . . . **CLC 16**
See also CA 124; 142; DLB 44

Mayakovski, Vladimir (Vladimirovich)
1893-1930 . . . . **TCLC 4, 18**
See also CA 104

Mayhew, Henry 1812-1887 . . . . . . **NCLC 31**
See also DLB 18, 55

Mayle, Peter 1939(?)- . . . . **CLC 89**
See also CA 139

Maynard, Joyce 1953- . . . . **CLC 23**
See also CA 111; 129

Mayne, William (James Carter)
1928- . . . . **CLC 12**
See also AAYA 20; CA 9-12R; CANR 37;
CLR 25; JRDA; MAICYA; SAAS 11;
SATA 6, 68

Mayo, Jim
See L'Amour, Louis (Dearborn)

Maysles, Albert 1926- . . . . **CLC 16**
See also CA 29-32R

Maysles, David 1932- . . . . **CLC 16**

Mazer, Norma Fox 1931- . . . . **CLC 26**
See also AAYA 5; CA 69-72; CANR 12,
32; CLR 23; JRDA; MAICYA; SAAS 1;
SATA 24, 67

Mazzini, Guiseppe 1805-1872 . . . . **NCLC 34**

McAuley, James Phillip
1917-1976 . . . . **CLC 45**
See also CA 97-100

McBain, Ed
See Hunter, Evan

McBrien, William Augustine
1930- . . . . **CLC 44**
See also CA 107

McCaffrey, Anne (Inez)
1926- . . . . . . **CLC 17; DAM NOV, POP**
See also AAYA 6; AITN 2; BEST 89:2;
CA 25-28R; CANR 15, 35, 55; DLB 8;
JRDA; MAICYA; MTCW; SAAS 11;
SATA 8, 70

McCall, Nathan 1955(?)- . . . . **CLC 86**
See also CA 146

McCann, Arthur
See Campbell, John W(ood, Jr.)

McCann, Edson
See Pohl, Frederik

McCarthy, Charles, Jr. 1933-
See McCarthy, Cormac
See also CANR 42; DAM POP

McCarthy, Cormac 1933- . . . . . **CLC 4, 57, 59**
See also McCarthy, Charles, Jr.
See also DLB 6, 143

McCarthy, Mary (Therese)
1912-1989 . . . . . . **CLC 1, 3, 5, 14, 24, 39,**
59; SSC 24
See also CA 5-8R; 129; CANR 16, 50;
DLB 2; DLBY 81; INT CANR-16;
MTCW

McCartney, (James) Paul
1942- . . . . **CLC 12, 35**
See also CA 146

McCauley, Stephen (D.) 1955- . . . . . **CLC 50**
See also CA 141

McClure, Michael (Thomas)
1932- . . . . **CLC 6, 10**
See also CA 21-24R; CANR 17, 46;
DLB 16

McCorkle, Jill (Collins) 1958- . . . . . . **CLC 51**
See also CA 121; DLBY 87

McCourt, James 1941- . . . . **CLC 5**
See also CA 57-60

McCoy, Horace (Stanley)
1897-1955 . . . . **TCLC 28**
See also CA 108; 155; DLB 9

McCrae, John 1872-1918 . . . . **TCLC 12**
See also CA 109; DLB 92

McCreigh, James
See Pohl, Frederik

McCullers, (Lula) Carson (Smith)
1917-1967 . . . . **CLC 1, 4, 10, 12, 48, 100;**
DA; DAB; DAC; DAM MST, NOV;
SSC 9, 24; WLC
See also AAYA 21; CA 5-8R; 25-28R;
CABS 1, 3; CANR 18;
CDALB 1941-1968; DLB 2, 7, 173;
MTCW; SATA 27

McCulloch, John Tyler
See Burroughs, Edgar Rice

McCullough, Colleen
1938(?)- . . . . **CLC 27; DAM NOV, POP**
See also CA 81-84; CANR 17, 46; MTCW

McDermott, Alice 1953- . . . . **CLC 90**
See also CA 109; CANR 40

McElroy, Joseph 1930- . . . . **CLC 5, 47**
See also CA 17-20R

McEwan, Ian (Russell)
1948- . . . . **CLC 13, 66; DAM NOV**
See also BEST 90:4; CA 61-64; CANR 14,
41; DLB 14; MTCW

McFadden, David 1940- . . . . **CLC 48**
See also CA 104; DLB 60; INT 104

McFarland, Dennis 1950- . . . . **CLC 65**

McGahern, John
1934- . . . . **CLC 5, 9, 48; SSC 17**
See also CA 17-20R; CANR 29; DLB 14;
MTCW

McGinley, Patrick (Anthony)
1937- . . . . **CLC 41**
See also CA 120; 127; CANR 56; INT 127

McGinley, Phyllis 1905-1978 . . . . . . **CLC 14**
See also CA 9-12R; 77-80; CANR 19;
DLB 11, 48; SATA 2, 44; SATA-Obit 24

McGinniss, Joe 1942- . . . . **CLC 32**
See also AITN 2; BEST 89:2; CA 25-28R;
CANR 26; INT CANR-26

McGivern, Maureen Daly
See Daly, Maureen

McGrath, Patrick 1950- . . . . **CLC 55**
See also CA 136

McGrath, Thomas (Matthew)
1916-1990 . . . . **CLC 28, 59; DAM POET**
See also CA 9-12R; 132; CANR 6, 33;
MTCW; SATA 41; SATA-Obit 66

McGuane, Thomas (Francis III)
1939- . . . . **CLC 3, 7, 18, 45**
See also AITN 2; CA 49-52; CANR 5, 24,
49; DLB 2; DLBY 80; INT CANR-24;
MTCW

McGuckian, Medbh
1950- . . . . **CLC 48; DAM POET**
See also CA 143; DLB 40

McHale, Tom 1942(?)-1982 . . . . **CLC 3, 5**
See also AITN 1; CA 77-80; 106

McIlvanney, William 1936- . . . . **CLC 42**
See also CA 25-28R; DLB 14

McIlwraith, Maureen Mollie Hunter
See Hunter, Mollie
See also SATA 2

McInerney, Jay
1955- . . . . **CLC 34; DAM POP**
See also AAYA 18; CA 116; 123;
CANR 45; INT 123

McIntyre, Vonda N(eel) 1948- . . . . . **CLC 18**
See also CA 81-84; CANR 17, 34; MTCW

McKay, Claude
. . . . **TCLC 7, 41; BLC; DAB; PC 2**
See also McKay, Festus Claudius
See also DLB 4, 45, 51, 117

McKay, Festus Claudius 1889-1948
See McKay, Claude
See also BW 1; CA 104; 124; DA; DAC;
DAM MST, MULT, NOV, POET;
MTCW; WLC

McKuen, Rod 1933- . . . . **CLC 1, 3**
See also AITN 1; CA 41-44R; CANR 40

McLoughlin, R. B.
See Mencken, H(enry) L(ouis)

McLuhan, (Herbert) Marshall
1911-1980 . . . . **CLC 37, 83**
See also CA 9-12R; 102; CANR 12, 34;
DLB 88; INT CANR-12; MTCW

McMillan, Terry (L.)
1951- . . . . **CLC 50, 61; DAM MULT,
NOV, POP**
See also AAYA 21; BW 2; CA 140

McMurtry, Larry (Jeff)
1936- . . . . **CLC 2, 3, 7, 11, 27, 44;
DAM NOV, POP**
See also AAYA 15; AITN 2; BEST 89:2;
CA 5-8R; CANR 19, 43;
CDALB 1968-1988; DLB 2, 143;
DLBY 80, 87; MTCW

McNally, T. M. 1961- . . . . **CLC 82**

McNally, Terrence
1939- . . . **CLC 4, 7, 41, 91; DAM DRAM**
See also CA 45-48; CANR 2, 56; DLB 7

McNamer, Deirdre 1950- . . . . **CLC 70**

McNeile, Herman Cyril 1888-1937
See Sapper
See also DLB 77

McNickle, (William) D'Arcy
1904-1977 . . . . . **CLC 89; DAM MULT**
See also CA 9-12R; 85-88; CANR 5, 45;
DLB 175; NNAL; SATA-Obit 22

McPhee, John (Angus) 1931- . . . . . . **CLC 36**
See also BEST 90:1; CA 65-68; CANR 20,
46; MTCW

McPherson, James Alan
1943- . . . . **CLC 19, 77**
See also BW 1; CA 25-28R; CAAS 17;
CANR 24; DLB 38; MTCW

McPherson, William (Alexander)
1933- . . . . **CLC 34**
See also CA 69-72; CANR 28;
INT CANR-28

Mead, Margaret 1901-1978 . . . . **CLC 37**
See also AITN 1; CA 1-4R; 81-84;
CANR 4; MTCW; SATA-Obit 20

Meaker, Marijane (Agnes) 1927-
See Kerr, M. E.
See also CA 107; CANR 37; INT 107;
JRDA; MAICYA; MTCW; SATA 20, 61

Medoff, Mark (Howard)
1940- . . . . **CLC 6, 23; DAM DRAM**
See also AITN 1; CA 53-56; CANR 5;
DLB 7; INT CANR-5

Medvedev, P. N.
See Bakhtin, Mikhail Mikhailovich

Meged, Aharon
See Megged, Aharon

Meged, Aron
See Megged, Aharon

Megged, Aharon 1920- . . . . **CLC 9**
See also CA 49-52; CAAS 13; CANR 1

Mehta, Ved (Parkash) 1934- . . . . **CLC 37**
See also CA 1-4R; CANR 2, 23; MTCW

Melanter
See Blackmore, R(ichard) D(oddridge)

Melikow, Loris
See Hofmannsthal, Hugo von

Melmoth, Sebastian
See Wilde, Oscar (Fingal O'Flahertie Wills)

Meltzer, Milton 1915- . . . . **CLC 26**
See also AAYA 8; CA 13-16R; CANR 38;
CLR 13; DLB 61; JRDA; MAICYA;
SAAS 1; SATA 1, 50, 80

Melville, Herman
1819-1891 . . . . . **NCLC 3, 12, 29, 45, 49;
DA; DAB; DAC; DAM MST, NOV;
SSC 1, 17; WLC**
See also CDALB 1640-1865; DLB 3, 74;
SATA 59

Menander
c. 342B.C.-c. 292B.C. . . . . **CMLC 9;
DAM DRAM; DC 3**
See also DLB 176

Mencken, H(enry) L(ouis)
1880-1956 . . . . **TCLC 13**
See also CA 105; 125; CDALB 1917-1929;
DLB 11, 29, 63, 137; MTCW

Mendelsohn, Jane 1965(?)- . . . . **CLC 99**
See also CA 154

Mercer, David
1928-1980 . . . . **CLC 5; DAM DRAM**
See also CA 9-12R; 102; CANR 23;
DLB 13; MTCW

Merchant, Paul
See Ellison, Harlan (Jay)

Meredith, George
1828-1909 . . **TCLC 17, 43; DAM POET**
See also CA 117; 153; CDBLB 1832-1890;
DLB 18, 35, 57, 159

Meredith, William (Morris)
1919- . . **CLC 4, 13, 22, 55; DAM POET**
See also CA 9-12R; CAAS 14; CANR 6, 40;
DLB 5

Merezhkovsky, Dmitry Sergeyevich
1865-1941 . . . . **TCLC 29**

Merimee, Prosper
1803-1870 . . . . **NCLC 6; SSC 7**
See also DLB 119

Merkin, Daphne 1954- . . . . **CLC 44**
See also CA 123

Merlin, Arthur
See Blish, James (Benjamin)

Merrill, James (Ingram)
1926-1995 . . . . **CLC 2, 3, 6, 8, 13, 18, 34,
91; DAM POET**
See also CA 13-16R; 147; CANR 10, 49;
DLB 5, 165; DLBY 85; INT CANR-10;
MTCW

Merriman, Alex
See Silverberg, Robert

Merritt, E. B.
See Waddington, Miriam

Merton, Thomas
1915-1968 . . **CLC 1, 3, 11, 34, 83; PC 10**
See also CA 5-8R; 25-28R; CANR 22, 53;
DLB 48; DLBY 81; MTCW

Merwin, W(illiam) S(tanley)
1927- . . . . . . **CLC 1, 2, 3, 5, 8, 13, 18, 45,
88; DAM POET**
See also CA 13-16R; CANR 15, 51; DLB 5,
169; INT CANR-15; MTCW

Metcalf, John 1938- . . . . **CLC 37**
See also CA 113; DLB 60

Metcalf, Suzanne
See Baum, L(yman) Frank

Mew, Charlotte (Mary)
1870-1928 . . . . **TCLC 8**
See also CA 105; DLB 19, 135

Mewshaw, Michael 1943- . . . . **CLC 9**
See also CA 53-56; CANR 7, 47; DLBY 80

Meyer, June
See Jordan, June

Meyer, Lynn
See Slavitt, David R(ytman)

Meyer-Meyrink, Gustav 1868-1932
See Meyrink, Gustav
See also CA 117

Meyers, Jeffrey 1939- . . . . **CLC 39**
See also CA 73-76; CANR 54; DLB 111

Meynell, Alice (Christina Gertrude Thompson)
1847-1922 . . . . **TCLC 6**
See also CA 104; DLB 19, 98

Meyrink, Gustav . . . . **TCLC 21**
See also Meyer-Meyrink, Gustav
See also DLB 81

Michaels, Leonard
1933- . . . . **CLC 6, 25; SSC 16**
See also CA 61-64; CANR 21; DLB 130;
MTCW

Michaux, Henri 1899-1984 . . . . . . **CLC 8, 19**
See also CA 85-88; 114

Michelangelo 1475-1564 . . . . **LC 12**

Michelet, Jules 1798-1874 . . . . **NCLC 31**

Michener, James A(lbert)
1907(?)- . . . . **CLC 1, 5, 11, 29, 60;
DAM NOV, POP**
See also AITN 1; BEST 90:1; CA 5-8R;
CANR 21, 45; DLB 6; MTCW

Mickiewicz, Adam 1798-1855 . . . . . **NCLC 3**

Middleton, Christopher 1926- . . . . . . **CLC 13**
See also CA 13-16R; CANR 29, 54;
DLB 40

Middleton, Richard (Barham)
1882-1911 . . . . **TCLC 56**
See also DLB 156

Montesquieu, Charles-Louis de Secondat
1689-1755 . . . . LC 7

Montgomery, (Robert) Bruce 1921-1978
See Crispin, Edmund
See also CA 104

Montgomery, L(ucy) M(aud)
1874-1942 . . . . TCLC 51; DAC;
DAM MST
See also AAYA 12; CA 108; 137; CLR 8;
DLB 92; DLBD 14; JRDA; MAICYA;
YABC 1

Montgomery, Marion H., Jr. 1925- . . CLC 7
See also AITN 1; CA 1-4R; CANR 3, 48;
DLB 6

Montgomery, Max
See Davenport, Guy (Mattison, Jr.)

Montherlant, Henry (Milon) de
1896-1972 . . . . CLC 8, 19; DAM DRAM
See also CA 85-88; 37-40R; DLB 72;
MTCW

Monty Python
See Chapman, Graham; Cleese, John
(Marwood); Gilliam, Terry (Vance); Idle,
Eric; Jones, Terence Graham Parry; Palin,
Michael (Edward)
See also AAYA 7

Moodie, Susanna (Strickland)
1803-1885 . . . . NCLC 14
See also DLB 99

Mooney, Edward 1951-
See Mooney, Ted
See also CA 130

Mooney, Ted . . . . CLC 25
See also Mooney, Edward

Moorcock, Michael (John)
1939- . . . . CLC 5, 27, 58
See also CA 45-48; CAAS 5; CANR 2, 17,
38; DLB 14; MTCW

Moore, Brian
1921- . . . . . . CLC 1, 3, 5, 7, 8, 19, 32, 90;
DAB; DAC; DAM MST
See also CA 1-4R; CANR 1, 25, 42; MTCW

Moore, Edward
See Muir, Edwin

Moore, George Augustus
1852-1933 . . . . TCLC 7; SSC 19
See also CA 104; DLB 10, 18, 57, 135

Moore, Lorrie . . . . CLC 39, 45, 68
See also Moore, Marie Lorena

Moore, Marianne (Craig)
1887-1972 . . . . CLC 1, 2, 4, 8, 10, 13, 19,
47; DA; DAB; DAC; DAM MST, POET;
PC 4
See also CA 1-4R; 33-36R; CANR 3;
CDALB 1929-1941; DLB 45; DLBD 7;
MTCW; SATA 20

Moore, Marie Lorena 1957-
See Moore, Lorrie
See also CA 116; CANR 39

Moore, Thomas 1779-1852 . . . . NCLC 6
See also DLB 96, 144

Morand, Paul 1888-1976 . . CLC 41; SSC 22
See also CA 69-72; DLB 65

Morante, Elsa 1918-1985 . . . . CLC 8, 47
See also CA 85-88; 117; CANR 35;
DLB 177; MTCW

Moravia, Alberto
1907-1990 . . . . CLC 2, 7, 11, 27, 46
See also Pincherle, Alberto
See also DLB 177

More, Hannah 1745-1833 . . . . NCLC 27
See also DLB 107, 109, 116, 158

More, Henry 1614-1687 . . . . LC 9
See also DLB 126

More, Sir Thomas 1478-1535 . . . . LC 10, 32

Moreas, Jean . . . . TCLC 18
See also Papadiamantopoulos, Johannes

Morgan, Berry 1919- . . . . CLC 6
See also CA 49-52; DLB 6

Morgan, Claire
See Highsmith, (Mary) Patricia

Morgan, Edwin (George) 1920- . . . . . CLC 31
See also CA 5-8R; CANR 3, 43; DLB 27

Morgan, (George) Frederick
1922- . . . . CLC 23
See also CA 17-20R; CANR 21

Morgan, Harriet
See Mencken, H(enry) L(ouis)

Morgan, Jane
See Cooper, James Fenimore

Morgan, Janet 1945- . . . . CLC 39
See also CA 65-68

Morgan, Lady 1776(?)-1859 . . . . . NCLC 29
See also DLB 116, 158

Morgan, Robin 1941- . . . . CLC 2
See also CA 69-72; CANR 29; MTCW;
SATA 80

Morgan, Scott
See Kuttner, Henry

Morgan, Seth 1949(?)-1990 . . . . CLC 65
See also CA 132

Morgenstern, Christian
1871-1914 . . . . TCLC 8
See also CA 105

Morgenstern, S.
See Goldman, William (W.)

Moricz, Zsigmond 1879-1942 . . . . . TCLC 33

Morike, Eduard (Friedrich)
1804-1875 . . . . NCLC 10
See also DLB 133

Mori Ogai . . . . TCLC 14
See also Mori Rintaro

Mori Rintaro 1862-1922
See Mori Ogai
See also CA 110

Moritz, Karl Philipp 1756-1793 . . . . . . LC 2
See also DLB 94

Morland, Peter Henry
See Faust, Frederick (Schiller)

Morren, Theophil
See Hofmannsthal, Hugo von

Morris, Bill 1952- . . . . CLC 76

Morris, Julian
See West, Morris L(anglo)

Morris, Steveland Judkins 1950(?)-
See Wonder, Stevie
See also CA 111

Morris, William 1834-1896 . . . . NCLC 4
See also CDBLB 1832-1890; DLB 18, 35,
57, 156

Morris, Wright 1910-... CLC 1, 3, 7, 18, 37
See also CA 9-12R; CANR 21; DLB 2;
DLBY 81; MTCW

Morrison, Chloe Anthony Wofford
See Morrison, Toni

Morrison, James Douglas 1943-1971
See Morrison, Jim
See also CA 73-76; CANR 40

Morrison, Jim . . . . CLC 17
See also Morrison, James Douglas

Morrison, Toni
1931- . . . . CLC 4, 10, 22, 55, 81, 87;
BLC; DA; DAB; DAC; DAM MST,
MULT, NOV, POP
See also AAYA 1; BW 2; CA 29-32R;
CANR 27, 42; CDALB 1968-1988;
DLB 6, 33, 143; DLBY 81; MTCW;
SATA 57

Morrison, Van 1945- . . . . CLC 21
See also CA 116

Morrissy, Mary 1958- . . . . CLC 99

Mortimer, John (Clifford)
1923- . . . . . . CLC 28, 43; DAM DRAM,
POP
See also CA 13-16R; CANR 21;
CDBLB 1960 to Present; DLB 13;
INT CANR-21; MTCW

Mortimer, Penelope (Ruth) 1918-... CLC 5
See also CA 57-60; CANR 45

Morton, Anthony
See Creasey, John

Mosher, Howard Frank 1943-... . . CLC 62
See also CA 139

Mosley, Nicholas 1923-... . . . . CLC 43, 70
See also CA 69-72; CANR 41; DLB 14

Mosley, Walter
1952- . . . . . CLC 97; DAM MULT, POP
See also AAYA 17; BW 2; CA 142;
CANR 57

Moss, Howard
1922-1987 . . . . CLC 7, 14, 45, 50;
DAM POET
See also CA 1-4R; 123; CANR 1, 44;
DLB 5

Mossgiel, Rab
See Burns, Robert

Motion, Andrew (Peter) 1952-... . . CLC 47
See also CA 146; DLB 40

Motley, Willard (Francis)
1909-1965 . . . . CLC 18
See also BW 1; CA 117; 106; DLB 76, 143

Motoori, Norinaga 1730-1801 . . . . NCLC 45

Mott, Michael (Charles Alston)
1930- . . . . CLC 15, 34
See also CA 5-8R; CAAS 7; CANR 7, 29

Mountain Wolf Woman
1884-1960 . . . . CLC 92
See also CA 144; NNAL

Moure, Erin 1955- . . . . CLC 88
See also CA 113; DLB 60

Mowat, Farley (McGill)
  1921- ...... **CLC 26; DAC; DAM MST**
  See also AAYA 1; CA 1-4R; CANR 4, 24,
  42; CLR 20; DLB 68; INT CANAR-24;
  JRDA; MAICYA; MTCW; SATA 3, 55

Moyers, Bill 1934- .... **CLC 74**
  See also AITN 2; CA 61-64; CANR 31, 52

Mphahlele, Es'kia
  See Mphahlele, Ezekiel
  See also DLB 125

Mphahlele, Ezekiel
  1919- ..... **CLC 25; BLC; DAM MULT**
  See also Mphahlele, Es'kia
  See also BW 2; CA 81-84; CANR 26

Mqhayi, S(amuel) E(dward) K(rune Loliwe)
  1875-1945 .... **TCLC 25; BLC;
      DAM MULT**
  See also CA 153

Mrozek, Slawomir 1930- .... **CLC 3, 13**
  See also CA 13-16R; CAAS 10; CANR 29;
  MTCW

Mrs. Belloc-Lowndes
  See Lowndes, Marie Adelaide (Belloc)

Mtwa, Percy (?)- .... **CLC 47**

Mueller, Lisel 1924- .... **CLC 13, 51**
  See also CA 93-96; DLB 105

Muir, Edwin 1887-1959 .... **TCLC 2**
  See also CA 104; DLB 20, 100

Muir, John 1838-1914 .... **TCLC 28**

Mujica Lainez, Manuel
  1910-1984 .... **CLC 31**
  See also Lainez, Manuel Mujica
  See also CA 81-84; 112; CANR 32; HW

Mukherjee, Bharati
  1940- .... **CLC 53; DAM NOV**
  See also BEST 89:2; CA 107; CANR 45;
  DLB 60; MTCW

Muldoon, Paul
  1951- .... **CLC 32, 72; DAM POET**
  See also CA 113; 129; CANR 52; DLB 40;
  INT 129

Mulisch, Harry 1927- .... **CLC 42**
  See also CA 9-12R; CANR 6, 26, 56

Mull, Martin 1943- .... **CLC 17**
  See also CA 105

Mulock, Dinah Maria
  See Craik, Dinah Maria (Mulock)

Munford, Robert 1737(?)-1783 .... **LC 5**
  See also DLB 31

Mungo, Raymond 1946- .... **CLC 72**
  See also CA 49-52; CANR 2

Munro, Alice
  1931- ...... **CLC 6, 10, 19, 50, 95; DAC;
      DAM MST, NOV; SSC 3**
  See also AITN 2; CA 33-36R; CANR 33,
  53; DLB 53; MTCW; SATA 29

Munro, H(ector) H(ugh) 1870-1916
  See Saki
  See also CA 104; 130; CDBLB 1890-1914;
  DA; DAB; DAC; DAM MST, NOV;
  DLB 34, 162; MTCW; WLC

Murasaki, Lady .... **CMLC 1**

Murdoch, (Jean) Iris
  1919- ...... **CLC 1, 2, 3, 4, 6, 8, 11, 15,
      22, 31, 51; DAB; DAC; DAM MST,
      NOV**
  See also CA 13-16R; CANR 8, 43;
  CDBLB 1960 to Present; DLB 14;
  INT CANR-8; MTCW

Murfree, Mary Noailles
  1850-1922 .... **SSC 22**
  See also CA 122; DLB 12, 74

Murnau, Friedrich Wilhelm
  See Plumpe, Friedrich Wilhelm

Murphy, Richard 1927- .... **CLC 41**
  See also CA 29-32R; DLB 40

Murphy, Sylvia 1937- .... **CLC 34**
  See also CA 121

Murphy, Thomas (Bernard) 1935- ... **CLC 51**
  See also CA 101

Murray, Albert L. 1916- .... **CLC 73**
  See also BW 2; CA 49-52; CANR 26, 52;
  DLB 38

Murray, Les(lie) A(llan)
  1938- .... **CLC 40; DAM POET**
  See also CA 21-24R; CANR 11, 27, 56

Murry, J. Middleton
  See Murry, John Middleton

Murry, John Middleton
  1889-1957 .... **TCLC 16**
  See also CA 118; DLB 149

Musgrave, Susan 1951- .... **CLC 13, 54**
  See also CA 69-72; CANR 45

Musil, Robert (Edler von)
  1880-1942 .... **TCLC 12, 68; SSC 18**
  See also CA 109; CANR 55; DLB 81, 124

Muske, Carol 1945- .... **CLC 90**
  See also Muske-Dukes, Carol (Anne)

Muske-Dukes, Carol (Anne) 1945-
  See Muske, Carol
  See also CA 65-68; CANR 32

Musset, (Louis Charles) Alfred de
  1810-1857 .... **NCLC 7**

My Brother's Brother
  See Chekhov, Anton (Pavlovich)

Myers, L. H. 1881-1944 .... **TCLC 59**
  See also DLB 15

Myers, Walter Dean
  1937- ..... **CLC 35; BLC; DAM MULT,
      NOV**
  See also AAYA 4; BW 2; CA 33-36R;
  CANR 20, 42; CLR 4, 16, 35; DLB 33;
  INT CANR-20; JRDA; MAICYA;
  SAAS 2; SATA 41, 71; SATA-Brief 27

Myers, Walter M.
  See Myers, Walter Dean

Myles, Symon
  See Follett, Ken(neth Martin)

Nabokov, Vladimir (Vladimirovich)
  1899-1977 ..... **CLC 1, 2, 3, 6, 8, 11, 15,
      23, 44, 46, 64; DA; DAB; DAC;
      DAM MST, NOV; SSC 11; WLC**
  See also CA 5-8R; 69-72; CANR 20;
  CDALB 1941-1968; DLB 2; DLBD 3;
  DLBY 80, 91; MTCW

Nagai Kafu .... **TCLC 51**
  See also Nagai Sokichi

Nagai Sokichi 1879-1959
  See Nagai Kafu
  See also CA 117

Nagy, Laszlo 1925-1978 .... **CLC 7**
  See also CA 129; 112

Naipaul, Shiva(dhar Srinivasa)
  1945-1985 ..... **CLC 32, 39; DAM NOV**
  See also CA 110; 112; 116; CANR 33;
  DLB 157; DLBY 85; MTCW

Naipaul, V(idiadhar) S(urajprasad)
  1932- .... **CLC 4, 7, 9, 13, 18, 37; DAB;
      DAC; DAM MST, NOV**
  See also CA 1-4R; CANR 1, 33, 51;
  CDBLB 1960 to Present; DLB 125;
  DLBY 85; MTCW

Nakos, Lilika 1899(?)- .... **CLC 29**

Narayan, R(asipuram) K(rishnaswami)
  1906- ...... **CLC 7, 28, 47; DAM NOV;
      SSC 25**
  See also CA 81-84; CANR 33; MTCW;
  SATA 62

Nash, (Frediric) Ogden
  1902-1971 .... **CLC 23; DAM POET**
  See also CA 13-14; 29-32R; CANR 34;
  CAP 1; DLB 11; MAICYA; MTCW;
  SATA 2, 46

Nathan, Daniel
  See Dannay, Frederic

Nathan, George Jean 1882-1958 ... **TCLC 18**
  See also Hatteras, Owen
  See also CA 114; DLB 137

Natsume, Kinnosuke 1867-1916
  See Natsume, Soseki
  See also CA 104

Natsume, Soseki .... **TCLC 2, 10**
  See also Natsume, Kinnosuke

Natti, (Mary) Lee 1919-
  See Kingman, Lee
  See also CA 5-8R; CANR 2

Naylor, Gloria
  1950- ..... **CLC 28, 52; BLC; DA; DAC;
      DAM MST, MULT, NOV, POP**
  See also AAYA 6; BW 2; CA 107;
  CANR 27, 51; DLB 173; MTCW

Neihardt, John Gneisenau
  1881-1973 .... **CLC 32**
  See also CA 13-14; CAP 1; DLB 9, 54

Nekrasov, Nikolai Alekseevich
  1821-1878 .... **NCLC 11**

Nelligan, Emile 1879-1941 .... **TCLC 14**
  See also CA 114; DLB 92

Nelson, Willie 1933- .... **CLC 17**
  See also CA 107

Nemerov, Howard (Stanley)
  1920-1991 .... **CLC 2, 6, 9, 36;
      DAM POET**
  See also CA 1-4R; 134; CABS 2; CANR 1,
  27, 53; DLB 5, 6; DLBY 83;
  INT CANR-27; MTCW

Neruda, Pablo
  1904-1973 ..... **CLC 1, 2, 5, 7, 9, 28, 62;
      DA; DAB; DAC; DAM MST, MULT,
      POET; HLC; PC 4; WLC**
  See also CA 19-20; 45-48; CAP 2; HW;
  MTCW

Nerval, Gerard de
1808-1855 ..... NCLC 1; PC 13; SSC 18

Nervo, (Jose) Amado (Ruiz de)
1870-1919 .... TCLC 11
See also CA 109; 131; HW

Nessi, Pio Baroja y
See Baroja (y Nessi), Pio

Nestroy, Johann 1801-1862 ...... NCLC 42
See also DLB 133

Neufeld, John (Arthur) 1938- ...... CLC 17
See also AAYA 11; CA 25-28R; CANR 11,
37, 56; MAICYA; SAAS 3; SATA 6, 81

Neville, Emily Cheney 1919- ...... CLC 12
See also CA 5-8R; CANR 3, 37; JRDA;
MAICYA; SAAS 2; SATA 1

Newbound, Bernard Slade 1930-
See Slade, Bernard
See also CA 81-84; CANR 49;
DAM DRAM

Newby, P(ercy) H(oward)
1918- .... CLC 2, 13; DAM NOV
See also CA 5-8R; CANR 32; DLB 15;
MTCW

Newlove, Donald 1928- .... CLC 6
See also CA 29-32R; CANR 25

Newlove, John (Herbert) 1938- ..... CLC 14
See also CA 21-24R; CANR 9, 25

Newman, Charles 1938- .... CLC 2, 8
See also CA 21-24R

Newman, Edwin (Harold) 1919- .... CLC 14
See also AITN 1; CA 69-72; CANR 5

Newman, John Henry
1801-1890 .... NCLC 38
See also DLB 18, 32, 55

Newton, Suzanne 1936- .... CLC 35
See also CA 41-44R; CANR 14; JRDA;
SATA 5, 77

Nexo, Martin Andersen
1869-1954 .... TCLC 43

Nezval, Vitezslav 1900-1958 ...... TCLC 44
See also CA 123

Ng, Fae Myenne 1957(?)- .... CLC 81
See also CA 146

Ngema, Mbongeni 1955- .... CLC 57
See also BW 2; CA 143

Ngugi, James T(hiong'o) .... CLC 3, 7, 13
See also Ngugi wa Thiong'o

Ngugi wa Thiong'o
1938- ..... CLC 36; BLC; DAM MULT,
NOV
See also Ngugi, James T(hiong'o)
See also BW 2; CA 81-84; CANR 27;
DLB 125; MTCW

Nichol, B(arrie) P(hillip)
1944-1988 .... CLC 18
See also CA 53-56; DLB 53; SATA 66

Nichols, John (Treadwell) 1940- .... CLC 38
See also CA 9-12R; CAAS 2; CANR 6;
DLBY 82

Nichols, Leigh
See Koontz, Dean R(ay)

Nichols, Peter (Richard)
1927- .... CLC 5, 36, 65
See also CA 104; CANR 33; DLB 13;
MTCW

Nicolas, F. R. E.
See Freeling, Nicolas

Niedecker, Lorine
1903-1970 .... CLC 10, 42; DAM POET
See also CA 25-28; CAP 2; DLB 48

Nietzsche, Friedrich (Wilhelm)
1844-1900 .... TCLC 10, 18, 55
See also CA 107; 121; DLB 129

Nievo, Ippolito 1831-1861 .... NCLC 22

Nightingale, Anne Redmon 1943-
See Redmon, Anne
See also CA 103

Nik. T. O.
See Annensky, Innokenty (Fyodorovich)

Nin, Anais
1903-1977 ...... CLC 1, 4, 8, 11, 14, 60;
DAM NOV, POP; SSC 10
See also AITN 2; CA 13-16R; 69-72;
CANR 22, 53; DLB 2, 4, 152; MTCW

Nishiwaki, Junzaburo 1894-1982 .... PC 15
See also CA 107

Nissenson, Hugh 1933- .... CLC 4, 9
See also CA 17-20R; CANR 27; DLB 28

Niven, Larry .... CLC 8
See also Niven, Laurence Van Cott
See also DLB 8

Niven, Laurence Van Cott 1938-
See Niven, Larry
See also CA 21-24R; CAAS 12; CANR 14,
44; DAM POP; MTCW

Nixon, Agnes Eckhardt 1927- ...... CLC 21
See also CA 110

Nizan, Paul 1905-1940 .... TCLC 40
See also DLB 72

Nkosi, Lewis
1936- ..... CLC 45; BLC; DAM MULT
See also BW 1; CA 65-68; CANR 27;
DLB 157

Nodier, (Jean) Charles (Emmanuel)
1780-1844 .... NCLC 19
See also DLB 119

Nolan, Christopher 1965- .... CLC 58
See also CA 111

Noon, Jeff 1957- .... CLC 91
See also CA 148

Norden, Charles
See Durrell, Lawrence (George)

Nordhoff, Charles (Bernard)
1887-1947 .... TCLC 23
See also CA 108; DLB 9; SATA 23

Norfolk, Lawrence 1963- .... CLC 76
See also CA 144

Norman, Marsha
1947- .... CLC 28; DAM DRAM
See also CA 105; CABS 3; CANR 41;
DLBY 84

Norris, Benjamin Franklin, Jr.
1870-1902 .... TCLC 24
See also Norris, Frank
See also CA 110

Norris, Frank
See Norris, Benjamin Franklin, Jr.
See also CDALB 1865-1917; DLB 12, 71

Norris, Leslie 1921- .... CLC 14
See also CA 11-12; CANR 14; CAP 1;
DLB 27

North, Andrew
See Norton, Andre

North, Anthony
See Koontz, Dean R(ay)

North, Captain George
See Stevenson, Robert Louis (Balfour)

North, Milou
See Erdrich, Louise

Northrup, B. A.
See Hubbard, L(afayette) Ron(ald)

North Staffs
See Hulme, T(homas) E(rnest)

Norton, Alice Mary
See Norton, Andre
See also MAICYA; SATA 1, 43

Norton, Andre 1912- .... CLC 12
See also Norton, Alice Mary
See also AAYA 14; CA 1-4R; CANR 2, 31;
DLB 8, 52; JRDA; MTCW; SATA 91

Norton, Caroline 1808-1877 ...... NCLC 47
See also DLB 21, 159

Norway, Nevil Shute 1899-1960
See Shute, Nevil
See also CA 102; 93-96

Norwid, Cyprian Kamil
1821-1883 .... NCLC 17

Nosille, Nabrah
See Ellison, Harlan (Jay)

Nossack, Hans Erich 1901-1978 ..... CLC 6
See also CA 93-96; 85-88; DLB 69

Nostradamus 1503-1566 .... LC 27

Nosu, Chuji
See Ozu, Yasujiro

Notenburg, Eleanora (Genrikhovna) von
See Guro, Elena

Nova, Craig 1945- .... CLC 7, 31
See also CA 45-48; CANR 2, 53

Novak, Joseph
See Kosinski, Jerzy (Nikodem)

Novalis 1772-1801 .... NCLC 13
See also DLB 90

Nowlan, Alden (Albert)
1933-1983 .. CLC 15; DAC; DAM MST
See also CA 9-12R; CANR 5; DLB 53

Noyes, Alfred 1880-1958 .... TCLC 7
See also CA 104; DLB 20

Nunn, Kem 19(?)- .... CLC 34

Nye, Robert
1939- .... CLC 13, 42; DAM NOV
See also CA 33-36R; CANR 29; DLB 14;
MTCW; SATA 6

Nyro, Laura 1947- .... CLC 17

Oates, Joyce Carol
1938- ...... CLC 1, 2, 3, 6, 9, 11, 15, 19,
33, 52; DA; DAB; DAC; DAM MST,
NOV, POP; SSC 6; WLC
See also AAYA 15; AITN 1; BEST 89:2;
CA 5-8R; CANR 25, 45;
CDALB 1968-1988; DLB 2, 5, 130;
DLBY 81; INT CANR-25; MTCW

Orwell, George
..... TCLC 2, 6, 15, 31, 51; DAB; WLC
See also Blair, Eric (Arthur)
See also CDBLB 1945-1960; DLB 15, 98

Osborne, David
See Silverberg, Robert

Osborne, George
See Silverberg, Robert

Osborne, John (James)
1929-1994 ..... CLC 1, 2, 5, 11, 45; DA;
DAB; DAC; DAM DRAM, MST; WLC
See also CA 13-16R; 147; CANR 21, 56;
CDBLB 1945-1960; DLB 13; MTCW

Osborne, Lawrence 1958- .... CLC 50

Oshima, Nagisa 1932- .... CLC 20
See also CA 116; 121

Oskison, John Milton
1874-1947 ..... TCLC 35; DAM MULT
See also CA 144; DLB 175; NNAL

Ossoli, Sarah Margaret (Fuller marchesa d')
1810-1850
See Fuller, Margaret
See also SATA 25

Ostrovsky, Alexander
1823-1886 .... NCLC 30, 57

Otero, Blas de 1916-1979......... CLC 11
See also CA 89-92; DLB 134

Otto, Whitney 1955-.............. CLC 70
See also CA 140

Ouida .... TCLC 43
See also De La Ramee, (Marie) Louise
See also DLB 18, 156

Ousmane, Sembene 1923- .... CLC 66; BLC
See also BW 1; CA 117; 125; MTCW

Ovid
43B.C.-18(?) ... CMLC 7; DAM POET;
PC 2

Owen, Hugh
See Faust, Frederick (Schiller)

Owen, Wilfred (Edward Salter)
1893-1918 ...... TCLC 5, 27; DA; DAB;
DAC; DAM MST, POET; WLC
See also CA 104; 141; CDBLB 1914-1945;
DLB 20

Owens, Rochelle 1936-............. CLC 8
See also CA 17-20R; CAAS 2; CANR 39

Oz, Amos
1939- .... CLC 5, 8, 11, 27, 33, 54;
DAM NOV
See also CA 53-56; CANR 27, 47; MTCW

Ozick, Cynthia
1928- .... CLC 3, 7, 28, 62; DAM NOV,
POP; SSC 15
See also BEST 90:1; CA 17-20R; CANR 23;
DLB 28, 152; DLBY 82; INT CANR-23;
MTCW

Ozu, Yasujiro 1903-1963 .... CLC 16
See also CA 112

Pacheco, C.
See Pessoa, Fernando (Antonio Nogueira)

Pa Chin .... CLC 18
See also Li Fei-kan

Pack, Robert 1929-.............. CLC 13
See also CA 1-4R; CANR 3, 44; DLB 5

Padgett, Lewis
See Kuttner, Henry

Padilla (Lorenzo), Heberto 1932-... CLC 38
See also AITN 1; CA 123; 131; HW

Page, Jimmy 1944-................ CLC 12

Page, Louise 1955-.............. CLC 40
See also CA 140

Page, P(atricia) K(athleen)
1916- .... CLC 7, 18; DAC; DAM MST;
PC 12
See also CA 53-56; CANR 4, 22; DLB 68;
MTCW

Page, Thomas Nelson 1853-1922.... SSC 23
See also CA 118; DLB 12, 78; DLBD 13

Paget, Violet 1856-1935
See Lee, Vernon
See also CA 104

Paget-Lowe, Henry
See Lovecraft, H(oward) P(hillips)

Paglia, Camille (Anna) 1947-...... CLC 68
See also CA 140

Paige, Richard
See Koontz, Dean R(ay)

Pakenham, Antonia
See Fraser, (Lady) Antonia (Pakenham)

Palamas, Kostes 1859-1943 .... TCLC 5
See also CA 105

Palazzeschi, Aldo 1885-1974...... CLC 11
See also CA 89-92; 53-56; DLB 114

Paley, Grace
1922- .... CLC 4, 6, 37; DAM POP;
SSC 8
See also CA 25-28R; CANR 13, 46;
DLB 28; INT CANR-13; MTCW

Palin, Michael (Edward) 1943-..... CLC 21
See also Monty Python
See also CA 107; CANR 35; SATA 67

Palliser, Charles 1947-........... CLC 65
See also CA 136

Palma, Ricardo 1833-1919........ TCLC 29

Pancake, Breece Dexter 1952-1979
See Pancake, Breece D'J
See also CA 123; 109

Pancake, Breece D'J.............. CLC 29
See also Pancake, Breece Dexter
See also DLB 130

Panko, Rudy
See Gogol, Nikolai (Vasilyevich)

Papadiamantis, Alexandros
1851-1911 .... TCLC 29

Papadiamantopoulos, Johannes 1856-1910
See Moreas, Jean
See also CA 117

Papini, Giovanni 1881-1956...... TCLC 22
See also CA 121

Paracelsus 1493-1541............. LC 14

Parasol, Peter
See Stevens, Wallace

Pareto, Vilfredo 1848-1923 .... TCLC 69

Parfenie, Maria
See Codrescu, Andrei

Parini, Jay (Lee) 1948- .... CLC 54
See also CA 97-100; CAAS 16; CANR 32

Park, Jordan
See Kornbluth, C(yril) M.; Pohl, Frederik

Parker, Bert
See Ellison, Harlan (Jay)

Parker, Dorothy (Rothschild)
1893-1967 .... CLC 15, 68;
DAM POET; SSC 2
See also CA 19-20; 25-28R; CAP 2;
DLB 11, 45, 86; MTCW

Parker, Robert B(rown)
1932- ...... CLC 27; DAM NOV, POP
See also BEST 89:4; CA 49-52; CANR 1,
26, 52; INT CANR-26; MTCW

Parkin, Frank 1940-.............. CLC 43
See also CA 147

Parkman, Francis, Jr.
1823-1893 .... NCLC 12
See also DLB 1, 30

Parks, Gordon (Alexander Buchanan)
1912- ... CLC 1, 16; BLC; DAM MULT
See also AITN 2; BW 2; CA 41-44R;
CANR 26; DLB 33; SATA 8

Parmenides
c. 515B.C.-c. 450B.C......... CMLC 22
See also DLB 176

Parnell, Thomas 1679-1718 .... LC 3
See also DLB 94

Parra, Nicanor
1914- ...... CLC 2; DAM MULT; HLC
See also CA 85-88; CANR 32; HW; MTCW

Parrish, Mary Frances
See Fisher, M(ary) F(rances) K(ennedy)

Parson
See Coleridge, Samuel Taylor

Parson Lot
See Kingsley, Charles

Partridge, Anthony
See Oppenheim, E(dward) Phillips

Pascal, Blaise 1623-1662 .... LC 35

Pascoli, Giovanni 1855-1912 ...... TCLC 45

Pasolini, Pier Paolo
1922-1975 .... CLC 20, 37; PC 17
See also CA 93-96; 61-64; DLB 128, 177;
MTCW

Pasquini
See Silone, Ignazio

Pastan, Linda (Olenik)
1932- .... CLC 27; DAM POET
See also CA 61-64; CANR 18, 40; DLB 5

Pasternak, Boris (Leonidovich)
1890-1960 ...... CLC 7, 10, 18, 63; DA;
DAB; DAC; DAM MST, NOV, POET;
PC 6; WLC
See also CA 127; 116; MTCW

Patchen, Kenneth
1911-1972 ... CLC 1, 2, 18; DAM POET
See also CA 1-4R; 33-36R; CANR 3, 35;
DLB 16, 48; MTCW

Pater, Walter (Horatio)
1839-1894 .... NCLC 7
See also CDBLB 1832-1890; DLB 57, 156

Paterson, A(ndrew) B(arton)
1864-1941 .... TCLC 32
See also CA 155

Pico della Mirandola, Giovanni
1463-1494 . . . . **LC 15**

Piercy, Marge
1936- . . . . **CLC 3, 6, 14, 18, 27, 62**
See also CA 21-24R; CAAS 1; CANR 13,
43; DLB 120; MTCW

Piers, Robert
See Anthony, Piers

Pieyre de Mandiargues, Andre 1909-1991
See Mandiargues, Andre Pieyre de
See also CA 103; 136; CANR 22

Pilnyak, Boris . . . . **TCLC 23**
See also Vogau, Boris Andreyevich

Pincherle, Alberto
1907-1990 . . . . . **CLC 11, 18; DAM NOV**
See also Moravia, Alberto
See also CA 25-28R; 132; CANR 33;
MTCW

Pinckney, Darryl 1953- . . . . **CLC 76**
See also BW 2; CA 143

Pindar 518B.C.-446B.C. . . . . **CMLC 12**
See also DLB 176

Pineda, Cecile 1942- . . . . **CLC 39**
See also CA 118

Pinero, Arthur Wing
1855-1934 . . . . . **TCLC 32; DAM DRAM**
See also CA 110; 153; DLB 10

Pinero, Miguel (Antonio Gomez)
1946-1988 . . . . **CLC 4, 55**
See also CA 61-64; 125; CANR 29; HW

Pinget, Robert 1919- . . . . **CLC 7, 13, 37**
See also CA 85-88; DLB 83

Pink Floyd
See Barrett, (Roger) Syd; Gilmour, David;
Mason, Nick; Waters, Roger; Wright,
Rick

Pinkney, Edward 1802-1828 . . . . . **NCLC 31**

Pinkwater, Daniel Manus 1941- . . . . **CLC 35**
See also Pinkwater, Manus
See also AAYA 1; CA 29-32R; CANR 12,
38; CLR 4; JRDA; MAICYA; SAAS 3;
SATA 46, 76

Pinkwater, Manus
See Pinkwater, Daniel Manus
See also SATA 8

Pinsky, Robert
1940- . . **CLC 9, 19, 38, 94; DAM POET**
See also CA 29-32R; CAAS 4; DLBY 82

Pinta, Harold
See Pinter, Harold

Pinter, Harold
1930- . . . . . **CLC 1, 3, 6, 9, 11, 15, 27, 58,
73; DA; DAB; DAC; DAM DRAM,
MST; WLC**
See also CA 5-8R; CANR 33; CDBLB 1960
to Present; DLB 13; MTCW

Piozzi, Hester Lynch (Thrale)
1741-1821 . . . . **NCLC 57**
See also DLB 104, 142

Pirandello, Luigi
1867-1936 . . . . . . **TCLC 4, 29; DA; DAB;
DAC; DAM DRAM, MST; DC 5;
SSC 22; WLC**
See also CA 104; 153

Pirsig, Robert M(aynard)
1928- . . . . **CLC 4, 6, 73; DAM POP**
See also CA 53-56; CANR 42; MTCW;
SATA 39

Pisarev, Dmitry Ivanovich
1840-1868 . . . . **NCLC 25**

Pix, Mary (Griffith) 1666-1709 . . . . . . **LC 8**
See also DLB 80

Pixerecourt, Guilbert de
1773-1844 . . . . **NCLC 39**

Plaidy, Jean
See Hibbert, Eleanor Alice Burford

Planche, James Robinson
1796-1880 . . . . **NCLC 42**

Plant, Robert 1948- . . . . **CLC 12**

Plante, David (Robert)
1940- . . . . **CLC 7, 23, 38; DAM NOV**
See also CA 37-40R; CANR 12, 36;
DLBY 83; INT CANR-12; MTCW

Plath, Sylvia
1932-1963 . . . . . **CLC 1, 2, 3, 5, 9, 11, 14,
17, 50, 51, 62; DA; DAB; DAC;
DAM MST, POET; PC 1; WLC**
See also AAYA 13; CA 19-20; CANR 34;
CAP 2; CDALB 1941-1968; DLB 5, 6,
152; MTCW

Plato
428(?)B.C.-348(?)B.C. . . . . . **CMLC 8; DA;
DAB; DAC; DAM MST**
See also DLB 176

Platonov, Andrei . . . . **TCLC 14**
See also Klimentov, Andrei Platonovich

Platt, Kin 1911- . . . . **CLC 26**
See also AAYA 11; CA 17-20R; CANR 11;
JRDA; SAAS 17; SATA 21, 86

Plautus c. 251B.C.-184B.C. . . . . **DC 6**

Plick et Plock
See Simenon, Georges (Jacques Christian)

Plimpton, George (Ames) 1927- . . . . . **CLC 36**
See also AITN 1; CA 21-24R; CANR 32;
MTCW; SATA 10

Plomer, William Charles Franklin
1903-1973 . . . . **CLC 4, 8**
See also CA 21-22; CANR 34; CAP 2;
DLB 20, 162; MTCW; SATA 24

Plowman, Piers
See Kavanagh, Patrick (Joseph)

Plum, J.
See Wodehouse, P(elham) G(renville)

Plumly, Stanley (Ross) 1939- . . . . . . **CLC 33**
See also CA 108; 110; DLB 5; INT 110

Plumpe, Friedrich Wilhelm
1888-1931 . . . . **TCLC 53**
See also CA 112

Poe, Edgar Allan
1809-1849 . . . . **NCLC 1, 16, 55; DA;
DAB; DAC; DAM MST, POET; PC 1;
SSC 1, 22; WLC**
See also AAYA 14; CDALB 1640-1865;
DLB 3, 59, 73, 74; SATA 23

Poet of Titchfield Street, The
See Pound, Ezra (Weston Loomis)

Pohl, Frederik 1919- . . . . . **CLC 18; SSC 25**
See also CA 61-64; CAAS 1; CANR 11, 37;
DLB 8; INT CANR-11; MTCW;
SATA 24

Poirier, Louis 1910-
See Gracq, Julien
See also CA 122; 126

Poitier, Sidney 1927- . . . . **CLC 26**
See also BW 1; CA 117

Polanski, Roman 1933- . . . . **CLC 16**
See also CA 77-80

Poliakoff, Stephen 1952- . . . . **CLC 38**
See also CA 106; DLB 13

Police, The
See Copeland, Stewart (Armstrong);
Summers, Andrew James; Sumner,
Gordon Matthew

Polidori, John William
1795-1821 . . . . **NCLC 51**
See also DLB 116

Pollitt, Katha 1949- . . . . **CLC 28**
See also CA 120; 122; MTCW

Pollock, (Mary) Sharon
1936- . . . . **CLC 50; DAC; DAM DRAM,
MST**
See also CA 141; DLB 60

Polo, Marco 1254-1324 . . . . **CMLC 15**

Polonsky, Abraham (Lincoln)
1910- . . . . **CLC 92**
See also CA 104; DLB 26; INT 104

Polybius c. 200B.C.-c. 118B.C. . . . . **CMLC 17**
See also DLB 176

Pomerance, Bernard
1940- . . . . **CLC 13; DAM DRAM**
See also CA 101; CANR 49

Ponge, Francis (Jean Gaston Alfred)
1899-1988 . . . . . **CLC 6, 18; DAM POET**
See also CA 85-88; 126; CANR 40

Pontoppidan, Henrik 1857-1943 . . . **TCLC 29**

Poole, Josephine . . . . **CLC 17**
See also Helyar, Jane Penelope Josephine
See also SAAS 2; SATA 5

Popa, Vasko 1922-1991 . . . . **CLC 19**
See also CA 112; 148

Pope, Alexander
1688-1744 . . . . . . **LC 3; DA; DAB; DAC;
DAM MST, POET; WLC**
See also CDBLB 1660-1789; DLB 95, 101

Porter, Connie (Rose) 1959(?)- . . . . . **CLC 70**
See also BW 2; CA 142; SATA 81

Porter, Gene(va Grace) Stratton
1863(?)-1924 . . . . **TCLC 21**
See also CA 112

Porter, Katherine Anne
1890-1980 . . . . . . **CLC 1, 3, 7, 10, 13, 15,
27; DA; DAB; DAC; DAM MST, NOV;
SSC 4**
See also AITN 2; CA 1-4R; 101; CANR 1;
DLB 4, 9, 102; DLBD 12; DLBY 80;
MTCW; SATA 39; SATA-Obit 23

Porter, Peter (Neville Frederick)
1929- . . . . **CLC 5, 13, 33**
See also CA 85-88; DLB 40

Porter, William Sydney   1862-1910
    See Henry, O.
    See also CA 104; 131; CDALB 1865-1917;
    DA; DAB; DAC; DAM MST; DLB 12,
    78, 79; MTCW; YABC 2

Portillo (y Pacheco), Jose Lopez
    See Lopez Portillo (y Pacheco), Jose

Post, Melville Davisson
    1869-1930 . . . . TCLC 39
    See also CA 110

Potok, Chaim
    1929- . . . . CLC 2, 7, 14, 26; DAM NOV
    See also AAYA 15; AITN 1, 2; CA 17-20R;
    CANR 19, 35; DLB 28, 152;
    INT CANR-19; MTCW; SATA 33

Potter, Beatrice
    See Webb, (Martha) Beatrice (Potter)
    See also MAICYA

Potter, Dennis (Christopher George)
    1935-1994 . . . . CLC 58, 86
    See also CA 107; 145; CANR 33; MTCW

Pound, Ezra (Weston Loomis)
    1885-1972 . . . . . . CLC 1, 2, 3, 4, 5, 7, 10,
       13, 18, 34, 48, 50; DA; DAB; DAC;
          DAM MST, POET; PC 4; WLC
    See also CA 5-8R; 37-40R; CANR 40;
    CDALB 1917-1929; DLB 4, 45, 63;
    MTCW

Povod, Reinaldo   1959-1994 . . . . CLC 44
    See also CA 136; 146

Powell, Adam Clayton, Jr.
    1908-1972 . . . . CLC 89; BLC;
                                  DAM MULT
    See also BW 1; CA 102; 33-36R

Powell, Anthony (Dymoke)
    1905- . . . . CLC 1, 3, 7, 9, 10, 31
    See also CA 1-4R; CANR 1, 32;
    CDBLB 1945-1960; DLB 15; MTCW

Powell, Dawn   1897-1965 . . . . CLC 66
    See also CA 5-8R

Powell, Padgett   1952- . . . . CLC 34
    See also CA 126

Power, Susan . . . . CLC 91

Powers, J(ames) F(arl)
    1917- . . . . CLC 1, 4, 8, 57; SSC 4
    See also CA 1-4R; CANR 2; DLB 130;
    MTCW

Powers, John J(ames)   1945-
    See Powers, John R.
    See also CA 69-72

Powers, John R. . . . . CLC 66
    See also Powers, John J(ames)

Powers, Richard (S.)   1957- . . . . CLC 93
    See also CA 148

Pownall, David   1938- . . . . CLC 10
    See also CA 89-92; CAAS 18; CANR 49;
    DLB 14

Powys, John Cowper
    1872-1963 . . . . CLC 7, 9, 15, 46
    See also CA 85-88; DLB 15; MTCW

Powys, T(heodore) F(rancis)
    1875-1953 . . . . TCLC 9
    See also CA 106; DLB 36, 162

Prager, Emily   1952- . . . . CLC 56

Pratt, E(dwin) J(ohn)
    1883(?)-1964 . . . . CLC 19; DAC;
                                   DAM POET
    See also CA 141; 93-96; DLB 92

Premchand . . . . TCLC 21
    See also Srivastava, Dhanpat Rai

Preussler, Otfried   1923- . . . . CLC 17
    See also CA 77-80; SATA 24

Prevert, Jacques (Henri Marie)
    1900-1977 . . . . CLC 15
    See also CA 77-80; 69-72; CANR 29;
    MTCW; SATA-Obit 30

Prevost, Abbe (Antoine Francois)
    1697-1763 . . . . LC 1

Price, (Edward) Reynolds
    1933- . . . . CLC 3, 6, 13, 43, 50, 63;
                           DAM NOV; SSC 22
    See also CA 1-4R; CANR 1, 37, 57; DLB 2;
    INT CANR-37

Price, Richard   1949- . . . . CLC 6, 12
    See also CA 49-52; CANR 3; DLBY 81

Prichard, Katharine Susannah
    1883-1969 . . . . CLC 46
    See also CA 11-12; CANR 33; CAP 1;
    MTCW; SATA 66

Priestley, J(ohn) B(oynton)
    1894-1984 . . . . CLC 2, 5, 9, 34;
                            DAM DRAM, NOV
    See also CA 9-12R; 113; CANR 33;
    CDBLB 1914-1945; DLB 10, 34, 77, 100,
    139; DLBY 84; MTCW

Prince   1958(?)- . . . . CLC 35

Prince, F(rank) T(empleton)   1912- . . CLC 22
    See also CA 101; CANR 43; DLB 20

Prince Kropotkin
    See Kropotkin, Peter (Aleksieevich)

Prior, Matthew   1664-1721 . . . . LC 4
    See also DLB 95

Pritchard, William H(arrison)
    1932- . . . . CLC 34
    See also CA 65-68; CANR 23; DLB 111

Pritchett, V(ictor) S(awdon)
    1900- . . . . CLC 5, 13, 15, 41;
                             DAM NOV; SSC 14
    See also CA 61-64; CANR 31; DLB 15,
    139; MTCW

Private 19022
    See Manning, Frederic

Probst, Mark   1925- . . . . CLC 59
    See also CA 130

Prokosch, Frederic   1908-1989 . . . . CLC 4, 48
    See also CA 73-76; 128; DLB 48

Prophet, The
    See Dreiser, Theodore (Herman Albert)

Prose, Francine   1947- . . . . CLC 45
    See also CA 109; 112; CANR 46

Proudhon
    See Cunha, Euclides (Rodrigues Pimenta) da

Proulx, E. Annie   1935- . . . . CLC 81

Proust, (Valentin-Louis-George-Eugene-)
    Marcel
    1871-1922 . . . . TCLC 7, 13, 33; DA;
              DAB; DAC; DAM MST, NOV; WLC
    See also CA 104; 120; DLB 65; MTCW

Prowler, Harley
    See Masters, Edgar Lee

Prus, Boleslaw   1845-1912 . . . . TCLC 48

Pryor, Richard (Franklin Lenox Thomas)
    1940- . . . . CLC 26
    See also CA 122

Przybyszewski, Stanislaw
    1868-1927 . . . . TCLC 36
    See also DLB 66

Pteleon
    See Grieve, C(hristopher) M(urray)
    See also DAM POET

Puckett, Lute
    See Masters, Edgar Lee

Puig, Manuel
    1932-1990 . . . . CLC 3, 5, 10, 28, 65;
                             DAM MULT; HLC
    See also CA 45-48; CANR 2, 32; DLB 113;
    HW; MTCW

Purdy, Al(fred Wellington)
    1918- . . . . CLC 3, 6, 14, 50; DAC;
                              DAM MST, POET
    See also CA 81-84; CAAS 17; CANR 42;
    DLB 88

Purdy, James (Amos)
    1923- . . . . CLC 2, 4, 10, 28, 52
    See also CA 33-36R; CAAS 1; CANR 19,
    51; DLB 2; INT CANR-19; MTCW

Pure, Simon
    See Swinnerton, Frank Arthur

Pushkin, Alexander (Sergeyevich)
    1799-1837 . . . . . NCLC 3, 27; DA; DAB;
           DAC; DAM DRAM, MST, POET;
                                 PC 10; WLC
    See also SATA 61

P'u Sung-ling   1640-1715 . . . . LC 3

Putnam, Arthur Lee
    See Alger, Horatio, Jr.

Puzo, Mario
    1920- . . . . . . CLC 1, 2, 6, 36; DAM NOV,
                                         POP
    See also CA 65-68; CANR 4, 42; DLB 6;
    MTCW

Pygge, Edward
    See Barnes, Julian (Patrick)

Pym, Barbara (Mary Crampton)
    1913-1980 . . . . CLC 13, 19, 37
    See also CA 13-14; 97-100; CANR 13, 34;
    CAP 1; DLB 14; DLBY 87; MTCW

Pynchon, Thomas (Ruggles, Jr.)
    1937- . . . . . CLC 2, 3, 6, 9, 11, 18, 33, 62,
       72; DA; DAB; DAC; DAM MST, NOV,
                         POP; SSC 14; WLC
    See also BEST 90:2; CA 17-20R; CANR 22,
    46; DLB 2, 173; MTCW

Pythagoras
    c. 570B.C.-c. 500B.C. . . . . CMLC 22
    See also DLB 176

Qian Zhongshu
    See Ch'ien Chung-shu

Qroll
    See Dagerman, Stig (Halvard)

Quarrington, Paul (Lewis)   1953- . . . . CLC 65
    See also CA 129

Reid, Christopher (John) 1949-..... **CLC 33**
See also CA 140; DLB 40

Reid, Desmond
See Moorcock, Michael (John)

Reid Banks, Lynne 1929-
See Banks, Lynne Reid
See also CA 1-4R; CANR 6, 22, 38;
CLR 24; JRDA; MAICYA; SATA 22, 75

Reilly, William K.
See Creasey, John

Reiner, Max
See Caldwell, (Janet Miriam) Taylor
(Holland)

Reis, Ricardo
See Pessoa, Fernando (Antonio Nogueira)

Remarque, Erich Maria
1898-1970 .... **CLC 21; DA; DAB; DAC;**
DAM MST, NOV
See also CA 77-80; 29-32R; DLB 56;
MTCW

Remizov, A.
See Remizov, Aleksei (Mikhailovich)

Remizov, A. M.
See Remizov, Aleksei (Mikhailovich)

Remizov, Aleksei (Mikhailovich)
1877-1957 .... **TCLC 27**
See also CA 125; 133

Renan, Joseph Ernest
1823-1892 .... **NCLC 26**

Renard, Jules 1864-1910 .... **TCLC 17**
See also CA 117

Renault, Mary.............. **CLC 3, 11, 17**
See also Challans, Mary
See also DLBY 83

Rendell, Ruth (Barbara)
1930- .... **CLC 28, 48; DAM POP**
See also Vine, Barbara
See also CA 109; CANR 32, 52; DLB 87;
INT CANR-32; MTCW

Renoir, Jean 1894-1979 .... **CLC 20**
See also CA 129; 85-88

Resnais, Alain 1922-.............. **CLC 16**

Reverdy, Pierre 1889-1960 .... **CLC 53**
See also CA 97-100; 89-92

Rexroth, Kenneth
1905-1982 ...... **CLC 1, 2, 6, 11, 22, 49;**
DAM POET
See also CA 5-8R; 107; CANR 14, 34;
CDALB 1941-1968; DLB 16, 48, 165;
DLBY 82; INT CANR-14; MTCW

Reyes, Alfonso 1889-1959 .... **TCLC 33**
See also CA 131; HW

Reyes y Basoalto, Ricardo Eliecer Neftali
See Neruda, Pablo

Reymont, Wladyslaw (Stanislaw)
1868(?)-1925 .... **TCLC 5**
See also CA 104

Reynolds, Jonathan 1942- .... **CLC 6, 38**
See also CA 65-68; CANR 28

Reynolds, Joshua 1723-1792 .... **LC 15**
See also DLB 104

Reynolds, Michael Shane 1937- .... **CLC 44**
See also CA 65-68; CANR 9

Reznikoff, Charles 1894-1976 .... **CLC 9**
See also CA 33-36; 61-64; CAP 2; DLB 28,
45

Rezzori (d'Arezzo), Gregor von
1914-...................... **CLC 25**
See also CA 122; 136

Rhine, Richard
See Silverstein, Alvin

Rhodes, Eugene Manlove
1869-1934 .... **TCLC 53**

R'hoone
See Balzac, Honore de

Rhys, Jean
1890(?)-1979 .... **CLC 2, 4, 6, 14, 19, 51;**
DAM NOV; SSC 21
See also CA 25-28R; 85-88; CANR 35;
CDBLB 1945-1960; DLB 36, 117, 162;
MTCW

Ribeiro, Darcy 1922-1997 .... **CLC 34**
See also CA 33-36R; 156

Ribeiro, Joao Ubaldo (Osorio Pimentel)
1941-.................... **CLC 10, 67**
See also CA 81-84

Ribman, Ronald (Burt) 1932- .... **CLC 7**
See also CA 21-24R; CANR 46

Ricci, Nino 1959-................. **CLC 70**
See also CA 137

Rice, Anne 1941- ..... **CLC 41; DAM POP**
See also AAYA 9; BEST 89:2; CA 65-68;
CANR 12, 36, 53

Rice, Elmer (Leopold)
1892-1967 .... **CLC 7, 49; DAM DRAM**
See also CA 21-22; 25-28R; CAP 2; DLB 4,
7; MTCW

Rice, Tim(othy Miles Bindon)
1944-...................... **CLC 21**
See also CA 103; CANR 46

Rich, Adrienne (Cecile)
1929- .... **CLC 3, 6, 7, 11, 18, 36, 73, 76;**
DAM POET; PC 5
See also CA 9-12R; CANR 20, 53; DLB 5,
67; MTCW

Rich, Barbara
See Graves, Robert (von Ranke)

Rich, Robert
See Trumbo, Dalton

Richard, Keith.................... **CLC 17**
See also Richards, Keith

Richards, David Adams
1950-................ **CLC 59; DAC**
See also CA 93-96; DLB 53

Richards, I(vor) A(rmstrong)
1893-1979 .... **CLC 14, 24**
See also CA 41-44R; 89-92; CANR 34;
DLB 27

Richards, Keith 1943-
See Richard, Keith
See also CA 107

Richardson, Anne
See Roiphe, Anne (Richardson)

Richardson, Dorothy Miller
1873-1957 .... **TCLC 3**
See also CA 104; DLB 36

Richardson, Ethel Florence (Lindesay)
1870-1946
See Richardson, Henry Handel
See also CA 105

Richardson, Henry Handel......... **TCLC 4**
See also Richardson, Ethel Florence
(Lindesay)

Richardson, John
1796-1852 .... **NCLC 55; DAC**
See also DLB 99

Richardson, Samuel
1689-1761 ...... **LC 1; DA; DAB; DAC;**
DAM MST, NOV; WLC
See also CDBLB 1660-1789; DLB 39

Richler, Mordecai
1931- .... **CLC 3, 5, 9, 13, 18, 46, 70;**
DAC; DAM MST, NOV
See also AITN 1; CA 65-68; CANR 31;
CLR 17; DLB 53; MAICYA; MTCW;
SATA 44; SATA-Brief 27

Richter, Conrad (Michael)
1890-1968 .... **CLC 30**
See also AAYA 21; CA 5-8R; 25-28R;
CANR 23; DLB 9; MTCW; SATA 3

Ricostranza, Tom
See Ellis, Trey

Riddell, J. H. 1832-1906 .... **TCLC 40**

Riding, Laura................... **CLC 3, 7**
See also Jackson, Laura (Riding)

Riefenstahl, Berta Helene Amalia 1902-
See Riefenstahl, Leni
See also CA 108

Riefenstahl, Leni................. **CLC 16**
See also Riefenstahl, Berta Helene Amalia

Riffe, Ernest
See Bergman, (Ernst) Ingmar

Riggs, (Rolla) Lynn
1899-1954 ..... **TCLC 56; DAM MULT**
See also CA 144; DLB 175; NNAL

Riley, James Whitcomb
1849-1916 ...... **TCLC 51; DAM POET**
See also CA 118; 137; MAICYA; SATA 17

Riley, Tex
See Creasey, John

Rilke, Rainer Maria
1875-1926 .... **TCLC 1, 6, 19;**
DAM POET; PC 2
See also CA 104; 132; DLB 81; MTCW

Rimbaud, (Jean Nicolas) Arthur
1854-1891 ...... **NCLC 4, 35; DA; DAB;**
DAC; DAM MST, POET; PC 3; WLC

Rinehart, Mary Roberts
1876-1958 .... **TCLC 52**
See also CA 108

Ringmaster, The
See Mencken, H(enry) L(ouis)

Ringwood, Gwen(dolyn Margaret) Pharis
1910-1984 .... **CLC 48**
See also CA 148; 112; DLB 88

Rio, Michel 19(?)-................. **CLC 43**

Ritsos, Giannes
See Ritsos, Yannis

Ritsos, Yannis 1909-1990..... **CLC 6, 13, 31**
See also CA 77-80; 133; CANR 39; MTCW

Ritter, Erika 1948(?)-............. **CLC 52**

Rivera, Jose Eustasio 1889-1928... **TCLC 35**
See also HW

Rivers, Conrad Kent 1933-1968..... **CLC 1**
See also BW 1; CA 85-88; DLB 41

Rivers, Elfrida
See Bradley, Marion Zimmer

Riverside, John
See Heinlein, Robert A(nson)

Rizal, Jose 1861-1896.......... **NCLC 27**

Roa Bastos, Augusto (Antonio)
1917-..... **CLC 45; DAM MULT; HLC**
See also CA 131; DLB 113; HW

Robbe-Grillet, Alain
1922-...... **CLC 1, 2, 4, 6, 8, 10, 14, 43**
See also CA 9-12R; CANR 33; DLB 83;
MTCW

Robbins, Harold
1916-............. **CLC 5; DAM NOV**
See also CA 73-76; CANR 26, 54; MTCW

Robbins, Thomas Eugene 1936-
See Robbins, Tom
See also CA 81-84; CANR 29; DAM NOV,
POP; MTCW

Robbins, Tom............. **CLC 9, 32, 64**
See also Robbins, Thomas Eugene
See also BEST 90:3; DLBY 80

Robbins, Trina 1938-............. **CLC 21**
See also CA 128

Roberts, Charles G(eorge) D(ouglas)
1860-1943.............. **TCLC 8**
See also CA 105; CLR 33; DLB 92;
SATA 88; SATA-Brief 29

Roberts, Elizabeth Madox
1886-1941................. **TCLC 68**
See also CA 111; DLB 9, 54, 102;
SATA 33; SATA-Brief 27

Roberts, Kate 1891-1985.......... **CLC 15**
See also CA 107; 116

Roberts, Keith (John Kingston)
1935-...................... **CLC 14**
See also CA 25-28R; CANR 46

Roberts, Kenneth (Lewis)
1885-1957................. **TCLC 23**
See also CA 109; DLB 9

Roberts, Michele (B.) 1949-........ **CLC 48**
See also CA 115

Robertson, Ellis
See Ellison, Harlan (Jay); Silverberg, Robert

Robertson, Thomas William
1829-1871.... **NCLC 35; DAM DRAM**

Robinson, Edwin Arlington
1869-1935........ **TCLC 5; DA; DAC;**
DAM MST, POET; PC 1
See also CA 104; 133; CDALB 1865-1917;
DLB 54; MTCW

Robinson, Henry Crabb
1775-1867................. **NCLC 15**
See also DLB 107

Robinson, Jill 1936-............. **CLC 10**
See also CA 102; INT 102

Robinson, Kim Stanley 1952-...... **CLC 34**
See also CA 126

Robinson, Lloyd
See Silverberg, Robert

Robinson, Marilynne 1944-........ **CLC 25**
See also CA 116

Robinson, Smokey................ **CLC 21**
See also Robinson, William, Jr.

Robinson, William, Jr. 1940-
See Robinson, Smokey
See also CA 116

Robison, Mary 1949-........ **CLC 42, 98**
See also CA 113; 116; DLB 130; INT 116

Rod, Edouard 1857-1910 .... **TCLC 52**

Roddenberry, Eugene Wesley 1921-1991
See Roddenberry, Gene
See also CA 110; 135; CANR 37; SATA 45;
SATA-Obit 69

Roddenberry, Gene .... **CLC 17**
See also Roddenberry, Eugene Wesley
See also AAYA 5; SATA-Obit 69

Rodgers, Mary 1931-............. **CLC 12**
See also CA 49-52; CANR 8, 55; CLR 20;
INT CANR-8; JRDA; MAICYA;
SATA 8

Rodgers, W(illiam) R(obert)
1909-1969 .... **CLC 7**
See also CA 85-88; DLB 20

Rodman, Eric
See Silverberg, Robert

Rodman, Howard 1920(?)-1985..... **CLC 65**
See also CA 118

Rodman, Maia
See Wojciechowska, Maia (Teresa)

Rodriguez, Claudio 1934-.......... **CLC 10**
See also DLB 134

Roelvaag, O(le) E(dvart)
1876-1931................. **TCLC 17**
See also CA 117; DLB 9

Roethke, Theodore (Huebner)
1908-1963 ...... **CLC 1, 3, 8, 11, 19, 46;**
DAM POET; PC 15
See also CA 81-84; CABS 2;
CDALB 1941-1968; DLB 5; MTCW

Rogers, Thomas Hunton 1927-..... **CLC 57**
See also CA 89-92; INT 89-92

Rogers, Will(iam Penn Adair)
1879-1935 ...... **TCLC 8; DAM MULT**
See also CA 105; 144; DLB 11; NNAL

Rogin, Gilbert 1929-.............. **CLC 18**
See also CA 65-68; CANR 15

Rohan, Koda .... **TCLC 22**
See also Koda Shigeyuki

Rohmer, Eric.................... **CLC 16**
See also Scherer, Jean-Marie Maurice

Rohmer, Sax .... **TCLC 28**
See also Ward, Arthur Henry Sarsfield
See also DLB 70

Roiphe, Anne (Richardson)
1935-...................... **CLC 3, 9**
See also CA 89-92; CANR 45; DLBY 80;
INT 89-92

Rojas, Fernando de 1465-1541 ...... **LC 23**

Rolfe, Frederick (William Serafino Austin
Lewis Mary) 1860-1913..... **TCLC 12**
See also CA 107; DLB 34, 156

Rolland, Romain 1866-1944...... **TCLC 23**
See also CA 118; DLB 65

Rolle, Richard c. 1300-c. 1349 ... **CMLC 21**
See also DLB 146

Rolvaag, O(le) E(dvart)
See Roelvaag, O(le) E(dvart)

Romain Arnaud, Saint
See Aragon, Louis

Romains, Jules 1885-1972.......... **CLC 7**
See also CA 85-88; CANR 34; DLB 65;
MTCW

Romero, Jose Ruben 1890-1952 ... **TCLC 14**
See also CA 114; 131; HW

Ronsard, Pierre de
1524-1585 .... **LC 6; PC 11**

Rooke, Leon
1934- .... **CLC 25, 34; DAM POP**
See also CA 25-28R; CANR 23, 53

Roosevelt, Theodore 1858-1919.... **TCLC 69**
See also CA 115; DLB 47

Roper, William 1498-1578.......... **LC 10**

Roquelaure, A. N.
See Rice, Anne

Rosa, Joao Guimaraes 1908-1967... **CLC 23**
See also CA 89-92; DLB 113

Rose, Wendy
1948- .... **CLC 85; DAM MULT; PC 13**
See also CA 53-56; CANR 5, 51; DLB 175;
NNAL; SATA 12

Rosen, Richard (Dean) 1949-....... **CLC 39**
See also CA 77-80; INT CANR-30

Rosenberg, Isaac 1890-1918....... **TCLC 12**
See also CA 107; DLB 20

Rosenblatt, Joe .... **CLC 15**
See also Rosenblatt, Joseph

Rosenblatt, Joseph 1933-
See Rosenblatt, Joe
See also CA 89-92; INT 89-92

Rosenfeld, Samuel 1896-1963
See Tzara, Tristan
See also CA 89-92

Rosenstock, Sami
See Tzara, Tristan

Rosenstock, Samuel
See Tzara, Tristan

Rosenthal, M(acha) L(ouis)
1917-1996 .... **CLC 28**
See also CA 1-4R; 152; CAAS 6; CANR 4,
51; DLB 5; SATA 59

Ross, Barnaby
See Dannay, Frederic

Ross, Bernard L.
See Follett, Ken(neth Martin)

Ross, J. H.
See Lawrence, T(homas) E(dward)

Ross, Martin
See Martin, Violet Florence
See also DLB 135

Ross, (James) Sinclair
1908- ...... **CLC 13; DAC; DAM MST;**
SSC 24

See also CA 73-76; DLB 88

Rossetti, Christina (Georgina)
1830-1894 ..... **NCLC 2, 50; DA; DAB;**
DAC; DAM MST, POET; PC 7; WLC
See also DLB 35, 163; MAICYA; SATA 20

Rossetti, Dante Gabriel
1828-1882 .... **NCLC 4; DA; DAB;**
DAC; DAM MST, POET; WLC
See also CDBLB 1832-1890; DLB 35

Rossner, Judith (Perelman)
1935- .... **CLC 6, 9, 29**
See also AITN 2; BEST 90:3; CA 17-20R;
CANR 18, 51; DLB 6; INT CANR-18;
MTCW

Rostand, Edmond (Eugene Alexis)
1868-1918 ..... **TCLC 6, 37; DA; DAB;**
DAC; DAM DRAM, MST
See also CA 104; 126; MTCW

Roth, Henry 1906-1995 .... **CLC 2, 6, 11**
See also CA 11-12; 149; CANR 38; CAP 1;
DLB 28; MTCW

Roth, Joseph 1894-1939 .... **TCLC 33**
See also DLB 85

Roth, Philip (Milton)
1933- ...... **CLC 1, 2, 3, 4, 6, 9, 15, 22,**
31, 47, 66, 86; DA; DAB; DAC;
DAM MST, NOV, POP; WLC
See also BEST 90:3; CA 1-4R; CANR 1, 22,
36, 55; CDALB 1968-1988; DLB 2, 28,
173; DLBY 82; MTCW

Rothenberg, Jerome 1931- .... **CLC 6, 57**
See also CA 45-48; CANR 1; DLB 5

Roumain, Jacques (Jean Baptiste)
1907-1944 .... **TCLC 19; BLC;**
DAM MULT
See also BW 1; CA 117; 125

Rourke, Constance (Mayfield)
1885-1941 .... **TCLC 12**
See also CA 107; YABC 1

Rousseau, Jean-Baptiste 1671-1741 ... **LC 9**

Rousseau, Jean-Jacques
1712-1778 .... **LC 14, 36; DA; DAB;**
DAC; DAM MST; WLC

Roussel, Raymond 1877-1933 ..... **TCLC 20**
See also CA 117

Rovit, Earl (Herbert) 1927- .... **CLC 7**
See also CA 5-8R; CANR 12

Rowe, Nicholas 1674-1718 .... **LC 8**
See also DLB 84

Rowley, Ames Dorrance
See Lovecraft, H(oward) P(hillips)

Rowson, Susanna Haswell
1762(?)-1824 .... **NCLC 5**
See also DLB 37

Roy, Gabrielle
1909-1983 .... **CLC 10, 14; DAB; DAC;**
DAM MST
See also CA 53-56; 110; CANR 5; DLB 68;
MTCW

Rozewicz, Tadeusz
1921- .... **CLC 9, 23; DAM POET**
See also CA 108; CANR 36; MTCW

Ruark, Gibbons 1941- .... **CLC 3**
See also CA 33-36R; CAAS 23; CANR 14,
31, 57; DLB 120

Rubens, Bernice (Ruth) 1923- ... **CLC 19, 31**
See also CA 25-28R; CANR 33; DLB 14;
MTCW

Rubin, Harold
See Robbins, Harold

Rudkin, (James) David 1936- ...... **CLC 14**
See also CA 89-92; DLB 13

Rudnik, Raphael 1933- .... **CLC 7**
See also CA 29-32R

Ruffian, M.
See Hasek, Jaroslav (Matej Frantisek)

Ruiz, Jose Martinez .... **CLC 11**
See also Martinez Ruiz, Jose

Rukeyser, Muriel
1913-1980 .... **CLC 6, 10, 15, 27;**
DAM POET; PC 12
See also CA 5-8R; 93-96; CANR 26;
DLB 48; MTCW; SATA-Obit 22

Rule, Jane (Vance) 1931- .... **CLC 27**
See also CA 25-28R; CAAS 18; CANR 12;
DLB 60

Rulfo, Juan
1918-1986 .... **CLC 8, 80; DAM MULT;**
HLC; SSC 25
See also CA 85-88; 118; CANR 26;
DLB 113; HW; MTCW

Rumi, Jalal al-Din 1297-1373 .... **CMLC 20**

Runeberg, Johan 1804-1877 ...... **NCLC 41**

Runyon, (Alfred) Damon
1884(?)-1946 .... **TCLC 10**
See also CA 107; DLB 11, 86, 171

Rush, Norman 1933- .... **CLC 44**
See also CA 121; 126; INT 126

Rushdie, (Ahmed) Salman
1947- .... **CLC 23, 31, 55, 100; DAB;**
DAC; DAM MST, NOV, POP
See also BEST 89:3; CA 108; 111;
CANR 33, 56; INT 111; MTCW

Rushforth, Peter (Scott) 1945- ..... **CLC 19**
See also CA 101

Ruskin, John 1819-1900 .... **TCLC 63**
See also CA 114; 129; CDBLB 1832-1890;
DLB 55, 163; SATA 24

Russ, Joanna 1937- .... **CLC 15**
See also CA 25-28R; CANR 11, 31; DLB 8;
MTCW

Russell, George William 1867-1935
See Baker, Jean H.
See also CA 104; 153; CDBLB 1890-1914;
DAM POET

Russell, (Henry) Ken(neth Alfred)
1927- .... **CLC 16**
See also CA 105

Russell, Willy 1947- .... **CLC 60**

Rutherford, Mark .... **TCLC 25**
See also White, William Hale
See also DLB 18

Ruyslinck, Ward 1929- .... **CLC 14**
See also Belser, Reimond Karel Maria de

Ryan, Cornelius (John) 1920-1974 ... **CLC 7**
See also CA 69-72; 53-56; CANR 38

Ryan, Michael 1946- .... **CLC 65**
See also CA 49-52; DLBY 82

Rybakov, Anatoli (Naumovich)
1911- .... **CLC 23, 53**
See also CA 126; 135; SATA 79

Ryder, Jonathan
See Ludlum, Robert

Ryga, George
1932-1987 .. **CLC 14; DAC; DAM MST**
See also CA 101; 124; CANR 43; DLB 60

S. S.
See Sassoon, Siegfried (Lorraine)

Saba, Umberto 1883-1957 .... **TCLC 33**
See also CA 144; DLB 114

Sabatini, Rafael 1875-1950 ...... **TCLC 47**

Sabato, Ernesto (R.)
1911- .... **CLC 10, 23; DAM MULT;**
HLC
See also CA 97-100; CANR 32; DLB 145;
HW; MTCW

Sacastru, Martin
See Bioy Casares, Adolfo

Sacher-Masoch, Leopold von
1836(?)-1895 .... **NCLC 31**

Sachs, Marilyn (Stickle) 1927- ..... **CLC 35**
See also AAYA 2; CA 17-20R; CANR 13,
47; CLR 2; JRDA; MAICYA; SAAS 2;
SATA 3, 68

Sachs, Nelly 1891-1970 .... **CLC 14, 98**
See also CA 17-18; 25-28R; CAP 2

Sackler, Howard (Oliver)
1929-1982 .... **CLC 14**
See also CA 61-64; 108; CANR 30; DLB 7

Sacks, Oliver (Wolf) 1933- .... **CLC 67**
See also CA 53-56; CANR 28, 50;
INT CANR-28; MTCW

Sade, Donatien Alphonse Francois Comte
1740-1814 .... **NCLC 47**

Sadoff, Ira 1945- .... **CLC 9**
See also CA 53-56; CANR 5, 21; DLB 120

Saetone
See Camus, Albert

Safire, William 1929- .... **CLC 10**
See also CA 17-20R; CANR 31, 54

Sagan, Carl (Edward) 1934-1996 .... **CLC 30**
See also AAYA 2; CA 25-28R; 155;
CANR 11, 36; MTCW; SATA 58

Sagan, Francoise .... **CLC 3, 6, 9, 17, 36**
See also Quoirez, Francoise
See also DLB 83

Sahgal, Nayantara (Pandit) 1927- ... **CLC 41**
See also CA 9-12R; CANR 11

Saint, H(arry) F. 1941- .... **CLC 50**
See also CA 127

St. Aubin de Teran, Lisa 1953-
See Teran, Lisa St. Aubin de
See also CA 118; 126; INT 126

Sainte-Beuve, Charles Augustin
1804-1869 .... **NCLC 5**

Saint-Exupery, Antoine (Jean Baptiste Marie
Roger) de
1900-1944 .... **TCLC 2, 56; DAM NOV;**
WLC
See also CA 108; 132; CLR 10; DLB 72;
MAICYA; MTCW; SATA 20

St. John, David
See Hunt, E(verette) Howard, (Jr.)

Saint-John Perse
See Leger, (Marie-Rene Auguste) Alexis
Saint-Leger

Saintsbury, George (Edward Bateman)
    1845-1933 .... **TCLC 31**
    See also DLB 57, 149

Sait Faik .... **TCLC 23**
    See also Abasiyanik, Sait Faik

Saki .... **TCLC 3; SSC 12**
    See also Munro, H(ector) H(ugh)

Sala, George Augustus .... **NCLC 46**

Salama, Hannu 1936- .... **CLC 18**

Salamanca, J(ack) R(ichard)
    1922- .... **CLC 4, 15**
    See also CA 25-28R

Sale, J. Kirkpatrick
    See Sale, Kirkpatrick

Sale, Kirkpatrick 1937- .... **CLC 68**
    See also CA 13-16R; CANR 10

Salinas, Luis Omar
    1937- ..... **CLC 90; DAM MULT; HLC**
    See also CA 131; DLB 82; HW

Salinas (y Serrano), Pedro
    1891(?)-1951 .... **TCLC 17**
    See also CA 117; DLB 134

Salinger, J(erome) D(avid)
    1919- .... **CLC 1, 3, 8, 12, 55, 56; DA;**
        DAB; DAC; DAM MST, NOV, POP;
                            SSC 2; WLC
    See also AAYA 2; CA 5-8R; CANR 39;
        CDALB 1941-1968; CLR 18; DLB 2, 102,
        173; MAICYA; MTCW; SATA 67

Salisbury, John
    See Caute, David

Salter, James 1925- .... **CLC 7, 52, 59**
    See also CA 73-76; DLB 130

Saltus, Edgar (Everton)
    1855-1921 .... **TCLC 8**
    See also CA 105

Saltykov, Mikhail Evgrafovich
    1826-1889 .... **NCLC 16**

Samarakis, Antonis 1919- .... **CLC 5**
    See also CA 25-28R; CAAS 16; CANR 36

Sanchez, Florencio 1875-1910 ..... **TCLC 37**
    See also CA 153; HW

Sanchez, Luis Rafael 1936- .... **CLC 23**
    See also CA 128; DLB 145; HW

Sanchez, Sonia
    1934- ...... **CLC 5; BLC; DAM MULT;**
                            PC 9
    See also BW 2; CA 33-36R; CANR 24, 49;
        CLR 18; DLB 41; DLBD 8; MAICYA;
        MTCW; SATA 22

Sand, George
    1804-1876 .... **NCLC 2, 42, 57; DA;**
        DAB; DAC; DAM MST, NOV; WLC
    See also DLB 119

Sandburg, Carl (August)
    1878-1967 .... **CLC 1, 4, 10, 15, 35; DA;**
        DAB; DAC; DAM MST, POET; PC 2;
                            WLC
    See also CA 5-8R; 25-28R; CANR 35;
        CDALB 1865-1917; DLB 17, 54;
        MAICYA; MTCW; SATA 8

Sandburg, Charles
    See Sandburg, Carl (August)

Sandburg, Charles A.
    See Sandburg, Carl (August)

Sanders, (James) Ed(ward) 1939- ... **CLC 53**
    See also CA 13-16R; CAAS 21; CANR 13,
        44; DLB 16

Sanders, Lawrence
    1920- .... **CLC 41; DAM POP**
    See also BEST 89:4; CA 81-84; CANR 33;
        MTCW

Sanders, Noah
    See Blount, Roy (Alton), Jr.

Sanders, Winston P.
    See Anderson, Poul (William)

Sandoz, Mari(e Susette)
    1896-1966 .... **CLC 28**
    See also CA 1-4R; 25-28R; CANR 17;
        DLB 9; MTCW; SATA 5

Saner, Reg(inald Anthony) 1931- .... **CLC 9**
    See also CA 65-68

Sannazaro, Jacopo 1456(?)-1530 ...... **LC 8**

Sansom, William
    1912-1976 ...... **CLC 2, 6; DAM NOV;**
                            SSC 21
    See also CA 5-8R; 65-68; CANR 42;
        DLB 139; MTCW

Santayana, George 1863-1952 ..... **TCLC 40**
    See also CA 115; DLB 54, 71; DLBD 13

Santiago, Danny .... **CLC 33**
    See also James, Daniel (Lewis)
    See also DLB 122

Santmyer, Helen Hoover
    1895-1986 .... **CLC 33**
    See also CA 1-4R; 118; CANR 15, 33;
        DLBY 84; MTCW

Santos, Bienvenido N(uqui)
    1911-1996 ...... **CLC 22; DAM MULT**
    See also CA 101; 151; CANR 19, 46

Sapper .... **TCLC 44**
    See also McNeile, Herman Cyril

Sapphire 1950- .... **CLC 99**

Sappho
    fl. 6th cent. B.C.- .... **CMLC 3;**
                            DAM POET; PC 5
    See also DLB 176

Sarduy, Severo 1937-1993 .... **CLC 6, 97**
    See also CA 89-92; 142; DLB 113; HW

Sargeson, Frank 1903-1982 .... **CLC 31**
    See also CA 25-28R; 106; CANR 38

Sarmiento, Felix Ruben Garcia
    See Dario, Ruben

Saroyan, William
    1908-1981 ..... **CLC 1, 8, 10, 29, 34, 56;**
        DA; DAB; DAC; DAM DRAM, MST,
                NOV; SSC 21; WLC
    See also CA 5-8R; 103; CANR 30; DLB 7,
        9, 86; DLBY 81; MTCW; SATA 23;
        SATA-Obit 24

Sarraute, Nathalie
    1900- .... **CLC 1, 2, 4, 8, 10, 31, 80**
    See also CA 9-12R; CANR 23; DLB 83;
        MTCW

Sarton, (Eleanor) May
    1912-1995 .... **CLC 4, 14, 49, 91;**
                            DAM POET
    See also CA 1-4R; 149; CANR 1, 34, 55;
        DLB 48; DLBY 81; INT CANR-34;
        MTCW; SATA 36; SATA-Obit 86

Sartre, Jean-Paul
    1905-1980 .... **CLC 1, 4, 7, 9, 13, 18, 24,**
        44, 50, 52; DA; DAB; DAC;
        DAM DRAM, MST, NOV; DC 3; WLC
    See also CA 9-12R; 97-100; CANR 21;
        DLB 72; MTCW

Sassoon, Siegfried (Lorraine)
    1886-1967 .... **CLC 36; DAB;**
        DAM MST, NOV, POET; PC 12
    See also CA 104; 25-28R; CANR 36;
        DLB 20; MTCW

Satterfield, Charles
    See Pohl, Frederik

Saul, John (W. III)
    1942- ...... **CLC 46; DAM NOV, POP**
    See also AAYA 10; BEST 90:4; CA 81-84;
        CANR 16, 40

Saunders, Caleb
    See Heinlein, Robert A(nson)

Saura (Atares), Carlos 1932- .... **CLC 20**
    See also CA 114; 131; HW

Sauser-Hall, Frederic 1887-1961.... **CLC 18**
    See also Cendrars, Blaise
    See also CA 102; 93-96; CANR 36; MTCW

Saussure, Ferdinand de
    1857-1913 .... **TCLC 49**

Savage, Catharine
    See Brosman, Catharine Savage

Savage, Thomas 1915- .... **CLC 40**
    See also CA 126; 132; CAAS 15; INT 132

Savan, Glenn 19(?)- .... **CLC 50**

Sayers, Dorothy L(eigh)
    1893-1957 ..... **TCLC 2, 15; DAM POP**
    See also CA 104; 119; CDBLB 1914-1945;
        DLB 10, 36, 77, 100; MTCW

Sayers, Valerie 1952- .... **CLC 50**
    See also CA 134

Sayles, John (Thomas)
    1950- .... **CLC 7, 10, 14**
    See also CA 57-60; CANR 41; DLB 44

Scammell, Michael 1935- .... **CLC 34**
    See also CA 156

Scannell, Vernon 1922- .... **CLC 49**
    See also CA 5-8R; CANR 8, 24, 57;
        DLB 27; SATA 59

Scarlett, Susan
    See Streatfeild, (Mary) Noel

Schaeffer, Susan Fromberg
    1941- .... **CLC 6, 11, 22**
    See also CA 49-52; CANR 18; DLB 28;
        MTCW; SATA 22

Schary, Jill
    See Robinson, Jill

Schell, Jonathan 1943- .... **CLC 35**
    See also CA 73-76; CANR 12

Schelling, Friedrich Wilhelm Joseph von
    1775-1854 .... **NCLC 30**
    See also DLB 90

Schendel, Arthur van 1874-1946 ... **TCLC 56**

Scherer, Jean-Marie Maurice 1920-
    See Rohmer, Eric
    See also CA 110

Schevill, James (Erwin) 1920- .... **CLC 7**
    See also CA 5-8R; CAAS 12

Serna, Ramon Gomez de la
See Gomez de la Serna, Ramon

Serpieres
See Guillevic, (Eugene)

Service, Robert
See Service, Robert W(illiam)
See also DAB; DLB 92

Service, Robert W(illiam)
1874(?)-1958 . . . . . . **TCLC 15; DA; DAC;**
DAM MST, POET; WLC
See also Service, Robert
See also CA 115; 140; SATA 20

Seth, Vikram
1952- . . . . **CLC 43, 90; DAM MULT**
See also CA 121; 127; CANR 50; DLB 120;
INT 127

Seton, Cynthia Propper
1926-1982 . . . . **CLC 27**
See also CA 5-8R; 108; CANR 7

Seton, Ernest (Evan) Thompson
1860-1946 . . . . **TCLC 31**
See also CA 109; DLB 92; DLBD 13;
JRDA; SATA 18

Seton-Thompson, Ernest
See Seton, Ernest (Evan) Thompson

Settle, Mary Lee 1918- . . . . **CLC 19, 61**
See also CA 89-92; CAAS 1; CANR 44;
DLB 6; INT 89-92

Seuphor, Michel
See Arp, Jean

Sevigne, Marie (de Rabutin-Chantal) Marquise
de 1626-1696 . . . . **LC 11**

Sewall, Samuel 1652-1730 . . . . **LC 38**
See also DLB 24

Sexton, Anne (Harvey)
1928-1974 . . . . **CLC 2, 4, 6, 8, 10, 15, 53;**
DA; DAB; DAC; DAM MST, POET;
PC 2; WLC
See also CA 1-4R; 53-56; CABS 2;
CANR 3, 36; CDALB 1941-1968; DLB 5,
169; MTCW; SATA 10

Shaara, Michael (Joseph, Jr.)
1929-1988 . . . . **CLC 15; DAM POP**
See also AITN 1; CA 102; 125; CANR 52;
DLBY 83

Shackleton, C. C.
See Aldiss, Brian W(ilson)

Shacochis, Bob . . . . **CLC 39**
See also Shacochis, Robert G.

Shacochis, Robert G. 1951-
See Shacochis, Bob
See also CA 119; 124; INT 124

Shaffer, Anthony (Joshua)
1926- . . . . **CLC 19; DAM DRAM**
See also CA 110; 116; DLB 13

Shaffer, Peter (Levin)
1926- . . . . . . **CLC 5, 14, 18, 37, 60; DAB;**
DAM DRAM, MST; DC 7
See also CA 25-28R; CANR 25, 47;
CDBLB 1960 to Present; DLB 13;
MTCW

Shakey, Bernard
See Young, Neil

Shalamov, Varlam (Tikhonovich)
1907(?)-1982 . . . . **CLC 18**
See also CA 129; 105

Shamlu, Ahmad 1925- . . . . **CLC 10**

Shammas, Anton 1951- . . . . **CLC 55**

Shange, Ntozake
1948- . . . . **CLC 8, 25, 38, 74; BLC;**
DAM DRAM, MULT; DC 3
See also AAYA 9; BW 2; CA 85-88;
CABS 3; CANR 27, 48; DLB 38; MTCW

Shanley, John Patrick 1950- . . . . **CLC 75**
See also CA 128; 133

Shapcott, Thomas W(illiam) 1935- . . **CLC 38**
See also CA 69-72; CANR 49

Shapiro, Jane . . . . **CLC 76**

Shapiro, Karl (Jay) 1913- . . **CLC 4, 8, 15, 53**
See also CA 1-4R; CAAS 6; CANR 1, 36;
DLB 48; MTCW

Sharp, William 1855-1905 . . . . **TCLC 39**
See also DLB 156

Sharpe, Thomas Ridley 1928-
See Sharpe, Tom
See also CA 114; 122; INT 122

Sharpe, Tom . . . . **CLC 36**
See also Sharpe, Thomas Ridley
See also DLB 14

Shaw, Bernard . . . . **TCLC 45**
See also Shaw, George Bernard
See also BW 1

Shaw, G. Bernard
See Shaw, George Bernard

Shaw, George Bernard
1856-1950 . . . **TCLC 3, 9, 21; DA; DAB;**
DAC; DAM DRAM, MST; WLC
See also Shaw, Bernard
See also CA 104; 128; CDBLB 1914-1945;
DLB 10, 57; MTCW

Shaw, Henry Wheeler
1818-1885 . . . . **NCLC 15**
See also DLB 11

Shaw, Irwin
1913-1984 . . . . **CLC 7, 23, 34;**
DAM DRAM, POP
See also AITN 1; CA 13-16R; 112;
CANR 21; CDALB 1941-1968; DLB 6,
102; DLBY 84; MTCW

Shaw, Robert 1927-1978 . . . . **CLC 5**
See also AITN 1; CA 1-4R; 81-84;
CANR 4; DLB 13, 14

Shaw, T. E.
See Lawrence, T(homas) E(dward)

Shawn, Wallace 1943- . . . . **CLC 41**
See also CA 112

Shea, Lisa 1953- . . . . **CLC 86**
See also CA 147

Sheed, Wilfrid (John Joseph)
1930- . . . . **CLC 2, 4, 10, 53**
See also CA 65-68; CANR 30; DLB 6;
MTCW

Sheldon, Alice Hastings Bradley
1915(?)-1987
See Tiptree, James, Jr.
See also CA 108; 122; CANR 34; INT 108;
MTCW

Sheldon, John
See Bloch, Robert (Albert)

Shelley, Mary Wollstonecraft (Godwin)
1797-1851 . . . . **NCLC 14, 59; DA; DAB;**
DAC; DAM MST, NOV; WLC
See also AAYA 20; CDBLB 1789-1832;
DLB 110, 116, 159; SATA 29

Shelley, Percy Bysshe
1792-1822 . . . . **NCLC 18; DA; DAB;**
DAC; DAM MST, POET; PC 14; WLC
See also CDBLB 1789-1832; DLB 96, 110,
158

Shepard, Jim 1956- . . . . **CLC 36**
See also CA 137; SATA 90

Shepard, Lucius 1947- . . . . **CLC 34**
See also CA 128; 141

Shepard, Sam
1943- . . . . **CLC 4, 6, 17, 34, 41, 44;**
DAM DRAM; DC 5
See also AAYA 1; CA 69-72; CABS 3;
CANR 22; DLB 7; MTCW

Shepherd, Michael
See Ludlum, Robert

Sherburne, Zoa (Morin) 1912- . . . . . . **CLC 30**
See also AAYA 13; CA 1-4R; CANR 3, 37;
MAICYA; SAAS 18; SATA 3

Sheridan, Frances 1724-1766 . . . . **LC 7**
See also DLB 39, 84

Sheridan, Richard Brinsley
1751-1816 . . . . **NCLC 5; DA; DAB;**
DAC; DAM DRAM, MST; DC 1; WLC
See also CDBLB 1660-1789; DLB 89

Sherman, Jonathan Marc . . . . **CLC 55**

Sherman, Martin 1941(?)- . . . . **CLC 19**
See also CA 116; 123

Sherwin, Judith Johnson 1936- . . . **CLC 7, 15**
See also CA 25-28R; CANR 34

Sherwood, Frances 1940- . . . . **CLC 81**
See also CA 146

Sherwood, Robert E(mmet)
1896-1955 . . . . . . **TCLC 3; DAM DRAM**
See also CA 104; 153; DLB 7, 26

Shestov, Lev 1866-1938 . . . . **TCLC 56**

Shevchenko, Taras 1814-1861 . . . . **NCLC 54**

Shiel, M(atthew) P(hipps)
1865-1947 . . . . **TCLC 8**
See also CA 106; DLB 153

Shields, Carol 1935- . . . . **CLC 91; DAC**
See also CA 81-84; CANR 51

Shields, David 1956- . . . . **CLC 97**
See also CA 124; CANR 48

Shiga, Naoya 1883-1971 . . . **CLC 33; SSC 23**
See also CA 101; 33-36R

Shilts, Randy 1951-1994 . . . . **CLC 85**
See also AAYA 19; CA 115; 127; 144;
CANR 45; INT 127

Shimazaki, Haruki 1872-1943
See Shimazaki Toson
See also CA 105; 134

Shimazaki Toson . . . . **TCLC 5**
See also Shimazaki, Haruki

Sholokhov, Mikhail (Aleksandrovich)
1905-1984 . . . . **CLC 7, 15**
See also CA 101; 112; MTCW;
SATA-Obit 36

Shone, Patric
See Hanley, James

Shreve, Susan Richards 1939- ...... **CLC 23**
See also CA 49-52; CAAS 5; CANR 5, 38;
MAICYA; SATA 46; SATA-Brief 41

Shue, Larry
1946-1985 ...... **CLC 52; DAM DRAM**
See also CA 145; 117

Shu-Jen, Chou 1881-1936
See Lu Hsun
See also CA 104

Shulman, Alix Kates 1932- ...... **CLC 2, 10**
See also CA 29-32R; CANR 43; SATA 7

Shuster, Joe 1914- .... **CLC 21**

Shute, Nevil .... **CLC 30**
See also Norway, Nevil Shute

Shuttle, Penelope (Diane) 1947- ..... **CLC 7**
See also CA 93-96; CANR 39; DLB 14, 40

Sidney, Mary 1561-1621 .... **LC 19**

Sidney, Sir Philip
1554-1586 ..... **LC 19; DA; DAB; DAC;
DAM MST, POET**
See also CDBLB Before 1660; DLB 167

Siegel, Jerome 1914-1996 .... **CLC 21**
See also CA 116; 151

Siegel, Jerry
See Siegel, Jerome

Sienkiewicz, Henryk (Adam Alexander Pius)
1846-1916 .... **TCLC 3**
See also CA 104; 134

Sierra, Gregorio Martinez
See Martinez Sierra, Gregorio

Sierra, Maria (de la O'LeJarraga) Martinez
See Martinez Sierra, Maria (de la
O'LeJarraga)

Sigal, Clancy 1926- .... **CLC 7**
See also CA 1-4R

Sigourney, Lydia Howard (Huntley)
1791-1865 .... **NCLC 21**
See also DLB 1, 42, 73

Siguenza y Gongora, Carlos de
1645-1700 .... **LC 8**

Sigurjonsson, Johann 1880-1919 ... **TCLC 27**

Sikelianos, Angelos 1884-1951 .... **TCLC 39**

Silkin, Jon 1930- .... **CLC 2, 6, 43**
See also CA 5-8R; CAAS 5; DLB 27

Silko, Leslie (Marmon)
1948- .... **CLC 23, 74; DA; DAC;
DAM MST, MULT, POP**
See also AAYA 14; CA 115; 122;
CANR 45; DLB 143, 175; NNAL

Sillanpaa, Frans Eemil 1888-1964... **CLC 19**
See also CA 129; 93-96; MTCW

Sillitoe, Alan
1928- .... **CLC 1, 3, 6, 10, 19, 57**
See also AITN 1; CA 9-12R; CAAS 2;
CANR 8, 26, 55; CDBLB 1960 to
Present; DLB 14, 139; MTCW; SATA 61

Silone, Ignazio 1900-1978 .... **CLC 4**
See also CA 25-28; 81-84; CANR 34;
CAP 2; MTCW

Silver, Joan Micklin 1935- .... **CLC 20**
See also CA 114; 121; INT 121

Silver, Nicholas
See Faust, Frederick (Schiller)

Silverberg, Robert
1935- .... **CLC 7; DAM POP**
See also CA 1-4R; CAAS 3; CANR 1, 20,
36; DLB 8; INT CANR-20; MAICYA;
MTCW; SATA 13, 91

Silverstein, Alvin 1933- .... **CLC 17**
See also CA 49-52; CANR 2; CLR 25;
JRDA; MAICYA; SATA 8, 69

Silverstein, Virginia B(arbara Opshelor)
1937- .... **CLC 17**
See also CA 49-52; CANR 2; CLR 25;
JRDA; MAICYA; SATA 8, 69

Sim, Georges
See Simenon, Georges (Jacques Christian)

Simak, Clifford D(onald)
1904-1988 .... **CLC 1, 55**
See also CA 1-4R; 125; CANR 1, 35;
DLB 8; MTCW; SATA-Obit 56

Simenon, Georges (Jacques Christian)
1903-1989 .... **CLC 1, 2, 3, 8, 18, 47;
DAM POP**
See also CA 85-88; 129; CANR 35;
DLB 72; DLBY 89; MTCW

Simic, Charles
1938- .... **CLC 6, 9, 22, 49, 68;
DAM POET**
See also CA 29-32R; CAAS 4; CANR 12,
33, 52; DLB 105

Simmel, Georg 1858-1918 .... **TCLC 64**

Simmons, Charles (Paul) 1924- ..... **CLC 57**
See also CA 89-92; INT 89-92

Simmons, Dan 1948-... **CLC 44; DAM POP**
See also AAYA 16; CA 138; CANR 53

Simmons, James (Stewart Alexander)
1933- .... **CLC 43**
See also CA 105; CAAS 21; DLB 40

Simms, William Gilmore
1806-1870 .... **NCLC 3**
See also DLB 3, 30, 59, 73

Simon, Carly 1945- .... **CLC 26**
See also CA 105

Simon, Claude
1913- .... **CLC 4, 9, 15, 39; DAM NOV**
See also CA 89-92; CANR 33; DLB 83;
MTCW

Simon, (Marvin) Neil
1927- .... **CLC 6, 11, 31, 39, 70;
DAM DRAM**
See also AITN 1; CA 21-24R; CANR 26,
54; DLB 7; MTCW

Simon, Paul (Frederick) 1941(?)- ... **CLC 17**
See also CA 116; 153

Simonon, Paul 1956(?)- .... **CLC 30**

Simpson, Harriette
See Arnow, Harriette (Louisa) Simpson

Simpson, Louis (Aston Marantz)
1923- .... **CLC 4, 7, 9, 32; DAM POET**
See also CA 1-4R; CAAS 4; CANR 1;
DLB 5; MTCW

Simpson, Mona (Elizabeth) 1957-... **CLC 44**
See also CA 122; 135

Simpson, N(orman) F(rederick)
1919- .... **CLC 29**
See also CA 13-16R; DLB 13

Sinclair, Andrew (Annandale)
1935- .... **CLC 2, 14**
See also CA 9-12R; CAAS 5; CANR 14, 38;
DLB 14; MTCW

Sinclair, Emil
See Hesse, Hermann

Sinclair, Iain 1943-.............. **CLC 76**
See also CA 132

Sinclair, Iain MacGregor
See Sinclair, Iain

Sinclair, Irene
See Griffith, D(avid Lewelyn) W(ark)

Sinclair, Mary Amelia St. Clair 1865(?)-1946
See Sinclair, May
See also CA 104

Sinclair, May .... **TCLC 3, 11**
See also Sinclair, Mary Amelia St. Clair
See also DLB 36, 135

Sinclair, Roy
See Griffith, D(avid Lewelyn) W(ark)

Sinclair, Upton (Beall)
1878-1968 ...... **CLC 1, 11, 15, 63; DA;
DAB; DAC; DAM MST, NOV; WLC**
See also CA 5-8R; 25-28R; CANR 7;
CDALB 1929-1941; DLB 9;
INT CANR-7; MTCW; SATA 9

Singer, Isaac
See Singer, Isaac Bashevis

Singer, Isaac Bashevis
1904-1991 .... **CLC 1, 3, 6, 9, 11, 15, 23,
38, 69; DA; DAB; DAC; DAM MST,
NOV; SSC 3; WLC**
See also AITN 1, 2; CA 1-4R; 134;
CANR 1, 39; CDALB 1941-1968; CLR 1;
DLB 6, 28, 52; DLBY 91; JRDA;
MAICYA; MTCW; SATA 3, 27;
SATA-Obit 68

Singer, Israel Joshua 1893-1944 ... **TCLC 33**

Singh, Khushwant 1915-.......... **CLC 11**
See also CA 9-12R; CAAS 9; CANR 6

Sinjohn, John
See Galsworthy, John

Sinyavsky, Andrei (Donatevich)
1925- .... **CLC 8**
See also CA 85-88

Sirin, V.
See Nabokov, Vladimir (Vladimirovich)

Sissman, L(ouis) E(dward)
1928-1976 .... **CLC 9, 18**
See also CA 21-24R; 65-68; CANR 13;
DLB 5

Sisson, C(harles) H(ubert) 1914-..... **CLC 8**
See also CA 1-4R; CAAS 3; CANR 3, 48;
DLB 27

Sitwell, Dame Edith
1887-1964 .... **CLC 2, 9, 67;
DAM POET; PC 3**
See also CA 9-12R; CANR 35;
CDBLB 1945-1960; DLB 20; MTCW

Sjoewall, Maj 1935-.............. **CLC 7**
See also CA 65-68

Sjowall, Maj
  See Sjoewall, Maj

Skelton, Robin 1925- . . . . **CLC 13**
  See also AITN 2; CA 5-8R; CAAS 5;
  CANR 28; DLB 27, 53

Skolimowski, Jerzy 1938- . . . . **CLC 20**
  See also CA 128

Skram, Amalie (Bertha)
  1847-1905 . . . . **TCLC 25**

Skvorecky, Josef (Vaclav)
  1924- . . . . **CLC 15, 39, 69; DAC;
                                              DAM NOV**
  See also CA 61-64; CAAS 1; CANR 10, 34;
  MTCW

Slade, Bernard . . . . **CLC 11, 46**
  See also Newbound, Bernard Slade
  See also CAAS 9; DLB 53

Slaughter, Carolyn 1946- . . . . **CLC 56**
  See also CA 85-88

Slaughter, Frank G(ill) 1908- . . . . . . **CLC 29**
  See also AITN 2; CA 5-8R; CANR 5;
  INT CANR-5

Slavitt, David R(ytman) 1935- . . . . **CLC 5, 14**
  See also CA 21-24R; CAAS 3; CANR 41;
  DLB 5, 6

Slesinger, Tess 1905-1945 . . . . **TCLC 10**
  See also CA 107; DLB 102

Slessor, Kenneth 1901-1971 . . . . **CLC 14**
  See also CA 102; 89-92

Slowacki, Juliusz 1809-1849 . . . . . **NCLC 15**

Smart, Christopher
  1722-1771 . . . **LC 3; DAM POET; PC 13**
  See also DLB 109

Smart, Elizabeth 1913-1986 . . . . **CLC 54**
  See also CA 81-84; 118; DLB 88

Smiley, Jane (Graves)
  1949- . . . . **CLC 53, 76; DAM POP**
  See also CA 104; CANR 30, 50;
  INT CANR-30

Smith, A(rthur) J(ames) M(arshall)
  1902-1980 . . . . **CLC 15; DAC**
  See also CA 1-4R; 102; CANR 4; DLB 88

Smith, Adam 1723-1790 . . . . **LC 36**
  See also DLB 104

Smith, Alexander 1829-1867 . . . . . **NCLC 59**
  See also DLB 32, 55

Smith, Anna Deavere 1950- . . . . **CLC 86**
  See also CA 133

Smith, Betty (Wehner) 1896-1972 . . . **CLC 19**
  See also CA 5-8R; 33-36R; DLBY 82;
  SATA 6

Smith, Charlotte (Turner)
  1749-1806 . . . . **NCLC 23**
  See also DLB 39, 109

Smith, Clark Ashton 1893-1961 . . . . **CLC 43**
  See also CA 143

Smith, Dave . . . . **CLC 22, 42**
  See also Smith, David (Jeddie)
  See also CAAS 7; DLB 5

Smith, David (Jeddie) 1942-
  See Smith, Dave
  See also CA 49-52; CANR 1; DAM POET

Smith, Florence Margaret 1902-1971
  See Smith, Stevie
  See also CA 17-18; 29-32R; CANR 35;
  CAP 2; DAM POET; MTCW

Smith, Iain Crichton 1928- . . . . **CLC 64**
  See also CA 21-24R; DLB 40, 139

Smith, John 1580(?)-1631 . . . . **LC 9**

Smith, Johnston
  See Crane, Stephen (Townley)

Smith, Joseph, Jr. 1805-1844 . . . . **NCLC 53**

Smith, Lee 1944- . . . . **CLC 25, 73**
  See also CA 114; 119; CANR 46; DLB 143;
  DLBY 83; INT 119

Smith, Martin
  See Smith, Martin Cruz

Smith, Martin Cruz
  1942- . . . . . **CLC 25; DAM MULT, POP**
  See also BEST 89:4; CA 85-88; CANR 6,
  23, 43; INT CANR-23; NNAL

Smith, Mary-Ann Tirone 1944- . . . . . **CLC 39**
  See also CA 118; 136

Smith, Patti 1946- . . . . **CLC 12**
  See also CA 93-96

Smith, Pauline (Urmson)
  1882-1959 . . . . **TCLC 25**

Smith, Rosamond
  See Oates, Joyce Carol

Smith, Sheila Kaye
  See Kaye-Smith, Sheila

Smith, Stevie . . . . **CLC 3, 8, 25, 44; PC 12**
  See also Smith, Florence Margaret
  See also DLB 20

Smith, Wilbur (Addison) 1933- . . . . . **CLC 33**
  See also CA 13-16R; CANR 7, 46; MTCW

Smith, William Jay 1918- . . . . **CLC 6**
  See also CA 5-8R; CANR 44; DLB 5;
  MAICYA; SAAS 22; SATA 2, 68

Smith, Woodrow Wilson
  See Kuttner, Henry

Smolenskin, Peretz 1842-1885 . . . . **NCLC 30**

Smollett, Tobias (George) 1721-1771 . . **LC 2**
  See also CDBLB 1660-1789; DLB 39, 104

Snodgrass, W(illiam) D(e Witt)
  1926- . . . . **CLC 2, 6, 10, 18, 68;
                                              DAM POET**
  See also CA 1-4R; CANR 6, 36; DLB 5;
  MTCW

Snow, C(harles) P(ercy)
  1905-1980 . . . . **CLC 1, 4, 6, 9, 13, 19;
                                              DAM NOV**
  See also CA 5-8R; 101; CANR 28;
  CDBLB 1945-1960; DLB 15, 77; MTCW

Snow, Frances Compton
  See Adams, Henry (Brooks)

Snyder, Gary (Sherman)
  1930- . . **CLC 1, 2, 5, 9, 32; DAM POET**
  See also CA 17-20R; CANR 30; DLB 5, 16,
  165

Snyder, Zilpha Keatley 1927- . . . . . . **CLC 17**
  See also AAYA 15; CA 9-12R; CANR 38;
  CLR 31; JRDA; MAICYA; SAAS 2;
  SATA 1, 28, 75

Soares, Bernardo
  See Pessoa, Fernando (Antonio Nogueira)

Sobh, A.
  See Shamlu, Ahmad

Sobol, Joshua . . . . **CLC 60**

Soderberg, Hjalmar 1869-1941 . . . . **TCLC 39**

Sodergran, Edith (Irene)
  See Soedergran, Edith (Irene)

Soedergran, Edith (Irene)
  1892-1923 . . . . **TCLC 31**

Softly, Edgar
  See Lovecraft, H(oward) P(hillips)

Softly, Edward
  See Lovecraft, H(oward) P(hillips)

Sokolov, Raymond 1941- . . . . **CLC 7**
  See also CA 85-88

Solo, Jay
  See Ellison, Harlan (Jay)

Sologub, Fyodor . . . . **TCLC 9**
  See also Teternikov, Fyodor Kuzmich

Solomons, Ikey Esquir
  See Thackeray, William Makepeace

Solomos, Dionysios 1798-1857 . . . **NCLC 15**

Solwoska, Mara
  See French, Marilyn

Solzhenitsyn, Aleksandr I(sayevich)
  1918- . . . . . . **CLC 1, 2, 4, 7, 9, 10, 18, 26,
                              34, 78; DA; DAB; DAC; DAM MST,
                                              NOV; WLC**
  See also AITN 1; CA 69-72; CANR 40;
  MTCW

Somers, Jane
  See Lessing, Doris (May)

Somerville, Edith 1858-1949 . . . . . . **TCLC 51**
  See also DLB 135

Somerville & Ross
  See Martin, Violet Florence; Somerville,
  Edith

Sommer, Scott 1951- . . . . **CLC 25**
  See also CA 106

Sondheim, Stephen (Joshua)
  1930- . . . . **CLC 30, 39; DAM DRAM**
  See also AAYA 11; CA 103; CANR 47

Sontag, Susan
  1933- . . . . **CLC 1, 2, 10, 13, 31;
                                              DAM POP**
  See also CA 17-20R; CANR 25, 51; DLB 2,
  67; MTCW

Sophocles
  496(?)B.C.-406(?)B.C. . . . . . **CMLC 2; DA;
             DAB; DAC; DAM DRAM, MST; DC 1**
  See also DLB 176

Sordello 1189-1269 . . . . **CMLC 15**

Sorel, Julia
  See Drexler, Rosalyn

Sorrentino, Gilbert
  1929- . . . . **CLC 3, 7, 14, 22, 40**
  See also CA 77-80; CANR 14, 33; DLB 5,
  173; DLBY 80; INT CANR-14

Soto, Gary
  1952- . . . . **CLC 32, 80; DAM MULT;
                                              HLC**
  See also AAYA 10; CA 119; 125;
  CANR 50; CLR 38; DLB 82; HW;
  INT 125; JRDA; SATA 80

Sudermann, Hermann 1857-1928 .. **TCLC 15**
See also CA 107; DLB 118

Sue, Eugene 1804-1857 .... **NCLC 1**
See also DLB 119

Sueskind, Patrick 1949- .... **CLC 44**
See also Suskind, Patrick

Sukenick, Ronald 1932- ..... **CLC 3, 4, 6, 48**
See also CA 25-28R; CAAS 8; CANR 32;
DLB 173; DLBY 81

Suknaski, Andrew 1942- .... **CLC 19**
See also CA 101; DLB 53

Sullivan, Vernon
See Vian, Boris

Sully Prudhomme 1839-1907 ...... **TCLC 31**

Su Man-shu .... **TCLC 24**
See also Su Chien

Summerforest, Ivy B.
See Kirkup, James

Summers, Andrew James 1942- ..... **CLC 26**

Summers, Andy
See Summers, Andrew James

Summers, Hollis (Spurgeon, Jr.)
1916- .... **CLC 10**
See also CA 5-8R; CANR 3; DLB 6

Summers, (Alphonsus Joseph-Mary Augustus)
Montague 1880-1948 .... **TCLC 16**
See also CA 118

Sumner, Gordon Matthew 1951- .... **CLC 26**

Surtees, Robert Smith
1803-1864 .... **NCLC 14**
See also DLB 21

Susann, Jacqueline 1921-1974 ...... **CLC 3**
See also AITN 1; CA 65-68; 53-56; MTCW

Su Shih 1036-1101 .... **CMLC 15**

Suskind, Patrick
See Sueskind, Patrick
See also CA 145

Sutcliff, Rosemary
1920-1992 .... **CLC 26; DAB; DAC;**
DAM MST, POP
See also AAYA 10; CA 5-8R; 139;
CANR 37; CLR 1, 37; JRDA; MAICYA;
SATA 6, 44, 78; SATA-Obit 73

Sutro, Alfred 1863-1933 .... **TCLC 6**
See also CA 105; DLB 10

Sutton, Henry
See Slavitt, David R(ytman)

Svevo, Italo
1861-1928 .... **TCLC 2, 35; SSC 25**
See also Schmitz, Aron Hector

Swados, Elizabeth (A.) 1951- .... **CLC 12**
See also CA 97-100; CANR 49; INT 97-100

Swados, Harvey 1920-1972 .... **CLC 5**
See also CA 5-8R; 37-40R; CANR 6;
DLB 2

Swan, Gladys 1934- .... **CLC 69**
See also CA 101; CANR 17, 39

Swarthout, Glendon (Fred)
1918-1992 .... **CLC 35**
See also CA 1-4R; 139; CANR 1, 47;
SATA 26

Sweet, Sarah C.
See Jewett, (Theodora) Sarah Orne

Swenson, May
1919-1989 .... **CLC 4, 14, 61; DA; DAB;**
DAC; DAM MST, POET; PC 14
See also CA 5-8R; 130; CANR 36; DLB 5;
MTCW; SATA 15

Swift, Augustus
See Lovecraft, H(oward) P(hillips)

Swift, Graham (Colin) 1949- .... **CLC 41, 88**
See also CA 117; 122; CANR 46

Swift, Jonathan
1667-1745 ...... **LC 1; DA; DAB; DAC;**
DAM MST, NOV, POET; PC 9; WLC
See also CDBLB 1660-1789; DLB 39, 95,
101; SATA 19

Swinburne, Algernon Charles
1837-1909 ...... **TCLC 8, 36; DA; DAB;**
DAC; DAM MST, POET; WLC
See also CA 105; 140; CDBLB 1832-1890;
DLB 35, 57

Swinfen, Ann .... **CLC 34**

Swinnerton, Frank Arthur
1884-1982 .... **CLC 31**
See also CA 108; DLB 34

Swithen, John
See King, Stephen (Edwin)

Sylvia
See Ashton-Warner, Sylvia (Constance)

Symmes, Robert Edward
See Duncan, Robert (Edward)

Symonds, John Addington
1840-1893 .... **NCLC 34**
See also DLB 57, 144

Symons, Arthur 1865-1945 .... **TCLC 11**
See also CA 107; DLB 19, 57, 149

Symons, Julian (Gustave)
1912-1994 .... **CLC 2, 14, 32**
See also CA 49-52; 147; CAAS 3; CANR 3,
33; DLB 87, 155; DLBY 92; MTCW

Synge, (Edmund) J(ohn) M(illington)
1871-1909 .... **TCLC 6, 37;**
DAM DRAM; DC 2
See also CA 104; 141; CDBLB 1890-1914;
DLB 10, 19

Syruc, J.
See Milosz, Czeslaw

Szirtes, George 1948- .... **CLC 46**
See also CA 109; CANR 27

Szymborska, Wislawa 1923- .... **CLC 99**
See also CA 154

T. O., Nik
See Annensky, Innokenty (Fyodorovich)

Tabori, George 1914- .... **CLC 19**
See also CA 49-52; CANR 4

Tagore, Rabindranath
1861-1941 .... **TCLC 3, 53;**
DAM DRAM, POET; PC 8
See also CA 104; 120; MTCW

Taine, Hippolyte Adolphe
1828-1893 .... **NCLC 15**

Talese, Gay 1932- .... **CLC 37**
See also AITN 1; CA 1-4R; CANR 9;
INT CANR-9; MTCW

Tallent, Elizabeth (Ann) 1954- ..... **CLC 45**
See also CA 117; DLB 130

Tally, Ted 1952- .... **CLC 42**
See also CA 120; 124; INT 124

Tamayo y Baus, Manuel
1829-1898 .... **NCLC 1**

Tammsaare, A(nton) H(ansen)
1878-1940 .... **TCLC 27**

Tan, Amy (Ruth)
1952- .... **CLC 59; DAM MULT, NOV,**
POP
See also AAYA 9; BEST 89:3; CA 136;
CANR 54; DLB 173; SATA 75

Tandem, Felix
See Spitteler, Carl (Friedrich Georg)

Tanizaki, Jun'ichiro
1886-1965 ...... **CLC 8, 14, 28; SSC 21**
See also CA 93-96; 25-28R

Tanner, William
See Amis, Kingsley (William)

Tao Lao
See Storni, Alfonsina

Tarassoff, Lev
See Troyat, Henri

Tarbell, Ida M(inerva)
1857-1944 .... **TCLC 40**
See also CA 122; DLB 47

Tarkington, (Newton) Booth
1869-1946 .... **TCLC 9**
See also CA 110; 143; DLB 9, 102;
SATA 17

Tarkovsky, Andrei (Arsenyevich)
1932-1986 .... **CLC 75**
See also CA 127

Tartt, Donna 1964(?)- .... **CLC 76**
See also CA 142

Tasso, Torquato 1544-1595 .... **LC 5**

Tate, (John Orley) Allen
1899-1979 .... **CLC 2, 4, 6, 9, 11, 14, 24**
See also CA 5-8R; 85-88; CANR 32;
DLB 4, 45, 63; MTCW

Tate, Ellalice
See Hibbert, Eleanor Alice Burford

Tate, James (Vincent) 1943- ... **CLC 2, 6, 25**
See also CA 21-24R; CANR 29, 57; DLB 5,
169

Tavel, Ronald 1940- .... **CLC 6**
See also CA 21-24R; CANR 33

Taylor, C(ecil) P(hilip) 1929-1981 ... **CLC 27**
See also CA 25-28R; 105; CANR 47

Taylor, Edward
1642(?)-1729 .... **LC 11; DA; DAB;**
DAC; DAM MST, POET
See also DLB 24

Taylor, Eleanor Ross 1920- .... **CLC 5**
See also CA 81-84

Taylor, Elizabeth 1912-1975 ... **CLC 2, 4, 29**
See also CA 13-16R; CANR 9; DLB 139;
MTCW; SATA 13

Taylor, Henry (Splawn) 1942- ...... **CLC 44**
See also CA 33-36R; CAAS 7; CANR 31;
DLB 5

Taylor, Kamala (Purnaiya) 1924-
See Markandaya, Kamala
See also CA 77-80

Tuohy, Frank . . . . **CLC 37**
See also Tuohy, John Francis
See also DLB 14, 139

Tuohy, John Francis   1925-
See Tuohy, Frank
See also CA 5-8R; CANR 3, 47

Turco, Lewis (Putnam)   1934- . . . **CLC 11, 63**
See also CA 13-16R; CAAS 22; CANR 24,
51; DLBY 84

Turgenev, Ivan
1818-1883 . . . . **NCLC 21; DA; DAB;**
DAC; DAM MST, NOV; DC 7; SSC 7;
WLC

Turgot, Anne-Robert-Jacques
1727-1781 . . . . **LC 26**

Turner, Frederick   1943- . . . . **CLC 48**
See also CA 73-76; CAAS 10; CANR 12,
30, 56; DLB 40

Tutu, Desmond M(pilo)
1931- . . . . . **CLC 80; BLC; DAM MULT**
See also BW 1; CA 125

Tutuola, Amos
1920- . . . . **CLC 5, 14, 29; BLC;**
DAM MULT
See also BW 2; CA 9-12R; CANR 27;
DLB 125; MTCW

Twain, Mark
. . . . . **TCLC 6, 12, 19, 36, 48, 59; SSC 6;**
WLC
See also Clemens, Samuel Langhorne
See also AAYA 20; DLB 11, 12, 23, 64, 74

Tyler, Anne
1941- . . . . **CLC 7, 11, 18, 28, 44, 59;**
DAM NOV, POP
See also AAYA 18; BEST 89:1; CA 9-12R;
CANR 11, 33, 53; DLB 6, 143; DLBY 82;
MTCW; SATA 7, 90

Tyler, Royall   1757-1826. . . . . **NCLC 3**
See also DLB 37

Tynan, Katharine   1861-1931 . . . . . . **TCLC 3**
See also CA 104; DLB 153

Tyutchev, Fyodor   1803-1873 . . . . . **NCLC 34**

Tzara, Tristan
1896-1963 . . . . **CLC 47; DAM POET**
See also Rosenfeld, Samuel; Rosenstock,
Sami; Rosenstock, Samuel
See also CA 153

Uhry, Alfred
1936- . . . . . **CLC 55; DAM DRAM, POP**
See also CA 127; 133; INT 133

Ulf, Haerved
See Strindberg, (Johan) August

Ulf, Harved
See Strindberg, (Johan) August

Ulibarri, Sabine R(eyes)
1919- . . . . **CLC 83; DAM MULT**
See also CA 131; DLB 82; HW

Unamuno (y Jugo), Miguel de
1864-1936 . . . **TCLC 2, 9; DAM MULT,**
NOV; HLC; SSC 11
See also CA 104; 131; DLB 108; HW;
MTCW

Undercliffe, Errol
See Campbell, (John) Ramsey

Underwood, Miles
See Glassco, John

Undset, Sigrid
1882-1949 . . . . **TCLC 3; DA; DAB;**
DAC; DAM MST, NOV; WLC
See also CA 104; 129; MTCW

Ungaretti, Giuseppe
1888-1970 . . . . **CLC 7, 11, 15**
See also CA 19-20; 25-28R; CAP 2;
DLB 114

Unger, Douglas   1952-. . . . . **CLC 34**
See also CA 130

Unsworth, Barry (Forster)   1930-. . . . **CLC 76**
See also CA 25-28R; CANR 30, 54

Updike, John (Hoyer)
1932- . . . . . . **CLC 1, 2, 3, 5, 7, 9, 13, 15,**
23, 34, 43, 70; DA; DAB; DAC;
DAM MST, NOV, POET, POP;
SSC 13; WLC
See also CA 1-4R; CABS 1; CANR 4, 33,
51; CDALB 1968-1988; DLB 2, 5, 143;
DLBD 3; DLBY 80, 82; MTCW

Upshaw, Margaret Mitchell
See Mitchell, Margaret (Munnerlyn)

Upton, Mark
See Sanders, Lawrence

Urdang, Constance (Henriette)
1922- . . . . **CLC 47**
See also CA 21-24R; CANR 9, 24

Uriel, Henry
See Faust, Frederick (Schiller)

Uris, Leon (Marcus)
1924- . . . . **CLC 7, 32; DAM NOV, POP**
See also AITN 1, 2; BEST 89:2; CA 1-4R;
CANR 1, 40; MTCW; SATA 49

Urmuz
See Codrescu, Andrei

Urquhart, Jane   1949-. . . . . **CLC 90; DAC**
See also CA 113; CANR 32

Ustinov, Peter (Alexander)   1921-. . . . **CLC 1**
See also AITN 1; CA 13-16R; CANR 25,
51; DLB 13

Vaculik, Ludvik   1926- . . . . **CLC 7**
See also CA 53-56

Valdez, Luis (Miguel)
1940- . . . . . **CLC 84; DAM MULT; HLC**
See also CA 101; CANR 32; DLB 122; HW

Valenzuela, Luisa
1938- . . . **CLC 31; DAM MULT; SSC 14**
See also CA 101; CANR 32; DLB 113; HW

Valera y Alcala-Galiano, Juan
1824-1905 . . . . **TCLC 10**
See also CA 106

Valery, (Ambroise) Paul (Toussaint Jules)
1871-1945 . . . . **TCLC 4, 15;**
DAM POET; PC 9
See also CA 104; 122; MTCW

Valle-Inclan, Ramon (Maria) del
1866-1936 . . . . . **TCLC 5; DAM MULT;**
HLC
See also CA 106; 153; DLB 134

Vallejo, Antonio Buero
See Buero Vallejo, Antonio

Vallejo, Cesar (Abraham)
1892-1938 . . . . **TCLC 3, 56;**
DAM MULT; HLC
See also CA 105; 153; HW

Vallette, Marguerite Eymery
See Rachilde

Valle Y Pena, Ramon del
See Valle-Inclan, Ramon (Maria) del

Van Ash, Cay   1918-. . . . . **CLC 34**

Vanbrugh, Sir John
1664-1726 . . . . **LC 21; DAM DRAM**
See also DLB 80

Van Campen, Karl
See Campbell, John W(ood, Jr.)

Vance, Gerald
See Silverberg, Robert

Vance, Jack . . . . **CLC 35**
See also Vance, John Holbrook
See also DLB 8

Vance, John Holbrook   1916-
See Queen, Ellery; Vance, Jack
See also CA 29-32R; CANR 17; MTCW

Van Den Bogarde, Derek Jules Gaspard Ulric
Niven   1921-
See Bogarde, Dirk
See also CA 77-80

Vandenburgh, Jane . . . . **CLC 59**

Vanderhaeghe, Guy   1951- . . . . **CLC 41**
See also CA 113

van der Post, Laurens (Jan)
1906-1996 . . . . **CLC 5**
See also CA 5-8R; 155; CANR 35

van de Wetering, Janwillem   1931- . . **CLC 47**
See also CA 49-52; CANR 4

Van Dine, S. S. . . . . **TCLC 23**
See also Wright, Willard Huntington

Van Doren, Carl (Clinton)
1885-1950 . . . . **TCLC 18**
See also CA 111

Van Doren, Mark   1894-1972. . . . . **CLC 6, 10**
See also CA 1-4R; 37-40R; CANR 3;
DLB 45; MTCW

Van Druten, John (William)
1901-1957 . . . . **TCLC 2**
See also CA 104; DLB 10

Van Duyn, Mona (Jane)
1921- . . . . **CLC 3, 7, 63; DAM POET**
See also CA 9-12R; CANR 7, 38; DLB 5

Van Dyne, Edith
See Baum, L(yman) Frank

van Itallie, Jean-Claude   1936-. . . . . . **CLC 3**
See also CA 45-48; CAAS 2; CANR 1, 48;
DLB 7

van Ostaijen, Paul   1896-1928 . . . . . **TCLC 33**

Van Peebles, Melvin
1932- . . . . **CLC 2, 20; DAM MULT**
See also BW 2; CA 85-88; CANR 27

Vansittart, Peter   1920-. . . . . **CLC 42**
See also CA 1-4R; CANR 3, 49

Van Vechten, Carl   1880-1964 . . . . . . **CLC 33**
See also CA 89-92; DLB 4, 9, 51

Van Vogt, A(lfred) E(lton)   1912-. . . . . **CLC 1**
See also CA 21-24R; CANR 28; DLB 8;
SATA 14

Varda, Agnes   1928- . . . . **CLC 16**
See also CA 116; 122

Vargas Llosa, (Jorge) Mario (Pedro)
1936- . . . . CLC 3, 6, 9, 10, 15, 31, 42, 85;
DA; DAB; DAC; DAM MST, MULT,
NOV; HLC
See also CA 73-76; CANR 18, 32, 42;
DLB 145; HW; MTCW

Vasiliu, Gheorghe   1881-1957
See Bacovia, George
See also CA 123

Vassa, Gustavus
See Equiano, Olaudah

Vassilikos, Vassilis   1933- . . . . CLC 4, 8
See also CA 81-84

Vaughan, Henry   1621-1695 . . . . LC 27
See also DLB 131

Vaughn, Stephanie . . . . CLC 62

Vazov, Ivan (Minchov)
1850-1921 . . . . TCLC 25
See also CA 121; DLB 147

Veblen, Thorstein (Bunde)
1857-1929 . . . . TCLC 31
See also CA 115

Vega, Lope de   1562-1635 . . . . LC 23

Venison, Alfred
See Pound, Ezra (Weston Loomis)

Verdi, Marie de
See Mencken, H(enry) L(ouis)

Verdu, Matilde
See Cela, Camilo Jose

Verga, Giovanni (Carmelo)
1840-1922 . . . . TCLC 3; SSC 21
See also CA 104; 123

Vergil
70B.C.-19B.C. . . . . . CMLC 9; DA; DAB;
DAC; DAM MST, POET; PC 12

Verhaeren, Emile (Adolphe Gustave)
1855-1916 . . . . TCLC 12
See also CA 109

Verlaine, Paul (Marie)
1844-1896 . . . . NCLC 2, 51;
DAM POET; PC 2

Verne, Jules (Gabriel)
1828-1905 . . . . TCLC 6, 52
See also AAYA 16; CA 110; 131; DLB 123;
JRDA; MAICYA; SATA 21

Very, Jones   1813-1880 . . . . NCLC 9
See also DLB 1

Vesaas, Tarjei   1897-1970 . . . . CLC 48
See also CA 29-32R

Vialis, Gaston
See Simenon, Georges (Jacques Christian)

Vian, Boris   1920-1959 . . . . TCLC 9
See also CA 106; DLB 72

Viaud, (Louis Marie) Julien   1850-1923
See Loti, Pierre
See also CA 107

Vicar, Henry
See Felsen, Henry Gregor

Vicker, Angus
See Felsen, Henry Gregor

Vidal, Gore
1925- . . . . . CLC 2, 4, 6, 8, 10, 22, 33, 72;
DAM NOV, POP
See also AITN 1; BEST 90:2; CA 5-8R;
CANR 13, 45; DLB 6, 152;
INT CANR-13; MTCW

Viereck, Peter (Robert Edwin)
1916- . . . . CLC 4
See also CA 1-4R; CANR 1, 47; DLB 5

Vigny, Alfred (Victor) de
1797-1863 . . . . . . NCLC 7; DAM POET
See also DLB 119

Vilakazi, Benedict Wallet
1906-1947 . . . . TCLC 37

Villiers de l'Isle Adam, Jean Marie Mathias
Philippe Auguste Comte
1838-1889 . . . . NCLC 3; SSC 14
See also DLB 123

Villon, Francois   1431-1463(?) . . . . PC 13

Vinci, Leonardo da   1452-1519 . . . . . . LC 12

Vine, Barbara . . . . CLC 50
See also Rendell, Ruth (Barbara)
See also BEST 90:4

Vinge, Joan D(ennison)
1948- . . . . CLC 30; SSC 24
See also CA 93-96; SATA 36

Violis, G.
See Simenon, Georges (Jacques Christian)

Visconti, Luchino   1906-1976 . . . . CLC 16
See also CA 81-84; 65-68; CANR 39

Vittorini, Elio   1908-1966 . . . . . CLC 6, 9, 14
See also CA 133; 25-28R

Vizinczey, Stephen   1933- . . . . CLC 40
See also CA 128; INT 128

Vliet, R(ussell) G(ordon)
1929-1984 . . . . CLC 22
See also CA 37-40R; 112; CANR 18

Vogau, Boris Andreyevich   1894-1937(?)
See Pilnyak, Boris
See also CA 123

Vogel, Paula A(nne)   1951- . . . . CLC 76
See also CA 108

Voight, Ellen Bryant   1943- . . . . CLC 54
See also CA 69-72; CANR 11, 29, 55;
DLB 120

Voigt, Cynthia   1942- . . . . CLC 30
See also AAYA 3; CA 106; CANR 18, 37,
40; CLR 13; INT CANR-18; JRDA;
MAICYA; SATA 48, 79; SATA-Brief 33

Voinovich, Vladimir (Nikolaevich)
1932- . . . . CLC 10, 49
See also CA 81-84; CAAS 12; CANR 33;
MTCW

Vollmann, William T.
1959- . . . . . . CLC 89; DAM NOV, POP
See also CA 134

Voloshinov, V. N.
See Bakhtin, Mikhail Mikhailovich

Voltaire
1694-1778 . . . . . LC 14; DA; DAB; DAC;
DAM DRAM, MST; SSC 12; WLC

von Daniken, Erich   1935- . . . . CLC 30
See also AITN 1; CA 37-40R; CANR 17,
44

von Daniken, Erich
See von Daeniken, Erich

von Heidenstam, (Carl Gustaf) Verner
See Heidenstam, (Carl Gustaf) Verner von

von Heyse, Paul (Johann Ludwig)
See Heyse, Paul (Johann Ludwig von)

von Hofmannsthal, Hugo
See Hofmannsthal, Hugo von

von Horvath, Odon
See Horvath, Oedoen von

von Horvath, Oedoen
See Horvath, Oedoen von

von Liliencron, (Friedrich Adolf Axel) Detlev
See Liliencron, (Friedrich Adolf Axel)
Detlev von

Vonnegut, Kurt, Jr.
1922- . . . . . . CLC 1, 2, 3, 4, 5, 8, 12, 22,
40, 60; DA; DAB; DAC; DAM MST,
NOV, POP; SSC 8; WLC
See also AAYA 6; AITN 1; BEST 90:4;
CA 1-4R; CANR 1, 25, 49;
CDALB 1968-1988; DLB 2, 8, 152;
DLBD 3; DLBY 80; MTCW

Von Rachen, Kurt
See Hubbard, L(afayette) Ron(ald)

von Rezzori (d'Arezzo), Gregor
See Rezzori (d'Arezzo), Gregor von

von Sternberg, Josef
See Sternberg, Josef von

Vorster, Gordon   1924- . . . . CLC 34
See also CA 133

Vosce, Trudie
See Ozick, Cynthia

Voznesensky, Andrei (Andreievich)
1933- . . . . CLC 1, 15, 57; DAM POET
See also CA 89-92; CANR 37; MTCW

Waddington, Miriam   1917- . . . . CLC 28
See also CA 21-24R; CANR 12, 30;
DLB 68

Wagman, Fredrica   1937- . . . . CLC 7
See also CA 97-100; INT 97-100

Wagner, Richard   1813-1883 . . . . NCLC 9
See also DLB 129

Wagner-Martin, Linda   1936- . . . . CLC 50

Wagoner, David (Russell)
1926- . . . . CLC 3, 5, 15
See also CA 1-4R; CAAS 3; CANR 2;
DLB 5; SATA 14

Wah, Fred(erick James)   1939- . . . . . . CLC 44
See also CA 107; 141; DLB 60

Wahloo, Per   1926-1975 . . . . CLC 7
See also CA 61-64

Wahloo, Peter
See Wahloo, Per

Wain, John (Barrington)
1925-1994 . . . . CLC 2, 11, 15, 46
See also CA 5-8R; 145; CAAS 4; CANR 23,
54; CDBLB 1960 to Present; DLB 15, 27,
139, 155; MTCW

Wajda, Andrzej   1926- . . . . CLC 16
See also CA 102

Wakefield, Dan   1932- . . . . CLC 7
See also CA 21-24R; CAAS 7

Wakoski, Diane
1937- .... CLC 2, 4, 7, 9, 11, 40;
DAM POET; PC 15
See also CA 13-16R; CAAS 1; CANR 9;
DLB 5; INT CANR-9

Wakoski-Sherbell, Diane
See Wakoski, Diane

Walcott, Derek (Alton)
1930- .... CLC 2, 4, 9, 14, 25, 42, 67, 76;
BLC; DAB; DAC; DAM MST, MULT,
POET; DC 7
See also BW 2; CA 89-92; CANR 26, 47;
DLB 117; DLBY 81; MTCW

Waldman, Anne 1945- .... CLC 7
See also CA 37-40R; CAAS 17; CANR 34;
DLB 16

Waldo, E. Hunter
See Sturgeon, Theodore (Hamilton)

Waldo, Edward Hamilton
See Sturgeon, Theodore (Hamilton)

Walker, Alice (Malsenior)
1944- .... CLC 5, 6, 9, 19, 27, 46, 58;
BLC; DA; DAB; DAC; DAM MST,
MULT, NOV, POET, POP; SSC 5
See also AAYA 3; BEST 89:4; BW 2;
CA 37-40R; CANR 9, 27, 49;
CDALB 1968-1988; DLB 6, 33, 143;
INT CANR-27; MTCW; SATA 31

Walker, David Harry 1911-1992.... CLC 14
See also CA 1-4R; 137; CANR 1; SATA 8;
SATA-Obit 71

Walker, Edward Joseph 1934-
See Walker, Ted
See also CA 21-24R; CANR 12, 28, 53

Walker, George F.
1947- .... CLC 44, 61; DAB; DAC;
DAM MST
See also CA 103; CANR 21, 43; DLB 60

Walker, Joseph A.
1935- .... CLC 19; DAM DRAM, MST
See also BW 1; CA 89-92; CANR 26;
DLB 38

Walker, Margaret (Abigail)
1915- .... CLC 1, 6; BLC; DAM MULT
See also BW 2; CA 73-76; CANR 26, 54;
DLB 76, 152; MTCW

Walker, Ted .... CLC 13
See also Walker, Edward Joseph
See also DLB 40

Wallace, David Foster 1962-....... CLC 50
See also CA 132

Wallace, Dexter
See Masters, Edgar Lee

Wallace, (Richard Horatio) Edgar
1875-1932 .... TCLC 57
See also CA 115; DLB 70

Wallace, Irving
1916-1990 ..... CLC 7, 13; DAM NOV,
POP
See also AITN 1; CA 1-4R; 132; CAAS 1;
CANR 1, 27; INT CANR-27; MTCW

Wallant, Edward Lewis
1926-1962 .... CLC 5, 10
See also CA 1-4R; CANR 22; DLB 2, 28,
143; MTCW

Walley, Byron
See Card, Orson Scott

Walpole, Horace 1717-1797 .... LC 2
See also DLB 39, 104

Walpole, Hugh (Seymour)
1884-1941 .... TCLC 5
See also CA 104; DLB 34

Walser, Martin 1927-............. CLC 27
See also CA 57-60; CANR 8, 46; DLB 75,
124

Walser, Robert
1878-1956 .... TCLC 18; SSC 20
See also CA 118; DLB 66

Walsh, Jill Paton................... CLC 35
See also Paton Walsh, Gillian
See also AAYA 11; CLR 2; DLB 161;
SAAS 3

Walter, Villiam Christian
See Andersen, Hans Christian

Wambaugh, Joseph (Aloysius, Jr.)
1937- .... CLC 3, 18; DAM NOV, POP
See also AITN 1; BEST 89:3; CA 33-36R;
CANR 42; DLB 6; DLBY 83; MTCW

Ward, Arthur Henry Sarsfield 1883-1959
See Rohmer, Sax
See also CA 108

Ward, Douglas Turner 1930-....... CLC 19
See also BW 1; CA 81-84; CANR 27;
DLB 7, 38

Ward, Mary Augusta
See Ward, Mrs. Humphry

Ward, Mrs. Humphry
1851-1920 .... TCLC 55
See also DLB 18

Ward, Peter
See Faust, Frederick (Schiller)

Warhol, Andy 1928(?)-1987........ CLC 20
See also AAYA 12; BEST 89:4; CA 89-92;
121; CANR 34

Warner, Francis (Robert le Plastrier)
1937- .... CLC 14
See also CA 53-56; CANR 11

Warner, Marina 1946-............. CLC 59
See also CA 65-68; CANR 21, 55

Warner, Rex (Ernest) 1905-1986.... CLC 45
See also CA 89-92; 119; DLB 15

Warner, Susan (Bogert)
1819-1885 .... NCLC 31
See also DLB 3, 42

Warner, Sylvia (Constance) Ashton
See Ashton-Warner, Sylvia (Constance)

Warner, Sylvia Townsend
1893-1978 .... CLC 7, 19; SSC 23
See also CA 61-64; 77-80; CANR 16;
DLB 34, 139; MTCW

Warren, Mercy Otis 1728-1814... NCLC 13
See also DLB 31

Warren, Robert Penn
1905-1989 .... CLC 1, 4, 6, 8, 10, 13, 18,
39, 53, 59; DA; DAB; DAC; DAM MST,
NOV, POET; SSC 4; WLC
See also AITN 1; CA 13-16R; 129;
CANR 10, 47; CDALB 1968-1988;
DLB 2, 48, 152; DLBY 80, 89;
INT CANR-10; MTCW; SATA 46;
SATA-Obit 63

Warshofsky, Isaac
See Singer, Isaac Bashevis

Warton, Thomas
1728-1790 .... LC 15; DAM POET
See also DLB 104, 109

Waruk, Kona
See Harris, (Theodore) Wilson

Warung, Price 1855-1911.......... TCLC 45

Warwick, Jarvis
See Garner, Hugh

Washington, Alex
See Harris, Mark

Washington, Booker T(aliaferro)
1856-1915 .... TCLC 10; BLC;
DAM MULT
See also BW 1; CA 114; 125; SATA 28

Washington, George 1732-1799...... LC 25
See also DLB 31

Wassermann, (Karl) Jakob
1873-1934 .... TCLC 6
See also CA 104; DLB 66

Wasserstein, Wendy
1950- .... CLC 32, 59, 90;
DAM DRAM; DC 4
See also CA 121; 129; CABS 3; CANR 53;
INT 129

Waterhouse, Keith (Spencer)
1929- .... CLC 47
See also CA 5-8R; CANR 38; DLB 13, 15;
MTCW

Waters, Frank (Joseph)
1902-1995 .... CLC 88
See also CA 5-8R; 149; CAAS 13; CANR 3,
18; DLBY 86

Waters, Roger 1944-.............. CLC 35

Watkins, Frances Ellen
See Harper, Frances Ellen Watkins

Watkins, Gerrold
See Malzberg, Barry N(athaniel)

Watkins, Gloria 1955(?)-
See hooks, bell
See also BW 2; CA 143

Watkins, Paul 1964-.............. CLC 55
See also CA 132

Watkins, Vernon Phillips
1906-1967 .... CLC 43
See also CA 9-10; 25-28R; CAP 1; DLB 20

Watson, Irving S.
See Mencken, H(enry) L(ouis)

Watson, John H.
See Farmer, Philip Jose

Watson, Richard F.
See Silverberg, Robert

Waugh, Auberon (Alexander) 1939- .. CLC 7
See also CA 45-48; CANR 6, 22; DLB 14

Waugh, Evelyn (Arthur St. John)
1903-1966 . . . . . . CLC 1, 3, 8, 13, 19, 27,
44; DA; DAB; DAC; DAM MST, NOV,
POP; WLC
See also CA 85-88; 25-28R; CANR 22;
CDBLB 1914-1945; DLB 15, 162; MTCW

Waugh, Harriet 1944- . . . . CLC 6
See also CA 85-88; CANR 22

Ways, C. R.
See Blount, Roy (Alton), Jr.

Waystaff, Simon
See Swift, Jonathan

Webb, (Martha) Beatrice (Potter)
1858-1943 . . . . TCLC 22
See also Potter, Beatrice
See also CA 117

Webb, Charles (Richard) 1939- . . . . . . CLC 7
See also CA 25-28R

Webb, James H(enry), Jr. 1946- . . . . CLC 22
See also CA 81-84

Webb, Mary (Gladys Meredith)
1881-1927 . . . . TCLC 24
See also CA 123; DLB 34

Webb, Mrs. Sidney
See Webb, (Martha) Beatrice (Potter)

Webb, Phyllis 1927- . . . . CLC 18
See also CA 104; CANR 23; DLB 53

Webb, Sidney (James)
1859-1947 . . . . TCLC 22
See also CA 117

Webber, Andrew Lloyd . . . . CLC 21
See also Lloyd Webber, Andrew

Weber, Lenora Mattingly
1895-1971 . . . . CLC 12
See also CA 19-20; 29-32R; CAP 1;
SATA 2; SATA-Obit 26

Weber, Max 1864-1920 . . . . TCLC 69
See also CA 109

Webster, John
1579(?)-1634(?) . . . . . . LC 33; DA; DAB;
DAC; DAM DRAM, MST; DC 2; WLC
See also CDBLB Before 1660; DLB 58

Webster, Noah 1758-1843 . . . . NCLC 30

Wedekind, (Benjamin) Frank(lin)
1864-1918 . . . . . . TCLC 7; DAM DRAM
See also CA 104; 153; DLB 118

Weidman, Jerome 1913- . . . . CLC 7
See also AITN 2; CA 1-4R; CANR 1;
DLB 28

Weil, Simone (Adolphine)
1909-1943 . . . . TCLC 23
See also CA 117

Weinstein, Nathan
See West, Nathanael

Weinstein, Nathan von Wallenstein
See West, Nathanael

Weir, Peter (Lindsay) 1944- . . . . CLC 20
See also CA 113; 123

Weiss, Peter (Ulrich)
1916-1982 . . . . CLC 3, 15, 51;
DAM DRAM
See also CA 45-48; 106; CANR 3; DLB 69,
124

Weiss, Theodore (Russell)
1916- . . . . CLC 3, 8, 14
See also CA 9-12R; CAAS 2; CANR 46;
DLB 5

Welch, (Maurice) Denton
1915-1948 . . . . TCLC 22
See also CA 121; 148

Welch, James
1940- . . . . . CLC 6, 14, 52; DAM MULT,
POP
See also CA 85-88; CANR 42; DLB 175;
NNAL

Weldon, Fay
1933- . . . . CLC 6, 9, 11, 19, 36, 59;
DAM POP
See also CA 21-24R; CANR 16, 46;
CDBLB 1960 to Present; DLB 14;
INT CANR-16; MTCW

Wellek, Rene 1903-1995 . . . . CLC 28
See also CA 5-8R; 150; CAAS 7; CANR 8;
DLB 63; INT CANR-8

Weller, Michael 1942- . . . . CLC 10, 53
See also CA 85-88

Weller, Paul 1958- . . . . CLC 26

Wellershoff, Dieter 1925- . . . . CLC 46
See also CA 89-92; CANR 16, 37

Welles, (George) Orson
1915-1985 . . . . CLC 20, 80
See also CA 93-96; 117

Wellman, Mac 1945- . . . . CLC 65

Wellman, Manly Wade 1903-1986 . . CLC 49
See also CA 1-4R; 118; CANR 6, 16, 44;
SATA 6; SATA-Obit 47

Wells, Carolyn 1869(?)-1942 . . . . . . TCLC 35
See also CA 113; DLB 11

Wells, H(erbert) G(eorge)
1866-1946 . . . . TCLC 6, 12, 19; DA;
DAB; DAC; DAM MST, NOV; SSC 6;
WLC
See also AAYA 18; CA 110; 121;
CDBLB 1914-1945; DLB 34, 70, 156;
MTCW; SATA 20

Wells, Rosemary 1943- . . . . CLC 12
See also AAYA 13; CA 85-88; CANR 48;
CLR 16; MAICYA; SAAS 1; SATA 18,
69

Welty, Eudora
1909- . . . . . . CLC 1, 2, 5, 14, 22, 33; DA;
DAB; DAC; DAM MST, NOV; SSC 1;
WLC
See also CA 9-12R; CABS 1; CANR 32;
CDALB 1941-1968; DLB 2, 102, 143;
DLBD 12; DLBY 87; MTCW

Wen I-to 1899-1946 . . . . TCLC 28

Wentworth, Robert
See Hamilton, Edmond

Werfel, Franz (V.) 1890-1945 . . . . . . TCLC 8
See also CA 104; DLB 81, 124

Wergeland, Henrik Arnold
1808-1845 . . . . NCLC 5

Wersba, Barbara 1932- . . . . CLC 30
See also AAYA 2; CA 29-32R; CANR 16,
38; CLR 3; DLB 52; JRDA; MAICYA;
SAAS 2; SATA 1, 58

Wertmueller, Lina 1928- . . . . CLC 16
See also CA 97-100; CANR 39

Wescott, Glenway 1901-1987 . . . . CLC 13
See also CA 13-16R; 121; CANR 23;
DLB 4, 9, 102

Wesker, Arnold
1932- . . . . CLC 3, 5, 42; DAB;
DAM DRAM
See also CA 1-4R; CAAS 7; CANR 1, 33;
CDBLB 1960 to Present; DLB 13;
MTCW

Wesley, Richard (Errol) 1945- . . . . . . CLC 7
See also BW 1; CA 57-60; CANR 27;
DLB 38

Wessel, Johan Herman 1742-1785 . . . . LC 7

West, Anthony (Panther)
1914-1987 . . . . CLC 50
See also CA 45-48; 124; CANR 3, 19;
DLB 15

West, C. P.
See Wodehouse, P(elham) G(renville)

West, (Mary) Jessamyn
1902-1984 . . . . CLC 7, 17
See also CA 9-12R; 112; CANR 27; DLB 6;
DLBY 84; MTCW; SATA-Obit 37

West, Morris L(anglo) 1916- . . . . . CLC 6, 33
See also CA 5-8R; CANR 24, 49; MTCW

West, Nathanael
1903-1940 . . . . . TCLC 1, 14, 44; SSC 16
See also CA 104; 125; CDALB 1929-1941;
DLB 4, 9, 28; MTCW

West, Owen
See Koontz, Dean R(ay)

West, Paul 1930- . . . . CLC 7, 14, 96
See also CA 13-16R; CAAS 7; CANR 22,
53; DLB 14; INT CANR-22

West, Rebecca 1892-1983 . . CLC 7, 9, 31, 50
See also CA 5-8R; 109; CANR 19; DLB 36;
DLBY 83; MTCW

Westall, Robert (Atkinson)
1929-1993 . . . . CLC 17
See also AAYA 12; CA 69-72; 141;
CANR 18; CLR 13; JRDA; MAICYA;
SAAS 2; SATA 23, 69; SATA-Obit 75

Westlake, Donald E(dwin)
1933- . . . . CLC 7, 33; DAM POP
See also CA 17-20R; CAAS 13; CANR 16,
44; INT CANR-16

Westmacott, Mary
See Christie, Agatha (Mary Clarissa)

Weston, Allen
See Norton, Andre

Wetcheek, J. L.
See Feuchtwanger, Lion

Wetering, Janwillem van de
See van de Wetering, Janwillem

Wetherell, Elizabeth
See Warner, Susan (Bogert)

Whale, James 1889-1957 . . . . TCLC 63

Whalen, Philip 1923- . . . . CLC 6, 29
See also CA 9-12R; CANR 5, 39; DLB 16

Wharton, Edith (Newbold Jones)
1862-1937 . . . . . . TCLC 3, 9, 27, 53; DA;
DAB; DAC; DAM MST, NOV; SSC 6;
WLC
See also CA 104; 132; CDALB 1865-1917;
DLB 4, 9, 12, 78; DLBD 13; MTCW

Wharton, James
See Mencken, H(enry) L(ouis)

Wharton, William (a pseudonym)
.... **CLC 18, 37**
See also CA 93-96; DLBY 80; INT 93-96

Wheatley (Peters), Phillis
1754(?)-1784 .... **LC 3; BLC; DA; DAC;
DAM MST, MULT, POET; PC 3; WLC**
See also CDALB 1640-1865; DLB 31, 50

Wheelock, John Hall 1886-1978 .... **CLC 14**
See also CA 13-16R; 77-80; CANR 14;
DLB 45

White, E(lwyn) B(rooks)
1899-1985 .. **CLC 10, 34, 39; DAM POP**
See also AITN 2, CA 13-16R; 116;
CANR 16, 37; CLR 1, 21; DLB 11, 22;
MAICYA; MTCW; SATA 2, 29;
SATA-Obit 44

White, Edmund (Valentine III)
1940- .... **CLC 27; DAM POP**
See also AAYA 7; CA 45-48; CANR 3, 19,
36; MTCW

White, Patrick (Victor Martindale)
1912-1990 .. **CLC 3, 4, 5, 7, 9, 18, 65, 69**
See also CA 81-84; 132; CANR 43; MTCW

White, Phyllis Dorothy James 1920-
See James, P. D.
See also CA 21-24R; CANR 17, 43;
DAM POP; MTCW

White, T(erence) H(anbury)
1906-1964 .... **CLC 30**
See also CA 73-76; CANR 37; DLB 160;
JRDA; MAICYA; SATA 12

White, Terence de Vere
1912-1994 .... **CLC 49**
See also CA 49-52; 145; CANR 3

White, Walter F(rancis)
1893-1955 .... **TCLC 15**
See also White, Walter
See also BW 1; CA 115; 124; DLB 51

White, William Hale 1831-1913
See Rutherford, Mark
See also CA 121

Whitehead, E(dward) A(nthony)
1933- .... **CLC 5**
See also CA 65-68

Whitemore, Hugh (John) 1936- ..... **CLC 37**
See also CA 132; INT 132

Whitman, Sarah Helen (Power)
1803-1878 .... **NCLC 19**
See also DLB 1

Whitman, Walt(er)
1819-1892 ..... **NCLC 4, 31; DA; DAB;
DAC; DAM MST, POET; PC 3; WLC**
See also CDALB 1640-1865; DLB 3, 64;
SATA 20

Whitney, Phyllis A(yame)
1903- .... **CLC 42; DAM POP**
See also AITN 2; BEST 90:3; CA 1-4R;
CANR 3, 25, 38; JRDA; MAICYA;
SATA 1, 30

Whittemore, (Edward) Reed (Jr.)
1919- .... **CLC 4**
See also CA 9-12R; CAAS 8; CANR 4;
DLB 5

Whittier, John Greenleaf
1807-1892 .... **NCLC 8, 59**
See also DLB 1

Whittlebot, Hernia
See Coward, Noel (Peirce)

Wicker, Thomas Grey 1926-
See Wicker, Tom
See also CA 65-68; CANR 21, 46

Wicker, Tom .... **CLC 7**
See also Wicker, Thomas Grey

Wideman, John Edgar
1941- .... **CLC 5, 34, 36, 67; BLC;
DAM MULT**
See also BW 2; CA 85-88; CANR 14, 42;
DLB 33, 143

Wiebe, Rudy (Henry)
1934- .... **CLC 6, 11, 14; DAC;
DAM MST**
See also CA 37-40R; CANR 42; DLB 60

Wieland, Christoph Martin
1733-1813 .... **NCLC 17**
See also DLB 97

Wiene, Robert 1881-1938........ **TCLC 56**

Wieners, John 1934- .... **CLC 7**
See also CA 13-16R; DLB 16

Wiesel, Elie(zer)
1928- ...... **CLC 3, 5, 11, 37; DA; DAB;
DAC; DAM MST, NOV**
See also AAYA 7; AITN 1; CA 5-8R;
CAAS 4; CANR 8, 40; DLB 83;
DLBY 87; INT CANR-8; MTCW;
SATA 56

Wiggins, Marianne 1947- .... **CLC 57**
See also BEST 89:3; CA 130

Wight, James Alfred 1916-
See Herriot, James
See also CA 77-80; SATA 55;
SATA-Brief 44

Wilbur, Richard (Purdy)
1921- ... **CLC 3, 6, 9, 14, 53; DA; DAB;
DAC; DAM MST, POET**
See also CA 1-4R; CABS 2; CANR 2, 29;
DLB 5, 169; INT CANR-29; MTCW;
SATA 9

Wild, Peter 1940- .... **CLC 14**
See also CA 37-40R; DLB 5

Wilde, Oscar (Fingal O'Flahertie Wills)
1854(?)-1900 .... **TCLC 1, 8, 23, 41; DA;
DAB; DAC; DAM DRAM, MST, NOV;
SSC 11; WLC**
See also CA 104; 119; CDBLB 1890-1914;
DLB 10, 19, 34, 57, 141, 156; SATA 24

Wilder, Billy .... **CLC 20**
See also Wilder, Samuel
See also DLB 26

Wilder, Samuel 1906-
See Wilder, Billy
See also CA 89-92

Wilder, Thornton (Niven)
1897-1975 ...... **CLC 1, 5, 6, 10, 15, 35,
82; DA; DAB; DAC; DAM DRAM,
MST, NOV; DC 1; WLC**
See also AITN 2; CA 13-16R; 61-64;
CANR 40; DLB 4, 7, 9; MTCW

Wilding, Michael 1942- .... **CLC 73**
See also CA 104; CANR 24, 49

Wiley, Richard 1944- .... **CLC 44**
See also CA 121; 129

Wilhelm, Kate .... **CLC 7**
See also Wilhelm, Katie Gertrude
See also AAYA 20; CAAS 5; DLB 8;
INT CANR-17

Wilhelm, Katie Gertrude 1928-
See Wilhelm, Kate
See also CA 37-40R; CANR 17, 36; MTCW

Wilkins, Mary
See Freeman, Mary Eleanor Wilkins

Willard, Nancy 1936- .... **CLC 7, 37**
See also CA 89-92; CANR 10, 39; CLR 5;
DLB 5, 52; MAICYA; MTCW;
SATA 37, 71; SATA-Brief 30

Williams, C(harles) K(enneth)
1936- .... **CLC 33, 56; DAM POET**
See also CA 37-40R; CAAS 26; CANR 57;
DLB 5

Williams, Charles
See Collier, James L(incoln)

Williams, Charles (Walter Stansby)
1886-1945 .... **TCLC 1, 11**
See also CA 104; DLB 100, 153

Williams, (George) Emlyn
1905-1987 ...... **CLC 15; DAM DRAM**
See also CA 104; 123; CANR 36; DLB 10,
77; MTCW

Williams, Hugo 1942- .... **CLC 42**
See also CA 17-20R; CANR 45; DLB 40

Williams, J. Walker
See Wodehouse, P(elham) G(renville)

Williams, John A(lfred)
1925- ... **CLC 5, 13; BLC; DAM MULT**
See also BW 2; CA 53-56; CAAS 3;
CANR 6, 26, 51; DLB 2, 33;
INT CANR-6

Williams, Jonathan (Chamberlain)
1929- .... **CLC 13**
See also CA 9-12R; CAAS 12; CANR 8;
DLB 5

Williams, Joy 1944- .... **CLC 31**
See also CA 41-44R; CANR 22, 48

Williams, Norman 1952- .... **CLC 39**
See also CA 118

Williams, Sherley Anne
1944- ..... **CLC 89; BLC; DAM MULT,
POET**
See also BW 2; CA 73-76; CANR 25;
DLB 41; INT CANR-25; SATA 78

Williams, Shirley
See Williams, Sherley Anne

Williams, Tennessee
1911-1983 ..... **CLC 1, 2, 5, 7, 8, 11, 15,
19, 30, 39, 45, 71; DA; DAB; DAC;
DAM DRAM, MST; DC 4; WLC**
See also AITN 1, 2; CA 5-8R; 108;
CABS 3; CANR 31; CDALB 1941-1968;
DLB 7; DLBD 4; DLBY 83; MTCW

Williams, Thomas (Alonzo)
1926-1990 .... **CLC 14**
See also CA 1-4R; 132; CANR 2

Williams, William C.
See Williams, William Carlos

Wouk, Herman
1915- .. **CLC 1, 9, 38; DAM NOV, POP**
See also CA 5-8R; CANR 6, 33; DLBY 82;
INT CANR-6; MTCW

Wright, Charles (Penzel, Jr.)
1935- .... **CLC 6, 13, 28**
See also CA 29-32R; CAAS 7; CANR 23,
36; DLB 165; DLBY 82; MTCW

Wright, Charles Stevenson
1932- .... **CLC 49; BLC 3;
DAM MULT, POET**
See also BW 1; CA 9-12R; CANR 26;
DLB 33

Wright, Jack R.
See Harris, Mark

Wright, James (Arlington)
1927-1980 .... **CLC 3, 5, 10, 28;
DAM POET**
See also AITN 2; CA 49-52; 97-100;
CANR 4, 34; DLB 5, 169; MTCW

Wright, Judith (Arandell)
1915- .... **CLC 11, 53; PC 14**
See also CA 13-16R; CANR 31; MTCW;
SATA 14

Wright, L(aurali) R. 1939-........ **CLC 44**
See also CA 138

Wright, Richard (Nathaniel)
1908-1960 .... **CLC 1, 3, 4, 9, 14, 21, 48,
74; BLC; DA; DAB; DAC; DAM MST,
MULT, NOV; SSC 2; WLC**
See also AAYA 5; BW 1; CA 108;
CDALB 1929-1941; DLB 76, 102;
DLBD 2; MTCW

Wright, Richard B(ruce) 1937- ...... **CLC 6**
See also CA 85-88; DLB 53

Wright, Rick 1945-.............. **CLC 35**

Wright, Rowland
See Wells, Carolyn

Wright, Stephen Caldwell 1946- .... **CLC 33**
See also BW 2

Wright, Willard Huntington 1888-1939
See Van Dine, S. S.
See also CA 115

Wright, William 1930-............ **CLC 44**
See also CA 53-56; CANR 7, 23

Wroth, LadyMary 1587-1653(?) ..... **LC 30**
See also DLB 121

Wu Ch'eng-en 1500(?)-1582(?)........ **LC 7**

Wu Ching-tzu 1701-1754 .... **LC 2**

Wurlitzer, Rudolph 1938(?)- ... **CLC 2, 4, 15**
See also CA 85-88; DLB 173

Wycherley, William
1641-1715 .... **LC 8, 21; DAM DRAM**
See also CDBLB 1660-1789; DLB 80

Wylie, Elinor (Morton Hoyt)
1885-1928 .... **TCLC 8**
See also CA 105; DLB 9, 45

Wylie, Philip (Gordon) 1902-1971... **CLC 43**
See also CA 21-22; 33-36R; CAP 2; DLB 9

Wyndham, John.............. **CLC 19**
See also Harris, John (Wyndham Parkes
Lucas) Beynon

Wyss, Johann David Von
1743-1818 .... **NCLC 10**
See also JRDA; MAICYA; SATA 29;
SATA-Brief 27

Xenophon
c. 430B.C.-c. 354B.C........ **CMLC 17**
See also DLB 176

Yakumo Koizumi
See Hearn, (Patricio) Lafcadio (Tessima
Carlos)

Yanez, Jose Donoso
See Donoso (Yanez), Jose

Yanovsky, Basile S.
See Yanovsky, V(assily) S(emenovich)

Yanovsky, V(assily) S(emenovich)
1906-1989 .... **CLC 2, 18**
See also CA 97-100; 129

Yates, Richard 1926-1992 ..... **CLC 7, 8, 23**
See also CA 5-8R; 139; CANR 10, 43;
DLB 2; DLBY 81, 92; INT CANR-10

Yeats, W. B.
See Yeats, William Butler

Yeats, William Butler
1865-1939 ..... **TCLC 1, 11, 18, 31; DA;
DAB; DAC; DAM DRAM, MST,
POET; WLC**
See also CA 104; 127; CANR 45;
CDBLB 1890-1914; DLB 10, 19, 98, 156;
MTCW

Yehoshua, A(braham) B.
1936- .... **CLC 13, 31**
See also CA 33-36R; CANR 43

Yep, Laurence Michael 1948- ...... **CLC 35**
See also AAYA 5; CA 49-52; CANR 1, 46;
CLR 3, 17; DLB 52; JRDA; MAICYA;
SATA 7, 69

Yerby, Frank G(arvin)
1916-1991 .... **CLC 1, 7, 22; BLC;
DAM MULT**
See also BW 1; CA 9-12R; 136; CANR 16,
52; DLB 76; INT CANR-16; MTCW

Yesenin, Sergei Alexandrovich
See Esenin, Sergei (Alexandrovich)

Yevtushenko, Yevgeny (Alexandrovich)
1933- .... **CLC 1, 3, 13, 26, 51;
DAM POET**
See also CA 81-84; CANR 33, 54; MTCW

Yezierska, Anzia 1885(?)-1970 ..... **CLC 46**
See also CA 126; 89-92; DLB 28; MTCW

Yglesias, Helen 1915-............ **CLC 7, 22**
See also CA 37-40R; CAAS 20; CANR 15;
INT CANR-15; MTCW

Yokomitsu Riichi 1898-1947 ...... **TCLC 47**

Yonge, Charlotte (Mary)
1823-1901 .... **TCLC 48**
See also CA 109; DLB 18, 163; SATA 17

York, Jeremy
See Creasey, John

York, Simon
See Heinlein, Robert A(nson)

Yorke, Henry Vincent 1905-1974 ... **CLC 13**
See also Green, Henry
See also CA 85-88; 49-52

Yosano Akiko 1878-1942.. **TCLC 59; PC 11**

Yoshimoto, Banana .... **CLC 84**
See also Yoshimoto, Mahoko

Yoshimoto, Mahoko 1964-
See Yoshimoto, Banana
See also CA 144

Young, Al(bert James)
1939- ..... **CLC 19; BLC; DAM MULT**
See also BW 2; CA 29-32R; CANR 26;
DLB 33

Young, Andrew (John) 1885-1971.... **CLC 5**
See also CA 5-8R; CANR 7, 29

Young, Collier
See Bloch, Robert (Albert)

Young, Edward 1683-1765.......... **LC 3**
See also DLB 95

Young, Marguerite (Vivian)
1909-1995 .... **CLC 82**
See also CA 13-16; 150; CAP 1

Young, Neil 1945-................ **CLC 17**
See also CA 110

Young Bear, Ray A.
1950- .... **CLC 94; DAM MULT**
See also CA 146; DLB 175; NNAL

Yourcenar, Marguerite
1903-1987 .... **CLC 19, 38, 50, 87;
DAM NOV**
See also CA 69-72; CANR 23; DLB 72;
DLBY 88; MTCW

Yurick, Sol 1925-................. **CLC 6**
See also CA 13-16R; CANR 25

Zabolotskii, Nikolai Alekseevich
1903-1958 .... **TCLC 52**
See also CA 116

Zamiatin, Yevgenii
See Zamyatin, Evgeny Ivanovich

Zamora, Bernice (B. Ortiz)
1938- ..... **CLC 89; DAM MULT; HLC**
See also CA 151; DLB 82; HW

Zamyatin, Evgeny Ivanovich
1884-1937 .... **TCLC 8, 37**
See also CA 105

Zangwill, Israel 1864-1926........ **TCLC 16**
See also CA 109; DLB 10, 135

Zappa, Francis Vincent, Jr. 1940-1993
See Zappa, Frank
See also CA 108; 143; CANR 57

Zappa, Frank.................... **CLC 17**
See also Zappa, Francis Vincent, Jr.

Zaturenska, Marya 1902-1982.... **CLC 6, 11**
See also CA 13-16R; 105; CANR 22

Zeami 1363-1443.................... **DC 7**

Zelazny, Roger (Joseph)
1937-1995 .... **CLC 21**
See also AAYA 7; CA 21-24R; 148;
CANR 26; DLB 8; MTCW; SATA 57;
SATA-Brief 39

Zhdanov, Andrei A(lexandrovich)
1896-1948 .... **TCLC 18**
See also CA 117

Zhukovsky, Vasily 1783-1852 .... **NCLC 35**

Ziegenhagen, Eric .... **CLC 55**

Zimmer, Jill Schary
See Robinson, Jill

Zimmerman, Robert
  See Dylan, Bob

Zindel, Paul
  1936- ..... **CLC 6, 26; DA; DAB; DAC;
        DAM DRAM, MST, NOV; DC 5**
  See also AAYA 2; CA 73-76; CANR 31;
  CLR 3, 45; DLB 7, 52; JRDA; MAICYA;
  MTCW; SATA 16, 58

Zinov'Ev, A. A.
  See Zinoviev, Alexander (Aleksandrovich)

Zinoviev, Alexander (Aleksandrovich)
  1922- .... **CLC 19**
  See also CA 116; 133; CAAS 10

Zoilus
  See Lovecraft, H(oward) P(hillips)

Zola, Emile (Edouard Charles Antoine)
  1840-1902 ...... **TCLC 1, 6, 21, 41; DA;
        DAB; DAC; DAM MST, NOV; WLC**
  See also CA 104; 138; DLB 123

Zoline, Pamela 1941- .... **CLC 62**

Zorrilla y Moral, Jose 1817-1893 .. **NCLC 6**

Zoshchenko, Mikhail (Mikhailovich)
  1895-1958 .... **TCLC 15; SSC 15**
  See also CA 115

Zuckmayer, Carl 1896-1977 .... **CLC 18**
  See also CA 69-72; DLB 56, 124

Zuk, Georges
  See Skelton, Robin

Zukofsky, Louis
  1904-1978 .... **CLC 1, 2, 4, 7, 11, 18;
        DAM POET; PC 11**
  See also CA 9-12R; 77-80; CANR 39;
  DLB 5, 165; MTCW

Zweig, Paul 1935-1984 .... **CLC 34, 42**
  See also CA 85-88; 113

Zweig, Stefan 1881-1942 .... **TCLC 17**
  See also CA 112; DLB 81, 118

Zwingli, Huldreich 1484-1531 .... **LC 37**

Cumulative Nationality Index

SSC Cumulative Title Index

Title Index

Title Index

Title Index

Title Index

Title Index